T0205256

Communications
in Computer and Information Science 1992

Editorial Board Members

Rationale

The CCIS series is devoted to the publication of proceedings of computer science conferences. Its aim is to efficiently disseminate original research results in informatics in printed and electronic form. While the focus is on publication of peer-reviewed full papers presenting mature work, inclusion of reviewed short papers reporting on work in progress is welcome, too. Besides globally relevant meetings with internationally representative program committees guaranteeing a strict peer-reviewing and paper selection process, conferences run by societies or of high regional or national relevance are also considered for publication.

Topics

The topical scope of CCIS spans the entire spectrum of informatics ranging from foundational topics in the theory of computing to information and communications science and technology and a broad variety of interdisciplinary application fields.

Information for Volume Editors and Authors

Publication in CCIS is free of charge. No royalties are paid, however, we offer registered conference participants temporary free access to the online version of the conference proceedings on SpringerLink (http://link.springer.com) by means of an http referrer from the conference website and/or a number of complimentary printed copies, as specified in the official acceptance email of the event.

CCIS proceedings can be published in time for distribution at conferences or as post-proceedings, and delivered in the form of printed books and/or electronically as USBs and/or e-content licenses for accessing proceedings at SpringerLink. Furthermore, CCIS proceedings are included in the CCIS electronic book series hosted in the SpringerLink digital library at http://link.springer.com/bookseries/7899. Conferences publishing in CCIS are allowed to use Online Conference Service (OCS) for managing the whole proceedings lifecycle (from submission and reviewing to preparing for publication) free of charge.

Publication process

The language of publication is exclusively English. Authors publishing in CCIS have to sign the Springer CCIS copyright transfer form, however, they are free to use their material published in CCIS for substantially changed, more elaborate subsequent publications elsewhere. For the preparation of the camera-ready papers/files, authors have to strictly adhere to the Springer CCIS Authors' Instructions and are strongly encouraged to use the CCIS LaTeX style files or templates.

Abstracting/Indexing

CCIS is abstracted/indexed in DBLP, Google Scholar, EI-Compendex, Mathematical Reviews, SCImago, Scopus. CCIS volumes are also submitted for the inclusion in ISI Proceedings.

How to start

To start the evaluation of your proposal for inclusion in the CCIS series, please send an e-mail to ccis@springer.com.

Haomiao Yang · Rongxing Lu
Editors

Frontiers in Cyber Security

6th International Conference, FCS 2023
Chengdu, China, August 21–23, 2023
Revised Selected Papers

Editors
Haomiao Yang ⓘ
University of Electronic Science
and Technology
Chengdu, China

Rongxing Lu ⓘ
University of New Brunswick
Fredericton, NB, Canada

ISSN 1865-0929   ISSN 1865-0937 (electronic)
Communications in Computer and Information Science
ISBN 978-981-99-9330-7   ISBN 978-981-99-9331-4 (eBook)
https://doi.org/10.1007/978-981-99-9331-4

This Springer imprint is published by the registered company Springer Nature Singapore Pte Ltd.
The registered company address is: 152 Beach Road, #21-01/04 Gateway East, Singapore 189721, Singapore

Paper in this product is recyclable.

Preface

This volume contains the cyber security research papers from the Sixth International Conference on Frontiers in Cyber Security (FCS 2023). The event was organized by the University of Electronic Science and Technology of China. This series, which started in 2018, brings together individuals in different research fields in cyber security to exchange ideas. These proceedings provide significant information on cutting-edge research and current topics in specific fields of cyber security.

As network technology has rapidly developed in recent years, an increasing number of cyber security threats have emerged. A variety of cyber-attack behaviors expose every common user to risks, including privacy leakage, property loss, etc. As a result, achieving cyber security has attracted unprecedented attention worldwide. The development of cyber security requires extensive communication. FCS, with its enduring theme of "Frontiers in Cyber Security", aims to disseminate the latest international breakthroughs in cyber security, emphasizing new trends and revolutionary technologies. In this volume, researchers have proposed and discussed their research achievements in areas such as privacy protection, cryptography, blockchain technology, machine learning security, information hiding, AI security, etc.

The FCS conference has been held six times since its inception in 2018. In these six events, FCS has enabled the sharing of innovative techniques and fostered multifaceted discussions in cyber security. Hundreds of researchers have shared and exchanged ideas with each other at the FCS conferences, which has promoted the development of cyber security. In 2023, FCS was held in Chengdu, China, and organized by the University of Electronic Science and Technology of China, which is one of the most important research institutes in China. FCS 2023 received 89 papers and finally accepted 44 papers. Reviewers were assigned 6 papers on average and each paper received 3.1 reviews. The type of peer review was double-blind in order to promote transparency and fairness. The conference received great attention from all over the world, with participants from different countries such as China, Japan, Norway, etc.

According to the accepted papers, the five topics of FCS 2023 were classified by reviewers as follows: Blockchain and Distributed Systems, Network Security and Privacy Protection, Cryptography and Encryption Techniques, Machine Learning and Security, and Internet of Things and System Security.

The proceedings editors wish to express their deepest gratitude to the dedicated Program Committee members, reviewers, and all contributors for upholding the conference's academic quality. We also sincerely thank Springer for their trust and for publishing the proceedings of FCS 2023.

October 2023

Haomiao Yang
Rongxing Lu

Organization

General Chairs

Hongwei Li	University of Electronic Science and Technology of China, China
Jianbing Ni	Queen's University, Canada

Program Chairs

Haomiao Yang	University of Electronic Science and Technology of China, China
Rongxing Lu	University of New Brunswick, Canada

Steering Chairs

Xiaosong Zhang	University of Electronic Science and Technology of China, China
Tsuyoshi Takagi	University of Tokyo, Japan
Fagen Li	University of Electronic Science and Technology of China, China
Hyunsung Kim	Kyungil University, South Korea

Local Chairs

Pin Yang	Sichuan University, China
Xiaohu Tang	Southwest Jiaotong University, China
Yimin Zhou	Chengdu University of Information Technology, China

Publicity Chairs

Guangquan Xu	Tianjin University, China
Emmanuel Ahene	KNUST, Ghana
Alzubair Hassan	University College Dublin, Ireland
Mohammad Zulkernine	Queen's University, Canada

Publication Chairs

Fagen Li   University of Electronic Science and Technology
                                of China, China
Xiaofen Wang   University of Electronic Science and Technology
                                of China, China

Financial Chair

Xiaolei Zhang   University of Electronic Science and Technology
                                of China, China

Web Chair

Dongyun Xue   University of Electronic Science and Technology
                                of China, China

Program Committee

Sokratis Katsikas   Norwegian University of Science and Technology,
                                Norway
Atsushi Takayasu   University of Tokyo, Japan
Weina Niu   University of Electronic Science and Technology
                                of China, China
Yijun Su   University of Chinese Academy of Sciences,
                                China
Yupu Hu   Xidian University, China
Zhenhua Liu   Xidian University, China
Tao Xiang   Chongqing University, China
Hui Zhu   Xidian University, China
Guangquan Xu   Tianjin University, China
Jian Xu   Northeastern University, China
Rongmao Chen   National University of Defense Technology,
                                China
Jun Shao   Zhejiang Gongshang University, China
Peng Xu   Huazhong University of Science and Technology,
                                China
Hongyu Yang   Civil Aviation University of China, China
Yan Zhang   University of Oslo, Norway

Pin Yang	Sichuan University, China
Chunxiang Xu	University of Electronic Science and Technology of China, China
Xiong Li	University of Electronic Science and Technology of China, China
Yimin Zhou	Chengdu University of Information Technology, China
Liang Zhao	Sichuan University, China
Lei Zhang	East China Normal University, China
Saqib Hakak	University of New Brunswick, Canada
Beibei Li	Sichuan University, China
Vasileios Gkioulos	Norwegian University of Science and Technology, Norway
Hyun Kim	Kyungil University, South Korea
Giedre Sabaliauskaite	Coventry University, UK
Lu Zhou	Xidian University, China
Xiaoguang Liu	Southwest Minzu University, China
Ling Xiong	Xihua University, China

Contents

Cryptography and Encryption Techniques

Machine Learning and Security

Internet of Things and System Security

Contents xx

Blockchain and Distributed Systems

Secure Cross-Chain Transaction for Medical Data Sharing in Blockchain-Based Internet of Medical Things

Bohao Jiang , Chaoyang Li(✉) , Yu Tang , and Xiangjun Xin

College of Software Engineering, Zhengzhou University of Light Industry, Zhengzhou 450001, China
lichaoyang@zzuli.edu.cn

Abstract. It is challenging to solve the phenomenon of "information and value island" caused by cross-chain operation in blockchain-based medical Internet of things; in this paper, a multi-link fusion model based on a relay chain is proposed. By constructing a relay alliance chain governed by multiple parties to manage the cross-chain network, the use of blockchain technology addresses issues related to data sharing and business collaboration between multiple institutional blockchain systems. The cross-chain system based on relay mode provides interactive services for heterogeneous blockchain systems. The security and stability of cross-chain transactions are guaranteed through cross-chain gateways and cross-chain interaction protocols. The basic types of cross-chain interaction are summarized, and the implementation process of cross-chain interaction based on intelligent contracts is formulated. Finally, multiple sets of experiments were conducted to verify the feasibility of the cross-chain the scheme and the performance indicators of the cross-chain system were evaluated. The cross-chain mechanism of blockchain based on a relay chain can provide secure and efficient cross-chain services; this approach is suitable for most current cross-chain scenarios.

Keywords: BIoMT · Cross-chain transactions · Cross-chain gateway

1 Introduction

The gradual transformation towards digitalization and informatization of medical services is underway, driven by the development of medical informatization. As an important data asset, medical data is constantly being analyzed and mined, which greatly promotes research and progress in the medical field. Information exchange and sharing between different organizations can make medical data play a higher value. Therefore, the demand for cross-regional and cross-institutional medical information sharing is increasing [1]. The blockchain-based Internet of medical things (BIoMT) not only aggregates scattered medical data generated by many smart devices but also combines blockchain to ensure that data and operation records cannot be tampered with, which solves the problem that traditional medical networking data cannot be shared across regions and institutions, and is easy to be tampered and leaked during sharing.

© The Author(s), under exclusive license to Springer Nature Singapore Pte Ltd. 2024
H. Yang and R. Lu (Eds.): FCS 2023, CCIS 1992, pp. 3–18, 2024.
https://doi.org/10.1007/978-981-99-9331-4_1

At present, more and more blockchain applications have appeared in more and more application scenarios, but technical challenges such as structure system, consensus algorithm, how to protect user privacy, smart contracts, system underlying performance, transaction throughput, and cross-chain transactions between different systems are still restricting the development of the industry and related fields [2]. Due to the differences in design concepts and smart contracts adopted by different blockchain projects, many heterogeneous blockchains have emerged, which directly leads to a large number of blockchains becoming new information islands. In an institutional chain setting, cross-chain technology can bridge the gap between different blockchain networks, enable data circulation and value transfer, and ultimately overcome information isolation [3, 4].

In the blockchain 3.0 stage, many researchers have proposed blockchain-based medical data privacy security schemes. Among them, literature [5] proposed a multi-level medical blockchain architecture, which was composed of a public chain and an alliance chain. The public chain is maintained by all medical institutions and mainly undertakes the interaction tasks between users and the system. At the same time, different types of medical institutions from different alliance chains combine attribute-based encryption technology to ensure medical data privacy. However, this scheme stores the data completely within the blockchain, which brings huge storage pressure to the institution. Zhu et al. [6] suggested a model and mechanism for sharing medical data securely based on blockchain technology. This mechanism uses an encryption algorithm to encrypt medical data and protect the privacy of hidden data. At the same time, patients can set access control policies to achieve secure data sharing so as to prevent unauthorized, illegal entities from obtaining the patient's medical data. Lu et al. [7] suggested This paper proposes a method to control data access control through blockchain to ensure data security, address the challenge of data sharing, and enhance sharing efficiency. On this basis, blockchain 3.0 ushered in technological innovation. However, using multi-chain transaction techniques between consortium and private blockchains requires dealing with trust and authentication issues between different institutional blockchain systems. Due to the differences between different blockchain networks (such as consensus algorithms or block structures), the main barriers to cross-chain port technology focus on secure auditing of cross-chain network access chains and ensuring the security of transactions between institutional blockchains and other blockchains involved in cross-chain transmission [8]. Is the current cross-link port technology facing a major challenge?

Based on the research discussed earlier, Evidently the proposed scheme mainly solves the problem of user identity management through a single blockchain [9]. Moreover, the existing smart contract platform does not necessarily meet the needs of the application and lacks flexibility and customization. Comparatively, there has been no research on specific schemes for cross-chain user identity management. The paper suggests a cross-chain identity authentication model that relies on the relay chain. The model uses the relay chain to establish a cross-chain user identity model to solve the problem of transaction information management under multiple blockchains. By constructing a public chain, the model uses the message passing protocol to establish a connection with the relevant organization chain in the multi-chain model. Theoretical analysis and security analysis show that the scheme has better security and transaction processing efficiency.

2 Multi-chain Fusion Model

The model framework is shown in Fig. 1, which targets the problems of trust transfer, cross-chain access, and privacy protection when users interact with cross-chain in multi-chain scenarios. The data sharing of medical data existing on different chains is realized, it guaranteed the privacy of shared data meanwhile changes the shortcomings of "information island" of blockchain. In this paper, a multi-chain fusion model is proposed, which includes a private chain that stores patients' personal medical data, a public chain that stores the research results of medical institutions, drug research and development data, etc., and a public chain ledger that stores medical operations and monitoring data of regulatory agencies.

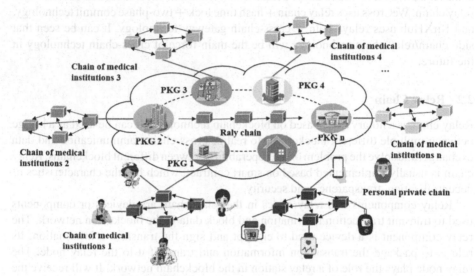

Fig. 1. Diagram of the multi-chain fusion model

2.1 Cross-Chain Technology

Among the many problems faced by blockchain, the interoperability between blockchains greatly limits the application space of blockchain. Whether it is a public chain or an alliance chain, cross-chain technology is the key to realising the Internet of value, and it is the bridge for the outward expansion and connection of blockchain. The mainstream cross-chain technologies include Notary schemes, Sidechains/relays, Hash-locking, and Distributed private key control. Cross-chain interaction can be divided into homogeneous chain cross-chain and heterogeneous chain cross-chain according to the different underlying technology platforms of the blockchain. The security mechanism, consensus algorithm, network topology, and block generation verification logic are consistent between homogeneous chains, and the cross-chain interaction between them is relatively simple. However, the cross-chain interaction of heterogeneous chains is relatively complex. For example, Bitcoin uses the PoW algorithm and Fabric uses the traditional deterministic consensus algorithm, whose block composition and deterministic guarantee mechanism are very different, and the direct cross-chain interaction mechanism is not easy to design. Cross-chain interaction between heterogeneous chains generally requires third-party auxiliary services to assist cross-chain interaction.

To achieve security and trust, cross-chain mechanisms and procedures must have some requirements, the most important of which is the atomicity of cross-chain transactions. For normal on-chain transactions, transactions need to be atomical-they need to be rolled back if they fail. The same is true for cross-chain transactions, where failure requires rolling back transactions involving two or more chains of the transaction.

At present, the most famous cross-chain projects in the public blockchain are Cosmos and Polkadot, both of which adopt a multi-chain and multi-layer architecture based on a relay chain. WeCross uses relay chain + hash time lock + two-phase commit technology, and BitXHub uses relay chain + cross-chain gateway technology. It can be seen that side chain/relay chain technology will be the main force of cross-chain technology in the future.

2.2 Relay Chain

Relay chain is a notary node based on blockchain technology. It can be used as a bridge between multiple different blockchains to realize cross-chain communication and data exchange, and solve the problem of interoperability between different blockchains. Relay chain is usually implemented based on smart contract, which has the characteristics of decentralization, transparency and security.

Relay components and relay nodes in the relay chain are devices or components used to transmit transaction information and block data in the blockchain network. The relay component is a device used to encrypt and sign the transaction information. Its role is to package the transaction information and transmit it to the relay node. The relay node plays the role of a relay station in the blockchain network. It will receive the transaction information from the relay component and forward it to other relay nodes or miner nodes, and will also receive the transaction information forwarded by other relay nodes or miner nodes and forward it. Through the forwarding of relay nodes, transaction information and block data can be propagated and synchronized in the entire blockchain network, thus ensuring the stable operation of the blockchain network. The role of these relay components and relay nodes is very important, because they can help to strengthen the security and reliability of the blockchain network, while also extending the coverage of the blockchain network and improving its efficiency and performance.

2.3 Multi-chain Description

The multi-chain structure comprises different categories of blockchains. These include the relay chain, user chain, and mechanism chain. The relay chain has been briefly described above. In this model, patients collect medical data through smart medical devices on the user chain, such as using a smartwatch to monitor heart rate in real-time, a thermometer to measure real-time body temperature, and all aspects of body health measured by home smart medical devices, which will be saved and uploaded to the patient's private chain in real-time. The corresponding other medical institutions can share the medical data of all parties through the alliance chain. The consortium blockchain of institutions includes medical institutions, insurance, banks, research institutions, government regulators and other blockchain institutions. Suppose that in the multi-chain fusion model, patient A needs to go to medical institution 1 for a physical examination. At this time, patient A needs to authorize institutional chain 1 to view the medical data shared by private user chain 1 through the relay chain so as to form this complete cross-chain data sharing.

2.4 Multi-chain Fusion Mechanism

According to the backbone chain The multi-chain fusion transaction model that utilizes the relay chain adopts a cross-chain model architecture. The multi-chain fusion model consists mainly of multiple private chains and public chain-ledgers. It includes the total chain, user chain and mechanism chain. As a relay chain, the main chain acts as a bridge between different blockchain networks and enables communication and interoperability between them and provides a security mechanism for transferring assets and data across chains. [10]. The responsibility for achieving access between different chains lies with the authentication of the system and the user. That's mainly used for medical data sharing between medical institutions (hospitals, insurance, government, patients) on different blockchains and complete records of operation records and data updates generated by different blockchain institutions. In this model, the patient can become a single institution on the blockchain and upload personal medical data to the private chain through smart medical devices, and the patient himself can authorize the custody of his data. Blockchain medical institutions include medical institutions, insurance, banks, scientific research institutions, and government regulators [11, 12].

3   Cross-Chain Transactions Process

The transaction flow is shown in the Fig. 2, which mainly contains cross-chain transactions, cross-chain identity authentication, consensus, gateway, interaction protocol standard.

3.1   Cross-Chain Transactions

The model presented in this paper based on blockchain adopts the relay chain cross-chain model architecture, then uses the relay chain as a trusted third party. Transaction execution: if institutional chain A wants to conduct cross-chain interaction with institutional chain B, when a user initiates a transaction request, the identity between the chains needs to be authenticated. Cross-chain requests are initiated between different blockchains and forwarded through cross-chain gateway and relay chain [13–15].

Different blockchains are different in encryption algorithms and block structures of their underlying platforms, so messages between different blockchains cannot communicate directly. Based on the gateway can convert the event data format thrown by different application chains into a unified structure. The protocol specifies the initiator chain, the

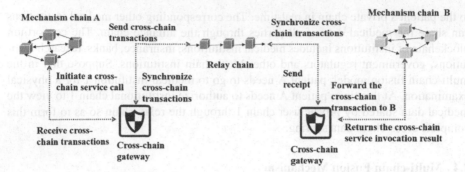

Fig. 2. The process of cross-chain transactions.

receiver chain, and the transaction mode, verification strategy, signature and much other information about the relevant cross-chain events. InterBlockchain Transfer Protocol (IBTP) facilitates communication and interaction between the mechanism chain and the relay chain as well as between different application chains in the multi-chain model. The transaction request of the application chain is converted to the IBTP structure through the gateway and submitted to the relay chain, and the relay chain performs the legitimacy verification and reliable routing of the cross-chain transaction through the IBTP content. IBTP messages are transmitted in P2P mode, and the main content of the message is encrypted with the public key of the other party to ensure that the message content is not stolen by the third party. At the same time, the call content is encrypted by the symmetric key negotiated between the cross-chain gateways and then sent to the relay chain to ensure the privacy of the transmitted call [16–18].

In the cross-chain system, when the business contract of the institutional chain a needs to perform relevant operations, it is realized by calling its management contract, also known as the Broker contract, through the contract. The request is caught by the Plugin that applies the chain, which then submits the request to the gateway. The network manager encapsulates the request IBTP and submits it to the relay chain. After verifying the validity of the request of agency chain A, the relay chain submits it to the destination gateway. The destination gateway eventually submits the request to the management contract (Broker) of institutional chain B. The management contract (Broker) then calls the request to the cross-chain business contract. The user Bob on the cross-chain business contract receives the relevant medical data provided by Alice on the institutional chain A. Figure 2 illustrates the specific process.

3.2 Cross-Chain Identity Authentication

The multi-chain fusion model mainly includes multiple private chains and public chain ledgers. There consists of three chains: the total chain, the user chain, and the mechanism chain. As a relay chain, the master chain's role is to manage and distribute unified identity credentials for users in the access cross-chain system and provide a trust delivery service mechanism for transactions. In the system, the responsibility of interaction access and identity verification of users is handled by the system itself. It is mainly used for medical data sharing among medical institutions (hospitals, insurance, government, patients) on different blockchains and complete records of operation records and data updates generated by institutions on different chains [19, 20]. In this model, a patient can become a single institution on a blockchain, uploading personal medical data to a private chain through smart medical devices, and the patient himself can authorize the custody of his data. Medical institutions on blockchain include medical institutions, insurance, banking, research institutions, government regulatory agencies, etc. After the cross-chain identity of these organizations on the blockchain is registered, they can apply for access to the system. When the users who have registered in the system need to add their identity information on other blockchains, they can update their identity and realize the association of identity information on multiple blockchains.

In the system, if an organization on a cross-chain system wants to interact with a user's medical data across the chain, the corresponding organization chain m needs to first send the request information with a digital signature to the user's private chain n through the cross-chain system, and the user's private chain n checks whether the digital signature is valid. If it is invalid, the zero-knowledge identity authentication process will be interrupted. If it is valid, authentication begins. After N times of zero-knowledge proof, if the verification is successful, the user's identity is proven to be credible, and the user is allowed to access his personal medical data.

3.3 Cross-Chain Consensus

The consensus algorithm of the relay chain is an indispensable and important component. The consensus algorithm is used to ensure the unity of the relay chain system, where the consistency includes the consistency of the transaction order, the consistency of the ledger, and the consistency of the node state. Due to the different cross-chain scenarios, the relay chain provides a pluggable plug-in mechanism for consensus algorithms to facilitate access to different kinds of consensus algorithms. For cross-chain scenarios, the tricky problem is that the adaptation of different kinds of consensus algorithm access is different. For the purpose of simplify the adaptation problem of different consensus algorithms, we adopt a plug-in mechanism, the role of the consensus algorithm is to package the transactions and the confirmation of blocks, and all the parts that operate on the consensus algorithm are encapsulated into the consensus algorithm plug-in, and a suitable plug-in interface is determined according to the requirements of the interaction between the relay chain and the consensus algorithm.

Taking the Raft consensus algorithm visited in this paper as an example, the transaction processing process through the consensus module is as follows:

Prepare interface: After receiving a transaction from a gRPC or Restful service, inject the received transaction into the transaction pool and sort it, then broadcast the transaction to the other nodes in the cluster. If the transaction exists before entering the transaction pool, the Prepare phase discards the transaction and does not broadcast it. Step interface: contains consensus block part. The Step interface receives four types of message structures: Consensus message type: and consensus message sent by Raft, the content of which mainly includes consensus log information, log index, current tenure information, etc. Broadcast transaction type: A transaction message that is broadcast by another node and accepted by the node will store the transaction in the transaction pool. Obtain transaction type: other nodes send request messages to obtain transactions.

If a node finds that some transactions do not exist in the transaction pool during the block generation phase, it will send a request message to the whole network to obtain lost transactions asynchronously. When the node receives the message and finds that the transaction is in the transaction pool or in the block's historical data, it sends the transaction to the node that lost the transaction. Response transaction type: Corresponding to the acquisition transaction type, the node that lost the transaction obtains the transaction sent by other nodes and deposits the transaction into the transaction pool for the block. Commit interface: Returns a channel containing the block structure information after the consensus is completed. ReportState interface: This is where the consensus algorithm plugin can do some finishing work for blocks.

3.4 Cross-Chain Gateway

In a typical transaction process, a cross-chain transaction is initiated with A as the initiator and B as the receiver, and the receipt is returned to application chain A after the execution on application chain B is completed. This is shown in Fig. 3.

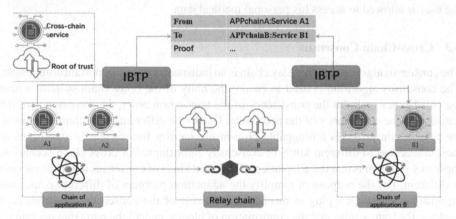

Fig.3. Based on the relay chain transaction graph

1) Listening for transactions

The transaction is initiated by the user and invokes the contract deployed on application chain A. If the contract receives a transaction request, it will send a cross-chain event in a specific format. The corresponding application chain plug-in will poll or subscribe to the cross-chain event, collect the Proof information (such as endorsement information in Fabric) on application chain A for the cross-chain event, and send it to the gateway listening module along with the IBTP packet. The monitor module does basic checks for cross-chain transactions, and the passed transactions can be submitted to the distribution module. When a problem occurs in a cross-chain transaction, the rollback operation is performed.

2) Distribution transaction

Once the monitoring module submits the transaction and the system receives it, the distribution module needs to be responsible for the specific transfer object of the transaction because the gateway supports different cross-chain modes. In relay mode, the distribution module sends transactions through the direct and relay chain's proxy modules. In the direct connection mode, it is possible to connect to the gateway of other application chains through the P2P network and send the corresponding transaction. The transactions in the relay chain mode participate in the consensus and are packaged into the block. Therefore, the relay chain light node module must synchronize and update the block header information. The synchronization module synchronizes all the transactions related to the relay chain block and its cross-chain gateway. For transactions synchronized by relay chain, it is also necessary to cooperate with light nodes to perform SPV verification of transactions to ensure the effectiveness of transactions.

3.5 Cross-Chain Interaction Protocol Standard

The general protocol IBTP specifies the initiator chain, receiver chain, and cross-chain transaction mode, verification strategy, signature and much other information of relevant cross-chain events and supports the interactive operation between the application chain and relay chain, application chain and application chain. Its structure is shown in the following table. The message of the application chain is converted into an IBTP structure through the gateway and submitted to the relay chain, and the relay chain performs the legitimacy verification and reliable routing of the cross-chain transaction through the IBTP content. Based on the IBTP, the gateway can convert the event data format thrown by different application chains into a unified structure. This is shown in Fig. 4.

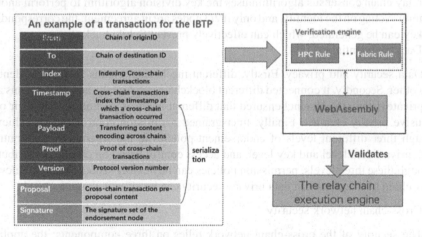

Fig. 4. Example transaction diagram of the IBTP structure

The cross-chain transfer protocol mainly focuses on the IBTP data structure, and the flow of the data structure between cross-chain transactions is based on several key features of the IBTP protocol: cross-chain service, cross-chain message proof and trust tree. Security performance analysis.

The paper suggests a multi-chain fusion model that relies on the relay chain, the network security of data transmission in the process of cross-chain transaction is ensured through the monitoring and acquisition operation of cross-chain gateways. The IBTP protocol enables secure transactions by facilitating interaction not only between the application chain and relay chain, but also among different application chains. This helps guarantee the security of transactions.

3.6 Security Analysis

This section provides security analysis for several common attack types in cross-chain network systems. For example, replay attack, internal and external data source attack, mutual authentication, man-in-the-middle attack, Sybil attack, generation attack, single point of failure, etc.

1) Man-in-the-middle attack: The communication data of the two sides of the communication is symmetrically encrypted by the session key, which solves the problem of private data leakage. Even if the data is hijacked, the attacker cannot decrypt the ciphertext to obtain valid information.
2) Replay attack: By intercepting and resending information, an adversary can deceive the system. In the proposed scheme, there are timestamps and sequence numbers as the basis of message freshness at different stages, such as cross-domain authentication and cross-chain transactions. Replay attacks can be easily identified if the system finds previously used random numbers or timeout timestamps in the message.
3) Sybil attack: In Sybil attack, the attacker relies on a single node with multiple identities to control the majority of nodes in the system to gain a voting advantage. The relay chain consensus algorithm uses the key division algorithm to perform anonymous voting on the identity, and only if 2/3 nodes are in agreement, the corresponding key can be generated, which can effectively prevent Sybil attacks
(1) Data confidentiality

Data security and privacy. Firstly, different mechanism chains are independent of each other. Secondly, it connected different blockchains separately, and relay chains and the private data in the channel ensured that different medical institutions had their own exclusive privacy channel. Finally, finer-grained permission control can be achieved through three different levels of endorsement policies in the smart contract: contract level, private data level and key level, and access control based on certificate attributes. Through these three levels, permission policies can be flexibly set according to relevant cross-chain transactions and data privacy security can be effectively guaranteed.

(2) Cross-chain network security

The security of the cross-chain network relies on three components: the application chain, the relay alliance chain, and the intermediate transmission channel. The application chain and relay alliance chain are partially protected by their own security mechanisms, and the security focuses on the intermediate transmission process between them. The transaction is a multi-step process to ensure atomicity and consistency, which involves multiple rounds of verification between the application chain and the relay consortium chain. The application chain events monitored, obtained and submitted to the relay alliance chain by the gateway are transactions that have been confirmed on the chain are trusted. The application chain can independently verify the events occurring in the relay alliance chain, eliminating the risk of the perpetrator tampering with the transaction instructions. Each transaction can only be transmitted in the network after passing through the cross-chain interaction protocol of the gateway, and the gateway is exclusive to an organization so that problems can be quickly detected. In summary, the secure communication between blockchains can be guaranteed.

(3) Cross-chain transactions security

Only when all the subordinate transaction of the transactions are completed the transaction will be successfully completed on the relay alliance chain and the application chain. If there is a problem in a sub-transaction, the corresponding rollback or cancellation of the transaction operation will be taken to ensure consistency and atomicity. The transactions and their subordinate transaction are recorded in a cross-chain transaction state table, which is managed by the state table alone, and different transactions do not interfere with each other to ensure isolation. As for persistence, blockchain data is inherently persistent. Only nodes of multiple organizations participating in the business can jointly endorse operating the mapping account, which ensures the security of cross-chain assets.

3.7 Performance Analysis

The performance analysis equipment configuration environment in this paper is shown in Table 1.

Table 1. Server configuration and fabric network configuration.

Guideline	configuration
operating system	Ubuntu 18. 04. 2 LTS
processor	Intel(R) Core(TM) i7-9750H CPU @ 2.60 GHz 2.60 GHz
RAM	16 GB
Hard disk	120 GB
Network bandwidth	10000 M/S
Fabric Version	V2.2.0
Consensus algorithm	Raft
Block generation mechanism	Batch Timeout: 2 s
	Max Message Count: 100
	Preferred Max Bytes: 2 MB
	Absolute Max Bytes: 98 MB

The system uses bitxhub's super-chain as the relay chain and its corresponding cross-chain gateway, and uses Hyperledger Fabric alliance chain as the application chain to build the cross-chain model architecture. Four of the nodes are selected, and the average response time of cross-chain transaction query and cross-chain transaction execution of the relay chain is calculated based on the time of receiving the cross-chain transaction to generate the block. The results are shown in Table 2.

Table 2. Efficiency of cross-chain transaction execution.

Node	Average response time/s	
	Transaction query	Cross-chain transactions
Node 1	2.684	3.157
Node 2	2.415	3.563
Node 3	2.457	4.941
Node 4	2.522	3.612

Apache JMeter is used as an automatic test and result report evaluation tool, and 300 cross-chain transaction execution response times in a certain period of time are tested by this tool. The test results are shown in Fig. 5.

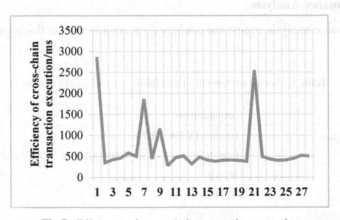

Fig.5. Efficiency of cross-chain transaction execution

The experiment in this section uses a server to build a Fabric network with 5 Orderer nodes AND 4 peer nodes (2 organizations, 2 nodes per organization) for testing, and the endorsement strategy is AND ('Org1.peer', 'Org2.peer'). The testing contract used in Fig. 6 is the officially provided marble case. Figure 5 illustrates that there is little performance difference between using private data within a channel and not using private data.

A total of 7 servers are used in the test in this section, of which three servers are used to build the relay alliance chain, two servers are used as the cross-chain gateway, and the other two servers are used to create two application chains, namely the Ethereum

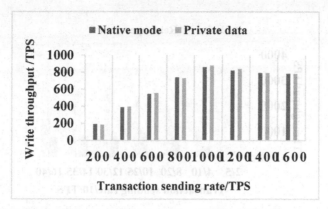

Fig.6. Performance comparison of using and without using private data

test network and the fabric alliance chain network, to simulate the real cross-chain scenario. There are three organizations in the relay alliance chain; one server deploys one organization, among which the sorting organization has five nodes, and the Ethereum organization and the fabric organization have four nodes each. The performance of four cross-chain contracts is tested. The transaction confirmation time of the application chain itself is not considered in the experiment, and the transaction is directly sent to the relay chain through the plug-in in the gateway. The investigation is set as follows: each group of tests sends transactions to the network for 1 min at a specific trade sending rate, and the number of clients is set to 10; that is, ten clients send transactions simultaneously. Figure 7 and Fig. 8 shows the throughput and latency of the read operation and write operation of asset exchange contract under different transaction sending rates. At first, the throughput of the write operation increases as the transaction sending rate increases, reaches the highest at 960TPS when the sending rate is 1000TPS, and then slightly decreases. At first, the average delay time decreases with the increase in the sending rate. When the sending rate exceeds 800TPS, the delay increases rapidly because when the transaction sending rate is higher than a certain level, there will be a backlog of outstanding transactions. The higher the sending rate is, the more backlog there will be, leading to an increase in the delay of transaction processing. The throughput of the read operation is the same as the sending rate, the maximum is maintained at about 3000TPS, and the delay is always held at 0.1s. The performance of the asset transfer, information payment and information exchange contracts is almost the same as that of the asset exchange contract and will not be shown separately.

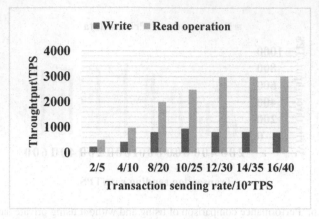

Fig.7. Throughput evaluation of asset exchange contract

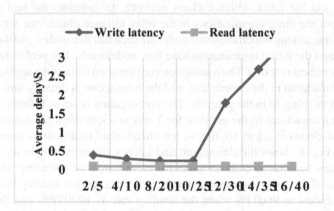

Fig.8. Delayed evaluation of asset exchange contracts

4 Conclusion

The paper introduces a multi-chain fusion model that utilizes a relay chain construction, which constructs a relay alliance chain to operate the entire cross-chain network in the way of chain governance. By using a gateway, interaction protocol, RAFT consensus algorithm, endorsement mechanism, channel allocation strategy, block weight allocation scheme and other technologies and schemes, the rules and ways of application chains participating in cross-chain interaction are formulated, which provide a safe and reliable technology platform for the interoperation between application chains. The gateway and the common protocol IBPT is utilized to enhance the security and privacy of cross-chain transactions. Finally, experiments and analysis show that the proposed multi-link fusion model has good performance and a high level of security.

Acknowledgements. This work was supported by the National Natural ScienceFoundation of China under Grant (No. 62272090), the Doctor Scientific Research Fund of Zhengzhou University of Light Industry (No. 2021BSJJ033), the Key Scientific Research Project of Colleges and Universities in Henan Province (CN) (No. 22A413010), the Foundation of State Key Laboratory of Public Big Data (No. PBD2023-25)

References

1. Kim, Y., Sun, J., Yu, H., Jiang, X.: Federated tensor factorization for computational phenotyping. In: KDD: Proceedings of the International Conference on Knowledge Discovery & Data Mining (2017)
2. Zhang, C., Zhu, L., Xu, C., Lu, R.: PPDP: an efficient and privacy-preserving disease prediction scheme in cloud-based e-healthcare system. Future Gener. Comput. Syst. **79**, 16–25 (2018)
3. Wang, C., Cheng, J., Sang, X., Li, G., Guan, X.: Privacy preserving in blockchain: state of the art and prospects. Computer Research and Development (2021)
4. Schulte, S., Sigwart, M., Frauenthaler, P., Borkowski, M.: Towards blockchain interoperability. In: Di Ciccio, C., Gabryelczyk, R., García-Bañuelos, L., Hernaus, T., Hull, R., Indihar Štemberger, M., Kő, A., Staples, M. (eds.) BPM 2019. LNBIP, vol. 361, pp. 3–10. Springer, Cham (2019). https://doi.org/10.1007/978-3-030-30429-4_1
5. Li, C., Dong, M., Li, J., Xu, G., Chen, X., et al.: Efficient medical big data management with keyword-searchable encryption in healthchain. IEEE Syst. J. **16**(4), 5521–5532 (2022)
6. Zhu, S., Li, C., Huang, R., Li, W.: Secure sharing model and mechanism of medical data based on block chain. Computer Technology and Development (2020)
7. Lu, X., Fu, S.: A trusted data access control scheme combining attribute based encryption and blockchain. Netinfo Secur. **21**, 7–14 (2021)
8. Malamas, V., Kotzanikolaou, P., Dasaklis, T.K., Burmester, M.: A Hierarchical Multi Blockchain for Fine Grained Access to Medical Data. IEEE Access **8**, 134393–134412 (2020)
9. Ma, Z., Meng, J., Wang, J., Shan, Z.: Blockchain based decentralized authentication modeling scheme in edge and IoT environment. IEEE Internet Things J. **8**(4), 2116–2123 (2020)
10. Li, C., Guo, Y., Dong, M., Xu, G., Chen, X., et al.: Efficient certificateless authenticated key agreement for blockchain-enabled internet of medical things. Comput. Mater. Continua **75**(1), 2043–2059 (2023)
11. Li, C., Zhang, T., Chen, X., Li, J.: An efficient anti-quantum lattice-based blind signature for blockchain-enabled systems. Inf. Sci. **546**, 253–264 (2021)
12. Li, F., Li, Z., Zhao, H.: Research on the progress of blockchain cross chain technology. J. Softw. **30**(6), 1649–1660 (2019)
13. Dong, G., Zhang, Z., Li, H., Bai, J., Hao, Y., et al.: Regulatory system architecture and key mechanisms of blockchain-based heterogeneous identity alliance. Commun. Technol. **53**(02), 401–413 (2020)
14. Li, C., Dong, M., Li, J., Xu, G., Chen, X., et al.: Healthchain: secure EMRs management and trading in distributed healthcare service system. IEEE Internet Things J. **8**(9), 7192–7202 (2020)
15. Shen, M., Liu, H., Zhu, L., Xu, K., Yu, H., et al.: Blockchain-assisted secure device authentication for cross-domain industrial IoT. IEEE J. Sel. Areas Commun. **38**(5), 942–954 (2020)
16. Li, C., Jiang, B., Guo, Y., Xin, X.: Efficient group blind signature for medical data anonymous authentication in blockchain-enabled IoMT. Comput. Mater. Continua **76**(1), 591–606 (2023)

17. Li, C., Dong, M., Xin, X., Li, J., Chen, X.B., Ota, K.: Efficient privacy-preserving in IoMT with blockchain and lightweight secret sharing. IEEE Internet Things J. **10**(24), 22051–22064 (2023)
18. Shao, S., Chen, F., Xiao, X., Gu, W., Lu, Y., et al.: IBE-BCIOT: an IBE based cross-chain communication mechanism of blockchain in IoT. World Wide Web **24**(5), 1665–1690 (2021)
19. Xie, T., Zhang, Y., Gai, K., Xu, L.: Cross-chain-based decentralized identity for mortgage loans. In: Qiu, H., Zhang, C., Fei, Z., Qiu, M., Kung, S.-Y. (eds.) KSEM 2021. LNCS (LNAI), vol. 12817, pp. 619–633. Springer, Cham (2021). https://doi.org/10.1007/978-3-030-82153-1_51
20. Zhang, H., Chen, X., Lan, X., Jin, H., Cao, Q.: BTCAS: a blockchain-based thoroughly cross-domain authentication scheme. J. Inf. Secur. Appl. **55**, 102538 (2020)

A Blockchain-Based Proxy Re-Encryption Scheme with Cryptographic Reverse Firewall for IoV

Chunhua Jin$^{(\boxtimes)}$, Zhiwei Chen, Wenyu Qin, Kaijun Sun, and Guanhua Chen

Faculty of Computer and Software Engineering, Huaiyin Institute of Technology, Huai'an 233003, China
xajch0206@163.com

Abstract. As the Internet of vehicles (IoV) technology develops, it promotes the intelligent interaction among vehicles, road side instrument, and the environment. Nevertheless, it also brings vehicle information security challenges. In recent years, vehicle data sharing is suffering to Algorithm Substitution Attacks (ASA), which means backdoor adversaries can carry out filtering attacks through data sharing. Therefore, this paper designs a blockchain-based proxy re-encryption scheme with a cryptographic reverse firewall (BIBPR-CRF) for IoV. In our proposal, the CRF can promise the internal safety of vehicle units. More specifically, it can prevent ASA attacks while ensuring chosen plaintext attack (CPA)-security. Meanwhile, the proxy re-encryption (PRE) algorithm can provide the confidential sharing and secure operation of data. Moreover, we use a consortium blockchain service center (CBSC) to store the first ciphertext and re-encrypt it with smart contracts on the blockchain, which can avoid single point of failure and achieve higher efficiency compared to proxy servers. Finally, we evaluate the performance of our scheme in terms of communication cost, computational cost, and energy consumption. Compared with the other three schemes, our proposal has the highest efficiency and is the most suitable for the IoV application.

Keywords: Internet of Vehicles · Proxy re-encryption · Blockchain-based · Security · Cryptographic reverse firewall

1 Introduction

IoV has been continuously developing in the era of big data. This technology allows vehicle sensors and roadside units to collect, analyze, and store data in real time. This capability enables vehicles to communicate with each other and service providers in a self-organized manner [1]. Meanwhile, IoV routing protocols are essential in monitoring connections to achieve high-quality communication between vehicles [2]. Ahmed Elkhalil et al. [3] proposed a method that takes advantage of RSUs attached to the Internet, which offers various data types to Vehicular Ad hoc Networks (VANET) users. In their paper, RSU, vehicle nodes,

H. Yang and R. Lu (Eds.): FCS 2023, CCIS 1992, pp. 19–33, 2024.
https://doi.org/10.1007/978-981-99-9331-4_2

and consortium blockchain service center are considered the underlying the architecture of IoV. The CBSC is responsible for storing, managing, verifying, and processing data collected by vehicle unit nodes and transmitted by sink nodes.

IoV utilizes wireless communication sensors installed in the vehicle to store local sensitive information through an onboard unit (OBU). Roadside Units (RSU) are wireless communication devices positioned in large numbers on both sides of roads and used as service providers for vehicles. The primary function of RSU is to collect ciphertexts sent by vehicles and transmit them to the CBSC for storage. Similarly, RSU sends user application information messages to the CBSC for identity verification and searching information. The Dedicated Short-Range Communications protocol (DSRC) is applied in Vehicular Ad hoc Networks (VANET) to communicate between vehicles and RSUs. Wireless sensor technology provides the vehicle's location, driving information status, and safety measures [4]. However, the rapid growth in Wireless Sensor Networks (WSNs) poses a significant challenge to the security of IoV. Thus, IoV must focus on processing significant amounts of data efficiently and protecting it from internal and external attacks that threaten data confidentiality, integrity, and privacy.

Blockchain is a way of storing and sharing data across different parties using encryption and verification methods [5]. It can achieve immutability because each block is linked to the previous one and has a unique code (hash) based on the SHA-256 algorithm. Blockchain has many applications in various fields, such as IoT, grid computing, IoV, medical systems, electronic voting, and WSN [6,7]. In blockchain, everyone keeps a copy of the same data and agrees on how to update it according to some rules. And it uses blocks as data units that cannot be changed or corrupted easily. The blocks are arranged in a chain-like structure using cryptography. A node (party) is chosen to record the transactions using a method called Proof of Stake (PoS). The other nodes also participate in storing, verifying, and maintaining the most recent block data. Once the data is confirmed, it can only be accessed by authorized parties. Therefore, blockchain has features such as openness, programmability, consistent data storage, and resistance to tampering and denial, which can be used to manage public information of vehicles in VANETs [8].

Cryptographic algorithms are supposed to work in a certain way, but sometimes they may be tampered with or compromised by an enemy. For instance, an insider attacker can launch an exfiltration attack, which means stealing secret information from any algorithm that has been hacked. This kind of attack was used by the NSA to access a lot of sensitive data from people by putting backdoors in cryptographic protocols, as revealed by the Snowden incident [9]. Other severe flaws in cryptographic modules have also shown that people's privacy is at risk. For example,Bellare et al. [10] studied a specific type of exfiltration attack called algorithm substitution attack (ASA), where an attacker can spy on users by changing an encryption scheme. They showed that this can be done with a standard scheme used on the Internet. One possible solution is to use cryptographic reverse firewalls (CRF), which were proposed by Mironov et al. [11] in 2015. CRF is a system for modifying messages from external networks sent or received by users. Therefore, even if an attacker intercepts a message from the backdoor, they cannot know the actual content of the message. However, we have designed a BIBRE-CRF scheme that allows someone to delegate their decryption permissions to others. We would like to know if we can combine CRF and PRE to protect data from leakage attacks. In this article, we explored this issue and provided a positive answer.

1.1   Related Work

PRE was proposed by Blaze et al. [12] In the PRE scheme, the data owner encrypts plaintext information into ciphertext and sends it to the proxy server. The proxy server re-encrypts the first ciphertext with the re-encrypt Key. The re-encrypted ciphertexts can be decrypted by data owner as well as recipient. In 2006, Matthew Green et al. [13] proposed an identity-based PRE. In this scheme, they proposed a scheme where a semi trusted proxy converts Alice's ciphertext into Bob's ciphertext without seeing the underlying plaintext. This approach solves the identity based PRE problem, where the data owner only need to know the identity of the recipient. It can also avoid certificate management issues in PKI environments. In 2021, Manikandan et al. [14] applied PRE algorithm to IoV and processed complex and subtle data by encoding information. The proposed approach solves the Double Decomposition Problem (DDP) using semi nearing, it can also solve the enormous difficulties encountered in searching for chaotic information, providing improved security with lesser computational overheads. To address security issues during communication, Green et al. [13] presented two identity-based PRE (IBPRE) schemes in the random oracle model. One is a unidirectional CPA-secure multihop PRE scheme, in which the ciphertext length increases linearly with the number of recipients. The second is a unidirectional CCA-secure single-hop PRE scheme, which utilizes signature technology. Then, Aloni et al. [15] proposed an article, "What about Bob? The Inadequacy of CPA Security for Proxy Re-encryption". They proposed an honest re-encryption attack (HRA), which is a strengthening of CPA security better captures the goals of PRE. Inspired by Aloni's scheme, Willy et al. [16] proved HRA-secure PRE in the standard model. They advanced the studies on HRA-secure PRE for the (Attribute-based) PRE setting. Their scheme formalized the definition of HRA-secure Key-Policy ABPRE and proposed a construction which is quantum-safe and secure in the standard model. However, many PRE schemes, especially IBPRE and ABPRE schemes, are not suitable for resource-constrained sensor devices in WBAN because the length of the ciphertext or re-encryption key is too long, and the computational cost is too high.

Fan et al. [17] designed a model in which the encrypted data is uploaded to the cloud, and access policies on the data are stored on the blockchain as transactions. And in 2019, Ahsan et al. [6] also proposed a blockchain-based PRE scheme for IoT data sharing. They established runtime dynamic smart contracts between the sensor and the data user without the involvement of a trusted third party. It also uses an efficient proxy re-encryption scheme that allows data to be visible only to the owner and the person present in the smart contract. Singh and Kim [18] presented a blockchain-based model for sharing data in vehicular networks and also enable secure communication among vehicles. However, the use of public blockchain does not work well in peer-to-peer (P2P) data sharing among vehicles due to the high cost involved in establishing a public blockchain in resource-constrained vehicles.

Considering that the proxy server may be malicious during data transmission and storage, it can forge information and transmit it to authorized parties. We can conclude that none of the above solutions can resist backdoor attacks. In 2015, a new concept named CRF was introduced by Mironov [11]. Even if a computer is compromised, the CRF can guarantee the security of the associated cryptographic scheme. And it can also prevent the leakage of confidential information from a compromised computer. Subsequently, Zhou et al. [19] proposed a certificateless public key encryption with CRF which is proved to achieve indistinguishable against chosen plaintext attack. And then, in 2022, they first proposed a new IBPRE scheme for cloud-assisted wireless body area networks [20]. This solution can avoid certificate management issues in PKI and also resist filtering attacks like ASA. Compared with above methods, the CRF is stackable. Users can set multiple CRFs, and their secret message's security can be guaranteed as long as at least one of the CRFs works correctly. Therefore, CRF is more universal and practical. This is the main reason why we chose the CRF to resist ASA in IBPRE.

1.2 Motivation and Contribution

In order to resist the backdoor attack of the IoV information sharing service and prevent the single point of failure problem of the cloud server, we construct a blockchain-based proxy re-encryption scheme with CRF. In this scheme, we use smart contracts on the blockchain to replace proxy servers for re-encryption computing, thus improving information security and computing efficiency. Compared with the existing IBPRE schemes, our scheme can meet the following characteristics simultaneously.

- We combine an efficient proxy re-encryption algorithm with blockchain technology to ensure the confidentiality, correctness, and unforgeability of IoV without relying on any trusted entities. In addition, the data is stored as ciphertexts on CBSC, so the security of the data, and user privacy will not be compromised.
- We use smart contracts on the blockchain for proxy re-encryption operations without questioning whether participants have changed information due to personal interests. At the same time, compared with the proxy server in the traditional way, this way of using smart contracts can avoid a single point of failure, improve security and also be very efficient.
- By extending the conventional IBPRE framework, we introduce the idea of the re-randomization in CRFs so that a re-encryption key that be re-randomized by a CRF does not match the ciphertexts stored in cloud servers. This process

is unrecognizable to entities other than the CRF. Therefore, the original re-encryption key and the updated re-encryption key are indistinguishable for attackers.

- It is able to resist exfiltration attacks (e.g. ASA) from backdoors, and exfilt-ration-resistant is provided. Currently, there is no solution for resisting the ASA. Through analyzing other resist-ASA methods, we found that the CRF is more versatile and practical because CRFs are stackable. The actual operation of CRFs is agnostic to the other entities. Meanwhile, ASA can be resisted if one CRF is not compromised. Exfiltration-resistant means if an adversary obtains the secret random number selected by a user, it will not be able to know the user's private messages.
- The proposed scheme has been proven to have strong security. Compared with similar schemes, our scheme has higher computation performance and lower communication overhead.

1.3 Organization

The Bilinear pairing, blockchain, samrt contract and CRF are introduced in Sect. 2. Our scheme is shown in Sect. 3. And we describe the analysis of the scheme in Sect. 4. We give the performance in Sect. 5. Finally, the conclusions are given in Sect. 6.

2 Preliminaries

In this section, we briefly introduce bilinear pairing, blockchain, smart contract, and properties of CRF.

2.1 Bilinear Pairing

Let G_1 and G_2 be two multiplication groups. Prime q is their order, and g is the generator of G_1. We can say $\hat{e} : G_1 \times G_1 \to G_2$ is a bilinear pairing if it meets the following properties:

1. Bilinearity: For $\forall (g_1, g_2) \in G_1$, $\forall (a, b) \in Z_q^*$, $\hat{e}(g_1^a, g_2^b) = \hat{e}(g_1, g_2)^{ab}$ must be true.
2. Non-degeneracy: For $\exists (g_1, g_2) \in G_1$ and 1_{G_2} be the identity element of G_2, there have $\hat{e}(g_1, g_2) \neq 1_{G_2}$.
3. Computability: For $\forall (g_1, g_2) \in G_1$, there is an effective algorithm to compute $\hat{e}(g_1, g_2)$.

2.2 Blockchain and Smart Contract

Blockchain is a kind of chain data structure that combines data blocks with time sequences [21]. A smart contract was a concept proposed by Nick Szabo [22], which is almost the same age as the internet. He defines a smart contract as a set of commitments defined in digital form, including agreements in which contract participants can execute these commitments automatically [23]. In this article, we refer to smart contracts as chaincodes, which are programs that are deployed and run on the blockchain network. The chaincode presets some conditions and rules to trigger the execution of the chaincode under certain events and conditions. The goal of it is to generate ledger data on the blockchain, which means that all operations on the blockchain data are completed by the chaincode. Moreover, security policies will be automatically invoked through chaincodes.

2.3   Cryptographic Reverse Firewall (CRF)

Let $\mathcal{W}$ be a CRF. $P = (receive, next, output)$ be a party, we can say $\mathcal{W}$ is a CRF for P if it meets the following properties. Here, r is an initial public parameter, m is the transmitted message.

$$\mathcal{W} \circ P := (receive_{\mathcal{W} \circ P}(\sigma, \mathcal{W}(m))),$$
$$next_{\mathcal{W} \circ P}(\sigma) = \mathcal{W}(next_P(\sigma)),$$
$$output_{\mathcal{W} \circ P}(\sigma) = output_P(\sigma).$$

A qualified CRF needs to satisty the following properties:

– Maintain functionality. If the user's computer works correctly, the CRF will not break the functionality of the cryptographic algorithms.
– Preserve security. No matter how the user's computer is disturbed by an attacker, the use of the CRF will remain as secure as the correct execution of cryptographic algorithms.
– Resist the exfiltration. No matter how to run the user's computer, the CRF will prevent the computer from leaking confidential information.

Functionality-Maintaining CRFs. Let $\mathcal{W}$ be a CRF. Meanwhile P is a party, $\mathcal{P}$ is a scheme, $\mathcal{F}$ is a function. We can say $\mathcal{W}$ maintains $\mathcal{F}$ for P in $\mathcal{P}$ if $\mathcal{W}^k \circ P$ maintain $\mathcal{F}$ for P in $\mathcal{P}$ for any polynomially bounded $k \geq 1$. When $P, \mathcal{P}, \mathcal{F}$ are clear, we can say $\mathcal{W}$ maintains functionality. Here, $\mathcal{W} \circ P = \mathcal{W} \circ (\mathcal{W}^{k-1} \circ P)$.

Weak Security-Preserving CRFs. $\mathcal{S}$ for P in $\mathcal{P}$ against $\mathcal{F}$-maintaining adversaries if $\mathcal{P}(P \Rightarrow \mathcal{W} \circ P^*)$ satisfies $\mathcal{S}$. When $P, \mathcal{P}, \mathcal{F}$, and $\mathcal{S}$ are clear, $\mathcal{W}$ maintains weak security. Here, P^* is the functionality-maintaining adversarial Implementation and $\mathcal{P}_{\mathcal{W} \circ P^*}$ means using $\mathcal{W} \circ P^*$ to replace P.

Weak Exfiltration-Resistant CRFs. Let $\mathcal{W}$ be a CRF. Meanwhile P is a party, $\mathcal{P}$ is a scheme, $\mathcal{F}$ is a function, $\mathcal{S}$ be a security requirement. We can say $\mathcal{W}$ is weak exfiltration-resistant for P_1 against P_2 in $\mathcal{P}$ if there is no probabilistic polynomial time adversary $\mathcal{A}$ can break the game **LEAK** $(\mathcal{P}, P_1, P_2, \mathcal{W}, \lambda)$. Here, λ is the security parameter, and P_2 is a $\mathcal{F}$-maintaining adversary.

3   Our Scheme

3.1   BIBPR-CRF

A BIBPR-CRF scheme consists of ten algorithms: $Setup$, $W_{PKG} \cdot Setup$, $KeyGen$, $W_{PKG} \cdot KeyGen$, Enc, $W_{DO} \cdot ENC$, $ReKeyGen$, $W_{DO} \cdot ReKeyGen$, $ReEnc$, and Dec.

- $Setup$: Given a security parameter k, this algorithm outputs a system public parameter par and a master secret key s.
- $W_{PKG} \cdot Setup$: PKG's CRF generates a random number algorithm. Given par', this algorithm outputs a new system public parameter par' under a random number.
- $KeyGen$: Given a user's ID, this algorithm outputs a user's public key Q_U and a private key SK_U (here $U \in \{DO, DR\}$).
- $W_{PKG} \cdot KeyGen$: W_{PKG} runs the algorithm to re-random user's private key and outputs a randomized user's private key SK'_U.
- Enc: Given a message M, par' and ID, this algorithm can output a ciphertext C_{DO}.
- $W_{DO} \cdot ENC$: It is a randomized encryption algorithm operated by the data owner's CRF W_{DO}. Given par' and C_{DO}, this algorithm outputs a randomized ciphertext C'_{DO}.
- $ReKeyGen$: Given a data receipt DR, this algorithm outputs a re-encryption key $rk_{ID_{DO} \to ID_{DR}}$ under par', the data receipt's public key PK_{DR} and the randomized data owner's private key SK_{DO}.
- $W_{DO} \cdot ReKeyGen$: W_{DO} runs the algorithm to re-random the re-encryption key $rk_{ID_{DO} \to ID_{DR}}$ and outputs a randomized $rk'_{ID_{DO} \to ID_{DR}}$.
- $ReEnc$: Given par', C'_{DO} and $rk'_{ID_{DO} \to ID_{DR}}$. This algorithm outputs a re-encrypted ciphertext C_{DR}.
- Dec: For ciphertexts encrypted only by the data owner, and re-encrypted ciphertexts encrypted jointly by the data owner and the smart contract on CBSC. There are two decryption steps:
  Non Re-encryptied ciphertext: Given par' and C'_{DO}, this algorithm outputs the corresponding plaintext under a random number and SK_{DO}.
  Re-encrypted ciphertext: Given par' and C_{DR}, this algorithm outputs the corresponding plaintext under the randomized receipt's private key SK'_{DR}.

This section mainly introduces our proposed scheme that one CRF W_{PKG} is deployed on a PKG's side and the other CRF is on a data owner's side. To provide CRFs for the PKG, we use the malleability of keys. The most important step is the operation on the PKG's public key P_{pub} and users' private key SK_U ($U \in \{DO, DR\}$). Here, DO and DR represent a data owner and a data recipient, respectively.

To provide CRFs for the data owner, our idea is to use the key's malleability in $W_{DO} \cdot ReKeyGen$ and encryption's re-randomization in $W_{DO} \cdot ENC$. These two processes can be seen as the re-randomization process of re-encrypted key and ciphertext. Here, par' is the necessary system parameter.

A BIBPR-CRF scheme is described as follows, which includes ten algorithm (Figs. 1 and 2).

Table 1. Explanation of symbols

Symbol	Description	Symbol	Description
G_1	An addition group	G_2	A multiplicative group
k	A security parameter	s	A master private key of PKG
P	A generator of G_1 and G_2	P_{pub}	A master public key of PKG
q	The prime order of G_1 and G_2	U	$U \in \{DO, DR\}$
H_i	A one-way hash function ($i = 1, 2$)	SK_U	U's private key
Q_U	U's public key	W_{PKG}	PKG's reverse firewall
W_{DO}	DO's reverse firewall	α	W_{PKG}'s random number
β	W_{DO}'s random number	r	DO's random number
$rk_{ID_{DO} \rightarrow ID_{DR}}$	Re-encrypt Key	C_{DO}	Ciphertext
$rk'_{ID_{DO} \rightarrow ID_{DR}}$	Re-randomized re-encrypt Key	C'_{DO}	Re-randomized ciphertext
C_{DR}	Re-encrypt ciphertext	M	Plaintext
$\hat{e}(P, P)$	Bilinear pairing operation		

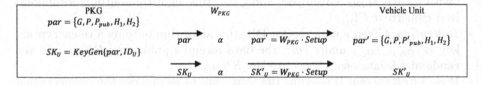

Fig. 1. A BIBPR-CRF scheme with a PKG's CRF

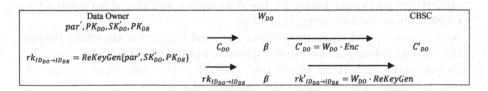

Fig. 2. A BIBPR-CRF scheme with a Data Owner's CRF

Setup: There is a security parameter k, PKG selects an additive group G_1 on the elliptic curve and a multiplicative group G_2, q is the order of the group and q is a prime number, and P is the generator of the group G_1 and G_2. Define three secure password hash functions $H_1 : \{0,1\}^* \rightarrow G_1$, $H_2 : G_2 \times \{0,1\}^* \rightarrow G_1$. PKG selects the system master key $s \in Z_q^*$ and calculates the corresponding master public key $P_{pub} = sP$. PKG sends system parameters $par = \{G, P, P_{pub}, H_1, H_2\}$ to W_{PKG} and keeps the master key s;

$W_{PKG} \cdot Setup$: W_{PKG} selects a random α to calculate $P'_{pub} = s\alpha P$ and sends $par' = \{G, P, P'_{pub}, H_1, H_2\}$ to all vehicle users;

$KeyGen$: Given a VU's $ID_U \in \{0,1\}^*$, PKG calculates its private key $SK_U = sQ_U$, here $Q_U = H_1(ID_U)$. Then PKG sends private key to its CRF W_{PKG};

$W_{PKG} \cdot KeyGen$: When PKG's CRF receives SK_U, it selects a random α and calculate $SK'_U = s\alpha Q_U$, and sends it to user in a secure way;

Enc: Given a message M, par', and Q_{DO}. DO selects a random $r \in Z_q^*$, generates $C_{DO} = \{C_1, C_2\} = \{rP, M \cdot \hat{e}(P'_{pub}, Q_{DO})^r\}$. Then DO sends this ciphertext C_{DO} to W_{DO};

$W_{DO} \cdot Enc$: When W_{DO} receives C_{DO}. It selects $\beta \in Z_q^*$ and generates a randomized ciphertext: $C'_{DO} = \{C'_1, C'_2\} = \{\beta P + C_1, C_2 \cdot \hat{e}(P'_{pub}, \beta Q_{DO})\}$. Whereafter, W_{DO} sends C'_{DO} to CBSC and saves it as meta-data;

$ReKeyGen$: Given a par', β and PK_{DR}. DO authorizes the legal rights of user DR by generating the proxy re-encryption key of DR: $rk_{ID_{DO} \to ID_{DR}} = H_2(\hat{e}(SK'_{DO}, Q_{DO}), ID_{DO}, ID_{DR}) - SK'_{DO}$. After that, DO sends it to W_{DO};

$W_{DO} \cdot ReKeyGen$: W_{DO} receives $rk_{ID_{DO} \to ID_{DR}}$ and further computes it to $rk'_{ID_{DO} \to ID_{DR}} = H_2(\hat{e}(SK'_{DO}, Q_{DO}), ID_{DO}, ID_{DR}) - SK'_{DO} - \beta Q_{DO}$, then sends it to CBSC.

$ReEnc$: After the smart constract on CBSC receives $rk'_{ID_{DO} \to ID_{DR}}$ and C'_{DO}, it will re-encrypt the ciphertext to

$$C_{DR} = \{C''_1, C''_2\}$$
$$= \{(r + \beta)P, M \cdot \hat{e}((r + \beta)P, (\alpha s + \beta)Q_{DO}) \cdot \hat{e}((r + \beta)P, H_2(\hat{e}(SK'_{DO}, Q_{DO}),$$

$$ID_{DO}, ID_{DR}) - SK'_{DO} - \beta Q_{DO})\}$$
$$= \{(r + \beta)P, M \cdot \hat{e}((r + \beta)P, H_2(\hat{e}(SK'_{DO}, Q_{DO}), ID_{DO}, ID_{DR}))\}$$

that can be decrypted by SK_{DR}.

Then the smart constract sends the re-randomized ciphertext to DR.

Dec: For C''_{DO} which can only be decrypted by the dataowner and C_{DR} which can only be decrypted by DR, there are two algorithms as follows:

Non re-encrypted ciphertext: When the data owner wants to decrypt the ciphertext, C_{DO} is first sent by smart contract to W_{DO}. Then, W_{DO} reverses $W_{DO} \cdot Enc$ by computing $C''_{DO} = \{D_1, D_2\} = \{C'_1, C'_2 \cdot \hat{e}(C'_1, -\beta Q_{DO})\} = \{(r + \beta)P, M \cdot \hat{e}((r + \beta)P, \alpha s Q_{DO})\}$. Then, W_{DO} sends it to DO. DO can encrypt the ciphertext:

$$M = D_2 / \hat{e}(D_1, SK'_{DR})$$

Re-encrypted ciphertext: When the recipient wants to decrypt the ciphertext, C_{DR} is sent by smart contract to DR, Then, DR can encrypt the ciphertext:

$$M = C_2^{''}/\hat{e}(C_1^{''}, H_2(\hat{e}(Q_{DO}, SK_{DR}'), ID_{DO}, ID_{DR}))$$

For the function of W_{PKG} in our scheme, it guarantees the confidentiality of a public parameter s and users' private key SK_U after PKG is compromised.

- **It can maintain functionality.** When the master secret key s is leaked, the adversary can forge the public parameter and obtain a user's private key by its identity. In our scheme, we use α to randomize s and SK_U for avoiding this situation. For the function of the W_{DO} in our scheme, we summarize the following parts.
- **It can resist information exfiltration.** Backdoor attacks can lead to information exfiltration. For example, when the random number r used for encryption is leaked, the adversary can use r to get the plaintext. However, the leakage of random numbers will lead to the leakage of user's secret information, which will not happen in our scheme. Because W_{DO} uses a random number β to randomize the ciphertext. Even if the adversary gets r, it cannot use it to obtain the user's private messages. Therefore, the CRF protects users' information confidentiality.
- **It can resist the forgery of the transmitted message by a malicious adversary.** A malicious adversary can forge the data owner and generates a spam M^* by computing $C_{DO}^* = Enc(par, PK_{DO}, M^*)$; $C_{DR}^* = ReEnc(par, rk_{ID_{DO} \to ID_{DR}}, C_{DO}^*)$, and sends C_{DR} to DR for misleading him. However, the malicious adversary forges fake ciphertexts that can be decrypted by DR, which will not happen in our scheme. Because the secret number β is used to randomize a re-encryption key. And our Re-encryption algorithm is performed through smart contracts. Therefore, the ciphertext C_{DR} corresponding to $rk_{ID_{DO} \to ID_{DR}}$ cannot be deduced only from PK_{DO}.

4   Analysis of the Scheme

In this section, we will explain the security analysis of our scheme.

Theorem 1. The CRFs for the PKG and data owner in our scheme maintain functionality, preserves weak security, and resists weak exfiltration. Resists weak exfiltration means when faced with an adversary who launches the ASA that does not affect normal functioning, our scheme can be resistant to information leakage.

Definition 1 (CPA security for BIBPR-CRF). We say that a BIBPR-CRF scheme is $(\epsilon, t, q_{sk}, q_{en}, q_{rk})$-CPA secure if no polynomially bounded adversary $\mathcal{A}$ has a non-negligible advantage against the challenger $\mathcal{C}$ in the $Game\triangle$. **Game LEAK** is a BIBPR-CRF ASA game, which means the adversary can replace any algorithm other than the algorithm parts of CRF operation, and then launch the attack on the system.

Definition 2 (Weak exfiltration-resistant for CRF). We say that a BIBPR-CRF protocol is weak $(\epsilon, t, q_{sk}, q_{re}, q_{rk})$-exfiltration-resistant secure if no polynomially bounded adversary $\mathcal{A}$ has a non-negligible advantage against the challenger $\mathcal{C}$ in the **Game LEAK**.

Proof. Due to the limited length of conference articles, the detailed security analysis can be found in the complete version, or you can contact the corresponding author.

5   Performance

In this section, we choose three CPA-secure PRE schemes that are IBP [20], P2B [24] and IPV2 [25], then compare the communication cost, computation cost, and energy consumption with them. First, for the communication cost, we use RK represent the re-encryption key, C_{DO} represents the ciphertext that only be decrypted by data owner, C_{DR} represents the ciphertext that only be decrypted by data receiver, $|G_1|$, $|G_2|$, and $|Z_q|$ represents the bits of an element in a cyclic addition group $|G_1|$, a multiplicative group $|G_2|$ and $|Z_q|$, respectively. n in P2B represents the number of sub-keys. For the computation cost, we use M to represent the point multiplication in G_1, use E to represent the exponentiation of G_2, and P represents pairing computation. Considering that these three computations take up most of the operation time, so that we can ignore other operations. As can be seen from Table 1, P2B is special in these schemes because it contains a variable n. The communication cost and computation cost of P2B will increase linearly with the increase of n. However, Sumana [24] pointed out that it needs not to set n be a very large number. In general, $n = 10$ will achieve the purpose of the leakage resilient. Even if $n = 10$, the communication cost and computation cost of P2B are much higher than other schemes. To maximize the advantage of P2B, we set $n = 1$ here.

We compare IBP, P2B and IPV2 with our scheme and give a quantitative analysis for them. In the same system environment, we use the equipment: ATmega128 8-bit processor, clocked at 7.3728 MHz, 4 KB RAM, and 128 KB ROM. From scheme [26], we can get the computational time of various kinds of computations: the pairing operation takes 1.9 s, the exponentiation operation in G_2 takes 0.9 s, and a point multiplication operation takes 0.81 s using the supersingular curve $y^2 + y = x^3 + x$ with an embedding degree 4 and implementing η_T pairing: $E(F_{2^{271}}) \times E(F_{2^{271}}) \rightarrow F_{2^{4 \cdot 271}}$, which is equivalent to the 80-bit security level. Therefore, in different phases, the communication and computational time of IBP, P2B, IPV2 and our scheme is shown in Table 2.

Assuming that the MICA2 has a power level of 3.0 V, the current draw during transmitting mode, active mode, and receiving mode is 27 mA, 8.0 mA, and 10.0 mA, respectively, with a data rate of 12.4 kbps. Therefore, in different phases, the computation time and total cost of IBP, P2B, IPV2 and our scheme is shown in Table 3.

For the communication cost, we use a curve over the the binary field $F_{2^{271}}$ with G_1 of 252 bits prime order. The size of an element in group G_1 is 542

Table 2. .

Performance Comparison				
Scheme	IBP [20]	P2B [24]	IPV2 [25]	Our
RekeyGen	5M+5E+2P	$(n+5)M^{-1}+M$	4M+7E+P	M+P
Enc	5M+6E+3P	5M-1	2M+6E+P	6M+3P
ReEnc	M+P	M+P	3M+E+8P	M+P
Dec	2M+2P	3M+3P	6M+6E+8P	M+2P
RK	$2\|G_1\|+\|G_2\|$	$2\|G_1\|+\|G_2\|+\|Z_q\|$	$5\|G_1\|+\|G_2\|+\|Z_q\|$	$\|G_2\|$
C_{DO}	$\|G_1\|+\|G_2\|$	$\|G_2\|$	$4\|G_1\|+\|G_2\|+\|Z_q\|$	$\|G_2\|$
C_{DR}	$2\|G_1\|+2\|G_2\|$	$\|G_2\|$	$5\|G_1\|+2\|G_2\|+2\|Z_q\|$	$\|G_2\|$

bits and can be reduced to 34 bytes by standard compression technique [27]. Similarly, the size of an element in group G_2 is 1084 bits and can be reduced to 136 bytes, the size of Z_p^* can be reduced to 32 bytes. Therefore, in terms of communication cost overhead during the ReKeyGen phase, IBP, P2B, IPV2, and our solutions are: $2|G_1| + |G_2| = 2*34 + 136\ bytes = 204\ bytes$, $|Z_p^*| + 2|G_1| + |G_2| = 32 + 2*34 + 136\ bytes = 236\ bytes$, $|Z_p^*| + 5|G_1| + |G_2| = 32 + 5*34 + 136\ bytes = 338\ bytes$, $|G_2| = 136\ bytes$, respectively. In terms of communication cost overhead during the C_{DO} phase, IBP, P2B, IPV2, and our solutions are: $|G_1| + |G_2| = 34 + 136\ bytes = 170\ bytes$, $|G_2| = 136\ bytes$, $|Z_p^*| + 4|G_1| + |G_2| = 32 + 4*34 + 136\ bytes = 304\ bytes$, $|G_2| = 136\ bytes$, respectively. And in terms of communication cost overhead during the C_{DR} phase, IBP, P2B, IPV2, and our solutions are: $2|G_1| + 2|G_2| = 2*34 + 2*136\ bytes = 340\ bytes$, $|G_2| = 136\ bytes$, $2|Z_p^*| + 5|G_1| + 2|G_2| = 2*32 + 5*34 + 2*136\ bytes = 506\ bytes$, $|G_2| = 136\ bytes$, respectively. In order to provide a clearer understanding of communication consumption, we can see the results as shown in Fig. 3.

Table 3. Computational time & Computation cost

Computational time (s)					Computation cost(mJ)
Scheme	RekeyGen	Enc	ReEnc	Dec	total
IBP [20]	12.35	15.15	2.71	5.42	887.64
P2B [24]	5.67	4.86	2.71	8.13	561.66
IPV2 [25]	11.44	8.92	18.53	25.46	1697.16
Our	2.71	10.56	2.71	4.61	521.82

For energy consumption, according to the evaluation approach in [26], we know the sensor node consumes $3 * 27 * 8/12400 = 0.052\ mJ$ to transmit one byte of data. Therefore, the communication energy consumption in processing of IBP , P2B, IPV2 and our scheme is $(204 + 170 + 340) * 0.052 = 37.128\ mJ$,

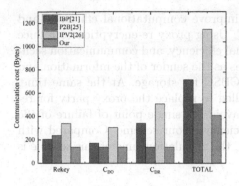
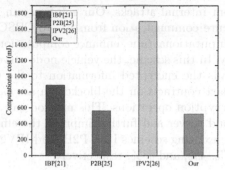

Fig. 3. Communication consumption.   **Fig. 4.** Computational cost.

$(136 + 136 + 236) * 0.052 = 26.416\ mJ$, $(506 + 304 + 338) * 0.052 = 59.696\ mJ$, and $(136 + 136 + 136) * 0.052 = 21.216\ mJ$. Based on the computational cost and the communication cost, the total energy consumption of these four schemes is $37.128 + 887.64 = 924.768\ mJ$, $26.416 + 561.66 = 588.076\ mJ$, $59.696 + 1697.16 = 1756.856\ mJ$, and $21.216 + 521.82 = 543.036\ mJ$, respectively. Figure 4 and Fig. 5 provide the sensor's computational cost and total energy consumption. Comparing the three schemes, our scheme has the lowest computational time and energy consumption.

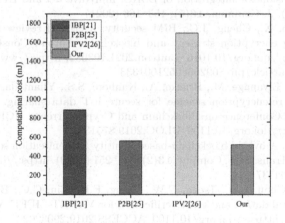

Fig. 5. Total energy consumption.

6 Conclusion

This paper proposes a new scheme to secure communication on IoV by using a BIBPR-CRF scheme. It is an excellent choice to protect wireless sensor networks from internal attacks. Our solution can improve computational efficiency and secure communication from VU to CBSC. Using proxy re-encryption to reduce computational time, enhance computational efficiency, and communication security. In this scheme, the vehicle node serves as the sender of the information and sends the encrypted information to the CBSC for storage. At the same time, smart contracts on the blockchain are called to replace the proxy party for re-encryption operations. This method can avoid the single point of failure of the cloud server and further improve the efficiency of our scheme. Compared with the existing schemes IBP, P2B, and IPV2, the calculation time of this scheme is 42%, 4%, and 68%, respectively.

References

1. Alam, K.M., Saini, M., Saddik, A.E.: Toward social internet of vehicles: concept, architecture, and applications. IEEE Access **3**, 343–357 (2015). https://doi.org/10.1109/ACCESS.2015.2416657
2. Alouache, L., Nguyen, N., Aliouat, M., Chelouah, R.: Survey on IoV routing protocols: security and network architecture. Int. J. Commun Syst **32**(2), e3849 (2019)
3. Elkhalil, A., zhang, J., Elhabob, R., Eltayieb, N.: An efficient signcryption of heterogeneous systems for internet of vehicles. J. Syst. Archit. **113**, 101885 (2021). https://doi.org/10.1016/j.sysarc.2020.101885, https://www.sciencedirect.com/science/article/pii/S1383762120301594
4. Hussain, S.M., Yusof, K.M.: Dynamic Q-learning and fuzzy CNN based vertical handover decision for integration of DSRC, mmWave 5G and LTE in internet of vehicles (IoV). J. Commun. **16**(5), 155–166 (2021)
5. Das, M., Tao, X., Cheng, J.C.: BIM security: a critical review and recommendations using encryption strategy and blockchain. Autom. Constr. **126**, 103682 (2021). https://doi.org/10.1016/j.autcon.2021.103682, https://www.sciencedirect.com/science/article/pii/S0926580521001333
6. Manzoor, A., Liyanage, M., Braeke, A., Kanhere, S.S., Ylianttila, M.: Blockchain based proxy re-encryption scheme for secure IoT data sharing. In: 2019 IEEE International Conference on Blockchain and Cryptocurrency (ICBC), pp. 99–103 (2019). https://doi.org/10.1109/BLOC.2019.8751336
7. Cui, Z., et al.: A hybrid blockchain-based identity authentication scheme for multi-WSN. IEEE Trans. Serv. Comput. **13**(2), 241–251 (2020). https://doi.org/10.1109/TSC.2020.2964537
8. Yang, Y.T., Chou, L.D., Tseng, C.W., Tseng, F.H., Liu, C.C.: Blockchain-based traffic event validation and trust verification for VANETs. IEEE Access **7**, 30868–30877 (2019). https://doi.org/10.1109/ACCESS.2019.2903202
9. Tang, Q., Yung, M.: Cliptography: Post-snowden cryptography. In: Proceedings of the 2017 ACM SIGSAC Conference on Computer and Communications Security, CCS 2017, pp. 2615–2616. Association for Computing Machinery, New York (2017). https://doi.org/10.1145/3133956.3136065
10. Bellare, M., Paterson, K.G., Rogaway, P.: Security of symmetric encryption against mass surveillance. In: Garay, J.A., Gennaro, R. (eds.) CRYPTO 2014. LNCS, vol. 8616, pp. 1–19. Springer, Berlin (2014). https://doi.org/10.1007/978-3-662-44371-2_1

11. Mironov, I., Stephens-Davidowitz, N.: Cryptographic reverse firewalls. In: Oswald, E., Fischlin, M. (eds.) EUROCRYPT 2015. LNCS, vol. 9057, pp. 657–686. Springer, Berlin (2015). https://doi.org/10.1007/978-3-662-46803-6_22
12. Blaze, M., Bleumer, G., Strauss, M.: Divertible protocols and atomic proxy cryptography. In: Nyberg, K. (ed.) EUROCRYPT 1998. LNCS, vol. 1403, pp. 127–144. Springer, Berlin (1998). https://doi.org/10.1007/bfb0054122
13. Green, M., Ateniese, G.: Identity-based proxy re-encryption. In: Katz, J., Yung, M. (eds.) ACNS 2007. LNCS, vol. 4521, pp. 288–306. Springer, Berlin (2007). https://doi.org/10.1007/978-3-540-72738-5_19
14. Manikandan, G., Perumal, R., Muthukumaran, V.: Secure data sharing based on proxy re-encryption for internet of vehicles using seminearring. J. Comput. Theor. Nanosci. **18**(1–2), 516–521 (2021)
15. Cohen, A.: What about bob? the inadequacy of CPA security for proxy reencryption. In: Lin, D., Sako, K. (eds.) PKC 2019. LNCS, vol. 11443, pp. 287–316. Springer, Cham (2019). https://doi.org/10.1007/978-3-030-17259-6_10
16. Susilo, W., Dutta, P., Duong, D.H., Roy, P.S.: Lattice-based HRA-secure attribute-based proxy re-encryption in standard model. In: Bertino, E., Shulman, H., Waidner, M. (eds.) Computer Security - ESORICS 2021. LNCS, vol. 12973, pp. 169–191. Springer, Heidelberg (2021). https://doi.org/10.1007/978-3-030-88428-4_9
17. Fan, K., Ren, Y., Wang, Y., Li, H., Yang, Y.: Blockchain-based efficient privacy preserving and data sharing scheme of content-centric network in 5G. IET Commun. **12**(5), 527–532 (2018)
18. Singh, M., Kim, S.: Branch based blockchain technology in intelligent vehicle. Comput. Netw. **145**, 219–231 (2018). https://doi.org/10.1016/j.comnet.2018.08.016, https://www.sciencedirect.com/science/article/pii/S1389128618308399
19. Zhou, Y., Guo, J., Li, F.: Certificateless public key encryption with cryptographic reverse firewalls. J. Syst. Archit. **109**, 101754 (2020)
20. Zhou, Y., Zhao, L., Jin, Y., Li, F.: Backdoor-resistant identity-based proxy re-encryption for cloud-assisted wireless body area networks. Inf. Sci. **604**, 80–96 (2022)
21. Swan, M.: Blockchain: Blueprint for a New Economy. O'Reilly Media Inc, Sebastopol (2015)
22. Szabo, N.: Formalizing and securing relationships on public networks. First monday (1997)
23. Wang, S., Yuan, Y., Wang, X., Li, J., Qin, R., Wang, F.Y.: An overview of smart contract: architecture, applications, and future trends. In: 2018 IEEE Intelligent Vehicles Symposium (IV), pp. 108–113. IEEE (2018)
24. Maiti, S., Misra, S.: P2b: privacy preserving identity-based broadcast proxy re-encryption. IEEE Trans. Veh. Technol. **69**(5), 5610–5617 (2020)
25. Sun, M., Ge, C., Fang, L., Wang, J.: A proxy broadcast re-encryption for cloud data sharing. Multimed. Tools Appl. **77**, 10455–10469 (2018)
26. Genç, Y., Afacan, E.: Implementation of new message encryption using elliptic curve cryptography over finite fields. In: 2021 International Congress of Advanced Technology and Engineering (ICOTEN), pp. 1–6. IEEE (2021)
27. Shim, K.A.: CPAS: an efficient conditional privacy-preserving authentication scheme for vehicular sensor networks. IEEE Trans. Veh. Technol. **61**(4), 1874–1883 (2012)

SCCT-DARS: Secure and Compliant Cryptocurrency Transactions in a Decentralized Anonymous Regulated System

Issameldeen Elfadul[1]([✉]), Lijun Wu[1], Rashad Elhabob[2], and Ahmed Elkhalil[3]

[1] School of Computer Science and Engineering, University of Electronic Science and Technology of China, Chengdu, Sichuan, China
issameldeen1234@yahoo.com

[2] School of Information and Software Engineering, University of Electronic Science and Technology of China, Chengdu, China

[3] School of Information Science and Technology, Southwest Jiaotong, Chengdu, Sichuan, China

Abstract. The Decentralized Anonymous Payment System (DAP) is considered to be one of the most successful and widely adopted blockchain applications. In spite of the high level of anonymity and security offered by these payment systems (DAP), their potential use for illicit activities can pose a threat to national security due to the inability to identify those involved or stop transactions. In this paper, we introduce Secure and Compliant Cryptocurrency Transactions in a Decentralized Anonymous Regulated System (SCCT-DARS), which aims to assure fulfillment of government regulations and supervision whereas preserving the confidentiality of transactions and the identities of transaction participants. The primary aspect of the suggested proposal is the utilization of the RSA accumulator in conjunction with the Schnorr protocol. This combination enables compliance with government regulations and provides a revocation mechanism in the event of regulation violations. Furthermore, to ensure transaction privacy and anonymity, our proposed system utilizes a combination of ring signatures, stealth addresses, and Pedersen commitments. Regarding security, our proposed protocol conforms to the existing state-of-the-art security requirements and achieves complete anonymity. In addition, the performance analysis demonstrates that our suggested protocol is still applicable and effective despite achieving complete anonymity.

Keywords: Decentralized Anonymous Payment Systems (DAP) · Government Regulations · Supervision · Anonymity · Privacy

1 Introduction

Blockchain, a decentralized and distributed public ledger, has recently gained substantial attention due to its immutability, openness, and transparency fea-

H. Yang and R. Lu (Eds.): FCS 2023, CCIS 1992, pp. 34–54, 2024.
https://doi.org/10.1007/978-981-99-9331-4_3

tures. Among the various applications of blockchain technology, the Decentralized Anonymous Payment System (DAP), commonly referred to as a cryptocurrency, emerges as a promising solution in the field of secure online payments. Monero [1] is one such DAP system that provides a high degree of anonymity and security by concealing the sender, receiver, and transaction amount. However, payment systems with a high-security level also have limitations. The extensive level of anonymity and security offered by such payment systems can pose a threat to the national security of countries due to the possibility of using it in illegal activities without the ability to identify those involved or stop their transactions [2]. Majumder et al. [3] stated that international terrorist organizations, such as the Islamic State, have used cryptocurrency to fund their operations. To combat the financing of terrorism, money laundering, and tax evasion, governments must verify the identity of cryptocurrency users as part of regulatory compliance [4]. Accordingly, Yanbing et al. [5] suggested a compromise approach aimed at striking a balance between delivering a strong level of security and the ability to enforce regulations that protect countries and prevent system misuse. In line with this suggestion, Chao et al. Introduced DCAP [6], a compromise solution that meets both security and regulatory needs while preserving user anonymity. However, this solution also has its own drawbacks, such as the requirement of a trusted third party (manager) who has the ability to reveal the identities of the parties involved in the transaction. Moreover, users must provide the trusted entity with their public key address as well as personal and business information, which can have catastrophic consequences if the trusted entity colludes with the validator node or hacker node and shares this sensitive information about its users.

1.1   Motivation and Contributions

Preserving user privacy and ensuring compliance with government regulations represent significant challenges, as highlighted in the literature review. Granting trusted third-party access to the user's public keys may constitute a major security breach. In a scenario where a user breaks the regulations or fails to meet government requirements, the trusted third party needs to know the actual public key of a user to initiate a revocation process. Furthermore, the trusted third party can access the sender and receiver's public keys. Consequently, if these keys were leaked or if the trusted third party decided to collude with the validator hacker node and share this information, it could lead to significant damage. Therefore, addressing these risks and vulnerabilities is critically important through developing a secure solution to protect user privacy and support regulatory compliance in cryptocurrency transactions.

Therefore, addressing these risks and vulnerabilities is critically important through developing a secure solution to protect user privacy and support regulatory compliance in cryptocurrency transactions.

These challenges motivated us to introduce Secure and Compliant Cryptocurrency Transactions in a Decentralized Anonymous Regulated (SCCT-DARS) System, which aims to ensure compliance with government regulations and supervision while preserving transaction privacy and transaction participants' anonymity. Precisely, our proposed SCCT-DARS system accomplishes the dual goals of enforcing regulations in addition to maintaining privacy and anonymity as follows:

1. Our SCCT-DARS system relies on a blind public key address to guarantee user anonymity when the user seeks permission from the certificate authority (government) to conduct transactions.
2. SCCT-DARS system uses the RSA accumulator to ensure that the user's permission to conduct transactions can be revoked in the event of violating regulations or failure to meet the financial requirements set by the government.
3. Our system utilizes a ring signature to protect the transaction sender's anonymity.
4. The system implements the stealth addresses to ensure unlinkability property and maintain the anonymity of the receiver.
5. Applying Pedersen's commitment to maintaining the privacy of transactions and ensuring that only the transaction participants can view the transferred amount.

1.2   Paper Organization

The remainder of the paper is structured as follows: In Sect. 2, we briefly discuss the related work regarding the security of cryptocurrencies and the regulations governing them. Section 3 presents a description of the network model, security standards, and cryptography materials. As a next step, Sect. 4 describes the detailed construction of our proposed SCCT-DARS system. The security assessment of our proposed system is presented in Sect. 5. The analysis of the proposed scheme is presented in Sect. 6 of the paper. Finally, we provide a conclusion and future work in Sect. 7.

2   Related Work

Decentralized payment systems (DPSs) have gained substantial attention in recent years as an alternative to traditional centralized financial systems. A key feature of DPSs is their use of blockchain technology, which provides a decentralized and transparent record of transactions. However, due to the open and transparent nature of the blockchain, early examples of DPSs such as Ethereum (ETH) [7] and Bitcoin [8] suffer from linkability and a lack of sufficient anonymity protection [9–11].

If addresses are linked, this can lead to de-anonymization and the revelation of the transaction participants' identities, especially when analysis services such as network-layer de-anonymization are used [12]. One notable solution to address the linkability problem is mixing services [13]. The main concept of mixing is to enable several users to construct a single transaction with multiple inputs and outputs simultaneously. This prevents a hacker node from linking the transaction input to its related output, even with the use of analytics services. However, mixing services have been criticized for the possibility of central trust entities stealing currencies or leak information about transaction participants. Mixcoin [14] is a solution that addresses the issue of currency theft and is compatible with Bitcoin. Duffield et al. introduced Dash [15], a mixing process that enhances participant anonymity by using multiple mixers instead of relying on a single mixer. TumbleBit [16] is a solution for payments using an untrusted intermediary called Tumbler. However, it has drawbacks, including the high financial fees charged for any mixing operation and the long time it takes to complete the mixing process.

Therefore, a new generation of cryptocurrencies, called Decentralized Anonymous Payment Systems (DAP), has been developed to address the flaws in mixer mechanisms. Monero [1] and Zerocash [17] are two of the most well-known DAP systems. They offer strong anonymity and privacy by hiding transaction details such as the sender, receiver, and transferred amount of the currency.

Despite the undeniable economic benefits of using cryptocurrencies, including both DPSs and DAPs [18,19], they have been used for illegal activities such as funding terrorism and money laundering [20,21]. As a result, countries have begun implementing regulations to organize the use of cryptocurrencies and prevent their use in criminal activities [22,23].

Several solutions have been proposed to achieve privacy and regulations. Yanbing et al. [5] suggested monitoring transactions through a central authority. However, their system allows the auditor to view the entire transaction history of a coin, which may pose a potential threat to user anonymity. Another solution applying regulations has been presented in SkyEye [24], where users encrypt their public information and provide proof to the regulator to show that they know the corresponding private information. However, the regulator can decrypt the data and reveal the identities of the participants.

RCash [25] presents an alternative regulatory approach by utilizing zero-knowledge proofs to set spending limits. However, the regulator is authorized to decrypt the public keys that serve as identifiers for transaction participants, and it knows the real-life identities corresponding to each public key address. Chao et al. developed a conditional anonymity payment system based on smart contracts to reconcile privacy and regulations [6]. However, one significant limitation of this approach is the involvement of a trusted party, a manager, who is authorized to disclose transaction participants' public keys, which could put users' privacy at risk. Furthermore, the visibility and observability of transferred coins by all users in the blockchain network led to the lack of sufficient confidentiality.

Finally, Table 1 comprehensively compares schemes that ensure compliance with government regulations and those that provide secure transaction privacy. Note that ●, ◖ , and ○ denotes full-featured, half-featured, and non-featured attributes, respectively.

Table 1. Transaction Privacy vs Compliance with Government Regulations

Scheme	Transaction Privacy			Supporting Regulation
	Sender Anonymity	Receiver Anonymity	Transferred Amount Privacy	
Bitcoin [8]	◖	◖	◖	○
Zerocash [17]	●	●	●	○
Monero [1]	●	●	●	○
DAPS [26]	◖	◖	●	●
[5]	◖	◖	◖	●
TumbleBit [16]	●	●	○	○

3   Preliminaries

Here we present the network model, the security standards, and the cryptography materials.

3.1   Network Model

In the network model for our proposed system, we have identified three key entities: Certificate Authority (CA), Participant, and Distributed Ledger Network. Furthermore, there are two types of communication that can be conducted within the system: On-chain communication and Off-chain communication, refer to Fig. 1.

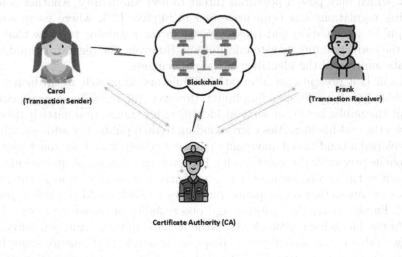

Fig. 1. The network model for the Secure and Compliant Cryptocurrency Transactions in a Decentralized Anonymous Regulated System (SCCT-DARS).

- Certificate Authority (CA): This is a trusted third party representing the state, CA ensures that the transaction participants comply with government regulations. In the first step, the participant supplies CA with their blind public key address as well as his personal and business information. Upon verifying that the participant meets the required legal and financial standards, the CA grants permission, also known as a certificate, confirming the participant's authorization to carry out financial transactions within the system.
- Participant: This category represents the main parties in the blockchain payment system responsible for sending or receiving cryptocurrency transactions. To initiate a transaction, a participant (also known as a user) must obtain permission, i.e., a certificate from CA to confirm compliance with the country's government regulations and financial standards. The certificate serves as permission for the user to engage in cryptocurrency transactions within the system.
- Distributed Ledger Network: This entity refers to the decentralized technology that utilizes blockchain for managing and storing ledger records over multiple nodes in a decentralized system.

3.2 Security Standards

Based on prior studies [9,11], our proposed SCCT-DARS system aims to achieve the following security properties:

- Privacy of the sender's identity and data integrity protection.
- Anti-linkability and the privacy of the receiver's identity.
- Compliance with government regulations and supporting the revocation of user permission.
- Transaction privacy.
- Collision prevention.

3.3 Cryptography Materials

1. *RSA accumulator:* In cryptography, the RSA accumulator is a primitive construct that effectively proves an element belongs to a given set of values [27–29]. It relies on modular exponentiation under strong RSA assumption. Formally, it can be defined as follows:
   Given a set $A = \{A_1, A_2, \ldots, A_n\}$ of random elements, the goal is to prove their membership in the accumulator.
   First, the set A is mapped to 2λ - bit prime number e through a collision-resistant hash function, i.e., $e_i = H_{prime}(A_i) \ \forall_i = \{1, \ldots, n\}$, respectively.
   Consequently, $Z = \{e_1, e_2, \ldots, e_n\}$ represent a set of mapped primes numbers.
   Next, commits to Z is the RSA accumulator, which can be calculated as

$$acc(Z) = g^{\prod_{e_i \in z} e_i} \ (mod \ N).$$

2. *Schnorr protocol:* Schnorr protocol is a zero-knowledge proof of discrete logarithm in a group of known order [30–32]. In formal terms, it can be summed up as follows:

   Let Z_N^* represents an RSA group, where a $\in Z_N$, $A = g^a \pmod{N}$, and $H_n\colon\{0,1\}^* \rightarrow Z_N$. The prover aims to convince the verifier that he knows the discrete logarithm of A base g, i.e., knowing a such that: $g^a = A$.

   The protocol consists of two algorithms:

   (a) *Prove algorithm (PR):* The prover conducts the following:
       $k \in_R Z_N$, $R = g^k \pmod{N}$, $c = H_n(g \mid A \mid R)$, $s = k + c \times a$.
       Sends the proof $\pi \leftarrow (c, s, R)$ to the verifier.

   (b) *Verification algorithm (VE):* Given $\pi = (c, s, R)$ and A, the verifier conducts the following:
       $c' = H_n(g \mid A \mid R)$, checks whether $c = c'$ and $g^s = A^c.R \pmod{N}$. If yes, accept. Otherwise, reject.

3. *Stealth address:* A stealth address is an extension of a Diffie-Hellman protocol, where two users or more without prior knowledge of each other generate a common secret value through the exchange of a public value on a public network [33,34].

   In our system, to achieve unlinkability and anonymity of the receiver's address, the sender does not directly transmit the cryptocurrencies to the receiver's address. Rather, on behalf of the receiver, the sender creates a temporary one-time public key address and transmits the cryptocurrencies to this address

   $$P_{stealth} = H_s(tU)P + V.$$

   While the receiver will be able to compute the one-time public key address $P_{stealth}$ as

   $$P'_{stealth} = H_s(uT)P + V.$$

4. *Ring signature:* A ring signature is a digital cryptographic signature that enables a user within a group to sign a message without revealing their identity [35,36]. By verifying the signature, the verifier can be certain that someone in the group has signed the message without being able to determine who specifically signed it. In our work, we utilize the LSAG ring signature [35].

5. *Pedersen Commitment:* The Pedersen commitment is a cryptographic protocol that enables the committer to commit to a secret value without revealing it [37,38]. At the same time, the verifier can check the validity of the commitment without knowing the secret value. Our system uses the Pedersen commitment to preserving transaction confidentiality by hiding the number of coins transferred. In technical terms, the Pedersen commitment can be described as follows:

   Given two generators of a group, points G and P, the committer creates a commitment to a secret value $x \in Z_l$ by randomly choosing a blind factor $s \in Z_l$ and computing the commitment as $C = xG + sP$.

   If given the equation $x_1 + x_2 = x_3$, where $x_1, x_2, x_3 \in Z_l$, then

   $$Commit(x_1) + Commit(x_2) = Commit(x_3).$$

$$C_1 + C_2 = C_3$$

Therefore

$$(x_1 + x_2)G + (s_1 + s_2)P = x_3 G + s_3 P.$$

4 Proposed SCCT-DARS System

Our proposed SCCT-DARS system employs the Unspent Transaction Output (UTXO) model to track currency ownership and ensure the validity of transactions while preserving participants' privacy by using Pedersen commitment. The UTXO model also provides an additional level of security against double-spending attack.

When a new transaction is created, the network verifies it by ensuring that the total value of the inputs is greater than the outputs and transaction fee. Mathematically, the validator node verifies $\sum$ (encrypted input values) $= \sum$ (encrypted output values).

4.1 The Technical Perspective

In this section, we will discuss the various stages and processes involved in our proposed digital currency system.

1. $PubP \leftarrow Setup(1^\lambda)$: This algorithm takes as input a security λ, and outputs the public parameters $PubP = \{(N, g), (P, \mathbb{G}, l, q, H_n, H_s, H_m, H_g, H_{prime})\}$, where the modulus N is the product of two unknown prime numbers, g $\in QR_N$ is the generator of the RSA accumulator, and QR_N denotes the quadratic residual group of the modulus N.
   E is an elliptic curve defined by the set of points (x, y) and satisfying a WeierstraB equation:
   $\{ E : y^2 = x^3 + ax + b \ (mod \ q), \quad \text{where } a, b, x, y \in F_q\}$.
   The generator P of the cyclic group $\mathbb{G}$ has the order l, the prime number $q > l$.
   The hash functions: $H_n : \{0,1\}^* \rightarrow Z_N$, $H_s : \{0,1\}^* \rightarrow F_q$, $H_m : \{0,1\}^* \rightarrow EC$, $H_g : \{P\}^* \rightarrow F_l^* \times \{P\}^*$, and $H_{prime} : \{0,1\}^* \rightarrow \{e : e \in \{0,1\}^{2\lambda} \wedge e \text{ is prime}\}$, it maps random elements to 2λ-bit primes.
2. *Create account stage:* In this stage, users are enrolled in the system.
   Initially, a user (say, Carol) is supplied with the public parameters $PubP$.
   Next, Carol selects her private key $q_c \in \mathbb{F}_l^*$ and calculates her corresponding public address $Q_c = q_c P$.
   Carol then creates a blinded version of her public address, Q_c', by multiplying her public address with the private key as $Q_c' = Q_c q$.
3. *Permission acquisition stage:*
   (a) Firstly, Carol uses off-chain communication to provide the CA with her blind public key address Q_c' along with her personal and business information. This is done to obtain proof allowing her to conduct a transaction.

(b) Next, CA reviews Carol's information and verifies that she is not on a block list and meets all government requirements. In light of this, she will be considered legally authorized to carry out the transaction.

(c) Following that, CA maps the blind public key address Q'_c into a prime number e_i through a hash function $e_i = H_{prime}(Q'_c)$.

(d) Next, to add e_i into $acc(Z)$, CA calculates the the new accumulator

$$acc(Z)' = (\ acc(Z)\ )^{e_i} \pmod N$$

Where $acc(Z)$ represents the original RSA accumulator before adding an element e_i, and $acc(Z)'$ represents the new RSA accumulator value after adding element e_i to $acc(Z)$.

(e) Subsequently, CA generates the witness $W_{e_i} = (acc(Z)')^{1/e_i} \pmod N$ to prove that an element e_i exists in the new accumulator $acc(Z)'$.

Note that, for security reasons (refer to Sect. 5.5), in our proposed system, the validator will not be provided with W_{e_i} or e_i to demonstrate that e_i exists in $acc(Z)'$. Instead, the validator will be given a zero-knowledge proof proving that e_i indeed exists in $acc(Z)'$.

(f) Afterward, to demonstrate in a zero-knowledge manner the knowledge of e_i such that

$$(W_{e_i})^{e_i} = acc(Z)' \pmod N \text{ hold },$$

CA conducts the following three steps :

i. Sample the secret $k \in Z_N$ and compute the commitment $R = g^k \pmod N$.

ii. Set $c = H_n(g \mid acc(Z)' \mid R)$.

iii. Compute $s = k + c\prod_{e_i \in z} e_i$.

(g) Finally, CA sends the proof $\pi \leftarrow (c, s, R)$ to Carol.

4. *Transaction creation stage:* During this stage, the transaction's sender, Carol, performs the following tasks: generating a receiver's one-time public key address, committing to the transfer amount, creating the signature, and attaching the necessary information.

(a) Generating a receiver's one-time public key address: As a security measure to maintain the anonymity of the receiver, coins are not sent directly to Frank's address. Instead, in each transaction, the sender, Carol, creates a new address $P_{stealth}$ for the receiver Frank, and then Carol transmits the coins to this address $P_{stealth}$ as described below:

Assume that the points U and V denote the receiver's public key addresses, i.e., $U = uP$, $V = vP$, u and v are the secret keys of U and B, respectively. Moreover, U and V are public to everyone.

If the sender, Carol, wants to transmit the coins to Frank, then she takes these actions:

i. Arbitrarily choose $t \in \mathbb{F}_l^*$ and compute $T = tP$.

ii. Generate the one-time public key address $P_{stealth}$ as

$$P_{stealth} = H_s(tU)P + V.$$

iii. Then, Carol assigns $P_{stealth}$ as the stealth address for Frank.

Note that, due to the Diffie-Hellman exchange, the secret value $tU = uT$, that is, $t(uP) = u(tP)$ can be calculated by both Carol and Frank.

(b) Committing to the transfer amount: As a security measure and to maintain transaction confidentiality, only the sender and receiver should be able to recognize the transmitted coins. At the same time, the validator node has to ensure that the sender cannot spend more than they possess, and it should remain unaware of how many input or output values the sender has sent or received.

To transmit x_1 coins, Carol executes Algorithm 1 (Commitment) and assigns its output as a message m, i.e., $m = C_{1,2}, C_{3,4}, X_{1,2}, X_{3,4}, S_{1,2}$, and $S_{3,4}$.

Algorithm 1. Commitment

Require: $P, H \in \mathbb{G}$, where P, H generate $\mathbb{G}$.
Ensure: Commit to secret values $x_1, x_2, x_3, x_4 \in \mathbb{Z}_l$, where input values x_1, x_2 equal output values x_3, x_4, i.e., $x_1 + x_2 = x_3 + x_4$.
1: Set $X_{1,2} = x_1 + x_2$ and $X_{3,4} = x_3 + x_4$.
2: Randomly choose the blind factors $s_1, s_2, s_3, s_4 \in \mathbb{Z}_l$, where $s_1 + s_2 = s_3 + s_4$ then set $S_{1,2} = s_1 + s_2$ and $S_{3,4} = s_3 + s_4$.
3: Compute the commitments C_1, C_2 for the input values x_1 and x_2 as $C_1 = x_1 G + s_1 P$, $C_2 = x_2 G + s_2 P$.
4: Combine commitments C_1, C_2 as $C_{1,2} = (x_1 + x_2)G + (s_1 + s_2)P$.
5: Compute the commitments C_3, C_4 for the output values x_3 and x_4 as $C_3 = x_3 G + s_3 P$, $C_4 = x_4 G + s_4 P$.
6: Combine commitments C_3, C_4 as $C_{3,4} = (x_3 + x_4)G + (s_3 + s_4)P$.
7: **Return as output:** $C_{1,2}, C_{3,4}, X_{1,2}, X_{3,4}, S_{1,2}$, and $S_{3,4}$.

(c) Creating the signature: To the transaction's commitment message m, where $m = C_{1,2}, C_{3,4}, X_{1,2}, X_{3,4}, S_{1,2}$, and $S_{3,4}$, without revealing which key among the set of keys has been used for the signature, Carol performs the following actions:

- Provide a set $N = \{Q_1, Q_2, Q_3\}$ of the public key addresses of a potential signer.
- Assuming that Carol's public/private key pair $(Q_2 = Q_c, q_2 = q_c)$ and her key-image β is given by the formula $\beta = q_2 H_m(Q_2)$, she proceeds with the following steps:
- Choose randomly $\varphi \in_R F_l$ then assign:
  - $L = \varphi P$.
  - $R = \varphi \, H_m(Q_2)$.
  - $C_3 \equiv H_s(m \parallel L_\varphi \parallel R_\varphi) \pmod{l}$.
- For $i = \pi + 1, \ldots, n, 1, \ldots \pi - 1$, choose randomly $\mu_1, \mu_3 \in_R F_l$, then assign:
  - $C_1 \equiv H_s(m \parallel \mu_3 P + C_3 Q_3 \parallel \mu_3 H_m(Q_3) + C_3 \beta) \pmod{l}$.

- $C_2 \equiv H_s(m \parallel \mu_1 P + C_1 Q_1 \parallel \mu_1 H_m(Q_1) + C_1 \beta \pmod{l}$.
- Compute $r_\pi = \varphi - C_\pi x_\pi \pmod{l}$.
  - Output the signature $\sigma = (C_1, s_1, \ldots, s_n, \beta)$.

(d) Attaching: Lastly, Carol attaches the following within the transaction:
  i. The message signature pair (m, σ).
  ii. The witness
$$W_{e_i} = acc(Z)^{1/e_i} \pmod{N}.$$
  iii. Zero-knowledge proof $\pi \leftarrow (c, s, R)$ to demonstrate that
$$(W_{e_i})^{e_i} = acc(Z) \pmod{N} \text{ hold}.$$

Then, Carol designates the receiver's address as
$$P_{stealth} = H_s(tU)P + V.$$

Next, she sends the transaction to the validator node to be verified.

5. *Distributed ledger-Adding transactions stage:* In this stage, the validator adds transactions to the distributed ledger. The process includes the subsequent steps:

(a) Verify the validity of the zero-knowledge proof: To ensure that CA has authorized Carol to conduct transactions, the validator verifies the validity of the zero-knowledge proof. Given $\pi \leftarrow (c, s, R)$ and $acc(Z)'$, the validator needs to demonstrate that the following equation holds:
$$(W_{e_i})^{e_i} = acc(Z)' \pmod{N}$$

To do this, the validator performs the following steps:
  - Computes $c' = H_n(g \mid acc(Z)' \mid R)$.
  - Checks whether $c = c'$ and
    $g^s = (acc(Z)')^c . R \pmod{N}$. If yes, accept. Otherwise, reject.

(b) Ensure that no double-spending occurs: The validator keeps a list of the whole key images employed to sign transactions.
Therefore, a validator examines the list to see whether $\beta = q_2 H_m(Q_2)$ exists. If β is found on the list, the validator classifies that as a double-spending try and rejects the transaction.
Otherwise, it continues to the next step.

(c) Verifies that Carol has sufficient coins in her balance: The validator must ensure that Carol has enough coins to cover her expenses, i.e., she cannot spend more than she possesses, while also maintaining transaction confidentiality. This validation process is achieved by executing Algorithm 2 (Verification of Sufficient Coins).

(d) Verify the validity of the ring signature $\mathcal{SIG}$: Assume that a message m, the message's signature $\sigma = (C_1, s_1, \ldots, s_n, \beta)$, and the set $N = \{Q_1, Q_2, Q_3\}$ of a potential signer are all provided, the validator conducts the followings:
As a beginning, compute C'_{i+1}
$C'_2 \equiv H_s(m \parallel \mu_1 P + C_1 Q_1 \parallel \mu_1 H_m(Q_1) + C_1 \beta \pmod{l}$.

Algorithm 2. Verification of Sufficient Coins

Require: $C_{1,2}$, $C_{3,4}$, $X_{1,2} = x_1 + x_2$, and $X_{3,4} = x_3 + x_4$.
Ensure: The validity of Carol's sufficient coins.
1: Compute $C'_{1,2} = (x_1 + x_2)G + (s_1 + s_2)P$.
2: Compute $C'_{3,4} = (x_3 + x_4)G + (s_3 + s_4)P$.
3: **if** $C'_{1,2} = C_{1,2}$ and $C'_{3,4} = C_{3,4}$
4:     Sufficient Coins Verified
5: **else**
6:     Reject Transaction
7: **end if then**

$$C'_3 \equiv H_s(m \parallel \mu_2 P + C'_2 Q_2 \parallel \mu_2 H_m(Q_2) + C'_2 \beta \pmod{l}.$$
$$C'_1 \equiv H_s(m \parallel \mu_3 P + C'_3 Q_3 \parallel \mu_3 H_m(Q_3) + C'_3 \beta \pmod{l}. \text{ Next, verify}$$
whether $C'_1 = C_1$. If it does, add transactions to the distributed ledger. If not, discard the transaction.

6. *Acquiring coins stage:* In the end, at receiving, Frank carries out the succeeding steps:
   (a) Calculate the one-time public key address $P'_{stealth}$ as

   $$P'_{stealth} = H_s(uT)P + V.$$

   As mentioned earlier, due to using the Diffie-Hellman exchange, the secret value $tU = uT$, which implies that, $t(uP) = u(tP)$. Consequently, we have $P_{stealth} = P'_{stealth}$.
   (b) Obtain the secret key δ of the one-time public key address $P'_{stealth}$ as

   $$\delta = H_s(uT) + v.$$

   (c) Finally, Frank re-sends the coins from the one-time public key address $P'_{stealth}$ to his address by conducting another transaction and signing it with the secret key δ.
7. *Revoke permission:* In cases where the user breaks the regulations or fails to meet government requirements, CA can revoke the user's permission.
   After a while, assuming Carol had broken a regulation, CA can revoke Carol's permission as follows:
   – First, CA maps the blind signature of Carol's public key $(\sigma, (r, s))$ to a prime number $e_i = H_{prime}(\sigma \mid r \mid s)$.
   – Following that, CA deletes e_i from $acc(Z)$ as follows:

   $$acc(Z)' = (\, acc(Z)\,)^{e_i^{-1} \mod \phi(N)} \pmod{N}.$$

   Where $acc(Z)$ represents the original RSA accumulator before deleting an element e_i, and $acc(Z)'$ represents the new RSA accumulator value after deleting element e_i from $acc(Z)$.
   – Next, as explained previously (Sect. 4.1.3.g), Carol received the proof $\pi \leftarrow (c, s, R)$ from the CA. When she decides to make another new transaction, she sends the transaction along with the proof $\pi \leftarrow (c, s, R)$ to the validator node for verification.

- Then, the validator verifies the validity of the zero-knowledge proof:
  Given $\pi \leftarrow (c, s, R)$ and $acc(Z)'$, the validator computes

$$c' = H_n(g \mid acc(Z)' \mid R)$$

and finds that

$$c \neq c'$$

and

$$g^s \neq (acc(Z)')^c.R \pmod{N}.$$

Consequently

$$(W_{e_i})^{e_i} = acc(Z)' \pmod{N} \text{ not hold.}$$

Reject the transaction.

5 Security Assessment

Our proposed system meets the security standards as follows:

- Privacy of the sender's identity and data integrity protection: The ring signature property provides the verifier with an assurance that a group member has signed the message while preventing the verifier from discerning the exact sender's key used to produce the signature. The difficulty of detecting the actual signer of the message, referred to as signer ambiguity, stems from the Decisional Diffie-Hellman Problem (DDHP) [35,39].
  Informally, DDHP is described as follows:
  Consider the cyclic group $\mathbb{G} = \{P^0, P^1, P^2, \ldots, P^{l-1}\}$ of order l with a generator P, and let a, b, and c be independently and uniformly chosen from the multiplicative group of integers modulo l. Then distinguishing between the distributions of (P^a, P^b, P^{ab}) and (P^a, P^b, P^z) is a complexity task. In other words, given (P^a, P^b, P^{ab}) as input, then determining whether $ab = z$ is a challenge.
  Formally, DDHP is defined as follows:
  1. Select $(x_1, x_2, x_3, x_4, x_5)$ from Z_l^*.
  2. Compute $(a_0 = P^{x_1}, b_0 = P^{x_2}, c_0 = P^{x_3})$ and compute $(a_1 = P^{x_4}, b_1 = P^{x_5}, c_1 = P^{x_4 x_5})$.
  3. Choose a random bit $b \in \{0, 1\}$.
  4. Let $(a, b, c) \equiv (a_b, b_b, c_b)$.
  We assert that there exists no adversary $\mathcal{A} \in \text{PPT}(k)$ such that

$$P[\mathcal{A}(P^a, P^b, P^c) = b] = \left(\frac{1}{2}\right) + \frac{1}{F(k)}$$

where $F(k)$ is a polynomial. In simpler terms, there is no adversary $\mathcal{A}$ that can successfully solve the Decisional Diffie-Hellman Challenge with a probability exceeding $1/2$ beyond that of random guessing. Therefore, the signer's identity remains secure.

Furthermore, one main property of digital signature is integrity. As a result, any change or tampering with the transaction after it has been signed will be detectable. Thus, the message's integrity, i.e., the transaction's integrity, is assured.

- Anti-linkability and the privacy of the receiver's identity: Stealth addresses [33] can be defined as an enhanced version of the Diffie-Hellman key exchange, allowing two or more parties to calculate a secret value by exchanging public values over an insecure channel.

  In our scheme, aiming to ensure the privacy of the receiver's identity, the sender avoids sending the coin directly to the receiver's address. Rather than sending the coin directly to the receiver's address, the sender generates a temporary address (referred to as a stealth address $P_{stealth}$), also known as a one-time public key address on behalf of the receiver, and then sends the coin to this particular address.

  Furthermore, to prevent linkability, in each transaction, the sender creates a different one-time address $P_{stealth}$ on behalf of the receiver and sends the funds to this address. This prevents transactions from being linked; even if the same sender makes multiple payments to the same receiver, they will not be linked to each other. As outlined in [33, 34], stealth addresses cab be defined as:

  Let U and V denote the receiver's public key addresses, where $U = uP$, $V = vP$, u and v are the secret keys of U and B, respectively. U and V are publicly published to all users. The sender selects a private key t, computes $T = tP$, and then transmits T to a receiver. Next the sender creates the one-time public key address $P_{stealth} = H_s(tU)P + V$. Due to the Diffie-Hellman exchange, the secret value $tU = uT$, that is, $t(uP) = u(tP)$, can be calculated by both parties. In light of that, the receiver will be able to compute the one-time public key address $P_{stealth}$ as $P'_{stealth} = H_s(uT)P + V$.

- Compliance with government regulations and supporting the revocation of user permission: Using the RSA accumulator ensures compliance with government regulations, and user permission can be revoked if regulations are violated.

- Transaction privacy: Due to the additively homomorphic of the Pedersen commitment, the verifier can perform the following check:
  Given $C_i = x_i G + s_i P$ for $(i = 1, 2, \ldots, l)$, then

$$\sum_{i=1}^{l} C_i = \sum_{i=1}^{l} x_i G + s_i P.$$

In simpler terms, this permits the validator node to verify that the committed input and output values are equal without the ability to disclose the exact values of those inputs or outputs.

- Collision prevention: In our scheme and to prevent collusion between the Certificate Authority (CA) and attacker node, when a user request permission

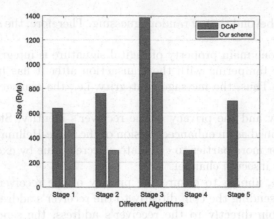

Fig. 2. Comparison of communication cost

from the CA to conduct transactions, they send their blind public key address Q'_c instead of their actual public key Q_c. This is done to prevent the possibility of cooperation between the CA and attacker nodes in case the CA decides to leak the user's public key to the attacker node. Moreover, the validator does not receive W_{e_i} nor e_i to verify the existence of e_i in $acc(Z)'$. Instead, we provide the validator with a zero-knowledge proof demonstrating the existence of e_i in $acc(Z)'$.

When the user, Carol, conducts a transaction, witness W_{e_i} and element e_i are embedded into the transaction and become visible to all nodes due to the openness feature of the blockchain. As the CA stores sensitive information about every user in its database, such as their names and jobs, there is a risk that this data may be leaked to the hacker node. Consequently, the hacker could exploit the leaked information to link between the user and W_{e_i}, e_i. This could be achieved through methods like side-channel analysis or artificial intelligence techniques, involving examining data patterns and narrowing down the analysis scope. In the end, these methods may facilitate de-anonymizing a user. To avoid such a scenario, the validator is provided with a zero-knowledge proof demonstrating the existence of e_i in $acc(Z)'$.

6   Performance Analysis

In this part, we comprehensively evaluate the proposed SCCT-DARS system and compare its performance to the DCAP [6] system. The evaluation includes aspects such as communication cost, security properties, and computation cost using a set of experimental evaluations. The experimental setup uses the PBC [40] library and is executed on a machine with an Intel(R) Core(TM) i7-7700 Processor and 8 GB of random-access memory, implemented in C++, and the underlying computational structure is the elliptic curve $y^2 = x^2 + x \pmod{p}$.

Table 2. Communication Cost Analysis Comparison.

No	Stage	DCAP	Our
1	Stage 1		
	Initialize	$\|\mathbb{G}\|$	$2\|\mathbb{G}\|$
	Registration	$2\|\mathbb{G}\|$	$2\|\mathbb{G}\|$
	Update	$2\|\mathbb{G}\|$	-
2	Stage 2		
	Proof	$5\|\mathbb{G}\|+6\|Z_q^*\|$	$2\|\mathbb{G}\|+2\|Z_q^*\|$
3	Stage 3		
	Transact	$10\|\mathbb{G}\|+5\|Z_q^*\|+v$	-
	One-time key	-	$\|\mathbb{G}\|$
	Pedersen	-	$4\|\mathbb{G}\|+4\|Z_q^*\|$
	Signature	-	$\|\mathbb{G}\|+4\|Z_q^*\|$
4	Stage 4		
	Verify	$2\|\mathbb{G}\|+2\|Z_q^*\|$	-
5	Stage 5		
	Smart Contract	$5\|\mathbb{G}\|+3\|Z_q^*\|$	-

6.1 Communication Cost Analysis

Suppose the size of every element in $\mathbb{QR}_N$ or $\mathbb{G}$ is 128 bytes, and the size of every element in Z_p or Z_n is 20 bytes. Let $\mid Z_p \mid$ and $\mid Z_n \mid$ stand for the bit length in Z_p, Z_n respectively, $\mid \mathbb{QR}_N \mid$ and $\mid \mathbb{G} \mid$ for the size of point in $\mathbb{QR}_N$, and $\mathbb{G}$ respectively, and - stand for the algorithm not present in the system.

It is important to mention that the value being transferred, denoted as v, has a maximum value of 2^{32}, and can thus be represented using 4 bytes.

The communication cost comparison between our proposed system and the DCAP [6] is based on five stages, namely: the sending address (stage 1), the permission acquisition stage, where the sender requests proof to enable the transaction (stage 2), the transaction issuance (stage 3), the verifying (stage 4), and the executing of the smart contract (stage 5). These stages represent the different steps in the communication process, and the cost associated with each step is evaluated and compared.

Based on Table 2 and Fig. 2, it is clear that our proposed system has the lowest communication cost compared to the DCAP [6].

6.2 Computation Cost Analysis

Consider the symbol $\mathbb{M}$ representing the multiplication operation, $\mathbb{E}$ representing the exponentiation operation, and - representing the algorithm not present in the system.

Table 3. Computation Cost Analysis Comparison.

No	Stage	DCAP	Our
1	Stage 1		
	Registration	4M	4M
	Update	2M	-
2	Stage 2		
	Proof	3M	M + 3E
3	Stage 3		
	Transact	9M	-
	One-time key	-	5M
	Pedersen Commitment	-	4M
	Signature	-	7M
4	Stage 4		
	Verify	13M	9M + 2E
5	Stage 5		
	Trace	M	-

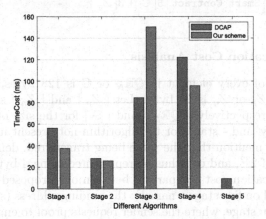

Fig. 3. Comparison of computation cost

The comparison between our proposed system and the DCAP [6] is based on the five stages, namely: creating the address (stage 1), the permission acquisition stage, where the sender requests proof to enable the transaction (stage 2), the transaction issuance (stage 3), the verifying (stage 4), and the executing of the smart contract (stage 5).

As illustrated in Table 3 and Fig. 3, our proposed scheme has minimal performance difference compared to the DCAP scheme [6].

6.3 Privacy and Security Analysis

This section deeply analyzes the privacy and security issues associated with our proposed system and DCAP [6]. It evaluates potential vulnerabilities and weaknesses in these systems and assesses compliance with relevant privacy regulations outlined in Security Standards.

Consider F_1, F_2, F_3, F_4, F_5, F_6, F_7, F_8, F_9, and F_{10} to represent the security features of data integrity protection, double-spend resistance, decentralized networks, compliance with government regulations, concealing the monetary value of the transaction, anti-linkability, unconditional anonymity, supporting the blinded public key submission, supporting the revocation of user permission, and eliminating the possibility of collision, respectively.

As illustrated in Table 4 , our system attains a considerable degree of fundamental security requirements while also granting the capability to revoke a user's authorization to perform transactions if they fail to abide by government regulations or abuse the service. Furthermore, unlike DCAP [6], our system eliminates the possibility of collusion between the CA and blockchain nodes.

It is important to acknowledge that there is a trade-off between security and performance in any algorithm design. Increasing the performance and efficiency of an algorithm may come at the cost of sacrificing or weakening its security properties; conversely, enhancing security measures may negatively impact the algorithm's performance. This is a crucial factor that should be considered when designing and implementing any system.

However, despite satisfying all of the essential security requirements outlined in the Security Assessment, our system still maintains reasonable performance results compared to the DCAP [6], as demonstrated in Tables 2 and 3. This highlights the careful consideration and balance that was taken into account during the design and implementation of our system to ensure that both security and performance were optimized.

Table 4. Security Features Comparison.

	F_1	F_2	F_3	F_4	F_5	F_6	F_7	F_8	F_9	F_{10}
DCAP	✓	✓	✓	✓	✗	✗	✗	✗	✓	✗
Our	✓	✓	✓	✓	✓	✓	✓	✓	✓	✓

7   Conclusion and Future Work

In this paper, we present Secure and Compliant Cryptocurrency Transactions in a Decentralized Anonymous Regulated System (SCCT-DARS). Our proposed system in this research seeks to align with government regulations, facilitate government supervision, and simultaneously protect transaction confidentiality and participant anonymity.

To ensure that the user meets the government regulations, we utilized an RSA accumulator combined with a zero-knowledge proof. We have implemented a ring signature technique to protect the sender's anonymity. To ensure transaction privacy, we have implemented the Pedersen commitment mechanism. A stealth address is utilized to ensure unlinkability and preserve the anonymity of the recipient in a transaction.

As part of our future efforts to improve the security of our system, we intend to expand the SCCT-DARS scheme and implement range proof to prevent cheating and fraudulent activities, precisely by preventing the commitment to negative values. Including range proof ensures that the secret committed value lies within a positive interval, thus avoiding manipulating the equation of the Peterson commitment.

Acknowledgments. This work was supported by the National Key Research and Development Program, under grants 2016QY13Z2302, and Sub Project of Independent Scientific Research Project, under grant ZZKY-ZX-03-02-04.

References

1. Alonso, K.M., Joancomartí, J.H.: Monero - privacy in the blockchain. Cryptology ePrint Archive, Paper 2018/535 (2018). https://eprint.iacr.org/2018/535
2. Shah, A.S., et al.: On the vital aspects and characteristics of cryptocurrency-a survey. IEEE Access **11**, 9451–9468 (2023)
3. Majumder, A., Routh, M., Singha, D.: A conceptual study on the emergence of cryptocurrency economy and its nexus with terrorism financing. In: The Impact of Global Terrorism on Economic and Political Development (2019)
4. Song, Y., Chen, B., Wang, X.-Y.: Cryptocurrency technology revolution: are bitcoin prices and terrorist attacks related? Financ. Innov. **9**(1), 1–20 (2023)
5. Wu, Y., Fan, H., Wang, X., Zou, G.: A regulated digital currency. Sci. China Inf. Sci. **62**, 1–12 (2019)
6. Lin, C., He, D., Huang, X., Khan, M.K., Choo, K.-K.R.: DCAP: a secure and efficient decentralized conditional anonymous payment system based on blockchain. IEEE Trans. Inf. Forensics Secur. **15**, 2440–2452 (2020)
7. Buterin, V., et al.: A next-generation smart contract and decentralized application platform. White Paper **3**(37), 2–1 (2014)
8. Bitcoin, N.S.: Bitcoin: a peer-to-peer electronic cash system. Decentralized Bus. Rev., 21260 (2008)
9. Quamara, S., Singh, A.K.: A systematic survey on security concerns in cryptocurrencies: state-of-the-art and perspectives. Comput. Secur. **113**, 102548 (2022)
10. Butler, S.: Cyber 9/11 will not take place: a user perspective of bitcoin and cryptocurrencies from underground and dark net forums. In: Groß, T., Viganò, L. (eds.) STAST 2020. LNCS, vol. 12812, pp. 135–153. Springer, Cham (2021). https://doi.org/10.1007/978-3-030-79318-0_8
11. Hellwig, D., Karlic, G., Huchzermeier, A.: Privacy and Anonymity, pp. 99–121. Springer, Cham (2020)
12. Koshy, P., Koshy, D., McDaniel, P.: An analysis of anonymity in bitcoin using P2P network traffic. In: Christin, N., Safavi-Naini, R. (eds.) FC 2014. LNCS, vol. 8437, pp. 469–485. Springer, Heidelberg (2014). https://doi.org/10.1007/978-3-662-45472-5_30

13. Chaum, D.L.: Untraceable electronic mail, return addresses, and digital pseudonyms. Commun. ACM **24**(2), 84–90 (1981)
14. Bonneau, J., Narayanan, A., Miller, A., Clark, J., Kroll, J.A., Felten, E.W.: Mixcoin: anonymity for bitcoin with accountable mixes. In: Christin, N., Safavi-Naini, R. (eds.) FC 2014. LNCS, vol. 8437, pp. 486–504. Springer, Heidelberg (2014). https://doi.org/10.1007/978-3-662-45472-5_31
15. Duffield, E., Diaz, D.: Dash: a privacycentric cryptocurrency (2015)
16. Heilman, E., Alshenibr, L., Baldimtsi, F., Scafuro, A., Goldberg, S.: Tumblebit: an untrusted bitcoin-compatible anonymous payment hub. Cryptology ePrint Archive (2016)
17. Sasson, E.B., et al.: Zerocash: decentralized anonymous payments from bitcoin. In: 2014 IEEE Symposium on Security and Privacy, pp. 459–474. IEEE (2014)
18. Rejeb, A., Rejeb, K., Keogh, J.G.: Cryptocurrencies in modern finance: a literature review. Etikonomi **20**(1), 93–118 (2021)
19. Makarov, I., Schoar, A.: Cryptocurrencies and decentralized finance (DeFi), Technical report, National Bureau of Economic Research (2022)
20. Teichmann, F.M.J., Falker, M.-C.: Cryptocurrencies and financial crime: solutions from Liechtenstein. J. Money Laundering Control **24**(4), 775–788 (2021)
21. Vassallo, D., Vella, V., Ellul, J.: Application of gradient boosting algorithms for anti-money laundering in cryptocurrencies. SN Comput. Sci. **2**(3), 1–15 (2021)
22. Chatzigiannis, P., Baldimtsi, F., Chalkias, K.: SoK: auditability and accountability in distributed payment systems. In: Sako, K., Tippenhauer, N.O. (eds.) ACNS 2021. LNCS, vol. 12727, pp. 311–337. Springer, Cham (2021). https://doi.org/10.1007/978-3-030-78375-4_13
23. Xue, L., Liu, D., Ni, J., Lin, X., Shen, X.S.: Enabling regulatory compliance and enforcement in decentralized anonymous payment. IEEE Trans. Dependable Secure Comput. **20**, 931–943 (2022)
24. Ma, T., Xu, H., Li, P.: SkyEye: a traceable scheme for blockchain. Cryptology ePrint Archive (2020)
25. Wüst, K., Kostiainen, K., Čapkun, V., Čapkun, S.: PRCash: fast, private and regulated transactions for digital currencies. In: Goldberg, I., Moore, T. (eds.) FC 2019. LNCS, vol. 11598, pp. 158–178. Springer, Cham (2019). https://doi.org/10.1007/978-3-030-32101-7_11
26. Wang, Z., Pei, Q., Liui, X., Ma, L., Li, H., Yu, S.: DAPS: a decentralized anonymous payment scheme with supervision. In: Wen, S., Zomaya, A., Yang, L.T. (eds.) ICA3PP 2019. LNCS, vol. 11945, pp. 537–550. Springer, Cham (2020). https://doi.org/10.1007/978-3-030-38961-1_46
27. Camenisch, J., Lysyanskaya, A.: Dynamic accumulators and application to efficient revocation of anonymous credentials. In: Yung, M. (ed.) CRYPTO 2002. LNCS, vol. 2442, pp. 61–76. Springer, Heidelberg (2002). https://doi.org/10.1007/3-540-45708-9_5
28. Li, J., Li, N., Xue, R.: Universal accumulators with efficient nonmembership proofs. In: Katz, J., Yung, M. (eds.) ACNS 2007. LNCS, vol. 4521, pp. 253–269. Springer, Heidelberg (2007). https://doi.org/10.1007/978-3-540-72738-5_17
29. Tomescu Nicolescu, I.A.: How to keep a secret and share a public key (using polynomial commitments). PhD thesis, Massachusetts Institute of Technology (2020)
30. Hao, F.: Schnorr non-interactive zero-knowledge proof, Technical report (2017)
31. Xue, R., Li, N.-H., Li, J.-T.: Algebraic construction for zero-knowledge sets. J. Comput. Sci. Technol. **23**(2), 166–175 (2008)
32. Soewito, B., Marcellinus, Y.: IoT security system with modified zero knowledge proof algorithm for authentication. Egypt. Inf. J. **22**(3), 269–276 (2021)

33. Yu, G.: Blockchain stealth address schemes. Cryptology ePrint Archive (2020)
34. Seguias, B.E.K.: Monero's building blocks part 10 of 10-stealth addresses (2018)
35. Liu, J.K., Wei, V.K., Wong, D.S.: Linkable spontaneous anonymous group signature for ad hoc groups. In: Wang, H., Pieprzyk, J., Varadharajan, V. (eds.) ACISP 2004. LNCS, vol. 3108, pp. 325–335. Springer, Heidelberg (2004). https://doi.org/10.1007/978-3-540-27800-9_28
36. Wang, L., Zhang, G., Ma, C.: A survey of ring signature. Front. Electr. Electron. Eng. China **3**, 10–19 (2008)
37. Singh, R., Dwivedi, A.D., Mukkamala, R.R., Alnumay, W.S.: Privacy-preserving ledger for blockchain and internet of things-enabled cyber-physical systems. Comput. Electr. Eng. **103**, 108290 (2022)
38. Wang, H., Liao, J.: Blockchain privacy protection algorithm based on Pedersen commitment and zero-knowledge proof. In: Proceedings of the 2021 4th International Conference on Blockchain Technology and Applications, pp. 1–5 (2021)
39. Seguias, B.E.K.: Monero's building blocks part 6 of 10-linkable spontaneous anonymous group (LSAG) signature scheme (2018)
40. Lynn, B., et al.: PBC library-pairing-based cryptography (2006). https://crypto.stanford.edu/pbc/. Accessed 27 Mar 2013

ODSC: A Unique Chameleon Hash-Based Application Framework for Blockchain Smart Contracts

Chenxi Xiong[1]📷, Ting Yang[1], and Hongqing Song[2](✉)

[1] University of Electronic Science and Technology of China, Chengdu 611731, China
202221081027@std.uestc.edu.cn, yting@uestc.edu.cn
[2] The Second Research Institute of CAAC, Chengdu 610041, China
songhongqing@caacetc.com

Abstract. Blockchain become a trust and secure environment for decentralized applications. The blockchain brings the benefits of tamper-resistant while also bringing on-chain overhead issues. With the development of blockchain smart contracts, securely reduce the on-chain data storage overhead is a very worthwhile research question. In this research, the Off-chain Data Storage based on Chameleon hash (ODSC), a unique framework for distributed system based on chameleon hash, supports code or stored data upgrades without changing on-chain data is presented. ODSC uses chameleon hash of data as index to ensure the index does not change during data modifying process while data can store outside of blockchain with authentication. The experimental results show ODSC has less on-chain storage than comparable frameworks. Additionally, ODSC has a far lower overhead than directly storing data in a smart contract.

Keywords: blockchain · storage · distributed system · smart contract · chameleon hash

1 Introduction

The size of blockchain-based decentralized apps can expanding quickly because of blockchain ledger structure. Every node must store the entire blockchain ledger data, which there will be a limit to on-chain data can store [1,2]. The data from decentralized applications is restricting the number of transactions as blockchain continues to grow. Thus, to build decentralized smart contracts and lower the price of on-chain data storage, a blockchain-based off-chain storage solution is needed.

Smart contract storage infrastructures have been proposed, Certledger [3], Smart Contract-based PKI (SCPKI) [4], and TrustCA [5] provide solutions for

Supported by the National Natural Science Foundation of China, Grant No (U2033212) and the Sichuan Science and Technology Program under grant No. 2022JDRC0006.

storing key-value data based on smart contract. However, these proposals are inefficient in terms of storage and have large headers. These proposals reduce on-chain storage overhead by storing data into InterPlanetary File System (IPFS) and then storing the index of data in blockchain. If data in IPFS need to be modified in these proposals, it is necessary to update new data and obtain a new index. The approach is practical for keeping Public Key Infrastructure (PKI) certificates that does not need to be updated for a while. But data often needs to be updated in apps. For example, domain name administrators must reassign domain name resolution information in Domain Name System (DNS). This will result in an additional overhead when updating the data stored in IPFS and sending transactions to call contracts. Namecoin [6] proposed a solution to build a new blockchain dedicated to storing and maintaining these key-value data. Nevertheless, existing blockchains can provide better security [7]. A framework to build off-chain data storage based on the existing public blockchain is required.

In this paper, propose a unique framework for building distributed application is proposed, what called ODSC. ODSC uses chameleon hash as an index to ensures that the index does not change after modifying data. ODSC reduces on-chain storage overhead and facilitates the storage of frequently updated data by storing data in application-based small-scale distributed storage. ODSC can be implemented based on the existing public blockchain that supports smart contract. The security of ODSC is guaranteed by the unforgeability of the chameleon hash and the transparency of blockchain. We used Go-lang to develop an ODSC-based demo program and verified the feasibility of the framework on Ethereum Sepolia testnet. The on-chain overhead of modifying data is also tiny.

2   Related Work

The Internet infrastructures based on trusted third-party (TTP) implementations have various problems due to their centralized design [8]. Therefore, in order to build these infrastructures without TTP, a decentralized architecture is reqiured. Many proposals have been proposed to build internet infrastructure based on blockchain.

Some proposals provided blockchain-based PKI implementation architectures. [3–5,9,10] proposed architectures based on smart contract to implement PKI. CertLedger [3] implemented certificate transparency and revocation transparency based on blockchain. SCPKI [4] built an attribute storage architecture. The full version stores attribute data in smart contract and the light version stores data on IPFS. TrustCA [5] implemented certificate transparency based on smart contract and utilizes IPFS to reduce the overhead of on-chain storage. IKP [9] designed a blockchain-based PKI enhancement that offers automatic responses to CA misbehavior and incentives for those who help detect misbehavior. It stored PKI-related data in smart contract, and designed detectors to monitor the logs of the smart contract to detect misbehavior of CAs. [10] designed blockchain-based PKI management framework for issuing, validating, and revoking certificates. This framework stores certificate data in smart contracts and constructs a chain of trust between contracts. These proposals use on-chain storage, which increases the overhead of on-chain storage. Some of them also use IPFS to reduce on-chain storage overhead, but it is inconvenient to modify stored data frequently.

There has also been other proposed blockchain-based storage framework. Saqib Ali [11] designed a decentralized data storage and access framework for PingER. It stores the file in P2P network, then packages the relevant information of the file as a transaction and sends it to blockchain. Shangping Wang uses Ethereum [12] smart contract to store encrypted parameters of files [13]. The proposed framework uses smart contract as a TTP, allowing users to decrypt files in cloud storage within a valid access period. These proposals use blockchain as a TTP to ensure that data cannot be modified and cannot be used to store modifiable data.

Namecoin [6], and Ethereum name service (ENS) [14] are blockchain-based domain name services. Namecoin [6] based on the code of Bitcoin [15] implements the storage of key-value data within its blockchain transaction database. Namecoin supports '.bit' address, public keys can be added to a domain to enable PKI. ENS [14] provides a domain name service based on Ethereum smart contracts. The resolution information of the domain name is stored in smart contract, which is on-chain storage. [6] proposed new chain to store data, but it is vulnerable to attacks. [14] stores data in smart contracts and its storage overhead on the chain is relatively large. There will be additional overhead when data has been modified.

3   Preliminaries

3.1   Chameleon Hash Based on Elliptic Curve

Chameleon hash was introduced in [16], which is the basis of ODSC. Elliptic curves can provide better security with the shorter private key, so we utilize elliptic curves to construct the chameleon hash function for implementing ODSC.

The chameleon hash is built upon an Abelian group G_p, where p is a large prime number. The cardinality of G_p should be divisible by a large prime number q [17] for security. A point O chosen from G_p as the base point. $x \in [1, q-1]$ is selected as the private key, and $y = xO$ calculated as the public key.

To compute the hash of a message m_1, h is used to map the message m_1 for a large integer. When computing the hash value of m_1 for the first time, a random number r_1 needs to be selected. Then the chameleon hash value $CH(m_1, y, r_1)$ of message m_1 can be computed as

$$CH(m_1, y, r_1) = h(m_1) \cdot O + r_1 \cdot y \tag{1}$$

When modifying the data corresponding to the chameleon hash, assuming that the new message is m_2, a new random number r_2 can be obtained through the collision finding algorithm $Find(m_1, r_1, m_2, x)$ as

$$Find(m_1, r_1, m_2, x) = (xr_1 + h(m_1) - h(m_2))x^{-1} \tag{2}$$

This is because need to ensure that $CH(m_1, y, r_1) = CH(m_2, y, r_2)$, expand the formula as

$$h(m_1) \cdot O + xr_1 \cdot O = h(m_2) \cdot O + xr_2 \cdot O \tag{3}$$

Therefore, the calculation formula of the collision algorithm can be derived. The output hash value will not be changed when updating the data. Only the holder of the private key x can generate a valid random number r_2, so the chameleon hash is unforgeable.

4   Framework Design

ODSC is used to store off-chain data, and it needs to rely on blockchain to store the digest of data to ensure credibility and transparency of data. Compared with other similar frameworks, ODSC can reduce the storage overhead on the chain, which is conducive to storing data that needs to be changed frequently.

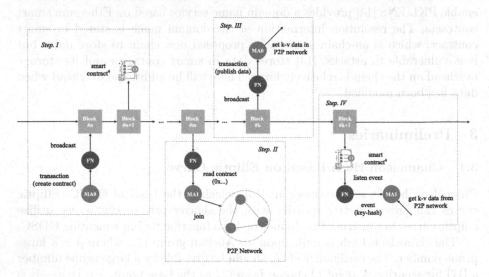

Fig. 1. ODSC overall workflow. It shows the workflow of ODSC, which is divided into four steps.

There are two different types of nodes in ODSC: (1) Full Node (FN), which runs the full node program of blockchain and can broadcast transaction. (2) Monitoring Agent (MA_n), which runs the framework, sends transactions to blockchain and monitors smart contract events through FN.

In addition, we need a smart contract to validate the nodes' permission. We will explain the purpose of this smart contract later and propose an ERC specification[1] that is beneficial for implementing ODSC-based applications.

---

[1] https://github.com/Chain-Lab/odsc-demo/blob/main/solidity/odsc-specification.
sol.

MA_n can deploy smart contract and manage the authority of the MA_n under the same application. A P2P network is built between MAs using Kademlia [18], and they all maintain a database to manage off-chain data. After illustrating the two types of nodes and smart contract in ODSC, the overall workflow of ODSC is shown in Fig. 1. The workflow has four steps as follows.

4.1 Contract Creation and Data Initialization

As the Step. I shown in Fig. 1. P2P protocol and creation of a smart contract on blockchain require a bootstrap node MA_0. MA_0 sends a transaction to blockchain through FN to create and initialize the smart contract. The developer develop smart contract and then deploys the compiled contract code by default method of blockchain. The data that the smart contract needs to initialize is *owner*, *boostrap* and *genesis*.

To limit the operation permission of the contract, MA_0 sets the *owner* attribute. Only the *owner* can modify the information in the smart contract. MA_0 fills *bootstrap* with its own connection information in P2P network. *genesis* is the index of genesis data, which is generated after MA_0 creates genesis data. Genesis data *gd* is created before MA_0 initializes the smart contract attributes. In other scenarios, *gd* can be set as required. After MA_0 creates *gd*, *signature* is generated by using the chameleon hash, and *signature* can be used for verification and as an index of the data. MA_0 will put *gd* to the P2P network and writes it to the smart contract during initialization.

Algorithm 1: Genesis data initialization

    Input: Private key *priv*
    Output: Genesis data *gd*
1   $gd \leftarrow NewData()$;
2   $gd.hash \leftarrow latestBlockHash$;
3   $gd.version \leftarrow 0$;
4   $sk \leftarrow ChameleonKey(priv)$;
5   $gd.index, gd.random \leftarrow sk.Signature(result)$;
6   $gd.list \leftarrow [sk.Address()]$;
7   output *result*

Fig. 2. Create genesis data algorithm

The pseudocode of the algorithm that creates the genesis data is shown in Fig. 2. For security, version and the latest block hash of blockchain must be set when the data is created and modified. *gd* contain a list, which is used to control data write permissions.

The distributed network running this framework will synchronize data on the network according to *list*. The index of *gd* is obtained through the chameleon hash, so MA_0 can change *list* in *gd* without affecting *gd.index*. Through the pseudocode of Fig. 2, we can know that the required attributes of genesis data *gd* are shown in Table 1.

Table 1. Genesis Data Initialization Attributes

Attribute	Type	Description
index	string	The chameleon output of genesis data
pubKey	string	Chameleon public key
random	stirng	Chameleon random number
blockHash	string	Latest block hash
timestamp	int	Timestamp when create
version	int	Data modification version
list	[]byte	Permission list in the application

4.2 Read Attribute and Connect P2P Network

The connection information bootstrap of the genesis node MA_0 is stored in the smart contract. But MA_0 may fail for abnormal reasons. According to bootstrap, a new node can discover other nodes and join the P2P network. The process for Step. II shown in Fig. 1 for new node MA_1 and MA_2 to join the P2P network are as follows.

1. MA_1 reads bootstrap from smart contract, then connects to MA_0;
2. MA_1 discover other nodes in the P2P network through MA_0 and built its routing table. Now other nodes can also discover other nodes through MA_1;
3. Another new node MA_2 wants to join the P2P network later, MA_2 can connect to MA_1 to discover other nodes in the P2P network.

New nodes such as MA_1 and MA_2 can call smart contract to record their connection information into the log. This can solve the single point of failure (SPOF) problem.

4.3 Manipulate Data and Call Contract

The node in an ODSC-based application needs to open a remote procedure call (RPC) [19] service to receive data operation commands. The RPC service is only exposed to the local command line interface (CLI) for security. There are three operations: create data, modify data and revoke data. When the node performs these three operations, it will emit an event on the smart contract. There are three types of events corresponding to data operations, which are *created*, *modified*, and *revoked*. Figure 3 shows the life cycle of data. After data is *created*, it undergoes a series of *modified* and finally is *revoked*.

Users can insert new data as Step. III in Fig. 1 by sending a message carrying the data to a node through RPC service. The node will create new data according to the pseudocode shown in Fig. 4 after receiving data. The attributes

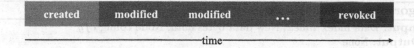

Fig. 3. Life cycle of a data

in a piece of data are similar to the attributes in genesis data shwon in Table 1. The difference is that *list* is replaced by an attribute named *data*.

Algorithm 2: Create new data

Input: Data bytes *data*, Node config *cfg*
Output: Data index *index*
1 *priv ← cfg.privateKey*;
2 *sk ← ChameleonKey(priv)*;
3 *newData ← NewData()*;
   // Get hash of the latest block from blockchain.
4 *newData.hash ← latestBlockHash*;
5 *newData.version ← 0*;
6 *newData.timestamp ← Time()*;
7 *newData.pubKey ← sk.Address()*;
8 *newData.data ← data*;
9 *newData.index, newData.random ← sk.Signature(newData)*;
10
11 *index ← sign*;
12 *CallSmartContract(created, index, random)*;
13 *PutDataToP2P(index, newData)*;
14 output *index*

Fig. 4. Create a new data algorithm

If a user needs to modify data, it is necessary to send a message carrying the data's *index* and new data bytes to the RPC interface of a node. After the node receives index and new data, it will modify data according to the pseudocode shown in Fig. 5.

According to the life cycle of data shown in Fig. 3, data can be revoked. Users can revoke data by sending a message carrying the index to the RPC interface of the node. As Step. III in Fig. 1, after the node receives the message, it will directly call the smart contract function and emit the revoked event.

Algorithm 3: Modify data

Input: Data index *index*, New data bytes *data*, Node config *cfg*
Output: None
1 *priv* ← *cfg.privateKey*;
2 *sk* ← *ChameleonKey(priv)*;
3 *orginData* ← *GetDataFromDB(index)*;
   // Get hash of the latest block from blockchain.
4 *newData* ← *copy(orginData)*;
5 *newData.hash* ← *latestBlockHash*;
6 *newData.version* ← *newData.version* + 1;
7 *newData.timestamp* ← *Time()*;
8 *newData.pubKey* ← *sk.Address()*;
9 *newData.data* ← *data*
10
11 *newData.random* ← *sk.reSignature(orginData, newData)*;
12 *CallSmartContract(modified, index, random)*;
13 *PutDataToP2P(index, newData)*;

Fig. 5. Modify data algorithm

4.4   Monitor Event and Synchronize Data

When an ODSC-based application runs, it will start a thread to monitor the events of the specified smart contract. The callback function corresponding to the event will be executed if an event is emitted. As mentioned above, there are three events in smart contract that correspond to the life cycle of data: *created*, *modified*, and *revoked*. Therefore, new nodes can traverse the log to synchronize data based on these events. New nodes can traverse the event log in the smart contract in turn to obtain data change records as the Step. IV shown in Fig. 1.

The *synchronize* workflow for a new node is shown in Fig. 6. New nodes append the traversed events to the task queue and then perform corresponding processing according to the type of events. During the *synchronize* process, new nodes need to synchronize data according to four conditions as follows.

- The *created* and *modified* events contain data's chameleon hash and a random number.
- The *revoked* event contains the chameleon hash of data, which can be revoked after verifying that the event was emitted by the creator of data.
- P2P networks only save the latest data. Therefore, when synchronizing data, mainly focus on the *modified* event, and use the last *modified* event to verify the data.
- If a piece of data has been revoked, the *modified* event is no longer valid.

Through the *synchronize* workflow, new nodes can update their data to latest. *index* and *random* of a data are used as parameters for the *created* event and *modified* event. Nodes in the P2P network take out *index* and *random* when monitoring events. The data can be obtained by using *index* as the key

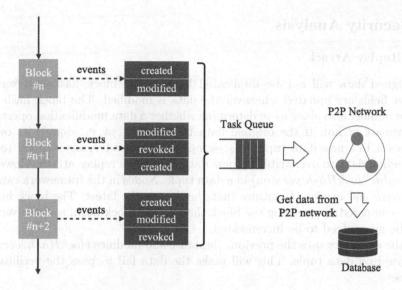

Fig. 6. Synchronize workflow

in the P2P network. The data is then deserialized to take out the public key contained within it. Nodes can use the random number and public key to check whether the value is valid. The validation workflow is shown in Fig. 7.

Algorithm 4: Verify data

> **Input:** Event *event*
> **Output:** Verify result *result*
> 1 $data \leftarrow GetDataFromP2P(event.index)$;
> 2 $strPublicKey \leftarrow data.pubKey$;
> 3 $pk \leftarrow ChameleonPublicKey(strPublicKey)$;
> 4 $result \leftarrow pk.Verify(event.index, event.random, data)$;
> 5 output $result$;

Fig. 7. Verify data algorithm

In addition to *created* and *modified* event, nodes also need to handle *revoked* event. If a *revoked* event with *index* as a parameter is monitored, the nodes in the P2P network will delete the data in their database and will not handle the event of the *index* in the future because the data has been revoked. To ensure that only the owner of the data can operate the data, other nodes will check whether the *modified* or *revoked* event is emitted by the creator of data.

5 Security Analysis

5.1 Replay Attack

The signed data will not be duplicated because the block hash and version number fields are updated whenever the data is modified. The block hash and version number also allow us to determine whether a data modification operation is legitimate or not. If the original data tuple is $(m_1, pk, r_1, sign_1)$, its owner modifies it to a new data tuple $(m_2, pk, r_2, sign_2)$. An adversary can try to use the original data to overwrite the new data to achieve replay attack. However, $m = (value|blockHash|version)$ in a data tuple. Nodes in the framework can use $blockHash$ and $version$ to ensure that the data is the latest. The block height can be compared by querying the block through the block hash, and the version must be guaranteed to be incremented.

If the adversary uses the previous signature and modifies $blockHash, version$ or $value$ in a data tuple. This will make the data fail to pass the verification because

$$CH(m, pk, r) \neq CH(m', pk, r) \tag{4}$$

This ensures that ODSC can defend against replay attack.

5.2 Data Security

There are five operations in ODSC: *genesis, create, modify, revoke* and *synchronize. genesis* is a single operation that is used to initialize ODSC, whose is similar to create. To prove these operations are secure, it is need to define four methods shown in Table 2. These methods can constitute the five data operations described above.

Table 2. Methods included in data operations

Method	Description
$MA_n Sign$	Sign data by chameleon hash
$MA_n Resign$	Re-sign data to keep index not change by chameleon hash
$Publish$	Publish data in P2P network
$Emit$	Emit event in smart contract

As mentioned above, *genesis* is the operation that can only be performed once by the genesis node, which corresponds to Step. I of Fig. 1. We assume that the genesis node is MA_0, its private key is sk_0, its public key is pk_0, and the permission list contained in genesis data is pl. In initializing ODSC, MA_0 constructs genesis data $gd = (pk_0, timestamp, version = 0, pl)$, then signs gd with chameleon hash to get index and random number by $index, r =$

$MA_0Sign(sk_0, gd)$. MA_0 constructs genesis message $gm = (gd, index, random)$. The operation of MA_0 at the time of *genesis* can be represented as

$$Publish(index, gm) \cap Emit(create, index, r) \tag{5}$$

With the operation, genesis node MA_0 writes index and random into smart contract. MA_0 publishes data gm to P2P network with *index*, then emits *created* event in smart contract with parameter *index* and *random*. According to the characteristics of the chameleon hash, only the genesis node MA_0 can generate valid *index* and *random* [16]. In addition, smart contract log is public, and blockchain transactions contain sender's information. Other nodes can use the information and smart contract log to verify whether the data on P2P network has been falsified. Therefore, the unforgeability of chameleon hash and the transparency of blockchain ensure that the genesis message gm is unalterable. The security in manipulate data and synchronize data is also based on the unforgeability of the chameleon hash and the transparency of blockchain.

The security of blokchain and elliptic curves based chameleon hash relies on the Elliptic Curve Discrete Logarithm Problem (ECDLP) [20]. Furthermore, the security of ODSC is based on ECDLP, a polynomial-time adversary can breach ODSC with negligible probability when the secret key length exceed 160 bits. In summary, the security of ODSC data can be guaranteed.

6 Experiments

6.1 Experimental Environment

We used Go-lang to develop an ODSC-based demo program[2]. The smart contract in demo program for testing is deployed on the Ethereum Sepolia testnet[3]. There are 15 nodes to test the functionality and performance of the program.

To ensure that the framework was feasible, we ran functional tests on the program. The program is also conducted performance testing in order to acquire quantifiable system.

6.2 Function Test

Following the completion of the node network deployment, we used the CLI tool to sequentially store files of 1kb, 5kb, 20kb, 50kb, 100kb, 200kb, 500kb, 1000kb, and 2000kb into the network. Because the file over 2000kb exceeds the default transfer size limit of the RPC interface, no larger files have been tested.

The demo program can create, modify, and revoke data in all tests. It is consistent with the expectations of ODSC.

---

[2] https://github.com/Chain-Lab/odsc-demo.
[3] Smart contract address is 0x42e87ba2470f5ef539037f250e5fd77a9155496a.

6.3 Performance Test

On-Chain Storage Consumption. Gas table contains the gas cost of different operations in Ethereum virtual machine (EVM). To precisely measure the storage cost of different on-chain storage methods, the cost of gas table has been modified[4] in go-ethereum for measuring, all none storage-related cost of operations are set to 1. Four types of contracts of different data storing methods are deployed on the local test node as follows.

1. Direct Storage: Receive encoded data, then store the data in smart contract.
2. On-chain NFT: Receive a Non-Fungible Tokens (NFT) token-id and encoded data, then store the data into a map of the smart contract. This map is a uint256 to string map, indicating the data resource corresponding to an NFT.
3. Off-chain NFT: Receive the NFT token-id and IPFS path, store the path into the map of the smart contract. The path points to the location of the corresponding image in IPFS.
4. ODSC: Receive the chameleon hash and random number, then emit event with them as parameters. The chameleon hash corresponds to the index of file in P2P network.

Table 3. Gas usage in different storage methods (Wei)

Storage	File size (kb)		
Method	10	25	50
Direct Storage	9227655	13398741	27703185
On-chain NFT	9230848	20290736	42856571
Off-chain NFT	62092	62092	62092
ODSC	1538	1538	1538

After storing data on these smart contracts respectively, we got the experimental results shown in Table 3.

Since the impact of computing operations is excluded from gas table, the experimental results can reflect the on-chain storage overhead of the storage method. From the gas usage of direct storage and on-chain NFT, the overhead of direct on-chain storage can be 6000 times the size of ODSC. Correspondingly, using off-chain storage has less storage overhead. Because only index information needs to be stored on-chain, the overhead of off-chain storage is also independent of file size. It can also be seen that ODSC has lower gas consumption than Off-chain NFT using IPFS. Through the experiment of on-chain storage overhead, ODSC can significantly reduce the on-chain storage overhead.

---

[4] https://github.com/Chain-Lab/odsc-demo/blob/main/experiment/gas_table/protocol_params.go.

Comparison. We obtained the gas usage of ODSC and other similar frameworks when creating, modifying, or revoking data. SCPKI, IKP, BGPCoin are used for comparison due to they have similar operations to ODSC.

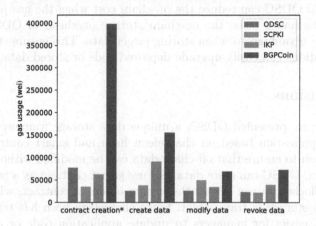

Fig. 8. Gas usage in similar frameworks

1. Contract creation: All blockchain-based frameworks need to deploy smart contract. Contract creation is the first step in framework initialization.
2. Create data: Insert new data into application. In ODSC-based application, data is stored in a small-scale P2P network. In other frameworks, data is stored in IPFS.
3. Modify data: Modify data for a specific index. After modifying data in corresponding storage, modify data's on-chain index.
4. Revoke data: Remove the corresponding data in application. Delete data of the corresponding index in storage, and marks the data as being revoked on blockchain.

Similar processes in SCPKI, IKP, and BGPCoin can be classified into these four operations for comparison. The comparison of gas usage data is shown in Fig. 8 to compare the differences in gas usage. The gas usage of contract creation was scaled down equally (divided by 10) to makes it easier to graph.

In Fig. 8 that ODSC uses less gas compared to other frameworks. The gas usage for contract creation is 119.3% higher than gas usage in SCPKI, which is related to the design of smart contract. Nevertheless, ODSC reduces the on-chain overhead by 31% compared to SCPKI, which consumes less gas. Since ODSC only needs to update the random number when modifying data, the gas usage in ODSC is 24.7% less than IKP. The gas usage when ODSC revokes data is 0.04% higher than SCPKI. This may be related to experimental error, but ODSC still has low on-chain storage overhead. By testing the gas usage and comparing it with similar frameworks, ODSC can reduce more on-chain storage overhead.

With the performance test result, ODSC can modify off-chain stored data in a convenient and safe manner, reducing on-chain storage overhead. In a production environment, higher security can be guaranteed if use the Ethereum mainnet. ODSC uses less gas than similar frameworks compared to the on-chain gas usage. It ensures that ODSC can reduce the on-chain cost when the gas price is high. Through performance tests, the on-chain storage overhead of ODSC is fixed, which is more advantageous when storing larger data. This ensures that ODSC-based applications can easily upgrade deployed code or stored data.

7 Conclusions

In this paper, we presented ODSC, a unique data storage framework for build distributed application based on chameleon hash and smart contract. It uses chameleon hash to ensure that off-chain data can be modified without changing on-chain index. ODSC can store data and use smart contract as a proxy in sub-pub mode. Blockchain can record the events of smart contract, which ensures that the data storage is transparent. Since chameleon hash has trapdoor, this makes ODSC easier for managers to update application code or stored data. The security of ODSC is guaranteed by the transparency of the blockchain itself and the unforgeability of transactions. This makes the data stored on the P2P network cannot be easily tampered with.

In order to verify the feasibility of ODSC, we used Go-lang to develop an ODSC-based demo program. After modifying the gas table of go-ethereum to avoid the gas impact of the operation, the on-chain storage overhead of ODSC and other smart contracts have been measured. ODSC significantly reduce on-chain data storage overhead, it has certain advantages over comparable frameworks. Therefore, ODSC can be used to develop some blockchain-based programs to store data off-chain with less overhead on-chain.

Nevertheless, ODSC relies on the consensus speed of the blockchain, which makes it unable to provide better real-time performance on existing public chains. Therefore, ODSC has limitations, it can only support some applications with low real-time requirements such as DNS, PKI, BGP, etc. With future blockchain technology development, ODSC can also be implemented based on high-performance or IoT blockchain. The improved ODSC and the high-performance blockchain can provide highly responsive services at that time.

References

1. Xu, C., Zhang, C., Xu, J., Pei, J.: SlimChain: scaling blockchain transactions through off-chain storage and parallel processing. Proc. VLDB Endowment **14**(11), 2314–2326 (2021)
2. Kumar, R., Marchang, N., Tripathi, R.: SMDSB: efficient off-chain storage model for data sharing in blockchain environment. In: Swain, D., Pattnaik, P.K., Athawale, T. (eds.) Machine Learning and Information Processing. AISC, vol. 1311, pp. 225–240. Springer, Singapore (2021). https://doi.org/10.1007/978-981-33-4859-2_24

3. Kubilay, M.Y., Kiraz, M.S., Mantar, H.A.: CertLedger: a new PKI model with certificate transparency based on blockchain. Comput. Secur. **85**, 333–352 (2019)
4. Al-Bassam, M.: SCPKI: a smart contract-based PKI and identity system. In: Proceedings of the ACM Workshop on Blockchain, Cryptocurrencies and Contracts, pp. 35–40 (2017)
5. Zhao, J., Lin, Z., Huang, X., Zhang, Y., Xiang, S.: TrustCA: achieving certificate transparency through smart contract in blockchain platforms. In: 2020 International Conference on High Performance Big Data and Intelligent Systems (HPBD&IS), pp. 1–6. IEEE (2020)
6. Namecoin, C.: Namecoin (2010)
7. Sayeed, S., Marco-Gisbert, H.: Assessing blockchain consensus and security mechanisms against the 51% attack. Appl. Sci. **9**(9), 1788 (2019)
8. Ali, F.S., Kupcu, A.: Improving PKI, BGP, and DNS using blockchain: a systematic review. arXiv preprint arXiv:2001.00747 (2020)
9. Matsumoto, S., Reischuk, R.M.: IKP: turning a PKI around with decentralized automated incentives. In: 2017 IEEE Symposium on Security and Privacy (SP), pp. 410–426. IEEE (2017)
10. Yakubov, A., Shbair, W., Wallbom, A., Sanda, D., et al.: A blockchain-based PKI management framework. In: The First IEEE/IFIP International Workshop on Managing and Managed by Blockchain (Man2Block) Colocated with IEEE/IFIP NOMS 2018, Tapei, Tawain 23–27 April 2018 (2018)
11. Ali, S., Wang, G., White, B., Cottrell, R.L.: A blockchain-based decentralized data storage and access framework for pinger. In: 2018 17th IEEE International Conference on Trust, Security and Privacy in Computing and Communications/12th IEEE International Conference on Big Data Science and Engineering (TrustCom/BigDataSE), pp. 1303–1308. IEEE (2018)
12. Wood, G., et al.: Ethereum: a secure decentralised generalised transaction ledger. Ethereum Proj. Yellow Pap. **151**(2014), 1–32 (2014)
13. Wang, S., Wang, X., Zhang, Y.: A secure cloud storage framework with access control based on blockchain. IEEE Access **7**, 112713–112725 (2019)
14. ENS, C.: ENS (2020)
15. Nakamoto, S.: Bitcoin: a peer-to-peer electronic cash system. Decentralized Bus. Rev., 21260 (2008)
16. Krawczyk, H., Rabin, T.: Chameleon hashing and signatures. Cryptology ePrint Archive (1998)
17. Blake, I., Seroussi, G., Smart, N.: Elliptic Curves in Cryptography, vol. 265. Cambridge University Press, Cambridge (1999)
18. Maymounkov, P., Mazières, D.: Kademlia: a peer-to-peer information system based on the XOR metric. In: Druschel, P., Kaashoek, F., Rowstron, A. (eds.) IPTPS 2002. LNCS, vol. 2429, pp. 53–65. Springer, Heidelberg (2002). https://doi.org/10.1007/3-540-45748-8_5
19. Nelson, B.J.: Remote Procedure Call. Carnegie Mellon University (1981)
20. Menezes, A.: Evaluation of security level of cryptography: the elliptic curve discrete logarithm problem (ECDLP). University of Waterloo 14 (2001)

Cross-Chain Identity Authentication for BIoMT with Multi-chain Fusion Mode

Chaoyang Li[1]([✉]) [iD], Kaifei Chen[2] [iD], Chaonan Shen[3] [iD], and Xiangjun Xin[1] [iD]

[1] College of Software Engineering, Zhengzhou University of Light Industry,
Zhengzhou 450001, China
lichaoyang@zzuli.edu.cn
[2] College of Food and Bioengineering, Zhengzhou University of Light Industry,
Zhengzhou 450001, China
[3] School of Software, Henan Finance University, Zhengzhou 451464, China

Abstract. Blockchain-based Internet of medical things (BIoMT) changes the traditional centralized management form to distributed for the healthcare systems, which promotes the value of medical data. However, there brings a new "data island" problem with the emergence of more and more chains. This paper first introduces a multi-chain fusion (MCF) model to establish a secure cross-chain transaction mechanism to solve this new centralized problem. Then, a cross-chain identity authentication (CCIA) protocol has been proposed, which contains two parts of user identity anonymization and anonymous identity authentication. Here, the former part helps to achieve identity information hiding in different chains, and the second part utilizes identity filing to check its validity. Moreover, the security analysis shows that the CCIA protocol can protect the privacy system and user. The performance evaluation show that the MCF model is efficient and practical. Therefore, the MCF model and CCIA protocol can well support cross-chain transactions to maximize the value of medical data.

Keywords: BIoMT · Multi-chain fusion · Cross-chain · Identity authentication

1 Introduction

The wide applications of blockchain technology bring revolutionary changes to traditional centralized healthcare systems [1], but the emergence of more and more chains has created a new centralized problem. This prevents patients from seeing a doctor across the medical institutions with their own electrical medical records and also limits the value of medical data. Therefore, the cross-chain transaction is a new direction for the blockchain-based Internet of medical things (BIoMT) [2].

Nowadays, four main cross-chain schemes are notary mechanisms, such as the side chain/relay, hash lock, and distributed private key control [3]. Among them, the side chain/relay mode is more costly and less efficient because it requires

H. Yang and R. Lu (Eds.): FCS 2023, CCIS 1992, pp. 70–81, 2024.
https://doi.org/10.1007/978-981-99-9331-4_5

waiting for the transactions Chain, making sure that no rollback will occur before confirming [4]. Hash locking ensures atomicity of cross-chain asset exchange, However, this method can support cross-chain asset exchange, but cannot achieve assets transfer or other forms of interaction [5]. Distributed private key control also needs to wait for the source chain transaction, and it isn't easy to develop. The notary public mechanism was introduced with a trusted third party acting as the validator and coordinator of cross-chain transactions, the transaction initiator is sent to the source chain after a transaction, and the notary verifies whether the transaction is valid by listening for events on the source chain [6]. After that, the target chain is notified to perform the corresponding operation, and the notary public group uses a specific consensus algorithm on the event to reach a consensus.

To achieve cross-chain transactions, it must verify the user's identity first [7]. Generally, the user's identity is anonymous showing in the transaction, which can protect the user's privacy when his medical data are transmitted to different chains along with the cross-chain transactions. Hence, the authentication of the user's anonymous identity is the essential guarantee of a valid cross-chain medical data exchange. Generally, there are three kinds of authentication methods: shared keys, biological characteristics, and a public key encryption algorithm [8]. The shared keys method is to utilize the key pre-shared between the server and the user for identification [9,10], the biological characteristics method is depended on a unique person's features of fingerprints, and iris [11], and the public key encryption algorithm method is to use the scheme of secure sockets layer or digital signature to perform identity authentication [12–15]. These three methods have different advantages, which are widely used in different situations. In blockchain-based healthcare systems, the public key encryption algorithm can help strange users verify others' identities using their public keys. In addition, there are also some new proposals for medical data privacy-preserving in BIoMT, such as lightweight secret sharing [16], quantum blockchain [17,18], AI-enabled authentication scheme [19], key agreement [20], etc. However, insecure cryptographic algorithms take threats to the user's privacy. Along with the continuous expansion of cross-institution medical data exchange demand, cross-chain identity authentication needs a more secure and efficient cryptographic protocol.

This paper focuses on the identity authentication problem in cross-chain transaction processes and introduces a multi-chain fusion (MCF) model first. This model can establish a secure cross-chain transaction mechanism to solve the new "data island" problem. Then, a cross-chain identity authentication (CCIA) protocol has been proposed. This scheme contains two parts of user identity anonymization and anonymous identity authentication. Moreover, the security analysis of CCIA protocol and performance evaluation of MCF model are presented.

2   Multi-chain Fusion Model

An MCF model based on a relay chain has been presented in this section as shown in Fig. 1. This model mainly consists of one parent chain (relay chain) and many child chains. The processes of cross-chain transactions can be divided into four parts: transaction generation, identity authentication, transaction verification, and transaction recordation.

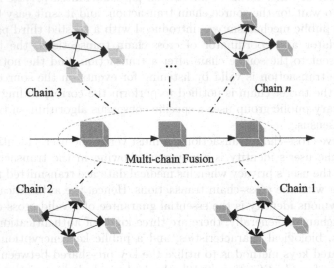

Fig. 1. Multi-chain fusion model.

(1) Transaction Generation. Different from the general signal chain system, this MCF model utilizes the relay chain to establish cross-chain transactions among different child chains. This relay chain plays the role of supporting cross-chain transactions and providing transaction consistency. The general user in one child chain initiates a new transaction when he wants to perform medical data exchange. This transaction composes of the basic information of the sender, receiver, medical data, and timestamp. It also contains the sender's identity filing and designated verifier signature. Here, identity filing is used for identity authentication, and the designated verifier signature prevents malicious data transmission.

(2) Identity Authentication. Identity authentication is the essential step for cross-chain transactions. The key generation centers (KGC) in these child chains compose of a union that takes responsibility for identity generation, identity authentication, and transaction verification. Every user obtains an anonymous identity from the KGC by a cross-chain identity authentication (CCIA) protocol first. When one user initiates a new transaction with the other user in the other child chain, the receiver performs identity authentication by the CCIA protocol. He utilizes identity filing to query the identity authentication to the key generation center in the original chain system. The manager checks the legality of this identity filing and sends back to results. Details of these identity authentication processes are given in the following section.

(3) Transaction Verification. Like the transaction verification processes in the general signal chain system, it must go through the steps of the pack, broadcast, audit, compare, and confirm. Here, the KGC union performs these verification processes, and this union also utilizes the consensus protocol of delegated proof of stake (DPoS) to maintain the MCF model-based system. When the packed temporary block passes these verification processes, the cross-chain transactions are verified to be legitimate.

(4) Transaction Recordation. This transaction recordation process contains two parts: child chain recordation and parent chain recordation. For legal cross-chain transactions, they should be recorded on the patent chain. Then, they also should be synchronized to the child chains corresponding to both transaction sides. Here, other child chains can choose not to synchronize these cross-chain transactions that are unrelated to them.

Here, this MCF model mainly focuses on the cross-chain identity privacy-preserving problem and establishes a secure channel for cross-chain transactions in the BIoMT. The following cross-chain identity authentication protocol plays an essential role in identity privacy-preserving among the cross-chain transaction processes.

3   Cross-Chain Identity Authentication Protocol

For identity privacy protection, this section proposes a cross-chain identity authentication protocol. This protocol mainly contains user identity anonymization and anonymous identity authentication.

3.1   User Identity Anonymization

Alice performs the following three steps to obtain an anonymous identity from the anonymous server and the simple workflow of user identity anonymization is shown in Fig. 2. This anonymous server is held by the parent chain, which takes responsibility for generating and managing anonymous identities.

- Alice random selects an anonymous parameter r_i, and sends a anonymous identity query $Q[ID_i] = E_{PK}(r_i||ID_i||Sig_{sk_i}(r_i)||t_1)$ to anonymous server. Here, PK is the public key of anonymous server, $Sig_{sk_-}(r_i)$ is the signature of r_i signed by Alice, sk_i is Alice's private key, and t_1 is the timestamp of this query;
- The anonymous server establishes an empty list L_i to store the anonymous identity query. After receiving the query on this anonymous parameter, it needs to check if r_i exists in the list first. If yes, it will ask Alice to resend a new query. If not, the anonymous server calculates $ID_i^* = h(ID_i * r_i)$. $h(\cdot)$ is a random hash function. Then, it will send $R[ID_i^*] = E_{pk_i}(ID_i^*||Sig_{SK}(ID_i^*)||t_2)$ to Alice, where pk_i is Alice's public key, $Sig_{SK}(ID_i^*)$ is the signature of ID_i^* signed by anonymous server, SK is the private key of anonymous server, and t_2 is the timestamp of this response.

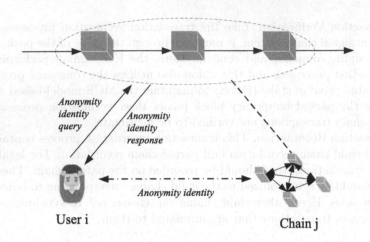

Fig. 2. User identity anonymization.

– Alice first checks whether $t_2 > t_1$ holds or not. If yes, she decrypts $R[ID_i^*]$ with sk_i, and obtains the anonymous identity ID_i^*.

Different medical chains aggregate a medical union as $M = M_1, M_2, ..., M_k$. Then, the anonymous server holds an anonymous identity list L_ID for Alice, and it performs the following Algorithm 1 to achieve user identity anonymization in different medical chains.

Algorithm 1. User identity anonymization

Input: Identity ID_i, Medical union M, Anonymous parameter list L_i, Anonymous identity list L_{ID}

Output: L_{ID}

1: Initiate $L_{ID} = \emptyset$
2: **for** $M_i \in M$ **do**
3:     User selects a random bit r_i as an anonymous parameter
4:     **if** r_i **then**
5:         Skip to step 3;
6:     **else**
7:         $r_i \in L_i$
8:         $ID_i^* = h(ID_i * r_i)$
9:         $ID_i^* \in L_{ID}$
10:    **end if**
11: **end for**

3.2   Anonymous Identity Authentication

Once Alice obtains the anonymous identity in the medical chain M_i, she can see a doctor in this medical institution and authorize the target user Bob to view her historical medical data. Here, the simple process of anonymous identity authentication is shown in Fig. 3, and the detailed descriptions are given below.

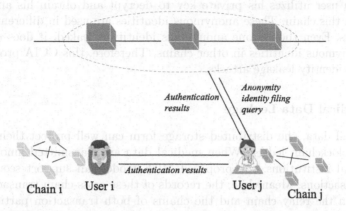

Fig. 3. Anonymous identity authentication.

- Alice sends the anonymous filing $F[ID_i^*] = E_{pk_j}(ID_i^* \| Sig_{sk_i}(ID_i^*) \| t_3)$ to the target user Bob j. Here, pk_j is the public key of Bob, $Sig_{sk_i}(ID_i^*)$ is the signature of ID_i^* signed by Alice, and t_3 is the timestamp of this anonymous filing;
- Bob sends $V[F] = E_{PK}(ID_i^* \| Sig_{sk_j}(ID_i^*) \| t_4)$ to the anonymous server for anonymous identity authentication . Here, $Sig_{sk_j}(ID_i^*)$ is the signature of ID_i^* signed by Bob, sk_j is the private key of Bob, and t_4 is the timestamp of this authentication information;
- The anonymous server check if ID_i^* exists in list L_{ID} after receiving the anonymous identity authentication query. If yes, it outputs $v_{ij} = 1$. If not, it outputs $v_{ij} = 0$. Then, the anonymous server returns the authentication results $C[v_{ij}] = E_{pk_j}(v_{ij} \| Sig_{SK}(v_{ij}) \| t_5)$ to Bob. Here, $Sig_{SK}(v_{ij})$ is the signature of v_{ij} signed by the anonymous server, and t_5 is the timestamp of this authentication information;
- Bob decrypts $C[v_{ij}]$ by his private key sk_j, and checks whether $t_5 > t_4 > t_3$ holds or not. If yes, he utilizes ID_i^* to store the medical data for Alice when $v_{ij} = 1$, but does not provide medical service for Alice when $v_{ij} = 0$. If not, the identity authentication fails.

4 Security Analysis

4.1 User Identity Leakage

When one user goes to another chain in a new medical institution, he first queries an anonymous identity with a random anonymous parameter r_i. The anonymous server generates an anonymous identity $ID_i^* = h(ID_i * r_i)$, and sends $R[ID_i^*] = E_{pk_i}(ID_i^*||Sig_{SK}(ID_i^*)||t_2)$ back to user with encryption method. It also establishes a list L_{ID} by the Algorithm 1 to store these anonymous identities. Then, this user utilizes his private key to decrypt and obtain his anonymous identity in this chain. These anonymous identities are used in different medical institutions. Even though one anonymous identity is leaked, it does not affect other anonymous identities in other chains. Therefore, this CCIA protocol can resist user identity leakage attacks.

4.2 Medical Data Leakage

For medical data, the distributed storage form can well protect their security with the blockchain ledger. When medical data are transmitted among different medical institutions, the proposed MCF model can support secure cross-chain transactions. Meanwhile, the records of these cross-chain transactions are recorded in the relay chain and the chains of both transaction parties, which improves the difficulty of tampering with medical data. Then, the proposed CCIA protocol provides another security guarantee for medical data as the user must pass the identity authentication first before he can view the medical data. Therefore, the proposed MCF model and CCIA protocol can resist user identity leakage attacks.

4.3 Cross-Chain Transaction Consistency

Based on the CCIA protocol, user identity privacy can be guaranteed among the cross-chain transaction processes in BIoMT. Meanwhile, the MCF model guarantees cross-chain transaction consistency. With the help of DPoS, the KGC union verifies the legitimacy of cross-chain transactions, and packed these transactions into the relay chain ledger. The cross-chain transactions are encrypted and recorded in the parent chain and both participants' child chains. This cross-chain transaction consistency mechanism guarantees the consistency of transaction data across different chains. No matter whether transaction tampering occurs in a child chain or parent chain, it can guarantee transaction security and consistency as it is impossible that one adversary can attack both the parent and child chains.

5 Performance Analysis

This evaluation of the MCF model and CCIA protocol. The performance environment is on a Windows 11 laptop with Intel(R) Core(TM) i7-9700 CPU 3.0 GHz and 16G RAM.

5.1 Cross-Chain Transaction Performance

For the MCF model in BIoMT, the transaction throughput and latency have been performed. The transaction throughput is one of the main items which shows the performance of this cross-chain algorithm. The throughputs of "Creat-Account", "Query", and "Transaction" are performed, and Fig. 4 shows the results. Meanwhile, the other item is transaction latency, and the performance results of the three same aspects are shown in Fig. 5. Here, the "CreatAccount" represents the generation rate of user registration, "Query" represents query times of cross-chain transaction origination, and "Transaction" represents the establishment transaction amounts. These results show that the MCF model can keep stable with increasing transaction numbers. For the three aspects, the "Query" is executed with high throughput by the low transaction latency and the "Transaction" is executed with low throughput by the high transaction latency.

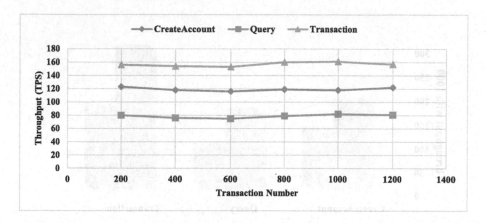

Fig. 4. Cross-chain transaction throughput.

Then, the comparison between the single-chain and this cross-chain concerning these two items is executed with the same transaction number 1000, and Fig. 6 and Fig. 7 give the results, respectively. Due to the identity authentication process, the throughput and latency of these transactions are all inferior to that in a single-chain. However, these results also show the proposed cross-chain identity authentication protocol is efficient as the difference between the cross-chain and single-chain systems is small. Moreover, the cross-chain is the development tendency of open and shared medical data, and the developments of cross-chain and identity authentication technologies will promote performance improvement of cross-chain medical data sharing.

5.2 Identity Authentication Efficiency

Time consumption has been considered for cross-chain identity authentication protocol performance in BIoMT. Here, three representative protocols have been

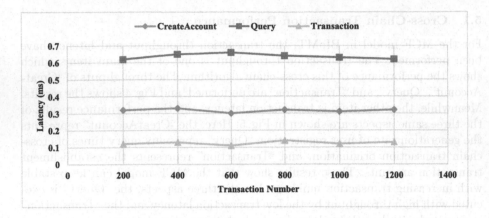

Fig. 5. Cross-chain transaction latency.

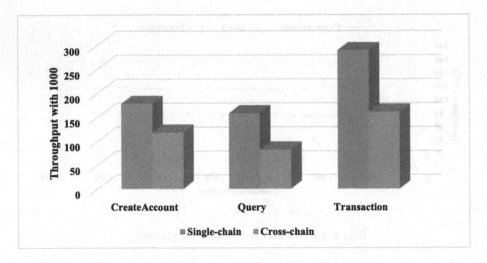

Fig. 6. Transaction throughput comparison.

selected for comparison, as the identity authentication with shared keys [9], with biological characteristics [9], and with a public key encryption algorithm [12]. Figure 7 gives the comparison results. Here, the protocol in Ref. [9] is based on the elliptic curve discrete logarithm problem, which has certain advantages of low time consumption with congruence operation. The protocol in Ref. [11] is based on the fingerprint template, which also has certain advantages of low time consumption by the biometric authentication method. The protocol in Ref. [12] is based on lattice assumption, which costs much time with big keys and complex matrix operations. But this scheme can provide anti-quantum attack properties for current information systems in the future universal quantum computer age. This paper utilizes public key encryption and signature algorithms to achieve

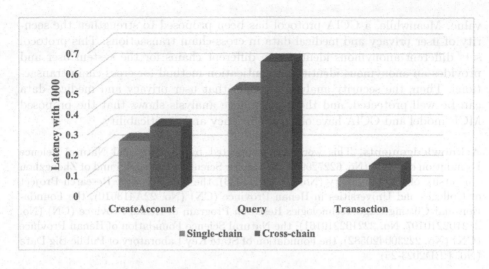

Fig. 7. Transaction latency comparison.

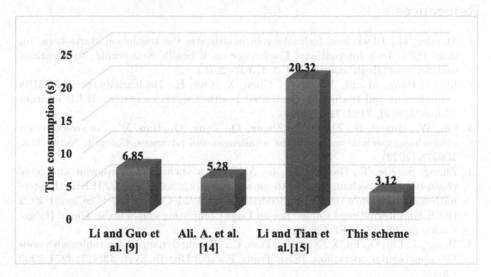

Fig. 8. Time consumption comparison for identity authentication.

cross-chain identity authentication, which costs the lowest time than similar protocols and shows a promising application in practice.

6 Conclusion

This paper focuses on the new "data island" problem and introduces an MCF model for cross-chain medical data-sharing in BIoMT. This model helps to establish a secure medical data-sharing mechanism and promotes the play of data value. Meanwhile, a CCIA protocol has been proposed to strengthen the security of user privacy and medical data in cross-chain transactions. This protocol sets different anonymous identities in different chains for the system user and provides an anonymous identity authentication method for cross-chain transactions. Then, the security analysis presents that user privacy and medical data can be well protected, and the performance analysis shows that the proposed MCF model and CCIA have obvious efficiency and practicability.

Acknowledgements. This work was supported by the National Natural Science Foundation of China (No. 62272090), the Doctor Scientific Research Fund of Zhengzhou University of Light Industry (No. 2021BSJJ033), the Key Scientific Research Project of Colleges and Universities in Henan Province (CN) (No. 22A413010), the Foundation and Cutting-Edge Technologies Research Program of Henan Province (CN) (No. 212102210107, No. 222102210161), the Natural Science Foundation of Henan Province (CN) (No. 222300420582), the Foundation of State Key Laboratory of Public Big Data (No. PBD2023-25)

References

1. Mettler, M.: Blockchain technology in healthcare: the revolution starts here. In: 2016 IEEE 18th International Conference on E-health Networking, Applications and Services (Healthcom), pp. 1–3. IEEE (2016)
2. Li, C., Dong, M., Li, J., Xu, G., Chen, X., Ota, K.: Healthchain: secure EMRs management and trading in distributed healthcare service system. IEEE Internet Things J. **8**(9), 7192–7202 (2020)
3. Ou, W., Huang, S., Zheng, J., Zhang, Q., Zeng, G., Han, W.: An overview on cross-chain: mechanism, platforms, challenges and advances. Comput. Netw. **218**, 109378 (2022)
4. Zhang, S., Xie, T., Gai, K., Xu, L.: ARC: an asynchronous consensus and relay chain-based cross-chain solution to consortium blockchain. In: 2022 IEEE 9th International Conference on Cyber Security and Cloud Computing (CSCloud)/2022 IEEE 8th International Conference on Edge Computing and Scalable Cloud (EdgeCom), pp. 86–92. IEEE (2022)
5. Wang, J., Liu, D., Fu, X., Xiao, F., Tian, C.: DHash: dynamic hash tables with non-blocking regular operations. IEEE Trans. Parallel Distrib. Syst. **33**(12), 3274–3290 (2022)
6. Xiong, A., Liu, G., Zhu, Q., Jing, A., Loke, S.W.: A notary group-based cross-chain mechanism. Digital Commun. Netw. **8**(6), 1059–1067 (2022)
7. Xue, L., Huang, H., Xiao, F., Wang, W.: A cross-domain authentication scheme based on cooperative blockchains functioning with revocation for medical consortiums. IEEE Trans. Netw. Serv. Manage. **19**(3), 2409–2420 (2022)
8. Xu, Y., et al.: An efficient identity authentication scheme with provable security and anonymity for mobile edge computing. IEEE Syst. J. **17**(1), 1012–1023 (2022)
9. Li, C., et al.: Efficient certificateless authenticated key agreement for blockchain-enabled internet of medical things. Comput. Mater. Continua **75**(1), 2043–2059 (2023)
10. Li, C., Dong, M., Li, J., Xu, G., Chen, X.B., Liu, W., Ota, K.: Efficient medical big data management with keyword-searchable encryption in healthchain. IEEE Syst. J. **16**(4), 5521–5532 (2022)

11. Ali, A., Baghel, V.S., Prakash, S.: A novel technique for fingerprint template security in biometric authentication systems. Vis. Comput., 1–15 (2022)
12. Li, C., Tian, Y., Chen, X., Li, J.: An efficient anti-quantum lattice-based blind signature for blockchain-enabled systems. Inf. Sci. **546**, 253–264 (2021)
13. Li, C., Xu, G., Chen, Y., Ahmad, H., Li, J.: A new anti-quantum proxy blind signature for blockchain-enabled Internet of Things. Comput. Mater. Continua **61**(2), 711–726 (2019)
14. Xin, X., Ding, L., Yang, Q., Li, C., Zhang, T., Sang, Y.: Efficient chain-encryption-based quantum signature scheme with semi-trusted arbitrator. Quantum Inf. Process. **21**(7), 246 (2022)
15. Li, C., Jiang, B., Guo, Y., Xin, X.: Efficient group blind signature for medical data anonymous authentication in blockchain-enabled IoMT. Comput. Mater. Continua **76**(1), 591–606 (2023)
16. Li, C., Dong, M., Xin, X., Li, J., Chen, X.B., Ota, K.: Efficient privacy-preserving in IoMT with blockchain and lightweight secret sharing. IEEE Internet Things J. **10**(24), 22051–22064 (2023)
17. Qu, Z., Zhang, Z., Zheng, M.: A quantum blockchain-enabled framework for secure private electronic medical records in Internet of Medical Things. Inf. Sci. **612**, 942–958 (2022)
18. Qu, Z., Meng, Y., Liu, B., Muhammad, G., Tiwari, P.: QB-IMD: a secure medical data processing system with privacy protection based on quantum blockchain for IoMT. IEEE Internet Things J. (2023). https://doi.org/10.1109/JIOT.2023.3285388
19. Adil, M., Khan, M.K., Jadoon, M.M., Attique, M., Song, H., Farouk, A.: An AI-enabled hybrid lightweight Authentication scheme for intelligent IoMT based cyber-physical systems. IEEE Trans. Netw. Sci. Eng. **10**(5), 2719–2730 (2022)
20. Chen, C.M., Liu, S., Li, X., Islam, S.H., Das, A.K.: A provably secure authenticated key agreement protocol for remote patient monitoring IoMT. J. Syst. Architect. **136**, 102831 (2023)

Blockchain-Based Signature Scheme with Cryptographic Reverse Firewalls for IoV

Chunhua Jin$^{(\boxtimes)}$, Wenwen Zhou, Lulu Li, Chang Liu, and Xiaobing Chen

Faculty of Computer and Software Engineering, Huaiyin Institute of Technology,
Huai'an 233003, China
xajch0206@163.com

Abstract. In recent years, research on Internet of Vehicles (IoV) has received widespread attention. However, widespread adoption of this technology faces various obstacles, such as data forgery. Ensuring authenticity of IoV data is crucial as malicious adversaries can manipulate or forge information, leading to security issues. Consequently, data transmission in IoV requires robust signatures. Identity-based signature (IBS) schemes have been proposed as an effective solution. However, traditional IBS schemes are unable to detect internal attackers, which may result in data leakage. To overcome this limitation, we append cryptographic reverse firewall (CRF) on this basis to design a secure and practicable IBS-CRF scheme which has the advantage of computational and communication cost. It is also proved to achieve existential unforgeability against chosen-message attacks (EUF-CMA) and resist internal attackers. Moreover, to further enhance security, a consortium blockchain is introduced, enabling organizations to establish consensus mechanisms and collectively manage and approve transactions. Eventually, we use pypbc library to implement it. The experimental results indicate that this scheme has the least running time. In a word, our blockchain-based IBS-CRF (BIBS-CRF) scheme is suitable for IoV environment.

Keywords: Cryptographic reverse firewall · Signature · Consortium blo-ckchain

1 Introduction

Over the past two decades, the emergence of IoV has sparked in society. It integrates two technological visions: vehicle's networking and vehicle's intelligence [1]. It can provide services for large cities or even a whole country, including road conditions, traffic congestion levels, and vehicular safety services [2]. IoV allows vehicles to be connected permanently to the Internet, forming an interconnected set [3]. Hence, IoV can make timely decisions to achieve smart driving by analyzing the data gathered from multiple sensors or other vehicles.

Up to now, IoV remains a hot topic of research. It has been applied to various applications such as intelligent transport and earthquake relief. Meanwhile, it has

H. Yang and R. Lu (Eds.): FCS 2023, CCIS 1992, pp. 82–95, 2024.
https://doi.org/10.1007/978-981-99-9331-4_6

combined with multifarious technical fields such as cloud computing, blockchain, etc. However, technology is a double-edged sword. As IoV grows better and better, more problems are revealed. In the field of intelligent transport, a malicious adversary can disguise as a "good man" to post false information. Therefore, it is urgent to ensure the availability and integrity of these information.

Given the state of affairs, an effective and secure signature scheme is necessary in IoV. To cope with the issue "forgery attack", all data transmitted in IoV should be signed. However, digital signature still cannot avoid internal attackers until scholars discover CRF. Recently, many scholars have extended application fields of CRF. Bossuat et al. [4] proposed a signed secure channel protocol based on Diffie-Hellman, on the basis of which succeeded in deploying a better performance CRF. Zhou et al. [5] designed a searchable public-key encryption with CRF for cloud storage. Kang et al. [6] brought CRF to web security space, being aimed to solve algorithm substitution attack or backdoor attack where web service would be subjected. Nevertheless, so far, no one has combined CRF with blockchain. Our BIBS-CRF scheme significantly reduces the need and dependence on certificate authority (CA) and ensures the non tamperability of data.

1.1 Motivation and Contribution

To resist internal attackers in IoV, we establish a secure and high-efficiency BIBS-CRF scheme. It is based upon modifications to Barreto's scheme [7].

The fivefold contributions of this paper are summarized as follows.

1. We construct an IBS scheme. IBS doesn't rely on cumbersome public key infrastructure (PKI) to key management and distribution. It can verify the identity of the signer through other authentication mechanisms without establishing and maintaining public key certificates.
2. We design two CRFs in the above IBS scheme. They are severally deployed on private key generator(PKG) and signer vehicles. PKG's CRF (PCRF) randomizes groups' generators, system public key, and vehicle private key in succession. It performs key malleable operation. Vehicle's CRF (VCRF) executes the same randomization algorithm on vehicle's private key and partial signature. Private keys and signatures are well-protected and not compromised.
3. To obtain a more secure and efficient scheme, we combine decentralized and non-tamperable consortium blockchain technology with signature algorithm. Updated system public parameters and vehicles' public keys are on the chain.
4. Compared with traditional schemes, we make a modification considering limited resources of vehicle units. Instead of relying on vehicle units for verification, we adopt road side units (RSU) as receivers for verification. This approach offers significant improvements in computational efficiency during the information communication process.
5. Our BIBS-CRF scheme can achieve EUF-CMA, maintain weakly security, and resist weakly exfiltration. Therefore, it possesses a high level of security.

1.2   Organization

The remainder of the paper is organized as follows. Related work is stated in Sect. 2. We present some definitions and calculation rules in Sect. 3. Our proposed BIBS-CRF scheme is described in Sect. 4. We conduct performance analysis in Sect. 5. Finally, we conclude this paper in Sect. 6.

2   Related Work

Digital signature has a promising development prospect as a significant application in the field of cryptography and has been used in more domains. In 1984, Shamir firstly presented the concept "Identity-Based Cryptograph (IBC)" [8] and designed an IBS scheme that adopted RSA algorithm. IBC simplifies key management and decreases the overhead of certificates. Therefore, the construction of IBS schemes becomes the focal point in modern cryptography. Over the years, various IBS schemes [9–13] have been successively utilized in many domains, such as cloud computing and wireless sensor networks.

The Snowden incident served as a warning to people about the significant threats performed by internal adversaries. Obviously, general digital signature schemes cannot resist such attacks. After Mironov and Stephens Devidowitz [14] first proposed CRF in 2015, this issue was clearly addressed. A CRF can be understood as a third-party set between a user and the outside world. This technology can ensure that even if the user's computer is attacked, the messages sent or received by the user will not be leaked [15].

In 2019, Zhou et al. [16] proposed two CRF protocols for identity-based encryption (IBE). One is a one-round encryption protocol with CRF used on the receiver. And the other is a two-loop encryption protocol, in which CRFs are deployed on both sender and receiver. They proved that these two protocols can resist the exfiltration of secret information. In 2020, Zhou et al. [15] designed a CRF protocol deployed on receiver and key generating center for certificateless public key encryption (CL-PKE), which has been proven to achieve indistinguishability against chosen plaintext attack. Compared with other CL-PKE schemes, it has the least communication cost. In 2023, to mitigate huge computational overhead in attribute-based encryption(ABE), Li et al. [17] constructed the online/offline multi-authority ABE with CRF scheme. This scheme not only uses CRF to resist backdoor attacks but also uses online/offline key generation, online/offline encryption, and outsourcing encryption technology to optimize computing efficiency.

During the same year, Jiang et al. [18] proposed a subversion-resistant public key encryption with keyword search(SR-PEKS) scheme based on CRF. In SR-PEKS, CRF sanitizes outputs of keyword generation derived from the server to resist subversion attack. Furthermore, it participates in a collaborative random-generating protocol to generate unbiased randomness for encryption, thus eliminating the subliminal channel.

2.1 Blockchain

Recently, blockchain has been applied in many domains [19–22], ranging from smart grid, healthcare, Internet of Things (IoT), IoV and so on, due to its immutability, decentralization and transparency. It is a distributed ledger managed by different entities and uses cryptographic methods to ensure transmission and access control [23].

In BIBS-CRF scheme, we adopt consortium blockchain. Its primary function is to establish a decentralized information sharing model among network nodes (namely RSUs). These RSUs are connected to each other through a peer-to-peer network. When a vehicle sends a message to the network, a node is chosen to encapsulate it into a transaction. Once the total number of transactions reaches a threshold value, these transactions are packaged into a block, which is then broadcasted to blockchain for consensus verification by other nodes. In the end, the selected node issues the block on blockchain after sanctioning the verification.

3 Preliminaries

3.1 Bilinear Groups

Definition 1 (Bilinear groups). Let consider groups $\mathbb{G}_1$, $\mathbb{G}_2$ and $\mathbb{G}_T$ of the same prime order p. P, Q are generators of $\mathbb{G}_1$ and $\mathbb{G}_2$ respectively. We make ($\mathbb{G}_1$, $\mathbb{G}_2$, $\mathbb{G}_T$) as bilinear map groups if there exists a bilinear map $\hat{e} : \mathbb{G}_1 \times \mathbb{G}_2 \to \mathbb{G}_T$ satisfying the following properties:

1. Bilinearity: $\forall (P, Q) \in \mathbb{G}_1 \times \mathbb{G}_2$, $\forall a, b \in \mathbb{Z}$, $\hat{e}(aP, bQ) = \hat{e}(P, Q)^{ab}$.
2. Non-degeneracy: $\forall P \in \mathbb{G}_1$, $Q \in \mathbb{G}_2$, $\hat{e}(P, Q) \neq 1_{\mathbb{G}_T}$ for $1_{\mathbb{G}_T}$ represents element identity in group $\mathbb{G}_T$.
3. Computability: $\forall (P, Q) \in \mathbb{G}_1 \times \mathbb{G}_2$, $\hat{e}(P, Q)$ is efficiently computable.
4. There exists an efficient, publicly computable (but not necessarily invertible) isomorphism $\psi : \mathbb{G}_2 \to \mathbb{G}_1$ such that $\psi(Q) = P$.

3.2 Identity-Based Signature

Definition 2 (Identity-Based Digital Signature). Identity-based signature ensures reliability of signer's identity and non-repudiation of signature. It has widespread applications in various fields, providing enhanced security for digital transactions. A generic identity-based signature scheme consists of four algorithms: *Setup, Extract, Sign, Verify.*

Setup: It is completed by PKG. The algorithm inputs a security parameter k and outputs a master key and system parameter *params*. This master key is kept secret.

Extract: It is completed by PKG that makes use of user's identity ID_u to generate corresponding private key S_u. S_u will be sent to the user in a secure channel.

Sign: It takes (*params*, ID_u, S_u, message M) as inputs and outputs a signature σ.

Verify: It takes (*params*, ID_u, M, σ) as inputs and outputs a correct symbol "⊤"(it represents σ is legal for message and identity) or an incorrect symbol"⊥"(it represents σ is illegal for message and identity).

All the algorithms mentioned above must adhere to conformance requirements of an identity-based signature system.

3.3   Cryptographic Reverse Firewall

Definition 3 (Cryptographic Reverse Firewall(CRF)). A CRF is a stateful algorithm denoted as $\mathcal{W}$, which takes its current state and a message as inputs and produces updated state and message as outputs. For a party P and a reverse firewall $\mathcal{W}$, we define $\mathcal{W} \circ P$ as the "composed" party, where $\mathcal{W}$ is applied to the incoming and outgoing messages of P. When the composed party participates in a protocol, the state of $\mathcal{W}$ is initialized with the public parameters. If $\mathcal{W}$ is composed of a party P, we call it a reverse firewall for P. There is no specific formula for the concept of reverse firewall, as it is a comprehensive security measure that involves multiple techniques and strategies. The implementation of a reverse firewall can vary depending on the organization's needs and the network environment.

Definition 4 (Functionality-maintaining). For any reverse firewall $\mathcal{W}$ and any party P, let $\mathcal{W}^1 \circ P = \mathcal{W} \circ P$, and for $k \geq 2$, let $\mathcal{W}^k \circ P = \mathcal{W} \circ (\mathcal{W}^{(k-1)} \circ P)$. For a protocol $\mathcal{P}$ that satisfies some functionality requirements $\mathcal{F}$, we say that a reverse firewall $\mathcal{W}$ maintains $\mathcal{F}$ for P in $\mathcal{P}$ if $\mathcal{W}^k \circ P$ maintains $\mathcal{F}$ for P in $\mathcal{P}$ for any polynomial bounded $k \geq 1$. When $\mathcal{F}$,P, $\mathcal{P}$ are clear, we simply say that $\mathcal{W}$ maintains functionality.

Definition 5 (Security-preserving). For a protocol $\mathcal{P}$ that satisfies some security requirements $\mathcal{S}$ and functionality $\mathcal{F}$ and a CRF $\mathcal{W}$.

1. $\mathcal{W}$ strongly preserves $\mathcal{S}$ for P in $\mathcal{P}$ if the protocol $P_P \rightarrow \mathcal{W} \circ \bar{P}$ satisfies $\mathcal{S}$.
2. $\mathcal{W}$ weakly preserves $\mathcal{S}$ for P in $\mathcal{P}$ if the protocol $P_P \rightarrow \mathcal{W} \circ \hat{P}$ satisfies $\mathcal{S}$.

Definition 6 (Exfiltration-Resistant). For a protocol $\mathcal{P}$ that satisfies functionality $\mathcal{F}$ and a reverse firewall $\mathcal{W}$, When $\mathcal{P}$, $\mathcal{F}$, party P_1 are clear, we simple say that $\mathcal{W}$ is strongly exfiltration-resistant against party P_2 or weakly exfiltration-resistant against P_2. In the special case when P_2 is empty, we say that W is exfiltration-resistant against eavesdroppers.

3.4   Difficult Problem

Definition 7 (q-Strong Diffie-Hellman($q - SDH$) problem). Let us consider bilinear map groups $(\mathbb{G}_1, \mathbb{G}_2, \mathbb{G}_T)$ and generators $P \in \mathbb{G}_1$ and $Q \in \mathbb{G}_2$.

The $q - SDH$ problem in the groups $(\mathbb{G}_1, \mathbb{G}_2)$ consists in, given a $(q+2)$-tuple $(P, Q, \alpha Q, \alpha^2 Q, ..., \alpha^q Q)$ as input, finding a pair $(c, \frac{1}{(c+\alpha)P})$ with $c \in \mathbb{Z}_p^*$.

4   Our Proposed BIBS-CRF Scheme

In this section, we propose the BIBS-CRF scheme for IoV that is based on Barreto's scheme [7] to resist internal attackers. Table 1 presents some frequently used notations.

Table 1. Notations and Descriptions

Notation	Description	Notation	Description
G_1, G_2, G_T	Bilinear map groups	k	A security param
H_1, H_2	Two different hash functions	$\psi()$	An isomorphism function
$e()$	A bilinear map	Q	The generator of G_2
P	The generator of G_1	s	System master key
Q_{pub}	System public key	ID	Vehicle identity
pk	Vehicle public key	sk	Vehicle private key
M	Message	σ	Signature

4.1   Details of Our Scheme

CRFs are deployed on PKG's side and vehicle's side in our scheme, which can be seen in the following Fig. 2, Fig. 3 and Fig. 4. To build the CRF for PKG, our idea is making use of keys' malleability. In Fig. 2 or Fig. 3, PCRF is not only used to rerandomize system parameters in case verifier accepts forged signatures, but also used to update vehicle's private key in case its leakage. VCRF rerandomizes the vehicle's private key to prevent malicious attackers from forging signatures. In Fig. 4, parameters (h, S) constitute a complete signature σ. VCRF is used to rerandomized S (a part of σ) in this place. Then blockchain periodically selects a leader node to validate the signature.

Our proposed scheme is made up of the following eight algorithms:

Setup: Given a security parameter k, PKG chooses bilinear map groups $(\mathbb{G}_1, \mathbb{G}_2, \mathbb{G}_T)$ of prime order $q(q > 2k)$, and hash functions $H_1 : \{0,1\}^* \to Z_p^*$, $H_2 : \{0,1\}^* \times \mathbb{G}_T \to \mathbb{Z}_p^*$; computes $g = \hat{e}(P, Q)$ where $P = \psi(Q)$ represents a generator of $\mathbb{G}_1$, where Q represents a generator of $\mathbb{G}_2$. It then randomly selects a master key $s \in \mathbb{Z}_p^*$, and calculates the system public key $Q_{pub} = sQ$. Special note that s is confidential. The public parameters are $pars = \{\mathbb{G}_1, \mathbb{G}_2, \mathbb{G}_T, P, Q, g, Q_{pub}, \hat{e}, \psi, H_1, H_2\}$.

PKeyMaul: When PKG's CRF PCRF receives $pars$, it selects $\alpha \in \mathbb{Z}_p^*$ independently and randomly, then calculates $Q' = \alpha Q$, $Q'_{pub} = \alpha Q_{pub} = \alpha sQ$. Therefore $pars' = \{\mathbb{G}_1, \mathbb{G}_2, \mathbb{G}_T, P, Q', g, Q'_{pub}, \hat{e}, \psi, H_1, H_2\}$ are published. Later, PCRF saves $pars'$ on blockchain.

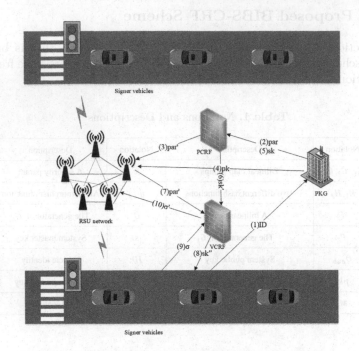

Fig. 1. Architecture overview of BIBS-CRF in IoV

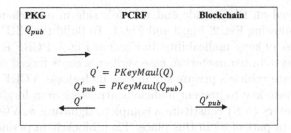

Fig. 2. Randomization operations of system public key

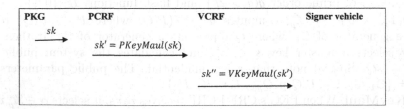

Fig. 3. Randomization operation of private key

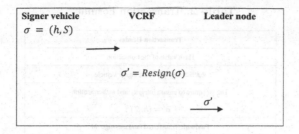

Fig. 4. Randomization operation of signature

Keygen: For a vehicle ID, the public key is $pk = H_1(ID)$. Its private key is $sk = \frac{1}{H_1(ID)+s}P$. sk will be sent to PCRF. Communication parties upload pk to blockchain for sake of avoiding data tampered.

RePKeyMaul: PCRF updates sk to $sk' = \frac{1}{\alpha} \times sk = \frac{1}{\alpha}(\frac{1}{H_1(ID)+s})P$ as a new private key. Then sk' is transmitted to VCRF.

VKeyMaul: VCRF receives sk', uses $\beta \in Z_p^*$ to re-randomize sk' to $sk'' = \beta \cdot sk' = \frac{\beta}{\alpha(H_1(ID)+s)}P$ and sends sk'' to signer vehicle.

Sign: In order to sign a message $M \in \{0,1\}^*$, the signer vehicle

(1) picks a random $x \in \mathbb{Z}_p^*$ and computes $r = g^x$
(2) sets $h = H_2(M, r) \in \mathbb{Z}_p^*$
(3) computes $S = (x+h)sk''$

The signature on M is $\sigma = (h, S)$.

Resign: Before verifier accepts signature, it passes VCRF which will re-randomize σ to $\sigma' = (h, S') = (h, \frac{1}{\beta}S)$. Subsequently, σ' will be transmitted to blockchain.

Verify: Upon receiving σ', the consortium blockchain selects a RSU_i using Algorithm 1(which is elaborated in [24]) from the nodes as a leader. Then the leader checks whether σ' is valid, according to the following equality: $h = H_2(M, \hat{e}(S', pk \cdot Q' + Q'_{pub})g^{-h})$. If the verification is successful, signature σ' and message M will be encapsulated as a transaction preserved on the consortium blockchain, as $T = (\sigma', pk, M)$. The transaction format is shown in Table 2. In a period time, multiple transactions will be packaged into a new block. The leader RSU_i generates a block, as shown in Table 3, in which contains the new transaction like Table 2. Then RSU_i broadcasts the block to other nodes for verifying with PBFT consensus algorithm.

Vital processes are described detailedly in Fig. 1, which helps us understand how CRF works intuitively and how the entire system runs. After rerandomization operations of CRF, updated data is either delivered to blockchain for storage or returned to signer for signature. Signature is similarly updated before transmitting to blockchain. Thus, a secure and efficient signature scheme is proposed. Ultimately, the leader RSU_i verifies the received signature whether it is

Table 2. Transaction Format

Transaction Header
Hash value of the transaction
Publich key pk of the signer vehicle
The signature to ensure integrity and authentication
$\sigma' = (h, S')$
Payload: Transferred raod message M

Table 3. Block Format

Block Header	
Version	Block version number
Previous Block Hash	Hash of previous block in the chain
Merkle Tree Root	Root hash of the transactions merkle tree
Timestamp	Creation time of this block
Block Payload	
List of Transactions	$\{T_i = (\sigma', PK_{ID}, M) \mid i = 1, ..., n\}$
Current Block Hash	Hash of current block in the chain

valid. The point that cannot be ignored in our system is that vehicles' public keys are all preserved on blockchain in case of information falsification.

In addition, what we can be aware of from Fig. 1 is that adversary has no ability to forge a legal signature accounting for unknown to random α and β. When verifiers receive a forged signature, they output an error symbol "⊥". Hence, it is beneficial for us to utilize CRF to impede information leakage caused by internal attackers in IoV.

4.2 Security Analysis

Theorem 1. *Our proposed BIBS-CRF scheme on the basis of an identity signature realizes EUF-CMA secure in the same way. In addition, reverse firewalls maintain functionality, weakly preserve security, and weakly resist exfiltration supposing that the original signature scheme [7] has EUF-CMA.*

Proof. We testify our scheme possessing these three properties. Due to the limited length of conference articles, the detailed security analysis can be found in the complete version, or you can contact the corresponding author.

The following game can prove BIBS-CRF scheme is EUF-CMA. What is worth noting is that these three algorithms: *Setup**, *Keygen**, *Sign** are tampered by adversary $\mathcal{A}$. It is a game between challenger $\mathcal{C}$ and adversary $\mathcal{A}$.

Init: $\mathcal{C}$ runs *Setup** algorithm to obtain PK and master key s, then runs *PKeyMaul* algorithm to obtain random number α and PK'. At last, $\mathcal{C}$ keeps s and α secret. It sends PK' to $\mathcal{A}$ at the same time.

Keygen Query: $\mathcal{A}$ selects an identity ID and has the right to get its corresponding private key sk. The challenger $\mathcal{C}$ executes *Keygen** algorithm and forwards the private key sk to adversary $\mathcal{A}$.

Sign Query: First of all, $\mathcal{A}$ presents an identity ID and a message M. Then $\mathcal{C}$ implements *Keygen** algorithm to gain sk, *RePKeyMaul* to gain sk', *VkeyMaul* to gain sk'', *Setup** algorithm to gain signature σ. Last $\mathcal{C}$ runs *Resign* algorithm to get σ'.

Forgery: The adversary $\mathcal{A}$ outputs (M^*, ID^*, σ^*). $\mathcal{A}$ will make success if the following three conditions are established: (1) Verify $(Q'_{pub}, ID^*, M^*, \sigma^*)$ is vaild; (2) $\mathcal{A}$ hasn't made an Keygen query on ID^*; (3) $\mathcal{A}$ hasn't made a sign query on (ID^*, M^*).

5   Performance Analysis

5.1   Theoretical Analysis

In this subsection, we analyze the performance of our BIBS-CRF scheme considering computational and communication cost. Compared with Barreto [7], Li [25], Yang Ou [26], the advantages of our scheme are ideally demonstrated. Li's scheme doesn't have CRF and is compared with the original scheme. Yang Ou's scheme is compared with ours.

The computational cost mainly consists of exponential operation, point multiplication operation, and paring operation. Other operations can be negligible contrasted to them. Thus, we use these operations to measure the computational cost. Here, Exp represents exponent operations; P represents pairing operations; PM represents point multiplication operations. Symbol × indicates that the scheme does not have this operation. Details are shown in table 4.

Table 4. Comparison of Schemes' Computational Cost

Operation	Barreto [7]	Li [25]	Yang Ou [26]	Ours
Setup	$PM + P$	×	Exp	$PM + P$
PKEM	×	×	$3Exp$	$2PM$
KeyGen	PM	$4PM + P$	$PM + 3Exp$	PM
RePKEM	×	×	×	PM
VKEM	×	×	Exp	PM
Sign	$PM + Exp$	$P + 4PM$	$2PM + 6Exp$	$PM + Exp$
Resign	×	×	×	PM
Verify	$PM + P$	$3P$	$4P$	$PM + P$

From Table 4, we can learn that PKEM denotes $PKeyMaul$ algorithm performed by PCRF, and similarly VKEM denotes $VKeyMaul$ algorithm performed by VCRF. Compared with [7] [25] [26], we can conclude that computational cost of our scheme is mainly increased by several point multiplication operations, which is caused by rerandomization operation of CRF. In addition, our scheme has less computational cost than Yang Ou [26]'s scheme which designs reverse firewalls in the same way. The augmentation of our scheme's computational cost is acceptable. For the communication cost, we make $|M|$ to indicate the number of bits of a message M, $|\mathbb{G}_1|$ to indicate the number of bits of an element in group $\mathbb{G}_1$, $|\mathbb{G}_2|$ to indicate the number of bits of an element in group $\mathbb{G}_2$, $|\mathbb{G}_T|$ to indicate the number of bits of an element in group $\mathbb{G}_T$ and $|u|$ to indicate the number of bits of an identity. In Table 4, comparisons among these algorithms in different schemes are taken on. It is noteworthy that the operation $Verify$ is only responsible for judging whether to accept or refuse signature, so its communication cost can be ignored. In view of the analysis from Table 5, we can conclude that the existence of CRF poses communication delay that is inevitable. And our scheme is based on blockchain that transmits parameters and spends communication cost as well. Although the cost of communication is raised, our scheme enhances security and resists exfiltration.

Table 5. Comparison of schemes' communication cost

Operation	Barreto [7]	Li [25]	Yang Ou [26]	Ours
Setup	$3|\mathbb{G}_T| + 3|\mathbb{G}_2| + 2|\mathbb{G}_1|$	$4|\mathbb{G}_1| + |\mathbb{G}_2|$	$(5 + |u| + |M|)|\mathbb{G}_1| + |\mathbb{G}_T|$	$3|\mathbb{G}_T| + 3|\mathbb{G}_2| + 2|\mathbb{G}_1|$
PKEM	×	×	$(10 + 2|u| + 2|M|)|\mathbb{G}_1| + 2|\mathbb{G}_T|$	$3|\mathbb{G}_T| + 4|\mathbb{G}_2| + 2|\mathbb{G}_1|$
KeyGen	$|u| + |\mathbb{G}_1|$	$3|\mathbb{G}_1| + |\mathbb{G}_2|$	$2|\mathbb{G}_1|$	$|u| + |\mathbb{G}_1|$
RePKEM	×	×	×	$|\mathbb{G}_1|$
VKEM	×	×	×	$|\mathbb{G}_1|$
Sign	$2|\mathbb{G}_1| + 2|\mathbb{G}_T| + |M|$	$4|\mathbb{G}_1| + |\mathbb{G}_2| + |M|$	$8|\mathbb{G}_1|$	$2|\mathbb{G}_1| + 2|\mathbb{G}_T| + |M|$
Resign	×	×	×	$|\mathbb{G}_1|$
Verify	×	×	×	×

5.2 Experimental Analysis

In this subsection, we implement Barreto [7], Zhou [16], Yang Ou [26] and our scheme by using pypbc library. We use type A pairing, which is set on an elliptic curve $y^2 = x^3 + x \bmod p$ in a finite field $\mathbb{E}(\mathbb{F}_p)$. In addition, we adopt the symmetrical pairings: $\mathbb{G} \times \mathbb{G} \to \mathbb{G}_T$. $\mathbb{G}$ is a cyclic addition group and $\mathbb{G}_T$ is a multiplicative group in $\mathbb{E}(\mathbb{F}_p)$. They have the same order q. The following execution environment is set up. Based on a specific security length, we set $q = 512$, $r = 160$. Symbol r represents the length of key and symbol q means the length of group element. The hash function is SHA-256. The experimental development is Python. The computer configuration of the schemes is Intel(R) Core(TM) i5-8250U CPU @ 1.60 GHz 1.80 GHz processor, 15.6 GB of RAM, 64-bit of Manjaro Linux operating system. To obtain more persuasive experimental results, we run these four schemes one hundred times severally, then take their average.

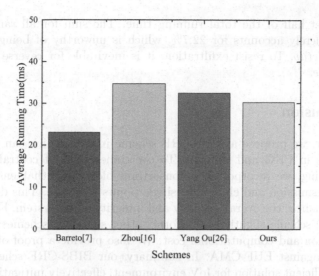

Fig. 5. Comparison of four schemes in average

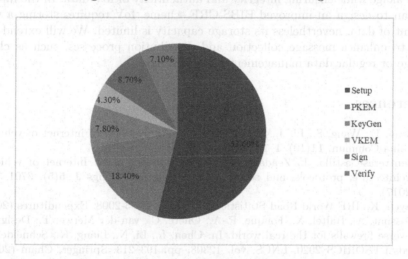

Fig. 6. Percentage of each part our proposed scheme

Next, we compare the total running time among three schemes via painting a histogram whose data originated from the above experiment. From analyzing Fig. 5, we can conclude that our scheme is more efficient than Zhou [16] and Yang Ou [26]'s schemes which are also digital signatures with CRF. Compared with the original scheme, there are some increases in running time as a result of the emergence of reverse firewalls in our scheme. Thus, I deem the augmentation is acceptable. The original scheme sacrifices security to improve efficiency. Meanwhile, we compare the running time ratio of each part of our scheme by drawing a pie chart. In Fig. 6, we can see that the operation *Setup* makes up

53.6%, almost half of the total running time. The sum for all randomization operations merely accounts for 22.7%, which is unworthy of being mentioned relative to *Setup*. To resist exfiltration, it is inevitable for reverse firewalls to consume time.

6 Conclusion

In this paper, we propose a BIBS-CRF scheme in IoV, which can resist internal attackers in PKG and vehicles. To overcome issues of centralization and data tampering, we incorporate a consortium blockchain that ensures secure message transmission and eliminates single points of failure. This decentralized approach enhances the overall security and integrity of the system. Furthermore, our proposed scheme slightly outperforms other signature schemes in terms of communication and computational cost. We also provide a proof of security of our scheme against EUF-CMA. In summary, our BIBS-CRF scheme offers a secure and efficient solution for IoV environment, effectively mitigating information leakage while ensuring integrity and authenticity of IoV data. In the future, we plan to design an improved BIBS-CRF scheme. IoV requires storing a vast amount of data, nevertheless its storage capacity is limited. We will extend our work to enhance message collection and distribution processes, such as cloud storage or regular data management and cleaning.

References

1. Yang, F., Wang, S., Li, J., Liu, Z., Sun, Q.: An overview of internet of vehicles. China Commun. **11**(10), 1–15 (2014)
2. Contreras-Castillo, J., Zeadally, S., Guerrero-Ibañez, J.A.: Internet of vehicles: architecture, protocols, and security. IEEE Internet Things J. **5**(5), 3701–3709 (2017)
3. Iaych, K.: IRF World Road Statistics 2010, Data 2003-2008. Expenditures (2010)
4. Bossuat, A., Bultel, X., Fouque, P.-A., Onete, C., van der Merwe, T.: Designing reverse firewalls for the real world. In: Chen, L., Li, N., Liang, K., Schneider, S. (eds.) ESORICS 2020. LNCS, vol. 12308, pp. 193–213. Springer, Cham (2020). https://doi.org/10.1007/978-3-030-58951-6_10
5. Zhou, Y., Hu, Z., Li, F.: Searchable public-key encryption with cryptographic reverse firewalls for cloud storage. IEEE Trans. Cloud Comput. **11**, 383–396 (2021)
6. Kang, B., Zhang, L., Yang, Y., Meng, X.: CRFs for digital signature and NIZK proof system in web services. In: Meng, W., Lu, R., Min, G., Vaidya, J. (eds.) ICA3PP 2022. LNCS, vol. 13777, pp. 192–213. Springer, Cham (2023). https://doi.org/10.1007/978-3-031-22677-9_11
7. Barreto, P.S.L.M., Libert, B., McCullagh, N., Quisquater, J.-J.: Efficient and provably-secure identity-based signatures and signcryption from bilinear maps. In: Roy, B. (ed.) ASIACRYPT 2005. LNCS, vol. 3788, pp. 515–532. Springer, Heidelberg (2005). https://doi.org/10.1007/11593447_28
8. Shamir, A.: Identity-based cryptosystems and signature schemes. In: Blakley, G.R., Chaum, D. (eds.) CRYPTO 1984. LNCS, vol. 196, pp. 47–53. Springer, Heidelberg (1985). https://doi.org/10.1007/3-540-39568-7_5

9. Kumar, M., Chand, S.: Escrow-less identity-based signature scheme with outsourced protection in cloud computing. Wireless Pers. Commun. **114**, 3115–3136 (2020)
10. Mezrag, F., Bitam, S., Mellouk, A.: An efficient and lightweight identity-based scheme for secure communication in clustered wireless sensor networks. J. Netw. Comput. Appl. **200**, 103282 (2022)
11. Zhou, Z., Gupta, B.B., Gaurav, A., Li, Y., Lytras, M.D., Nedjah, N.: An efficient and secure identity-based signature system for underwater green transport system. IEEE Trans. Intell. Transp. Syst. **23**(9), 16161–16169 (2022)
12. Ramadan, M., Liao, Y., Li, F., Zhou, S.: Identity-based signature with server-aided verification scheme for 5G mobile systems. IEEE Access **8**, 51810–51820 (2020)
13. Ullah, S.S., et al.: A lightweight identity-based signature scheme for mitigation of content poisoning attack in named data networking with internet of things. IEEE Access **8**, 98910–98928 (2020)
14. Mironov, I., Stephens-Davidowitz, N.: Cryptographic reverse firewalls. In: Oswald, E., Fischlin, M. (eds.) EUROCRYPT 2015. LNCS, vol. 9057, pp. 657–686. Springer, Heidelberg (2015). https://doi.org/10.1007/978-3-662-46803-6_22
15. Zhou, Y., Guan, Y., Zhang, Z., Li, F.: Cryptographic reverse firewalls for identity-based encryption. In: Shen, B., Wang, B., Han, J., Yu, Y. (eds.) FCS 2019. CCIS, vol. 1105, pp. 36–52. Springer, Singapore (2019). https://doi.org/10.1007/978-981-15-0818-9_3
16. Zhou, Y., Guo, J., Li, F.: Certificateless public key encryption with cryptographic reverse firewalls. J. Syst. Architect. **109**, 101754 (2020)
17. Li, J., Fan, Y., Bian, X., Yuan, Q.: Online/offline MA-CP-ABE with cryptographic reverse firewalls for IoT. Entropy **25**(4), 616 (2023)
18. Jiang, C., Xu, C., Zhang, Z., Chen, K.: SR-PEKS: subversion-resistant public key encryption with keyword search. IEEE Trans. Cloud Comput. **11**, 3168–3183 (2023)
19. Mollah, M.B., et al.: Blockchain for future smart grid: a comprehensive survey. IEEE Internet Things J. **8**(1), 18–43 (2020)
20. Shahnaz, A., Qamar, U., Khalid, A.: Using blockchain for electronic health records. IEEE Access **7**, 147782–147795 (2019)
21. Alsharari, N.: Integrating blockchain technology with internet of things to efficiency. Int. J. Technol. Innovation Manag. (IJTIM) **1**(2), 01–13 (2021)
22. Kapassa, E., Themistocleous, M., Christodoulou, K., Iosif, E.: Blockchain application in internet of vehicles: challenges, contributions and current limitations. Future Internet **13**(12), 313 (2021)
23. Pavithran, D., Shaalan, K., Al-Karaki, J.N., Gawanmeh, A.: Towards building a blockchain framework for IoT. Clust. Comput. **23**(3), 2089–2103 (2020)
24. Zhang, H., Wang, J., Ding, Y.: Blockchain-based decentralized and secure keyless signature scheme for smart grid. Energy **180**, 955–967 (2019)
25. Li, T., Wang, H., He, D., Yu, J.: Permissioned blockchain-based anonymous and traceable aggregate signature scheme for industrial internet of things. IEEE Internet Things J. **8**(10), 8387–8398 (2020)
26. Ouyang, M., Wang, Z., Li, F.: Digital signature with cryptographic reverse firewalls. J. Syst. Architect. **116**, 102029 (2021)

Network Security and Privacy Protection

A Hierarchical Asynchronous Federated Learning Privacy-Preserving Framework for IoVs

Rui Zhou[1], Xianhua Niu[1(✉)], Ling Xiong[1], Yangpeng Wang[1], Yue Zhao[2], and Kai Yu[3]

[1] School of Computer and Software Engineering, Xihua University, Chengdu, China
niuxh@mail.xhu.edu.cn
[2] Science and Technology on Communication Security Laboratory, Chengdu, China
[3] Railway Eryuan Engineering Group Co. Ltd., Chengdu, Sichuan, China

Abstract. Data sharing plays a crucial role in the Internet of Vehicles, as it greatly enhances the driving experience for users. Federated Learning (FL) has shown good advantages and efficiency in knowledge sharing among vehicles. However, due to the uncertainty of the IoVs, the existing federated learning frameworks cannot meet the high-precision, fast convergence, and high fault tolerance requirements in the learning process. To address these issues, this paper proposes a hierarchical federated learning framework for IoVs environment that combines synchronous and asynchronous methods to improve machine learning performance in the Internet of Vehicles environment. The proposed asynchronous algorithm can improve the accuracy of the global model via controlling the proportion of parameters submitted by users. In addition, to improve the reliability of the parameters, our framework provides a malicious node exclusion algorithm to improve the reliability of the parameters. It effectively reduces the adverse impact of malicious parameters on the global model. Finally, lightweight pseudonym is used in the proposed framework to ensure the privacy of participants' identities. The experimental results demonstrate that the proposed framework achieves high learning accuracy and fast convergence speed. Additionally, it effectively defends against poisoning attacks and ensures the protection of participants' identity privacy.

Keywords: Hierarchical federated learning · Privacy-preserving · IoVs · Data sharing

1 Introduction

Recently, with the rapid development of transportation and communication technologies, related infrastructure has been built and improved rapidly [1,2]. The

This research was funded in part by the National Natural Science Foundation of China under Grant U20B2049 and U20B2046, and in part by the Key Research and Development Project of Sichuan Province of China under Grant 2022YFG0172.

development of Intelligent City and Intelligent Transportation has raised the requirements for road traffic efficiency as well as safety. Internet of Vehicles (IoVs) have become a current research hotspot due to the rapid development of transportation and communication technologies. In vehicle networking scenarios, data is generated by vehicles as they are being driven. Real-time data is also collected by roadside unit(RSU) nodes and shared among entities, forming a critical component of achieving traffic intelligence.

With the prevalence of mobile vehicles in the IoVs, a diverse range of data types such as trajectory, traffic information, and multimedia data are incessantly generated. The efficient and effective utilization of this substantial volume of data poses a significant challenge in enhancing driving experience and providing high-quality services in the IoVs. Google has proposed a federated learning algorithm that allows for data sharing without the original data leaving local devices. [2]. Previous studies in Telematics have effectively integrated FL and IoVs to prevent privacy breaches during data sharing [3] [4]. In synchronous FL, aggregation nodes must wait for all participants to complete local training before aggregation can take place [5]. The computational and communication resources as well as the data quantity usually vary among the multiple end nodes, causing them to submit the model parameters at different times after each round of local training. This issue leads to slow nodes, which may suffer from the "falling runner" problem, resulting in a longer time to train the global model [6]. Asynchronous FL algorithms have been proposed based on exponential moving average (EMA) [7] which can reduce the training time. However, the high frequency of fast node updates in this algorithm can result in the final global model deviating from the convergence direction of other models. Additionally, some studies have suggested using a weighted aggregation approach based on the number of interactions [8], but this approach does not account for the quality of the uploaded models. Poor quality models are given larger weighting factors, leading to lower convergence efficiency of the global model.

The majority of the aforementioned schemes solely employ either synchronous or asynchronous FL. However, these schemes are plagued with either low training efficiency or convergence issues. Therefore, this paper proposes a scheme that combines hierarchical FL and privacy protection by utilizing both synchronous and asynchronous FL. To safeguard the privacy of participating vehicles, a pseudonym technique is employed while a weighted aggregation approach is designed to combine model accuracy and training speed and address the shortcomings of previous works. To summarize, the contributions of this paper are as follows:

- To address the shortcomings of the exponential moving average algorithm, a new asynchronous FL aggregation algorithm is proposed that incorporates accuracy and time dimension considerations to weight the aggregation model parameters, eliminating the undesirable effects of outdated weights and also reducing the undesirable effects of low accuracy model parameters.
- To enhance the model's learning accuracy and convergence speed, we present a novel hierarchical FL framework by synergistically combining synchronous

and asynchronous FL. Our experiments show that our method outperforms traditional FL.

- To protect vehicle privacy, we design a lightweight pseudonym algorithm to protect the identity privacy of participating vehicles, which can achieve the effect of communicating one pseudonym in one round.

2   Related Work

There have been rapid developments in communication technologies, particularly in the area of device-to-device (D2D) communication, which wireless networks have widely adopted. Nishiyama et al. [9] introduced the idea of a multi-hop communication network system that can be used in various wireless communication contexts. Numerous studies have explored D2D communication and these form the foundation for efficient and reliable sharing of resources in IoVs, allowing users to share resources through vehicle-to-vehicle (V2V) communication. Moreover, the emergence of machine learning presents new opportunities for sharing information resources in IoVs.Dai et al. [10] incorporated both AI and blockchain technologies into wireless networks and proposed a secure and intelligent framework for resource sharing. While it enhances the security and efficiency of resource sharing, Conventional AI depends on pooling data for training purposes and is not applicable in the distributed environment of IoVs.

In this regard, FL serves as a privacy-preserving approach of machine learning for distributed edge intelligence [11]. It enables participants to learn collaboratively and generate predictive models that are applicable to all participants.In the traditional FL process, the nodes responsible for edge training are referred to as workers, while the nodes responsible for aggregation are called servers. Workers and servers share the learned knowledge and build a shared model between the workers and servers. The objective of FL is to minimize the global loss function [12]. Incentive mechanisms are used to motivate participants to contribute their local data to the shared model. The existing research on FL focuses on privacy preservation. In the paper by Samarakoon [13], the authors propose a Federated Learning-based framework for vehicle communication where vehicles act as workers and send their learned results to the nearby RSUs. In traditional FL processes, each worker obtains the global model from the server and pushes the updates to the server, respectively [14] [13]. The server synchronizes the parameters received from all workers and aggregates them into a global model in traditional synchronous FL approaches [10]. However, this method has higher communication costs and takes longer to train due to slow nodes. Asynchronous FL, on the other hand, overcomes this limitation and ensures that the training continues within the expected time, even if some workers fail. Two examples of asynchronous FL schemes are proposed in the literature. In [15], an algorithm based on node selection and asynchronous aggregation is introduced. Meanwhile, [7] presents an asynchronous aggregation algorithm utilizing an exponential sliding average. This algorithm is especially efficient when dealing with high communication delay and heterogeneous networks. The current research on IoVs predominantly focuses on single-layer architectures that involve multiple entities. However, it is evident that a multi-layer architecture would be better suited for IoVs.

In order to achieve secure and efficient knowledge sharing in IoVs, it is necessary to improve the existing FL algorithm and framework. A hierarchical Federated Learning framework for IoVs is designed using a combination of synchronous and asynchronous aggregation.

3   Preliminaries

3.1   System Model

Fig. 1 illustrates a hierarchical Federated Learning framework for knowledge sharing, comprising three entities: vehicles, RSU, and Central Aggregation Server (CA). The proposed framework utilizes a combination of Top-layer Federated Learning (TFL) and multiple Bottom-layer Federated Learning (BFL) to aggregate distinct environmental data for knowledge sharing. TFL employs asynchronous Federated learning, while BFL utilizes synchronous Federated Learning.

- **Vehicle** In this framework, vehicles serve as edge nodes, collecting data from vehicles and training their local models during the FL process. Afterward, vehicles upload their model gradients to the intermediate layer RSU.
- **RSU** The RSU collects and aggregates the model gradients from the bottom vehicle nodes and can also collect the available data near it. In our framework, the RSU is not only the aggregation server of BFL but also the data provider and trainer in TFL.
- **CA** The CA collects the gradients uploaded by the intermediate layer RSUs and performs top aggregation processes to produce a global model.

3.2   Threat Models

This paper considers two threat models in its application scenario: the Identity Privacy Violation Model and the Security Threat Model.

- **Privacy threat model** The privacy threat model in this article assumes that RSUs are semi-honest entities, exhibiting both honesty and curiosity. RSUs are motivated to deduce the true identity of a vehicle by analyzing the data uploaded by the vehicle.
- **Security threat model** In the security threat model of connected vehicles, there may be malicious vehicles that can compromise the global model. These malicious vehicles upload malicious training samples that can affect the convergence direction of the global model.

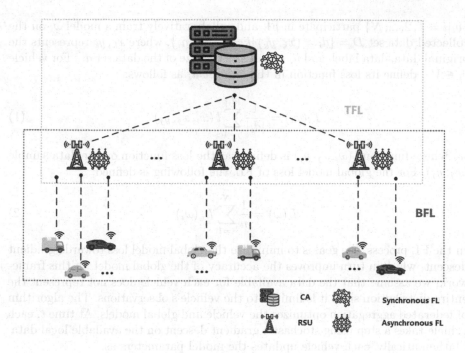

Fig. 1. System model

3.3 Security and Privacy Requirements

In the hypothetical IoVs scenario, the security requirements that need to be met are as follows:

- **Identity privacy protection** Based on the information transmitted by the vehicle within the channel, an attacker is unable to recover the true identity of the sender.
- **Unlinkability** In the scenario where multiple messages are sent through the same vehicle, it is impossible for an attacker to link the messages to the sender.
- **Resist poisoning attacks** It can resist poisoning attacks on global models by malicious vehicles. This means that the system is designed to be resilient to attacks where malicious vehicles upload bad data to the global model in an attempt to skew the results.

3.4 Federated Learning

We use Federated Learning to achieve model training at the vehicle layer. vehicles are responsible for collecting data from their surroundings as Federated Learning training set. Each vehicle acts as a worker in the FL, which is named as BFL, and implements the learning process through its own On-Board Unit.In the proposed scheme, it is assumed that there are N vehicles and vehicles $V =$

$\{v_i | i = 1, 2, ..., N\}$ participate in FL and collaboratively train a model ω_i on the collected data set $D = \{d_i = (x_k, y_k) | k = 1, 2, ...n_i\}$, where x_k, y_k represents the original data, data label, and n_i represents the size of the data set d_i. For vehicle $v_i \in V$, define its loss function in the dataset d_i as follows:

$$L_i(\omega_i) = \frac{1}{|d_i|} \sum_{j=1}^{|d_i|} l(\omega_i, x_j, y_j) \tag{1}$$

where function $l(\omega_i, x_j, y_j)$ is defined as the loss function on the data sample (x_j, y_j). For the global model loss of FL, the following is defined:

$$L(\omega) = \frac{1}{n} \sum_{i=1}^{N} L_i(\omega_i) \tag{2}$$

In the FL process, the goal is to minimize the global model loss towards gradient descent, which in turn improves the accuracy of the global model. In this framework, we assume that the data available for each vehicle does not represent the entire distribution since it is limited to the vehicle's observations. The algorithm of federated aggregation optimizes the vehicle and global models. At time t, each vehicle takes a step using stochastic gradient descent on the available local data. Mathematically, each vehicle updates the model parameters as:

$$\omega_t^i = \omega_t - \eta \cdot \nabla L_i(\omega_{t-1}, d_i) \tag{3}$$

where $\nabla L_i(\omega_{t-1}, d_i)$ and η represent the gradient descent and learning rate, respectively. d_i is the data collected by the vehicle. And ω_t^i and ω_t represent the vehicle learning model parameters and RSU model for the t round, respectively.

4   The Proposed Scheme

4.1   Initialization Phase

The current phase is mainly carried out by the CA to generate a series of system parameters. The specific process is as follows:

- Randomly select two large prime numbers p and q, and choose a q-order additive cyclic group G with its generator denoted as P.
- Choose a random number $SK_{CA} \in Z_q^*$ as the private key of the CA, and compute $PK_{CA} = SK_{CA} \cdot P$ as the public key of the CA.
- Choose a secure one-way hash function $H: g \to Z_q^*$, $g \in G$.
- The CA publicly announces the system's public parameters: $\{P, PK_{CA}, H\}$

In this paper, a privacy protection method based on pseudonym is designed to achieve that the RSU side can only use the data, but can't know exactly where the data comes from that specific vehicle. The interaction process is shown in Fig. 2.

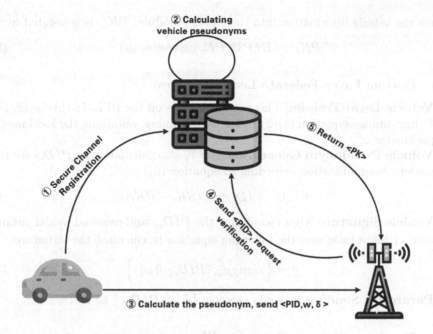

Fig. 2. Pseudonym interaction process

In the multi-round learning process of the FL framework, the fixed pseudonym may lead to the leakage of model parameters. To address this privacy concern, this paper proposes to use the $BIP32$ [17] algorithm as the pseudonym update algorithm. With this approach, each round of the learning process is assigned a new pseudonym, which can effectively protect the privacy of the data uploaded by each node. This "one round one pseudonym" mechanism prevents the leakage of model parameters and ensures the privacy of the FL process.

4.2 Vehicle Registration

- **Registration** The vehicle i selects the private key seed to generate the root private key SK_{root} and the root chain code $chain_{root}$, then calculates the root public key $PK_{root} = SK_{root} \cdot P$ and sends $\langle PK_{root}, chain_{root}, ID_i \rangle$ to the CA for vehicle registration via a secure channel. Notably, both the CA and V_i will use the $BIP32$ [17] algorithm to facilitate updates to SK_{root} and PK_{root}.
- **Pseudonym Generation** CA generates the pseudonyms to be used for Vehicle i according to the following formula:

$$PID_{v_i} = ID_i \oplus H\left(SK_{CA} \cdot PK_{v_i}\right) \qquad (4)$$

where H is the hash function. $(PID_{v_i}, PK_{v_i}, ID_i)$ represents the information of the vehicle, $(PID_{v_i}, PK_{v_i}, ID_i) = \left(PID_{v_i^z}, PK_{v_i^z}, ID_i\right)$, where $z \in \{1, ...\mu\}$. CA stores the vehicle information into the storage module. PK_{v_i} is generated by:

$$PK_{v_i} = BIP32(PK_{root}, chain_{root}) \tag{5}$$

4.3 Bottom Layer Federate Learning Phase

- **Vehicle Local Training** This section focuses on the BFL. In this layer, the V_i first utilizes equation (1)(2)(3) for local training, obtaining the local model parameter ω_t^i.
- **Vehicle Pseudonym Generation** The V_i also calculates the $PID_{v_i^z}$ for the current communication according to equation (6)

$$PID_{v_i} = ID_i \oplus H\left(SK_{v_i} \cdot PK_{CA}\right) \tag{6}$$

- **Vehicle Signature** After calculating the $PID_{v_i^z}$ and required model parameter ω_t^i the vehicle uses the following equation to calculate the signature:

$$\delta = \left\{ sign_{SK_{v_i^z}}(PID_{v_i^z} \parallel \omega_t^i) \right\} \tag{7}$$

- **Parameter Sending** V_i sends message $\left\{\delta, \omega_t^i, PID_{v_i^z}\right\}$ to RSU.

4.4 Top Layer Federate Learning Phase

- **Signature Verification** RSU receives $\left\{\delta, \omega_t^i, PID_{v_i^z}\right\}$ from the vehicle and uses $PID_{v_i^z}$ to retrieve the corresponding $PK_{v_i^z}$ on the CA. The RSU verifies the signature δ using $PK_{v_i^z}$ from the CA. If the verification is successful, it proceeds to the next operation. In contrast, when verification fails, it rejects the message.
- **Malicious Vehicle Node Elimination** We use the Multi-KRUM [18] algorithm to implement the exclusion of malicious data. Assume that G is the total amount of model parameters uploaded by vehicles under an RSU and f is the total amount of Byzantine parameters. The sum of each parameter and the Euclidean distance to the nearest $G - f - 2$ parameters is calculated as the score of that model parameter according to the following equation.

$$M(x) = \sum_{x \to y} \|\bar{w}_x - \bar{w}_y\| \tag{8}$$

where ω_y denotes the $G - f - 2$ closest vectors (neighbors) of ω_x. Finally, the $G - f$ model parameters with the lowest scores are selected as legitimate updates for aggregation.
- **RSU Aggregation** After completing the local training, the vehicle sends the model parameters to a nearby RSU, and after completing the exclusion of malicious data, the aggregation is executed according to the following equation:

$$\omega_t^r = \frac{1}{|N_t|} \sum_{i=1}^{|N_t|} \omega_t^i \tag{9}$$

where N_t is the number of vehicles involved in aggregation in round t.

- **RSU Local Training** The RSU can collect information from the environment to participate in FL. After the malicious vehicle is eliminated. Each RSU updates its own model parameters in the following manner:

$$\omega_t^j = \omega_t^r - \eta \cdot \nabla L_j \left(\omega_{t-1}^r, d_j \right) \tag{10}$$

where ω_t^j is the model parameter of the RSU after BFL aggregation and d_j is the surrounding data collected by the RSU. After RSU finishes training, it uploads the model parameters to the CA, which executes the aggregation algorithm and finishes generating the global model.

- **Model Parameter Storage** Assuming that the weight aggregation is $W = \left\{ \omega_t^1, \omega_t^2, ..., \omega_t^k \right\}$ at time t, denote RSU node 1 by ω_t^1, while leaving the summary of version t in the parameter server. If node 1 sends an update ω_{t+1}^1 at the next moment, the weight summary will update the corresponding position of node 1, i.e. $W = \left\{ \omega_{t+1}^1, \omega_t^2, ..., \omega_t^k \right\}$. This approach ensures that outdated update weights are included. In this process, the parameters of each parameter server are stored separately to preserve the latest weights of all nodes. This method improves the drawback of simple aggregated storage of parameter servers in two ways. Firstly, it effectively restricts the high-frequency updates of fast-running nodes. Secondly, it maximizes the overall weights' guarantee to prevent the generation of severely biased fast-node training data in the high-frequency updates environment. As a result, this method improves the model's overall convergence performance.

- **Weighting Factor Calculation and CA Aggregation** This framework retains the latest uploaded weights from all RSU, increases the independence of fast and slow nodes, and effectively limits the high-frequency updates of fast nodes while reducing the lagging influence of slow nodes. Building on this, a weighted aggregation mechanism based on version number and model accuracy is proposed to better adapt to different practical situations. At the time of aggregation, the difference between the latest version provided by different RSUs and the latest version recorded on the Central Aggregator (CA) is calculated. The weighting factor of the time dimension is calculated according to the following formula:

$$T(j) = (v_{latest} - v_j + 1)^{-\beta} \tag{11}$$

where $T(j)$ represents the time-dimensional weighting factor representing RSU number j, v_j represents the version of the parameter uploaded by RSU number j, v_{latest} is the latest version saved by CA, and β is the hyperparameter, $\beta \in (0, 1)$.

Meanwhile CA will calculate the accuracy of the received model parameters from RSU_j on the common test set and design the aggregated weighting coefficients of the quality dimensions based on the accuracy.

$$Acc(j) = Accuracy(\omega^j) \tag{12}$$

where $Accuracy(*)$ is the calculated function of the accuracy of the test model over the public test set, and $Acc(j)$ is the accuracy of the model uploaded by RSU_j.

Finally, we designed a weight score $s(j)$ for the model, and $s(j)$ was calculated according to the following equation:

$$s(j) = Acc(j) \cdot T(j) \tag{13}$$

In order to keep the weights expected to be constant, they need to be normalized according to the following equation:

$$S(j) = \frac{s(j)}{\sum_{j=1}^{k} (v_{latest} - v_j + 1)^{-\beta} \cdot Acc(j)} \tag{14}$$

The algorithm proposed in this paper features a more flexible and accurate weighted aggregation mechanism, as demonstrated by the formula presented above. This mechanism enables the dynamic calculation of appropriate weights for aggregating each weight based on its version and accuracy during the aggregation process. The specific aggregation formula is given below:

$$\omega_{latest} = \sum_{j=1}^{k} \left(S(j) \cdot \omega^j \right) \tag{15}$$

The proposed hierarchical federated learning algorithm is illustrated in Algorithm 1.

5 Security Analysis

This section presents an informal security analysis of the HASFL system.

- **Identity Privacy Protection** During vehicle registration, the identity information is securely transmitted, ensuring its confidentiality. In the data upload phase, the true identity of the vehicle is concealed using a pseudonym, which can only be decrypted by the CA from intercepted messages. Consequently, the privacy of vehicle identity information is effectively preserved.

- **Unlinkability** Each time the vehicle sends a message, it generates a new kana for communication. Since the pseudonym is associated with the vehicle's chain code, connecting two messages sent by the same vehicle requires knowledge of the vehicle's root chain code and root public key. However, within this solution, only the CA and the vehicle possess this information. Consequently, the scheme fulfills the security requirements of non-linkage.

- **Resist Poisoning Attacks** The framework demonstrates robustness against poisoning attacks through the utilization of the MULTI-KRUM algorithm. This algorithm effectively identifies and eliminates malicious parameters prior to their participation in the global aggregation process, thereby preventing their inclusion in the global model.

Algorithm 1: Hierarchical federated learning algorithm

---

1 Initialization: N Vehicles, M RSUs, Learning rate η, Hyperparameters β, SK_{CA}, PK_{CA}, SK_{root}, $Chain_{root}$, H ;

2 **Vehicle executes:**

3   $D^v \longleftarrow Vehicle_n$ collects surrounding data as local training batch

4 **for** *each local epoch* **do**

5   **for** *batch* $d \in D^r$ **do**

6 | learning model $\omega^r \longleftarrow \omega^r - \eta \cdot \bigtriangledown L(\omega^r, d)$

7   **end**

8   Generate PID

9 **end**

10 Return: ω^v and PID to RSU

11 **RSU executes:**

12   $C_m \longleftarrow$ learning model set of Vehicles collected by RSU_m

13 **for** *each Vehicle in* C_m **do**

14   Verify PID

15   Calculate Multi-krum score $M(x)$

16 **end**

17 $C_f \longleftarrow$ valid learning model set of Vehicles filtered by Multi-KRUM

18 **for** *each Vehicle in* C_f **do**

19     $\omega^r \longleftarrow \frac{1}{|N_t|} \sum_{i=1}^{|N_t|} \omega_i^v$

20 **end**

21 $D^r \longleftarrow RSU_m$ collects surrounding data as further training batch

22 **for** *each local epoch* **do**

23   **for** *batch* $d \in D^v$ **do**

24 | learning model $\omega^v \longleftarrow \omega^v - \eta \cdot \bigtriangledown L(\omega^v, d)$

25   **end**

26 **end**

27 Return: ω^r to CA

28 **CA executes:**

29   $w_m \longleftarrow$ learning model set of RSU

30 CA store w_m

31 **for** *each* RSU_j *in* W_m **do**

32   calculate accuracy $A(j)$ and time $T(j)$

33     $S(j) = \frac{A(j) \cdot T(j)}{\sum_{j=1}^{M} A(j) \cdot T(j)}$

34 **end**

35 $\omega_{global} = \sum_{j=1}^{k} (S(j) \cdot \omega_j)$

36 Output:global learning model ω_{global}

---

6 Experimental Results and Analysis

This section presents simulation experiments and performance evaluation of the HASFL framework for IoVs. The results demonstrate the effectiveness of the system, including the hierarchical Federated Learning approach that combines both synchronous and asynchronous modes to optimize the loss function and accuracy. Furthermore, we evaluate the effectiveness of the error-removal algorithm incorporated in the framework by comparing the scheme with and without the error-removal algorithm. Finally, we compare our scheme with two other vehicular FL approaches to demonstrate its superiority.

6.1   Parameter Setting

- **Network Initialization:** Our simulation scenario consisted of a complex area with dimensions of 1500 m × 1000 m on the SUMO map, incorporating 10 RSUs within the CA.
- **Dataset:** We evaluate our experiments on the MNIST dataset, a sample of which are images containing numbers that simulate the fragmented information and application profiles generated by vehicles while driving. Each instance is a 28 × 28 single-channel picture with 10 different categories. The dataset is split into 100 shards, and the shards are ssigned to 100 providers. The edge data sharing task is to share the computing results on the local data of each data provider.

6.2   Results and Analysis

To assess the feasibility of the HASFL framework, we conducted experiments using 30, 60, and 100 vehicles, while keeping the number of RSUs fixed at 10. We initially evaluated the accuracy and loss of our proposed scheme using the MNIST dataset with various numbers of data providers. The resulting accuracy and loss values are presented in Fig. 3 and Fig. 4. Our findings indicate that high accuracy can be achieved with different numbers of vehicles participating in the training, and that the more vehicles that participate, the higher the accuracy. Furthermore, the loss results demonstrate that they can converge to very low values. Therefore, we can confirm that our scheme can achieve convergence and find a stable final solution in a limited computation time, regardless of the number of participating vehicles. In conclusion, our experiments have confirmed the feasibility of the proposed system.

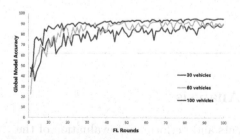

Fig. 3. The accuracy with various numbers of data providers

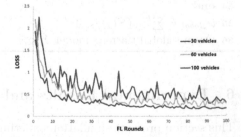

Fig. 4. The loss results with various numbers of data providers

We conducted experiments to assess the impact of malicious nodes on Federated Learning and to evaluate the performance of our error-removal algorithm. Specifically, we used 100 vehicles and 10 RSUs, while assuming the presence of 30 malicious vehicle nodes. We compared the accuracy of our proposed scheme with and without the error-removal algorithm. As shown in Fig. 5, the accuracy of our proposed scheme without the error-removal algorithm increased with the number of training rounds, peaked at round 23, and then declined. However, the inclusion of our error-removal algorithm enabled the framework to achieve convergence of about 95%.

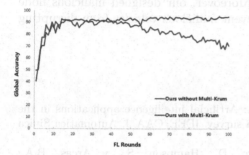 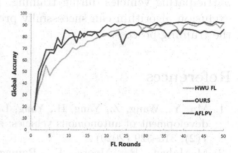

Fig. 5. Model accuracy with and without error-removal algorithm

Fig. 6. Performance comparison with existing solutions

We conducted a performance comparison of our proposed scheme with two other algorithms: the hierarchical synchronous Federated Learning Algorithm (HWU FL) and the non-hierarchical Asynchronous Federated Learning Algorithm (AFLPV). As shown in Fig. 6, our proposed scheme exhibits a faster convergence speed and higher average accuracy than HWU FL. Although our proposed scheme converges at a slower rate than AFLPV, it achieves a significantly higher stable accuracy than AFLPV. Our results effectively demonstrate that hierarchical Federated Learning performs better than traditional non-hierarchical Federated Learning, and a combination of synchronous and asynchronous aggregation updates performs better than fully synchronous aggregation updates in an IoVs scenario.

In conclusion, the hierarchical Federated Learning algorithm proposed in this paper surpasses the traditional FL algorithm. This is because the hierarchical algorithm utilizes an intermediate layer to collect knowledge from the bottom of the network and then reprocesses it by combining its own data. This process enhances the relevance of all data and reflects group intelligence, which ultimately improves the learning accuracy. Moreover, the asynchronous weighting approach based on interaction rounds and model accuracy can speed up the convergence of the system. The advantages of our scheme are crucial for traffic scenarios, especially for future intelligent transportation systems, where multiple vehicles and RSUs cooperate to predict or analyze traffic conditions.

7 Conclusion

This paper addresses the challenge of knowledge sharing in the Internet of Vehicles (IoVs) scenario. A hierarchical federated learning framework is proposed that allows both vehicles and RSUs to contribute effectively. A synchronous and asynchronous combined method is designed, and a more accurate weighting coefficient is computed based on the comprehensive model accuracy and interaction frequency to facilitate asynchronous weighted aggregation. The experimental results demonstrate the effectiveness of our approach in terms of both accuracy and convergence speed. To ensure identity privacy, pseudonyms are used for the participating vehicles during training. Moreover, our designed malicious node exclusion algorithm can successfully prevent malicious vehicles from disrupting the training process.

References

1. Ma, Y., Wang, Z., Yang, H., Yang, L.: Artificial intelligence applications in the development of autonomous vehicles: a survey. IEEE/CAA J. Automatica Sinica **7**(2), 315–329 (2020)
2. McMahan, B., Moore, E., Ramage, D., Hampson, S., y Arcas, B.A.: Communication-efficient learning of deep networks from decentralized data. In: Artificial Intelligence and Statistics, pp. 1273–1282. PMLR (2017)
3. Liang, F., Yang, Q., Liu, R., Wang, J., Sato, K., Guo, J.: Semi-synchronous federated learning protocol with dynamic aggregation in internet of vehicles. IEEE Trans. Veh. Technol. **71**(5), 4677–4691 (2022)
4. Kong, X., et al.: A federated learning-based license plate recognition scheme for 5G-enabled internet of vehicles. IEEE Trans. Industr. Inf. **17**(12), 8523–8530 (2021)
5. Lyu, L., et al.: Towards fair and privacy-preserving federated deep models. IEEE Trans. Parallel Distrib. Syst. **31**(11), 2524–2541 (2020)
6. Xie, C., Koyejo, S., Gupta, I.: Asynchronous federated optimization. arXiv preprint arXiv:1903.03934 (2019)
7. Lian, X., Zhang, W., Zhang, C., Liu, J.: Asynchronous decentralized parallel stochastic gradient descent. In: International Conference on Machine Learning, pp. 3043–3052. PMLR (2018)
8. Huang, J., et al.: AFLPC: an asynchronous federated learning privacy-preserving computing model applied to 5G–V2X. Secur. Commun. Netw. **2022** (2022)
9. Nishiyama, H., Ito, M., Kato, N.: Relay-by-smartphone: realizing multihop device-to-device communications. IEEE Commun. Mag. **52**(4), 56–65 (2014)
10. Dai, Y., Xu, D., Maharjan, S., Chen, Z., He, Q., Zhang, Y.: Blockchain and deep reinforcement learning empowered intelligent 5G beyond. IEEE Netw. **33**(3), 10–17 (2019)
11. Lu, Y., Huang, X., Dai, Y., Maharjan, S., Zhang, Y.: Federated learning for data privacy preservation in vehicular cyber-physical systems. IEEE Netw. **34**(3), 50–56 (2020)
12. Kang, J., Xiong, Z., Niyato, D., Xie, S., Zhang, J.: Incentive mechanism for reliable federated learning: a joint optimization approach to combining reputation and contract theory. IEEE Internet Things J. **6**(6), 10700–10714 (2019)

13. Samarakoon, S., Bennis, M., Saad, W., Debbah, M.: Federated learning for ultra-reliable low-latency V2V communications. In: 2018 IEEE Global Communications Conference (GLOBECOM), pp. 1–7. IEEE (2018)

14. Kim, H., Park, J., Bennis, M., Kim, S.L.: Blockchained on-device federated learning. IEEE Commun. Lett. **24**(6), 1279–1283 (2019)

15. Feyzmahdavian, H.R., Aytekin, A., Johansson, M.: An asynchronous mini-batch algorithm for regularized stochastic optimization. IEEE Trans. Autom. Control **61**(12), 3740–3754 (2016)

16. Lian, X., Zhang, W., Zhang, C., Liu, J.: Asynchronous decentralized parallel stochastic gradient descent. In: International Conference on Machine Learning, pp. 3043–3052. PMLR (2018)

17. Lin, C., He, D., Huang, X., Kumar, N., Choo, K.K.R.: BCPPA: a blockchain-based conditional privacy-preserving authentication protocol for vehicular ad hoc networks. IEEE Trans. Intell. Transp. Syst. **22**(12), 7408–7420 (2021)

18. Blanchard, P., Mhamdi, E., Guerraoui, R., Stainer, J.: Machine learning with adversaries: byzantine tolerant gradient descent. In: Neural Information Processing Systems (2017)

A Secure Mutual Authentication Scheme for Wireless Communication

Jie Song, Xiangyu Pan, and Fagen Li[✉]

School of Computer Science and Engineering, University of Electronic Science
and Technology of China, Chengdu 611731, China
fagenli@uestc.edu.cn

Abstract. With the rapid development of network technology, the number of mobile devices is increasing at a phenomenal speed. However, many wireless communications are established on public wireless networks, which makes it a challenge to ensure the message confidentiality and user privacy. Besides, mobile devices usually have limited resources. It is necessary to design a secure and efficient cryptographic scheme for wireless communication. In this paper, we propose an identity-based mutual authentication scheme for resource-constrained mobile devices. With the help of random oracle model, we show that the scheme is provably secure under extended Canetti-Krawczyk (eCK) security model. Finally, through comparative experiments with six related works, we demonstrate that the proposed scheme is the most suitable for resource-constrained mobile devices in wireless communications.

Keywords: Mutual authentication · Identity-based cryptography · Key exchange · Mobile devices · Wireless communication

1 Introduction

In recent years, 5th generation (5G) network has been gradually popularized with the rapid development of network technology. Meanwhile, a large quantity of emerging applications based on wireless network are integrated into people's daily life. Vehicle ad hoc networks (VANETs) improve the transportation efficiency and driving safety by providing reliable information services for vehicles [32]. Wireless body area networks (WBANs) collect real-time biomedical data through the sensors placed in or around patients' bodies and send it to remote medical personnel for diagnosis [27]. Unmanned aerial vehicle (UAV) technology has been filtering down to ordinary consumers, which can be used for aerial photography, media filming, package delivery, emergency rescue and so forth [33]. Since most applications like the above are established on public wireless networks, the messages transmitted may be intercepted, modified, replayed etc.

Supported by Sichuan Science and Technology Program (Grant No. 2022YFG0172 and 2022ZHCG0037).

H. Yang and R. Lu (Eds.): FCS 2023, CCIS 1992, pp. 114–130, 2024.
https://doi.org/10.1007/978-981-99-9331-4_8

In those cases, users' privacy data can be revealed and the validity of messages cannot be guaranteed. It is crucial to ensure the security of wireless communication, which includes user authentication, data confidentiality, message integrity, privacy preservation and so on. In addition, most mobile devices are considered to have relatively low computation power and small storage space. Therefore, it is necessary to design a cryptographic scheme with high security and efficiency for wireless communication. To reduce the cost of mobile devices, we propose an identity-based mutual authentication scheme for wireless communication. Then, we prove that the proposed scheme is secure under the well-known extended Canetti-Krawczyk (eCK) [12] security model. Through comparison with related works, our scheme is the most suitable for resource-constrained mobile devices in wireless communications.

Related works are discussed in Sect. 2. Section 3 describes preliminaries. Then, we give the concrete construction of the scheme and provide the security analysis in Sect. 4 and 5, respectively. In Sect. 6, we show the comparison results between our scheme with other schemes. Finally, we conclude this paper in Sect. 7.

2   Related Works

Shim [23] introduced an identity-based signature scheme and constructed a conditional privacy-preserving authentication scheme for vehicular sensor networks. The authentication scheme could also support batch verification process. Subsequently, Liu et al. [14] found that [23] was proved only secure against chosen-identity and no-message attack and it had non-negligible error in batch verification. To reduce the computation overhead of message processing in VANET, He et al. [10] designed a pairing-free authentication scheme with conditional privacy protection. To achieve secure communication and driver privacy in a vehicular sensor network, Lo and Tsai [16] developed an identity-based signature scheme and proposed a novel anonymous authentication scheme. To deal with the issue that too many valid identities were held by one user to protect identity privacy, Wang and Yao [26] presented a local identity-based anonymous message authentication protocol based on a hybrid authentication scheme. However, the aforementioned works were designed to support one-way authentication.

In 2008, Yang and Chang [30] put forward an identity-based remote mutual authentication scheme on elliptic curve cryptosystem (ECC). Their scheme also supported a session key agreement between two participants. Later, Yoon and Yoo [31] found out that [30] was not secure against impersonation attack and could not satisfy perfect forward secrecy. They provided an improved scheme which not only solved the security issues in [30] but also reduced computation overhead. In 2012, He et al. [5] came up with a more efficient identity-based remote mutual authentication scheme. It was proved secure under random oracle model (ROM). In the next year, Chou et al. [4] introduced two authentication with key agreement schemes, which included a two-party and three-party identity-based mutual authentication scheme respectively. They claimed that the two schemes were able to achieve strong notions of security. Unfortunately, Farash and Attari [7] demonstrated that two schemes in [4] were both insecure against impersonation attack. Besides, they presented an improved one to eliminate the security flaws of the first scheme in [4]. Wang and Zhang [27] came up with an anonymous authentication scheme for WBANs and analyzed the security by means of BAN [2] logic. However, Wu et al. [29] demonstrated that [27] was vulnerable to impersonation attack and presented another anonymous authentication scheme under ROM. To provide secure communication in mobile healthcare social networks (MHSNs), He et al. [8] introduced a framework for handshake scheme in MHSNs and proposed a cross-domain handshake scheme which supported symptoms-matching in MHSNs. However, the communication cost in [8] was too expensive. Odelu et al. [20] presented a new provably secure authenticated key agreement scheme for smart grid. They demonstrated that the scheme was secure under Canetti-Krawczyk (CK) [3] model. However, it suffers from denial of service (DoS) attack since the smart meter must send a third message to complete the session. Saeed et al. [22] put forward an authentication key agreement scheme for wireless sensor networks and proved it secure under extended Canetti-Krawczyk (eCK) [12] model. Kumar and Chand [11] designed an identity-based anonymous authentication and key agreement protocol for WBAN, and they showed that the protocol was provably secure under BRP [1] model. Unfortunately, it could not provide perfect forward secrecy because an attacker was able to recover the ephemeral key after a key extraction query, and then calculate the session key.

Besides, Mezrag et al. [18] and Fanian et al. [6] proposed clustering mechanism to extend the wireless sensor networks lifetime. Mezrag et al. [19] presented an identity-based authentication and key agreement scheme, which achieved all desirable security properties of key agreement and prevented specific cyberattacks on clustered wireless sensor networks. Wang et al. [25], Tao et al. [24] and Liu et al. [15] researched cross-domain authentication key agreement protocol for heterogeneous cryptosystem, where the protocol initiator used PKI and the responder used IBC. However, the communication cost in the above three protocol was too expensive due to too many interaction rounds. Li et al. [13] and He et al. [9] studied on heterogeneous anonymous mutual authentication, where the protocol initiator belonged to IBC while the responder belonged to PKI. Zhang et al. [33] and Wazid et al. [28] worked on lightweight remote authentication protocols for UAV communications.

3   Preliminaries

3.1   Bilinear Pairing

$\mathbb{G}_1$ is an additive group with order q and $\mathbb{G}_2$ is a multiplicative group with order q, where q is a large prime number. $\hat{e} : \mathbb{G}_1 \times \mathbb{G}_1 \to \mathbb{G}_2$ is a bilinear map and it satisfies the following three properties.

- Bilinearity: $\hat{e}(rP, sQ) = \hat{e}(P, Q)^{rs}$ for any $r, s \in \mathbb{Z}_q^*$ and $P, Q \in \mathbb{G}_1$.

- Non-degeneracy: $\hat{e}(P,Q) \neq 1_{\mathbb{G}_2}$ for any $P, Q \in \mathbb{G}_1$, where $1_{\mathbb{G}_2}$ is the identity element of $\mathbb{G}_2$.
- Computability: $\hat{e}(P,Q)$ can be computed efficiently for any $P, Q \in \mathbb{G}_1$.

3.2   Collusion Attack Algorithm with k Traitors (k-CAA) Problem

Given $(h_1, h_2, ..., h_k) \in \mathbb{Z}_q^*$ and $(P, sP, (s+h_1)^{-1}P, (s+h_2)^{-1}P, ..., (s+h_k)^{-1}P) \in \mathbb{G}_1$, it is difficult to compute $(s+h)^{-1}P$ for some $h \in \mathbb{Z}_q^*$.

3.3 q-Strong Diffie-Hellman (q-SDH) Problem

Given a generator $P \in \mathbb{G}_1$ and q elements $(sP, s^2P, ..., s^qP) \in \mathbb{G}_1$, finding a pair $(t, (s+t)^{-1}P)$ is hard.

3.4   Computational Diffie-Hellman (CDH) Problem

Given two randomly selected $rP, sP \in \mathbb{G}_1$, it is difficult to compute rsP.

3.5   System Architecture

The communication system model is depicted in Fig. 1. It is composed of the three participants, namely PKG, User A and User B. All users should register with PKG. It verifies a user's identity and generates a long-term secret key based on the identity. A and B is the initiator and responder of the scheme, respectively. They intend to achieve mutual authentication.

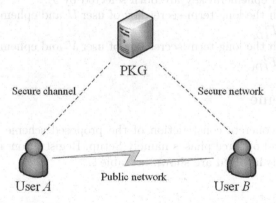

Fig. 1. Communication system model

3.6   Security Model

We adopt the well-known extended Canetti-Krawczyk [12] (eCK) security model. Let $\Gamma_{ID_U}^i$ denote user U's i-th session. We say that $\Gamma_{ID_U}^i$ is accepted if the proposed scheme is finished successfully in the session. Every accepted session has a session key K, a session identification sid. We say that session $\Gamma_{ID_U}^i$ and session $\Gamma_{ID_V}^j$ are partnered if they share a same K and a same sid. The eCK security model can be defined by a game played by an adversary $\mathcal{F}$ and a challenger $\mathcal{C}$ as follows.

$\mathcal{F}$ is allowed to adaptively query the following oracles.

- $H_i(M)$: It takes as input M and returns a random hash value.
- Send($\Gamma_{ID_U}^i, m$): It simulates that user U receives message m and replies with the corresponding message according to the proposed scheme.
- Extract(ID_i): It reveals the long-term secret key of ID_i.
- Ephemeral Key Reveal($\Gamma_{ID_U}^i$): It reveals the ephemeral key chosen by user U in $\Gamma_{ID_U}^i$.
- Reveal($\Gamma_{ID_U}^i$): It reveals the session key of $\Gamma_{ID_U}^i$.
- Test($\Gamma_{ID_U}^i$): This query can be issued only once. It randomly chooses a bit $b \in \{0, 1\}$. If $b = 0$, it responds with a random $K \in \mathbb{G}_2$; Otherwise, it responds with the session key of $\Gamma_{ID_U}^i$.

When $\mathcal{F}$ finishes the query phase, it outputs a bit $b' \in \{0, 1\}$ as the guess of b. $\mathcal{F}$ wins the game if $b' = b$ and $\Gamma_{ID_U}^i$ is accepted and clean. Assume that $\Gamma_{ID_U}^i$ and $\Gamma_{ID_V}^j$ are partnered, we say that $\Gamma_{ID_U}^i$ is clean if neither of the following conditions is met.

1. User U or V is an adversary-controlled party. It means that the long-term secret key and ephemeral key are both selected by $\mathcal{F}$.
2. $\mathcal{F}$ reveals both the long-term secret key of user U and ephemeral key chosen by user U in $\Gamma_{ID_U}^i$.
3. $\mathcal{F}$ reveals both the long-term secret key of user V and ephemeral key chosen by user V in $\Gamma_{ID_V}^j$.

4   Our Scheme

We provide the concrete construction of the proposed scheme in this section, which is composed of three phases namely Setup, Registration and Authentication. The symbols involved are shown in Table 1.

4.1   Setup

According to security parameter λ, PKG sets public parameters pp as follows.

1. It selects a large prime number q, a q-order additive group $\mathbb{G}_1$, a q-order multiplicative group $\mathbb{G}_2$, a bilinear pairing $\hat{e} : \mathbb{G}_1 \times \mathbb{G}_1 \to \mathbb{G}_2$ satisfying the properties in Sect. 3.1. P is a generator of $\mathbb{G}_1$ and $g = \hat{e}(P, P)$ is a generator of $\mathbb{G}_2$.

Table 1. Symbols and descriptions

Symbol	Description
λ	Security parameter
pp	Public parameters
q	A large prime number
$\hat{e}$	A bilinear map from $\mathbb{G}_1$ to $\mathbb{G}_2$
$\mathbb{G}_1$	An additive group with order q
$\mathbb{G}_2$	A multiplicative group with order q
P	A generator in $\mathbb{G}_1$
g	A generator in $\mathbb{G}_2$
H_i	The i-th Hash function
P_{pub}/s	Master public/secret key pair
ID_U	The identity of user U
S_{ID_U}	The long-term secret key of user U

2. It selects five secure one-way hash functions: $H_i : \{0,1\}^* \to \mathbb{Z}_q^*$, where $i = 1$ to 5.
3. It chooses master secret key $s \in \mathbb{Z}_q^*$ and calculates master public key $P_{pub} = sP$.

Finally, PKG publishes public parameters $pp = \{q, \mathbb{G}_1, \mathbb{G}_2, P, g, \hat{e}, H_1, H_2, H_3, H_4, H_5, P_{pub}\}$ and keeps s secret.

4.2 Registration

User A sends its identity ID_A to PKG for registration. PKG takes as input s and ID_A, then calculates a long-term secret key S_{ID_A} for user A.

$$S_{ID_A} = \frac{1}{s + H_1(ID_A)} P$$

PKG transmits S_{ID_A} to user A secretly. After receiving S_{ID_A}, user A computes $s_A = H_2(ID_A, S_{ID_A})$. Similarly, user B registers with PKG for its long-term secret key S_{ID_B} and calculates s_B.

4.3 Authentication

After both users register with PKG, they start a communication session for mutual authentication.

1. In the beginning, user A randomly picks $r_A \in \mathbb{Z}_q^*$ and calculates

$$T_A = (r_A + s_A)(H_1(ID_B)P + P_{pub}),$$

$$K_A = g^{(r_A + s_A)},$$

$$h_1 = H_3(ID_A, T_A, K_A),$$

$$\sigma_A = (r_A + s_A + h_1)S_{ID_A},$$

$$c_A = H_4(K_A, ID_B) \oplus (ID_A, \sigma_A),$$

then delivers message $m_1 = (T_A, c_A)$ to user B through an open public network.

2. Upon receiving message m_1, user B first computes

$$K_A = \hat{e}(S_{ID_B}, T_A),$$

and recovers the sender's identity and the corresponding signature

$$(ID_A, \sigma_A) = c_A \oplus H_4(K_A, ID_B).$$

Then user B calculates

$$h_1 = H_3(ID_A, T_A, K_A),$$

and verifies the validity of the signature

$$\hat{e}(\sigma_A, H_1(ID_A)P + P_{pub}) = g^{h_1} K_A$$

If the above equation does not hold, the verification fails and user B abandons the session. Otherwise, the authentication of user A is completed. Afterwards, user B randomly selects $r_B \in \mathbb{Z}_q^*$ and does the following computations.

$$K_B = g^{r_B + s_B}, K_{BA} = K_A^{r_B + s_B},$$

$$h_2 = H_5(ID_A, ID_B, K_A, K_B, K_{BA}).$$

Then user B accepts K_{BA} as the session key and transmits $m_2 = (K_B, h_2)$ back to user A.

3. After receiving message m_2 from user B, user A computes

$$K_{AB} = K_B^{r_A + s_A},$$

then verifies the following equation.

$$h_2 = H_5(ID_A, ID_B, K_A, K_B, K_{AB})$$

If it holds, the authentication of user B is finished and user A accepts K_{AB} as the session key. Otherwise, user A closes the session.

4.4 Correctness

We prove the correctness of our scheme as below. User B computes

$$K_A = \hat{e}(S_{ID_B}, T_A)$$
$$= \hat{e}(\frac{1}{s + H_1(ID_B)}P, (r_A + s_A)(H_1(ID_B)P + P_{pub}))$$
$$= \hat{e}(P, P)^{(r_A + s_A)}$$
$$= g^{(r_A + s_A)},$$
$$h_1 = H_3(ID_A, T_A, K_A),$$

then user B verifies the validity of σ_A as follows.

$$\hat{e}(\sigma_A, H_1(ID_A)P + P_{pub})$$
$$= \hat{e}((r_A + s_A + h_1)\frac{1}{s + H_1(ID_A)}P, H_1(ID_A)P + P_{pub})$$
$$= \hat{e}(P, P)^{(r_A + s_A + h_1)}$$
$$= K_A g^{h_1}$$

After that, user B calculates the session key as

$$K_{BA} = K_A^{(r_B + s_B)} = g^{(r_A + s_A)(r_B + s_B)}.$$

In the side of user A, it calculates the session key as

$$K_{AB} = K_B^{(r_A + s_A)} = g^{(r_B + s_B)(r_A + s_A)} = K_{BA}.$$

5 Security Analysis

5.1 Mutual Authentication (MA)

Theorem 1. *If the k-CAA problem is difficult, the proposed scheme can achieve initiator-to-responder authentication.*

Proof. If there is a probabilistic polynomial time (PPT) adversary $\mathcal{F}$ who can forge a valid intialization message, we can construct another PPT algorithm $\mathcal{C}$ using $\mathcal{F}$ as a subroutine to solve the given k-CAA instance $(q_1, q_2, ..., q_k, P, sP, (s+q_1)^{-1}P, (s+q_2)^{-1}P, ..., (s+q_k)^{-1}P)$. $\mathcal{C}$'s task is to find a pair $(q^*, (s+q^*)^{-1}P)$ for some $q^* \in \mathbb{Z}_q^*$. $\mathcal{C}$ sets the challenge initiator identity as ID^*, generates public parameters $pp = \{q, \mathbb{G}_1, \mathbb{G}_2, P, g, P_{pub} = sP\}$ and sends pp to $\mathcal{F}$.

Without loss of generality, we suppose that Send and Extract queries are preceded by an H_1 query, and k is larger than the number of H_1 query. $\mathcal{C}$ generates initially empty lists L_{H_1}, L_{H_2}, L_{H_3}, L_{H_4} and L_{H_5} to store the query results of five hash functions respectively. $\mathcal{C}$ answers $\mathcal{F}$'s queries as follows.

- $H_1(ID_i)$: If $ID_i = ID^*$, $\mathcal{C}$ responds with q^*. Otherwise, $\mathcal{C}$ answers with q_i and adds $(ID_i, q_i, (s+q_i)^{-1}P)$ to L_{H_1}.
- $H_2(m_i)$: $\mathcal{C}$ randomly chooses $s_i \in \mathbb{Z}_q^*$, answers with s_i and adds (m_i, s_i) to L_{H_2}.
- $H_3(m_i)$: $\mathcal{C}$ randomly chooses $h_{1i} \in \mathbb{Z}_q^*$, answers with h_{1i} and adds (m_i, h_{1i}) to L_{H_3}.
- $H_4(m_i)$: $\mathcal{C}$ randomly chooses $k_i \in \mathbb{Z}_q^*$, answers with k_i and adds (m_i, k_i) to L_{H_4}.
- $H_5(m_i)$: $\mathcal{C}$ randomly chooses $h_{2i} \in \mathbb{Z}_q^*$, answers with h_{2i} and adds (m_i, h_{2i}) to L_{H_5}.
- Send$(\Gamma_{ID_U}^i, m)$: If $ID_U = ID^*$ and $m = $ 'Start', $\mathcal{C}$ randomly selects $r, h \in \mathbb{Z}_q^*$, calculates

$$T = rq^*P + rP_{pub} - hq_V P - hP_{pub},$$

$$K = \hat{e}(\frac{1}{s+q_V}P, T),$$

$$\sigma = \frac{r}{s+q_V}P,$$

$$c = H_4(K, ID_V) \oplus (ID^*, \sigma)$$

and answers with (T, c), where V is the responder in $\Gamma_{ID_U}^i$. Otherwise, $\mathcal{C}$ answers according to the specification of the proposed scheme. In both cases, (T, c) is a valid initialization message.
- Extract(ID_i): $\mathcal{C}$ finds $(ID_i, q_i, (s+q_i)^{-1}P)$ from L_{H_1} and answers with $(s+q_i)^{-1}P$. Here $\mathcal{F}$ is not allowed to query ID^*.
- Ephemeral-Key-Reveal$(\Gamma_{ID_U}^i)$: $\mathcal{C}$ answers with the corresponding ephemeral key chosen by user U in $\Gamma_{ID_U}^i$.
- Reveal$(\Gamma_{ID_U}^i)$: $\mathcal{C}$ answers with the session key of $\Gamma_{ID_U}^i$.
- Test$(\Gamma_{ID_U}^i)$: $\mathcal{C}$ randomly chooses a bit $b \in \{0,1\}$. If $b = 0$, $\mathcal{C}$ answers with a random $K \in \mathbb{G}_2$; Otherwise, $\mathcal{C}$ answers with the session key of $\Gamma_{ID_U}^i$.

After query phase, $\mathcal{F}$ forges a valid initialization message (T_A, c_A) from ID^* to ID_V. We replays $\mathcal{C}$ with the same tape but different choices of H_3, as in forking lemma [21], so that $\mathcal{F}$ outputs another valid initialization message (T_A', c_A'). $\mathcal{C}$ first recovers (K_A, σ_A) and (K_A', σ_A') from two messages respectively, then computes h_1 and h_1' respectively. Finally, $\mathcal{C}$ calculates $S_{ID^*} = (h_1 - h_1')(\sigma_1 - \sigma_2)$, and outputs S_{ID^*} as the solution of the given k-CAA problem. □

Theorem 2. *If the DL problem and 1-SDH problem are difficult, the proposed scheme can achieve responder-to-initiator authentication.*

Proof. Assume that an adversary $\mathcal{F}$ intercepts an initialization message (T_A, c_A) from user A to user B, $\mathcal{F}$ tries to forges a valid response message from user B to user A. Due to the collision resistance of hash functions, $\mathcal{F}$ has to extract the correct K_A from T_A. There are three cases that $\mathcal{F}$ can recover K_A successfully, which are shown below.

Case 1: $\mathcal{F}$ just guesses the right value of h_2.

Case 2: $\mathcal{F}$ extracts s from $P_{pub} = sP$ so that $\mathcal{F}$ is able to compute user B's long-term secret key $S_{ID_B} = (s + H_1(ID_B))^{-1}P$ and recover K_A.

Case 3: $\mathcal{F}$ calculates $S_{ID_B} = (s + H_1(ID_B))^{-1}P$ and recover K_A.

Apparently the probability of Case 1 is $1/2^\lambda$, which is a negligible number. Since DL problem and 1-SDH problem are difficult, Case 2 and 3 can hardly happen. To sum up, forging a valid response message is hard to achieve.   □

Based on Theorem 1 and Theorem 2, no adversary can forge a valid initialization message or a valid response message. Therefore, mutual authentication is achieved.

5.2 Key Agreement

From Sect. 4.4, it can be easily seen that user A and user B finally agree on a same session key if the proposed scheme is executed successfully.

5.3 Session Key Security (SKS)

Theorem 3. *If k-CAA, DL, 1-SDH and DBDH problems are difficult to solve, the proposed scheme is able to satisfy SKS under eCK security model.*

Proof. An adversary $\mathcal{F}$ can get advantage in attacking SKS of the proposed scheme in the following two cases:

Case 1: $\mathcal{F}$ intercepts and forges authentication transcripts, which means $\mathcal{F}$ may impersonate a user.

Case 2: $\mathcal{F}$ does not alter any transcripts.

From Sect. 5.1 we can get that, if k-CAA, DL and 1-SDH problems are difficult, the probability of $\mathcal{F}$ forging a valid message is negligible. Therefore, The advantage in Case 1 is negligible too.

Then we discuss Case 2. Given an instance of DBDH problem (aP, bP, cP, X), $\mathcal{C}$ needs to decide if $X = \hat{e}(P, P)^{abc}$. $\mathcal{C}$ selects $s \in \mathbb{Z}_q^*$, generates public parameters $pp = \{q, \mathbb{G}_1, \mathbb{G}_2, P, g, P_{pub} = sP\}$ and sends pp to $\mathcal{F}$. $\mathcal{C}$ guesses α such that $\mathcal{F}$ queries Test with the α-th session.

Without loss of generality, we suppose that Send and Extract queries are preceded by an H_1 query. $\mathcal{C}$ generates initially empty lists L_{H_1}, L_{H_2}, L_{H_3}, L_{H_4} and L_{H_5} to store the query results of five hash functions respectively. $\mathcal{C}$ answers queries as follows.

- $H_1(ID_i)$: $\mathcal{C}$ randomly chooses $q_i \in \mathbb{Z}_q^*$, responds with q_i and adds (ID_i, q_i) to L_{H_1}.
- $H_2(m_i)$: $\mathcal{C}$ randomly chooses $s_i \in \mathbb{Z}_q^*$, answers with s_i and adds (m_i, s_i) to L_{H_2}.
- $H_3(m_i)$: $\mathcal{C}$ randomly chooses $h_{1i} \in \mathbb{Z}_q^*$, answers with h_{1i} and adds (m_i, h_{1i}) to L_{H_3}.

- $H_4(m_i)$: $\mathcal{C}$ randomly chooses $k_i \in \mathbb{Z}_q^*$, answers with k_i and adds (m_i, k_i) to L_{H_4}.
- $H_5(m_i)$: $\mathcal{C}$ randomly chooses $h_{2i} \in \mathbb{Z}_q^*$, answers with h_{2i} and adds (m_i, h_{2i}) to L_{H_5}.
- Send($\Gamma_{ID_U}^i, m$): When $\mathcal{F}$ queries the the α-th session, $\mathcal{C}$ calculates

$$T_U = (s + H_1(ID_V))aP, K_U = \hat{e}(aP, P),$$

$$h_1 = H_3(ID_U, T_U, K_U),$$

$$\sigma_U = \frac{1}{s + H_1(ID_U)}(aP + h_1 P),$$

$$c_U = H_4(K_U, ID_V) \oplus (ID_U, \sigma_U),$$

and answers (T_U, c_U) as the initialization message. $\mathcal{C}$ then computes

$$K_V = \hat{e}(bP, cP), K_{VU} = X,$$

$$h_2 = H_5(ID_U, ID_V, K_U, K_V, K_{VU}),$$

and answers (K_V, h_2) as the response message. Otherwise, $\mathcal{C}$ answers according to the specification of the proposed scheme.
- Extract(ID_i): $\mathcal{C}$ finds (ID_i, q_i) from L_{H_1} and answers with $(s + q_i)^{-1}P$.
- Ephemeral-Key-Reveal($\Gamma_{ID_U}^i$): $\mathcal{C}$ answers with the corresponding ephemeral key chosen by user U in $\Gamma_{ID_U}^i$.
- Reveal($\Gamma_{ID_U}^i$): $\mathcal{C}$ answers with the session key of $\Gamma_{ID_U}^i$.
- Test($\Gamma_{ID_U}^i$): If $\mathcal{F}$ queries the α-th session, $\mathcal{C}$ answers with X. Otherwise, $\mathcal{C}$ randomly chooses a bit $b \in \{0, 1\}$. If $b = 0$, $\mathcal{C}$ answers with a random $K \in \mathbb{G}_2$; If $b = 1$, $\mathcal{C}$ answers with the session key of $\Gamma_{ID_U}^i$.

The probability of $\mathcal{F}$ querying Test with the α-th session is at least $1/q_S$, where q_S is the maximum number of Send query. If $\mathcal{F}$ can win the game with a non-negligible advantage ϵ, $\mathcal{C}$ is able to solve the given DBDH problem with an advantage larger than $(1/q_S)\epsilon$.   □

5.4 Perfect Forward Secrecy (PFS)

If S_{ID_A} and S_{ID_B} are revealed, the attacker can calculate $s_A = H_1(ID_A, S_{ID_A})$ and $s_B = H_1(ID_B, S_{ID_B})$. It can get $K_B = g^{(r_B + s_B)}$ from transcripts and recover $K_A = g^{(r_A + s_A)}$ from T_A, then compute g^{r_A} and g^{r_B}. However, it is not capable of computing the session key $g^{(r_A + s_A)(r_B + s_B)}$ based on K_A and K_B due to the CDH problem. Only if the attacker gets r_A or r_B, it can calculates the session key. Nevertheless, it is difficult for the attacker to derive r_A or r_B because of the DL problem. Therefore, perfect forward secrecy is achieved.

5.5 Identity Privacy

The transcript of a session consists of two messages, (T_A, c_A) and (K_B, h_2). Only c_A contains the identity information of user A. However, an attacker is not able to extract ID_A from c_A since it cannot extract K_A from T_A without knowing user B's long-term secret key S_{ID_B}. Hence, the identity privacy is preserved.

5.6   Resistance Against Attacks

Since the proposed scheme is proved capable of satisfying mutual authentication, impersonation attack and man-in-the-middle attack will not work.

Owing to the collision resistance of hash functions, the proposed scheme can defend against replay attack if we add two timestamps to H_3 and H_5 respectively.

For the responder B, the session will be immediately abandoned if the verification equation does not hold. If B successfully responds message m_2, the proposed scheme is finished in B's side. For the initiator A, if A does not receive message m_2 from B within a set time interval after A sends message m_1, A closes the session. In other words, the proposed scheme is secure against DoS attack.

Even if an attacker has the access to the ephemeral keys (r_A, r_B), the session key is secure since the attacker does not know two users' long-term secret keys (S_{ID_A}, S_{ID_B}) and is not able to compute s_A or s_B. Therefore, the proposed scheme can resist against ephemeral key compromise attack.

6   Comparison

We compare the proposed scheme with six related works [8,9,11,20,22,29] in terms of security, computation overhead and communication cost. Table 2 shows the security comparison. SP-1, SP-2, SP-3, SP-4, SP-5, SP-6 and SP-7 denote seven security properties respectively, namely MA, SKS, PFS, identity privacy, resistance against replay attack, resistance against DoS attack and resistance against ephemeral key compromise attack. Our scheme can satisfy all security properties even under eCK model while other schemes cannot.

Table 2. Security comparison

Scheme	SP-1	SP-2	SP-3	SP-4	SP-5	SP-6	SP-7	Security model
[29]	Yes	Yes	No	Yes	Yes	Yes	No	BRP
[9]	Yes	Yes	Yes	Yes	Yes	Yes	No	BRP
[8]	Yes	Yes	Yes	Yes	Yes	Yes	No	BRP
[22]	Yes	Yes	Yes	No	Yes	Yes	No	CK
[20]	Yes	Yes	Yes	Yes	Yes	No	No	CK
[11]	Yes	Yes	No	Yes	Yes	Yes	No	BRP
Ours	Yes	Yes	Yes	Yes	Yes	Yes	Yes	eCK

We show the comparison of computation overhead in Table 3. T_{mtp}, T_{bp}, T_{pm} and T_e denote the time of a map-to-point function, a bilinear map, a point multiplication and an exponentiation respectively. In Table 3, we neglect other fast operations such as hash function, point addition, XOR etc.

The comparison of communication cost is shown in Table 4. $|\mathbb{G}_1|$, $|\mathbb{G}_2|$, $|\mathbb{Z}_q^*|$ and $|ID|$ are the length of an element in $\mathbb{G}_1$, an element in $\mathbb{G}_2$, an element in $\mathbb{Z}_q^*$ and an identity respectively.

Table 3. Computation overhead

Scheme	Initiator	Responder
[29]	$3T_{pm} + 2T_e$	$T_{bp} + 3T_{pm} + 2T_e$
[9]	$T_{mtp} + 4T_{pm}$	$T_{mtp} + 2T_{bp} + 4T_{pm}$
[8]	$6T_{pm}$	$6T_{pm}$
[22]	$6T_{pm}$	$6T_{pm}$
[20]	$2T_{pm} + 2T_e$	$2T_{bp} + 2T_{pm} + T_e$
[11]	$4T_{pm}$	$6T_{pm}$
Ours	$3T_{pm} + 2T_e$	$2T_{bp} + T_{pm} + 3T_e$

Table 4. Communication cost

Scheme	Initialization message	Response message	Rounds
[29]	$3|\mathbb{G}_1| + |\mathbb{Z}_q^*| + |ID|$	$|\mathbb{G}_2| + |\mathbb{Z}_q^*|$	2
[9]	$2|\mathbb{G}_1| + |ID|$	$|\mathbb{G}_1| + |\mathbb{Z}_q^*|$	2
[8]	$3|\mathbb{G}_1| + 3|\mathbb{Z}_q^*| + 2|ID|$	$3|\mathbb{G}_1| + 3|\mathbb{Z}_q^*| + 2|ID|$	3
[22]	$2|\mathbb{G}_1| + 2|\mathbb{Z}_q^*| + |ID|$	$2|\mathbb{G}_1| + 2|\mathbb{Z}_q^*| + |ID|$	2
[20]	$2|\mathbb{G}_1| + 3|\mathbb{Z}_q^*| + |ID|$	$|\mathbb{G}_2| + |\mathbb{Z}_q^*|$	3
[11]	$3|\mathbb{G}_1| + |\mathbb{Z}_q^*| + |ID|$	$|\mathbb{G}_1| + |\mathbb{Z}_q^*|$	2
Ours	$2|\mathbb{G}_1| + |ID|$	$|\mathbb{G}_2| + |\mathbb{Z}_q^*|$	2

We did the experiments on a computer with 3.60 GHz AMD Ryzen 5 3600 CPU, 16.0 GB memory and Windows 10 operating system. We used type-A curve in PBC library [17], which is an elliptic curve $y^2 = x^3 + x$ over $\mathbb{F}_p$ based on a prime order $p \equiv 3 \mod 4$. Figure 2, 3 and 4 depict the experimental results under 80, 112 and 128 security strength respectively. Under 80 security strength, the total computation overheads of seven schemes are 20.8 ms, 38.5 ms, 30.0 ms, 33.0 ms, 19.3 ms, 26.2 ms and 18.6 ms respectively. Under 112 security strength, the total computation overheads of seven schemes are 75.4 ms, 163.1 ms, 105.8 ms, 110.0 ms, 72.5 ms, 90.9 ms and 73 ms respectively. Under 128 security strength, the total computation overheads of seven schemes are 177 ms, 434 ms, 234 ms, 238 ms, 179 ms, 198 ms and 183 ms respectively.

It can be seen that, our scheme performs better than [8,11,22] in every aspect. The communication cost of [9] is the same as ours, but its computation overhead is higher much than ours and it cannot resist against ephemeral key compromise attack under eCK model. [29] and [20] have similar computation overhead as ours. However, [29] cannot provide PFS and resistance against ephemeral key compromise attack under eCK model. [20] is not able to defend against DoS attack and ephemeral key compromise attack under eCK model. In addition, our scheme has the lowest computation overhead under 80 security strength

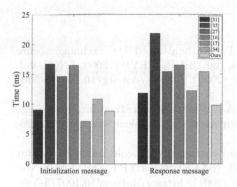

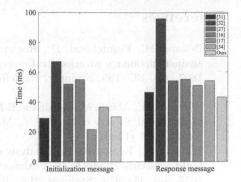

Fig. 2. 80 security strength   **Fig. 3.** 112 security strength

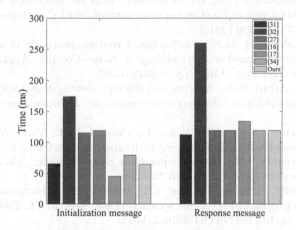

Fig. 4. 128 security strength

while has the highest security and lowest communication cost. It means that our scheme is the most suitable for resource-constrained mobile devices in wireless communications.

7   Conclusion

In this paper, we propose a mutual authentication scheme for wireless communications. We prove that the proposed scheme can achieve mutual authentication, session key security, perfect forward secrecy, identity privacy and resistance against various attacks under eCK model. Besides, through comparative experiments, we demonstrate that the proposed scheme is the most suitable for mobile devices with limited resources.

References

1. Bellare, M., Pointcheval, D., Rogaway, P.: Authenticated key exchange secure against dictionary attacks. In: Preneel, B. (ed.) EUROCRYPT 2000. LNCS, vol. 1807, pp. 139–155. Springer, Heidelberg (2000). https://doi.org/10.1007/3-540-45539-6_11

2. Burrows, M., Abadi, M., Needham, R.M.: A logic of authentication. In: Proceedings of the Royal Society of London. A. Mathematical and Physical Sciences, vol. 426, pp. 233–271 (1989)

3. Canetti, R., Krawczyk, H.: Analysis of key-exchange protocols and their use for building secure channels. In: Pfitzmann, B. (ed.) EUROCRYPT 2001. LNCS, vol. 2045, pp. 453–474. Springer, Heidelberg (2001). https://doi.org/10.1007/3-540-44987-6_28

4. Chou, C.H., Tsai, K.Y., Lu, C.F.: Two id-based authenticated schemes with key agreement for mobile environments. J. Supercomput. **66**, 973–988 (2013)

5. Debiao, H., Jianhua, C., Jin, H.: An id-based client authentication with key agreement protocol for mobile client-server environment on ECC with provable security. Inf. Fusion **13**, 223–230 (2012)

6. Fania, F., Rafsanjani, M.K.: Cluster-based routing protocols in wireless sensor networks: a survey based on methodology. J. Netw. Comput. Appl. **142**, 111–142 (2019). https://doi.org/10.1016/j.jnca.2019.04.02

7. Farash, M.S., Attari, M.A.: A secure and efficient identity-based authenticated key exchange protocol for mobile client-server networks. J. Supercomput. **69**, 395–411 (2014)

8. He, D., Kumar, N., Wang, H., Wang, L., Choo, K.K.R., Vinel, A.: A provably-secure cross-domain handshake scheme with symptoms-matching for mobile healthcare social network. IEEE Trans. Dependable Secure Comput. **15**, 33–645 (2018). https://doi.org/10.1109/TDSC.2016.2596286

9. He, D., Zeadally, S., Kumar, N., Lee, J.H.: Anonymous authentication for wireless body area networks with provable security. IEEE Syst. J. **11**, 2590–2601 (2017). https://doi.org/10.1109/JSYST.2016.2544805

10. He, D., Zeadally, S., Xu, B., Huang, X.: An efficient identity-based conditional privacy-preserving authentication scheme for vehicular ad hoc networks. IEEE Trans. Inf. Forensics Secur. **10**, 2681–2691 (2015). https://doi.org/10.1109/TIFS.2015.2473820

11. Kumar, M., Chand, S.: A lightweight cloud-assisted identity-based anonymous authentication and key agreement protocol for secure wireless body area network. IEEE Syst. J. **15**, 2779–2786 (2021). https://doi.org/10.1109/JSYST.2020.2990749

12. LaMacchia, B., Lauter, K., Mityagin, A.: Stronger security of authenticated key exchange. In: Susilo, W., Liu, J.K., Mu, Y. (eds.) ProvSec 2007. LNCS, vol. 4784, pp. 1–16. Springer, Heidelberg (2007). https://doi.org/10.1007/978-3-540-75670-5_1

13. Li, F., Wang, J., Zhou, Y., Jin, C.: A heterogeneous user authentication and key establishment for mobile client-server environment. Wireless Netw. **26**, 913–924 (2020)

14. Liu, J.K., Yuen, T.H., Au, M.H., Susilo, W.: Improvements on an authentication scheme for vehicular sensor networks. Expert Syst. Appl. **41**, 2559–2564 (2014). https://doi.org/10.1016/j.eswa.2013.10.003

15. Liu, X., Ma, W.: CDAKA: a provably-secure heterogeneous cross-domain authenticated key agreement protocol with symptoms-matching in TMIS. J. Med. Syst. **42**, 1–15 (2018)
16. Lo, N.W., Tsai, J.L.: An efficient conditional privacy-preserving authentication scheme for vehicular sensor networks without pairings. IEEE Trans. Intell. Transp. Syst. **17**, 1319–1328 (2016). https://doi.org/10.1109/TITS.2015.2502322
17. Lynn, B., et al.: Pairing-based cryptography library (2013). https://crypto.stanford.edu/pbc/
18. Mezrag, F, Bitam, S., Mellouk, A.: Secure routing in cluster-based wireless sensor networks. In: 2017 IEEE Global Communications Conference, pp. 1–6. GLOBECOM (2017)
19. Mezrag, F., Bitam, S., Mellouk, A.: An efficient and lightweight identity-based scheme for secure communication in clustered wireless sensor networks. J. Netw. Comput. Appl. **200**, 103282 (2022). https://doi.org/10.1016/j.jnca.2021.103282
20. Odelu, V., Das, A.K., Wazid, M., Conti, M.: Provably secure authenticated key agreement scheme for smart grid. IEEE Trans. Smart Grid **9**, 1900–1910 (2016)
21. Pointcheval, D., Stern, J.: Security arguments for digital signatures and blind signatures. J. Cryptol. **13**, 361–396 (2001). https://doi.org/10.1007/s001450010003
22. Saeed, M.E.S., Liu, Q.Y., Tian, G.: AKAIoTs: authenticated key agreement for internet of things. Wireless Netw. **25**, 3081–3101 (2019)
23. Shim, K.A.: An efficient conditional privacy-preserving authentication scheme for vehicular sensor networks. IEEE Trans. Veh. Technol. **61**, 1874–1883 (2012). https://doi.org/10.1109/TVT.2012.2186992
24. Tao, F., Shi, T., Li, S.: Provably secure cross-domain authentication key agreement protocol based on heterogeneous signcryption scheme. In: 2020 IEEE 4th Information Technology, Networking, Electronic and Automation Control Conference (ITNEC), vol. 1, pp. 2261–2266 (2020). https://doi.org/10.1109/ITNEC48623.2020.9084710
25. Wang, C., Liu, C., Niu, S., Wang, X.: An authenticated key agreement protocol for cross-domain based on heterogeneous signcryption scheme. In: 2017 13th International Wireless Communications and Mobile Computing Conference (IWCMC), pp. 723–728 (2017). https://doi.org/10.1109/IWCMC.2017.7986374
26. Wang, S., Yao, N.: LIAP: a local identity-based anonymous message authentication protocol in VANETs. Comput. Commun. **112**, 154–164 (2017)
27. Wang, C., Zhang, Y.: New authentication scheme for wireless body area networks using the bilinear pairing. J. Med. Syst. **39**, 1–8 (2015)
28. Wazid, M., Das, A.K., Kumar, N., Vasilakos, A.V., Rodrigues, J.J.P.C.: Design and analysis of secure lightweight remote user authentication and key agreement scheme in internet of drones deployment. IEEE Internet Things J. **6**, 3572–3584 (2019). https://doi.org/10.1109/JIOT.2018.2888821
29. Wu, L., Zhang, Y., Li, L.: Efficient and anonymous authentication scheme for wireless body area networks. J. Med. Syst. **40**, 134 (2016)
30. Yang, J.H., Chang, C.C.: An ID-based remote mutual authentication with key agreement scheme for mobile devices on elliptic curve cryptosystem. Comput. Secur. **28**, 138–143 (2009). https://doi.org/10.1016/j.cose.2008.11.008

31. Yoon, E.Y., Yoo, K.Y.: Robust id-based remote mutual authentication with key agreement scheme for mobile devices on ECC. In: 2009 International Conference on Computational Science and Engineering, vol. 2, pp. 633–640 (2009). https://doi.org/10.1109/CSE.2009.363

32. Zhang, C., Lin, X., Lu, R.,Ho, P-H.: RAISE: an efficient RSU-aided message authentication scheme in vehicular communication networks. In: 2008 IEEE International Conference on Communications, pp. 451–1457 (2008). https://doi.org/10.1109/ICC.2008.281

33. Zhang, Y., He, D., Li, L., Chen, B.: A lightweight authentication and key agreement scheme for internet of drones. Comput. Commun. **154**, 455–464 (2020). https://doi.org/10.1016/j.comcom.2020.02.067

A Multi-tab Webpage Fingerprinting Method Based on Multi-head Self-attention

Lixia Xie[1], Yange Li[1], Hongyu Yang[1,2(✉)], Ze Hu[2], Peng Wang[1], Xiang Cheng[3,4], and Liang Zhang[5]

[1] School of Computer Science and Technology, Civil Aviation University of China, Tianjin 300300, China
yhyxlx@hotmail.com
[2] School of Safety Science and Engineering, Civil Aviation University of China, Tianjin 300300, China
[3] School of Information Engineering, Yangzhou University, Yangzhou 225127, China
[4] Information Security Evaluation Center of Civil Aviation, Civil Aviation University of China, Tianjin 300300, China
[5] School of Information, The University of Arizona, Tucson, AZ 85721, USA

Abstract. The Tor anonymous communication network can provide Internet anonymous access function, making it challenging for network regulators to track the webpages visited by users. However, webpage fingerprinting, a commonly used passive traffic analysis technology, can identify webpages by monitoring and analyzing the near-end traffic of users. Currently, most existing webpage fingerprinting methods assume that users only open a single tab to access one webpage, which is not realistic, while multi-tab methods have limitations in utilizing mixed areas and the number of identified webpages. To solve the above limitations, this paper proposes a Multi-head Self-attention-based Multi-tab Webpage Fingerprinting (MSMWF) method on Tor, which designs a reasonable network structure according to the type of mixed webpages in multi-tab webpage traffic sequence. First, sequence embedding and block division are performed on the original multi-tab webpage traffic sequence to generate the embedded vector. Then, three sets of self-attention heads are used to extract the global features of the three types of mixed webpages, which can effectively use the correlation between different regions of the multi-tab sequences to identify the corresponding webpages. Experimental results demonstrate that MSMWF outperforms baseline methods in identifying multi-tab webpages and performs well in various experimental scenarios.

Keywords: Tor · Multi-tab Webpage Fingerprinting · Multi-head Self-attention

1 Introduction

Currently, Tor is the largest anonymous communication system with the largest number of users. By utilizing data forwarding, content encryption, and traffic confusion to hide the communication content and relationship, it provides ordinary users the ability to

© The Author(s), under exclusive license to Springer Nature Singapore Pte Ltd. 2024
H. Yang and R. Lu (Eds.): FCS 2023, CCIS 1992, pp. 131–140, 2024.
https://doi.org/10.1007/978-981-99-9331-4_9

access the Internet anonymously and cover up their network communication source and target [1, 2]. This makes it difficult to track and locate users, leading to an increase in anonymous abuse and malicious activities, which is the pain point and difficulty of network supervision. Webpage fingerprinting (WF) [3] is a typical passive traffic analysis method. It collects and extracts the fingerprint information of the target webpage by monitoring the near-end traffic of the Tor client, uses the fingerprint information to construct a model, and applies it to the latest monitored webpage traffic to identify the webpage visited by the user. It helps network regulatory and law enforcement departments to effectively obtain evidence and accurately crack down on anonymous communication crimes.

Most early studies focused on single-tab WF, assuming that users only visit one webpage each time they open the browser, and the traffic accessing that webpage can be fully collected. In practice, many users tend to open multiple tabs to access multiple webpages simultaneously. During this process, traffic from different webpages is mixed, causing interference in WF. Therefore, single-tab WF methods that rely on complete single webpage traffic often fail in multi-tab browsing scenarios [4].

In multi-tab webpage browsing scenarios, there are generally three types of multi-tab webpage traffic sequences, including apart traffic sequences, continuous traffic sequences, and overlapping traffic sequences. To use a unified method to handle all types of multi-tab webpage traffic sequences above, we merged three types of multi-tab webpage traffic sequences and classified the single webpage within them. The webpages in multi-tab webpage traffic sequences are divided into three categories according to different mixing forms. The first webpage, its tail mixed with other webpages. The middle webpages, their head and tail mixed with other webpages. The last webpage, its head mixed with other webpages.

This paper proposes MSMWF, a multi-tab webpage fingerprinting method based on multi-head self-attention for Tor. MSMWF is designed to improve the performance of WF by perceiving the correlation between different regions in multi-tab sequences and paying more attention to key information. In summary, the main contributions of this paper are as follows:

- We propose a sequence embedding and block division method for multi-tab webpage traffic sequences. The embedding vector that preserves the original order of users browsing the webpage is extracted from the original multi-tab webpage traffic sequence through sequence embedding. Then, the embedding vector is divided into blocks to further separate sequences belonging to different webpages.
- We propose a multi-head self-attention-based global feature extraction method. We have set up three encoders based on multi-head self-attention, which correspond to different mixed types of webpages in multi-tab sequences. To extract more suitable global features, each encoder perceives the correlation between each sequence block and pays different attention to each sequence block.
- Experiments show that the proposed MSMWF has outstanding performance in multi-tab WF. MSMWF uses the same network architecture to recognize all types of multi-tab webpages, which improves the practicality of WF research.

2 Related Work

Traditional single-tab WF methods use manually designed features and machine learning methods. Such as k-NN [5], k-fingerprinting [6], CUMUL [7], and so on. With the development of neural networks and related technology, the WF methods based on neural network has gradually surpassed traditional methods based on manual feature extraction [8]. Siriam et al. [9] proposed a single-tab Deep Fingerprinting (DF) method. They built a deep convolutional neural network model with complex architecture. However, the assumption that users only browse on a single tab is not always true as most users tend to open multiple webpages simultaneously.

Zou et al. [2] pointed out that weakening the user behavior hypothesis is one of the keys to practical WF. Some multi-tab WF methods use manually designed features to identify split points, and then recognize webpages based on the partial sequence after segmentation [10–12]. Xu et al. [12] proposed a multi-tab WF method based on split point recognition (denoted as Xu-Splitting). Xu-Splitting uses the BalanceCascade algorithm [13] to address data imbalance in split point recognition and XGBoost [14] to identify split points between overlapping webpages. But this method discards all traffic after the split point and only classifies the first visited webpage, and the classification effect will be reduced by the errors in the segmentation traffic process. Later, some research attempts to bypass the problem of split point recognition and directly use the information of the entire multi-tab webpage traffic sequence to identify webpages. Cui et al. [15] proposed a sectioning algorithm (denoted as Cui-Sectioning). Cui-Sectioning divides a traffic sequence into sections, predicts each section, and uses a majority vote to determine the final predicted webpage category. However, this method only treats the mixed regions of multi-tab sequences equally with other regions, which can lead to information confusion. Guan et al. [16] proposed a Block Attention Profiling Model (BAPM), focusing on overlapping webpage traffic. BAPM generates a tab-aware representation, divides the traffic into blocks, applies self-attention analysis to group blocks of the same webpage, and identifies multiple webpages simultaneously in the global view. However, when the number of webpages increases, the number of attention heads needs to be dynamically adjusted, which makes the network structure unstable.

In conclusion, the current multi-tab WF method has problems with mixed regions being unable to be effectively utilized and the limited number of recognizable webpages. MSMWF addresses these issues by leveraging multi-head self-attention for global feature extraction to maximize the utilization of mixed regions and optimize the network structure to accommodate various mixed webpage scenarios.

3 Proposed Methodology

The proposed method MSMWF is composed of three parts: sequence embedding, block division, and multi-tab WF. Multi-tab WF is mainly implemented through multi-head self-attention-based global feature extraction. The overview of MSMWF is shown in Fig. 1.

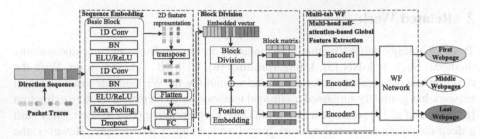

Fig. 1. The overview of MSMWF.

3.1 Sequence Embedding

The dimension of the original multi-tab direction sequence is usually large, so convolutional neural networks are first used for sequence embedding. The convolutional basic block of this network contains two one-dimensional convolutional layers, each of which has batch normalization and activation operations, which can effectively accelerate the training process of deep networks. The max pooling layer and dropout operation in each basic block can effectively prevent overfitting and help optimize the model. In particular, the ELU activation function [17] is used in the first basic block to learn negative values in the direction sequence. The number of channels of four connected convolutional basic blocks increases gradually, enabling the extraction of different levels of two-dimensional feature representations from the original one-dimensional direction sequence. Each row in the two-dimensional feature representation represents the features obtained by the convolution of the original sequence on one channel in the original order. Therefore, transposing and flattening it can preserve the original relative positions of each webpage sequence. The last two fully connected layers are used for dimensionality reduction to generate the embedded vector. Sequence embedding can not only explore the potential features of multi-tab webpage traffic sequence but also preserve the original order in which users browse webpages.

3.2 Block Division

Dividing the embedded vector after sequence embedding into blocks to generate a block matrix helps separate features belonging to different webpages. Too many or too few blocks can affect recognition performance. If the number of blocks is too small and the size of the blocks is too large, each block will contain more mixed parts of different webpages, and the connection between each block and the single webpage will become more chaotic. If the number of blocks is too large and the size of the blocks is too small, the webpage features contained in each small block are not obvious, making it more difficult to group blocks with strong correlations. After experimental verification, the number of blocks selected in this paper is 16. Since the parallel operation of the attention mechanism ignores the position information of the sequence, the corresponding position information is supplemented by adding a fixed position embedding based on the sine function and cosine function [18].

3.3 Multi-tab WF

The architecture of the encoders and WF network in multi-tab WF is shown in Fig. 2.

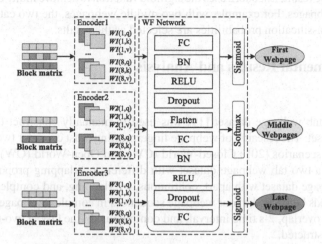

Fig. 2. The architecture of multi-tab WF.

Three multi-head self-attention-based encoders are established to extract global features for different types of webpages in multi-tab webpage traffic sequences. Encoder1 captures features for the first visited webpage with a mixed tail, Encoder2 handles the middle webpages with mixed heads and tails, and Encoder3 focuses on the last visited webpage with a mixed head. Each encoder perceives the correlation between blocks, and blocks with strong correlation promote the classification of the same type of webpage, while blocks with weak correlation are to some extent ignored. And the parameters are continuously updated based on predicted losses so that each block of the sequence receives different levels of attention. For example, after model iteration training, Encoder1 will pay more attention to the header blocks with strong correlation and less attention to the mixed blocks in the middle, while the blocks of other unrelated webpages will receive the least attention, which can achieve reasonable utilization of information in each block.

The WF network builds the fully connected layers, uses different activation functions to output the classification probability, and realizes the classification of different mixed types of webpages. The classification methods for three types of webpages are:

$$webpage_{first} = \text{softmax}(MultiHead_{first}) \tag{1}$$

$$webpage_{middle} = \text{sigmoid}(MultiHead_{middle}) \tag{2}$$

$$webpage_{last} = \text{softmax}(MultiHead_{last}) \tag{3}$$

where softmax (.) represents the normalized exponential function and sigmoid (.) represents the activation function. $MultiHead_{first}$, $MultiHead_{middle}$, and $MultiHead_{last}$ represent global features extracted by Encoder1, Encoder2, and Encoder3 and passed through the fully connected layers, respectively.

Encoder1 and Encoder3 extract global features for the classification of the first and last webpages, respectively, using the softmax function. The highest probability category is chosen as the result. Encoder2 uses the sigmoid function to achieve multi-classification of middle webpages. For example, with two middle webpages, the two categories with the highest classification probabilities are selected as the results.

4   Experimental Results and Analysis

4.1   Dataset

Wang single-tab webpage dataset [19] was used to manually construct the multi-tab webpage dataset. The research of webpage fingerprinting must consider two recognized experimental scenarios [20] : Closed-World (CW) and Open-World (OW). In the CW, we construct a two-tab webpage dataset with different overlapping proportions and a four-tab webpage dataset with apart, continuous, overlapping, and complex types. The mixing methods between the four webpage sequences in complex webpages here are as follows: 10% overlap, 2-s time interval, and continuous. In the OW, a two-tab webpage dataset is constructed.

4.2   Performance Metrics

We use accuracy, macro average precision (macro_P), and macro average recall (macro_R) as performance metrics. Accuracy refers to the proportion of correctly classified samples in all testing sequences. In multi-classification, when calculating the precision and recall of a certain category, it is necessary to consider that category as a positive category and all other categories as negative categories. The macro_P and macro_R comprehensively consider the classification effect of each category and calculate the arithmetic mean of precision and recall of all webpage categories respectively.

4.3   Closed-World Experiments and Analysis

To validate the effectiveness of MSMWF, BAPM [16], Cui-Sectioning [15], Xu-Splitting [12], and Multi-DF are chosen as comparison methods in the experiments. Multi-DF is a deformation of the single-tab WF method DF [9], adapted for multi-tab browsing by changing the activation function of the last layer to sigmoid and using binary cross-entropy loss as the loss function. In the CW, the results of two-tab WF with different overlapping proportions are shown in Table 1.

The following conclusions can be obtained by observing the experimental results:

1. The experimental results indicate that MSMWF outperforms comparison methods. And it maintains stable recognition effectiveness with increasing overlapping proportions. It utilizes sequence embedding networks to explore features in multi-tab webpage traffic sequences while preserving the original access order. It uses a set of self-attention heads to extract global features from a class of webpage sequences, allowing the model to pay more attention to the regions related to its classification target, and integrate the correlation features of multiple subspaces, thereby improving the performance of WF.

2. The recognition performance of Multi-DF is not ideal all the time, indicating that the single-tab WF method cannot be directly applied to multi-tab browsing scenarios. As the overlap proportion increases, the recognition accuracy of Xu-Splitting significantly decreases. Cui-Sectioning treats all regions in the sequence equally, and mixed regions containing the information of multiple webpages confuse the recognition results. BAPM achieves high accuracy in recognizing the first webpage by utilizing separate self-attention heads to extract features from each webpage in a multi-tab sequence. However, its accuracy is lower for webpages with high overlap proportions and mixed heads due to limitations in the convolutional network and single-head attention mechanism in extracting comprehensive global features.

3. The header information is crucial in WF because users need to establish a connection with the server at the beginning of accessing a webpage, and there are more outgoing requests from the client to the server. The information transmitted during this period helps to distinguish different webpages. Because the head of the last webpages is mixed with the previous webpage, the head information cannot be fully utilized, resulting in lower recognition accuracy than the first webpage.

Table 1. Results of two-tab WF with different overlapping proportions.

Overlapping proportion		10%	20%	30%	40%	50%
Metrics		Accuracy	Accuracy	Accuracy	Accuracy	Accuracy
First Webpage	Multi-DF	68.1%	60.9%	64.2%	62.2%	56.7%
	Xu-Splitting	81.1%	71.9%	64.4%	54.4%	42.5%
	Cui-Sectioning	36.7%	35.0%	38.4%	36.4%	37.6%
	BAPM	96.6%	96.8%	95.8%	95.9%	94.5%
	MSMWF	**96.8%**	**97.4%**	**95.9%**	**96.6%**	**96.1%**
Last Webpage	Multi-DF	61.2%	56.6%	58.3%	55.6%	52.7%
	Xu-Splitting	27.0%	22.1%	19.2%	15.7%	15.4%
	Cui-Sectioning	30.7%	30.1%	31.9%	30.6%	29.3%
	BAPM	81.1%	80.1%	78.2%	77.1%	78.9%
	MSMWF	**92.9%**	**93.8%**	**92.7%**	**91.8%**	**92.7%**

To verify the generalization ability of MSMWF, four-tab WF experiments were conducted on apart, continuous, overlapping, and complex webpages. The experimental results are shown in Table 2. The Top-2 accuracy is used to evaluate the recognition performance of the second and third webpages. The experimental results show that MSMWF has good recognition performance for various types of multi-tab webpages, proving that this method has good robustness and can uniformly recognize all types of multi-tab webpages traffic sequences. In addition, because the mixed region of the middle and last webpages in the apart and continuous type webpage sequence does not

Table 2. Results of four-tab WF in CW.

Sequence type	First Webpage Accuracy	Second Webpage Top-2 Accuracy	Third Webpage Top-2 Accuracy	Last Webpage Accuracy
apart	98.8%	92.3%	91.0%	94.4%
continuous	98.7%	89.7%	90.7%	93.6%
overlapping	98.4%	84.3%	84.4%	91.9%
complex	97.7%	87.3%	90.5%	95.6%

overlap with other webpage sequences, its recognition results are superior to those of the corresponding positions in the overlapping webpage sequence.

4.4 Open-World Experiments and Analysis

The results of the two-tab WF in OW are shown in Table 3. In the OW scenario, all unmonitored webpages are regarded as a single category, so the results of this experiment are evaluated on 51 categories. MSMWF achieves the highest accuracy and macro_P, but slightly lower macro_R on the first webpage. Analysis of the test dataset reveals that MSMWF misclassifies some monitored webpages as unmonitored ones due to data imbalance caused by the high ratio of unmonitored webpages to monitored ones (approximately 50:1). Xu-Splitting and Cui-Sectioning have lower macro_R rates, indicating that they are more susceptible to data imbalance.

Table 3. Results of the two-tab WF in OW.

Methods	First Webpage			Last Webpage		
	Accuracy	macro_P	macro_R	Accuracy	macro_P	macro_R
Multi-DF	65.1%	60.7%	72.3%	52.4%	42.4%	33.7%
Xu-Splitting	55.2%	58.0%	25.7%	31.1%	2.5%	2.3%
Cui-Sectioning	49.5%	51.7%	22.2%	44.6%	40.4%	17.0%
BAPM	94.6%	91.5%	**94.4%**	81.5%	74.8%	70.7%
MSMWF	**96.1%**	**91.9%**	93.3%	**89.1%**	**79.2%**	**80.8%**

4.5 Ablation Experiments and Analysis

We designed two ablation experiments to verify the importance of each component, and the experimental results are shown in Fig. 3. MSMWF\E&D refers to removing sequence embedding and block division from MSMWF, while MSMWF\S refers to removing multi-head self-attention-based global feature extraction from MSMWF.

Due to the ability of sequence embedding and block division to mine the potential features of mixed regions and separate them from other regions, the effective utilization of mixed regions is achieved, and the head information in this region is an important feature for the recognition of the last webpage with mixed head. Therefore, the recognition accuracy of MSMWF\E&D for the last webpage significantly decreases. MSMWF\S is equivalent to degenerating into a simple multi-tab classifier, with a significant decrease in recognition accuracy.

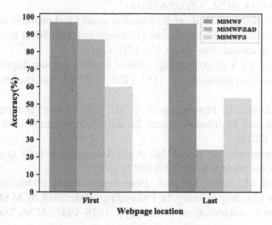

Fig. 3. Results of ablation experiments.

5 Conclusion and Future Works

The proposed MSMWF addresses limitations in handling mixed regions and the number of identified webpages. MSMWF first extracts potential features from the original direction sequence using sequence embedding. It then divides the embedded vector into blocks and adds position encoding to separate webpage features, and employs multi-head self-attention-based encoders to extract global features. The WF network generates the final recognition results. Experimental results demonstrate that MSMWF can identify all types of multi-tab webpage traffic sequences using the same network architecture and can adapt to the situation where more webpages are mixed.

In the future, we can attempt to future weaken the experimental assumptions of existing methods to enhance the practicality of WF.

Acknowledgment. This work was supported by the National Natural Science Foundation of China (Grant No. 62201576), the Civil Aviation Joint Research Fund Project of the National Natural Science Foundation of China (Grant No. U1833107), the Fundamental Research Funds for the Central Universities (Grant No. 3122022050), and the Open Fund of the Information Security Evaluation Center of Civil Aviation University of China (ISECCA-202202).

References

1. Zhao, N.F., Su, J.S., Zhao, B.T., et al.: A survey on hidden service location technologies in anonymous communication system. Chinese J. Comput. **45**(2), 393–411 (2022)

2. Zou, H.F., Su, J.S., Wei, Z.T., et al.: A review of the research of website fingerprinting identification and defense. Chinese J. Comput. **45**(10), 2243–2278 (2022)
3. Sun, X.F., Huang, A.S., Luo, X.T., et al.: Webpage fingerprinting identification on tor: a survey. J. Comput. Res. Dev. **58**(8), 1773–1788 (2021)
4. Juarez, M., Afroz, S., Acar, G., et al.: A critical evaluation of website fingerprinting attacks. In: Proceedings of the 2014 ACM SIGSAC Conference on Computer and Communications Security, pp. 263–274. ACM, AZ, USA (2014)
5. Wang, T., Cai, X., Nithyanand, R., et al.: Effective attacks and provable defenses for website fingerprinting. In: 23rd {USENIX} Security Symposium ({USENIX} Secu-rity 14), pp. 143–157. USENIX Association, San Diego, CA, USA (2014)
6. Hayes, J., Danezis, G.: k-fingerprinting: a robust scalable website fingerprinting technique. In: USENIX security symposium, pp. 1187–1203. USENIX Association, Austin, TX, USA (2016)
7. Panchenko, A., Lanze, F., Pennekamp, J., et al.: Website fingerprinting at internet scale. In: 23rd Network and Distributed System Security Symposium (NDSS), pp. 1–15. ISOC, California, USA (2016)
8. Rimmer, V., Preuveneers, D., Juarez, M., et al.: Automated website fingerprinting through deep learning. arXiv preprint arXiv:1708.06376 (2017)
9. Sirinam, P., Imani, M., Juarez, M., et al.: Deep fingerprinting: undermining website finger-printing defenses with deep learning. In: Proceedings of the 2018 ACM SIGSAC Conference on Computer and Communications Security, pp. 1928–1943. ACM, Toronto, ON, Canada (2018)
10. Gu, X., Yang, M., Luo, J.: A novel website fingerprinting attack against multi-tab browsing behavior. In: 19th International Conference on Computer Supported Cooperative Work in Design (CSCWD), pp. 234–239. IEEE, Calabria, Italy (2015)
11. Wang, T., Goldberg, I.: On realistically attacking tor with website fingerprinting. Proc. Priv. Enhancing Technol. **2**(4), 21–36 (2016)
12. Xu, Y., Wang, T., Li, Q., et al.: A multi-tab website fingerprinting attack. In: Proceedings of the 34th Annual Computer Security Applications Conference, pp. 327–341. IEEE, San Juan, PR, USA (2018)
13. Liu, X.Y., Wu, J., Zhou, Z.H.: Exploratory undersampling for class-imbalance learning. IEEE Trans. Syst. Man, Cybern. Part B **39**(2), 539–550 (2008)
14. Chen, T., Guestrin, C.: XGBoost: A Scalable Tree Boosting System. arXiv preprint arXiv: 1603.02754, (2016)
15. Cui, W., Chen, T., Fields, C., et al.: Revisiting assumptions for website fingerprinting attacks. In: Proceedings of the 2019 ACM Asia Conference on Computer and Communications Security, pp. 328–339. ACM, London, UK (2019)
16. Guan, Z., Xiong, G., Gou, G., et al.: BAPM: block attention profiling model for multi-tab website fingerprinting attacks on tor. In: Annual Computer Security Applications Conference, pp. 248–259. IEEE, USA (2021)
17. Clevert, D.A., Unterthiner, T., Hochreiter, S.: Fast and accurate deep network learning by exponential linear units (elus). arXiv preprint arXiv:1511.07289 (2015)
18. Vaswani, A., Shazeer, N., Parmar, N., et al.: Attention is all you need. In: Advances in Neural Information Processing Systems, vol. 30, pp. 5998–6008 (2017)
19. Wang, T., Goldberg, I.: {Walkie-Talkie}: an efficient defense against passive website finger-printing attacks. In: USENIX Security Symposium. pp. 1375–1390. USENIX Association, Vancouver, BC, Canada (2017)
20. Wang, Y., Xu, H., Guo, Z., et al.: SnWF: website fingerprinting attack by ensembling the snapshot of deep learning. IEEE Trans. Inf. Forensics Secur. **17**(1), 1214–1226 (2022)

Improving Accuracy of Interactive Queries in Personalized Differential Privacy

Mingjie Lu[1]([⊠]) and Zhenhua Liu[1,2]

[1] School of Mathematics and Statistics, Xidian University, Xi'an 710071, China
1831536879@qq.com
[2] State Key Laboratory of Cryptology, P.O. Box 5159, Beijing 100878, China

Abstract. Privacy-preserving data publishing has been an important research field in the era of big data. Various privacy protection schemes have been proposed to balance privacy and utility. Personalized differential privacy (PDP) is especially noteworthy as it offers stronger privacy guarantees, taking into account the diverse privacy requirements of users. However, existing PDP mechanisms produce query results with low accuracy, which leads to poor data utility. Specifically, PDP is realized by sampling data and invoking on differential privacy, thus the problem of poor accuracy in differential privacy itself is brought into PDP. Interactive queries is a natural setting in differentially private publishing scenarios. Considering the need for interactive queries in PDP, we firstly establish a privacy budget allocation method by equalizing the common privacy budget and then recycling the remaining privacy budget, and then propose a combined mechanism to answer multiple queries. As accurately, for each round of query, there is a high probability that user's data with high record sensitivity will not be sampled, thereby reducing the overall sensitivity. And a smaller noise is added according to the corresponding allocated privacy budget. Finally, the combined mechanism is proved to meet the privacy demands, and the experiment results executing on synthetic datasets and real datasets demonstrate that the combined mechanism under the privacy budget method can achieve better accuracy than the traditional mechanisms.

Keywords: Personalized differential privacy · interactive queries · privacy budget allocation · accuracy · sampling data

---

This work is supported by the Natural Science Basic Research Plan in Shaanxi Province of China under Grant No. 2022JZ-38, the Fundamental Research Funds for the Central Universities under Grant No. QTZX23001, the National Natural Science Foundation of China under Grant No. 61807026, the Plan For Scientific Innovation Talent of Henan Province under Grant No. 184100510012, and in part by the Program for Science and Technology Innovation Talents in the Universities of Henan Province under Grant No. 18HASTIT022.

1   Introduction

Privacy is a personal attribute, and when certain attributes are exposed by a group, they may not be considered as privacy. For example, a hospital releases a report stating that smokers have a higher chance of getting lung cancer, which is not privacy-sensitive information. However, if Alice is known to be a smoker, her personal privacy is compromised as there is a probability that she may get lung cancer. To protect privacy, organizations often release data for analysis after processing it to provide statistical information. However, attackers can still use differential attacks to infer individual information. For instance, if attackers know Alice's presence in a medical database, they can query the number of people with cancer and the number of people, including Alice, with cancer. By subtracting the answers, the privacy information related to Alice can be exposed.

Differential privacy (DP) [6] provides one of the strongest guarantees for analyzing aggregated data, even when the adversary has access to all information about anyone other than the target. A common approach to achieve DP is to add a random noise to the aggregation analysis result. DP ensures that the aggregation results are insensitive to the absence or present of each user's data. Consequently, attackers can not distinguish the result of queries including a particular user or not. However, a limitation of DP is that DP provides only a uniform level of privacy and ignores the fact that different individuals usually have different privacy requirements for their personal data.

Personalized differential privacy [16] has been proposed to address different privacy needs for users. A center collects data of each user and returns an inquiry based on the corresponding privacy budget. One possible approach to achieve Privacy-Differential Privacy (PDP) is a two-step procedure. The first step involves non-uniform sampling at the individual tuple level based on a privacy threshold. In the second step, a DP mechanism with a privacy budget equal to the threshold is invoked and executed on the sampled set. The other is a direct approach that is analogous to the exponential mechanism which applies a real-valued score function based on the number of data that would need to be modified in the original dataset to obtain the target result. Accuracy can benefit from the privacy budget tightly related to individuals. One major reason is that if both dp and pdp are to be satisfied, the minimum privacy budget among the users needs to be selected, which will reduce the utility of the data. At the same time, when users have the ability to adjust the level of privacy protection for their own data, they are more willing to contribute their data for analysis.

Moreover, there are two natural settings involved in differentially private publishing scenarios - interactive and non-interactive [29]. In the interactive setting, the center accepts an online query that cannot be issued until the previous queries have been published. In the non-interactive setting, all queries are accepted at one time and the corresponding disturbed results are published simultaneously.

Despite the substantial progress in PDP, PDP still faces the problem of poor accuracy. One of the major reasons is that the realization of PDP is a combination of sampling and DP, and then the low precision of DP itself is inherited to

PDP. It makes no sense to analyze the query results with low precision. As a practical online question-and-answer method, interactive data publishing technology has aroused a lot of research. Nevertheless, there are no analysis for interactive queries in personalized differential privacy. With the challenges above, we are aware of the critical importance of constructing an interactive query mechanism in personalized differential privacy with high precision.

1.1   Related Works

Differential Privacy. Dwork *et al.* [6] proposed the concept of differential privacy that provides uniform protection ((ϵ,0)-indistinguishability) for everyone. Due to the consideration of arbitrary adjacent data sets, differential privacy can not offer highly accurate results.

One way to improve precision of differential privacy is to relax privacy protection. Dwork *et al.* [8] gave (ϵ, δ)-indistinguishability by introducing a slack parameter δ, which essentially guarantees that the probability that any individual suffers privacy loss exceeding ϵ is bounded by δ. Furthermore, Dwork *et al.* [2] introduced a novel relaxation of differential privacy known as concentrated differential privacy. This relaxation offers improved accuracy compared to differential privacy and provides tighter bounds on expected loss compared to (ϵ,δ)-differential privacy. In addition, Gehrke *et al.* [10] proposed crowd-blending privacy, which relaxes differential privacy by adding a condition that a person blends in a crowd of k people.

Another way is to optimize the noise distribution. Nissim *et al.* [20] presented a new definition of sensitivity named local sensitivity. Local sensitivity only considers datasets that are adjacent to the actual dataset, so the noise that is added to aggregation query results can be significantly reduced. Subsequently, Huang *et al.* [13] proposed the concept of record sensitivity to improve the utility. In particular, each data record is allocated a personalized sampling probability that data records whose presence or absence has a high influence on the final result are specified a relatively small sampling probability. Since the number of records with high sensitivity is reduced, the amount of added noise is also reduced, leading to improved accuracy.

Personalized Differential Privacy. Alaggan *et al.* [1] proposed heterogeneous differential privacy, which was the first work considered the privacy preferences of users. However, their stretching mechanism cannot be applied to some aggregate functions (e.g. *median, min/max*) or some types of queries. To overcome these problems, Jorgensen *et al.* [16] designed two novel mechanisms to reach personalized differential privacy. The first mechanism introduces a threshold value to compute each tuple's sampling probability, and then invokes the original differential privacy based on the sampling result. The second is a direct approach by modifying the score function of the exponential mechanism. For the second mechanism of PDP, Niu *et al.* [21] proposed the utility aware personalized exponential mechanism by distinguishing the same score functions to improve data utility.

To improve the utility, Li *et al.* [18] proposed two partition-based mechanisms: privacy aware and utility-based partitioning. When the number of blocks of a partition is predefined, the dynamic programming problem is used to find the optimal partition to minimize the waste of privacy budget and maximize the utility. Whereupon Niu *et al.* [22] proposed utility-aware sampling mechanism, which reuses the remaining privacy budget by multiple rounds of sampling. Furthermore, Qu *et al.* [23] presented a personalized model based on *generative adversarial nets* (GAN) to achieve differential privacy and enhance spatial-temporal private data sharing. Recently, a large number of work [3–5,14,17,23,25,26] considered personalized differential privacy in various scenarios.

Interactive Data Releasing. In terms of interactive data releasing, Dwork *et al.* [6] firstly proposed the Laplace mechanism, where the Laplace distribution noise is added to the corresponding true results to realize differential privacy protection. For the Laplace mechanism, a certain privacy budget is consumed during each query, and differential privacy protection is no longer provided when the privacy budget is exhausted.

From the aspect of increasing the number of queries, Roth *et al.* [24] defined the median mechanism, which categorizes all queries into hard and easy queries, and adds noise only to the hard queries. The results of the easy queries are derived from the results of the hard queries. Furthermore, Hardt *et al.* [12] proposed *Private Multiplicative Weights* (PMW) mechanism, which works by setting an initial threshold. When the difference between the results of the current round and the results of the previous round does not exceed the threshold, the current query result is published. Otherwise, the previous query result is reused. Based on PMW, Gupta *et al.* [11] gave a new *Iterative Database Construction* (IDC) algorithm that is similar to PMW. The initial data set is a subset randomly selected from the original data set. When the difference between the current query result and the previous query result is greater than the threshold, the initial data set is updated until the difference is less than the threshold.

Although the above interactive data publishing algorithm improves the number of data publishing, the algorithm cannot give a reasonable privacy budget allocation scheme. A reasonable privacy budget allocation scheme can improve not only the number of queries, but also the availability of query results. Wu *et al.* [28] proposed a parametric density estimation algorithm using *Gaussian mixtures model* (GMM), where the overall privacy budget and the initial privacy budget are initialized, and the remaining privacy budget is evenly distributed to subsequent queries. Subsequently, Dwork [7] provided two ideas for privacy budget allocation in differential privacy k-means algorithm. If the number of iterations is fixed, the privacy budget is evenly divided. Otherwise, the algorithm employs the bisection method.

1.2   Our Motivation and Contributions

In order to fill the gap of interactive query scheme in personalized differential privacy, we establish a privacy budget allocation method for interactive queries in personalized differential privacy first. Inspired by the minimum mechanism [16], we propose a combined mechanism that equalizes the common privacy budget to invoke DP and then recycles the remaining privacy budget to invoke PDP. Specifically, we utilize the *Personalized Sampling Laplace Mechanism* (PSLM) to reduce sensitivity during the rounds of queries invoking DP. Based on the data obtained from the last round of sampling using PSLM, we then invoke PDP to perform the final round of queries. Due to the reduction of sensitivity, the scale of noise distribution is reduced, so the perturbation results can obtain higher accuracy.

The main contributions of this paper are summarized as below:

1. We establish a privacy budget allocation method for interactive queries in personalized differential privacy, which equalizes the common privacy budget and then recycles the remaining privacy budget based on the sequential composition theorem.
2. Based on the privacy budget allocation method, we propose a combined mechanism that combines PSLM and PDP to answer the accepted queries.
3. Due to the combination of differential privacy with higher accuracy, the results of each round of inquiries are more accurate in the proposed privacy allocation method.
4. The privacy of the proposed mechanism is theoretically proven, and its accuracy is experimentally demonstrated.

2 Preliminaries

2.1 System Model

The system model consists of three parties: the users, the center and the requestors [21]. As shown in Fig. 1, a user $u(u = 1, \cdots, n)$ sends her or his sensitive data d_u and a personal privacy budget demand ϵ_u to the center, where the privacy budget ϵ_u represents the degree to which the user u wants to protect the sensitive data d_u. The higher the privacy budget is, the lower the protection degree is, and vice versa. The center will protect the users' sensitive data set $D = \{d_1, \cdots, d_n\}$ according to the corresponding privacy budget set $\Phi = \{\epsilon_1, \cdots, \epsilon_n\}$. If a requestor submits a query to the center for learning statistical information about the dataset, then the center will return a query result back to the requestor. It is assumed that the requestor is not fully trusted by the users and center. In other words, the requestor wants to infer from the query results whether a specified user has submitted her or his data. Generally, the center needs to perturb the query results, so that the requestor cannot infer some sensitive information about a single user.

2.2 Differential Privacy

Differential privacy is one of the strongest privacy preservation methods, which can capture a strong privacy intuition: if one data record has a limited influence

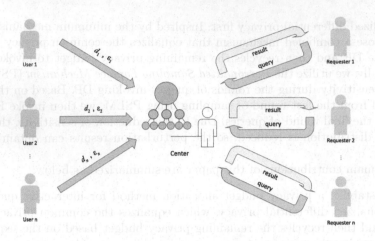

Fig. 1. Personalized differential privacy.

on the outputs of one mechanism, then it is difficult to extract some information about the record from the outputs. To that end, differentially private mechanisms can guarantee that their outputs are insensitive to any particular data record in datasets. That is, the presence or absence of any data record has a limited influence on differentially private mechanisms' outputs. Furthermore, the presence or absence is captured by the concept of neighboring database. Specifically, two datasets D and D' are neighboring, denoted by $D \sim D'$, if D differs D' by only one data record.

Definition 1. *(Dataset [16]). A dataset $D \subset \mathcal{D}$ is a set of tuples $D = \{d_1, \cdots, d_i, \cdots\}$ from universe $\mathcal{D}$, where data $d_i \in A_1 \times \cdots \times A_s \times \mathcal{U}$, A_i are attributes, and $\mathcal{U}$ denotes the universe of users. We write d_u to denote the data associated with user u.*

For differential privacy and personalized differential privacy, there is a notion of neighboring dataset. We say that two datasets are neighboring if one is a subset of the other and the larger one contains exactly one more data.

Definition 2. *(Neighboring datasets [16]). Two datasets $D, D' \subset \mathcal{D}$ are said to be neighboring, or neighbors, denoted $D \sim D'$, if $D \subset D'$ and $|D'| = |D| + 1$. Let $D \overset{t}{\sim} D'$ denote that D and D' are neighbors, $t \in D'$, but $t \notin D$.*

Definition 3. *(ϵ-Differential privacy [6]). A mechanism $\mathcal{M} : D \to \mathcal{R}$ satisfies ϵ-differential privacy, if for all pairs $D \sim D' \subset \mathcal{D}$ and any set $\mathcal{O} \subset \mathcal{R}$ of any outputs, then*

$$\Pr[\mathcal{M}(D) \in \mathcal{O}] \leq e^\epsilon \Pr[\mathcal{M}(D') \in \mathcal{O}].$$

Definition 3 protects against that, for example, if an adversary who knows the full inputs except for one tuple t and the outputs, the adversary are still unable to deduce even whether t is in the input.

The mechanism M is associated with global sensitivity. Global sensitivity measures the maximal change on the result of a query when removing one record from the dataset D [7].

Definition 4. *(Global Sensitivity [9]). For any aggregation query function f: $D \rightarrow \mathcal{R}^d$, the global sensitivity of the function is*

$$\Delta f = \max_{D \sim D'} \|f(D) - f(D')\|_1.$$

To satisfy the differential privacy definition, the Laplace mechanism is usually utilized. The Laplace mechanism is suitable for numeric output and relies on the Laplace noise distribution scale.

Theorem 1. *(Laplace mechanism [9]). For an aggregation query function f, Laplace mechanism returns $f(D) + \mathcal{N}$, where $\mathcal{N}$ is drawn from $Lap(\frac{\Delta f}{\epsilon})$, the mean of Laplace distribution and its scale are 0 and $\frac{\Delta f}{\epsilon}$, and Δf denotes the sensitivity of the function f.*

For an aggregation query function f, it can be any aggregation function, such as count, average, sum and others.

Theorem 2. *(Sequential composition theorem [19]). Let $M_1, M_2, \cdots, M_k$ be k algorithms that satisfy ϵ_1-DP, ϵ_2-DP, $\cdots$, ϵ_k-DP, respectively. Publish $r =< r_1, r_2, \cdots, r_k >$ that satisfies $(\sum_{i=1}^{k} \epsilon_i)$-DP, i.e., that is, the sequence $M_i(D)$ provides $(\sum_{i=1}^{k} \epsilon_i)$-DP.*

2.3 Personalized Sampling Laplace Mechanism

Personalized sampling Laplace mechanism is an optimized mechanism in differential privacy that assigns a personalized sampling probability to each data record, so that the sensitivity is reduced. Consequently, the accuracy can be improved.

Record sensitivity is an extension of local sensitivity and measures the maximum impact of a single piece of data on the results of an aggregated query.

Definition 5. *(Record sensitivity [13]). Given a dataset D, a function f, and $x_u \in D$ that corresponds to the data record of a user u, record sensitivity is defined:*

$$RS_{d_u} = |f(D_{+d_u}) - f(D_{-d_u})|,$$

where D_{+d_u} means that there exists a record d_u in the dataset D, and D_{-d_u} means that there is no record d_u in the dataset D.

Definition 6. *(Sampling probability [13]). For a function $f : D \rightarrow \mathcal{R}^d$, a dataset $D \subset \mathcal{D}$, and a balance parameter c, the center computes each user's record sensitivity. Let $RS(D)$ denote the procedure that independently samples each tuple $d_u \in D$ with probability*

$$\pi_{d_u} = \begin{cases} \frac{1-e^{\epsilon}}{1-e^{\epsilon \frac{RS_{d_u}}{c}}}, & RS_{d_u} \geq c; \\ 1, & RS_{d_u} < c. \end{cases}$$

The selection of the balance parameter c is based on the record sensitivity. According to the sampling probability $\{\pi_{d_u} | d_u \in D\}$, we get a new dataset $RS(D) = \bar{D}$, and then set $r_1 = f(\bar{D}) + Lap(\frac{c}{\epsilon})$.

Given a privacy level ϵ and the balance parameter c, the personalized sampling Laplace mechanism satisfies

$$\frac{\mathcal{M}(D_{-d_u})}{\mathcal{M}(D_{+d_u})} \leq e^{\epsilon \frac{RS_{d_u}}{c}} \text{ and } \frac{\mathcal{M}(D_{+d_u})}{\mathcal{M}(D_{-d_u})} \leq e^{\epsilon \frac{RS_{d_u}}{c}}.$$

2.4   Personalized Differential Privacy

Being different from traditional differential privacy, PDP makes use of a *privacy specification*, in which each user can specify the privacy preference for her or his data.

Definition 7. *(Privacy specification [16]). A privacy specification is a mapping from users to personal privacy preferences, where a smaller value represents a stronger privacy preference. The symbol $\Phi = (\epsilon_1, \cdots, \epsilon_n)$ is used to denote the set of privacy budgets for all users U, and Φ^u is used to denote the privacy budget of user u.*

Definition 8. *(Personalized differential privacy [16]). For a privacy demand set Φ, a randomized mechanism $\mathcal{M}$ satisfies Φ-PDP if for any D and D' differing at most one arbitrary user u, and for an arbitrary set of possible outputs of $\mathcal{M}$, we have*

$$\Pr[\mathcal{M}(D) \in \mathcal{O}] \leq e^{\Phi^u} \Pr[\mathcal{M}(D') \in \mathcal{O}].$$

Sampling can get a subset from a dataset. Computing query results on sampled data rather than the original dataset can introduce more randomness to meet the privacy requirements specified by individuals. We describe the sample mechanism [16] below.

Definition 9. *(Sample mechanism [16]). For a function $f : D \rightarrow R$, a dataset $D \subset \mathcal{D}$, a privacy budget set $\Phi = (\epsilon_1, \cdots, \epsilon_n)$ and a sampling threshold t, $S(D, \Phi, t)$ denotes a procedure that independently samples each tuple $d \in D$ with probability*

$$\pi_u(t) = \begin{cases} \frac{e^{\epsilon_u} - 1}{e^t - 1}, & \epsilon_u < t; \\ 1, & otherwise. \end{cases}$$

According to the sampling probability $\{\pi_u(t) | d \in D\}$, we get a new dataset $S(D, \Phi, t) = \tilde{D}$, and then set $r_2 = f(\tilde{D}) + Lap(\frac{\Delta f}{t})$. The output of the sample mechanism can be defined as:

$$SM_f(D, \Phi, t) = DP_t^f(S(D, \Phi, t)),$$

where DP_t^f is any t-differential private mechanism that computes the function f.

3   The Proposed Scheme Construction

In this section, we firstly present the framework of the privacy budget allocation, then a detailed description of the combined mechanism (CM) under the
framework is proposed. In the end, the privacy of the combined mechanism is
analyzed.

3.1   Privacy Budget Allocation

It is assumed that there are T rounds in the interactive queries. Inspired by the
method of equalizing the privacy budget [7], we select the smallest privacy budget
denoted by ϵ_{min} according to the privacy budget set $\Phi = (\epsilon_1, \cdots, \epsilon_n)$ submitted
by all users, and then split it equally among the first $T - 1$ rounds. For each
round, $\frac{\epsilon_{min}}{T-1}$ privacy budget is consumed. At last, the remaining privacy budget
is consumed for the T-th query. Depending on the privacy budget allocated, the
first $T - 1$ rounds call differential privacy and the last round calls personalized
differential privacy. The whole idea of the privacy budget allocation setting is
shown in Fig. 2.

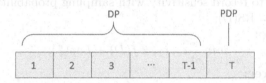

Fig. 2. Privacy budget allocation.

3.2   The Combined Mechanism

Under the method of the proposed privacy budget allocation, we put forward the
Combined Mechanism (CM), and then apply it to the privacy budget allocation
setting proposed above. For convenience, we consider the special case of only
querying twice, and it's easy to generalize to T queries. The sampling results of
the T-th query are based on the sampling results of the $(T-1)$-th query, and the
sampling probability is based on the remaining privacy budgets.

The combined mechanism that answers two round of queries consists of five
phases as shown in Algorithm 1. In phase one, the raw database is sampled
according to record sensitivity by assigning a specific sampling probability to
each user. A Laplace mechanism is then invoked in phase two to deal with the
sampled data and publish the corresponding disturbed answer. In phase three,
each user's privacy budget is updated. The data at the end of the first round
of sampling is sampled again according to the updated privacy budget, and
the differential privacy mechanism described in phase four and five is called to
process the second round sampling results. In the end, the second disturbed
answer is published.

Algorithm 1: CM Mechanism.

Require:

        A query function f,

        A dataset D,

        A Laplace mechanism M,

        A privacy preference Φ,

        A balance parameter c,

        A threshold t.

Ensure:

        The noise answer r.

1: **Phase one:**

2: For $x_i \in D$ do:

3: Compute record sensitivity RS_{d_u}:
$$RS_{d_u} = |f(D_{+d_u}) - f(D_{-d_u})|,$$

4: Compute the first round sampling probability π_{d_u}:
$$\pi_{d_u} = \begin{cases} \dfrac{1-e^{\epsilon}}{1-e^{\epsilon\frac{RS_{d_u}}{c}}}, & RS_{d_u} \geq c, \\ 1, & RS_{d_u} < c; \end{cases}$$

5: End for.

6: According to record sensitivity with sampling probability $\{\pi_{d_u}|d_u \in D\}$, namely $\bar{D}= \mathrm{RS}(D)$;

7: **Phase two:**

8: Define $\epsilon_{min} = \min\limits_{u\in\{1,\cdots,n\}} \epsilon_u, r_1 = f(\bar{D}) + Lap(\frac{c}{\epsilon})$;

9: **Phase three:**

10: Update everyone's privacy budget:

    if $RS_{x_u} < c$, then
$$\bar{\Phi}^u = \Phi^u - \epsilon\frac{RS_{d_u}}{c},$$

    else if $RS_{d_u} \geq c$, then
$$\bar{\Phi}^u = \Phi^u - \epsilon.$$

We get a new privacy budget set $\bar{\Phi}$, and the corresponding remaining privacy budget of user u is expressed as $\bar{\epsilon}_u$. From the new privacy budget set $\bar{\Phi}$, the set of sampled data is denoted as $\bar{\Phi}_s$, and the other is denoted as $\bar{\Phi}_{ns}$;

11: **Phase four:**

12: For $x_u \in \bar{D}$ do:

13: Compute the second round sampling probability $\pi_u(t)$:
$$\pi_u(t) = \begin{cases} \dfrac{e^{\bar{\epsilon}_u}-1}{e^t-1}, & \bar{\epsilon}_u < t, \\ 1, & otherwise; \end{cases}$$

14: End for.

15: The second round's sampling probability $\{\pi_u(t)|d_u \in \bar{D}\}$ is then used to sample from $\bar{D}$, resulting in a new dataset $\tilde{D} = S'(\bar{D})$;

16: **Phase five:**

17: Define $\Delta_f = \max\limits_{d_u \in \tilde{D}} RS_{d_u}, r_2 = f(\tilde{D}) + Lap(\frac{\Delta_f}{t})$;

18: **Return** $r = (r_1, r_2)$.

The first round of sampling is based on user data's record sensitivity and a balance parameter c, which balances sampling errors and noise errors. When a user's record sensitivity is large, a relatively small sampling probability is used to reduce noise errors. For records with sensitivity smaller than c, the sampling probability is 1 to minimize sampling errors. Conversely, for records with sensitivity greater than c, the sampling probability is inversely proportional to their sensitivity to reduce noise errors.

It has been shown that the balance parameter c can be used as sensitivity [13]. Then, using the privacy budget ϵ and balance parameter c, the Laplace mechanism is invoked to answer the query and obtain the perturbed data for the first round. To enhance accuracy, the minimum privacy budget of the entire user universe, ϵ, is chosen to optimize each user's privacy requirement. In extreme cases where each user has the same privacy budget, personalized differential privacy degenerates into standard differential privacy. However, the simple application of the Laplace mechanism may not yield highly accurate results.

After the first round of data processing, the remaining privacy budget is calculated according to the privacy budget that has been already consumed.

The second round of sampling result is based on the result of the first round of sampling, the remaining privacy budget calculated above, and a threshold value t. The threshold value t also plays a role of balancing the sampling errors and noise errors. When $t = \max_{x_i \in \bar{D}} \bar{\Phi}^i$, the combined mechanism exactly satisfies each user's privacy requirement. When $t = \min_{x_i \in \bar{D}} \bar{\Phi}^i$, the combined mechanism will collapse down to the minimum baseline mechanism [16], where each data will be sampled, but the combined mechanism does not gain any benefit from personalized privacy preferences. Often, a larger threshold t may introduce excessive noise due to high sampling errors, while a smaller t may result in excessive noise due to high noise errors [16]. Thus an optimal threshold value needs to be chosen carefully.

In the end, the Laplace mechanism with threshold t is invoked again to process the result of the second round of sampling and obtain the perturbed data for the second round. With this, the two disturbed answer from both rounds of queries are fully published.

Figure 3 illustrates an example of dataset sampling. The left side shows the sampled (yellow) and not sampled (gray) data in the first round, while the right side represents the consumed privacy budget (orange) and the remaining privacy budget (green) after the first round of queries. The red dashed lines on both sides indicate the balance parameter and the threshold, respectively. The process begins by calculating the record sensitivity for each user based on the query function. A balance parameter c is selected, which is equal to the record sensitivity of User 3. Users 1, 5, and n have record sensitivities greater than the balance parameter, resulting in their sampling probabilities being less than 1, represented by equal-length orange bars in the right graph. After the first round of sampling, Users 1, 2, 3, and 4 are chosen, with Users 2 and 4 consuming relatively smaller privacy budgets. A threshold value t is optimally selected from

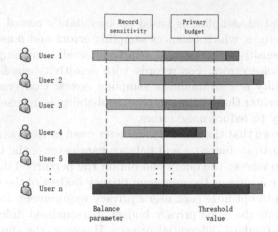

Fig. 3. The combined mechanism. (Color figure online)

the remaining privacy budget. Finally, the second round of sampling is performed based on the remaining privacy budget, threshold t, and the data from the first round of sampling.

3.3 Privacy Analysis

In this section, the combined mechanism is analyzed according to its privacy. We first introduce the following theorems proposed in [13] and [16], then get our theorem that shows the combined mechanism satisfies Φ-PDP.

Theorem 3. *The personalized sampling Laplace mechanism satisfies ϵ-differential privacy. Specifically, if $RS_{d_u} \geq c$, then*

$$\Pr[PSLM_f(D_{+d_u}) \in \mathcal{O}] \leq e^{\epsilon} \cdot \Pr[PSLM_f(D_{-d_u}) \in \mathcal{O}].$$

Otherwise,

$$\Pr[PSLM_f(D_{+d_u}) \in \mathcal{O}] \leq e^{\epsilon \cdot \frac{RS_{d_u}}{c}} \Pr[PSLM_f(D_{-d_u}) \in \mathcal{O}]$$
$$\leq e^{\epsilon} \cdot \Pr[PSLM_f(D_{-d_u}) \in \mathcal{O}].$$

Theorem 4. *The sampling mechanism SM_f satisfies Φ-PDP, Specifically, for $\Phi^u \geq t$,*

$$\Pr[SM_f(D, \Phi, t) \in \mathcal{O}] \leq e^{t} \cdot \Pr[SM_f(D_{-d_u}, \Phi, t) \in \mathcal{O}]$$
$$\leq e^{\Phi^u} \cdot \Pr[SM_f(D_{-d_u}, \Phi, t) \in \mathcal{O}];$$

for $\Phi^u < t$,

$$\Pr[SM_f(D, \Phi, t) \in \mathcal{O}] \leq e^{\Phi^u} \cdot \Pr[SM_f(D_{-d_u}, \Phi, t) \in \mathcal{O}].$$

Theorem 5. *The combined mechanism CM satisfies Φ-PDP.*

Due to limited space, please refer to Appendix A and B for the proof of Theorem 5 and utility analysis.

4   Simulation Experiments

Since the previous $T - 1$ rounds all applied PSLM on differential privacy, the fact that the results of the previous $T - 1$ rounds were more accurate than the laplace mechanism. In this section, the comparison of the T-th round of the combined mechanism and the sampling mechanism is given. The experiments are performed on the synthetic databases and real datasets [15, 27].

The balance parameter c is selected to minimize errors between sampled and actual data, and it varies depending on the aggregate function databases. In experiments, for better performance, c is set above 90% of record sensitivities. It's assumed that privacy requirements in synthetic databases and the real dataset are uniformly distributed from 0 to 1. To optimize results and find the best threshold, we explore values of t from 0.1 to 1.

The first experiment involves using synthetic databases to compare the mechanism's performance across different types of datasets. Synthetic data allows us to generate datasets with varying characteristics conveniently. To ensure a more intuitive comparison of the mechanism's performance, we conduct experiments on synthetic databases and use the same threshold value for each dataset.

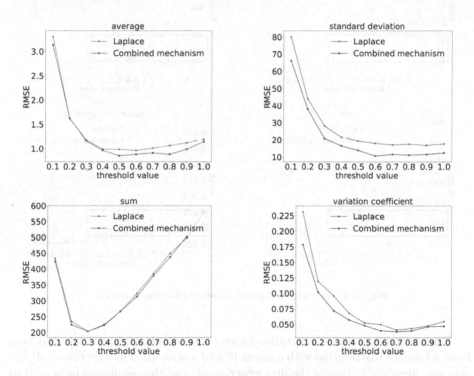

Fig. 4. Error comparisons of Normal distribution data

In the first experiment, using synthetic databases with 100 records drawn from a normal distribution (mean = 10, standard deviation = 10), we compare the proposed mechanism to the sample mechanism based on Root-Mean-Squared Error (RMSE) [13]. The experiment is repeated 500 times to obtain average results. Figure 4 displays the experiment results, indicating that the combined mechanism outperforms the original one. For instance, with a threshold of 0.5, the average function achieves a minimum error of 0.3, and the combined mechanism shows a 50% improvement over the sampling mechanism. The proposed mechanism also demonstrates an approximate 40% improvement in the standard deviation function with a threshold of 0.6. The sum function does not exhibit significant improvement, but the proposed mechanism performs similarly to the original one. Regarding the variation coefficient function, the combined mechanism achieves the optimal value in the range of 0.6 to 0.8, representing some improvement compared to the sampling mechanism.

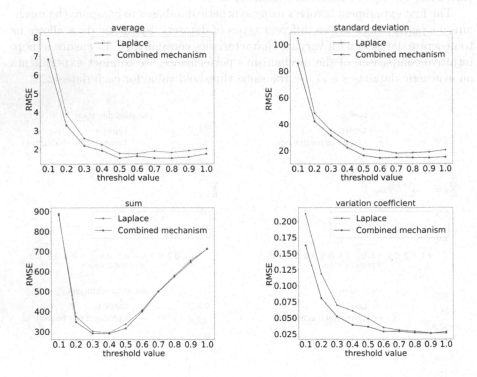

Fig. 5. Error comparisons of Laplace distribution data

The second experiment also utilizes a synthetic database, where data is drawn from a Laplace distribution with a mean 10 and a scale 10. The experimental process was identical to that of the first experiment, and the results are presented in Fig. 5. In comparison to the normal distribution, the Laplace distribution tends to generate extreme values more frequently. Evidently, the presence of extreme values results in a higher mean square error for the query results of the four functions on data obeying the Laplace distribution, as compared to the query results on data obeying the normal distribution. Under this circumstance, the proposed approach yields better results compared to the Laplace distribution.

In the last experiment, the database used is from the Data Curation Network End User Survey [15], a real dataset. It consists of the processed dataset from the 2021 End User Survey conducted by the Data Curation Network. The survey was distributed to depositors within six Data Curation Network institutions' repositories: Cornell University eCommons, Duke University Research Data Repository, Johns Hopkins University Data Archive, Illinois Data Bank, University of Illinois, University of Michigan Deep Blue Data, and the Data Repository for the University of Minnesota (*!DRUM!*). The survey included researchers who had deposited a dataset with repositories at these institutions between January 1, 2019, and March 15, 2021. The attribute chosen for analysis is the "duration" attribute, which contains 65 records. The results are presented in Fig. 6. All four functions used in the experiment show significantly improved error results compared to the synthetic dataset.

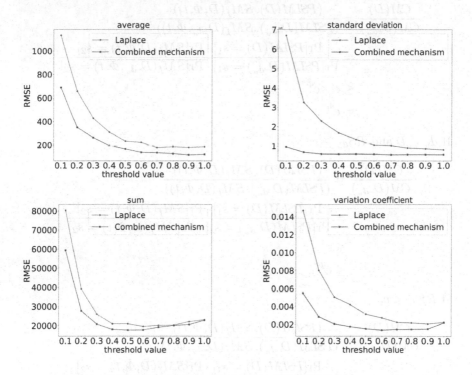

Fig. 6. Error comparisons of real data 2

5   Conclusion

In this paper, we have established a privacy budget allocation method for interactive queries in personalized differential privacy, proposed a combination mechanism that merges personalized sampling Laplace mechanism into personalized differential privacy, and proved that the proposed mechanism meets the privacy requirements. Furthermore, four experiments compared with the sample mechanism demonstrated that the proposed mechanism in the privacy budget allocation method for interactive queries can improve the accuracy of query results.

A   Security Proof of Theorem 5

Proof. The data in D can be divided into selected in $\bar{D}$ or not. Moreover, the data selected in $\bar{D}$ can also be divided into whose record sensitivity is less than c or greater than c. Data with a recorded sensitivity less than c will definitely be sampled into $\bar{D}$, while data with a recorded sensitivity greater than c will be sampled into $\bar{D}$ with a certain probability. The details are as follows.

If $d_u \in \bar{D}$ and $RS_{d_u} \geq c$:

$$
\begin{aligned}
\frac{CM(D)}{CM(D_{-d_u})} &= \frac{(PSLM(D), SM_f(\bar{D}, \bar{\Phi}, t))}{(PSLM(D_{-d_u}), SM_f(\bar{D}_{-d_u}, \bar{\Phi}, t))} \\
&= \frac{\Pr[PSLM(D) = s_1] \cdot \Pr[SM_f(\bar{D}, \bar{\Phi}, t) = s_2]}{\Pr[PSLM(D_{-d_u}) = s_1] \cdot \Pr[SM_f(\bar{D}_{-d_u}, \bar{\Phi}, t) = s_2]} \\
&\leq e^\epsilon \cdot e^{\bar{\Phi}u} \\
&= e^{\Phi u}.
\end{aligned}
$$

If $d_u \notin \bar{D}$ and $RS_{d_u} \geq c$:

$$
\begin{aligned}
\frac{CM(D)}{CM(D_{-d_u})} &= \frac{(PSLM(D), SM_f(\bar{D}, \bar{\Phi}, t))}{(PSLM(D_{-d_u}), SM_f(\bar{D}, \bar{\Phi}, t))} \\
&= \frac{\Pr[PSLM(D) = s_1] \cdot \Pr[SM_f(\bar{D}, \bar{\Phi}, t) = s_2]}{\Pr[PSLM(D_{-d_u}) = s_1] \cdot \Pr[SM_f(\bar{D}, \bar{\Phi}, t) = s_2]} \\
&\leq e^\epsilon \\
&\leq e^{\Phi u}.
\end{aligned}
$$

If $RS_{d_u} < c$:

$$
\begin{aligned}
\frac{CM(D)}{CM(D_{-d_u})} &= \frac{(PSLM(D), SM_f(\bar{D}, \bar{\Phi}, t))}{(PSLM(D_{-d_u}), SM_f(\bar{D}_{-d_u}, \bar{\Phi}, t))} \\
&= \frac{\Pr[PSLM(D) = s_1] \cdot \Pr[SM_f(\bar{D}, \bar{\Phi}, t) = s_2]}{\Pr[PSLM(D_{-d_u}) = s_1] \cdot \Pr[SM_f(\bar{D}_{-d_u}, \bar{\Phi}, t) = s_2]} \\
&\leq e^{\frac{RS_{d_u}}{c}} \cdot e^{\bar{\Phi}u} \\
&= e^{\Phi u}.
\end{aligned}
$$

B   Utility Analysis

Intuitively, the first round of sampling reduces the values with high sensitivity to records, which leads to a reduction in the added noise when the differential privacy step is performed in the second round of sampling. As a result, the accuracy of the results generated by the combined mechanism can be improved.

According to the privacy budget allocation method above, we have the following equations about privacy:

$$SM_f(D, \Phi, t) \Longleftrightarrow (\mathcal{M}_\epsilon^f(D), \mathcal{M}_{t'}^f(RS(D, \Phi - \epsilon, t'))),$$
$$CM(D) \Longleftrightarrow (\mathcal{M}(f, \bar{D}, \frac{c}{\epsilon}), \mathcal{M}_{t'}^f(RS(\bar{D}, \bar{\Phi}, t'))),$$

where $t - \epsilon$ is denoted as t' and $\bar{\Phi}^u \geq \Phi - \epsilon$. It has been show in [13], if the balance parameters are chosen appropriately, the accuracy of the model can be improved significantly. Therefore, our objective is to compare the accuracy of the second result obtained from the combined mechanism with that of the sampling mechanism.

The total errors are caused by sampling errors and noise errors. To obtain high accuracy, $|f(D) - f(\tilde{D})|$ needs to be small. In other words, if for the aggregate function $f(x)$, $f(D)$ can approximate $f(\tilde{D})$ well, and then the accuracy could be improved because the sampling errors go down. The balance parameter c is to balance sampling errors and noise errors. $c = \arg\min_c \beta$. The original mechanism is viewed as a special case of the combined mechanism. When balance parameter c is big enough, each record will be sampled in the first round of sampling. That is to say, the combined mechanism degenerates into the original mechanism. This means the combined mechanism is better than the original mechanism in terms of accuracy if the balance parameter is selected properly.

References

1. Alaggan, M., Gambs, S., Kermarrec, A.M.: Heterogeneous differential privacy. J. Priv. Confidentiality **7** (2015). https://doi.org/10.29012/jpc.v7i2.652
2. Bun, M., Steinke, T.: Concentrated differential privacy: simplifications, extensions, and lower bounds. In: Hirt, M., Smith, A. (eds.) TCC 2016. LNCS, vol. 9985, pp. 635–658. Springer, Heidelberg (2016). https://doi.org/10.1007/978-3-662-53641-4_24
3. Cai, H., Ye, F., Yang, Y., Zhu, Y., Li, J.: Towards privacy-preserving data trading for web browsing history. In: 2019 IEEE/ACM 27th International Symposium on Quality of Service (IWQoS), pp. 1–10 (2019). https://doi.org/10.1145/3326285.3329060
4. Cui, L., Qu, Y., Yu, S., Gao, L., Xie, G.: A trust-grained personalized privacy-preserving scheme for big social data. In: 2018 IEEE International Conference on Communications (ICC), pp. –6 (2018). https://doi.org/10.1109/ICC.2018.8422439
5. Deldar, F., Abadi, M.: PDP-SAG: personalized privacy protection in moving objects databases by combining differential privacy and sensitive attribute generalization. IEEE Access **7**, 85887–85902 (2019). https://doi.org/10.1109/ACCESS.2019.2925236

6. Dwork, C.: Differential privacy. In: Encyclopedia of Cryptography and Security (2006)
7. Dwork, C.: A firm foundation for private data analysis. Commun. ACM **54**(1), 86–95 (2011). https://doi.org/10.1145/1866739.1866758
8. Dwork, C., Kenthapadi, K., McSherry, F., Mironov, I., Naor, M.: Our data, ourselves: privacy via distributed noise generation. In: Vaudenay, S. (ed.) EUROCRYPT 2006. LNCS, vol. 4004, pp. 486–503. Springer, Heidelberg (2006). https://doi.org/10.1007/11761679_29
9. Dwork, Cynthia, McSherry, Frank, Nissim, Kobbi, Smith, Adam: Calibrating noise to sensitivity in private data analysis. In: Halevi, Shai, Rabin, Tal (eds.) TCC 2006. LNCS, vol. 3876, pp. 265–284. Springer, Heidelberg (2006). https://doi.org/10.1007/11681878_14
10. Gehrke, J., Hay, M., Lui, E., Pass, R.: Crowd-blending privacy. In: Safavi-Naini, R., Canetti, R. (eds.) CRYPTO 2012. LNCS, vol. 7417, pp. 479–496. Springer, Heidelberg (2012). https://doi.org/10.1007/978-3-642-32009-5_28
11. Gupta, A., Roth, A., Ullman, J.: Iterative constructions and private data release. In: Cramer, R. (ed.) TCC 2012. LNCS, vol. 7194, pp. 339–356. Springer, Heidelberg (2012). https://doi.org/10.1007/978-3-642-28914-9_19
12. Hardt, M., Rothblum, G.N.: A multiplicative weights mechanism for privacy-preserving data analysis. In: 2010 IEEE 51st Annual Symposium on Foundations of Computer Science, pp. 61–70 (2010). https://doi.org/10.1109/FOCS.2010.85
13. Huang, W., Zhou, S., Zhu, T., Liao, Y.: Privately publishing internet of things data: Bring personalized sampling into differentially private mechanisms. IEEE Internet Things J. **9**(1), 80–91 (2022). https://doi.org/10.1109/JIOT.2021.3089518
14. Iftikhar, M., Wang, Q., Li, Y.: dK-personalization: publishing network statistics with personalized differential privacy. In: Gama, J., Li, T., Yu, Y., Chen, E., Zheng, Y., Teng, F. (eds.) PAKDD 2022. LNCS, vol. 13280, pp. 194–207. Springer, Cham (2022). https://doi.org/10.1007/978-3-031-05933-9_16
15. Johnston, L., et al.: Value of curation survey. https://doi.org/10.13020/04ee-q089
16. Jorgensen, Z., Yu, T., Cormode, G.: Conservative or liberal? Personalized differential privacy. In: 2015 IEEE 31st International Conference on Data Engineering, pp. 1023–1034 (2015). https://doi.org/10.1109/ICDE.2015.7113353
17. Kang, H., Ji, Y., Zhang, S.: Enhanced privacy preserving for social networks relational data based on personalized differential privacy. Chin. J. Electron. **31**, 741–751 (2022). https://doi.org/10.1049/cje.2021.00.274
18. Li, H., Xiong, L., Ji, Z., Jiang, X.: Partitioning-based mechanisms under personalized differential privacy. In: Kim, J., Shim, K., Cao, L., Lee, J.-G., Lin, X., Moon, Y.-S. (eds.) PAKDD 2017. LNCS (LNAI), vol. 10234, pp. 615–627. Springer, Cham (2017). https://doi.org/10.1007/978-3-319-57454-7_48
19. McSherry, F.: Privacy integrated queries: an extensible platform for privacy-preserving data analysis. Commun. ACM **53**(9), 89–97 (2010). https://doi.org/10.1145/1810891.1810916
20. Nissim, K., Raskhodnikova, S., Smith, A.: Smooth sensitivity and sampling in private data analysis. In: Proceedings of the Thirty-Ninth Annual ACM Symposium on Theory of Computing, STOC 2007, pp. 75–84. Association for Computing Machinery, New York (2007). https://doi.org/10.1145/1250790.1250803
21. Niu, B., Chen, Y., Wang, B., Cao, J., Li, F.: Utility-aware exponential mechanism for personalized differential privacy. In: 2020 IEEE Wireless Communications and Networking Conference (WCNC), pp. 1–6 (2020). https://doi.org/10.1109/WCNC45663.2020.9120532

22. Niu, B., Chen, Y., Wang, B., Wang, Z., Li, F., Cao, J.: Adapdp: adaptive personalized differential privacy. In: IEEE INFOCOM 2021 - IEEE Conference on Computer Communications, pp. 1–10 (2021). https://doi.org/10.1109/INFOCOM42981.2021.9488825

23. Qu, Y., Yu, S., Zhou, W., Tian, Y.: Gan-driven personalized spatial-temporal private data sharing in cyber-physical social systems. IEEE Trans. Netw. Sci. Eng. 7(4), 2576–2586 (2020). https://doi.org/10.1109/TNSE.2020.3001061

24. Roth, A., Roughgarden, T.: Interactive privacy via the median mechanism. In: Proceedings of the Forty-Second ACM Symposium on Theory of Computing, STOC 2010, pp. 765–774. Association for Computing Machinery, New York (2010). https://doi.org/10.1145/1806689.1806794

25. Tian, F., Zhang, S., Lu, L., Liu, H., Gui, X.: A novel personalized differential privacy mechanism for trajectory data publication. In: 2017 International Conference on Networking and Network Applications (NaNA), pp. 61–68 (2017). https://doi.org/10.1109/NaNA.2017.47

26. Wang, Z., et al.: Personalized privacy-preserving task allocation for mobile crowdsensing. IEEE Trans. Mob. Comput. 18(6), 1330–1341 (2019). https://doi.org/10.1109/TMC.2018.2861393

27. Wright, S., et al.: Data curation network end user survey. https://doi.org/10.13020/DZQP-KS53

28. Wu, Y., Wu, Y., Peng, H., Zeng, J., Chen, H., Li, C.: Differentially private density estimation via gaussian mixtures model. In: 2016 IEEE/ACM 24th International Symposium on Quality of Service (IWQoS), pp. 1–6 (2016). https://doi.org/10.1109/IWQoS.2016.7590445

29. Zhu, T., Li, G., Zhou, W., Yu, P.S.: Differentially private data publishing and analysis: a survey. IEEE Trans. Knowl. Data Eng. 29(8), 1619–1638 (2017). https://doi.org/10.1109/TKDE.2017.2697856

VPSearch+: Achieving Verifiability for Privacy-Preserving Multi-keyword Search Without Client Storage Overhead

Li Gong[1]($\boxtimes$), Ao Liu[1], Long He[1], Xinbo Ban[1], and Hang Chen[2]

[1] The Second Research Institute of CAAC, Chengdu 610042, China
{gongli,helong}@caacsri.com
[2] Sichuan Province Airport Group Co. Ltd., Chengdu 610202, China

Abstract. Searchable Encryption (SE) makes it possible to query encrypted data stored on the cloud server while ensuring data and queries privacy. Most SE schemes assume that the cloud server is "honest-but-curious", that is the cloud server strictly follow the specified protocol or algorithm, they don't consider whether the results returned by the cloud server is really correct. In practical, in order to reduce the calculation cost, it is possible that the cloud server only completes part of the computing tasks of the protocol and returns wrong computing results to users. Therefore, it is very important for users to be able to verify the search results returned by the cloud server. To address above problem, we explore a Verifiable Privacy-preserving multi-keyword Search without client storage overhead scheme in this paper, called VPSearch+, which integrating symmetric-key hidden vector encryption with a privacy-preserving multi-keyword search scheme. Compared with TDSC'18 scheme, our proposed scheme can verify the search results quickly without storing a local copy of the outsourced data, radically reducing the storage overhead of the client in the verifiable SE scheme. Finally, the security analysis proves the high security of our model, and extensive experiments conducted on real-world dataset demonstrate that the proposed scheme can achieve better performance in terms of efficiency and storage overhead.

Keywords: Dynamic Searchable Encryption · Verifiability · Multi-Keyword Search · Privacy-Preserving

1 Introduction

Cloud computing has completely changed the traditional computation model by providing elastic computation and storage resources. For save costs and improve query efficiency, more and more data owner outsource local data and query task to the cloud server. These advantages make cloud computing flourish, but also raising some challenges about the outsourced data security and privacy [1]. The cloud server is an untrusted medium entity that makes a profit by providing powerful computation and storage resources, and it has the incentive to steal outsourced private data and gain profits from it. To protect data privacy, the data owner usually encrypt sensitive data before

© The Author(s), under exclusive license to Springer Nature Singapore Pte Ltd. 2024
H. Yang and R. Lu (Eds.): FCS 2023, CCIS 1992, pp. 160–175, 2024.
https://doi.org/10.1007/978-981-99-9331-4_11

outsourcing to the cloud server. However, how to perform computation and keyword search directly on encrypted data has become a new challenge. So far, only fully homomorphic encryption [2] can achieve arbitrary computations over encrypted data, but its high computation cost and complex interactions makes it inefficient and impractical.

Song et al. [3] proposed first searchable encryption (SE) scheme to support keyword search on encrypted data in 2000, and a few years later Boneh et al. [4] proposed first public-key searchable encryption (PKSE). More recent a series of SE schemes have achieved trade-off among data security, query efficiency and functionality, i.e., single-keyword search [5–7], and multi-keyword search [8–10]. Unfortunately, all of these schemes assume that the cloud server will follow the designated protocol honestly, that is, honest-but-curious model, so these schemes do not consider whether the computation results returned by the cloud server is authentic. In practice, the cloud server may run only part of the protocol and return wrong computation results to the search user due to system failure or in order to reduce computation cost. Thus, the keywords search results returned by the cloud server cannot be completed trusted. Therefore, it's important for the search user to be able to verify whether the keyword search results over encrypted data are trusted, especially for very critical computation results.

Our Contribution. In this paper, we explore how to achieve privacy-preserving multi-keyword search over encrypted cloud data based on verification. Different from the honest-but-curious server assumption in most privacy-preserving keyword search schemes, in this scheme, the cloud server is assumed a "semi-honest" entity, where the cloud server may run only part of the delegated computation task and return erroneous results to reduce computation costs.

To this end, we adapt the symmetric-key hidden vector encryption (SHVE) from [11] to support verifiability for privacy-preserving multi-keyword search. The original hidden vector encryption (HVE) [12] is designed based on public-key cryptography, which is computationally expensive and inefficient. Therefore, this paper decide to adopt symmetric-key HVE.

The main contributions of our model can be summarized as below:

- We proposed a scheme for privacy-preserving multi-keyword search over encrypted cloud based verification under the "semi-honest" cloud server model. It is realized by integrating the symmetric-key hidden vector encryption technique with a privacy-preserving multi-keyword searchable encryption scheme. The verification process of this scheme is very efficient because it only relies on symmetric-key hidden vector encryption.
- Based on the above technique and structure, we achieve a verifiable searchable encryption scheme (VPSearch+) over outsourced cloud data without storing any the outsourced data or its label locally, radically reducing the storage costs of the search user client in the verifiable SE scheme.
- We make a detailed comparative analysis on verifiability, privacy and efficiency of VPSearch+ with some of existing verifiable schemes. Specifically, we implement schemes under the Enron email dataset and the experimental results show that VPSearch+ is very efficient on keyword search and search results verification.

2 Related Work

In recent years, experts have investigated the rich properties of SE, e.g. multi-keyword search [13, 14], forward and backward privacy [7, 15], and verifiability [16–18].

Mathiyalahan et al. [19] first applied the Merkle Patricia Tree (MPT) in the cloud computing. The MPT tree was proposed to reduce the storage cost of the index structure in the Merkle hash tree scheme. Through The index is constructed using a compressed prefix tree including three node types to reduce the depth and width of the tree. However, in this solution, the space cost of the cloud server providing search result authentication information to the data user is relatively high, and the demand for communication overhead is relatively large. Liu et al. [17] proposed a searchable encryption scheme based on aggregate key and result verification, which allows each authorized user to retrieve encrypted documents and use the aggregate key to verify the correctness of the retrieval results. However, the key aggregation of this scheme is based on bilinear mapping, which leads to certain defects in efficiency, especially when the amount of data is large, its efficiency limitation is more obvious.

Zhang et al. [20] proposed a SSE scheme that supports search result verification, which proposed a new multi-set-hash function primitive data structure, and realizes the verifiability of retrieval results through incremental hash operations. Ge et al. [21] proposed a verifiable SSE scheme based on Accumulative Authentication Tag (AAT), which allows users to locally verify the correctness of the ciphertext returned by the cloud server. However, this scheme only supports single-keyword search, and the ciphertext index constructed from the original data needs to be decrypted on the cloud server, which has a great risk of injection attacks and sensitive data leakage. Wan et al. extended the integer field in the scheme [16] to the real number field, combined with the searchable encryption scheme MRSE [13] proposed by Cao et al. to support multi-keyword query retrieval, proposed a polynomial function arithmetic based The results of the circuit validate the SE scheme, VPSearch [18]. However, this scheme needs to save the copy label $L_i(i = 1, 2, ..., n)$ locally of the outsourced data (where n is the size of the data), so the storage overhead of the client is positively correlated with the size of the data.

3 Preliminaries

3.1 Symmetric-Key Hidden Vector Encryption

Predicate encryption is a research notion for public-key cryptography. It supports search queries on encrypted data, and provides a new fine-grained access control scheme. In 2007, D. Boneh and B. Waters proposed Hidden Vector Encryption (HVE) [12]. In order to combine with our model, we decided to adopt symmetric-key HVE(SHVE) [11].

The details as follows, an instantiation of a SHVE consists of four PPT algorithms:

- $SHVE.Setup(1^\lambda) \rightarrow (sk)$: Input a security parameter λ and output a relevant secret key which uniformly samples $sk \xleftarrow{\$} \{0, 1\}^\lambda$.

- *SHVE.KeyGen(sk, p ∈ {0,1}^n) → s*: Input the secret key sk and a predicate vector $p = (p_1, ..., p_n)$, P is defined as a collection of all 1 positions in p, i.e $P = \{l_i \in [n] \mid p_{l_i} = 1\}$ and let these positions be $l_1 < l_2 < ... < l_{|x|}$, $K \xleftarrow{\$} \{0,1\}^\lambda$. The details of this algorithm are as follows:

$$b_0 = \oplus_{i \in [\|P\|]} (F(sk, p_{l_i} \| l_i)) \oplus K$$
$$b_1 = Sym.Enc(K, 0^\lambda)$$

In the end, the algorithm outputs the key:

$$s = (b_0, b_1, P)$$

- *SHVE.Enc(sk, q ∈ {0,1}^n) → r*: Input the secret key sk and a index vector $q = (q_1, ..., q_n)$, for each $l \in [n]$, $r_l = F(sk, q_l \| l)$. Finally, outputs the ciphertext:

$$r = (\{r_l\}_{l \in [n]})$$

- *SHVE.Query(s, r)*: Input the key s and the ciphertext r, the details of this algorithm calculation are detailed below:

$$K_0 = \left(\oplus_{i \in [\|P\|]} r_{l_i} \right) \oplus b_0$$
$$\delta = Sym.Dec(K_0, b_1)$$

If $\delta = 0^\lambda$, this algorithm outputs 'true', otherwise, outputs 'false'.

The correctness of the above algorithm is verified as following. Let $r = (\{r_l\}_{l \in [n]})$ be the ciphertext of index vector $q = (q_1, ..., q_n)$ and $s = (b_0, b_1, P)$ be a key generated by predicate vector $p = (p_1, ..., p_n)$. We discuss the following scenarios:

- If output 'true', we have $p_{l_i} = q_{l_i}$ for each $i \in [\|P\|]$. We can get the following relationship:

$$K_0 = \left(\oplus_{i \in [\|P\|]} r_{l_i} \right) \oplus b_0 = K$$
$$\delta = Sym.Dec(K_0, b_1)$$
$$= 0^\lambda$$

- If output 'false', we have $p_{l_i} \neq q_{l_i}$ for some $i \in [\|P\|]$. We can get the following relation:

$$K_0 = \left(\oplus_{i \in [\|P\|]} r_{l_i} \right) \oplus b_0 \neq K$$
$$\delta \neq Sym.Dec(K_0, b_1)$$
$$\neq 0^\lambda$$

This is the verification of the correctness of the SHVE scheme. We will utilize the SHVE to construct our VPSearch+ scheme.

3.2 Verifiable Search Scheme

Definition 1 (Verifiable multi-keyword Search (VPSearch+) scheme). A verifiable multi-keyword search scheme is a tuple of six polynomial-time algorithms i.e., Setup, IndexBuild, TrapdoorGen, Auth, Search, Verify:

- $\mathbf{K} \leftarrow$ Setup(1^λ) is the probabilistic key generation algorithm run by the data owner. It takes a random security parameter λ, outputs a key set $\mathbf{K}$.
- $(I, C) \leftarrow$ IndexBuild$(\mathbf{K}, F, W)$ is the probabilistic index building algorithm run by the data owner. It takes the key set $\mathbf{K}$, the documents F and the keyword dictionary W, outputs the encrypted data C and the corresponding secure index I.
- $T_{\widetilde{w}} \leftarrow$ TrapdoorGen$(\mathbf{K}, \widetilde{w} = (w_1 \wedge w_2 \wedge \ldots \wedge w_m), W)$ is the probabilistic trapdoor generation algorithm run by the search user. It takes the key set $\mathbf{K}$, the searched keywords $\widetilde{w}$ and the keyword dictionary W, outputs the trapdoor $T_{\widetilde{w}}$.
- $(T_D, T_Q) \leftarrow$ Auth$(\mathbf{K}, D_1, Q_1)$ is the probabilistic authentication tags generation algorithm run by the data owner or the search user. It takes the key set $\mathbf{K}$, the plaintext index D_1 and the plaintext trapdoor Q_1, outputs T_D as the authentication tag for D_1, outputs T_Q as the verification tag for Q_1.
- $(C(\widetilde{w}), T_{D_{\widetilde{w}}}) \leftarrow$ Search$(T_{\widetilde{w}}, I, C)$ is the search algorithm run by the cloud server. It takes the trapdoor $T_{\widetilde{w}}$, the secure index I and the encrypted data C, and outputs the ciphertext set $C(\widetilde{w})$ and the corresponding authentication tags $T_{D_{\widetilde{w}}}$.
- $(accept, reject) \leftarrow$ Verify$(T_{D_{\widetilde{w}}}, T_Q)$ is the verification algorithm run by the search user. It takes the authentication tags $T_{D_{\widetilde{w}}}$ and the verification tag T_Q, and outputs a verification result "accept" or "reject".

4 Problem Formulation

4.1 System Model

As illustrated in Fig. 1, in our system model, we consider three basic entities.

- *Cloud Server*: The cloud server is an untrusted medium entity with powerful computation and storage resources, which stores data owner's outsourced authentication tags, documents and corresponding indexes. When the search user sends a search request to the cloud server, it would execute the request and then return the corresponding search result (i.e., tag and encrypted data). But the entity is dishonest, i.e, the cloud server may some motivation to run only part of the protocol and return wrong calculation results to the search user, such as system failure or in order to reduce computation overhead.
- *Data owner*: The data owner outsources the encrypted raw documents and corresponding indexes to the cloud server. To protect the data privacy and search pattern, some encryption primitives are used to encrypt raw documents and corresponding indexes, generate authentication tags for the index. After that, the data owner outsources the authentication tags, encrypted data and indexes to the cloud server. Then she sends the key set to the search user.

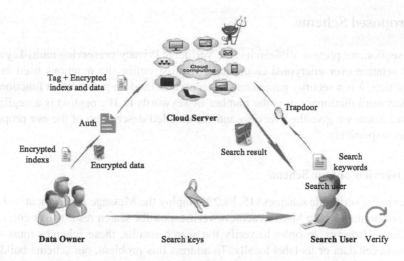

Fig. 1. System model

- *Search user*: When the search user want to search the data for some keywords, she will generate secure trapdoor(i.e., search token) based on the search keywords and the key set and then sends trapdoor to the cloud server for executing this request. The cloud server performs search based on the trapdoor and returns the corresponding ciphertext search results. Finally, the search user receives the search results, verifies the authentication tags, and decrypts the correct search results with the symmetric key.

4.2 Security Requirements

Based on the above threat models, we define the following security requirements:

- *Verifiablity*: This solution requires the cloud server to be able to return a tag that proves the correctness of the multi-keyword search result, and the search user can verify the correctness of the result according to the tag returned by the cloud server *without* storing the outsourced data locally.
- *Confidentiality of Data*: Considering the privacy of documents and indexes, all plaintexts of documents and the indexes must not be identifiable except the data owner and authorized search users.
- *Privacy Protection of Index and Trapdoor*: As discussed in our model, indexes are constructed based on keyword dictionary and data owner's documents, trapdoors are generated based on search users' search key and search keywords, respectively. So if the server can get some contents of indexes and trapdoors, it may be able to infer the association between search keyword and encrypted documents. Therefore, the contents of indexes and trapdoors should be not identified by the server.
- *Unlinkability of Trapdoors*: The trapdoors generated by any two search requests should be different, even if the keywords of the two requests are the same.

5 Proposed Scheme

In this section, we present VPSearch+, the Verifiable Privacy-preserving multi-keyword Search scheme over encrypted cloud data. We first define the notations used in our construction, λ is a security parameter, $\mathbf{F}$ is a pseudo-random permutation function, W is the keyword dictionary, n is the number of keywords in W, $\mathrm{negl}(\lambda)$ is a negligible function. Then, we give the overview and the detailed description of the our proposed scheme, respectively.

5.1 Overview of Our Scheme

Some existing verifiable schemes [15, 18, 22] employ the Message Authentication Code (MAC) or homomorphic MAC to achieve verification for search results over encrypted cloud data. However, in order to verify the search results, these schemes must store the outsourced data or its label locally. To address this problem, our scheme builds on the privacy-preserving multi-keyword searchable encryption scheme in [13], which is integrated with symmetric-key HVE to achieve both verifiability and privacy without storing any the outsourced data or its label locally. The main reason for choosing this scheme is that its multi-keyword searches operation is based on vector inner product, which fully supports symmetric-key HVE.

As shown in Fig. 1, the data owner first encrypts the plaintext data and indexes, generates and encrypts authentication tags with symmetric-key HVE, then authentication tags and the encrypted indexes and data are uploaded to the cloud server, the key set is sent to the search user. Next, the search user can generate secure trapdoor and send to the cloud server. At the same time, the search user also generates tag for trapdoor with symmetric-key HVE to verify the authentication tags returned from the cloud server. With the trapdoor, the cloud server can execute the search request and then return the corresponding tag and encrypted data.

After that, we give the overview of core algorithms of scheme [13]. The data owner firstly encrypts the document set $F = (F_1, F_2, ..., F_N)$, for F_i, its index D_i is constructed as an m-dimensional binary vector. $D_i[j]$ is set to 1 if this document contains the jth keyword in the keyword dictionary W; otherwise, it is set as 0. Similarly, the trapdoor Q is also an m-dimensional binary vector, $Q_{[i]}$ is set to 1 if i-th keyword of dictionary is in the search keywords set $\widetilde{w}$; otherwise, it is set as 0. Then the index D_i and the trapdoor Q are encrypted using matrix multiplication, i.e., $\widetilde{D}_i = M^T D_i$ and $\widetilde{Q} = M^{-1}Q$ where M is a invertible matric. After that, the index D_i is extended to $D_i = (D_i, 1)$, the trapdoor Q is extended to $Q = (rQ, t)$, where r is random number. Finally, the cloud server calculates the query result as $R = r(D_i \cdot Q) + t$, if $R > 0$, the corresponding encrypted index and document will be returned.

We apply symmetric-key HVE on the index D_i and the trapdoor Q to generate authentication tags T_D and T_Q, respectively. Then the search user executes the verification algorithm locally over the authentication tags, which the architecture is shown in Fig. 2. Since symmetric-key HVE only uses one-way function and inner products without any public key operation, the verification process is computationally efficient.

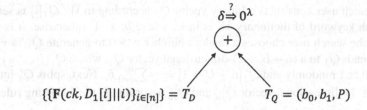

$$\{\{F(ck, D_1[i]\|i)\}_{i\in[n]}\} = T_D \qquad T_Q = (b_0, b_1, P)$$

Fig. 2. Architecture of verification algorithm with symmetric-key HVE. D_1 is the plaintext document index and Q is the search trapdoor

5.2   VPSearch+: Verifiable Privacy-Preserving Multi-keyword Search Based on Symmetric-Key HVE

Now, we describe our proposed verifiable privacy-preserving multi-keyword search scheme in detail, called VPSearch+. VPSearch+ consists the following six polynomial-time algorithms i.e., Setup, IndexBuild, TrapdoorGen, Auth, Search, Verify.

- Setup($1^\lambda, n$): It takes a random security parameter λ and the number of keywords n in keyword dictionary W. The data owner generates random key set $\mathbf{K} = \{S, M_1, M_2, ck, msk\}$, where S is a $(n + U + 1)$-dimensional binary vector, M_1 and M_2 are two $(n + U + 1) \times (n + U + 1)$ invertible matrices, and U is the number of dummy keywords, ck is the PRP function key and msk is the symmetric key used to encrypted documents, respectively. Then the data owner sends $\mathbf{K}$ to the search user through a secure channel.
- IndexBuild($\mathbf{K}, F, W$): This algorithm takes the key set $\mathbf{K}$, the plaintext documents F and the keyword dictionary W, outputs the encrypted data C, the secure index I and the authentication tags for outsourcing to the cloud server. The index vector for document F_i are processed as follows:

  The data owner constructs a binary vector subindex D_1 for F, $D_1[j]$ is set to 1 if this document contains the jth keyword in the keyword dictionary W; otherwise, it is set as 0. Then extends D_1 to a $(n + U + 1)$-dimensional vector D_1', where $D_1'[n + 1] = \varepsilon_1, \ldots, D_1'[n + U] = \varepsilon_U, D_1'[n + U + 1] = 1$ and ε_i is a random number. Next, splits D_1' into tow $(n + U + 1)$-dimensional vector D_{1a}' and D_{1b}' according to the following rule:

$$\begin{cases} D_{1a}'[i] = D_{1b}'[i] = D_1'[i] \ S[i] = 0 \\ D_1'[i] = D_{1a}'[i] + D_{1b}'[i] \ S[i] = 1 \end{cases} \tag{1}$$

Then the data owner encrypts the subindex (D_{1a}', D_{1b}') using the matrices M_1 and M_2: $\widetilde{D_1} = (M_1^T D_{1a}', M_2^T D_{1b}')$, encrypts document F with symmetric algorithm: $C \leftarrow Sym \cdot \text{Enc}(msk, F)$ and generates authentication tags by the Auth algorithm: $T_D \leftarrow \text{VPSearch+.Auth}(ck, D_1)$. Finally, $(\widetilde{D_1}, C, T_D)$ will be uploaded to the cloud server.
- TrapdoorGen($\mathbf{K}, \widetilde{w} = (w_1 \wedge w_2 \wedge \ldots \wedge w_m), W$): It takes the key set $\mathbf{K}$, the search keywords $\widetilde{w}$ and the keyword dictionary W, outputs the secure trapdoor $T_{\widetilde{w}}$. In order to protect the privacy of search keywords, the process is as follows:

The search user constructs a binary vector Q_1 according to W, $Q_1[i]$ is set to b_i if the j-th keyword of dictionary W is in $\widetilde{w}$, where $b_i = 1$; otherwise, it is set as 0. Next, the search user chooses a random number $r > 0$ to generate $Q_1 = r \cdot Q_1$. Then extends Q_1 to a $(n + U + 1)$-dimensional vector Q_1', where $Q_1'[j]_{n+1 \leq j \leq n+U}$ is set to 0 or 1 randomly and $Q_1'[n + U + 1] = -\sum_{i=1}^{m} b_i$. Next, splits Q_1' into tow $(n + U + 1)$-dimensional vector Q_{1a}' and Q_{1b}' according to the following rule:

$$\begin{cases} Q_1'[i] = Q_{1a}'[i] + Q_{1b}'[i] \ S[i] = 0 \\ Q_{1a}'[i] = Q_{1b}'[i] = Q_1'[i] \ S[i] = 1 \end{cases} \tag{2}$$

Finally, the search user encrypts the search trapdoor as $\widehat{Q_1} = (M_1^{-1} Q_{1a}', M_2^{-1} Q_{1b}')$, and sends trapdoor $T_{\widetilde{w}} = \{\widehat{Q_1}\}$ to the cloud server.

- Auth(K, D_1, Q_1): This algorithm takes the index D_1 and generates authentication tag T_D, then uploads T_D to the cloud server. In addition, the search user will generate tag T_Q for trapdoor Q_1 and verify the authentication tags of search result returned by the cloud server, which are processed as follows:

For index D_1, where $D_1[i]$ indicates whether the i-th keyword of dictionary W is in the document. This algorithm constructs authentication tag T_D as follows:

$$\begin{cases} T_{D_i} = \mathbf{F}(ck, D_1[i] \| i) \\ T_D = \left(\{T_{D_i}\}_{i \in [n]} \right) \end{cases} \tag{3}$$

For trapdoor Q_1, where $Q_1[i]$ indicates whether the i-th keyword of dictionary W is in the search keywords. This algorithm constructs tag T_Q as follows:

$$\begin{cases} b_0 = \oplus_{i \in [P]]} (\mathbf{F}(ck, Q_1[i] \| i)) \oplus K \\ b_1 = \text{Sym.Enc}(K, 0^\lambda) \end{cases} \tag{4}$$

where P is defined as a collection of all 1 positions in Q_1, i.e., $P = \{i \in [n] \mid Q_1[i] = 1\}$. Finally, the search user generates the tag for Q_1 as $T_Q = (b_0, b_1, P)$.

- Search($T_{\widetilde{w}}$, $\widetilde{D_1}$): It takes the trapdoor $T_{\widetilde{w}}$, the secure index $\widetilde{D_1}$, and outputs a ciphertext set $C(\widetilde{w})$ and the corresponding authentication tags $T_{D_{\widetilde{w}}}$. Then for each secure index $\widetilde{D_1}$, this algorithm calculates the query results as follows:

$$\begin{aligned} R_1 &= \widetilde{D_1} \cdot \widehat{Q_1} = \left(M_1^T D_{1a}', M_2^T D_{1b}' \right) \cdot \left(M_1^{-1} Q_{1a}'', M_2^{-1} Q_{1b}'' \right) \\ &= D_a' \cdot Q_a'' + D_b' \cdot Q_b'' \\ &= D' \cdot Q'' \\ &= r \left(D_1 \cdot Q_1 + \sum_{i=1}^{V} \varepsilon_i - \sum_{i=1}^{m} b_i \right) \end{aligned}$$

If $R_1 \geq 0$, the corresponding ciphertext document C and the authentication tag T_D will be add to the ciphertext set $C(\widetilde{w})$ and the authentication tags $T_{D_{\widetilde{w}}}$, respectively. Finally, $C(\widetilde{w})$ and $T_{D_{\widetilde{w}}}$ will be returned.

- Verify($T_{D_{\widetilde{w}}}$, T_Q): It takes the authentication tags $T_{D_{\widetilde{w}}}$ and the verification tag T_Q. Then the search user invokes $SHVE.Query(T_{D_{\widetilde{w}}}, T_Q)$ to obtain the result, processes is shown as follow:

$$K_0 = \left(\oplus_{i \in [|P|]} T_{D_i}\right) \oplus b_0$$
$$\delta = Sym \cdot Enc\,(K_0, b_1) \tag{5}$$
$$= 0^\lambda$$

Where P is a collection of all 1 positions in Q_1, i.e., $P = \{i \in [n] \mid Q_1[i] = 1\}$. If Eq.(5) is satisfied (i.e., $\delta = 0^\lambda$), the search user accepts the corresponding ciphertext document C as the search result; otherwise rejects the result.

Theorem 1. *The result returned by the cloud server is correct if Eq. (5) is valid.*

Proof. Assume the authentication tag T_D returned by the cloud server and the corresponding index D_1 satisfy the retrieval logic of the trapdoor Q_1, where $Q_1[i] = D_1[i]$ for all $i \in [|P|]$. Therefore, there will be

$$K_0 = \left(\oplus_{i \in [|P|]} T_{D_i}\right) \oplus b_0 = K$$
$$\delta = Sym \cdot Dec\,(K_0, b_1)$$
$$= Sym \cdot Dec\,(K, b_1) \tag{6}$$
$$= 0^\lambda$$

Therefore, the result returned by the cloud server is correct if Eq. (5) is valid.

6 Security Analysis

The security requirements of this scheme are given in Sect. 4.2, including the verifiability, the confidentiality of data, the privacy protection of index and trapdoor, and the unlinkability of trapdoors. Next, we will prove the security requirements of this scheme one by one.

6.1 Verifiablity

For a cloud service that may be "semi-honest" or "dishonest", it needs to reduce its operating costs as much as possible and maximize its revenue. If there is no result verification mechanism in this algorithm, in order to save the computational cost, the cloud server may randomly return a wrong retrieval result without doing any calculation when it receives the query request.

The verifiability of our scheme completely depends on the correctness of the SHVE algorithm in the authorization phase. The only entities involved in the authorization phase are the data owner and the search user and these are two "completely honest" entities. Therefore, as long as the Auth and Verify is strictly implemented, this scheme can ensure that the search user can correctly verify the authentication label returned by the cloud server without the storage overhead of local copy of the outsourced data, that is, it can ensure the verifiability of the query result.

6.2 Confidentiality of Data

Since the cloud server is defined as a "semi-honest" entity, in order to ensure the confidentiality of the original data, the plaintext data will be encrypted by using a symmetric encryption algorithm (e.g., AES), and then the ciphertext of the data will be outsourced to the cloud server. The security of AES algorithm has been fully proved in [13]. Any entity can not recover the encrypted data without the symmetric key msk, and msk is generated by the data owner and shared with the search user through a secure channel, any unauthorized user or malicious adversary can not obtain any information about msk. Therefore, our scheme is able to guarantee the confidentiality of data.

6.3 Privacy Protection of Index and Trapdoor

Our proposed model is constructed based on the MRSE [13], so its also inherits the security of the it. As described in Sect. 4.2, all index vectors are generated by the data owner based on the plaintext data and keyword dictionary, all trapdoor vectors are generated by the search user based on the search keywords and keyword dictionary, after encrypted and uploaded to the cloud server. If the cloud server only knows the data ciphertext, index ciphertext and trapdoor ciphertext, does not know M_1 and M_2, it is impossible to recover the plaintext of the index and trapdoor in PPT time.

Therefore, in the known ciphertext model, this scheme can achieve the privacy protection of index and trapdoor. In the known background model, in addition to the ciphertext data, the adversary also knows more background knowledge, such as the links between trapdoors and some other information. In [23], a known plaintext attack (KPA) adversary is proposed, which assumes that the KPA adversary knows some plaintext-ciphertext pairs and tries to recover the trapdoor vectors and index vectors. Next, we try to analyze the security of our scheme against KPA adversary.

Theorem 2. *VPSearch+ can resist KPA attack if the adversary doesn't know the random number r of each trapdoor.*

Proof. Assume the adversary known a set of plaintext-ciphertext pairs plaintext, for each query vector Q, will be encrypted $\widetilde{Q} = \left(M_1^{-1}Q', M_2^{-1}Q''\right)$ with M_1 and M_2. And then calculated with index $\widetilde{D} = \left(M_1^T D_1', M_2^T D''\right)$ as follows:

$$
\begin{aligned}
\widetilde{D} \cdot \widetilde{Q} &= \left(M_1^T D', M_2^T D''\right) \cdot \left(M_1^{-1}Q', M_2^{-1}Q'\right) \\
&= M_1^T D' \cdot M_1^{-1}Q' + M_2^T D'' \cdot M_2^{-1}Q' \\
&= \left(M_1^T\right)^T D' \cdot M_1^{-1}Q' + \left(M_2^T\right)^T D'' \cdot M_2^{-1}Q' \\
&= (D')^T Q' + (D'')^T Q'' \\
&= r \left(D \cdot Q + \sum_{i=1}^{V} \varepsilon_i - \sum_{i=1}^{m} b_i\right)
\end{aligned}
\tag{7}
$$

If the adversary can get the plaintext of the query vector Q, there are $(n + U + 2)$ (i.e. r and $(n + U + 1)$-dimensional index vector D) unknowns in Eq. (7). If the random number r in each query vector are all the same, the adversary can get the $(n + U + 2)$ unknowns through establish $(n+U+2)$ equalities. However, in the MRSE scheme with noise, the random number r in each query vector are randomly generated. Therefore, there are $(2n + 2U + 3)$ unknowns $((n + U + 2)\, r$ and $(n + U + 1)$-dimensional $D)$ in the $(n + U + 2)$ equalities established by the adversary. Therefore, even if the adversary knows the plaintext of the $(n + u + 2)$ query vectors and the corresponding inner calculation results, the index vector D also cannot be recovered. Similarly, if the adversary has get a set of plaintext-ciphertext pairs of index vectors, it is also impossible to recover the query vector. The proof process is similar to the above, and will not be repeated.

6.4 Unlinkability of Trapdoors

The unlinkability of trapdoors means that the trapdoors generated by any two queries should be different, even if the keywords of the two queries are exactly the same. In TrapdoorGen, random numbers r and t are to ensure the randomness of the trapdoor. Even if the keywords of the two queries are exactly the same, the random numbers generated in the two trapdoor are almost impossible to be the same. Therefore, the unlinkability of trapdoor can be achieved.

7 Performance Evaluation

For evaluate our scheme, we implemented it in Java. Data owner and all search users' code be implemented on a desktop computer with a single Intel(R) Core(TM) i7-8565U 1.99GHz CPU, 8 GB RAM, Lenovo Air 13IWL 500G running Windows 10. The server's code be implemented on a Lenovo server which has Intel(R) Xeon(R) E5-2620 2.10 GHZ CPU, 16 GB RAM, 256SSD, 1 TB mechanical hard disk running on the Ubuntu 18.04 operating system.

7.1 Dataset

We evaluated the performance of our scheme using the well-known Enron email dataset [24]. This dataset contains email data from more than 150 users, about 517,413 plaintext files of 429MB. We wrote a code to pro-process these data, including removing irrelevant data, counting the quantitative relationship between keywords and documents, keyword extraction and deduplication, and so on. Finally, we extracted 160,097 keywords 7,082,725 document/keyword pairs.

Figure 3 illustrates the relationship between keywords and documents in the inverted index view. From Fig. 3, we can see that only a small number of documents contain many keywords, and most documents contain no more than 100 keywords. Therefore, it can be inferred that most search will not return a large number of ciphertext documents.

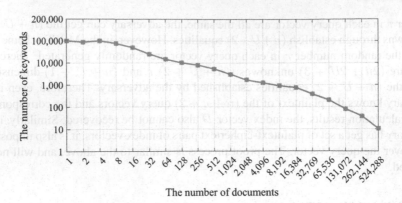

The number of documents

Fig. 3. The statistical information of Enron email dataset

7.2 Computation Overhead

As shown in Fig. 4, this figure fully demonstrates the computation overhead between our proposed scheme and the TDSC'18 scheme. This results show that our proposed scheme has great advantages in the Auth, Search and Verify. The computation of the verification is all focused on the local search user and its power is limited, so the computation overhead is particularly important for the whole query process. Figure 4(f) reflect our proposed scheme VPSearch+'s advantage in the verification process. It can be seen from the figure that the computation overhead of the verification of VPSearch+ and [18] is positively correlated with the number of documents, but obviously, the verification overhead of VPSearch+ is much smaller.

7.3 Storage Overhead

The storage overhead of VPSearch+ is mainly includes three entities: data owner, search user and cloud server. A comparison of VPSearch+ with TDSC'18 [18] as shown in Table 1. As can be seen from Table 1, in our proposed scheme, the search user does not need to have any storage overhead for the outsourced documents and their labels locally.

Table 1. Storage overhead

Scheme	Data Owner	Search User	Cloud Server
[18]	$O(2n^2 + n + N)$	$O(2n^2 + n + N)$	$O(2n + 2N)$
VPSearch+	$O(2n^2 + n)$	$O(2n^2 + n)$	$O(2n + 2N)$

n is the size of keyword dictionary, N is the number of document.

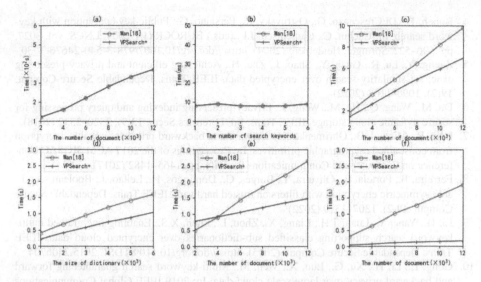

Fig. 4. Computation overhead. (a) Comparison with IndexBuild time. (b) Comparison with TrapdoorGen time. (c) Comparison with index Auth time. (d) Comparison with Auth time. (e) Comparison with Search time. (f) Comparison with Verify time.

8   Conclusion

Designing verifiable searchable encryption is very important for privacy-preserving data outsourcing. In this paper, we designed a verifiable privacy-preserving multi-keyword searchable encryption scheme. VPSearch+ utilized the symmetric-key hidden vector encryption technique to achieve its verifiability, and without storing any the outsourced data or its label locally, radically reducing the storage costs of the search user client in the verifiable SE scheme. Security analysis shows that the scheme can achieve multi-keyword search while ensuring the verifiability and the privacy protection of index and trapdoor. Finally, the experimental results show that the authorization and verification process of our proposed scheme is efficient.

Acknowledgements. This work was partially supported by CAAC Security Capacity Building Project (AQNL2021RJS02).

References

1. Ren, K., Wang, C., Wang, Q.: Security challenges for the public cloud. IEEE Internet Comput. **16**(1), 69–73 (2012)
2. Gentry, C.: Fully homomorphic encryption using ideal lattices. In: Proceedings of the Forty-First Annual ACM Symposium on Theory of Computing, pp. 169–178 (2009)
3. Song, D.X., Wagner, D., Perrig, A.: Practical techniques for searches on encrypted data. In: Proceedings of S&P, pp. 44–55. IEEE (2000)

4. Boneh, D., Di Crescenzo, G., Ostrovsky, R., Persiano, G.: Public key encryption with keyword search. In: Cachin, C., Camenisch, J.L. (eds.) EUROCRYPT 2004. LNCS, vol. 3027, pp. 506–522. Springer, Heidelberg (2004). https://doi.org/10.1007/978-3-540-24676-3_30
5. Zheng, Y., Lu, R., Guan, Y., Shao, J., Zhu, H.: Achieving efficient and privacy-preserving exact set similarity search over encrypted data. IEEE Trans. Dependable Secure Comput. 19(2), 1090–1103 (2022)
6. Du, M., Wang, Q., He, M., Weng, J.: Privacy-preserving indexing and query processing for secure dynamic cloud storage. IEEE Trans. Inf. Forensics Secur. 13(9), 2320–2332 (2018)
7. Bost, R., Minaud, B., Ohrimenko, O.: Forward and backward private searchable encryption from constrained cryptographic primitives. In: Proceedings of the 2017 ACM SIGSAC Conference on Computer and Communications Security, pp. 1465–1482 (2017)
8. Ferreira, B., Portela, B., Oliveira, T., Borges, G., Domingos, H., Leitao, J.: Boolean searchable symmetric encryption with filters on trusted hardware. IEEE Trans. Dependable Secure Comput. 19(2), 1307–1319 (2022)
9. Li, H., Yang, Y., Luan, T.H., Liang, X., Zhou, L., Shen, X.S.: Enabling fine-grained multi-keyword search supporting classified sub-dictionaries over encrypted cloud data. IEEE Trans. Dependable Secure Comput. (2015). https://doi.org/10.1109/TDSC.2015.2406704
10. Gong, L., Li, H., Xu, G., Luo, X., Wen, M.: Multi-keyword search guaranteeing forward and backward privacy over large-scale cloud data. In: 2019 IEEE Global Communications Conference (GLOBECOM), pp. 1–6 (2019)
11. Lai, S., et al.: Result pattern hiding searchable encryption for conjunctive queries. In: Proceedings of the 2018 ACM SIGSAC Conference on Computer and Communications Security (2018)
12. Boneh, D., Waters, B.: Conjunctive, subset, and range queries on encrypted data. In: Vadhan, S.P. (ed.) TCC 2007. LNCS, vol. 4392, pp. 535–554. Springer, Heidelberg (2007). https://doi.org/10.1007/978-3-540-70936-7_29
13. Cao, N., Wang, C., Li, M., Ren, K., Lou, W.: Privacy-preserving multi-keyword ranked search over encrypted cloud data. IEEE Trans. Parallel Distrib. Syst. 25(1), 222–233 (2014)
14. Li, H., Liu, D., Dai, Y., Luan, T.H., Shen, X.S.: Enabling efficient multi-keyword ranked search over encrypted mobile cloud data through blind storage. IEEE Trans. Emerg. Top. Comput. 3(1), 127–138 (2014)
15. Bost, R., Fouque, P.-A., Pointcheval, D.: Verifiable dynamic symmetric searchable encryption: optimality and forward security. Cryptology ePrint Archive (2016)
16. Fiore, D., Gennaro, R., Pastro, V.: Efficiently verifiable computation on encrypted data. In: Proceedings of the 2014 ACM SIGSAC Conference on Computer and Communications Security, pp. 844–855 (2014)
17. Liu, Z., Li, T., Li, P., Jia, C., Li, J.: Verifiable searchable encryption with aggregate keys for data sharing system. Futur. Gener. Comput. Syst. 78, 778–788 (2018)
18. Wan, Z., Deng, R.H.: VPSearch: achieving verifiability for privacy-preserving multi-keyword search over encrypted cloud data. IEEE Trans. Dependable Secure Comput. 15(6), 1083–1095 (2018)
19. Mathiyalahan, S., Manivannan, S., Nagasundaram, M., Ezhilarasie, R.: Data integrity verification using MPT (Merkle Patricia Tree) in cloud computing. Int. J. Eng. Technol. 7(2.24), 500–503 (2018)
20. Zhang, Z., Wang, J., Wang, Y., Su, Y., Chen, X.: Towards efficient verifiable forward secure searchable symmetric encryption. In: Sako, K., Schneider, S., Ryan, P.Y.A. (eds.) ESORICS 2019. LNCS, vol. 11736, pp. 304–321. Springer, Cham (2019). https://doi.org/10.1007/978-3-030-29962-0_15
21. Ge, X., et al.: Towards achieving keyword search over dynamic encrypted cloud data with symmetric-key based verification. IEEE Trans. Dependable Secure Comput. 18(1), 490–504 (2021)

22. Jiang, X., Yu, J., Yan, J., Hao, R.: Enabling efficient and verifiable multi-keyword ranked search over encrypted cloud data. Inf. Sci. **403**, 22–41 (2017)
23. Lin, W., Wang, K., Zhang, Z., Chen, H.: Revisiting security risks of asymmetric scalar product preserving encryption and its variants. In: 2017 IEEE 37th International Conference on Distributed Computing Systems (ICDCS), pp. 1116–1125. IEEE (2017)
24. Cohen, W.W.: Enron email dataset (2005). Internet: https://www.cs.cmu.edu/enron/. Accessed 25 May 2008

Security-Enhanced Function Privacy Attribute-Based Encryption

Xinmin Li[✉], Leyou Zhang, and Xuanyang Hou

School of Mathematics and Statistics, Xidian University, Xi'an 710071, China
21071212629@stu.xidian.edu.cn

Abstract. Attribute-based encryption is the extension of identity-based encryption. It associates ciphertext and user private key with attributes to flexibly represent access structure to achieve fine-grained access control. However, at present, most ABE schemes focus on data privacy protection, while ignoring the user's private key, which is an important part of privacy disclosure. Based on the concept of function privacy of IBE, the definition of function privacy attribute-based encryption is given. Additionally, through the analysis of the well known fuzzy identity encryption scheme, we show why the existing work does not support function privacy. To achieve the function privacy, this paper shows how to use "extract-add-combine" to transform the existing work to an security-enhanced scheme. We also present the security proof of the modified scheme.

Keywords: attribute-based encryption · function privacy · fuzzy identity-based encryption

1 Introduction

With the prosperity of cloud technology, more and more local users choose to encrypt local important data and store it to the remote cloud to realize data sharing for specific user group. However, there are many uncontrollable factors in this storage method. How to ensure the privacy of encrypted data and realize function privacy when malicious users steal the secret key is a very important and challenging work. This requires the scheme to achieve data privacy on the one hand and function privacy on the other.

In identity-based encryption schemes, if the adversary obtains a private key and has already obtained some prior information, such as a small set of users to which the private key belongs. Then the adversary can determine the owner of

This work was supported in part by the National Nature Science Foundation of China under Grant 61872087 and Grant 51875457; in part by the Key Foundation of National Natural Science Foundation of China under Grant U19B2021; and in part by the Key Research and Development Program of Shaanxi under Program 2022GY-028 and Program 2022GY-050.

the private key by sequentially using the user public key in user set to encrypt the message and then testing whether the obtained private key decrypt successfully. To avoid such private keys from compromising user privacy, Boneh et al. [7] proposed function privacy of IBE.

In ABE, the private key no longer matches the user's identity, but is embedded with user's attributes to enable fine-grained access control that matches cloud sharing environment. The local user encrypts the confidential data using ABE so that only users whose attributes embedded in their private keys match the access policy in the ciphertext can perform decryption. If ABE cannot support function privacy, then an adversary who steals the private key may learn the attributes embedded in it through some analysis and leak the user privacy. Most existing ABE schemes only focus on data confidentiality and ignore function privacy, an important part of disclosure of user privacy, so we propose a security-enhanced function privacy ABE to avoid such privacy disclosure.

2   Related Work

Identity-based encryption (IBE) [1], which Shamir inventively proposed for the first time in 1984, is where ABE has its roots. Sahai and Waters proposed a fuzzy IBE [2] with choose plaintext security in 2005. In fuzzy IBE, the unique identification in IBE is extended to an attribute set composed of multiple attributes. When using biological information as the unique identification in IBE, there will inevitably be some noise. The biggest advantage of the scheme in [2] is that it has certain error tolerance and can decrypt ciphertext encrypted with slightly different metrics of the same biological characteristic. In addition in [2], Sahai and Waters proposed the concept of attributed-based encryption for the first time. Each user corresponds to a specific set of attributes, which is also the fundamental difference between this scheme and IBE. User ω wants to decrypt the message encrypted with public key of ω', if and only if their attribute sets meet the preset condition under a certain metric. Subsequently, Goyal et al. [3] and Bethencourt et al. [4] proposed two paradigms of ABE, KP-ABE and CP-ABE, respectively.

Shen et al. [5] proposed a predicate encryption that protects predicate privacy, requiring the token not to divulge any information embedded in the query predicate. Agrawal et al. [6] proposed a new UC-style SMIN security definition based on data and functional privacy, and demonstrated that it is extremely secure against a large number of real-world attacks. On the basis of data privacy, Boneh et al. [7] put forward a new concept of function privacy of IBE, which requires that the decryption key associated with the identity cannot reveal any identity-related information, beyond the absolute minimum necessary. Boneh et al. [8] extended the function privacy framework and improved the function privacy of IBE in [7]. Datta et al. [9] proposed a functional privacy scheme in private key setting for inner product function encryption based on prime order group, which achieves the strongest indistinguishability. Brakerski et al. [10] proposed a general transformation that can convert non-function-privacy functional encryption in a variety enough function class into function-privacy functional encryption. Overcome the drawback that some private-key setting function privacy schemes only work with a limited classes of functions(such as inner products) and can only meet a limited degree of function privacy.

Song et al. [11] proposed an ABE in which the attribute audit function and key generation are separated. The key generation center cannot know the user's attributes to protect the user privacy during the key generation process. Lin et al. [12] proposed a multi-user CP-ABE scheme for medical cloud system that allows keyword search. To safeguard patient privacy, it allows users to search in the cloud system using keywords. Zuo et al. [13] proposed a blockchain based CP-ABE scheme for cloud data security sharing. The scheme does not rely on any trusted third party and records the user's behavior on a tamper-proof blockchain. Li et al. [14] proposed a CP-ABE scheme that uses policy hiding to hide the attributes in the access policy, which protects the data confidentiality of cloud IoT and user privacy. Aiming at the function privacy, user input privacy and calculation correctness of the cloud involved in outsourced computing, Song et al. [15] use homomorphic encryption and other technologies to realize the input and function privacy of matrix functions.

3   Preliminaries

Definition 1. *Min-entropy [7]: Let $H_\infty(X) = -log(max_x Pr[X = x])$ be the minimum-entropy of X, where X is a random variable.*

Definition 2. *k-source [7]: A random variable X is called $k-source$, if $H_\infty(X) \geq k$. A T-dimensional random variable $Y = (Y_1, Y_2, \cdots, Y_T)$ is called $(k_1, \cdots, k_T) - source$ [7], if each component Y_i of Y is $k_i - source$. That is, $H_\infty(Y_i) \geq k_i$ is required when each component appears as a variable alone. A T-dimensional random variable Y is called $(T, k) - block - source$ [7], if for each $i \in [T]$ and under the condition $\{Y_k = y_k\}_{k \in [1 \cdots i-1]}$, Y_k is $k-source$.*

Definition 3. *Universal Hashing [7]: F is the set of functions $f : D_1 \rightarrow D_2$, where f is hash function and $|D_1| > |D_2|$. If*

$$\Pr_{f \leftarrow F, \forall a \neq b \in D_1} [f(a) = f(b)] = \frac{1}{|D_2|}$$

then F is called the universal hashing.

Definition 4. *Statistical distance [16]: For two random variable X_1 and X_2 defined on a finite field $\mathscr{F}$, the statistical distance between X_1 and X_2 defined on $\mathscr{F}$ is*

$$SD(X_1, X_2) = \frac{1}{2} \Sigma_{x \in \mathscr{F}} |Pr[X_1 = x] - Pr[X_2 = x]|$$

Lemma 1. *If F is a universal hashing as defined above, $Y = (Y_1, \cdots, Y_T)$ is a $(T, k) - block - source(k \geq log|D_2| + 2log(\frac{1}{\epsilon}) + \Theta(1))$ random variable, then the distribution $(F_1, F_1(Y_1), \cdots, F_T, F_T(Y_T))_{(F_1, \cdots, F_T) \leftarrow F^T}$ and uniform distribution on $(F \times D_2)^T$ is ϵT-close.*

Lemma 2. *If F is a universal hashing as defined above, $\boldsymbol{Y} = (Y_1, \cdots . Y_T)$ is a $(k_1, \cdots, k_T) - source(k_i \geq i \cdot log|D_2| + 3log(\frac{1}{\epsilon}) + \Theta(1))$ random variable, then the distribution $(F_1, F_1(Y_1), \cdots, F_T, F_T(Y_T))_{(F_1, \cdots, F_T) \leftarrow F^T}$ and uniform distribution on $(F \times D_2)^T$ is $2\epsilon T$-close.*

Definition 5. *Real-or-Random function privacy oracle [7](ROR^{FP}): ROR^{FP} takes triple $(mode, msk, I)$ as input, where $mode \in \{real, rand\}$. msk is the master secret key, and $I = (i_1, i_2, \cdots, i_T) \in U^T$, where U is the complete set of attribute. If the mode $= real$, ROR^{FP} will take the attribute vector I as input. If the mode $= random$, ROR^{FP} will randomly select a vector $(i_1, i_2, \cdots, i_T)$ from U^T as input. Then ROR^{FP} invokes the key generation algorithm to generate the key for each component $i_1, i_2, \cdots, i_T$ in the input vector, and finally obtains an attribute private key vector $(sk_{i1}, sk_{i2}, \cdots, sk_{iT})$.*

Definition 6. *Function privacy adversary [7]: $X \in \{(T, k) - block, (k_1, \cdots, k_T)\}$. An adversary that is allowed to interact with the ROR^{FP} for the attribute vector I (each I is an $X-source$) and can obtain a private key vector generated by the ROR^{FP} is called an $X-Source$ function privacy adversary.*

Definition 7. *Data privacy [7]: In an ABE scheme $\prod$ over attribute set U, if there is a negligible value $\epsilon(\lambda)$ for any data private PPT adversary $\mathscr{A}$ such that*

$$Adv_{\prod,A}^{DP}(\lambda) = |Pr[Expt_{DP,\prod,A}^{0}(\lambda) = 1] - Pr[Expt_{DP,\prod,A}^{1}(\lambda) = 1]| \leq \epsilon(\lambda)$$

hold, then $\prod$ is data privacy. $Expt_{DP,\prod,A}^{b}(\lambda)$ $(b \in \{0, 1\})$ is defined:

1. *The adversary $\mathscr{A}$ announces a identity id^* to challenge.*
2. *$Setup(1^\lambda) \rightarrow (pp, msk)$.*
3. *$A^{KeyGen(msk,\cdot)}(1^\lambda, pp) \rightarrow SK$.*
4. *$Enc(id^*, pp, m_b^*) \rightarrow C^*$.*
5. *output b'.*

Let S be the identity set that $\mathscr{A}$ asked for the private key in step 3. If there is no $id \in S$ such that $|id \cap id^*| \geq d$, output b', otherwise output $\perp$.

Definition 8. *Function privacy [7]: For $X \in \{(T, k) - block, (k_1, \cdots, k_T)\}$. In an ABE scheme $\prod$, if there is a negligible value $\epsilon(\lambda)$ for any PPT function privacy adversary $\mathscr{A}$*

$$Adv_{\prod,A}^{FP}(\lambda) = |Pr[Expt_{FP,\prod,A}^{real}(\lambda) = 1] - Pr[Expt_{FP,\prod,A}^{random}(\lambda) = 1]| \leq \epsilon(\lambda)$$

holds, then the scheme $\prod$ satisfies statistically $X-Source$ function privacy. $Expt_{FP,\prod,A}^{mode}(\lambda)$ defined below:

1. *$Setup(1^\lambda) \rightarrow (pp, msk)$.*
2. *$A^{ROR^{FP}} \rightarrow b$.*
3. *output b.*

Definition 9. *DBDH assumption [7]: Let G and G_T are two cyclic groups. Both groups have the order of large prime p. $e : G \times G \to G_T$ is a non degenerate computable bilinear mapping. The DBDH assumption is that distribution $(g, g^a, g^b, g^c, e(g,g)^{abc})_{\leftarrow R\{a,b,c\}}$ and distribution $(g, g^a, g^b, g^c, e(g,g)^z)_{\leftarrow R\{a,b,c,z\}}$ are computationally indistinguishable.*

4   System Definition and Security Model

4.1   Formal Definition

$Setup(1^\lambda) \to pp, msk$: Take the security parameter λ as input, output public parameter pp and master secret key msk.

$KeyGen(msk, \omega) \to SK$: Input msk, identity ω, output the private key SK of ω.

$Enc(\omega', pp, m) \to C$: Input ω', pp, and plaintext m, output ciphertext C.

$Dec(SK, pp, C) \to m$: Input SK of ω, pp, and ciphertext C as input, output m if and only if $|\omega \cap \omega'| \geq d$.

4.2   Security Model

Init. The adversary $\mathscr{A}$ declares the identity α he wants to challenge.

Setup. Challenger C runs $setup(1^\lambda)$. Then, C sends the public parameters to $\mathscr{A}$ and keeps the master key.

Phase1. The $\mathscr{A}$ is allowed to query the hash function value of an attribute i in ω, and the corresponding private key of i, with one restriction $|\omega \cap \alpha| \leq d$.

H-queries. The $\mathscr{A}$ queries the hash function value of attribute i, C calculates hash value $h(i)$ and sends $h(i)$ to $\mathscr{A}$.

Secret key queries. The $\mathscr{A}$ queries the secret key extraction. $\mathscr{A}$ sends an attribute i to C, and C sends its corresponding secret key to $\mathscr{A}$.

Phase2. Same as phase 1.

Challenge. $\mathscr{A}$ sends two message m_0, m_1 to challenger, C sends C^* to $\mathscr{A}$.

Guess. $\mathscr{A}$ guesses the value of b, and outputs b'.

5   Why ABE Can Not Support Function Privacy

In this section, we will show why ABE can not support function privacy by analyzing the well-known FIBE [2] and how to transform it into a function privacy FIBE. FIBE has both similarities and differences with traditional IBE. In FIBE, each user is associated with a specific set of attributes, each of which corresponds to an attribute secret key. When the distance between a user with identity ω and a user with identity ω' is within a certain range through some measure, ω can use its own private key to decrypt messages encrypted by $\omega's$ public key, because of the error tolerance of FIBE.

In FIBE, ω is used to represent the user identity, and ω is also used as a set of attributes owned by the user. Each attribute in ω can be regard as a numerical value $i \in U$, and the attribute private key is $D_i = g^{\frac{q(i)}{t_i}}$, where U is the attribute universe, g is a generator of group G, t_i is a master secret key corresponding to i, and $q(i)$ is the value of $q(x)$ when $x = i$. $q(x)$ is a polynomial associated with user. $g^{q(i)}$ can be regarded as mapping an attribute i to an element in G. The mapping process of all attributes can be viewed as a hash function $H : U \rightarrow G$, and the corresponding secret key of each attribute i is $D_i = H(i)^{\frac{1}{t_i}}$. Consider that the adversary asks for ROR^{FP} with a distribute circuit, which samples uniformly distributed attributes. The most significant bit of $e(g^{\frac{1}{t_i}}, H(i))$ is 0. It is obvious that the distribution not only has almost full entropy, but also can be represented by a polynomial size circuit with given common parameters. For $D_i = H(i)^{\frac{1}{t_i}}$, adversary outputs 0, if and only if the most significant bit of $e(g, D_i)$ is 0. Otherwise, the adversary outputs 1. From the properties of bilinear mapping, $e(g, D_i) = e(g, H(i)^{\frac{1}{t_i}}) = e(g^{\frac{1}{t_i}}, H(i))$. The adversary has $\frac{1}{2}$ advantage to select the *real mode* from the *random mode* of ROR Oracle, so this scheme does not meet the function privacy defined above.

The "extract-add-combine" method [7] is used to transform the FIBE without function privacy into one with function privacy. The master secret key generation and public parameter generation in the setup phase of the modified scheme are the same as those in the original scheme. The difference is that a hash function is added in the setup phase of the modified scheme to map an attribute i to an element in G.

The first step is "extract", which is carried out in the key generation phase. Instead of directly generating attribute private key corresponding to the attribute i, the key generation algorithm first uses the randomly selected seed s and applies the strong random extractor to the attribute i to obtain $i_s \overset{def}{=} Ext(i, s)$. The secret key sk_i of the attribute i in the modified scheme consists of the selected seed s and i_s. This step ensures the function privacy of the modified scheme: as long as the attributes are taken from a fully unpredictable distribution, the distribution (s, i_s) is statistically close to the uniform distribution, so (s, i_s) does not reveal any information of i. However, this step may damage the data confidentiality of the original scheme. For example, when the definition of the random extractor is highly non-injective, an adversary with a secret key pair (s, i_s) may find $i \neq i'$ but $Ext(i, s) = Ext(i', s)$. In this case, the same privacy key pair is legal for two different attributes, which is in contradiction with the data privacy of the original scheme. In order to solve this problem, the extractor is required to be at least anti-collision.

The second step is "add", which is carried out in the encryption phase. In the "extract" step, the secret key of original scheme has been changed, and it is related to the seed s that are randomly chosen. The encryption algorithm cannot know the selected seed, so the decryption algorithm is required to successfully decrypt the ciphertext no matter which seed is selected. This problem can be solved by "add" ciphertext components.

The third step is "combine", which is carried out in the decryption phase. Due to the "add" step, the ciphertext is some components related to the seed s. Regardless of the seed used, new decryption algorithm need to be able to join ciphertext components in a specified way and perform correct decryption.

6 Construction of the Function Privacy ABE

6.1 Fuzzy Identity-Based Encryption Supporting Function Privacy

Set security parameter λ, attribute universe U. Let $GroupGen$ be a parameter generation algorithm. λ can be used to determine the size of p, for example p can be taken as λ bit.

Setup: $GroupGen$ takes security parameter 1^λ as input and outputs G, G_T, e, p, g. p is a large prime, G and G_T are two groups of order p, and g is a generator of G. $e : G \times G \to G_T$ is a bilinear map. Set a hash function $H : U \to G^l$ (based on random oracle), which maps each attribute $i \in U$ to G^l. For each $i \in U$, random exponent $t_i \in Z_p^*$ is selected and $T_i = g^{t_i}$ is calculated. The public parameter and master secret key are $pp = (H, g, p, e, \{T_i\}_{i \in U})$ and $msk = (t_i)_{i \in U}$ respectively.

KeyGen: Identity $\omega \subseteq U$ is a set of some attributes. For each attribute $i \in \omega$, $H(i) = (h_{i1}, h_{i2}, \cdots, h_{il}) \in G^l$. An extractor seed $s = (s_{i1}, s_{i2}, \cdots, s_{il}) \in Z_p^l$ is randomly selected. The private key $sk_i = (s, z_i)$ consists of two parts: the seed s and $z_i = (Ext(H(i), s))^{t_i}$, where $Ext(H(i), s) = Ext((h_{i1}, \cdots, h_{il}), (s_{i1}, \cdots, s_{il})) = \prod_{j=1}^l h_{ij}^{s_{ij}}$. The private key of ω is $SK = \{sk_i\}_{i \in \omega}$.

Encrypt: The encryption algorithm takes the public key of ω', public parameter, and plaintext as input. $t \in Z_p^*$ is randomly selected. The definition of the ciphertext with additional fragments is as follows

$$C = (\omega', C_0 = g^t, \{C_{ij} = e(T_i, H(i))^t \cdot m\}_{i \in \omega', j \in [l]})$$

Decrypt: When $|\omega \cap \omega'| \geq d$, ω can use his own private key to decrypt the ciphertext encrypted using $\omega's$ public key. First, choose any subset S of $\omega \cap \omega'$ that contains d elements. Then, the private key and the ciphertext components are combined to compute $D_1 = \prod_{i \in S, j \in [l]} C_{ij}^{s_{ij}}$ and $D_2 = \prod_{i \in S} e(C_0, z_i)$ respectively. Finally, calculate $m = (D_1/D_2)^{(\sum_{i \in S, j \in [l]} s_{ij})^{-1}}$.

Correctness:

$$D_1 = \prod_{i \in S, j \in [l]} C_{ij}^{s_{ij}}$$

$$= \prod_{i \in S, j \in [l]} e(T_i, H(i))^{ts_{ij}} \cdot m^{s_{ij}}$$

$$= \prod_{i \in S, j \in [l]} e(g^{t_i}, h_{ij})^{ts_{ij}} \cdot m^{\sum_{i \in S, j \in [l]} s_{ij}}$$

$$D_2 = \prod_{i \in S} e(C_0, z_i)$$

$$= \prod_{i \in S} e(g^t, (\prod_{j \in [l]} h_{ij}^{s_{ij}})^{t_i})$$

$$= \prod_{i \in S, j \in [l]} e(g^t, h_{ij}^{s_{ij}})^{t_i}$$

$$D_1 / D_2 = m^{\sum_{i \in S, j \in [l]} s_{ij}}$$

Therefore, as long as $\sum_{i \in S, j \in [l]} s_{ij} \neq 0 \ (mod \ p)$(an event which occurs with probability $1 - 1/p$ over the randomness of **KeyGen**), the message can be correctly reconstructed by computing $(D_1 / D_2)^{(\sum_{i \in S, j \in [l]} s_{ij})^{-1}}$.

6.2   Proof of Security

Theorem 1. *If there is an adversary that can break the data privacy of the scheme, a simulator based on random oracle model can be constructed to solve the DBDH assumption with a non-negligible advantage.*

Proof. For each $b \in \{0, 1\}$, define $Expt_0^b$ to be equal to $Expt_{DP,\Pi,A}^b(\lambda)$ in Definition 7, except in the 4th step. In the 4th step of $Expt_0^b$, the challenge ciphertext is $(C_0^*, \{u_{ij}^*\}_{j \in [k]}, \{C_{ij}^*\}_{j \in [k+1,l]})$, where $\{u_{ij}^*\}_{j \in [k]}$ are independently and uniformly distributed elements in G_T. Define $Expt_i^b$ to be equal to $Expt_0^b$. In particular, in $Expt_l^0$ and $Expt_l^1$, C_0^* is chosen uniformly from G, $u_{i1}^*, \cdots, u_{il}^*$ are chosen uniformly from G_T, the view of adversary $\mathscr{A}$ is independent of b. Therefore, $Expt_l^0 = Expt_l^1$. Assume $\mathscr{A}$ can distinguish $Expt_k^b$ and $Expt_{k+1}^b$ for $0 \leq k \leq l-1$ and $b \in \{0, 1\}$ with at least ϵ advantage, then we can construct a simulator $\mathscr{B}$ that sovles the DBDH assumption with at least $\frac{1}{2}\epsilon$ as follows.

Init. Adversary $\mathscr{A}$ announces an identity α to be challenged.

Setup. Simulator $\mathscr{B}$ randomly selects $\tilde{t}_1, \cdots, \tilde{t}_{|U|} \in Z_p^*$. For $i \in \alpha$, $\mathscr{B}$ sets $T_i = g^{\tilde{t}_i}$. For $i \in U - \alpha$, $\mathscr{B}$ sets $T_i = A \cdot g^{\tilde{t}_i}$, which implies $t_i = a + \tilde{t}_i$. Simulator $\mathscr{B}$ sends the public key $PK = \{H, g, p, e, T_1, \cdots, T_{|U|}\}$ to $\mathscr{A}$.

Phase 1. Adversary $\mathscr{A}$ can make oracle and secret key queries for attributes contained in identity γ, requiring that the set overlap between γ and α is less than d.

H-queries. Simulator $\mathscr{B}$ keeps a list H^{list} of triples, $H^{list} = (i, \boldsymbol{h}_i, \boldsymbol{\alpha}_i)$. i is an attribute, $\boldsymbol{h}_i$ is the hash value of i, and $\boldsymbol{\alpha}_i$ is a random vector. Each component in $\boldsymbol{h}_i = (h_{i1}, h_{i2}, \cdots, h_{il})$ is an element in G. Each component in $\boldsymbol{\alpha}_i = (\alpha_{i1}, \alpha_{i2}, \cdots, \alpha_{il})$ is an element in Z_p. Simulator $\mathscr{B}$ replies to the adversary $\mathscr{A}$'s each hash query as follows:

1. If $i \in H^{list}$, simulator $\mathscr{B}$ replies to $\mathscr{A}$ with $H(i) = \boldsymbol{h}_i = (h_{i1}, h_{i2}, \cdots, h_{il})$.
2. If $i \notin H^{list}$ and $i \in \alpha \cap \gamma$, simulator $\mathscr{B}$ samples $\boldsymbol{\alpha}_i \leftarrow Z_p^l$ and computes $h_{i(k+1)} = B \cdot g^{\alpha_{i(k+1)}} = g^b \cdot g^{\alpha_{i(k+1)}}$. Then $\mathscr{B}$ computes other components of $\boldsymbol{h}_i$, $h_{ij} = g^{\alpha_{ij}} (i \in \alpha \cap \gamma, j \in [l] \backslash k+1)$.
3. If $i \notin H^{list}$ and $i \in \gamma - (\alpha \cap \gamma)$, simulator $\mathscr{B}$ samples $\boldsymbol{\alpha}_i \leftarrow Z_p^l$ and computes $h_{ij} = g^{\alpha_{ij}} (i \in \gamma - (\alpha \cap \gamma), j \in [l])$.

Finally $\mathscr{B}$ sends $\boldsymbol{h}_i$ to $\mathscr{A}$ and inserts the new triple into list H^{list}.

Secret Key Queries. When adversary $\mathscr{A}$ queries the secret key of γ, simulator $\mathscr{B}$ performs **H-queries** first to obtain the triple $(i, \boldsymbol{h}_i, \boldsymbol{\alpha}_i)$.

1. If $i \in \alpha \cap \gamma$, $\mathscr{B}$ samples $s_{i1}, s_{i2}, \cdots, s_{il} \leftarrow Z_p$ and computes

$$z_i = B^{\tilde{t}_i s_{i(k+1)}} \cdot g^{\tilde{t}_i s_{i(k+1)} \alpha_{i(k+1)}} \cdot \prod_{j \in [l], j \neq k+1} g^{\tilde{t}_i s_{ij} \alpha_{ij}}$$

2. If $i \in \gamma - (\alpha \cap \gamma)$, $\mathscr{B}$ samples $s_{i1}, s_{i2}, \cdots, s_{il} \leftarrow Z_p$ and computes

$$z_i = \prod_{j=1}^{l} A^{s_{ij} \alpha_{ij}} \cdot \prod_{j=1}^{l} g^{s_{ij} \alpha_{ij} \tilde{t}_i}$$

Then simulator $\mathscr{B}$ calculates $sk_i = (s_{i1}, \cdots, s_{il}, z_i)$ for each $i \in \gamma$, and sends $SK = \{sk_i\}_{i \in \gamma}$ as the secret key for γ to $\mathscr{A}$. The distribution of the private key generated by $\mathscr{B}$ is the same as the original scheme.

Challenge. When adversary $\mathscr{A}$ chooses two plaintext messages m_0^*, m_1^* with the same length, simulator $\mathscr{B}$ tosses a fair coin $b \in \{0, 1\}$ and sets $C_0^* = C$. Next, $\mathscr{B}$ sets $C_{ik+1}^* = Z \cdot e(C^{\tilde{t}_i}, B) e(A \cdot g^{\tilde{t}_i}, C^{\alpha_{i(k+1)}}) \cdot m_b^*$ and $C_{ij}^* = e(A, B)^{\alpha_{ij}} \cdot m_b^*$ ($j \in \{k+2, \cdots, l\}$). Simulator $\mathscr{B}$ returns $C^* = (\alpha, C_0^*, \{C_{ij}^*\}_{i \in \alpha, j \in [l]})$ as challenge ciphertext, where $\{C_{ij}^*\}_{j \in \{1, \cdots, k\}}$ are independently and randomly selected from G_T and $\{C_{ij}^*\}_{j \in \{k+1, \cdots, l\}}$ follows the above calculation procedure.

If Z is a DBDH tuple, $Z = e(g, g)^{abc}$, then

$$C_{ik+1}^* = Z \cdot e(C^{\tilde{t}_i}, B) e(A \cdot g^{\tilde{t}_i}, C^{\alpha_{i(k+1)}}) \cdot m_b^* = e(g, g)^{abc} e(g^{\tilde{t}_i}, g^b)^c e(g^a g^{\tilde{t}_i}, g^{\alpha_{i(k+1)}})^c \cdot m_b^*$$

$$= e(g^a, g^b)^c e(g^{\tilde{t}_i}, g^b)^c e(g^a g^{\tilde{t}_i}, g^{\alpha_{i(k+1)}})^c \cdot m_b^* = (e(g^a g^{\tilde{t}_i}, g^b) e(g^a g^{\tilde{t}_i}, g^{\alpha_{i(k+1)}}))^c \cdot m_b^*$$

$$= (e(g^a g^{\tilde{t}_i}, g^b g^{\alpha_{i(k+1)}}))^c \cdot m_b^* = e(g^{t_i}, h_{ik+1})^t \cdot m_b^*$$

$(C_0^*, C_{i1}^*, \cdots, C_{il}^*)_{i \in \alpha, j \in [l]}$ is identically distributed to the challenge in $Expt_i^b$. If Z is a random 4-tuple, $(C_0^*, C_{i1}^*, \cdots, C_{il}^*)_{i \in \alpha, j \in [l]}$ is identically distributed to the challenge in $Expt_{i+1}^b$.

Guess. Adversary $\mathscr{A}$ guesses the value of b. If $b' = b$, $\mathscr{B}$ will guess that it is getting a DBDH tuple. If $b' \neq b$, $\mathscr{B}$ will guess that it is getting a random 4-tuple. Define event P as the simulator is given a DBDH tuple and event $\bar{P}$ as the simulator is given a random 4-tuple.

In the case where simulator is given a random 4-tuple, adversary $\mathscr{A}$ gains no information about b. Therefore, $Pr[b = b'|\bar{P}] = \frac{1}{2}$. In the case where simulator is given a DBDH tuple, the adversary $\mathscr{A}$ is given an is given a well-formed ciphertext, and in this case $\mathscr{A}$ has the advantage of ϵ as defined. Therefore, $Pr[b = b'|P] = \frac{1}{2} + \epsilon$. The overall advantage of $\mathscr{B}$ is

$$\frac{1}{2} Pr[b = b'|\bar{P}] + \frac{1}{2} Pr[b = b'|P] - \frac{1}{2} = \frac{1}{2}\epsilon$$

6.3   Proof of Function Privacy

Lemma 3. *The proposed scheme satisfies the statistical function privacy in the random oracle model for* $X \in \{(T, k) - block, (k1, \cdots, k_T)\}$.

Proof. Let variable $X \in \{(T, k) - block, (k1, \cdots, k_T)\}$. Supposing $\mathscr{A}$ is a computationally unbounded $X-source$ function privacy adversary, it is allowed to query the $Real - or - Random$ function privacy oracle ROR^{FP} with number of polynomial time $Q_{ROR}(\lambda)$. It can be proved that the distribution of the experiment $Expt_{FP,A}^{real}$ and the distribution of the experiment $Expt_{FP,A}^{random}$ are statistically close from the perspective of $\mathscr{A}$. That is, the two are computationally indistinguishable from the perspective of $\mathscr{A}$. $View_{real}$ and $View_{random}$ are used to represent the distribution that $\mathscr{A}$ can get in the two cases.

The hash function $H : U \rightarrow G^l$ is modeled as a random oracle, so the distribution above can be limited to the condition that the hash function in the attribute space is injective. For $\boldsymbol{I} \in U^T$, $H(\boldsymbol{I}) \overset{def}{=} (H(i_1), \cdots, H(i_T))$. The restriction H is injective, which ensures that any $X-source$ $\boldsymbol{I} = (i_1, \cdots, i_T) \in U^T$ mapped by H is $X-Source$ over $(G^l)^T$.

Define $\boldsymbol{I} = (i_1, \cdots, i_T)$ is an $X-source$ random variable, and $\mathscr{A}$ uses this vector to query the function privacy oracle machine ROR^{FP}. Then $\mathscr{A}$ can get

$$View_{mode} = ((s_{11}, \cdots, s_{1l}, (\prod_{j=1}^{l} h_{1j}^{s_{1j}})), \cdots, (s_{T1}, \cdots, s_{Tl}, (\prod_{j=1}^{l} h_{Tj}^{s_{Tj}})))$$

where $mode \in \{real, rand\}$, $s_{ij} \leftarrow Z_p$. If the $mode$ of the ROR^{FP} is $real$, $\mathscr{A}$ obtains the real private key vector of $\boldsymbol{I}$. If the $mode$ of the ROR^{FP} is $random$, $\mathscr{A}$ obtains the secret key vector corresponding to an attribute vector randomly and uniformly selected by the oracle machine from the attribute universe U. The distribution of the two modes of *mode* can be proved that it is statistically close to the uniform distribution.

Function set $\{f_{s1,\cdots,sl} : G^l \rightarrow G\}_{s1,\cdots,sl \in Z_p}$ is a universal hashsing, where function is defined as $f_{s1,\cdots,sl}(h_1,\cdots,h_l) = \prod_{j=1}^{l} h_j^{s_j}$. By lemma1 and lemma2, it can be obtained that the statistical distance between $View_{real}$ and uniform distribution is negligible under the security parameter λ. Because the uniform distribution on the attribute universe U is $(T,k) - block - source$ and $(k_1,\cdots,k_T) - source$, the statistical distance between $View_{random}$ and uniform distribution is negligible. Therefore, the *real* and *random* modes of the ROR^{FP} are computationally indistinguishable from the perspective of $\mathscr{A}$. So

$$|Pr[Expt_{FP,\Pi,A}^{real}(\lambda) = 1] - Pr[Expt_{FP,\Pi,A}^{random}(\lambda) = 1]| \leq v(\lambda)$$

is established, and the scheme meets the statistical function privacy.

Table 1. Time overhead comparison.

Scheme	Setup	KeyGen	Enc	Dec
Modified scheme	$\|U\|E$	$l\|\omega'\|E$	$l\|\omega'\|P + (l\|\omega'\| + 1)E$	$l\|S\|E + \|S\|P$
Original scheme	$\|U\|E + P$	$\|\omega\|E$	$(\|\omega'\| + 1)E$	$\|S\|P$

Table 2. Functional Comparison

Scheme	Setting mode	Data Privacy	Function Privacy	Complexity Assumption
[9]	Private-key setting	Full	Full	SXDH
[17]	Public-key setting	Selective	×	q-DPBDHE2
[18]	Public-key setting	Selective	×	q-GDH
Our scheme	Public-key setting	Selective	Statistical	DBDH

7   Comparison

Compared with the time cost of the original scheme [2], we find that the modified scheme only performs exponential operation in the setup phase, and the operating cost at this stage is reduced compared to the original scheme. However, due to the addition of some "ciphertext fragments" to achieve function privacy, the modified scheme adds other costs than the original scheme at other stages.

Table 1 gives specific comparison result. $|*|$ indicates the number of elements in a set, ω and ω' indicate the user identity, S represents the intersection of ω and ω, U represents the complete set of system attributes, and E and P represent the time cost of exponential and pair operation, respectively.

In addition to comparing with the scheme before modification, we also compare the proposed scheme with three other schemes. The scheme in [9] achieves full function privacy in the private-key setting and full security data privacy is achieved. ABE schemes in [17] and [18] can achieve selective security of data but do not support function privacy. The proposed scheme can achieve selective security of data and statistical function privacy in public-key setting. Table 2 demonstrates the comparison of the four schemes.

8   Conclusion

The current society attaches more and more importance to privacy protection, which requires the scheme to meet not only data confidentiality but also function privacy. In this paper, the concept of statistical function privacy attribute-based encryption is presented. "extract-add-combine" is used to transform the non function privacy scheme FIBE into a function privacy scheme. The proposed scheme supports statistical function privacy in the public-key setting, which requires that the entropy of the distribution to which the private key is belongs must be greater than a predetermined minimum entropy, that is, the function privacy in public-key setting is greatly limited. Function privacy in private-key setting does not require such a precondition. In the future work, we hope to weaken the prerequisite restriction of function privacy in the public-key setting as much as possible, and achieve a more optimized compromise between the security and efficiency of the scheme.

References

1. Shamir, A.: Identity-based cryptosystems and signature schemes. In: Blakley, G.R., Chaum, D. (eds.) CRYPTO 1984. LNCS, vol. 196, pp. 47–53. Springer, Heidelberg (1985). https://doi.org/10.1007/3-540-39568-7_5
2. Sahai, A., Waters, B.: Fuzzy identity-based encryption. In: Cramer, R. (ed.) EURO-CRYPT 2005. LNCS, vol. 3494, pp. 457–473. Springer, Heidelberg (2005). https://doi.org/10.1007/11426639_27
3. Goyal, V., Pandey, O., Sahai, A., Waters, B.: Attribute-based encryption for fine-grained access control of encrypted data. In: Proceedings of the 13th ACM Conference on Computer and Communications Security, Alexandria, Virginia, USA, pp. 89–98. Association for Computing Machinery (2006)
4. Bethencourt, J., Sahai, A., Waters, B.: Ciphertext-policy attribute-based encryption. In: 2007 IEEE Symposium on Security and Privacy (SP 2007), Berkeley, CA, USA, pp. 321–334. IEEE (2007)
5. Shen, E., Shi, E., Waters, B.: Predicate privacy in encryption systems. In: Reingold, O. (ed.) TCC 2009. LNCS, vol. 5444, pp. 457–473. Springer, Heidelberg (2009). https://doi.org/10.1007/978-3-642-00457-5_27

6. Agrawal, S., Agrawal, S., Badrinarayanan, S., Kumarasubramanian, A., Prabhakaran, M., Sahai, A.: Functional encryption and property preserving encryption: new definitions and positive results. Cryptology ePrint Archive
7. Boneh, D., Raghunathan, A., Segev, G.: Function-private identity-based encryption: hiding the function in functional encryption. In: Canetti, R., Garay, J.A. (eds.) CRYPTO 2013. LNCS, vol. 8043, pp. 461–478. Springer, Heidelberg (2013). https://doi.org/10.1007/978-3-642-40084-1_26
8. Boneh, D., Raghunathan, A., Segev, G.: Function-private subspace-membership encryption and its applications. In: Sako, K., Sarkar, P. (eds.) ASIACRYPT 2013. LNCS, vol. 8269, pp. 255–275. Springer, Heidelberg (2013). https://doi.org/10.1007/978-3-642-42033-7_14
9. Datta, P., Dutta, R., Mukhopadhyay, S.: Functional encryption for inner product with full function privacy. In: Cheng, C.-M., Chung, K.-M., Persiano, G., Yang, B.-Y. (eds.) PKC 2016. LNCS, vol. 9614, pp. 164–195. Springer, Heidelberg (2016). https://doi.org/10.1007/978-3-662-49384-7_7
10. Brakerski, Z., Segev, G.: Function-private functional encryption in the private-key setting. J. Cryptol. **31**, 202–225 (2018)
11. Song, Y., Wang, H., Wei, X., Wu, L.: Efficient attribute-based encryption with privacy-preserving key generation and its application in industrial cloud. Secur. Commun. Netw. (2019)
12. Lin, H.Y., Jiang, Y.R.: A multi-user ciphertext policy attribute-based encryption scheme with keyword search for medical cloud system. Appl. Sci. **11**(1), 63 (2020)
13. Zuo, Y., Kang, Z., Xu, J., Chen, Z.: BCAS: a blockchain-based ciphertext-policy attribute-based encryption scheme for cloud data security sharing. Int. J. Distrib. Sens. Netw. **17**(3), 1–16 (2021)
14. Li, J., Zhang, Y., Ning, J., Huang, X., Poh, G.S.: Attribute based encryption with privacy protection and accountability for CloudIoT. IEEE Trans. Cloud Comput. **10**(2), 762–773 (2022)
15. Song, B., Zhou, D., Wu, J., Yuan, X., Zhu, Y., Wang, C.: Protecting function privacy and input privacy in the publicly verifiable outsourcing computation of polynomial functions. Future Internet **15**(4), 1–19 (2023)
16. Håstad, J., Impagliazzo, R., Levin, L.A., Luby, M.: A pseudorandom generator from any one-way function. SIAM J. Comput **28**(1999), 1364–1396 (1999)
17. Huang, K.Q.: Online/offline revocable multi-authority attribute-based encryption for edge computing. In: 2020 12th International Conference on Measuring Technology and Mechatronics Automation (ICMTMA), Phuket, Thailand, pp. 563–568. IEEE (2020)
18. Sethia, D., Sahu, R., Yadav, S., Kumar, R.: Attribute revocation in ECC-based CP-ABE scheme for lightweight resource-constrained devices. In: 2021 International Conference on Communication, Control and Information Sciences (ICCISc), Idukki, India, pp. 1–6. IEEE (2021)

Certificateless Ring Signcryption Scheme with Conditional Privacy Protection in Smart Grid

Shuanggen Liu[✉][iD], Zhentao Liu[iD], Jueqin Liang[iD], Wanju Zhang[iD], and Zirong Heng[iD]

School of Cyberspace Security, Xi'an University of Posts and Telecommunications, Shaanxi, China
liushuanggen201@xupt.edu.cn

Abstract. In the context of smart grids, bidirectional transmission of electricity information enables real-time electricity generation tailored to consumer needs. However, ensuring user privacy during data collection has emerged as a significant concern with the proliferation of data collection and transmission capabilities. Existing solutions such as group signature and pseudonym systems have limitations, such as lack of trustworthiness in group signature administrators and increased system costs associated with pseudonym storage. To address these drawbacks, this paper proposes a certificateless ring signcryption scheme with conditional privacy protection based on the SM2 algorithm. The scheme efficiently enables users to ring signcryption transmitted messages, thereby concealing the sender's identity from the message receiver. This approach resolves the privacy concerns mentioned earlier. In addition, tracking algorithm and batch verification algorithm have been designed to improve computational efficiency while also providing the ability for trusted parties to track malicious users. This scheme achieves conditional privacy preservation while avoiding substantial storage costs for power resources. Compared to the latest available programmes, our proposed scheme offers enhanced efficiency and lower communication costs. It represents a novel and effective solution for privacy protection in smart grids, ensuring secure data transmission while minimizing system overhead.

Keywords: Conditional privacy preservation · Smart grid · SM2 algorithm · Certificateless ring signcryption · Traceability · Batch verification

1 Introduction

Smart Grids (SG) provide electricity in a more reliable, efficient and secure way, more economical, more efficient and more future-proof than traditional grids. SG sends information through the smart grid system to the power control centre,

Supported by National Natural Science Foundation of China under Grant.

which processes the information upon receipt, obtains customer-specific data and controls the transmission of electricity to the customer. In this process, the communication between the smart meter and the power control centre (CC) is bidirectional. If attackers disguise themselves as legitimate customers and transmit malicious information to a service node, they can disrupt the normal operation of the SG and cause damage. In addition, a proliferation of users in the SG can cause response delays, degrade the quality of service and increase the computational pressure on central resources. Therefore, it is a key issue for SG to effectively address the problem of tracking down malicious users while ensuring the confidentiality and integrity of their private data when communicating with each other between users and service nodes.

Privacy issues in smart grids are divided into two main areas: data privacy and user privacy. The main solutions for protecting user identity privacy include adding pseudonyms, group signatures, and ring signatures. Among these three approaches, adding pseudonyms results in excessive storage requirements and high communication latency. In group signatures, fairness of the administrator needs to be guaranteed; otherwise, the anonymity of the signature may be compromised. Ring signatures are more suitable than the other two methods due to their unique characteristics for it.

The concept of ring signcryption proposed in the paper [1] is an improvement on ring signatures, making ring signatures and encryption simultaneous, disguising the efficiency. Since then, more and more ring signcryption schemes have been proposed. They are mainly based on elliptic curves and improve computational efficiency by reducing the number of bilinear pairs or simplifying the algorithm.

In traditional Public Key Infrastructure (PKI) based ring signcryption schemes, it is assumed that the PKI is a trusted authority (TRA) that generates and distributes keys for all members of the scheme through a certificate mechanism. However, if the PKI is compromised, the security of the information becomes questionable, raising concerns about key security. Therefore, it is essential to design the scheme in a way that addresses these issues while retaining the advantages of an identity-based scheme. To meet this requirement, we introduce a certificateless ring signcryption(CLRSC) scheme based on certificateless public key cryptography, where the user's private key consists of a partial private key generated by the secret key generation center (KGC) and a secret value chosen by the user.

The SM2 encryption algorithm is one of the public key encryption algorithms based on elliptic curve cryptography. It is widely used due to its high speed and security. Various SM2-based encryption and signature algorithms are currently used in various fields. The scheme is more secure than traditional public key encryption of the same length and does not require bilinear pairs, making encryption simpler and more suitable for various encryption scenarios.

To solve the aforementioned problems, we propose certificateless ring signcryption scheme for CPPA using the SM2 algorithm and ring signcryption. Specifically, this paper has four main contributions:

1. First, based on the SM2 algorithm, we propose a certificateless ring signcryption scheme with conditional privacy protection authentication (CPPA) functionality in SG, addressing the privacy protection of users.
2. Second, to prevent malicious users from causing damage to the smart grid, we propose a traceable algorithm for tracking malicious users. This algorithm does not require additional stored information but simply reports this information to a trusted third party (TRA) when a malicious user is found, thus completing the tracking process.
3. Third, the scheme is resistant to both internal and external adversary attacks through a certificateless component, and its security is fully proven using a stochastic metaphorical machine model. The scheme is ensured to be more secure compared to other schemes.
4. Finally, the efficiency analysis shows that the scheme proposed in this paper not only reduces the communication cost, but also improves the computational efficiency compared with other schemes. At the same time, we have added more functions that are more suitable for smart grid than existing solutions.

2   Related Works

In recent years, privacy protection in the smart grid has been extensively discussed and researched by scholars worldwide, leading to significant progress in the field. The concept of "smart grid" was first proposed by the Electric Power Research Institute (EPRI) in 2001. In 2016, Tan et al. [2] divided the data cycle of the smart grid into four phases: data generation, data collection, data storage, and data processing. They discussed and analyzed the security vulnerabilities and solutions in each phase and highlighted future research directions in the smart grid domain. Subsequent researchers have proposed various solutions to address privacy protection issues in the smart grid.

For example, in 2017, Morello et al. [3] introduced the development trends of the smart grid and elaborated on research directions that can enhance its security. Ferrag et al. [4] conducted a comprehensive survey in 2018, focusing on privacy protection schemes in smart grids released between 2013 and 2017. They classified these schemes into different categories and provided suggestions for further research.

In 2019, Gai et al. [5] proposed a data sharing method that combines blockchain and edge computing technologies to address privacy protection and energy security in the smart grid. In the same year, they also proposed a privacy protection scheme utilizing alliance chains in the smart grid [6]. Li et al. made a study of ring signcryption secrets that could be verified in batch. Kumar et al. [7] summarized and classified real network attack events in traditional power grids and presented new research ideas for the future of the smart grid. Guan et al. [8] proposed an efficient communication scheme for data privacy in the smart grid without relying on a trusted center. Kong et al. [9] proposed a group blind signature scheme with privacy protection for the smart grid.

Researchers have also explored cryptographic algorithms, such as SM2, and applied them to ring signature schemes and signcryption algorithms with multiple characteristics. Ring signatures, which provide spontaneity and unconditional anonymity, are widely used in fields such as email, smart grids, and electronic trading. Ring signatures can be categorized as those under the public key infrastructure system, identity-based ring signatures, and certificateless ring signatures. The concept of the ring signcryption algorithm was first proposed by Huang et al. [10], and subsequent scholars have developed various ring signcryption schemes and applied them in scenarios such as the Internet of Things and the Internet of Vehicles.

In recent years, researchers have proposed several privacy protection schemes applied to SG. Zhang et al. [11] proposed a decentralized privacy protection scheme for SG, while Cai et al. [12] introduced a ring signcryption scheme for VANET (Vehicular Ad hoc Networks) to address privacy protection. Wu et al. [13] proposed an authentication scheme based on the SM2 algorithm for the smart grid, and Guo et al. [19] presented a bilinear pair based certificateless ring signcryption scheme. In the following years, Guo et al. [14] proposed a ring signcryption scheme with tracking function for VANET, and Chakraborty et al. [15] explored potential applications of smart meters in the protection and monitoring of distribution systems.

In 2022, Yu et al. [16,17] constructed two anti-quantum ring signcryption schemes and a ring signcryption scheme based on identity. These schemes contribute to enhancing privacy protection in the smart grid and exploring the potential of quantum-resistant cryptographic techniques.In 2023, Du et al. [21] improved on the ring signcryption scheme proposed by Cai et al. [12].

3   Preliminaries

3.1   Hardness Assumption

Definition 1. *(Elliptic Curve Computational Diffie-Hellman Problem (ECCD-HP)). Given point G is taken as the base point on the finite field of elliptic curve $E(a, b)$, and the value of aP and bP is known. The value of abP cannot be solved effectively in the polynomial time.*

Definition 2. *(Elliptic Curve Discrete Logarithm Problem (ECDLP)). Given any two points P, Q on the elliptic curve $E(a, b)$ in the additive group $(G, +)$ of order q, the value x satisfying the equation $Q = x \cdot P$ is cannot be solved in polynomial time.*

3.2   Formal Definition

The scheme is divided into eight algorithms, which are completed by the following four entities: KGC, TRA, ID_s, ID_r.

1. *Setup*: TRA and KGC to execute the setup process. Inputs the security parameter k, returns the system parameters $params$, master tracking key mtk and master public key mpk.
2. *Set − SV*: User inputs the identity ID_i, and then outputs T_i and a secret value t_i for the user ID_i.
3. *Extract − PSK*: The algorithm input T_i, then, KGC produces the partial private key d_i and d_i for ID_i.
4. *Generate − PK*: After verifying d_i, the user ID_i generates a public-private key pair through d_i and t_i, and exposes the public key PK_i.
5. *Signcryption*: User ID_s executes the signcryption algorithm, and uses $params$, sk_s, PK_r and L to signcrypt the message m.
6. *Verification*: It inputs the ciphertext σ received, and the ring listed L. The algorithm outputs 1 if the signcryption σ is valid, otherwise it outputs 0.
7. *Unsigncryption*: If the verification result is 1. The verifier uses L and sk_r decrypt the σ to get the message m.
8. *Tracking*: When the identity of the signer ID_s needs to be traced, the trusted third party TRA can find the real identity of the signer ID_s through σ and L.

3.3 System Model

This scheme consists of five main entities: Key generation center KGC, trusted authority TRA, control center CC and user.

1. KGC: It is responsible for generating keys for users, regional gateways and power suppliers in the smart grid.
2. TRA: It is responsible for approving power request information from users. When malicious users are found, the tracking algorithm can be used to query the true identity for the malicious users.
3. CC: The verifier in the scheme, responsible for collecting and verifying the received user data, and realizing real-time monitoring, load balancing, billing and pricing functions.
4. User: The signer in the scheme. In the smart grid, the user is usually a smart device, such as a smart meter. $User_i$ sends power consumption data to the control center through the regional gateway.

In this section, the detailed design in smart grid is as follows, and some relevant symbols are shown in Table 1.

3.4 Threat Model

The certificateless ring signcryption mainly faces two main types of attacks. The first type of attacker A_I is one with a malicious user on the ring. This type of attacker unaware the master private key of the system, but can replace the public key of any user when generating the ring signcryption. The second type of attacker A_{II} is a spiteful KGC. The attacker knows the master private key of

Table 1. Notations and meanings

Notations	Meanings
k	The security parameter
q	The order of G
P	The generator of G
G	Additive group on elliptic curve
H_1, H_2, H_3, H_4	Hash functions
mtk	The master trace key of TRA
T_{pub}	The public key of TRA
msk	The master private key of KGC
mpk	The master public key of KGC
ID_i	The real identity of user i
d_i	The partial private key of user ID_i
sk_i	The private key of ID_i
PK_i	The public key of ID_i
m	A power consumption message
L	Public key collection
I	A tracking mark
TS	A timestamp
σ	Encrypted ciphertext

the system, but does not have the ability to replace the public key of any user. We define seven kinds of metaphor machines that can be queried by A_I and A_{II}. The definitions of these seven oracles and their run times are shown below.:

1. Query-H_i: After entering the value to query, output the output corresponding to the hash. The number of runs is q_{H_i}.
2. Query-PSK: For query the partial private key, after entering the ID_i, output the corresponding partial private key psk_i. The number of runs is q_{PSK}.
3. Query-SK: For query the private key, Enter the ID_i of the public key PK_i that has not been replaced to obtain the corresponding private key sk_i. The number of runs is q_{SK}.
4. Query-PK: After entering the ID_i, output the corresponding PK_i. The number of runs is q_{PK}.
5. Replace-PK: C inputs tuple (ID_i, T'), the challenger substitutes T_i with T_i'. The number of runs is q_R.
6. Query-RSC: After entering tuple (ID_r, ID_s, m), C gets the corresponding ciphertext. The number of runs is q_{RSC}.
7. Query-USC: Input tuple (σ, ID_r), C obtains the decrypted ciphertext. The number of runs is q_{USC}.

Definition 3. *If the advantage of opponent C with polynomial time algorithm in Game 1 and Game 2 can be overlooked, the scheme in this paper is security for IND-CLRSC-CCA2.*

Proof. The requirements for A_I success are as follows:

1. A_I cannot query Query-PK of ID_r.
2. A_I cannot query Query-PSK of ID_r, if its public key has been substituted.
3. A_I cannot pair tuple (σ, ID_s, ID_r) perform Query-USC.

Challenge: Coutputs two different messages $m_b(b \in \{0,1\})$ with the same length, signer ID_s and verifier ID_r, forwards them. Challenger random selects $b \in \{0,1\}$ and execute signcryption algorithm with the tuple (m_b, ID_s, ID_r). Then, the challenger sends σ to A_I.

Guess: A_I guessing b' after allow the query is executed adaptively in the query stage. If $b' = b$, A_I win.

The advantages of A_I are as follows:

$$Adv_{A_I}^{IND-CLRSC-CCA2} = Pr[A_I \ wins]$$

Game 2: A_{II} and challenger C play the following games:

Setup: Challenger C, execute the setting algorithm, get *params* and *msk*, and then give them to A_{II}.

Query: A_{II} can implement the query what ware mentioned as above. In addition, the following restrictions must be satisfied:

1. A_{II} carried out Query-SK for ID_r.
2. A_{II} cannot carried out Query-USC for tuple (σ, ID_s, ID_r).

Challenge: A_{II} outputs two different messages with the same length m_0 and m_1, the sender ID_s and the receiver ID_r, then forward them. The challenger C picked a random bit $b \in \{0,1\}$, use the tuple (m_b, ID_s, ID_r) to execute the signal encryption algorithm. Later, σ is sent back to A_{II} by the challenger.

Guess: A_{II} guessing b' after allow the query is executed adaptively in the query stage. If $b' = b$, A_{II} win the Game 2.

The advantages of A_{II} are described as:

$$Adv_{A_{II}}^{IND-CLRSC-CCA2} = Pr[A_{II} \ wins].$$

Definition 4. *CLRSC scheme is security for EUF-CLRSC-CMA2, if the advantage of the polynomial opponent in the Game 3 and Game 4 can be ignored.*

Proof. **Game 3:** A_I and a challenger C play the following games:

Setting: Same as Game 1.

Query: A_I can execute the query of all oracles defined in this stage above. In addition, the following conditions have to be fulfilled.

1. A_I cannot obtain the tuple (σ, m) with the sender ID_s and the receiver ID_r during the Query-RSC.

2. A_I as ID_s cannot execute Query-SK.

If the public key of ID_s has been replaced, A_I cannot query Query-PSK.

Forgery: A_I forwards new tuple (σ, m, ID_r). The challenger C uses tuple (σ, m, ID_r) to run the unsigncryption algorithm, if the algorithm output is absent $\bot$, then A_I will win Game 3.

The advantages of A_I are represented as follows:

$$Adv_{A_I}^{EUF-CLRSC-CMA2} = Pr[A_I \ wins].$$

Game 4: A_{II} and Challenger C play the following games:

Setting: Same as Game 2.

Query: A_{II} can implement the query what ware mentioned as above in this stage. In addition, the following conditions have to be fulfilled.

1. A_{II} cannot carried out Query-RSC for tuple (σ, m) with sender ID_s and receiver ID_r.
2. A_{II} cannot carry out Query-SK for ID_s.

Forgery: A_{II} inputs new tuple (σ, m, ID_r). the challenger C uses tuple (σ, m, ID_r) to runs unsigncryption algorithm, if the algorithm output is absent $\bot$, then A_{II} will win Game 4.

The advantages of A_{II} are described as follows:

$$Adv_{A_{II}}^{EUF-CLRSC-CMA2} = Pr[A_{II} \ wins].$$

3.5   Security Performance

Considering the real situation of smart grid, this proposal should satisfy the following characteristics.

1. Message validation: The ciphertext is secured and not compromised.
2. Traceability: TRA can recover the identity of the malicious sender from the malicious message.
3. Confidentiality. No one can decrypt the ciphertext and obtain the plaintext except the message receiver.
4. Anonymity: Except for TRA, no one can track the sender by analysis of the message transmitted.
5. Replay attack resistance: Assuming that an attacker intercepts the message, analyzes it and resends it after a certain delay, the message will not pass authentication.

4   CPPA Scheme in SG

The implementation process of our proposed scheme is as follows:

1. **Setup**(1^k) $\rightarrow$ ($params, msk, mpk, mtk$): Enter the security parameter k, KGC and TRA to perform the following steps:

(a) The KGC selects $p, q > 2^k$ is a large prime number, F_p is a finite field. Elliptic curve equation $E : y^2 = x^3 + ax + b \bmod p$ is defined on F_p. The points satisfying the equation form an Abelian group marked with G, whose order is q, and P is the base point of group G.

(b) The KGC picks $x \in Z_q^*$ randomly as the master private key msk, computes $P_{pub} = xP$ as the master public key mpk.

(c) The KGC sets security hash functions H_1, H_2, H_3, H_4, where $H_1 : \{0,1\}^* \rightarrow Z_q^*$, $H_2 : G \times G \rightarrow \{0,1\}^l$, $H_3 : \{0,1\}^l \times G \rightarrow Z_q^*$, $H_4 : \{0,1\}^* \rightarrow Z_q^*$. The length of message is l.

(d) The TRA randomly chooses $k \in Z_q^*$, computes $T_{pub} = kP$ as the master track key mtk.

(e) The KGC publishes the system parameters $params = \{p, q, G, P, P_{pub}, T_{pub}, H_1, H_2, H_3, H_4\}$ to all users.

2. **Set** $-$ **SV**$(ID_i) \rightarrow (t_i, T_i)$: User ID_i randomly picks a secret value $t_i \in Z_q^*$ and computes $T_i = t_i P$. And then, sends T_i to the KGC.

3. **Extract** $-$ **PSK**$(params, T_i) \rightarrow (d_i, R_i)$: After receiving T_i, the KGC randomly generates a number $r_i \in Z_q^*$ and computes $R_i = r_i P$, $u_i = H_1(ID_i, T_i, R_i, P_{pub})$, $d_i = r_i + u_i x$, where d_i as the partial private key. Then, KGC publicizes R_i and forwards $D_i = (d_i, R_i)$ to the user ID_i via communication channel.

4. **Generate** $-$ **PK**$(T_i, R_i) \rightarrow (sk_i, PK_i)$: User ID_i acquires D_i and tests the effectiveness of d_i by formulae: $d_i P = R_i + H_1(ID_i, T_i, R_i, P_{pub})P_{pub}$.

If fails, the user will return to the beginning. If the equation is true, user ID_i will obtain part of the private key d_i and set the private key $sk_i = t_i + d_i$ and the public key $PK_i = sk_i P$.

5. **Signcryption**$(params, sk_s, PK_r, L, m) \rightarrow \sigma$: The sender ID_s completes the following steps.

(a) The user ID_s form a ring identity set $L = ID_1, ID_2, \ldots, ID_n$, obtain the corresponding public key of the members in the ring, where ID_s must be included in the L.

(b) The user ID_s randomly picks $d \in Z_q^*$, computes $A = d \cdot P$, $B = d \cdot PK_r$.

(c) ID_s performs the following formulas, where $\oplus$ is the XOR operator, I is the tracking mark and m is the power-related information: $C = H_2(B, L) \oplus m$, $\beta = H_3(C, A)$, $I = (sk_s + \beta t_s)T_{pub}$, $a = H_4(L, C, m, I)$.

(d) The user ID_s randomly picks numbers $k_s \in Z_q^*$ and computes $Z_s = k_s \cdot P$, $s_s = ((1 + sk_s)^{-1}(k_s - a \cdot sk_s)) \bmod q$.

(e) ID_s randomly picks numbers $s_i \in Z_q^*$ for $i = 1, \ldots, s-1, s+1, \ldots, n$ and computes the following formulas
   i. $Z_* = (\sum_{i=1, i \neq s}^{n} s_i)P + \sum_{i=1, i \neq s}^{n} [(s_i + a)PK_i]$
   ii. $Y = Z_* + Z_s$

(f) Add the timestamp TS to the ciphertext σ. After that, the final ciphertext σ will be send to the specified receiver ID_r. The final ciphertext is shown below

$$\sigma = \{C, \{s_1, s_2, \ldots, s_n\}, A, L, I, Y, TS\}.$$

6. **Verification** and **Unsigncryption**$(params, \sigma, sk_r) \to m$: After receiving the ciphertext σ, the receiver ID_r firstly confirms the validity of c_7 through the formula $|c_7 - TS_{cur}| \leq \triangle TS$, where $\triangle TS$ represents the set maximum effective time interval, TS_{cur} is the current timestamp. If the equation does not hold, ID_r will discard the message.

   (a) ID_r needs to check $c_{2(i)} \in Z_q^*(1 \leq i \leq n)$. If not, ID_r will trash the message and report to the TRA.

   (b) Then, the receiver ID_r makes computations $B' = sk_r \cdot c_3$, $m' = c_1 \oplus H_2(B', c_4)$.

   (c) The receiver ID_r computes $a' = H_4(c_4, c_1, m', c_5)$, $Y' = (\sum_{i=1}^n c_{2(i)})P + \sum_{i=1}^n [(c_{2(i)} + a')PK_i]$.

   (d) ID_r needs to check $Y' = c_6$. If not, ID_r report to TRA and discard the message. If true, ID_r is sure that the ciphertext σ is correct and receives it.

7. **BatchVerification**$(params, \sigma^j, sk_r) \to m^j$: A batch verification algorithm has been designed to improve the efficiency of verification. When the verifier ID_r receives m ciphertexts $\sigma^j = \{c_1^j, c_2^j, c_3, c_4, c_5^j, c_6^j, c_7^j\}_{j=1,2,\ldots,m}$ at the same time, it can prove the correctness of these ciphertexts in batch by the following formulas:

   (a) Check $c_{2(i)} \in Z_q^*(1 \leq i \leq n)$. If not, ID_r will trash these messages and report to the TRA.

   (b) $B' = sk_r \cdot c_3$,

   (c) $m^j = c_1^j \oplus H_2(B', c_4)$

   (d) $a^j = H_4(c_4, c_1^j, m^j, c_5)$

   (e) $\hat{Y} = \sum_{j=1}^m c_6$

   (f) $\hat{Y}' = (\sum_{i=1}^n \sum_{j=1}^m c_{2(i)}^j)P + \sum_{i=1}^n [\sum_{j=1}^m (c_{2(i)}^j + a^{j'})PK_i]$

   Check $\hat{Y}' = \hat{Y}$. If not, ID_r will trash these messages and report to the TRA. If true, ID_r is sure that these ciphertexts $\sigma^j(j = 1, 2, \ldots, m)$ is correct and receives it.

8. **Tracking**$(\sigma, ID_r) \to (ID_s)$: When the message does not pass verification, the receiver can report the situation to TRA. It can also monitor the entire smart grid to detect possible malicious behavior. When receiving the reported information, TRA can used the following formula to recover the user ID_j who qualify for malicious behavior from the ring set $L = \{ID_1, ID_2, \ldots, ID_n\}$: $k^{-1}I = PK_j + H_3(c_1, c_3)T_j$.

5   Safety Analysis

In the section, we provide a detailed analysis of the security of the above scheme.

5.1   Correctness

Unsigncryption:

$$
\begin{aligned}
m^{'} &= c_1 \oplus H_2(B^{'}, c_5) \\
&= H_2(B, L) \oplus m \oplus H_2(sk_r \cdot A, L) \\
&= H_2(B, L) \oplus H_2(B, L) \oplus m \\
&= m
\end{aligned}
$$

Verification:

$$
\begin{aligned}
Y^{'} &= (\sum_{i=1}^{n} c_{2(i)})P + \sum_{i=1}^{n}[(c_{2(i)} + a')PK_i] \\
&= c_{2(s)}P + (c_{2(s)} + a)PK + (\sum_{i=1,i\neq s}^{n} c_{2(i)})P + \sum_{i=1,i\neq s}^{n}[(c_{2(i)} + a)PK_i] \\
&= Z_s + Z_* \\
&= Y
\end{aligned}
$$

Tracking:

$$
\begin{aligned}
k^{-1}I &= PK_j + H_3(C, A)T_j \\
sk_j + \beta t_j &= sk_j + H_3(C, A)t_j \\
\beta &= H_3(C, A)
\end{aligned}
$$

To sum up the programme is correct.

5.2   Confidentiality

Theorem 1. *The ECCDHP can be solved with the probability $\varepsilon' \geq (1 - \frac{q_{USC}}{2^k})\frac{\varepsilon}{e(q_{PSK}+q_{SK}+q_R)}$ by a simulator C, in which k the security parameter and e expresses as the base of natural logarithm.*

Proof. The proof of this paper is similar to paper [14], and the detailed proof can be referred to it.

Theorem 2. *If a Type II opponent A_{II} can play a non-negligible advantage ε in Game 2 to successful attack IND-CLRSC-CCCA2. The ECCDHP can reach its solution by algorithm C with probability $\varepsilon' \geq (1 - \frac{q_{USC}}{2^k})\frac{\varepsilon}{e q_{PSK}}$.*

Proof. The proof of this paper is similar to paper [14], and the detailed proof can be referred to it.

5.3   Unforgeability

Theorem 3. *If a Type I opponent A_I can play a non-negligible advantage ε in Game 3 to successful attack EUF-CLRSC-CMA2. The ECDLP can be solution by probability $\varepsilon' \geq \frac{\varepsilon}{e(q_{PSK}+q_{SK}+q_R)}$ by a simulator C.*

Proof. The proof of this paper is similar to paper [14], and the detailed proof can be referred to it.

Theorem 4. *If a Type II opponent A_{II} can play a non-negligible advantage ε in Game 4 to successful attack EUF-CLRSC-CMA2. The ECDLP can be solution by probability $\varepsilon' \geq \frac{\varepsilon}{eq_{PSK}}$ by a simulator C.*

Proof. The proof of this paper is similar to paper [14], and the detailed proof can be referred to it.

5.4   Anonymity

The verifier performs the same operation on each public key when verifying the ciphertext and cannot tell the difference between the real signer and the others.

5.5   Traceability

After receiving the I in the suspicious signcrypt, search L to confirm the identity ID_i of the true signer by satisfying the equation $k^{-1}I = PK_i + H_3(C,A)T_i$. The k^{-1} in the equation is only known by TRA, so in the proposed CLRSC scheme, conditional anonymity is guaranteed.

5.6   Replay Attack Resistance

Each correct ciphertext contains a timestamp TS. After receiving the ciphertext, the verifier first checks the timestamp TS. If not, ID_r rejects σ. Which ensures that the intercepted returned message cannot successfully pass the ID_r verification.

6   Activity Analysis

In smart grid, in addition to paying attention to the security of user data privacy, we also need to consider the efficiency of scheme implementation. We compare this scheme with Scheme [11,14,20,21] in terms of security, This scheme is compared with schemes. [11,14,20,21] in terms of security, computing cost and communication cost.

6.1   Computational Cost Analysis

The device configuration for our simulation is as follows: Intel(R) Core i5-1335U, 16GB, Windows 10 operating system; code running environment is Ubuntu 18.04. By using the miracle [18] and JPBC, we define the following symbols corresponding to different computing operations and list the respective time consumption, as seen in Table 2. To facilitate comparison of different algorithms, we set the security level to 80 bytes.

Table 2. Execution time of encryption operation.

Operation	Operation represented by the symbol	Executing time (ms)
T_h	a hash-to-point operation	4.874
T_e	a bilinear pairing operation	3.536
T_{Gm}	a scale multiplication operation in G_1	1.587
T_m	a scale multiplication operation in G	0.413

We analyzed our proposed scheme and four other CPPA schemes [11, 14, 20, 21], calculate separately the consumption required for a single message in terms of key generation, signcryption, unsigncryption, batch verification and tracking. Assume that there are n ring members and m ciphertexts. The specific calculation results are shown in Table 3.

Table 3. Computing efficiency of five CLRSC schemes.

Schemes	Ken Gen	Signcryption	Unsigncryption	Batch verification	Tracking
Liu [20]	$1T_h$	$(n+1)T_{Gm}$	$nT_{Gm} + 2T_e$	$(n+m)T_{Gm} + 2T_e$	$2T_e$
Zhang [11]	$6T_m$	$(2n+3)T_m$	$(n+1)T_m$	$(n+1)T_m$	–
Guo [14]	$4T_m$	$(4n+3)T_m$	$(4n+2)T_m$	$(4n+2)mT_m$	$3T_m$
Du [21]	$1T_{Gm} + 1T_h$	$(n+3)T_{Gm} + 1T_e$	$nT_{Gm} + 4T_e$	–	$2T_{Gm} + 2T_e$
Our scheme	$4T_m$	$(n+4)T_m$	$(n+1)T_m$	$(n+1)T_m$	$2T_m$

In addition to meeting the most basic safety requirements, our solutions add additional functionality. Table 4 compares our scheme with five other schemes in terms of security features and analysis. Our solution meets the functionality needed in the smart grid while addressing the user's privacy protection.

We can use scientific calculations to determine the time required for key generation, signcryption, unsigncryption, batch verification, and tracking. Assuming that $n = m = 5$. Through Fig. 1, we can then clearly compare the efficiency of these five schemes.

From the above analysis, it is clear that the solution in this paper has all the functions required for application in smart grid. Compared to existing solutions, our solution is more efficient in all phases and more comprehensive in its functionality.

Table 4. Safety analysis of five CLRSC schemes.

Schemes	Liu [20]	Zhang [11]	Guo [14]	Du [21]	Our scheme
Tracking	✓	✗	✓	✓	✓
Replay attack resistance	✗	✓	✓	✓	✓
Certificateless	✗	✓	✓	✗	✓
Formal security analysis	✗	✓	✓	✓	✓
Pseudonym-less	✗	✓	✓	✓	✓
Batch verification	✓	✓	✓	✗	✓
Pairing-less	✗	✓	✓	✗	✓
Efficiency	✗	✓	✗	✗	✓

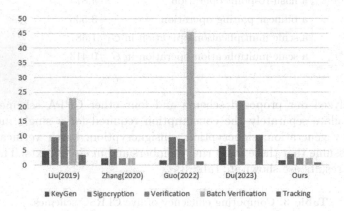

Fig. 1. Comparative efficiency in stages (n = m = 5)

6.2 Computational Cost Analysis

In this section, we will analyze the communication cost of these schemes. In the previous section, we set the lengths of $\hat{p}$ and $\bar{p}$ to 64 bytes and 20 bytes, respectively, and we can obtain the lengths of the elements in G_1 and G to 128 bytes and 40 bytes, respectively, and use $|G_1|$ and $|G|$ to denote the length of the elements in them. In addition to this, $|H|$ indicates that the output value corresponding to the hash function is 20 bytes, and $|TS|$ indicates that the size of the timestamp is 4 bytes. Since these schemes are ring signcrypttion schemes, we only compare the size of the public-private key pair and the size of the ring signature, and do not calculate the set of messages and ring members. The comparison results are shown in Table 5.

To make a clearer comparison of the communication costs, we set the number of ring members at 5 to better show the differences between the schemes. Combining Table 5, we can calculate the following. The communication overheads for these five options Liu, Zhang, Guo, Du and this paper are 772, 364, 244, 900 and 224 respectively.

Table 5. Communication cost analysis of five CLRSC schemes.

Schemes	Private key size	Public key size	Communication overhead (bytes)
Liu [20]	$\|G_1\| = 128$ bytes	$\|G_1\| = 128$ bytes	$(n+1)\|G_1\| + \|TS\| = 128n + 132$ bytes
Zhang [11]	$2\|Z_q^*\| = 40$ bytes	$2\|G\| = 80$ bytes	$(n+3)\|G\| + 2\|Z_q^*\| + \|TS\| = 40n + 164$bytes
Guo [14]	$2\|Z_q^*\| = 40$ bytes	$2\|G\| = 80$ bytes	$3\|G_1\| + (n+1)\|Z_q^*\| + \|TS\| = 20n + 144$bytes
Du [21]	$\|G_1\| = 128$ bytes	$\|G_1\| = 128$ bytes	$(n+2)\|G_1\| + \|TS\| = 128n + 260$bytes
Our scheme	$\|Z_q^*\| = 20$ bytes	$\|G\| = 40$ bytes	$3\|G\| + n\|Z_q^*\| + \|TS\| = 20n + 124$bytes

The analysis in this section shows that the communication cost of our scheme is slightly higher than [14], which is significantly better than [11,20,21]. Therefore, the cost of this paper is lower than existing schemes and fits the needs of smart grids.

7 Conclusion

In this paper we propose a CLRSC scheme with CPPA functionality in SG. It can better protect user privacy during the information transfer. When a malicious user appears among the communication members, the tracking algorithm can quickly identify the malicious user. We demonstrate through security analysis that the scheme can resist the threat of external attacks and internal malicious KGC. Compared with the existing CLRSC, our scheme without bilinear pairing and is faster. In the future, we will conduct more research on aggregated ring signcryptions and add aggregation features to improve applicability.

Acknowledgements. This work was supported by National Natural Science Foundation of China under Grant (NO. 62102311).

References

1. Rivest, R.L., Shamir, A., Tauman, Y.: How to leak a secret. In: Boyd, C. (ed.) ASIACRYPT 2001. LNCS, vol. 2248, pp. 552–565. Springer, Heidelberg (2001). https://doi.org/10.1007/3-540-45682-1_32
2. Tan, S., De, D., Song, W.Z., et al.: Survey of security advances in smart grid: a data driven approach. IEEE Commun. Surv. Tutor. 19(1), 397–422 (2016)
3. Morello, R., De Capua, C., Fulco, G., et al.: A smart power meter to monitor energy flow in smart grids: the role of advanced sensing and IoT in the electric grid of the future. IEEE Sens. J. 17(23), 7828–7837 (2017)
4. Ferrag, M.A., Maglaras, L.A., Janicke, H., et al.: A systematic review of data protection and privacy preservation schemes for smart grid communications. Sustain. Urban Areas 38, 806–835 (2018)
5. Gai, K., Wu, Y., Zhu, L., et al.: Permissioned blockchain and edge computing empowered privacy-preserving smart grid networks. IEEE Internet Things J. 6(5), 7992–8004 (2019)
6. Gai, K., Wu, Y., Zhu, L., et al.: Privacy-preserving energy trading using consortium blockchain in smart grid. IEEE Trans. Ind. Inf. 15(6), 3548–3558 (2019)

7. Kumar, P., Lin, Y., Bai, G., et al.: Smart grid metering networks: a survey on security, privacy and open research issues. IEEE Commun. Surv. Tutor. **21**(3), 2886–2927 (2019)
8. Guan, A., Guan, D.J.: An efficient and privacy protection communication scheme for smart grid. IEEE Access **8**, 179047–179054 (2020)
9. Kong, W., Shen, J., Vijayakumar, P., et al.: A practical group blind signature scheme for privacy protection in smart grid. J. Parallel Distrib. Comput. **136**, 29–39 (2020)
10. Huang, X., Susilo, W., Mu, Y., et al.: Identity-based ring signcryption schemes: cryptographic primitives for preserving privacy and authenticity in the ubiquitous world. In: 19th International Conference on Advanced Information Networking and Applications (AINA 2005) Volume 1 (AINA papers), vol. 2, pp. 649–654. IEEE (2005)
11. Zhang, S., Rong, J., Wang, B.: A privacy protection scheme of smart meter for decentralized smart home environment based on consortium blockchain. Int. J. Electr. Power Energy Syst. **121**, 106140 (2020)
12. Cai, Y., Zhang, H., Fang, Y.: A conditional privacy protection scheme based on ring signcryption for vehicular ad hoc networks. IEEE Internet Things J. **8**(1), 647–656 (2020)
13. Wu, K., Cheng, R., Cui, W., et al.: A lightweight SM2-based security authentication scheme for smart grids. Alex. Eng. J. **60**(1), 435–446 (2021)
14. Guo, R., Xu, L., Li, X., et al.: An efficient certificateless ring signcryption scheme with conditional privacy-preserving in VANETs. J. Syst. Architect. **129**, 102633 (2022)
15. Chakraborty, S., Das, S., Sidhu, T., et al.: Smart meters for enhancing protection and monitoring functions in emerging distribution systems. Int. J. Electr. Power Energy Syst. **127**, 106626 (2021)
16. Yu, H., Shi, J.: Certificateless multi-source signcryption with lattice. J. King Saud Univ.-Comput. Inf. Sci. **34**(10), 10157–10166 (2022)
17. Yu, H., Wang, W., Zhang, Q.: Certificateless anti-quantum ring signcryption for network coding. Knowl.-Based Syst. **235**, 107655 (2022)
18. MIRACL cryptographic SDK (2021). https://github.com/miracl/MIRACL. Accessed 29 Oct 2021
19. Guo, H., Deng, L.: Certificateless ring signcryption scheme from pairings. Int. J. Netw. Secur. **22**(1), 102–111 (2020)
20. Liu, F., Wang, Q.: IBRS: an efficient identity-based batch verification scheme for VANETs based on ring signature. In: 2019 IEEE Vehicular Networking Conference (VNC), pp. 1–8. IEEE (2019)
21. Du, H., Wen, Q., Zhang, S., et al.: An improved conditional privacy protection scheme based on ring signcryption for VANETs. IEEE Internet Things J. https://doi.org/10.1109/JIOT.2023.3279896

Byzantine-Robust Privacy-Preserving Federated Learning Based on DT-PKC

Wenhao Jiang, Shaojing Fu[✉], Yuchuan Luo, Lin Liu, and Yongjun Wang

College of Computer, National University of Defense Technology, Changsha, China
fushaojing@nudt.edu.cn

Abstract. Federated Learning (FL) offers a solution that enables multiple clients to jointly train machine learning models while maintaining data privacy by only uploading model information instead of local data. However, some studies show that attackers can infer users' row data and member information from the model gradients. Researchers have proposed a number of FL schemes for privacy protection, among which the typical method uses homomorphic encryption to update the model gradients directly on ciphertext. In this scenario, all clients often share identical private keys, which can pave the way for encrypted model data interception and subsequent information theft by unauthorized users. More seriously, these methods only consider the issue of privacy disclosure, ignoring the problem of Byzantine attacks in FL. Addressing both privacy breaches and Byzantine attacks remains a challenge. In this paper, we aim to address the aforementioned problems by proposing a homomorphic encryption-based Byzantine robust learning framework termed Secure-Krum Federated Learning (SKFL). The SKFL uses random noise additive mask to combine the revised Distributed Double-Trap Public Key Cryptosystem (DT-PKC) and the improved Krum algorithm for the first time, which can protect user privacy and resist Byzantine attacks. The results of our experiments on diverse real-world datasets, demonstrate the efficacy of SKFL in protecting client privacy in a federated learning environment, while resisting poisoning attacks when no more than 50% Byzantine clients are present.

Keywords: Federated learning · Privacy protection · Byzantine robustness · Homomorphic encryption · Additive mask

1 Introduction

The exposure of user privacy has resulted in hefty fines for numerous Internet enterprises. Various laws and regulations have emerged in the world today to regulate the management and use of data. Consequently, data are kept under strict control in different enterprises and organizations leading to such data inaccessible for sharing, thus forming "data islands" isolated from each other.

To mitigate the issue of "data islands" and ensure user privacy, Federated Learning has emerged as a promising solution. It enables participants to train

© The Author(s), under exclusive license to Springer Nature Singapore Pte Ltd. 2024
H. Yang and R. Lu (Eds.): FCS 2023, CCIS 1992, pp. 205–219, 2024.
https://doi.org/10.1007/978-981-99-9331-4_14

on local data and upload updated gradients to a server to obtain a global model while preserving data security. During Federated Learning, clients only upload gradients while keeping raw data locally to protect data privacy and security.

Nevertheless, Federated Learning still faces security challenges such as privacy breaches and poisoning attacks. Geiping et al. [8] propose a gradient inversion attack, which enables determination of clients' raw data based on shared gradients. Additionally, the member inference attack proposed in [18] establishes a way to determine whether specific data was contributed by certain clients during the training process. Depending on the target of the attacker, Byzantine attacks can be divided into targeted [9] and non-targeted [3] poison attacks. For gradient inversion attacks and member inference attacks, the adversary exploits the model gradients in plaintext to obtain privacy information without knowing the user's local data. In Byzantine attacks, the adversary uploads malicious gradients to corrupt or control the average model. When faced with privacy breaches and Byzantine attacks at the same time, some existing schemes emerge with flaws. To solve the above problems, we propose a SKFL scheme that combines homomorphic encryption technology with Krum aggregation algorithm to protect user privacy and resist Byzantine attacks.

Some existing schemes assume server can be completely trust and resist the effect of Byzantine clients by calculations in plaintext domain. For example, the Krum algorithm [7] enhances Byzantine robustness based on Euclidean distance similarity, but it's unrealistic to know the number of Byzantine clients in advance. Therefore, in this paper, we improve the algorithm, applying homomorphic encryption and mask technology to enable the algorithm to combat Byzantine attacks when malicious users' number is unknown, while protecting user data privacy. Specifically, the paper's main contributions include:

1. We propose a new Secure-Krum Federated Learning (SKFL) framework, which utilizes the revised Double-trap Public Key Isomeric Encryption System (DT-PKC) to protect user privacy and the improved Krum algorithm to resist Byzantine attacks in global training.
2. To incorporate DT-PKC and Krum algorithm, we propose an additive masking technology based on random noise for the first time, which is able to solve the privacy leakage problem of Krum algorithm in plaintext domain and the problem of distinguishing Byzantine users in ciphertext domain.
3. Our experiments using the typical datasets MNIST and Fashion-MNIST show that SKFL can resist Byzantine attacks without incurring additional overhead. Besides, the theoretically analyses demonstrate that SKFL can protect user privacy from servers and other clients throughout the process.

2   Related Work

FL requires clear model data to ensure Byzantine robustness, which could leads to privacy breaches for users. Blanchard et al. proposed Krum [4] robust polymerization scheme to solve the problem of poisoning attack. In this scheme, by calculating the distance between gradients and selecting the client closest to the sum of other clients as the global model, it can resist poisoning attacks to a certain extent, but the accuracy of the results is not high. Based on this, Guerraoui et al. [11] propose a Bulyan polymerization scheme to calculate the polymerization gradient instead of selecting one client. However, both of these schemes require the attacker to have a relatively small presence on the client side. In order to improve Byzantine robustness, Yin et al. [19] proposed a scheme based on the Median and a scheme based on the median Trimmed Mean.

However, invisible data for privacy makes it difficult to distinguish between Byzantine and benign users. Secure Multi-Party Computing Technology [5] (MPC) enables multiple parties to contribute to data analysis without compromising privacy. It ensures that each party holds part of the data and that the analysis can be performed without revealing individual data. However, the data overhead for communication between client and server is high. Multi-Party Homomorphic Encryption Technology [15] (MHE) secures data privacy by converting plaintext data to ciphertext before sharing it, allowing computation on the encrypted data. Trusted implementation of environmental technologies [12] (TEE) involves the deployment of trusted hardware to facilitate secure data entry, which is beneficial where other technologies are not feasible or practical. Differential Privacy Technology [17] (DP) achieves data privacy protection by introducing noise to the dataset, which makes it more difficult for the adversary to identify data sources while preserving the accuracy of the dataset. Although it enhances security, it negatively impacts the final training model efficacy.

Researchers have conducted some studies on the balance between privacy and robustness. So et al. [1] propose the first single-server Byzantine-resilient secure FL framework (BREA) for secure aggregation. BREA is based on an integrated, randomly-quantified, verifiable approach to outlier detection and secure model aggregation while ensuring reliability, privacy, and convergence of FL. Liu et al. [14] proposed an asynchronous local differential privacy mechanism by using a well-designed noise and cloud malicious node detection mechanism to mitigate the label flipping attacks of malicious nodes while maintaining data privacy. Bernstein et al. [2] voting, thus ensuring that a single participant does not have too much power. Chang et al. [6] designed Cronus, a powerful collaborative machine learning framework that defends against toxic attacks on federated learning through strong knowledge transfer between black-box native models. However, this framework is limited because it reduces accuracy and has higher computational costs. In practice, the aforementioned scheme involves transmitting the symbols representing the gradient vectors to the server, which potentially exposes the submodels to information leakage. Although Byzantine algorithms have been a primary focus in federated learning research, the issue of data privacy protection has largely been overlooked. Consequently, there is a critical need to investigate methodologies for enhancing the robustness of federated learning against Byzantine adversaries while simultaneously safeguarding user privacy. This research endeavor holds significant importance and offers valuable theoretical insights.

3 Preliminaries

3.1 Improved Krum Algorithm

Krum algorithm procedure: (1) Initialization: Negotiation model and various required parameters; (2) The server distributes the global parameter w to all clients; (3) For each client C_i, model w_i is trained at the same time and then uploaded to the server; (4) After the server receives the gradients, the distance between the two calculation model gradient vector $d_{i,j} = ||w_i - w_j||^2$. (5) n is the total number of users, f is the number of Byzantine clients, and $2f + 2 < n$. For each model w_i, select the nearest $n - f - 1$ distance to it, i.e. $d_{i,1}, d_{i,2}, \ldots, d_{i,i-1}, d_{i,i+1}, \ldots, d_{i,n}$, the smallest $n - f - 1$, may as well be set as $d_{i,1}, d_{i,2}, \ldots, d_{i,n-f-1}$, and then add up as the score $Kr(i) = \sum_{j=1}^{n-f-1} d_{i,j}$ of this model w_i; (6) After calculating the scores of all models, find out the model w^* with the lowest score; (7) Broadcast w^* to clients as a global model.

The changes made in this paper are as follows: (i) In step (5), the minimum $n - f - 1$ distances are no longer selected, but all distances are summarized, so as to solve the problem of unknown Byzantine client number f in advance. At the same time, this paper can solve the attack against Krum [4], that is, all malicious client model gradients are set to be the same; (ii) In step (3), the public key pk is used to encrypt the w_i before uploading, and the encrypted noise is added to the homomorphism of the ciphertext model through the Noise-Adding Server and partial decryption is performed. The noise model is obtained from the Computing Server, and then the noise is eliminated through the process of distance calculation. The detailed process can be seen in Sect. 5, Section B.

3.2 Modified DT-PKC Scheme

Partial homomorphic encryption [13,16] is an encryption algorithm satisfying one of additive homomorphism or multiplicative homomorphism, such as Paillier scheme, ElGamal scheme and RSA algorithm, etc. The Distributed Two Trapdoors Public-Key Cryptosystem (DT-PKC) [10] used in this paper is derived from BCP algorithm. In this scheme, some improvements are made to the scheme of homomorphic operation under multi-key constructed by BCP algorithm. The main key $\lambda = \frac{lcm(p-1,q-1)}{2}$, which can decrypt the ciphertext encrypted by any public key, is divided into two parts λ_1 and λ_2, so that each part cannot be decrypted separately. This solves the security problem that arises when the central server has the master key.

In SKFL, the original DT-PKC algorithm is modified, no longer dividing by 2 and $\lambda = lcm(p - 1, q - 1)$ when generating Carmichael number λ, to prevent the possibility of decryption failure of the strong private key.

The plaintext space of DT-PKC cryptosystem is Z_N and the ciphertext space is Z_N^2. The algorithm mainly includes seven parts: **KeyGen**, **Enc**, **WDec**, **SDec**, **SKeyS**, **PSDec1** and **PSDec2**.

DT-PKC has additive homomorphism. Therefore, it also supports addition and scalar multiplication operations on ciphertext.

4 Problem Setup

4.1 System Model

1. **Clients(C):** C_i is the data owner in federated learning and holds a weak private key λ_{C2}, which can complete local training and data encryption and decryption, in order to benefit from the global model. At the same time, C_i may be malicious, attempting to destroy or control the federated learning system through Byzantine attacks, with the expectation of intercepting other client data (Fig. 1).

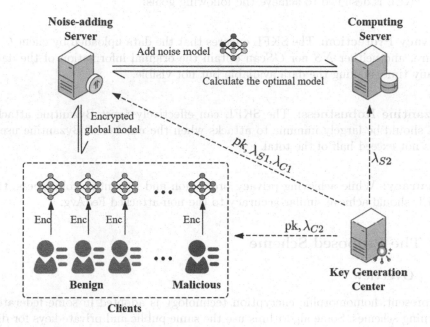

Fig. 1. System Model

2. **Noise-adding server(NS):** NS directly communicates with the client, holding two weak keys λ_{C1} and λ_{S1}, which are used to partially decrypt the global model and the noise model respectively, and there is a group of randomly generated noise data. NS receives model ciphertext gradients from the clients in a round of iteration, performs homomorphic addition operation with the encrypted noise model, partially decrypts and sends them to CS, the computing server, and finally distributes the global model cooperatively with CS.

3. **Computing Server(CS):** CS holding a weak key λ_{S2}, which can fully decrypt the ciphertext from NS after partial decryption. However, the plaintext obtained by CS is the result of noisy data, and it does not have noise model, so it cannot obtain the privacy information of the client. The noise can be eliminated by calculation and the optimal global model can be found.

4. **Key Generation Center(KGC)**: The KGC initializes a set of key data, generates public and private key pairs, and destroys private keys, keeping and publishing only the public key pk. In order to avoid the separate decryption of NS or CS, the main key is divided into two parts, λ_{S1} and λ_{S2}, and distributed to NS and CS. Then the master key is divided into other two parts, λ_{C1} and λ_{C2}, which are different from the previous two parts, and distributed to NS and C_i for client decryption of the global model.

4.2 Design Goals

The SKFL is designed to achieve the following goals:

Privacy Protection: The SKFL ensures that the data uploaded by client C is secure, and neither NS nor CS can obtain the original information of the data at any time, making the data available but not visible.

Byzantine Robustness: The SKFL can effectively resist Byzantine attacks and should be largely immune to attacks when the number of Byzantine users does not exceed half of the total.

Accuracy: While achieving privacy protection and Byzantine robustness, the SKFL should achieve similar accuracy to the non-attacked FedAvg.

5   The Proposed Scheme

5.1   Overview

At present, homomorphic encryption technology is adopted in some federated learning schemes. Some algorithms use the same public and private keys for different clients in order to ensure accurate homomorphic operation in ciphertext, such as Paillier algorithm adopted by traditional FL scheme for privacy protection. As a result, the data of the whole system may be mastered by the attacker after a user discloses the private key to the attacker. And the data of the client may be decrypted after being intercepted by other users, resulting in privacy disclosure at the C level of the client, as shown in the Fig. 2.

SKFL uses DT-PKC public key encryption algorithm. The client can only decrypt the ciphertext which partially decrypted from the server. Otherwise, even if C_i intercepts other users' ciphertext, C_i cannot decrypt it independently. Meanwhile, DT-PKC splits the strong private key into two parts, ensuring that NS or CS cannot decrypt separately. In a typical FL scenario, if the user colludes with the server, the user data is easily leaked on the server side. In SKFL, user information cannot be recovered because the server has only part of the private key, even if the client colludes with one of the servers, it cannot be fully decrypted.

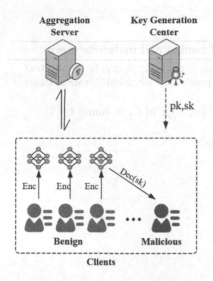

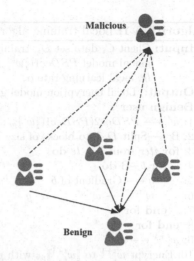

Fig. 2. The client decrypts the cipher-text after intercepting it.

Fig. 3. The distance between Byzantine clients and other clients is large.

Our scheme assumes that the client's data set is independent and identically distributed (i.i.d), and finds out the optimal model in every round from all the trained clients' models through calculation in ciphertext as the global model, so as to resist Byzantine attacks. The SKFL defaults that the data uploaded by Byzantine users is deviated from the general public. Whether it is random noise attack or label flipping attack, its parameters will be far away from the parameter group range of normal users (Fig. 3), so it will be discarded due to the high value of evaluation $Kr(i)$.

5.2 Details of SKFL

The whole process of SKFL consists of four aspects: system initialization, local training, secure calculation of optimal model and secure distribution of global model. We describe the processes below.

System Initialization: Key generation and distribution are mainly carried out in this stage. KGC first locally generates N, the product of large prime numbers p and q, with $\lambda(N)$ as the Carmichael function value of N, and splits the strong private key λ into two weak private keys λ_{C1} and λ_{C2}, which are securely transmitted to NS and CS for collaborative decryption. Then, the strong private key λ is divided into other two weak private keys λ_{S1} and λ_{S1}, which are transmitted to NS and C_i respectively for collaborative decryption. g is a generator of N of order λ, which generates a random number sk less than $\frac{N}{4}$ and calculates h. $\{N, g, h\}$ is used as the public key pk and the private key sk is destroyed. Once the above tasks are completed, the KGC can be taken offline.

Algorithm 1: Local training algorithm of benign and malicious users

---

Input: Client C_i data set D_i, training rounds t, partially decrypted ciphertext
      global model $PSDec1(\llbracket w^t \rrbracket_{pk}, \lambda_{S1})$, public key pk, local iteration times
      le, local learning rate α.

Output: Local encryption model gradients $\llbracket w_i^{t+1} \rrbracket_{pk}$ of C_i at round $t + 1$

Benign user :

1: $w^t \longleftarrow PSDec2(PSDec1(\llbracket w^t \rrbracket_{pk}, \lambda_{S1}), \lambda_{S2})$

2: B $\longleftarrow$ Split D_i into blocks of size B

3: **for** $iter$ from 1 to le **do**

4:    **for** $b \in$ B **do**

5:       $g \longleftarrow$ Gradient of b

6:       $w^{iter} \longleftarrow w^{iter-1} - \alpha \cdot g$

7:    **end for**

8: **end for**

9: $w_i^{t+1} \longleftarrow w^{le}$

10: Encrypt w_i^{t+1} to $\llbracket w_i^{t+1} \rrbracket_{pk}$ with pk

Random noise attack :

1: $w_i^{t+1} \longleftarrow$ Use noise to generate a set of data of the same size

2: Encrypt w_i^{t+1} to $\llbracket w_i^{t+1} \rrbracket_{pk}$ with pk

Label flipping attack :

1: $w^t \longleftarrow PSDec2(PSDec1(\llbracket w^t \rrbracket_{pk}, \lambda_{S1}), \lambda_{S2})$

2: B $\longleftarrow$ Split D_i into blocks of size B

3: **for** $iter$ from 1 to le **do**

4:    **for** $b \in$ B **do**

5:       $label(b) \longleftarrow 9 - label(b), label(b) \in [0,9]$

6:       $g \longleftarrow$ Gradient of b

7:       $w^{iter} \longleftarrow w^{iter-1} - \alpha \cdot g$

8:    **end for**

9: **end for**

10: $w_i^{t+1} \longleftarrow w^{le}$

11: Encrypt w_i^{t+1} to $\llbracket w_i^{t+1} \rrbracket_{pk}$ with pk

---

Algorithm 2: NS Adds Noise

Input: Ciphertext model $\llbracket w_i^{t+1} \rrbracket_{pk}$ from client C_i, number of clients
      participating in aggregation n, public key pk, random noise r, weak
      private key λ_{S1}.

Output: Partial decryption noise model $PSDec1(\llbracket w^{t+1} + r \rrbracket_{pk}, \lambda_{S1})$

1: Encrypt r to $\llbracket r \rrbracket_{pk}$ with pk

2: **for** i from 1 to n **do**

3:    $\llbracket w_i^{t+1} + r \rrbracket_{pk} \longleftarrow \llbracket w_i^{t+1} \rrbracket_{pk} \cdot \llbracket r \rrbracket_{pk}$

4:    $PSDec1(\llbracket w_i^{t+1} + r \rrbracket_{pk}, \lambda_{S1})$

5: **end for**

Local Training: Assume that the total number of users is n, the number of training rounds is t, the number of Byzantine users is m and $n > 2m$. In the phase of local training, NS partially decrypts the global model as $PSDec1$ with λ_{C1} and sends it to C_i. For all $i \in [1, n]$, C_i can decrypt the global model w_t using the weak private key λ_{C2}. After that, user C_i trained local model w_i^{t+1} with global model w^t and local data set D_i, and uploaded updated model gradients just like traditional FL model. To protect data privacy, client C_i with the public key pk encrypts local model gradients w_i^{t+1} to $[\![w_i^{t+1}]\!]_{pk}$ and sends it to the NS. The process of local training can be described by Algorithm 1. In label flipping attack, because the label values of data set are 0 to 9, 9 minus the label value is used as its flip value.

Algorithm 3: CS calculates the optimal model

Input: The partially decrypted noise model $PSDec1([\![w_i^{t+1} + r]\!]_{pk}, \lambda_{S1})$ from
   NS , the weak private key λ_{S2}, and the number of clients participating
   in the aggregation n.
Output: Optimal model index x
1: $w_i^{t+1} + r \longleftarrow PSDec2(PSDec1([\![w_i^{t+1} + r]\!]_{pk}, \lambda_{S1}), \lambda_{S2})$
2: **for** i from 1 to n **do**
3:    $l_i \longleftarrow 0$
4:    **for** j from 1 to n **do**
5:       $w_{i,j} \longleftarrow (w_i^{t+1} + r) - (w_j^{t+1} + r)$
6:       $d_{i,j} = sum(|w_{i,j} \cdot w_{i,j}|)$
7:       $l_i \longleftarrow l_i + d_{i,j}$
8:    **end for**
9:    $Kr(i) \longleftarrow l_i$
10: **end for**
11: $x \longleftarrow argmin(Kr(x))$

Secure Calculation of Optimal Model: At this stage, server CS calculates optimal model w^* from w_i^{t+1}, $i \in [1, n]$ as a global model of $t + 1$ round, which is securely transmitted to each client. This stage also includes step decryption of distance information and calculation of distance sum. In order to simulate the real federated learning environment, we set the ratio of Byzantine clients as b, so their number is $n \cdot b$, and the proportion of users participating in a round of training is f. In each round of training, random $|nf|$ (integer) client to participate in the aggregate. After receiving the encryption parameter $[\![w_i^{t+1}]\!]_{pk}$ of n users, the NS begins to aggregate. First, NS randomly generates noise model r and encrypts it to $[\![r]\!]_{pk}$. Then, NS multiplies each ciphertext parameter by ciphertext noise model, gets $[\![w_i^{t+1} + r]\!]_{pk}$, and partially decrypts it with the weak private key λ_{S1}, gets $PSDec1([\![w_i^{t+1} + r]\!]_{pk}, \lambda_{S1})$ and sends it to CS. For each client C_i, CS decrypts the other part of $PSDec2(PSDec1([\![w_i^{t+1} + r]\!]_{pk}, \lambda_{S1}), \lambda_{S2})$ with λ_{S2} to get the intermediate vector. For each C_i and all C_j

except C_i, calculate the difference $w_{i,j} = (w_i + r) - (w_j + r) = w_i - w_j$ between the model gradient vectors in pairs. Then, square and sum the internal elements of the vector. For client C_i and C_j distance $d_{i,j}$, namely $d_{i,j} = sum(|w_{i,j} \cdot w_{i,j}|)$. For each model gradient w_i, calculate the distance from all other model gradients $\{d_{i,1}, d_{i,2}..., d_{i,n}\}$, and then added together as the evaluation value $Kr(i) = \sum_{j=1}^{n} d_{i,j}$ of w_i in this model. After calculating the evaluation values of all models, the client model w_x^{t+1} corresponding to model $argmin(Kr(x))$ with the smallest value of evaluation is found out as the global model of the next round.

Algorithm 4: Distribution global model

Input: The optimal model index x, the number of clients participating in the aggregation n, the server weak private key λ_{C1}, λ_{C2}.

Output: Global model w_x^{t+1}

1: CS: x is optimal model
2: **for** i from 1 to n **do**
3:    NS: send $PSDec1(\llbracket w_x^{t+1} \rrbracket_{pk}, \lambda_{C1})$ to C_i
4:    $w_x^{t+1} \longleftarrow PSDec2(PSDec1(\llbracket w_x^{t+1} \rrbracket_{pk}, \lambda_{C1}), \lambda_{C2})$
5:    C_i: get w_x^{t+1}
6: **end for**

Secure Distribution of the Global Model: CS informs NS that the global model in the next round is x after calculating. The model w_x^{t+1} kept in the NS is in encrypted form, so NS uses the weak private key λ_{C1} to partially decrypt $\llbracket w_x^{t+1} \rrbracket_{pk}$ and sends it to C_i. C_i with λ_{C2} can completely decrypt to get the global model w_x^{t+1}.

6 Security Analysis

This paper puts forward the following theorems and gives proofs.

Theorem 1. *In the SKFL, the DT-PKC public key encryption system can ensure the privacy security of the local model gradients of the client, and achieve confidentiality for semi-honest servers.*

Proof. DT-PKC is based on the decision Diffie-Hellman (DDH) hypothesis, which has been proved to be semantically secure [10]. Meanwhile, in DT-PKC encryption, the strong private key $MK = \lambda$ is randomly divided into two weak private keys λ_1 and λ_2. Unless the attacker obtains the key on both servers at the same time, the strong private key λ cannot be recovered, and it is difficult to breach the protection of both servers. This means that it cannot restore plaintext. The process of this scheme can be expressed as follows: (1) $C_i \longrightarrow NS$:

Because NS has only weak private key and does not collude with CS, it cannot decrypt and obtain model gradient information. (2) NS: $[\![w_i]\!]_{pk} \cdot [\![r]\!]_{pk}$, the random noise model is only stored in NS, so that C_i and CS cannot know. The gradients of the model w_i is invisible for CS. (3) CS: $(w_i + r) - (w_j + r)$. In the process of calculating distance to find the optimal model w^*, CS can only get the difference between the two models, from which the original information of the model cannot be acquired. (4) $NS \longrightarrow C_i$: $PSDec1([\![w_x^{t+1}]\!]_{pk}, \lambda_{C1})$, NS only knows the i value corresponding to the optimal model, and partially decrypts w^* and sends it to the clients, unable to obtain gradient information.

Theorem 2. *In the original DT-PKC scheme, the strong private key λ sometimes caused decryption to fail, but the improved scheme does not.*

Proof. In the original DT-PKC scheme, $\lambda = lcm(p-1, q-1)/2$, where $p = 2p'+1$ and $q = 2q' + 1$. p, q, p', q' are all prime numbers. So λ can be written as: $\lambda = lcm(p-1, q-1)/2 = p'q'$. Because g is a generator of order $\frac{(p-1)(q-1)}{2}$, that is, $g^{\frac{(p-1)(q-1)}{2}} = 1 \bmod n$. It is easy to know that $\frac{(p-1)(q-1)}{2} = 2p'q' = 2\lambda$, so $g^{2\lambda} = 1 \bmod n$. From the properties of the Carmichael function, if $w^\lambda = 1 \bmod n$, $w^{n\lambda} = 1 \bmod n^2$. So in this situation, $g^{2n\lambda} = 1 \bmod n^2$. As we know, $[\![m]\!]_{pk} = \{T_1, T_2\}$, where $T_1 = h^r(1 + mN) \bmod N^2$, $T_2 = g^r \bmod N^2$. When decrypting with a strong private key λ, $T_1^\lambda \bmod N^2 = g^{\lambda\theta r}(1 + mN\lambda) \bmod N^2$ where θ and r are all random numbers. It means, $\theta \cdot r$ does not have to be even, and only when $\theta \cdot r = 2k, k \in Z_N \longrightarrow g^{\lambda\theta r}(1 + mN\lambda) \bmod N^2 = 1$. To solve this problem, we define $\lambda = lcm(p-1, q-1) = 2p'q'$ in SKFL. In this case, θ and r can take any number to satisfy the following equation: $g^{\lambda\theta r}(1 + mN\lambda) \bmod N^2 = 1$, which can ensure decryption success.

7   Experiment and Result Analysis

7.1   Experimental Setting

All experiments in this paper were run on a host equipped with Ubuntu 18.04, Intel(R) Core(TM) i7-12700H 2.30 GHz CPU and 16 GB RAM. The client and server were simulated by different processes.

Data Sets and Models: In this paper, the multi-layer perceptron (MLP) model is used to test the effect of two image classification task data sets: (i) MNIST data set: The training set consisted of 60,000 handwritten 0–9 pictures with 28×28 pixels; the test set consisted of 10,000 pictures with the same size, and the proportion of each of these 10 digits was 10%. Because they are handwritten by staff, the same numbers will vary from picture to picture.(ii)Fashion-MNIST data set: The only difference is that Fashion-MNIST data set contains ten categories of grayscale clothing images.

In these two data sets, we set each client to have a random 600 training data sets and a random 100 test data sets that do not cross each other to simulate the independent and identical distribution. In this paper, the experiment set the total number of clients $n = 100$, the proportion of clients participating in training in each round $f = 0.1$, the learning rate $\alpha = 0.01$, the SGD momentum set to 0.5, the number of local training iterations $le = 10$, the block size $B = 10$, and the total training rounds $T = 10$. b represents the percentage of Byzantine clients in n clients.

Table 1. Accuracy and influence of two kinds of attacks on MNIST data set under different proportions of Byzantine clients

Scheme (attack)	Byzantine client ratio (acc & inf)							
	10%		20%		30%		40%	
BaseLine	0.938		0.941		0.948		0.951	
SKFL (targeted attack)	0.925	1.3%	0.930	1.1%	0.934	1.4%	0.938	1.3%
FedAvg (targeted attack)	0.926	1.2%	0.922	2.0%	0.901	4.9%	0.860	9.6%
SKFL (untargeted attack)	0.926	1.2%	0.937	0.4%	0.944	0.5%	0.948	0.3%
FedAvg (untargeted attack)	0.511	45.5%	0.381	59.5%	0.322	66.0%	0.283	70.2%

Attack Setting: This paper considers non-targeted attacks and targeted attacks on Byzantine clients. For non-targeted attacks, the Byzantine client does not need to train the model, but directly uses random noise to generate a set of arbitrary gradients as the aggregate participants. For targeted attacks, the Byzantine client carries out label flipping attack, that is, the label value l in the training set is flipped to $N - l - 1$, $l \in 0, 1, ...N$, N is the number of label types. In order to test the defense effect of this scheme under different proportions of Byzantine clients b, set b to increase by 1% from 0 until it reaches 49%.

BaseLine Settings: In the design goals, we proposed that while achieving privacy protection and Byzantine robustness, the SKFL should be as similar as possible to FedAvg in the case of no attacks and maintain normal accuracy. Therefore, a baseline was set to represent the accuracy of FedAvg schemes without attacks for comparison.

7.2   Experimental Result

Through experiments, we demonstrate that the SKFL can achieve the design goals presented in Sect. 4: privacy protection, Byzantine robustness, and accuracy.

$$inf = \frac{acc_{Baseline} - acc_A}{acc_{Baseline}} \tag{1}$$

We use inf, which represents the influence of Byzantine clients on solution A to judge the degree of influence, where $acc_{Baseline}$ represents the accuracy of the baseline, and acc_A represents the accuracy of solution A. In order to improve the training effect, we used a group of correct data sets for pre-training before NS distribute the global model in first round. Table 1 respectively show the defense effects of SKFL on the MNIST datasets. In the case of targeted and non-targeted attacks by different percentages of Byzantine clients, SKFL and FedAvg differ significantly after ten iterations. The corresponding curves are shown in Fig. 4 and Fig. 5. Intuitively, when the number of Byzantine clients increases, the proportion of benign users will decrease, and the test accuracy of the global model should also decrease. However, regardless of targeted or non-targeted attacks, the SKFL can maintain high accuracy under less than 50% Byzantine client ratio.

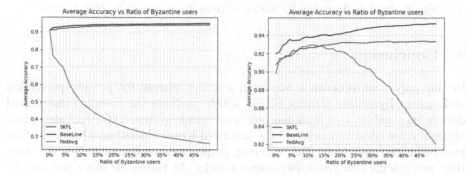

Fig. 4. Average Accuracy Vs Ration of Byzantine users of MNIST.

First, this is because the modified Krum algorithm always finds one benign client from all clients as the global model, directly eliminating the influence of Byzantine clients. We find that SKFL has a better defense effect against random noise attacks than label flipping attacks. We speculate that the reason is that in label flipping attacks, the model gradients of malicious users are more normal than those of random models.

The predicted results are within the range of tag sets and the distance from other users is smaller than that of random models. The average model generated by Fedavg is not affected much. As for the random model generated by random noise attack, though a small number of Byzantine clients can reduce the accuracy of the average model a lot. With the increase of malicious users, the prediction accuracy will be affected more. But because it deviates significantly from the benign user base, SKFL can eliminate up to 50% of such Byzantine clients and not be affected at all. Secondly, the DT-PKC algorithm and the random noise additive mask protect the privacy of users.

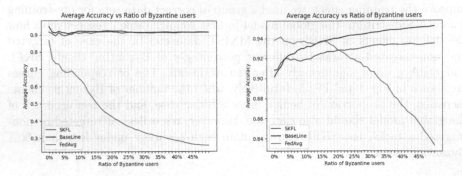

Fig. 5. Average Accuracy Vs Ration of Byzantine users of Fashion-MNIST.

8   Conclusion

In this paper, we propose a federated learning scheme for privacy protection and against Byzantine attacks, SKFL, which combines the modified distributed double-trap public key homomorphic encryption system DT-PKC algorithm, random noise additive mask and the improved Krum algorithm. Multiple experiments on two data sets with different proportions of Byzantine clients show that our scheme can resist Byzantine attacks. At the same time, the double-trapdoor nature of SKFL prevents model data leakage at all levels. However, the large number of model gradients to encrypt and decrypt leads to the high time cost. How to package ciphertext while maintaining homomorphism is a technology worth studying in the future. As for the non-independent and uniformly distributed data sets on the client side, we leave them for later exploration.

References

1. So, J., Güler, B., Avestimehr, A.S.: Byzantine-resilient secure federated learning. IEEE J. Sel. Areas Commun. **39**(7), 2168–2181 (2021)
2. Bernstein, J., Zhao, J., Azizzadenesheli, K., Anandkumar, A.: signSGD with majority vote is communication efficient and fault tolerant (2019)
3. Bhagoji, A.N., Chakraborty, S., Mittal, P., Calo, S.B.: Analyzing federated learning through an adversarial lens. CoRR abs/1811.12470 (2018). http://arxiv.org/abs/1811.12470
4. Blanchard, P., Mhamdi, E.M.E., Guerraoui, R., Stainer, J.: Machine learning with adversaries: byzantine tolerant gradient descent. In: NIPS 2017: Proceedings of the 31st International Conference on Neural Information Processing Systems (2017)
5. Bonawitz, K., Ivanov, V., Kreuter, B., Marcedone, A., McMahan, H.B.: Practical secure aggregation for federated learning on user-held data. CoRR abs/1611.04482 (2016). http://dblp.uni-trier.de/db/journals/corr/corr1611.htmlBonawitzIKMMPRS16
6. Chang, H., Shejwalkar, V., Shokri, R., Houmansadr, A.: Cronus: robust and heterogeneous collaborative learning with black-box knowledge transfer (2019)

7. Fung, C., Yoon, C.J.M., Beschastnikh, I.: Mitigating sybils in federated learning poisoning. CoRR abs/1808.04866 (2018). http://arxiv.org/abs/1808.04866
8. Geiping, J., Bauermeister, H., Dröge, H., Moeller, M.: Inverting gradients - how easy is it to break privacy in federated learning? In: Proceedings of the 34th International Conference on Neural Information Processing Systems, NIPS 2020. Curran Associates Inc., Red Hook (2020)
9. Li, H., Ditzler, G.: Targeted data poisoning attacks against continual learning neural networks. In: 2022 International Joint Conference on Neural Networks (IJCNN) (2022)
10. Liu, X., Deng, R.H., Choo, K.K.R., Weng, J.: An efficient privacy-preserving outsourced calculation toolkit with multiple keys. IEEE Trans. Inf. Forensics Secur. **11**(11), 2401–2414 (2016). https://doi.org/10.1109/TIFS.2016.2573770
11. Mhamdi, E.M.E., Guerraoui, R., Rouault, S.: The hidden vulnerability of distributed learning in byzantium, vol. 80, pp. 3521–3530 (2018). https://proceedings.mlr.press/v80/mhamdi18a.html
12. Mo, F., Haddadi, H., Katevas, K., Marin, E., Perino, D., Kourtellis, N.: PPFL: privacy-preserving federated learning with trusted execution environments. In: Proceedings of the 19th Annual International Conference on Mobile Systems, Applications, and Services, MobiSys 2021, pp. 94–108. Association for Computing Machinery, New York (2021). https://doi.org/10.1145/3458864.3466628
13. Paillier, P.: Public-key cryptosystems based on composite degree residuosity classes. In: Stern, J. (ed.) EUROCRYPT 1999. LNCS, vol. 1592, pp. 223–238. Springer, Heidelberg (1999). https://doi.org/10.1007/3-540-48910-X_16
14. Liu, Y., Zhao, R., Kang, J., Yassine, A., Niyato, D., Peng, J.: Towards communication-efficient and attack-resistant federated edge learning for industrial Internet of Things. ACM Trans. Internet Technol. **22**(3), 1–22 (2022)
15. Sav, S., et al.: POSEIDON: privacy-preserving federated neural network learning. CoRR abs/2009.00349 (2020). https://arxiv.org/abs/2009.00349
16. Shejwalkar, V., Houmansadr, A.: Manipulating the byzantine: optimizing model poisoning attacks and defenses for federated learning. In: 28th Annual Network and Distributed System Security Symposium, NDSS 2021, Virtually, 21–25 February 2021. The Internet Society (2021)
17. Shokri, R., Shmatikov, V.: Privacy-preserving deep learning (conference paper). In: Proceedings of the ACM Conference on Computer and Communications Security, pp. 1310–1321 (2015)
18. Truex, S., Liu, L., Gursoy, M.E., Yu, L., Wei, W.: Demystifying membership inference attacks in machine learning as a service. IEEE Trans. Serv. Comput. **14**(6), 2073–2089 (2019)
19. Yin, D., Chen, Y., Ramchandran, K., Bartlett, P.L.: Byzantine-robust distributed learning: towards optimal statistical rates. CoRR abs/1803.01498 (2018). http://arxiv.org/abs/1803.01498

Updatable and Dynamic Searchable Symmetric Encryption Scheme with Forward and Backward Privacy

Huijuan Qiu[1($\boxtimes$)] and Zhenhua Liu[1,2]

[1] School of Mathematics and Statistics, Xidian University, Xi'an 710071, China
1670478515@qq.com, zhualiu@hotmail.com
[2] State Key Laboratory of Cryptology, P.O. Box 5159, Beijing 100878, China

Abstract. Dynamic searchable symmetric encryption (*DSSE*) enables search and modification on encrypted data. While considerable efforts have been dedicated to achieving forward and backward privacy in *DSSE*, the potential adverse consequences of key corruption or exposure have been overlooked. In this paper, we introduce the updatability into *DSSE* to resist the key exposure attacks, propose a new concept named updatable and dynamic searchable symmetric encryption (*U&D-SSE*), and establish $\mathcal{L}$-adaptive security model tailored to the update environment. Then we construct a *U&D-SSE* scheme with token inference, where a ciphertext can be updated by a token and a key can be inferred in bi-direction. Furthermore, a *U&D-SSE* scheme with token-free inference is proposed to achieve no-directional key update through indistinguishable obfuscation. Finally, both schemes are proven to be secure in the $\mathcal{L}$-adaptive security model, and ensuring the preservation of forward and backward privacy.

Keywords: Dynamic searchable symmetric encryption · Key exposure · Indistinguishability obfuscation · Forward privacy · Backward privacy

1 Introduction

As a cloud computing model, cloud storage securely stores data across multiple virtual servers hosted by a third party, enables intelligent integration of all storage resources, provides small businesses with agility, cost savings, security,

Supported by the Natural Science Basic Research Plan in Shaanxi Province of China under Grant No. 2022JZ-38, the Fundamental Research Funds for the Central Universities under Grant No. QTZX23001, the National Natural Science Foundation of China under Grant No. 61807026, the Plan For Scientific Innovation Talent of Henan Province under Grant No. 184100510012, and in part by the Program for Science and Technology Innovation Talents in the Universities of Henan Province under Grant No. 18HASTIT022.

and simplicity, while empowers large enterprises to achieve scalability, persistent cost-saving capabilities, and centralized data leak prevention. Moreover, legitimate users can effortlessly access their data anytime and from anywhere using any Internet-connected device connected to the cloud.

To ensure privacy, the data owner tends to store the encrypted data in the cloud. However, the encryption operation could impede flexible access for both valid users and even the data owner. Searchable symmetric encryption (SSE) was proposed to enable the searchability on the encrypted data. In practice, DSSE is more appealing as it offers data owners additional functionalities, such as remote data addition or deletion.

Generally, data owners will securely store their private keys in their devices. However, these devices may be inadvertently lost, maliciously stolen, or even vulnerable to powerful side-channel attacks (e.g. [1]), leading to partial leakage or complete loss of private keys. This poses a significant threat to data security, and searchable encryption is not immune to such risks. In fact, as noted in the NIST guideline $SP800 - 57$ [2], "re-keying" can impact the length of a cryptoperiod. Numerous techniques have been proposed to counter key compromise attacks, including forward-secure, key-insulated, intrusion-resilient cryptography, and updatable encryption (UE). Among these, UE stands out as it allows transferring of ciphertexts from the old key to the new key without revealing the underlying data.

However, to the best of our knowledge, limited research has addressed the issue of searchable encryption for the key-exposure problem. Abdalla et al. [3] proposed temporary keyword search (PETKS), allowing the server to search ciphertexts using a trapdoor during the same cryptoperiod. Tang [4] introduced a forward secure public-key encryption with keyword search (PEKS) by preventing old token searches for the newly added data. However, neither of these approaches includes a specific key update feature. Until 2018, for the first time, Anada et al. [5] considered to update the key in PEKS scheme. But their ciphertexts are updated mechanically only by decrypting and then re-encrypting. Therefore, exploring more flexible ways of updating in DSSE is a pertinent consideration.

1.1 Related Works

- *The forward and backward privacy of DSSE.* Symmetric searchable encryption was first introduced by Song et al. [6], which goes through the process from static search to dynamic search. The first DSSE scheme was introduced by Kamara et al. [7], boasting sublinear search performance but inadvertently leaking the hash value of modified document keywords. To address this issue, Kamara et al. [8] made further advancements, mitigating leakage at the expense of increased server space complexity. Subsequently, Cash et al. [9] devised a dynamic scheme optimized for managing large data sets. In the realm of DSSE, a crucial objective is to ensure that dynamic modifications do not divulge any additional information.

1) Forward privacy has become an essential attribute for *DSSE* in countering the file-injection attack. Stefanov et al. [10] initially introduced forward privacy and built an *ORAM*-inspired dynamic scheme. Bost [11] defined forward privacy formally and constructed a highly efficient scheme based on trapdoor permutation (*TDP*), offering optimal search and modification complexity. Nevertheless, *TDP* relies on asymmetric encryption primitive. As an advancement, Wei et al. [12] introduced a symmetric encryption primitive called the "key-based blocks chain" (*KBBC*) technique to build a forward privacy searchable encryption scheme *FSSE*, which allows for storing the key of the current block in the previous block, enhancing the overall security and efficiency of the system.

2) Backward privacy was first formally defined by Bost et al. [13], with three types of leakage (Type-I to Type-III) ranked from the most secure to the least secure. They also proposed four efficient *DSSE* schemes, including Janus, focusing on achieving both forward and backward privacy. Then Chamani et al. [14] built three schemes with forward-and-backward security, while Sun et al. [15] improved Janus to get Janus++ scheme by symmetric puncturable encryption (*SPE*). In short, the much more practical schemes are those with forward and Type-III backward privacy.

- *The inference function of update token.* Updatable encryption is proposed to minimize the impact of key corruption on the encrypted data. Boneh et al. [16] clearly came up with the concept of updatable encryption for the first time. Furthermore, update functionality has been added for different types of cryptographic schemes by Ananth et al. [17] such as signature, encryption, and classical protocols. Since then, there has been a boom [18,20–25] in the updatable encryption. The influence of token on the direction of ciphertext and key update has also been widely studied.

1) Effect of token on ciphertext: Update token can be used to update the old ciphertext. But token can also be used to degrade ciphertext. That is, ciphertext at the epoch e can be deduced from the corrupted token and the ciphertext at the epoch $e+1$. If an adversary obtains the private key at the corresponding epoch, it can easily win the game. Lehmann et al. [20] presented the effect of token inference on the direction of challenge ciphertext update. In practice, only bi-directional ciphertext update is implemented. Until 2022, Nishimaki [25] constructed the first uni-directional ciphertext update scheme based on *LWE*.

2) Effect of token on key: Similarly, a token can be used to upgrade or downgrade key. Specifically, there are three types of key update according to the inference direction: uni-directional, bi-directional and no-directional. After many collisions of views, Nishimaki [25] make a significant advancement in 2022 by subdividing uni-directional key updates into two categories: forward-leak and backward-leak, proposed the first updatable encryption scheme UE_{iO} with no-directional key update. According to Nishimaki, the combination of backward-leak uni-directional key update and uni-directional ciphertext update is strictly stronger than other forms, and backward-leak uni-directional key update is equivalent to no-directional key update, which contradicts the findings in [24].

1.2   Our Motivation and Contributions

- *The necessity of updating in DSSE.* Typically, the key is stored in a trusted device to safeguard the confidentiality of ciphertext. However, the longer the key is utilized, the higher the potential risk it poses. Many dynamic searchable encryption schemes prioritize forward and backward privacy, which unfortunately cannot address the issue of private key leakage. $\Sigma o\varphi o\varsigma$ currently stands as one of the most efficient *DSSE* schemes; nevertheless, it heavily relies on one-way *TDP*. As an improvement, the *KBBC* technique [12] can achieve higher performance and broader application scopes by incorporating a mechanism that stores the key of the current block in the preceding block. This approach ensures forward privacy for newly added data blocks, with the exception of the head pointer Key^*, which is retained by the data owner. Once the private key is corrupted, forward privacy will no longer be guaranteed. So it becomes crucial to contemplate updating keys and ciphertexts as a measure to reduce the impact of key corruption.

- *The importance of flexible updating.* The crudest update method in searchable encryption is that data owner sends the secret keys to cloud server [5], where the server can use the old key to decrypt any ciphertext and index, and then use the new key to complete the re-encryption process. Clearly, this operation violates data security. Another simplest and most straightforward way to implement update in searchable encryption is that data owner downloads all ciphertexts from the server, then decrypt, re-encrypt, upload new ciphertexts and indexes to cloud server, which is also unrealistic. To make update more realistic, we introduce a new form of symmetric encryption by adding an update protocol to the original *DSSE* scheme, where ciphertexts can be updated with an update token.

- *The impact of token inference.* Ideally, a token should solely be used to update the ciphertext from the old epoch to the new epoch. The epoch is determined by the valid time of the key. Terribly, in the proposed update protocol, the update token possesses additional functionality due to directionality. Meaning that an adversary can upgrade and downgrade both the ciphertext and the key between two epochs using the corrupted tokens, namely the bi-directional ciphertext updates and key updates. Let's take *U&D-SSE* scheme with token inference as an example. Assume that the adversary corrupts a token Δ_{e+1} and the key uk_e. At first sight it has no effect on our scheme. But if the adversary gets K_ω^e by some guessed ω, then he will get K_ω^{e+1} with Δ_{e+1}. So even though the ciphertext has been updated to epoch $e + 1$ and deleted immediately, the server would learn what $ind\|op$ is. To mitigate the impact of token inference on the update protocol, we utilize an indistinguishable obfuscator to conceal the token during the update process and return the updated result. As a result, a *U&D-SSE* scheme with token-free inference is constructed.

A comparison of the proposed schemes with prior works is provided in Table 1. Beside the schemes themselves, we believe this work leads to a new attempt to resist leakage in *DSSE*. To sum up, the main contributions are as follows.

Table 1. A brief comparison of the proposed schemes with the existing schemes

Scheme	FP	BP	Updatable	Token.(key)	Token.(ct)
$\Sigma o\varphi o\varsigma$ [11]	✓	×	×	–	–
FSSE [12]	✓	×	×	–	–
Π_{KI}/Π_{KE} [5]	–	–	✓	uni	uni
Aura [19]	✓	✓	×	–	–
U&D-SSE^1	✓	✓	✓	uni	bi
U&D-SSE^2	✓	✓	✓	no	uni

Note: *U&D-SSE*^{1} is the *U&D-SSE* scheme with token inference, and *U&D-SSE*^{2} is the *U&D-SSE* scheme with token-free inference. *FP*, *BP*, *Token.*(key) and *Token.*(ct) indicate forward privacy, backward privacy, the effect of token on ciphertext, and the effect of token on key, respectively. Specifically, *uni* denotes token can only complete updating, *bi* means token can complete updating and degrading, and *no* denotes token has no effect on keys.

1) **Introduce the updatability into *DSSE*.** To mitigate the problem of private key corruption in *DSSE*, we add the updatability into *DSSE*, define the syntax of *U&D-SSE*. Then to characterize the leakage of key corruption and update process, we introduce leakage function $\mathcal{L}^{upd}$, and allow any adversary to query corruption and update oracles to build $\mathcal{L}$-adaptive security model.

2) **Propose a *U&D-SSE* scheme with token inference.** By exploiting the *KBBC* technology, we present the first *U&D-SSE* scheme with token inference, which surpasses simple re-encryption processes. Consequently, the updated database reamins fully searchable with the new private key, and a token can bi-directionally update or infer a key and a ciphertext.

3) **Construct a *U&D-SSE* scheme with token-free inference.** As an improvement, we propose a *U&D-SSE* scheme with token-free inference, enabling no-directional key updates by concealing a key within the obfuscation program using $i\mathcal{O}$. Thus the inference of an update token to the secret key in the initial construction can be avoid.

2 Preliminaries

2.1 Notations

In this paper, *blk* is a data block, T is an integer that represents the maximum number of epochs, e is the current epoch during T, and ts is a timestamp that starts at 0 and increases with each query. Denote e^* as the challenge epoch and Δ_e as an update token at the epoch e.

2.2 Basic Primitives

Puncturable Pseudorandom Function (PPRF) [25]. Given two sets $\mathcal{P} = \{0,1\}^{n(\lambda)}$ and $\mathcal{R} = \{0,1\}^{m(\lambda)}$, a pseudorandom function $PRF : K \times \mathcal{P} \to \mathcal{R}$, and a puncture algorithm $Punc : K \times \overline{\mathcal{P}} \to \overline{\mathcal{R}}$ for two subsets $\overline{\mathcal{P}} \subseteq \mathcal{P}$ and $\overline{\mathcal{R}} \subseteq \mathcal{R}$, where $K \leftarrow \{0,1\}^\lambda$, and $n(\lambda), m(\lambda)$ are two efficiently computable functions. Then a puncturable pseudorandom function *PPRF* is consisted of a tuple of algorithms (*PRF*, *Punc*) that satisfies the following two conditions.

1. *Functionality preserving under puncturing*: For all polynomial size subset $\{x_i\}_{i\in[k]}$ of $\mathcal{P}$ and $x \in \mathcal{P}\backslash\{x_i\}_{i\in[k]}$, we have

$$\Pr\left[PRF(K,x) = PRF(K^*,x) : K \leftarrow \{0,1\}^\lambda, K^* \leftarrow Punc(K,\{x_i\}_{i\in[k]})\right] = 1.$$

2. *Pseudorandomness at the punctured points*: For all polynomial size subset $\{x_i\}_{i\in[k]}$ of $\mathcal{P}$, and any PPT adversary $\mathcal{A}$, it holds that

$$Adv_{PRF,\mathcal{A}}^{PPRF} := \Pr[\mathcal{A}(K^*, \{PRF(K,x_i)\}_{i\in[k]}) = 1] - \Pr[\mathcal{A}(K^*,\mathcal{U}^k) = 1] \leq negl(\lambda),$$

where $K \leftarrow \{0,1\}^\lambda, K^* \leftarrow Punc(K,\{x_i\}_{i\in[k]})$, and $\mathcal{U}$ denotes the uniform distribution over $\mathcal{R}$.

Indistinguishability Obfuscation ($i\mathcal{O}$) [26]. For a circuit class $\{C_\lambda\}(\lambda \in N)$, a PPT algorithm $i\mathcal{O}$ is an indistinguishability obfuscator that satisfies the following two conditions.

1. *Functionality*: For any security parameter $\lambda\in N$, circuit $C\in C_\lambda$, and input x, we have that
$$\Pr[C'(x) = C(x)|C' \leftarrow i\mathcal{O}(C,\lambda)] = 1.$$

2. *Indistinguishability*: For any PPT distinguisher $\mathcal{D}$ and $C_0, C_1 \in C_\lambda$, if $\forall x$, $\Pr[C_0(x) \neq C_1(x) \cap |C_0| = |C_1|] \leq negl(\lambda)$, then the following holds

$$Adv_{i\mathcal{O},\mathcal{D}}(\lambda) := \left| \Pr\left[\mathcal{D}(i\mathcal{O}(C_0,\lambda)) = 1\right] - \Pr\left[\mathcal{D}(i\mathcal{O}(C_1,\lambda)) = 1\right] \right| \leq negl(\lambda).$$

Key-Based Block Chain (KBBC) [12]. A key-based block chain $\mathcal{BC}$ has the capability to link arbitrary number of blocks while concealing their relations. Each data block is of the form $blk = (id, value, key, ptr)$, where $(id, value)$ means data identifier and data value of the current block blk, and (key, ptr) refers to encryption key and identifier of its next data block, respectively. Once the key for the header block is corrupted, the forward privacy of $KBBC$ cannot be guaranteed. Generally, the $KBBC$ technique involves adding data block and searching data as follows.

1. *AddHead*($\mathcal{BC}, id, value, 1^\lambda$) is an algorithm performed by data owner to add a new block into $\mathcal{BC}$. Data owner chooses a random key k from $\{0,1\}^\lambda$, retrieves $(\mathcal{BC}.head.key, \mathcal{BC}.head.ptr)$ of the current header block in the chain, encrypts $(value, \mathcal{BC}.head.key, \mathcal{BC}.head.ptr)$ by k, and stores the ciphertext in $\mathcal{BC}.id$. After completing the adding, the owner updates and shares the stored header block information (id, k) with data user for retrieval, deletes the old header block information, and returns a block blk to cloud server.

2. *Retrieve*($\mathcal{BC}, id, k$) is an algorithm run by cloud server to search the corresponding data. After receiving the search information (id, k) from data user, this algorithm takes an identifier id and a key k as inputs, finds a block blk by the identifier id, uses the key k to decrypt the block blk to obtain key $blk.key$ and identifier $blk.ptr$ of the next data block, and returns the current $value$ to the data user. Then this algorithm uses $(blk.key, blk.ptr)$ to repeat the above operation, until $blk.ptr = \bot$.

3 Formal Updatable and Dynamic Searchable Symmetric Encryption

In this section, we introduce the formal definition and the security model for updatable and dynamic searchable symmetric encryption (*U&D-SSE*).

3.1 System Framework

There are three entities in the system framework of updatable and dynamic searchable symmetric encryption, as shown in Fig. 1.

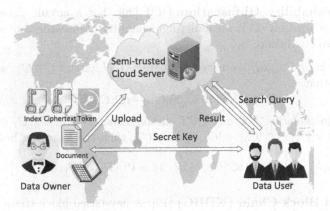

Fig. 1. System framework of *U&D-SSE*

- **Data Owner.** Data owner (*DO*) uses a key to encrypt some documents and search keywords into ciphertexts and indexes, respectively. As the need arises, *DO* can dynamically modify the database by adding or deleting some ciphertexts and indexes, and update the database by sending an update token to update these ciphertexts and indexes. In addition, if the data owner needs to share the data with others, they can transmit the secret key to the intended data users through a secure channel.
- **Cloud Server.** Cloud server (*CS*) can faithfully perform the operations for data owners or users, such as storing, searching, modifying and updating. For a particular keyword, cloud server searches the documents by matching the encrypted index, and then sends the searched results back to data user. After receiving an update token from *DO*, *CS* periodically executes the update algorithm to update the stored ciphertexts and delete the old ciphertexts.
- **Data User.** A valid data user (*DU*) is an entity who can access to the outsourced data and issue search queries. When *DU* generates a search query embedded with the desired search keyword and submits the query to cloud server, she or he can decrypt the ciphertext returned by cloud server with

the secret key to obtain the corresponding documents. Upon receiving an updated key from DO, the data user must exclusively utilize the new key for posting search queries and decrypting the ciphertexts.

3.2 Syntax

Definition 1 *(Updatable and dynamic searchable symmetric encryption). An U&D-SSE scheme consists of an algorithm Setup and three protocols {Modify, Update, Search} executed by data owner, data user, and cloud server.*

- *$Setup(1^\lambda, \mathcal{DB}) \to (\mathcal{EDB}_0, uk_0)$ is an algorithm run by data owner to establish an encrypted database that supports keyword search. This algorithm takes a security parameter 1^λ and a database $\mathcal{DB}$ as inputs, and outputs a tuple of $(\mathcal{EDB}_0, uk_0)$, which means an encrypted database and an initial key of data owner, respectively.*
- *$Modify(uk_e, op, inp; \mathcal{EDB}_e) \to \big(Modify_{DO}(uk_e, op, inp); Modify_{CS}(\mathcal{EDB}_e)\big)$ is a protocol between data owner and cloud server to support the modifying operation. For DO, the algorithm $Modify_{DO}(uk_e, op, inp)$ takes the current key uk_e, the operation op, and an input inp (parsed as the index and a set of keywords $\mathcal{W}$) as inputs, and outputs a modification of encrypted database. For CS, the algorithm $Modify_{CS}(\mathcal{EDB}_e)$ stores the modified database into $\mathcal{EDB}_e$.*
- *$Update(uk_e; \mathcal{EDB}_e) \to \big(Update_{DO}(uk_e); Update_{CS}(\mathcal{EDB}_e)\big)$ is a protocol between data owner and cloud server to support the update operation. For DO, the algorithm $Update_{DO}(uk_e)$ takes the key uk_e as input, and outputs a new key uk_{e+1} at the next epoch and a special token $\triangle_{e+1}$ for CS. After receiving $\triangle_{e+1}$, CS runs $Update_{CS}(\mathcal{EDB}_e)$ and outputs the updated database.*
- *$Search(uk_e, \omega; \mathcal{EDB}_e) \to \big(Search_{DU}(uk_e, \omega); Search_{CS}(\mathcal{EDB}_e)\big)$ is a protocol between data user and cloud server to perform a search query at the epoch e. For DU, the algorithm $Search_{DU}(uk_e, \omega)$ takes the key uk_e, and the keyword ω as inputs, and returns a query que. For CS, the algorithm $Search_{CS}(\mathcal{EDB}_e)$ takes $\mathcal{EDB}_e$ and the query que as inputs, and outputs the search results SR.*

Correctness. An *U&D-SSE* scheme is correct if the search protocol *Search* always returns a correct result with an overwhelming probability for each query. At the same time, the update of a valid $\mathcal{EDB}_e$ from the epoch e to epoch $e+1$ yields a valid encrypted database $\mathcal{EDB}_{e+1}$, which can be searched by DU under the new key uk_{e+1} at the epoch $e+1$.

3.3 Security Models

We firstly define the family of leakage functions to capture the leakage caused by executing three protocols, which can be used to formalize the adaptive security. Let Q^* record plaintexts (inp, e) by which an adversary can generate a ciphertext at the epoch e. After the key uk_e has been corrupted, the adversary can also obtain the underlying plaintext of *U&D-SSE*, which also contained in Q^*.

Leakage Functions. The leakage function $\mathcal{L}$ [13,15] maintains a list QU of all queries issued up to now, containing search queries (ts, ω) and modification queries (ts, op, inp) to capture the leakage during search and modification:

- $sp(\omega) = \{ts : (ts, \omega) \in QU\}$: List of timestamps that leaks which search queries are related to the same keyword ω.
- $TimeDB(\omega) = \{(ts, ind)|(ts, add, (\omega, ind)) \in QU$ and ind has not been deleted$\}$: List of all existing documents matching ω and the timestamps they were inserted into the database.
- $TimeMod(\omega) = \{ts|(ts, add, (\omega, ind)) \cup (ts, del, (\omega, ind)) \in QU\}$: List of timestamps of all modifications on ω.

If a private key is corrupted and not updated in time, $\mathcal{A}$ can decrypt to obtain the underlying plaintext or initiate a modification query maliciously. In addition, the ciphertexts before and after the update will also expose some information, which can be used to launch attacks by $\mathcal{A}$. To formalize the definition of leakages from key corruption and update process, we introduce three types of leakage functions at the current epoch e as follows.

- $KeyCor(e')$: List of the plaintexts of the encrypted databases. When the key at the epoch e' has been corrupted, $\mathcal{A}$ can decrypt all ciphertexts updated to the epoch e'. Assume that $c_1 \in \mathcal{EDB}_{e'}$ is obtained by encrypting (op, inp) at the epoch e_1 and updated to the epoch e', then $KeyCor(e') = \{(op, inp)|e' \leq e\}$.
- $KeyMod(e)$: List of the modification queries issued after the current epoch key has been corrupted. The adversary $\mathcal{A}$ can utilize the corrupted key to issue a modification query at will, which can be used to launch a malicious attack. Let $KeyMod(e) = \{(e, op, inp)|(inp, e) \in Q^*\}$.
- $KeyUpd(e)$: List of the timestamps and relationships between the corresponding ciphertexts before and after the update, which can be used to get some information by $\mathcal{A}$. At the same time, $\mathcal{A}$ can also use a corrupted token to infer the key and ciphertexts. Assume that a ciphertext $c_{e''}$ is generated at the epoch e'', then $KeyUpd(e) = \{(e'', e)|c_e$ is updated from $c_{e''}$ at the epoch $e\}$.

$\mathcal{L}$-Adaptive Security. The $\mathcal{L}$-adaptive security [13] is portrayed by simulating the security games between *U&D-SSEReal* and *U&D-SSEIdeal*, and taking $\mathcal{L} = (\mathcal{L}^{Stp}, \mathcal{L}^{Srch}, \mathcal{L}^{Mod})$ as the input to a simulator $\mathcal{S}$. In order to describe the information leaked to the adversary $\mathcal{A}$ during the update, a function $\mathcal{L}^{Upd}$ is introduced to characterize the leakage caused by any operation that occurs before and after the update, which can be depicted by three leakage functions: *KeyCor*, *KeyMod*, *KeyUpd*. More formally, we consider the following security games, and the details are expressed in Appendix B.

- *U&D-SSEReal*$_{\mathcal{A}}(\lambda)$: At the epoch e, $\mathcal{A}$ initially chooses a database $\mathcal{DB}$, and calls $Setup(1^\lambda, \mathcal{DB})$ to generate $\mathcal{EDB}_e$. Then $\mathcal{A}$ adaptively performs the search queries, modification queries, and update queries before and after the key is compromised at the epoch e. By running $Search(uk_e, \omega; \mathcal{EDB}_e)$, $Modify(uk_e, op, inp; \mathcal{EDB}_e)$, and $Update_{CS}(\triangle_{e+1}, \mathcal{EDB}_e)$, then $\mathcal{A}$ can output a bit $b \in \{0, 1\}$ based on the results of the queries.

- $U\&D\text{-}SSEIdeal_{\mathcal{A},\mathcal{S},\mathcal{L}}(\lambda)$: $\mathcal{A}$ chooses a database $\mathcal{DB}$, and receives $\mathcal{EDB}_e$ generated by the simulator $\mathcal{S}(\mathcal{L}^{Stp}(\mathcal{DB}))$. Then $\mathcal{A}$ adaptively performs the search, modification and update queries, respectively. The simulator $\mathcal{S}$ outputs a transcript by using the leakage functions $\mathcal{L}^{Srch}$, $\mathcal{L}^{Mod}$, and $\mathcal{L}^{Upd}$. Eventually, $\mathcal{A}$ outputs a bit $b \in \{0,1\}$.

The $\mathcal{L}$-adaptive security states that any PPT adversary $\mathcal{A}$ cannot distinguish between real and ideal games at any epoch e. However, if $KeyUpd(e) \neq null$, $\mathcal{A}$ can obtain information from the update of the ciphertexts and indexes, and the $\mathcal{L}$-adaptive security will be broken. Thus the condition $KeyUpd(e) = null$ is necessary. Formally, the $\mathcal{L}$-adaptive security of $U\&D\text{-}SSE$ is shown below.

Definition 2 *($\mathcal{L}$-Adaptive Security of U&D-SSE). Given a leakage function $\mathcal{L} = (\mathcal{L}^{Stp}, \mathcal{L}^{Srch}, \mathcal{L}^{Mod}, \mathcal{L}^{Upd})$, a U&D-SSE scheme is said to be $\mathcal{L}$-adaptively secure at the epoch e, if for any PPT adversary $\mathcal{A}$ that makes a polynomial $q(\lambda)$ of queries and $KeyUpd(e) = null$, there exists an efficient simulator $\mathcal{S}$ such that:*

$$\left| \Pr\left[U\&D\text{-}SSEReal_{\mathcal{A}}(\lambda) = 1\right] - \Pr\left[U\&D\text{-}SSEIdeal_{\mathcal{A},\mathcal{S},\mathcal{L}}(\lambda) = 1\right] \right| \leq negl(\lambda).$$

4 Construction of Updatable and Dynamic Searchable Symmetric Encryption

Due to the severe consequences of key exposure in $DSSE$, an updatable and dynamic searchable symmetric encryption scheme is constructed, building upon Wei's scheme [12], which features bi-directional key updates. Moreover, to address the potential issue of tokens inferring keys in the initial construction, we introduce a novel $U\&D\text{-}SSE$ scheme with token-free inference, incorporating a key update mechanism that is non-directional.

4.1 *U&D-SSE* with Token Inference

Construction. F is a pseudorandom function, G is a group of order q (a λ-bit prime) with a generator g, and $A[\omega]$ denotes the number of times that ω has been searched. $H_1 : \{0,1\}^\lambda \times \{0,1\}^{\log|w|+1} \to Z_q$, $H_2 : \{0,1\}^\lambda \times \{0,1\}^\mu \to \{0,1\}^\lambda$. Let $blk_i^{(j)}$ mean the ciphertext generated at the epoch i is updated j times.

- **Setup:**
  1) DO chooses a random key $uk_0 \xleftarrow{\gamma} \{0,1\}^\lambda$ and sets $A[\omega] \leftarrow 0$ for all ω.
  2) Select a random transformation $\pi_1 : \{0,1\}^* \to G$ and a mapping function $\pi_2 : G \to \{0,1\}^{2\lambda+\mu}$, and replace each ω with $\omega\|0$ in $\mathcal{DB}$.
  3) Pick an empty tree $\mathcal{EDB}$ and a set W that stores the information of the header block.
- **Modify**$(uk_e, op, inp; \mathcal{EDB}_e)$:
  1) DO executes $Modify_{DO}(uk_e, op, inp)$ with the following steps:
     (a) Parse inp as (ind, ω) to compute $K_\omega^e \leftarrow H_1(uk_e, \omega, A[\omega])$ at epoch e.
     (b) Retrieve $(id, key_e) \leftarrow \left(W(\omega\|A[\omega]).id, W(\omega\|A[\omega]).key\right)$.

(c) Choose $id^* \overset{\gamma}{\leftarrow} \{0,1\}^\mu$ and $r \overset{\gamma}{\leftarrow} \{0,1\}^\lambda$ to compute $key_e^* \leftarrow F_{uk_e}(r)$.

(d) Generate $blk_e^{(0)} = (id^*, P\|Q) \leftarrow (id^*, [(key_e\|id) \oplus mask_e]$
$\|\pi_2([\pi_1(ind\|op)]^{K_\omega^e}))$, where $mask_e \leftarrow H_2(key_e^*, id^*)$.

(e) Send the data block $blk_e^{(0)}$ to CS, and DO replaces (id, key_e) with $\big(W(\omega\|A[\omega]).id, W(\omega\|A[\omega]).key\big) \leftarrow (id^*, key_e^*)$ locally.

2) CS performs $Modify_{CS}(\mathcal{EDB}_e)$ to insert the block $blk_e^{(0)}$ into $\mathcal{EDB}_e$.

- **Update**$(uk_e; \mathcal{EDB}_e)$:

  1) DO chooses a new key $uk_{e+1} \leftarrow \{0,1\}^\lambda$ and executes $Update_{DO}(uk_e)$:
     (a) Compute $K_\omega^{e+1} \leftarrow H_1(uk_{e+1}, \omega, A[\omega])$.
     (b) Retrieve $(id, key_e) \leftarrow \big(W(\omega\|A[\omega]).id, W(\omega\|A[\omega]).key\big)$.
     (c) Compute $K_\omega^e \leftarrow H_1(uk_e, \omega, A[\omega])$ and $mask_e \leftarrow H_2(key_e, id)$.
     (d) Select $r' \overset{\gamma}{\leftarrow} \{0,1\}^\lambda$, and compute $key_{e+1} \leftarrow F_{uk_{e+1}}(r')$ and $mask_{e+1} \leftarrow H_2(key_{e+1}, id)$.
     (e) Let $\big(W(\omega\|A[\omega]).id, W(\omega\|A[\omega]).key\big) \leftarrow (id, key_{e+1})$.
     (f) Generate $\triangle_{e+1}^1 \leftarrow K_\omega^{e+1}/K_\omega^e$ and $\triangle_{e+1}^2 \leftarrow mask_{e+1} \oplus mask_e$.
     (g) Send $(\triangle_{e+1}^1, \triangle_{e+1}^2, key_e, id)$ to CS.

  2) CS updates blk_e to blk_{e+1} with $Update_{CS}(\mathcal{EDB}_e)$ as follows:
     (a) Retrieve $blk_i^{(j)}$ from $blk_i^{(j)} \leftarrow \mathcal{EDB}.id$, where $i + j = e$.
     (b) Update $blk_i^{(j+1)}.P$ with $blk_i^{(j+1)}.P = blk_i^{(j)}.P \oplus \triangle_{e+1}^2$.
     (c) Update $blk_i^{(j+1)}.Q$ with $blk_i^{(j+1)}.Q = \pi_2\{[\pi_2^{-1}blk_i^{(j)}.Q]^{\triangle_{e+1}^1}\}$.
     (d) Find the next block from $blk_i^{(j)}.P \oplus H_2(key_e, id) \to id'\|key'$ to generate other $blk_i^{(j+1)}.Q$ parts as (c).

- **Search**$(uk_e, \omega; \mathcal{EDB}_e)$:

  1) DU carries out $Search_{DU}(uk_e, \omega)$ to retrieve (id, key_e) from $\big(W(\omega\| A[\omega]).id, W(\omega\|A[\omega]).key\big)$ and sends (id, key_e) to CS.

  2) CS returns the search results SR as in $Search_{CS}(\mathcal{EDB}_e)$:
     (a) Compute $mask_e \leftarrow H_2(key_e, id)$ with (id, key_e) returned by DU.
     (b) Retrieve $blk_i^{(j)}$ from $\mathcal{EDB}_e$ with id.
     (c) If $i + j = e$, then store $SR_i \leftarrow blk_i^{(j)}.Q$ and get $(blk_i^{(j)}.ptr, blk_i^{(j)}.key)$ from $blk_i^{(j)}.P \oplus mask_e \to id'\|key'$. Otherwise return $\perp$, until $blk_i^{(j)}.ptr == \perp$.

  3) DU decrypts SR to get $ind_i\|op_i$ as follows:
     (a) $\pi_1^{-1}\big([\pi_2^{-1}(SR_i)]^{1/K_\omega^e}\big) \to (ind_i\|op_i)$.
     (b) Run $Modify(uk_e, add, inp)$ by $A[\omega] := A[\omega] + 1$ again to re-encrypt document indices.

The reason why other $blk_i^{(j)}.P$ is not updated in the blocks is that $key\|id$ is available to cloud server and $mask_e$ is generated by two random strings key_e and id, so the corruption of uk_e has no effect on other $blk_i^{(j)}.P$. Furthermore, an intuitive example is shown in Fig. 2. Assume that there are three data blocks $(blk_1^{(0)}, i)$ containing keyword ω at the epoch $e = 1$, and only one block need to be inserted at the next epoch, where $i \in \{1, 2, 3\}$ denotes the i-th block. Then $blk_1^{(1)}.Q \leftarrow \pi_2\big([\pi_2^{-1}(blk_1^{(0)}.Q)]^{\triangle_2^1}\big)$, the value of P in the third block $(blk_1^{(0)}, 3)$ is updated to $blk_1^{(1)}.P \leftarrow (blk_1^{(0)}.P) \oplus \triangle_2^2$, and $blk_1^{(1)}.P = blk_1^{(0)}.P$ in the rest blocks.

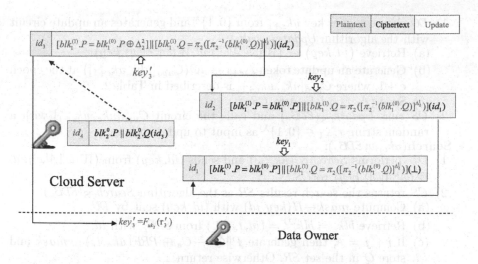

Fig. 2. An intuitive example about *U&D-SSE*

4.2   *U&D-SSE* with Token-Free Inference

In *U&D-SSE* scheme with token inference, it is clear that if $\mathcal{A}$ corrupts both $\triangle_{e+1}^1$ and K_ω^e (guessed by the corrupted key uk_e and ω), $\mathcal{A}$ can infer K_ω^{e+1}, which will increase $\mathcal{A}$'s advantage of decrypting the ciphertext at the latest epoch. Therefore, the functionality of token inference should be avoided, and indistinguishable obfuscation make the proposed no-directional key update scheme more sense.

Construction. $A[\omega]$ denotes the number of times that a keyword ω has been searched and F is a pseudorandom function. Let $PRG : \{0,1\}^\lambda \rightarrow \{0,1\}^{2\lambda}$, $PRF : \{0,1\}^\lambda \times \{0,1\}^{2\lambda} \rightarrow \{0,1\}^l$, $H : \{0,1\}^\lambda \times \{0,1\}^\mu \rightarrow \{0,1\}^l$, and (E, D) is a normal symmetric encryption and decryption algorithm.

- **Setup**: It is the same as *U&D-SSE* with token inference.
- **Modify**$(uk_e, op, inp; \mathcal{EDB}_e)$:
  1) *DO* executes $Modify_{DO}(uk_e, op, inp)$ to generate a data block $blk_e^{(0)}$ as follows.
     - (a) Choose $r_e \in \{0,1\}^\lambda$, and compute $t_e = PRG(r_e)$, $y_e = PRF(uk_e, t_e)$.
     - (b) Retrieve $(id, key) \leftarrow \big(W(\omega\|A[\omega]).id, W(\omega\|A[\omega]).key\big)$.
     - (c) Choose $id^* \xleftarrow{\gamma} \{0,1\}^\mu$ and $r \xleftarrow{\gamma} \{0,1\}^\lambda$, and compute $key^* \leftarrow F_{uk_e}(r)$.
     - (d) Generate $blk_e^{(0)} = \big(id^*, t_e, y_e \oplus mask \oplus [(key\|id)\|E_{uk_e}(ind\| op\|A[\omega])]\big)$, where $mask \leftarrow H(key^*, id^*)$, and update (id, key) in map $\big(W(\omega\|A[\omega]).id, W(\omega\|A[\omega]).key\big)$ with $\big(W(\omega\|A[\omega]).id, W(\omega\|A[\omega]). key\big) \leftarrow (id^*, key^*)$.
     - (e) Send the data block $blk_e^{(0)}$ to *CS*.
  2) *CS* performs $Modify_{CS}(\mathcal{EDB}_e)$ and inserts $blk_e^{(0)}$ into $\mathcal{EDB}_e$.
- **Update**$(uk_e; \mathcal{EDB}_e)$:

1) DO chooses a new key uk_{e+1} from $\{0,1\}^\lambda$ and generates an update circuit with the algorithm $Update_{DO}(uk_e)$:

   (a) Retrieve $(id, key) \leftarrow (W(\omega\|A[\omega]).id, W(\omega\|A[\omega]).key)$.

   (b) Generate an update token $\triangle_{e+1} \leftarrow iO(C_{upd}[uk_e, uk_{e+1}])$ at the epoch $e+1$, where $C_{upd}[uk_e, uk_{e+1}]$ is described in Table 2.

   (c) Send $(\triangle_{e+1}, id, key)$ to CS.

2) CS runs $Update_{CS}(\mathcal{EDB}_e)$ and calls the circuit $C_{upd}[uk_e, uk_{e+1}]$ with a random string $r_{e+1} \in \{0,1\}^\lambda$ as input to update blk_e.

- **Search**$(uk_e, \omega; \mathcal{EDB}_e)$:

1) DU performs $Search_{DU}(uk_e, \omega)$ and sends (id, key) from $(W(\omega\|A[\omega]).id,$ $W(\omega\|A[\omega]).key)$ to CS.

2) CS returns the search results SR as the algorithm $Search_{CS}(\mathcal{EDB}_e)$.

   (a) Compute $mask \leftarrow H(key, id)$ with (id, key) sent by DU.

   (b) Retrieve $blk_e = blk_i^{(j)} = (id, t_e, C_e)$ from $\mathcal{EDB}_e$ with id.

   (c) If $i + j = e$, then generate $P\|Q \leftarrow C_e \oplus PRF(uk_e, t_e) \oplus mask$ and store Q in the set SR. Otherwise return $\bot$.

   (d) Find the next block by $P.ptr$, repeat the above until $P.ptr == \bot$, and send SR to DU.

3) DU can get $ind_i\|op_i$ from $D_{uk_e}(SR)$ and run $Modify(uk_e, add, inp)$ by $A[\omega] := A[\omega] + 1$ again to re-encrypt document indices.

Since the secret keys uk_e and uk_{e+1} are subtly embedded in the token by using the indistinguishable obfuscation technique on the punctured program, there is no way to infer uk_{e+1} (resp. uk_e) from uk_e (resp. uk_{e+1}) and $\triangle_{e+1}$. That is to say, the tokens are not helpful for upgrading and degrading keys. Thus the proposed scheme can implement no-directional key update.

Correctness. The output of the update algorithm **Update**$(uk_e; \mathcal{EDB}_e)$ is exactly the same as that of the algorithm **Modify**$(uk_e, op, inp; \mathcal{EDB}_e)$ by the definition of $C_{upd}[uk_e, uk_{e+1}]$, so the search protocol **Search** always returns a correct result with an overwhelming probability for each query. Once the secret key uk_e has been updated, the trapdoors generated from old keys cannot search keywords due to $i+j \neq e$, which will return $\bot$. Thus, the correctness for $U\&D$-SSE with token-free inference holds.

5   Security Analysis

In this section, we will put forward the $\mathcal{L}$-adaptive security of $U\&D$-SSE scheme with token-free inference. Since $U\&D$-SSE scheme with token-free inference is an enhancement of the first construction in terms of update direction, the security and the proofs of them are similar.

Theorem 1. *If F and PRF are two secure pseudorandom functions, PRG is a secure pseudorandom generator, hash function H is modeled as a random oracle outputting l bit, we define $\mathcal{L}_{U\&D\text{-}SSE} = (\mathcal{L}_{U\&D\text{-}SSE}^{Srch}, \mathcal{L}_{U\&D\text{-}SSE}^{Mod}, \mathcal{L}_{U\&D\text{-}SSE}^{Upd})$, where $\mathcal{L}_{U\&D\text{-}SSE}^{Srch}(\omega) = (sp(\omega), TimeDB(\omega), TimeMod(\omega))$, $\mathcal{L}_{U\&D\text{-}SSE}^{Mod}(op, \omega, ind) = op$, $\mathcal{L}_{U\&D\text{-}SSE}^{Upd} = (KeyCor(e'), KeyMod(e), KeyUpd(e))$, and $KeyUpd(e) = null$, then the proposed $U\&D$-SSE scheme is $\mathcal{L}_{U\&D\text{-}SSE}$-adaptive-secure.*

Table 2. The description of program $C_{upd}[uk_e, uk_{e+1}]$

Program 1 Update algorithm $C_{upd}[uk_e, uk_{e+1}]$

Hardwired:
> uk_e, uk_{e+1}.

Input:
>   A random seed $r_{e+1} \in \{0,1\}^\tau$, id, key and blk_e.

Compute:
>   1) Retrieve $blk_e = (id, t_e, C_e)$ from $\mathcal{EDB}_e$ with id
>   2) $u = P\|Q_e = C_e \oplus PRF(uk_e, t_e) \oplus H(id, key)$
>   3) $Q_{e+1} \leftarrow E_{uk_{e+1}}[D_{uk_e}(Q_e)], u' = [P\|Q_{e+1}] \oplus mask$
>   4) $t_{e+1} = PRG(r_{e+1})$, $y_{e+1} = PRF(uk_{e+1}, t_{e+1})$
>   5) $blk_{e+1} \leftarrow (id, t_{e+1}, C_{e+1}) = (id, t_{e+1}, y_{e+1} \oplus u')$
>   6) Insert blk_{e+1} into $\mathcal{EDB}_{e+1}$, and delete blk_e
>   7) Find the next block with $P.ptr$
>   8) Repeat the above until $P.ptr == \perp$

Output:
>   A ciphertext blk_{e+1}.

Actually, the condition $KeyUpd(e) = null$ states that the fresh ciphertext generated by the modification algorithm **Modify** is indistinguishable from the updated ciphertext generated by the update algorithm **Update**. In short, it doesn't matter whether the simulator $\mathcal{S}$ encrypts $\overline{inp}$ with the key uk_e(case $b = 0$) or updates $\overline{\mathcal{EDB}}$ with $\triangle_e$(case $b = 1$), and the final result has the same form and does not reveal "age"(number of updates), thus the proposed schemes satisfy $KeyUpd(e) = null$. Formally, the condition can be described as follows.

Definition 3 *(KeyUpd(e) = null of U&D-SSE).* *An U&D-SSE scheme is said to satisfy $KeyUpd(e) = null$ iff for any valid PPT adversary $\mathcal{A}$, the advantage function*

$$Adv_{U\&D\text{-}SSE,\mathcal{A}}^{KeyUpd(e)=null} = \left| \Pr[Exp_{U\&D\text{-}SSE,\mathcal{A}}^{KeyUpd(e)=null} = 1] - \frac{1}{2} \right| \leq negl(\lambda)$$

is negligible, where $Exp_{U\&D\text{-}SSE,\mathcal{A}}^{KeyUpd(e)=null}$ is defined as Table 3.

Fact 1. If $i\mathcal{O}$, *PPRF* satisfy definitions in Sect. 2.2, then *U&D-SSE* scheme with token-free inference satisfy $KeyUpd(e) = null$ in the no-directional key updates setting. That is

$$Adv_{U\&D\text{-}SSE,\mathcal{A}}^{KeyUpd(e)=null}(\lambda) \leq negl(\lambda).$$

The behaviors of the available oracles are shown in Table 4 in the Appendix A, and the proof of Theorem 1 and Fact 1 is shown in Appendix C.

Forward Privacy. A $\mathcal{L}$-adaptive-secure *U&D-SSE* scheme is forward privacy iff $\mathcal{L}^{Mod}(op, inp) = \mathcal{L}'(op, (ind_i, u_i))$, where $\mathcal{L}'$ is stateless. Since the proposed two

Table 3. The condition of $KeyUpd(e) = $ null for $U\&D\text{-}SSE$

$Exp_{U\&D-SSE,\mathcal{A}}^{KeyUpd(e)=null}(1^{\lambda})$:

     do Setup

         $(\overline{inp}, \overline{\mathcal{EDB}}) \xleftarrow{r} \mathcal{A}^{\mathcal{O}.Modify,\mathcal{O}.Next,\mathcal{O}.Corr,\mathcal{O}.Upd(\mathcal{EDB}_{e-1})}(\lambda)$

         $e^* := e;\ flag := 1;\ b \xleftarrow{r} \{0,1\}$

         if $(\overline{\mathcal{EDB}}, e^* - 1) \notin E$ or $(\overline{inp}, e^*) \notin Q^*$ then return $\perp$

         if $b = 0$ then $\mathcal{EDB}_{e^*}^* \xleftarrow{r} Modify(uk_{e^*}, add, \overline{inp})$

         else $\mathcal{EDB}_{e^*}^* \xleftarrow{r} Update_{CS}(\triangle_e^*, \overline{\mathcal{EDB}})$

         $b' \xleftarrow{r} \mathcal{A}^{\mathcal{O}.Next,\mathcal{O}.Corr,\mathcal{O}.Upd(\mathcal{EDB}_{e-1}),\mathcal{O}.Upd\widetilde{C}}(\mathcal{EDB}^*)$

         if $K^* \cap C^* \neq \varnothing$ then $twf \leftarrow 1$

         if $twf = 1$ then $b' \xleftarrow{r} \{0,1\}$

         if $b = b'$ then return 1

Note: $flag = 1$ denote $\mathcal{A}$ has issued a challenge query, otherwise $flag = 0$.

schemes are constructed on the basis of the key-based blocks chain technique, which can provide forward privacy for the newly added block because its next block identifier id is encrypted by data owner randomly, and the updated ciphertext is indistinguishable from the encrypted ciphertext, the modified entries cannot be linked with the previous modify and search queries.

Backward Privacy. A $\mathcal{L}$-adaptive-secure $U\&D\text{-}SSE$ scheme is modify pattern revealing backward privacy [13] iff $\mathcal{L}^{Srch}(\omega) = \mathcal{L}'(TimeDB(\omega), TimeMod(\omega))$, $\mathcal{L}^{Mod}(op, \omega, ind) = \mathcal{L}''(op, \omega)$, where $\mathcal{L}'$ and $\mathcal{L}''$ are stateless. In the first construction, we change $ind\|op$ to $\pi_2([\pi_1(ind\|op)]^{K_\omega^e})$ with the corresponding key K_ω^e, so that it is unable to recover $ind\|op$ from the retrieval result for the server while retrieving. Analogously, the ciphertext in the enhanced construction is $y_e \oplus mask \oplus [key\|id\|E_{uk_e}(ind\|op\|A[\omega])]$, and two document indices are re-encrypted after each search, so the proposed two schemes are backward privacy.

6 Conclusions

We have proposed two U&D-SSE schemes to mitigate the risk of secret key exposure. Importantly, the U&D-SSE scheme with token-free inference has no-directional key update, which avoids the ability of tokens to infer keys. At the same time, the proposed two schemes can effectively achieve forward and backward privacy. Compared to the outstanding scheme [5], which updates ciphertext by decrypting and then re-encrypting, our proposed schemes rotate ciphertexts using update tokens, offering a more efficient approach. Furthermore, a sophisticated $i\mathcal{O}$ tool is utilized in the update process, making the construction of an efficient U&D-SSE scheme an intriguing area for future research.

A   Leakage Sets

The bookkeeping techniques are widely used in *UE* [20, 22, 25]. In order to use these techniques to track the information gained by $\mathcal{A}$ in *U&D-SSE*, we have made the following adjustments and the behavior of oracles are defined in Table 4.

1. $\mathcal{K}$: List of epochs when $\mathcal{A}$ corrupted the epoch key via $\mathcal{O}.Corr$.
2. $\mathcal{T}$: List of epochs when $\mathcal{A}$ corrupted the update token via $\mathcal{O}.Corr$.
3. $\mathcal{C}$: List of epochs when $\mathcal{A}$ obtained challenge-equal ciphertexts via $\mathcal{O}.Chall$ or $\mathcal{O}.Upd\widetilde{C}$.
4. E: List of non-challenge ciphertexts $(cnt, \mathcal{EDB}_e, e)$ returned via $\mathcal{O}.Modify$ or $\mathcal{O}.Upd$, where cnt means a query index incremented by each call of $\mathcal{O}.Modify$.
5. $\widetilde{E}$: List of challenge-equal ciphertexts $(\mathcal{EDB}_e^*, e^*)$ obtained by $\mathcal{O}.Chall$ or $\mathcal{O}.Upd\widetilde{C}$.
6. $\widetilde{Q}^*$: List of challenge plaintexts $\{(\overline{inp}, e^*), (\overline{inp}_1, e^*)\}$, where $(\overline{inp}, \overline{\mathcal{EDB}})$ is the query to $\mathcal{O}.Chall$ and $\overline{inp}_1$ is the underlying plaintext of $\overline{\mathcal{EDB}}$.

The leakage sets $\mathcal{K}^*, \mathcal{C}^*, E^*, \widetilde{E}^*$ can be inferred by token inference.

Table 4. The behavior of oracles in the process of querying

$\underline{Setup(1^\lambda)}$:

$(\mathcal{DB}, uk_0, \sigma_0) \leftarrow Setup()$

$\triangle_0 := \perp; e, cnt, twf := 0$

$E, \widetilde{E}, C, K, T := \emptyset$

$\underline{\mathcal{O}.Modify(op, inp)}$

$cnt := cnt + 1$

if $inp \in \widetilde{Q}^*$ then

    return $\perp$

if $op = Add$ then

    $\mathcal{EDB}_e \leftarrow Modify(uk_e, add, inp; \mathcal{EDB}_e)$

if $op = Del$ then

    $\mathcal{EDB}_e \leftarrow Modify(uk_e, del, inp; \mathcal{EDB}_e)$

$E := E \cup (cnt, \mathcal{EDB}_e, e)$

return $\mathcal{EDB}_e$

$\underline{\mathcal{O}.Next(\,)}$

$e := e + 1$

$(uk_e, \triangle_e) \leftarrow Update_{DO}(uk_{e-1})$

if $flag = 1$ then

    $\mathcal{EDB}_e^* \leftarrow Update_{CS}(\triangle_e, \mathcal{EDB}_{e-1}^*)$

$\underline{\mathcal{O}.Upd(\mathcal{EDB}_{e-1})}$

if $(j, \mathcal{EDB}_{e-1}, e - 1) \notin E$, then

    return $\perp$

$\mathcal{EDB}_e \leftarrow Update_{CS}(\triangle_e, \mathcal{EDB}_{e-1})$

$E := E \cup (cnt, \mathcal{EDB}_e, e)$

$\underline{\mathcal{O}.Corr(crp, \hat{e})}$

if $\hat{e} > e$ then

    return $\perp$

if $crp = key$ then $K := K \cup \hat{e}$

    return $K_{\hat{e}}$

if $crp = token$ then $T := T \cup \hat{e}$

    return $\triangle_{\hat{e}}$

$\underline{\mathcal{O}.Chall(\overline{inp}, \overline{\mathcal{EDB}})}$

if $flag = 1$ then

    return $\perp$

$flag=1; \; e^* := e$

if $(\overline{\mathcal{EDB}}, e^* - 1; \overline{\mathcal{EDB}}_1) \notin E$ then

    return $\perp$

if $b = 0$ then

    $\mathcal{EDB}_{e^*}^* \leftarrow Modify(uk_{e^*}, add, \overline{inp})$

else $\mathcal{EDB}_{e^*}^* \leftarrow Update_{CS}(\triangle_{e+1}^*, \overline{\mathcal{EDB}})$

$C := C \cup e^*$

$\widetilde{E} := \widetilde{E} \cup (\mathcal{EDB}_{e^*}^*, e^*)$

return $\mathcal{EDB}_{e^*}^*$

$\underline{\mathcal{O}.Upd\widetilde{C}()}$

if $flag = 0$ then

    return $\perp$

$C := C \cup e$

$\widetilde{E} := \widetilde{E} \cup (\mathcal{EDB}_e^*, e)$

return $\mathcal{EDB}_e^*$

B   The Adaptive Security of *U&D-SSE*

The $\mathcal{L}$-adaptive security is defined by the indistinguishable of the two *U&D-SSEReal* and *U&D-SSEIdeal* games as Table 5.

Table 5. *U&D-SSEReal* and *U&D-SSEIdeal* security games. Boxes highlight the differences in the games.

$U\&D-SSEReal_{\mathcal{A}}(\lambda,q)$	$U\&D-SSEIdeal_{\mathcal{A},\mathcal{S},\mathcal{L}}(\lambda,q)$
1. $\mathcal{DB} \leftarrow \mathcal{A}()$	1. $\mathcal{DB} \leftarrow \mathcal{A}()$
2. $(\mathcal{EDB}_e) \leftarrow \boxed{Setup(\mathcal{DB})}$	2. $(\mathcal{EDB}_e) \leftarrow \boxed{\mathcal{S}(\mathcal{L}^{stp}(\mathcal{DB}))}$
3. $Transcript \leftarrow (\mathcal{DB}, \mathcal{EDB}_e)$	3. $Transcript \leftarrow (\mathcal{DB}, \mathcal{EDB}_e)$
4. for $k = 1$ to q do	4. for $k = 1$ to q do
5. $QU_k = (type_k, param_k) \leftarrow$ $\mathcal{A}(Transcript)$	5. $QU_k = (type_k, param_k) \leftarrow$ $\mathcal{A}(Transcript)$
6. if $type_k = Modify$ then	6. if $type_k = Modify$ then
7. $R_k \leftarrow \boxed{Modify(op, inp; \mathcal{EDB}_e)}$	7. $R_k \leftarrow \boxed{\mathcal{S}(\mathcal{L}^{Mod}(op, inp))}$
8. if $type_k = Search$ then	8. if $type_k = Search$ then
9. $R_k \leftarrow \boxed{Search(\omega; \mathcal{EDB}_e)}$	9. $R_k \leftarrow \boxed{\mathcal{S}(\mathcal{L}^{Srch}(que))}$
10. else $(type_k = Update)$ then	10. else $(type_k = Update)$ then
11. $R_k \leftarrow \boxed{Update_{CS}(uk_e, uk_{e+1}; \mathcal{EDB}_e)}$	11. $R_k \leftarrow \boxed{\mathcal{S}(\mathcal{L}^{Upd}(e \text{ or } e'))}$
12. end if	12. end if
13. Append (QU_k, R_k) to $Transcript$.	13. Append (QU_k, R_k) to $Transcript$.
14. end for	14. end for
15. $b \leftarrow \mathcal{A}(Transcript)$	15. $b \leftarrow \mathcal{A}(Transcript)$
16. return b	16. return b

C   Security Proof

In the following, we mainly prove Theorem 1, means that the $\mathcal{L}$-adaptive security of *U&D-SSE* scheme with token-free inference, who is an enhancement of the first construction in terms of update direction.

Proof. In this proof, $\mathcal{A}$ is a probabilistic polynomial-time adversary who tries to break the security of *U&D-SSE* scheme, the simulator $\mathcal{S}$ is responsible for generating the transcripts for $\mathcal{A}$.

Game G_0: The first experiment G_0 is exactly corresponding to the real world game $U\&D-SSEReal_{\mathcal{A}}^{U\&D-SSE}(\lambda)$, such that

$$\Pr[U\&D-SSEReal_{\mathcal{A}}^{U\&D-SSE}(\lambda) = 1] = \Pr[G_0 = 1]. \tag{1}$$

Game G_1: It is just like G_0 except that: we choose some random strings instead of using pseudorandom functions F and *PRF*. That is to say, for an identifier id^*, S chooses two random strings $t_e^c \in \{0,1\}^n$ and $y_e^c \in \{0,1\}^l$, and stores (id^*, t_e^c, y_e^c) in a table D. When querying F to generate key_e^* for (ω, id^*), S chooses a new random string $key_e^* \in \{0,1\}^\lambda$ if (ω, id^*) is never queried before, and stores it in the key table *KD*. Otherwise, return the key corresponding to (ω, id^*) in *KD*. Therefore, if the adversary $\mathcal{A}$ can distinguish G_1 from G_0, then we can build a reduction and there exists an adversary $\mathcal{B}_1$, who can distinguish between F, *PRF* and the truly random functions:

$$\left| \Pr[G_1 = 1] - \Pr[G_0 = 1] \right| \leq Adv_{\mathcal{B}_1}^{PRF,F}(\lambda). \tag{2}$$

Game G_2: This game is identical to G_1, except that we model H as a random oracle, and only *Modify* is adjusted and the rest is the same as before.
$Modify(uk_e, op, inp; \mathcal{EDB}_e)$: (Suppose the number of blocks containing ω is c)

- Data owner:
  1) $((id_0, mask_0, key_0), \cdots, (id_c, mask_c, key_c), c) \leftarrow W(\omega \| A[\omega])$
  2) $id_{c+1} \xleftarrow{\gamma} \{0,1\}^\mu$, $key_{c+1} \xleftarrow{\gamma} \{0,1\}^\lambda$, $mask_{c+1} \xleftarrow{\gamma} \{0,1\}^l$
  3) $W(\omega \| A[\omega]) \leftarrow ((id_0, mask_0, key_0), \cdots, (id_{c+1}, mask_{c+1}, key_{c+1}), c+1)$
  4) $((id_0, t_0^e, y_0^e), \cdots, (id_c, t_c^e, y_c^e)) \leftarrow D$, $t_{c+1}^e \in \{0,1\}^n$, $y_{c+1}^e \in \{0,1\}^l$
  5) $D \leftarrow ((id_0, t_0^e, y_0^e), \cdots, (id_{c+1}, t_{c+1}^e, y_{c+1}^e))$
  6) $blk_e^{(0)} \leftarrow (id_{c+1}, t_{c+1}^e, y_{c+1}^e \oplus mask_{c+1} \oplus [key_c \| id_c \| E_{uk_e}(ind \| op \| A[\omega]))$,
     and send the block $blk_e^{(0)}$ to the server.
- Cloud server: Insert the block $blk_e^{(0)}$ into the tree $\mathcal{EDB}_e$.

So we have

$$\Pr[G_2 = 1] = \Pr[G_1 = 1]. \tag{3}$$

Simulator: Before emulation, we need to make sure that the update process does not reveal the age of the ciphertext. Otherwise, the adversary can easily distinguish the real game from the ideal game through the acquired information. In other words, the condition $KeyUpd(e) = null$ needs to be satisfied, which can be guaranteed with Fact 1. So the simulator can directly be derived from Game G_2. What remains to do is to replace the direct use of the searched keyword ω by min $sp(\omega)$, meaning that the search trapdoor about ω in this game is generated by using the search pattern $sp(\omega)$. So G_2 and $U\&D\text{-}SSEIdeal_{\mathcal{A},\mathcal{S},\mathcal{L}}(\lambda)$ will be identical games, the only difference being that, instead of the keyword ω, S uses the counter $\omega = min\ sp(\omega)$ uniquely mapped from ω. Hence we get that:

$$\Pr[G_2 = 1] = \Pr[U\&D\text{-}SSEIdeal_{\mathcal{A},\mathcal{S},\mathcal{L}}^{U\&D\text{-}SSE}(\lambda) = 1]. \tag{4}$$

Conclusion: By combining all the distinguishing advantages from all the games, there exists a PPT adversary $\mathcal{B}_1$ such that the advantage against the proposed *U&D-SSE* scheme is:

$$\left| \Pr[U\&D\text{-}SSEReal_{\mathcal{A}}^{U\&D\text{-}SSE}(\lambda)] - \Pr[U\&D\text{-}SSEIdeal_{\mathcal{A},\mathcal{S},\mathcal{L}}^{U\&D\text{-}SSE}(\lambda)] \right| \leq Adv_{\mathcal{B}_1}^{PRF,F}(\lambda).$$

The proof of Fact 1 is similar to [25], and due to space limitations, we will present the proof in the full version.

References

1. Kocher, P.C.: Timing attacks on implementations of Diffie-Hellman, RSA, DSS, and other systems. In: Koblitz, N. (ed.) CRYPTO 1996. LNCS, vol. 1109, pp. 104–113. Springer, Heidelberg (1996). https://doi.org/10.1007/3-540-68697-5_9
2. Barker, E., Dang, Q.: NIST special publication 800-57 part 1, revision 4: recommendation for key management. Technical report, NIST **16** (2016). https://csrc.nist.gov/publications/detail/sp/800-57-part-1/rev-4/archive/2016-01-28
3. Abdalla, M., et al.: Searchable encryption revisited: consistency properties, relation to anonymous IBE, and extensions. In: Shoup, V. (ed.) CRYPTO 2005. LNCS, vol. 3621, pp. 205–222. Springer, Heidelberg (2005). https://doi.org/10.1007/11535218_13
4. Tang, Q.: Towards forward security properties for PEKS and IBE. In: Foo, E., Stebila, D. (eds.) ACISP 2015. LNCS, vol. 9144, pp. 127–144. Springer, Cham (2015). https://doi.org/10.1007/978-3-319-19962-7_8
5. Anada, H., Kanaoka, A., Matsuzaki, N., Watanabe, Y.: Key-updatable public-key encryption with keyword search: models and generic constructions. In: Susilo, W., Yang, G. (eds.) ACISP 2018. LNCS, vol. 10946, pp. 341–359. Springer, Cham (2018). https://doi.org/10.1007/978-3-319-93638-3_20
6. Song, D.X., Wagner, D., Perrig, A.: Practical techniques for searches on encrypted data. In: Proceeding 2000 IEEE Symposium on Security and Privacy, S&P 2000, pp. 44–55. IEEE (2000). https://doi.org/10.1109/SECPRI.2000.848445
7. Kamara, S., Papamanthou, C., Roeder, T.: Dynamic searchable symmetric encryption. In: Proceedings of the 2012 ACM Conference on Computer and Communications Security, CCS 2012, pp. 965–976. ACM (2012). https://doi.org/10.1145/2382196.2382298
8. Kamara, S., Papamanthou, C.: Parallel and dynamic searchable symmetric encryption. In: Sadeghi, A.-R. (ed.) FC 2013. LNCS, vol. 7859, pp. 258–274. Springer, Heidelberg (2013). https://doi.org/10.1007/978-3-642-39884-1_22
9. Cash, D., et al.: Dynamic searchable encryption in very-large databases: data structures and implementation. In: Proceedings of the 2014 Network and Distributed System Security Symposium, NDSS 2014 (2014). https://doi.org/10.14722/ndss.2014.23264
10. Stefanov, E., Papamanthou, C., Shi, E.: Practical dynamic searchable encryption with small leakage. In: Proceedings of the 2014 Network and Distributed System Security Symposium, NDSS 2014 (2014). https://doi.org/10.14722/ndss.2014.23298
11. Bost, R.: Σοφος: forward secure searchable encryption. In: Proceedings of the 2016 ACM SIGSAC Conference on Computer and Communications Security, CCS 2016, pp. 1143–1154. ACM (2016). https://doi.org/10.1145/2976749.2978303
12. Wei, Y., Lv, S., Guo, X., Liu, Z., Huang, Y., Li, B.: FSSE: forward secure searchable encryption with keyed-block chains. Inf. Sci. **500**, 113–126 (2019). https://doi.org/10.1016/j.ins.2019.05.059

13. Bost, R., Minaud, B., Ohrimenko, O.: Forward and backward private searchable encryption from constrained cryptographic primitives. In: Proceedings of the 2017 ACM SIGSAC Conference on Computer and Communications Security, CCS 2017, pp. 1465–1482. ACM (2017). https://doi.org/10.1145/3133956.3133980

14. Chamani, J.G., Papadopoulos, D., Papamanthou, C., Jalili, R.: New constructions for forward and backward private symmetric searchable encryption. In: Proceedings of the 2018 ACM SIGSAC Conference on Computer and Communications Security, CCS 2018, pp. 1038–1055. ACM (2018). https://doi.org/10.1145/3243734.3243833

15. Sun, S.F., et al.: Practical backward-secure searchable encryption from symmetric puncturable encryption. In: Proceedings of the 2018 ACM SIGSAC Conference on Computer and Communications Security, CCS 2018, pp. 763–780. ACM (2018). https://doi.org/10.1145/3243734.3243782

16. Boneh, D., Lewi, K., Montgomery, H., Raghunathan, A.: Key homomorphic PRFs and their applications. In: Canetti, R., Garay, J.A. (eds.) CRYPTO 2013. LNCS, vol. 8042, pp. 410–428. Springer, Heidelberg (2013). https://doi.org/10.1007/978-3-642-40041-4_23

17. Ananth, P., Cohen, A., Jain, A.: Cryptography with updates. In: Coron, J.-S., Nielsen, J.B. (eds.) EUROCRYPT 2017. LNCS, vol. 10211, pp. 445–472. Springer, Cham (2017). https://doi.org/10.1007/978-3-319-56614-6_15

18. Everspaugh, A., Paterson, K., Ristenpart, T., Scott, S.: Key rotation for authenticated encryption. In: Katz, J., Shacham, H. (eds.) CRYPTO 2017. LNCS, vol. 10403, pp. 98–129. Springer, Cham (2017). https://doi.org/10.1007/978-3-319-63697-9_4

19. Sun, S., et al.: Practical non-interactive searchable encryption with forward and backward privacy. In: Proceedings of the 2021 Network and Distributed System Security Symposium, NDSS 2021 (2021). https://doi.org/10.14722/ndss.2021.24162

20. Lehmann, A., Tackmann, B.: Updatable encryption with post-compromise security. In: Nielsen, J.B., Rijmen, V. (eds.) EUROCRYPT 2018. LNCS, vol. 10822, pp. 685–716. Springer, Cham (2018). https://doi.org/10.1007/978-3-319-78372-7_22

21. Klooß, M., Lehmann, A., Rupp, A.: (R)CCA secure updatable encryption with integrity protection. In: Ishai, Y., Rijmen, V. (eds.) EUROCRYPT 2019. LNCS, vol. 11476, pp. 68–99. Springer, Cham (2019). https://doi.org/10.1007/978-3-030-17653-2_3

22. Boyd, C., Davies, G.T., Gjøsteen, K., Jiang, Y.: Fast and secure updatable encryption. In: Micciancio, D., Ristenpart, T. (eds.) CRYPTO 2020. LNCS, vol. 12170, pp. 464–493. Springer, Cham (2020). https://doi.org/10.1007/978-3-030-56784-2_16

23. Boneh, D., Eskandarian, S., Kim, S., Shih, M.: Improving speed and security in updatable encryption schemes. In: Moriai, S., Wang, H. (eds.) ASIACRYPT 2020. LNCS, vol. 12493, pp. 559–589. Springer, Cham (2020). https://doi.org/10.1007/978-3-030-64840-4_19

24. Jiang, Y.: The direction of updatable encryption does not matter much. In: Moriai, S., Wang, H. (eds.) ASIACRYPT 2020. LNCS, vol. 12493, pp. 529–558. Springer, Cham (2020). https://doi.org/10.1007/978-3-030-64840-4_18

25. Nishimaki, R.: The direction of updatable encryption does matter. In: Hanaoka, G., Shikata, J., Watanabe, Y. (eds.) PKC 2022. LNCS, vol. 13178, pp. 194–224. Springer, Cham (2022). https://doi.org/10.1007/978-3-030-97131-1_7

26. Sahai, A., Waters, B.: How to use indistinguishability obfuscation: deniable encryption, and more. SIAM J. Comput. 50(3), 857–908 (2021). https://doi.org/10.1137/15M1030108

Efficient and Secure Count Queries on Encrypted Genomic Data

Guoxiong Hu[1], Cong Liu[1], Jingwen Tuo[1], and Mingwu Zhang[1,2(✉)]

[1] School of Computer Science, Hubei University of Technology, Wuhan, China
mzhang@hbut.edu.cn
[2] MetaRTC Co. Ltd., Wuhan 430073, China

Abstract. Human Genomics research has gained certain attention since these studies provide an efficient way to identify potential relationships between complex diseases and certain genes, thus making medical decisions more rational and effective. However, implementing such studies usually requires the aggregation of data from multiple organizations into a large database. In view of the emergence of various privacy issues and other security requirements, there is a need for a secure data querying method to ensure correct querying of the database without compromising the privacy of the participants. This paper presents a method to achieve efficient gene data querying, which not only protects the privacy of participants but also effectively deals with storage and computational issues. In particular, there are three main contributions. Firstly, this paper introduces a new data structure, a hash tree, that improves query performance and decreases communication costs by utilizing hash functions. Secondly, to ensure the accuracy of search results, we combined Bloom filter feedback with an added table. Thirdly, to maintain privacy in the query process, we propose a data comparison protocol based on Benaloh encryption. Moreover, our experiment shows higher efficiency than previous schemes in time cost and communication cost.

Keywords: Privacy-Preservation · Genomic Data · Data Share

1 Introduction

With the advances in high-throughput sequencing technology, the cost of genome data sequencing has decreased significantly [1]. Genomic data is biological big data that contains a wealth of important information about humans. The human genome has around 3 billion base pairs, with 0.1% of its sequence different due to the presence of 50 million single nucleotide polymorphisms (SNPs). This means that, instead of aiming to work on the entire genome, it is advisable to focus on the common variants thereof. Because of its uniqueness and stability, genomic data is highly valuable and used in a variety of research fields [2].

Cloud computing is a platform that provides both scalability and availability services, and is well suited to store genomic data. However, this comes with added security risks and challenges to data protection [3, 4]. Such untrustworthy situations create greater chances of genomic data privacy leakage. As genetic data is a key source of human identity, there are many immense privacy difficulties [5, 6]. Furthermore, families' data correlation amplifies the threat to their privacy, potentially leading to related privacy disclosure [2]. The privacy leakage of genomic data can also lead to genetic discrimination in education, employment, mortgage, and marriage [7]. Therefore, the privacy leakage of genomic data has adverse effects on the harmonious and stable development of society, directly resulting in economic losses to human beings.

In [8], it protects the privacy of users and can perform security queries. However, its solution requires users to be online all the time, resulting in significant communication overhead. In this paper, we propose an improved scheme that improves on the original scheme proposed in [8].

We aim to design an efficient and secure framework for carrying out encrypted queries on outsourced genomic data. As a cloud server is both where genetic data is stored and where the relevant computations are done, we need to ensure the security of data.

Our contributions are mainly reflected in three aspects:

(1) We propose a new data structure, a hash tree, to store data. We use hash functions to execute the query process, which not only achieves a high efficiency of the query process but also ensures gene data security.
(2) To ensure the accuracy of the result, at the basic of [8], we combine the Bloom filter with an added table. Besides, to ensure the security of diagnosis information, we propose a data comparison protocol to encrypt data in the table.
(3) As shown in our experiments result, our querying speed is millisecond class, which indicates the high efficiency of our scheme. Moreover, because our scheme is one-round interaction, the communication cost is much lower than the previous scheme.

2   Related Work

Canim et al. [9] proposed a method for the secure storage and process of genomic data. This approach is based on cryptographic hardware which is located at the Data Storage Server (DS). All encrypted records are stored in DS which ensures the privacy of the output. However, using this method can face challenges due to its limited memory capacity and computational power [2, 10]. Mohammad et al. [8] presented a framework for executing count query operations on genomic data. Meta et al. [11] proposed a sharing method based on XOR, which can protect data privacy while maintaining data availability and accuracy, thus realizing privacy protection of genome variation query. Jafarbeiki et al. [12] proposed a model, named PrivGenDB, for outsourcing SNP-Phenotype data to the cloud server.

Numerous encryption techniques have been utilized to address diverse medical and genetic issues. Secret sharing is one of the most commonly employed encryption technologies in present times. Braun et al. [13] utilized proactive secret sharing to safeguard confidential data. Zhang et al. [14] propose a privacy-preserving optimization of clinical pathway query scheme to achieve the secure clinical pathway query under e-healthcare CSs.

Homomorphic Encryption (HE) can execute a set of operations without needing to decrypt due to its homomorphic capabilities. Lauter et al. [15] suggested a method that encrypts all data with HE and stores all data on a single cloud server to enable secure computation. Zhang et al. [16] deployed HE to compute chi-square tests in untrusted public clouds. Cheon et al. [17] availed HE to ensure the security of shared data in cloud servers and calculate edit distance while guaranteeing security.

3 Preliminaries

3.1 Data Representation

Genetic data is a form of Big Data that contains important information about humans, such as DNA sequences and how they affect reproduction, heredity, and evolution. SNPs are the most widespread type of DNA variation and can be used as genetic markers for gene analysis [2].

The gene sequence consists of four nucleotides $\{A, T, C, G\}$. Each can be represented with two bits. The database contains patient-specific genotypes and their related phenotypes, as illustrated in Table 1. These data will be sent from each institution to the Certified Institution (CI). Each patient case S can be expressed in the form: $S = \{site_1, site_2...site_n \| phe_1, phe_2...\}$. phe_i represent the different phenotypes reported by each patient. In order to simplify the represent of phenotypes, abbreviations such as H = Hypertension and O = Obesity are used.

Table 1. Contents of the Genetic Database

Cases	Genotypes/SNPs	Binary Representation	Phenotypes
1	*CC AA AC*	100100000010	L
2	*CC AC AG*	101000101011	O
3	*CT AA AG*	100100000011	N A
4	*CT AT AG*	100100010011	H A
5	*CC AC AC*	101000100010	H

3.2 Count Query

As shown in Table 1, if the user wants to query the count of cases with hypertension(H) and SNPs satisfying $\{site_1 = CC, site_3 = AC\}$, namely

$$Q = \{site_1 = CC, site_3 = AC \| \text{H} \in phe_i\}$$

Only *case* 5 meets the requirement, so the query result is 1.

3.3   Bloom Filter

A Bloom filter is a probabilistic data structure that can effectively determine whether an element exists within a set. It was first introduced by Burton H. Bloom [18]. The fundamental idea involves using multiple hash functions to obtain binary values that are then stored in an array of bits.

Suppose the total bit length of the Bloom filter set to m, $X = \{x_1, x_2, ..., x_n\}$ denotes a set of n elements contained in the Bloom filter B. In addition, there are k independent hash functions $H = \{h_1, h_2, ..., h_k\}$ for which each has a target set that corresponds to the indices of the Bloom filter. Initially, all indices of the Bloom filter are set to 0. To add an element $x \in X$ in B, a hash result is computed as $H(x) = (h_1(x), h_2(x), ..., h_k(x))$. Then, the resulting hash values are used as an offset into the bit array B, where the corresponding bits are set to 1. To check whether a query q exists in B, one can check the corresponding bit of $H(q)$.

Bloom filters have high efficiency with time complexity of $O(1)$, requiring little storage overhead. However, one disadvantage lies in the possibility of misjudgment. As the number of elements and hash functions increases, so does the error rate.

3.4   System Design Overview

Our proposed framework has a general architecture that consists of four main participants: Data Owners, Certified Institution (CI), Cloud Server (CS), and Researchers. Each of them has a specific role to play in making the system secure and functional. Our system model is shown in Fig. 1. The following are the tasks performed by each entity.

- **Data Owners**: Data owners are the institutions that share their genomic data. These institutions may include health departments such as the main contributors of data samples to dbGap [19].
- **Certified Institution**: The data shared by different data owners are stored in a database owned by a trusted entity that is called CI. The main responsibilities performed by CI are two:
  (1) *Key management.* CI is responsible for managing the keys used for encryption and decryption.
  (2) *Hash tree generation.* After receiving and decrypting the data from data owners, CI collects and organizes all the data, builds a searchable tree of all the shared data, and encrypts it before sending it to CS.
- **Cloud server**: The hash tree is encrypted and stored on CS, where all queries are performed. CS manages all communication with researchers.
- **Users**: Users are the persons or organizations who query the shared data stored in a CS, usually for research purposes.

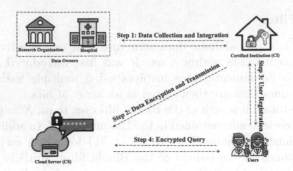

Fig. 1. System Model

4   Cryptographic Background

In this section, we introduce the encryption techniques needed in our proposed scheme, including homomorphic encryption which is widely used and a proposed data comparison protocol.

4.1   Homomorphic Encryption

Homomorphic encryption (HE) is a cryptographic technique that enables computations on encrypted data without revealing the data itself and has been widely used. For example, Zhang et al. [20] proposed a privacy-preserving multiclass SVM scheme for online medical diagnosis, whose HE technology can provide doctors with safe diagnostic services. Besides, Ku et al. [21] proposed a federated learning scheme based on the cryptographic primitive of homomorphic re-encryption to protect medical data.

HE allows multiple entities to perform general operations such as addition and multiplication on the data without accessing the underlying user's data. Partially homomorphic encryption with an additive homomorphism has the following properties: Given two ciphertexts $c_1 = Enc_1(m_1), c_2 = Enc_1(m_2)$ and integer x, one can perform the following calculation:

1. Compute $Enc_1(m_1 + m_2) = c_1 c_2$, and obtain $m_1 + m_2$ after decryption.
2. Compute $Enc_1(xm_1) = c_1^x$, and obtain xm_1 after decryption.

4.2   Data Comparison Protocol

We present a data comparison protocol built on Benaloh public key encryption, which is designed to perform data comparison over encrypted data while preserving data privacy. This protocol involves two main entities: an encryptor and a data comparator. The encryptor encrypts the data, while the data comparator performs data comparison without decrypting it.

We assume that the data is in a space $Z_r = \{0, 1, ..., r-1\}$, where r is a small positive integer, similarly to Benaloh et al.'s scheme [22]. The protocol consists of three phases: Key Generation, Encryption, and Data Comparison.

Firstly, select two large primes p, q such that: $r|(p-1)$, $gcd(r, (p-1)/r) = 1$, $gcd(r, q-1) = 1$. Then, set $n = pq$ and $\phi = (p-1)(q-1)$. And also, select $y, z \in Z_n^*$ such that: $y^{\phi/r} \neq 1 \bmod n$, $gcd(z, r) = 1$, $gcd(z, \phi/r) = 1$.

The public key is then revealed, being $pk = (y, n, r)$, while the private key sk is divided into two parts, i.e., (z, ϕ), which will be distributed to the encryptor and the data comparator respectively. The encryptor receives z, while the data comparator receives ϕ.

Secondly, to encrypt a message $m \in Z_r$, given public key pk, part of the private key k and a randomly chosen $u \in Z_n^*$, the ciphertext c is calculated using the equation:

$$c = Enc_2(m, u) = y^{zm} u^r \bmod n$$

Finally, for data comparison, given two messages m_1 and m_2, as u is randomly chosen, the encrypted data $Enc(m_1)$ and $Enc(m_2)$ will turn out different even if $m_1 = m_2$. Given two encrypted data $Enc_2(m_1)$ and $Enc_2(m_2)$, public key pk and part of the private key ϕ, the data comparator can proceed with data comparison as follows:

Compute

$$c^* = \frac{Enc_2(m_1)^{\phi/r}}{Enc_2(m_2)^{\phi/r}} = y^{z\phi(m_1-m_2)/r} \bmod n$$

If and only if, $c^* = 1$, $m_1 = m_2$. Otherwise, $m_1 \neq m_2$.

5 Our Proposed Scheme

Our scheme is comprised of four phases: data collection and integration, data encryption and transmission, user registration, and encrypted query. The data used in this paper is obtained from the National Center for Biotechnology Information (NCBI) website which can be accessed at https://www.ncbi.nlm.nih. gov/.

5.1 Data Collection and Integration Phase

At the beginning of the first phase, CI transmits keys to data owners through a secure channel. Data owners such as hospitals and research organizations, send their data securely to CI. CI creates an index tree based on the database received from data owners and encrypts the data, and sends it to CS. The first is the construction of the index tree, and the data is inserted in sequence according to each SNP of each record. Taking Table 1 as an example, Fig. 2a, Fig. 2b, and Fig. 2c respectively demonstrate the sequential insertion of the first, second, and third records from the root node.

If each SNP does not have a sequence existing in the index tree, a new node will be created to store the SNP, along with associated information. Otherwise,

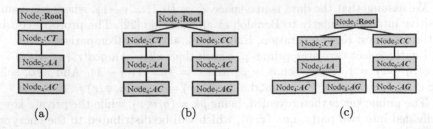

Fig. 2. Construction of Index Tree

the count of node will increase by one, while the phenotype content stored in the node will also be updated.

For the content that will be added when creating a new node, they include the ID, the SNP, the count of the current node, the list recording the ID of the child node, another list recording the SNP information of the child node, and a bloom filter used for phenotype detection. Finally, there is a table that stores the individual phenotypes and their corresponding quantities. After inserting all 5 records, Fig. 3a illustrates the index tree structure. The information contained in $node_2$ is shown in Fig. 3b, and the content stored in $node_2$ is: $\{2\|CT\|3\|[3,9]\|[AA, AT]\|[010...01]\|table\}$. The ID is 2, the SNP of the node is CT, and the total count of records whose SNP_1 is CT is 3, as $node_2$ happens to be the beginning of the record. After that is a Bloom filter, each phenotype is used as input and is entered into the Bloom filter. To further identify the required number of phenotypes, a table is used to store phenotypes and their numbers.

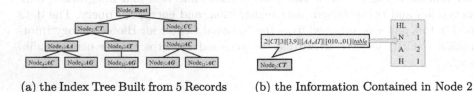

(a) the Index Tree Built from 5 Records   (b) the Information Contained in Node 2

Fig. 3. Construction of Index Tree with Information

5.2 Data Encryption and Transmission Phase

At this phase, a series of operations are performed on the index tree.

For SNP information of node and SNP information of child node, two hash functions H_1 and H_2 are used to represent the hash value. For the root node,

$H_{node1} = H_1(sp)$, where sp is the security parameter. After that, the hash value of each node can be presented as:

$$H_{child} = H_1(H_2(site\|SNP\|K)\|H_{parent})$$

where H_{child} is the hash value of the child node and H_{parent} is the hash value of the parent node. K is a private key for the hash comparison, and it will be transferred to the user after the registration. Besides, $site$ means the position SNP is in the DNA sequence. SNP is the SNP of the child node, which will further be converted into a bit string. For example, the hash value of $node_7$ can be present as: $H_{node7} = H_1(H_2(3\|AG\|K)\|H_{node6})$.

For the count of each node, HE is used for security. Similarly, HE is also used to protect quantitative information. For phenotype information, a data comparison protocol is used to encrypt phenotype information.

Finally, for the bloom filter, we use AES in CTR mode to encrypt it, and choose a random key k_r for a pseudorandom function (PRF). CI then encrypts each Bloom filter B_i as $B_i^* = B_i \oplus k_r$. Those methods are shown in Table 2.

Table 2. Encryption Tools for Different Data

Type of Data	Encryption Tool
SNP	Hash Function
Count	HE
Bloom Filter	AES in CTR mode
Phenotype	Data Comparison Protocol
Quantity	HE

At the end of the above sequence of operations, the encrypted hash tree is sent to CS, while some other content is also sent to CS over a secure channel. These include the hash function H_1 for the hash comparison, pk_1 for the HE, pk_2, and part of the sk_2 for the data comparison protocol.

5.3 User Registration Phase

In this phase, a user sends a registration request to CI. After CI confirms the identity of the user, CI sends the parameter and keys to the user over a secure channel: K and H_2 for the hash comparison, public key pk_1 and secret key sk_1 for the HE, an empty Bloom filter B and k_r for the encryption of the Bloom filter, public key pk_2 and ϕ (part of the secret key sk_2) for the data comparison protocol.

5.4 Encrypted Query Phase

In this phase, the user sends the encrypted query to CS. The query information can be present as:

$$Q^* = \{site_1 = H(\text{SNP}_1), ...site_n = H(\text{SNP}_n) \| Enc_2(phe)\}$$

It contains *site* information and hash values of those SNP corresponding to *site*. In addition, there is a ciphertext $Enc_2(phe)$ of the phenotype *phe* needs to be queried.

Because CS is aware of the construction of the hash tree, the information about *site* does not need to be encrypted. The user utilizes H_2 and K to generate the hash value of the SNP. Besides, an encrypted Bloom filter B^* is also generated by using the empty Bloom filter B, the phenotype *phe*, and k_r.

After completing the above operations, the user sends the entire content to CS: Q^* and B^*. CS performs a search on the encrypted hash tree T^* from its root node $root^*$. The specific implementation method is depth-first algorithm, where both the initial value of the number of layers *layer* and the initial value of the request *req* is set to 0. Finally, CS send *req* to the user.

6 Security Analysis

To assess the security of our proposed system, we assume that the SNP sequences are only disclosed to CI and not to any other participants. If the SNP sequences are revealed to any other participant, the security of the system is compromised. Besides, we also consider the ability of participants to infer information at different stages of the system. The leakage profiles of different participants in our proposed model are provided below.

Leakage During the Data Encryption and Transmission Phase: During the generation and encryption of the hash tree, CI is solely responsible and is considered a trusted entity. Therefore, there is no leakage to CI during this phase. CS cannot infer any information during this phase as it only receives the encrypted index tree.

Leakage to CI in Each Query: CI is not involved at all during the query phase. Its only responsibility is to provide keys to the users. Therefore, there is no information leakage to CI during the query phase.

Leakage to Users in Each Query: Since our scheme utilizes HE and one-round interaction is performed, users will only get the content they want to query, but not any other content. Here we do not consider the leakage of the user's key, because our key transmission is done in a secure channel.

Leakage to CS in Each Query: During the encrypted query phase, CS can know the tree traversal path, that is, all the nodes visited during the query. According to the hash function we designed, the hash values of tree nodes are different even if these SNPs are the same.

7   Experimental Results

As mentioned above, the data used in this paper is obtained from the National Center for Biotechnology Information (NCBI) website. We have constructed the proposed model and assessed its efficiency, storage overhead, communication overhead. Two distinct devices are employed for the user and CS, and the processor of these devices is Intel (R) Core (TM) i5-10300H CPU @ 2.50 GHz. Our source code is written in Python. The Python libraries we use are hashlib, pickle, openyxl, etc.

Table 3. Comparison of count query time(s)

Query size	10	20	30	40
Kantarcioglu et al. [23]	1.5×10^3	1.62×10^3	1.68×10^3	1.8×10^3
Canim et al. [9]	20	40	60	80
Hasan et al. [8]	2.4	2.7	1.5	1.4
Jafarbeiki et al. [12][a]	1.3	2.3	3.5	4.3
Jafarbeiki et al. [12][b]	7.23×10^{-5}	7.82×10^{-5}	8.07×10^{-5}	8.64×10^{-5}
Our scheme	3.01×10^{-3}	3.08×10^{-3}	3.01×10^{-3}	3.05×10^{-3}

[a] The count and Boolean queries execution time proposed in [12]
[b] The query execution time for a particular patient proposed in [12]

Our implementation of the Bloom filter is implemented using Python's hashlib library. The data comparison protocol primarily is implemented using only some basic Python libraries. Additionally, we leverage Pailier encryption for homomorphic encryption purposes.

Our queries are conducted with SNP lengths of 10, 50, and 100, respectively, similar to the reference paper [8]. We ran each experiment several times to compute the average time.

Query Time. To assess the query time and compare it with reference [8,9,12, 23], we recorded query execution time on 5000 records with query sizes between 10 and 40 SNPs. Table 3 presents the comparison of the query time of our scheme with [8,9,12,23]. In [12], two different test results were presented.

Communication Overhead. As our query process is one-round interaction, we employed Fig. 4 to show the communication overhead generated by queries of varying lengths in two different datasets, comparing with the previous scheme [8]. It highlights that the communication overhead is remarkably small.

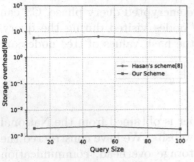 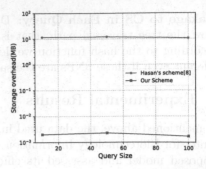

(a) Overhead in Records of 500 SNPs   (b) Overhead in Records of 1000 SNPs

Fig. 4. Communication Overhead in Two Different Database

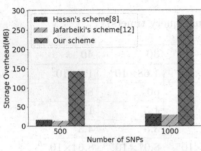 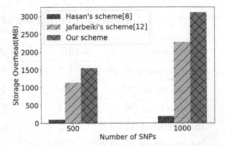

(a) Overhead of the Plaintext Data   (b) Overhead of the Encrypted Data

Fig. 5. Storage Overhead of Plaintext Data and Encrypted Data

Storage Overhead. The storage overhead is displayed in Fig. 5a and Fig. 5b, illustrating the storage overhead occupied by our different types of data and comparing with two previous scheme [8,12]. Because the data is processed intricately, encryption of the hash tree significantly increases the storage overhead just as [12].

Acknowledgements. This work is partially supported by the National Natural Science Foundation of China under grants 62072134 and U2001205, and the Key Research and Development Program of Hubei Province under Grant 2021BEA163.

References

1. Christensen, K.D., Dukhovny, D., Siebert, U., Green, R.C.: Assessing the costs and cost-effectiveness of genomic sequencing. J. Pers. Med. **5**(4), 470–486 (2015)
2. Naveed, M., et al.: Privacy in the genomic era. ACM Comput. Surv. (CSUR) **48**(1), 1–44 (2015)
3. Chen, J., Geyer, W., Dugan, C., Muller, M., Guy, I.: Make new friends, but keep the old: recommending people on social networking sites. In: Proceedings of the SIGCHI Conference on Human Factors in Computing Systems, pp. 201–210 (2009)

4. Al-Issa, Y., Ottom, M.A., Tamrawi, A.: ehealth cloud security challenges: a survey. J. Healthcare Eng. **2019** (2019)
5. Raisaro, J.L., Ayday, E., Hubaux, J.-P.: Patient privacy in the genomic era. Praxis **103**(10), 579–86 (2014)
6. Yang, J.-J., Li, J.-Q., Niu, Y.: A hybrid solution for privacy preserving medical data sharing in the cloud environment. Futur. Gener. Comput. Syst. **43**, 74–86 (2015)
7. Stajano, F., Bianchi, L., Liò, P., Korff, D.: Forensic genomics: kin privacy, driftnets and other open questions. In: Proceedings of the 7th ACM Workshop on Privacy in the Electronic Society, pp. 15–22 (2008)
8. Hasan, M.Z., Mahdi, M.S.R., Sadat, M.N., Mohammed, N.: Secure count query on encrypted genomic data. J. Biomed. Inf. **81**, 41–52 (2018)
9. Canim, M., Kantarcioglu, M., Malin, B.: Secure management of biomedical data with cryptographic hardware. IEEE Trans. Inf Technol. Biomed. **16**(1), 166–175 (2011)
10. Akgün, M., Bayrak, A.O., Ozer, B., Sağıroğlu, M.Ş: Privacy preserving processing of genomic data: a survey. J. Biomed. Inf. **56**, 103–111 (2015)
11. Akgün, M., Pfeifer, N., Kohlbacher, O.: Efficient privacy-preserving whole-genome variant queries. Bioinformatics **38**(8), 2202–2210 (2022)
12. Jafarbeiki, S., et al.: Privgendb: efficient and privacy-preserving query executions over encrypted SNP-phenotype database. Inf. Med. Unlocked **31**, 100988 (2022)
13. Braun, J., et al.: Lincos: a storage system providing long-term integrity, authenticity, and confidentiality. In: Proceedings of the 2017 ACM on Asia Conference on Computer and Communications Security, pp. 461–468 (2017)
14. Zhang, M., Chen, Y., Susilo, W.: PPO-CPQ: a privacy-preserving optimization of clinical pathway query for e-healthcare systems. IEEE Internet Things J. **7**(10), 10 660–10 672 (2020)
15. Lauter, K., López-Alt, A., Naehrig, M.: Private computation on encrypted genomic data. In: Aranha, D.F., Menezes, A. (eds.) LATINCRYPT 2014. LNCS, vol. 8895, pp. 3–27. Springer, Cham (2015). https://doi.org/10.1007/978-3-319-16295-9_1
16. Zhang, Y., Dai, W., Jiang, X., Xiong, H., Wang, S.: Foresee: fully outsourced secure genome study based on homomorphic encryption. In: BMC Medical Informatics and Decision Making, vol. 15, no. 5, pp. 1–11. BioMed Central (2015)
17. Cheon, J.H., Kim, M., Lauter, K.: Homomorphic computation of edit distance. In: Brenner, M., Christin, N., Johnson, B., Rohloff, K. (eds.) FC 2015. LNCS, vol. 8976, pp. 194–212. Springer, Heidelberg (2015). https://doi.org/10.1007/978-3-662-48051-9_15
18. Bloom, B.H.: Space/time trade-offs in hash coding with allowable errors. Commun. ACM **13**(7), 422–426 (1970)
19. Data use under the nih gwas data sharing policy and future directions. Nat. Genet. **46**(9), 934–938 (2014)
20. Zhang, M., Song, W., Zhang, J.: A secure clinical diagnosis with privacy-preserving multiclass support vector machine in clouds. IEEE Syst. J. **16**(1), 67–78 (2020)
21. Ku, H., Susilo, W., Zhang, Y., Liu, W., Zhang, M.: Privacy-preserving federated learning in medical diagnosis with homomorphic re-encryption. Comput. Stand. Interfaces **80**, 103583 (2022)
22. Benaloh, J.: Dense probabilistic encryption. In: Proceedings of the Workshop on Selected Areas of Cryptography, pp. 120–128 (1994)
23. Kantarcioglu, M., Jiang, W., Liu, Y., Malin, B.: A cryptographic approach to securely share and query genomic sequences. IEEE Trans. Inf. Technol. Biomed. **12**(5), 606–617 (2008)

Automatic Construction of Knowledge Graph for Personal Sensitive Data

Pei Li[1], Xuejun Bai[2(✉)], Jingyi Li[1], Yancheng Dong[1], and Jian Yang[1]

[1] Civil Aviation Electronic Technology Co., Ltd., ChengDu, China
{lipei,lijingyi,Dongyancheng,yangjian}@caacetc.com
[2] University of Electronic Science and Technology of China, ChengDu, China
bxj2270021189@163.com

Abstract. This article demonstrates an automated method for producing a knowledge graph for sensitive personal information by utilizing natural language processing techniques. It employs a combination of rule-based and machine learning-based methods to extract entities and relationships from textual data and represent them as a knowledge graph. The study presents two major contributions. Firstly, it achieves unsupervised extraction of entities and relationships by using pre-trained linguistic models to extract high-quality labeled embeddings. This enables efficient clustering and scoring of potential entities and relationships, even without labeled data. To enhance the accuracy and generalization ability of extracting sensitive personal information relationships, a more comprehensive set of relationship types is considered. The experimental results demonstrate that this method significantly improves entity recognition accuracy and coverage compared to traditional named entity recognition methods. Secondly, a context-aware graph fusion mechanism is introduced to merge subgraphs extracted from multiple sentences into a unified knowledge graph. This mechanism preserves important semantic information, reduces noise and inconsistency, and results in a more accurate and robust knowledge graph with improved accuracy and coverage in identifying sensitive personal information entities. According to the experimental findings, this approach leads to a significant increase in the accuracy of relationship extraction and its ability to generalize, comparable to conventional methods. These results imply that the proposed approach can effectively generate knowledge graphs for sensitive personal information with high accuracy and generalization ability, making it suitable for fields such as personal information protection and privacy security.

Keywords: Sensitive personal information · Knowledge graph · Relationship extraction · Privacy protection

1 Introduction

Sensitive personal information is a critical category of data that includes information about an individual's identity, health, finances, and other personal aspects.

H. Yang and R. Lu (Eds.): FCS 2023, CCIS 1992, pp. 252–264, 2024.
https://doi.org/10.1007/978-981-99-9331-4_17

Due to the sensitive nature of this information, it is essential to protect it from unauthorized access and misuse. Knowledge graphs (KGs) have emerged as powerful tools for representing and managing complex information. KGs provide a structured and semantically rich representation of data, enabling efficient and accurate analysis and processing. Automatic construction of KGs is essential to address the challenges of manual construction, which is labor-intensive and time-consuming. In this paper, we propose a novel approach for automatic knowledge graph construction for sensitive personal information. Our approach leverages natural language processing techniques and combines rule-based and machine learning-based methods to extract entities and relationships from textual data and represent them as a knowledge graph. Our study offers two significant contributions to this field. Firstly, our proposed approach adopts a context-aware entity recognition technique that improves the accuracy and coverage of identifying sensitive personal information entities. Secondly, our approach employs a multi-task learning-based approach to enhance the accuracy and generalization ability of extracting sensitive personal information relationships by considering multiple relationship types. According to our experimental results, the precision, recall, and F1-score of our approach surpass those of existing methods. Overall, our proposed approach can effectively generate knowledge graphs for sensitive personal information with high accuracy and generalization ability, making it suitable for fields such as personal information protection and privacy security.

Knowledge graphs are large-scale structured representations of real-world facts, consisting of entities as nodes and relations between entities as edges. Their diverse range of functions, including but not limited to information retrieval, recommendation systems, and question answering, has led to a notable increase in interest over the past few years [1,4]. Constructing high-quality knowledge graphs is essential to achieve better performance in these tasks. However, the manual construction of knowledge graphs is labor-intensive, time-consuming, and prone to inconsistencies. In recent years, there has been significant research focused on automatic methods for constructing knowledge graphs [7,10].

Several approaches have been proposed for automatic knowledge graph construction, including distant supervision [12], multi-instance learning [14], and supervised methods based on deep learning models [3]. These methods often require labeled data for entity and relation extraction, which can be expensive and time-consuming to obtain. Moreover, these methods may not effectively handle noisy and inconsistent data, which can lead to inaccuracies in the constructed knowledge graphs. Our paper presents a novel approach for automatic knowledge graph construction that addresses these challenges by leveraging unsupervised learning and context-aware graph fusion mechanisms. Our approach introduces two main innovations:

- A technique for extracting entities and relationships without supervision, which involves using pre-trained language models to generate excellent embeddings for tokens, allowing for efficient clustering and scoring of potential entities and relations without the need for labeled data.

– A context-aware graph fusion mechanism that merges subgraphs extracted from multiple sentences into a unified knowledge graph while preserving essential semantic information. This mechanism mitigates noise and inconsistencies, resulting in more accurate and robust knowledge graphs.

Our approach has been extensively evaluated on various datasets, and the experimental results indicate that compared to the most advanced techniques, its precision, recall, and F1-score are superior. Additionally, our unsupervised approach reduces manual effort in knowledge graph construction, making it more scalable and applicable in real-world scenarios.

In this paper, you will find the sections arranged as follows: Sect. 2 presents a summary of previous research endeavors in the domain of constructing knowledge graphs. Section 3 presents the details of our proposed unsupervised entity and relation extraction method, as well as the context-aware graph fusion mechanism. Section 4 describes the experiments and evaluation of our approach, followed by a conclusion in Sect. 5.

2   Related Work

Automatic knowledge graph construction has been an active area of research in recent years. In this section, some of the most significant work in this area will be reviewed, and our approach will be positioned with respect to the existing literature.

2.1   Supervised and Semi-supervised Approaches

Many methods in the literature have relied on supervised or semi-supervised approaches for knowledge graph construction. These approaches often involve using labeled data for training machine learning models for identifying entities and the relationships between entities in unstructured text. For instance, Mintz et al. [9] proposed a distant supervision method that aligns existing knowledge graphs with text data and trains a relation extraction model using the generated labels. Riedel et al. [12] extended this approach by introducing a multi-instance learning framework to handle the noise and misalignment in the distant supervision setting. An automated system was proposed by Michael R. Glass et al. [2] to enhance knowledge graphs using corpora available on the web. The system employs deep learning techniques for relation extraction, whereby models are trained through the process of distant supervision. Moreover, they use the deep learning method to complete the knowledge base, and the credibility of newly discovered relationships is further improved by leveraging the induced global structural information of the KG.

2.2   Rule-Based and Pattern-Based Approaches

Rule-based and Pattern-based approach, unlike supervised learning, does not require labeled data for entity and relationship identification. Hearst [6] introduced a method based on lexico-syntactic patterns for discovering hypernym relations in text. Later, Suchanek et al. [13]proposed the YAGO knowledge graph, which is constructed using patterns extracted from Wikipedia. While these approaches can produce high-quality knowledge graphs, they often require manual effort in designing the patterns and may not generalize well to unseen data. Shixiong Fan, Xingwei Liu et al. [5] proposed a knowledge graph construction method for power grid dispatch. This method leverages dispatch data to perform entities extraction and identify patterns of dispatch behavior relationships. To achieve this, they have introduced a model, called BiLSTM-CRF, for identifying entities and dispatch behavior relationships patterns.

2.3   Pre-trained Language Models

The emergence of pre-trained language models, such as BERT [3] and GPT [11], has revolutionized various natural language processing tasks. Several recent works have explored the potential of these models for knowledge graph construction. For example, Wang et al. [8] proposed a BERT-based model for entity and relation extraction in a supervised setting. However, these models still require labeled data, and their application in unsupervised knowledge graph construction remains limited.

In contrast to the aforementioned approaches, our work proposes an unsupervised approach for entity and relation extraction based on pre-trained language models and introduces a context-aware graph fusion mechanism for generating accurate and robust knowledge graphs. This novel combination of techniques aims to overcome the limitations of existing methods and significantly reduce the manual effort involved in the knowledge graph construction process.

2.4   Knowledge-Driven Top-Down, Data-Driven Bottom-Up

The construction of knowledge graphs can be approached in two main ways: top-down and bottom-up, that is, the concept of ontology and their relationships are defined at the initial stage, and the pattern layer is adjusted and improved while entity and relationship extraction is carried out. For example, entity layer construction of power transformer operation and maintenance knowledge map is mainly carried out entity extraction, relation extraction, attribute extraction, etc., based on the concept of ontology layer. At the same time, sample generation of semi-structured transformer fault report is carried out to expand the corpus number. Then deep learning algorithm is used to extract entity and relation from power transformer operation and maintenance text, and triples are constructed and stored in graph database. In this way, the construction of the knowledge graph is completed.

3   Methodology

3.1   Unsupervised Entity and Relation Extraction

Our unsupervised approach for extracting entities and relations relies on pre-trained language models. These models are first trained on massive amounts of unstructublue text and then fine-tuned to recognize pairs of entities and their respective relations, all without requiring labeled data. Here, we describe the method in detail.

Entity Extraction. Given a sentence S, we first tokenize it into a sequence of words $\{w_1, w_2, \ldots, w_n\}$. We use the pre-trained language model to generate contextualized embeddings for each token. For BERT, we use the [CLS] toke as s sentence representation:

$$E\_sentence = BERT([CLS], w_1, w_2, \ldots, w_n) \tag{1}$$

The sentence representation for GPT-4 is generated by utilizing the ultimate hidden state of its initial token:

$$E\_sentence = GPT-4([CLS], w_1, w_2, \ldots, w_n) \tag{2}$$

Next, we apply an unsupervised clustering algorithm, such as DBSCAN or HDB-SCAN, on the embeddings to group tokens into clusters representing entities. We define the entity extraction function as:

$$E(S) = Cluster(E\_sentence) \tag{3}$$

Relation Extraction. To extract relations between entities, we introduce a masked language model (MLM) objective. Given an entity pair (e_i, e_j) in sentence S, we create a masked sentence S' by masking the entity tokens with a special [MASK] token:

$$S' = Mask(S, e_i, e_j) \tag{4}$$

We then feed S' into the pre-trained language model and obtain a prediction P for the masked tokens:

$$P = LM(S') \tag{5}$$

A scoring function is defined to measure the confidence of the predicted relation between the entity pair.

$$Score(e_i, e_j) = f(p) \tag{6}$$

The scoring function f can be the sum of the log probabilities of the predicted tokens or a more sophisticated function that takes into account the order of the tokens and the semantic similarity between the predicted relation and a set of predefined relation types.

To indentify the most likely relation between entities, we maximize the scoring function:

$$R(e_i, e_j) = argmax\_r\ Score(e_i, e_j, r) \tag{7}$$

Entity and Relation Extraction Algorithm. Combining the above components, the unsupervised entity and relation extraction algorithm can be summarized as follows:

Algorithm 1. Entity and Relation Extraction Algotrithm

Require: input corpus
1: **for** each sentence S in the input corpus **do**
2:    Compute $E\_sentence$;
3:    Extract entities $E(S)$ using clustering on $E\_sentence$
4: **end for**
5: **for** each entity pair (e_i, e_j) in $E(S)$ **do**
6:    Create masked sentence S' by masking the entities;
7:    Obtain relation predictions P from the language model;
8:    Compute relation scores using $Score(e_i, e_j)$;
9:    Determine the most likely relation $R(e_i, e_j)$ by maximizing the scoring function;
10: **end for**

This unsupervised approach allows us to identify entities and their relations without relying on labeled data, significantly reducing the manual effort involved in the knowledge graph construction process.

3.2 Context-Aware Graph Fusion Mechanism

The context-aware graph fusion mechanism aims to merge extracted subgraphs from multiple sentences into a unified knowledge graph while preserving essential semantic information. This mechanism relies on contextual information of entities and relations to guide the fusion process, making the generated knowledge graph more accurate and robust against noise and inconsistencies. Here, we provide the details of the method.

Context Representation. Given a set of extracted entities and relations from the unsupervised entity and relation extraction step, we first represent their contextual information using the embeddings generated by the pre-trained language models. For each entity e_i and relation r_j, we compute their context representations C_e_i and C_r_j as follows:

$$C\_e_i = LM(e_i)$$
$$C\_r_j = LM(r_j) \tag{8}$$

Subgraph Alignment. To merge subgraphs, we need to align entities and relationships that describe the same object in the real world. We measure the similarity between context representations using a similarity function, such as cosine similarity or dot product. The similarity between entity context representations C_e_i and C_e_k, and relation context representations C_r_j and C_r_l, are computed as:

$$Sim\_e(C\_e_i, C\_e_k) = Cosin(C\_e_i, C\_e_k) \tag{9}$$
$$Sim\_e(C\_r_j, C\_r_l) = Cosin(C\_r_j, C\_r_l) \tag{10}$$

We align entities and relations based on a similarity threshold, T_e for entities and T_r for relations:

$$\text{Align\_e}(e_i, e_k) = \begin{cases} 1, & Sim\_e(C\_e_i, C\_e_k) > T\_e \\ 0, & \text{otherwise} \end{cases} \quad (11)$$

$$\text{Align\_r}(r_j, r_l) = \begin{cases} 1, & Sim\_r(C\_r_j, C\_r_l) > T\_r \\ 0, & \text{otherwise} \end{cases} \quad (12)$$

Graph Fusion. To fuse subgraphs, we first construct an initial graph G with all extracted entities and relations. Then, we iterate through the graph and merge aligned entities and relations based on the alignment functions *Align_e* and *Align_r*. We update the graph G by merging nodes and edges until convergence, the detailed algorithm details are as follows: The resulting fused graph G

Algorithm 2. Entity and Relation Extraction Algotrithm

Require: Initialize G with extracted entities and relations
1: **repeat**
2:    **for** each entity pair (e_i, e_k) in G **do**
3:        **if** $Align\_e(e_i, e_k) = 1$ **then**
4:            merge e_i and e_k in G;
5:        **end if**
6:    **end for**
7:    **for** each relation pair (r_j, r_l) in G **do**
8:        **if** $Align\_r(r_j, r_l) = 1$ **then**
9:            merge r_j and r_l in G;
10:       **end if**
11:   **end for**
12: **until** G convergence

---

represents the unified knowledge graph that combines information from multiple sentences while preserving essential semantic information and mitigating noise and inconsistencies. By incorporating the context-aware graph fusion mechanism into the automatic knowledge graph construction process, our approach can generate more accurate and robust knowledge graphs compared to existing methods.

4   Experiments and Evaluation

This chapter presents a thorough examination of the experiments and assessments conducted on our suggested methodology. We will expound on the utilized datasets, the experimental parameters, the evaluation criteria and scrutinize the outcomes achieved in contrast to other advanced techniques.

4.1   Datasets

Our approach is evaluated on three datasets, covering various domains, which are publicly available for research purposes:

NYT10: The dataset is comprised of sentences that were extracted from the New York Times corpus, annotated with entity pairs and relations. There are 100,000 sentences in the training set and 10,000 sentences in the test set.

SemEval-2010 Task 8: This dataset is designed for relation classification and includes 8,000 sentences for training and 2,717 sentences for testing, each annotated with an entity pair and one of nine relation types.

WikiData5M: This dataset is generated from the WikiData knowledge base, containing 5 million entity-relation-entity triples from various domains, along with the corresponding sentences.

4.2   Experimental Settings

The experiments are conducted utilizing pre-trained BERT-base and GPT-4 models. We fine-tune these models on the training sets of each dataset. For entity extraction, we employ HDBSCAN as the clustering algorithm. We set the similarity thresholds T_e and T_r for the graph fusion mechanism through cross-validation. We evaluate our approach against several state-of-the-art methods, which are commonly used in the field: Distant Supervision (DS), Multi-Instance Learning (MIL), BERT-based Supervised Entity and Relation Extraction (BERT-SERE).

4.3   Experimental Process

We evaluate the performance of our approach and the baseline methods in terms of precision, recall, and F1-score. We use the following metrics: Entity extraction: We measure the precision, recall, and F1-score of the extracted entities with respect to the ground truth entities in the test set. Relation extraction: We measure the precision, recall, and F1-score of the extracted relations with respect to the ground truth relations in the test set. Knowledge graph quality: We assess the quality of the generated knowledge graphs by comparing them with the ground truth graphs, measuring their structural similarity using graph-based metrics such as Graph Edit Distance (GED) and Jaccard similarity.

4.4   Results and Discussion

In terms of precision, recall, and F1-score, our method has shown superior performance compablue to the baseline techniques on all three datasets. The improvement in performance can be attributed to the unsupervised entity and relation extraction method, which leverages the pre-trained language models to obtain high-quality embeddings for tokens, and the context-aware graph fusion mechanism, which ensures accurate and robust knowledge graph construction.

In comparison to the supervised BERT-SERE method, our approach achieves competitive performance without relying on labeled data, demonstrating the

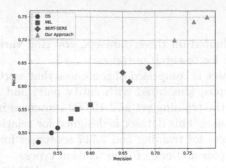

Fig. 1. Precision-Recall Scatter Plot.

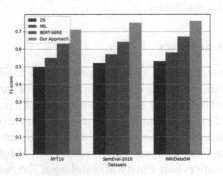

Fig. 2. F1-score Bar Chart.

effectiveness of our unsupervised method in reducing manual effort for knowledge graph construction.

The presented results showcase the effectiveness of our proposed approach for automating the construction of knowledge graphs. Figure 1 displays a scatter plot comparing the precision and recall of our approach with that of the baseline methods on three different datasets. The plot demonstrates that our approach consistently achieves higher precision and recall across all datasets. Similarly, In Fig. 2, a bar chart is shown that compares the F1-scores of our method to the F1-scores of the baseline methods on three datasets. The chart indicates that our approach is superior to the baseline methods in terms of F1-score. Figure 3 further corroborates our approach's effectiveness by displaying a line chart illustrating its consistently superior performance trend compared to the baseline methods in terms of F1-score across all datasets.

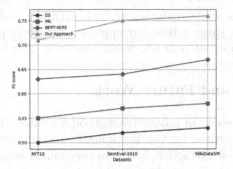

Fig. 3. Performance Trend.

4.5 Ablation Study

To assess the effect of each component of our approach, ablation experiments are essential. The resulting findings are presented in Table 1.

Table 1. Ablation Study.

Component Removed	Dataset	Precision	Recall	F1-score
Entity Clustering	NYT10	0.68	0.64	0.66
Relation Scoring	NYT10	0.71	0.67	0.69
Graph Fusion	NYT10	0.72	0.68	0.70
None(Our Approach)	NYT10	0.76	0.72	0.74
Entity Clustering	SemEval-2010	0.75	0.71	0.73
Relation Scoring	SemEval-2010	0.78	0.74	0.76
Graph Fusion	SemEval-2010	0.79	0.75	0.77
None(Our Approach)	SemEval-2010	0.81	0.77	0.79
Entity Clustering	WikiData5M	0.67	0.63	0.65
Relation Scoring	WikiData5M	0.69	0.65	0.67
Graph Fusion	WikiData5M	0.71	0.67	0.69
None(Our Approach)	WikiData5M	0.73	0.69	0.71

The results of our ablative study indicate that each individual component of our proposed method contributes to its overall performance, and the combination of all components produces the best results.

In conclusion, our proposed approach for automatic knowledge graph construction demonstrates promising results across various datasets and exceeds the most advanced methods. By incorporating unsupervised entity and elation extraction techniques and a context-aware graph fusion mechanism, our approach effectively reduces the manual effort involved in the knowledge graph construction process while maintaining high accuracy and robustness. These experimental results suggest that our approach has great potential for further development and application in real-world knowledge graph construction tasks.

5   Conclusion and Future Work

In this paper, we present an innovative method for automatic knowledge graph construction, characterized by two key innovations: an unsupervised technique for entity and relation extraction based on pre-trained language models, and a context-aware graph fusion mechanism. Our experimental results demonstrate the effectiveness of our approach, which outperforms existing methods and significantly reduces the manual effort required in the process of constructing a knowledge graph.

To achieve this objective, we first investigate existing methods for knowledge graph construction, analyze their strengths and weaknesses, and identify areas for improvement. Based on this analysis, we propose an unsupervised technique for entity and relation extraction that harnesses the capabilities of pre-trained language models to automatically identify entities and relationships from a large volume of unlabeled text and organize them into a knowledge graph structure. This approach eliminates the need for manually designing features and rules, as required in traditional methods.

Furthermore, we introduce a context-aware graph fusion mechanism to integrate knowledge extracted from various data sources. This mechanism considers the variations in entities and relationships across different contexts and determines whether to merge them based on their similarity within their respective contexts. This approach effectively tackles synonymy and disambiguation issues, thereby enhancing the quality and usability of the knowledge graph.

To validate the effectiveness of our proposed method, we conducted experiments on multiple datasets and compared the results with existing methods. The experimental results revealed that our approach outperforms existing methods across various evaluation metrics, particularly in terms of precision and recall for entity and relationship extraction. Additionally, we analyzed the advantages of our approach in reducing manual effort, such as automating the processes of knowledge extraction and fusion, thereby reducing the dependence on human-annotated data.

In summary, this paper presents an innovative method for automatic knowledge graph construction that effectively tackles the challenges of entity and relationship extraction, as well as knowledge fusion. We anticipate that this method will offer valuable insights for future research and applications in the field of knowledge graph construction.

In future research, we intend to explore the integration of external knowledge bases and ontologies to further enhance the quality of the constructed knowledge graphs. Additionally, we plan to investigate the potential of our approach in other natural language processing tasks, such as sentiment analysis and more.

Acknowledgment. The authors are grateful to the National Key R&D Program of China for supporting this research under the project "Privacy protection for individual rights in data." This project provided the necessary funding and resources to conduct this study, which has greatly contributed to the development of knowledge in the field. The authors also appreciate the efforts of all project members who have contributed to this research. Their valuable insights and constructive feedback have been instrumental in shaping the direction of this work.

References

1. Bordes, A., Usunier, N., Garcia-Duran, A., Weston, J., Yakhnenko, O.: Translating embeddings for modeling multi-relational data. Adv. Neural Inf. Process. Syst. **26** (2013)
2. Dash, S., Glass, M.R., Gliozzo, A., Canim, M., Rossiello, G.: Populating web-scale knowledge graphs using distantly supervised relation extraction and validation. Information **12**(8), 316 (2021)
3. Devlin, J., Chang, M.W., Lee, K., Toutanova, K.: Bert: pre-training of deep bidirectional transformers for language understanding. arXiv preprint arXiv:1810.04805 (2018)
4. Dong, X., et al.: Knowledge vault: a web-scale approach to probabilistic knowledge fusion. In: Proceedings of the 20th ACM SIGKDD International Conference on Knowledge Discovery and Data Mining, pp. 601–610 (2014)
5. Fan, S., et al.: How to construct a power knowledge graph with dispatching data? Sci. Program. **2020**, 1–10 (2020)
6. Hearst, M.A.: Automatic acquisition of hyponyms from large text corpora. In: COLING 1992: The 14th International Conference on Computational Linguistics, vol. 2 (1992)
7. Ji, G., He, S., Xu, L., Liu, K., Zhao, J.: Knowledge graph embedding via dynamic mapping matrix. In: Proceedings of the 53rd Annual Meeting of the Association for Computational Linguistics and the 7th International Joint Conference on Natural Language Processing, vol. 1: Long papers, pp. 687–696 (2015)
8. Liu, X., Tu, Z., Wang, Z., Xu, X., Chen, Y.: A crowdsourcing-based knowledge graph construction platform. In: Hacid, H., et al. (eds.) ICSOC 2020. LNCS, vol. 12632, pp. 63–66. Springer, Cham (2021). https://doi.org/10.1007/978-3-030-76352-7_9
9. Mintz, M., Bills, S., Snow, R., Jurafsky, D.: Distant supervision for relation extraction without labeled data. In: Proceedings of the Joint Conference of the 47th Annual Meeting of the ACL and the 4th International Joint Conference on Natural Language Processing of the AFNLP, pp. 1003–1011 (2009)
10. Nickel, M., Murphy, K., Tresp, V., Gabrilovich, E.: A review of relational machine learning for knowledge graphs. Proc. IEEE **104**(1), 11–33 (2015)
11. Radford, A., Narasimhan, K., Salimans, T., Sutskever, I., et al.: Improving language understanding by generative pre-training (2018)
12. Riedel, S., Yao, L., McCallum, A.: Modeling relations and their mentions without labeled text. In: Balcázar, J.L., Bonchi, F., Gionis, A., Sebag, M. (eds.) ECML PKDD 2010. LNCS (LNAI), vol. 6323, pp. 148–163. Springer, Heidelberg (2010). https://doi.org/10.1007/978-3-642-15939-8_10

13. Suchanek, F.M., Kasneci, G., Weikum, G.: Yago: a core of semantic knowledge. In: Proceedings of the 16th International Conference on World Wide Web, pp. 697–706 (2007)
14. Surdeanu, M., Tibshirani, J., Nallapati, R., Manning, C.D.: Multi-instance multi-label learning for relation extraction. In: Proceedings of the 2012 Joint Conference on Empirical Methods in Natural Language Processing and Computational Natural Language Learning, pp. 455–465 (2012)

Cryptography and Encryption Techniques

Heterogeneous Aggregate Signature for Unmanned Aerial Vehicles

Xiangyu Pan and Fagen Li(✉)

School of Computer Science and Engineering, University of Electronic Science and Technology of China, Chengdu 611731, China
fagenli@uestc.edu.cn

Abstract. In recent years, internet of things (IoT) technology has become an indispensable part of people's lives. At the same time, the application field of unmanned aerial vehicle (UAV) technology is gradually expanding with the development of network technology. However, it has always been a challenge to ensure the communication security of UAVs since their communications are established on public wireless networks. Besides, with the increase of the types and number of UAVs, secure batch authentication for UAVs becomes particularly important. Although aggregate signature is an appropriate approach, the existing aggregate signature schemes are not feasible for UAVs from different cryptosystems since they were all designed in a homogeneous cryptosystem. In this paper, we propose a heterogeneous aggregate signature scheme HAS and present its security proofs. We also provide the experimental results of HAS and other five related works. It demonstrates that HAS is efficient and feasible for UAVs with limited resources.

Keywords: Batch authentication · Heterogeneous cryptosystem · Aggregate signature · Unmanned aerial vehicle

1 Introduction

The applications of unmanned aerial vehicle (UAV) technology has become more and more extensive with the rapid development of internet of things (IoT) and network technology [17]. Lots of companies produce UAVs for different purposes like express delivery, news report, traffic supervision and so forth. For instance, an UAV captures a traffic jam at a crossroad, it can inform the nearest ground station (GS) immediately. However, UAV communications depend on open wireless network, which makes it face varieties of threats such as eavesdropping, impersonation, tampering and repudiation etc. No matter what an UAV is used for, the communication security of UAV must be safeguarded. The communication of UAV mainly consists of UAV-to-UAV (U2U) and UAV-to-GS (U2G) [11], we focus on the latter in this paper.

Supported by Sichuan Science and Technology Program (Grant No. 2021YFG0157 and 2022ZHCG0037).

Digital signature is an appropriate method for authentication. A secure digital signature scheme can provide three main properties, namely integrity, authentication, and non-repudiation. In order to improve the efficiency of multi-user authentication, Boneh et al. [1] put forward the concept of aggregate signature in 2003. n different users sign n different messages to generate n different signatures respectively, an aggregate signature scheme makes it possible to aggregate these n signatures into a single signature. Meanwhile, the receiver can verify the validity of the single signature to check whether the n senders have signed the n different messages.

With the increasing popularization of UAV technology, many UAVs with various functions will be built by different companies. That is to say, for the communication security of UAVs, there may exists a lot of UAVs belonging to different cryptosystems in a certain area. However, the existing aggregate signature schemes are all designed in a homogeneous cryptosystem. It is expensive for a verifier to setup three sets of cryptosystems. In addition, the resources of an UAV are relatively limited. The computation overhead and communication cost on UAV's side should be reduced as much as possible. In this paper, we propose a heterogeneous aggregate signature scheme, which enables UAVs from different cryptosystems to authenticate to a GS. We prove its security with the help of random oracle model (ROM). In addition, the experimental results of HAS and other five related works are provided, which demonstrates that HAS is efficient and feasible for UAVs with limited resources.

Related works are discussed in Sect. 2. Section 3 describes preliminaries. In Sect. 4, we present the concrete construction of HAS and its security proofs. After that, the performance of our scheme is shown in Sect. 5. Security analysis are provided in Sect. 6. Finally, we summarize the paper in Sect. 7.

2   Related Works

Since UAV technology began to expand from military field to civil field, many different new challenges appear [16]. Due to the fact that UAV communication is established on open wireless network, the communication security of UAV has attracted much attention of researchers [5,8,9]. Cyber attacks are the main threats of UAV communication [10,14], there are several cryptographic protocols especially designed for UAV communication. Ozmen and Yavuz [21] put forward an efficient public key infrastructure (PKI) based framework for UAVs, which was feasible for UAVs with limited computation power. Khan et al. [13] proposed a signcryption scheme in identity-based cryptosystem (IBC) employing multiaccess edge computing to ensure the security of UAV communication. Won et al. [29,30] presented two efficient signcryption tag key encapsulation protocols in certificateless cryptosystem (CLC).

To solve the problem of batch authentication, Boneh et al. [1] first put forward the concept of aggregate signature and security models for it. To minimize the total information needed to verify in a signature scheme, Gentry and Ramzan [6] proposed the first aggregate signature scheme in IBC environment. The first certificateless aggregate signature scheme were introduced by Gong et al. [7] in the next year. However, these three schemes are all inefficient because the number of bilinear pairings increases linearly with the number of users. Wen and Ma [28] came up with an efficient aggregate signature scheme in PKI. The number of pairing operations in verification phase is independent of the number of signatures. Shim [24] proposed an identity-based aggregate signature schemes with constant pairing computations. Recently, to eliminate the use of certificates in PKI and the key-escrow problem in IBC, most aggregate signature schemes were proposed in CLC environment. Xiong et al. [33] introduced a certificateless aggregate signature scheme with constant pairing operations. But shortly afterwards, Cheng et al. [3] found an attack on [33], which shows it not capable of achieving existential unforgeability against chosen-message attack (EUF-CMA). They proposed an improved scheme and proved it secure against 'malicious-but-passive' KGC attack with the help of ROM. Cui et al. [4] proposed a no-pairing certificateless aggregate signature scheme for vehicular ad-hoc network (VANET). Later, Kamil and Ogundoyin [20] pointed out the drawbacks in Cui et al.'s scheme that it is not secure against type II adversary. Then they put forward a provably secure certificateless aggregate signature scheme for VANETs without pairings. Their scheme can meet the security requirements for VANETs while supporting conditional privacy preservation. In order to provide the anonymous authentication with preserved privacy and security in VANETs, Thumbur et al. [25] presented a privacy-preserving certificateless aggregate signature scheme for VANETs. Kumar et al. [15] introduced a certificateless aggregate signature scheme to provide the medical data privacy and integrity in healthcare wireless sensor networks. To ensure the communication and data security of healthcare wireless sensor networks and protect patient privacy, Xie et al. [32] presented an improved certificateless aggregate signature scheme after analyzing the drawbacks of [15]. Recently, Wang et al. [27] proposed a conditional privacy-preserving certificateless aggregate signature scheme for authentication in VANETs. Moreover, they proved its security in the standard model.

Chen et al. [2], Ma et al. [19] and Verma et al. [26] researched on certificate-based cryptosystem (CBC) aggregate signature, which is an extension of CLC aggregate signature. Particularly, Wu et al. [31] put forward a novel attack namely fully chosen-key attacks. To explain that, the security model they defined is different from the traditional security models of aggregate signature schemes. The adversary's goal in their security model is to forge a valid aggregate signature while there exists at least one invalid individual signature. Although they gave a solution to this kind of attack, it is inefficient or even more time-consuming.

3 Preliminaries

3.1 System Architecture

There are six main entities in the system architecture, including UAVs, a trace authority (TRA), a certificate authority (CA), a private key generator (PKG), a key generation center (KGC) and a ground station (GS).

- UAVs: UAVs from different cryptosystems are the senders in this system, they intend to authenticate to a GS.
- TRA: To protect UAVs' identity privacy, it is responsible for generating pseudo identities for UAVs based on their real identities.
- CA: It issues certificates for UAVs in PKI.
- PKG: It extracts secret keys for UAVs In IBC.
- KGC: It generates partial secret keys for UAVs in CLC.
- GS: It is the verifier of the signatures sent from UAVs in this system.

Here the TRA, the CA and the PKG are modeled as trusted authorities while the KGC is a semi-trusted authority.

3.2   Bilinear Pairing

$\mathbb{G}$ is an additive group with order q and $\mathbb{G}_T$ is a multiplicative group with order p, where p is a large prime number. $\hat{e} : \mathbb{G} \times \mathbb{G} \to \mathbb{G}_T$ is a bilinear map and it satisfies the following three properties.

1. Bilinearity: $\hat{e}(aP, bQ) = \hat{e}(P, Q)^{ab}$ for any $a, b \in \mathbb{Z}_p^*$ and $P, Q \in \mathbb{G}$.
2. Non-degeneracy: $\hat{e}(P, Q) \neq 1_{\mathbb{G}_T}$ for any $P, Q \in \mathbb{G}$.
3. Computability: $\hat{e}(P, Q)$ can be computed with efficiency for any $P, Q \in \mathbb{G}$.

3.3   Computational Diffie-Hellman (CDH) Problem

Given group $\mathbb{G}$ of prime order p, a generator $P \in \mathbb{G}$ and two elements $aP, bP \in \mathbb{G}$, where a, b are randomly selected from $\mathbb{Z}_p^*$, it is difficult to compute abP.

4   The Proposed Scheme

In the first subsection, a concrete heterogeneous aggregate signature scheme HAS is proposed. Moreover, we provide its security proofs in the second subsection. The symbols and their descriptions are shown in Table 1.

4.1   Concrete Construction

- Setup: Given a security parameter λ, it chooses a p-order additive group $\mathbb{G}$, a p-order multiplicative group $\mathbb{G}_T$ and a bilinear map $\hat{e}: \mathbb{G} \times \mathbb{G} \to \mathbb{G}_T$. Then it randomly selects two generators P and Q of $\mathbb{G}$, three collision-resistant hash functions: $H_0 : \{0,1\}^* \to \{0,1\}^n$, $H_1 : \{0,1\}^* \to \mathbb{G}$, $H_2 : \{0,1\}^* \to \mathbb{Z}_p^*$.
  - Trace authority: The TRA picks a random number $s \in \mathbb{Z}_p^*$ as its secret key, then publishes $T_{pub} = sP$.
  - Certificate authority: The CA's initialization is omitted since we omit the process of registration in PKI-KG.
  - Private key generator: The PKG chooses $s_1 \in \mathbb{Z}_p^*$ randomly as its secret key and publishes the corresponding public key $P_{pub1} = s_1 P$.

Table 1. Notations

Symbol	Description
RID_i/ID_i	Real identity/pseudo identity
spp	System public parameters
m_i/σ_i	Message/signature
T_{pub}/s	The TRA's public/secret key pair
P_{pub1}/s_1	The PKG's public/secret key pair
P_{pub2}/s_2	The KGC's public/secret key pair
pk_i/sk_i	ID_i's public/secret key pair in PKI
S_{ID_i}	ID_i's secret key in IBC
upk_i/usk_i	ID_i's user public/secret key pair in CLC
psk_i	ID_i's partial secret key in CLC
λ	Security parameter
p	A large prime number
$\mathbb{G}/\mathbb{G}_T$	An additive/multiplicative group with order p
P, Q	Two generators in $\mathbb{G}$
n	The length of an identity

- Key generation center: The KGC randomly selects $s_2 \in \mathbb{Z}_p^*$ as its secret key and publishes the corresponding public key $P_{pub2} = s_2 P$.
- PIDG: An UAV$_i$ with real identity RID_i picks $r_i \in \mathbb{Z}_p^*$ randomly and computes $R_i = r_i P$, then sends (R_i, RID_i) to the TRA. After receiving the request, the TRA first checks the validity of RID_i. If it is valid, the TRA computes RID_i's pseudo identity $ID_i = RID_i \oplus H_0(sR_i, t_i, T_{pub})$, where t_i is the expiration date of ID_i. Next, the TRA returns (ID_i, t_i) to UAV$_i$ through a secure channel and saves (ID_i, R_i, t_i) in its database in case of disputes. Note that UAV$_i$ can verify whether the equation $ID_i = RID_i \oplus H_0(r_i T_{pub}, t_i, T_{pub})$ holds to check the validity of ID_i. The TRA can trace ID_i's real identity by calculating $RID_i = ID_i \oplus H_0(sR_i, t_i, T_{pub})$ while others cannot.
- PKI-KG: In PKI, an UAV$_i$ with pseudo identity ID_i randomly chooses its secret key $sk_i = x_i \in \mathbb{Z}_p^*$, computes the corresponding public key $pk_i = x_i P$ and submits pk_i together with ID_i to the CA to register a certificate.
- IBC-KG: In IBC, an UAV$_i$ sends its pseudo identity ID_i to the PKG. the PKG calculates ID_i's secret key as $S_{ID_i} = s_1 H_1(ID_i)$.
- CLC-KG: In CLC, an UAV$_i$ first sends its pseudo identity ID_i to the KGC. The KGC computes ID_i's partial secret key as $psk_i = s_2 H_1(ID_i)$. Next, UAV$_i$ picks its user secret key $usk_i = x_i \in \mathbb{Z}_p^*$ and generates its public key $upk_i = x_i P$. ID_i's secret key is (psk_i, usk_i).
- Sign: This algorithm is composed of three subalgorithm namely PKI-Sign, IBC-Sign and CLC-Sign, which represent the signature generation algorithm in PKI, IBC and CLC respectively.

- PKI-Sign: An UAV$_i$ with pseudo identity ID_i in PKI picks $r_i \in \mathbb{Z}_p^*$ randomly, calculates

$$R_i = r_i P, h_i = H_2(ID_i, m_i, T_i, R_i), S_i = (r_i + h_i sk_i)Q$$

The signature is $\sigma_i = (R_i, S_i)$. UAV$_i$ sends $(ID_i, m_i, \sigma_i, T_i)$ to the GS, where T_i is a timestamp.

- IBC-Sign: An UAV$_i$ in IBC chooses $r_i \in \mathbb{Z}_p^*$ randomly, calculates

$$R_i = r_i P, h_i = H_2(ID_i, m_i, T_i, R_i), S_i = S_{ID_i} + h_i r_i P_{pub1}$$

The signature is $\sigma_i = (R_i, S_i)$. UAV$_i$ sends $(ID_i, m_i, \sigma_i, T_i)$ to the GS.

- CLC-Sign: An UAV$_i$ in CLC selects $r_i \in \mathbb{Z}_p^*$ randomly, calculates

$$R_i = r_i P, h_i = H_2(ID_i, m_i, T_i, R_i), S_i = psk_i + h_i r_i P_{pub2} + (r_i + h_i usk_i)Q$$

The signature is $\sigma_i = (R_i, S_i)$. UAV$_i$ sends $(ID_i, m_i, \sigma_i, T_i)$ to the GS.

- IV: This algorithm consists of three individual signature verification subalgorithm namely PKI-IV, IBC-IV and CLC-IV.
  - PKI-IV: Receiving $(ID_i, m_i, \sigma_i = (R_i, S_i), T_i)$ from an UAV in PKI, GS calculates $h_i = H_2(ID_i, m_i, T_i, R_i)$ and checks the following equation.

$$\hat{e}(S_i, P) = \hat{e}(R_i + h_i pk_i, Q)$$

  - IBC-IV: After receiving $(ID_i, m_i, \sigma_i, T_i)$ from an UAV in IBC, GS calculates $h_i = H_2(ID_i, m_i, T_i, R_i)$ and checks the following equation.

$$\hat{e}(S_i, P) = \hat{e}(H_1(ID_i) + h_i R_i, P_{pub1})$$

  - CLC-IV: After receiving $(ID_i, m_i, \sigma_i, T_i)$ from an UAV in CLC, GS calculates $h_i = H_2(ID_i, m_i, T_i, R_i)$ and checks the following equation.

$$\hat{e}(S_i, P) = \hat{e}(H_1(ID_i) + h_i R_i, P_{pub2}) \cdot \hat{e}(R_i + h_i upk_i, Q)$$

- HASV: When receiving n tuples of $(ID_i, m_i, \sigma_i, T_i)$ including j tuples from PKI, k tuples from IBC and l tuples from CLC respectively $(n = j + k + l)$, the GS first computes $h_i = H_2(ID_i, m_i, T_i, R_i)$ for $i = 1$ to n and $S = \sum_{i=1}^{n} S_i$. Next, for the j signature from UAVs in PKI, the GS computes $A = \sum_{i=1}^{j} (R_i + h_i pk_i)$. For the k signatures from UAVs in IBC, the GS computes $B = \sum_{i=1}^{k} (H_1(ID_i) + h_i R_i)$. For the l signatures from UAVs in CLC, the GS computes $C_1 = \sum_{i=1}^{l} (H_1(ID_i) + h_i R_i)$ and $C_2 = \sum_{i=1}^{l} (R_i + h_i upk_i)$. After that, the GS checks whether the following equation holds:

$$\hat{e}(S, P) = \hat{e}(B, P_{pub1}) \cdot \hat{e}(C_1, P_{pub2}) \cdot \hat{e}(A + C_2, Q)$$

If the equation above is correct, the GS accept the heterogeneous aggregate signature. Otherwise, the signature is invalid and the GS rejects it. It can be easily seen that our scheme can also work in a homogeneous cryptosystem.

4.2   Security Proofs

Our scheme is existential unforgeable against any PPT forgers iff the PKI part, IBC part and CLC part of HAS are all capable of achieving existential unforgeability. We provide the security proofs for the three cryptosystems respectively.

Theorem 1. *With the help of ROM, if the PKI part of HAS (EUF-CMA in PKI) is compromised by a PPT adversary $\mathcal{A}_1$ with a non-negligible advantage ϵ within time t, the CDH assumption can be solved in an expected time of $t' \leq t + (3q_S + 1)t_{sm}$ with a same advantage ϵ, where q_S and t_{sm} denotes the number of query $\mathcal{O}_S$ and the time of a scalar multiplication in $\mathbb{G}$ respectively.*

Proof. In PKI, if there exists an adversary $\mathcal{A}_1$ who can win Game I within time t, we are able to construct an efficient algorithm $\mathcal{C}$ taking $\mathcal{A}_1$ as a subalgorithm to break the CDH assumption. Given a CDH tuple $\{p, \mathbb{G}, aP, bP\}$, $\mathcal{C}$ simulates Game I with $\mathcal{A}_1$ to solve the CDH problem as follows.

1. $\mathcal{C}$ generates a p-order additive group $\mathbb{G}$, two generators P, $Q = bP$, a hash function $H_2 : \{0,1\}^* \to \mathbb{Z}_p^*$ and a bilinear map $\hat{e} : \mathbb{G} \times \mathbb{G} \to \mathbb{G}_T$, where $\mathbb{G}_T$ is a p-order multiplicative group. $\mathcal{C}$ sets the challenge public key as $pk^* = aP$, and the corresponding pseudo identity is ID^*. Finally, $\mathcal{C}$ sends $spp = \{p, \mathbb{G}, \mathbb{G}_T, P, Q\}$ and (pk^*, ID^*) to $\mathcal{A}_1$.
2. $\mathcal{A}_1$ can issue a polynomial number of queries to the following two oracles.
   - **Hash function H_2 $\mathcal{O}_{H_2}$:** $\mathcal{C}$ creates a list L_{H_2} to maintain the query results of H_2. Every time $\mathcal{A}_1$ submits a query (ID_i, m_i, T_i, R_i), $\mathcal{C}$ first checks L_{H_2} if there exists a tuple $(ID_i, m_i, T_i, R_i, h_i)$ on L_{H_2}. If so, $\mathcal{C}$ retrieves h_i and answers $\mathcal{A}_1$ with h_i. Otherwise, $\mathcal{C}$ picks a random $h_i \in \mathbb{Z}_p^*$, answers with h_i and adds the new tuple $(ID_i, m_i, T_i, R_i, h_i)$ to L_{H_2}.
   - **Sign $\mathcal{O}_S$:** $\mathcal{A}_1$ submits (pk_i, m_i, T_i) to $\mathcal{C}$. $\mathcal{C}$ selects $r_i, h_i \in \mathbb{Z}_p^*$ randomly, calculates $S_i = r_i Q, R_i = r_i P - h_i pk_i$. Next, $\mathcal{C}$ checks whether there is a tuple $(ID_i, m_i, T_i, R_i, h_i)$ in L_{H_2}. If so, $\mathcal{C}$ chooses another $r_i, h_i \in \mathbb{Z}_p^*$ and calculates again. Until there is no such tuple in L_{H_2}, $\mathcal{C}$ adds $(ID_i, m_i, T_i, R_i, h_i)$ to L_{H_2} and responds with $\sigma_i = (R_i, S_i)$. The signature is valid because it satisfies the verification equation.
3. After the query phase, $\mathcal{A}_1$ outputs a signature. The three conditions of forking lemma [22] are satisfied, so if $\mathcal{A}_1$ is an efficient forger, $\mathcal{C}$ can obtain two valid signature tuples $(pk^*, m_1, R_1, h_1, S_1)$ and $(pk^*, m_2, R_2, h_2, S_2)$, where $m_1 = m_2$ and $R_1 = R_2$. Therefore, $\mathcal{C}$ can compute $(h_2 - h_1)^{-1}(S_2 - S_1) = abP$. $\mathcal{C}$ outputs it as the solution to the given CDH problem.

Theorem 2. *With the help of ROM, if the IBC part of HAS (EUF-CMA in IBC) is compromised by a PPT adversary $\mathcal{A}_2$ with a non-negligible advantage ϵ within time t, the CDH assumption can be solved in an expected time of $t' \leq t + (q_{H_1} + q_{KE} + 3q_S + 3)t_{sm}$ with an advantage $\epsilon' \geq \epsilon/4q_{KE}$, where q_{H_1}, q_{KE}, q_S and t_{sm} denotes the number of query $\mathcal{O}_{H_1}, \mathcal{O}_{KE}, \mathcal{O}_S$ and the time of a scalar multiplication in $\mathbb{G}$ respectively.*

Proof. In IBC, if there exists an adversary $\mathcal{A}_2$ can win Game II within a polynomial time t, we are able to construct an efficient algorithm $\mathcal{C}$ taking $\mathcal{A}_2$ as a subalgorithm to break CDH assumption. Given a CDH tuple $\{p, \mathbb{G}, aP, bP\}$, $\mathcal{C}$ simulates Game II with $\mathcal{A}_2$ to solve the CDH problem as follows.

1. $\mathcal{C}$ executes the initialization algorithm to generate a p-order additive group $\mathbb{G}$, two generators P, Q, two hash functions $H_1 : \{0,1\}^* \to \mathbb{G}$, $H_2 : \{0,1\}^* \to \mathbb{Z}_p^*$ and a bilinear map $\hat{e} : \mathbb{G} \times \mathbb{G} \to \mathbb{G}_T$, where $\mathbb{G}_T$ is a p-order multiplicative group. Then $\mathcal{C}$ sets master public key as $P_{pub1} = aP$. Finally, $\mathcal{C}$ sends $spp = \{p, \mathbb{G}, \mathbb{G}_T, P, Q, P_{pub1}\}$ to $\mathcal{A}_2$.

2. $\mathcal{A}_2$ can issue a polynomial number of queries to the following four oracles.

   - **Hash function H_1 $\mathcal{O}_{H_1}$:** $\mathcal{C}$ generates a list L_{H_1} to maintain the query results of H_1. Every time $\mathcal{A}_2$ submits an ID_i, $\mathcal{C}$ retrieves and responds with Q_{ID_i} if there is a tuple $(ID_i, t_i, c_i, Q_{ID_i})$ in L_{H_1}. Otherwise, $\mathcal{C}$ picks $c_i \in \{0,1\}$ randomly ($\Pr[c_i = 0] = \delta$). If $c_i = 0$, $\mathcal{C}$ chooses $t_i \in \mathbb{Z}_p$, calculates $Q_{ID_i} = t_i bP$, responds with Q_{ID_i} and adds the tuple $(ID_i, t_i, c_i, Q_{ID_i})$ to L_{H_1}. If $c_i = 1$, $\mathcal{C}$ chooses $t_i \in \mathbb{Z}_p^*$, calculates $Q_{ID_i} = t_i P$, responds with Q_{ID_i} and adds the tuple $(ID_i, t_i, c_i, Q_{ID_i})$ to L_{H_1}.

   - **Hash function H_2 $\mathcal{O}_{H_2}$:** The same in the proof of **Theorem** 1.

   - **Key extraction $\mathcal{O}_{KE}$:** $\mathcal{A}_2$ submits an ID_i to $\mathcal{C}$. $\mathcal{C}$ first applies ID_i to $\mathcal{O}_{H_1}$ and retrieves the corresponding tuple $(ID_i, t_i, c_i, Q_{ID_i})$. If $c_i = 0$, $\mathcal{C}$ aborts. Otherwise, $\mathcal{C}$ computes $S_{ID_i} = t_i P_{pub1}$ and returns back. Note that the probability of not aborting in this phase is at least $(1 - \delta)^{q_{KE}}$.

   - **Sign $\mathcal{O}_S$:** $\mathcal{A}_2$ submits (ID_i, m_i, T_i) to $\mathcal{C}$. $\mathcal{C}$ first applies ID_i to $\mathcal{O}_{H_1}$ and retrieves the corresponding tuple $(ID_i, t_i, c_i, Q_{ID_i})$. $\mathcal{C}$ selects $r_i, h_i \in \mathbb{Z}_p^*$ randomly, calculates $R_i = r_i P - h_i^{-1} Q_{ID_i}$, $S_i = h_i r_i P_{pub1}$. Next, $\mathcal{C}$ checks whether there is a tuple $(ID_i, m_i, T_i, R_i, h_i)$ in L_{H_2}. If so, $\mathcal{C}$ chooses another $r_i, h_i \in \mathbb{Z}_p^*$ and calculates again. Until there is no such tuple in L_{H_2}, $\mathcal{C}$ adds $(ID_i, m_i, T_i, R_i, h_i)$ to L_{H_2} and responds with $\sigma_i = (R_i, S_i)$. The signature is valid because it satisfies the verification equation.

3. After the query phase, $\mathcal{A}_2$ outputs a signature. The three conditions of forking lemma [22] are satisfied, so if $\mathcal{A}_2$ is an efficient forger, $\mathcal{C}$ can obtain two valid signature tuples $(ID^*, m_1, R_1, h_1, S_1)$ and $(ID^*, m_2, R_2, h_2, S_2)$, where $m_1 = m_2$ and $R_1 = R_2$. $\mathcal{C}$ applies ID^* to $\mathcal{O}_{H_1}$ and retrieves the corresponding tuple $(ID^*, t_i, c_i, Q_{ID_i})$. If $c_i = 1$, $\mathcal{C}$ aborts. Otherwise, $\mathcal{C}$ computes $(h_2^{-1} - h_1^{-1})^{-1}(h_2^{-1}S_2 - h_1^{-1}S_1) = abP$. $\mathcal{C}$ outputs it as the solution to the given CDH problem. Note that the probability of not aborting in this phase is larger than δ. Therefore, $\mathcal{C}$'s advantage of solving CDH assumption is $\epsilon' \geq (1 - \delta)^{q_{KE}} \cdot \delta \cdot \epsilon$. Let $\delta = 1/q_{KE}$, then we have

$$\epsilon' \geq (1 - \frac{1}{q_{pskE}})^{q_{pskE}} \cdot \frac{1}{q_{pskE}} \cdot \epsilon \geq \frac{\epsilon}{4q_{pskE}}$$

Since ϵ is non-negligible, ϵ' is non-negligible too.

Theorem 3. *With the help of ROM, the CLC part of HAS is capable of achieving EUF-CMA if the CDH problem is intractable.*

Proof. This theorem will be proved by the composition of **Lemma** 1 and **Lemma** 2.

Lemma 1. *If a type I adversary $\mathcal{A}_3$ can break the CLC part of HAS-U2G (EUF-CMA-I in CLC) in a polynomial time t with a non-negligible advantage ϵ, there exists an efficient algorithm to solve the CDH problem within a time $t' \leq t + (q_{H_1} + q_{Cu} + q_{pskE} + 6q_S + 4)t_{sm}$ with an advantage $\epsilon' \geq \epsilon/4q_{pskE}$, where q_{H_1}, q_{Cu}, q_{pskE}, q_S and t_{sm} denotes the number of query $\mathcal{O}_{H_1}$, $\mathcal{O}_{Cu}$, $\mathcal{O}_{pskE}$, $\mathcal{O}_S$ and the time of a scalar multiplication in $\mathbb{G}$ respectively.*

Proof. In CLC, if there is a type I adversary $\mathcal{A}_3$ can win Game III within a polynomial time, we are able to construct an efficient algorithm $\mathcal{C}$ making use of $\mathcal{A}_3$ to crack the CDH assumption. Given a CDH tuple $\{p, \mathbb{G}, aP, bP\}$, $\mathcal{C}$ simulates Game III with $\mathcal{A}_3$ to solve the CDH problem as follows.

1. $\mathcal{C}$ executes Setup to generate a p-order additive group $\mathbb{G}$, two generators P, $Q = cP$ (c is randomly picked in $\mathbb{Z}_p^*$), two hash functions $H_1 : \{0,1\}^* \to \mathbb{G}$, $H_2 : \{0,1\}^* \to \mathbb{Z}_p$ and a bilinear map $\hat{e} : \mathbb{G} \times \mathbb{G} \to \mathbb{G}_T$, where $\mathbb{G}_T$ is a p-order multiplicative group. Then $\mathcal{C}$ sets master public key as $P_{pub2} = aP$. Finally, $\mathcal{C}$ sends $spp = \{p, \mathbb{G}, \mathbb{G}_T, P, Q, P_{pub2}\}$ to $\mathcal{A}_3$.
2. $\mathcal{A}_3$ can issue a polynomial number of queries to the following five oracles.
   - **Hash function H_1 $\mathcal{O}_{H_1}$:** The same in the proof of **Theorem** 2.
   - **Hash function H_2 $\mathcal{O}_{H_2}$:** The same in the proof of **Theorem** 1.
   - **Create user $\mathcal{O}_{Cu}$:** $\mathcal{C}$ creates a list L_U. After receiving an ID_i from $\mathcal{A}_3$, $\mathcal{C}$ first searches L_U for (ID_i, upk_i, usk_i). If it is found, $\mathcal{C}$ answers with upk_i. Otherwise, $\mathcal{C}$ selects $usk_i \in \mathbb{Z}_p^*$ randomly, calculates $upk_i = usk_i P$, adds (ID_i, upk_i, usk_i) to L_U and responds with upk_i.
   - **Replace user public key $\mathcal{O}_{Rupk}$:** After receiving $\{ID_i, upk_i'\}$ from $\mathcal{A}_3$, $\mathcal{C}$ searches L_U for (ID_i, upk_i, usk_i). If it is found, $\mathcal{C}$ replaces this tuple with a new one $(ID_i, upk_i', \perp)$, where $\perp$ is the symbol of empty. Otherwise, $\mathcal{C}$ simply adds $(ID_i, upk_i', \perp)$ to L_U.
   - **User secret key extraction $\mathcal{O}_{uskE}$:** $\mathcal{A}_3$ submits an ID_i to $\mathcal{C}$. $\mathcal{C}$ checks if there is a tuple (ID_i, upk_i, usk_i) in L_U. If so, $\mathcal{C}$ retrieves and answers with usk_i. Otherwise, $\mathcal{C}$ applies ID_i to $\mathcal{O}_{Cu}$ and responds with usk_i.
   - **Partial secret key extraction $\mathcal{O}_{pskE}$:** $\mathcal{A}_3$ submits an ID_i to $\mathcal{C}$. $\mathcal{C}$ first applies ID_i to $\mathcal{O}_{H_1}$ and retrieves the corresponding $(ID_i, t_i, c_i, Q_{ID_i})$. If $c_i = 0$, $\mathcal{C}$ aborts. Otherwise, $\mathcal{C}$ computes $psk_i = t_i P_{pub2}$ and returns back. The probability of not aborting in this phase is at least $(1 - \delta)^{q_{pskE}}$.
   - **Sign $\mathcal{O}_S$:** $\mathcal{A}_3$ submits (ID_i, m_i, T_i) to $\mathcal{C}$. $\mathcal{C}$ first applies ID_i to $\mathcal{O}_{H_1}$ and $\mathcal{O}_{Cu}$, retrieves the corresponding tuple $(ID_i, t_i, c_i, Q_{ID_i})$ and (ID_i, upk_i, usk_i). Then $\mathcal{C}$ selects $r_i, h_i \in \mathbb{Z}_p^*$ randomly, computes $R_i = r_i P - h_i^{-1} Q_{ID_i}$, $S_i = h_i r_i P_{pub2} + r_i Q + h_i c upk_i - h_i^{-1} c Q_{ID_i}$. Next, $\mathcal{C}$ checks whether there is a tuple $(ID_i, m_i, T_i, R_i, h_i)$ in L_{H_2}. If so, $\mathcal{C}$ chooses another $r_i, h_i \in \mathbb{Z}_p^*$ and calculates again. Until there is no such tuple in

L_{H_2}, $\mathcal{C}$ adds $(ID_i, m_i, T_i, R_i, h_i)$ to L_{H_2} and responds with $\sigma_i = (R_i, S_i)$. In addition, the signature is valid because it satisfies the verify equation.

3. The three conditions of forking lemma [22] are satisfied, so if $\mathcal{A}_3$ is an efficient forger, $\mathcal{C}$ can obtain two valid signature tuples $(ID^*, m_1, R_1, h_1, S_1)$ and $(ID^*, m_2, R_2, h_2, S_2)$, where $m_1 = m_2$ and $R_1 = R_2$. $\mathcal{C}$ applies ID^* to $\mathcal{O}_{H_1}$ and retrieves the tuple $(ID^*, t_i, c_i, Q_{ID_i})$. If $c_i = 1$, $\mathcal{C}$ aborts. Otherwise, $\mathcal{C}$ can compute $(h_2^{-1} - h_1^{-1})^{-1}(h_2^{-1}S_2 - h_1^{-1}S_1) - cR_1 = abP$. $\mathcal{C}$ outputs it as the solution to the given CDH problem. Note that the probability of not aborting in this phase is larger than δ. Therefore, $\mathcal{C}$'s advantage of solving the CDH assumption is $\epsilon' \geq (1 - \delta)^{q_{pskE}} \cdot \delta \cdot \epsilon$. Let $\delta = 1/q_{pskE}$, then we have

$$\epsilon' \geq (1 - \frac{1}{q_{pskE}})^{q_{pskE}} \cdot \frac{1}{q_{pskE}} \cdot \epsilon \geq \frac{\epsilon}{4q_{pskE}}$$

Since ϵ is non-negligible, ϵ' is non-negligible too. ∎

Lemma 2. *If a type II adversary $\mathcal{A}_4$ can break the CLC part of HAS-U2G (EUF-CMA-II in CLC) in a polynomial time t with a non-negligible advantage ϵ, there exists an efficient algorithm to solve the CDH problem within a time $t' \leq t + (q_{H_1} + q_{Cu} + 6q_S + 4)t_{sm}$ with an advantage $\epsilon' \geq \epsilon/4q_{uskE}$, where q_{H_1}, q_{Cu}, q_S, q_{uskE} and t_{sm} denotes the number of query $\mathcal{O}_{H_1}$, $\mathcal{O}_{Cu}$, $\mathcal{O}_S$, $\mathcal{O}_{uskE}$ and the time of a scalar multiplication in $\mathbb{G}$ respectively.*

Proof. In CLC, if there is a type II adversary $\mathcal{A}_4$ can win Game IV within a polynomial time t, we are able to construct an efficient algorithm $\mathcal{C}$ making use of $\mathcal{A}_4$ to crack the CDH assumption. Given a CDH tuple $\{p, \mathbb{G}, aP, bP\}$, $\mathcal{C}$ simulates Game IV with $\mathcal{A}_4$ to solve the CDH problem as follows.

1. $\mathcal{C}$ executes Setup to generate a p-order additive group $\mathbb{G}$, two generators P, $Q = aP$, two hash functions $H_1 : \{0,1\}^* \to \mathbb{G}$, $H_2 : \{0,1\}^* \to \mathbb{Z}_p^*$ and a bilinear map $\hat{e} : \mathbb{G} \times \mathbb{G} \to \mathbb{G}_T$, where $\mathbb{G}_T$ is also a p-order group. Then $\mathcal{C}$ picks a random $s_2 \in \mathbb{Z}_p^*$ as master secret key and sets master public key as $P_{pub2} = s_2 P$. Finally, $\mathcal{C}$ sends $spp = \{p, \mathbb{G}, \mathbb{G}_T, P, Q, P_{pub2}\}$ and s_2 to $\mathcal{A}_4$.
2. $\mathcal{A}_4$ can issue a polynomial number of queries to the following five oracles.
   - **Hash function H_1 $\mathcal{O}_{H_1}$:** $\mathcal{C}$ generates a list L_{H_1}. Every time $\mathcal{A}_4$ submits an ID_i, $\mathcal{C}$ retrieves and responds with Q_{ID_i} if there is a tuple (ID_i, t_i, Q_{ID_i}) in L_{H_1}. Otherwise, $\mathcal{C}$ picks $t_i \in \mathbb{Z}_p^*$ randomly, calculates $Q_{ID_i} = t_i P$, adds (ID_i, t_i, Q_{ID_i}) to L_{H_1} and answers with Q_{ID_i}.
   - **Hash function H_2 $\mathcal{O}_{H_2}$:** The same in the proof of **Theorem** 1.
   - **Create user $\mathcal{O}_{Cu}$:** $\mathcal{C}$ creates a list L_U. After receiving an ID_i from $\mathcal{A}_4$, $\mathcal{C}$ first searches L_U for a tuple $(ID_i, c_i, upk_i, usk_i)$. If it is found, $\mathcal{C}$ answers with upk_i. Otherwise, $\mathcal{C}$ picks $c_i \in \{0,1\}$ randomly ($\Pr[c_i = 0] = \delta$). If $c_i = 1$, $\mathcal{C}$ selects $usk_i \in \mathbb{Z}_p^*$ randomly, calculates $upk_i = usk_i P$, adds the new tuple $(ID_i, c_i, upk_i, usk_i)$ to L_U and responds with upk_i. Otherwise, $\mathcal{C}$ selects $usk_i \in \mathbb{Z}_p^*$ randomly, adds the new tuple $(ID_i, c_i, upk_i = usk_i bP, usk_i)$ and responds with upk_i.

- **User secret key extraction** $\mathcal{O}_{uskE}$: $\mathcal{A}_4$ submits an ID_i to $\mathcal{C}$. $\mathcal{C}$ checks if there is a tuple (ID_i, upk_i, usk_i) in L_U. If not, $\mathcal{C}$ applies ID_i to $\mathcal{O}_{Cu}$ and retrieves the corresponding tuple $(ID_i, c_i, upk_i, usk_i)$. If $c_i = 0$, $\mathcal{C}$ aborts. Otherwise, $\mathcal{C}$ answers with usk_i. The probability of not aborting in this phase is at least $(1 - \delta)^{q_{uskE}}$.
- **Sign** $\mathcal{O}_S$: $\mathcal{C}$ applies ID_i to $\mathcal{O}_{H_1}$ and $\mathcal{O}_U$, retrieves the tuple (ID_i, t_i, Q_{ID_i}) and $(ID_i, c_i, upk_i, usk_i)$. Then $\mathcal{C}$ selects $r_i, h_i \in \mathbb{Z}_p^*$ randomly, computes $R_i = r_i P - h_i upk_i$, $S_i = s_2 H_1(ID_i) + s_2 h_i R_i + r_i Q$. Next, $\mathcal{C}$ checks whether there is a tuple $(ID_i, m_i, T_i, R_i, h_i)$ in L_{H_2}. If so, $\mathcal{C}$ chooses another $r_i, h_i \in \mathbb{Z}_p^*$ and calculates again. Until there is no such tuple in L_{H_2}, $\mathcal{C}$ adds $(ID_i, m_i, T_i, R_i, h_i)$ to L_{H_2} and responds with $\sigma_i = (R_i, S_i)$. The signature is valid because it satisfies the verification equation.

3. The three conditions of forking lemma [22] are satisfied, so if $\mathcal{A}_4$ is an efficient forger, $\mathcal{C}$ can obtain two valid signature tuples $(ID^*, m_1, R_1, h_1, S_1)$ and $(ID^*, m_2, R_2, h_2, S_2)$, where $m_1 = m_2$ and $R_1 = R_2$. $\mathcal{C}$ applies ID^* to $\mathcal{O}_U$ and retrieves the corresponding tuple $(ID^*, c_i, upk_i, usk_i)$. If $c_i = 1$, $\mathcal{C}$ aborts. Otherwise, $\mathcal{C}$ can compute $(h_2 - h_1)^{-1}(S_2 - S_1) - s_2 R_1 = abP$. $\mathcal{C}$ outputs it as the solution to the given CDH problem. Note that the probability of not aborting in this phase is larger than δ. Therefore, $\mathcal{C}$'s advantage of solving the CDH assumption is $\epsilon' \geq (1 - \delta)^{q_{uskE}} \cdot \delta \cdot \epsilon$. Let $\delta = 1/q_{uskE}$, then we have

$$\epsilon' \geq (1 - \frac{1}{q_{uskE}})^{q_{uskE}} \cdot \frac{1}{q_{uskE}} \cdot \epsilon \geq \frac{\epsilon}{4 q_{uskE}}$$

Since ϵ is non-negligible, ϵ' is non-negligible too. ∎

5   Comparison

In this section, our scheme is compared with five related works, including WM [28], SMLWM [23], YLWC [34], TRRGRP [25] and KLL [12]. We provide the main computation overhead of single signature in Table 2. T_{bp}, T_{mtp} and T_{pm} denote the time of a bilinear pairing, a map-to-point hash function and a point multiplication respectively. In Table 2, in order to show the comparison more intuitively, we divide our scheme into three parts namely HAS-PKI, HAS-IBC and HAS-CLC. They represent the PKI part, IBC part and CLC part of HAS respectively. In terms of each cryptosystem, our scheme is no less efficient than others except for [25]. In Table 3, we provide the main computation overhead of aggregate signature. For simplicity, we assume that there are $3n$ senders in other five works while there are n senders in each cryptosystem ($3n$ in total) in our scheme. In Table 4, we show the comparison of communication cost. $\mathbb{G}$, $\mathbb{Z}_p$ and ID denote the length of an element in $\mathbb{G}$, an element in $\mathbb{Z}_p$ and an identity respectively. Similarly, we divide our scheme into three parts in Table 4. We can see that in both PKI and CLC parts, our scheme has the lowest communication cost. While in IBC, the communication cost of our scheme is the same as [23] and [34]. We provide the comparison of security in Table 5. SG-1, SG-2, SG-3, SG-4,

Table 2. Theoretical computation overhead (single signature)

Schemes	Cryptosystem	Sign	Verify
WM [28]	PKI	$2T_{pm}$	$2T_{bp} + T_{pm}$
HAS-PKI	PKI	$2T_{pm}$	$2T_{bp} + T_{pm}$
SMLWM [23]	IBC	$2T_{pm} + T_{mtp}$	$3T_{bp} + 2T_{mtp}$
YLWC [34]	IBC	$3T_{pm}$	$2T_{bp} + T_{pm} + T_{mtp}$
HAS-IBC	IBC	$2T_{pm}$	$2T_{bp} + T_{pm} + T_{mtp}$
TRRGRP [25]	CLC	$2T_{pm}$	$3T_{pm}$
KLL [12]	CLC	$5T_{pm} + 2T_{mtp}$	$5T_{bp} + 2T_{pm} + 4T_{mtp}$
HAS-CLC	CLC	$3T_{pm}$	$3T_{bp} + 2T_{pm} + T_{mtp}$

Table 3. Theoretical computation overhead (Aggregate signature, $3n$ senders)

Schemes	Cryptosystem	Aggregate verify
WM [28]	PKI	$2T_{bp} + 3nT_{pm}$
SMLWM [23]	IBC	$(6n + 1)T_{bp} + 6nT_{mtp}$
YLWC [34]	IBC	$(3n + 1)T_{bp} + 3nT_{pm} + 3nT_{mtp}$
TRRGRP [25]	CLC	$(6n + 1)T_{pm}$
KLL [12]	CLC	$(3n + 4)T_{bp} + 6nT_{pm} + (9n + 1)T_{mtp}$
Ours	Heterogeneous	$4T_{bp} + 4nT_{pm} + 2nT_{mtp}$

SG-5 and SG-6 denote integrity, authentication, non-repudiation, identity privacy, identity traceability and resistance against attacks respectively. Obviously, [25,34] and our scheme satisfy all security goals while others cannot.

With the help of PBC library [18], we conducted comparative experiments on a computer with 3.60 GHz AMD Ryzen 5 3600 CPU, 16.0 GB memory and Windows 10 operating system. We used type-A curve in PBC library. It is an elliptic curve $y^2 = x^3 + x$ over $\mathbb{F}_q$ where $q \equiv 3 \bmod 4$. $\mathbb{Z}_p$ and $\mathbb{F}_q$ are set to 160 bits long and 512 bits long respectively. In the experiments, we take into account all operations including randomness generation, XOR, point addition, hash function, point multiplication, bilinear map and map-to-point function. Figure 1 shows the computation overhead of single signature. On the sender's side, HAS-PKI is nearly the same as [28]. HAS-IBC is 48.6% and 27.8% more efficient than [23] and [34] respectively. HAS-CLC is 66.2% more efficient than [12] but 27.8% less efficient than [25]. In Fig. 2, we set the number of senders to $3n$ (n senders in each cryptosystem in our scheme). It can be easily seen that our scheme is less efficient than [28] and [25] but more efficient than others.

Table 4. Communication cost

Schemes	Cryptosystem	Key size	Message length
WM [28]	PKI	$\mathbb{G}+\mathbb{Z}_p$	$3\mathbb{G}$
Ours	PKI	$\mathbb{G}+\mathbb{Z}_p$	$2\mathbb{G}+ID$
SMLWM [23]	IBC	$\mathbb{G}+ID$	$2\mathbb{G}+ID$
YLWC [34]	IBC	$\mathbb{G}+ID$	$2\mathbb{G}+ID$
Ours	IBC	$\mathbb{G}+ID$	$2\mathbb{G}+ID$
TRRGRP [25]	CLC	$3\mathbb{G}+2\mathbb{Z}_p$	$3\mathbb{G}+\mathbb{Z}_p+ID$
KLL [12]	CLC	$3\mathbb{G}+ID$	$4\mathbb{G}+2\mathbb{Z}_p+ID$
Ours	CLC	$2\mathbb{G}+\mathbb{Z}_p+ID$	$2\mathbb{G}+ID$

Table 5. Security

Schemes	SG-1	SG-2	SG-3	SG-4	SG-5	SG-6
WM [28]	✓	✓	✓	✗	✗	✓
SMLWM [23]	✓	✓	✓	✗	✗	✓
YLWC [34]	✓	✓	✓	✓	✓	✓
TRRGRP [25]	✓	✓	✓	✓	✓	✓
KLL [12]	✓	✓	✓	✗	✗	✓
Ours	✓	✓	✓	✓	✓	✓

Although our scheme is less efficient than [28] and [25,28] cannot provide identity privacy and traceability while the communication cost of [25] is much higher than ours. In addition, our scheme supports the authentication of UAVs from heterogeneous cryptosystems while others cannot. To sum up, our scheme is efficient and feasible for UAVs from heterogeneous cryptosystems.

6 Security Analysis

- Integrity: Owing to the collision resistance of H_2, if any m_i or σ_i has been altered, the aggregate signature cannot pass the verification.
- Authentication: Since each UAV uses its secret key to sign a message and the GS takes all UAVs' public keys as input to run HASV, authentication can be achieved if the aggregate signature passes the verification.
- Non-repudiation: Everyone can check whether a signature is sent from ID_i by applying ID_i's public key to the individual verify algorithm, since only ID_i has the corresponding secret key.
- Identity privacy: A pseudo identity ID_i is generated by the TRA, nobody can recover the real identity RID_i without knowing the TRA's secret key s.
- Identity traceability: The TRA can retrieve the real identity RID_i of any valid pseudo identity ID_i based on its database and secret key s.

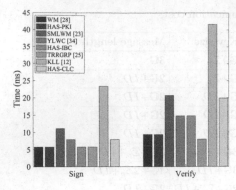
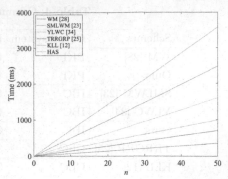

Fig. 1. Computation overhead (Single signature)

Fig. 2. Computation overhead (Aggregate signature)

- Resistance against attacks: Forgery attack can be prevented by authentication. Integrity guarantees that the message will not be tampered with. Because the input of H_2 contains a timestamp T_i, our scheme is secure against replay attack. Authentication and integrity together ensure that HAS-U2G can resist against man-in-the-middle attack.

7   Conclusion

In this paper, in view of the development of IoT and UAV technology, we have discussed the significance of batch authentication for UAVs. We proposed a heterogeneous aggregate signature scheme HAS from UAVs in different cryptosystems to a GS and proved its security. The experiments we carried out demonstrates that HAS is efficient and feasible for UAVs with limited resources. We consider to research on a more efficient heterogeneous aggregate signature scheme without pairing operation in future works.

References

1. Boneh, D., Gentry, C., Lynn, B., Shacham, H.: Aggregate and verifiably encrypted signatures from bilinear maps. In: Biham, E. (ed.) EUROCRYPT 2003. LNCS, vol. 2656, pp. 416–432. Springer, Heidelberg (2003). https://doi.org/10.1007/3-540-39200-9_26
2. Chen, J., Hao, Y., Huang, Z.: Secure certificate-based aggregate signature scheme. Comput. Eng. Appl. **49**, 60–64 (2013)
3. Cheng, L., Wen, Q., Jin, Z., Zhang, H., Zhou, L.: Cryptanalysis and improvement of a certificateless aggregate signature scheme. Inf. Sci. **295**, 337–346 (2015). https://doi.org/10.1016/j.ins.2014.09.065
4. Cui, J., Zhang, J., Zhong, H., Shi, R., Xu, Y.: An efficient certificateless aggregate signature without pairings for vehicular ad hoc networks. Inf. Sci. **451–452**, 1–15 (2018). https://doi.org/10.1016/j.ins.2018.03.060

5. He, D., Chan, S., Guizani, M.: Drone-assisted public safety networks: the security aspect. IEEE Commun. Mag. **55**(8), 218–223 (2017). https://doi.org/10.1109/MCOM.2017.1600799CM

6. Gentry, C., Ramzan, Z.: Identity-based aggregate signatures. In: Yung, M., Dodis, Y., Kiayias, A., Malkin, T. (eds.) PKC 2006. LNCS, vol. 3958, pp. 257–273. Springer, Heidelberg (2006). https://doi.org/10.1007/11745853_17

7. Gong, Z., Long, Y., Hong, X., Chen, K.: Two certificateless aggregate signatures from bilinear maps. In: Eighth ACIS International Conference on Software Engineering, Artificial Intelligence, Networking, and Parallel/Distributed Computing (SNPD 2007), vol. 3, pp. 188–193 (2007). https://doi.org/10.1109/SNPD.2007.132

8. He, D., Chan, S., Guizani, M.: Communication security of unmanned aerial vehicles. IEEE Wirel. Commun. **24**(4), 134–139 (2017). https://doi.org/10.1109/MWC.2016.1600073WC

9. He, S., Wu, Q., Liu, J., Hu, W., Qin, B., Li, Y.-N.: Secure communications in unmanned aerial vehicle network. In: Liu, J.K., Samarati, P. (eds.) ISPEC 2017. LNCS, vol. 10701, pp. 601–620. Springer, Cham (2017). https://doi.org/10.1007/978-3-319-72359-4_37

10. Javaid, A.Y., Sun, W., Devabhaktuni, V.K., Alam, M.: Cyber security threat analysis and modeling of an unmanned aerial vehicle system. In: 2012 IEEE Conference on Technologies for Homeland Security (HST), pp. 585–590 (2012). https://doi.org/10.1109/THS.2012.6459914

11. Jawhar, I., Mohamed, N., Al-Jaroodi, J., Agrawal, D.P., Zhang, S.: Communication and networking of UAV-based systems: classification and associated architectures. J. Netw. Comput. Appl. **84**, 93–108 (2017). https://doi.org/10.1016/j.jnca.2017.02.008

12. Kar, J., Liu, X., Li, F.: Cl-ass: an efficient and low-cost certificateless aggregate signature scheme for wireless sensor networks. J. Inf. Secur. Appl. **61**, 102905 (2021). https://doi.org/10.1016/j.jisa.2021.102905. https://www.sciencedirect.com/science/article/pii/S2214212621001319

13. Khan, M., et al.: Multiaccess edge computing empowered flying ad-hoc networks with secure deployment using identity-based generalized signcryption scheme. Mob. Inf. Syst. **2020** (2020). https://doi.org/10.1155/2020/8861947

14. Kim, A., Wampler, B., Goppert, J., Hwang, I., Aldridge, H.: Cyber attack vulnerabilities analysis for unmanned aerial vehicles. In: Infotech@Aerospace 2012 (2012). https://doi.org/10.2514/6.2012-2438

15. Kumar, P., Kumari, S., Sharma, V., Sangaiah, A.K., Wei, J., Li, X.: A certificateless aggregate signature scheme for healthcare wireless sensor network. Sustain. Comput. Inf. Syst. **18**, 80–89 (2018). https://doi.org/10.1016/j.suscom.2017.09.002

16. Li, B., Zhao, S., Miao, R., Zhang, R.: A survey on unmanned aerial vehicle relaying networks. IET Commun. **15**, 1262–1272 (2021). https://doi.org/10.1049/cmu2.12107

17. Lin, C., He, D., Kumar, N., Choo, K.K.R., Vinel, A., Huang, X.: Security and privacy for the internet of drones: challenges and solutions. IEEE Commun. Mag. **56**, 64–69 (2018). https://doi.org/10.1109/MCOM.2017.1700390

18. Lynn, B., et al.: Pairing-based cryptography library (2013). https://crypto.stanford.edu/pbc/

19. Ma, X., Shao, J., Zuo, C., Meng, R.: Efficient certificate-based signature and its aggregation. In: Liu, J.K., Samarati, P. (eds.) ISPEC 2017. LNCS, vol. 10701, pp. 391–408. Springer, Cham (2017). https://doi.org/10.1007/978-3-319-72359-4_23

20. Ogundoyin, S., Kamil, I.: An improved certificateless aggregate signature scheme without bilinear pairings for vehicular ad hoc networks. J. Inf. Secur. Appl. **44**, 184–200 (2018). https://doi.org/10.1016/j.jisa.2018.12.004

21. Ozmen, M.O., Yavuz, A.A.: Dronecrypt - an efficient cryptographic framework for small aerial drones. In: MILCOM 2018 - 2018 IEEE Military Communications Conference (MILCOM), pp. 1–6 (2018). https://doi.org/10.1109/MILCOM.2018. 8599784

22. Pointcheval, D., Stern, J.: Security arguments for digital signatures and blind signatures. J. Cryptol. **13** (2001). https://doi.org/10.1007/s001450010003

23. Shen, L., Ma, J., Liu, X., Wei, F., Miao, M.: A secure and efficient id-based aggregate signature scheme for wireless sensor networks. IEEE Internet Things J. **4**(2), 546–554 (2017). https://doi.org/10.1109/JIOT.2016.2557487

24. Shim, K.A.: An id-based aggregate signature scheme with constant pairing computations. J. Syst. Softw. **83**, 1873–1880 (2010). https://doi.org/10.1016/j.jss.2010. 05.071

25. Thumbur, G., Rao, G.S., Reddy, P.V., Gayathri, N.B., Reddy, D.V.R.K., Padmavathamma, M.: Efficient and secure certificateless aggregate signature-based authentication scheme for vehicular ad hoc networks. IEEE Internet Things J. **8**(3), 1908–1920 (2021). https://doi.org/10.1109/JIOT.2020.3019304

26. Verma, G.K., Singh, B.B., Kumar, N., Chamola, V.: CB-CAS: certificate-based efficient signature scheme with compact aggregation for industrial internet of things environment. IEEE Internet Things J. **7**(4), 2563–2572 (2020). https://doi.org/10. 1109/JIOT.2019.2944632

27. Wang, H., Wang, L., Zhang, K., Li, J., Luo, Y.: A conditional privacy-preserving certificateless aggregate signature scheme in the standard model for vanets. IEEE Access **10**, 15605–15618 (2022)

28. Wen, Y., Ma, J.: An aggregate signature scheme with constant pairing operations. In: 2008 International Conference on Computer Science and Software Engineering, vol. 3, pp. 830–833 (2008). https://doi.org/10.1109/CSSE.2008.941

29. Won, J., Seo, S., Bertino, E.: Certificateless cryptographic protocols for efficient drone-based smart city applications. IEEE Access **5**, 3721–3749 (2017). https:// doi.org/10.1109/ACCESS.2017.2684128

30. Won, J., Seo, S.H., Bertino, E.: A secure communication protocol for drones and smart objects. In: ASIACCS 2015 - Proceedings of the 10th ACM Symposium on Information, Computer and Communications Security, pp. 249–260 (2015). https://doi.org/10.1145/2714576.2714616

31. Wu, G., Zhang, F., Shen, L., Guo, F., Susilo, W.: Certificateless aggregate signature scheme secure against fully chosen-key attacks. Inf. Sci. **514**, 288–301 (2020). https://doi.org/10.1016/j.ins.2019.11.037

32. Xie, Y., Li, X., Zhang, S., Li, Y.: *iclas*?: an improved certificateless aggregate signature scheme for healthcare wireless sensor networks. IEEE Access **7**, 15170–15182 (2019). https://doi.org/10.1109/ACCESS.2019.2894895

33. Xiong, H., Guan, Z., Chen, Z., Li, F.: An efficient certificateless aggregate signature with constant pairing computations. Inf. Sci. **219**, 225–235 (2013). https://doi.org/ 10.1016/j.ins.2012.07.004

34. Yang, X., Liu, R., Wang, M., Chen, G.: Identity-based aggregate signature scheme in vehicle ad-hoc network. In: 2019 4th International Conference on Mechanical, Control and Computer Engineering (ICMCCE), pp. 1046–10463 (2019). https:// doi.org/10.1109/ICMCCE48743.2019.00233

Secure Arbitrated Quantum Signature Scheme with Bell State

Tianyuan Zhang , Chaoyang Li , and Xiangjun Xin

College of Software Engineering, Zhengzhou University of Light Industry,
Zhengzhou 450002, China
xin_xiang_jun@126.com

Abstract. Recent researches on quantum signatures has no formal proof. Based on the Bell state and key-controlled hash function, an arbitrated quantum signature (AQS) scheme with formal proof is presented. In this scheme, the signer gets the quantum signature by encoding/encrypting Bell states, the encoded/encrypted states are swapped according to the protocol. The signature verification is performed by a trusted arbitrator. Arbitrator decoding/decrypting the swapped quantum states and comparing the decrypted message with the output of the key-controlled hash function to verify the validity of the signature. The security proof of the scheme reduces to the fundamental assumption of quantum mechanics: The indistinguishability of any two unknown quantum states. And its unforgeability can be formally proved with a security model under a chosen-message attack. Therefore, its security can be supported by a formal proof.

Keywords: arbitrated quantum signature · security model · chosen-message attack · unforgeability · formal security proof

1 Introduction

Quantum cryptography and its related fields have received significant attention since the advent of quantum mechanics in the early 20th century. The greatest discovery of Quantum cryptography was the quantum key distribution protocol [1](QKDP), that makes key becomes more secure. Much of the early work in quantum cryptography focused on this concept's "Fundamental Structure", but later developments saw the "Practical Use" such as quantum signature schemes.

The concept of quantum signature was first proposed in 2001 by Gottesman and Chuang [5], which was a milestone in the development of quantum cryptography. This article proposes for the first time using quantum states as a medium for signature, and the security of the quantum signature scheme is endorsed by the properties of quantum mechanics. Since then, researchers have made significant progress in this area, with various quantum signature schemes [8,9,12–17] proposed over the years.

A more practical quantum signature scheme is the so-called arbitrated quantum signature (AQS) scheme. AQS scheme was first proposed in 2002 by Zeng

© The Author(s), under exclusive license to Springer Nature Singapore Pte Ltd. 2024
H. Yang and R. Lu (Eds.): FCS 2023, CCIS 1992, pp. 283–294, 2024.
https://doi.org/10.1007/978-981-99-9331-4_19

et al. [14]. The goal of AQS is to provide a secure way for two parties, known as the signer and the receiver, to sign messages in the presence of a trusted third party, known as the arbitrator.

An area of active research has been on the security of the AQS scheme. While most AQS scheme is designed to be resistant to certain types of attacks, such as eavesdropping attacks [6] and intercept-resend attack [4], there are still potential vulnerabilities that could be exploited by adversaries.

Such as, Xia et al. presented semi-quantum blind signature [11] are proved insecure [2], because the signer and receiver can obtain the secret key through collusion. Specifically, such security vulnerabilities have commonalities: These AQS schemes have no security model. Our AQS scheme is to fill this gap with formal secure proof.

Improvements to our AQS scheme include:

1. Entangled Bell states as the information transmission medium.
2. Proved the existential unforgeability against chosen-message attacks (EU-ACMA) with a formal security model.
3. Random oracle model is involved in security proof.
4. Efficiency of our protocol is calculated and compared with existing Bell state protocol.

2 Preliminaries

For a clearer understanding of our scheme, some notations that appear in our scheme are presented below:

2.1 Classical Bits and Operations

1. Let $x = (x_1, x_2, \cdots, x_y)$ stand for a y-length sequence x, quantum or classical, is composed of $x_1, x_2, \cdots, x_y$ in order.
2. Let "$||$" stand for the classical-bits concatenate.
3. Let "$\oplus$" stand for the bitwise XOR.
4. Let key-controlled hash function $f_k : \{0,1\}^* \longmapsto \{0,1\}^{2n}$ as Eq. (1) follow:

$$f_k(m) = hash(k||m||k), \forall m \in \{0,1\}^* \tag{1}$$

where $hash()$ is a classical hash function have a uniform outputs $2n$-bits length.

2.2 Quantum States and Operations

Let 4 Pauli operators

$$\sigma_{00} \equiv I \equiv \begin{pmatrix} 1 & 0 \\ 0 & 1 \end{pmatrix}, \tag{2}$$

$$\sigma_{01} \equiv X \equiv \begin{pmatrix} 0 & 1 \\ 1 & 0 \end{pmatrix}, \tag{3}$$

$$\sigma_{10} \equiv iY \equiv \begin{pmatrix} 0 & -1 \\ 1 & 0 \end{pmatrix}, \tag{4}$$

$$\sigma_{11} \equiv Z \equiv \begin{pmatrix} 1 & 0 \\ 0 & -1 \end{pmatrix}. \tag{5}$$

Let 4 Bell states

$$|\Phi^+\rangle \equiv \frac{|00\rangle + |11\rangle}{\sqrt{2}}, \tag{6}$$

$$|\Psi^+\rangle \equiv \frac{|01\rangle + |10\rangle}{\sqrt{2}}, \tag{7}$$

$$|\Phi^-\rangle \equiv \frac{|00\rangle - |11\rangle}{\sqrt{2}}, \tag{8}$$

$$|\Psi^-\rangle \equiv \frac{|01\rangle - |10\rangle}{\sqrt{2}}. \tag{9}$$

Let quantum one-time pad encryption function $E_k : \{0,1\}^{2n} \longmapsto \{|0\rangle, |1\rangle\}^{2n}$ and decryption function $D_k : \{|0\rangle, |1\rangle\}^{2n} \longmapsto \{0,1\}^{2n}$ can be found in Eq. (10) and Eq. (11), where k is a secret key with length $2n; x, y$ denotes plain-text and cipher-text, respectively:

$$E_k(x) = \bigotimes_{i=1}^{2n} E_k(x)_i = \bigotimes_{i=1}^{2n} |k_i \oplus x_i\rangle \tag{10}$$

$$D_k \left(\bigotimes_{i=1}^{2n} |y_i\rangle \right) = (y_1 \oplus k_1)||(y_2 \oplus k_2)|| \cdots (y_{2n} \oplus k_{2n}) \tag{11}$$

2.3 Encoding and Decoding Process with Bell State

The perform-measure process, specifically performing the Pauli operator on Bell state first particle and measuring it, can be regarded as encoding/decoding for 2-classical-bits. Taking a Bell state $|\Psi^-\rangle$ as an example, see in Eq. (12).

$$(\sigma_{00} \otimes I) |\Psi^-\rangle = |\Psi^-\rangle$$
$$(\sigma_{01} \otimes I) |\Psi^-\rangle = |\Phi^-\rangle$$
$$(\sigma_{10} \otimes I) |\Psi^-\rangle = |\Phi^+\rangle \tag{12}$$
$$(\sigma_{11} \otimes I) |\Psi^-\rangle = |\Psi^+\rangle$$

Following the above example, we denote an encoding procedure for 2-bits information on $|\Psi^-\rangle$ as $\sigma_{|\Psi^-\rangle} : \{00, 01, 10, 11\} \longmapsto \{|\Psi^-\rangle, |\Phi^-\rangle, |\Phi^+\rangle, |\Psi^+\rangle\}$.

The decoding procedure on Bell state can be considered as a measuring procedure. The measurement results through inverse mapping can be obtained from the 2-bits information. The Encoding/Decoding procedure are shown in Table 1.

Table 1. Encoding & Decoding for $|\Psi^-\rangle$ to Bell states Table.

Classical message to be encoded	Quantum message to be decoded
00	$|\Psi^-\rangle$
01	$|\Phi^-\rangle$
10	$|\Phi^+\rangle$
11	$|\Psi^+\rangle$

2.4   Detectable Eavesdropping Communication

The detectable eavesdropping quantum communication process in this paper is defined as the following two steps:

DEC1: Before the message sender Tom sends the quantum states sequence, which in basic $\{|0\rangle, |1\rangle\}$ for communication, he prepares decoy particles which randomly distributed within $\{|-\rangle, |+\rangle\}$ first. Then Tom randomly inserts them into the quantum sequence. Finally, Tom sends the sequence to receiver Kate. Note that Tom records the positions and states of every decoy particle inserted.

DEC2: After receiver Kate announces that she has completed receiving the sequence, Tom publishes the position and state of all decoy particles. Then, Kate measures all the decoy particles using $\{|+\rangle, |-\rangle\}$ basis. If the error rate exceeds the predetermined threshold, we can assert that eavesdropping occurred during communication.

3   Our AQS Scheme

There are three partners participated in our AQS scheme: Alice demands to generate a signature $|S\rangle$ on message m and sends it to signature receiver Bob; Bob demands verification if $|S\rangle$ is or not the signature of m by queries arbitrator Trent; Trent as a trusted arbitrator demands to assist Bob to verify $|S\rangle$.

These partners generate and verify a valid signature by executing the AQS protocol. The protocol consists of three procedures: The initialization procedure, the signing procedure, and the verification procedure.

These three procedures are shown below:

3.1 Initialization Procedure

Init-1. These three partners prepare $n |\Psi^-\rangle$. To distinguish the internal order of entangled Bell state particles, Alice's denotes as $|\Psi^-\rangle_{AB}^n$, Bob's denotes as $|\Psi^-\rangle_{CD}^n$ and Trent's denotes as $|\Psi^-\rangle_{EF}^n$. Note that every subscript A,B,C,D,E or F can be regarded as a n-length particle sequence. In the following text, we use $|AB\rangle^n$ to represented quantum sequence $|A\rangle^n$ and $|B\rangle^n$, even if states of $|AB\rangle^n$ are transformed by unitary operators or are sent. So do with $|C\rangle^n$, $|D\rangle^n$, $|E\rangle^n$ and $|F\rangle^n$.

Init-2. Alice shares secret key $skA = (skA_1, skA_2, \cdots, skA_{2n})$ with Trent by the secure quantum key distribution protocol (QKDP) [1]. Bob shares secret key $skB = (skB_1, skB_2, \cdots, skB_{2n})$ with Trent following the same protocol [1].

Init-3. Alice yields $f_{skA}(m)$ of the message to be signed m by calcuates the key-controlled hash function f_{skA} with her key skA. Then she divide $f_{skA}(m)$ into 2-bits pair sequence and gets $n2$-bits sequence Seq.

$$
\begin{aligned}
f_{skA}(m) &= (f_{skA}(m)_1, f_{skA}(m)_2, \cdots, f_{skA}(m)_{2n}) \\
&= hash(skA\|m\|skA)
\end{aligned}
\tag{13}
$$

$$
\begin{aligned}
Seq &= (Seq_1, Seq_2, \cdots, Seq_n) \\
&= ((f_{skA}(m)_1, f_{skA}(m)_2)_1, (f_{skA}(m)_3, f_{skA}(m)_4)_2, \cdots, \\
&\quad (f_{skA}(m)_{2n-1}, f_{skA}(m)_{2n})_n)
\end{aligned}
\tag{14}
$$

3.2 Signing Procedure

Sign-1. Alice uses $\sigma_{|\Psi^-\rangle}$ encodes all 2-bits of Seq and gets $|AB\rangle^n$.

$$
\begin{aligned}
|AB\rangle^n &= (|AB\rangle_1, |AB\rangle_2, \cdots, |AB\rangle_n) \\
|AB\rangle_i &= \sigma_{|AB\rangle_i}(Seq_i)
\end{aligned}
\tag{15}
$$

Sign-2. The three partners swap their quantum sequences like Fig. 1 shown below. Note that the swapping process is got involved with detectable eavesdropping communication, see Sect. 2.4. If eavesdroppings are detected, the protocol should be terminated.

After swapping, Alice holds $|AF\rangle^n$, Bob holds $|CB\rangle^n$ and Trent holds $|ED\rangle^n$.

Sign-3. After swapping process, Alice Bob and Trent holding different quantum sequences like Fig. 2 shown below. Then Alice measures $|AF\rangle^n$ with Bell basis, and she gets AF^n by decodes measuring results according to Table 1, after that she encrypts AF^n uses quantum one-time pad encryption see Eq. (10) and sends

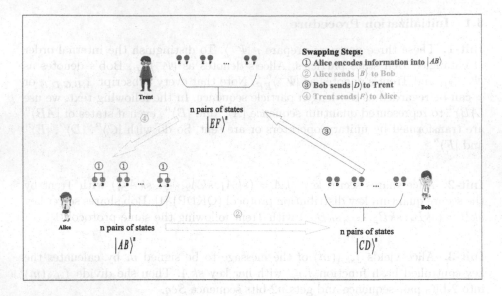

Fig. 1. Swapping process between three partners

encrypted results $E_{skA}(AF^n)$ as the signature of message m to Trent, finally she sends m to Bob and Trent, too. Note that the communication of encrypted results is got involved with detectable eavesdropping communication, see Sect. 2.4. If eavesdroppings are detected, the protocol should be terminated.

3.3   Verification Procedure

Verify-1. Bob measures $|CB\rangle^n$ with Bell basis, then he gets CB^n by decodes measuring results according to Table 1, after that he encrypts CB^n uses quantum one-time pad encryption see Eq. (10) and sends encrypted results $E_{skB}(CB^n)$ to Trent. Note that the sending process is also got involved with detectable eavesdropping communication, see Sect. 2.4. If eavesdroppings are detected, the protocol should be terminated.

Verify-2. Trent measures $|ED\rangle^n$, after that he does the decryption following Eq. (10), then he gets $CB^{n'}$ and $AF^{n'}$. Through Table 1, Trent can get the quantum sequences of $|CB\rangle^{n'}$ and $|AF\rangle^{n'}$, so that Trent is able to estimate $|ED\rangle^{n'}$ by the two quantum sequences.

Verify-3. Trent calculates $f_{skA}(m)'$ see Eq. (13) and gets Seq' see Eq. (14), then he can verify previous estimate about $\left|ED'\right\rangle^{n'}$ by checks Table 2. The checking sub-procedure is:

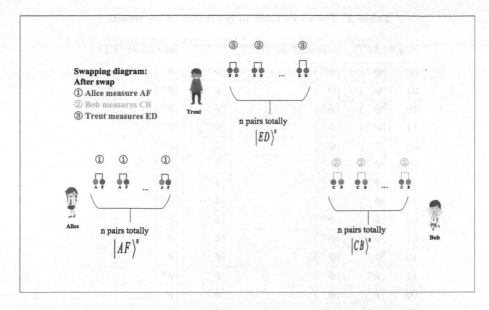

Fig. 2. After Swapping quantum sequence holding situation between three partners

1. Trent takes one of Seq' and one of corresponding $|AF\rangle^n$ to checks table and gets intermediate $|BE\rangle^n$.
2. Trent takes $|BE\rangle^n$ and corresponding $|CB\rangle^n$ to checks table and gets an $\left|ED'\right\rangle^n$ as an estimated value.
3. Trent compares the estimated value and the measured value of each $|ED\rangle_i^n$.
4. Unless all compares are passed, the check is not passed.

If the check is passed, the signature is considered valid; if not, the signature is considered invalid.

4 Security Analysis

Our AQS scheme's security analysis will be carried out in three aspects: The security of the secret keys, the unforgeability of the security model under a chosen-message attack and The intercept-measure-resend resistance of our AQS.

4.1 The Security of the Secret Keys

As our scheme executes, Trent shares secret keys skA, skB with Alice and Bob, respectively. Because of the sharing protocol [1] is unconditionally secure, which is proved by [10].

It's not difficult to see that our quantum one-time pad encryption function Eq. (10) can break through unless an adversary makes exponential attempts.

Table 2. The check table to get intermediate results

Seq'_i	$|AF\rangle^{n'}_i$	intermediate $|BE\rangle^n_i$	$|CB\rangle^{n'}_i$	estimated $|ED'\rangle^n_i$
00	$|\Psi^-\rangle$	$|\Psi^-\rangle$	$|\Psi^-\rangle$	$|\Psi^-\rangle$
01	$|\Psi^-\rangle$	$|\Phi^-\rangle$	$|\Psi^-\rangle$	$|\Phi^-\rangle$
10	$|\Psi^-\rangle$	$|\Phi^+\rangle$	$|\Psi^-\rangle$	$|\Phi^+\rangle$
11	$|\Psi^-\rangle$	$|\Psi^+\rangle$	$|\Psi^-\rangle$	$|\Psi^+\rangle$
00	$|\Phi^-\rangle$	$|\Phi^-\rangle$	$|\Phi^-\rangle$	$|\Psi^-\rangle$
01	$|\Phi^-\rangle$	$|\Psi^-\rangle$	$|\Phi^-\rangle$	$|\Phi^-\rangle$
10	$|\Phi^-\rangle$	$|\Psi^+\rangle$	$|\Phi^-\rangle$	$|\Phi^+\rangle$
11	$|\Phi^-\rangle$	$|\Phi^+\rangle$	$|\Phi^-\rangle$	$|\Psi^+\rangle$
00	$|\Phi^+\rangle$	$|\Phi^+\rangle$	$|\Phi^+\rangle$	$|\Psi^-\rangle$
01	$|\Phi^+\rangle$	$|\Psi^+\rangle$	$|\Phi^+\rangle$	$|\Phi^-\rangle$
10	$|\Phi^+\rangle$	$|\Psi^-\rangle$	$|\Phi^+\rangle$	$|\Phi^+\rangle$
11	$|\Phi^+\rangle$	$|\Phi^-\rangle$	$|\Phi^+\rangle$	$|\Psi^+\rangle$
00	$|\Psi^+\rangle$	$|\Psi^+\rangle$	$|\Psi^+\rangle$	$|\Psi^-\rangle$
01	$|\Psi^+\rangle$	$|\Phi^+\rangle$	$|\Psi^+\rangle$	$|\Phi^-\rangle$
10	$|\Psi^+\rangle$	$|\Phi^-\rangle$	$|\Psi^+\rangle$	$|\Phi^+\rangle$
11	$|\Psi^+\rangle$	$|\Psi^-\rangle$	$|\Psi^+\rangle$	$|\Psi^+\rangle$

Thus, the secret keys skA, skB can not be cracked in the initialization procedure and encrypted communication process.

During the signing procedure, three partners swap the quantum sequences. Sequence $|B\rangle^n$ contains the information about key-controlled hash value. The next theorem-proof is in order to prove the adversary cannot get any information from quantum sequence $|B\rangle^n$.

Theorem 1. *For any positive polynomial $q(.)$ and two different quantum sequences $|P\rangle$ and $|Q\rangle$, if their trace distance $D(\rho_P, \rho_Q) < \frac{1}{q(.)}$, the quantum sequences cannot be distinguish. [7, 12]*

Theorem 2. *Each state of the quantum sequence $|B\rangle^n$ has the same reduced density operator.*

Proof. During the initialization procedure, Alice computes the key-controlled hash $f_{skA}(m)$, which has a uniform output.

By Eq. (15) and Eq. (12), the density operator of $|AB\rangle^n$ is computed as below:

$$\rho_{|AB\rangle_i^n} = \frac{1}{4} \sum_{x_i, y_i \in \{0,1\}} \left(\sigma_{x_i y_i} \bigotimes I\right) |AB\rangle_i^n \langle AB|_i^n \left(\sigma_{x_i y_i} \bigotimes I\right)^\dagger$$

$$= \frac{1}{4} \left(\left(\sigma_{00} \bigotimes I\right) |AB\rangle_i^n \langle AB|_i^n \left(\sigma_{00} \bigotimes I\right)^\dagger \right.$$

$$+ \left(\sigma_{01} \bigotimes I\right) |AB\rangle_i^n \langle AB|_i^n \left(\sigma_{01} \bigotimes I\right)^\dagger$$

(16)

$$+ \left(\sigma_{10} \bigotimes I\right) |AB\rangle_i^n \langle AB|_i^n \left(\sigma_{10} \bigotimes I\right)^\dagger$$

$$\left. + \left(\sigma_{11} \bigotimes I\right) |AB\rangle_i^n \langle AB|_i^n \left(\sigma_{11} \bigotimes I\right)^\dagger \right)$$

$$= \frac{I}{4}$$

Thus, the reduced density operator of $|B\rangle^n$ can be calcuated by calcuates partial trace $tr_B(\rho_{|AB\rangle_i^n})$

$$\rho_{|AB\rangle_i^n}^2 = tr_B(\rho_{|AB\rangle_i^n})$$

$$= tr_B(\frac{I}{4})$$

(17)

$$= \frac{I}{2}$$

□

Above all, no adversary is able to extract information about secret keys skA, skB from the communication.

4.2 Unforgeability of Our AQS Scheme

In the following subsection, the existential unforgeability against chosen-message attacks (EU-ACMA) is proved.

Formal Security Model. A formally proven security model is introduced first. This model is a simulation of the above scheme, but the signatory has been replaced with a challenger, and the receiver has been replaced with an adversary. A game is also introduced to express the probability adversary could forge successfully. For a clearer understanding of the simulating procedures of the game are shown below:

Initialization: Challenger Alice, adversary Bob shares secret key K_A, K_B with trusted arbitrator Trent, respectively. Three partners prepares $|\Psi^-\rangle^n$, respectively.

Signature Query: Bob adaptively prepares polynomial $p = O(poly(*))$ messages $m_1, m_2, \cdots, m_n$ and asks Alice to generate n messages' signature. To replies the signature, Alice asks for Random Oracle RO. RO tosses a coin and makes a different move; note that the coin facing down with practicability $p = \frac{1}{n}$ RO always records his move whether the coin is facing up or down:

1. if coin faces up, RO retrieves records if Alice asked this message before, for the message has not queried before: RO responses $p \, |\Psi^-\rangle$ states as sequence $|AB\rangle^p$.
2. if coin faces down, RO prepares p random states as sequence $|AB\rangle^p$.

Alice does the normal protocol as usual (including encoding sequences $|AB\rangle^p$, swapping sequences, measuring sequences $|AF\rangle^p$, etc.).

Forgery: After Bob asks p messages, assume Bob has the ability to forge successfully with probability ε. And he does forge successfully. Thus he generates a valid signature. When it comes to verifying procedure, the forging signature verifies by RO and the coin facing down. Then the game terminates.

Review this game, the forger Bob forges successfully. That means Bob distinguishes the unknown quantum states (caused by the coin facing down) with probability $Pr = \varepsilon \cdot (1 - \frac{1}{p})^p \cdot \frac{1}{p}$. Obviously, $Pr \geq \frac{\varepsilon}{e \times p}$ is a Non-neglected probability. That violates the principles of quantum mechanics.

4.3   The Intercept-measure-resend Resistance of Our AQS

An quantum adversary, we generally call him/her Eve, who conducts intercept-measure-resend attack is describing as follows. Eve intercepts and measures qubits sending on the channel, on the basis of measuring results Eve sends elaborately selected qubits to original recipient. According to the analysis of the above subsections, no adversary is able to extract information about secret keys from the communication process. That is to say, Eve can intercepts and measures the qubits, but it is in vain. In a word, our AQS scheme have a totally resistance under intercept-measure-resend attack.

5   Conclusion

The previous research has barely contained the security model of AQS schemes. These securities are also not formally proven. This means no sufficient proof can support their security against EU-ACMA.

Incidentally, we have expounded the qubit-efficiency of our AQS scheme here.

We consider the number of qubits transmitted for pure-signature as the numerator and the total qubits number transmitted on the channel(excluding the qubits for eavesdropping detection) as the denominator, then the qubit-efficiency η can be express by Eq. (18)

$$\eta = \frac{len(signature)}{len(signature) + len(non - signature)} \tag{18}$$

The efficiency compared with other AQS schemes is shown as Table 3.

Table 3. Efficiency comparing with other AQS

Schemes	Have security model	Provably secure	Need entanglement particles	Qubit-efficiency
[3]	No	No	Yes	33%
[4]	No	Yes	Yes	25%
ours	Yes	Yes	Yes	18.2%

According to the Table 3, our AQS scheme have the secure model under chosen messages attack, while the others have no secure model. Another point where we are ahead of our peers is provably secure of our AQS.

In a word, our scheme expenses a limited efficiency in exchange for better quantum-based security.

Acknowledgements. This work was supported by the National Natural Science Foundation of China under Grant 62272090, the Key Scientific Research Project of Colleges and Universities in Henan Province (CN) (No. 22A413010), the Doctor Scientific Research Fund of Zhengzhou University of Light Industry (No. 2021BSJJ033), the Foundation of State Key Laboratory of Public Big Data (No. PBD2023-25).

References

1. Bennett, C.H., Brassard, G.: Quantum cryptography: public key distribution and coin tossing. arXiv preprint arXiv:2003.06557 (2020)
2. Cao, J., Xin, X., Li, C., Li, F.: Security analysis and improvement of a blind semi-quantum signature. Int. J. Theor. Phys. **62**(4), 87 (2023)
3. Ding, L., Xin, X., Yang, Q., Sang, Y.: Security analysis and improvements of XOR arbitrated quantum signature-based GHZ state. Mod. Phys. Lett. A **37**(02), 2250008 (2022)
4. Gao, F., Qin, S.J., Guo, F.Z., Wen, Q.Y.: Cryptanalysis of the arbitrated quantum signature protocols. Phys. Rev. A **84**(2), 022344 (2011)
5. Gottesman, D., Chuang, I.: Quantum digital signatures. arXiv preprint arXiv:quant-ph/0105032 (2001)
6. Guo, W., Zhang, J.Z., Li, Y.P., An, W.: Multi-proxy strong blind quantum signature scheme. Int. J. Theor. Phys. **55**, 3524–3536 (2016)
7. Li, Y., Chong, X., Bao, L.: Quantum probabilistic encryption scheme based on conjugate coding. China Commun. **10**(2), 19–26 (2013)
8. Liang, X.Q., Wu, Y.L., Zhang, Y.H., Wang, S.S., Xu, G.B.: Quantum multi-proxy blind signature scheme based on four-qubit cluster states. Int. J. Theor. Phys. **58**, 31–39 (2019)
9. MeiLing, Z., YuanHua, L., Min, N., QingJi, Z., Dong, Z.: Arbitrated quantum signature of quantum messages with a semi-honest arbitrator. Int. J. Theor. Phys. **57**(5), 1310–1318 (2018)
10. Shor, P.W., Preskill, J.: Simple proof of security of the bb84 quantum key distribution protocol. Phys. Rev. Lett. **85**(2), 441 (2000)

11. Xia, C., Li, H., Hu, J.: A semi-quantum blind signature protocol based on five-particle GHZ state. Eur. Phys. J. Plus **136**(6), 633 (2021)
12. Xin, X., Ding, L., Zhang, T., Yang, Q., Li, C.: Provably secure arbitrated-quantum signature. Quant. Inf. Process. **21**(12), 390 (2022)
13. Xin, X., He, Q., Wang, Z., Yang, Q., Li, F.: Security analysis and improvement of an arbitrated quantum signature scheme. Optik **189**, 23–31 (2019)
14. Zeng, G., Keitel, C.H.: Arbitrated quantum-signature scheme. Phys. Rev. A **65**(4), 042312 (2002)
15. Zhang, K.J., Zhang, W.W., Li, D.: Improving the security of arbitrated quantum signature against the forgery attack. Quant. Inf. Process. **12**(8), 2655–2669 (2013)
16. Zhang, L., Sun, H.W., Zhang, K.J., Jia, H.Y.: An improved arbitrated quantum signature protocol based on the key-controlled chained CNOT encryption. Quant. Inf. Process. **16**(3), 1–15 (2017)
17. Zou, X., Qiu, D., Mateus, P.: Security analyses and improvement of arbitrated quantum signature with an untrusted arbitrator. Int. J. Theor. Phys. **52**(9), 3295–3305 (2013)

AFHPS: An Authorized Function Homomorphic Proxy Signature Scheme with Sampling Batch Verification

Lin Li, Xiaofen Wang[⊠], and Ting Chen

University of Electronic Science and Technology of China, Chengdu 610000, China
202221080624@std.uestc.edu.cn, {xfwang,brokendragon}@uestc.edu.cn

Abstract. Homomorphic signature allows any entity to generate a valid signature of new data without a secret key on behalf of the data owner (DO) by performing homomorphic operations on authenticated data. However, general homomorphic signature schemes have two problems: (i) the original signatures are generated by the DO, which may be computationally expensive; and (ii) the linear function f is randomly selected by the aggregator and cannot be specified by the DO, which limits the application scenarios of homomorphic signature. To address the problems above, in this paper we propose an authorized function homomorphic proxy signature scheme with sampling batch verification (AFHPS). Our scheme combines the advantages of homomorphic signature, proxy signature and functional signature, which enables DO to delegate the ability of signature of the original messages and the specified linear function f to the proxy signer and control its behavior. A concrete construction of our scheme is given in this paper, and we prove that it is secure under the co-CDH assumption. In addition, we show how to apply our scheme to realize authentication in blockchain.

Keywords: homomorphic signature · proxy signature · functional signature · sampling batch verification

1 Introduction

Since the concept of homomorphic signature was proposed by Rivest [1] in 2000, homomorphic signature has attracted more and more attention. Homomorphic signature means that any entity is allowed to perform homomorphic operations on the authenticated data to generate a new data and obtain a valid signature of the new data without a secret key. With this particularity, homomorphic signature has a wide range of theoretical research space and high application value. In 2009, Boneh et al. [2] proposed a linear homomorphic signature scheme applied to network coding to solve the problem of pollution attacks. Since then, homomorphic signature has developed from single-key schemes to multi-key schemes, from certificate-based schemes to certificateless schemes, from network coding to electronic medical field, and the homomorphic signature theory space has been

© The Author(s), under exclusive license to Springer Nature Singapore Pte Ltd. 2024
H. Yang and R. Lu (Eds.): FCS 2023, CCIS 1992, pp. 295–308, 2024.
https://doi.org/10.1007/978-981-99-9331-4_20

unprecedentedly developed [3–10]. However, for an entity with relatively poor computing power, the work of generating signatures for multiple messages is very time-consuming, and all the above schemes have this problem.

For the signer with weak computing power, the signature right can be delegated to a third party with strong computing power, which is also known as proxy signature [11]. In recent years, many proxy signature schemes have been proposed [12–15], which can effectively transfer signature right and are suitable for a variety of application scenarios. However, most proxy signature schemes assume that the proxy signer is honest, which is too strong because the proxy signer is not completely trusted in some application scenarios. At the same time, for the proxy signature of a single message, it is easy for the verifier to verify whether the proxy signer has signed honestly, but it is very inefficient to verify the proxy signature of multiple messages one by one. In addition, it is worth nothing that the current proxy signature schemes do not have homomorphic property.

The concept of functional signature was first proposed by Boyle in 2013 and a general architecture of functional signature [16] is given. This technology means that the Data Owner (DO) generates the specified function f, functional signature key sk_f, signature key sk and message m, and gives them to a third party. The third party carries out the calculation and generates the operation result $m^* = f(m)$ and the signature of the message m. The verifier can verify the calculation result and behavior of the third party according to the above information. Accordingly, many scholars have proposed a variety of functional signature schemes [17–19], but these schemes have a common problem, that is, the verifier will calculate $f(m)$ again when verifying the result. If the verifier is an entity with low computing power, it will cause the calculation of $f(m)$ to be very time-consuming and lose the meaning of the functional signature.

Our Contributions. In this paper, we synthesize the above problems and construct an authorized function homomorphic proxy signature scheme with sampling batch verification. Specifically, our contributions are summarized as follows:

- Our scheme has the advantages of both homomorphic signature and proxy signature. Our scheme combines homomorphic signature with KPW proxy signature scheme [20]. This method can not only reduce the local computing overhead of entities, but also make the proxy signature have the property of homomorphism.
- The signature verification phase of our scheme includes the verification of computing behavior of proxy signer. In the above functional signature schemes, the verifier needs to calculate $m^* = f(m)$ again, where m^* is the calculation result sent by the proxy signer, and $f(m)$ is calculated locally by the verifier. When the function f has many parameters, additional computational overhead will be introduced. On the contrary, our scheme takes the function f as the input of signature verification and achieves the purpose of verifying homomorphic signature and proxy signer's computing behavior through a verification equation.

- Our scheme does not need to dictate that proxy signer must be completely honest. After the DO entrusts the messages and authorization information to the proxy signer, the proxy signer may not honestly sign the message content specified by the DO due to computing costs or other reasons. Our scheme adopts sampling verification to verify the computing behavior. The idea is a compromise between simple aggregate authentication of proxy signature and batch verification, which can effectively solve the problem of tampered data passing verification in simple aggregation authentication and low efficiency of batch verification.

Organization. The organization of the rest of this paper is as follows. We review the existing homomorphic signature, proxy signature and functional signature schemes in Related Works. We introduce the knowledge needed in Preliminaries. The system model and security model are presented in System Model And Security Model and the construction and security proof of algorithm are proposed in Construction. Then, in Applications Discussion, we discuss its application in blockchain and UAVs. Finally, we conclude this paper in Conclusion.

2   Related Works

2.1   Homomorphic Signature

Homomorphic signature means that any entity is allowed to perform homomorphic operations on the authenticated messages to generate a new data and obtain a valid signature of the new data without a secret key. Specifically, DO has a string of messages $m = (m_1, m_2, \ldots, m_n)$ and generates the original signatures $\sigma = (\sigma_1, \sigma_2, \ldots, \sigma_n)$. An aggregator can use m and σ to generate aggregated message $m = \sum_{i=1}^{n} f_i m_i$ and homomorphic signature $\sigma = \prod_{i=1}^{n} \sigma_i^{f_i}$, where f_i is an integer. Boneh et al. [2] proposed a linear homomorphic signature scheme applied to network coding in 2009. The intermediate routing node in the scheme, that is, an aggregator, can linearly random code several packet vectors $(v_1, v_2, \ldots, v_n)$ received to generate an aggregated vector $v = \sum_{i=1}^{n} f_i v_i$, and the signatures $(\sigma_1, \sigma_2, \ldots, \sigma_n)$ of the above vectors are correspondingly linear aggregated to generate a homomorphic signature $\sigma = \prod_{i=1}^{n} \sigma_i^{f_i}$, and then the σ and v are forwarded, where f_i is an integer randomly selected by intermediate routing node. This scheme can resist the pollution attacks in network coding and improve the network throughput and robustness. However, the linear aggregation function $f = (f_1, f_2, \ldots, f_n)$ in this scheme is randomly selected and is not specified by DO, which makes the scheme limited in similar cloud computing scenarios. Guo et al. [3] proposed an authorized function homomorphic signature scheme, in which the linear function f is specified by DO instead of randomly selected, so the homomorphic signature scheme can be applied to the field of outsourced computation and solve the problem existing in Boneh's scheme. Recently, some scholars have proposed multi-key homomorphic signature scheme [5] and certificateless homomorphic signature scheme [6], which greatly enrich the theory of homomorphic signature. However, for entities with weak computing power, the work of generating the original message signatures in the above schemes will be very time-consuming.

2.2 Proxy Signature

Another related notion is proxy signature, in which DO can designate a proxy signer to generate valid signatures on behalf of DO. This concept was first proposed by Mambo et al. [11], and many proxy signature schemes suitable for different scenarios have emerged successively, such as proxy signature scheme with authorized certificate [20], threshold proxy signature scheme [21], multi-proxy signature scheme [22] and so on. For compactness, the authors of [12] combined the advantages of aggregate signature and proxy signature, and first proposed the concept and scheme of aggregate proxy signature, but the scheme does not have homomorphic property. Recently, Xu et al. [23] proposed an efficient certificateless designated verifier proxy signature scheme and applied it to Smart City. However, to the best of our knowledge, most proxy signature schemes have no homomorphism. In our scheme, we combine the homomorphic signature with the proxy signature and propose a homomorphic proxy signature scheme, which extends the application scenarios of homomorphic signature and proxy signature.

2.3 Functional Signature

Boyle et al. [16] proposed the concept of functional signature for the first time, in which DO hands out a specified function f and message m to allow a specified proxy to calculate $f(m)$ and verifier could verify the computing behavior of the proxy. The authors of [17] proposed a decentralized functional signature scheme, in which there are multiple authorities and each one is able to certify a specific function. Liu et al. [18] proposed a distributed functional signature scheme, which adopts the idea of secret sharing and divides the signing key of function f into n shares and distributes them to n different parties. Only when all $f_i(m)$ is provided can the final $f(m)$ be recovered, where $f_i(m)$ is a sub secret. But the problem with the above schemes is that the verifier will calculate $f(m)$ again. This can be time-consuming if the verifier is an entity with weak computing power.

3 Preliminaries

3.1 Bilinear Groups and Hardness Assumption

Bilinear Groups. Let G_1 and G_2 be two cyclic groups of large prime order q, $e : G_1 \times G_1 \to G_2$ be a symmetric pairing, it satisfies the following properties:

- Bilinearity: $e(g^a, h^b) = e(g, h)^{ab} = e(g^b, h^a)$, for all $g, h \in G_1$ and $a, b \in Z_q$.
- Non-degeneration: Assuming g and h are the generators of G_1, then $e(g, h)$ is a generator of G_2, i.e., $e(g, h) \neq 1$.
- Computability: $\forall g, h \in G_1$, $e(g, h)$ can be efficiently calculated.

Hardness Assumption. Given three randomly chosen elements $g_1, g_2, g_2{}^a \in G_1$ for some unknown $a \in Z_q$, calculate $g_1{}^a \in G_1$.

Let $Adv_{\mathcal{A},G_1}^{co-CDH} = Pr[g_1{}^a \leftarrow \mathcal{A}(g_1, g_2, g_2{}^a)]$ be the probability of a PPT adversary solving the co-CDH problem. We say that the co-CDH problem is hard in G_1 if no PPT adversary has non-negligible probability $Adv_{\mathcal{A},G_1}^{co-CDH}$.

3.2   Notions

Here, we give the key concepts and representation symbols of this paper, as shown in Table 1.

Table 1. Notation Definitions

Variable	Definition
DO	Data Owner
sk_D, sk_p	secret keys of DO and proxy signer
pk_D, pk_p	public keys of DO and proxy signer
(G_1, G_2)	bilinear groups
g_1, g_2	two generators of G_1
Z_q^*	$\{1, 2, ..., q-1\}$
H_1, H_2	hash functions
$\{0,1\}^*$	a sequence of binary number
m_w	an authorization information
x_p	secret key of proxy signature
y_p	public key of proxy signature
(σ, r)	a signature
σ_{m_w}	a warrant of authorization information
$\hat{m}$	aggregated message
$\hat{\sigma}$	homomorphic signature

3.3   Homomorphic Signature

In this paper, a homomorphic signature scheme consists of five PPT algorithms.

- Setup: Taking as input a security parameter 1^λ and a maximum length of data l, the algorithm outputs the system parameter *params*.
- KeyGen: This algorithm takes as input *params*, and outputs two pairs of keys (sk, pk) of DO and proxy signer.
- Sign: The algorithm takes as input sk, message m and an indicator i. This algorithm outputs a signature σ_i.

- Eval: The algorithm takes as input messages $m = (m_1, m_2, \ldots, m_n)$, signatures $\sigma = (\sigma_1, \sigma_2, \ldots, \sigma_n)$ and a linear function $f = (f_1, f_2, \ldots, f_n)$. The algorithm outputs an aggregated message $\hat{m}$ and a homomorphic signature $\hat{\sigma}$.

- Verify: This algorithm takes as input $m = (m_1, m_2, \ldots, m_n)$, $\sigma = (\sigma_1, \sigma_2, \ldots, \sigma_n)$, $\hat{m}$, $\hat{\sigma}$, a linear function f and public key pk. This algorithm outputs a bit $b \in \{0,1\}$ indicating whether the $\hat{\sigma}$ is correct or not.

3.4   KPW Proxy Signature

In this paper, we use the KPW proxy signature scheme [20] to construct our scheme. KPW proxy signature scheme consists of five PPT algorithms.

- ProxyGen: DO generates a random number $k \in_R Z_q$, and compute $K = g^k \bmod q$. DO concatenates m_w and K, and hashes the result: $e = h(m_w, K)$, where the information on the delegation should be described in a warrant m_w. After that, DO computes $C_{m_w} = sk_D \times e + k \bmod q$.

- ProxyDelivery: DO gives (m_w, C_{m_w}, K) to a proxy signer in a secure manner.

- ProxyVer: Proxy signer confirms $e = h(m_w, K)$ and $g^{C_{m_w}} = pk_D^e \times K \bmod q$. After confirming the validity of (m_w, C_{m_w}, K), the proxy signer calculates an alternative proxy signature key $x_p = C_{m_w} + sk_p \times e \bmod q$, where sk_p is the secret key of the proxy signer.

- ProxySign: For signing a message m, the proxy signer uses the x_p to execute the ordinary signing operation. Then the proxy signature on m is $(m, Sign_{x_p}(m), K, m_w)$.

- Verify: The verifier first calculates $e = h(m_w, K)$ and $y_p = (pk_D \times pk_p)^e \times K \bmod q$, and checks the correctness of m_w, where y_p is public key of proxy signature and pk_p is public key of proxy signer. Then uses the signature verification algorithm to verify the signature $Sign_{x_p}(m)$.

4   System Model and Security Model

4.1   Formal Definition

Our authorized function homomorphic signature scheme with sampling batch verification consists of seven PPT algorithms, as follows.

- Setup $(1^\lambda, l)$: On input a security parameter 1^λ and an integer l, this algorithm outputs system parameter *params*.

- KeyGen *(params)*: On input system parameter, DO and proxy signer run this algorithm, which outputs DO's key (sk_D, pk_D) and proxy signer's key (sk_p, pk_p).

- Delegation (m_w, sk_D): On input an authorization information $m_w = (m, f = (f_1, f_2, \ldots, f_n), pk_p)$ and DO's secret key sk_D, where $f_i \in Z_q^*$. This algorithm outputs an authorization warrant $\sigma_{m_w} = (C_{m_w}, K_0)$.

- PKeyGen($m_w, \sigma_{m_w}, pk_D, sk_p, pk_p$): On input an authorization information m_w, an authorization warrant σ_{m_w}, DO's public key pk_D and proxy signer's key (sk_p, pk_p), this algorithm outputs a pair of proxy signature key (x_p, y_p). The secret key x_p is kept by proxy signer, and the public key y_p is published.
- PSign (x_p, m, i): On input the proxy signature secret key x_p, a message m and an indicator i. This algorithm is run by proxy signer and outputs a signature (σ_i, r_i) on m, where r_i is selected randomly.
- Eval($m_w, \{\sigma_i, r_i\}_1^n$): On input an authorization information m_w and n signatures $\{\sigma_i, r_i\}_1^n$ from the same DO, this algorithm outputs the evaluated $\hat{m} = f(\boldsymbol{m})$ and homomorphic signature $\hat{\sigma} = \prod_{i=1}^n \sigma_i^{f_i}$.
- Pverify $(m_w, \{\sigma_i, r_i\}_1^n, \sigma_{m_w}, \hat{m}, \hat{\sigma}, pk_D, y_p)$: On input the authorization information m_w, n signatures $\{\sigma_i, r_i\}_1^n$, the authorization warrant σ_{m_w}, the evaluated message $\hat{m}$, homomorphic signature $\hat{\sigma}$, DO's public key pk_D and proxy signature public key y_p. This algorithm verifies correctness of homomorphic signature $\hat{\sigma}$ and calculation behavior.

4.2   System Model

Our scheme consists of three parts: DO, Proxy Signer and Verifier. The detailed work of these three parties is as follows.

- DO: DO is the data owner and is responsible for generating the authorization information m_w and the signature σ_{m_w} of the authorization information.
- Proxy Signer: The proxy signer is semi-honest and responsible for generating proxy signature key and proxy signatures $\{\sigma_i, r_i\}_1^n$ for messages $\boldsymbol{m}$ specified by DO, using authorized function f to linearly aggregate messages and generate homomorphic signature $\hat{\sigma}$ for aggregated message.
- Verifier: The verifier is mainly responsible for verifying the correctness of homomorphic signature and calculation behavior of proxy signer.

4.3   Security Model

We only consider one type of unforgeability in our scheme: proxy signature unforgeability. Proxy signature unforgeability means that, except the proxy signer, anyone else including DO cannot generate a valid proxy signature on behalf of the proxy signer. At the same time, the verifier will verify the authorization information and include the authorized function f in the homomorphic signature verification, so even if the existing signature is used for other function operations, it cannot be verified successfully.

We suppose that the adversary $\mathcal{A}$ could obtain the delegation from DO, but it does not know secret key of the proxy signer. The adversary $\mathcal{A}$ can adaptively query the hash values of messages. Then, the simulator $\mathcal{S}$ returns the hash values of the messages queried by the adversary. And adversary $\mathcal{A}$ could also adaptively query the signatures of messages. As a response, the simulator $\mathcal{S}$ returns the signatures of the messages queried by the adversary. Finally, the adversary $\mathcal{A}$ sends the forged signature to the $\mathcal{S}$. The detailed security model is as follows.

- Setup: The simulator $\mathcal{S}$ sets an instance of co-CDH to simulate the signature algorithm. $\mathcal{S}$ generates a pair of keys for proxy signature and sends the public key to $\mathcal{A}$.
- Hash Query: $\mathcal{A}$ can make a serious of queries for the hash values of messages. $\mathcal{S}$ uses the random oracle to generate the hash values of messages specified by $\mathcal{A}$ and sends them to $\mathcal{A}$.
- Sign Query: $\mathcal{A}$ can also make some queries for the signatures of messages adaptively. $\mathcal{S}$ uses the simulated signature algorithm to generate the signatures of messages queried by $\mathcal{A}$ and returns them to $\mathcal{A}$.
- Forgery: After having some hash values and signatures, $\mathcal{A}$ forges the signature σ^* of an unqueried message m^* and sends the forged result to $\mathcal{S}$.

The adversary $\mathcal{A}$ wins the game if PVerify $(\sigma^*, m^*, y_p) = 1$, and m^* does not appear in sign queries.

5 Construction

5.1 Specific Algorithm

Below we show a concrete construction of our scheme.

- Setup $(1^\lambda, l)$: Let (G_1, G_2) be bilinear groups satisfying $|G_1| = |G_2| = q$, where q is a prime number, g_1 and g_2 be the generators of G_1. The bilinear map is given by $e : G_1 \times G_1 \to G_2$. Define hash functions $H_1 : \{0, 1\}^* \to Z_q^*$, $H_2 : \{0, 1\}^* \times \{0, 1\}^* \to G_1$. H_2 will be viewed as random oracle in security proof. The security parameter is λ. l is the maximum length of data. The system parameter is $params = (G_1, G_2, q, g_1, g_2, e, \lambda, l, H_1, H_2)$.
- KeyGen $(params)$: DO sets a secret key $sk_D = x_0$, where x_0 is randomly selected in Z_q^*. Then DO computes the public key $pk_D = g_2^{x_0}$. The proxy signer randomly selects an $x_B \in Z_q^*$ as the secret key $sk_p = x_B$ and computes the public key $pk_p = g_2^{x_B}$.
- Delegation (m_w, sk_D): DO sets an authorization information $m_w = (\boldsymbol{m}, f, pk_p)$, where $\boldsymbol{m} = (m_1, m_2, \ldots, m_n)$ is a message vector authorized by DO, $f = (f_1, f_2, \ldots, f_n)$ is a linearly function authorized by DO and pk_p is the public key of proxy signer. Then DO randomly selects a $k_0 \in Z_q^*$ and computes $K_0 = g_2^{k_0}$. Finally, DO computes the signature C_{m_w} of m_w, where $C_{m_w} = x_0 \times H_1(\boldsymbol{m}\|f\|pk_p) + k_0$. This algorithm outputs warrant $\sigma_{m_w} = (C_{m_w}, K_0)$.

- PKeyGen($m_w, \sigma_{m_w}, pk_D, sk_p, pk_p$): After receiving the (m_w, σ_{m_w}) sent by DO, proxy signer first verifies the equation $g_2^{C_{m_w}} = pk_D^{H_1(m\|f\|pk_p)} \times K_0$ holds. If the authentication passes, the authorization information m_w is granted by DO. Then proxy signer computes public and secret key of proxy signature: $x_p = C_{m_w} + x_B \times H_1(m\|f\|pk_p)$, $y_p = g_2^{x_p} = (pk_D \times pk_p)^{H_1(m\|f\|pk_p)} \times K_0$. This algorithm outputs the secret key and public key (x_p, y_p) of proxy signature.
- PSign (x_p, m, i): Given a message m, the proxy signer selects a random number $r_i \in Z_q^*$, then computes $\sigma_i = (H_2(m, r_i) \times g_1^m)^{x_p}$. Finally, this algorithm outputs $(m, (\sigma_i, r_i))$.
- Eval($m_w, \{\sigma_i, r_i\}_1^n$): Given $m_w = (m, f, pk_p)$ and signatures $\{\sigma_i, r_i\}_1^n$ of $m = (m_1, m_2, \ldots, m_n)$, the proxy signer first computes $\hat{m} = \sum_{i=1}^n f_i m_i$, then generates the signature of $\hat{m}$: $\hat{\sigma} = \prod_{i=1}^n \sigma_i^{f_i}$. This algorithm output $(\hat{m}, \hat{\sigma})$.
- Pverify $(m_w, \{\sigma_i, r_i\}_1^n, \sigma_{m_w}, \hat{m}, \hat{\sigma}, pk_D, y_p)$: Verifier first verifies the equation $g_2^{C_{m_w}} = pk_D^{H_1(m\|f\|pk_p)} \times K_0$ holds. If the verification passes, the authorization information m_w is granted by DO. Then verifier verifies the signature of a single message using random sampling batch verification algorithm: verifier selects k random numbers $\alpha = (\alpha_{i_1}, \alpha_{i_2}, \ldots, \alpha_{i_k})$ and k messages from $m = (m_1, m_2, \ldots, m_n)$ randomly, where k is $1 \leq k \leq n$. Then verifier computes $m' = \sum_{i=i_1}^{i_k} \alpha_i m_i$ and $\sigma' = \prod_{i=i_1}^{i_k} \sigma_i^{\alpha_i}$, verifies the equation $e(\sigma', g_2) = e(g_1^{m'} \times \prod_{i=i_1}^{i_k} H_2(m_i, r_i)^{\alpha_i}, y_p)$ holds. If true, the proxy signer has honestly signed the messages specified by DO. Finally, the verifier verifies the equation $e(\hat{\sigma}, g_2) = e(g_1^{\hat{m}} \times \prod_{i=1}^n H_2(m_i, r_i)^{f_i}, y_p)$. If the verification passes, it means that the proxy signer has honestly calculated the messages using the authorized function f specified by DO.

5.2   Correct Analysis

Theorem 1. The proposed scheme is correct.

Proof. For a single signature verification, the correctness of the verification is proved as follows:

$$
\begin{aligned}
& e(\sigma_i, g_2) \\
=\; & e((H_2(m, r_i) \times g_1^m)^{x_p}, g_2) \\
=\; & e(H_2(m, r_i) \times g_1^m, g_2^{x_p}) \\
=\; & e(H_2(m, r_i) \times g_1^m, y_p)
\end{aligned}
\tag{1}
$$

For homomorphic signature verification, the correctness of the verification is proved as follows:

$$e(\hat{\sigma}, g_2) = e(\prod_{i=1}^{n} \sigma_i^{f_i}, g_2)$$

$$= e(\prod_{i=1}^{n} ((H_2(m_i, r_i) \times g_1^{m_i})^{x_p})^{f_i}, g_2)$$

$$= e(\prod_{i=1}^{n} (H_2(m_i, r_i) \times g_1^{m_i})^{f_i}, g_2^{x_p})$$

$$= e(\prod_{i=1}^{n} (H_2(m_i, r_i)^{f_i} \times g_1^{f_i m_i}), g_2^{x_p}) \qquad (2)$$

$$= e(\prod_{i=1}^{n} g_1^{f_i m_i} \times \prod_{i=1}^{n} H_2(m_i, r_i)^{f_i}, g_2^{x_p})$$

$$= e(g_1^{\sum_{i=1}^{n} f_i m_i} \times \prod_{i=1}^{n} H_2(m_i, r_i)^{f_i}, y_p)$$

$$= e(g_1^{\hat{m}} \times \prod_{i=1}^{n} H_2(m_i, r_i)^{f_i}, y_p)$$

5.3   Security Proof

Theorem 2. The proposed scheme is unforgeable against chosen message attacks under the co-CDH assumption.

Proof. Suppose $\mathcal{A}$ is a probabilistic polynomial time adversary who is capable to break the proposed scheme with non-negligible probability. $\mathcal{S}$ is a simulator who aims to compute g_1^a given a co-CDH instance (g_1, g_2, g_2^a). $\mathcal{S}$ can obtain the solution of the co-CDH instance by playing the following interactive game with $\mathcal{A}$.

- Setup: $\mathcal{S}$ receives the co-CDH challenge $\{g_1, g_2, g_2^a\}$ and must output g_1^a. $\mathcal{S}$ sets $g_1 = g_1$, $g_2 = g_2$, $y = g_2^a$. The secret key a is not known to $\mathcal{A}$.
- Hash Query: When $\mathcal{A}$ submits a fresh query $H_2(m_i, r_i)$ for random m_i, $\mathcal{S}$ generates random values r_i and p. $\mathcal{S}$ then stores $\{m_i, r_i, p\}$ in $H - list$ and returns $H_2(m_i, r_i) = g_1^{p+r_i}$. If m_i was queried before, $\mathcal{S}$ searches for the existing record from $H - list$ and returns the same $H_2(m_i, r_i) = g_1^{p+r_i}$.
- Sign Query: When $\mathcal{A}$ submits a signing query for m_i, we assume the hash query has already been made. If not, $\mathcal{S}$ goes ahead and computes the hash query first. In either case, $\mathcal{S}$ can recover $\{m_i, r_i, p\}$ from $H - list$ and let $\sigma_i = (H_2(m_i, r_i) \times g_1^{m_i})^a = (g_1^{p+r_i} \times g_1^{m_i})^a = (g_1^{p+r_i+m_i})^a$ and returns it.

- Forgery: Suppose $\mathcal{A}$ produces a valid $(m^*, (\sigma^*, r^*))$ pair where the signature of m^* is never queried by $\mathcal{A}$ before, if $r^* = r_i$ $\mathcal{S}$ aborts; if $r^* \neq r_i$, $\mathcal{S}$ goes ahead to solve the co-CDH assumption:

$$
\begin{aligned}
&(\frac{\sigma^*}{\sigma_i})^{\frac{1}{r^*+m^*-(r_i+m_i)}} \\
&= (\frac{g_1^{p+r^*+m^*}}{g_1^{p+r_i+m_i}})^{\frac{a}{r^*+m^*-(r_i+m_i)}} \\
&= (g_1^{r^*+m^*-(r_i+m_i)})^{\frac{a}{r^*+m^*-(r_i+m_i)}} \\
&= g_1^a
\end{aligned}
\tag{3}
$$

However, the above result obviously contradicts the hardness of co-CDH, since based on the assumption of co-CDH, it is intractable to solve within polynomial time. In other words, the assumption, that $\mathcal{A}$ is a PPT adversary who is capable to break the proposed scheme with non-negligible probability, is not true.

6 Applications Discussion

Recently, UAVs are widely used in various fields including military, industry, agriculture and so on, with advantages due to economies of scale. However, due to the characteristics of short battery life, weak computing power and limited storage of UAVs, it is difficult and inconvenient to share and storage data among UAVs. Fortunately, the rapid development of decentralized blockchain has effectively solved the problem of data sharing and storage of UAVs, which makes a UAV store its own data in blockchain for other UAVs to use. In addition, in some special scenarios, UAVs need to calculate the collected data before storing them in blockchain. To reduce computing overhead, data processing can be leveraged using cloud computing technology. But the problem is, how to ensure that the cloud server has specified the calculation of the messages specified by the UAVs. In more details, if the cloud server stores the wrong calculation results in the blockchain, then other UAVs will be difficult to detect.

In order to solve this problem, we will show how to use AFHPS to achieve data authentication and ensure the correctness of the computing behavior and calculation results of the cloud server.

The application of our scheme in the field of blockchain and UAVs is shown in Fig. 1.

At first, UAV_1 uploads authorization information to the blockchain, where authorization information includes data, linear function, and public key of cloud computing center.

The cloud computing center reads authorization information from the blockchain. First, the cloud computing center verifies the integrity of the authorization information. If the verification passes, it generates the proxy signature key, and uses the key to calculate the signatures of data. At the same time, the cloud computing center calculates aggregated data based on the linear authorized function

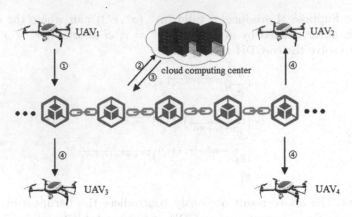

① Upload data and authorization information
② Read data and calculate, generate the corresponding signatures
③ Submit the aggregated result and signatures
④ Read data, verify the aggregated result and signatures

Fig. 1. The application in the field of blockchain and UAVs.

contained in the authorization information and generates homomorphic signature of the aggregated result. Finally, the cloud computing center submits the signatures of original messages, aggregated result and homomorphic signature to the blockchain.

When other UAVs access the aggregated result, first verify that the authorization information is correct. If correct, the random sampling batch verification algorithm is used to further check the proxy signature of a single message generated by the cloud computing center. If the verification equation holds, other UAVs can assume that the cloud computing center has honestly signed the data in the blockchain. Next, UAVs will verify the aggregated result and homomorphic signature. Finally, under the premise of verification, UAVs can use the aggregated data to complete the set task.

AFHPS can ensure the integrity of data in the blockchain. Because of adopting the way of signature batch verification, when the cloud computing center stores wrong information, UAVs could detect them with low computational overhead. At the same time, with the use of blockchain, the storage overhead of UAVs is also reduced.

7 Conclusion

In this paper, we introduce the notion of authorized function homomorphic proxy signature with sampling batch verification, which enables the data owner to delegate the signature ability of the original messages and the specified calculation function to the proxy signer and control its behavior. We give a concrete construction, which is based on homomorphic signature, proxy signature and functional signature. Then we prove that our scheme satisfies the unforgeability. Finally, we discuss its application in UAVs and blockchain.

References

1. Rivest, R.L.: Two signature schemes. Talk given October 17, 2000 at Cambridge University (2000)
2. Boneh, D., Freeman, D., Katz, J., Waters, B.: Signing a linear subspace: signature schemes for network coding. In: Jarecki, S., Tsudik, G. (eds.) PKC 2009. LNCS, vol. 5443, pp. 68–87. Springer, Heidelberg (2009). https://doi.org/10.1007/978-3-642-00468-1_5
3. Guo, Q., Huang, Q., Yang, G.: Authorized function homomorphic signature. Comput. J. **61**(12), 1897–1908 (2018)
4. Zhang, Y., Jiang, Y., Li, B., Zhang, M.: An efficient identity-based homomorphic signature scheme for network coding. In: Barolli, L., Zhang, M., Wang, X.A. (eds.) EIDWT 2017. LNDECT, vol. 6, pp. 524–531. Springer, Cham (2018). https://doi.org/10.1007/978-3-319-59463-7_52
5. Aranha, D.F., Pagnin, E.: The simplest multi-key linearly homomorphic signature scheme. In: Schwabe, P., Thériault, N. (eds.) LATINCRYPT 2019. LNCS, vol. 11774, pp. 280–300. Springer, Cham (2019). https://doi.org/10.1007/978-3-030-30530-7_14
6. Chang, J., Ji, Y., Shao, B., Xu, M., Xue, R.: Certificateless homomorphic signature scheme for network coding. IEEE/ACM Trans. Netw. **28**(6), 2615–2628 (2020)
7. Li, Y., Zhang, F., Liu, X.: Secure data delivery with identity-based linearly homomorphic network coding signature scheme in IoT. IEEE Trans. Serv. Comput. **15**(4), 2202–2212 (2020)
8. Lin, C., Xue, R., Huang, X.: Linearly homomorphic signatures with designated combiner. In: Huang, Q., Yu, Yu. (eds.) ProvSec 2021. LNCS, vol. 13059, pp. 327–345. Springer, Cham (2021). https://doi.org/10.1007/978-3-030-90402-9_18
9. Gu, Y., Shen, L., Zhang, F., Xiong, J.: Provably secure linearly homomorphic aggregate signature scheme for electronic healthcare system. Mathematics **10**(15), 2588 (2022)
10. Li, Y., Zhang, M., Zhang, F.: Structure-preserving linearly homomorphic signature with designated combiner for subspace. In: Information Security and Privacy: 27th Australasian Conference, ACISP 2022, Wollongong, NSW, Australia, 28–30 November 2022, Proceedings, pp. 229–243. Springer, Heidelberg (2022). https://doi.org/10.1007/978-3-031-22301-3_12
11. Mambo, M., Usuda, K., Okamoto, E.: Proxy signatures for delegating signing operation. In: Proceedings of the 3rd ACM Conference on Computer and Communications Security, pp. 48–57 (1996)
12. Li, J., Kim, K., Zhang, F., Chen, X.: Aggregate proxy signature and verifiably encrypted proxy signature. In: Susilo, W., Liu, J.K., Mu, Y. (eds.) ProvSec 2007. LNCS, vol. 4784, pp. 208–217. Springer, Heidelberg (2007). https://doi.org/10.1007/978-3-540-75670-5_15
13. Cao, F., Cao, Z.: A secure identity-based multi-proxy signature scheme. Comput. Electr. Eng. **35**(1), 86–95 (2009)
14. Debiao, H., Jianhua, C., Jin, H.: An id-based proxy signature schemes without bilinear pairings. Ann. Telecommun.-annales des télécommunications **66**, 657–662 (2011)

15. Verma, G.K., Singh, B., Kumar, N., Obaidat, M.S., He, D., Singh, H.: An efficient and provable certificate-based proxy signature scheme for IIoT environment. Inf. Sci. **518**, 142–156 (2020)
16. Boyle, E., Goldwasser, S., Ivan, I.: Functional signatures and pseudorandom functions. In: Krawczyk, H. (ed.) PKC 2014. LNCS, vol. 8383, pp. 501–519. Springer, Heidelberg (2014). https://doi.org/10.1007/978-3-642-54631-0_29
17. Liang, B., Mitrokotsa, A.: Decentralised functional signatures. Mob. Netw. Appl. **24**, 934–946 (2019)
18. Liu, M., Wang, L., Wu, Q., Song, J.: Distributed functional signature with function privacy and its application. Secur. Commun. Netw. **2021**, 1–14 (2021)
19. Guo, Q., Huang, Q., Ma, S., Xiao, M., Yang, G., Susilo, W.: Functional signatures: new definition and constructions. Sci. China Inf. Sci. **64**, 1–13 (2021)
20. Kim, S., Park, S., Won, D.: Proxy signatures, revisited. In: Han, Y., Okamoto, T., Qing, S. (eds.) Information and Communications Security: First International Conference, ICIS 1997 Beijing, China, 11–14 November 1997 Proceedings 1, pp. 223–232. Springer, Heidelberg (1997). https://doi.org/10.1007/bfb0028478
21. Sun, H.-M., Lee, N.-Y., Hwang, T.: Threshold proxy signatures. IEE Proc.-Comput. Dig. Techn. **146**(5), 259–263 (1999)
22. Hwang, S.J., Shi, C.H.: A simple multi-proxy signature scheme (2000)
23. Xu, Z., Luo, M., Vijayakumar, P., Peng, C., Wang, L.: Efficient certificateless designated verifier proxy signature scheme using UAV network for sustainable smart city. Sustain. Urban Areas **80**, 103771 (2022)

ASEV: Anonymous and Scored-Based E-Voting Protocol on Blockchain

Fang Li(✉), Xiaofen Wang, Tao Chen, Lin Li, and Hao Huang

University of Electronic Science and Technology of China, Chengdu 611731, China
{202121080531,vageous}@std.uestc.edu.cn, xfwang@uestc.edu.cn

Abstract. E-voting protocols based on the blockchain can ensure secure and fair voting without a trusted third party. Nonetheless, the majority of current blockchain-based voting protocols only permit yes/no voting for a single candidate. This paper proposes an electronic voting protocol utilizing blockchain technology that supports score voting for multiple candidates. Compared with conventional yes/no voting methods, the main challenges of score-based voting are how to ensure that the score assigned for each candidate by a voter is in a defined range, the sum of scores voted by one voter is a predefined constant and the privacy of the voting scores is protected. In our protocol, two types of zero-knowledge proofs, i.e., zero-knowledge proof for set membership (ZKSM) and zero-knowledge sum proof (ZKSP) are used to satisfy the two key requirements of the score constraint. Meanwhile, based on the distributed ElGamal encryption algorithm and Paillier algorithm, we design a novel encryption algorithm to encrypt the ballots, which improves the efficiency of computing the voting results while supporting robustness so that even if some voters abstain or cast invalid votes, the voting results can still be directly computed by each voter without restarting the protocol. The security analysis shows that our voting protocol achieves maximal ballot secrecy, anonymity, eligibility, resistance against multi-voting, robustness, and dispute-freeness. The performance analysis demonstrates the effectiveness and practicality of our voting protocol.

Keywords: Score-based Voting · Blockchain · Zero-knowledge Proof · Self-Tallying

1 Introduction

Voting serves as an equitable and efficient mechanism for making decisions, thus, playing a critical role in contemporary society. With the emergence and development of blockchain technology, numerous blockchain-based electronic voting protocols have been proposed. Blockchain [1] is a decentralized, tamper-proof, and traceable distributed ledger that can increase the security and transparency of the voting scheme while reducing reliance on third-party organizations in traditional electronic voting.

© The Author(s), under exclusive license to Springer Nature Singapore Pte Ltd. 2024
H. Yang and R. Lu (Eds.): FCS 2023, CCIS 1992, pp. 309–322, 2024.
https://doi.org/10.1007/978-981-99-9331-4_21

In 2017, McCorry et al. [2] proposed the first decentralized self-tallying electronic voting protocol based on blockchain. By utilizing smart contracts, their solution effectively eliminated the need for a trusted third party in the voting process. Afterward, a subsequent study [3] proposed an Ethereum-based voting system that provided privacy protection, eligibility, and fairness for voters. Unfortunately, both systems [2,3] are only suitable for small-scale board voting. Li et al. [4] developed a blockchain-based self-tallying electronic voting protocol in Internet of Things (IoT) environment. This innovative solution addressed key requirements such as fairness, dispute-freeness, and ballot privacy, but did not account for true abstentions and incurred a higher tallying overhead.

Existing research on electronic voting has mostly focused on yes/no voting with multiple candidates for single-seat elections, with little attention paid to flexible voting paradigms [5]. However, score voting electoral systems are widely used in various elections, where voters rate each candidate with a score, the scores are summed or averaged, and the candidate with the highest score is elected. Cramer et al. [6] first introduced this problem in 1996 and proposed a "1-out-of-m" multi-candidate voting scheme in 2000. However, its computational complexity is too high, and thus it is not suitable for practical use. Yang et al. [7] proposed a blockchain-based self-tallying system to support score voting. However, in their system if more than one abstention occurs, the tally calculations are inherently very complex. Dery et al. [8] designed a score-based voting protocol that can implement five different voting rules. However, this protocol incurs high computational and communication costs due to certain score-based algorithms and MPC-based tally schemes.

In this paper, we propose a blockchain-based voting protocol supporting score voting that simultaneously achieves full decentralization, self-tallying, legitimacy, robustness and can resist multi-voting. Specifically, the contributions are summarized as below:

- We propose a scored-based voting protocol based on blockchain and homomorphic encryption, which can achieve decentralized multi-candidate scored-based voting with self-tallying function. The protocol also allows voters to cast anonymous and unlinkable electronic ballots securely.
- Our protocol proposes two types of zero-knowledge proofs, i.e., zero-knowledge proof for set membership (ZKSM) [9] and zero-knowledge sum proof (ZKSP) [10]. These proofs allow voters to prove the validity of their ballots to verifiers without revealing the specific content of their votes, i.e., prove that each evaluation score in the ballot is within a defined range and that the sum of the scores of each ballot is equal to a predefined constant.
- Our protocol achieves maximum ballot secrecy and robustness. Based on the distributed ElGamal encryption algorithm [11] and Paillier algorithm [12], we have designed a novel encryption algorithm to encrypt the ballots, so that the vote of each voter can be kept confidential as long as all other voters in the voting group do not collude. In our protocol, even if some voters abstain or cast invalid ballots, the voting result can still be calculated directly by each voter without restarting the protocol.

2 Preliminaries

2.1 Score-Based Voting

Score-based voting is a method of election that involves the use of a scorestyle ballot. In this type of voting, voters are required to assign a certain number of points within a specified range, such as 0 to 5 or 1 to 10, to each candidate. The total score for each ballot must be equal to a predetermined number set by the election organization. After the vote casting, the scores of each candidate are tallied and then the individual with the highest total score is elected.

An example is shown in Fig. 1 to demonstrate the ballot of score-based voting. There are three candidates and the total evaluation score in each ballot must add up to 6. A voter can choose to allocate their votes equally across all candidates (as seen in ballot 1); or to only support one candidate (as seen in ballot 2); or to assign various scores to different candidates (as seen in ballot 3). It is clear that score-based voting is more versatile than the traditional 'yes-or-no' voting found in many existing works [13,14].

Ballot 1	
A	2
B	2
C	2

Ballot 2	
A	0
B	6
C	0

Ballot 3	
A	1
B	2
C	3

Fig. 1. Score-based election instructions for three voters and three candidates.

2.2 One-Time Ring Signature

In electronic voting systems, one of the main issues is anonymity, i.e., the relationship between the voter and his ballot cannot be disclosed. We adopt the one-time ring signature (OTRS) proposed by Nicolas van Saberhagen [15,16], which ensures that a voter with one key pair can sign a ballot only once.

The parameters in OTRS are defined as follows [17]: F_q is a cyclic group with a prime number q as its order, $E(F_q)$ refers to an elliptic curve defined over the finite group F_q. The base point of the curve $E(F_q)$ is represented by G, while the order of the base point is denoted by l. Assuming that H_s is a cryptographic hash function that maps a binary sequence with arbitrary length to a finite field F module q, and H_p is a cryptographic hash function that maps finite field points on an elliptic curve to themselves.

Signature Generation (SG). In the scheme where a legal signer possesses a private key x_s associated with the public key P_s, where $s \in [n]$, and a set of public keys $\{P_i\}_{i \in [n]}$ is given, the signer generates a "key image" denoted as $I = x_s H_p(P_s)$. Then, the signer applies the transformations to the key image.

$$L_i = \begin{cases} q_i G, & i = s \\ q_i G + w_i P_i, & i \neq s \end{cases} \tag{1}$$

and

$$R_i = \begin{cases} q_i H_p(P_i), & i = s \\ q_i H_p(P_i) + w_i I, & i \neq s, \end{cases} \tag{2}$$

where q_i and w_i are random numbers from the $[1, ..., l]$, the signer then computes

$$c = H_s(m, L_1, ..., L_n, R_1, ..., R_n) \tag{3}$$

$$c_i = \begin{cases} w_i, & i \neq s \\ c - \sum_{i=1}^n c_i \pmod{l}, & i = s \end{cases} \tag{4}$$

$$r_i = \begin{cases} q_i, & i \neq s \\ q_s - c_s x, & i = s \end{cases} \tag{5}$$

Then, the one-time ring signature is generated as

$$\sigma = (I, c_1, ..., c_n, r_1, ..., r_n) \tag{6}$$

Signature Verification (SV). Any verifier can calculate the transformations

$$\begin{cases} L_i' = r_i G + c_i P_i \\ R_i' = r_i H_p(P_i) + c_i I \end{cases}, i \in [n] \tag{7}$$

then checks whether the following equation holds true or not:

$$\sum_{i=1}^n c_i = H_s(m, L_1', ..., L_n', R_1', ..., R_n') \tag{8}$$

3   System Model and Security Requirement

3.1   System Model

The framework of ASEV is shown in Fig. 2, which contains four kinds of entities, i.e. a blockchain platform, an election organizer (EO), a set of candidates and a set of voters.

- Blockchain: The blockchain has the responsibility of storing all public parameters and encrypted ballots, and executing smart contracts.

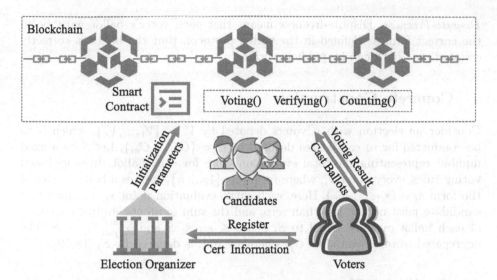

Fig. 2. The framework of the blockchain-based self-tallying voting system.

- Election organizer: The election organizer is responsible for initializing the voting system and announcing important parameters, creating and publishing smart contracts, and verifying voters' identity.
- Candidates: Candidates refers to a group of qualified individuals eligible for election participation.
- Voters: A collection of eligible users who have been granted the right to vote in an election and who are required to cast their ballots by the deadline, otherwise they are considered to have abstained.

3.2 Security Requirements

Maximal Ballot Secrecy. The encrypted ballot B_i of a voter ensures that no information about his original vote is revealed to anyone.

Anonymity. Anonymity requires that the correspondence between voter identity and ballot be kept secret.

Eligibility. Only successfully registered voters can submit their ballots.

Resistance Against Multi-voting. In the voting process, each voter can only vote once. If a voter casts more than one ballot, only one of them can be included in the calculation of the voting result.

Self-tallying. Once all ballots have been cast, any voter in the system can calculate the result of the voting.

Robustness. In the self-tallying voting system, robustness means that the voting result is counted correctly even if some voters do not vote or cast illegal ballots.

Dispute-Freeness. Dispute-freeness means that each voter's ballot must be in the correct form as defined in the voting protocol, that the ballot is correctly counted, and both can be publicly verified.

4   Concrete Construction

Consider an election with n voters denoted by $V = \{V_1, ..., V_n\}$, which is to be conducted for m candidates denoted by $C = \{C_1, ... C_m\}$. Let S be a fixed number representing the total evaluation score for each ballot. In score-based voting rules, every voter V_i, where $i \in [n] := \{1, ..., n\}$, creates a ballot vector of the form $s_i = (s_{i1}, ..., s_{im})$. Here, each single evaluation point s_{ij} assigned to a candidate must not be less than zero, and the sum of all the evaluation points of each ballot must be equal to S, i.e., $0 \leqslant s_{ij} \leqslant S$ and $\sum_{j=1}^{m} s_{ij} = S$. The aggregated score of candidate C_j, where $j \in [m]$, is denoted by S_j [18,19].

4.1   Registering Phase

During this phase, each voter V_i submits a registration request, his identity ID_i and other evidence to the election organization ***EO***. Upon ***EO*** verifying the authenticity of the information provided, V_i can participate in the voting. Then ***EO*** initializes the voting and publishes the system parameters, and voters generate their public keys.

Setup$(k) \rightarrow (params, \lambda)$: *Setup* algorithm generates the system's public parameters $params = (N, g, \mathbb{G})$ by taking the security parameter k as input, where $N = pq$ (p and q are two large primes of equal length), $g \in \mathbb{G}$ is an element with an order that is a non-zero multiple of N. The group $\mathbb{G}$ is defined as $\mathbb{Z}_{N^2}^*$. Additionally, ***EO*** securely sends the secret parameter $\lambda = lcm(p - 1, q - 1)$ to V_i, and publics the public parameters *params*.

KeyGen$(k) \rightarrow (x_i, y_i)$: Taken a security parameter k as input, the voter V_i chooses a random number $x_i \in \mathbb{Z}_p^*$ as his private key, and computes his public key $y_i = g^{x_i}$.

4.2   Voting Phase

During the voting phase, each voter V_i decides his choices and generates an encrypted ballot, a one-time ring signature, and corresponding zero-knowledge proof. Then V_i submits the ballot and signature, along with the zero-knowledge proof to the blockchain.

Vote$(x_i, \{s_{ij}\}_{j \in [m]}, \{y_i\}_{i \in [n]}) \rightarrow (B_i, \sigma_i, \Pi_{B_i})$: This algorithm is operated by each voter V_i. V_i chooses an score s_{ij} for each candidate $C_j, j \in [m]$. It is required that $0 \leqslant s_{ij} \leqslant S$ and $\sum_{j=1}^{m} s_{ij} = S$. Taking V_i's secret key x_i, score $\{s_{ij}\}_{j \in [m]}$ and the public keys $\{y_i\}_{i \in [n]}$ as input, V_i generates a encrypted ballot $B_i =$

Algorithm 1: Zero-knowledge proof for set membership (ZKSM)

Input   : The voter V_i's public key y_i and encrypted ballot $B_i = (b_{i1}, ..., b_{im})$
Output : $\Pi^1_{V_i} = (\Pi^{11}_{V_i}, ..., \Pi^{1m}_{V_i})$

begin

    for $j=1$ *to* m **do**

        choose random

        $\rho, e_\alpha, d_\alpha \in \mathbb{Z}_p^*, \alpha \in [0, S] \setminus \{k\}$

        calculate

        $a_\alpha = g^{e_\alpha} y_i^{\lambda d_\alpha}$

        $b_\alpha = w_i^{e_\alpha} (\frac{b_{ij}}{g^{s_{i\alpha}}})^{\lambda d_\alpha}$

        $a_k = g^\rho$

        $b_k = w_i^\rho$

        for $\tau \in [0, S]$ **do**

            Set

            $a_\tau = g^{e_\tau} y_i^{\lambda d_\tau}; \; b_\tau = w_i^{e_\tau} (\frac{b_{ij}}{g^{s_{i\tau}}})^{\lambda d_\tau}$

        end

        calculate

        $c = H(b_{ij}, \{a_\tau, b_\tau\}_{\tau \in [0, S]})$

        $d_k = c - \sum_{\alpha \in [0, S] \setminus \{k\}} d_\alpha$

        $e_k = \rho - \lambda x_i d_k$

        $\Pi^{1j}_{V_i} = (b_{ij}, c, \{a_\tau, b_\tau, d_\tau, e_\tau\}_{\tau \in [0, S]})$

    end

    return $\Pi^1_{V_i} = (\Pi^{11}_{V_i}, ..., \Pi^{1m}_{V_i})$

end

Algorithm 2: Zero-knowledge sum proof (ZKSP)

Input   : The voter V_i's public key y_i and encrypted ballot $B_i = (b_{i1}, ..., b_{im})$
Output : $\Pi^2_{V_i}$

begin

    choose random

    $\tilde{x}_i \in \mathbb{Z}_p^*$

    calculate

    $\tilde{y}_i = g^{\tilde{x}_i}$

    $\tilde{b}_i = w_i^{\lambda m \tilde{x}_i}$

    $c = H(y_i, \tilde{y}_i, \prod_{j=1}^m b_{ij}, \tilde{b}_i)$

    $\bar{x}_i = \tilde{x}_i - c x_i$

    return $\Pi^2_{V_i} = (y_i, \tilde{y}_i, \bar{x}_i, \prod_{j=1}^m b_{ij}, \tilde{b}_i, c)$

end

$(b_{i1}, ..., b_{im})$. To guarantee the privacy of score set $\{s_{ij}\}_{j \in [m]}$, V_i encrypts each s_{ij} as $b_{ij} = w_i^{x_i} g^{s_{ij}} r_{ij}^N \pmod{N^2}$, where $w_i = \prod_{j=1}^{i-1} y_j / \prod_{j=i+1}^{n} y_j$, and $r_{ij} \in \mathbb{Z}_p^*$ is a random number.

Then voter V_i generates a ring signature σ_i on B_i by running $OTRS.SG$ algorithm. Next, V_i runs Algorithm 1 to prove that the encrypted score is in the predefined range (i.e., $\{s_{ij}\} \in [0, S]$). Then, V_i proves $\sum_{j=1}^{m} s_{ij} = S$ through the Algorithm 2. The Π_{B_i} for the ballot B_i is denoted as $\Pi_{B_i} = \{\Pi_{V_i}^1, \Pi_{V_i}^2\}$. Finally, V_i submits $B_i \| \sigma_i$ and the proof Π_{B_i} to blockchain.

Algorithm 3: Verification of proof $\Pi_{V_i}^1$ generated by Algorithm 1

Input : The voter V_i's proof $\Pi_{V_i}^1 = (\Pi_{V_i}^{11}, ..., \Pi_{V_i}^{1m})$
Output : 0 or 1

begin
  for *j=1 to m* **do**
    if $c \neq \sum_{\tau=0}^{S} d_\tau$ **then**
      return 0
    end
    for $\tau \in [0, S]$ **do**
      if $(a_\tau \neq g^{e_\tau} y_i^{\lambda d_\tau}) \| (b_\tau \neq w_i^{e_\tau} (\frac{b_{ij}}{g^{s_{i\tau}}})^{\lambda d_\tau})$ **then**
        return 0
    end
  end
  return 1
end

Algorithm 4: Verification of proof $\Pi_{V_i}^2$ generated by Algorithm 3

Input   : The voter V_i's proof $\Pi_{V_i}^2 = (y_i, \tilde{y}_i, \tilde{x}_i, \prod_{j=1}^{m} b_{ij}, \tilde{b}_i, c)$
Output : 0 or 1

begin
  if $(c \neq H(y_i, \tilde{y}_i, \prod_{j=1}^{m} b_{ij}, \tilde{b}_i)) \| (\tilde{y}_i \neq (y_i)^c g^{x_i}) \|$
  $(\tilde{b}_i \neq (\prod_{j=1}^{m} b_{ij}/g^S)^{\lambda c} \cdot w_i^{\lambda m \tilde{x}_i})$ **then**
    return 0
  else
    return 1
  end
end

4.3 Counting Phase

In the counting phase, the *Verify* algorithm is executed to verify the validity of the ZKPs and signatures. The voting result is computed in two scenarios: i) if all voters cast their ballots honestly, the *Tally* algorithm is executed; ii) if some voters abstain from voting, the *Tally-abandon* algorithm is executed.

$Verify(B_i, \{y_i\}_{i\in[n]}, \sigma_i, \Pi_{B_i}) \to \{0,1\}$: This algorithm can be run by any party, which takes the voter V_i's encrypted ballot B_i and public key y_i, the corresponding signature σ_i and the zero-knowledge proof Π_{B_i} as input, and runs $OTRS.SV$ algorithm to check whether the ring signature σ_i of the ballot is valid and first used by checking whether the key image I_i has existed. And checks whether the ballot is in the right form through Algorithm 3 and Algorithm 4. It outputs 1 if both are correct and 0 otherwise.

$Tally\left(\{B_i\}_{i\in[n]}, \lambda\right) \to \{S_1, ..., S_m\}$: This algorithm, run by any voter, takes all the ballots $\{B_i\}_{i\in[n]}$ and λ as input, and computes $b_j = \prod_{i=1}^{n} b_{ij} = \prod_{i=1}^{n} w_i^{x_i} g^{s_{ij}} r_{ij}^N \pmod{N^2} = g^{\sum_{i=1}^{n} s_{ij}} \left(\prod_{i=1}^{n} r_{ij}\right)^N \pmod{N^2}$ and $b_j^\lambda \pmod{N^2} = g^{\lambda \sum_{i=1}^{n} s_{ij}} \pmod{N^2}$. Then the voting result S_j of the candidate C_j can be computed as $S_j = \sum_{i=1}^{n} s_{ij} = L\left(b_j^\lambda\right) \cdot L^{-1}\left(g^\lambda\right) \pmod{N}$, where $L(x) = \frac{(x-1)}{N}$ is a function of x.

$Tally\text{-}abandon\left(\{B_i\}_{i\in D\subseteq[1,n]}, \lambda\right) \to \left\{\hat{S}_1, ..., \hat{S}_m\right\}$: We assume that D is the set of voters who submitted valid ballots in the voting phase, and $|D| < n$. To compute the final result of the voting, each voter V_i, who is in D, publishes $\hat{w}_i^{x_i}$, where $\hat{w}_i = \left(\prod_{j\in\{i+1,\cdots,n\}\backslash D} y_j\right)/\left(\prod_{j\in\{1,\cdots,i-1\}\backslash D} y_j\right)$, and computes the voting result from all valid ballots as $\hat{S}_j = \sum_{i\in D} s_{ij} = L\left(\hat{b}_j^\lambda\right) \cdot L^{-1}\left(g^\lambda\right) \pmod{N}$, where $\hat{b}_j = \prod_{i\in D} \hat{w}_i^{x_i} b_{ij} = \prod_{i\in D} \hat{w}_i^{x_i} w_i^{x_i} g^{s_{ij}} r_{ij}^N \pmod{N^2} = g^{\sum_{i\in D} s_{ij}} \left(\prod_{i\in D} r_{ij}\right)^N \pmod{N^2}$.

5 Security Analysis

5.1 Maximal Ballot Secrecy

Each ballot must be encrypted before submission. We use distributed ElGamal encryption and Paillier encryption algorithm, both of which are semantically secure. During the verification phase, zero-knowledge proofs ensure that the verification process does not leak any information about the ballots. In addition, the tallying is performed on the ciphertext state of the ballots using homomorphic operations. Therefore, individual ballots do not reveal any useful information about the voter's choices.

5.2   Anonymity

The signature of voter V_i on his encrypted ballot B_i takes the form $\sigma_i = (I_i, c_i^1, ..., c_i^n, r_i^1, ..., r_i^n)$, where I_i does not reveal V_i's public key, and c_i^j and r_i^j obfuscate V_i's identity with other voters in the voter group. Thus, with the information provided by σ, it is only possible to determine whether V_i is a member of the voter group, but not his specific identity [20].

5.3   Eligibility

In the registration phase, the ring public key P_i of all valid voters is stored on the blockchain. When voting, voters must sign the ballot with their ring private key. However, an adversary without a ring private key cannot generate a valid signature, so his submitted ballot will be discarded in the counting phase.

5.4   Resistance Against Multi-voting

The key image in the signature σ_i is used to resist multi-voting. To generate a valid σ_i, V_i must calculate the I_i as required, and the I_i in different signatures of V_i is the same. When there are multiple ballots on the blockchain corresponding to the same I_i, only one ballot is kept.

5.5   Self-tallying

The result can be calculated by any party in the system without additional help after all voters have cast their ballots. If all voters submit the correct ballot, the result is $S_j = \sum_{i=1}^n s_{ij} = L\left(b_j^\lambda\right) \cdot L^{-1}\left(g^\lambda\right) \pmod{N}$. If some voters abstain, the legal voters can still calculate the result as $\hat{S}_j = \sum_{i \in D} s_{ij} = L\left(\hat{b}_j^\lambda\right) \cdot L^{-1}\left(g^\lambda\right)$ $\pmod{N}$ from the uploaded ballots.

5.6   Robustness

Our protocol allows for voter abstention, which means that even if some voters choose not to cast or cast improperly, the voting results can still be accurately calculated by running the *Tally-abandon* algorithm without requiring a restart of the protocol.

5.7   Dispute-Freeness

Our protocol employs blockchain as a credible bulletin board to ensure that none of the ballots can be modified. The use of zero-knowledge proof guarantees that the ballots are generated in the correct format and can be publicly verified. In the event of any dispute, voters can retrieve their ballots and corresponding zero-knowledge proofs from the blockchain to verify them.

6 Implementation Analysis

6.1 Theoretical Analysis

The computational efficiency of a blockchain-based voting protocol that supports score voting depends mainly on the voting and counting phases. This section presents a theoretical analysis of the computational cost of the voting and counting processes, as indicated in Table 1. Below are the definitions of the parameters. Let n be the number of voters and m the number of candidates. The total evaluation points in each ballot is represented as S. We denote the execution time for the multiplication operation as t_m; the execution time for the exponential operation as t_e; the execution time for hash calculation as t_h.

In the voting phase, the ballot generation time for each candidate is $3t_e + 2t_m$. The overhead of σ increases with the value of n, whereas the zero-knowledge proof (ZKP) for B_i grows with m and S. The verification overhead for the signature and ZKP also increases with n and m, respectively. The Tally algorithm is dominated by multiplication and exponentiation calculations, and it increases linearly with m. It is noteworthy that the value of t_m is considerably smaller than t_e such that Tally is efficient. However, in case of abandonment, the Tally-abandon algorithm is more complex than that of the Tally, including additional multiplication calculations.

Table 1. Computation Cost of ASEV.

Algorithms	Parameter	Computation Cost
Vote	B_i	$m \cdot (3t_e + 2t_m)$
	σ_i	$nt_m + 2t_h$
	$\Pi^1_{V_i}$	$m \cdot [(4S+2)t_e + (2S)t_m + t_h]$
	$\Pi^2_{V_i}$	$2t_e + mt_m + t_h$
Verify	σ_i	$4nt_m + (n+1)t_h$
	$\Pi^1_{V_i}$	$m(4S)t_e$
	$\Pi^2_{V_i}$	$4t_e + 2mt_m + t_h$
Tally	$\{S_1, ..., S_m\}$	$m(nt_m + 2t_e)$
Tally-abandon	$\{\hat{S}_1, ..., \hat{S}_m\}$	$2m(nt_m + t_e)$

6.2 Experiment Analysis

The performance evaluation of ASEV will be conducted from two perspectives: firstly, the comparison of time consumption in the voting and counting stages for different numbers of voters, and secondly, the comparison of time consumption in the voting and counting stages for different numbers of candidates.

Experiment Setup. We conduct the experiments on a 64bits Ubuntu-20.04 equipped with the 12th Gen Intel(R) Core(TM) i9-12900K (3.2 GHz). Our codes are in python with the Pypbc library. For ease of comparison, the execution time of the operations are summarized as follows.

- t_m: the computation cost of multiplication operation in $\mathbb{G}$, which is approximately 0.0016 ms.
- t_e: the computation cost of exponentiation operation in $\mathbb{G}$, which is approximately 0.0209 ms.
- t_h: the computation cost of hash calculation related to $\mathbb{G}$, which is approximately 0.0067 ms.

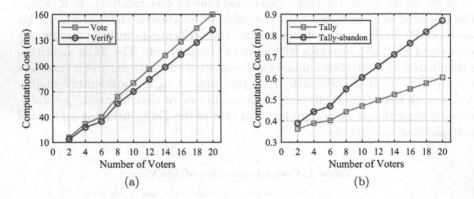

Fig. 3. Computation cost of different numbers of voters ($m = 8, S = 10$).

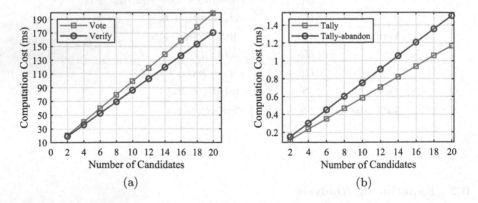

Fig. 4. Computation cost of different numbers of candidates ($n = 10, S = 10$).

Implementation Results. Figure 3 displays the time consumption of voting and counting stages among different numbers of voters when the number of candidates is 8. It can be observed from the figure that among the four algorithms the most expensive one is *Vote*, due to the fact that $\Pi_{V_i}^1$ dominates and is the most complex zero-knowledge proof among all. The most efficient algorithm is *Tally*, which is consistent with our theoretical analysis, as it does not require zero-knowledge proofs and the equation for vote counting is proportional to the product of voters' ballots and linear with the number of voters.

Figure 4 shows the comparison of time consumption in the voting and counting stages for different numbers of candidates when the number of voters is 10. The time for calculating the voting result in this system does not exceed 1 ms when the number of candidates increases to 12. The experimental results indicate that as the number of candidates increases, the time consumption in both the voting and counting stages increases linearly.

7   Conclusion

In this paper, we constructed a blockchain-based self-tallying electronic voting protocol that enables voters to assign arbitrary scores to different candidates in a predefined range. This scoring voting scheme is rarely implemented in existing electronic voting solutions with privacy-preserving mechanisms. The security analysis shows that our voting protocol achieves the maximal ballot secrecy, anonymity, eligibility, resistance against multi-voting, robustness, and dispute-freeness. The performance analysis demonstrates the effectiveness and practicality of our self-tallying voting protocol. In our future work, we will improve the zero-knowledge proof of encrypted ballots, which is one of the difficulties in voting protocols.

References

1. Nakamoto, S.: Bitcoin: a peer-to-peer electronic cash system. Decentralized Bus. Rev. 21260 (2008)
2. McCorry, P., Shahandashti, S.F., Hao, F.: A smart contract for boardroom voting with maximum voter privacy. In: Kiayias, A. (ed.) FC 2017. LNCS, vol. 10322, pp. 357–375. Springer, Cham (2017). https://doi.org/10.1007/978-3-319-70972-7_20
3. Hardwick, F.S., Gioulis, A., Akram, R.N., Markantonakis, K.: E-voting with blockchain: an e-voting protocol with decentralisation and voter privacy. In: 2018 IEEE International Conference on Internet of Things (iThings) and IEEE Green Computing and Communications (GreenCom) and IEEE Cyber, Physical and Social Computing (CPSCom) and IEEE Smart Data (SmartData), pp. 1561–1567. IEEE (2018)
4. Li, Y., et al.: A blockchain-based self-tallying voting protocol in decentralized IoT. IEEE Trans. Dependable Secure Comput. **19**(1), 119–130 (2020)
5. Cramer, R., Gennaro, R., Schoenmakers, B.: A secure and optimally efficient multi-authority election scheme. Eur. Trans. Telecommun. **8**(5), 481–490 (1997)
6. Cramer, R., Franklin, M., Schoenmakers, B., Yung, M.: Multi-authority secret-ballot elections with linear work. In: Maurer, U. (ed.) EUROCRYPT 1996. LNCS, vol. 1070, pp. 72–83. Springer, Heidelberg (1996). https://doi.org/10.1007/3-540-68339-9_7

322   F. Li et al.

7. Yang, Y., Guan, Z., Wan, Z., Weng, J., Pang, H.H., Deng, R.H.: Priscore: blockchain-based self-tallying election system supporting score voting. IEEE Trans. Inf. Forensics Secur. **16**, 4705–4720 (2021)
8. Dery, L., Tassa, T., Yanai, A.: Fear not, vote truthfully: secure multiparty computation of score based rules. Expert Syst. Appl. **168**, 114434 (2021)
9. Benarroch, D., Campanelli, M., Fiore, D., Gurkan, K., Kolonelos, D.: Zero-knowledge proofs for set membership: efficient, succinct, modular. In: Borisov, N., Diaz, C. (eds.) FC 2021. LNCS, vol. 12674, pp. 393–414. Springer, Heidelberg (2021). https://doi.org/10.1007/978-3-662-64322-8_19
10. Xie, T., Zhang, J., Zhang, Y., Papamanthou, C., Song, D.: Libra: succinct zero-knowledge proofs with optimal prover computation. In: Boldyreva, A., Micciancio, D. (eds.) CRYPTO 2019. LNCS, vol. 11694, pp. 733–764. Springer, Cham (2019). https://doi.org/10.1007/978-3-030-26954-8_24
11. ElGamal, T.: A public key cryptosystem and a signature scheme based on discrete logarithms. IEEE Trans. Inf. Theory **31**(4), 469–472 (1985)
12. Paillier, P.: Public-key cryptosystems based on composite degree residuosity classes. In: Stern, J. (ed.) EUROCRYPT 1999. LNCS, vol. 1592, pp. 223–238. Springer, Heidelberg (1999). https://doi.org/10.1007/3-540-48910-X_16
13. Yu, B., et al.: Platform-independent secure blockchain-based voting system. In: Chen, L., Manulis, M., Schneider, S. (eds.) ISC 2018. LNCS, vol. 11060, pp. 369–386. Springer, Cham (2018). https://doi.org/10.1007/978-3-319-99136-8_20
14. Camenisch, J., Kiayias, A., Yung, M.: On the portability of generalized schnorr proofs. In: Joux, A. (ed.) EUROCRYPT 2009. LNCS, vol. 5479, pp. 425–442. Springer, Heidelberg (2009). https://doi.org/10.1007/978-3-642-01001-9_25
15. Rivest, R.L., Shamir, A., Tauman, Y.: How to leak a secret. In: Boyd, C. (ed.) ASIACRYPT 2001. LNCS, vol. 2248, pp. 552–565. Springer, Heidelberg (2001). https://doi.org/10.1007/3-540-45682-1_32
16. van Saberhagen, N.: Cryptonote v 2.0 (2013)
17. Lai, W.-J., Hsieh, Y.-C., Hsueh, C.-W., Wu, J.-L.: Date: a decentralized, anonymous, and transparent e-voting system. In: 2018 1st IEEE International Conference on Hot Information-centric Networking (HotICN), pp. 24–29. IEEE (2018)
18. Lu, S., Li, Z., Miao, X., Han, Q., Zheng, J.: PIWS: private intersection weighted sum protocol for privacy-preserving score-based voting with perfect ballot secrecy. IEEE Trans. Comput. Soc. Syst. (2022)
19. Alshehri, A., Baza, M., Srivastava, G., Rajeh, W., Alrowaily, M., Almusali, M.: Privacy-preserving e-voting system supporting score voting using blockchain. Appl. Sci. **13**(2), 1096 (2023)
20. Mundhe, P., Yadav, V.K., Singh, A., Verma, S., Venkatesan, S.: Ring signature-based conditional privacy-preserving authentication in VANETs. Wirel. Pers. Commun. **114**, 853–881 (2020)

A New Self-dual BKZ Algorithm Based on Lattice Sieving

Xixuan Deng[1,2] and Huiwen Jia[1,2(✉)]

[1] School of Mathematics and Information Science, Key Laboratory of Information Security, Guangzhou University, Guangzhou, China
hwjia@gzhu.edu.cn
[2] Guangzhou Center for Applied Mathematics, Guangzhou University, Guangzhou, China

Abstract. Lattice reduction algorithm is an important algorithm for solving lattice Shortest Vector Problem (SVP), which makes it the primary tool for evaluating the security of lattice-based cryptographic schemes. Lattice reduction algorithm's running time and memory depend on the SVP-Oracle used as a subroutine. In this work, we use lattice sieving algorithm as the SVP-Oracle, combined with the Self-Dual BKZ algorithm, to design a new lattice reduction algorithm. Compared to the previous implementations based on enumeration algorithm, our new algorithm can produce more accurate results in less time. In addition, our new algorithm maintains the same computational performance as the state-of-the-art, i.e. the pump and jump BKZ.

Keywords: Lattice reduction algorithm · Security evaluation · Self-Dual BKZ · Lattice sieving

1 Introduction

Lattice-based cryptography has emerged as one of the most attractive areas due to its excellent properties such as resistance to quantum attacks and algorithmic simplicity. Currently, lattice-based cryptographic schemes are mostly based on Learning With Errors (LWE) problem [21] and Short Integer Solution (SIS) problem [1]. Both problems can be reduced to SVP and solved using the lattice reduction algorithm. Therefore, improving the lattice reduction algorithm is an important task for the security evaluation of lattice-based cryptography.

The lattice reduction algorithm can be broadly divided into two categories: One is the Block-Korkine-Zolotarev (BKZ) algorithm [23], which inputs a lattice basis and blocksizes β and outputs a reduced lattice basis with short vectors of length related by β. Due to its excellent performance in practice, the BKZ algorithm has become the most widely used algorithm. There are many improvements to the BKZ algorithm such as BKZ2.0 [8], Progressive BKZ [5], DeepBKZ [17]. Another algorithm is Self-Dual BKZ algorithm [16], which is based on slide

H. Yang and R. Lu (Eds.): FCS 2023, CCIS 1992, pp. 323–336, 2024.
https://doi.org/10.1007/978-981-99-9331-4_22

reduction [11]. Different with original BKZ algorithm, the slide reduction algorithm works on primal lattice basis and dual lattice basis. In theory, the slide reduction algorithm performs better, but in real experiments it does not perform as well as the BKZ algorithm. In 2016, Micciancio and Walter combined the characteristics of BKZ algorithm and slide reduction, proposed the Self-Dual BKZ algorithm, and it yields an excellent approximation factors. However, its output quality still has a small gap with the BKZ algorithm for the same inputs.

The efficiency of BKZ algorithms depends on the SVP-Oracle used in the algorithm. The main algorithms used are the enumeration algorithm [20] and the sieving algorithm [2]. Sieving has a better time complexity in theory but performs poorly in practice, hence many BKZ algorithms use enumeration. However, sieving has developed rapidly in recent years, and its performance has improved significantly [6,7,9,14,18]. In the Dramstart Lattice Challenge, sieving holds a top position on the challenge list [22].

Considering the development of sieving, in this work, we combine sieving with Self-Dual BKZ and design our new algorithm. Then, according to the feature of the sieving, we modify the preprocessing steps and the termination conditions of the algorithm. We test our algorithm in the SVP challenge and ideal lattice challenge [19] (the ideal lattice structure is never used). The results indicate that, compared to previous implementation, our algorithm takes less time to achieve the same or better results, making it more usable.

2   Preliminaries

2.1   Notations

$\mathbb{R}$ and $\mathbb{Z}$ respectively represents the set of real numbers and the set of integers. All vectors are denoted by bold lower case letters and should be read as column vectors. Matrices are denoted by bold capital letters. We write matrix $\mathbf{B}$ as $\mathbf{B} = [\mathbf{b}_0, \mathbf{b}_1, ..., \mathbf{b}_{d-1}]$ where $\mathbf{b}_i$ is the i-th row vector of $\mathbf{B}$. All the indices in this article start from zero. $\langle, \rangle$ denotes the inner product of vectors. Norms in this paper are Euclidean and denoted as $\| \cdot \|$.

2.2   Lattice and Related Definitions

Definition 1 (Lattice). *A lattice $\mathcal{L}$ is a discrete subgroup of $\mathbb{R}^d$. A lattice $\mathcal{L}$ generated by a basis $\mathbf{B}$ which is a set of linearly independent vectors $\{\mathbf{b}_0, \mathbf{b}_1, ..., \mathbf{b}_{d-1}\}$ as $\mathcal{L}(\mathbf{B}) = \{\sum_{i=0}^{d-1} v_i \cdot \mathbf{b}_i \mid v_i \in \mathbb{Z}\}$. Where d is the dimension of the lattice and n is the rank of the lattice. If $d = n$, the lattice is called a full rank lattice, and if $n \geq 2$, the lattice has an infinite basis. For ease of explanation, in the following definition we will use the full rank lattice.*

Definition 2 (Gram-Schmidt Orthogonalization and Projective Sublattice). *For a given lattice basis $\mathbf{B}$, we define its Gram-Schmidt orthogonal basis $\mathbf{B}^* = [\mathbf{b}_0^*, \mathbf{b}_1^*, ..., \mathbf{b}_{d-1}^*]$ where $\mathbf{b}_i^* = \sum_{j=0}^{i-1} \mu_{ij} \mathbf{b}_j^*$ and $\mu_{ij} = \frac{\langle \mathbf{b}_i, \mathbf{b}_j^* \rangle}{\|\mathbf{b}_j^*\|^2}$. The* *determinant of the lattice is $det(\mathcal{L}(\mathbf{B})) = \prod_0^{d-1} \parallel \mathbf{b}_i^* \parallel$. We denote the orthogonal projection by $\pi_i : \mathbb{R}^d \to span(\mathbf{b}_0, \mathbf{b}_1, ..., \mathbf{b}_{i-1})^{\perp}$ for $i \in \{0, 1, 2, .., d-1\}$, and π is used as the identity map. Denote the local projected sublattice $\mathcal{L}_{[l:r]} = (\pi_l(\mathbf{b}_l), ..., \pi_l(\mathbf{b}_{r-1})))$ and the basis is $\mathbf{B}_{[l:r]}$.*

Definition 3 (Dual Lattice). *For a lattice $\mathcal{L}$, the dual lattice of $\mathcal{L}$ is defined as: $\tilde{\mathcal{L}} = \{\mathbf{w} \in span(\mathcal{L}) | \langle \mathbf{w}, \mathbf{v} \rangle \in \mathbb{Z}$ for all $\mathbf{v} \in \mathcal{L}\}$. It is a classical fact that $det(\tilde{\mathcal{L}}) = det(\mathcal{L})^{-1}$. For a lattice basis $\mathbf{B}$, denote $\mathbf{D}$ as the unique matrix so that $\mathbf{B}^{\mathbf{T}}\mathbf{D} = \mathbf{D}^{\mathbf{T}}\mathbf{B} = \mathbf{I}$. Then $\tilde{\mathcal{L}}(\mathbf{B}) = \mathcal{L}(\mathbf{D})$ and $\mathbf{D}$ is the dual lattice basis of $\mathbf{B}$. Given a lattice basis $\mathbf{B}$, its dual basis $\mathbf{D}$ is computable in polynomial time, but requires at least $\Omega(d^3)$ bit operations using matrix inversion.*

Definition 4 (Shortest Vector Problem). *The Shortest Vector Problem (SVP) is given a lattice basis $\mathbf{B}$, find the shortest no-zero vector in $\mathcal{L}(\mathbf{B})$. We use $\lambda_1(\mathcal{L})$ as the norm of the shortest vector. The definition also applies to sublattice and projected sublattice. In this work we named the SVP-Oracle as the algorithm for solving the SVP.*

Definition 5 (SVP Reduction and Dual SVP Reduction). *In this work, we will often modify the lattice basis $\mathbf{B}$ to make that satisfied $\alpha \parallel \mathbf{b}_0 \parallel \leq \lambda_1(\mathcal{L}(\mathbf{B}))$ for some $\alpha \leq 1$, we denote this process as SVP reduction. Moreover, the dual SVP reduction is to modify the basis $\mathbf{B}$ such that its dual basis $\mathbf{D}$ satisfies $\alpha \parallel \mathbf{d}_{d-1} \parallel \leq \lambda_1(\tilde{\mathcal{L}}(\mathbf{B}))$.*

Definition 6 (Hermite's Constant). *Minkowski's theorem relates the length of the shortest vector in a lattice to its dimension, it states $\lambda_1(\mathcal{L}(\mathbf{B})) \leq \sqrt{\gamma_d} det(\mathcal{L}(\mathbf{B}))^{1/d}$. The γ_d is Hermite's constant states $\Omega(d) \leq \gamma_d \leq d$.*

Definition 7 (Gaussian Heuristic). *There is another way to evaluate the length of the shortest vector in a lattice. According to the Gaussian heuristic, we can predict the shortest vector lengths as: $\lambda_1(\mathcal{L}) \approx \sqrt{d/2\pi e} \cdot det(\mathcal{L}(\mathbf{B}))^{1/d}$.*

2.3 Lattice Reduction

Lattice reduction is the process of taking a basis for a given lattice $\mathcal{L}$ and finding subsequent basis of $\mathcal{L}$ with shorter and closer to orthogonal vectors. Generally, the solution of the SVP is typically obtained by selecting the first vector in the output of the lattice reduction algorithm. Here we recall several lattice reduction algorithms and the definitions of reduced basis.

Definition 8 (LLL). *The LLL algorithm [15] is a polynomial-time reduction algorithm. A basis $\mathbf{B}$ can be defined as an LLL reduced basis if it satisfies the following two definitions:*

$$(\forall 0 \leq i \leq d-1, j < i) \quad \mu_{i,j} \leq \frac{1}{2} \tag{1}$$

$$(\forall 0 \leq i < d) \quad \varepsilon \parallel \mathbf{b}_i^* \parallel^2 \leq \parallel \mathbf{b}_{i+1}^* \parallel^2 + \mu_{i+1,i}^2 \parallel \mathbf{b}_i^* \parallel \tag{2}$$

where $\varepsilon \in (\frac{1}{4}, 1]$ is a reduction parameter. A d-dimension LLL reduced basis theoretically has a short vector with a approximation factor $\delta_0 = (4/3)^{(d-1)/4d}$. But in practice, LLL algorithm performs better [12].

Definition 9 (BKZ). *The BKZ algorithm [23] can be seen as a generalisation of the LLL algorithm to larger blocksizes. An BKZ-β reduced basis satisfies two definitions:*

$$(\forall 0 \le i \le d-1, j < i) \quad \mu_{i,j} \le \frac{1}{2} \tag{3}$$

$$\| \mathbf{b}_i^* \| \le \lambda_1(\mathcal{L}_{[i:min(i+\beta,d)]}) \tag{4}$$

When $\beta = 2$, the BKZ reduction can be seen as LLL reduction. When $\beta = d$, it calls HKZ reduction. HKZ reduction is the strongest reduced basis in theory, but it is difficult to achieve in experiment. The blocksizes β is the most important parameter in BKZ algorithm. During the BKZ reduction process, it is necessary to repeatedly call the SVP-Oracle in the β-sublattice. Therefore, the blocksizes is closely related to the algorithm's running time and output quality. For a BKZ-β reduced basis, the $\mathbf{b}_0$ satisfies $\| \mathbf{b}_0 \| \le 2\gamma_\beta^{\frac{d-1}{2(\beta-1)} + \frac{3}{2}} \cdot det(\mathbf{B})^{1/d}$. A brief description of the BKZ algorithm is given in Algorithm 1.

Algorithm 1. The Block Korkin-Zolotarev (BKZ) algorithm

Input: A basis $\mathbf{B} = [\mathbf{b}_0, \mathbf{b}_1, ..., \mathbf{b}_{d-1}]$, a blocksizes $\beta \in \{2, ..., d\}$.
Output: The basis $[\mathbf{b}_0, \mathbf{b}_1, ..., \mathbf{b}_{d-1}]$ is BKZ-β reduced.
1: Compute the Gram-Schmidt triangular matrix μ and $\| \mathbf{b}_0^* \|^2, \| \mathbf{b}_1^* \|^2, ..., \| \mathbf{b}_{d-1}^* \|^2$

2: $z \leftarrow 0; j \leftarrow 0;LLL(\mathbf{b}_0, \mathbf{b}_1, ..., \mathbf{b}_{d-1})$ //LLL reduce the input basis and update μ
3: **while** $z < d - 1$ **do**
4:     $j \leftarrow (j \mod (d-1)) + 1; k \leftarrow min(j + \beta - 1, d); h \leftarrow min(k+1, d)$
5:     $v \leftarrow$ SVP-Oracle $(\mu_{[j,k]}, \| \mathbf{b}_j^* \|, ..., \| \mathbf{b}_k^* \|)$
6:     **if** $v \ne (1, 0, ..., 0)$ **then**
7:         $z \leftarrow 0;$ LLL$(\mathbf{b}_0, ..., \sum_{i=j}^k v_i \mathbf{b}_i, \mathbf{b}_j, ..., \mathbf{b}_h, \mu)$
8:     **else**
9:         $z \leftarrow z + 1$;LLL$(\mathbf{b}_0, ..., \mathbf{b}_h, \mu)$
10:    **end if**
11: **end while**
12: **return** $\mathbf{B}$

Definition 10 (Slide Reduction). *There is a variant reduction algorithm called slide reduction [11]. Slide reduction also requires parameter blocksizes k, but k must be divided by dimensions d. The Algorithm 2 is a brief description of slide reduction algorithm.*

The slide reduction includes two processes. First, it calls SVP-Oracle on the projected sublattice of the primal lattice, and moves the whole after an SVP-Oracle has finished. Then call SVP-Oracle on the projected sublattic of the dual

---

Algorithm 2. slide reduction

Input: A basis $\mathbf{B} = [\mathbf{b}_0, \mathbf{b}_1, ..., \mathbf{b}_{d-1}]$, a blocksize k and need $d = nk$
Output: A slide reduced basis $[\mathbf{b}_0, \mathbf{b}_1, ..., \mathbf{b}_{d-1}]$ with blocksize k.
1: **while** $\mathbf{B}$ is modified by the loop **do**
2:     **while** $\mathbf{B}$ is modified by the loop **do**
3:         LLL $(\mathbf{B})$;
4:         **for** each $i \in [0, d-1]$ **do**
5:             SVP reduction $\mathbf{B}_{[ik+1, ik+k]}$;
6:         **end for**
7:     **end while**
8:     **for** each $i \in [0, d-2]$ **do**
9:         Dual SVP reduction $\mathbf{B}_{[ik+1, ik+k]}$;
10:    **end for**
11: **end while**
12: **return** $\mathbf{B}$

---

lattice. The slide reduction can be proved to be terminate in polynomial time. The slide reduction outputs basis is satisfy $\| \mathbf{b}_0 \| \leq \gamma_k^{\frac{d-1}{2(k-1)}} \cdot det(\mathbf{B})^{1/d}$. *It can be observed that the approximation factor is slightly better than BKZ algorithm. However, slide reduction has been reported to be greatly inferior to BKZ in experiments [12].*

3 Self-dual BKZ and Pump

3.1 Self-dual BKZ

In order to bridge the gap between theory and practice and to better realise the theoretical benefits of slide reduction, Micciancio and Walter design the Self-Dual BKZ algorithm [16]. The Algorithm 3 is the pseudo code of Self-Dual BKZ.

Algorithm 3. Self-Dual BKZ

Input: A basis $\mathbf{B} = [\mathbf{b}_0, \mathbf{b}_1, ..., \mathbf{b}_{d-1}]$, a blocksizes k
Output: A k-reduced basis $\mathbf{B}'$
1: **do:**
2:     **for** $i = 0, 1, ..., d - k$
3:         SVP reduction $\mathbf{B}_{[i, i+k+1]}$ using SVP-Oracle
4:     **for** $i = d - k + 1, ..., 0$
5:         Dual SVP reduction $\mathbf{B}_{[i, i+k+1]}$ using SVP-Oracle
6: **while** $\mathbf{B}$ is modified
7: **return** $\mathbf{B}$

Like slide reduction, Self-Dual BKZ also works on the primal lattice basis and the dual lattice basis. However, in Self-Dual BKZ, the reduction context is only moved one dimension at a time. At the end of the algorithm, it outputs a $k-$reduced basis that satisfies the following definition:

Definition 11. *A basis* $\mathbf{B} = [\mathbf{b}_0, ..., \mathbf{b}_d]$ *is* k-reduced *if either* $n < k$, *or it satisfies the following conditions:*

- $\| b_k^* \|^{-1} = \lambda_1(\tilde{\mathcal{L}}(\mathbf{B}_{[0,k]}))$, *and*
- *for some SVP reduced basis* $\tilde{\mathbf{B}}$ *of* $\mathcal{L}(\mathbf{B}_{[0,k]})$, $\pi_2([\tilde{\mathbf{B}}|\mathbf{B}_{[k+1,d]}])$ *is* $k-$reduced.

Then they prove that the worst case output quality of Self-Dual BKZ is at least as good as the worst case behaviour of BKZ using the following theorem:

Theorem 1. *If* $\mathbf{B}$ *is* $k-$reduced, *then* $\lambda_1(\mathbf{B}_{[0,k]}) \leq \gamma_k^{\frac{d-1}{2(k-1)}} \cdot det(\mathbf{B})^{1/d}$.

This theorem has been proved in [16]. However, according to the experimental comparison between BKZ and Self-Dual BKZ, there is still a small gap in the accuracy of the results obtained by these two algorithms. But as the blocksizes increases, the gap tends to decreases.

3.2 The General Sieve Kernel and Pump

In this part, we give a brief introduction of The General Sieve Kernel (G6K) and Pump algorithm. G6K is an abstract state machine that supports different lattice sieving algorithms and lattice reduction stage [4]. The basic stage of G6K is Pump, an SVP-Oracle that finds short lattice vectors whose projection vector is the shortest in corresponding projection sublattice. A description of Pump is given in Algorithm 4.

It can be seen that Pump is not a specific algorithm, but a class of strategies that support multiple sieving algorithms. Pump combines two methods that have greatly improved sieving in practice [9,14]. Compared to the previous Sieving and enumeration, G6K is not just an oracle for solving SVP. It summarises previous algorithms and computational strategies, making it easy to implement new ideas on it. The records for the Darmstadt Lattice Challenges are currently held by G6K and its variants [22].

3.3 Self-dual BKZ Based on Pump

The latest implementation of Self-Dual BKZ is based on enumeration [16]. Considering the excellent performance of sieving, we use Pump as the SVP-Oracle and Dual SVP-Oracle in Self-Dual BKZ. We then add a preprocessing step to the algorithm before the actual execution. Finally, we modify the algorithm's termination condition to better match the sieving algorithm. Our algorithm is described in Algorithm 5.

Algorithm 4. Pump

Input: B, κ, β, $ds = f, stn = 30$
Output: a reduce basis **B**
1: $r = \kappa + \beta; l = max\{\kappa + f + 1, r - stn\}; lib = \kappa; L = \emptyset$
2: LLL($\mathbf{B}_{[\kappa,r]}$)
3: $L =$ Gauss Sieve($\mathbf{B}_{[l,r]}, L$)
4: **while** $l > \kappa + f$ **do**
5:     extend all vectors in list L 1 dimension , l=l-1
6:     $L =$ Sieve ($\mathbf{B}_{[l,r]}, L$)
7: **end while**
8: **while** $d > 1$ & $ilb < \kappa + ds$ **do**
9:     BL = best lifts (L) //base on insertion function compute a insert position
10:    **if** BL $\neq \emptyset$ **then**
11:        ii = BL.index (max (BL)) //Find the best insert position
12:        Insert $\mathbf{v}_{ii}$ into local project basis $\mathbf{B}_{[\kappa,r]}$
13:        ilb = ii+1
14:    **else**
15:        shrink all $\mathbf{v} \in L$ 1 dimension
16:    **end if**
17:    $L=$ Sieve ($\mathbf{B}_{[l,r]}, L$)
18:    l=l+1
19: **end while**
20: **return B**

Algorithm 5. Self-Dual BKZ with Pump (SDBP)

Input: A lattice basis **B**, a blocksizes range $\{k_1, k_2, ..., k_n\}$
Output: A k_n-reduced basis $\mathbf{B}'$
1: **for** each $k_i \in \{k_1, k_2, , ..., k_n\}$ **do**
2:     **for** $i = 0, 1, ..., k_i$:
3:         **Pump** ($\mathbf{B}_{[i:k_i+i]}$)
4:     **end for**
5:     **for** $i = d - k_i + 1, ..., 0$:
6:         **Pump** ($\tilde{\mathbf{B}}_{[i,i+k_i-1]}$)
7:     **end for**
8: **end for**
9: **return B**

Small Blocksizes BKZ as Preprocessing. Before the actual execution of the algorithm, we use a small blocksizes BKZ as preprocessing, which takes a negligible time compared to the total algorithm running time. It can provide a better basis than the initial basis. In other words, when the algorithm actually begin, the vectors of the input lattice basis are shorter and closer together orthogonally, and this can speed up the sieving.

Sieving as SVP-Oracle. The core idea of sieving is to generate a list to store lattice vectors, and generate new short vectors based on the calculation between vector pairs. So the main limitation to the performance of the sieving is the space complexity, but with the development of hardware, the advantages of the sieving are gradually being reflected.

Pump can find the shortest vector in an n dimension sublattice instead of searching in the whole d dimension lattice, which is the key to its computational efficiency. This relies on dimension for free [9] and progressive sieve [14]. The main idea of dimension for free is to use the sieving lattice vectors that contain some information of the lattice:

$$L := Sieve(\mathcal{L}_n) = \{\mathbf{x} \in \mathcal{L}_n| \parallel \mathbf{x} \parallel \leq \sqrt{4/3} \cdot gh(\mathcal{L}_n)\}$$

If the projection of the target vector $\mathbf{s}$ satisfies $\pi_d(\mathbf{s}) \leq \sqrt{4/3} \cdot gh(\mathcal{L}_n)$ then it can recover $\mathbf{s}$ in the n-dimension sublattice. This condition depends on the input lattice basis, so preprocessing is required. During the execution of Pump, the dimension of sieving increase gradually instead of directly running the sieving on the entire sublattice. This ensures that when the execution approaches the whole sublattice, the sieving's list already contains many short lattice vectors. It can make the Sieving more efficient on the whole sublattice.

Progressively Increase the Blocksizes and Modify the Abort Condition. Unlike the original Self-Dual BKZ, we use the strategy of G6K: gradually increase the blocksizes until to the target number. This also changes the termination condition of the algorithm. In the original Self-Dual BKZ, if the lattice basis is not improved after multiple checks, it will abort the algorithm process. Since the sieving is a randomized algorithm, each increase in sieving dimension will generate new short vectors, even if they are not the target vector. These short vectors are still meaningful for subsequent calculations. Hence we modify the termination condition, and the algorithm will not abort until the last SVP-Oracle is completed.

4   Experiments

For an experiment comparison, we implement SDBP using G6K's Pump [3], and the sieving algorithm in Pump is HK3-Sieve [13]. Our test lattice basis include ideal lattice and SVP Challange lattice, both are generated from Darmstadt Lattice Challenges [22] with seed 0. Our operating environment is based on Intel Xeon 6226R and Nvidia RTX3080Ti. We define the approximation factor $\phi = \parallel \mathbf{b}_0 \parallel /(\sqrt{d/2\pi e} \cdot det(\mathcal{L})^{1/d})$. Based on that the experimental results are measured.

4.1   Compare with Self-dual BKZ in FPLLL

In order to test the improvement of our algorithm, we compare it with the previous implementation and report our results in Table 1, 2, 3, 4, 5 and 6. To compare the time cost by the FPLLL's Self-Dual BKZ [24] and our SDBP, we choose some blocksizes as input parameters of FPLLL's Self-Dual BKZ, get the short vector of its output, and compute the approximation factor ϕ. Then we try to get a close (or better) result by our SDBP in the same lattice basis. Considering that sieving is a randomization algorithm, each parameter was run 7 times and then the average was calculated as the final result.

Table 1. Compare the running time of FPLLL's Self-Dual BKZ and SDBP achieve the same (or better) approximation factor ϕ in 100-dimension ideal lattice with index 101

	FPLLL	SDBP	FPLLL	SDBP	FPLLL	SDBP	FPLLL	SDBP
ϕ	1.391	1.399	1.336	1.327	1.278	1.254	1.260	1.152
Running time (s)	270	158	318	173	8594	719	86654	2840
Blocksizes	40	(40:55)	41	(40:56)	45	(40:70)	50	(40:80)

Table 2. Same as Table 1, but in 110-dimension ideal lattice with index 121

	FPLLL	SDBP	FPLLL	SDBP	FPLLL	SDBP	FPLLL	SDBP
ϕ	1.517	1.516	1.415	1.415	1.301	1.263	1.327	1.326
Running time (s)	288	70	1938	535	18862	2235	158143	1035
Blocksizes	40	(40:47)	43	(40:63)	47	(40:80)	50	(40:70)

Table 3. Same as Table 1, but in 120-dimension ideal lattice with index 248

	FPLLL	SDBP	FPLLL	SDBP	FPLLL	SDBP	FPLLL	SDBP
ϕ	1.630	1.601	1.574	1.521	1.582	1.559	1.576	1.374
Running time (s)	287	128	1936	940	4859	425	151696	2683
Blocksizes	40	(40:50)	43	(40:67)	45	(40:60)	50	(40:80)

We tested our SDBP algorithm in ideal lattice with algebraic structure and integer lattice without algebraic structure, choosing 3 sets of lattice dimensions between 100 and 120 and 4 sets of blocksizes between 40 and 50. The results indicate that compare to the previous Self-Dual BKZ which is based on enumeration, our SDBP can obtain approximate (or even better) output in less time though with larger blocksizes. However, given that time is the most significant factor affecting the practical use of algorithms, we believe that using larger blocksizes is acceptable.

Table 4. Same as Table 1, but in 100 dimension SVP Challenge lattice

	FPLLL	SDBP	FPLLL	SDBP	FPLLL	SDBP	FPLLL	SDBP
ϕ	1.391	1.384	1.368	1.324	1.304	1.262	1.267	1.219
Running time (s)	304	42	893	157	15100	808	79323	1734
Blocksizes	40	(40:45)	43	(40:55)	47	(40:70)	50	(40:80)

Table 5. Same as Table 1, but in 110 dimension SVP Challenge lattice

	FPLLL	SDBP	FPLLL	SDBP	FPLLL	SDBP	FPLLL	SDBP
ϕ	1.509	1.467	1.444	1.424	1.382	1.383	1.388	1.274
Running time (s)	428	181	4897	268	16391	1039	164718	2353
Blocksizes	40	(40:55)	45	(40:58)	47	(40:70)	50	(40:80)

Table 6. Same as Table 1, but in 120 dimension SVP Challenge lattice

	FPLLL	SDBP	FPLLL	SDBP	FPLLL	SDBP	FPLLL	SDBP
ϕ	1.662	1.652	1.566	1.543	1.445	1.439	1.484	1.437
Running time (s)	336	100	1741	417	30259	2851	139032	1881
Blocksizes	40	(40:48)	43	(40:60)	47	(40:80)	50	(40:75)

4.2   Compare to Pump-and-Jump BKZ

In this part, we will compare the differences between Dual BKZ and Original BKZ in practical experiments. Our choice for comparison is G6K's default BKZ algorithm which is called Pump and Jump BKZ (pnj-BKZ). The pnj-BKZ also use Pump as SVP-Oracle, and it was the best performing algorithm for the present. Same as before, for each parameter we run 7 times to calculate the average values as the result. Based on the result of the experiment, we created the Fig. 1, Table 7 and Table 8.

Similarly, we test our SDBP on different sets of lattice dimensions and blocksizes. There are 6 sets of lattices and 7 sets of blocksizes. Our SDBP has a similar running time to the pnj-BKZ. But in terms of output quality, there is a small gap between the pnj-BKZ and the SDBP. As the blocksizes increases, the gap shows a decreasing trend. According to [16] these two algorithms will intersect at blocksizes 80. However, considering the effect of sieving on the blocksizes, we predict that the intersection point of SDBP and pnj-BKZ might be greater than 80. This is an issue that still needs to be researched for further optimisation.

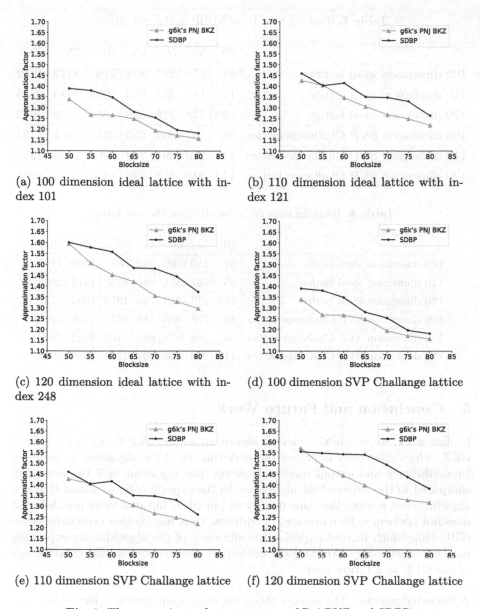

(a) 100 dimension ideal lattice with index 101

(b) 110 dimension ideal lattice with index 121

(c) 120 dimension ideal lattice with index 248

(d) 100 dimension SVP Challange lattice

(e) 110 dimension SVP Challange lattice

(f) 120 dimension SVP Challange lattice

Fig. 1. The approximate factor compare of Pnj-BKZ and SDBP

Table 7. Running time (s) of SDBP in the test lattice

	50	55	60	65	70	75	80
100 dimension ideal lattice	91	158	297	524	719	1173	1912
110 dimension ideal lattice	111	181	357	655	1035	1483	2235
120 dimension ideal lattice	128	228	425	858	1389	1938	2683
100 dimension SVP Challange lattice	90	157	304	550	808	1161	1734
110 dimension SVP Challange lattice	114	200	391	749	1066	1552	2353
120 dimension SVP Challange lattice	112	232	417	836	1235	1881	2978

Table 8. Running time (s) of pnj-BKZ in the test lattice

	50	55	60	65	70	75	80
100 dimension ideal lattice	81	150	290	565	887	1409	2186
110 dimension ideal lattice	95	181	351	667	973	1613	2569
120 dimension ideal lattice	115	213	419	793	1373	1995	2731
100 dimension SVP Challange lattice	84	158	308	580	947	1450	2217
110 dimension SVP Challange lattice	96	188	377	690	1102	1623	2609
120 dimension SVP Challange lattice	115	216	404	804	1214	1949	2998

5 Conclusion and Future Work

In this work, we use lattice sieving algorithm as the SVP-Oracle in Self-Dual BKZ, which effectively improves the performance of the algorithm in terms of time efficiency and output quality. However, our algorithm still has some gap compared to the current best algorithm. In the experiments, we found that our algorithm can achieve the same quality as pnj-BKZ, but due to its instability, it does not perform well on average. In addition, G6K has another version based on GPU [10], which further improves the efficiency of the algorithm by exploiting hardware technology. We leave the optimized implementation taking advantage of the GPU as a future work.

Acknowledgement. The authors thank the anonymous reviewers for helpful comments and suggestions. This work was supported by the National Key Research and Development Program of China (Grant No. 2021YFB3100200).

References

1. Ajtai, M.: Generating hard instances of lattice problems. In: Proceedings of the Twenty-Eighth Annual ACM Symposium on Theory of Computing, pp. 99–108 (1996)

2. Ajtai, M., Kumar, R., Sivakumar, D.: A sieve algorithm for the shortest lattice vector problem. In: Proceedings of the Thirty-Third Annual ACM Symposium on Theory of Computing, STOC 2001, pp. 601–610. Association for Computing Machinery, New York (2001). https://doi.org/10.1145/380752.380857

3. Albrecht, M.R.: The General Sieve Kernel. https://github.com/fplll/g6k

4. Albrecht, M.R., Ducas, L., Herold, G., Kirshanova, E., Postlethwaite, E.W., Stevens, M.: The general sieve kernel and new records in lattice reduction. In: Ishai, Y., Rijmen, V. (eds.) EUROCRYPT 2019. LNCS, vol. 11477, pp. 717–746. Springer, Cham (2019). https://doi.org/10.1007/978-3-030-17656-3_25

5. Aono, Y., Wang, Y., Hayashi, T., Takagi, T.: Improved progressive BKZ algorithms and their precise cost estimation by sharp simulator. In: Fischlin, M., Coron, J.-S. (eds.) EUROCRYPT 2016. LNCS, vol. 9665, pp. 789–819. Springer, Heidelberg (2016). https://doi.org/10.1007/978-3-662-49890-3_30

6. Becker, A., Ducas, L., Gama, N., Laarhoven, T.: New directions in nearest neighbor searching with applications to lattice sieving, pp. 10–24 (2016). https://epubs.siam.org/doi/abs/10.1137/1.9781611974331.ch2

7. Becker, A., Gama, N., Joux, A.: Speeding-up lattice sieving without increasing the memory, using sub-quadratic nearest neighbor search. Cryptology ePrint Archive, Paper 2015/522 (2015). https://eprint.iacr.org/2015/522

8. Chen, Y., Nguyen, P.Q.: BKZ 2.0: better lattice security estimates. In: Lee, D.H., Wang, X. (eds.) ASIACRYPT 2011. LNCS, vol. 7073, pp. 1–20. Springer, Heidelberg (2011). https://doi.org/10.1007/978-3-642-25385-0_1

9. Ducas, L.: Shortest vector from lattice sieving: a few dimensions for free. In: Nielsen, J.B., Rijmen, V. (eds.) EUROCRYPT 2018. LNCS, vol. 10820, pp. 125–145. Springer, Cham (2018). https://doi.org/10.1007/978-3-319-78381-9_5

10. Ducas, L., Stevens, M., van Woerden, W.: Advanced lattice sieving on GPUs, with tensor cores. In: Canteaut, A., Standaert, F.-X. (eds.) EUROCRYPT 2021. LNCS, vol. 12697, pp. 249–279. Springer, Cham (2021). https://doi.org/10.1007/978-3-030-77886-6_9

11. Gama, N., Nguyen, P.Q.: Finding short lattice vectors within mordell's inequality. In: Proceedings of the 40th Annual ACM Symposium on Theory of Computing, Victoria, British Columbia, Canada, 17–20 May 2008 (2008)

12. Gama, N., Nguyen, P.Q.: Predicting lattice reduction. In: Smart, N. (ed.) EUROCRYPT 2008. LNCS, vol. 4965, pp. 31–51. Springer, Heidelberg (2008). https://doi.org/10.1007/978-3-540-78967-3_3

13. Herold, G., Kirshanova, E.: Improved algorithms for the approximate k-list problem in euclidean norm. In: Fehr, S. (ed.) PKC 2017. LNCS, vol. 10174, pp. 16–40. Springer, Heidelberg (2017). https://doi.org/10.1007/978-3-662-54365-8_2

14. Laarhoven, T., Mariano, A.: Progressive lattice sieving. In: Lange, T., Steinwandt, R. (eds.) PQCrypto 2018. LNCS, vol. 10786, pp. 292–311. Springer, Cham (2018). https://doi.org/10.1007/978-3-319-79063-3_14

15. Lenstra, H., Lenstra, A.K., Lovász, L.: Factoring polynomials with rational coefficients (1982)

16. Micciancio, D., Walter, M.: Practical, predictable lattice basis reduction. In: Fischlin, M., Coron, J.-S. (eds.) EUROCRYPT 2016. LNCS, vol. 9665, pp. 820–849. Springer, Heidelberg (2016). https://doi.org/10.1007/978-3-662-49890-3_31

17. Nakamura, S., Ikematsu, Y., Yasuda, M.: Dynamic self-dual DeepBKZ lattice reduction with free dimensions. In: Giri, D., Buyya, R., Ponnusamy, S., De, D., Adamatzky, A., Abawajy, J.H. (eds.) Proceedings of the Sixth International Conference on Mathematics and Computing. AISC, vol. 1262, pp. 377–391. Springer, Singapore (2021). https://doi.org/10.1007/978-981-15-8061-1_30

18. Nguyen, P.Q., Vidick, T.: Sieve algorithms for the shortest vector problem are practical. J. Math. Cryptol. **2**(2), 181–207 (2008). https://doi.org/10.1515/JMC.2008.009

19. Plantard, T., Schneider, M.: Creating a challenge for ideal lattices. Cryptology ePrint Archive, Paper 2013/039 (2013). https://eprint.iacr.org/2013/039

20. Pohst, M.: On the computation of lattice vectors of minimal length, successive minima and reduced bases with applications. ACM SIGSAM Bull. **15**(1), 37–44 (1981)

21. Regev, O.: On lattices, learning with errors, random linear codes, and cryptography. In: Proceedings of the Thirty-Seventh Annual ACM Symposium on Theory of Computing, pp. 84–93 (2005)

22. Schneider, M., Gama, N.: Darmstadt SVP Challenges (2010). https://www.latticechallenge.org/svp-challenge/index.php

23. Schnorr, C.P., Euchner, M.: Lattice basis reduction: improved practical algorithms and solving subset sum problems. In: Budach, L. (ed.) FCT 1991. LNCS, vol. 529, pp. 68–85. Springer, Heidelberg (1991). https://doi.org/10.1007/3-540-54458-5_51

24. development team, T.F.: fplll, a lattice reduction library, Version: 5.4.4 (2023). https://github.com/fplll/fplll

A Certificateless Designated Verifier Sanitizable Signature

Yonghua Zhan[1], Bixia Yi[1], Yang Yang[1,2(✉)], Renjie He[1], and Rui Shi[3]

[1] School of Computer and Big Data, Fuzhou University, Fuzhou, Fujian, China
[2] School of Computing and Information Systems, Singapore Management University,
Singapore, Singapore
yang.yang.research@gmail.com
[3] Beijing Electronic Science and Technology Institute, Beijing, China

Abstract. Sanitizable Signature is a digital signature variant that
enables modification operations, allowing sanitizers to alter the signed
data in a regulated manner without requiring any interaction with the
original signer. It is widely used in scenarios such as healthcare data
privacy protection, social networks, secure routing, etc. In existing sanitizable signature schemes, anyone can verify the validity and authenticity
of the sanitized message, which results in costly certificate management
overhead or complicated key escrow problems. To address these challenges, a designated verifier certificateless sanitizable signature scheme is
proposed. This scheme introduces the concept of a designated verifier into
sanitizable signatures, allowing sanitizers to specify verifier for the sanitized message. Only the specified verifiers can verify the validity of the
message/signature pair, ensuring that the message information remains
confidential to parties other than the designated verifiers. Security analysis demonstrates that the proposed scheme satisfies the properties of
unforgeability, immutability, privacy and non-transferability. Comparative analysis demonstrates that the proposed scheme provides additional
support for designated verifiers compared to traditional sanitizable signature schemes, while eliminating certificate management and key escrow
issues. We have conducted an experiment, and the results demonstrate
that the proposed scheme displays excellent efficiency.

Keywords: Data Sharing · Sanitizable Signature · Certificateless ·
Designated Verifier

1 Introduction

Given the swift advancement and integration of technologies such as cloud computing, big data, and the Internet of Things (IoT), data is being shared among
various users and organizations, and its value is becoming increasingly significant. However, as data empowers and enables intelligence, it also faces severe
privacy protection challenges. To strengthen the management and protection
of data, many countries have enacted relevant laws and regulations. Examples

© The Author(s), under exclusive license to Springer Nature Singapore Pte Ltd. 2024
H. Yang and R. Lu (Eds.): FCS 2023, CCIS 1992, pp. 337–352, 2024.
https://doi.org/10.1007/978-981-99-9331-4_23

include China's "Data Security Law of the People's Republic of China" and "Personal Information Protection Law of the People's Republic of China," the European Union's General Data Protection Regulation (GDPR), and the United States' Health Insurance Portability and Accountability Act (HIPAA) for medical data security [3]. These regulations aim to establish sound data security governance systems and enhance data security capabilities.

Digital signatures play a crucial role in cryptographic techniques, guaranteeing the authenticity and integrity of data. Any slight modification to signed data will result in the failure of signature verification. While digital signatures provide a solid security foundation for identity authentication and data integrity, they also limit the ability to make reasonable modifications to signed data in certain application scenarios, hindering users from flexibly and efficiently utilizing documents. For example, when the government discloses documents, sensitive data involving personal information and national secrets often need to be redacted. If traditional digital signature schemes are used to sign the documents, citizens are unable to verify the authenticity of the disclosed information due to the partial modification of the document's data. To ensure the validity of the modified document, it would require the signer to re-sign it. If there are numerous versions of modified documents, this method would incur significant computational overhead. Similarly, in scenarios such as electronic health records [8,14], multimedia forensics, e-commerce, and smart grids, using only traditional digital signature schemes cannot efficiently verify the validity of shared sub-documents. To address this issue, sanitizable signatures provide an effective solution [1].

Sanitizable Signature permits a semi-trusted intermediary, referred to as the sanitizer, to meticulously and non-interactively modify the signed data, all the while retaining the capability to generate a new signature that can be validated effectively. It ensures the integrity and authenticity of shared data and enables the flexible hiding of specific sensitive information based on different data sharing scenarios and recipients, thus ensuring data security while harnessing the value of the data and promoting the development of data-driven applications.

Sanitizable signatures enable the hiding of sensitive data by the sanitizer for privacy protection. However, in practice, the unmodified parts of the sanitized document may still contain private information. Unfortunately, most sanitizable signature schemes do not consider the risk of information leakage from these unmodified parts during the data sharing process. Taking medical data as an example, after a doctor signs an electronic medical record, the patient can act as the sanitizer to hide sensitive information before submitting the sanitized record to an insurance company for claims processing. At this point, the insurance company may sell the patient's medical information to interested parties, and any other party that obtains the sanitized document can verify its validity, posing a severe privacy threat to the patient. Therefore, it is necessary to adopt a Designated Verifier mechanism to limit the scope of data verification and ensure that only specific recipients can authenticate and validate the integrity of the shared data [2,11].

Sanitizable signatures are typically based on traditional public key cryptography, requiring a trusted certificate authority to issue certificates for authenticating user public keys. As the number of users increases, this leads to expensive certificate management overhead. To tackle this issue, several identity-based sanitizable signature schemes [7,10,12,13] and attribute-based sanitizable signature schemes [4,6] have been proposed. The former uses unique public identity information of users, such as ID numbers, phone numbers, and email addresses, as public keys, while the latter associates ciphertext and keys with attribute sets and access structures. However, these schemes face the issue of key escrow. The Private Key Generation Center (PKG) holds the master key for generating all user private keys, making the security of user keys entirely dependent on the PKG. This poses significant challenges to data privacy protection. Certificateless cryptography, on the other hand, offers a solution to the key escrow problem. In certificateless cryptography, the Key Generation Center (KGC) collaborates with users to generate complete private keys, eliminating the need for a central authority like the PKG [5,9,15].

Contribution. The primary contributions of this paper can be succinctly summarized as follow: addressing the issues of data leakage by data sharing parties in sanitizable signature schemes, as well as the challenges of certificate management and key escrow, we propose a designated verifier certificateless sanitizable signature scheme based on the idea of Universal Designated Verifier Signatures (UDVS).

- Firstly, the signer generates a message and signs it, and then sends it to the sanitizer via a secure channel. The sanitizer acts as both the sanitizer of the message and the holder of the UDVS signature. They specify the designated verifier for the sanitized message and its signature according to their specific requirements. Only the designated verifier can validate and have confidence in the validity of the message and its signature, ensuring that the message information remains confidential to parties other than the designated verifier.
- Secondly, the proposed scheme builds upon certificateless signatures, eliminating the necessity for complex certificate management and resolving the key escrow issue.
- Thirdly, by conducting formal security analysis, we establish that the scheme effectively safeguards against malicious users and a malicious Key Generation Center (KGC), ensuring unforgeability, immutability, privacy, and non-transferability.
- Fourthly, both experimental results and theoretical analysis substantiate that the performance of the proposed scheme surpasses that of comparable schemes in terms of efficiency and effectiveness.

2 System Model and Security Goals

2.1 System Model

Figure 1 illustrates the system model of the proposed scheme in this chapter. The system consists of four entities: Key Generation Center (KGC), Signer, Sanitizer, and Verifier. Each entity is defined as follows:

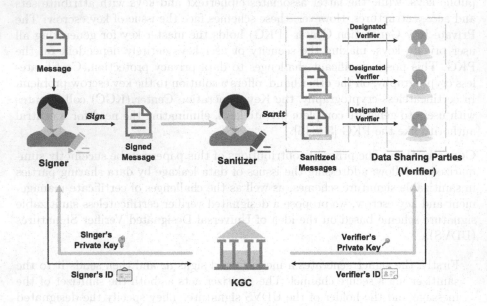

Fig. 1. System Model

- **Key Generation Center (KGC):** The Key Generation Center (KGC) assumes the responsibility of system initialization and generates the corresponding key pairs based on user identities. A segment of the user's private key is securely transmitted through a protected channel.
- **Signer:** The Signer assumes the responsibility for generating and signing message. They can define the content that can be sanitized and send the message and its signature to the Sanitizer through a secure channel.
- **Sanitizer:** The Sanitizer can sanitize sensitive data in the shared message, generate a new signature, and specify the Verifier to validate the sanitized message and its signature.
- **Verifier:** The Verifier is assigned by the data sharing party. Only the designated Verifier can validate the authenticity of the corresponding message.

2.2 Security Goals

In order to facilitate secure data sharing effectively, this scheme aims to accomplish the following objectives:

- **Unforgeability:** Only the signer, sanitizer, and designated verifier can generate valid signatures. No one else can forge a valid signature.
- **Immutability:** The sanitizer cannot modify the data blocks in the message that are not allowed to be sanitized.
- **Privacy:** Privacy guarantees that only the signer and sanitizer possess information regarding the sanitized portions of the data, preventing anyone else from obtaining such details.
- **Non-Transferability:** The designated verifier lacks the ability to prove the validity of the signature to third parties.

These objectives play a critical role in ensuring the security and integrity of the shared data while preserving the privacy of sensitive information.

3 The Proposed Scheme

3.1 Overview

This scheme implements a certificateless sanitizable signature scheme with designated verifiers, using the concepts of certificateless signatures and universal designated verifier signatures. In this scheme, the signer and verifiers obtain the certificateless signature key pair from the Key Generation Center (KGC). The signer first computes the certificateless signature on the message m and generates auxiliary information aux required for sanitization. The message/signature pair (m, s) and aux are then transmitted to the sanitizer through a secure channel. In the universal designated verifier signature scheme, the sanitizer assumes the role of the "signature holder". Upon receiving (m, s), the sanitizer first verifies its validity. If valid, the sanitizer utilizes the auxiliary information to sanitize the document, resulting in a sanitized document m' and a certificateless signature σ'. The sanitizer then designates a verifier for the message/signature pair (m', σ') and generates a designated verifier signature σ'' for it. This yields a message/signature pair (m', σ'') that can only be verified by the designated verifier.

3.2 Detail

The specific algorithm for the designated verifier sanitizable signature without certificates scheme is as follow:

$(pp, msk) \leftarrow Setup(\lambda)$. Input the security parameter λ, the KGC executes the $Setup$ algorithm to generate the system's public parameters PP and the system master key msk.

- Let the bilinear pairing $e : \mathbb{G} \times \mathbb{G} \to \mathbb{G}_T$, where $\mathbb{G}$ and $\mathbb{G}_T$ are respectively cyclic groups of prime order q for addition and multiplication. Let P be the generator of $\mathbb{G}$.
- Select the hash function $h_1 : \{0,1\}^* \to \mathbb{Z}_q^*$ and $H_1, H_2 : \{0,1\}^* \to \mathbb{G}^*$.
- Randomly choose $s \in \mathbb{Z}_p^*$, then let $msk = s$ and compute the main public key $P_{pub} = sP$

KGC keeps the msk in secret and output the system public parameter $pp = \{q, e, \mathbb{G}, \mathbb{G}_T, P, P_{pub}, h_1, h_2, H_1, H_2, H_3\}$.

$(pk_{Sig/Vrf}, sk_{Sig/Vrf}) \leftarrow KGen(pp, msk, ID_{Sig/Vrf})$. Input pp, msk and the identity of the signer ID_{Sig}, KGC interacts with the signer to execute the $KGen$ algorithm to generate the secret key pair (pk_{Sig}, sk_{Sig}) of the signer.

- Generating the secret value: the signer randomly chooses the secret value $s_{Sig} \in \mathbb{Z}_q^*$ and compute $P_{Sig} = s_{Sig}P$, $Q_{Sig} = H_1(ID_{Sig}||P_{Sig})$, and then sends Q_{Sig} to KGC.
- Generating public key: the signer generates the public key $pk_{Sig} = (P_{Sig}, Q_{Sig})$.
- Generating partial secret key: KGC computes the partial secret key of the signer $d_{Sig} = sQ_{Sig}$, and sends it to the signer through a secure channel.
- Generating private key: the signer generates the private key $sk_{Sig} = (d_{Sig}, s_{Sig})$.

And finally we get the secret key pair (pk_{Sig}, sk_{Sig}) of the signer.

Similarly, KGC interacts with the verifier and executes $(pk_{Vrf}, sk_{Vrf}) \leftarrow KGen(pp, msk, ID_{Vrf})$ to obtain the verifier's key pair (pk_{Vrf}, sk_{Vrf}).

$(m, \sigma, aux) \leftarrow Sign(pp, m, pk_{Sig}, sk_{Sig}, ID_{Sig}, ADM)$. Input the system public parameter pp, message m, the secret key pair (pk_{Sig}, sk_{Sig}), the identity of the signer ID_{Sig} and ADM, the signer executes $Sign$ algorithm to generate the signature σ for m, and generates the required aux for the sanitizable data blocks.

- Divide m to n data blocks $m = m_1||m_2||...||m_n$.
- For each data block $m_i (i \in [1, n])$, randomly chooses $t_i \in \mathbb{Z}_q^*$ and computes the signature for m_i as follow: Compute $T_i = t_iP$, $\alpha_i = h_1(ID_{Sig}||P_{Sig}||m_i||T_i)$ and $W = H_2(P_{pub})$. Then compute $\sigma_i = d_{Sig} + \alpha_i \cdot t_i \cdot W + s_{Sig} \cdot W = d_{Sig} + (\alpha_i \cdot t_i \cdot s_{Sig}) \cdot W$. And for each $i \in ADM$, computes the transformation value $\chi_i = t_i \cdot W$.
- Finally, the signer obtains he message/signature pair (m, σ) and aux, where $\sigma = (\{\sigma_i\}_{i \in [1,n]}, \{T_i\}_{i \in [1,n]})$, $aux = (\{\chi_i\}_{i \in ADM}, ADM)$. The signer sends them to the sanitizer through a secure channel.

$0/1 \leftarrow Verify(pp, m, \sigma, pk_{Sig}, ID_{Sig})$. Input the system public parameter pp, original message/signature pair (m, σ), the public key $pk_{Sig} = (P_{Sig}, Q_{Sig})$

of the signer and the identity of the signer ID_{Sig}, the sanitizer executes $Verify$ algorithm to authenticate the validity of the message/signature pair (m, σ).

The sanitizer computes $W = H_2(P_{pub})$. For each $i \in [1, n]$, computes $\alpha_i = h_1(ID_{Sig}||P_{Sig}||m_i||T_i)$. And then computes $\sigma = \Sigma_{i=1}^{n}\sigma_i, T = \Sigma_{i=1}^{n}\alpha_i \cdot T_i$ and verifies:

$$e(\sigma, P) = e(P_{pub}, Q_{Sig})^n \cdot e(T, W) \cdot e(P_{Sig}, W)^n \tag{1}$$

is satisfied or not. If the condition is true, it indicates that (m, σ) is a valid message/signature pair and the output is 1. Otherwise, the output is 0.

$(m', \sigma') \leftarrow Sanit(pp, m, \sigma, pk_{Sig}, ID_{Sig}, MOD, aux)$. Input the system public parameter pp, original message/signature pair (m, σ), the public key $pk_{Sig} = (P_{Sig}, Q_{Sig})$ of the original signer, the identity of the signer ID_{Sig}, the description MOD of the data block to be sanitized and aux, the sanitizer executes $Sanit$ algorithm to sanitize the message m and generates a valid signature σ' for the sanitized message m'.

- If $ADM(MOD) = 0$, output $\perp$.
- Sanitize m to obtain $m' = MOD(m) = \{m'\}_{i \in [1, n]}$, where for $i \in MOD, m'_i \neq m_i$. Otherwise $m'_i = m_i$.
- For each data block $m'_i (i \in [1, n])$, compute sanitized signature σ': If $i \notin MOD$, then $\sigma'_i = \sigma_i$; if $i \in MOD$, then computes $\alpha'_i = h_1(ID_{Sig}||P_{Sig}||m_i||T_i)$ and $\alpha'_i = h_1(ID_{Sig}||P_{Sig}||m'_i||T_i)$, then $\sigma'_i = \sigma_i - \alpha_i \cdot \chi_i + \alpha'_i \cdot \chi_i = \sigma_i + (\alpha'_i - \alpha_i) \cdot \chi_i$.

After the sanitization, fo each $i \in [1, n], \sigma'_i = d_{Sig} + \alpha'_i \cdot t_i \cdot W + s_{Sig} \cdot W$. And finally, the sanitizer obtains the sanitized message/signature pair (m', σ'), where $\sigma' = (\{\sigma'_i\}_{i \in [1, n]}, \{T_i\}_{i \in [1, n]})$.

$(m', \sigma'') \leftarrow DSign(pp, m', \sigma', pk_{Vrf})$. Input the system public parameter pp, sanitized message/signature pair (m', σ') and the public key $pk_{Vrf} = (P_{Vrf}, Q_{Vrf})$ of the designated verifier, the sanitizer execute $DSign$ to assign verifier to (m', σ').

For each signature $\sigma'_i (i \in [1, n])$, the sanitizer compute $\bar{\sigma}_i = e(\sigma', P_{Vrf})$. Finally, it outputs the message/signature pair (m', σ'') of the designated verifier, where $\sigma'' = (\{\bar{\sigma}_i\}_{i \in [1, n]}, \{T_i\}_{i \in [1, n]})$.

$0/1 \leftarrow DVerify(pp, m', \sigma'', pk_{Sig}, ID_{Sig}, sk_{Vrf})$. Input the system public parameter pp, message/signature pair (m', σ'') of the designated verifier, the public key of the signer $pk_{Sig} = (P_{Sig}, Q_{Sig})$, the identity of the signer ID_{Sig} and the private key of the designate verifier $sk_{Vrf} = (d_{Vrf}, s_{Vrf})$, the designated verifier execute $DVerify$ algorithm to authenticate the validity of the message/signature pair (m', σ'').

The designated verifier computes $W = H_2(P_{pub})$. For each $i \in [1, n]$, computes $\alpha'_i = h_1(ID_{Sig}||P_{Sig}||m'_i||T_i)$. And then computes $\bar{\sigma} = \Pi_{i=1}^{n}\bar{\sigma}_i, T = \Sigma_{i=1}^{n}\alpha_i \cdot T_i$, and verifies:

$$\bar{\sigma} = [e(P_{pub}, Q_{Sig})^n \cdot e(T', W) \cdot e(P_{Sig}, W)^n]^{s_{Vrf}} \tag{2}$$

is satisfied or not. If the condition is true, it indicates that (m', σ'') is a valid message/signature pair and the output is 1. Otherwise, the output is 0.

3.3   Security Analysis

Unforgeability. This scheme exhibits unforgeability against adaptive chosen message attacks and selective identity attacks. Below, we provide security analysis for forgery attacks from two types of adversaries: $\mathcal{A}_I$ and $\mathcal{A}_{II}$. Assuming a Computational Diffie-Hellman (CDH) problem instance is given $(P, Q_1 = aP, Q_2 = bP, Q_3 = abP)$.

For $\mathcal{A}_I$ type forgeries, the attacker does not have access to the master key s of the system but can replace a legitimate public key of the user. Let's assume an $\mathcal{A}_I$ attacker replaces the public key $pk_s = (P_s, Q_s)$ of a legitimate user ID_s with $pk_s^* = (P_s^*, Q_s^*)$. Using the replaced public key, the attacker successfully forges a signature (m^*, σ^*) for a message m. Let $P_{pub} = Q_1 = aP, Q_s^* = \vartheta_s Q_2 = \vartheta_s bP, W = \omega P$. Computes $\sigma = \Sigma_{i=1}^n \sigma_i, T = \Sigma_{i=1}^n \alpha_i \cdot T_i$, and then sign and verify the equation $e(\sigma, P) = e(P_{pub}, Q_{Sig})^n \cdot e(T, W) \cdot e(P_{Sig}, W)^n$ is satisfied. We have:

$$e(\sigma_i^*, P) = e(P_{pub}, Q_S) \cdot e(\alpha_i^* \cdot T_i, W) \cdot e(P_S, W)$$
$$\Rightarrow e(P_{pub}, Q_S) = e(\sigma_i^*, P) \cdot [e(\alpha_i^* \cdot T_i, W) \cdot e(P_S, W)]^{-1}$$
$$\Rightarrow e(aP, \vartheta_s bP) = e(\sigma_i^*, P) \cdot [e(\alpha_i^* \cdot T_i, \omega P) \cdot e(P_S, \omega P)]^{-1}$$
$$\Rightarrow e(\vartheta_S \cdot abP, P) = e(\sigma_i^*, P) \cdot [e(\omega \cdot \alpha_i^* \cdot T_i, P) \cdot e(\omega \cdot P_S, P)]^{-1}$$
$$\Rightarrow abP = \vartheta_S^{-1}(\sigma_i^* - \omega \cdot \alpha_i^* \cdot T_i - \omega \cdot P_S)$$

By successfully solving the CDH problem using adversary $\mathcal{A}_I$, the CDH problem itself is resolved. However, the CDH problem is a difficult problem that cannot be currently solved in the real world. Therefore, the forgery attack by adversary $\mathcal{A}_I$ cannot succeed.

For adversary $\mathcal{A}_{II}$, this particular adversary possesses access to the system master key s, but lacks the capability to substitute legitimate the public keys of the user. Suppose an $\mathcal{A}_{II}$ adversary successfully performs a forgery attack using the public key $pk_s = (P_s, Q_s)$ of user ID_s on message m, resulting in a forged signature (m^*, σ^*). Let $P_s = Q_1 = aP, W = \omega bP$. Computes $\sigma = \Sigma_{i=1}^n \sigma_i, T = \Sigma_{i=1}^n \alpha_i \cdot T_i$, and then sign and verify the equation $e(\sigma, P) = e(P_{Pub}, Q_{Sig})^n \cdot e(T, W) \cdot e(P_{Sig}, W)^n$ is satisfied. We have:

$$e(\sigma_i^*, P) = e(P_{pub}, Q_S) \cdot e(\alpha_i^* \cdot T_i, W) \cdot e(P_S, W)$$
$$\Rightarrow e(P_S, W) = e(\sigma_i^*, P) \cdot [e(P_{pub}, Q_S) \cdot e(\alpha_i^* \cdot T_i, W)]^{-1}$$
$$\Rightarrow e(aP, \omega bP) = e(\sigma_i^*, P) \cdot [e(sP, Q_S) \cdot e(\alpha_i^* \cdot T_i, W)]^{-1}$$
$$\Rightarrow e(\omega \cdot abP, P) = e(\sigma_i^*, P) \cdot [e(sQ_S, P) \cdot e(\alpha_i^* \cdot t_i \cdot W, P)]^{-1}$$
$$\Rightarrow abP = (\omega)^{-1}(\sigma_i^* - sQ_S - \alpha_i^* \cdot t_i \cdot W)$$

The adversary $\mathcal{A}_{II}$, as a subroutine, successfully solves the CDH problem. However, it is based on the security assumption that the CDH problem is difficult and currently unsolved in the real world. Therefore, the forgery attack by the adversary $\mathcal{A}_{II}$ cannot be successful.

Immutability. In this scheme, only the data blocks that are allowed to be sanitized that $i \in ADM$, have corresponding computation transformation values χ_i. Data blocks that are not allowed to be sanitized do not have corresponding χ_i values in the scheme. If the sanitizer wants to sanitize the data block, it needs to compute $\sigma_i' = \sigma_i - \alpha_i \cdot \chi_i + \alpha_i' \cdot \chi_i = \sigma_i + (\alpha_i' - \alpha_i) \cdot \chi_i$, which requires the transformation value χ_i, while the data blocks that are not allowed to be sanitized $\sigma_i' = d_{Sig} + \alpha_i' \cdot t_i \cdot W + s_{Sig} \cdot W = d_{Sig} + \alpha_i' \cdot \chi_i + s_{Sig} \cdot W$, cannot obtain the value of t_i through computation, and $\chi_i = t_i \cdot W$ can be regard as a Discrete Logarithm (DL) problem. According to the DL problem, the Sanitizer cannot obtain t_i. Therefore, the Sanitizer is unable to perform sanitization on these data blocks. As a result, the proposed scheme satisfies the immutability property.

Privacy. Verification parties must not have the ability to deduce sensitive information from the sanitized message/signature pairs. Because this scheme is designated for specific verification parties, the confirmation of the validity of the message/signature pairs is restricted solely to the designated parties, and cannot be accomplished by any other entity, and therefore, the information that has been sanitized cannot be recovered. However, for the designated verification parties, the message/signature pairs (m', σ'') do not involve information about the sanitized part of the message $m_i(m_i \neq m_i')$. As a result, this scheme meets the privacy requirement.

Non-transferability. Non-Transferability refers to the property that given a message/signature pair (m', σ'') for a designated verifier, no one other than the designated verifier can determine whether (m', σ'') was generated by the sanitizer or the designated verifier, even if they have knowledge of all users' private keys. This is because the designated verifier can simulate the generation of a signature counterpart σ^*, and this counterpart cannot be distinguished from the signature σ'' output by the sanitizer. The process of the designated verifier simulating the signature is as follows:

The designated verifier computes $W = H_2(P_{pub})$. For each $i \in [1, n]$, randomly chooses $T_i^* \in \mathbb{G}$ and computes $\alpha_i^* = h_1(ID_{Sig}||P_{Sig}||m_i'||T_i^*)$. Then computes $T^* = \Sigma_{i=1}^n \alpha_i^* \cdot T_i^*$, and outputs a signature counterpart $\sigma^* = \bar{\sigma}^*, \{T_i^*\}_{i \in [1,n]}$ for the message m', where $\bar{\sigma}^* = e(s_{Vrf} \cdot P_{pub}, Q_{Sig})^n \cdot e(s_{Vrf} T^*, W) \cdot e(s_{Vrf} \cdot P_{Sig}, W)^n$. This counterpart satisfied the correctness:

$$
\begin{aligned}
\bar{\sigma}^* &= e(s_{Vrf} \cdot P_{pub}, Q_{Sig})^n \cdot e(s_{Vrf} \cdot T^*, W) \cdot e(s_{Vrf} \cdot P_{Sig}, W)^n \\
&= e(P_{pub,Q_{Sig}})^{s_{Vrf} \cdot n} \cdot e(T^*, W)^{s_{Vrf}} \cdot e(P_{Sig}, W)^{s_{Vrf} \cdot n} \\
&= [e(Q_{Sig}, P_{pub})^n \cdot e(T^*, W) \cdot e(P_{Sig}, W)^n]^{s_{Vrf}}
\end{aligned}
$$

Therefore, for message m', the designated verifier generates a signature counterpart σ^* that is indistinguishable from the signature σ'' produced by the sanitizer.

4 Performance Analysis

In this section, we conduct a comparison between our scheme and the identity-based revocable proxy signature scheme [13] and the certificateless revocable proxy signature scheme [16] in terms of theoretical and experimental evaluations.

4.1 Theory Comparison

Table 1. Function Comparison

Scheme	Unforgeability	Immutability	Certificate Management Problems	Key Escrow Problems	Designated verifier
[13]	✓	×	✓	×	×
[16]	–	✓	✓	✓	×
Ours	✓	✓	✓	✓	✓

Table 1 shows the difference of the features between our proposed scheme and the related purifiable signature schemes [13] and [16]. The following analysis is conducted on these features:

- Unforgeability is a fundamental and important property that ensures that individuals without the signing key cannot generate valid signatures. Scheme [13] and our proposed scheme both satisfy this property, while scheme [16] does not define or discuss this property.
- Immutability ensures that the sanitizer can only sanitize data within the range specified by the signer. In scheme [13], the signer computes transformation values for sanitization, and the sanitizer with access to these values can modify any data block, violating the property of immutability. Scheme [16] and our proposed scheme both satisfy this property.
- Traditional public key encryption involves users generating public/private key pairs and having their public keys certified by a Certification Authority (CA), resulting in expensive certificate management overhead. Scheme [13] is based on identity-based cryptography, while schemes [16] and our proposed scheme are based on certificateless cryptography, eliminating this problem.
- The identity-based scheme [13] relies on a private key generator (PKG) to generate the private keys for the user, resulting in a key escrow problem. The certificateless cryptography schemes [16] and our proposed scheme do not have this problem.
- Only designated verifiers are allowed to verify the validity of message/signature pairs. Except for our proposed scheme, the other two sanitizable signature schemes do not support designated verifiers.

Based on the aforementioned information, we can conclude that our proposed scheme surpasses existing schemes in several aspects. It eliminates the need for costly certificate management, resolves the challenges associated with key escrow, guarantees non-forgeability and immutability, and provides support for designated verifiers.

Table 2. Single Execution Time of Each Operation

Notations	Description	Single execution time (ms)
$pair$	The operation of bilinear pairing	4.50315
$Exp_{\mathbb{G}_T}$	The exponentiation operation on $\mathbb{G}_T$	0.55745
$Mul_{\mathbb{G}_T}$	The multiplication operation on $\mathbb{G}_T$	0.00515
$Add_{\mathbb{G}}$	The addition operation on $\mathbb{G}$	0.04015
$Mul_{\mathbb{G}}$	The multiplication operation on $\mathbb{G}$	0.04015
$Hash_{\mathbb{G}}$	The hash operation on $\mathbb{G}$	18.6542

Due to the computational overhead mainly focused on operations in groups $\mathbb{G}$ and $\mathbb{G}_T$, operations on $\mathbb{Z}_q$ are ignored in this context. To directly compare the computational costs of different schemes, we tested the execution time of various operations based on the JPBC library. The experimental environment consists of an Intel(R) Core(TM) i7-10875H CPU @ 2.30 GHz, 16 GB RAM, and Windows 10(x64) OS. Table 2 provides the symbol descriptions and the time overhead of single executions for various operations. Additionally, the number of data blocks is represented as n, the size of the set of data blocks that can be sanitized (ADM) is denoted as l_{adm}, and the size of the set of data blocks to be sanitized (MOD) is denoted as l_{mod}.

Table 2 presents a comparison of the computational costs between the sanitizable signature scheme [13], the scheme [16], and the proposed scheme. Since the scheme [13] and the scheme [16] do not support specified verifier, only the proposed scheme provides the costs for the specified verifier signature algorithm and the specified verifier verification algorithm. From the table, it can be observed that the costs of signature and verification are linearly related to the number of data blocks, denoted as n. The cost of sanitization exhibits a linear relationship with either the number of blocks that can be sanitized (l_{adm}) or the number of blocks to be sanitized (l_{mod}). In the proposed scheme, the costs associated with designated verifier signature and designated verifier verification also demonstrate a linear increase as the number of data blocks, n, grows.

In the signature generation phase, compared to scheme [13], the proposed scheme reduces n $Add_{\mathbb{G}}$ operations, $(n - l_{adm})$ $Mul_{\mathbb{G}}$ operations, and $(2n - 1)$ $Hash_{\mathbb{G}}$ operations. Compared to scheme [16], the proposed scheme reduces n $Mul_{\mathbb{G}}$ operations and $(n - 1)$ $Hash_{\mathbb{G}}$ operations. Since both $Hash_{\mathbb{G}}$ and $Mul_{\mathbb{G}}$ have significant costs, overall, the proposed scheme exhibits significantly lower signature generation costs compared to scheme [13] and scheme [16].

In the sanitization phase, since $l_{mod} \leq l_{adm} \leq n$, the computing consumption of our scheme and scheme [13] are the same and generally lower than scheme [16]. In the verification phase, the proposed scheme reduces computational costs compared to scheme [13] by $2Add_{\mathbb{G}} + Mul_{\mathbb{G}} + (n-1)Hash_{\mathbb{G}} - Mul_{\mathbb{G}_T} - Exp_{\mathbb{G}_T} - Pair$, and this difference increases linearly with n. The proposed scheme also reduces computing consumption compared to scheme [16] by $nAdd_{\mathbb{G}} + 2Mul_{\mathbb{G}} + (n-1)Hash_{\mathbb{G}} - Mul_{\mathbb{G}_T} - 2Exp_{\mathbb{G}_T} - Pair$, and this difference also increases linearly with n.

Overall, Our proposed scheme exhibits lower overhead compared to scheme [13] and scheme [16], and the difference between them increases linearly with the increase in n. Furthermore, our scheme surpasses both scheme [13] and scheme [16] in terms of security and functionality.

Table 3. Computation Cost Comparison Between Sanitizable Signature Scheme

Algorithm	[13]	[16]	Ours
Signature	$2nAdd_{\mathbb{G}} + 3nMul_{\mathbb{G}} + 2nHash_{\mathbb{G}}$	$nAdd_{\mathbb{G}} + (3n + l_{adm})Mul_{\mathbb{G}} + nHash_{\mathbb{G}}$	$nAdd_{\mathbb{G}} + (2n + l_{adm})Mul_{\mathbb{G}} + Hash_{\mathbb{G}}$
Verification	$2nAdd_{\mathbb{G}} + (n+1)Mul_{\mathbb{G}} + nHash_{\mathbb{G}} + Mul_{\mathbb{G}_T} + Exp_{\mathbb{G}_T} + 3Pair$	$(3n-2)Add_{\mathbb{G}} + (n+2)Mul_{\mathbb{G}} + nHash_{\mathbb{G}} + Mul_{\mathbb{G}_T} + 3Pair$	$(2n-1)Add_{\mathbb{G}} + nMul_{\mathbb{G}} + Hash_{\mathbb{G}} + 2Mul_{\mathbb{G}_T} + 2Exp_{\mathbb{G}_T} + 4Pair$
Sanitization	$l_{mod}Add_{\mathbb{G}} + l_{mod}Mul_{\mathbb{G}}$	$l_{adm}Add_{\mathbb{G}} + l_{adm}Mul_{\mathbb{G}}$	$l_{mod}Add_{\mathbb{G}} + l_{mod}Mul_{\mathbb{G}}$
Designated verifier signature	–	–	$nPair$
Designated verifier verification	–	–	$(n-1)Add_{\mathbb{G}} + nMul_{\mathbb{G}} + Hash_{\mathbb{G}} + (n+1)Mul_{\mathbb{G}_T} + 3Exp_{\mathbb{G}_T} + 3Pair$

4.2 Experiment Comparison

In this section, we conducted performance testing of our proposed scheme using the JPBC library and compared it with scheme [13] and scheme [16]. The experiments were conducted on an Intel(R) Core(TM) i7-10875H CPU @ 2.30 GHz, 16 GB RAM, and Windows 10 (x64) OS. All three schemes were implemented based on the supersingular curve SS512, which achieves an 80-bit security level.

Figure 2 shows the computational overhead of each algorithm in our scheme. For this test, we set the number of data block n, to 50, and the total number of blocks that can be sanitized, l_{adm}, and the total number of blocks to be sanitized, l_{mod}, both to 20. As shown in Fig. 2, the required time for signature, verification, sanitization, designated verifier, and designated verifier verification algorithms were 0.92 s, 0.41 s, 0.15 s, 0.21 s, and 0.41 s, respectively. Among them, the signature algorithm has the highest overhead, while the verification algorithm and the designated verifier verification algorithm have similar overheads.

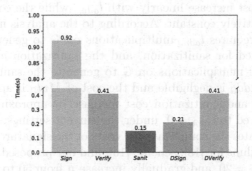

Fig. 2. Algorithm Computation Cost of This Scheme

Figure 3a demonstrates the impact of the number of data blocks, n, on the computational overhead of our proposed scheme. With $l_{adm} = 20$, we gradually increase n from 50 to 300 and test the computational overhead of each algorithm. It can be observed that the sanitization overhead remains constant and unaffected by n. On the contrary, the computational overhead of the remaining algorithms experiences a linear increase as n increases. According to the analysis in Table 3, the signature, verification, and designated verifier verification algorithms involve time-consuming $Mul_{\mathbb{G}}$ and $Hash_{\mathbb{G}}$, resulting in higher computational overhead compared to the designated verifier signature algorithm, which only requires $Pair$ operations. Additionally, among the signature overhead, verification overhead, and designated verifier verification overhead, the coefficient of $Mul_{\mathbb{G}}$ is larger, indicating a more pronounced growth trend in the signature overhead.

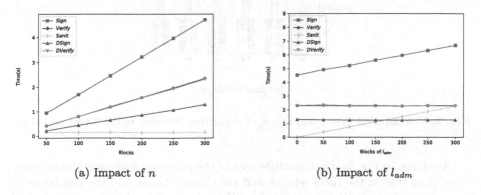

(a) Impact of n (b) Impact of l_{adm}

Fig. 3. Impact of n and l_{adm}

Figure 3b demonstrates the impact of the total number of sanitizable data blocks, l_{adm}, on the computational cost of our scheme. We set n = 300 and gradually increase l_{adm} from 0 to 300, while keeping $l_{mod} = l_{adm}$. We test the computational cost of various algorithms. It shows that only the signature cost and sanitization cost increase linearly with l_{adm}, while the costs of other algorithms remain relatively constant. According to the analysis in Table 3, the signature algorithm requires l_{adm} multiplications on $\mathbb{G}$ to generate the auxiliary information required for sanitization, and the sanitization algorithm requires l_{adm} additions and multiplications on $\mathbb{G}$ to generate the sanitizable signature. Since the cost of $Add_{\mathbb{G}}$ is negligible and the cost of $Mul_{\mathbb{G}}$ is approximately 8ms, the signature cost and sanitization cost increase by approximately 2.4s when $l_{adm} = 300$ compared to $l_{adm} = 0$, under the current settings.

Figure 4 illustrates the computational costs of the signature, verification, and sanitization algorithms for [13], scheme [16], and our proposed scheme. Here, we set $l_{adm} = 50$, $l_{mod} = 20$, and gradually increase n from 50 to 300.

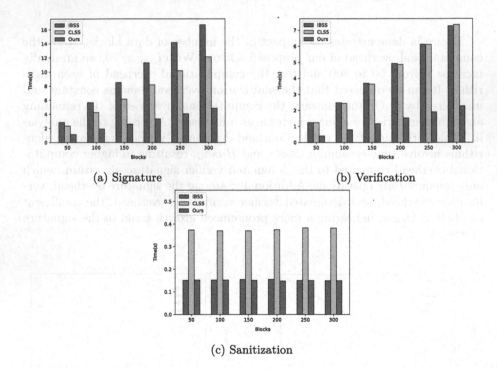

(a) Signature   (b) Verification

(c) Sanitization

Fig. 4. Computation Cost Comparison of Algorithm Between IBBS, CLSS and Ours

As shown in Fig. 4a, the signature cost of the proposed scheme is significantly lower than that in the IBSS scheme and the CLSS scheme, and the gap between them increases with the increase of n. When n = 300, the signature cost of our proposed scheme is approximately 11.8 s less than the IBSS scheme and approximately 7.3 s less than the CLSS scheme.

As shown in Fig. 4b, the cost in verification of the IBSS scheme and the CLSS scheme remains similar, while the verification cost of the proposed scheme is significantly lower than these two schemes. Moreover, this difference increases noticeably with the increase of n, which is consistent with the analysis in Table 3. When $n = 300$, the difference between our proposed scheme and the IBSS scheme is approximately 4.98 s, and the difference between our proposed scheme and the CLSS scheme is approximately 5.07 s.

As shown in Fig. 4c, the sanitization cost of the proposed scheme is the same as that in the IBSS scheme and both are lower than the CLSS scheme. According to the analysis in Table 3, the sanitization cost of our proposed scheme and the IBSS scheme is related to l_{mod}, while the CLSS scheme depends on l_{adm}. Therefore, when $l_{adm} \geq l_{mod}$, the sanitization cost of the CLSS scheme is the highest among the three schemes. When $l_{adm} = l_{mod}$, the sanitization cost is the same for all three schemes.

Through experimental comparisons, it can be observed that the performance of our proposed solution is not inferior and even superior to existing sanitizable signature schemes. Our approach is based on certificateless signatures, which avoids the key escrow issue present in the IBSS scheme. In comparison to the CLSS scheme, our solution incorporates an additional mechanism for designated verifiers, addressing the concern of information leakage on the verifier's side and further ensuring the privacy and security of shared data.

5   Conclusion

In order to ensure the privacy of shared data, our proposed sanitizable signature scheme addresses the issues of information leakage by data sharers, the costly certificate management overhead, and the potential security risks associated with key escrow in existing schemes.

Firstly, our solution introduces a certificateless approach for sanitizable signatures. The public key is derived from the public information of the user, and the private key is generated jointly by the user and the KGC, eliminating the need for a dedicated organization to manage user certificates and preventing the compromise of user private keys by the KGC, thus safeguarding data security.

Secondly, our scheme supports designated verifiers. After generating multiple sanitized versions of a message based on different usage scenarios, the sanitizer can designate a verifier for each version. The designated verifier represents the current data sharer, ensuring that only the sharer can verify the validity of the corresponding sanitized message, thereby preventing the leakage of message information to others.

Finally, through theoretical and experimental comparisons with similar sanitizable signature schemes, we have demonstrated that our proposed scheme offers improved security and functionality, while also being more efficient than existing solutions.

References

1. Bilzhause, A., Pöhls, H.C., Samelin, K.: Position paper: the past, present, and future of sanitizable and redactable signatures. In: Proceedings of the 12th International Conference on Availability, Reliability and Security, pp. 1–9 (2017)
2. Deng, L., Yang, Y., Gao, R.: Certificateless designated verifier anonymous aggregate signature scheme for healthcare wireless sensor networks. IEEE Internet Things J. **8**(11), 8897–8909 (2021)
3. Centers for Disease Control and Prevention: HIPAA privacy rule and public health. Guidance from CDC and the US department of health and human services. MMWR Morb. Mortal. Weekly Rep. **52**(Suppl. 1), 1–17 (2003)
4. Hou, H., Ning, J., Zhao, Y., Deng, R.H.: Fine-grained and controllably editable data sharing with accountability in cloud storage. IEEE Trans. Dependable Secure Comput. **19**(5), 3448–3463 (2021)
5. Hussain, S., Ullah, S.S., Ali, I., Xie, J., Inukollu, V.N.: Certificateless signature schemes in industrial internet of things: a comparative survey. Comput. Commun. **181**, 116–131 (2022)
6. Liu, X., Ma, J., Xiong, J., He, T., Li, Q.: Attribute-based sanitizable signature scheme in cloud computing environment. J. Electron. Inf. Technol. **36**(7), 1749–1754 (2014)
7. Liu, Z., Ren, L., Li, R., Liu, Q., Zhao, Y.: Id-based sanitizable signature data integrity auditing scheme with privacy-preserving. Comput. Secur. **121**, 102858 (2022)
8. Ma, J., Liu, J., Huang, X., Xiang, Y., Wu, W.: Authenticated data redaction with fine-grained control. IEEE Trans. Emerg. Top. Comput. **8**(2), 291–302 (2017)
9. Ma, K., et al.: An efficient certificateless signature scheme with provably security and its applications. IEEE Syst. J. (2023)
10. Ming, Y., Shen, X., Peng, Y.: Identity-based sanitizable signature scheme in the standard model. In: Zhu, R., Zhang, Y., Liu, B., Liu, C. (eds.) ICICA 2010. CCIS, vol. 105, pp. 9–16. Springer, Heidelberg (2010). https://doi.org/10.1007/978-3-642-16336-4_2
11. Ng, S., Tauber, T., Cheung, L.: ECDSA-compatible privacy preserving signature with designated verifier. In: 2021 IEEE 5th International Conference on Cryptography, Security and Privacy (CSP), pp. 84–89. IEEE (2021)
12. Shen, W., Qin, J., Yu, J., Hao, R., Hu, J.: Enabling identity-based integrity auditing and data sharing with sensitive information hiding for secure cloud storage. IEEE Trans. Inf. Forensics Secur. **14**(2), 331–346 (2018)
13. Xu, Y., Ding, L., Cui, J., Zhong, H., Yu, J.: PP-CSA: a privacy-preserving cloud storage auditing scheme for data sharing. IEEE Syst. J. **15**(3), 3730–3739 (2020)
14. Xu, Z., Luo, M., Kumar, N., Vijayakumar, P., Li, L.: Privacy-protection scheme based on sanitizable signature for smart mobile medical scenarios. Wirel. Commun. Mob. Comput. **2020** (2020)
15. Xu, Z., Wu, L., Li, L., He, D.: A new certificateless generalized designated verifier aggregate signature scheme. J. Commun. (2017)
16. Zhang, W., Yan, Y., Wu, Y., Hu, J.: Certificateless revocable proxy signature scheme in cloud storage. Comput. Syst. Appl. **1**, 281–287 (2022)

An Inner Product Function Encryption Scheme for Secure Distance Calculation

Gang Tan[1], Yuzhu Wang[1], Jing Wang[1], and Mingwu Zhang[1,2]($\boxtimes$)

[1] School of Computer Science and Information Security, Guilin University of Electronic Technology, Guilin 541004, China
[2] School of Computer Science, Hubei University of Technology, Wuhan 430068, China
mzhang@hbut.edu.cn

Abstract. With the continuous advancement of cloud computing, an increasing amount of data is being entrusted to Cloud Service Providers (CSPs) for hosting. Nonetheless, this trend has also raised concerns regarding data privacy. To ensure the protection of data privacy, it is advisable to encrypt the data prior to uploading. Functional Encryption (FE) is a novel multifunctional encryption paradigm that enables fine-grained access control over encrypted data stored on CSPs. By utilizing restricted functional keys, users can acquire knowledge of specific functions of encrypted messages while keeping other message information concealed. Inner product computation is a potent and straightforward functional within FE that can fulfill the requirements of numerous specific applications. This paper proposes an inner product function encryption scheme for secure distance calculation, enabling users to obtain the inner product functional value of encrypted data based on their location predicates. This distinctive FE scheme addresses the concern of location privacy protection, particularly in contact tracing applications for infectious disease cases.

Keywords: Secure Distance Calculation · Inner Product Functional Encryption · Fine-Grained Access Control

1 Introduction

Over the past decades, numerous cryptographic primitives have been introduced, including Identity-based Encryption (IBE) [1–3], Attribute-based Encryption (ABE) [4–6] and Predicate Encryption (PE) [7–9] to provide fine-grained access control, which is an ideal feature for modern applications. Functional Encryption (FE) [10–13] is a novel public key encryption paradigm that enables fine-grained and non-interactive access control to encrypted data. FE empowers an authorized authority to generate a master secret key msk, and subsequently, the possessor of the master secret key can generate the decryption key sk_f for function f. By utilizing the master public key mpk, a message x can be encrypted into a ciphertext ct. Subsequently, Users can decrypt the ciphertext ct using the

H. Yang and R. Lu (Eds.): FCS 2023, CCIS 1992, pp. 353–369, 2024.
https://doi.org/10.1007/978-981-99-9331-4_24

functional decryption key sk_f to obtain the result of the function $f(x)$. Unlike traditional encryption, FE solely discloses the functional result $f(x)$ without revealing any other information about the message, rendering it highly suitable for cloud computing scenarios where encrypted data can be safely stored on untrusted servers, and functional decryption keys can be distributed to other users or Cloud Service Providers (CSPs) for data computation to mitigate the risk of information leakage.

A pragmatic and specialised FE scheme has garnered considerable attention in the cryptography community. Recent studies [14,15] have exhibited the feasibility of executing circuit computations of general polynomial size. Abdalla et al. [16] proposed the Inner Products Functional Encryption (IPFE) scheme, which is specifically designed for real-world scenarios and can calculate the value of any polynomial [16,18,19]. IPFE specialises in computing inner product functional values, which is a valuable statistical technique that can provide weighted averages. It has become an essential tool for the construction of FE schemes related to key and ciphertext vectors.

Secure distance calculation is a rapidly expanding field in mobile applications, with the potential to improve the efficiency and personalization of services in various domains, including public safety, healthcare, and transportation. However, the use of this technology raises significant concerns about user location privacy. When enjoying location-based services, users must share their location information with CSPs, which could compromise sensitive personal data and be exploited by malicious third parties. This highlights the need for robust secure distance calculation protection mechanisms when implementing location-based services. Even if users have confidence in the CSPs, they are still vulnerable to network attacks and internal employee self-interest, which could result in the disclosure of their location information.

This paper proposes a novel scheme, an inner product function encryption scheme for secure distance calculation, to protect the privacy of user location. By utilizing IPFE, users can encrypt their location and transmit it to the CSP, which can perform specific distance calculations directly on the ciphertext. This allows for evaluation and filtering while also ensuring location privacy, with a particular application scenario in the context of infectious diseases. The CSP can utilize IPFE to calculate the inner product functional value of the encrypted location vector and key vector and compare it with a predefined threshold to alert relevant users to take appropriate action to control the spread of the virus.

1.1 Related Works

As general circuits are impractical for FE, Abdalla et al. [16] proposed the first simple FE scheme for inner products to achieve an efficient FE scheme based on standard assumptions. They constructed two selectively secure IPFE schemes based on Decisional Diffie-Hellman (DDH) assumption and Learning with Errors (LWE) assumptions, respectively. In [17], Tomida introduced the first IPFE scheme with rigorous security proofs. Although the inner product is not as powerful as general circuits, it is still a valuable functionality that can be utilized for statistical computation, biometric authentication, and more [16,20]. The concept of unboundedness plays a crucial role in the field of Attribute-Based Encryption (ABE) and has been studied extensively. Tomida and Takashima defined and implemented unbounded IPFE in [26], while Dufour Sans and Pointcheval proposed unbounded IPFE schemes in [27].

However, the selective security model is less desirable than the adaptive security model. To address this issue, Wee and Agrawal [21,24] proposed selective or semi-adaptive IPFE schemes based on DDH. Subsequently, Agrawal et al. [19,25] proposed an adaptively secure IPFE scheme based on the assumptions of DDH, LWE, and Decisional Composite Residuosity (DCR). This improved the security of IPFE schemes and provided a more robust protection mechanism for location privacy. Their significant contribution went beyond adaptive security and included the development of the first IPFE scheme based on the DCR assumption. At the same time, references [21,24,25] investigated simulation-based security of IPFE to enhance its security.

The DCR-based IPFE scheme can handle inner products modulo p by utilizing groups that simplify the discrete logarithm problem, which is a notable advantage. Unlike DDH-based IPFE schemes, the DCR-based scheme relies on groups where solving the discrete logarithm problem is challenging, thereby increasing the security of the scheme. Castagnos et al. [21] proposed an adaptively secure and more efficient IPFE scheme constructed over modulo p using class groups. Their scheme is similar to the DCR-based IPFE scheme in that both use a group where the discrete logarithm problem is easy, which is due to the class groups. In [22,23], the External Diffie-Hellman (XDH) assumption is introduced as a natural extension of the DDH assumption, which improves the security of the scheme based on hard assumptions and serves as the basis for the subsequent security proof of our proposed scheme.

1.2 Contributions

In order to provide a full understanding of the content and significance of our paper, we outline three main contributions below:

- We have introduced and formally defined a novel primitive for distance computation that uses inner product function encryption to achieve secure distance computation. By using inner product function encryption, our proposed method achieves secure distance computation in ciphertext while preserving the privacy of the user's location information.
- The inner product function encryption scheme proposed in this paper for secure distance computation is instantiated based on the asymmetric XDH assumption, and it is shown to withstand chosen plaintext attacks in the standard model under the asymmetric XDH assumption.
- To illustrate the concept discussed above, we present two potential applications of our techniques in the context of privacy-preserving location information sharing.

1.3　Organization

This paper is structured into five chapters. First, in Sect. 2, we provide a comprehensive explanation of the fundamental concepts and principles underlying IPFE. Second, in Sect. 3, we present our scheme, including its definition, construction, and security proofs. This chapter provides a detailed technical description of our proposed scheme, including the cryptographic primitives and algorithms used in its implementation. We have also performed a security analysis of the scheme, demonstrating its resistance to chosen plaintext attacks. In Sect. 4, we explore the application of our scheme to real-world scenarios. We demonstrated the versatility and applicability of our scheme in various application scenarios. Finally, in Sect. 5, we summarise the contributions and limitations of the paper and propose future research directions and goals for the development of this field.

2　Preliminaries

This section serves as a foundational introduction to the basic terms and symbols used in our paper. We provide a comprehensive overview of bilinear mappings and XDH assumptions, which are fundamental to our security assumptions. Next, we provide a detailed explanation of the standard definition of Euclidean distance, which plays a critical role in the computation of inner products in our proposed scheme. In addition, we provide a detailed explanation of the definition, correctness, and security proof of inner product functional encryption, which is a key component of our scheme.

2.1　Nations

To help the reader understand of the notations used in our paper, we have compiled a comprehensive list of important notations in Table 1.

2.2　Bilinear Mapping

A bilinear pairing group is defined by the tuple $(\mathbb{G}_1, \mathbb{G}_2, \mathbb{G}_T, g, h, q, e)$, where q is a prime number that is related to the security parameter λ. The groups $\mathbb{G}_1$, $\mathbb{G}_2$, and $\mathbb{G}_T$ are three cyclic groups of order q, where g and h being generators of $\mathbb{G}_1$ and $\mathbb{G}_2$, respectively. The mapping $e : \mathbb{G}_1 \times \mathbb{G}_2 \to \mathbb{G}_T$ is bilinear if it satisfies the following conditions:

- **Bilinearity**: The mapping $e : \mathbb{G}_1 \times \mathbb{G}_2 \to \mathbb{G}_T$ is bilinear if the equation $e\left(g^a, h^b\right) = e\left(g, h\right)^{ab}$ holds for any $g \in \mathbb{G}_1$, $h \in \mathbb{G}_2$, and $a, b \in \mathbb{Z}_q^*$.
- **Non-degeneracy**: There exist $g \in \mathbb{G}_1$ and $h \in \mathbb{G}_2$ such that $c\left(g, h\right) \neq 1$.
- **Computability**: For any $g \in \mathbb{G}_1$ and $h \in \mathbb{G}_2$, there exists a polynomial-time algorithm to effectively compute the bilinear mapping $e(g, h)$.

Table 1. Notations used in paper

Notation	Description
λ	a security parameter
$\mathbf{x}$	the vector $\mathbf{x} = (x_1, ..., x_n)$
$\mathbf{y}$	the vector $\mathbf{y} = (y_1, ..., y_n)$
$\langle , \rangle$	inner product operator
n	the length of encoded vectors
$e(.,.)$	a nondegradable bilinear mapping
g	a generator of $\mathbb{G}_1$
h	a generator of $\mathbb{G}_2$
$\mathbb{G}_1$	a cyclic group of order p
$\mathbb{G}_2$	a cyclic group of order p
q	a big prime number
D_i	the i-th distribution of XDH assumption
$\triangle_{\mathbf{x},\mathbf{y}}$	Euclidean distance between vector $\mathbf{x}$ and vector $\mathbf{y}$

2.3   External Diffie-Hellman (XDH)

Assume that the Computational Diffie-Hellman (CDH) assumption is intractable in both $\mathbb{G}_1$ and $\mathbb{G}_2$. The XDH assumption states that the DDH assumption is also intractable in $\mathbb{G}_1$. Specifically, it assumes the existence of two distributions as follows:

$$D_1 := \left(g, g^a, g^b, h, g^{ab}\right), D_2 := \left(g, g^a, g^b, h, T\right), \qquad (1)$$

where $g \in \mathbb{G}_1$, $h \in \mathbb{G}_2$, $a, b \in \mathbb{Z}_q^*$, and $T \in \mathbb{G}_1$ are selected uniformly and randomly.

Let $\mathcal{A}$ be an algorithm, and define $Adv_{\mathcal{A}}^{\text{XDH}}$ as the advantage of $\mathcal{A}$ in distinguishing between the two distributions

$$Adv_{\mathcal{A}}^{\text{XDH}} = \left| Pr\left[\mathcal{A}\left(g, g^a, g^b, h, g^{ab}\right) = 1\right] - Pr\left[\mathcal{A}\left(g, g^a, g^b, h, T\right) = 1\right]\right|, \qquad (2)$$

where we choose $\left(g, g^a, g^b, h, g^{ab}\right)$ from D_1, and $\left(g, g^a, g^b, h, T\right)$ from D_2.

We say that an algorithm $\mathcal{C}$ has an advantage $Adv_{\mathcal{A}}^{\text{XDH}} = \epsilon$ in solving the XDH problem in asymmetric pairing if $\mathcal{C}$ outputs a bit in $\{0, 1\}$ and this is true if the probability is

$$\left| Pr\left[\mathcal{C}\left(g, g^a, g^b, h, g^{ab}\right) = 0\right] - Pr\left[\mathcal{C}\left(g, g^a, g^b, h, T\right) = 0\right]\right| \geq \epsilon, \qquad (3)$$

where the probability is taken over the random choice of the generator $g \in \mathbb{G}_1$, $h \in \mathbb{G}_2$, the exponents $a, b \in \mathbb{Z}_q^*$, $T \in \mathbb{G}_1$, and the random bit selected by $\mathcal{C}$.

2.4   Euclidean Distance Metric

To compute an inner product between two vectors can be treated in the same way as computing the distance between two points. A common distance measure is the Euclidean distance, defined as the square root of the sum of the squares of the differences between the corresponding dimensions of two points in the Euclidean n-space. Let $\mathbf{x} = (x_1, ..., x_n)$ and $\mathbf{y} = (y_1, ..., y_n)$ be two points in the Euclidean n-space, then the Euclidean distance between $\mathbf{x}$ and $\mathbf{y}$ is defined as:

$$\triangle_{\mathbf{x},\mathbf{y}} = \sqrt{\sum_{i=1}^{n} (x_i - y_i)^2}, \tag{4}$$

where x_i and y_i are the coordinates of the points $\mathbf{x}$ and $\mathbf{y}$ in the ith dimension, respectively.

We will be using the following two formulas:

$$\langle \mathbf{x}, \mathbf{y} \rangle = |\mathbf{x}| \, |\mathbf{y}| \cos(\theta), \tag{5}$$

$$(\mathbf{x} - \mathbf{y})^2 = |\mathbf{x}|^2 + |\mathbf{y}|^2 - 2 |\mathbf{x}| \, |\mathbf{y}| \cos(\theta). \tag{6}$$

By combining the above formulas, we utilized the square of the distance as the metric to simplify the calculations. Hence, we obtain:

$$\begin{aligned}
\triangle_{\mathbf{x},\mathbf{y}}^2 &= \sum_{i=1}^{n} (x_i - y_i)^2 \\
&= (\mathbf{x} - \mathbf{y})^2 \\
&= |\mathbf{x}|^2 + |\mathbf{y}|^2 - 2 \langle \mathbf{x}, \mathbf{y} \rangle,
\end{aligned}$$

where $\langle \cdot, \cdot \rangle$ represents the inner product. This formula transforms the problem of calculating the Euclidean distance into the problem of calculating the inner product of vectors, which is crucial for the inner product computation in our proposed scheme.

2.5   Inner Product Functional Encryption (IPFE)

The IPFE scheme is defined as a tuple that consists of the following four algorithms IPFE = (Setup, Encrypt, KeyGen, Decrypt):

- **Setup** $(1^\lambda, n) \rightarrow (mpk, msk)$: This algorithm takes the security parameter 1^λ and the length n of the vector as input, and outputs the master public key mpk and the master secret key msk.
- **Encrypt** $(mpk, \mathbf{x}) \rightarrow ct$: This algorithm takes the master public key mpk and the vector $\mathbf{x}$ that is to be encrypted as input, and outputs the ciphertext ct.
- **KeyGen** $(msk, \mathbf{y}) \rightarrow sk_{\mathbf{y}}$: This algorithm takes the master secret key msk and the vector $\mathbf{y}$ as input, and outputs the functional decryption key $sk_{\mathbf{y}}$.
- **Decrypt** $(ct, sk_{\mathbf{y}}) \rightarrow \langle \mathbf{x}, \mathbf{y} \rangle$ or $\bot$: This algorithm takes the functional decryption key $sk_{\mathbf{y}}$ and the ciphertext ct as input, and outputs either $\langle \mathbf{x}, \mathbf{y} \rangle$ or $\bot$ after decryption.

Correctness: The correctness property must satisfy the following requirement

$$Pr \left[\text{Decrypt}\,(ct, sk_{\mathbf{y}}) = \langle \mathbf{x}, \mathbf{y} \rangle \, \middle| \, \begin{array}{c} (mpk, msk) \leftarrow \text{Setup}\,(1^{\lambda}, n) \\ sk_{\mathbf{y}} \leftarrow \text{KeyGen}\,(msk, \mathbf{y}) \\ ct \leftarrow \text{Encrypt}\,(mpk, \mathbf{x}) \end{array} \right] = 1 - neg(1^{\lambda}).$$

Security: In the condition of selective security against indistinguishable chosen plaintext attacks (IND-sCPA), the security model for IPFE consists of six stages: Init, Setup, Phase 1, Challenge, Phase 2, and Guess. It is a game that is played between the challenger $\mathcal{C}$ and the adversary $\mathcal{A}$. The security game is defined as follows:

- **Init**: The adversary $\mathcal{A}$ generates two random vectors $\mathbf{x}_0$, and $\mathbf{x}_1 \in \mathcal{X}$ and sends them to the challenger $\mathcal{C}$.
- **Setup**: The challenger $\mathcal{C}$ generates the master public key mpk and the master secret key msk by running Setup $(1^{\lambda}, n)$ and sends the master public key mpk to the adversary $\mathcal{A}$.
- **Phase 1**: The adversary $\mathcal{A}$ is limited to making a polynomial number of key queries for a non-zero key vector $\mathbf{y} \in \mathcal{Y} \setminus \{\mathbf{0}\}$, under the condition that $\langle \mathbf{x}_0, \mathbf{y} \rangle = \langle \mathbf{x}_1, \mathbf{y} \rangle$. If requested, the challenger $\mathcal{C}$ will generate the corresponding functional decryption key $sk_{\mathbf{y}}$ and provide it to $\mathcal{A}$.
- **Challenge**: To initiate the challenge phase, the challenger $\mathcal{C}$ randomly selects a bit $\beta \in \{0,1\}$ and encrypts the corresponding message vector $\mathbf{x}_{\beta}$ into a challenge ciphertext $ct_{\mathbf{x}_{\beta}} \leftarrow \text{Encrypt}\,(mpk, \mathbf{x}_{\beta})$. Subsequently, the challenger transmits the challenge ciphertext to the adversary $\mathcal{A}$.
- **Phase 2**: Using the constraint from Phase 1, the adversary $\mathcal{A}$ continues to request keys for additional key vectors.
- **Guess**: Finally, the adversary $\mathcal{A}$ produces an output bit $\beta' \in \{0,1\}$. The adversary $\mathcal{A}$ wins the game if $\beta' = \beta$; otherwise, the adversary $\mathcal{A}$ loses the game.

For a probabilistic polynomial time (PPT) adversary $\mathcal{A}$, the adversary's advantage is defined as follows:

$$Adv_{\text{IPFE},\mathcal{A}}^{\text{IND-sCPA}}\,(1^{\lambda}) := Pr \left[\beta' = \beta \, \middle| \, \begin{array}{c} (mpk, msk) \leftarrow \text{Setup}\,(1^{\lambda}, n) \\ sk_{\mathbf{y}} \leftarrow \mathcal{A}^{\text{KeyGen}(msk, \cdot)}\,(\mathbf{y}) \\ \beta \xleftarrow{\$} \{0,1\} \\ ct_{\mathbf{x}_{\beta}} \leftarrow \text{Encrypt}\,(mpk, \mathbf{x}_{\beta}) \\ \beta' \leftarrow \mathcal{A}^{\text{Decrypt}(sk_{\mathbf{y}}, \cdot)}\,(ct_{\mathbf{x}_{\beta}}) \end{array} \right] - \frac{1}{2}.$$

Here, $Adv_{\text{IPFE},\mathcal{A}}^{\text{IND-sCPA}}$ represents the adversary's advantage. IPFE is considered IND-sCPA secure if the advantage $Adv_{\text{IPFE},\mathcal{A}}^{\text{IND-sCPA}}$ of any PPT adversary $\mathcal{A}$ in the IND-sCPA security game is negligibly small.

3   Our Scheme

3.1   Definition

An inner product function encryption scheme for secure distance calculation can be represented as a tuple $\mathcal{IPFE} = $ (Setup, Encrypt, KeyGen, Decrypt) consisting of the following four algorithms:

- **Setup** $(1^\lambda, n) \rightarrow (msk, mpk)$: This algorithm takes the security parameter 1^λ and the vector length n as inputs and generates the master public key mpk and the master secret key msk as output.

- **Encrypt** $(mpk, \text{LBS}, \mathbf{x}) \rightarrow CT_\mathbf{x}^{\text{LBS}}$: This algorithm takes the master public key mpk, the location-based service LBS, and the vector $\mathbf{x} = (x_1, \ldots, x_n)$ as input. By utilizing the Euclidean distance measure, we can construct a new vector $\mathbf{x}'$ that is well suited for inner product evaluation, represented as $\mathbf{x}' = \left(|\mathbf{x}|^2, 1, x_1, \ldots, x_n\right)$. Subsequently, we employ this new vector to transform the ciphertext $CT_\mathbf{x}^{\text{LBS}}$ into $CT_{\mathbf{x}'}^{\text{LBS}}$.

- **KeyGen** $(msk, \text{LBS}', \mathbf{y}) \rightarrow sk_\mathbf{y}^{\text{LBS}'}$: This algorithm takes the master secret key msk, the location information LBS$'$ of the key holder, and the vector $\mathbf{y} = (y_1, \ldots, y_n)$ as inputs. Using the Euclidean distance measure, we can construct a new vector $\mathbf{y}'$ that is suitable for inner product evaluation, defined as $\mathbf{y}' = \left(1, |\mathbf{y}|^2, -2y_1, \ldots, -2y_n\right)$. Then, we use this new vector to transform the functional decryption key $sk_\mathbf{y}^{\text{LBS}'}$ into $sk_{\mathbf{y}'}^{\text{LBS}'}$.

- **Decrypt** $\left(sk_{\mathbf{y}'}^{\text{LBS}'}, CT_{\mathbf{x}'}^{\text{LBS}}\right) \rightarrow \langle \mathbf{x}', \mathbf{y}' \rangle$ or $\bot$: This algorithm takes the functional decryption key $sk_{\mathbf{y}'}^{\text{LBS}'}$ and the ciphertext $CT_{\mathbf{x}'}^{\text{LBS}}$ as inputs. If LBS $\neq$ LBS$'$, the decryption algorithm will most likely fail and return an error symbol $\bot$. The decryption of $CT_{\mathbf{x}'}^{\text{LBS}}$ is done with $sk_{\mathbf{y}'}^{\text{LBS}'}$, both of which are capable of computing the square of the distance, $\langle \mathbf{x}', \mathbf{y}' \rangle = (\mathbf{x} - \mathbf{y})^2$, between the two points.

Correctness: The correctness requirement is defined as follows:

$$Pr\left[\text{Decrypt}\left(sk_{\mathbf{y}'}^{\text{LBS}'}, CT_{\mathbf{x}'}^{\text{LBS}}\right) = \langle \mathbf{x}', \mathbf{y}' \rangle \, \middle| \, \begin{array}{l} (msk, mpk) \leftarrow \text{Setup}\left(1^\lambda, n\right) \\ sk_{\mathbf{y}'}^{\text{LBS}'} \leftarrow \text{KeyGen}\left(msk, \text{LBS}', \mathbf{y}'\right) \\ CT_{\mathbf{x}'}^{\text{LBS}} \leftarrow \text{Encrypt}\left(mpk, \text{LBS}, \mathbf{x}'\right) \end{array} \right]$$
$$= 1 - neg(1^\lambda).$$

Security: The IND-sCPA security model of our scheme consists of six stages: Init, Setup, Phase 1, Challenge, Phase 2, and Guess. This model defines a game between the challenger $\mathcal{C}$ and the adversary $\mathcal{A}$, which is described as follows:

- **Init**: The adversary $\mathcal{A}$ selects two challenge message vectors $\mathbf{x}_0'$ and $\mathbf{x}_1'$ from the message space $\mathcal{X}$, and sends them to the challenger $\mathcal{C}$. Here, $\mathbf{x}_0'$ and $\mathbf{x}_1'$ are arbitrary vectors in $\mathcal{X}$.

- **Setup**: The challenger $\mathcal{C}$ generates the master public key mpk and the master secret key msk by running the Setup algorithm, and then sends the master public key mpk to the adversary $\mathcal{A}$.
- **Phase 1**: The adversary $\mathcal{A}$ can make a polynomial number of key requests on a key vector $\mathbf{y}' \in \mathcal{Y} \setminus \{\mathbf{0}\}$, subject to the restriction that $\langle \mathbf{x}'_0, \mathbf{y}' \rangle = \langle \mathbf{x}'_1, \mathbf{y}' \rangle$. Subsequently, the challenger $\mathcal{C}$ generates a functional decryption key $sk_{\mathbf{y}'}^{\mathrm{LBS}}$ and sends it to the adversary $\mathcal{A}$.
- **Challenge**: The challenger $\mathcal{C}$ selects a random bit $\beta \in \{0,1\}$ and generates a challenge ciphertext $CT_{\mathbf{x}'_\beta}^{\mathrm{LBS}} \leftarrow \mathrm{Encrypt}\left(mpk, \mathrm{LBS}, \mathbf{x}'_\beta\right)$, which is then sent to the adversary $\mathcal{A}$. The following restrictions apply:
  1. Requests with the same location information LBS cannot be repeated.
  2. If $\mathrm{LBS} = \mathrm{LBS}'$, which means that the queried location information LBS is the same as the challenged location information LBS', then the following condition must hold: $\langle \mathbf{x}'_0 - \mathbf{x}'_1, \mathbf{y}' \rangle = 0$.
- **Phase 2**: In Phase 2, the adversary $\mathcal{A}$ requests keys for additional key vectors, subject to the restrictions imposed in Phase 1.
- **Guess**: At the end of the game, the adversary $\mathcal{A}$ produces an output bit $\beta' \in \{0,1\}$. The adversary wins the game if $\beta' = \beta$, and loses otherwise.

The advantage of a PPT adversary $\mathcal{A}$ is defined as follows:

$$Adv_{\mathcal{IPFE},\mathcal{A}}^{\mathrm{IND\text{-}sCPA}}\left(1^\lambda\right) := Pr \left| \beta' = \beta \left| \begin{array}{c} (msk, mpk) \leftarrow \mathrm{Setup}\left(1^\lambda, n\right) \\ sk_{\mathbf{y}'}^{\mathrm{LBS}} \leftarrow \mathcal{A}^{\mathrm{KeyGen}(\mathrm{LBS},\mathbf{y}')}(msk) \\ \beta \xleftarrow{\$} \{0,1\} \\ CT_{\mathbf{x}'_\beta}^{\mathrm{LBS}} \leftarrow \mathrm{Encrypt}\left(mpk, \mathrm{LBS}, \mathbf{x}'_\beta\right) \\ \beta' \leftarrow \mathcal{A}^{\mathrm{Decrypt}\left(sk_{\mathbf{y}'}^{\mathrm{LBS}},\cdot\right)}\left(CT_{\mathbf{x}'_\beta}^{\mathrm{LBS}}\right) \end{array} \right. \right| - \frac{1}{2}.$$

If the advantage $Adv_{\mathcal{IPFE},\mathcal{A}}^{\mathrm{IND\text{-}sCPA}}$ of any PPT adversary $\mathcal{A}$ is negligible, then our scheme is considered to be secure under IND-sCPA.

3.2 Construction

Setup $(1^\lambda, n)$: The algorithm sets the master public key mpk and the master secret key msk using the security parameter 1^λ and the vector length parameter n. It selects random integers $(\alpha, a_0, a_1, \ldots, a_n) \in \left(\mathbb{Z}_q^*\right)^{n+2}$, and sets them as follows:

$$g_1 = g^{a_1}, \ldots, g_n = g^{a_n};$$
$$h_1 = h^{a_1}, \ldots, h_n = h^{a_n}, h_0 = h^{a_0}.$$

The algorithm generates and publishes the master public key mpk as follows:

$$mpk = (g, g_1, \ldots, g_n, e(g, h_0)).$$

The master secret key msk is generated and set as follows:

$$msk = (\alpha, h, h_0, h_1, \ldots, h_n, e(g, h)).$$

Encrypt $(mpk, \text{LBS}, \mathbf{x})$: The algorithm takes the master public key mpk, the location-based service LBS, and the message vector $\mathbf{x} = (x_1, \ldots, x_n) \in \mathcal{X}$ as input, where $\mathcal{X}$ is the message space. By using the Euclidean distance, we can set a new vector $\mathbf{x}'$ that is suitable for inner product evaluation as $\mathbf{x}' = \left(|\mathbf{x}|^2, 1, x_1, \ldots, x_n\right)$. Then the encryption algorithm selects a random integer $s \in \mathbb{Z}_q^*$ and computes the following ciphertext:

$$ct_1 = g^s,$$
$$ct_{2,i} = g^{x_i}(g_i)^s \ (1 \leq i \leq n),$$
$$ct_3 = e(g, h_0^{\text{LBS}})^s.$$

The final ciphertext generated by the encryption algorithm is:

$$CT_{\mathbf{x}'}^{\text{LBS}} := \{\text{LBS}, ct_1, (ct_{2,1}, \ldots, ct_{2,n}), ct_3\}.$$

KeyGen $(msk, \text{LBS}', \mathbf{y})$: This algorithm takes the master secret key msk, the location information LBS$'$ of the key holder, and the vector $\mathbf{y} = (y_1, \ldots, y_n) \in \mathcal{Y} \setminus \{\mathbf{0}\}$ as inputs, where $\mathcal{Y}$ is the key space. By using the Euclidean distance, we can set a new vector $\mathbf{y}'$ that is suitable for inner product evaluation as $\mathbf{y}' = \left(1, |\mathbf{y}|^2, -2y_1, \ldots, -2y_n\right)$. Then the algorithm sets $R = \prod_{i=1}^n (y_i)^\alpha$, and calculates the following:

$$sk_1 = h_0^{\text{LBS}} \prod_{i=1}^n (h_i)^{y_i R}, \ sk_2 = h^R, sk_3 = e(g, h)^R.$$

To obtain the functional decryption key, the algorithm outputs the following:

$$sk_{\mathbf{y}'}^{\text{LBS}'} := (sk_1, sk_2, sk_3, \mathbf{y}').$$

Decrypt $\left(sk_{\mathbf{y}'}^{\text{LBS}'}, CT_{\mathbf{x}'}^{\text{LBS}}\right)$: To decrypt the given ciphertext $CT_{\mathbf{x}'}^{\text{LBS}}$ with the functional decryption key $sk_{\mathbf{y}'}^{\text{LBS}'} := (sk_1, sk_2, sk_3, \mathbf{y}')$, the decryption algorithm computes the following:

$$\langle \mathbf{x}', \mathbf{y}' \rangle = \log_{sk_3} \left\{ e(ct_1, sk_1)^{-1} \cdot e\left(\prod_{i=1}^n (ct_{2,i})^{y_i}, sk_2\right) \cdot ct_3 \right\}.$$

Correctness: To verify the correctness of our scheme, given the ciphertext $CT_{\mathbf{x}'}^{\mathrm{LBS}}$ and the functional decryption key $sk_{\mathbf{y}'}^{\mathrm{LBS}'}$ as defined above, the following procedure can be used:

$$\langle \mathbf{x}', \mathbf{y}' \rangle = \log_{sk_3} \left\{ e\left(ct_1, sk_1\right)^{-1} \cdot e\left(\prod_{i=1}^{n} (ct_{2,i})^{y_i}, sk_2\right) \cdot ct_3 \right\}$$

$$= \log_{sk_3} \left\{ e\left(g^s, h_0^{\mathrm{LBS}} \prod_{i=1}^{n} (h_i)^{y_i R}\right)^{-1} \cdot e\left(\prod_{i=1}^{n} (g^{x_i} (g_i)^s)^{y_i}, h^R\right) \cdot e\left(g, h_0^{\mathrm{LBS}}\right)^s \right\}$$

$$= \log_{sk_3} \left\{ e\left(g^s, h_0^{\mathrm{LBS}}\right)^{-1} \cdot e\left(g^s, \prod_{i=1}^{n} (h^{a_i})^{y_i R}\right)^{-1} \cdot e\left(\prod_{i=1}^{n} (g^{x_i y_i}), h^R\right) \right\}$$

$$+ \log_{sk_3} \left\{ e\left(\prod_{i=1}^{n} (g^{a_i s y_i}), h^R\right) \cdot e\left(g, h_0^{\mathrm{LBS}}\right)^s \right\}$$

$$= \log_{sk_3} \left\{ e(g, h_0^{\mathrm{LBS}})^{-s} \cdot e(g, h)^{-Rs \sum_{i=1}^{n} a_i y_i} \cdot e(g, h)^{R \sum_{i=1}^{n} x_i y_i} \right\}$$

$$+ \log_{sk_3} \left\{ e(g, h)^{Rs \sum_{i=1}^{n} a_i y_i} \cdot e(g, h_0^{\mathrm{LBS}})^s \right\}$$

$$= \log_{sk_3} \left\{ e(g, h)^{R \langle \mathbf{x}', \mathbf{y}' \rangle} \right\}.$$

The decryption algorithm finally obtains $\langle \mathbf{x}', \mathbf{y}' \rangle$ that satisfies the following equation:

$$\langle \mathbf{x}', \mathbf{y}' \rangle = \log_{sk_3} \left\{ e(g, h)^{R \langle \mathbf{x}', \mathbf{y}' \rangle} \right\}$$

$$= \log_{e(g,h)^R} \left\{ e(g, h)^{R \langle \mathbf{x}', \mathbf{y}' \rangle} \right\}$$

$$= \langle \mathbf{x}', \mathbf{y}' \rangle.$$

When the inner product value of $\langle \mathbf{x}', \mathbf{y}' \rangle$ is non-zero, the Euclidean distance metric $\triangle_{\mathbf{x}, \mathbf{y}}$ can be utilized to measure the distance between the corresponding locations. If the computed distance value falls within the predetermined threshold, it can be inferred that the user's locations are correlated. In particular, a non-zero inner product indicates that the two vectors have similarities in certain dimensions. The Euclidean distance metric can provide a more comprehensive assessment of the differences between two vectors by measuring the distribution of their similarities throughout the entire vector. If the calculated Euclidean distance value is smaller than the preset threshold, it indicates that the difference between the two vectors is small, and their locations are correlated. This information can be utilized for distance calculation.

3.3   Proof of Security

Assuming that the XDH assumption is hard, then our scheme can achieve IND-sCPA security. If an adversary $\mathcal{A}$ breaks the IND-sCPA security of our scheme with a non-negligible advantage of ϵ, a challenger $\mathcal{C}$ can be constructed to solve the XDH assumption with a non-negligible advantage of $\frac{\epsilon}{2}$. The interaction process between $\mathcal{A}$ and $\mathcal{C}$ is described below:

- **Init:** The adversary $\mathcal{A}$ selects a location-based service LBS* and sends two challenge vectors $\mathbf{x}_0'$ and $\mathbf{x}_1' \in \mathcal{X}$ to the challenger $\mathcal{C}$.
- **Setup:** The challenger $\mathcal{C}$ first chooses random exponents $\left(\alpha, a_0, a_1', \ldots, a_n'\right) \in \mathbb{Z}_q^*$ and defines the following:

$$\mathbf{x}' = \mathbf{x}_0', g_i = g^{ax_{1,i}}g^{-ax_{0,i}}g^{a_i'},$$

$$h_0 = h^{a_0}, h_i = h^{ax_{1,i}}h^{-ax_{0,i}}h^{a_i'}.$$

To simulate the system, the following parameters are specified:

$$\left\{a_i = ax_{1,i} - ax_{0,i} + a_i'\right\}_{i=1}^n.$$

Next, the challenger $\mathcal{C}$ sends the following master public key mpk to the adversary $\mathcal{A}$:

$$mpk = (g_1, \ldots, g_n, e(g, h_0)).$$

The corresponding master secret key msk can be computed as follows:

$$msk = (\alpha, h, h_0, \{h_i\}_{i=1}^n, e(g, h)),$$

where $\{h_i\}_{i=1}^n$ is unknown to the challenger $\mathcal{C}$.

- **Phase 1:** The adversary $\mathcal{A}$ adaptively requests secret key queries for the key vector $\mathbf{y}' \in \mathcal{Y} \setminus \{\mathbf{0}\}$ subject to the constraint that $\langle \mathbf{x}_0', \mathbf{y}' \rangle = \langle \mathbf{x}_1', \mathbf{y}' \rangle$, and the maximum number of queries is polynomially bounded. The challenger $\mathcal{C}$ computes $R = \prod_{i=1}^n (\mathbf{y})^\alpha$ and sets the following:

$$sk_1 = h_0^{\text{LBS}} \prod_{i=1}^n \left(h^{a_i' y_i R}\right), sk_2 = h^R, sk_3 = e(g, h)^R.$$

If the key vector $\mathbf{y}'$ satisfies $\langle \mathbf{x}_0', \mathbf{y}' \rangle - \langle \mathbf{x}_1', \mathbf{y}' \rangle = 0$, then the correct distribution of the key $(sk_1, sk_2, sk_3, \mathbf{y}')$ in the algorithm is as follows:

$$sk_1 = h_0^{\text{LBS}} \prod_{i=1}^n \left(h^{a_i' y_i R}\right) = h_0^{\text{LBS}} h^{a(\langle \mathbf{x}_0', \mathbf{y}' \rangle - \langle \mathbf{x}_1', \mathbf{y}' \rangle)R} \prod_{i=1}^n h^{a_i' y_i R}$$

$$= h_0^{\text{LBS}} \prod_{i=1}^n h^{a(x_{1,i}y_i - x_{0,i}y_i)R} \prod_{i=1}^n h^{a_i' y_i R} = h_0^{\text{LBS}} \prod_{i=1}^n \left(h^{ax_{1,i}}h^{-ax_{0,i}}h^{a_i'}\right)^{y_i R}$$

$$= h_0^{\text{LBS}} \prod_{i=1}^n (h^{a_i})^{y_i R} = h_0^{\text{LBS}} \prod_{i=1}^n (h_i)^{y_i R}.$$

Thus, the secret key $(sk_1, sk_2, sk_3, \mathbf{y}')$ defined above satisfies the following property:

$$sk_1 = h_0^{\text{LBS}} \prod_{i=1}^n (h_i)^{y_i R}, sk_2 = h^R, sk_3 = e(g, h)^R.$$

As the secret key $sk_{\mathbf{y'}}^{\mathrm{LBS}} := (sk_1, sk_2, sk_3, \mathbf{y'})$ for $\mathbf{y'}$ satisfies the definition, it is valid. The challenger $\mathcal{C}$ then sends $sk_{\mathbf{y'}}^{\mathrm{LBS}}$ to the adversary $\mathcal{A}$.

- **Challenge**: If the adversary $\mathcal{A}$ successfully completes Phase 1, the challenger $\mathcal{C}$ sets the following:

$$ct_1 = g^b, \left\{ ct_{2,i} = g^{x_i} T^{x_{1,i} - x_{0,i}} g^{a_i' b} \right\}_{i=1}^n, ct_3 = e(g^b, h_0^{\mathrm{LBS}}).$$

If $s = b$ and $T = g^{ab}$, the correct distribution of the ciphertext $\{ct_1, (ct_{2,1}, \ldots, ct_{2,n}), ct_3\}$ for the message vector $\mathbf{x'}$ computed by the algorithm is as follows:

$$ct_{2,i} = g^{x_i} T^{x_{1,i} - x_{0,i}} g^{a_i' b} = g^{x_i} \left(g^{ab}\right)^{x_{1,i} - x_{0,i}} g^{a_i' b}$$

$$= g^{x_i} g^{ab(x_{1,i} - x_{0,i})} g^{a_i' b} = g^{x_i} g^{a x_{1,i} b} g^{-a x_{0,i} b} g^{a_i' b}$$

$$= g^{x_i} g^{a_i b} = g^{x_i} (g_i)^b.$$

Thus, the ciphertext $\{ct_1, (ct_{2,1}, \ldots, ct_{2,n}), ct_3\}$ defined above satisfies the following property:

$$ct_1 = g^s, ct_{2,i} = g^{x_i} (g_i)^s, ct_3 = e(g, h_0^{\mathrm{LBS}})^s.$$

This satisfies the definition, and the challenger $\mathcal{C}$ sends the ciphertext $CT_{\mathbf{x'}}^{\mathrm{LBS}} := \{\mathrm{LBS}, ct_1, (ct_{2,1}, \ldots, ct_{2,n}), ct_3\}$ to the adversary $\mathcal{A}$.

- **Phase 2**: The adversary $\mathcal{A}$ continuously requests secret keys for additional key vectors with the same restrictions as in Phase 1.
- **Guess**: If $\beta' = \beta$, the challenger $\mathcal{C}$ outputs 1 to indicate that $T = g^{ab}$; otherwise, $\mathcal{C}$ outputs 0 to indicate that $T \neq g^{ab}$.

The following analysis concerns the probability of the challenger $\mathcal{C}$ successfully solving the XDH assumption. Let $success$ denote the event of $\mathcal{C}$ successfully solving the XDH assumption, $\gamma = 1$ denote $T = g^{ab}$, and $\gamma = 0$ denote $T \neq g^{ab}$. Hence, we have:

$$Pr[success] = Pr[success|\gamma = 1]Pr[\gamma = 1] + Pr[success|\gamma = 0]Pr[\gamma = 0]$$

$$= \frac{1}{2} \cdot \left(\frac{1}{2} + \epsilon\right) + \frac{1}{2} \cdot \frac{1}{2}$$

$$= \frac{1}{2} + \frac{\epsilon}{2}.$$

In the above equation, if $T = g^{ab}$ (with a probability of $\frac{1}{2}$), the challenger $\mathcal{C}$ perfectly simulates the game, and the adversary $\mathcal{A}$ wins the game with a probability of $\frac{1}{2} + \frac{\epsilon}{2}$. On the other hand, if $T \neq g^{ab}$, $\mathcal{C}$ cannot simulate the game, and $\mathcal{A}$ wins the game with a probability of only $\frac{1}{2}$. In summary, the advantage of the challenger $\mathcal{C}$ in solving the XDH assumption can be expressed as follows:

$$Adv_{\mathcal{C}}^{\mathrm{XDH}} = Pr[success] - \frac{1}{2} = \frac{\epsilon}{2}.$$

Since ϵ is non-negligible in our assumption, $Adv_{\mathcal{C}}^{\mathrm{XDH}}$ is also non-negligible. Thus, if the adversary $\mathcal{A}$ breaks the IND-sCPA security of our scheme with non-negligible advantage, the challenger $\mathcal{C}$ will solve the XDH assumption with non-negligible advantage.

4   Discussion and Application

This chapter explores a variety of real-world applications that can be developed and implemented using secure distance calculation. By exploring these applications, readers can gain a deeper understanding of the potential of our scheme and its impact on our daily lives.

4.1   Contact Tracing

To demonstrate the versatility of our scheme, we present an application that utilizes it to measure the distance between two points. The computation of the inner product between two vectors can be equivalent to the calculation of the distance between two points. To illustrate, consider the distance between two points represented by vectors $\mathbf{x}' = \left(|\mathbf{x}|^2, 1, x_1, \ldots, x_n\right)$ and $\mathbf{y}' = \left(|\mathbf{y}|^2, 1, y_1, \ldots, y_n\right)$. The Euclidean distance formula can be utilized to calculate this distance as follows: $\triangle_{\mathbf{x},\mathbf{y}} = \sqrt{\sum_{i=1}^{n}(x_i - y_i)^2}$.

In our scheme, we can decrypt the ciphertext $CT_{\mathbf{x}'}^{\mathrm{LBS}}$ with the secret key $sk_{\mathbf{y}'}^{\mathrm{LBS}}$ based on the user's location service. Then we can compute the squared Euclidean distance $\triangle_{\mathbf{x}',\mathbf{y}'}^2$ between the two vectors $\mathbf{x}'$ and $\mathbf{y}'$. Our scheme helps to identify close contacts of infectious diseases while preserving the privacy of the individuals involved. Assuming that each element of the vector represents the user's location information, our scheme computes the value of the inner product between itself and an infected individual, without directly accessing the infected individual's location data. By computing the inner product of their encrypted location information and the encrypted location information of the infected person, users can identify potential contact with the infected person while preserving the privacy of the individuals involved. Therefore, our scheme offers a promising approach for contact tracing and other distance calculations that require privacy-preserving computations.

4.2   Chat Recommendation

By incorporating our scheme into nearby chat applications enables users to filter out other nearby users, while keeping their own location information confidential. In this scenario, if a vector represents a person's location information, users can determine the differences in their location with respect to others, without revealing their own location information. This allows users to determine their distance from others based on distance calculations and conduct online chats based on relative location distance while protecting their privacy. As a result, users can determine the proximity of others and start a conversation based on their relative location, all while maintaining the protection of their privacy. This methodology can also be extended to a range of location-based services, including location-based advertising or tailored recommendations. By evaluating the inner product and encrypting the inner product function, our scheme promotes secure and efficient distance computation while maintaining user privacy.

5 Conclusion

In this paper, we present a novel scheme that based on inner product functional encryption technology that is capable of encrypting and protecting user location information, thereby achieving secure distance calculation. Unlike conventional location-based service schemes, it does not reveal the user's actual location information. Instead, the scheme conceals it through encryption, which can only be decrypted by similar locations users with access to the location information. In the security proof of our scheme, we demonstrate its resilience against chosen plaintext attacks in the standard model, based on the asymmetric XDH assumption. The potential applications of our scheme are numerous, including contact tracing for infectious diseases, but there is still room for improvement in terms of security. Future research directions should focus on constructing more secure schemes, such as adaptively secure and simulation-based secure schemes, to further enhance the security of our scheme.

References

1. Shamir, A.: Identity-based cryptosystems and signature schemes. In: Blakley, G.R., Chaum, D. (eds.) CRYPTO 1984. LNCS, vol. 196, pp. 47–53. Springer, Heidelberg (1985). https://doi.org/10.1007/3-540-39568-7_5
2. Boneh, D., Franklin, M.: Identity-based encryption from the weil pairing. In: Kilian, J. (ed.) CRYPTO 2001. LNCS, vol. 2139, pp. 213–229. Springer, Heidelberg (2001). https://doi.org/10.1007/3-540-44647-8_13
3. Boneh, D., Boyen, X.: Efficient selective identity-based encryption without random oracles. J. Cryptol. **24**, 659–693 (2011)
4. Waters, B.: Ciphertext-policy attribute-based encryption: an expressive, efficient, and provably secure realization. In: Catalano, D., Fazio, N., Gennaro, R., Nicolosi, A. (eds.) PKC 2011. LNCS, vol. 6571, pp. 53–70. Springer, Heidelberg (2011). https://doi.org/10.1007/978-3-642-19379-8_4
5. Goyal, V., Pandey, O., Sahai, A., et al.: Attribute-based encryption for fine-grained access control of encrypted data. In: Proceedings of the 13th ACM Conference on Computer and Communications Security, pp. 89–98 (2006)
6. Lewko, A., Okamoto, T., Sahai, A., Takashima, K., Waters, B.: Fully secure functional encryption: attribute-based encryption and (hierarchical) inner product encryption. In: Gilbert, H. (ed.) EUROCRYPT 2010. LNCS, vol. 6110, pp. 62–91. Springer, Heidelberg (2010). https://doi.org/10.1007/978-3-642-13190-5_4
7. Katz, J., Sahai, A., Waters, B.: Predicate encryption supporting disjunctions, polynomial equations, and inner products. In: Smart, N. (ed.) EUROCRYPT 2008. LNCS, vol. 4965, pp. 146–162. Springer, Heidelberg (2008). https://doi.org/10.1007/978-3-540-78967-3_9

8. Okamoto, T., Takashima, K.: Hierarchical predicate encryption for inner-products. In: Matsui, M. (ed.) ASIACRYPT 2009. LNCS, vol. 5912, pp. 214–231. Springer, Heidelberg (2009). https://doi.org/10.1007/978-3-642-10366-7_13

9. Gay, R., Méaux, P., Wee, H.: Predicate encryption for multi-dimensional range queries from lattices. In: Katz, J. (ed.) PKC 2015. LNCS, vol. 9020, pp. 752–776. Springer, Heidelberg (2015). https://doi.org/10.1007/978-3-662-46447-2_34

10. Garg, S., et al.: Candidate indistinguishability obfuscation and functional encryption for all circuits. SIAM J. Comput. **45**(3), 882–929 (2016)

11. Boneh, D., Sahai, A., Waters, B.: Functional encryption: definitions and challenges. In: Ishai, Y. (ed.) TCC 2011. LNCS, vol. 6597, pp. 253–273. Springer, Heidelberg (2011). https://doi.org/10.1007/978-3-642-19571-6_16

12. Goldwasser, S., et al.: Reusable garbled circuits and succinct functional encryption. In: Proceedings of the Forty-Fifth Annual ACM Symposium on Theory of Computing (2013)

13. O'Neill, A.: Definitional issues in functional encryption. Cryptology ePrint Archive (2010)

14. Garg, S., et al.: Candidate indistinguishability obfuscation and functional encryption for all circuits. SIAM J. Comput. **45**(3), 882–929 (2016)

15. Garg, S., et al.: Fully Secure Functional Encryption without Obfuscation. IACR Cryptology ePrint Archive 2014, p. 666 (2014)

16. Abdalla, M., et al.: Simple functional encryption schemes for inner products. Cryptology ePrint Archive (2015)

17. Tomida, J.: Tightly secure inner product functional encryption: multi-input and function-hiding constructions. Theoret. Comput. Sci. **833**, 56–86 (2020)

18. Agrawal, S., Libert, B., Stehlé, D.: Fully secure functional encryption for inner products, from standard assumptions. In: Robshaw, M., Katz, J. (eds.) CRYPTO 2016. LNCS, vol. 9816, pp. 333–362. Springer, Heidelberg (2016). https://doi.org/10.1007/978-3-662-53015-3_12

19. Attrapadung, N., Libert, B.: Functional encryption for inner product: achieving constant-size ciphertexts with adaptive security or support for negation. In: Nguyen, P.Q., Pointcheval, D. (eds.) PKC 2010. LNCS, vol. 6056, pp. 384–402. Springer, Heidelberg (2010). https://doi.org/10.1007/978-3-642-13013-7_23

20. Kim, S., Lewi, K., Mandal, A., Montgomery, H., Roy, A., Wu, D.J.: Function-hiding inner product encryption is practical. In: Catalano, D., De Prisco, R. (eds.) SCN 2018. LNCS, vol. 11035, pp. 544–562. Springer, Cham (2018). https://doi.org/10.1007/978-3-319-98113-0_29

21. Castagnos, G., Laguillaumie, F., Tucker, I.: Practical fully secure unrestricted inner product functional encryption modulo p. In: Peyrin, T., Galbraith, S. (eds.) ASIACRYPT 2018. LNCS, vol. 11273, pp. 733–764. Springer, Cham (2018). https://doi.org/10.1007/978-3-030-03329-3_25

22. Uzunkol, O., Kiraz, M.S.: Still wrong use of pairings in cryptography. Appl. Math. Comput. **333**, 467–479 (2018)

23. Chen, J., Lim, H.W., Ling, S., Wang, H., Wee, H.: Shorter IBE and signatures via asymmetric pairings. In: Abdalla, M., Lange, T. (eds.) Pairing 2012. LNCS, vol. 7708, pp. 122–140. Springer, Heidelberg (2013). https://doi.org/10.1007/978-3-642-36334-4_8

24. Abdalla, M., Gay, R., Raykova, M., Wee, H.: Multi-input inner-product functional encryption from pairings. In: Coron, J.-S., Nielsen, J.B. (eds.) EUROCRYPT 2017. LNCS, vol. 10210, pp. 601–626. Springer, Cham (2017). https://doi.org/10.1007/978-3-319-56620-7_21

25. Agrawal, S., Libert, B., Maitra, M., Titiu, R.: Adaptive simulation security for inner product functional encryption. In: Kiayias, A., Kohlweiss, M., Wallden, P., Zikas, V. (eds.) PKC 2020. LNCS, vol. 12110, pp. 34–64. Springer, Cham (2020). https://doi.org/10.1007/978-3-030-45374-9_2

26. Tomida, J., Takashima, K.: Unbounded inner product functional encryption from bilinear maps. Jpn. J. Ind. Appl. Math. **37**, 723–779 (2020)

27. Dufour-Sans, E., Pointcheval, D.: Unbounded inner-product functional encryption with succinct keys. In: Deng, R.H., Gauthier-Umaña, V., Ochoa, M., Yung, M. (eds.) ACNS 2019. LNCS, vol. 11464, pp. 426–441. Springer, Cham (2019). https://doi.org/10.1007/978-3-030-21568-2_21

Efficient Non-interactive Zero-Knowledge Proof for Graph 3-Coloring Problem

Haitao Zhan[1], Dongyang Bai[1], Yuzhu Wang[1], and Mingwu Zhang[1,2,3(✉)]

[1] School of Computer Science and Information Security, Guilin University of
Electronic Technology, Guilin 541004, China
[2] MetaRTC Co. Ltd., Wuhan 430073, China
[3] School of Computer Science, Hubei University of Technology,
Wuhan 430068, China
mzhang@hbut.edu.cn

Abstract. Zero-knowledge proof (ZKP) has a crucial role in the construction of cryptographic protocols and privacy protection. One of the
core research components of zero-knowledge proof is the NP-complete
(NPC) problem. This paper focus on a classic NPC problem graph 3-
coloring problem (3-GCP). Firstly, we propose a non-interactive zero-
knowledge (NIZK) proof scheme for the 3-GCP. In our scheme, the prover
generates a proof π for each edge based on the graph and the coloring
scheme. The verifier then chooses whether to trust the provers' proof
based solely on π. This is the non-interaction between the prover and the
verifier. Moreover, we optimize this scheme for efficiency based on the
idea of homomorphic encryption. It allows each execution of the scheme
to prove a vertex in the graph. Finally, we present the security analysis
and computational cost of our solution, which again demonstrates that
our solution is feasible.

Keywords: Non-interactive proof · Privacy protection · Computation
zero-knowledge · Commitment

1 Introduction

The concept of zero-knowledge proof was first introduced by Goldwasser, Micali,
and Rackoff [18]. Informally, a zero-knowledge proof is essentially a protocol
involving two or more parties, that is, a sequence of steps that two or more
parties need to take in order to complete a task. It requires that the prover be
able to convince the verifier that he has a secret piece of evidence w related to a
given public input x, but that the proof procedure does not reveal any information about w to the verifier. Since their introduction, zero-knowledge proofs have
occupied an important place in contemporary cryptography. Not only does it provide strong support as a cryptographic primitive to implement the analysis and

This work is supported by the National Natural Science Foundation of China under
grants 62072134 and U2001205, and the Key projects of Guangxi Natural Science Foundation under grant 2019JJD170020, and the Key Research and Development Program
of Hubei Province under Grant 2021BEA163.

construction of various cryptographic protocols, but its proof methods have also become widely used methods. It has used in domains as diverse as anonymous voting and identity authentication [29,30], witness encryption [17,32], Smart contracts [2] and other aspects.

A classical example of a zero-knowledge proof is the 3-GCP, which is also known to be an NPC problem. We say that a graph G is 3-colorable if one can color the vertices of G with 3 colors in such a way that any two adjacent vertices receive two different colors. A zero-knowledge proof of the 3-coloring problem for a graph requires that if the prover knows a 3-coloring scheme χ for the graph G, then he must be able to convince the verifier that he has the χ and that the verifier does not get any useful information about χ in the course of the proof. Zero-knowledge proofs for 3-GCP have been extensively studied. Several recent works [3,12] have given some proof schemes based on substitution technology. However, it still suffers from numerous problems. First, during the verification process, the verifier needs to send the challenge value. It requires both parties to be online at the same time, which is infeasible for some scenarios. Then, each run of the protocol is capable of proving only one edge of the graph, which means that the protocol requires a large number of runs. This significantly adds to the computational cost.

In some cases, zero-knowledge proofs rely on commitment schemes. A commitment is a cryptographic primitive that is often a fundamental ingredient of various cryptographic protocols. The cryptographic commitment involves two players, the committer and the verifier, and is divided into a commitment generation phase and a commitment opening phase. In the commitment generation phase, the committer select a sensitive data v, compute the corresponding commitment c, and then send the commitment c to the verifier. With the commitment c, the verifier determines that the commitr can only have one way to interpret the data v, which has not yet been decrypted and cannot be broken. In the commitment opening phase, the committer announces the explicit text of data v and other relevant parameters, and the verifier repeats the computation process of commitment generation, comparing whether the newly generated commitment is consistent with the previously received commitment c. If it is consistent, the verification is successful, otherwise it fails. The currently used commitment schemes are: bit commitment based on pseudo-randomn generator [26], hash commitment based on unidirectionality of hash function [9], Pedersen commitment based on discrete logarithm problem [25], bit commitment based on symmetric cryptographic utility [15], etc. Inspired by the idea of homomorphic encryption [1], in this paper we use Fujisaki-Okamoto (FO) commitment [16] based on the discrete logarithm assumption to construct a zero-knowledge proof scheme. It allows each execution of the scheme to prove a vertex in the graph, significantly reducing the number of runs and the computational cost of the scheme.

1.1 Contribution

In this paper, we first give and construct a non-interacting zero-knowledge proof scheme for 3-GCP based on the discrete logarithm assumption. In this scheme, we make it possible for the prover and the verifier not to be online at the same time by using knowledge in the cyclic group with secret order technology [28]. We then optimize the scheme according to the idea of homomorphic encryption, such that each execution of the scheme proves a vertex in the graph, thus reducing the computational cost.

- Provide formal definitions and security concepts for the non-interactive zero-knowledge proof scheme for the 3-GCP.
- Based on the discrete logarithm assumption, we construct an efficient non-interactive zero-knowledge proof scheme for the 3-GCP. Then inspired by the idea of homomorphic encryption, we optimize the scheme such that there is no interaction between the prover and verifier. In terms of computational cost, compared to $O(nm\lambda)$ commitments of [21] and $O(n + m\lambda)$ commitments of [12], our scheme only needs to generate $O(n + m)$ commitments, where n is the total number of vertices of the graph G, m is the total number of edges of the graph G, and λ is the security parameter.
- We give a security analysis of our constructed scheme and show that our scheme achieves computational soundness and computational zero-knowledge. In our scheme, we use FO commitment based on the discrete logarithm assumption for each vertex in the graph. Due to the binding of the commitment scheme, if the prover does not have quantum computing power, the verifier will reject the proof of the prover with overwhelming probability when the prover does not know a specific 3-coloring scheme. Moreover, the prover uses a randomly chosen value for each commitment in the proof phase to improve zero-knowledge. Also due to the hiding of the commitment scheme, the verifier cannot obtain any knowledge of the graph 3-coloring scheme unless the verifier is able to break the discrete logarithm problem.

1.2 Related Work

Interactive proof systems have been used extensively in the study of NPC problems since they were proposed by Goldwasser, Micali, and Rackoff [18]. In fact, due to the graph theory as the main source of NPC problems, some computational zero-knowledge proof techniques based on different graph problems such as isomorphism, diffeomorphism, clustering, independent sets, etc. have been proposed [14,19,20]. However, the application scenario is limited by the fact that interactive proof systems require both the prover and the verifier to be online. In 1986, Amos Fiat and Adi Shamir proposed the Fiat-Shamir transformation [13], which can convert an interactive zero-knowledge proof system to a non-interactive zero-knowledge proof system by a hash function. Recently, Chris Peikert et al. [27] constructed a non-interactive zero-knowledge proof system for NP languages that uses hash functions to apply the Fiat-shamir transform in a reasonable way to achieve non-interactivity. The concept of non-interactive zero-knowledge proofs is proposed by Blum et al. in [5]. Protocols implemented through non-interactive zero-knowledge proofs significantly save protocol execution time and improve the efficiency of protocol operation. This is important in applications such as blockchain, anonymous verifiable voting, and secure exchange of digital assets.

As a classical NPC problem, the zero-knowledge proof sketch for the 3-GCP is given by Brasaard and Crepéau [7]. Later, Kilian [21] proposed an efficient zero-knowledge proof system for the 3-GCP. The protocol is based on the implementation of "notary envelopes" using "ideal bit commitment" and "pair-blob". In the protocol, the prover uses bit commitment and XOR operations to color the vertices of the graph G. Subsequently the verifier sends a random challenge edge $e_{ij}(v_i, v_j)$ to the prover. After receiving the edge e_{ij} the prover proves that $v_i \neq v_j$ without exposing any information about v_i and v_j. However, this protocol is not non-interactive, which means that both the prover and the verifier must be online. Secondly, a malicious prover can color the graph with more than three colors, which means that the soundness of the protocol does not hold. In order to solve this problem, Ehsan Ebrahimi [12] proposed a bit commitment scheme based on the Learning Parity with Noise (LPN) problem and used it to construct an interactive zero knowledge proof system. In the scheme the prover does not reveal the specific color of the vertices, but proves that the two vertices are colored differently by an inequality protocol with a much reduced number of commitments. However, this scheme is still interactive and in order to achieve negligible soundness errors, the protocol must be run in large numbers, which leads to the generation of a large number of commitments and is not efficient. In addition, Cheng-Long Li et al. [22] generated a quantum randomness service [4,24] random number certified by the leak-free Bell test and conceived a non-interactive zero-knowledge proof system for the three-color problem using this technical system. Unfortunately, their solution is still interactive. In our work, the proof scheme satisfies non-interactivity, computational soundness, and computational zero-knowledge. Also, in terms of computational cost, the proof sends only $O(n + m)$ commitments to the verifier, where n is the total number of vertices of the graph.

1.3 Organization

Section 2 is dedicated to notations, key technologies and definitions needed in this paper. We provide formal definitions and security concepts for non-interactive zero-knowledge proof scheme of the 3-GCP in Sect. 3. In Sect. 4, we first construct a computational zero-knowledge non-interactive proof system for proving the 3-GCP. We then optimize the scheme so that each run of the proof Algorithm completes a zero-knowledge proof for all edges associated with any one vertex in the graph. Finally, we conclude in Sect. 5.

2 Preliminaries

2.1 Notations

Let $\mathbb{R}$, $\mathbb{Z}$, $\mathbb{N}$ be the set of real numbers, integers and natural numbers, respectively, and a universe of 3-Coloring scheme $\mathcal{K}$. If S is a finite set then $x \xleftarrow{\$} S$ is the operation of picking an element uniformly from S. In this paper, we use χ to denote a 3-coloring scheme, where $\chi \xleftarrow{\$} \mathcal{K}$. For a natural number n, $[n]$ means the set $\{1, \ldots, n\}$. N is a large composite number and the factorization of N is unknown. $\mathbb{Z}_N^*$ is an integer group under multiplication modulo N without the factors of N, and $\mathbb{G}$ is a cyclic subgroup of $\mathbb{Z}_N^*$ with a large order. Integers g and h are generators of $\mathbb{G}$, $h = g^L \bmod N$ and L is unknown to anyone except the parameter generator, where $L \in \mathbb{Z}$. We denote by $[a, b]$ that the secret number v lies between a and b, a is a lower bound and b is an upper bound for the given range. If s_1 and s_2 are two strings of characters, then $s_1 \parallel s_2$ represents the concatenation of string s_1 and string s_2. $Pr[P : V]$ is the probability that the predicate P holds true where free variables in P are assigned according to the program in V. Unless otherwise stated, we use λ as a safety parameter throughout the paper. A nonnegative function $negl(\lambda) = 1/o(\lambda^t)$ is called negligible, which vanishes faster than any polynomial of degree t, $\forall t \in \mathbb{N}$.

2.2 The Fujisaki-Okamoto Commitment Scheme

In this paper we use FO commitment scheme [16] as our commitment scheme. To make things easier, we denote the commitment to v in the base (g, h) by $Com(v, r) = g^v h^r \bmod N$, where r is randomly selected over $\mathbb{Z}$.

$Com(v, r)$ is considered by Boudot to be a statistically secure commitment Scheme [6]. Informally, the prover $\mathcal{P}$ is unable to generate the same commitment for two values v_1 and v_2, such that $v_1 \neq v_2$ unless $\mathcal{P}$ can factor N or solve the discrete logarithm of g in base h or the discrete logarithm of h in base g. In other words, $\mathcal{P}$ finds v_1, v_2, r_1, r_2 where $v_1 \neq v_2$ such that $Com(v, r)$ is computationally infeasible. Similarly, we say that the commitment does not statistically reveal any information about the secret to the verifier, because any two commitments are statistically indistinguishable for the verifier. Formally, there exists a simulator S^* that generates statistically indistinguishable commitments without knowledge of the v from those generated by the real commitment of the $\mathcal{P}$.

Definition 1. *secret order principle. N is a large composite with unknown factorization and $\mathbb{G}$ is a cyclic subgroup of $\mathbb{Z}_N^*$ with a large order. It is hard to calculate any multiple of the order of $\mathbb{G}$ if factorization of N is hard.*

The secret ordering principle is based on the large integer decomposition problem. This principle implies that it is computationally infeasible to compute arbitrary multiples of subgroup order as long as the factorization of mod N is intractable. And it also guarantees the binding and uniqueness of the prover to the committed integers. The security of the FO commitment [16] is based on this principle.

2.3 Knowledge of Discrete Logarithm in a Cyclic Group with a Secret Order (KDLCGSO)

KDLCGSO can be seen as a variant of the schnorr protocol [29], which enables a party to prove knowledge of integers v and r to satisfy $g^v h^r = y \bmod N$. In [23] KDLCGSO is most basic and important proof primitive. In [8], the author also uses this primitive to prove that the number of commitments is a square.

Let $y = g^v h^r \bmod N$ be the common input, and we denote $\mathcal{P}$ as the prover and $\mathcal{V}$ as the verifier. $\mathcal{P}$ wants to convince $\mathcal{V}$ that he/she knows a secret $v \in \mathbb{Z}$. KDLCGSO is described in Table 1.

The following KDLCGSO is a non-interactive zero-knowledge proof protocol. In contrast to the interactive KDLCGSO, it implements the non-interactive feature by using the Fiat-Shamir transformation to generate challenges. Note that the KDLCGSO used in this paper is the non-interactive version unless otherwise stated. The KDLCGSO proof satisfies computational soundness and computational zero-knowledge, where the soundness of the KDLCGSO proof relies on Theorem 1.

Table 1. KDLCGSO.

1) $\mathcal{P} \rightarrow \mathcal{V}$: $\qquad\qquad\qquad R = g^a h^b$
   where a and b are randomly chosen from a large set of integers.

2) $\mathcal{P} \rightarrow \mathcal{V}$: $\qquad\qquad\qquad x = \mathcal{H}(y \| R)$
   where $\mathcal{H}(\cdot)$ is a secure hash function

3) $\mathcal{P} \rightarrow \mathcal{V}$: $\qquad\qquad\qquad S_1 = a + xv$
   $\qquad\qquad\qquad\qquad\qquad\quad S_2 = b + xr$

4) $\mathcal{V}$ verification:
   $\qquad\qquad\qquad\qquad\quad g^{S_1} h^{S_2} = \alpha \cdot y^x$

Theorem 1. *Even if the order of g and h are secret, there is still a polynomial algorithm to calculate integers v and r to satisfy $g^v h^r = y \bmod N$.*

The earliest formal proof of the theorem appeared in [16], but the same author [10] finds out that the analysis in [16] is incomplete. No formal proof of theorem 1 is available until [11]. Proof of theorem 1 is quite complex, proof of theorem 1 is not repeated here and interested readers are referred to [11].

In [6,23], KDLCGSO is used as a cryptographic primitive for other protocols. In [6], "proof that two commitments hide the same secret" and "proof that a committed number is a square" are combinations of two KDLCGSO proofs sharing the same secret logarithms. In [23], to proof that a committed number is a square is the same as in [6] and employs two combined KDLCGSO proofs. The soundness of them all depends on theorem 1. We follow the syntax in [28] and proof that two commitments hide the same secret is denoted as $EL(v, r_1, r_2 | g_1, h_1, g_2, h_2 | A, B)$. The EL proof is a kind of zero-knowledge proof protocol and is used to verify whether two commitments A and B where $A = g_1^v h_1^{r_1} \bmod N$ and $B = g_2^v h_2^{r_2} \bmod N$ hiding the same secret v or not. Proof that a committed number is a square is denoted as $SQR(v, r | g, h | A)$, The SQR function is a zero-knowledge proof and is used to verify whether the commitment $A = g^{v^2} h^r \bmod N$ hiding the square secret v^2 or not.

2.4   Committed Integer Lies in a Specific Interval (RG)

RG proof was first proposed by Brickell and others in [8]. This proof is used to verify whether the secret number in commitment lies in a specific interval or not. Such kind of proofs are intensively used in several schemes: electronic cash systems, group signatures, publicly verifiable secret sharing schemes, and other zero-knowledge protocols. We denote this proof as $RG(v, r|g, h|A|[a, b])$, and the RG proof is a kind of zero-knowledge proof and is used to verify that the commitment $A = g^v h^r \bmod N$ hides an integer v that lies in a particular interval $[a, b]$. The specific implementations of the proof protocol is not provided here. They can be found in [31].

Here we will introduce a variant of the RG proof, which we call the PRG proof. In fact, for a commitment $A = g^v h^r \bmod N$ we find that Tsai et al. transform the proof that v is in $[a, b]$ into a proof that a number c related to v is greater than 0 when constructing the RG proof. For a commitment $B = g^m h^r \bmod N$, we write its PRG proof as $PRG(m, r|g, h|B)$, which means that the secret number m hidden in the commitment B is a positive integer. For easy understanding, we briefly discuss the process of PRG as follows: where (g, h, B) can be regarded as public parameters, and $\mathcal{P}$ is the prover and $\mathcal{V}$ is the verifier.

- $\mathcal{P}$:
  1) Pick a big random non-zero integer x and a integer r', compute $C = B^{x^2} h^{r'} \bmod N$.
  2) Run the SQR protocol to get $SQR_1(x, r'|B, h|C)$.
  3) Randomly choose an integer α such that $\alpha^2 < mx^2$ (If not, reselect α until the condition is met) and calculate $\beta = mx^2 - \alpha^2$.
  4) set two positive integers r_1 and r_2 such that $r_1 + r_2 = rx^2 + r'$, and calculate $D = g^{\alpha^2} h^{r_1} \bmod N, E = g^\beta h^{r_2} \bmod N$.
  5) Run the SQR protocol to get $SQR_2(\alpha, r_1|g, h|D)$ and publish: $\pi = (C, D, E, SQR_1, SQR_2, \beta)$.
- $\mathcal{V}$ check:
  - Is C equal to $D \times E$, SQR_1, SQR_2 and is β greater than 0.

If $\mathcal{V}$ can pass the above proofs, then the $\mathcal{V}$ will believe that the secret m hidden by that commitment B is a positive integer. Simply put, SQR_1 ensures that the secret number in C is the product of m and a square number, so we have $m > 0$ when $mx^2 > 0$. And because $C = D \times E$, that is, $mx^2 = \alpha^2 + \beta$, and $\beta > 0$, so $m > 0$.

3   Definition of NIZK Proof for 3-GCP

In this section, we provide the formal definition and security concept of the non-interactive zero-knowledge proof scheme for the 3-GCP.

Definition 2. *Non-interactive zero-knowledge proof arguments for 3-GCP. A NIZK proof argument for 3-GCP consists of three polynomial (possibly randomized) algorithms Setup Prove and Verify described below.*

- $pk \leftarrow Setup(1^\lambda)$ The polynomial algorithm $Setup$ takes as input the security parameter λ and returns public parameter pk.
- $\pi \leftarrow Prove(\chi, pk)$ The polynomial algorithm $Prove$ takes as input the parameter pk and the 3-coloring scheme $\chi \xleftarrow{\$} \mathcal{K}$ and returns the proof π.
- $b \leftarrow Verify(\pi, pk)$ The verification algorithm $Verify$ on inputs pk and π, returns a bit b that indicates the accept (when $b = 1$) or the reject (when $b = 0$).

The NIZK proof argument for 3-GCP typically satisfies three security properties: correctness, soundness, and zero-knowledge. We explain this in more detail below.

Correctness. The correctness property states that an honest prover can follow the protocol and convince the verifier by all proofs that it owns a 3-coloring scheme χ of the graph G.

Definition 3. *Correctness of NIZK proof argument for 3-GCP. Let NIZK proof argument for the 3-GCP = (Setup, Prove, Verify) be a non-interactive zero-knowledge proof arguments for the 3-GCP. If for all security parameters λ, a NIZK proof argument for 3-GCP = (Setup, Prove, Verify) satisfies the correctness property for any valid 3-color scheme $\chi \xleftarrow{\$} \mathcal{K}$ of the graph G, the following probabilities are satisfied.*

$$Pr\left[Verify(\pi, pk) = 1 : \begin{array}{c} pk \xleftarrow{\$} Setup(1^\lambda) \\ \pi \xleftarrow{\$} Prove(\chi, pk) \end{array}\right] \geq 1 - negl(\lambda)$$

Soundness. The soundness property states that if the proof passes with non-negligible probability, then $\chi \xleftarrow{\$} \mathcal{K}$ must be a valid 3-coloring scheme of the graph G and known by the prover.

Definition 4. *Soundness of NIZK proof argument for 3-GCP. Let NIZK proof argument for the 3-GCP = (Setup, Prove, Verify) be a non-interactive zero-knowledge proof arguments for the 3-GCP. A NIZK proof argument for the 3-GCP = (Set, Pro, Ver) satisfies the soundness property if there exists a PPT simulator S and for any λ such that the following probabilistic is negligible.*

$$Pr\left[Verify(\pi, pk) = 1 \wedge \chi \notin \mathcal{K} : \begin{array}{c} pk \xleftarrow{\$} Setup(1^\lambda) \\ \pi \xleftarrow{\$} Prove(\chi, pk) \end{array}\right] \leqslant negl(\lambda)$$

Zero-Knowledge. The zero-knowledge property states that a polynomially bounded malicious verifier cannot obtain any information about the knowledge χ. No one can obtain the secret unless the verifier discloses it.

Definition 5. *Zero-knowledge of NIZK proof argument for 3-GCP. Let NIZK proof argument for the 3-GCP = (Set, Pro, Ver) be a non-interactive zero-knowledge proof argument for the 3-GCP. A NNIZK proof argument for the 3-GCP = (Setup, Prove, Verify) satisfies the zero-knowledge property if there exists a PPT simulator S^* and for all security parameter λ, adversaries $\mathcal{A}$, such that the following probabilistic is negligible.*

$$Pr\left[b = b' : \begin{array}{c} pk \xleftarrow{\$} Setup(1^\lambda) \\ b \xleftarrow{\$} (0,1); \chi \xleftarrow{\$} \mathcal{A}(pk) \\ \pi_1 \xleftarrow{\$} Prove(\chi, pk); \pi_0 \xleftarrow{\$} S^*(pk) \\ b' \xleftarrow{\$} \mathcal{A}(pk, \pi_b) \end{array}\right] - \frac{1}{2} \leqslant negl(\lambda)$$

4 Our Construction for the NIZK Proof of 3-GCP

In this section, first, we construct a NIZK proof scheme for 3-GCP that achieves non-interaction between the prover and the verifier, and we present a security analysis of the scheme. Second, we optimize the scheme based on the idea of homomorphic encryption and give a general construction in which the optimized scheme preserves the non-interactivity of the original scheme and is more efficient.

4.1 Construction 1

We say a graph $G(V, E)$, where $|V| = n$, $|E| = m$, is 3-colorable if there exists a map $\chi : V \rightarrow \{01, 10, 11\}$ such that for any edge $e_{ij}(v_i, v_j) \in E$, $\chi(v_i) \neq \chi(v_j)$, where $i \in [n], j \in [n]$ and $i \neq j$ that is, the two vertices of any one edge are mapped to different colors. For convenience, in this paper we directly denote the mapping $\chi(v_i)$ of v_i by v_i if not specifically stated. The core idea behind the scheme is that graph $G(V, E)$ is 3-colorable if and only if $|v_i - v_j| > 0$ i.e.$(v_i - v_j)^2 > 0$ for all $e_{ij}(v_i, v_j) \in E$ and $v_i \in [1, 3]$, $v_j \in [1, 3]$. If we directly use $(v_i - v_j)^2$ in our scheme, it may leak the information about v_i and v_j with high probability. Therefore we compute $\varphi^2(v_i - v_j)^2$, where $\varphi \xleftarrow{\$} \mathbb{Z}$. So, when $\varphi^2(v_i - v_j)^2 > 0$, $|v_i - v_j| > 0$.

Our construction scheme contains 3 Algorithms, namely $Setup_1, Prove_1$, and $Verify_1$, whose formal descriptions are provided in Algorithms 1, 2, and 3, respectively. It is worth noting that the graph $G(V, E)$, where $|V| = n$, $|E| = m$, is common to all, but the prover $\mathcal{P}$ knows a 3-coloring scheme χ of the graph G. In the scheme, the trusted third party usually runs Algorithm 1 and returns the Public Key pk to $\mathcal{P}$ and the verifier $\mathcal{V}$. In fact, the public Key pk output in Algorithm 1 is the parameter (g, h, N) of the FO commitment and the graph G and then $\mathcal{P}$ run Algorithm 2 to generate the proof π.

Algorithm 1. Setup: $Setup_1(1^\lambda) \to pk$

Input: The security parameter λ.
Output: The Public Key $pk = (g, h, N, G)$
The trusted third party inputs the security parameter:

1. Pick a large composite number N such that $N = pq$, where p and q are prime factors.
2. Find an element $g \in \mathbb{Z}_N^*$ with a large order and calculate $h = g^L \bmod N$, where $L \in \mathbb{Z}$.
3. Return the pubilc key $pk = (g, h, N, G)$ to $\mathcal{P}$ and $\mathcal{V}$.

Algorithm 2. Prove: $Prove_1(\chi, pk) \to \pi$

Input: The 3-coloring scheme χ and the public key pk.
Output: The proof π.
$\mathcal{P}$ generates a proof π based on the χ and the pk:

1. First pick n large random integer $r_1, \ldots, r_n$, and then generate a commitment c_k for each vertex v_k in graph G based on the χ and generate a range proof RG_k for each commitment c_k, where $k = 1, \ldots, n$.

$$c_k = g^{v_k} h^{r_k} \bmod N$$
$$RG_k(v_k, r_k | g, h | c_k | [1, 3])$$

2. Randomly selects an edge $e_{ij}(v_i, v_j)$ in graph G to generate a commitment c_{t_1} representing the color difference between two vertices of the edge $e_{ij}, (i, j \in [n])$.

$$c_{t_1} = c_i / c_j \bmod N$$

3. Pick a random integer r' to compute a commitment c_{t_2}, then utilizes c_{t_1} and c_{t_2} to make an EL Proof.

$$c_{t_2} = c_{t_1}^{v_i - v_j} h^{r'} \bmod N$$
$$EL_1(v_i - v_j, \ r_i - r_j, \ r' | g, \ h, \ c_{t_1}, \ h | c_{t_1}, \ c_{t_2})$$

4. Randomly pick a big integer φ that is not zero and an integer r'', calculate a commitment c_{t_3} and generate an SQR proof for it.

$$c_{t_3} = c_{t_2}^{\varphi^2} h^{r''} \bmod N$$
$$SQR_1(\varphi, \ r'' | c_{t_2}, \ h | c_{t_3})$$

5. Run PRG Protocol to get $PRG_1(\varphi^2(v_i - v_j)^2, \ ((r_i - r_j)(v_i - v_j) + r')\varphi^2 + r'' | g, \ h | c_{t_3})$, and set the $\pi_1 = (c_i, c_j, RG_i, RG_j, c_{t_1}, c_{t_2}, c_{t_3}, EL_1, SQR_1, PRG_1)$.
6. Repeat steps 1-5(edges already selected are no longer selected) $m - 1$ times to generate the proof $\pi = (\pi_1, \ldots, \pi_m)$ and return the π to $\mathcal{V}$.

Upon receiving the proof π sent back by $\mathcal{P}$, $\mathcal{V}$ runs Algorithm 3 to verify π. $\mathcal{V}$ takes each π_ρ ($\rho \in [m]$), respectively, as an input to Algorithm 3. Algorithm 3 returns a bit b that indicates the accept (when $b = 1$) or the reject (when $b = 0$) after each verification, and the $\mathcal{V}$ accepts the proof π only if the verification result of each π_ρ is accepted, otherwise it is rejected.

Algorithm 3. Verify: $Verify_1(\pi_\rho, pk) \rightarrow b$

Input: The public key pk and the proof π_ρ.
Output: A bit b representing acceptance or rejection.
The $\mathcal{V}$ performs validation based on π_ρ (the edge is e_{ij}) and pk:

1. Verify RG_i, RG_j and checks whether

$$c_{t_1} = c_i/c_j \bmod N$$

   if RG_i, RG_j passes and $c_{t_1} = c_i/c_j \bmod N$ then proceed to the next step, otherwise return $b = 0$ and halt
2. Verify EL_1, SQR_1, and PRG_1, setting $b = 1$ if all validations pass, and $b = 0$ otherwise, and finally return b.

Lemma 1. *Correctness: If the prover knows a 3-coloring χ of G, then the verifier $\mathcal{V}$ always accepts the solution.*

Proof. Satisfaction of the verifications are as follows.

- If the prover $\mathcal{P}$ provides an actual 3-coloring χ and strictly follows the proof Algorithm 2, then RG_i and RG_j immediately pass the verification and $c_{t_1} = c_i/c_j$. Therefore, step 1 is satisfied.
- As $c_{t_1} = c_i/c_j = g^{v_i - v_j} h^{r_i - r_j} \bmod N$ and $c_{t_2} = c_{t_1}^{v_i - v_j} h^{r'} \bmod N$ both commit the same value. So EL_1 is correct. Again, SQR_1 and PRG_1 are correct, so step 2 is satisfied and Algorithm 3 returns $b = 1$.

Ultimately, since all proofs π_ρ are accepted by Algorithm 3, the proof π passes successfully, so our scheme satisfies the correctness property.

Lemma 2. *Soundness: If the proof π passes successfully the verifications with a non-negligible probability, the prover knows a $\chi \in \mathcal{K}$ of G.*

Proof. Based on the difficulty of solving discrete logarithm problem and the integer factorization problem, FO commitment has the property of secret binding. It is impossible for a polynomial prover to calculate integers a_1, a_2, b_1 and b_1 such that $A = g^{a_1} h^{b_1} \bmod N$, $B = g^{a_2} h^{b_2} \bmod N$ and $(a_1, b_1) \neq (a_2, b_2)$. It means that after the prover publishes the commitment, the prover has a negligible probability to change the secret number and to generate the same commitment. Thus, the passing of the verification in step 1 shows that all vertices in the G are mapped to the set $\{1,2,3\}$, i.e. the whole graph G does not have a fourth color. Similarly, due to the binding nature of the FO commitment, if $SQR_1(\varphi, r''|c_{t_2}, h|c_{t_3})$ is verified to pass, then the prover must have used a square number φ^2 to generate c_{t_3}. Also because

$$c_{t_1} = c_i/c_j \bmod N$$

$$c_{t_2} = c_{t_1}^{v_i - v_j} h^{r'} \bmod N$$

If $EL_1(v_i - v_j, r_i - r_j, r'|g, h, c_{t_1})$ verification passed. The number of secrets hidden in the commitment c_{t_2} must be $(v_i - v_j)^2$, that is, the hidden number in commitment c_{t_3} is $\varphi^2(v_i - v_j)^2$. So when the PRG_1 passes verification, it proves that the prover not only knows the secret number hidden in c_{t_3}, but that this number must be positive, i.e. the two vertices of the edge are mapped with different colors. Therefore, our scheme provides the property of soundness.

Lemma 3. *Zero-knowledge: During the verification process, the verifier learns nothing about the prover's solution.*

Proof. Based on the difficulty of solving the discrete logarithm problem and the integer factorization problem, FO commitment has the property of secret hinding. This means that for any two commitments $A = g^{a_1} h^{b_1} \bmod N$, $B = g^{a_2} h^{b_2} \bmod N$ generated by FO commitment, $A = g^{a_1} h^{b_1} \bmod N$, $B = g^{a_2} h^{b_2} \bmod N$ are indistinguishable for a PPT adversaries $\mathcal{A}$, i.e., $\mathcal{A}$ does not obtain any useful information to distinguish the two commitments. We assume that there exists a PPT simulator S^* and a prover $\mathcal{P}$ a verifier $\mathcal{V}$. $\mathcal{P}$ uses the secret number v to generate the commitment c and the simulator S^* to generate the promise c^*, where r, v^*, r^* are randomly selected from $\mathbb{Z}$.

$$c = g^v h^r \bmod N$$

$$c^* = c = g^{v^*} h^{r*} \bmod N$$

Because of $h = g^L \bmod N$, Therefore for $c^* = g^{v^*} h^{r*} \bmod N$ there must exist an r_1 such that $c^* = g^v h^{r_1} \bmod N$. More precisely, c and c^* are viewed as generating from the same secret number v. Therefore, $\mathcal{V}$ cannot distinguish real proof and simulative proof. This proof process also applies to our scheme, so our scheme has zero-knowledge property.

4.2 Construction 2

In this section, we present our improved scheme from the previous section. For the graph $G(V, E)$, our scheme from the previous section does not rely on iso-morphic techniques to generate proofs, which means that proof generation no longer requires a large number of commitments, enabling a significant reduction in proof size and verification time. But each of its subproofs $\pi_\rho, \rho \in [m]$ is still able to prove only that the difference between the two vertices corresponding to one edge is not zero. We therefore propose an improved scheme which is able to prove a vertex perfectly for each subproof $\pi_\rho, i \in [m]$. Informally, each

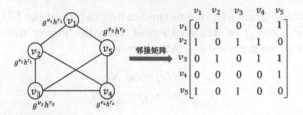

Fig. 1. Graphs with vertex commitment G

subproof can simultaneously prove that the difference between the two vertices corresponding to each edge associated with that vertex is not zero.

As shown in Fig. 1, the graph $G(V, E)$, where $|V| = n$, $|E| = m$, the same scheme as above, we use FO commitment to hide the coloring of each vertex. For example, $c_i = g^{v_i} h^{r_i} \bmod N$ is a commitment to vertex v_i, where $i \in [n]$. For convenience, we use a graph with only five vertices for illustration and a matrix to represent the undirected graph G, so we are only concerned with the half of the matrix that is diagonal. The central idea of the scheme is that for any vertex on the graph G, it is possible to generate a proof that all edges incident to that vertex have their two vertices colored differently. For the sake of comprehension, we choose vertex v_1 for illustration. We want to be able to generate a commitment $c_{v_1} = g^{(v_1-v_2)(v_1-v_5)} h^R \bmod N$ for the vertex v_1. Above the diagonal of the adjacency matrix, vertex v_1 is connected to vertices v_2 and vertex v_5, respectively. Hence, we treat the commitments corresponding to all neighboring vertices of the vertex v_1 as follows.

$$c_{1,2} = (c_1/c_2) = g^{v_1-v_2} h^{r_1-r_2} \bmod N$$
$$c_{1,5} = (c_1/c_5) = g^{v_1-v_5} h^{r_1-r_5} \bmod N$$

Ultimately we calculate

$$c_{v_1} = c_{1,2}{}^{v_1-v_5} h^{r_{v_1}} \bmod N$$
$$= g^{(v_1-v_2)(v_1-v_5)} h^{(r_1-r_2)(v_1-v_5)+r_{v_1}} \bmod N$$

If it is proved that the commitment value in c_{v_1} is not zero i.e. $(v_1 - v_2)(v_1 - v_5) \neq 0$, it implies that the vertex v_1 does not have the same coloring as all the vertices adjacent to it. Then, we cross out the edge associated with vertex v_1 from the graph G to form a new graph G' and repeat the above proof. Finally, we finish the proof of the graph G when the newly formed graph does not have any edges in it. The detailed process of the scheme is as follows.

Similar to construction 1, during the Setup phase, the trusted third party usually runs Algorithm 1 and returns the public key $pk = (g, h, N, G(V, E))$ to the prover $\mathcal{P}$ and the verifier $\mathcal{V}$. For the G, let $|V| = n$ and $|E| = m$ and $\mathcal{P}$ knows a 3-coloring χ of G. The formal description of Prove and Verify Algorithms, namely $Prove_2$, $Verify_2$ are provided in Algorithm 4 and 5, respectively.

Algorithm 4. Prove: $Prove_2(\chi, pk) \to \pi$

Input: The 3-coloring scheme χ and the public key pk.
Output: The proof π.
$\mathcal{P}$ generates a proof π based on the χ and the pk:

1. Compute for all vertices in the graph G.

$$c_z = g^{v_z} h^{r_z} \bmod N$$
$$RG_z(v_z, r_z | g, h | c_z | [1, 3])$$

where r_z is randomly chooses by $\mathcal{P}$, $z \in [n]$.

2. Uniformly selects a vertex from the graph G and notes it as v_1. Assume that there are k vertices including v_1 as mutual neighbors and compute commitments $c_{1,i}$ ($i \in [k]$ and $i \neq 1$) representing the color difference between the two vertex v_1 and v_i.

$$c_{1,i} = (c_1/c_i) = g^{v_1 - v_i} h^{r_1 - r_i} \bmod N$$
$$c_{1,3} = (c_1/c_3) = g^{v_1 - v_3} h^{r_1 - r_3} \bmod N$$
$$\vdots$$
$$c_{1,k} = (c_1/c_k) = g^{v_1 - v_k} h^{r_1 - r_k} \bmod N$$

3. Utilizes $c_{1,i}$ calculate, $i \in [k]$.

$$c_{v_1,1} = c_{1,2}{}^{v_1 - v_3} h^{r'_1} \bmod N = g^{(v_1 - v_2)(v_1 - v_3)} h^{R_1} \bmod N$$
$$c_{v_1,2} = c_{v_1,1}{}^{v_1 - v_4} h^{r'_2} \bmod N = g^{(v_1 - v_2)(v_1 - v_3)(v_1 - v_4)} h^{R_2} \bmod N$$
$$\vdots$$
$$c_{v_1,k-2} = c_{v_1,k-3}{}^{v_1 - v_k} h^{r'_{k-2}} \bmod N = g^{(v_1 - v_2) \cdots (v_1 - v_k)} h^{R_{k-2}} \bmod N$$
$$c_{v_1,k-1} = c_{v_1,k-2}{}^{(v_1 - v_2) \cdots (v_1 - v_k)} h^{r'_{k-1}} \bmod N = g^{(v_1 - v_2) \cdots (v_1 - v_k)^2} h^{R_{k-1}} \bmod N$$

where R_j is denoted as the index of h in $c_{v_1,j}$, $j \in [k-1]$, for example $c_{v_1,1}$: $R_1 = (r_1 - r_2)(v_1 - v_3) + r'_1$, and r'_i is randomly and uniformly selected by $\mathcal{P}$.

4. Utilizes $c_{v_1,j}$, $c_{1,i}$ to make EL Proof, $i \in [k]$ and $j \in [k-1]$.

$$EL_1((v_1 - v_3), r'_1, r_1 - r_3 | c_{1,2}, h, g, h | c_{v_1,1}, c_{1,3})$$
$$EL_2((v_1 - v_4), r'_2, r_1 - r_4 | c_{v_1,1}, h, g, h | c_{v_1,2}, c_{1,4})$$
$$\vdots$$
$$EL_{k-2}((v_1 - v_k), r'_{k-2}, r_1 - r_k | c_{v_1,k-3}, h, g, h | c_{v_1,k-2}, c_{1,k})$$
$$EL_{k-1}((v_1 - v_2) \cdots (v_1 - v_k), r'_{k-1}, R_{k-2} | c_{v_1,k-2}, h, g, h | c_{v_1,k-1}, c_{v_1,k-2})$$

5. Randomly pick a large integer φ that is not zero and an integer r', calculate and make a SQR Proof.

$$c_{v_1,k} = c_{v_1,k-1}{}^{\varphi^2} h^{r'} \bmod N$$
$$SQR_1(\varphi, r' | c_{v_1,k-1}, h | c_{v_1,k})$$

6. Run PRG Protocol to get $PRG_1(\varphi^2((v_1 - v_2) \cdots (v_1 - v_k))^2, R_{k-1}\varphi^2 + r' | g, h | c_{t_3})$, and set $\pi_1 = (c_1, \cdots, c_k, RG_1, \cdots, RG_k, c_{1,2}, \cdots, c_{1,k}, c_{v_1,1}, \cdots, c_{v_1,k}, EL_1, \cdots, EL_{k-1}, SQR_1, PRG_1)$.

7. Cross out the edge associated with vertex v_1 from the graph G to form a new graph G' and repeat the steps 2-6, and until there are no edges in the newly formed graph. Assuming η ($\eta < n$) repetitions, and return the $\pi = (\pi_1, \cdots, \pi_\eta)$ to $\mathcal{V}$.

Algorithm 5. Verify: $Verify_2(\pi_\rho, pk) \to b$

Input: The public key pk and the proof π_ρ.
Output: A bit b representing acceptance or rejection.
The $\mathcal{V}$ performs validation based on π_ρ and pk:

1. Verify RG_i for all $i \in [k]$, and checks whether

$$c_{1,2} = (c_1/c_2) = g^{v_1-v_2} h^{r_1-r_2} \bmod N$$
$$c_{1,3} = (c_1/c_3) = g^{v_1-v_3} h^{r_1-r_3} \bmod N$$
$$\vdots$$
$$c_{1,k} = (c_1/c_k) = g^{v_1-v_k} h^{r_1-r_k} \bmod N$$

   if all RG_i pass and $c_{1,j} = c_1/c_j \bmod N$ for all j ($j \in [k]$ and $j \neq 1$) then continue to the next step otherwise return $b = 0$ and halts.
2. Verify all EL_i ($i \in [k-1]$), SQR_1, and PRG_1, if all validations pass then set $b = 1$ otherwise set $b = 0$ and finally returns b.

This scheme is an improvement on construction 1, and its security properties simply follow the security properties of construction 1. Therefore, we do not give the proof process in detail here. Similarly, like construction 1, this scheme has the property of non-interactivity, i.e., the prover and verifier do not need to be online at the same time to complete the proof.

Efficiency. In the Algorithm 4, Step 1 only needs to be performed once and the steps 2–6 need to be repeated η ($\eta < n$) times. In total, the step 1 of the Algorithm 4 consists of n commitments and execution of the steps 2–6 needs $O(m)$ commitments. Furthermore, our scheme allows us to generate just 1 SQR proof and 1 PRG proof for each vertex in the graph G. In fact, due to our selection of vertices, isolated vertices appear in the process of forming new graphs, and these isolated vertices do not require us to make proofs. This leads to the fact that we need to generate SQR and PRG proofs that are smaller than n. Moreover, our scheme only needs to generate $O(n + m)$ commitments that is a significant improvement compared to $O(nm\lambda)$ commitments of [21] and $O(n + m\lambda)$ commitments of [12], where λ is the security parameter.

5   Conclusion

In this paper, we propose a non-interactive zero-knowledge proof scheme for the 3-GCP. Compared with [12,21] our scheme does not need to generate a large number of commitments and is non-interactive, which makes it a better application scenario. In addition, we optimize the scheme so that it can prove one vertex of the graph per run, and it is more efficient compared to [12], requiring only a small number of runs to generate a proof for the entire graph.

References

1. Acar, A., Aksu, H., Uluagac, A.S., Conti, M.: A survey on homomorphic encryption schemes: theory and implementation. ACM Comput. Surv. (CSUR) **51**(4), 1–35 (2018)
2. Alupotha, J., Boyen, X.: Practical UC-secure zero-knowledge smart contracts. Cryptology ePrint Archive (2022)
3. Bick, A., Kol, G., Oshman, R.: Distributed zero-knowledge proofs over networks. In: Proceedings of the 2022 Annual ACM-SIAM Symposium on Discrete Algorithms (SODA), pp. 2426–2458. SIAM (2022)
4. Bierhorst, P., et al.: Experimentally generated randomness certified by the impossibility of superluminal signals. Nature **556**(7700), 223–226 (2018)
5. Blum, M., De Santis, A., Micali, S., Persiano, G.: Noninteractive zero-knowledge. SIAM J. Comput. **20**(6), 1084–1118 (1991)
6. Boudot, F.: Efficient proofs that a committed number lies in an interval. In: Preneel, B. (ed.) EUROCRYPT 2000. LNCS, vol. 1807, pp. 431–444. Springer, Heidelberg (2000). https://doi.org/10.1007/3-540-45539-6_31
7. Brassard, G., Crepeau, C.: Non-transitive transfer of confidence: a perfect zero-knowledge interactive protocol for sat and beyond. In: 27th Annual Symposium on Foundations of Computer Science (SFCS 1986), pp. 188–195. IEEE (1986)
8. Brickell, E.F., Chaum, D., Damgård, I.B., van de Graaf, J.: Gradual and verifiable release of a secret (extended abstract). In: Pomerance, C. (ed.) CRYPTO 1987. LNCS, vol. 293, pp. 156–166. Springer, Heidelberg (1988). https://doi.org/10.1007/3-540-48184-2_11
9. Coron, J.-S., Dodis, Y., Malinaud, C., Puniya, P.: Merkle-Damgård revisited: how to construct a hash function. In: Shoup, V. (ed.) CRYPTO 2005. LNCS, vol. 3621, pp. 430–448. Springer, Heidelberg (2005). https://doi.org/10.1007/11535218_26
10. Damgård, I.: On σ-protocols. Lecture Notes, University of Aarhus, Department for Computer Science, p. 84 (2002)
11. Damgård, I., Fujisaki, E.: A statistically-hiding integer commitment scheme based on groups with hidden order. In: Zheng, Y. (ed.) ASIACRYPT 2002. LNCS, vol. 2501, pp. 125–142. Springer, Heidelberg (2002). https://doi.org/10.1007/3-540-36178-2_8
12. Ebrahimi, E.: Post-quantum efficient proof for graph 3-coloring problem. Cryptology ePrint Archive (2021)
13. Fiat, A., Shamir, A.: How to prove yourself: practical solutions to identification and signature problems. In: Odlyzko, A.M. (ed.) CRYPTO 1986. LNCS, vol. 263, pp. 186–194. Springer, Heidelberg (1987). https://doi.org/10.1007/3-540-47721-7_12
14. Firsov, D., Unruh, D.: Zero-knowledge in easycrypt. Cryptology ePrint Archive (2022)
15. Fridrich, J.: Symmetric ciphers based on two-dimensional chaotic maps. Int. J. Bifurcat. Chaos **8**(06), 1259–1284 (1998)
16. Fujisaki, E., Okamoto, T.: Statistical zero knowledge protocols to prove modular polynomial relations. In: Kaliski, B.S. (ed.) CRYPTO 1997. LNCS, vol. 1294, pp. 16–30. Springer, Heidelberg (1997). https://doi.org/10.1007/BFb0052225
17. Garg, S., Gentry, C., Sahai, A., Waters, B.: Witness encryption and its applications. In: Proceedings of the Forty-Fifth Annual ACM Symposium on Theory of Computing, pp. 467–476 (2013)
18. Goldwasser, S., Micali, S., Rackoff, C.: The knowledge complexity of interactive proof systems. SIAM J. Comput. **18**(1), 186–208 (1989)

19. Grilo, A.B., Slofstra, W., Yuen, H.: Perfect zero knowledge for quantum multi-prover interactive proofs. In: 2019 IEEE 60th Annual Symposium on Foundations of Computer Science (FOCS), pp. 611–635. IEEE (2019)
20. Hart, E., McGinnis, J.A.: Physical zero-knowledge proofs for flow free, hamiltonian cycles, and many-to-many k-disjoint covering paths. arXiv preprint arXiv:2202.04113 (2022)
21. Kilian, J.: A note on efficient zero-knowledge proofs and arguments. In: Proceedings of the Twenty-Fourth Annual ACM Symposium on Theory of Computing, pp. 723–732 (1992)
22. Li, C.L., et al.: Device-independent-quantum-randomness-enhanced zero-knowledge proof. arXiv preprint arXiv:2111.06717 (2021)
23. Lipmaa, H.: On diophantine complexity and statistical zero-knowledge arguments. In: Laih, C.-S. (ed.) ASIACRYPT 2003. LNCS, vol. 2894, pp. 398–415. Springer, Heidelberg (2003). https://doi.org/10.1007/978-3-540-40061-5_26
24. Liu, Y., et al.: Device-independent quantum random-number generation. Nature **562**(7728), 548–551 (2018)
25. Metere, R., Dong, C.: Automated cryptographic analysis of the pedersen commitment scheme. In: 7th International Conference on Mathematical Methods, Models, and Architectures for Computer Network Security. Newcastle University (2017)
26. Naor, M.: Bit commitment using pseudo-randomness. In: Brassard, G. (ed.) CRYPTO 1989. LNCS, vol. 435, pp. 128–136. Springer, New York (1990). https://doi.org/10.1007/0-387-34805-0_13
27. Peikert, C., Shiehian, S.: Noninteractive zero knowledge for NP from (plain) learning with errors. In: Boldyreva, A., Micciancio, D. (eds.) CRYPTO 2019. LNCS, vol. 11692, pp. 89–114. Springer, Cham (2019). https://doi.org/10.1007/978-3-030-26948-7_4
28. Peng, K., Bao, F.: An efficient range proof scheme. In: 2010 IEEE Second International Conference on Social Computing, pp. 826–833. IEEE (2010)
29. Schnorr, C.P.: Efficient signature generation by smart cards. J. Cryptol. **4**, 161–174 (1991)
30. Takabatake, Y., Kotani, D., Okabe, Y.: An anonymous distributed electronic voting system using zerocoin. IEICE Tech. Rep. **116**(282), 127–131 (2016)
31. Tsai, Y.C., Tso, R., Liu, Z.Y., Chen, K.: An improved non-interactive zero-knowledge range proof for decentralized applications. In: 2019 IEEE International Conference on Decentralized Applications and Infrastructures (DAPPCON), pp. 129–134. IEEE (2019)
32. Yu, J.: Towards malicious security of private coin honest verifier zero knowledge for NP via witness encryption. In: Guo, F., Huang, X., Yung, M. (eds.) Inscrypt 2018. LNCS, vol. 11449, pp. 586–606. Springer, Cham (2019). https://doi.org/10.1007/978-3-030-14234-6_31

Cloud-Aided Scalable Revocable IBE with Ciphertext Update from Lattices in the Random Oracle Model

Yanhua Zhang[1][✉], Ximeng Liu[2], Yupu Hu[3], and Huiwen Jia[4]

[1] Zhengzhou University of Light Industry, Zhengzhou 450001, China
yhzhang@email.zzuli.edu.cn
[2] Fuzhou University, Fuzhou 350108, China
[3] Xidian University, Xi'an 710071, China
yphu@mail.xidian.edu.cn
[4] Guangzhou University, Guangzhou 510006, China
hwjia@gzhu.edu.cn

Abstract. Cloud-aided scalable revocable identity-based encryption with ciphertext update (CA-RIBE-CU), first introduced by Wang et al. in 2017 and the first lattice-based instantiation constructed by Zhang et al. in 2021, offer significant advantages over previous identity revocation mechanisms when considering the scenario of secure data sharing in the cloud setting. In this primitive, the receiver can utilize the short-term decryption keys to decrypt all encrypted data sent to him or her, meanwhile, the ciphertexts stored in the cloud will update to new ones with the aided of an untrusted cloud service provider (CSP) and without any interaction with the data owners, and thus, the revoked receivers cannot access to both previously and subsequently shared data, that is, to achieve both identity revocation and ciphertext update simultaneously for IBE.

In this paper, inspired by the first quantum resistant construction of CA-RIBE-CU by Zhang et al. in FCS 2021, we propose a new lattice-based CA-RIBE-CU scheme in the random oracle model (ROM). We also adopt the two interesting tools "hybrid ciphertexts" and "hybrid short-term decryption keys" proposed by Zhang et al. to enable constant ciphertexts and simplified ciphertexts update. Differently, instead of using a super-lattice to issue the long-term private keys and the time update keys, our new construction is based on the main technique for lattice basis delegation without dimension increase, which benefits the new CA-RIBE-CU scheme with much shorter items in almost all keys and final ciphertexts, thus enriching the research of lattice-based revocable IBE.

Keywords: Identity-based encryption · Lattices · Identity revocation · Ciphertext update · Random oracle model

1 Introduction

Identity-based encryption (IBE) was first introduced by Shamir [24] in CRYPTO 1984, which eliminates the necessity for public-key infrastructure in conventional

© The Author(s), under exclusive license to Springer Nature Singapore Pte Ltd. 2024
H. Yang and R. Lu (Eds.): FCS 2023, CCIS 1992, pp. 387–403, 2024.
https://doi.org/10.1007/978-981-99-9331-4_26

public-key cryptosystems. Identity revocation, one of the fundamental issues in IBE, was first discussed by Boneh and Franklin [5], and a naive solution that a trusted private key generator (PKG) periodically issues new private key for each non-revoked user in each time period was suggested. Unfortunately, this solution is impractical, as PKG's workload grows linearly in the number of system users.

The first scalable IBE construction with identity revocation, or simply revocable IBE (RIBE) scheme, was creatively proposed by Boldyreva et al. [6] in CCS 2008, in which a binary tree based revocation method [18] is adopted and the PKG's workload is only logarithmic in the number of system users. In particular, the time key update is exactly executed for all non-revoked receivers through a public channel. However, when considering a practical application of RIBE, there is a serious problem that the ciphertexts generated for some receiver, but prior to the receiver's revocation, remain available to the revoked receiver who owns the old short-term decryption keys which are enough to decrypt those ciphertexts. Thus, this problem may be undesirable for the multi-user applications, such as the scenario of secure data sharing in the cloud setting.

To solve identity revocation and ciphertexts update problems simultaneously in a practical manner, the notion of cloud-aided scalable RIBE with ciphertext update (CA-RIBE-CU) was introduced by Wang et al. [29] in 2017, in which the receiver can utilize short-term decryption keys to decrypt all encrypted data sent to him or her, meanwhile, the ciphertexts stored in the cloud will update to new ones with the aided of an untrusted cloud service provider (CSP) and without any interaction with data owners, and thus, the revoked receivers cannot access to both previously and subsequently shared data. To be more specific, a CA-RIBE-CU primitive is carried out as follows: once the system is set up, a trusted PKG issues a long-term private key to the receiver. A time update key is generated by PKG and sent to all receivers (the CSP will re-encrypt all ciphertexts for the receiver at the end of each time period no matter he or she is revoked or not, thus, no time update key is involved in ciphertexts update) through a public channel at each time period. The CSP does ciphertexts update on the encrypted data stored in it to new ones, and the old ones are completely deleted. Because only a non-revoked receiver can obtain the valid short-term decryption key and no revoked receiver can decrypt the new ciphertexts (including the former, current and the latter ciphertexts) sent to him or her. It is worthy to be mentioned that a similar revocation method called RIBE with server-aided ciphertext evolution (RIBE-SA-CE) was introduced by Sun et al. [26] in 2020, in which the time update keys have to be sent to CSP and all receivers simultaneously.

Apart from introducing these two new primitives, Wang et al. [29] and Sun et al. [26] described the pairing-based instantiations of CA-RIBE-CU and RIBE-SA-CE, respectively. However, both constructions will be insecure once the quantum computers become a reality [25]. Encouragingly, the first lattice-based RIBE-SA-CE was constructed by Zhang et al. [33] in Inscrypt 2021. Although the second scheme in [33] achieves the decryption key exposure resistance (DKER) property, a default security requirement for RIBE since it was introduced by Seo and Emura [23] in PKC 2013, the significant shortcoming of Zhang et al. [33] is a rather low efficiency, that is, the whole encryptions and ciphertexts update processings are considerably sophisticated and the bit-size of final ciphertexts is linear in the length of each receiver's identity, because both sender and CSP utilize a double encryption mechanism which has to re-encrypt the same temporary ciphertext (i.e., an encryption of original message) for all nodes on path(id), the path from a leaf node (a receiver with identity id is assigned to this node) to the root node of binary tree (BT). Shortly afterwards, by creatively adopting two interesting tools called "hybrid ciphertexts" and "hybrid short-term decryption keys", Zhang et al. [31] constructed the first lattice-based CA-RIBE-CU scheme in the standard model (SM) in FCS 2021 to resolve the problems of Zhang et al. [33]. In addition, with a new treatment of identity and time period spaces, their scheme has fewer items in the public parameters and the master secret key.

In this paper, inspired by the clear advantages of CA-RIBE-CU that support identity revocation and ciphertexts update simultaneously, we also bring it into the world of lattices and construct the lattice-based CA-RIBE-CU in the random oracle model (ROM) by adopting a different technique called lattice basis delegation without dimension increase, to further explore to reduce keys-size and final ciphertexts-size than before and enrich the field of CA-RIBE-CU.

RELATED WORKS. The first scalable RIBE scheme was introduced by Boldyreva et al. [6] in CCS 2008, whose constriction is creatively designed by combining a fuzzy IBE [22] and a complete subset (CS) methodology [18]. Subsequently, an adaptively secure RIBE scheme and an RIBE with DKER, based on pairings, were proposed by Libert and Vergnaud [14] and Seo and Emura [23], respectively. To resist quantum attacks, the lattice-based RIBE without DKER, the lattice-based RIBE with bounded (and unbounded) DKER and an adaptively secure scheme in the quantum ROM were proposed by Chen et al. [7], Takayasu and Watanabe [28], Katsumata et al. [10], Wang et al. [30] and Takayasu [27], respectively.

The study of outsourcing RIBE was initiated by Li et al. [12] in 2015, in which a semi-trusted CSP is adopted to update each non-revoked receiver's time key. Liang et al. [13] also attempted to solve these same problems mentioned earlierly in this work by using proxy re-encryption technique, however, exactly as it was shown in [29], the construction of [13] cannot resist the re-encryption key forgery attack and the collusion attack. Subsequently, to overcome the main decryption challenges for non-revoked receivers only with a limited resource, Qin et al. [20] introduced a new revocation mechanism called server-aided RIBE (SA-RIBE), in which almost all of workloads on receivers are delegated to an untrusted CSP. Inspired by the primitives of Li et al. [12] and Qin et al. [20], Dong et al. [8] and Nguyen et al. [19] constructed the first lattice-based outsourcing RIBE scheme and the first lattice-based SA-RIBE scheme, respectively. Soon after, the generic constructions of RIBE with CS and subset difference techniques and server-aided revocable hierarchical IBE were respectively proposed by Ma and Lin [16], Lee [11] and Liu and Sun [15]. In particular, by providing a modification of Dong et al. [8] and simplifying the design of Nguyen et al. [19], a secure lattice-based outsourcing RIBE and a simplified lattice-based SA-RIBE were proposed by Zhang et al. [32] and Zhang et al. [34], respectively.

OUR CONTRIBUTIONS AND TECHNIQUES. In this paper, we introduce the first construction of lattice-based CA-RIBE-CU in ROM. We inherit and extend the main security and efficiency advantages of Wang et al.'s model and Zhang et al.'s lattice-based CA-RIBE-CU scheme in SM: the ciphertexts can be updated to new ones with the aided of untrusted CSP and without any interaction with data owners or PKG, meanwhile, the revoked receivers cannot access to all the former, current, and the latter shared data in CSP. Furthermore, the final ciphertexts also enjoys constant size and encryptions and ciphertexts update processings are simpler, not linear in the length of identities and without a burdensome double encryption mechanism as in Zhang et al. [33]. As for previous lattice-based RIBE schemes [7,10,19,27,28,30–34], our new construction only works for one-bit message, but the multi-bit version can be easily achieved by adopting a standard transformation technique introduced in [1,9]. Interestingly, based on the main technique for lattice basis delegation without dimension increase, first introduced by Agrawal et al. [2] in the construction of hierarchical IBE (HIBE) scheme, our new construction has much shorter items in the public parameters and enjoys much shorter keys-size and final ciphertexts-size than before (including the first lattice-based CA-RIBE-CU in SM), and it is provable secure under the classical learning with errors (LWE) hardness assumption.

As in [31], each receiver's long-term private key of our construction includes a trapdoor matrix, thus having a relatively large bit-size. A standard asymptotic comparison among the lattice-based RIBE schemes [7,8,10,19,27,28,30–34] and ours is shown in Table 1, and the detailed comparison between the lattice-based CA-RIBE-CU scheme in SM [31] and ours is shown in Table 2.

Table 1. Comparison of Lattice-Based RIBE Schemes.

Schemes	$|token|$	$|sk_{id}|$	$|uk_t|$	$|dk_{id,t}|$	$|ct_{id,t}|$	CU	DKER	Model
[7]	–	$\mathcal{O}(\log N) \cdot \tilde{\mathcal{O}}(n)$	$\Delta_0 \cdot \tilde{\mathcal{O}}(n)$	$\tilde{\mathcal{O}}(n)$	$\tilde{\mathcal{O}}(n)$	no	no	SM
[19]	$\mathcal{O}(\log N) \cdot \tilde{\mathcal{O}}(n)$	$\tilde{\mathcal{O}}(n^2)$	$\Delta_0 \cdot \tilde{\mathcal{O}}(n)$	$\tilde{\mathcal{O}}(n)$	$\tilde{\mathcal{O}}(n)$	no	Unbounded	SM
[28]	–	$d \cdot \mathcal{O}(\log N) \cdot \tilde{\mathcal{O}}(n)$	$\Delta_0 \cdot \tilde{\mathcal{O}}(n)$	$\tilde{\mathcal{O}}(n)$	$\tilde{\mathcal{O}}(n)$	no	Bounded	SM
[8]	$\mathcal{O}(N) \cdot \tilde{\mathcal{O}}(n^2)$	$\mathcal{O}(\log N) \cdot \tilde{\mathcal{O}}(n^2)$	$\Delta_0 \cdot \tilde{\mathcal{O}}(n^2)$	$\tilde{\mathcal{O}}(n^2)$	$\tilde{\mathcal{O}}(n)$	no	no	SM
[10]	–	$\tilde{\mathcal{O}}(n^2)$	$\Delta_0 \cdot \tilde{\mathcal{O}}(n)$	$\tilde{\mathcal{O}}(n)$	$\tilde{\mathcal{O}}(n)$	no	Unbounded	SM
[30]	–	$\tilde{\mathcal{O}}(n^2)$	$\Delta_0 \cdot \tilde{\mathcal{O}}(n)$	$\tilde{\mathcal{O}}(n)$	$\tilde{\mathcal{O}}(n)$	no	Unbounded	SM
[27]	–	$d \cdot \mathcal{O}(\log N) \cdot \tilde{\mathcal{O}}(n)$	$\Delta_0 \cdot \tilde{\mathcal{O}}(n)$	$\tilde{\mathcal{O}}(n)$	$\tilde{\mathcal{O}}(n)$	no	Bounded	QROM
[33]	–	$\tilde{\mathcal{O}}(n^2)$	$\Delta_0 \cdot \tilde{\mathcal{O}}(n)$	$\tilde{\mathcal{O}}(n)$	$\mathcal{O}(\log N) \cdot \tilde{\mathcal{O}}(n)$	yes	Unbounded	SM
[31]	–	$\tilde{\mathcal{O}}(n^2)$	$\Delta_0 \cdot \tilde{\mathcal{O}}(n)$	$\tilde{\mathcal{O}}(n)$	$\tilde{\mathcal{O}}(n)$	yes	Unbounded	SM
[32]	$\mathcal{O}(N) \cdot \tilde{\mathcal{O}}(n^2)$	$\mathcal{O}(\log N) \cdot \tilde{\mathcal{O}}(n^2)$	$\Delta_0 \cdot \tilde{\mathcal{O}}(n^2)$	$\tilde{\mathcal{O}}(n^2)$	$\tilde{\mathcal{O}}(n)$	no	Unbounded	SM
[34]	$\mathcal{O}(\log N) \cdot \tilde{\mathcal{O}}(n)$	$\tilde{\mathcal{O}}(n^2)$	$\Delta_0 \cdot \tilde{\mathcal{O}}(n)$	$\tilde{\mathcal{O}}(n)$	$\tilde{\mathcal{O}}(n)$	no	Unbounded	SM
Ours	–	$\tilde{\mathcal{O}}(n^2)$	$\Delta_0 \cdot \tilde{\mathcal{O}}(n)$	$\tilde{\mathcal{O}}(n)$	$\tilde{\mathcal{O}}(n)$	yes	Unbounded	ROM

Note: n is security parameter, $N = poly(n)$ is the maximum numbers of system users, $\Delta_0 = \mathcal{O}(r \log \frac{N}{r})$ where r is the number of revoked receivers, and d is the number of private keys stored in each node over path(id); $|\cdot|$ denotes the bit-size, token is a token, sk_{id} is long-term private key, uk_t is time update key, $dk_{id,t}$ is short-term decryption key, and $ct_{id,t}$ is ciphertext; QROM denotes quantum ROM, and "–" means that there is no this item in the corresponding scheme.

Table 2. Comparison of Lattice-Based CA-RIBE-CU Schemes.

Schemes	$|pp|$	$|sk_{id}|$	$|uk_t|$	$|dk_{id,t}|$	$|ct_{id,t}|$	Model
[31]	$(4nm+2n)\Delta_1$	$(4m^2+2mn+2m)\Delta_1$	$2m\Delta_0\Delta_1$	$7m\Delta_1$	$(12m+3n-2)\Delta_1$	SM
Ours	$(2nm+2n)\Delta_1$	$(m^2+mn+m)\Delta_1$	$m\Delta_0\Delta_1$	$3m\Delta_1$	$(6m+3n-2)\Delta_1$	ROM

Note: pp is public parameter; $\Delta_0 = \mathcal{O}(r\log\frac{N}{r})$, $\Delta_1 = \lceil\log q\rceil$.

As a high level, the design method of our lattice-based CA-RIBE-CU scheme in ROM is similar to the first lattice-based instantiation of Zhang et al. [31] in the sense that we also adopt a lattice-based RIBE scheme [7] and a lattice-based two-level HIBE scheme [1] as the basic building blocks. Differently, instead of using a super-lattice to issue long-term private keys and time update keys, a technique for lattice basis delegation without dimension increase [2] is introduced, from which PKG can issue a series of shorter trapdoor matrices and shorter public vectors to all receivers. This enables that much shorter items are included in the public parameters and shorter keys-size and final ciphertexts-size.

Similarly, we also adopt the two interesting tools called "hybrid ciphertexts" and "hybrid short-term decryption keys", first introduced by Katsumata et al. [10] in the construction of lattice-based RIBE with DKER, to resolve the problems of sophisticated encryptions and ciphertexts update processings of Zhang et al. [33]. We now introduce how these tools work in our scheme: the receivers are first issued by PKG a hybrid long-term private key which includes a series of short vectors and a short HIBE trapdoor, that is, $sk_{id} = ((e_{id,\theta})_{\theta\in path(id)}, \mathbf{R}_{\mathbf{A}_{\tilde{id}}})$, in which $\mathbf{R}_{\mathbf{A}_{\tilde{id}}}$ is used to sample a short $e_{\tilde{id},t}$ as one part of the short-term decryption key $dk_{id,t} = (e_{id,\theta\in(path(id)\cap KUNodes(BT,RL,t))}, e_{t,\theta\in(path(id)\cap KUNodes(BT,RL,t))}, e_{\tilde{id},t})$ for each time period independently from the previous time periods. Here, $\tilde{id}$ is a virtual identity of the real id, which we will explain latter. The data owner encrypts the one-bit message $m \in \{0,1\}$ under HIBE and RIBE to obtain a hybrid ciphertext of the form $ct_{id,t=t_0} = (id, t_0, c_0, \mathbf{c}_{00}, \mathbf{c}_{01}, \mathbf{c}_{02})$, where c_0 is the ciphertext component carrying m. The ciphertext $ct_{id,t}$ is then sent to CSP, and the untrusted CSP could honestly update $ct_{id,t}$ to a new $ct_{id,t'=t_k} = (id, t_0, t_k, c_k, \mathbf{c}_{00}, \mathbf{c}_{01}, \mathbf{c}_{01}, \mathbf{c}_{k0}, \mathbf{c}_{k1}, \mathbf{c}_{k2})$ for the new time period $t' > t$. Once receiving $ct_{id,t'}$ from CSP, the non-revoked receiver id should be able to recover the original message m.

In the constructions of Zhang et al. [31] and [34], the virtual identity method was adopted to remove some items in the public parameters of previous schemes, we also adopt it in our new construction and recall how it works: both identity space $\mathcal{I}$ and time period space $\mathcal{T}$ are treated as a subset of $\mathbb{Z}_q^n\backslash\{\mathbf{0}_n\}$, a virtual identity $\tilde{\mathcal{I}}$ satisfying $\mathcal{I}\cap\tilde{\mathcal{I}} = \emptyset$ and $|\mathcal{I}| = |\tilde{\mathcal{I}}|$ is introduced. Especially, there is a one-to-one correspondence between a real identity $id \in \mathcal{I}$ and a virtual identity $\tilde{id} \in \tilde{\mathcal{I}}$. A simple instance can be given as follows: define $\mathcal{I} = \{1\} \times \mathbb{Z}_q^{n-1}$, a real identity $id = (1, id_1, \cdots, id_n) \in \mathcal{I}$, we define a new space $\tilde{\mathcal{I}} = \{-1\}\times\mathbb{Z}_q^{n-1}$ which satisfies $|\mathcal{I}| = |\tilde{\mathcal{I}}| = q^{n-1}$ and the virtual identity $\tilde{id} = (-1, id_1, \cdots, id_n)$. The time period space $\mathcal{T} = \{0, 1, \cdots, t_{max} - 1\}$ is encoded into the set $\{2\} \times \mathbb{Z}_q^{n-1}$.

ORGANIZATION. In Sect. 2, we review the definition of CA-RIBE-CU and some knowledge on lattices. A lattice-based CA-RIBE-CU in ROM is described and analyzed in Sect. 3. In the final Sect. 4, we conclude our whole paper.

2   Definition and Security Model

Table 3 refers to the notations used in this paper.

Table 3. Notations of This Paper.

Notations	Definition
$\Lambda_q^{\perp}(\mathbf{A}), \Lambda_q^{\mathbf{u}}(\mathbf{A})$	q-ary orthogonal lattice Λ defined by a parity-check $\mathbf{A}$, and its shift
$\mathcal{D}_{\Lambda,s,\mathbf{c}}$	discrete Gaussian distribution over Λ with center $\mathbf{c}$ and a parameter $s > 0$
$\overset{\$}{\leftarrow}$	sampling uniformly at random
$\|\cdot\|, \|\cdot\|_\infty$	Euclidean norm ℓ_2, infinity norm ℓ_∞
mod q	$(-(q-1)/2, (q-1)/2]$
$\log e$	logarithm of e with base 2
ppt	probabilistic polynomial-time

2.1   Cloud-Aided Scalable Revocable IBE with Ciphertext Update

We now review the definition and security model of CA-RIBE-CU, introduced by Wang et al. [29]. A CA-RIBE-CU is an extension of RIBE that supports identity revocation, additionally, delegating the ciphertexts update to an untrusted CSP which is normally assumed to perform correct operations and return the correct results. A trusted PKG first derives the master secret key (msk) and the public parameters (pp), then issues a long-term private key sk_{id} for each receiver with an identity id and a time update key uk_t with a time period t by using msk, meanwhile, uk_t is sent to all receivers publicly, and PKG maintains a revocation list (RL) to record the state information on revoked receivers. CSP periodically transforms a ciphertext for a receiver id with time t into a new one for $t' > t$ no matter id is revoked or not. To decrypt a ciphertext $ct_{id,t}$ which specifies an identity id and time t (if it is a re-encrypted ciphertext, an original encryption time t_0 is also given), the non-revoked receiver id combines long-term private key sk_{id} and update key uk_t (and uk_{t_0}) to derive a short-term decryption key $dk_{id,t}$ (and dk_{id,t_0}). The system model of CA-RIBE-CU is shown in Fig. 1.

Definition 1. *A CA-RIBE-CU involves 4 distinct entities: PKG, CSP, senders, and receivers, associated with an identity space $\mathcal{I}$, time space $\mathcal{T}$, message space $\mathcal{M}$, and consists of 8 polynomial-time algorithms which are described as follows:*

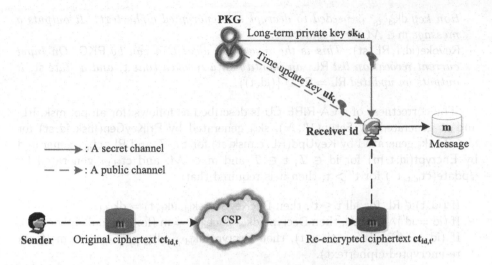

Fig. 1. System Model of CA-RIBE-CU.

- Setup($1^n, N$): *This is the setup algorithm run by a trusted* PKG. *On input a system security parameter n and the maximal number of users N, it outputs a master secret key* msk, *the public parameters* pp, *a user revocation list* RL *(initially $\emptyset$), and a state* st. *Note:* msk *is kept in secret by* PKG, *and* pp *is made public and as an implicit input of all other algorithms.*
- PriKeyGen(msk, id, st): *This is the key generation algorithm run by* PKG. *On input an identity* id, *master secret key* msk, *and a state* st, *it outputs a long-term private key* sk_{id} *and an updated state* st.
- KeyUpd(RL, t, msk, st): *This is the key update algorithm run by* PKG. *On input current revocation list* RL, *the time period* t, *master secret key* msk, *and a state* st, *it outputs a time update key* uk_t.
- DecKeyGen(sk_{id}, uk_t, t): *This is the decryption key generation algorithm run by the receiver* id. *On input a long-term private key* sk_{id}, *a corresponding time update key* uk_t *(or $\perp$), and current time* t, *it outputs a short-term decryption key* $dk_{id,t}$ *(or $\perp$ indicating that* id *has been revoked). Note: to decrypt a re-encrypted ciphertext, an original encryption time* t_0 *and time update key* uk_{t_0} *is also needed to compute the short-term decryption key* dk_{id,t_0}.
- Encrypt(id, t, m): *This is the encryption algorithm run by the sender. On input a receiver's identity* id, *encryption time period* t, *and a message* m. *It outputs a ciphertext* $ct_{id,t}$.
- Update($ct_{id,t}, t'$): *This is the ciphertext update algorithm run by the untrusted* CSP. *On input a ciphertext* $ct_{id,t}$ *(no matter it is an original ciphertext or a re-encrypted ciphertext) with identity* id *and time* t, *and a new time period* $t' > t$, *it outputs a re-encrypted ciphertext* $ct_{id,t'}$.
- Decrypt($dk_{id',t'}, ct_{id,t}$): *This is the decryption algorithm run by the receiver. On input a ciphertext* $ct_{id,t}$ *and a decryption key* $dk_{id',t'}$ *(the short-term decryp-*

tion key dk_{id',t_0} *is needed to decrypt a re-encrypted ciphertext). It outputs a message* $m \in \mathcal{M}$, *or a symbol* $\perp$.

- Revoke(id, t, RL, st): *This is the revocation algorithm run by* PKG. *On input current revocation list* RL, *an identity* id, *a revoked time* t, *and a state* st, *it outputs an updated* $RL = RL \cup \{(id, t)\}$.

The correctness of a CA-RIBE-CU is described as follows: for all pp, msk, RL, and st generated by Setup($1^n, N$), sk_{id} generated by PriKeyGen(msk, id, st) for $id \in \mathcal{I}$, uk_t generated by KeyUpd(RL, t, msk, st) for $t \in \mathcal{T}$ and RL, $ct_{id,t}$ generated by Encrypt(id, t, m) for $id \in \mathcal{I}$, $t \in \mathcal{T}$ and $m \in \mathcal{M}$, and $ct_{id,t''}$ generated by Update($ct_{id,t}, t''$) for $t'' > t$, then it is required that:

- If $(id, t) \notin RL$ for all $t \leq t'$, then DecKeyGen(sk_{id}, uk_t, t) = $dk_{id,t}$.
- If $(id = id') \wedge (t = t')$, then Decrypt($dk_{id',t'}, ct_{id,t}$) = m (for original ciphertext).
- If $(id = id') \wedge (t'' = t' > t)$, then Decrypt($dk_{id',t'}, dk_{id',t}, ct_{id,t''}$) = m (for a re-encrypted ciphertext).

A CA-RIBE-CU is an extension of RIBE and should satisfy the indistinguishability under the chosen-plaintext attack (IND-CPA) security of RIBE to guarantee message hiding security against an attacker $\mathcal{A}$ who may own a long-term private key (e.g., a revoked receiver). Wang et al. [29] defined semantic security against adaptive-revocable-identity-time and chosen-plaintext attacks for CA-RIBE-CU. Here, as in [31], we consider selective-revocable-identity-time security (a weaker notion was initially suggested by Boldyreva et al. [6], subsequently by Chen et al. [7], Nguyen et al. [19], Katsumata et al. [10] and Zhang et al. [31], in which $\mathcal{A}$ sends a challenge pair (id*, t*) (for original challenge ciphertext, t* is a single time period; for re-encrypted challenge ciphertext, $t^* = (t_0^*, t_k^*)$ is a time period vector) to the challenger $\mathcal{C}$ before the execution of Setup($1^n, N$).

In the IND-CPA security model of CA-RIBE-CU, $\mathcal{A}$ can request the long-term private key, time update key, identity revocation, short-term decryption key, and ciphertext update queries. One of the most restrictions is that if $\mathcal{A}$ has requested a long-term private key for the challenge identity id*, then id* must be revoked before (or at) the time update key query of challenge time t*. Finally, $\mathcal{A}$'s goal is to determine that the challenge ciphertxet is completely random, or correctly encrypted on the challenge message m* corresponding to (id*, t*).

Definition 2. *The* IND-CPA *security of* CA-RIBE-CU *is described as follows:*

- Intial: *The attacker* $\mathcal{A}$ *declares a challenge identity and time pair* (id*, t*).
- Setup: *The challenger* $\mathcal{C}$ *runs* Setup($1^n, N$) *to obtain* (msk, pp, RL, st). *Note:* RL *is initially* $\emptyset$, $\mathcal{C}$ *keeps* msk *in secret and provides* pp *to* $\mathcal{A}$.
- Query phase 1: *The query-answer between* $\mathcal{A}$ *and* $\mathcal{C}$ *is described in Table 4:*

Table 4. The Query-Answer between $\mathcal{A}$ and $\mathcal{C}$.

	PriKenGen($\cdot$)	KeyUpd($\cdot$)	DecKeyGen($\cdot$)	Update	Revoke($\cdot$)
$\mathcal{A}$	id	RL, t	id, t	$ct_{id,t}, t'$	RL, id, t
$\mathcal{C}$	sk_{id}	uk_t	$dk_{id,t}$	$ct_{id,t'}$	RL = RL $\cup$ {(id, t)}

Note: the oracles share st and these queries are with some restrictions defined later.

- Challenge: $\mathcal{A}$ submits a challenge $m^* \in \mathcal{M}$. $\mathcal{C}$ samples a bit $b \xleftarrow{\$} \{0,1\}$. If $b = 0$, $\mathcal{C}$ returns a challenge ciphertext $ct^*_{id^*,t^*}$ by running Encrypt(id^*, t^*, m^*) or Update(Encrypt(id^*, t_0^*, m^*), t_k^*), otherwise, a random $ct^*_{id^*,t^*} \xleftarrow{\$} \mathcal{U}$.
- Query phase 2: $\mathcal{A}$ makes additional queries as before with the same restrictions.
- Guess: $\mathcal{A}$ outputs a bit $b^* \in \{0,1\}$, and wins if $b^* = b$.

In the above game, the following restrictions should be satisfied:

- KeyUpd($\cdot$) and Revoke($\cdot$) must be queried in a non-decreasing order of time.
- Revoke($\cdot$) cannot be queried at t if KeyUpd($\cdot$) has been queried at t.
- Revoke($\cdot$) must be queried on id^* at $t \le t^*$ (or $t \le t_k^*$) if PriKenGen($\cdot$) has been queried on id^*.
- DecKeyGen($\cdot$) cannot be queried at t if KeyUpd($\cdot$) has not been queried at t.
- DecKeyGen($\cdot$) cannot be queried on (id^*, t^*) (or (id^*, t_k^*)), and in Update query, $t < t'$.

The advantage of $\mathcal{A}$ is defined as $\text{Adv}^{\text{IND-CPA}}_{\text{CA-RIBE-CU}, \mathcal{A}}(n) = |\Pr[b^* = b] - 1/2|$, and a CA-RIBE-CU is IND-CPA secure if $\text{Adv}^{\text{IND-CPA}}_{\text{CA-RIBE-CU}, \mathcal{A}}(n)$ is negligible in the security parameter n.

2.2 Lattices

In this subsection, we recall the knowledge on integer lattice Λ.

Lemma 1 ([9]). *For $q \ge 2$, $m \ge 2n\lceil \log q \rceil$, assume that the columns of $\mathbf{A} \in \mathbb{Z}_q^{n \times m}$ generate $\mathbb{Z}_q^n$, let $\epsilon \in (0, 1/2)$, $s \ge \eta_\epsilon(\Lambda_q^\perp(\mathbf{A}))$, then the followings hold:*

1. *For $\mathbf{e} \xleftarrow{\$} \mathcal{D}_{\mathbb{Z}^m, s}$, the statistical distance between $\mathbf{u} = \mathbf{A}\mathbf{e} \bmod q$ and $\mathbf{u}' \xleftarrow{\$} \mathbb{Z}_q^n$ is at most 2ϵ.*

2. *For $\mathbf{e} \xleftarrow{\$} \mathcal{D}_{\mathbb{Z}^m, s}$, then $\Pr[\|\mathbf{e}\|_\infty \le \lceil s \cdot \log m \rceil]$ holds with a larger probability.*

Lemma 2 ([3,4,17]). *Let $n \ge 1$, $q \ge 2$, $m = 2n\lceil \log q \rceil$, there is a ppt algorithm TrapGen(q, n, m) that returns $\mathbf{A} \in \mathbb{Z}_q^{n \times m}$ statistically close to an uniform matrix in $\mathbb{Z}_q^{n \times m}$ and a trapdoor $\mathbf{R_A}$ for $\Lambda_q^\perp(\mathbf{A})$.*

Gentry et al. [9] showed an algorithm to sample short vectors from a discrete Gaussian distribution, and an improvement was proposed in [17]. Meanwhile, to delegate a trapdoor for a lattice with fixed dimension was given in [2].

Lemma 3 ([9,17]). *Let $n \geq 1$, $q \geq 2$, $m = 2n\lceil \log q \rceil$, given $\mathbf{A} \in \mathbb{Z}_q^{n \times m}$, a trapdoor $\mathbf{R_A}$ for $\Lambda_q^\perp(\mathbf{A})$, a parameter $s = \omega(\sqrt{n \log q \log n})$, and a vector $\mathbf{u} \in \mathbb{Z}_q^n$, there is a ppt algorithm $\mathsf{SamplePre}(\mathbf{A}, \mathbf{R_A}, \mathbf{u}, s)$ returning a shorter vector $\mathbf{e} \in \Lambda_q^{\mathbf{u}}(\mathbf{A})$ sampled from a distribution statistically close to $\mathcal{D}_{\Lambda_q^{\mathbf{u}}(\mathbf{A}), s}$.*

Lemma 4 ([2]). *Let $q > 2$, $m = 2n\lceil \log q \rceil$, $s' \geq \sqrt{n \log q} \cdot \omega(\sqrt{\log m})$, given $\mathbf{A} \in \mathbb{Z}_q^{n \times m}$ who can generate $\mathbb{Z}_q^n$, a trapdoor $\mathbf{R_A}$ for $\Lambda_q^\perp(\mathbf{A})$, an invertible matrix $\mathbf{R} \in (\mathcal{D}_{\mathbb{Z}^m, s'})^m$, a parameter $s > \|\widetilde{\mathbf{R_A}}\| \cdot s' \cdot \sqrt{m} \cdot \omega(\log^{1.5} m)$, there is a ppt algorithm $\mathsf{BasisDel}(\mathbf{A}, \mathbf{R}, \mathbf{R_A}, s)$ returning a trapdoor $\mathbf{R_B}$ for $\Lambda_q^\perp(\mathbf{B} = \mathbf{A}\mathbf{R}^{-1})$, especially, $\|\widetilde{\mathbf{R_B}}\| \leq \|\widetilde{\mathbf{R_A}}\| \cdot m^{1.5} \cdot \omega(\log^{1.5} m)$.*

Lemma 5 ([2]). *Let $q > 2$, $m = 2n\lceil \log q \rceil$, $s' \geq \sqrt{n \log q} \cdot \omega(\sqrt{\log m})$, given $\mathbf{A}$ who can generate $\mathbb{Z}_q^n$, there is a ppt algorithm $\mathsf{SampleRwithBasis}(\mathbf{A}, s')$ returning a matrix $\mathbf{R} \in (\mathcal{D}_{\mathbb{Z}^m, s'})^m$ and a trapdoor $\mathbf{R_B}$ for $\Lambda_q^\perp(\mathbf{B} = \mathbf{A}\mathbf{R}^{-1})$, especially, $\|\widetilde{\mathbf{R_B}}\| \leq \mathcal{O}(\sqrt{n \log q})$.*

We recall the learning with errors (LWE) problem, introduced by Regev [21].

Definition 3. *The LWE problem is defined as follows: given a random $\mathbf{s} \xleftarrow{\$} \mathbb{Z}_q^n$, a distribution χ over $\mathbb{Z}$, let $\mathcal{A}_{\mathbf{s}, \chi}$ be the distribution $(\mathbf{A}, \mathbf{A}^\top \mathbf{s} + \mathbf{e})$ where $\mathbf{A} \xleftarrow{\$} \mathbb{Z}_q^{n \times m}$, $\mathbf{e} \xleftarrow{\$} \chi^m$, and to make distinguish between $\mathcal{A}_{\mathbf{s}, \chi}$ and $\mathcal{U} \xleftarrow{\$} \mathbb{Z}_q^{n \times m} \times \mathbb{Z}_q^m$.*
Let $\beta \geq \sqrt{n} \cdot \omega(\log n)$, for a prime power q, given a β-bounded χ, the LWE problem is as least as hard as the shortest independent vectors problem $\mathsf{SIVP}_{\widetilde{\mathcal{O}}(nq/\beta)}$.

3 Our Lattice-Based CA-RIBE-CU Scheme in ROM

3.1 Description of the Scheme

As in [31], our new lattice-based CA-RIBE-CU also consists of 8 polynomial-time algorithms: Setup, PriKeyGen, KeyUpd, DecKeyGen, Encrypt, Update, Decrypt and Revoke. Let identity space $\mathcal{I} = \{1\} \times \mathbb{Z}_q^{n-1}$, time space $\mathcal{T} = \{2\} \times \mathbb{Z}_q^{n-1}$, and one-bit message space $\mathcal{M} = \{0, 1\}$. The main algorithms are described as follows:

– Setup($1^n, N$): On input a security parameter n and the maximal number of users $N = poly(n)$, set a prime $q = \widetilde{\mathcal{O}}(n^5)$, $m = 2n\lceil \log q \rceil$, two Gaussian parameters $s' = \widetilde{\mathcal{O}}(\sqrt{m})$, $s = \widetilde{\mathcal{O}}(m^4)$, and a norm bound $\beta = \widetilde{\mathcal{O}}(\sqrt{n})$ for a distribution χ. The PKG specifies the following steps:

1. Run TrapGen(q, n, m) twice to get $\mathbf{A} \in \mathbb{Z}_q^{n \times m}$ with a trapdoor $\mathbf{R_A}$, $\mathbf{B} \in \mathbb{Z}_q^{n \times m}$ with a trapdoor $\mathbf{R_B}$, and sample $\mathbf{u} \xleftarrow{\$} \mathbb{Z}_q^n$.

2. Sample a collision-resistance hash function $\mathcal{G} : \{0,1\}^* \to (\mathcal{D}_{\mathbb{Z}^m, s'})^m$.

3. Set the sate $\mathsf{st} = \mathsf{BT}$ that BT is with at least N leaf nodes, and the initial revocation list $\mathsf{RL} = \emptyset$.

4. Set public parameters $\mathsf{pp} = (\mathbf{A}, \mathbf{B}, \mathbf{u}, \mathcal{G})$, and the master secret key $\mathsf{msk} = (\mathbf{R_A}, \mathbf{R_B})$.

5. Output $(\mathsf{pp}, \mathsf{msk}, \mathsf{RL}, \mathsf{st})$, where msk is kept in secret by PKG, and pp is made public and as an implicit input of all other algorithms.

– PriKeyGen($\mathsf{msk}, \mathsf{id}, \mathsf{st}$): On input an identity $\mathsf{id} \in \mathcal{I}$, the master secret key msk and the state st. The PKG specifies the following steps:

1. Set id to an unassigned leaf node of BT, and for each $\theta \in \mathsf{path}(\mathsf{id})$, if $\mathbf{u}_{1,\theta}, \mathbf{u}_{2,\theta}$ are undefined, then sample $\mathbf{u}_{1,\theta} \xleftarrow{\$} \mathbb{Z}_q^n$, set $\mathbf{u}_{2,\theta} = \mathbf{u} - \mathbf{u}_{1,\theta}$, and store $(\mathbf{u}_{1,\theta}, \mathbf{u}_{2,\theta})$ in node θ.

2. Define $\mathbf{A}_{\mathsf{id}} = \mathbf{A}\mathcal{G}(\mathsf{id})^{-1} \in \mathbb{Z}_q^{n \times m}$, and $\mathbf{A}_{\widetilde{\mathsf{id}}} = \mathbf{A}\mathcal{G}(\widetilde{\mathsf{id}})^{-1} \in \mathbb{Z}_q^{n \times m}$.

3. Run SamplePre($\mathbf{A}_{\mathsf{id}}$, BasisDel($\mathbf{A}, \mathcal{G}(\mathsf{id})^{-1}, \mathbf{R_A}, s$), $\mathbf{u}_{1,\theta}, s$) to generate $\mathbf{e}_{\mathsf{id},\theta} \in \mathbb{Z}^m$ satisfying $\mathbf{A}_{\mathsf{id}} \mathbf{e}_{\mathsf{id},\theta} = \mathbf{u}_{1,\theta} \bmod q$.

4. Run BasisDel($\mathbf{A}, \mathcal{G}(\widetilde{\mathsf{id}})^{-1}, \mathbf{R_A}, s$) to generate a trapdoor $\mathbf{R}_{\mathbf{A}_{\widetilde{\mathsf{id}}}}$ for $\Lambda_q^{\perp}(\mathbf{A}_{\widetilde{\mathsf{id}}})$.

5. Output an updated st, and $\mathsf{sk}_{\mathsf{id}} = ((\theta, \mathbf{e}_{\mathsf{id},\theta})_{\theta \in \mathsf{path}(\mathsf{id})}, \mathbf{R}_{\mathbf{A}_{\widetilde{\mathsf{id}}}})$.

– KeyUpd($\mathsf{RL}, \mathsf{t}, \mathsf{msk}, \mathsf{st}$): On input a time $\mathsf{t} \in \mathcal{T}$, the master secret key msk, a revocation list RL and the state st. The PKG specifies the following steps:

1. Define $\mathbf{B}_{\mathsf{t}} = \mathbf{B}\mathcal{G}(\mathsf{t})^{-1}$, for each $\theta \in \mathsf{KUNodes}(\mathsf{BT}, \mathsf{RL}, \mathsf{t})$, retrieve $\mathbf{u}_{2,\theta}$.

2. Run SamplePre($\mathbf{B}_{\mathsf{t}}$, BasisDel($\mathbf{B}, \mathcal{G}(\mathsf{t})^{-1}, \mathbf{R_B}, s$), $\mathbf{u}_{2,\theta}, s$) to generate $\mathbf{e}_{\mathsf{t},\theta} \in \mathbb{Z}^m$ satisfying $\mathbf{B}_{\mathsf{t}} \mathbf{e}_{\mathsf{t},\theta} = \mathbf{u}_{2,\theta} = \mathbf{u} - \mathbf{u}_{1,\theta} \bmod q$.

3. Output $\mathsf{uk}_{\mathsf{t}} = (\theta, \mathbf{e}_{\mathsf{t},\theta})_{\theta \in \mathsf{KUNodes}(\mathsf{BT}, \mathsf{RL}, \mathsf{t})}$.

– DecKeyGen($\mathsf{sk}_{\mathsf{id}}, \mathsf{uk}_{\mathsf{t}}, \mathsf{t}$): On input a long-term private key $\mathsf{sk}_{\mathsf{id}} = ((\theta, \mathbf{e}_{\mathsf{id},\theta})_{\theta \in \mathsf{path}(\mathsf{id})}, \mathbf{R}_{\mathbf{A}_{\widetilde{\mathsf{id}}}})$, a time t and current update key $\mathsf{uk}_{\mathsf{t}} = (\theta, \mathbf{e}_{\mathsf{t},\theta})_{\theta \in \mathsf{KUNodes}(\mathsf{BT}, \mathsf{RL}, \mathsf{t})}$. The receiver id specifies the following steps:

1. If $\mathsf{path}(\mathsf{id}) \cap \mathsf{KUNodes}(\mathsf{BT}, \mathsf{RL}, \mathsf{t}) = \emptyset$, return $\perp$ and abort.

2. Otherwise, define $\mathbf{A}_{\widetilde{\mathsf{id}},\mathsf{t}} = \mathbf{A}_{\widetilde{\mathsf{id}}}\mathcal{G}(\mathsf{t})^{-1} \in \mathbb{Z}_q^{n \times m}$.

3. Run SamplePre($\mathbf{A}_{\widetilde{\mathsf{id}},\mathsf{t}}$, BasisDel($\mathbf{A}_{\widetilde{\mathsf{id}}}, \mathcal{G}(\mathsf{t})^{-1}, \mathbf{R}_{\mathbf{A}_{\widetilde{\mathsf{id}}}}, s$), $\mathbf{u}, s$) to generate $\mathbf{e}_{\widetilde{\mathsf{id}},\mathsf{t}} \in \mathbb{Z}^m$ satisfying $\mathbf{A}_{\widetilde{\mathsf{id}},\mathsf{t}} \mathbf{e}_{\widetilde{\mathsf{id}},\mathsf{t}} = \mathbf{u} \bmod q$.

4. Pick $\theta \in (\mathsf{path}(\mathsf{id}) \cap \mathsf{KUNodes}(\mathsf{BT}, \mathsf{RL}, \mathsf{t}))$ (only one θ exists), and return $\mathsf{dk}_{\mathsf{id},\mathsf{t}} = (\mathbf{e}_{\mathsf{id},\theta}, \mathbf{e}_{\mathsf{t},\theta}, \mathbf{e}_{\widetilde{\mathsf{id}},\mathsf{t}})$.

– Encrypt($\mathsf{id}, \mathsf{t}_0, m$): On input an identity $\mathsf{id} \in \mathcal{I}$, a time $\mathsf{t}_0 \in \mathcal{T}$, and a message $m \in \{0,1\}$. The sender specifies the following steps:

1. Define $\mathbf{A}_{\mathsf{id}} = \mathbf{A}\mathcal{G}(\mathsf{id})^{-1}$, $\mathbf{B}_{\mathsf{t}_0} = \mathbf{B}\mathcal{G}(\mathsf{t}_0)^{-1}$, and $\mathbf{A}_{\widetilde{\mathsf{id}},\mathsf{t}_0} = \mathbf{A}\mathcal{G}(\widetilde{\mathsf{id}})^{-1} \mathcal{G}(\mathsf{t}_0)^{-1}$.

2. Sample $\mathbf{s}_{00}, \mathbf{s}_{01} \xleftarrow{\$} \mathbb{Z}_q^n$, $e_0 \xleftarrow{\$} \chi$, and $\mathbf{e}_{00}, \mathbf{e}_{01}, \mathbf{e}_{02} \xleftarrow{\$} \chi^m$.

3. Set $\mathbf{c}_{00} = \mathbf{A}_{\mathsf{id}}^{\mathrm{T}} \mathbf{s}_{00} + \mathbf{e}_{00} \bmod q \in \mathbb{Z}_q^m$, $\mathbf{c}_{01} = \mathbf{B}_{\mathsf{t}_0}^{\mathrm{T}} \mathbf{s}_{00} + \mathbf{e}_{01} \bmod q \in \mathbb{Z}_q^m$, and $\mathbf{c}_{02} = \mathbf{A}_{\widetilde{\mathsf{id}},\mathsf{t}_0}^{\mathrm{T}} \mathbf{s}_{01} + \mathbf{e}_{02} \bmod q \in \mathbb{Z}_q^m$.

4. Compute $c_0 = \mathbf{u}^{\mathrm{T}}(\mathbf{s}_{00} + \mathbf{s}_{01}) + e_0 + m \lfloor \frac{q}{2} \rfloor \bmod q$.

    5. Output $\mathsf{ct}_{\mathsf{id},t_0} = (\mathsf{id}, t_0, c_0, \mathbf{c}_{00}, \mathbf{c}_{01}, \mathbf{c}_{02}) \in (\{1\} \times \mathbb{Z}_q^{n-1}) \times (\{2\} \times \mathbb{Z}_q^{n-1}) \times \mathbb{Z}_q \times (\mathbb{Z}_q^m)^3$.

– Update($\mathsf{ct}_{\mathsf{id},t}, t'$): Two cases need to be considered according to $\mathsf{ct}_{\mathsf{id},t}$.

1. On input an original ciphertext $\mathsf{ct}_{\mathsf{id},t} = \mathsf{ct}_{\mathsf{id},t_0} = (\mathsf{id}, t_0, c_0, \mathbf{c}_{00}, \mathbf{c}_{01}, \mathbf{c}_{02})$ and a new time $t' = t_1 > t_0$. The CSP specifies the following steps:

    1.1. Define $\mathbf{A}_{\widetilde{\mathsf{id}},t'=t_1} = \mathbf{A}\mathcal{G}(\widetilde{\mathsf{id}})^{-1}\mathcal{G}(t_1)^{-1}$.

    1.2. Sample $\mathbf{s}_{10}, \mathbf{s}_{11} \xleftarrow{\$} \mathbb{Z}_q^n$, and $\mathbf{e}_{10}, \mathbf{e}_{11}, \mathbf{e}_{12} \xleftarrow{\$} \chi^m$.

    1.3. Set $\mathbf{c}_{10} = \mathbf{A}_{\mathsf{id}}^{\mathrm{T}}\mathbf{s}_{10} + \mathbf{e}_{10} \bmod q \in \mathbb{Z}_q^m$, $\mathbf{c}_{11} = \mathbf{B}_{t'}^{\mathrm{T}}\mathbf{s}_{10} + \mathbf{e}_{11} \bmod q \in \mathbb{Z}_q^m$, and $\mathbf{c}_{12} = \mathbf{A}_{\widetilde{\mathsf{id}},t'}^{\mathrm{T}}\mathbf{s}_{11} + \mathbf{e}_{12} \bmod q \in \mathbb{Z}_q^m$.

    1.4. Compute $c_1 = c_0 + \mathbf{u}^{\mathrm{T}}(\mathbf{s}_{10} + \mathbf{s}_{11}) \bmod q$.

    1.5. Output $\mathsf{ct}_{\mathsf{id},t'=t_1} = (\mathsf{id}, t_0, t_1, c_1, \mathbf{c}_{00}, \mathbf{c}_{01}, \mathbf{c}_{02}, \mathbf{c}_{10}, \mathbf{c}_{11}, \mathbf{c}_{12}) \in (\{1\} \times \mathbb{Z}_q^{n-1}) \times (\{2\} \times \mathbb{Z}_q^{n-1})^2 \times \mathbb{Z}_q \times (\mathbb{Z}_q^m)^6$. *Note*: $(\mathbf{s}_{10}, \mathbf{s}_{11})$ should be stored in secret by CSP.

2. On input a $k - 1$ ($k \geq 2$) times re-encrypted ciphertext $\mathsf{ct}_{\mathsf{id},t} = \mathsf{ct}_{\mathsf{id},t_{k-1}} = (\mathsf{id}, t_0, t_{k-1}, c_{k-1}, \mathbf{c}_{00}, \mathbf{c}_{01}, \mathbf{c}_{02}, \mathbf{c}_{(k-1)0}, \mathbf{c}_{(k-1)1}, \mathbf{c}_{(k-1)2})$ and a new time $t' = t_k > t$. The CSP specifies the following steps:

    2.1. Define $\mathbf{A}_{\widetilde{\mathsf{id}},t'=t_k} = \mathbf{A}_{\widetilde{\mathsf{id}}}\mathcal{G}(t_k)^{-1}$.

    2.2. Sample $\mathbf{s}_{k0}, \mathbf{s}_{k1} \xleftarrow{\$} \mathbb{Z}_q^n$, and $\mathbf{e}_{k0}, \mathbf{e}_{k1}, \mathbf{e}_{k2} \xleftarrow{\$} \chi^m$.

    2.3. Set $\mathbf{c}_{k0} = \mathbf{A}_{\mathsf{id}}^{\mathrm{T}}\mathbf{s}_{k0} + \mathbf{e}_{k0} \bmod q \in \mathbb{Z}_q^m$, $\mathbf{c}_{k1} = \mathbf{B}_{t'}^{\mathrm{T}}\mathbf{s}_{k0} + \mathbf{e}_{k1} \bmod q \in \mathbb{Z}_q^m$, and $\mathbf{c}_{k2} = \mathbf{A}_{\widetilde{\mathsf{id}},t'}^{\mathrm{T}}\mathbf{s}_{k1} + \mathbf{e}_{k2} \bmod q \in \mathbb{Z}_q^m$.

    2.4. Retrieve $(\mathbf{s}_{(k-1)0}, \mathbf{s}_{(k-1)1})$ (it is always pre-defined in the re-encrypted time t_{k-1}), and compute $c_k = c_{k-1} + \mathbf{u}^{\mathrm{T}}((\mathbf{s}_{k0} - \mathbf{s}_{(k-1)0}) + (\mathbf{s}_{k1} - \mathbf{s}_{(k-1)1})) = c_0 + \mathbf{u}^{\mathrm{T}}(\mathbf{s}_{k0} + \mathbf{s}_{k1}) \bmod q$.

    2.5. Output $\mathsf{ct}_{\mathsf{id},t'} = (\mathsf{id}, t_0, t_k, c_k, \mathbf{c}_{00}, \mathbf{c}_{01}, \mathbf{c}_{02}, \mathbf{c}_{k0}, \mathbf{c}_{k1}, \mathbf{c}_{k2}) \in (\{1\} \times \mathbb{Z}_q^{n-1}) \times (\{2\} \times \mathbb{Z}_q^{n-1})^2 \times \mathbb{Z}_q \times (\mathbb{Z}_q^m)^6$. *Note*: $(\mathbf{s}_{k0}, \mathbf{s}_{k1})$ is stored in secret by CSP.

– Decrypt($\mathsf{dk}_{\mathsf{id}',t'}, \mathsf{ct}_{\mathsf{id},t}$): Two cases need to be considered according to $\mathsf{ct}_{\mathsf{id},t}$.

1. On input an original ciphertext $\mathsf{ct}_{\mathsf{id},t} = \mathsf{ct}_{\mathsf{id},t_0} = (\mathsf{id}, t_0, c_0, \mathbf{c}_{00}, \mathbf{c}_{01}, \mathbf{c}_{02})$, and a short-term decryption key $\mathsf{dk}_{\mathsf{id}',t'} = (\mathbf{e}_{\mathsf{id}',\theta}, \mathbf{e}_{t',\theta}, \mathbf{e}_{\widetilde{\mathsf{id}'},t'})$, $\theta \in (\mathsf{path}(\mathsf{id}') \cap \mathsf{KUNodes}(\mathsf{BT}, \mathsf{RL}, t'))$. The receiver id' specifies the following steps:

    1.1. If $(\mathsf{id} \neq \mathsf{id}') \vee (t \neq t')$, return $\bot$ and abort.

    1.2. Otherwise, compute $w_0 = c_0 - \mathbf{e}_{\mathsf{id},\theta}^{\mathrm{T}}\mathbf{c}_{00} - \mathbf{e}_{t,\theta}^{\mathrm{T}}\mathbf{c}_{01} - \mathbf{e}_{\widetilde{\mathsf{id}},t}^{\mathrm{T}}\mathbf{c}_{02} \bmod q$.

    1.3. Output $\lfloor \frac{2}{q}w_0 \rceil \in \{0,1\}$.

2. On input a $k \geq 1$ times re-encrypted ciphertext $\mathsf{ct}_{\mathsf{id},t} = \mathsf{ct}_{\mathsf{id},t_k} = (\mathsf{id}, t_0, t_k, c_k, \mathbf{c}_{00}, \mathbf{c}_{01}, \mathbf{c}_{02}, \mathbf{c}_{k0}, \mathbf{c}_{k1}, \mathbf{c}_{k2})$, and a short-term decryption key $\mathsf{dk}_{\mathsf{id}',t'} = (\mathbf{e}_{\mathsf{id}',\theta_k}, \mathbf{e}_{t',\theta_k}, \mathbf{e}_{\widetilde{\mathsf{id}'},t'})$, $\theta_k \in (\mathsf{path}(\mathsf{id}') \cap \mathsf{KUNodes}(\mathsf{BT}, \mathsf{RL}, t'))$. The receiver id' specifies the following steps:

    2.1. If $(\mathsf{id} \neq \mathsf{id}') \vee (t = t_k \neq t')$, return $\bot$ and abort.

    2.2. Otherwise, retrieve uk_{t_0} (it is always sent to receivers publicly by PKG).

2.3. Define $\mathbf{A}_{\widetilde{id},t_0} = \mathbf{A}_{\widetilde{id}} \mathcal{G}(t_0)^{-1}$, and run $\mathsf{SamplePre}(\mathbf{A}_{\widetilde{id},t_0}, \mathsf{BasisDel}(\mathbf{A}_{\widetilde{id}},$ $\mathcal{G}(t_0)^{-1}, \mathbf{R}_{\mathbf{A}_{\widetilde{id}}}, s), \mathbf{u}, s)$ to generate $\mathbf{e}_{\widetilde{id},t_0} \in \mathbb{Z}^m$ satisfying $\mathbf{A}_{\widetilde{id},t_0} \mathbf{e}_{\widetilde{id},t_0} = \mathbf{u} \bmod q$.

2.4. Pick $\theta_0 \in (\mathsf{path}(id) \cap \mathsf{KUNodes}(\mathsf{BT}, \mathsf{RL}, t_0))$, and return a new short-term decryption key $\mathsf{dk}_{id,t_0} = (\mathbf{e}_{id,\theta_0}, \mathbf{e}_{t_0,\theta_0}, \mathbf{e}_{\widetilde{id},t_0})$.

2.5. Compute $w_0 = c_k - \mathbf{e}_{id,\theta_0}^{\mathrm{T}} \mathbf{c}_{00} - \mathbf{e}_{t_0,\theta_0}^{\mathrm{T}} \mathbf{c}_{01} - \mathbf{e}_{\widetilde{id},t_0}^{\mathrm{T}} \mathbf{c}_{02} - \mathbf{e}_{id,\theta_k}^{\mathrm{T}} \mathbf{c}_{k0} - \mathbf{e}_{t,\theta_k}^{\mathrm{T}} \mathbf{c}_{k1} - \mathbf{e}_{\widetilde{id},t}^{\mathrm{T}} \mathbf{c}_{k2} \bmod q$.

2.6. Output $\lfloor \frac{2}{q} w_0 \rceil \in \{0,1\}$.

- $\mathsf{Revoke}(id, t, \mathsf{RL}, \mathsf{st})$: On input current revocation list RL, an identity id, a time t, and a state $\mathsf{st} = \mathsf{BT}$. The PKG specifies the following steps:

  1. Add (id, t) to RL for all nodes associated with id.
  2. Output an updated $\mathsf{RL} = \mathsf{RL} \cup \{(id,t)\}$.

3.2 Analysis

Efficiency: The efficiency aspect of our scheme with $N = poly(n)$ is as follows:

- The bit-size of public parameters pp is is $(2nm + n + n)\log q = \widetilde{\mathcal{O}}(n^2)$.
- The long-term private key sk_{id} consists of a trapdoor matrix of bit-size $\widetilde{\mathcal{O}}(n^2)$, and a series of short vectors of bit-size $\widetilde{\mathcal{O}}(n)$.
- The time update key uk_t has bit-size $\mathcal{O}(r \log \frac{N}{r}) \cdot \widetilde{\mathcal{O}}(n)$ where r is the number of revoked receivers.
- The ciphertext $\mathsf{ct}_{id,t}$ has bit-size $(3(n-1) + 1 + 6m)\log q = \widetilde{\mathcal{O}}(n)$ at most.
- The short-term decryption key $\mathsf{dk}_{id,t}$ has bit-size $\widetilde{\mathcal{O}}(n)$.

By the above analysis, though as in the lattice-based CA-RIBE-CU in SM [31], our lattice-based CA-RIBE-CU in ROM enjoys the same asymptotic efficiency for the public parameters pp, the long-term private key sk_{id}, time update key uk_t, the short-term decryption key $\mathsf{sk}_{id,t}$, and the ciphertext $\mathsf{ct}_{id,t}$, in our new scheme, two matrices over $\mathbb{Z}_q^{n \times m}$ has been removed from pp, the trapdoor matrix is over $\mathbb{Z}^{m \times m}$ (not $\mathbb{Z}^{2m \times 2m}$) and the short vectors are over $\mathbb{Z}^m$ (not $\mathbb{Z}^{2m}$) in sk_{id}, similarly, the short vectors are over $\mathbb{Z}^m$ (not $\mathbb{Z}^{2m}$) in uk_t and $\mathsf{dk}_{id,t}$, and six vectors are over $\mathbb{Z}_q^m$ (not $\mathbb{Z}_q^{3m}$) in our ciphertext (including the original ciphertext and the re-encrypted ciphertext). The only shortcoming is that two trapdoor matrices are included in msk as in Zhang et al. [33]. On the whole, our new lattice-based CA-RIBE-CU in ROM enjoys a much higher efficiency.

Correctness: If our lattice-based CA-RIBE-CU in ROM is operated correctly as specified, and the receiver id is not revoked at $t \in \mathcal{T}$, then $\mathsf{dk}_{id,t} = (\mathbf{e}_{id,\theta}, \mathbf{e}_{t,\theta}, \mathbf{e}_{\widetilde{id},t})$ satisfies $\mathbf{A}_{id}\mathbf{e}_{id,\theta} = \mathbf{u}_{1,\theta} \bmod q$, $\mathbf{B}_t\mathbf{e}_{t,\theta} = \mathbf{u}_{2,\theta} \bmod q$, and $\mathbf{A}_{\widetilde{id},t}\mathbf{e}_{\widetilde{id},t} = \mathbf{u} \bmod q$. In the decryption algorithm, the non-revoked receiver id tries to derive m by using $\mathsf{dk}_{id,t} = (\mathbf{e}_{id,\theta}, \mathbf{e}_{t,\theta}, \mathbf{e}_{\widetilde{id},t})$ (and $\mathsf{dk}_{id,t_0} = (\mathbf{e}_{id,\theta_0}, \mathbf{e}_{t_0,\theta_0}, \mathbf{e}_{\widetilde{id},t_0})$).

- If the ciphertext is an original one, $\mathsf{ct}_{\mathsf{id},t=t_0} = (\mathsf{id}, t_0, c_0, \mathbf{c}_{00}, \mathbf{c}_{01}, \mathbf{c}_{02})$, compute

$$
\begin{aligned}
w_0 &= c_0 - \mathbf{e}_{\mathsf{id},\theta}^{\mathrm{T}} \mathbf{c}_{00} - \mathbf{e}_{t,\theta}^{\mathrm{T}} \mathbf{c}_{01} - \mathbf{e}_{\widetilde{\mathsf{id}},t}^{\mathrm{T}} \mathbf{c}_{02} = \mathbf{u}^{\mathrm{T}}(\mathbf{s}_{00} + \mathbf{s}_{01}) + e_0 + \mathsf{m}\lfloor\tfrac{q}{2}\rfloor \\
&\quad - \underbrace{(\mathbf{A}_{\mathsf{id}}\mathbf{e}_{\mathsf{id},\theta} + \mathbf{B}_t\mathbf{e}_{t,\theta})^{\mathrm{T}}\mathbf{s}_{00}}_{=\mathbf{u}^{\mathrm{T}}\mathbf{s}_{00}} - \mathbf{e}_{\mathsf{id},\theta}^{\mathrm{T}}\mathbf{e}_{00} - \mathbf{e}_{t,\theta}^{\mathrm{T}}\mathbf{e}_{01} - \underbrace{(\mathbf{A}_{\widetilde{\mathsf{id}},t}\mathbf{e}_{\widetilde{\mathsf{id}},t})^{\mathrm{T}}\mathbf{s}_{01}}_{=\mathbf{u}^{\mathrm{T}}\mathbf{s}_{01}} - \mathbf{e}_{\widetilde{\mathsf{id}},t}^{\mathrm{T}}\mathbf{e}_{02} \\
&= \mathsf{m}\lfloor\tfrac{q}{2}\rfloor + \underbrace{e_0 - \mathbf{e}_{\mathsf{id},\theta}^{\mathrm{T}}\mathbf{e}_{00} - \mathbf{e}_{t,\theta}^{\mathrm{T}}\mathbf{e}_{01} - \mathbf{e}_{\widetilde{\mathsf{id}},t}^{\mathrm{T}}\mathbf{e}_{02}}_{\text{error}}
\end{aligned}
$$

According to our parameters settings, it can be checked that the error term error is bounded by $q/5$ (i.e., $\|\text{error}\|_\infty < q/5$), thus, we have the conclusion $\lfloor\tfrac{2}{q}w_0\rceil = \mathsf{m}$ with overwhelming probability.

- If the ciphertext is a $k \geq 1$ times re-encrypted one, $\mathsf{ct}_{\mathsf{id},t=t_k} = (\mathsf{id}, t_0, t_k, c_k, \mathbf{c}_{00}, \mathbf{c}_{01}, \mathbf{c}_{02}, \mathbf{c}_{k0}, \mathbf{c}_{k1}\mathbf{c}_{k2})$.

  1. Compute

$$
\begin{aligned}
w_k &= c_k - \mathbf{e}_{\mathsf{id},\theta_k}^{\mathrm{T}} \mathbf{c}_{k0} - \mathbf{e}_{t,\theta_k}^{\mathrm{T}} \mathbf{c}_{k1} - \mathbf{e}_{\widetilde{\mathsf{id}},t}^{\mathrm{T}} \mathbf{c}_{k2} = c_0 + \mathbf{u}^{\mathrm{T}}(\mathbf{s}_{k0} + \mathbf{s}_{k1}) \\
&\quad - \underbrace{(\mathbf{A}_{\mathsf{id}}\mathbf{e}_{\mathsf{id},\theta_k} + \mathbf{B}_t\mathbf{e}_{t,\theta_k})^{\mathrm{T}}\mathbf{s}_{k0}}_{=\mathbf{u}^{\mathrm{T}}\mathbf{s}_{k0}} - \mathbf{e}_{\mathsf{id},\theta_k}^{\mathrm{T}}\mathbf{e}_{k0} - \mathbf{e}_{t,\theta_k}^{\mathrm{T}}\mathbf{e}_{k1} - \underbrace{(\mathbf{A}_{\widetilde{\mathsf{id}},t}\mathbf{e}_{\widetilde{\mathsf{id}},t})^{\mathrm{T}}\mathbf{s}_{k1}}_{=\mathbf{u}^{\mathrm{T}}\mathbf{s}_{k1}} - \mathbf{e}_{\widetilde{\mathsf{id}},t}^{\mathrm{T}}\mathbf{e}_{k2} \\
&= \mathbf{u}^{\mathrm{T}}(\mathbf{s}_{00} + \mathbf{s}_{01}) + e_0 + \mathsf{m}\lfloor\tfrac{q}{2}\rfloor \underbrace{- \mathbf{e}_{\mathsf{id},\theta_k}^{\mathrm{T}}\mathbf{e}_{k0} - \mathbf{e}_{t,\theta_k}^{\mathrm{T}}\mathbf{e}_{k1} - \mathbf{e}_{\widetilde{\mathsf{id}},t}^{\mathrm{T}}\mathbf{e}_{k2}}_{\text{error}'}
\end{aligned}
$$

  2. Retrieve uk_{t_0}, define $\mathbf{A}_{\widetilde{\mathsf{id}},t_0} = \mathbf{A}_{\widetilde{\mathsf{id}}}\mathcal{G}(t_0)^{-1}$, and run SamplePre $(\mathbf{A}_{\widetilde{\mathsf{id}},t_0}, \mathsf{BasisDel}(\mathbf{A}_{\widetilde{\mathsf{id}}}, \mathcal{G}(t_0)^{-1}, \mathbf{R}_{\mathbf{A}_{\widetilde{\mathsf{id}}}}, s), \mathbf{u}, s)$ to generate $\mathbf{e}_{\widetilde{\mathsf{id}},t_0} \in \mathbb{Z}^m$ satisfying $\mathbf{A}_{\widetilde{\mathsf{id}},t_0}\mathbf{e}_{\widetilde{\mathsf{id}},t_0} = \mathbf{u} \bmod q$.

  3. Return a new short-term decryption key $\mathsf{dk}_{\mathsf{id},t_0} = (\mathbf{e}_{\mathsf{id},\theta_0}, \mathbf{e}_{t_0,\theta_0}, \mathbf{e}_{\widetilde{\mathsf{id}},t_0})$ where $\theta_0 \in (\mathsf{path}(\mathsf{id}) \cap \mathsf{KUNodes}(\mathsf{BT}, \mathsf{RL}, t_0))$.

  4. Compute

$$
\begin{aligned}
w_0 &= w_k - \mathbf{e}_{\mathsf{id},\theta_0}^{\mathrm{T}} \mathbf{c}_{00} - \mathbf{e}_{t_0,\theta_0}^{\mathrm{T}} \mathbf{c}_{01} - \mathbf{e}_{\widetilde{\mathsf{id}},t_0}^{\mathrm{T}} \mathbf{c}_{02} = \mathbf{u}^{\mathrm{T}}(\mathbf{s}_{00} + \mathbf{s}_{01}) + e_0 + \mathsf{m}\lfloor\tfrac{q}{2}\rfloor + \text{error}' \\
&\quad - \underbrace{(\mathbf{A}_{\mathsf{id}}\mathbf{e}_{\mathsf{id},\theta_0} + \mathbf{B}_t\mathbf{e}_{t_0,\theta_0})^{\mathrm{T}}\mathbf{s}_{00}}_{=\mathbf{u}^{\mathrm{T}}\mathbf{s}_{00}} - \mathbf{e}_{\mathsf{id},\theta_0}^{\mathrm{T}}\mathbf{e}_{00} - \mathbf{e}_{t_0,\theta_0}^{\mathrm{T}}\mathbf{e}_{01} - \underbrace{(\mathbf{A}_{\widetilde{\mathsf{id}},t_0}\mathbf{e}_{\widetilde{\mathsf{id}},t_0})^{\mathrm{T}}\mathbf{s}_{01}}_{=\mathbf{u}^{\mathrm{T}}\mathbf{s}_{01}} - \mathbf{e}_{\widetilde{\mathsf{id}},t_0}^{\mathrm{T}}\mathbf{e}_{02} \\
&= \mathsf{m}\lfloor\tfrac{q}{2}\rfloor + \underbrace{e_0 + \text{error}' - \mathbf{e}_{\mathsf{id},\theta_0}^{\mathrm{T}}\mathbf{e}_{00} - \mathbf{e}_{t_0,\theta_0}^{\mathrm{T}}\mathbf{e}_{01} - \mathbf{e}_{\widetilde{\mathsf{id}},t_0}^{\mathrm{T}}\mathbf{e}_{02}}_{\text{error}}
\end{aligned}
$$

According to our parameters settings, it can be checked that error is bounded by $q/5$ (i.e., $\|\text{error}\|_\infty < q/5$), thus, we have the conclusion $\lfloor\tfrac{2}{q}w_0\rceil = \mathsf{m}$ with overwhelming probability.

Security: For the IND-CPA security of our new lattice-based CA-RIBE-CU scheme, we show the following theorem.

Theorem 1. *Our lattice-based* CA-RIBE-CU *scheme in* ROM *is* IND-CPA *secure if the* LWE *assumption holds.*

The proofs have been omitted due to lack of space, for any interested reader, please contact the corresponding author for the full version.

4 Conclusion

In this paper, we propose a new lattice-based CA-RIBE-CU scheme in ROM. In comparison with previous lattice-based constructions of RIBE, our scheme enjoys a significant advantage in terms of ciphertext security when considering a secure data sharing in the cloud setting, and the revoked receivers cannot access to both previously and subsequently shared data. Instead of using a super-lattice to issue long-term private keys and time update keys, our new construction is based on the main technique for lattice basis delegation without dimension increase, which benefits the new construction with much shorter items in almost all keys and final ciphertexts, thus enriching the research of lattice-based RIBE.

Acknowledgments. The authors would like to thank the anonymous reviewers of FCS 2023 for their very helpful comments, and this research was supported by Henan Key Laboratory of Network Cryptography Technology (No.LNCT2022-A09), International Cultivation of Henan Advanced Talents (2023026) and The Key Scientific Research Project of Higher Education of Henan Province (22A520047).

References

1. Agrawal, S., Boneh, D., Boyen, X.: Efficient lattice (H)IBE in the standard model. In: Gilbert, H. (ed.) EUROCRYPT 2010. LNCS, vol. 6110, pp. 553–572. Springer, Heidelberg (2010). https://doi.org/10.1007/978-3-642-13190-5_28

2. Agrawal, S., Boneh, D., Boyen, X.: Lattice basis delegation in fixed dimension and shorter-ciphertext hierarchical IBE. In: Rabin, T. (ed.) CRYPTO 2010. LNCS, vol. 6223, pp. 98–115. Springer, Heidelberg (2010). https://doi.org/10.1007/978-3-642-14623-7_6

3. Ajtai, M.: Generating hard instances of lattice problems (Extended Abstract). In: STOC, pp. 99–108. ACM (1996). https://doi.org/10.1145/237814.237838

4. Alwen, J., Peikert, C.: Generating shorter bases for hard random lattices. Theor. Comput. Syst. **48**(3), 535–553 (2011). https://doi.org/10.1007/s00224-010-9278-3

5. Boneh, D., Franklin, M.: Identity-based encryption from the Weil pairing. In: Kilian, J. (ed.) CRYPTO 2001. LNCS, vol. 2139, pp. 213–229. Springer, Heidelberg (2001). https://doi.org/10.1007/3-540-44647-8_13

6. Boldyreva, A., Goyal, V., Kumar, V.: Identity-based encryption with efficient revocation. In: CCS, pp. 417–426. ACM (2008). https://doi.org/10.1145/1455770.1455823

7. Chen, J., Lim, H.W., Ling, S., Wang, H., Nguyen, K.: Revocable identity-based encryption from lattices. In: Susilo, W., Mu, Y., Seberry, J. (eds.) ACISP 2012. LNCS, vol. 7372, pp. 390–403. Springer, Heidelberg (2012). https://doi.org/10.1007/978-3-642-31448-3_29

8. Dong, C., Yang, K., Qiu, J., et al.: Outsouraced revocable identity-based encryption from lattices. Trans. Emerg. Telecommun. Technol. e3529 (2018). https://doi.org/10.1002/ett.3529
9. Gentry, C., Peikert, C., Vaikuntanathan, V.: Trapdoor for hard lattices and new cryptographic constructions. In: STOC, pp. 197–206. ACM (2008). https://doi.org/10.1145/1374376.1374407
10. Katsumata, S., Matsuda, T., Takayasu, A.: Lattice-based revocable (Hierarchical) IBE with decryption key exposure resistance. In: Lin, D., Sako, K. (eds.) PKC 2019. LNCS, vol. 11443, pp. 441–471. Springer, Cham (2019). https://doi.org/10.1007/978-3-030-17259-6_15
11. Lee, K.: A generic construction for revocable identity-based encryption with subset difference methods. PLoS ONE 15(9), e0239053 (2020). https://doi.org/10.1371/journal.pone.o239053
12. Li, J., Li, J., Chen, X., et al.: Identity-based encryption with outsourced revocation in cloud computing. IEEE Trans. Comput. 64(2), 426–437 (2015). https://doi.org/10.1109/TC.2013.208
13. Liang, K., Liu, J.K., Wong, D.S., Susilo, W.: An efficient cloud-based revocable identity-based proxy re-encryption scheme for public clouds data sharing. In: Kutyłowski, M., Vaidya, J. (eds.) ESORICS 2014. LNCS, vol. 8712, pp. 257–272. Springer, Cham (2014). https://doi.org/10.1007/978-3-319-11203-9_15
14. Libert, B., Vergnaud, D.: Adaptive-ID secure revocable identity-based encryption. In: Fischlin, M. (ed.) CT-RSA 2009. LNCS, vol. 5473, pp. 1–15. Springer, Heidelberg (2009). https://doi.org/10.1007/978-3-642-00862-7_1
15. Liu, Y., Sun, Y.: Generic construction of server-aided revocable hierarchical identity-based encryption. In: Wu, Y., Yung, M. (eds.) Inscrypt 2020. LNCS, vol. 12612, pp. 73–82. Springer, Cham (2021). https://doi.org/10.1007/978-3-030-71852-7_5
16. Ma, X., Lin, D.: Generic constructions of revocable identity-based encryption. In: Liu, Z., Yung, M. (eds.) Inscrypt 2019. LNCS, vol. 12020, pp. 381–396. Springer, Cham (2020). https://doi.org/10.1007/978-3-030-42921-8_22
17. Micciancio, D., Peikert, C.: Trapdoors for lattices: simpler, tighter, faster, smaller. In: Pointcheval, D., Johansson, T. (eds.) EUROCRYPT 2012. LNCS, vol. 7237, pp. 700–718. Springer, Heidelberg (2012). https://doi.org/10.1007/978-3-642-29011-4_41
18. Naor, D., Naor, M., Lotspiech, J.: Revocation and tracing schemes for stateless receivers. In: Kilian, J. (ed.) CRYPTO 2001. LNCS, vol. 2139, pp. 41–62. Springer, Heidelberg (2001). https://doi.org/10.1007/3-540-44647-8_3
19. Nguyen, K., Wang, H., Zhang, J.: Server-aided revocable identity-based encryption from lattices. In: Foresti, S., Persiano, G. (eds.) CANS 2016. LNCS, vol. 10052, pp. 107–123. Springer, Cham (2016). https://doi.org/10.1007/978-3-319-48965-0_7
20. Qin, B., Deng, R.H., Li, Y., Liu, S.: Server-aided revocable identity-based encryption. In: Pernul, G., Ryan, P.Y.A., Weippl, E. (eds.) ESORICS 2015. LNCS, vol. 9326, pp. 286–304. Springer, Cham (2015). https://doi.org/10.1007/978-3-319-24174-6_15
21. Regev, O.: On lattices, learning with errors, random linear codes, and cryptography. In: STOC, pp. 84–93. ACM (2005). https://doi.org/10.1145/1060590.1060603
22. Sahai, A., Waters, B.: Fuzzy identity-based encryption. In: Cramer, R. (ed.) EUROCRYPT 2005. LNCS, vol. 3494, pp. 457–473. Springer, Heidelberg (2005). https://doi.org/10.1007/11426639_27

23. Seo, J.H., Emura, K.: Revocable identity-based encryption revisited: security model and construction. In: Kurosawa, K., Hanaoka, G. (eds.) PKC 2013. LNCS, vol. 7778, pp. 216–234. Springer, Heidelberg (2013). https://doi.org/10.1007/978-3-642-36362-7_14

24. Agrawal, S., Boneh, D., Boyen, X.: Lattice basis delegation in fixed dimension and shorter-ciphertext hierarchical IBE. In: Rabin, T. (ed.) CRYPTO 2010. LNCS, vol. 6223, pp. 98–115. Springer, Heidelberg (2010). https://doi.org/10.1007/978-3-642-14623-7_6

25. Shor, P.: Polynomial-time algorithms for prime factorization and dislogarithms on a quantum computer. SIAN J. Comput. 26(5), 1485–1509 (1997). https://doi.org/10.1016/j.tcs.2020.02.03

26. Sun, Y., Mu, Y., Susilo, W., et al.: Revocable identity-based encryption with server-aided ciphertext evolution. Theor. Comput. Sci. 2020(815), 11–24 (2020). https://doi.org/10.1016/j.tcs.2020.02.03

27. Takayasu, A.: Adaptively secure lattice-based revocable IBE in the QROM: compact parameters, tight security, and anonymity. Des. Codes Cryptogr. (2021). https://doi.org/10.1007/s10623-021-00895-3

28. Takayasu, A., Watanabe, Y.: Lattice-based revocable identity-based encryption with bounded decryption key exposure resistance. In: Pieprzyk, J., Suriadi, S. (eds.) ACISP 2017. LNCS, vol. 10342, pp. 184–204. Springer, Cham (2017). https://doi.org/10.1007/978-3-319-60055-0_10

29. Wang, C., Li, Y., Fang, J., et al.: Cloud-aided scalable revocable identity-based encryption scheme with ciphertext update. Concurr. Comput. Pract. Exp. 2017(29), e4035 (2017). https://doi.org/10.1002/cpe.4035

30. Wang, S., Zhang, J., He, J., Wang, H., Li, C.: Simplified revocable hierarchical identity-based encryption from lattices. In: Mu, Y., Deng, R.H., Huang, X. (eds.) CANS 2019. LNCS, vol. 11829, pp. 99–119. Springer, Cham (2019). https://doi.org/10.1007/978-3-030-31578-8_6

31. Zhang, Y., Liu, X., Hu. Y., et al.: Cloud-aided scalable revocable identity-based encryption with ciphertext update from lattices. In: Cao, C., et al. (eds.) FCS 2021. CCIS, vol. 1558, pp. 269–287. Springer, Singapore (2021). https://doi.org/10.1007/978-981-19-0523-0_18

32. Zhang, Y., Liu, X., Hu. Y., et al.: On the analysis of the outsourced revocable identity-based encryption from lattices. In: Yang, M., Chen, C., Liu, Y. (eds.) NSS 2021. LNCS, vol. 13401, pp. 79–99. Springer, Cham (2021). https://doi.org/10.1007/978-3-030-92708-0_5

33. Zhang, Y., Liu, X., Hu, Y., Jia, H.: Revocable identity-based encryption with server-aided ciphertext evolution from lattices. In: Yu, Yu., Yung, M. (eds.) Inscrypt 2021. LNCS, vol. 13007, pp. 442–465. Springer, Cham (2021). https://doi.org/10.1007/978-3-030-88323-2_24

34. Zhang, Y., Liu, X., Hu. Y., et al.: Simplified server-aided revocable identity-based encryption from lattices. In: Ge, C., Guo, F. (eds.) ProvSec 2022. LNCS, vol. 13600, pp. 71–87. Springer, Cham (2022). https://doi.org/10.1007/978-3-031-20917-8_6

Heterogeneous Signcryption Scheme with Equality Test for Internet of Vehicles

Chunhua Jin[✉], Wenyu Qin, Zhiwei Chen, Kaijun Sun[✉], Guanhua Chen, and Jinsong Shan

Faculty of Computer and Software Engineering, Huaiyin Institute of Technology, Huai'an 233003, China
xajch0206@163.com, sunkaijun2020@163.com

Abstract. By collecting and using vehicle dynamic data from sensors on vehicles, Internet of Vehicles (IoV) has greatly enhanced the convenience and intelligence of users' transportation. However, the data transmission in IoV may compromise user privacy by revealing sensitive information such as location and identity. To address this problem, many signcryption schemes are proposed. Although most existing signcryption schemes can ensure user privacy, they fail to support communication among devices with heterogeneous cryptosystems and cannot enable ciphertext equality test. To overcome these limitations, we present a heterogenous signcryption scheme with equality test, named CP-HSCET. This scheme allows an IoV device in certificateless (CLC) environment to signcrypt messages and transport them to the management center in public key infrastructure (PKI)-based environment, hence achieving higher universality. Moreover, it supports equality test on ciphertexts, which allows a semi-honest third-party (usually a cloud server) to verify if the ciphertexts with different public key have the same plaintexts without unsigncrypting them, thereby enhancing the availability of our scheme. Finally, we compare the proposed scheme with the other four schemes. The result shows that the proposal is significantly superior to other schemes in terms of computation cost and total energy consumption. Therefore, our scheme is the most suitable for IoV environments, in which most of the devices have lower computational power.

Keywords: Internet of vehicles · Heterogeneous cryptosystem · Equality test · Signcryption

1 Introduction

IoV refers to the interconnection of vehicles, road infrastructure, and mobile devices, enabling seamless communication and collaboration between these entities [1]. The development of the IoV has been driven by the increasing demand for intelligent transportation systems, which aim to improve road safety, reduce traffic congestion, and enhance the overall driving experience [2]. In the IoV, vehicles are equipped with sensors, cameras, and other communication devices

H. Yang and R. Lu (Eds.): FCS 2023, CCIS 1992, pp. 404–418, 2024.
https://doi.org/10.1007/978-981-99-9331-4_27

that collect and transmit data in real-time. This data is used to monitor traffic conditions, optimize routing, and provide drivers with real-time information about road conditions and hazards. Additionally, vehicles can communicate with each other and with road infrastructure, such as traffic lights, to coordinate their movements and avoid collisions. At the same time, vehicles can send their data to a cloud server managed by the traffic control center for safekeeping. In the event of a traffic incident, the relevant data can be retrieved from the cloud server and used as evidence [3]. The communication network in IoV consists of various technologies, such as Vehicle-to-Vehicle (V2V), Vehicle-to-Roadside Units (V2R), Vehicle-to-Personal devices (V2P), Vehicle-to-Sensors (V2S), and Vehicle-to-Infrastructure of cellular networks (V2I). These communication technologies use different frequencies, data rates, and protocols, which pose significant security challenges in protecting the sensitive data transmitted in the IoV.

In the context of cloud-assisted IoV, maintaining the confidentiality and privacy of transmitted data is crucial. To achieve this, encryption then outsourcing seems to be a promising approach. However, this approach greatly hinders the availability of IoV data as searching for encrypted data is difficult. A straightforward solution is to download all the uploaded data to a local machine, decrypt and then search for it, which can be time-consuming. To address the challenge of balancing data confidentiality and searchability, a public key encryption scheme with keyword search (PKE-KS) has been proposed [4]. This scheme enables users to retrieve data from the cloud server without having to decrypt it by exploiting keywords. Although PKE-KS provides a search functionality over ciphertexts, it has a drawback in that it can only perform the search if the keyword and the uploaded data are encrypted using the same public key. To address this issue, Yang et al. [5] proposed the public key encryption with equality test (PKEET) scheme. The PKEET scheme allows the cloud server to conduct an equality test on ciphertexts encrypted with different public keys, making it possible to overcome the limitation of the PKE-KS scheme.

In IoV communication, the open nature of the transmission channels makes it easy for adversaries to intercept, manipulate, or delete data. This result in a lack of guarantees for data integrity and authentication. In order to settle this issue, Wang et al. [6] proposed a signcryption scheme with equality test. It can perform the encryption and signature operations in a single logical step and achieve authentication, integrity, non-repudiation and confidentiality, simultaneously. In addition, a remote server can determine whether two ciphertexts signcrypt the same underlying plaintext. However, the entities of the scheme are in the same cryptosystem and not suitable for the actual environment. To resolve this problem, Hou et al. [7] presented a heterogeneous signcryption scheme with equality test (HTSC-ET). Their scheme allows a sensor in PKI to communicate with a user in IBC. Moreover, a cloud server can perform the equivalence test on signcrypted ciphertext or encrypted ciphertext, or both encrypted/signcrypted ciphertext. Later, Xiong et al. [8] constructed an HSCIP-ET scheme from IBC to PKI. The proposed scheme can conduct the equality test on diverse ciphertexts to guarantee the integrity, authentication, unforgeability, and confidentiality of the transmitted messages. In addition, it can be proven secure in the random oracle model (ROM). However, IBC has the key escrow problem since the public key generator (PKG) knows all entities' private keys. Certificateless cryptography (CLC) [9] solves this problem perfectly, where the Key Generation Center (KGC) produces a partial secret key for the entity, while the entity creates the remaining portion of their private key. Due to the heterogeneous nature of IoV, designing an HSC-ET scheme where the vehicle sensors are in CLC while the server is in PKI is an overwhelming choice as it can be well-suited to this environment. For vehicle sensors, CLC does not involve key escrow problem and public key certificate management problem. For servers, PKI is widely adopted.

1.1 Motivation and Contribution

The motivation of this paper is to enable the cloud server to perform equivalence tests between signcrypted ciphertexts, regardless of whether the signcryption uses the same or different private keys. Furthermore, since the collected data is transmitted through a public channel, which is susceptible to various attacks such as tampering and deletion, the paper also addresses the need to provide authentication, integrity, non-repudiation, and confidentiality. To ensure the security of IoV, which is a heterogeneous network, an SC-ET algorithm based on heterogeneous systems is employed. The specific contributions are stated as follows.

1. We introduce a new cryptographic scheme called CP-HSCET, which combines the features of heterogeneous signcryption and equality test. CP-HSCET allows vehicle sensors in CLC that eliminates the need for certificate management and key escrow as well as the management center in PKI that is widely adopted. It also admits a cloud server to support an equivalence test on distinct ciphertexts without having any knowledge of the underlying plaintext.
2. With CPHSC-ET, we aim to enhance the security of cloud-based data transmission and ensure confidentiality, integrity, non-repudiation, and authentication.
3. The suggested scheme provides flexibility by allowing it to switch between two encryption modes: PKI-based encryption and heterogeneous signcryption. This flexibility ensures that the scheme can be adapted to different scenarios and requirements, making it a more versatile and practical solution. Moreover, this switching capability does not compromise the security or efficiency of the scheme.
4. For security, this construction satisfies the indistinguishability against adaptive chosen ciphertext attacks (IND-CCA2) and one-way security against adaptive chosen-ciphertext attacks (OW-CCA2) under the bilinear Diffie-H ellman inversion problem (BDHIP) as well as existential unforgeability against adaptive chosen messages attacks (EUF-CMA) under the q-strong Diffie-Hellman problem (q-SDHP) and modified inverse computational Diffie-Hellm an problem (m-ICDHP) in the random oracle model.

5. For performance analysis, we compare the proposed scheme with the other four schemes. The comparison result indicates that it only occupies less than 46.52%, 54.39%, 60.82% and 37.35% of other schemes in terms of computation overhead, respectively. And for the total energy consumption, it only occupies below 45% of the other plans at 30 ciphertexts. Therefore, our scheme has the highest efficiency and is the most suitable for IoV environments, in which most of the devices have lower computational power.

1.2   Related Work

Three related works called secure search encryption for IoV, public key encryption with equality test (PKEET) and public key signcryption with equality test (PKSET) are described as follows.

Feng et al. [10] presented an attribute-based encryption with parallel outsourced decryption scheme for edge intelligent IoV. A tree access structure based on Spark and MapReduce is applied to edge intelligent IoV, which can significantly improve the speed of outsourced decryption. Jiang et al. [11] provided an attribute-based data access control scheme for IoV. In their scheme, they deploy fog nodes in the data access area to provide location-based keys and assist in vehicle decryption. Additionally, they employ a blockchain system to publish public parameters, which ensures the transparency and reliability of our system. Li et al. [12] presented a proxy re-encryption scheme with equality test for IoV. Their construction not only achieves the fine-grained delegation, but also provides ciphertext equality test by a cloud server. In order to solve the issues of transmission latency and insufficient computing capacity, Xiong et al. [13] designed a group attribute-based encryption with equality test scheme for autonomous transportation systems. Their design enables sensors installed in vehicles to encrypt traffic data with a specific access policy, allowing only users possessing the required attributes to access the encrypted data. Additionally, the construction also can realize ciphertext search function by providing equality tests. Tan et al. [14] proposed a cloud-edge collaboration searchable data sharing scheme for IoV. The blockchain technology is used to store the hash value of the data ciphertext and the search index of the keyword. In addition, they also utilize attribute-based searchable encryption to provide fine-grained access control and keyword search functionality. To solve the high computational complexity issue of attribute-based encryption (ABE) scheme, Zhen et al. [15] proposed a multiauthority attribute keyword search scheme which is based on the cloud-edge-end collaboration model and can achieve efficient and secure fine-grained keyword retrieval for IoV data.

Boneh et al. [4] first introduced the concept of PKE-KS. Their construction allows the server to recognize any messages that include a particular keyword, without gaining access to any other information contained in the message. But it just supports the search function for ciphertexts encrypted utilizing the same public key. To tackle this problem, Yang et al. [5] presented the primitive of PKEET, which allows anyone to perform an equivalence test to verify if two ciphertexts were generated using different public keys but have the same plaintext. Tang et al. [16] presented a fine-grained authorization PKEET scheme. Two users must work together to generate a token that grants the semi-trusted proxy permission to perform an equality test between the ciphertexts on the same encrypted data. Later, Tang et al. [17] designed a primitive named all-or-nothing PKEET which means that the proxy can execute equality test on both two entities' ciphertexts if he can obtain the ciphertexts of them. However, the above-mentioned schemes incur certificate management issues. To settle this problem, Ma et al. [18] put forward an IBC-PKEET scheme using bilinear pairing. Their scheme supports the sender utilizing the receiver's identity to encrypt keywords. Moreover, the cloud server can execute an equality test on ciphertexts from different entities. However, their scheme utilizes the time-consuming bilinear pairing operation, so they incur more computation overhead. Later, Wu et al. [19] gave an improved IBC-PKEET scheme, which consumes less computation overhead during the design phase. As there exists the key escrow issue in IBC cryptosystem, CLC-PKEET scheme [20] has been proposed which can avoid the issues in IBC and PKI, and the server can execute the equality test on two entities' ciphertexts in the case of unknown the contents of their plaintexts. Later, Hassan et al. [21] presented a fine-grained access control equality test scheme. It means that the cloud server can perform search functionality according to four types of authorizations. Zhao et al. [22] designed a CLC-PKEET scheme. Their construction allows a cloud server to do the equality test on ciphertext and can be well applied in IoV scenario.

The above-mentioned schemes are only support equality test for encryption schemes, there also exist signcryption schemes that support equality test. Signcryption [23] is a cryptographic primitive that combines the functionalities of encryption and signature in a single logical step, which is known as "signature-then-encryption". It has significantly reduced the computational overhead when compared to the traditional approaches where encryption and signature are performed separately. Wang et al. [6] gave a first public key signcryption scheme with equality test (PKSC-ET). Later, Lin et al. [24] gave a generic PKSC-ET construction. Their design can be adapted to support IBC setting. This modification allows for greater flexibility and applicability to various scenarios. Inspired by their construction, Xiong et al. [7] proposed an IBC-PKEET scheme. Their scheme inherits the advantage of signcryption and equality test. They also provide formal security proof which is very important for algorithm design. However, previous methods have focused on supporting only one system, leaving the unaddressed issues of supporting heterogeneous systems. Xiong et al. [8] presented two HSC-PKEET schemes. However, their scheme has an inherent problem in IBC. In 2023, Hou et al. [25] provided a heterogeneous online/offline signcryption with equality test (HOOSC-PKEET). They utilize the online/offline method to reduce computational overhead. It means that the lightweight operation is done in online phase, while the heavy operation is done in offline phase. In addition, the equality test function is also achieved to check whether two ciphertexts contain the same plaintext. Shao et al. [26] presented an HSC-ET scheme that is from CLC to PKI. However, their scheme is inefficient since the time-consuming bilinear pairing operation is utilized in signcryption algorithm.

1.3 Organization

The rest of this paper is arranged as follows. Preliminaries are introduced in Sect. 2. An efficient CP-HSCET scheme is designed in Sect. 3. Security analysis is given in Sect. 4. Performance is shown in Sect. 5. Finally, the conclusion are given in Sect. 6.

2 Preliminaries

Here, we introduce bilinear pairings and difficult problems as follows.

2.1 Bilinear Pairings

Let G_1, G_2 be an additive group and a multiplicative group, respectively. G_1 as well as G_2 have the same prime order p. P is a generator of G_1. A bilinear pairing is a map $e : G_1 \times G_1 \to G_2$ with the following properties:

1. Bilinearity: $e(aP, bQ) = e(P, Q)^{ab}$ for all $P, Q \in G_1, a, b \in Z_p^*$.
2. Non-degeneracy: There exists $P, Q \in G_1$ such that $e(P, Q) \neq 1$.
3. Computability: There is an efficient algorithm to compute $e(P, Q)$ for all $P, Q \in G_1$

The modified Weil and Tate pairings are the admissible maps ([27] offers more information).

2.2 Difficult Problems

Definition 1. *Given G_1 and G_2, p, P and e as the above definition,*

- *The bilinear Diffie-Hellman inversion (BDHI) problem in (G_1, G_2, e) is to compute $e(P, P)^{1/\alpha}$ given $(P, \alpha P)$ in which $\alpha \in \mathbb{Z}_p^*$.*
- *The q-strong Diffie-Hellman (q-SDH) problem in (G_1, G_2, e) is to search a pair $(\omega, \frac{1}{\alpha+\omega}P) \in \mathbb{Z}_p^* \times G_1$ given $(P, \alpha P, \alpha^2 P, ..., \alpha^q P)$ in which $\alpha \in \mathbb{Z}_p^*$.*
- *The modified inverse computational Diffie-Hellman (m-ICDH) problem in G_1 is to compute $(a + b)^{-1}P$ given (P, aP, bP) in which $a, b \in \mathbb{Z}_p^*$.*

3 A CP-HSCET Scheme

In this section, we first define the formal model of CP-HSCET scheme, in which the sender is in CLC environment and the receiver is in PKI environment.

Table 1. Notations

Symbol	Description	Symbol	Description
G_1	An addition group	$\{0,1\}^*$	A string of arbitrary length
G_2	A multiple group	s	A master private key of KGC
P	A generator of G_1	P_{pub}	A master public key of KGC
p	The prime order of G_1 and G_2	g	A element in group G_1, in which $g = e(P, P)$
e	A bilinear pairing	ID_s	An identity of the sender
k	A security parameter	x_s	A secret value of the sender with identity ID_s
H_i	A one way hash function ($i=1,2,3,4$)	PK_s	A public key of the sender with identity ID_s
D_s	A partial private key of identity ID_s	$PK_r = (PK_1, PK_2)$	A public key of the receiver
SK_s	A full private key of the sender with identity ID_s	$SK_r = (SK_1, SK_2)$	A private key of the receiver
$\{0,1\}^*$	A string of arbitrarily length	E	A function
PK_α	A public key of CA	td_r	A trapdoor

3.1 The Proposed Scheme

Our construction is composed of the following eight algorithms. Table 1 shows the main notations.

Setup: G_1, G_2, P, p and e are given as in Sect. 2. H_1, H_2, H_3, H_4 are four hash functions, in which $H_1 : \{0,1\}^* \rightarrow \mathbb{Z}_p^*$, $H_2 : G_1 \rightarrow \mathbb{Z}_p^*$, $H_3 : G_2 \rightarrow \mathbb{Z}_p^*$, and $H_4 : G_2 \rightarrow \{0,1\}^*$. KGC selects a master key $s \in \mathbb{Z}_p^*$ and sets $P_{pub} = sP$. It also calculates $g = e(P, P)$. KGC keeps s secret and publishes system parameters $(G_1, G_2, e, p, g, P, P_{pub}, H_1, H_2, H_3, H_4)$. Here, a function E is defined. We assume that PK_α is the public key of CA. If $PK_r = PK_\alpha$ and $E(PK_r) = 1$, our construction is a signcryption scheme. If $PK_r \neq PK_\alpha$ and $E(PK_r) = 0$, our construction is only a public key encryption scheme.

Partial-Private-Key-Extract: On inputting a sender's identity ID_s, KGC calculates his partial private key

$$D_s = \frac{1}{H_1(ID_s) + s} P$$

as well as transmits D_s to the sender by a secure approach. As in [28], an online Transport Layer Security (TLS) approach or an offline approach can be utilized to transmit the partial private key D_s to the sender.

Set-Secret-Value: On inputting a sender's identity ID_s, The sender selects a random $x_s \in \mathbb{Z}_p^*$ as its secret value and calculates its public key $PK_s = x_s(H_1(ID_s)P + P_{pub})$.

Set-Private-Key: On inputting a secret key x_s and a partial private key D_s, the sender calculates its full private key $S_s = \frac{1}{x_s + H_2(PK_s)} D_s$.

Extract-PKI: A receiver in PKI selects two random values x_1, x_2, and calculates his private keys $SK_r = (SK_1, SK_2) = (\frac{1}{x_1}P, \frac{1}{x_2}P)$ as well as the corresponding public keys $PK_r = (PK_1, PK_2) = (x_1 P, x_2 P)$.

Trapdoor: On inputting the receiver's private key $SK_r = (SK_1, SK_2)$, the receiver sets the trapdoor as $td = SK_2$.

Signcryption: On inputting a sender's identity ID_s, public key PK_s and private key S_s, a receiver's public key $PK_r = (PK_1, PK_2)$ and a message m, the sender executes the following steps:

1. Select $\alpha_1, \alpha_2 \in \mathbb{Z}_p^*$, and compute $r_1 = g^{\alpha_1}$, $r_2 = g^{\alpha_2}$.
2. Compute $h = H_3(m, r_1, r_2, ID_s, PK_s, PK_1, PK_2)$.
3. Compute $C_1 = E(PK_r)(\alpha_1 + h)S_s$.
4. Compute $C_2 = \alpha_1 PK_1$.
5. Compute $C_3 = \alpha_2 PK_2$.
6. Compute $C_4 = \alpha_2 H_1(m) \oplus H_4(r_2)$.
7. Compute $C_5 = m \| \alpha_2 \oplus H_5(r_1)$.
8. Output $\sigma = (C_1, C_2, C_3, C_4, C_5)$.

Unsigncryption: On inputting a sender's identity ID_s and public key PK_s, a receiver's private key $SK_r = (SK_1, SK_2)$, and a ciphertext σ, the receiver executes the following steps:

1. Compute $r_1 = e(C_2, SK_1)$, $r_2 = e(C_3, SK_2)$.
2. Recover $m \| \alpha_2 = C_5 \oplus H_5(r_1)$.
3. Compute $h = H_3(m, r_1, r_2, ID_s, PK_s, PK_1, PK_2)$.
   - If $E(PK_r) = 0$, we check if $C_4 \oplus (\alpha_2 H_1 m) = H_4(r_2)$. If yes, output m; otherwise, output $\perp$.
   - If $E(PK_r) = 1$, we check if $C_4 \oplus (\alpha_2 H_1(m)) = H_4(r_2)$ and only if $r_1 = e(C_1, PK_s + H_2(PK_s)(H_1(ID_s)P + P_{pub}))g^{-h}$ holds. If yes, output m; otherwise, output $\perp$.

Test: On inputting a ciphertext $\sigma_\mu = (C_{1\mu}, C_{2\mu}, C_{3\mu}, C_{4\mu}, C_{5\mu})$, trapdoor td_μ, another ciphertext $\sigma_\nu = (C_{1\nu}, C_{2\nu}, C_{3\nu}, C_{4\nu}, C_{5\nu})$ and trapdoor td_ν, a cloud server executes the following steps:

1. Compute $r_{2\mu} = e(C_{3\mu}, td_{2\mu})$ and $r_{2\nu} = e(C_{3\nu}, td_{2\nu})$.
2. Then compute $X_\mu = C_{4\mu} \oplus H_4(r_{2\mu})$ and $X_\nu = C_{4\nu} \oplus H_4(r_{2\nu})$.
3. Check if $r_{2\mu}^{X_\nu} = r_{2\nu}^{X_\mu}$. If yes, $m_\mu = m_\nu$.

3.2   Consistency

The consistency can be easily verified by the following equation.

$$
\begin{aligned}
r_1 &= e(C_1, PK_s + H_2(PK_s)(H_1(ID_s)P + P_{pub}))g^{-h} \\
&= e((\alpha_1 + h)\frac{1}{x_s + H_2(PK_s)}\frac{1}{H(ID_s) + s}P, x_s(H_1(ID_s) + P)P + H_2(PK_s)(H_1(ID_s + s)P)g^{-h} \\
&= e((\alpha_1 + h)P, P)g^{-h} \\
&= e(P, P)^{\alpha_1} \\
&= r_1
\end{aligned}
$$

$$r_{2\mu} = e(C_{3\mu}, SK_{2\mu})$$

$$= e(\alpha_{2\mu}PK_{2\mu}, \frac{1}{x_{2\mu}}P)$$

$$= e(\alpha_{2\mu}x_{2\mu}P, \frac{1}{x_{2\mu}}P)$$

$$= e(P, P)^{\alpha_{2\mu}}$$

$$r_{2\nu} = e(C_{3\nu}, SK_{2\nu})$$

$$= e(\alpha_{2\nu}PK_{2\nu}, \frac{1}{x_{2\nu}}P)$$

$$= e(\alpha_{2\nu}x_{2\nu}P, \frac{1}{x_{2\nu}}P)$$

$$= e(P, P)^{\alpha_{2\nu}}$$

$$r_{2\mu}^{X_\nu} = e(P, P)^{\alpha_{2\mu}X_\nu}$$

$$= e(P, P)^{\alpha_{2\mu}(C_{4\nu} \oplus H_4(r_{2\nu}))}$$

$$= e(P, P)^{\alpha_{2\mu}\alpha_{2\nu}H_1(m_\nu)}$$

$$= e(P, P)^{\alpha_{2\nu}X_\mu}$$

$$= r_{2\nu}^{X_\mu}$$

According to the above equation, we can get $m_\mu = m_\nu$.

4   Security

The following Theorems 1, 2 and 3 show that the proposed scheme satisfies IND-CCA2, OW-CCA and EUF-CMA security.

Theorem 1: *If an attacker $\mathcal{A}$ is against the security of Definition 2 who has an advantage ϵ', an algorithm $\mathcal{C}$ can settle the BDHI problem for $q = q_{H_1}$ with an advantage $\epsilon' \geq \frac{\epsilon}{(2q_{H_3}+q_{H_5})}(1 - \frac{q_u}{2^k})$ in time $t' \leq t + O(q_u)t_p + 0(q_u q_{H_3})t_e$, in which t_e is the time for an exponentiation operation in G_2 and t_p is the time for one pairing operation.*

Theorem 2: *If an attacker $\mathcal{A}$ is against the security of Definition 3 who has an advantage ϵ', an algorithm $\mathcal{C}$ can settle the BDHI problem for $q = q_{H_1}$ with an advantage $\epsilon' \geq \frac{\epsilon}{(2q_{H_3}+q_{H_5})}(1 - \frac{q_u}{2^k})$ in time $t' \leq t + O(q_u)t_p + O(q_u q_{H_3})t_e$, in which t_e is the time for an exponentiation operation in G_2 and t_p is the time for one pairing operation.*

Theorem 3: *Our construction is EUF-CMA secure under the q-SDH and m-ICDH assumptions in the random oracle model.*

Due to the limited length of conference articles, the detailed security analysis can be found in the complete version, or you can contact the corresponding author.

5   Performance

This section presents a comparative analysis of our scheme and other existing schemes [22, 26, 29, 30]. The comparison result is shown in Table 2, where $\mathcal{O}_p$, $\mathcal{O}_e$, $\mathcal{O}_{pm}$ denotes the point multiplication operation in G_1, the pairing operation and the point multiplication operation in G_2, SC denotes the signcryption algorithm and USC denotes the unsigncryption algorithm. Considering the different environments of different schemes, we have calculated the cryptosystem of the communication parties of each scheme. CLC-PKI means that the sender is in CLC cryptosystem and the receiver is in PKI cryptosystem. Finally, We calculate the size of public keys (PK), ciphertexts (C) and trapdoor (TD) in the five schemes. Note that, since both the receiver and sender need to know the other party's public key, the size of PK is the total length of both parties' public keys. In order to more accurately evaluate the performance of these schemes, we have implemented them and will comprehensively compare them in terms of computation overhead and energy consumption in the rest of the section.

Table 2. Comparison of existing schemes

	SC			USC			Test			Direction	Size of		
	$\mathcal{O}_p$	$\mathcal{O}_e$	$\mathcal{O}_{pm}$	$\mathcal{O}_p$	$\mathcal{O}_e$	$\mathcal{O}_{pm}$	$\mathcal{O}_p$	$\mathcal{O}_e$	$\mathcal{O}_{pm}$		PK	C	TD
Rashad [29]	6	4	0	4	6	1	3	0	0	CLC-CLC	$6|G_1|$	$3|G_1|+|Z_P^*|$	$|G_1|$
Shao [26]	2	2	5	2	0	6	4	0	6	CLC-PKI	$4|G_1|$	$4|G_1|+|Z_P^*|$	$|Z_P^*|$
Zhao [22]	2	2	3	2	0	2	4	0	2	PKI-PKI	$4|G_1|$	$3|G_1|+2|Z_P^*|$	$|G_1|+|Z_P^*|$
Wang [30]	1	5	0	2	3	2	2	2	4	PKI-PKI	$4|G_1|$	$3|G_1|+|Z_P^*|$	0
Ours	0	2	3	3	1	1	2	2	0	CLC-PKI	$3|G_1|$	$3|G_1|+2|Z_P^*|$	$|G_1|$

To evaluate the efficiency of our scheme, we implement the above schemes with the pypbc library on a 1G RAM, 2-core virtual machine, whose host is an intel(R) core(TM) i7-9750H CPU @ 2.60 GHz machine with 16G RAM. In addition, we use the Type-A pairing over super-singular elliptic curve $E(F_P)$: $y^2 = x^3 + x$ to achieve the same security level as 1024-bit RSA. The group size p is 512 *bits*. The computation time of the above schemes is shown in Fig. 1, where GK denotes generate Key phase, SC denotes signcryption phase, and USC denotes unsigncryption phase. Easily, we can find that our scheme has the highest efficiency in the real-time running phase, with only about one-third of the computational cost of other schemes. Our scheme has a slightly higher cost than wang [30] only in the phase that does not require repeated runs, which is because Wang [30] is based on IBC cryptosystem and has low security. In terms of overall running time, our scheme also outperforms the other schemes by 46.52%, 54.39%, 60.82%, and 37.35%, respectively. We further calculated

Table 3. Computation energy comparison

Schemes	Setup (ms)	GK(ms)		SC (ms)	USC (ms)	Test (ms)	Power (mW)	Usage (ms/s)	Total Time(ms)	CEC (mJ)
		sender	receiver							
Rashad [29]	7.376	6.243	7.629	18.253	12.178	2.877	1540	984	54.557	82.674
Shao [26]	14.300	2.579	3.321	12.399	13.515	13.903	1520	972	60.018	88.673
Zhao [22]	17.553	14.363	12.532	13.132	7.085	9.809	1550	983	74.474	113.472
Wang [30]	10.512	0.992	2.500	12.426	11.943	8.203	1530	970	46.575	69.121
Ours	7.698	4.242	5.082	4.599	5.852	1.705	1530	985	29.178	43.972

* CEC: Computation energy consumption.

the time required for each scheme to signcrypt multiple ciphertexts. As shown in Fig. 1, the gap between our scheme and the other schemes widens as the number of ciphertexts increases. At 100 ciphertexts, the computational cost of our scheme is only about 35% of others. Finally, we present the computational energy consumption comparison in Table 3, where *Power* and *Usage* denotes the power and CPU usage of the algorithm process. So we have $E_T = Power * Usage * Time$. As we can clear see, our scheme has the lowest energy consumption. Therefore, considering that the computing nodes in the IoV environment are mostly devices with lower computing power, our scheme is more suitable for this scenario.

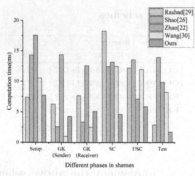

(a) Computation time

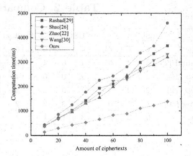

(b) Computation time comparison

Fig. 1. Comparison of computation overhead

Table 4. Total energy consumption comparison

Schemes	Size of(bytes)			Power (mW)	Transport Rate(Mbps)	energy consumption(mJ)	
	PK	C	TD			Communication	Total
Rashad [29]	384	256	64	792	54	0.021	82.694
Shao [26]	256	320	64	792	54	0.021	88.694
Zhao [22]	256	320	128	792	54	0.021	113.492
Wang [30]	256	256	0	792	54	0.015	69.136
ours	192	320	64	792	54	0.017	43.989

For the communication cost, we calculate the size of data transmitted of the five schemes. The statistical results are shown in Table 4. In our experimental environment, $|G_1| = 512bits$, and $|Z_p^*| = 512bits$. Therefore, we can obtain the number of transmitted bytes for each scheme as follows: In Rashad [29], the user needs to transport $10|G_1| + |Z_p^*| = 10 * 512 + 512 = 5632bits = 704bytes$ messages; In Shao [26], the user needs to transport $8|G_1| + 2|Z_p^*| = 8 * 512 + 2 * 512 = 5120bits = 640bytes$ messages; In Zhao [22], the user needs to transport $8|G_1| + 3|Z_p^*| = 8 * 512 + 3 * 512 = 5632bits = 704bytes$ messages; In Wang [30], the user needs to transport $7|G_1| + |Z_p^*| = 7 * 512 + 512 = 4096bits = 512bytes$ messages; And in our scheme, the user needs to transport $7|G_1| + 2|Z_p^*| = 7*512 + 2 * 512 = 4608bits = 576bytes$ messages. Moreover, we select the ESP8266EX WI-FI model as the network card for communication, which operates at a voltage of 3.3V, a current of 0.24A, and can achieve a data transfer rate of 51Mbps. It has been widely used in IoV devices. With the help of above parameter, we can obtain the communication energy consumption $E_c = Sizeof(PK + C + TD)/TransportRate * Power$ and Total energy consumption $E_T = E_c + CEC$. The energy consumption of the schemes is shown in Table 4. As we can clearly see, the proposed scheme has the lowest total energy consumption among the five schemes.

We also analyze the relationship between the total energy consumption of the scheme and the number of ciphertexts. The analysis result is clearly illustrated in Fig. 2. As the number of ciphertexts increases, the energy consumption of our scheme shows a linear growth trend. The gap between its energy consumption and other schemes also grows gradually, and stabilizes at below 45% of others at the 30 keywords.

In summary, our scheme is significantly superior to other schemes in terms of security attributes, computational overhead, and energy consumption. Considering that the nodes in the vehicle network are mostly car cameras, car sensors and other low computing power IoV devices, our scheme is more suitable for IoV environments.

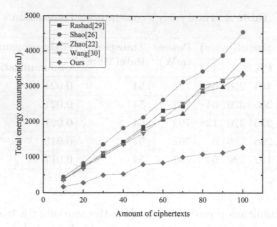

Fig. 2. Total energy consumption comparison

6   Conclusion

In this paper, we propose an efficient CP-HSCET scheme. In our scheme, the sender is usually IoV devices in CLC environment, which eliminates certificate management problem in PKI and key escrow problem in IBC, and the receiver is usually the management center in PKI environment. Furthermore, our scheme allows an authenticated cloud server to check the equality of ciphertexts without unsigncrypting them. Finally, we give a detailed and rigorous comparison result in terms of computation overhead and total energy consumption. For the computation overhead, our scheme has reduced by 46.52%, 54.39%, 60.82%, and 37.35% compared to the other four schemes, respectively. And for total energy consumption, it also reduces by 46.81%, 50.40%, 61.24%, and 36.37%, respectively. Therefore, our scheme has the highest efficiency, and is the most suitable for IoV environments, in which most of the devices have lower computational power.

Acknowledgements. This work is supported by the Graduate Practice Innovation Program of Jiangsu Province (grant no. SJCX23_1860), and the Graduate Science and Technology Innovation Program of Huaiyin Institute of Technology (grant no. HGYK202123).

References

1. Taslimasa, H., Dadkhah, S., Neto, E.C.P., Xiong, P., Ray, S., Ghorbani, A.A.: Security issues in internet of vehicles (IoV): a comprehensive survey. Internet Things 100809 (2023)
2. Ji, B., et al.: Research on optimal intelligent routing algorithm for IoV with machine learning and smart contract. Digit. Commun. Netw. **9**(1), 47–55 (2023)
3. Ijemaru, G.K., Ang, L.M., Seng, K.P.: Transformation from IoT to IoV for waste management in smart cities. J. Netw. Comput. Appl. **204**, 103393 (2022)

4. Boneh, D., Di Crescenzo, G., Ostrovsky, R., Persiano, G.: Public key encryption with keyword search. In: Cachin, C., Camenisch, J.L. (eds.) EUROCRYPT 2004. LNCS, vol. 3027, pp. 506–522. Springer, Heidelberg (2004). https://doi.org/10.1007/978-3-540-24676-3_30

5. Yang, G., Tan, C.H., Huang, Q., Wong, D.S.: Probabilistic public key encryption with equality test. In: Pieprzyk, J. (ed.) CT-RSA 2010. LNCS, vol. 5985, pp. 119–131. Springer, Heidelberg (2010). https://doi.org/10.1007/978-3-642-11925-5_9

6. Wang, H.: Unrestricted identity-based aggregate signcryption in the standard model from multilinear maps. Cryptology ePrint Archive (2014)

7. Xiong, H., et al.: Heterogeneous signcryption with equality test for IIoT environment. IEEE Internet Things J. 8(21), 16142–16152 (2020)

8. Xiong, H., Hou, Y., Huang, X., Zhao, Y., Chen, C.M.: Heterogeneous signcryption scheme from IBC to PKI with equality test for WBANs. IEEE Syst. J. 16(2), 2391–2400 (2021)

9. Xiang, D., Li, X., Gao, J., Zhang, X.: A secure and efficient certificateless signature scheme for internet of things. Ad Hoc Netw. 124, 102702 (2022)

10. Feng, C., Yu, K., Aloqaily, M., Alazab, M., Lv, Z., Mumtaz, S.: Attribute-based encryption with parallel outsourced decryption for edge intelligent IoV. IEEE Trans. Veh. Technol. 69(11), 13784–13795 (2020)

11. Jiang, M., Wang, H., Zhang, W., Qin, H., Sun, X.: Location-based data access control scheme for internet of vehicles. Comput. Electr. Eng. 86, 106716 (2020)

12. Li, W., Jin, C., Kumari, S., Xiong, H., Kumar, S.: Proxy re-encryption with equality test for secure data sharing in internet of things-based healthcare systems. Trans. Emerg. Telecommun. Technol. 33(10), e3986 (2022)

13. Xiong, H., Wang, H., Meng, W., Member, K.H.Y.: Attribute-based data sharing scheme with flexible search functionality for cloud assisted autonomous transportation system. IEEE Trans. Ind. Inform. (2023)

14. Tan, X., Cheng, W., Huang, H., Jing, T., Wang, H.: Edge-aided searchable data sharing scheme for IoV in the 5G environment. J. Syst. Architect. 136, 102834 (2023)

15. Zhen, Y., Chui, Y., Zhang, P., Liu, H.: Multiauthority attribute-based keyword search over cloud-edge-end collaboration in IoV. Wirel. Commun. Mob. Comput. 2022 (2022)

16. Tang, Q.: Public key encryption schemes supporting equality test with authorisation of different granularity. Int. J. Appl. Cryptogr. 2(4), 304–321 (2012)

17. Tang, Q.: Public key encryption supporting plaintext equality test and user-specified authorization. Secur. Commun. Netw. 5(12), 1351–1362 (2012)

18. Ma, S.: Identity-based encryption with outsourced equality test in cloud computing. Inf. Sci. 328, 389–402 (2016)

19. Wu, L., Zhang, Y., Choo, K.K.R., He, D.: Efficient and secure identity-based encryption scheme with equality test in cloud computing. Futur. Gener. Comput. Syst. 73, 22–31 (2017)

20. Qu, H., Yan, Z., Lin, X.J., Zhang, Q., Sun, L.: Certificateless public key encryption with equality test. Inf. Sci. 462, 76–92 (2018)

21. Hassan, A., Wang, Y., Elhabob, R., Eltayieb, N., Li, F.: An efficient certificateless public key encryption scheme with authorized equality test in healthcare environments. J. Syst. Architect. 109, 101776 (2020)

22. Zhao, Y., Hou, Y., Chen, Y., Kumar, S., Deng, F.: An efficient certificateless public key encryption with equality test toward internet of vehicles. Trans. Emerg. Telecommun. Technol. 33(5), e3812 (2022)

418   C. Jin et al.

23. Nayak, P., Swapna, G.: Security issues in IoT applications using certificateless aggregate signcryption schemes: an overview. Internet Things 100641 (2022)

24. Lin, X.J., Sun, L., Qu, H.: Generic construction of public key encryption, identity-based encryption and signcryption with equality test. Inf. Sci. **453**, 111–126 (2018)

25. Hou, Y., Cao, Y., Xiong, H., Song, Y., Xu, L.: An efficient online/offline heterogeneous signcryption scheme with equality test for IoVs. IEEE Trans. Veh. Technol. (2023)

26. Shao, H., Niu, S., Hu, Y.: Heterogeneous signcryption scheme with equality test from CLC to PKI for internet of vehicles. In: 2022 3rd International Conference on Electronics, Communications and Information Technology (CECIT), pp. 340–345. IEEE (2022)

27. Boneh, D., Franklin, M.: Identity-based encryption from the weil pairing. SIAM J. Comput. **32**(3), 586–615 (2003)

28. Yang, Y., Zhang, R., et al.: High efficiency secure channels for a secure multiparty computation protocol based on signal. Secur. Commun. Netw. **2023** (2023)

29. Elhabob, R., Zhao, Y., Sella, I., Xiong, H.: An efficient certificateless public key cryptography with authorized equality test in IIoT. J. Ambient Intell. Humaniz. Comput. **11**, 1065–1083 (2020)

30. Wang, Y., Pang, H., Deng, R.H., Ding, Y., Wu, Q., Qin, B.: Securing messaging services through efficient signcryption with designated equality test. Inf. Sci. **490**, 146–165 (2019)

An Improved Updatable Signature Scheme with Weakened Token

Jiacheng Zhou[1]($\boxtimes$) and Zhenhua Liu[1,2]

[1] School of Mathematics and Statistics, Xidian University, Xi'an 710071, China
1587228735@qq.com
[2] State Key Laboratory of Cryptology, P.O. Box 5159, Beijing 100878, China

Abstract. Updatable signatures (US) play a crucial role in cloud storage scenarios by providing the functionality to update signatures and resisting key compromise attacks. In PKC 2021, Cini et al. proposed the first updatable signature scheme, where an update token was granted more power than necessary. To restrict access to the token, various techniques such as leakage profiles were employed. Without such restrictions, an adversary could easily forge a new valid signature without compromising a new signing key. In this paper, we improve Cini et al.'s signature and its security via weakening the functionality of update token. Specifically, we propose a change in the way the update token is generated, involving both the signer and the server. Initially, a Diffie-Hellman key exchange protocol is executed between the signer and the server to establish a secret value. This secret value is then embedded by the signer into the update token generation process, ensuring that only those possessing the secret value can update a signature using the update token. Furthermore, we employ the technique of indistinguishability obfuscation to minimize the information leaked by the weakened token. This enhancement allows the improved updatable signature scheme to achieve no-directional key update and uni-directional signature update. Finally, we present an enhanced security model without leakage profiles restricting an adversary, where the adversary is allowed to corrupt update tokens and signing keys freely except a signing key at the challenge epoch, and prove the improved scheme to be secure.

Keywords: Updatable signature · Weakened token · Indistinguishability obfuscation · No-directional key updates

Supported by the Natural Science Basic Research Plan in Shaanxi Province of China under Grant No. 2022JZ-38, the Fundamental Research Funds for the Central Universities under Grant No. QTZX23001, the National Natural Science Foundation of China under Grant No. 61807026, the Plan For Scientific Innovation Talent of Henan Province under Grant No. 184100510012, and in part by the Program for Science and Technology Innovation Talents in the Universities of Henan Province under Grant No. 18HASTIT022.

1   Introduction

In recent years, the significant growth in data volume has led to the emergence of a new storage mode known as cloud storage. In this scenario, data owners can generate and store their data in cloud servers, allowing data users to access it anytime and anywhere via the Internet. This storage mode offers improved storage efficiency, and virtualization techniques further enhance it by eliminating storage space waste, automatically reallocating data, and improving storage space utilization. Additionally, these techniques provide load balancing and redundancy functions, ensuring the confidentiality and authenticity of data stored on cloud servers through encryption and signature methods.

However, when secret keys used for data encryption or signing are compromised, data owners must update their keys. Simultaneously, the corresponding data stored in the cloud server needs to be updated as well. A direct solution to this issue (for encryption/signature, respectively) is to first generate new secret keys, then download all data in cloud, decrypt/verify using the old keys, and encrypt/sign with the updated keys, finally, upload all the updated data to cloud. However, this approach would incur significant computational and storage costs for the data owner. In order to reduce the computation required for updating data in the cloud, a new primitive called updatable encryption (UE) has emerged, followed by updatable signature (US) schemes.

UE has been widely studied since its introduction by Boneh et al. [3]. The main technique behind UE is key rotation, where users periodically change their old encryption keys to new ones and generate tokens for the cloud server. These tokens are then used to convert the ciphertexts (data encrypted under the old key) into new ones (data encrypted under the new key). This approach eliminates the need for the user to download any data, as the cloud server is responsible for updating the stored data. This significantly reduces the computational costs for the user. The development of UE greatly influenced US.

Many notions of signature contained implicitly key update or/and signature update function, such as signature with re-randomizable key [10], key-updatable signature [13] or key-updating signature [15]. However, none of the above works provided a definitional framework until Cini et al. [6]. Inspired by Lehmann et al. [18] and Boyd et al. [5], Cini et al. constructed a US scheme based on key-homomorphic primitive. Their work adopted the same updating patten as UE proposed in [18], which means a user periodically changes her or his old signing key to a new one, and generates a token for cloud server to convert the old signature to new one. However, in this patten, anyone who gets the update token can use it to update any old valid signature, which means that a malicious user can also perform updating operation when he obtains the update token. This patten gives an update token more than needed power, as only cloud server is supposed to perform updating operation. And this makes it indispensable to use leakage profiles in security model to limit the adversary's ability. Otherwise, it would be easy for any adversary to forge a valid signature. Despite leakage profiles serving as an effective technique for security analysis, they can lead to inconsistencies between the security model and the actual situation.

1.1   Related Works

In 2013, Boneh et al. [3] explicitly proposed the notion of updatable encryption for the first time. Later, Everspaugh et al. [9] provided a systematic study for ciphertext-dependent UE. Based on the above works, Boneh et al. [2] enhanced the definition of confidentiality and integrity by requiring that the update algorithm should not leak any information about the ciphertext. For ciphertext-independent update, Lehmann et al. [18] formally introduced two security notions in the sequential manner: encryption indistinguishability and update indistinguishability. Furthermore, Klooß et al. [16] enhanced the security from CPA to (R)CCA. The same year, Boyd et al. [5] proposed the definition of indistinguishable updatable encryption (IND-UE), which requires that the ciphertexts generated by the encryption algorithm should be indistinguishable from that by the update algorithm.

In addition to improving security, the direction of update is gradually refined. Lehmann et al. [18] discussed the directionality for the first time, and put forward the notions of uni-directional update and bi-directional update to capture the ability of the token to update (downgrade) the ciphertext or key to the new (old) epoch. Jiang [14] drew a counterintuitive conclusion: uni-directional update and bi-directional update are equivalent under the same security notion, and proposed no-directional key update setting, where the update token cannot update or downgrade key. Moreover, in 2022 Nishimaki [20] subdivided uni-directional key update into forward-leak and backward-leak, and proposed the first updatable encryption scheme $UE_{i\mathcal{O}}$ with no-directional key update (following which we construct a no-directional signature scheme).

In 2023, Miao et al. [19] realized uni-directional UE and PRE from a new generic primitive called key and plaintext homomorphic encryption, which firstly achieved backwards-leak uni-directional key update and uni-directional ciphertext update based on less structured assumptions. Actually the classification of update direction can be seen as the classification of the information leaked by the update token, the more information the update token leaked, the more things it can be used to do, e.g., update/downgrade the signing key and/or signature.

As for updatable signature (US), key-updatable signature [13] or key-updating signature [15] proposed in context of secure messaging, allowed to update key and obtain signature under updated key, but both works did not consider signature update. Similarly, Fleischhacker et al. [10] proposed a novel primitive called signature scheme with re-randomizable key, which allows to re-randomize secret key and public key separately but consistently, and they gave two instantiations of the primitive based on Schnorr's signature scheme [23] and Hofheinz and Kiltz's signature scheme [12]. Their work considered key update, but did not consider signature update.

Later, key-homomorphic signature by Derler and Slamanig [7] simultaneously covered key update and signature update. But Derler et al. only considered the updatable (they called adaptability) properties functional-wise and focused on using it to construct primitives such as ring signature schemes, (universal) designated verifier signature schemes, they did not consider security in the sense of update, not to mention update direction. Recently, Cini et al. [6] gave a comprehensive framework for US and UMAC, and constructed US from key-homomorphic (KH) signatures. However, they only considered bi-directional key and signature update, and stressed that no-directional US did not seem to be as desirable as UE. The reason is that upgrading an old signature was necessary for correctness (thus cannot be prevented), and preventing downgrading the key or signature back to the previous epoch was only required if old public keys were not revoked which is the scenario in Poettering et al. [21].

In 2022, Poettering et al. [21] introduced a new cryptographic primitive sequential digital signature (SDS) and defined the strong, rigorous security models that captured forward security as well as self-enforcement. There was no update token in their work, as Poettering et al. did not consider updating the existing signatures. Instead, they stored all the public keys to verify corresponding signatures.

1.2   Our Motivation and Contributions

In Cini et al. [6], assume an adversary has corrupted an old signing key sk_{e-1}. If it obtains an update token Δ_e, it could trivially forge a valid signature under a new signing key sk_e, for any message m, by first using sk_{e-1} to generate a valid signature σ_{e-1} at the epoch $e-1$, and then updating it to σ_e with the help of Δ_{e-1}. This attack works well even in no-directional key update and uni-directional signature update model. Moreover it seems impractical to prevent the adversary from getting an update token if the update token is sent in plaintext. And if the update token is encrypted and sent to the server secretly, it is meaningless to consider the information leaked by the token, as no one except the server can obtain the token.

After receiving an update token, the server can update the signature in the cloud storage by using the token. Therefore, a natural idea is that the user and the server collaborate to generate an update token, contradict to the previous patten that the user generated the token alone. Specifically, the server and the user negotiate a secret value. Then the user embeds the secret value into the update token without which the token cannot be used to update any signature. Under this framework, the update token is weakened. Furthermore, by limiting the information leaked by the token to make it no-directional key update, the above forging attack can be resisted, even the adversary is allowed to corrupt the update token freely. To sum up, the main contributions are as follows.

1. **Analyze the security of Cini et al.'s updatable signature.** We notice that in Cini et al.'s updatable signature, when an adversary has corrupted an old epoch signing key and an update token, she or he can first generate a signature about any message by using the old epoch signing key, and then use the update token to update the signature to get a valid signature corresponding to a new epoch signing key. At the same time, the adversary can infer a new epoch signing key from the corrupted old signing key and the update token, and then sign any message. The important reason why the adversary

can forge a new signature is that the update token is bi-directional and is given more than needed power.

2. **Propose an improved updatable signature scheme with weakened token.** To resist against the above forgery, a possible solution is to weaken the function of the update token. Firstly, we enhance the security model of updatable signature by omitting the leakage profiles and providing any adversary more freedom in accessing update tokens and keys, which is more in line with the reality. Then we construct an improved updatable signature scheme with weakened token by using indistinguishability obfuscator and puncturable pseudorandom function, which can achieve no-directional key update and uni-directional signature update. Finally, we prove that the proposed scheme is secure under the enhanced security model.

Table 1. A brief comparison of our construction with the existing schemes

Scheme	key/sig	Dir.(key)	Dir.(sig)	Leakage Profiles	US-EUF-CMA	EUF-US
JS [13]	key	–	–	–	–	–
JMM [15]	key	–	–	–	–	–
FKMSS [10]	key	–	–	–	–	–
DS [7]	both	bi	bi	–	–	–
CRSS [6]	both	bi	bi	✓	✓	×
Ours	both	no	uni	×	✓	✓

Note: The column key/sig indicates that whether key and/or signature updates are taken into account by the schemes. Dir.(key) and Dir.(sig) indicate the key update direction and signature update direction, respectively. The EUF-US security model is an enhanced version of the US-EUF-CMA security model.

2 Preliminaries

We give some notations and introduce some basic primitives in this section.

2.1 Notations

The notations are shown in Table 2.

Table 2. Notation description

Notations	Descriptions
t_e	A secret value at the epoch e
$negl(\cdot)$	A negligible function
e^*	The challenge epoch
$K_e\{t_e\}$	A punctured key with punctured point t_e
Δ	An update token
$[N]$	The integer set from 1 to N
$C_{upd}[sk_{e+1}, pk_e]$	An update program with fixed constants $[sk_{e+1}, pk_e]$ at the epoch e
$\mathbb{Z}_p$	The additive group of integers modulo p

2.2   Basic Primitives

Pseudorandom Generator (PRG). A PRG [11] is an efficient and deterministic algorithm for generating a longer and unpredictable "uniform-looking" string based on a short and uniform string called the seed. PRG is pseudorandom if no efficient distinguisher $\mathcal{D}$ can differentiate whether it is a string outputted by PRG or a string randomly chosen.

Definition 1 *(Pseudorandom generator). Let $l(\cdot)$ be a polynomial and PRG be a deterministic polynomial-time algorithm such that for any input $s \in \{0,1\}^n$ with any n, the result $PRG(s)$ is a string of length $l(n)$. PRG is called a pseudorandom generator if the following conditions hold:*

1. *(Expansion) For any n, it holds that $l(n) > n$.*
2. *(Pseudorandomness) For any PPT algorithm, there is a negligible function $negl(\lambda)$ such that*

$$\Big| \Pr\left[\mathcal{D}(PRG(s)) = 1\right] - \Pr\left[\mathcal{D}(r) = 1\right] \Big| \le negl(\lambda),$$

where the first probability is taken over uniform choice of $s \in \{0,1\}^n$ and the randomness of $\mathcal{D}$, and the second probability is taken over uniform choice of $r \in \{0,1\}^{l(n)}$ and the randomness of $\mathcal{D}$. Generally, $l(\cdot)$ is referred to as an expansion factor of PRG.

Puncturable Pseudorandom Function (PPRF). PPRF [22] is one of simple constrained pseudorandom functions. Any PPT adversary is allowed to have a polynomial scale input set first. Even if the adversary is given a punctured key that can be used to compute all values of function at inputs that are not in the given set, it is difficult to distinguish between a value of function for input in the given set and a random element of equal length to the value.

Definition 2 *(Puncturable pseudorandom function). A PRF $F : \mathcal{K} \times \{0,1\}^k \to \{0,1\}^{k'}$ is a puncturable pseudorandom function if there is a key space $\mathcal{K}$, an additional punctured key space $\mathcal{K}_p$, and three polynomial time algorithms F.Key, F.Puncture and F.Eval that satisfy the following properties.*

1. *(Functionality preserved under puncturing) For any PPT adversary $\mathcal{A}$ such that $\mathcal{A}(1^\lambda)$ outputs a set $S \subseteq \{0,1\}^{k(\lambda)}$, then for any $x \in \{0,1\}^{k(\lambda)}$ and $x \notin S$:*

$$\Pr\left[F.Eval(K,x) = F.Eval(K(S),x) : K \leftarrow F.Key(1^\lambda),\right.$$
$$\left. K\{S\} \leftarrow F.Puncture(K,S)\right] = 1,$$

where $K \in \mathcal{K}$ and $K\{S\}) \in \mathcal{K}_p$.
2. *(Pseudorandom at punctured points) For any PPT adversary $(\mathcal{A}_1, \mathcal{A}_2)$ such that $\mathcal{A}_1(1^\lambda)$ outputs a set $S \subseteq \{0,1\}^{k(\lambda)}$, considering an experiment with $\forall x \in S$, $F.Eval(K,x) \in \{0,1\}^{k'}$, where $K \leftarrow F.Key(1^\lambda)$, and the punctured key $K\{S\} \leftarrow F.Puncture(K,S)$, then:*

$$\Big| \Pr\left[\mathcal{A}_2(K\{S\}, x, F.Eval(K\{S\},x)) = 1\right]$$
$$- \Pr\left[\mathcal{A}_2(K\{S\}, x, y \leftarrow \{0,1\}^{k'}) = 1\right] \Big| \le negl(\lambda).$$

For convenience, in the following sections F.Eval(K, x) and F.Puncture(K, S) are denoted by F(K, x) and K{S}, respectively.

Bilinear Maps. Let $\mathbb{G}$ and $\mathbb{G}_T$ be two multiplicative cyclic groups of prime order p and g be a generator of $\mathbb{G}$.

Definition 3. *A bilinear map [4] is a map $\tilde{e}: \mathbb{G} \times \mathbb{G} \to \mathbb{G}_T$ satisfying the following properties:*

- *Bilinearity: For all $u, v \in \mathbb{G}$, and $a, b \in \mathbb{Z}_p$, $\tilde{e}(u^a, v^b) = \tilde{e}(u, v)^{ab}$.*
- *Non-degeneracy: $\tilde{e}(g, g) \neq 1_{\mathbb{G}_T}$.*
- *Computability: For all $u, v \in \mathbb{G}$, bilinear pairing $\tilde{e}(u, v)$ be effectively calculated in polynomial time.*

Definition 4 *(Computational Diffie-Hellman (CDH) problem). For a group $\mathbb{G}$ of prime order p with a generator g, define the advantage $\mathrm{Adv}_{\mathbb{G},\mathcal{A}}^{CDH}$ [4] of an adversary $\mathcal{A}$ as*

$$\mathrm{Adv}_{\mathbb{G},\mathcal{A}}^{CDH} = \Pr\left[y = h^a | a \leftarrow \mathbb{Z}_p, h \leftarrow \mathbb{G}, y \leftarrow \mathcal{A}(g, g^a, h)\right],$$

where the probability is taken over the random choice of $\mathcal{A}$ and the random selection of a, h. CDH is hard if no adversary exists such that $\mathrm{Adv}_{\mathbb{G},\mathcal{A}}^{CDH} \geq negl(\lambda)$.

Indistinguishability Obfuscator $(i\mathcal{O})$. As a weakening solution to virtual black-box confusion, $i\mathcal{O}$ was first proposed by Barak et al. [1] in 2001 to ensure that any two circuits with the same functionality are indistinguishable after confusion. Popularly, $i\mathcal{O}$ is a relatively efficient program. The input of this program is a circuit C to be confused, and the output is an indistinguishable obfuscated program $i\mathcal{O}(C)$ of the input circuit, which is defined as follows.

Definition 5 *(Indistinguishability Obfuscation). A uniform PPT machine iO is called as an indistinguishability obfuscation for a circuit class $\{C_\lambda\}$ if the following two conditions are satisfied:*

1. *(Preserving functionality) For a security parameter $\lambda \in N$, any $C \in C_\lambda$, and any input x, the following formula holds,*

$$\Pr\left[C'(x) = C(x): \ C' \leftarrow i\mathcal{O}(\lambda, C)\right] = 1.$$

2. *(Indistinguishability of obfuscation) For any PPT distinguisher $\mathcal{D}$, there exists a negligible function $negl(\lambda)$ such that the following holds: for a security parameter $\lambda \in N$ and any pair of circuits $C_0, C_1 \in C_\lambda$ with $|C_0| = |C_1|$, we have that if $C_0(x) = C_1(x)$ for any input x, then*

$$\left| \Pr\left[\mathcal{D}(i\mathcal{O}(\lambda, C_0)) = 1\right] - \Pr\left[\mathcal{D}(i\mathcal{O}(\lambda, C_1)) = 1\right] \right| \leq negl(\lambda).$$

2.3 Diffie-Hellman Key Exchange Protocol

In 1976, Diffie and Hellman [8] introduced a key exchange protocol based on the discrete logarithm problem. In this protocol, Alice and Bob will negotiate a random secret value for their private-key system over a public and authenticated channel. A cyclic group $\mathbb{G}$ of order p and a generator g are set as public parameters. Alice chooses a random integer $a \in \mathbb{Z}_p$ and sends g^a to Bob. Similarly, Bob sends g^b to Alice for random $b \in \mathbb{Z}_p$. They can obtain a sharing secret value g^{ab}.

For simplicity, we use the algorithm $US.Kex(params, r_1, r_2)$ to describe the protocol executed by two parties, e.g., Alice and Bob, where $params$ refers to all the public parameters (i.e.,$(\mathbb{G}, p, g)$), needed in executing the protocol, r_1 represents any value that Alice sends to Bob (i.e., g^a), and r_2 that Bob sends to Alice (i.e., g^b). An honest execution of the protocol will result in an element $g^{ab} \in \mathbb{G}$ shared by Alice and Bob. Moreover, as proposed by Krawczyk [17] in CRYPTO 2010, for a group $\mathbb{G}$ where the Decisional Diffie-Hellman is known to fail (such as in bilinear group), and only the CDH assumption is hold, a random oracle $H : \mathbb{G} \rightarrow \{0,1\}^n$ is needed for transforming the input source g^{ab} to a string $H(g^{ab})$ that is indistinguishable from a uniform string in $\{0,1\}^n$.

2.4 Cini et al.'s Updatable Signature

In this subsection, we review the updatable signature scheme $(US.Setup, US.Sig, US.Ver, US.Next, US.Update)$ proposed by Cini et al. [6] as follows.

- $US.Setup(1^\lambda, n)$: A signer first chooses a full-domain hash function $H_0 : \{0,1\}^* \rightarrow \mathbb{G}$, and runs the group-generation algorithm $G(1^\lambda)$ to obtain $(\mathbb{G}, \mathbb{G}_T, p)$, where $\mathbb{G}$ and $\mathbb{G}_T$ are groups of order p, and g is a generator of $\mathbb{G}$. Then the signer chooses a random value $sk_0 \in \mathbb{Z}_p$, computes $pk_0 = g^{sk_0}$, and sends pk_0 to the server.
- $US.Sig(sk_e, m)$: The signer takes a message m and sk_e as inputs, and outputs a message-signature pair $(m, \sigma_e = H_0(m)^{sk_e})$.
- $US.Ver(m, \sigma_e, pk_e)$: A verifier verifies the validity of the message-signature pair by testing if $e(H_0(m), pk_e) = e(\sigma_e, g)$. If the equation holds, then the verifier outputs 1. Otherwise output 0.
- $US.Next(pk_e, sk_e, \Delta_{e+1})$: When the epoch is to update, the signer randomly chooses $\Delta_{e+1} \in \mathbb{Z}_p$, computes $sk_{e+1} = sk_e + \Delta_{e+1}$ and public key $pk_{e+1} = g^{sk_{e+1}}$, and sends pk_{e+1} and Δ_{e+1} to the server.
- $US.Update(m, \Delta_{e+1}, \sigma_e)$: The server computes $\sigma_{e+1} = \sigma_e \cdot H_0(m)^{\Delta_{e+1}}$ and outputs an updated message-signature pair (m, σ_{e+1}).

In Cini et al.'s scheme [6], it is trivial to forge a valid signature of a message m for any adversary who has corrupted the old epoch signing key sk_e. Since the update token Δ_{e+1} is bi-directional, the adversary first computes $\sigma_e = H_0(m)^{sk_e}$, and updates it to obtain $\sigma_{e+1} = H_0(m)^{\Delta_{e+1} \cdot \sigma_e}$ by using Δ_{e+1}. And the adversary can also compute $sk_{e+1} = sk_e + \Delta_{e+1}$, and sign the message m by computing $\sigma_{e+1} = H(m)^{sk_{e+1}}$.

To solve this problem, the functionality of update token has to be weakened, as discussed in Sect. 1.2. The idea is that a signer and the cloud server utilize a technique (e.g. Diffie-Hellman key exchange protocol [8]) to negotiate a secret value, and the signer uses the secret value to generate an update token for the server. To update an old and valid signature, one needs to have both the update token and the secret value.

3   Updatable Signature with Weakened Token and Enhanced Security Model

In this section, we now introduce the formal definition of updatable signature with weakened token (US-WT) and the enhanced security models.

3.1   Formal Definition

Updatable signature with weakened token (US-WT) is a tuple of PPT algorithms $US.Setup, US.Sig, US.Ver, US.Next, US.SVex, US.Update$ as follows.

- $US.Setup(\lambda, N)$: A signer chooses a security parameter λ, a secret value $t_0 \in \{0,1\}^{2n}$, and the maximum number of epochs $N \in 2^\lambda$ as inputs, and outputs a public-secret key pair (pk_0, sk_0) at the initial epoch 0.
- $US.Sig(sk_e, m, t_e)$: The signer takes the secret key sk_e, the secret value t_e at the epoch e and a message $m \in M$ as inputs, and outputs a message-signature pair (m, σ_e).
- $US.SVex()$: To perform update at the epoch e, the signer and the server negotiate a secret value t_{e+1}, which will be used to generate an update token Δ_{e+1} and update a signature.
- $US.Next(pk_e, sk_e, t_{e+1})$: In addition to the signing key and public key at the epoch e, the signer also takes the secret value t_{e+1} as inputs, and outputs a new key pair (pk_{e+1}, sk_{e+1}) and an update token Δ_{e+1} at the epoch $e + 1$.
- $US.Update(m, \sigma_e, \Delta_{e+1}, t_{e+1})$: The cloud server takes the message-signature pair (m, σ_e), the token Δ_{e+1} as well as the secret value t_{e+1} as inputs, and outputs an updated message-signature pair (m, σ_{e+1}).
- $US.Ver(m, pk_e, \sigma_e)$: A verifier takes the message-signature pair (m, σ_e) at the epoch e and the corresponding public key pk_e as inputs, and outputs a verdict $b \in \{0,1\}$.

Correctness of Updatable Signature. At any epoch $e \leq N$, for any valid public-secret key pair (pk_e, sk_e) and $US.Sig(sk_e, m, t_e) \to \sigma_e$, it holds that $US.Ver(pk_e, m, \sigma_e) = 1$ [6]. Furthermore, at any $e \leq N - 1$, for a valid message-signature pair (m, σ_e), $US.Next(pk_e, sk_e, t_{e+1}) \to (pk_{e+1}, sk_{e+1}, \Delta_{e+1})$, and for $US.Update(\Delta_{e+1}, m, \sigma_e, t_{e+1}) \to (m, \sigma_{e+1})$, we have that

$$\Pr[US.Ver(pk_{e'}, m, \sigma_{e'}) \neq 1] \leq \varepsilon(\lambda)$$

holds, for any $e' \in [N]$, where $\varepsilon(\lambda) = negl(\lambda)$. If $\varepsilon(\lambda) = 0$, then the signature is called to be perfectly correct.

3.2 Enhanced Security Model

In the original security model [6] of updatable signature, an adversary $\mathcal{A}$ was granted to access $\mathcal{O}.Next(\cdot)$, $\mathcal{O}.Corr(handle, \hat{e})$, $\mathcal{O}.Upd$, $\mathcal{O}.Sig$ and $\mathcal{O}.Ver$ oracles. To exclude trivial winnings, leakage profiles are used to prevent the adversary $\mathcal{A}$ from obtaining some keys and tokens of specific epoch. As discussed before, it is not appropriate or realistic to limit the adversary's access to the keys and tokens. However, if the limitation is omitted, then it is trivial to forge a valid signature. The problem above is actually due to the information leaked from an update token, and that using the update token alone can implement the update function. Thus, if the token does not leak any information (i.e., it can not be used to update or downgrade a signing key, which is exactly in the no-directional key update setting), and it is infeasible to use the update token solely to update any signature (i.e., in the weakened token model), then the token would be useless for the adversary, so it can be corrupted by the adversary without any limitation. The enhanced security model is actually aiming at this model, which combines no-directional key update with weakened token (i.e., no-directional US-WT).

We introduce a global state $\mathcal{S} = (K, S)$, and $\hat{e}$ represents the current epoch. $K = \{e \in [N]\}$ denotes all epochs that the adversary queried $\mathcal{O}.Corr(key, e)$, and $S = \{(e, m, \sigma_e)_{e \in [N]}\}$ denotes all tuples that the adversary queried the signing oracle $\mathcal{O}.Sig(m, e)$ at epoch e or $\mathcal{O}.Upd(m, \sigma_{e-1})$ at epoch $e - 1$. The oracles that the adversary has accessed to are defined in Table 3.

Table 3. The behavior of oracles in the eEUF-US game

$\mathcal{O}.Sign(m, e)$:	$\mathcal{O}.Corr(handle, e)$:
$(m, \sigma_e) \xleftarrow{r} US.Sig(sk_e, m, t_e)$	if $e > \hat{e}$
set $S := S \cup \{(e, m, \sigma_e)\}$	return $\perp$,
return (m, σ_e)	if $handle = key$
	set $K := K \cup \{e\}$
$\mathcal{O}.Next(\ )$:	return sk_e,
$\hat{e} := \hat{e} + 1$	if $handle = token$
$(\Delta_{\hat{e}}, k_{\hat{e}}) \xleftarrow{r} US.Next(pk_{\hat{e}-1}, sk_{\hat{e}-1}, t_{\hat{e}})$	return Δ_e.
$k_{\hat{e}} = (pk_{\hat{e}}, sk_{\hat{e}})$	$\mathcal{O}.Upd(\sigma_{e-1}, m)$:
return $pk_{\hat{e}}$.	if $US.Ver(pk_{e-1}, \sigma_{e-1}, m) = 0$
	return $\perp$
	else $\sigma_e \leftarrow US.Update(m, \sigma_{e-1}, \Delta_e, t_e)$
$\mathcal{O}.Ver(m, \sigma_e)$:	set $S := S \cup \{(e, m, \sigma_e)\}$
$b \xleftarrow{r} US.Ver(m, pk_e, \sigma_e)$	return σ_e
return b.	

Existential Unforgeability for Updatable Signature (EUF-US). This notion is actually similar to US-EUF-CMA proposed in [6], except that there is no leakage profiles. The adversary is valid unless he corrupts the challenge-epoch signing key sk_{e^*}. Informally, the EUF-US notion ensures that no PPT adversary can non-trivially forge signatures even when the adversary adaptively compromises a number of keys and tokens. A scheme Σ is EUF-US secure if any PPT adversary succeeds in the following experiment only with negligible probability.

The experiment starts by computing the initial tuple (keys and secret value for epoch 0) $(pk_0, sk_0, t_0) \leftarrow US.Setup(\lambda, N)$. During the experiment, via the oracles, the adversary may query signatures for any epoch e up to the current epoch $\hat{e}$, iterate to the next epoch $\hat{e} + 1$. The adversary may also update signatures, and corrupt tokens or keys for any epoch e up to the current epoch $\hat{e}$. Eventually, the adversary outputs a message-signature pair $(m^*, \sigma_{e^*}^*)$, at epoch $e^* \in [N]$, and succeeds if $US.Ver(pk_{e^*}, m^*, \sigma_{e^*}^*) = 1$ and the adversary is valid, which means $e^* \notin K$ and $(e^*, m^*, \sigma_{e^*}^*) \notin S$.

Definition 6 *(EUF-US). A scheme Σ is EUF-US secure iff for any valid PPT adversary $\mathcal{A}$, the advantage function:*

$$Adv_{\Sigma, \mathcal{A}}^{EUF-US}(\lambda, N) := \Pr[Exp_{\Sigma, \mathcal{A}}^{EUF-US}(\lambda, N) = 1]$$

is negligible in λ, where $Exp_{\Sigma, \mathcal{A}}^{EUF-US}(\lambda, N)$ is defined in Table 4.

Table 4. The EUF-US security notion for Σ

$$
\boxed{
\begin{array}{l}
Exp_{\Sigma, \mathcal{A}}^{EUF-US}(\lambda, N): \\
\quad (pk_0, sk_0) \leftarrow Setup(\lambda, N) \\
\quad \text{set } K := S := \emptyset \\
\quad (m^*, \sigma_{e^*}^*) \leftarrow \mathcal{A}^{\mathcal{O}.Next, \mathcal{O}.Corr, \mathcal{O}.Upd, \mathcal{O}.Sign, \mathcal{O}.Ver} \\
\quad \text{return 1 if } US.Ver(pk_{e^*}, m^*, \sigma_{e^*}^*) = 1 \text{ and} \\
\quad (e^* \notin K) \wedge [(e^*, m^*, \sigma_{e^*}^*) \notin S].
\end{array}
}
$$

4   Construction of the Improved Updatable Signature Scheme with Weakened Token

4.1   Scheme Description

Inspired by Cini et al.'s scheme [6] and Nishimaki's scheme [20], we propose an improve updatable signature scheme Σ_{US} with weakened token, which achieves no-directional key update and uni-directional signature update.

Let $PRG : \{0,1\}^n \rightarrow \{0,1\}^{2n}$, $PPRF : \mathcal{K} \times \{0,1\}^{2n} \rightarrow \mathbb{Z}_p$ (Note that by definition, the output of $PPRF$ is a string of length k', however, we can use some techniques like encode or hash function to map the string to $\mathbb{Z}_p$ space. We omit here for simplicity). The detailed scheme is described as follows:

Table 5. The description of update circuit C_{upd}

Circuit 1 Update Circuit C_{upd}

Constant:

sk_{e+1} and pk_e.

Input:

A message-signature pair (m, σ_e) and a secret value t_{e+1}
1) Compute $b = US.Ver(m, \sigma_e, pk_e)$.
2) if $b = 1$,
3) Compute $y = PPRF(sk_{e+1}, t_{e+1})$,
4) Compute $\sigma_{e+1} = H_0(m)^y$.
5) Else return $\perp$.

Output:

A message-signature pair $(m, \sigma_{e+1} = H_0(m)^y)$.

- $US.Setup(1^\lambda, N)$: The signer runs a group-generation algorithm $G(1^\lambda)$ to obtain $(\mathbb{G}, \mathbb{G}_T, p)$, where $\mathbb{G}$ and $\mathbb{G}_T$ are groups with prime order p, and g is a generator of $\mathbb{G}$. Then the signer chooses two full-domain hash functions $H_0 : \{0,1\}^* \to \mathbb{G}$, $H_1 : \mathbb{G} \to \{0,1\}^n$. $\tilde{e}$ is a bilinear map $\tilde{e} : \mathbb{G} \times \mathbb{G} \to \mathbb{G}_T$. Then the signer chooses $t_0 \in \{0,1\}^{2n}$ and a puncturable pseudorandom function key $sk_0 = K_0 \in \mathcal{K}$ for $PPRF$, computes $pk_0 = g^{PPRF(sk_0, t_0)}$. Finally, the signer outputs $pk_0, H_0, H_1, paramas = (g, p), \tilde{e}$.
- $US.Sig(m, sk_e, t_e)$: At epoch e, the signer computes $y = PPRF(sk_e, t_e)$, and outputs a message-signature pair (m, σ_e), where $\sigma_e = H_0(m)^y$.
- $US.Ver(m, \sigma_e, pk_e)$: A verifier can verify the validity of the message-signature pair (m, σ_e) by testing whether $\tilde{e}(H_0(m), pk_e) = \tilde{e}(\sigma_e, g)$. If the equation holds, then the verification algorithm outputs 1, which means that the message-signature pair is valid. Otherwise, outputs 0, and it is invalid.
- $US.SVex(params)$: The server and the signer randomly choose two values $a_e, b_e \in \mathbb{Z}_p$ respectively, and execute Diffie-Hellman protocol, i.e., execute the algorithm $US.Kex(params, g^{a_e}, g^{b_e})$ and get the shared element $g_e = g^{a_e \cdot b_e}$. Then they compute the same random string $r_e = H_1(g_e) \in \{0,1\}^n$, and obtain an secret value $t_{e+1} = PRG(r_e) \in \{0,1\}^{2n}$.
- $US.Next(pk_e, t_{e+1})$: The signer firstly randomly chooses $sk_{e+1} \in \mathcal{K}$, computes $pk_{e+1} = g^{PPRF(sk_{e+1}, t_{e+1})}$ and $\Delta_{e+1} = i\mathcal{O}(C_{upd}[pk_e, sk_{e+1}])$ ($C_{upd}[pk_e, sk_{e+1}]$ is an update circuit described in Table 5), where the update token is implied by the program $i\mathcal{O}(C_{upd}[pk_e, sk_{e+1}])$. Then the signer sends pk_{e+1} and Δ_{e+1} to the server.
- $US.Update(m, \sigma_e, t_{e+1}, \Delta_{e+1})$: The server enters the message-signature pair (m, σ_e) and the secret value t_{e+1} into the program Δ_{e+1}. The program first verifies if the message-signature pair is valid, i.e., the program computes $b = US.Ver(m, \sigma_e, pk_e)$. If $b = 1$ the program outputs the updated message-signature pair (m, σ_{e+1}), where $\sigma_{e+1} = H_0(m)^{PPRF(sk_{e+1}, t_{e+1})}$, i.e., $(m, \sigma_{e+1}) \leftarrow i\mathcal{O}(C_{upd}[pk_e, sk_{e+1}](m, \sigma_e, t_{e+1}))$. Else the program outputs $\perp$.

Remarks on the Construction. The proposed scheme is based on the bi-directional updatable signature scheme in [6] which is based on the BLS signature scheme. To make it no-directional, we follow the idea of Nishimaki [20]. In Nishimaki's scheme, the update token is a program confused by $i\mathcal{O}$. And The program implicitly contains both the old epoch secret key and the new epoch secret key (their scheme is in symmetric setting). Update operation is actually performed by first decrypting an old ciphertext with the old secret key and then re-encrypting with the new secret key. However, in US scheme, when updating a signature, the server first verifies the validity of the old signature using the old epoch public key and then re-signs the message with the new epoch signing key. In BLS signature scheme, signature for message m is generated by $H_0(m)^{sk}$, where sk is the signing key. In order to make BLS signature scheme no-directional, the key generation algorithm is broke into two steps: the signer firstly chooses a *PPRF* key K, then generates a secret value t, signature is generated by $H_0(m)^{PPRF(K,t)}$. In this way, $i\mathcal{O}$ can be used to confuse the secret key K. Now, the adversary has to corrupt both the update token and the corresponding secret value to perform update function, which we think is more difficult than before, and both parts are updated separately. Further, the secret value is a pseudorandom string, keeping it secret would be easier compared to keeping the whole update token secret, which means the proposed scheme works better than simply encrypting the update token using an additional encryption scheme, and also saves the cost for extra key management of the additional encryption scheme.

4.2 Correctness and Directionality

In this section, the correctness and directionality of the proposed scheme is presented, including the update direction of key and signature.

Correctness. It is easy to show the correctness of the proposed updatable signature scheme due to the property of the bilinear map. For a valid message-signature pair $(m, \sigma = H_0(m)^{PPRF(sk_e, t_e)})$ and the corresponding public key $pk_e = g^{PPRF(sk_e, t_e)}$, the equation $\tilde{e}(H_0(m), pk_e) = \tilde{e}(\sigma_e, g)$ always hold. Further the output of the update algorithm $US.Update(m, \sigma_e, t_{e+1}, \Delta_{e+1})$ is exactly the same as the signing algorithm $US.Sig(m, sk_{e+1}, t_{e+1})$, so its correctness also holds.

No-directional Key Updates. How the token is generated determines the update direction of the key and the signature. In the scheme, token is generated by the algorithm $US.Next(pk_e, t_{e+1})$, it only takes the previous epoch public key pk_e and the new epoch signing key sk_{e+1} as inputs, so it is impossible to infer the previous signing key from the token due to the security of the underlying BLS signature scheme. Besides, the new epoch signing key is confused by $i\mathcal{O}$, there is no way to obtain the sk_{e+1} from sk_e and Δ_{e+1}, due to the security of indistinguishability obfuscator.

Uni-directional Signature Updates. Similarly, as the tokens only contains the previous epoch public key pk_e, it is infeasible to downgrade a signature to the previous epoch due to the security of the BLS signature scheme.

5 Unforgeability

In this section, the unforgeability of the proposed scheme Σ_{US} can be guaranteed in the following theorem.

Theorem 1. *If $i\mathcal{O}$, PRG, and PPRF satisfy their definitions, respectively, then Σ_{US} is EUF-US secure. That is, $Adv_{\Sigma_{US},\mathcal{A}}^{EUF-US} \leq negl(\lambda)$.*

We modify the proof line of Nishimaki [20] to fit into US setting, and prove that the scheme is secure under our EUF-US security model. The EUF-US security of Σ_{US} can be reduced to the CDH problem, by embedding CDH instance into the EUF-US experiment. The intuition is that, we firstly change the public key of the challenge epoch e^* of EUF-US experimrnt, then replace pk_{e^*} with an item of CDH instance. So that, any adversary who can forge a valid signature is able to solve the CDH problem. In order to insert the CDH instance at epoch e^*, the public key $g^{PPRF(sk_e,t_e^*)}$ is indistinguishable with g^a for a chosen randomly should be proved first. The puncturable character of the PPRF can be used to dig out the value $PPRF(sk_e,t_e^*)$ from the token and preserve the token's functionality to make it look like the not punctured token (using $i\mathcal{O}$) for the adversary. Note that as t^{e^*} is generated by executing key exchange protocol between the signer and the server, so we assume that the adversary does not know the secret t_e^*, if he knows, he can easily distinguish the punctured and not punctured token by just entering the secret t_e^*. After this work, as the token does not contain any information of the value $PPRF(sk_e,t_e^*)$, it is independent of its corresponding public key $g^{PPRF(sk_e,t_e^*)}$, so the public key can be replaced with g^a. Then the rest work of this reduction is similar to proving the security of the BLS signature scheme. The details can be found in Appendix A.

6 Conclusions

We have presented a definitional framework called updatable signature with weakened token (US-WT) which is based on the US construction proposed by Cini et al. [6]. And we have constructed an improve updatable signature scheme Σ_{US} with weakened token, which achieves no-directional key updates and uni-directional signature updates. And the proposed scheme has been proved secure under our enhanced security model. The proposed scheme uses $i\mathcal{O}$ technique, and is based on BLS signature scheme which is secure under random oracle model. So how to construct a scheme that is efficient and secure in the standard model would be an interest research direction.

A   Security proof of Theorem 1

Let N be the upper bound of the epoch number. We construct a sequence of hybrid games.

Hyb_i: This is the same as $Exp^{EUF\text{-}US}_{\Sigma_{US},\mathcal{A}}(\lambda, N)$ except the following differences: when the adversary sends a query to $\mathcal{O}.Next$ at the epoch j,

- for $j < i$, return an honestly generated pk_{j+1},
- for $j \geq i$, we randomly choose $a \in \mathbb{Z}_p$ and return $pk = g^a$.

Thus Hyb_{N+1} is just $Exp^{EUF\text{-}US}_{\Sigma_{US},\mathcal{A}}(\lambda, N)$.

Hyb'_i: This is the same as Hyb_i except that the game chooses $e^* \in [N]$, which serves as the challenge epoch. If the adversary finally forges a signature at the epoch $e \neq e^*$, the game aborts. So Hyb'_i equals Hyb_i with probability $1/(N+1)$. Our goal is to prove $\left| \Pr[Hyb'_{i+1} = 1] - \Pr[Hyb'_i = 1] \right| \leq negl_1(\lambda)$.

Lemma 1. *If there exist iO, PRG, and PPRF that satisfy their respective definitions, it holds that* $\left| \Pr[Hyb'_{i+1} = 1] - \Pr[Hyb'_i = 1] \right| \leq negl_1(\lambda)$.

Proof. We define a sequence of games.

Game-0: This game chooses a random coin $coin \leftarrow \{0,1\}$. If $coin = 0$, it simulates Hyb'_i. Otherwise, it simulates Hyb'_{i+1}. That is to say, if $coin = 1$, a real pk_{i+1} for the $\mathcal{O}.Next$ query is sent at the epoch i, and if $coin = 0$, $pk = g^a$ is sent for a uniform $a \in \mathbb{Z}_p$. We define an event E_x as that the adversary correctly guesses $coin$ in **Game-x**.

Game-1: This is the same as **Game-0** except that we modify the answer to the $\mathcal{O}.Next$ query at the epoch i for $coin = 1$. It chooses $t_{i+1} \leftarrow \{0,1\}^{2n}$ instead of computing $t_{i+1} = PRG(r_{i+1})$.

Game-2: This is the same as **Game-1** except that we modify the token generation at the epoch $i + 1$. It computes a punctured key $sk_{i+1}\{t_{i+1}\} \leftarrow Punc(sk_{i+1}, t_{i+1})$ and $\Delta^{punctured}_{i+1} = iO(C_{upd}[pk_i, sk_{i+1}\{t_{i+1}\}])$ instead of Δ_{i+1}. The description of $C_{upd}[pk_i, sk_{i+1}\{t_{i+1}\}]$ is given in Table 6.

Game-3: This is the same as **Game-2** except we modify pk_{i+1} for the $\mathcal{O}.Next$ query at the epoch i for $coin = 1$. It chooses a uniform $a \in \mathbb{Z}_p$, and returns $pk_{i+1} = g^a$.

Table 6. The description of update circuit $C_{upd}[pk_i, sk_{i+1}\{t_{i+1}\}]$

Circuit 1 Update Circuit $C_{upd}[pk_i, sk_{i+1}\{t_{i+1}\}]$

Constant:

pk_i and $sk_{i+1}\{t_{i+1}\}$

Input:

A message-signature pair (m, σ_i), the secret value t_{i+1},

1) Compute $b = US.Ver(m, \sigma_i, pk_i)$.
2) If $b = 1$,
3) Compute $y = PPRF(sk_{i+1}\{t_{i+1}\}, t_{i+1})$.
4) Output $(m, \sigma_{i+1} = H_0(m)^y)$.
5) Else return $\bot$.

Output: A message-signature pair (m, σ_{i+1}).

By the definition of **Game-0**, we have $\Pr[E_0] = |\Pr[Hyb'_{i+1} = 1] - \Pr[Hyb'_i = 1]|$. In addition, since pk_{i+1} for $coin = 1$ is equal to $coin = 0$ in **Game-3**, it trivially holds that $\Pr[E_3] \leq negl(\lambda)$. Thus, to complete the proof of Lemma 1, we need to prove the Propositions 1, 2, 3 below.

Proposition 1. *It holds that* $\left|\Pr[E_1] - \Pr[E_0]\right| \leq \mathrm{Adv}^{prg}_{\mathcal{B}_1, PRG}(\lambda)$.

Proposition 2. *It holds that* $\left|\Pr[E_2] - \Pr[E_1]\right| \leq \mathrm{Adv}^{i\mathcal{O}}_{\mathcal{B}_2, i\mathcal{O}}(\lambda)$.

Proposition 3. *It holds that* $\left|\Pr[E_3] - \Pr[E_2]\right| \leq \mathrm{Adv}^{pprf}_{\mathcal{B}_3, PPRF}(\lambda)$.

We give the proofs of Propositions 1 to 3 below.

Proof of Proposition 1. It is easy to obtain this proposition since the only difference between these games is the answer to $\mathcal{O}.Next$ query for $coin = 1$ at the epoch i, the answer either equals $t_{i+1} \leftarrow \{0, 1\}^{2n}$ or $t_{i+1} = PRG(r_{i+1})$. Note that r_{i+1} is not used in any other part. This value is an internal randomness to generate a secret t_{i+1}. Thus, the proposition holds according to the security of PRG.

Proof of Proposition 2. The difference between these games is the token $\Delta^{punctured}_{i+1}$ or Δ_{i+1}. If the two circuits $C_{upd}[pk_i, sk_{i+1}]$ and $C_{upd}[pk_i, sk_{i+1}\{t_{i+1}\}]$ are functionally equivalent, we obtain the statement by using $i\mathcal{O}$ security.

The two programs are different if $t_{i+1} = PRG(r_{i+1})$ since in $\Delta^{punctured}_{i+1}$ we use a punctured key $sk_{i+1}\{t_{i+1}\}$ (other parts are completely the same). However, since $r_{i+1} \in \{0, 1\}^n$, for a random $t_{i+1} \in \{0, 1\}^{2n}$, $t_{i+1} = PRG(r_{i+1})$ happens only with $1/2^n$. Thus, these two circuits are functionally equivalent with probability $1 - 1/2^n$. By using $i\mathcal{O}$ security, we complete the proof.

Proof of Proposition 3. We construct an adversary $\mathcal{B}$ for PPRF by using a distinguisher $\mathcal{A}$ for these two games. $\mathcal{B}$ chooses $t_{i+1} \in \{0, 1\}^{2n}$, then sends it to the challenger of PPRF and receives $(sk_{i+1}\{t_{i+1}\}, y)$. $\mathcal{B}$ sets (implicitly) $sk_{i+1} = sk_{i+1}\{t_{i+1}\}$, computes public key $pk_{i+1} = g^y$, and simulates the game for $\mathcal{A}$.

If $y = PPRF(sk_{i+1}, t_{i+1})$, we are in **Game-2**. If $y \leftarrow \mathbb{Z}_p$, we are in **Game-3**. Therefore, if $\mathcal{A}$ distinguishes the two games, $\mathcal{B}$ can break the security of PPRF. This completes the proof.

Now we have proved that $\big| \Pr[Hyb'_{i+1} = 1] - \Pr[Hyb'_i = 1] \big| \leq negl_1(\lambda)$. we use Hyb'_0 for simplicity (that is in this game all pk_i for $i > 0$ are generated by random choosing $a \in \mathbb{Z}_p$ and returning $pk = g^a$).

Lemma 2. *Let $\mathbb{G}$ be a CDH-hard group of prime order p, and g be a generator of $\mathbb{G}$. If there exists an adversary that can succeed in Hyb'_0 with non-negligible advantage, then we could construct an algorithm $\mathcal{B}$ that can solve a CDH problem with non-negligible probability.*

Proof. This part is close to the proof for BLS signature [4] scheme. Let q_H denote the number of queries that the adversary makes at most to the hash function H_0. Suppose the adversary $\mathcal{A}$ is a forger that succeeds in Hyb'_0 with probability ϵ, which means $\mathcal{A}$ output a valid signature at the epoch e^* with probability ϵ. We show how to construct an algorithm $\mathcal{B}$ that solves a CDH problem with probability at least $1/q_H \cdot \epsilon$.

$\mathcal{B}$ is given $g, g^a, h \in \mathbb{G}$, whose goal is to output h^a. $\mathcal{B}$ will simulate a challenger and interact with $\mathcal{A}$ at the epoch e^* as follows (Note that at other epochs $\mathcal{B}$ simulates for $\mathcal{A}$ honestly).

Setup. Algorithm $\mathcal{B}$ starts by giving $\mathcal{A}$ the generator g and the public key g^{a+r}, where r is random in $\mathbb{Z}_p$ chosen by $\mathcal{B}$.

H-queries. At any time the adversary $\mathcal{A}$ can query the random oracle H_0. To respond to these queries, $\mathcal{B}$ maintains a list of tuples $\langle M_j, w_j, b_j, c_j \rangle$ as explained below. We refer to this list as H_0-list. The list is initially empty. When $\mathcal{A}$ queries the oracle H_0 at a point $M_i \in \{0,1\}^*$, the algorithm $\mathcal{B}$ responds as follows:
1. If the query M_i already appears in H_0-list in a tuple $\langle M_i, w_i, b_i, c_i \rangle$, then the algorithm $\mathcal{B}$ responds with $H_0(M_i) = w_i \in \mathbb{G}$.
2. Otherwise, $\mathcal{B}$ generates a random coin $c_i \in \{0, 1\}$, so that $\Pr[c_i = 0] = 1/q_H$.
3. $\mathcal{B}$ picks a random $b_i \in \mathbb{Z}_p$ and computes $w_i \leftarrow (h^{1-c_i} \cdot g^{b_i}) \in \mathbb{G}$.
4. $\mathcal{B}$ adds the tuple $\langle M_j, w_j, b_j, c_j \rangle$ to H_0-list and responds to $\mathcal{A}$ by setting $H_0(M_i) = w_i$. Note that w_i is uniform in $\mathbb{G}$ and is independent of $\mathcal{A}$'s current view as required.

Signature queries. Let M_i be a signature query issued by $\mathcal{A}$. For epochs $e \in [0, N]\backslash\{e^*\}$, $\mathcal{B}$ generates sk_e, pk_e itself, and so it can easily answer the signature query of $\mathcal{A}$. At the epoch e^*, $\mathcal{B}$ responds to this query as follows:
1. $\mathcal{B}$ runs the above algorithm for responding to H_0-queries to obtain $w_i \in \mathbb{G}$ such that $H_0(M_i) = w_i$. Let $\langle M_i, w_i, b_i, c_i \rangle$ be the corresponding tuple in H_0-list. If $c_i = 0$, then $\mathcal{B}$ reports failure and terminates.

2. Otherwise, we know $c_i = 1$ and hence $w_i = g^{b_i} \in \mathbb{G}$. Define $\sigma_i = g^{a \cdot b_i} \cdot g^{r \cdot b_i} \in \mathbb{G}$. Observe that $\sigma_i = w_i^{a+r}$, and therefore σ_i is a valid signature on M_i under the public key. $\mathcal{B}$ gives σ_i to $\mathcal{A}$.

Update-queries. Let M_i, σ_i be an update query issued by $\mathcal{A}$. At the epochs $e \in [0, N] \backslash \{e^* - 1, e^*\}$, $\mathcal{B}$ generates sk_e, pk_e, Δ_e its self, and so it can easily answer the update query of $\mathcal{A}$. At the epochs $e^* - 1, e^* + 1$, due to the indistinguishability between the signatures generated by $US.Update$ and $US.Sig$, $\mathcal{B}$ responds to this query with an answer of the signature query for M_i.

Output. Eventually, $\mathcal{A}$ produces a message-signature tuple (M_f, σ_f) such that no signature query was issued for M_f. If there is no tuple in H_0-list containing M_f, then $\mathcal{B}$ issues a query itself for $H_0(M_f)$ to ensure that such a tuple exists. We assume σ_f is a valid signature on M_f under the given public key. If it is not, $\mathcal{B}$ reports failure and terminates. Next, $\mathcal{B}$ finds the tuple $\langle M_f, w, b, c \rangle$ in H_0-list. If $c = 1$, then $\mathcal{B}$ reports failure and terminates. Otherwise, $c = 0$ and therefore $H_0(M_f) = w = h \cdot g^b$. Hence, $\sigma = h^{a+r} \cdot g^{b(a+r)}$. Then $\mathcal{B}$ outputs the required h^a as $h^a \leftarrow \sigma / (h^r \cdot g^{a \cdot b} \cdot g^{r \cdot b})$.

Finally, we get that the adversary can succeed in Hyb_0' with negligible probability due to the CDH hard problem [4]. More formally, $\Pr[Hyb_0' = 1] \le negl_2(\lambda)$. From Lemma 1, we have

$$\left| \Pr[Hyb_0' = 1] - \Pr[Hyb_{N+1}' = 1] \right| \le N \cdot negl_1(\lambda),$$

$$\Pr[Hyb_{N+1}' = 1] \le N \cdot negl_1(\lambda) + negl_2(\lambda)$$

Thus,

$$\Pr[Exp_{\Sigma_{US}, \mathcal{A}}^{EUF\text{-}US} EUF\text{-}US(\lambda, N) = 1] \le negl(\lambda),$$

where $negl(\lambda) = (N + 1) \cdot (N \cdot negl_1(\lambda) + negl_2(\lambda))$.

References

1. Barak, B., et al.: On the (Im)possibility of obfuscating programs. In: Kilian, J. (ed.) CRYPTO 2001. LNCS, vol. 2139, pp. 1–18. Springer, Heidelberg (2001). https://doi.org/10.1007/3-540-44647-8_1

2. Boneh, D., Eskandarian, S., Kim, S., Shih, M.: Improving speed and security in updatable encryption schemes. In: Moriai, S., Wang, H. (eds.) ASIACRYPT 2020. LNCS, vol. 12493, pp. 559–589. Springer, Cham (2020). https://doi.org/10.1007/978-3-030-64840-4_19

3. Boneh, D., Lewi, K., Montgomery, H., Raghunathan, A.: Key homomorphic PRFs and their applications. In: Canetti, R., Garay, J.A. (eds.) CRYPTO 2013. LNCS, vol. 8042, pp. 410–428. Springer, Heidelberg (2013). https://doi.org/10.1007/978-3-642-40041-4_23

4. Boneh, D., Lynn, B., Shacham, H.: Short signatures from the Weil pairing. In: Boyd, C. (ed.) ASIACRYPT 2001. LNCS, vol. 2248, pp. 514–532. Springer, Heidelberg (2001). https://doi.org/10.1007/3-540-45682-1_30

5. Boyd, C., Davies, G.T., Gjøsteen, K., Jiang, Y.: Fast and secure updatable encryption. In: Micciancio, D., Ristenpart, T. (eds.) CRYPTO 2020. LNCS, vol. 12170, pp. 464–493. Springer, Cham (2020). https://doi.org/10.1007/978-3-030-56784-2_16

6. Cini, V., Ramacher, S., Slamanig, D., Striecks, C., Tairi, E.: Updatable signatures and message authentication codes. In: Garay, J.A. (ed.) PKC 2021. LNCS, vol. 12710, pp. 691–723. Springer, Cham (2021). https://doi.org/10.1007/978-3-030-75245-3_25

7. Derler, D., Slamanig, D.: Key-homomorphic signatures: definitions and applications to multiparty signatures and non-interactive zero-knowledge. Des. Codes Cryptogr. **87**(6), 1373–1413 (2019). https://doi.org/10.1007/s10623-018-0535-9

8. Diffie, W., Hellman, M.: New directions in cryptography. IEEE Trans. Inf. Theory **22**(6), 644–654 (1976). https://doi.org/10.1109/TIT.1976.1055638

9. Everspaugh, A., Paterson, K., Ristenpart, T., Scott, S.: Key rotation for authenticated encryption. In: Katz, J., Shacham, H. (eds.) CRYPTO 2017. LNCS, vol. 10403, pp. 98–129. Springer, Cham (2017). https://doi.org/10.1007/978-3-319-63697-9_4

10. Fleischhacker, N., Krupp, J., Malavolta, G., Schneider, J., Schröder, D., Simkin, M.: Efficient unlinkable sanitizable signatures from signatures with re-randomizable keys. In: Cheng, C.-M., Chung, K.-M., Persiano, G., Yang, B.-Y. (eds.) PKC 2016. LNCS, vol. 9614, pp. 301–330. Springer, Heidelberg (2016). https://doi.org/10.1007/978-3-662-49384-7_12

11. Håstad, J., Impagliazzo, R., Levin, L.A., Luby, M.: A pseudorandom generator from any one-way function. SIAM J. Comput. **28**(4), 1364–1396 (1999). https://doi.org/10.1137/S0097539793244708

12. Hofheinz, D., Kiltz, E.: Programmable hash functions and their applications. In: Wagner, D. (ed.) CRYPTO 2008. LNCS, vol. 5157, pp. 21–38. Springer, Heidelberg (2008). https://doi.org/10.1007/978-3-540-85174-5_2

13. Jaeger, J., Stepanovs, I.: Optimal channel security against fine-grained state compromise: the safety of messaging. In: Shacham, H., Boldyreva, A. (eds.) CRYPTO 2018. LNCS, vol. 10991, pp. 33–62. Springer, Cham (2018). https://doi.org/10.1007/978-3-319-96884-1_2

14. Jiang, Y.: The direction of updatable encryption does not matter much. In: Moriai, S., Wang, H. (eds.) ASIACRYPT 2020. LNCS, vol. 12493, pp. 529–558. Springer, Cham (2020). https://doi.org/10.1007/978-3-030-64840-4_18

15. Jost, D., Maurer, U., Mularczyk, M.: Efficient ratcheting: almost-optimal guarantees for secure messaging. In: Ishai, Y., Rijmen, V. (eds.) EUROCRYPT 2019. LNCS, vol. 11476, pp. 159–188. Springer, Cham (2019). https://doi.org/10.1007/978-3-030-17653-2_6

16. Klooß, M., Lehmann, A., Rupp, A.: (R)CCA secure updatable encryption with integrity protection. In: Ishai, Y., Rijmen, V. (eds.) EUROCRYPT 2019. LNCS, vol. 11476, pp. 68–99. Springer, Cham (2019). https://doi.org/10.1007/978-3-030-17653-2_3

17. Krawczyk, H.: Cryptographic extraction and key derivation: the HKDF scheme. In: Rabin, T. (ed.) CRYPTO 2010. LNCS, vol. 6223, pp. 631–648. Springer, Heidelberg (2010). https://doi.org/10.1007/978-3-642-14623-7_34

18. Lehmann, A., Tackmann, B.: Updatable encryption with post-compromise security. In: Nielsen, J.B., Rijmen, V. (eds.) EUROCRYPT 2018. LNCS, vol. 10822, pp. 685–716. Springer, Cham (2018). https://doi.org/10.1007/978-3-319-78372-7_22

19. Miao, P., Patranabis, S., Watson, G.: Unidirectional updatable encryption and proxy re-encryption from DDH. In: Boldyreva, A., Kolesnikov, V. (eds.) Public-Key Cryptography – PKC 2023. PKC 2023. LNCS, vol. 13941, pp. 368–398. Springer, Cham (2023). https://doi.org/10.1007/978-3-031-31371-4_13

20. Nishimaki, R.: The direction of updatable encryption does matter. In: Hanaoka, G., Shikata, J., Watanabe, Y. (eds.) Public-Key Cryptography – PKC 2022. PKC 2022. LNCS, vol. 13178, pp. 194–224. Springer, Cham (2022). https://doi.org/10.1007/978-3-030-97131-1_7
21. Poettering, B., Rastikian, S.: Sequential digital signatures for cryptographic software-update authentication. In: Atluri, V., Di Pietro, R., Jensen, C.D., Meng, W. (eds.) Computer Security – ESORICS 2022. ESORICS 2022. LNCS, vol. 13555, pp. 255–274. Springer, Cham (2022). https://doi.org/10.1007/978-3-031-17146-8_13
22. Sahai, A., Waters, B.: How to use indistinguishability obfuscation: deniable encryption, and more. SIAM J. Comput. **50**(3), 857–908 (2021). https://doi.org/10.1137/15M1030108
23. Schnorr, C.P.: Efficient identification and signatures for smart cards. In: Brassard, G. (ed.) CRYPTO 1989. LNCS, vol. 435, pp. 239–252. Springer, New York (1990). https://doi.org/10.1007/0-387-34805-0_22

A Pairing-Based Certificateless Authenticated Searchable Encryption with MTI Guarantees

Mohammed Raouf Senouci[1]([✉]), Abdelkader Senouci[2], and Fagen Li[1]

[1] School of Computer Science and Engineering, University of Electronic Science and Technology of China, Chengdu 611731, People's Republic of China
senoucimedraouf@gmail.com, fagenli@uestc.edu.cn
[2] Faculty of Engineering and Environment, Northumbria University, Newcastle, UK
abdelkader.senouci@northumbria.ac.uk

Abstract. Nowadays, users prefer to encrypt their sensitive data before outsourcing it to the cloud. although, performing the encryption assures the data privacy, but it jeopardizes the search functionality. Public key encryption with keyword search (PEKS) is a potential solution for addressing this problem. However, most PEKS schemes are either inefficient, or susceptible to some type of attack(s) (i.e. inside keyword guessing attack, outside keyword guessing attack, ... etc.). Therefore, we propose a sustainable certificateless authenticated encryption system with keyword search scheme. To the best of our knowledge, the proposed scheme considers the multi-trapdoor indistinguishability in the certificateless primitive. Moreover, a thorough security analysis shows that our scheme also guarantees the security against both online and offline keyword guessing attacks. Finally, based on the performance analysis results, we find that the suggested scheme is efficient and outperforms the other schemes.

Keywords: authenticated searchable encryption · multi-trapdoor indistinguishability · keyword guessing attack · certificateless encryption · bilinear pairing

1 Introduction

Cloud storage technology has gotten a lot of attention in recent years, applications. Nonetheless, using encryption is a mandatory step for ensuring the privacy of the users sensitive data.

Boneh et al. [1] offered the first PEKS scheme, which is constructed on a bilinear map to meet the aim of searching through ciphertext without disclosing any information about the plaintext. However, the search difficulty in this technique is proportionally linear with the amount of encrypted keywords in each document. Furthermore, a secure connection is required to broadcast trapdoors.

To address this issue, Baek et al. [2] proposed a secure channel-free PEKS approach in which the trapdoor is communicated via a public channel utilizing the cloud's public/private keys.

Later, Byun et al. [3] discovered that contemporary PEKS schemes are vulnerable to an offline keyword guessing attack since keywords are quite often chosen from a much narrower range than passwords and users are accustomed to searching for documents using distinctive frequently used words. However, Rhee et al. [4] pointed out that PEKS schemes require a secure channel to deliver the trapdoor, which make them impractical in real world scenarios, where constructing such a secure channel is a difficult task to accomplish. Moreover, they also pointed out that when removing the secure channel, the schemes become susceptible to an offline keyword guessing attack (OKGA). To eliminate this problem, the authors proposed the notion of secure channel free, that is also referred to as PEKS with a designated server. Ma et al. [5] proposed a public key encryption scheme with equality testing that incorporate an authorization mechanism for the user to control the comparison of its ciphertexts with others. another variant that made an attempt in solving the secure channel problem is presented by Fang et al. in [6]. The authors presented a secure channel free PEKS scheme that is robust against keyword guessing attacks under the standard model.

However, the aforementioned solutions either have a key management or a key escrow problem. Peng et al. [7] first describe the concept of certificateless public key encryption with keyword search to remedy these limitations (CLPEKS). Wu et al. [8] later demonstrate that Peng et al.'s scheme is vulnerable to an offline keyword guessing attack. Senouci et al. [9] proposed a certificateless public key encryption with keyword search that withstand both offline and online keyword guessing attacks which can be performed by either an inside or an outside adversaries. Moreover, to prevent against the inside keyword guessing attack (IKGA), Huang et al. [10] establish the notion of public key authenticated encryption with keyword search (PAEKS). The proposed scheme permit the sender in encrypting and authenticating each keyword separately. Wu et al. [11] point out that most of the PEKS schemes are either based on public key infrastructure, or identity-based encryption, which suffers from the certificate management problem, and key escrow problem. In contrast, He et al. [12] proposed a certificateless public key authenticated encryption with keyword search scheme, which they claimed that is secure against IKGA. Zhang et al. [13] proposed a deniably authenticated searchable encryption scheme based on blockchain for medical image data sharing. Ma et al. [14] proposed a certificateless searchable encryption scheme for mobile healthcare system. Later, Wu et al. [15] showed that He et al.'s scheme [12] is incorrect, and Ma et al.'s scheme [14] is susceptible to keyword guessing attacks. Qin et al. [16] proposed a public key authenticated encryption with keyword search, which claimed to be secure against outside chosen multi. ciphertext attacks. Yang et al. [17] proposed a certificateless public key searchable encryption with multi-trapdoor privacy. Senouci et al. [18] proposed a certificateless encryption with keyword search, that is secure channel free, and does not require using the bilinear pairing operations which are known to be computationally intensive cryptographic procedures.

1.1   Contributions

In this work, we propose a sustainable certificateless authenticated encryption with keyword search scheme, and prove that guarantees all the security requirements, namely, offline keyword guessing attack, online keyword guessing attack, and multi-trapdoor indistinguishability.

The proposed scheme support single keyword search, meaning that each ciphertext generated by the sender contains a distinct keyword. However, in the case of the trapdoor, the receiver can search for a file using some keyword. This latter could be used by the receiver again to retrieve the same file in the future. Thus, one or more trapdoor(s) that sent by the receiver could contain the same keyword. In this scenario, the multi-trapdoor indistinguishability should be the best security guarantee that we must guarantee. Therefore, the outlines of our contributions are provided as follows:

- We proposed a searchable encryption scheme that extends the certificateless primitive, this achieved by splitting the private key of a user into two part. The first part is a partial private key, and it is generated by the KGC. While the second part is a secret key that a user chooses.
- Moreover, the proposed scheme enables both the sender and the receiver to authenticate the ciphertext and the trapdoor, respectively. This approach makes the possibility for an adversary in forging a valid ciphertext or trapdoor a difficult task. Thus, it will guarantee the security against both offline keyword guessing attack, and online keyword guessing attacks.
- In addition, we consider the multi-trapdoor indistinguishability in the certificateless primitive. Therefore, we define the security model, and we prove that the proposed scheme is semantically secure in the random oracle model under the Computational Bilinear Diffie-Hellman (CDH) assumption.
- Finally, we compare the proposed scheme with other schemes in terms of security guarantees, computational overheads, and communication costs. The aim of the comparison yields to a conclusion that our scheme has better security guarantees, and more efficient than other schemes.

1.2   Paper Organization

The rest of the paper is organized as follows. In Sect. 2, we start by giving a concrete implementation of the scheme, and we show its correctness. In Sect. 3, we first prove that the proposed scheme is secure against both online and offline keyword guessing attacks, followed by defining the security model used, and finishing by proving that the scheme is semantically and guarantees the multi-trapdoor indistinguishability in the certificateless primitive. In Sect. 4, we evaluate the performance of the proposed scheme with other schemes in terms of security guarantees, computational overheads, and communication costs. Moreover, in Sect. 5 we present a possible application for the proposed scheme in real life. Finally, we conclude the paper in Sect. 6.

2 Our Scheme

As depicted in Fig. 1, the system model has the following four entities, namely: Key Generation Center (KGC), Sender (S), Receiver (R) and Cloud Server (CS).

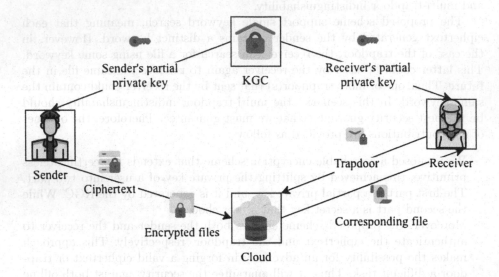

Fig. 1. CLPAEKS system architecture

These entities will execute the following probabilistic polynomial-time algorithms:

- $(s, prms) \leftarrow$ **Setup**(λ): Given a security parameter λ, KGC selects an additive cyclic group G_1 and a multiplicative cyclic group G_2 of the same order $q > 2^\lambda$. It also chooses an element P as a generator of G_1, a bilinear pairing function $\hat{e} : G_1 \times G_1 \rightarrow G_2$, a random number $s \in Z_q^*$ as the master secret key. Moreover, KGC selects four different cryptographic hash functions: $h_1 : \{0,1\}^* \rightarrow Z_q^*$, $h_2 : \{0,1\}^* \times G_1 \times G_1 \rightarrow G_1$, and $h_3 : G_2 \times G_1 \times G_1 \rightarrow Z_q^*$. Finally, KGC publishes the system parameters $prms = \{\lambda, G_1, G_2, \hat{e}, P, h_1, h_2, h_3\}$ and keeps the master secret key s secretly.
- $psk_U \leftarrow$ **ExtractPartialPrivateKey**$(prms, id_U)$: KGC executes the following steps for each user U.
    1. Takes the system parameters $prms$ and the sender's identity $id_S \in \{0,1\}^*$ as input. KGC computes $psk_S = s \cdot h_1(id_S) \cdot P$. Then, it returns psk_S to the sender.
    2. Takes the system parameters $prms$ and the receiver's identity $id_R \in \{0,1\}^*$ as input. KGC computes $psk_R = s \cdot h_1(id_R) \cdot P$. Then, it returns psk_R to the receiver.
- $x_U \leftarrow$ **SetSecretValue**(): This algorithm is performed by each user U as follows:

1. The sender chooses a random number $x_S \in Z_q^*$ as its secret value.
2. The receiver chooses a random number $x_R \in Z_q^*$ as its secret value.

- $sk_U \leftarrow$ **SetPrivateKey**(psk_U, x_U): This algorithm is performed by each user U as follows:
  1. Takes a sender's partial private key psk_S and a secret value x_S. The sender sets $sk_S = (psk_S, x_S)$ as its private key.
  2. Takes a receiver's partial private key psk_R and a secret value x_R. The receiver sets $sk_R = (psk_R, x_R)$ as its private key.
- $pk_U \leftarrow$ **SetPublicKey**$(prms, x_U)$: This algorithm is performed by each user U as follows:
  1. Takes the system parameters $prms$ and a sender's secret value x_S. The sender computes $pk_S = x_S \cdot P$, and sets pk_S as its public key.
  2. Takes the system parameters $prms$ and a receiver's secret value x_R. The receiver computes $pk_R = x_R \cdot P$, and sets pk_R as its public key.
- $C_w \leftarrow$ **GenerateCiphertext**$(prms, sk_S, pk_S, pk_R, w)$: The sender takes the system parameters $prms$, the sender's private key $sk_S = (psk_S, x_S)$, the sender's public key pk_S, the receiver's public key pk_R, and the keyword w as input. Then, it performs the following:
  1. The sender computes $K_1 = x_S \cdot pk_R$, and $K_2 = h_1(id_R) \cdot psk_S$.
  2. Finally, the sender returns the ciphertext $C_w = h_2(w, K_1, K_2)$.
- $T_w \leftarrow$ **GenerateTrapdoor**$(prms, sk_R, pk_R, pk_S, w')$: The receiver takes the system parameters $prms$, the receiver's private key $sk_R = (psk_R, x_R)$, the receiver's public key pk_R, the sender's public key pk_S, and the keyword w' as input. Then, it performs the following:
  1. The receiver computes $K_1' = x_R \cdot pk_S$, and $K_2' = h_1(id_S) \cdot psk_R$.
  2. The receiver chooses a random number $r \in Z_q^*$, and computes $T_1 = r \cdot P$.
  3. The receiver computes $T_2 = h_3(A, pk_S, pk_R)$, where $A = \hat{e}(K_3', r \cdot P)$, and $K_3' = h_2(w', K_1', K_2')$.
  4. Finally, the receiver returns the trapdoor $T_w = (T_1, T_2)$.
- $\top \backslash \bot \leftarrow$ **SearchTest**$(prms, pk_S, pk_R, C_w, T_w)$: The cloud takes the system parameters $prms$, the sender's public key pk_S, the receiver's public key pk_R, the ciphertext C_w, and the trapdoor $T_w = (T_1, T_2)$ as input. Then, it performs the following:
  1. The cloud computes $T_2' = h_3(B, pk_S, pk_R)$, where $B = \hat{e}(C_w, T_1)$.
  2. The cloud returns $\top$ if the equation $T_2' = T_2$ holds. Otherwise, it returns $\bot$.

Correctness. Let C_w be the ciphertext of the keyword w, and T_w be the trapdoor of the keyword w'. First, we know that $K_1 = x_S \cdot pk_R = x_S \cdot x_R \cdot P = x_R \cdot pk_S$, thus $K_1 = K_1'$. Moreover, $K_2 = h_1(id_R) \cdot psk_S = h_1(id_S) \cdot h_1(id_R) \cdot s \cdot P = h_1(id_S) \cdot psk_R$, thus $K_2 = K_2'$. Therefore, If $w = w'$, then $C_w = h_2(w, K_1, K_2) = h_2(w', K_1', K_2') = K_3'$. Subsequently, we will have the following: $T_1 = r \cdot P$, and $A = \hat{e}(K_3', r \cdot P) = \hat{e}(C_w, r \cdot P) = B$. Moreover, $T_2 = h_3(A, pk_S, pk_R) = h_3(B, pk_S, pk_R) = T_2'$. Hence, the proposed scheme is sound.

3   Security Analysis

In this section, we first prove that the proposed scheme is secure against both offline and online keyword guessing attacks. Next, we describe the security model for the proposed scheme. Finally, we prove that our scheme is resilient against different keyword guessing attacks, and provides multi-trapdoor indistinguishability guarantees.

3.1   Keyword Guessing Attack Guarantees

Theorem 1. *If DL problem is intractable, then the proposed scheme is secure against both offline and online keyword guessing attacks.*

Proof: The proof of Theorem 1 is concluded from Lemma 1 and Lemma 2.   □

Lemma 1. *If DL is intractable, then the proposed scheme is secure against offline keyword guessing attack.*

Proof: An offline keyword guessing attack is the possibility of generating a valid ciphertext by an adversary. This attack can be feasible iff the following steps are successfully performed:

We recall tat the ciphertext equations are: $C_w = h_2(w, K_1, K_2)$, where $K_1 = x_S \cdot pk_R$, and $K_2 = h_1(id_R) \cdot psk_S$.

- **Step1**: Computing the correct value for K_1. This can be achieved using either the following methods:
  - By setting $K_1 = x_R \cdot pk_S$ as a reference, the adversary must solve the DL problem to extract the correct value for x_R.
  - By setting $K_1 = x_S \cdot pk_R$ as a reference, the adversary must solve the DL problem to extract the correct value for x_S.
- **Step2**: Computing the correct value for K_2. We know that $K_2 = h_1(id_R) \cdot psk_S$ and $psk_S = s \cdot h_1(id_S) \cdot P$. Thus, by setting $K_2 = s \cdot h_1(id_S) \cdot h_1(id_R) \cdot P$ as a reference, the adversary must solve the DL problem to extract the correct value of s. Note that this step can be skipped only in the case where the adversary is a malicious KGC, because it gets hold of the master secret key s.

After performing the previous steps, the adversary now has all the required components to execute an offline keyword attack using its keywords of choice.   □

Lemma 2. *If DL is intractable, then the proposed scheme is secure against online keyword guessing attack.*

Proof: An online keyword guessing attack is the possibility of generating a valid trapdoor by an adversary.

We recall tat the ciphertext equations are: $T_1 = r \cdot P$, $T_2 = h_3(A, pk_S, pk_R)$, where $A = \hat{e}(K_3', r \cdot P)$, $K_3' = h_2(w', K_1', K_2')$, $K_1' = x_R \cdot pk_S$, and $K_2' = h_1(id_S) \cdot psk_R$. Hence, similar to the proof of Lemma 1, this attack can be feasible iff the correct value of K_1' and K_2' computed correctly. We omit the proof details here.   □

3.2 Security Model

In certificateless cryptography [19], we have an adversary of Type1, and an adversary of Type2. The former cannot access the system's master key, but it can replace any user's public key. While the latte cannot replace user's public key, but it can access the system's master key.

We define the security model of our proposed scheme by the following game (i.e. Game 1). This game guarantees the multi-trapdoor indistinguishability (MTI) as introduced in [16,17], and it is performed between a simulator S and an adversary A.

First, we define some helper oracles. These oracles can be queried by the adversary A, and are controlled by the simulator S as follows:

- *CreateUser*: On receiving a user's identity id_u as input, a public key pk_u is returned if id_u has already been created. Otherwise, a new record for id_u will be created by producing a private/public key pair (sk_u, pk_u) and then pk_u is returned.
- *ExtPartialPrivateKey*: On receiving a user's identity id_u as input, a partial private key psk_u is returned.
- *ExtPrivateKey*: On receiving a user's identity id_u as input, a private key x_u is returned.
- *RequestPublicKey*: On receiving a user's identity id_u as input, a public key pk_u is returned.
- *ReplacePublicKey*: If the adversary A is an adversary of Type2, then S will simply ignore the request due the restriction that the adversary is not allowed to replace any user's public key. Otherwise, it will expect receiving a user's identity id_u and a new public key pk'_u as input. Then, it will replace the old pubic key pk_u with the new one pk'_u.
- *GenerateCiphertext*: On receiving a sender's identity id_S, a receiver's identity id_R, and a keyword w as input; S computes and outputs the corresponding ciphertext C_w.
- *GenerateTrapdoor*: On receiving a sender's identity id_S, a receiver's identity id_R, and a keyword w' as input; S computes and outputs the corresponding trapdoor T_w.

Game 1 (MTI Security). *This game is played between a simulator S and an adversary A as follows:*

- **Init.** Given a security parameter λ, S runs the **Setup**(λ) algorithm and obtain the system parameters $prms$ and the master secret key s. Then, it will act as follows:
  - If the adversary A is an adversary of Type1, then S will return only $prms$.
  - Else if the adversary A is an adversary of Type2, then S will return both $prms$ and s.
- **Phase1.** During this phase, A is allowed to adaptively query the previously defined oracles simulated by S.

- **Challenge.** at some point, the adversary $\mathcal{A}$ outputs a sender's identity id_S^*, a receiver's identity id_R^*, and two distinct tuples of keywords $\boldsymbol{w_0} = (w_{0,1}^*, w_{0,2}^* \ldots, w_{0,n}^*)$ and $\boldsymbol{w_1} = (w_{1,1}^*, w_{1,2}^* \ldots, w_{1,n}^*)$. Next, $\mathcal{S}$ chooses a random bit $b \in \{0,1\}$, and for each $w_{b,i}^*$ it chooses a random number $r \in Z_q^*$, computes and returns the corresponding trapdoor $T_{w_{b,i}^*} = GenerateTrapdoor(sk_S^*, pk_S^*, pk_R^*, w_{b,i}^*)$. In addition, this query is subject to the following restrictions:
  - The adversary is not allowed to query the ciphertext oracle with the challenge keywords $w_{b,i}^*$, the challenge sender's identity id_S^*, and the challenge receiver's identity id_R^*.
  - Moreover, the adversary is not allowed to query the trapdoor oracle with the challenge keywords $w_{b,i}^*$, the challenge sender's identity id_S^*, and the challenge receiver's identity id_R^*.
- **Phase2.** $\mathcal{A}$ can continue probing $\mathcal{S}$ for more queries as it did in **Phase1**, with the only limitation that $w_i \notin \{w_{0,1}^*, \ldots, w_{0,n}^*, w_{1,1}^*, \ldots, w_{1,n}^*\}$.
- **Guess.** $\mathcal{A}$ outputs a bit $b' \in \{0,1\}$, then $\mathcal{S}$ outputs $\eta' = 0$ if $b' = b$. Otherwise, it outputs $\eta' = 1$.

Theorem 2. *The proposed scheme is semantically secure in the random oracle model under the CDH assumption, and guarantees the multi-trapdoor indistinguishability.*

Proof: Suppose that an adversary $\mathcal{A}$ is able to break the proposed scheme during the Game 1. Then, we can construct an efficient algorithm $\mathcal{S}$ which uses $\mathcal{A}$ as a subroutine to solve the CDH problem. Given a parameter of bilinear group $(\hat{e}, G_1, G_2, P)$ and an instance of CDH problem (P, aP, bP, X), where $a, b \in Z_q^*$ are random choices known only to the $\mathcal{S}$, and X is either abP or a random element of G_2. Next, $\mathcal{S}$ will simulate the environment as follows:

- **Init.** Given a security parameter λ, $\mathcal{S}$ runs the **Setup**(λ) algorithm and obtain the system parameters $prms$ and the master secret key s. Next, it chooses $l, m \in \{1, 2, \ldots, q_{CU}\}$ randomly as the guesses of the i-th, and the j-th of the $CreateUser$ queries initiated by the adversary $\mathcal{A}$. These guesses correspond to the sender's challenge identity $id_S^\diamond$, and the receiver's challenge identity $id_R^\diamond$, respectively. Finally, $\mathcal{S}$ will acts as follows:
  - If the adversary $\mathcal{A}$ is an adversary of Type1, then $\mathcal{S}$ will return only $prms$.
  - Else if the adversary $\mathcal{A}$ is an adversary of Type2, then $\mathcal{S}$ will return both $prms$ and s.
- **Phase1.** $\mathcal{A}$ adaptively query the following oracles that are simulated by $\mathcal{S}$.
  - h_1Query: On receiving a user's identity $id_u \in \{0,1\}^*$, $\mathcal{S}$ randomly chooses an element from Z_q^* as the output of $h_1(id_u)$.
  - h_2Query: $\mathcal{S}$ keeps a list L_{h_2} that is empty initially. On receiving a sender's identity $id_S \in \{0,1\}^*$, a receiver's identity $id_R \in \{0,1\}^*$, a keyword $w \in \{0,1\}^*$, and two elements $K_1, K_2 \in G_1$ as input. First, $\mathcal{S}$ checks if the entry (w, K_1, K_2) already exists in L_{h_2}, then it returns the corresponding $h_2(w, K_1, K_2)$. Otherwise, it acts as follows:

* S obtains the tuples (i, id_S, sk_S, pk_S) and (j, id_R, sk_R, pk_R) by invoking $CreateUser(id_S)$ and $CreateUser(id_R)$, respectively.
* If $\{i, j\} = \{l, m\}$ and $\hat{e}(K_1, P) = \hat{e}(pk_S, pk_R)$ and $\hat{e}(K_2, s \cdot P) = \hat{e}(psk_S, psk_R)$, then S returns abP as the answer of this query.
* Otherwise, S chooses a random element from G_1 as the value of $h_2(w, K_1, K_2)$, adds the tuple $(w, K_1, K_2, h_2(w, K_1, K_2))$ to L_{h_2}, and returns $h_2(w, K_1, K_2)$ to $\mathcal{A}$.

- h_3Query: On receiving an element A from G_2, and two element K_1 and K_2 from G_1, S randomly chooses a number from Z_q^* as the output of this query.

- $CreateUser$: S maintains a list L_{CU} that is empty initially. On receiving a user's identity $id_u \in \{0,1\}^*$ as input. First, S checks if the entry id_u already exists in L_{CU}, then it returns the corresponding user's public key pk_u. Otherwise, it acts as follows:
    * If $id_u = id_S^\diamond$, S returns $pk_u = aP$ and appends the tuple $(id_u, \perp, \perp, aP)$ to L_{CU}.
    * Else if $id_u = id_R^\diamond$, S returns $pk_u = bP$ and appends the tuple $(id_u, \perp, \perp, bP)$ to L_{CU}.
    * Otherwise, S chooses a number $x_u \in Z_q^*$ and an element $psk_u \in G_1$, randomly. Then, it returns $pk_u = x_u \cdot P$ and adds the tuple (id_u, psk_u, x_u, pk_u) to L_{CU}.

- $ExtPartialPrivateKey$: On receiving a user's identity $id_u \in \{0,1\}^*$ as input. First, S obtains the tuple (id_u, psk_u, x_u, pk_u) by invoking $CreateUser(id_u)$. Next, it checks if $psk_u \neq \perp$, then it returns psk_u. Otherwise, it returns random bit η' and aborts.

- $ExtPrivateKey$: On receiving a user's identity $id_u \in \{0,1\}^*$ as input. First, S obtains the tuple (id_u, psk_u, x_u, pk_u) by invoking $CreateUser(id_u)$. Next, it checks if $x_u \neq \perp$, then it returns x_u. Otherwise, it returns random bit η' and aborts.

- $RequestPublicKey$: On receiving a user's identity $id_u \in \{0,1\}^*$ as input. First, S obtains the tuple (id_u, psk_u, x_u, pk_u) by invoking $CreateUser(id_u)$. Next, it returns the value pk_u.

- $ReplacePublicKey$: On receiving a user's identity $id_u \in \{0,1\}^*$ and a new public key pk_u' as input. S will act as follows:
    * If the adversary $\mathcal{A}$ is an adversary of Type2, then S will simply ignore the request due the restriction that the adversary is not allowed to replace any user's public key.
    * Else if the adversary $\mathcal{A}$ is an adversary of Type1, then S first obtains the tuple (id_u, psk_u, x_u, pk_u) by invoking $CreateUser(id_u)$. Next, it updates the old entry found in L_{CU} with the new tuple $(id_u, psk_u, \perp, pk_u')$.

- $GenerateCiphertext$: On receiving a sender's identity $id_S \in \{0,1\}^*$, a receiver's identity $id_R \in \{0,1\}^*$, a cloud's identity $id_C \in \{0,1\}^*$, and a keyword $w \in \{0,1\}^*$ as input. S performs the following steps:

* It obtains the tuples (id_S, psk_S, x_S, pk_S), and (id_R, psk_R, x_R, pk_R) by invoking
  $CreateUser(id_S)$, and $CreateUser(id_R)$, respectively.
* If $id_S \notin \{id_S^\diamond, id_R^\diamond\}$ or $id_R \notin \{id_S^\diamond, id_R^\diamond\}$, then $\mathcal{S}$ computes $K_1 = x_S \cdot pk_R$, $K_2 = h_1(id_R) \cdot psk_S$, and $C_w = h_2(w, K_1, K_2)$.
* Otherwise, it outputs a random bit η' and aborts.

- $GenerateTrapdoor$: On receiving a sender's identity $id_S \in \{0,1\}^*$, a receiver's identity $id_R \in \{0,1\}^*$, and a keyword $w' \in \{0,1\}^*$ as input. $\mathcal{S}$ performs the following steps:
  * It obtains the tuples (id_S, psk_S, x_S, pk_S), and (id_R, psk_R, x_R, pk_R) by invoking
    $CreateUser(id_S)$, and $CreateUser(id_R)$, respectively.
  * If $id_S \notin \{id_S^\diamond, id_R^\diamond\}$ or $id_R \notin \{id_S^\diamond, id_R^\diamond\}$, then $\mathcal{S}$ chooses a random number $r \in Z_q^*$, computes $K_1' = x_R \cdot pk_S$, $K_2' = h_1(id_S) \cdot psk_R$, $K_3' = h_2(w', K_1', K_2')$, $A = \hat{e}(K_3', r \cdot P)$, $T_1 = r \cdot P$, and $T_2 = h_3(A, pk_S, pk_R)$.
  * Otherwise, it outputs a random bit η' and aborts.

- **Challenge.** at some point, the adversary $\mathcal{A}$ outputs a sender's identity id_S^*, a receiver's identity id_R^*, and two distinct tuples of keywords $\boldsymbol{w}_0 = (w_{0,1}^*, w_{0,2}^* \ldots, w_{0,n}^*)$ and $\boldsymbol{w}_1 = (w_{1,1}^*, w_{1,2}^* \ldots, w_{1,n}^*)$. Next, $\mathcal{S}$ chooses a random bit $b \in \{0,1\}$, and for each $w_{b,i}^*$ it chooses a random number $r \in Z_q^*$, computes the corresponding trapdoor $T_{w_{b,i}^*} = (T_{1,i}, T_{2,i})$, where $T_{1,i} = r_i \cdot P$, $T_{2,i} = h_3(\hat{e}(X_i, r_i \cdot P), pk_S^*, pk_R^*)$, and $X_i = h_2(w_{b,i}^*, x_R^* \cdot pk_S^*, h_1(id_S^*) \cdot psk_R^*)$. We should emphasize that each of challenged keywords $w_{b,i}^*$ should never exist in L_{h_2}, as the adversary is forbidden to query both the ciphertext oracle and the trapdoor oracle with $w_{b,i}^*$. This is because the adversary will be able to break the CDH problem directly.
- **Phase2.** $\mathcal{A}$ can continue probing $\mathcal{S}$ for more queries as it did in **Phase1**, with the only limitation that $w_i \notin \{w_{0,1}^*, \ldots, w_{0,n}^*, w_{1,1}^*, \ldots, w_{1,n}^*\}$.
- **Guess.** $\mathcal{A}$ outputs a bit $b' \in \{0,1\}$, then $\mathcal{S}$ outputs $\eta' = 0$ if $b' = b$. Otherwise, it outputs $\eta' = 1$.

Let E_1 be the event of terminating the simulation. This event can occur in the case where $\mathcal{S}$ finds that the challenged identities are incorrect. The probability of nonoccurence is $n \cdot q_{h_2}/q_{cu}(q_{cu} - 1)$. Next, assuming that $\mathcal{B}$ does not abort during the gem, then we will have following cases:

- If $X = abP$, then the view of $\mathcal{A}$ is the same as in a real attack. Therefore, the probability of $\mathcal{A}$ to win the above game is $Adv_{\mathcal{A}}^{MTI} = |\Pr[b' = b] - \frac{1}{2}|$.
- Else if X is randomly selected from G_1, then the value of $h_2(w, K_1, K_2)$ is also a random element from G_1. Therefore, the probability of $\mathcal{A}$ to win the above game is $\frac{1}{2}$.

Moreover, the advantage of $\mathcal{S}$ in solving the CDH problem is as follows:

$$
\begin{aligned}
\Pr[\eta' = \eta] &= \Pr[\eta' = \eta | E_1]\Pr[E_1] + \Pr[\eta' = \eta | \neg E_1]\Pr[\neg E_1] \\
&= \frac{1}{2} + (\Pr[\eta' = 0 | \neg E_1 \wedge \eta = 0]\Pr[\eta = 0] \\
&\quad + \Pr[\eta' = 1 | \neg Abort \wedge \eta = 1] - \frac{1}{2})\Pr[\neg E_1] \\
&\geq \frac{1}{2} + (\frac{1}{2}(Adv_{\mathcal{A}}^{MT-IND}(\lambda) + \frac{1}{2}) + \frac{1}{2} \cdot \frac{1}{2} - \frac{1}{2})\Pr[\neg E_1] \\
&\geq \frac{1}{2} + \frac{1}{2}Adv_{\mathcal{A}}^{MT-IND}(\lambda)\Pr[\neg E_1]
\end{aligned}
$$

It follows that $Adv_{\mathcal{S}}^{CDH} = |\Pr[\eta' = \eta] - \frac{1}{2}| \geq \frac{1}{2}Adv_{\mathcal{A}}^{MT-IND}(\lambda)\Pr[\neg E_1]$. Thus, $\mathcal{S}$ breaks the CDH problem with a probability at least $Adv_{\mathcal{S}}^{CDH} \geq \frac{n \cdot q_{H2}}{2q_{cu} \cdot (q_{cu}-1)} \cdot Adv_{\mathcal{A}}^{MT-IND}(\lambda)$. □

4   Performance Analysis

In this part, we use performance measures (such as: security guarantees, computational overheads, and communication costs), to evaluate the effectiveness of the scheme proposed in this work compared to other solutions proposed in [11,15] and [17].

4.1   Security Guarantees

In this segment, we will review the security guarantees that proposed scheme offers compared to the other schemes presented in [11,15] and [17]. From Table 1, we can clearly see that proposed scheme guarantees all the security requirements, namely, secure channel free (SCF), inside keyword guessing attack (IKGA), outside keyword guessing attack (OKGA), trapdoor indistinguishability[1] (T-IND), and multi-trapdoor indistinguishability (MT-IND).

Table 1. Security comparison

Schemes	SCF	IKGA	OKGA	T-IND	MT-IND
[11]	✓	✓		✓	
[15]	✓	✓		✓	
[17]	✓	✓	✓	✓	
Ours	✓	✓	✓	✓	✓

---

[1] If a scheme guarantees the multi-trapdoor indistinguishability (MT-IND), then this implies that the scheme also guarantees trapdoor indistinguishability (TD-IND).

4.2   Computation and Communication Costs

We start this subsection by presenting the configuration used to validate the different schemes. We choose a Type-A pairing, which uses the curve $y^2 = x^3 + x$ over a field F_q for some prime $q \equiv 3 \bmod 4$. Then, by utilizing the PBC library [20], we set the group order $r = 256$ bits, the order of the base field $q = 3072$ bits, and we use the SHA-256 as the general hash function, as suggested by NIST report in [21].

In addition, the benchmark has been done using a MacBook with Dual-Core Intel Core i 5@ 1.8 GHz and 8 GB of RAM memory, running macOS Big Sur version 11.6. The different basic operation symbols and their running time[2] are as follows: T_{mm}: The running time for a modular multiplication (0.0005 ms), T_{sm}: The running time for a scalar multiplication (22.2317 ms), T_{ma}: The running time for a modular operation (0.0005 ms), T_{pa}: The running time for a point addition (0.0539 ms), T_{bp}: The running time for a bilinear pairing operation (23.1499 ms), T_{exp}: The running time for an point exponentiation (0.0066 ms), T_{hz}: The running time for a Hash-To-Z_q^* operation (254.6800 ms), and T_{hp}: The running time for a Hash-To-Point operation (56.4113 ms).

According to Table 2 and Fig. 2a, by comparison with [11,15] and [17], the running times for the algorithm $GenerateCiphertext$ of the proposed scheme have fallen by 18.27%, 71,41% and 62.21%, respectively. In addition, the running time of the $GenerateTrapdoor$ algorithm of the proposed scheme has decreased by 19.09% and 60.92% compared to time in [11] and [15], respectively. Moreover, for the $SearchTest$ algorithm, we can clearly see that the running time of the proposed is much faster than the one presented in [11,15] and [17], where the running times have diminished by 68.59%, 68.89% and 64.35%, respectively.

Moreover, from Table 2 and Fig. 2b, we clearly see that the ciphertext size of the proposed scheme has reduced to half compared to the scheme [11], and by 66.67% compared to the schemes [15] and [17]. In addition, the trapdoor size has reduced by 48.00% compared to the scheme [11], and by 45.83% compared to the schemes [15] and [17].

Therefore, the proposed scheme is more efficient, and has a better overall communication cost.

5   Application

Searchable encryption could be adopted in the transportation sector in various ways. For example, let us consider a scenario where the sender is a vehicle equipped with sensors that collect traffic data such as traffic density, speed, and location. The receiver could be a traffic management system that needs to access this data to optimize traffic flow and reduce congestion.

In the scenario depicted in Fig. 3, the sender (vehicle) collects traffic data and generates a ciphertext based on the data, then uploads it to the cloud server.

---

[2] We execute each operation 10000 times, collect the timing of each execution, then we calculate the average of the running time.

Table 2. Computation and communication costs

Schemes	Computation costs (ms)			Communication costs ($bits$)	
	Ciphertext	Trapdoor	Test	Ciphertext	Trapdoor
[11]	$2T_{hz} + T_{hp} + T_{mm} + T_{ma} + 5T_{sm} + 3T_{pa} = 366.0144$	$2T_{hz} + T_{hp} + 2T_{mm} + T_{ma} + 7T_{sm} + 4T_{pa} + T_{bp} = 466.9435$	$3T_{sm} + 2T_{pa} + T_{ma} + T_{hz} + 2T_{bp} = 179.6326$	$2|G_1| = 6144$	$|G_1| + |G_2| + |Z_q^*| = 6400$
[15]	$2T_{exp} + 3T_{bp} + 3T_{hp} + 3T_{sm} = 1046.2688$	$2T_{bp} + T_{exp} + 3T_{hp} + 3T_{sm} = 966.7076$	$2T_{exp} + 2T_{bp} + T_{sm} = 181.3541$	$2|G_1| + |G_2| = 9216$	$2|G_1| = 6144$
[17]	$3T_{sm} + 3T_{mm} + 3T_{bp} + 2T_{hp} + 3T_{hz} + 2T_{exp} + T_{pa} = 791.6640$	$3T_{mm} + 2T_{pa} + T_{hz} + 4T_{sm} + T_{bp} = 145.4540$	$T_{pa} + 2T_{bp} + T_{exp} + T_{sm} = 158.2581$	$2|G_1| + |G_2| = 9216$	$2|G_1| = 6144$
Ours	$2T_{sm} + T_{hz} + T_{hp} = 299.1500$	$3T_{sm} + 2T_{hz} + T_{hp} + T_{bp} = 377.7996$	$T_{bp} + T_{hz} = 56.4179$	$|G_1| = 3072$	$|G_1| + |Z_q^*| = 3328$

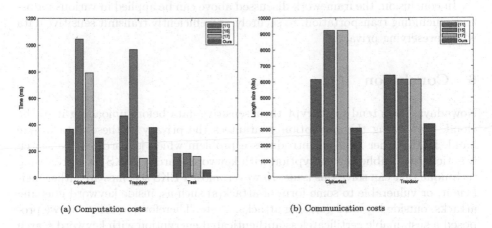

(a) Computation costs (b) Communication costs

Fig. 2. Experiment results

The receiver (traffic management system) generates a trapdoor based on the required traffic data and sends it to the cloud server as a search query. The cloud server then searches its database of ciphertexts for matches, and returns the corresponding data to the receiver.

Using a searchable encryption scheme, sensitive traffic data can be securely and efficiently transmitted from the data owner to the data receiver while preserving privacy. Additionally, the use of a cloud server allows for scalability, as the system can handle a large volume of data from multiple vehicles.

A real-world application of the scenario is in a smart city where traffic management systems can be optimized to improve traffic flow and reduce congestion. This framework can be used to collect and analyze traffic data from various sources, including buses, taxis, and private vehicles, to identify congested areas and adjust traffic signals. This could lead to a reduction in travel time, fuel consumption, and greenhouse gas emissions, resulting in a more sustainable and efficient transportation system.

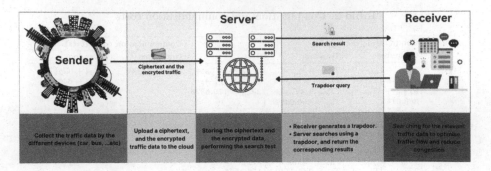

Fig. 3. The application of CLPAEKS

In conclusion, the framework discussed above can be applied in various industries, including transportation, to securely and efficiently transmit sensitive data while preserving privacy.

6   Conclusion

Nowadays, users tend to encrypt their sensitive data before uploading it to the cloud. Performing the encryption guarantees the privacy of these data in one hand. In the other hand, it introduces a problem which jeopardizes the search functionality. Public key encryption with keyword search (PEKS) is a promising technique that can solve this issue. However, most PEKS schemes are either inefficient, or vulnerable to some form of attack(s) such as, inside keyword guessing attacks, outside keyword guessing attacks,... etc. Therefore, in this work we proposed a sustainable certificateless authenticated encryption with keyword search scheme. a rigorous security analysis proved that our scheme can withstand both an online and offline keyword guessing attacks. Moreover, the proposed scheme can guarantee the multi-trapdoor indistinguishability in the certificateless primitive. Finally, the performance analysis performed yields to the conclusion that the proposed scheme is efficient and outperforms the other schemes.

References

1. Boneh, D., Di Crescenzo, G., Ostrovsky, R., Persiano, G.: Public key encryption with keyword search. In: Cachin, C., Camenisch, J.L. (eds.) EUROCRYPT 2004. LNCS, vol. 3027, pp. 506–522. Springer, Heidelberg (2004). https://doi.org/10.1007/978-3-540-24676-3_30
2. Baek, J., Safavi-Naini, R., Susilo, W.: Public key encryption with keyword search revisited. In: Gervasi, O., Murgante, B., Laganà, A., Taniar, D., Mun, Y., Gavrilova, M.L. (eds.) ICCSA 2008. LNCS, vol. 5072, pp. 1249–1259. Springer, Heidelberg (2008). https://doi.org/10.1007/978-3-540-69839-5_96

3. Byun, J.W., Rhee, H.S., Park, H.-A., Lee, D.H.: Off-line keyword guessing attacks on recent keyword search schemes over encrypted data. In: Jonker, W., Petković, M. (eds.) SDM 2006. LNCS, vol. 4165, pp. 75–83. Springer, Heidelberg (2006). https://doi.org/10.1007/11844662_6

4. Rhee, H.S., Park, J.H., Susilo, W., Lee, D.H.: Trapdoor security in a searchable public-key encryption scheme with a designated tester. J. Syst. Softw. **83**, 763–771 (2010). https://doi.org/10.1016/J.JSS.2009.11.726

5. Ma, S., Huang, Q., Zhang, M., Yang, B.: Efficient public key encryption with equality test supporting flexible authorization. IEEE Trans. Inf. Forensics Secur. **10**, 458–470 (2015). https://doi.org/10.1109/TIFS.2014.2378592

6. Fang, L., Susilo, W., Ge, C., Wang, J.: Public key encryption with keyword search secure against keyword guessing attacks without random oracle. Inf. Sci. **238**, 221–241 (2013). https://doi.org/10.1016/J.INS.2013.03.008

7. Peng, Y., Cui, J., Peng, C., Ying, Z.: Certificateless public key encryption with keyword search. China Commun. **11**, 100–113 (2014). https://doi.org/10.1109/CC.2014.7004528

8. Wu, T.Y., Meng, F., Chen, C.M., Liu, S., Pan, J.S.: On the security of a certificateless searchable public key encryption scheme. Adv. Intell. Syst. Comput. **536**, 113–119 (2016). https://doi.org/10.1007/978-3-319-48490-7_14

9. Senouci, M.R., Benkhaddra, I., Senouci, A., Li, F.: An efficient and secure certificateless searchable encryption scheme against keyword guessing attacks. J. Syst. Archit. **119**, 102271 (2021). https://doi.org/10.1016/J.SYSARC.2021.102271

10. Huang, Q., Li, H.: An efficient public-key searchable encryption scheme secure against inside keyword guessing attacks. Inf. Sci. **403–404**, 1–14 (2017). https://doi.org/10.1016/J.INS.2017.03.038

11. Wu, L., Zhang, Y., Ma, M., Kumar, N., He, D.: Certificateless searchable public key authenticated encryption with designated tester for cloud-assisted medical internet of things. Annales des Telecommunications/Ann. Telecommun. **74**, 423–434 (2019). https://doi.org/10.1007/S12243-018-00701-7

12. He, D., Ma, M., Zeadally, S., Kumar, N., Liang, K.: Certificateless public key authenticated encryption with keyword search for industrial internet of things. IEEE Trans. Ind. Inform. **14**, 3618–3627 (2018). https://doi.org/10.1109/TII.2017.2771382

13. Zhang, Y.L., Wen, L., Zhang, Y.J., Wang, C.F.: Deniably authenticated searchable encryption scheme based on blockchain for medical image data sharing. Multimed. Tools Appl. **79**, 27075–27090 (2020). https://doi.org/10.1007/S11042-020-09213-W

14. Ma, M., He, D., Khan, M.K., Chen, J. Certificateless searchable public key encryption scheme for mobile healthcare system. Comput. Electr. Eng. **65**, 413–424 (2018). https://doi.org/10.1016/J.COMPELECENG.2017.05.014

15. Wu, B., Wang, C., Yao, H.: Security analysis and secure channel-free certificateless searchable public key authenticated encryption for a cloud-based internet of things. PLOS ONE **15**, e0230722 (2020). https://doi.org/10.1371/JOURNAL.PONE.0230722

16. Qin, B., Chen, Y., Huang, Q., Liu, X., Zheng, D.: Public-key authenticated encryption with keyword search revisited: Security model and constructions. Inf. Sci. **516**, 515–528 (2020). https://doi.org/10.1016/J.INS.2019.12.063

17. Yang, G., Guo, J., Han, L., Liu, X., Tian, C.: An improved secure certificateless public-key searchable encryption scheme with multi-trapdoor privacy. Peer-to-Peer Network. Appl. **15**, 503–515 (2022). https://doi.org/10.1007/S12083-021-01253-9

454   M. R. Senouci et al.

18. Senouci, M.R., Benkhaddra, I., Senouci, A., Li, F.: A provably secure free-pairing certificateless searchable encryption scheme. Telecommun. Syst. (2022). https://doi.org/10.1007/s11235-022-00912-3
19. Al-Riyami, S.S., Paterson, K.G.: Certificateless public key cryptography. In: Laih, C.-S. (ed.) ASIACRYPT 2003. LNCS, vol. 2894, pp. 452–473. Springer, Heidelberg (2003). https://doi.org/10.1007/978-3-540-40061-5_29
20. PBC library - pairing-based cryptography. https://crypto.stanford.edu/pbc/
21. Keylength - NIST report on cryptographic key length and cryptoperiod (2020). https://www.keylength.com/en/4/

Machine Learning and Security

Anomaly Detection Method for Integrated Encrypted Malicious Traffic Based on RFCNN-GRU

Huiqi Zhao[✉], Yaowen Ma, Fang Fan, and Huajie Zhang

School of Intelligent Equipment, Shandong University of Science and Technology,
Tai'an 271000, China
zhqskd@163.com

Abstract. Although a lot of work has been devoted to the identification of malicious traffic, the identification methods for encrypted malicious traffic are few and weakly targeted, and traditional machine learning and single deep learning anomaly detection methods have been unable to achieve good results in encrypted malicious traffic. Therefore, this paper proposes an integrated deep learning anomaly detection method based on encrypted malicious traffic time series information according to the importance of features, which only considers statistical data and encrypted malicious traffic time series characteristics, without decrypting or using any payload information, so as to achieve high accuracy of encrypted malicious traffic anomaly detection. The integrated model is constructed by 1D Convolutional Neural Network, Gate Recurrent Unit and Random Forest. By analyzing the most informative features in encrypted network traffic data, the classification output value of the single feature group trained by CNN-GRU model is combined with the output probability of Random Forest Classifier according to weight. Ultimately, our model will select the detection class with the highest average output in the total classifier. The proposed RFCNN-GRU model can achieve high precision and strong robustness of encrypted malicious traffic anomaly detection under multi-classification.

Keywords: Encrypt malicious traffic · Abnormal detection · Timing information · RFCNN-GRU

1 Introduction

With the popularization of the Internet and the expansion of its application scope, network attacks have also become a serious security threat. Therefore, researchers continue to improve network intrusion detection technology and have achieved remarkable results [1–5]. However, due to the increasing demand for security and privacy protection, encrypted communication has become more and more common in the network, and has gradually become an important means of data protection. For certain types of traffic, encryption has even become a mandatory requirement of the law. Gartner has predicted that by 2021, 83% of traffic will be encrypted. It seems that the proportion of encrypted

H. Yang and R. Lu (Eds.): FCS 2023, CCIS 1992, pp. 457–471, 2024.
https://doi.org/10.1007/978-981-99-9331-4_30

traffic has far exceeded expectations. As of early 2023, up to 98% of web traffic will be encrypted. According to Google's network monitoring data, encrypted traffic accounts for more than 95% of the traffic flowing through Google servers [6].

Encrypted traffic was once considered the best security choice for online browsing and conducting business. However, with the development of network technology, most of today's network threats are also lurking in encrypted channels. Attackers use encryption technology to wrap malicious code on the surface In order to evade the detection and identification of the security protection system in the seemingly normal communication traffic on the Internet, so as to achieve the attack and intrusion on the target network. This attack method is highly stealthy and deceptive, and can effectively evade traditional network security protection measures, posing a huge challenge and threat to network security. According to Gartner statistics, more than 70% of malicious network attacks in 2020 used encrypted traffic technology, and encrypted attack traffic has gradually become an important means and link for APT attack organizations to attack. Zscaler released the "2022 State of Encryption Attack Report" [7], which analyzed 24 billion threats in a year from the beginning of the fourth quarter of 2021 to the end of the third quarter of 2022, revealing that HTTPS traffic including SSL and TLS details of the threat. The report shows that attacks using encrypted channels continue to rise from 57% in 2020 to more than 85% in 2022. Therefore, it is of great practical significance to efficiently identify encrypted malicious traffic. With more and more Internet applications implementing various encryptions at the network layer, transport layer, and application layer, from the perspective of network traffic, a hidden and opaque Internet world is being constructed. Traditional methods based on payload content analysis are becoming more and more ineffective, and more advanced machine learning and deep learning encrypted malicious traffic anomaly detection methods are receiving widespread attention.

2   Related Works

Identifying encrypted malicious traffic involves a complex task of massive data processing and analysis, which brings great challenges to anomaly detection. Compared with the traffic characteristics of the plaintext, the encrypted traffic characteristics change greatly, and cannot be detected and identified through the traditional attack payload matching method. At the same time, there are great differences between the encryption methods and encapsulation formats of different encryption protocols, which need to be considered specifically. Detection and discrimination strategy [8].

In recent years, researchers at home and abroad have conducted research on network-encrypted malicious traffic [9–14], and have made certain achievements. Shekhawat et al. [15] considered the problem of feature analysis in detail, applied three machine learning techniques to the problem of distinguishing malicious encrypted HTTP traffic from benign encrypted traffic, and obtained results comparable to previous work; Wang et al. [16] concluded A machine learning method for encrypted malicious traffic detection, analyzing and combining data sets from 5 different sources to generate a comprehensive and fair data set, implementing and comparing 10 encrypted malicious traffic detection algorithms, providing follow-up researchers Reference; Then a new concept of encrypted traffic characteristics specially used for encrypted malicious traffic analysis was proposed. A two-layer detection framework was formed by deep learning and traditional machine learning algorithms [17], which had good results on selected data sets.; Chen et al. [18] proposed an improved density peak clustering algorithm based on grid screening, custom center decision value and mutual neighbor degree, using a three-stage hierarchical sampling method to sample encrypted traffic data Further in-depth inspection of encrypted malicious traffic; Ferriyan et al. [19] proposed a method TLS2Vec to detect encrypted malicious traffic based on transport layer security hand-shake and payload function, without waiting for the traffic session to complete while protecting privacy; Yang et al. [20] proposed Deep Q Network and deep The encrypted traffic sample generation method of convolution generative confrontation network learns new samples from the training samples of encrypted traffic, so that the model has cer-tain self-learning and adaptive capabilities; Wang et al. [21] combined the two-layer attention mechanism of spatio-temporal features, Using 1D-CNN and BiGRU to extract the spatial features in encrypted traffic data packets and the temporal features between encrypted flows, respectively, has a good effect on fine-grained encrypted malicious traffic detection performance.

However, there are still problems to be solved and technologies that need to be improved urgently in the current research on the anomaly detection of encrypted mali-cious traffic. First, the real encrypted malicious traffic samples are fewer and the pro-portion is uneven, and the unbalanced data set will cause falsely high accuracy. In fact, the generalization ability of the model decreases, and the accuracy rate will not reflect the real performance of the model; second, the correlation between the feature vectors in the continuous time slots of encrypted malicious traffic is not fully utilized, and the traditional machine learning method or even a single The neural network model can no longer satisfy the in-depth mining of encrypted traffic feature information. The main contributions of this paper to the above problems are: Constructing a RFCNN-GRU model that can fully capture the correlation of feature vectors in timing information and analyzing the relationship between the three groups of features of packet group-ing, inter-arrival time, and packet flow in the detection of encrypted malicious traffic anomalies. The importance of features, finally, the output value of each feature group under the CNN-GRU model and the output probability of the random forest classifier are combined according to the weight to output the detection class with the highest average output in the total classifier; The undersampling method combined with the data set selective integration method constructs a multi-category encrypted malicious attack balance data set to demonstrate the advancement of the method proposed in this paper.

3 Encrypted Traffic Characteristics

The increasing amount of encrypted traffic in network traffic makes it more difficult to identify network traffic. In traditional network security, most threats come from plaintext traffic, such as HTTP, TCP, and UDP traffic. Although these protocols may also be used to launch attacks or transmit malicious data, they themselves have exposed some information between the two parties in the communication. In contrast, encrypted traffic not only protects the content of the communication, but also hides the metadata in the communication. The characteristic of encrypted traffic is that its payload or header fields are highly random and unpredictable, which makes traditional signature or rule-based detection methods unable to work effectively. Therefore, researchers began to try to extract statistical features and temporal features from encrypted traffic and apply them to machine learning or deep learning models [22–27].

Traffic features include statistical features and time series features. Statistical features mainly refer to features related to traffic size, distribution, frequency, etc., such as packet size distribution, transmission rate, traffic direction, etc. Statistical features have no specific restrictions on encrypted traffic. Experts in the field of traffic analysis have conducted in-depth research on statistical features of traffic, and found that statistical features are effective for traffic classification [22, 23].

However, some current research results cannot obtain good detection results in the anomaly detection of encrypted malicious traffic based on statistical characteristics, and many malicious attack methods may be more relevant to the characteristics of time series information. By analyzing the encrypted traffic, extracting the packet size on the timeline, inter-arrival time series, and data flow distribution data to obtain the important characteristics of the packet. The relevant characteristics are quite different in encrypted and unencrypted traffic. For the packet size distribution, the packet size in encrypted traffic usually has different distribution methods and ranges; for the interarrival time distribution, the interarrival time in encrypted traffic is usually larger than Plaintext traffic is more random; flow duration for encrypted traffic is typically longer than plaintext traffic for packet flow-related characteristics because it requires encryption and decryption operations for each packet.

Due to the continuous development of encryption algorithms and protocols, the detection accuracy of traditional machine learning and single deep learning methods may decrease over time. Therefore, it is also necessary to continuously update the feature set and train the model to improve the detection accuracy. In addition, because the characteristics of encrypted traffic make it difficult to conduct in-depth analysis and auditing, in some specific scenarios, it may be necessary to use other more complex technologies to achieve accurate identification and analysis of encrypted malicious traffic, where timing features are important in anomaly detection The application has gradually emerged [24–27].

4 Anomaly Detection Method of Encrypted Traffic Based on RFCNN-GRU Model

4.1 Encrypted Malicious Traffic Balance Dataset Construction

Constructing encrypted malicious traffic data sets is one of the most important tasks in the field of network communication security, but in current practical applications, the imbalance of encrypted malicious traffic data sets is extremely prominent. Encrypted malicious traffic imbalance refers to the imbalance in the number of samples between benign and malicious traffic types or malicious traffic types, such as a certain attack type has too many samples while other attack types have fewer samples. The imbalance of encrypted malicious traffic may lead to insufficient training of deep learning models, affecting the performance and accuracy of the models. Therefore, corresponding measures need to be taken to solve the imbalance problem of encrypted malicious traffic. Currently commonly used methods for processing unbalanced datasets include:

Under-sampling: Under-sampling is a technique for balancing a dataset by removing excess samples. This method can randomly delete a part of excessive samples so that all samples have a similar number. The under-sampling method is relatively simple and easy to implement, but some useful information may be lost, resulting in a decrease in model performance.

Oversampling: Oversampling is a technique for balancing a dataset by duplicating samples. This method can replicate too few samples so that all samples are of similar size. The oversampling method can increase the number of samples, but it may lead to the problem of overfitting so that the machine learning model cannot adapt to the new data well.

SMOTE (Synthetic Minority Over-sampling Technique): SMOTE is an algorithm based on the over-sampling technique [28], which balances the dataset by synthesizing minority class samples. When SMOTE is oversampling, it does not simply copy the minority class samples, but generates some new synthetic samples by calculating the gap between adjacent data points to maintain the diversity of the original data set and reduce the risk of overfitting.

However, in the model training process of encrypted malicious traffic anomaly detection, the more important point is the authenticity of the data. Real data provides real traffic characteristics in order to obtain a better detection rate. Among the above-mentioned currently commonly used methods for processing unbalanced datasets, the SMOTE algorithm, threshold-based sampling strategies, and meta-learning methods may neutralize the authenticity of the data, and a single under-sampling method may lose some useful information, resulting in a decline in model performance. Oversampling methods can lead to overfitting. In order to solve the extremely unbalanced problem of the current encrypted malicious traffic data set, this paper adopts the under-sampling method combined with the method of multi-data set integration to construct the data set. Among them, the normal traffic comes from the CICIDS2017 data set [29], which has a high degree of complexity and diversified network traffic, the malicious attack traffic part comes from CICIDS2017, and the rest comes from the attack traffic of CSE-CIC-IDS2018 [30]. Encrypted malicious traffic balance dataset. The proportion of attack samples before and after processing the balanced data set is shown in Fig. 1.

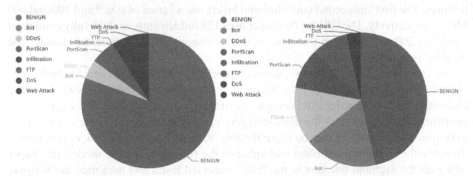

Fig. 1. A. On the left is the distribution of data samples before balance processing; B. The right side is the distribution of data samples before balance processing.

462 H. Zhao et al.

4.2 CNN-GRU Model

The deep learning architecture in this paper mainly uses the Convolutional Neural Network (CNN) and the Gated Recurrent Unit (GRU) for sequence classification. In our model, a 1D Convolutional Neural Network is applied to time-series features of encrypted malicious traffic to capture the correlation between feature vectors in consecutive time slots. The more traditional CNNs were chosen because they are good at recognizing simple patterns in data, and then using these simple patterns to generate more complex patterns in higher-level layers. Since encrypted malicious traffic itself cannot take advantage of the content characteristics of the payload, we hope to obtain directional features from fewer fragments of the overall timing features, so that it can also produce good training results in data fragments that are not highly correlated.

Gated Recurrent Units (GRUs) serve as a recurrent neural network that extends traditional feed-forward neural networks to sequences of variable length. GRUs handle these variable-length sequences by maintaining a hidden state whose activation depends on previous states. In this way, GRUs are able to adaptively capture correlations from time series data.

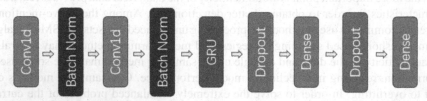

Fig. 2. Initially constructed CNN-GRU model. Including two layers of 1D Convolutional Neural Network, the Gated Recurrent Unit, and two layers of Fully Connected Layers.

In this paper, the preliminary deep learning model constructed by combining the Convolutional Neural Network and the Gated Recursive Unit to capture the features of the encrypted malicious traffic features is shown in Fig. 2. The model uses packet grouping, inter-arrival times, and data flow correlations represented in the time series as features. The first and second convolutional layers use a kernel of size 3 and 200 and 400 filters, respectively. The GRU in this paper uses 128 hidden units, and the fully connected layer has 200 and 9 hidden units, respectively, where 9 is the number of classes. The detailed parameters are shown in Table 1.

In order to reduce overfitting, dropout processing is required between fully connected layers. Finally, because the Sigmoid activation function has smooth nonlinear characteristics, it can reduce the complexity of the model and reduce the occurrence of overfitting. Combined with the multi-category classification characteristics of the Softmax function, the model can be more flexibly adapted to different task requirements. To solve the overfitting problem and enhance the robustness of the model, this paper first uses the Sigmoid function in the fully connected layer, and then uses the Softmax function in the output layer. In addition, the model introduces an early stopping mechanism, and sets the loss value of the verification set as a monitoring parameter. When the

Table 1. Initial CNN-GRU neural network structure.

Layer(type)	Input Shape	Output Shape
conv1d_1	(64, 30, 2)	(64, 28, 200)
batch_normalization_1	(64, 28, 200)	(64, 28, 200)
conv1d_2	(64, 28, 200)	(64, 26, 400)
batch_normalization_2	(64, 26, 400)	(64, 26, 400)
gru_1	(64, 26, 400)	(64, 128)
dropout_1	(64, 128)	(64, 128)
dense_1	(64, 128)	(64, 200)
dropout_2	(64, 200)	(64, 200)
dense_2	(64, 200)	(64, 9)

loss occurs in consecutive rounds and is no longer optimized, the training is stopped to improve the model's recognition effect and generalization ability.

4.3 CNN-GRU Model Ensemble Random Forest Optimization

The Gated Recurrent Unit and Convolutional Neural Network deep learning model preliminarily constructed above are still lacking in generalization ability and robustness. When there are many potential categories, the baseline GRU has high deviation and has a certain Performs poorly on unknown attack types with noise. In order to solve this problem, this paper introduces the random forest method with high recognition in the current research results to optimize the model through integration.

The architecture diagram of the RFCNN-GRU integrated model is shown in Fig. 3. Instead of training a single classifier on all three features, this paper creates separate classifiers to learn each feature of the ensemble approach. The rationale for the model is that each deep learning architecture can be trained to recognize different signals such that the ensemble of the three is robust over many possible signals. The final ensemble classifier in this paper simply selects the class with the highest Softmax probability after averaging among the three individual classes. In order to solve the problem of high deviation, the random forest method is integrated. In order to reduce the complexity of the model, the initial deep learning model is modified, a CNN layer is deleted, and only the dropout layer is processed for the inter-arrival time feature to speed up the training time.

The random forest classifier achieves more than 90% of the 10-fold cross-validation accuracy. To this end, this paper creates an ensemble of random forests using the optimal deep learning classifiers constructed above. This requires averaging the Softmax output from the CNN-RNN ensemble above with the log probability output from the Random Forest classifier provided by scikit-learn. Let RF(x), D1(x), D2(x), and D3(x) be the output probabilities of the random forest, packet grouping, data flow characteristics, and arrival time training classifiers, respectively. The final combined classifier is equivalent to selecting the predicted class with the highest average output among the four total classifiers. The weight formula of the combination classifier is shown in the following Formula 1.

$$P = \alpha * \sigma(RF) + \beta * \sigma(D_1) + \gamma * \sigma(D_2) + \delta * \sigma(D_3) \tag{1}$$

Among them, P is the prediction class with the highest average output, α, β, γ, δ, are constants, and the performance index of encrypted malicious traffic anomaly detection is given in the integrated model based on the preliminary single feature, $\sigma(RF)$, $\sigma(D_1)$, $\sigma(D_2)$ and $\sigma(D_3)$ are random forest, data packet grouping, data flow characteristics, and arrival time prediction values respectively.

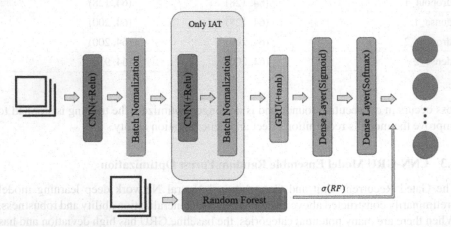

Fig. 3. RFCNN-GRU integrated model architecture diagram.

5 Experiment and Result Analysis

5.1 Experimental Configuration

All experiments in this section run on Windows 10 operating system. In terms of hardware, the CPU is 11th Gen Intel Core i7-11800H, and the memory is 16 GB. The experiment is accelerated by an NVIDIA RTX3060 with 6 GB of video memory. In terms of software, all experiments are completed using PyTorch.

5.2 Benchmark Model

In order to verify that the integrated deep learning model proposed in this paper has significant effectiveness in the multi-classification task of encrypted malicious traffic anomaly detection, the comparison model in this paper selects the machine learning method with good effect at present: Random Forest and K-nearest neighbor algorithm, unintegrated deep learning Gate Recurrent Unit and 1D Convolutional Neural Network model. In addition, the effects of the CNN-GRU model proposed by relevant scholars and the Long Short Term Memory model on anomaly detection of multiple classifications on the dataset in this paper are compared. By comparing their accuracy rate, accuracy rate, recall rate and F1 score values, the advanced nature of the proposed method is verified.

5.3 Evaluation Criteria

The evaluation indicators of traditional anomaly detection models include four main indicators: precision, accuracy, recall, and F1-score. In the specific detection results, T (true) and F (false) represent data that are classified correctly or incorrectly, respectively. P (positive) and N (negative) respectively indicate whether the prediction result of the detection system is abnormal data or normal data. All data in the dataset must be classified into four categories: TP, TN, FP, and FN. Only TP indicates that the classification result of the system contains abnormal attack data, and the classification result is correct; TN indicates that the classification result of the system is positive and correct; FP indicates that although the classification result is wrong, the system predicts that the data is abnormal attack data; FN indicates that although the classification result is not correct, the system predicts the data as normal. The classification result of the model to the data is represented by a confusion matrix, as shown in the following Table 2.

Table 2. List of predicted and actual situations.

Category	Predicted Positive Class	Predict Negative Class
Actual Positive Category	TP	FN
Actual Negative Category	FP	TN

The accuracy rate describes the ratio of the number of correctly predicted samples to the total number of samples, and the calculation formula is as follows:

$$\text{Accuracy} = \frac{TP + TN}{TP + FP + TN + FN} \tag{2}$$

Accuracy describes the ratio of the number of classes predicted to be positive to the number of classes actually predicted to be positive, the calculation formula is as follows:

$$\text{Precision} = \frac{TP}{TP + FP} \tag{3}$$

The recall rate describes that the number of predicted positive classes is actually the ratio of the number of positive classes to the number of all positive classes, and the calculation formula is as follows:

$$\text{Recall} = \frac{TP}{TP + FN} \tag{4}$$

The F1 score describes the size of the harmonic mean between precision and recall, and is calculated as follows:

$$F_1 - \text{score} = \frac{2 \times \text{recall} \times \text{precision}}{\text{recall} + \text{precision}} \tag{5}$$

5.4 Experimental Results and Analysis

Data Preprocessing
In this paper, data cleaning, feature extraction, feature selection, and data standardization are performed on the constructed encrypted malicious traffic data set to improve data quality and reduce noise, so as to maximize the performance and accuracy of the deep learning model. The data cleaning stage integrates data and eliminates illegal data, and cleans dirty data with NULL and Infiniti and illegal floating-point numbers in the data set out of the sample set. The initial data set is the original captured real data packet extracted by the open source tool CIC-flowmeter, and eighty-four statistical features are extracted. Considering the invisible characteristics of some encrypted traffic features and the time complexity of model training, the data set features are finally divided into packet grouping features, data flow features, and inter-arrival time series features under timing information. In the data normalization stage, one-hot encoding is performed on the non-numeric features in the discrete features, and Min-Max Normalization is used to normalize the input vector. The formula for Min-Max normalization is as follows, where x is the value before normalization, x_{max} and x_{min} represent the maximum and minimum values of the features in the data set, respectively.

$$x' = \frac{x - x_{min}}{x_{max} - x_{min}} \tag{6}$$

The preprocessed data set is divided into a training set and a test set. According to the number of samples in the data set and continuous experimental attempts in the early stage, this paper uses 70% of the samples for model training and 30% of the samples for testing the model. The statistics of various attack samples in the training set and test set are shown in Table 3.

Table 3. Statistics of samples of each category in the training set and test set.

	BENIGN	Bot	DDoS	PortScan	Infiltration	FTP	DoS	WebAttack
Train	524660	201710	153481	111251	65169	33355	36749	23738
Test	224854	86447	65778	47679	27930	14295	15749	10175

Feature Importance Evaluation
Before starting to compare the RFCNN-GRU deep learning method of feature integration, regarding the weight setting, we did relevant experiments to compare the classification of single features in the RF-CNNGRU model for packet grouping features, data flow features, and inter-arrival time series features. Effect to obtain the basis and specific value of the weight division. The evaluation indicators are precision, accuracy, recall and F1-score. Figure 4 shows the comparison of experimental results of three single-group features under the RFCNN-GRU model.

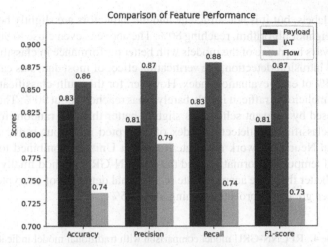

Fig. 4. Index comparison of a single-group feature under the RF-CNNGRU model.

Through the index comparison, it can be seen that the single-group feature of the inter-arrival time is higher than the single-group feature of packet grouping and data packet flow in terms of precision, accuracy, recall rate, and F1-score index, so the feature is the most important, while The feature importance of the packet flow is the weakest, so the weight of the combined classifier is specified according to the feature importance during feature integration, as shown in the following Formula 7.

$$P = \frac{1}{2} * \sigma(RF) + \frac{1}{6}\sigma(D_1) + \frac{1}{4}\sigma(D_2) + \frac{1}{12}\sigma(D_3) \tag{7}$$

Among them, the P combination classifier predicts the total probability value of multi-classification, $\sigma(RF)$ is the prediction probability value of the random forest classifier, and $\sigma(D_1)$, $\sigma(D_2)$, and $\sigma(D_3)$ are respectively based on the packet grouping characteristics and the inter-arrival time Features, data flow features single-group feature input RF-CNNGRU model prediction probability value.

Model Comparison Results
This article compares the proposed integrated model with a single 1D-CNN, GRU, LSTM model, and a traditional machine learning model with better results, and further verifies that the proposed RFCNN-GRU-based feature integration encrypted traffic anomaly detection method has a certain degree of advancement. The evaluation indicators are still precision, accuracy, recall, or F1-score, and the verification data is shown in Table 4. From the data in the table, it can be clearly concluded that the k-neighbor algorithm is the worst in terms of precision, accuracy, recall and F1 score, and the accuracy rate of less than 80% can further verify the importance of feature vector correlation extraction under time series information. Similar to the 1D Convolutional Neural Network, Gated Recurrent Unit and Long-term Short-term Memory Network, all capture the correlation between temporal

features and labels, but it is not sufficient, and the indicators are slightly better than the k-Nearest Neighbor algorithm, reaching 80%. The above is even close to 90%; Random forest has always been one of the models with better performance in classification tasks. In traditional intrusion detection, the verification effect of most data sets can even reach more than 95% of each evaluation index. However, for the multi-classification problem of encrypted malicious traffic, it is only barely It has reached about 90%; The CNN-GRU model proposed by relevant scholars is slightly better than the random forest method in the multi-classification detection index of encrypted malicious traffic after the 1D Convolutional Neural Network and Gate Recurrent Unit are combined to capture the correlation of temporal information; and the RFCNN-GRU method finally proposed in this paper is better than The accuracy rate of abnormal detection of encrypted malicious traffic has been greatly improved, reaching about 95%.

Table 4. RFCNN-GRU model comparison with traditional model indicators.

Model	Accuracy	Precision	Recall	F1-score
Random-Forest	0.89	0.90	0.89	0.88
k-NN	0.78	0.76	0.77	0.75
1D-CNN	0.88	0.85	0.86	0.84
GRU	0.89	0.91	0.90	0.89
LSTM	0.82	0.84	0.83	0.83
CNN-GRU	0.91	0.91	0.90	0.91
RFCNN-GRU	0.96	0.94	0.95	0.95

In order to more intuitively reflect the indicator gap between the models, a comparison chart of the visual evaluation indicators of each model is drawn, as shown in Fig. 5.

It is not difficult to see that due to the encryption of malicious traffic, the available features of the random forest and k-neighbor algorithms are significantly reduced, and a single deep learning model cannot fully extract the correlation between statistical features and time series features, so it is impossible to achieve future-proof analysis. Accuracy of Encrypted Malicious Traffic Detection. However, compared with the traditional model, the CNN-GRU model initially constructed in this paper has improved the visual indicators for the detection and classification of encrypted malicious traffic anomalies. There has been a significant improvement. It is more comprehensively verified that the RFCNN-GRU-based integrated encrypted malicious traffic anomaly detection method proposed in this paper has certain advanced.

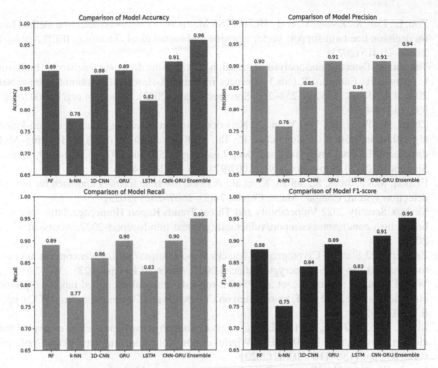

Fig. 5. Comparison chart of evaluation indicators of each model.

6 Conclusions and Future Work

The integrated deep learning anomaly detection method based on encrypted malicious traffic time series information proposed in this paper has good results in encrypted malicious traffic that has been learned in multiple categories. Constructing a balanced data set of malicious attack samples makes the accuracy index more meaningful for reference. The final model optimized by the 1D Convolutional Neural Network and the Gated Recurrent Unit integrated Random Forest realizes the encryption of malicious traffic under multi-classification by analyzing the most informative features of encrypted network traffic data. The high precision and strong robustness of anomaly detection have made some explorations for further improving the detection effect of encrypted malicious traffic. In the future work, there are still technical problems in anomaly detection of encrypted malicious traffic that need to be solved urgently. The detection of unknown attacks has always been a major difficulty in the field of anomaly detection of malicious attacks. Therefore, it is necessary to continue to explore encryption on the basis of current research detection methods for unknown attacks.

References

1. Qazi, E.U.H., Faheem, M.H., Zia, T.: HDLNIDS: hybrid deep-learning-based network intrusion detection system. Appl. Sci. **13**(8), 4921 (2023)

2. Zou, L., Luo, X., Zhang, Y., et al.: HC-DTTSVM: a network intrusion detection method based on decision tree twin support vector machine and hierarchical clustering. IEEE Access **11**, 21404–21416 (2023)
3. Takeda, A.: Detection and analysis of intrusion attacks using deep neural networks. In: Barolli, L., Miwa, H., Enokido, T. (eds.) Advances in Network-Based Information Systems. NBiS 2022. LNNS, vol. 526, pp. 258–266. Springer, Cham (2022). https://doi.org/10.1007/978-3-031-14314-4_26
4. Zhang, Y., Wang, D., Wu, Y., et al.: Network intrusion detection based on apriori-kmeans algorithm. In: Jain, L.C., Kountchev, R., Tai, Y., Kountcheva, R. (eds.) 3D Imaging–Multidimensional Signal Processing and Deep Learning. SIST, vol. 297, pp. 101–109. Springer, Singapore (2022). https://doi.org/10.1007/978-981-19-2448-4_10
5. Farooq, M.S., Abbas, S., Sultan, K., et al.: A fused machine learning approach for intrusion detection system. Comput. Mater. Contin. **74**(2), 2607–2623 (2023)
6. Skybox Security 2022 Vulnerability and Threat Trends Report Homepage. https://www.skyboxsecurity.com/resources/report/vulnerability-threat-trends-report-2022. Accessed 12 Apr 2023
7. Zscaler 2022 State of Cryptographic Attacks Report. https://info.zscaler.com/resources-industry-reports-the-state-of-encrypted-attacks-2022. Accessed 16 Apr 2023
8. Wu, H., Cui, C., Cheng, G., et al.: PSCM: towards practical encrypted unknown protocol classification. In: 2022 IEEE Symposium on Computers and Communications (ISCC), pp. 1–6. IEEE (2022)
9. Liu, J., Xiao, Q., Jiang, Z., et al.: Effectiveness evaluation of evasion attack on encrypted malicious traffic detection. In: 2022 IEEE Wireless Communications and Networking Conference (WCNC), pp. 1158–1163. IEEE (2022)
10. Liu, J., Wang, L., Hu, W., et al.: Spatial-temporal feature with dual-attention mechanism for encrypted malicious traffic detection. Secur. Commun. Netw. **2023** (2023)
11. Zheng, J., Zeng, Z., Feng, T.: GCN-ETA: high-efficiency encrypted malicious traffic detection. Secur. Commun. Netw. **2022**, 1–11 (2022)
12. Tang, Z., Wang, J., Yuan, B., et al.: Markov-GAN: Markov image enhancement method for malicious encrypted traffic classification. IET Inf. Secur. **16**(6), 442–458 (2022)
13. Zhou, Y., Shi, H., Zhao, Y., et al.: Identification of encrypted and malicious network traffic based on 1D convolutional neural networkal neural network. J. Cloud Comput. **12**(1), 1–10 (2023)
14. Ren, G., Cheng, G., Fu, N.: Accurate encrypted malicious traffic identification via traffic interaction pattern using graph convolutional network. Appl. Sci. **13**(3), 1483 (2023)
15. Shekhawat, A.S., Di Troia, F., Stamp, M.: Feature analysis of encrypted malicious traffic. Expert Syst. Appl. **125**, 130–141 (2019)
16. Wang, Z., Fok, K.W., Thing, V.L.L.: Machine learning for encrypted malicious traffic detection: approaches, datasets and comparative study. Comput. Secur. **113**, 102542 (2022)
17. Wang, Z., Thing, V.L.L.: Feature mining for encrypted malicious traffic detection with deep learning and other machine learning algorithms. Comput. Secur. **128**, 103143 (2023)
18. Chen, L., Gao, S., Liu, B., et al.: THS-IDPC: a three-stage hierarchical sampling method based on improved density peaks clustering algorithm for encrypted malicious traffic detection. J. Supercomput. **76**, 7489–7518 (2020)
19. Ferriyan, A., Thamrin, A.H., Takeda, K., et al.: Encrypted malicious traffic detection based on Word2Vec. Electronics **11**(5), 679 (2022)
20. Yang, J., Liang, G., Li, B., et al.: A deep-learning-and reinforcement-learning-based system for encrypted network malicious traffic detection. Electron. Lett. **57**(9), 363–365 (2021)
21. Wang, L., Cheng, J., Zhang, R., et al.: Spatio-temporal feature encryption malicious traffic detection via attention mechanism. In: 2022 IEEE 10th International Conference on Information, Communication and Networks (ICICN), pp. 51–56. IEEE (2022)

22. Yan, H., He, L., Song, X., et al.: Bidirectional statistical feature extraction based on time window for tor flow classification. Symmetry **14**(10), 2002 (2022)
23. Shi, Z., Luktarhan, N., Song, Y., et al.: TSFN: a novel malicious traffic classification method using BERT and LSTM. Entropy **25**(5), 821 (2023)
24. Lee, J.M., Kim, J.D.: A generative model for traffic demand with heterogeneous and spatiotemporal characteristics in massive Wi-Fi systems. Electronics **11**(12), 1848 (2022)
25. Tang, H., Wang, Q., Jiang, G.: Time series anomaly detection model based on multi-features. Comput. Intell. Neurosci. **2022** (2022)
26. Park, J., Park, Y., Kim, C.I.: TCAE: temporal convolutional autoencoders for time series anomaly detection. In: 2022 Thirteenth International Conference on Ubiquitous and Future Networks (ICUFN), pp. 421–426. IEEE (2022)
27. Xu, L., Ding, X., Zhao, D., et al.: A three-dimensional ResNet and transformer-based approach to anomaly detection in multivariate temporal-spatial data. Entropy **25**(2), 180 (2023)
28. Chawla, N.V., Bowyer, K.W., Hall, L.O., et al.: SMOTE: synthetic minority over-sampling technique. J. Artif. Intell. Res. **16**, 321–357 (2002)
29. Sharafaldin, I., Lashkari, A.H., Ghorbani, A.A.: Toward generating a new intrusion detection dataset and intrusion traffic characterization. ICISSp **1**, 108–116 (2018)
30. Malaiya, R.K., Kwon, D., Suh, S.C., et al.: An empirical evaluation of deep learning for network anomaly detection. IEEE Access **7**, 140806–140817 (2019)

TimeGAN: A Novel Solution to Imbalanced Encrypted Traffic Datasets

Hao Liu, Yong Zeng[✉], Tianci Zhou, Zhihong Liu, and Jianfeng Ma

Xidian University, Xi'an 710126, Shaanxi, People's Republic of China
yzeng@mail.xidian.edu.cn

Abstract. Currently, the performance of machine learning-based encrypted traffic recognition models is always unsatisfactory on imbalanced datasets. Existing methods neglected the time series features in the traffic. To solve this problem, this paper proposes TimeGAN, an encrypted traffic time series feature generation model based on dilated convolutional network. Our model not only adopts the advantages of generative adversarial networks (GANs) to model the distribution of time series features of encrypted traffic, but also adopts the structure of dilated convolutional network, which can characterize the causal sequence relationship of traffic sending behavior and generate traffic time series feature data that is closest to the real distribution. We evaluated the performance of the model on three public datasets, and the results showed that our model outperformed all existing models.

Keywords: Encrypted traffic · Imbalanced dataset · Dilated convolution · GAN

1 Introduction

With the rapid development of the Internet, encrypted traffic is widely used in network environments. Encrypted traffic identification has become an important component of network traffic analysis [1]. Existing research mainly uses encrypted traffic features combined with machine learning models to classify traffic. These studies first extract feature information from the transmission process of encrypted traffic into feature vectors, and then input the feature vectors into machine learning models for classification to achieve encrypted traffic identification.

However, the accuracy of encrypted traffic identification is often limited by the problem of data imbalance [2]. The problem of data imbalance in encrypted traffic refers to the difference in the number of samples of each category of traffic in the encrypted traffic dataset, with some minority class samples being insufficient. This leads to low recognition ability of machine learning models on minority class encrypted traffic samples, which damages the overall classification performance.

The main reason for the impact of data imbalance on traffic classification performance in encrypted traffic is that most machine learning models use back-propagation algorithm for parameter updating and model tuning. Each round

H. Yang and R. Lu (Eds.): FCS 2023, CCIS 1992, pp. 472–486, 2024.
https://doi.org/10.1007/978-981-99-9331-4_31

of iteration requires randomly sampling a certain proportion of samples from the dataset. In this process, the majority class is more likely to be selected, and therefore the weight of the majority class will continue to increase in back-propagation, making the model more and more biased towards the majority class. On the contrary, the probability of selecting the minority class is low in the back-propagation algorithm, and it is extremely easy to be influenced by the majority class samples. As the training process is repeated, the machine learning model will ultimately completely bias towards the majority class and ignore the minority class.

To address this issue, there are mainly three approaches [3] proposed in existing research, there are: data sampling, model improvement, and using GANs to generate small sample traffic data.

The main idea of data sampling techniques [4,5] is to balance the distribution of data by oversampling or undersampling. However, the quality of generated samples from the sampling scheme is highly dependent on the selected sample center points. If the feature data selected as the sampling basis is inappropriate, it may make it difficult for the model to characterize the distribution state of this type of sample. Therefore, the above solution is not widely applicable.

The method of model improvement [6–8] based on model refinement mainly improves the accuracy of detection by adding attention mechanisms to the model or using multi-modal model structures to learn the distribution characteristics of small sample traffic data. However, this will increase the complexity of the model, and models that are too complex often lead to overfitting, making it difficult for the model to have better classification performance in practical applications.

The method of generating small sample data [9–13] involves using GANs to learn the distribution characteristics of the sample data through adversarial learning. The networks are trained to generate data from the perspective of the data distribution, which enhances the representation effect of the small sample flow. By using GANs, the distribution characteristics of encrypted traffic data can be fully learned, and the networks can generate the required flow feature data according to the pattern, resulting in a good representation effect.

Based on the ideas above, to capture the feature of temporal sequence sending behavior we propose TimeGAN, a generative adversarial model for generating encrypted traffic time series features based on dilated convolution. In particular, we embedded a dilated convolutional network structure into TimeGAN, which can adaptively learn the distribution characteristics of small sample traffic features and use these features to generate more realistic small sample flow data in generation stage. The dilated convolutional network is a convolutional neural network model that is friendly to the calculation of temporal features. It not only allows the model to focus on the temporal distribution characteristics of the features, but also can model traffic features at a lower time complexity compared with models such as RNN and LSTM. Overall, TimeGAN can improve the representation effectiveness of traffic data from the perspectives of sample quantity and feature distribution, thus enhancing the classifier's ability to classify small sample traffic. The contributions of our work are as follows:

- **Time series based:** We propose an enhancement to the GAN model by incorporating the dilated convolutional network which can capture the causal relationship of temporal features in network traffic. This structure aids in representing traffic data with an adaptive encoding model, leading to better classification of imbalanced traffic datasets.
- **SOTA performance:** We evaluate our model on three imbalanced network traffic datasets. We use TimeGAN to fill in missing data and generate additional samples which can enhance the representation capability of small samples. Finally, we get state of the art (SOTA) results on three datasets and demonstrate the effectiveness and advantages of our model.

2 Related Works

There are three main approaches for dealing with imbalanced encrypted traffic data: data sampling, model improvement, and generating small samples. This article will introduce each of these methods separately.

Data Sampling: Data sampling includes oversampling and undersampling. The main idea of oversampling is to generate similar data based on some rules from the original small sample traffic data, aiming to increase the amount of data and make the model focus on the small sample classes. The main strategy for undersampling is to select some of the data from the large sample traffic data and combine it with the small sample data to create a new dataset. In practice, the main approach is oversampling or a combination of both oversampling and undersampling. Pan et al. [4] addressed the problem of imbalanced distribution of encrypted traffic data using the SMOTE oversampling technique. The main idea of this oversampling technique is to generate similar traffic data based on the k-nearest neighbors of the target sample, thereby generating small sample traffic data and improve accuracy. Chen et al. [5] first used the SMOTE oversampling model to supplement the small sample data, and then further identified the encrypted traffic using a clustering model that maximizes mutual information and an SVM feature classification model. Although the studies mentioned above have solved the problem of imbalanced distribution of traffic data to some extent using oversampling techniques, the quality of the generated traffic data based on the sampling strategy is highly dependent on the selected sample center points, so the effect of the studies above is not stable.

Model Improvement: The main idea of improving the traffic distribution imbalance through model improvement is to use multi-modal model structures to learn the distribution characteristics of small sample traffic. Tang et al. [6] adopted a multi-model coupling scheme to solve the problem of imbalanced distribution, where they integrated multiple models and finally coupled the classification results of each model to achieve identification of small sample traffic data. Wu et al. [7] proposed a traffic classification model DNN-BTF, which combines CNN and RNN networks and can further utilize traffic features based on the combination of temporal and spatial features, thereby improving classification efficiency. Zhang et al. [8] constructed the parallel cross-correlation neural network PCCN, which significantly improved the characterization ability of small sample traffic by fusing the flow characteristics learned by two branch networks, thereby solving the problem of uneven distribution. However, model integration and algorithm improvement inevitably increase the complexity of the model, and the model with too much complexity often leads to overfitting.

GAN for Traffic Data Generation: The main idea of using GAN to generate small sample data to solve the problem of imbalanced traffic data is to use GAN for adversarial learning of the distribution characteristics of sample data, and generate data from the perspective of data distribution to enhance the representation effect of small sample traffic. Guo et al. [11] proposed ITCGAN, which uses a combination of one-dimensional convolutional neural networks and linear layers to construct a generative adversarial network (GAN), and then generates the first 784 bytes of encrypted traffic data packets to solve the problem of small sample representation of traffic. Wang et al. [9] converted traffic data packets into binary byte vectors and used a GAN model to generate the overall content of the data packets, surpassing ITCGAN in terms of the number of classification categories and accuracy. Wang et al. [10] used a generative network model with constraint conditions to constrain the traffic data generated by the GAN model, and the experimental results were significantly better than oversampling schemes such as ROS and SMOTE. Sychugov et al. [12] used WGAN to generate traffic samples. Compared with the original GAN model, the improved WGAN can better solve the problem of gradient disappearance in the original model, and therefore has better training effects. Li et al. [13] constructed input vectors based on the sending characteristics of data packets in network flow sequences, and then used a GAN model to generate obfuscated traffic data to evade traffic inspection.

The above research shows that GANs can fully learn the distribution characteristics of encrypted traffic data, and thus generate the required traffic feature data based on patterns. In addition, existing methods neglected the time series features of the traffic. Therefore, this study also focuses on the advantages of GAN models in order to build causal relationships of traffic temporal features and better address the problem of imbalanced encrypted traffic data.

3 Background Knowledge

In this chapter we introduce the relevant knowledge of GANs and causal dilated convolution.

3.1 WGAN

In 2014, Goodfellow et al. [14] first proposed the generative adversarial network (GAN), which provided a new way to generate data samples. By training two models: the generator (G) and the discriminator (D), GAN can generate completely new data based on the existing sample distribution. In this process, the

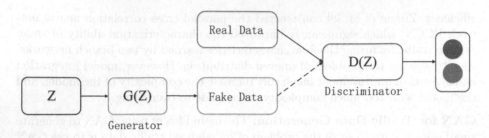

Fig. 1. Generative Adversarial Network

generator and discriminator can reach Nash equilibrium through games and generate high-quality samples that are difficult to distinguish from the original data (Fig. 1).

In 2017, Martin et al. [15] proposed an improvement to the GAN model, which mainly targets the loss function of the traditional GAN model. They analyzed the structure and loss function of the original GAN and proposed that the optimal solution of the original GAN model is mainly achieved by calculating JS divergence. However, in the actual training process, JS divergence will inevitably make the loss function tend to a constant during training, resulting in the problem of gradient disappearance. Therefore, they used Wasserstein distance as the loss function of the model. This distance function can estimate the minimum cost required for noise data to be transformed into real data samples, rather than measuring the distance between the generated data distribution and the real data distribution. By modifying the loss function, the GAN model is easier to train. The loss function of WGAN after improvement can be expressed by the following formula.

$$W(G, D) = \frac{1}{K} \sup E_{x \sim p_{\text{duta}}(x)}[f(x)] - E_{z \sim p_z(z)}[f(x)] \tag{1}$$

3.2 Dilated Convolutional Network

In previous deep learning research, researchers often believed that RNN or LSTM is more suitable for processing sequences, especially time series problems. However, in the actual application process, RNN and LSTM often require more training time to process longer sequences due to their structural features. Moreover, they are prone to the problem of gradient disappearance during training. Therefore, some studies have proposed using improved convolutional network models to process sequence problems. Causal convolutional networks can increase the receptive field by moving the convolution window, thereby achieving the correlation between sequence features. This structure has superior performance in processing time series problems.

From the structure in Fig. 2, it can be seen that the output of each layer is obtained by the input of this position in the previous layer and the input of the previous position. After the model is stacked multiple times, the causal

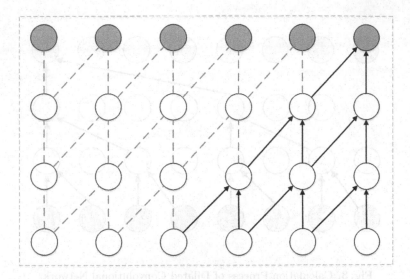

Fig. 2. Calculation Process of Causal Convolutional Network

connections established with previous positions become stronger, thereby solving the problem of time prediction using convolutional networks. However, this structure also has a disadvantage: the expansion speed of the causal convolution receptive field is too slow. If a larger range of causal feature associations needs to be achieved, multiple layers of network structures need to be stacked. However, this will also bring high time complexity and gradient disappearance problems. To further improve this problem, some studies have proposed a dilated convolution structure. This structure achieves fast expansion of causal convolution by skipping some units in the hidden layer of the causal convolution network, thereby solving the problem of deep stacking of causal convolution models.

Figure 3 shows the structure of the dilated convolution network. In the schematic diagram, by skipping some data in the middle hidden layer, the receptive field of the data is doubled in the same four-layer model. The structure of the dilated convolution solves the problem of too many model layers caused by the slow expansion of the causal convolution receptive field, thereby saving the model's computing resources and ensuring the robustness of the model during training.

4 Model

In this section, we show how to construct the feature sequence and the structure of TimeGAN.

4.1 Feature Construction

For the collected voice traffic packets, we first select and construct the features. The features are labeled as a tuple of the form $< s, d >$, where s represents the

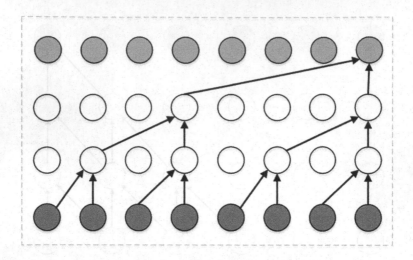

Fig. 3. Calculation Process of Dilated Convolutional Network

size of the packets and d represents the sending directions of the packets. We specify that the sending direction of packets sent from the smart speaker to the server is represented as 1, and the opposite direction is represented as -1.

The features of the traffic packets are integrated for different voice commands, and we will get the sequence of packet features, which can be expressed as follow.

$$F_c = << s_1, d_1 >, < s_2, d_2 >, \ldots, < s_n, d_n >>$$

where s_i and d_i represent the size and transmission direction of the $i-th$ packet. Based on the above data format, we can integrate the input traffic features into the following form. The data format contains both transmission direction and packet size.

Data Format: $SD_p = < s_1 * d_1, s_2 * d_2, \ldots, s_n * d_n >$

4.2 Our Model

In the previous section, this article mainly introduced the relevant background knowledge of GANs and Causal Convolutions. The intrinsic correlation and distribution characteristics of encrypted traffic behavior features can be modeled by relying on GAN models and deep neural network structures, so as to construct this feature. Therefore, this study proposes a GAN based on Temporal Feature Encoding (TimeGAN). This algorithm can use causal convolution structure to encode and construct the causal distribution characteristics of traffic sending behavior.

Figure 4 shows the basic structure of TimeGAN. The model is divided into two main parts. The generator G(z) is mainly constructed by a one-dimensional deconvolution oversampling model, and the discriminator D(z) is mainly constructed by an dilated convolutional model. The model first trains the discriminator with real traffic data, then generates Gaussian noise and inputs it into the

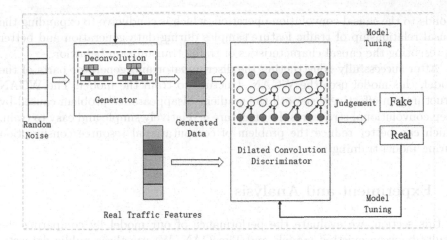

Fig. 4. Model Structure of TimeGAN

generator to construct "fake" traffic data. Finally, the generated traffic data is given to the discriminator for judgment, and the model is trained according to the results.

The main function of the discriminator shown in Fig. 4 is to extract the temporal distribution characteristics of encrypted traffic sequence features and then distinguish the traffic samples generated by the generator according to the distribution of each traffic temporal feature. This helps the generator to encode temporal features. In this model, we use an dilated convolutional model to construct the temporal features of encrypted traffic. The dilated convolutional model can model the causal relationship of temporal features and extract the hidden features of traffic sending behavior. In Sect. 3 of this study, we have explained that modeling the distribution characteristics of encrypted traffic temporal features can further analyze the behavioral differences of different traffic during transmission, thereby providing a basis for accurate classification of traffic. Therefore, using dilated convolutional encoding for the temporal features of traffic sending can further judge the effect of the generator and improve the authenticity of generated samples.

The main function of the generator shown in Fig. 4 is to generate encrypted traffic sample data based on the input Gaussian noise. In the generator, this model uses a one-dimensional deconvolution structure to expand Gaussian noise into encrypted traffic temporal feature data. Deconvolution, also known as transposed convolution, is the opposite of convolution operation. It can generate or restore high-dimensional data based on low-dimensional input data. In this model, using deconvolution as the main structure of the generator has two reasons: (1) Compared with traditional linear layers, the operation structure of convolutional layers makes it possible to construct feature data for generating non-linear features. This also provides the possibility of further establishing complex relationships between features. (2) The deconvolution operation corresponds to the causal convolution operation, which is conducive to expanding the causal relationship of traffic feature samples during data generation and better representing the causal characteristics of traffic transmission behavior.

After successfully constructing the discriminator and generator parts of the model, this model uses the WGAN structure to train the model. The WGAN structure can effectively smooth the gradient disappearance problem caused by deep convolutional structures. Its structure is relatively simple and easy to train, which can better reduce the problem of computational resource consumption during model training.

5 Experiment and Analysis

In this section, we evaluate the performance of our model by comparing the results between existing models and TimeGAN. We use three public datasets, namely, CIC-AAGM2017 [16], CIC-AndMAL2017 [17] and ISCX-nonTor2016 [18]. Please note that, all these datasets are imbalanced, the distribution of these datasets are shown in Table 1, Table 2 and Table 3. For existing models, we choose SMOTE and FLOWGAN. As we summarized in Sect. 2, FLOWGAN proposed by Wang et al. [9] converts traffic data packets into binary byte vectors and uses a GAN model to generate the overall content of the data packets. SMOTE [19] according to the idea of random oversampling to generate approximate data of original samples.

Table 1. CIC-AAGM2017 dataset distribution

Traffic type	#Encrypted flow sequence	Proportion (%)
Benign	44258	58.41%
Adware	30968	40.87%
General Malware	539	7.29%
Total	75765	100%

5.1 Evaluation Metrics

For evaluation metrics, we use Accuracy, F_1 score and mAP [20]. These indicators are commonly used in the field of machine learning to evaluate the classification performance of models. They not only reflect the overall accuracy of the model's classification samples, but also reflect the classification performance of the classification model on all categories and the degree of attention the model pays to data in each category.

Table 2. CIC-AndMAL2017 dataset distribution

Traffic type	#Encrypted flow sequence	Proportion (%)
Adware	68728	26.88%
Ransomware	69112	27.03%
SMSMalware	44299	17.32%
Scareware	73538	28.77%
Total	255677	100%

Table 3. ISCX-nonTor2016 dataset distribution

Traffic type	#Encrypted flow sequence	Proportion
Audio	864	4.28%
Browsing	9215	45.67%
Chat	119	0.58%
Email	152	0.75%
FTP	2317	11.48%
P2P	6496	32.19%
Video	820	4.06%
Voip	191	0.99%
Total	20174	100%

5.2 Experiment Results and Analysis

In this section, we verify the effectiveness of the TimeGAN model by using it
to fill three imbalanced traffic datasets. We will compare the effectiveness of
TimeGAN with other models to demonstrate its effectiveness.

From the results shown in Table 4, it can be seen that directly applying the
classification model to the three imbalanced datasets does not lead to satisfactory
identification results. Especially, the F1 and mAP indicators of the model have
relatively low values on all three datasets, indicating that the traffic data of small
sample classes has not been correctly classified.

Figure 5 shows the specific classification results, where (a)–(c) represent
the confusion matrices of the proposed model on the CIC-AAGM2017, CIC-
AndMAL2017, and ISCX-nonTor2016 datasets, respectively. As shown in (a) of
Fig. 5, it can be observed that all 108 flow data in the General Malware category
of the CIC-AAGM2017 dataset were misclassified. Similarly, the SMSMalware
category in CIC-AndMAL2017 and the Audio, Chat, and Video categories in
ISCX-nonTor2016 also encountered this problem. This indicates that the classification model struggles to accurately represent small-scale traffic data.

Table 4. Classification accuracy before data balance

	CIC-AAGM2017	CIC-AndMAL2017	ISCX-nonTor2016
Accuracy	83.55%	67.91%	74.24%
F1	0.8095	0.6467	0.7191
mAP	0.6968	0.5036	0.3621

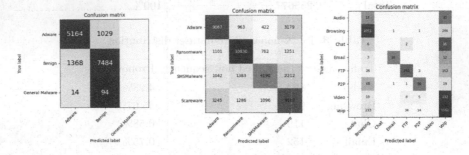

Fig. 5. Confusion Matrix

Next, we use the TimeGAN model to fill and balance the dataset. In view of the sample size of the original dataset, we appropriately undersample the samples in the larger categories and generate samples in the smaller categories to achieve a balanced traffic data sample. We balance the number of each type of sample in the CIC-AAGM2017 dataset to 30,000, balance the number of each type of sample in the CIC-AndMal2017 dataset to 60,000, and balance the number of each type of sample in the ISCX-nonTor2016 dataset to 6,000, to achieve absolute balance in the original sample distribution. In addition, we also compare our model with the SMOTE model and the FLOWGAN model to demonstrate the advantages of our proposed model.

Table 5. Experiment Result (Accuracy)

	TimeGAN	SMOTE	FLOWGAN
CIC-AAGM2017	99.96%	96.02%	79.23%
CIC-AndMal2017	81.47%	64.17%	75.07%
ISCX-nonTor2016	97.49%	92.69%	93.64%

Table 5 shows the comparison of TimeGAN, SMOTE, and FLOWGAN in terms of accuracy. First, it can be seen from the experimental results that, under the condition of using the same adaptive encoding model to encode and classify traffic time series features, the prediction accuracy of the TimeGAN model on the three datasets has increased by 16.4%, 13.96%, and 23.22%, respectively, compared to the original imbalanced set with a Gaussian distribution. This indicates that TimeGAN can effectively improve the prediction accuracy. Secondly, by comparing the classification results horizontally on the same dataset, it can be seen that TimeGAN has significant advantages over the other two models in handling imbalanced data. This indicates that compared to SMOTE sample generation method relying on clustering and FLOWGAN generation algorithm using linear layers to generate traffic samples, TimeGAN can better capture the distribution characteristics and causal relationships of traffic data features, thereby generating more helpful traffic data for small sample representation.

Table 6. Experiment Result (F1 and mAP)

	TimeGAN		SMOTE		FLOWGAN	
	F1	mAP	F1	mAP	F1	mAP
CIC-AAGM2017	0.9996	0.9994	0.9602	0.9354	0.7525	0.6976
CIC-AndMAL2017	0.8142	0.7118	0.6413	0.5050	0.7521	0.6313
ISCX-nonTor2016	0.9550	0.9553	0.9279	0.8724	0.9366	0.8866

Table 6 presents a comparison of TimeGAN, SMOTE, and FLOWGAN in terms of F1 and mAP scores. The data in the table shows that the TimeGAN oversampling model performs significantly better than the SMOTE oversampling model and the FLOWGAN model in both of these evaluations, with a more significant improvement in the mAP score. Therefore, it can be concluded that the TimeGAN model's classification performance across all categories is significantly better than the other two models, and it also demonstrates the reliability of generating sample data.

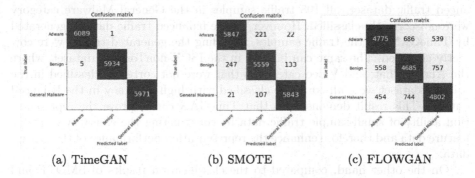

(a) TimeGAN   (b) SMOTE   (c) FLOWGAN

Fig. 6. CIC-AAGM2017 Confusion Matrix

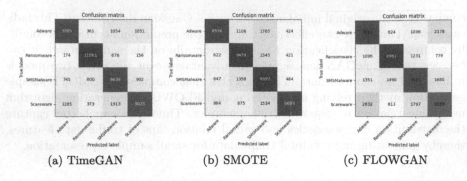

(a) TimeGAN   (b) SMOTE   (c) FLOWGAN

Fig. 7. CIC-AndMAL2017 Confusion Matrix

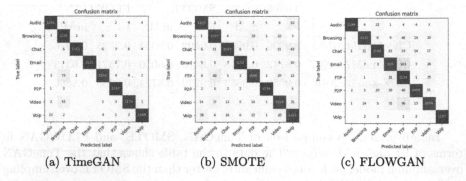

(a) TimeGAN   (b) SMOTE   (c) FLOWGAN

Fig. 8. ISCX-nonTor2016 Confusion Matrix

Figure 6, 7 and 8 show the confusion matrices of the classification results using the CIC-AAGM2017 dataset as an example. Compared with the experimental results on the imbalanced traffic dataset shown in Fig. 5, in the imbalanced traffic dataset, all 108 traffic samples in the General Malware category were not correctly classified. However, in the balanced traffic dataset generated by TimeGAN, all the traffic samples, including the generated traffic, were correctly classified. The same can be seen in the ISCX-nonTor2016 dataset, where the Audio, Chat, and Video categories that were not correctly classified in the original dataset were all correctly classified with high accuracy in the balanced dataset. This result demonstrates that TimeGAN can improve the representation ability of small-sample traffic data by constructing the causality of traffic feature data and therefore enhance the representation performance of the feature data.

On the other hand, compared to the classification results of SMOTE and FLOWGAN, TimeGAN also shows significant improvement in the classification performance across all categories. In CIC-AndMal2017 dataset, the classification results of SMOTE oversampling show that over 3000 data points in each category are misclassified. Although this is improved in the FLOWGAN model, there still exists large bias in the prediction results for the SMSMalware category. In contrast, the TimeGAN model shows significantly better prediction results for each category compared to these two models, demonstrating its advantage in dealing with imbalanced flow data.

6   Conclusion

This paper proposes a TimeGAN model based on time series feature encoding for the existing encrypted traffic dataset with Gaussian distribution. The model uses an dilated network to encode the causal relationship of traffic time series features and further uses the model to generate traffic sending behavior features to solve the problem of insufficient recognition of small sample traffic with Gaussian distribution in encrypted traffic datasets. In the experimental part, this paper combines the encrypted traffic generation model with the adaptive coding model to achieve accurate identification of encrypted traffic data and compares it with relevant research schemes. The proposed flow generation algorithm can adaptively learn the feature distribution of encrypted traffic, thereby improving the prediction accuracy.

Acknowledgements. We would like to thank the anonymous reviewers for their careful reading of our manuscript and their constructive comments.

References

1. Aceto, G., Ciuonzo, D., Montieri, A., Pescapè, A.: Mimetic: mobile encrypted traffic classification using multimodal deep learning. Comput. Netw. **165**, 106944 (2019). https://doi.org/10.1016/j.comnet.2019.106944. https://www.sciencedirect.com/science/article/pii/S1389128619304669
2. Japkowicz, N., Stephen, S.: The class imbalance problem: a systematic study. Intell. Data Anal. **6**(5), 429–449 (2002)
3. Vu, L., Van Tra, D., Nguyen, Q.U.: Learning from imbalanced data for encrypted traffic identification problem. In: Proceedings of the 7th Symposium on Information and Communication Technology, SoICT 2016, pp. 147–152. Association for Computing Machinery, New York (2016). https://doi.org/10.1145/3011077.3011132
4. Wang, P., Chen, X.: SAE-based encrypted traffic identification method. Comput. Eng. **44**(11), 140–147 (2018)
5. Xuejiao, C., Pan, W., Shidong, L.: Key technology research of SSL encrypted application identification under imbalance of application class. Telecommun. Sci. **31**(12), 2015355 (2016)
6. Tang, Z., Zeng, X., Chen, J.: Multi-model coupling method for imbalanced network traffic classification based on clustering. Int. J. High Perform. Comput. Networking **16**(1), 26–35 (2020)
7. Wu, Y., Tan, H., Qin, L., Ran, B., Jiang, Z.: A hybrid deep learning based traffic flow prediction method and its understanding. Transp. Res. **90**(MAY), 166–180 (2018)
8. Zhang, Y., Chen, X., Guo, D., Song, M., Teng, Y., Wang, X.: PCCN: parallel cross convolutional neural network for abnormal network traffic flows detection in multi-class imbalanced network traffic flows. IEEE Access **7**, 119904–119916 (2019)

9. Wang, Z., Wang, P., Zhou, X., Li, S., Zhang, M.: FLOWGAN: unbalanced network encrypted traffic identification method based on GAN. In: 2019 IEEE International Conference on Parallel & Distributed Processing with Applications, Big Data & Cloud Computing, Sustainable Computing & Communications, Social Computing & Networking (ISPA/BDCloud/SocialCom/SustainCom), pp. 975–983. IEEE (2019)

10. Wang, P., Li, S., Ye, F., Wang, Z., Zhang, M.: PacketCGAN: exploratory study of class imbalance for encrypted traffic classification using CGAN. In: ICC 2020–2020 IEEE International Conference on Communications (ICC), pp. 1–7. IEEE (2020)

11. Guo, Y., Xiong, G., Li, Z., Shi, J., Cui, M., Gou, G.: Combating imbalance in network traffic classification using GAN based oversampling. In: 2021 IFIP Networking Conference (IFIP Networking), pp. 1–9. IEEE (2021)

12. Sychugov, A., Grekov, M.: Using wasserstein generative adversarial networks to create network traffic samples. In: AIP Conference Proceedings, vol. 2402, p. 050070. AIP Publishing LLC (2021)

13. Li, J., Zhou, L., Li, H., Yan, L., Zhu, H.: Dynamic traffic feature camouflaging via generative adversarial networks. In: 2019 IEEE Conference on Communications and Network Security (CNS), pp. 268–276. IEEE (2019)

14. Goodfellow, I., et al.: Generative adversarial networks. Commun. ACM 63(11), 139–144 (2020)

15. Arjovsky, M., Chintala, S., Bottou, L.: Wasserstein generative adversarial networks. In: International Conference on Machine Learning, pp. 214–223. PMLR (2017)

16. Lashkari, A.H., Kadir, A.F.A., Gonzalez, H., Mbah, K.F., Ghorbani, A.A.: Towards a network-based framework for Android malware detection and characterization. In: 2017 15th Annual Conference on Privacy, Security and Trust (PST), p. 233-23309 (2017)

17. Lashkari, A.H., Kadir, A.F.A., Taheri, L., Ghorbani, A.A.: Toward developing a systematic approach to generate benchmark Android malware datasets and classification. In: 2018 International Carnahan Conference on Security Technology (ICCST), pp. 1–7 (2018)

18. Lashkari, A.H., Draper-Gil, G., Mamun, M.S.I., Ghorbani, A.A., et al.: Characterization of Tor traffic using time based features. In: ICISSp, pp. 253–262 (2017)

19. Chawla, N.V., Bowyer, K.W., Hall, L.O., Kegelmeyer, W.P.: SMOTE: synthetic minority over-sampling technique. J. Artif. Int. Res. 16(1), 321–357 (2002)

20. Mitchell, T.: Machine Learning. McGraw-Hill Education (1997)

Secure Steganography Scheme Based on Steganography Generative Adversarial Network

Guangxu Pan$^{(\boxtimes)}$, Zhongpeng Yang, and Yong Ma

Civil Aviation Chengdu Electronic Technology Co., Ltd., Chengdu 610041, China
1312503948@qq.com

Abstract. Taking into consideration the security concerns surrounding steganography due to the infiltration of dense images during the image stealth process, this article proposes the addition of a noise layer between the embedded information and decoding information of the SteGAN model in order to train the dense image to resist noise attacks. To improve the stabilization of the discriminator's training, the principle of spectral normalization is applied to mitigate the convergence speed of the discriminator. This will enable the networks to continue training and enhance the confrontation between stealth and stealth analysis. Finally, the model is trained on the COCO dataset. The experimental results reveal that the dense image obtained through noise layer training performs well in terms of imperceptibility, with a decoding accuracy rate of more than 90% for all confidential images trained by the noise, except for JPEG compression. Moreover, it can effectively protect against the detection of stealth analysis tools.

Keywords: Image Steganography · Steganography Generative Adversarial Network · Spectral normalization · Steganographic analysis

1 Introduction

In the field of steganography, robustness is a critical component of steganographic security. It serves as a key indicator of the carrier image's ability to withstand attacks and maintain the integrity of the encoded information. Ideally, the carrier image should remain intact during transmission to the decoder, but noise attacks can cause damage in the form of cropping, compression, or addition. Despite these potential attacks, the decoder must still be able to accurately extract the secret information. This reflects the robustness of the carrier image and can be an important factor in assessing the security of steganography.

Volkhonskiy et al. were the first to propose combining Generative Adversarial Networks (GAN) with information steganography, and proposed the Steganographic Generative Adversarial Networks (SGAN) [1] model, which Yang et al. improved the embedding simulation network (TES) in ASDL-GAN [2] for the problem that it is difficult to back propagate, and used Tanh simulator instead of it, and considering the ability of the discriminator to resist steganalysis, channels are added to the discriminator so that it can resist steganalysis detection against channels. The structure of encoding-decoding network has similarity with steganography in that both fuse the data first and then extract them. Hayes et al. combined the encoding-decoding structure with information steganography and proposed Steganography Generative Adversarial Network (SteGAN) [3] information steganography model. Using common carrier images with embedded information as binary information as input to generate steganographic images, but too much steganographic information embedded in the model during training will lead to the problem of gradient disappearance of the model, which cannot be trained for a long time, resulting in low quality of the generated steganographic images. Zhu et al. proposed another steganographic model of generative adversarial network, Hiding Data with Deep Networks (HiDDeN) [4]. This model has a similar network structure as SteGAN, and is characterized by adding a noise layer to the information embedding process to train the noise on the carrier image, making it resistant to noise attacks and capable of decoding with high accuracy even after noise attacks.

Some steganographic models perform the steganographic task in an idealized situation without considering the possible attacks on the carrier image in the process of transmission, and, when the steganographic capacity of the model is increased, the quality of the carrier image is improved, but it is also vulnerable to attacks by third parties to corrupt the carrier image to obtain secret information, and the attacks on the image generally involve noise, so in this paper A noise layer is incorporated between the encoder and decoder of the SteGAN model, which is used to simulate the attacks that the carrier image may suffer during transmission, hoping to improve the robustness of the carrier image by training the model to make it resistant to distortions generated by various noises; and to stabilize the training of the discriminator network so that it can converge stably and generate adversaries to optimize the network [5]. Therefore, the Robust Steganography Generative Adversarial Network (RS-GAN), a secure steganography scheme based on Steganography Generative Adversarial Network is proposed.

2 Solutions

2.1 SteGAN

Figure 1 depicts the SteGAN model, a three-way adversarial system containing a generator (Alice), a discriminator (Bob), and a steganalysis (Eve). Alice creates a carrier image by merging a carrier image with a random binary sequence of secret messages and sends it to Bob to extract the confidential information from the carrier image. Meanwhile, Eve functions as a steganographic analyzer, detecting the presence of the secret message in the received image to evaluate the steganographic security.

In continuous adversarial learning, Alice learns to conceal secret information in any carrier image, while Bob fine-tunes the steganography algorithm by parsing Alice's carrier image to accurately recover the information. Eve optimizes the network structure, making it easier to differentiate between carrier and steganography images and counteracts Alice and Bob through the adversarial game to enhance their learning ability. The ultimate goal is to achieve a Nash equilibrium between the two sides.

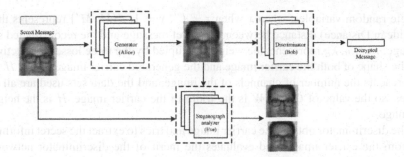

Fig. 1. SteGAN model diagram

The objective function of SteGAN is expressed as:

$$\min_{G} \max_{D} \max_{S} V(S, D, G) = E_{X \sim P_{data}(X)}(logD(x)) + E_{z \sim P_{noise}(z)}$$
$$(log(1 - D(G(z)))) + E_{z \sim P_{noise}(z)}(logS(Stego(G(z)))) + log(1 - S(G(z))) \tag{1}$$

G is the generator network; D is the discriminator network; S is the steganography analyzer; $Stego(x)$ denotes the result of embedding secret information in the carrier; $P_{data}(x)$ is the image data distribution; x is the real data sample of the training set; $P_{noise}(z)$ is the carrier image distribution; z denotes random noise; $E_{x \sim p_{data}(x)}$ denotes the expectation of the sample data; $E_{z \sim p_{noise}(z)}$ denotes the expectation of the generated data.

The information embedding process of SteGAN is done when training the generator network, and the secret information extraction process is implemented when training the discriminator network, and their respective loss functions can be written as:

$$L_{Bob}(\theta_A, \theta_B, M, C) = d(M, B(\theta_B, C')) = d(M, B(\theta_B, A(\theta_A, C, M))) =$$
$$d(M, M') = \left(\sum_{i=1}^{n} (M_i - M_{i'})^2\right)^{\frac{1}{2}}, \tag{2}$$

$$L_{Eve}(\theta_E, C, C') = -y \cdot \log(\theta_E, x) - (1 - y) \cdot \log(1 - E(\theta_E, x)), \tag{3}$$

$$L_{Alice}(\theta_A, C, M) = \lambda_A \cdot d(C, C') + \lambda_B \cdot L_{Bob} + \lambda_E \cdot L_{Eve}(\theta_E, C'). \tag{4}$$

In this equation, represents the parameters of Alice, Bob, and Eve, respectively; is the steganographic information; is the carrier image; is the carrier image; represents the output of Alice on and; represents the output of Bob on; represents the output of Eve on and; and are both discrete random variables, when, 0 when,1; represents the EL (Euclidean Distance) distance between the secret message and the reconstructed secret message; represents the weights occupied by the three losses, respectively. In this equation, θ_A, θ_B, θ_E represents the parameters of Alice, Bob, and Eve, respectively; M is the steganographic information; C is the carrier image; C' is the carrier image; $A(\theta_A, C, M)$ represents the output of Alice on C and M; $B(\theta_B, C')$ represents the output of Bob on C'; $E(\theta_A, C, C')$ represents the output of Eve on C and C'; x and y are both discrete random variables, when x when $x = C'$, $y = 1$; $d(M, M')$ represents the EL (Euclidean Distance) distance between the secret message and the reconstructed secret message; λ_A, λ_B, λ_E represents the weights occupied by the three losses, respectively.

The shape of both the carrier image and the generated carrier image is $C \times H \times W$, C represents the number of channels of the image, and the data sets used are all color images, so the value of C is 3; W is the width of the carrier image; H is the height of the image.

The discriminator obtains the carrier image and tries to extract the secret information M' from the carrier image, and evaluates the merit of the discriminator network by judging the difference between M and M'.

The steganography analyzer plays the role of discriminative classification in the model, it receives carrier image and carrier image as input and determines whether the image is a carrier image or a carrier image from these two types of images.

2.2 Design of Noise Layer

(1) Dropout noise

In the process of transmitting a carrier image, the first consideration should be the random distortion caused by noise. When designing this module, we assume that some pixels of the carrier image will be lost. To introduce random noise, we replace the lost pixels with pixels of the same position in the carrier image. The replaced pixels are invisible to the human perception system, but play a crucial role in encoding the secret message. During decoding, the decoder extracts as much information as possible and learns to deal with the redundant information in the carrier image. The distortion ratio can be regulated by controlling the intensity factor p, which ranges from 0 to 1.

(2) Cropout noise

The Cropout operation uses the same idea as the Dropout operation, and takes the same p-value to control the distortion ratio. The similarity is that both are the result of pixel replacement, using the pixels of the carrier image to replace the pixels of the carrier image.

(3) Crop noise

The cropping operation is to crop the dense image according to a certain ratio to get a noisy image, and the cropped image/dense image is called the cropping ratio, which is denoted by k and takes a value between 0 and 1.

(4) Gaussian noise

Gaussian noise, as the name implies, is associated with a Gaussian distribution, and the probability density function of this noise follows a Gaussian distribution. Gaussian noise is widely used, not only in electronics, but also often in digital images. In this paper, we use Gaussian noise to add noise to images, using a 3×3 Gaussian filter templates, with the center of the template as the coordinate origin for sampling [6]. The coordinates of the template at each position, as shown in Fig. 2 below, where the i-axis (same position as the x-axis) is horizontal to the right and the j-axis (opposite direction to the y-axis) is vertical to the bottom, and the Gaussian two-dimensional function is shown in Eq. 5, where σ denotes the intensity coefficient, and the specific values are described in the experimental section.

$$G(x, y) = \frac{1}{2\pi\sigma^2} e^{-\frac{x^2+y^2}{2\sigma^2}}, \tag{5}$$

(-1,1)	(0,1)	(1,1)
(-1,0)	(0,0)	(1,0)
(-1, -1)	(0, -1)	(1, -1)

Fig. 2. 2D Gaussian distribution function and corresponding (x,y) coordinate values in the 3 * 3 filter

(5) JPEG compression

we use an approximate simulation of JPEG compression in HiDDeN, where the quantization value is theoretically equivalent in terms of information to limit the amount of information that can pass through the "channel". In order to limit the amount of information that can be passed through a particular frequency domain channel, noise layers were created to simulate JPEG compression. These layers apply a DCT transform using a span 8 convolutional layer, with each filter corresponding to a fundamental vector in the DCT transform. Thus, the network activation represents the DCT domain coefficients of the encoded image. Masks are then applied to the DCT coefficients to limit the information flow; higher frequency coefficients are more likely to be discarded, simulating JPEG differentiable compression as in Fig. 3. Then, transposed convolution is used to generate the noisy image for the inverse DCT transform.

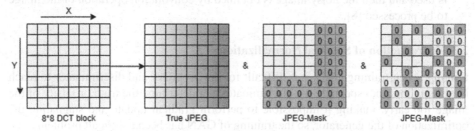

Fig. 3. Simulated JPEG Differentiable Compression

In summary, JPEG compresses an image by performing a discrete cosine transform (DCT) to give a grid of frequency components, which are then quantized, while higher frequency components are quantized more aggressively, with bright red indicating stronger quantization. The DCT transform can be implemented as a single span of 8 convolutional layers with a fixed 64 filters based on the DCT, but due to the quantization step, JPEG compression is indistinguishable due to the quantization step. Therefore, two different approximations are used to train the model, JPEG-Mask zeroes out a fixed set of high frequency coefficients, while JPEG-Drop zeroes out the channels with a higher probability of descent.

Call the corresponding layers JPEG-Mask and JPEG-Drop. JPEG-Mask applies a fixed mask, keeping only 25 low-frequency DCT coefficients in the Y-channel and 9 in the U, V-channel (immediately after JPEG, more information is also kept in the Y-channel). The other coefficients are set to zero. In real JPEG compression, the coarser the quantization of a coefficient, the more likely that coefficient will be zeroed out in the simulation of the neural network. Both methods are successful in generating models that are robust to real JPEG compression.

(6) Pepper noise

In the most common noise in digital images, pepper noise is considered one of them, in fact, pepper noise is two kinds of noise, one is pepper noise, the other is salt noise, from the naming of its characteristics can be seen, the former will generally produce black noise, belonging to low gray noise, the latter will produce white noise, belonging to high gray noise, but usually both appear at the same time, generally by the image sensor, transmission channel and decoding processing, etc. produced by the black and white see the bright and dark spots of noise, in the image to see is black and white miscellaneous dots [7].

(7) Mean filtered noise

The common use of mean filtering is noise reduction, where a simple average of the pixels included in the filter mask field is calculated, but mean filtering has some limitations and can have the negative effect of blurring edges, which is caused by sharp changes in image grayscale that create image edges. Mean filtering has another important role when roughly describing an image that needs to be blurred, where smaller objects in the image will blend in with the background and larger objects will become speckle-like and easy to detect. In this paper, the common mean filter is used and then the noisy image is obtained by convolution operation of the image to be processed [8].

2.3   Introduction of Spectral Normalization

Usually, when training GAN, it is difficult for the generator and discriminator to reach Nash equilibrium, especially the discriminator can determine the truth or falsity of the image too early, making it impossible to perform gradient update and stagnating the optimization of the generator, so the training of GAN has been a difficult problem to be solved.

Spectral normalization decomposes the parameters W of each layer of the neural network as SVD and then limits its maximum singular value to 1, dividing by the maximum singular value of W after each update of W. The maximum stretching factor of each layer for the input x does not exceed 1 [9].

$$\frac{g_l(x) - g_l(y)}{x - y} \leq 1, \tag{6}$$

For the whole neural network $f(x) = g_N(g_{N-1}(\ldots g_1(x)\ldots))$ naturally satisfies the Lipschitz continuity as well.

The power iteration initializes a random $\hat{u}$ and then iterates $\hat{u}$ and $\hat{v}$ according to the following equation:

$$\hat{v} = \frac{W^T \hat{u}}{\|W^T \hat{u}\|_2}, \hat{u} = \frac{W^T \hat{v}}{\|W^T \hat{v}\|_2} \tag{7}$$

The maximum singular value W of the final matrix $\sigma(W)$ can be obtained from $\hat{u}$ and $\hat{v}$ as follows:

$$\sigma(W) \approx \hat{u} W^T \hat{v}, \tag{8}$$

After obtaining $\sigma(W)$, the network performs a spectral normalization of the parameter W W for each update of the parameters:

$$W = \frac{W}{\sigma(W)}, \tag{9}$$

The spectral normalization constraint, which constrains the Lipschitz constant of the discriminator by constraining the spectral norm of the weight matrix of each layer of the network of the discriminator of the GAN, enhances the stability of the GAN during the training process [10].

2.4 RS-GAN Model Structure

After describing the noise produced by the noise layer, this paper inserts the noise layer between the generator and the discriminator to simulate noise attacks. Additionally, the discriminator uses spectral normalization to enhance encoder training stability. The model construction is displayed in Fig. 4.

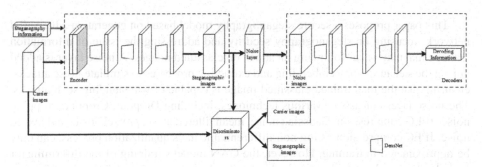

Fig. 4. RS-GAN model

After embedding the steganographic data into the carrier image, the encoder introduces noise into the image using a predefined noise layer. The distorted image is then decoded by the decoder to retrieve the secret information. The decoder then compares the retrieved information with the embedded information to generate loss values that are used to train the encoder. Meanwhile, the discriminator analyzes the received images to distinguish between the embedded and non-embedded ones. The network structure of the discriminator is illustrated in Fig. 5.

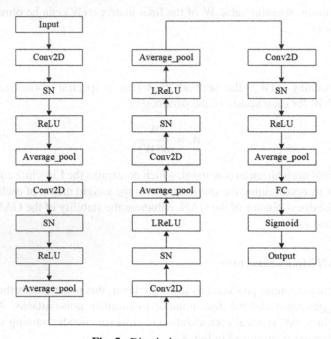

Fig. 5. Discriminator structure

This paper proposes a secure steganography model based on generative adversarial network, focusing on steganography security and addressing the issue of information leakage that may occur following an attack on classified images. A noise layer is added during the steganography embedding and extraction processes to simulate noise attacks, ensuring that the final trained classified image is capable of withstanding such attacks. The noise layer consists of various techniques, including Dropout, Cropout, cropping noise, JPEG compression, Gaussian noise, mean filtered noise, pretzel noise, and hybrid noise. JPEG compression, being non-differentiable in its quantization process, can only be approximated in training. However, the GAN model's training of the discriminator often leads to gradient explosions, making network optimization and the quality of generated carrier images difficult to achieve. To stabilize the network training, we incorporate spectral normalization into the discriminator network structure.

3 Training of Models

The experiments were run on a server with an Intel(R) Xeon(R) CPU E5–2620 v3 @2.40 GHz processor, using 64 GByte of memory, with an operating system of NVIDIA Tesla T4 GPU and Ubuntu 16.04. The RS-GAN model was trained and evaluated using the COCO dataset. The COCO dataset is The COCO dataset is a large, rich object detection, segmentation, and captioning dataset with more than 1.5 million individuals in the entire dataset. Therefore, the COCO dataset is very large and complex [11], which can well confirm the performance of the RS-GAN model proposed in this paper. The COCO dataset is preprocessed and cropped to a size of 360 × 360 images.

4 Experimental Results and Analysis

4.1 Steganography Capacity

The formula for calculating the steganographic capacity is shown in (10).

$$K = \frac{Q}{N \times N}, \tag{10}$$

Q is the number of bits of secret information (random information);N is the pixel value of the image. A Q-bit random message is connected to each sample of each data set, varying the size of the message Q to test the limit of the amount of information that can be effectively hidden in the carrier image. The dataset used consists of 32 pixels by 32-pixel images, which corresponds to a steganographic capacity of approximately 0.1 bpp to 0.7 bpp when setting Q to 100 to 700.

The results of comparing the steganographic capacity of RSGAN with other models are shown in Table 1. The maximum capacity of RSGAN can reach 0.6 bpp, while the maximum capacity of other steganographic models is 0.4 bpp, which means that the embedding capacity of RSGAN model can be increased by 50% compared with other models.

Table 1. Model capacity comparison

	RSGAN	HiDDeN	SteGAN	SGAN
Number of image bits /bit	32	16	32	64
Steganography capacity /bpp	0.6	0.2	0.4	0.4

4.2 Imperceptibility

Maintaining good image quality after a noise attack is crucial, with imperceptibility being a key characteristic. Evaluation metrics such as MSE, PSNR, and SSIM from the previous section are still used for evaluation criteria. As shown in Fig. 6, the carrier image is trained by combining different types of noise, divided into two layers, with the top layer being the carrier image and the bottom layer containing the carrier image along with various noise types.

The results of Dropout, Cropout, cropping noise, Gaussian noise, JPEG compression, pretzel noise, mean filter, and mixed noise training are displayed from left to right in each column of the figure. Each type of noise is trained separately to produce steganographic images that are resistant to specific noise attacks. However, when trained together, the resulting images can resist most noise attacks. The training parameters used for each noise type vary, mainly corresponding to different noise coefficients. For instance, in Dropout, the pixel loss ratio is set to 0.3 during training, while in Cropout, the pixel loss ratio is set based on block operation, with crop noise set to 0.03 during training. In Gaussian noise, the fuzzy noise coefficient is set to 2.0. The coefficients set for each noise layer greatly impact the decoding accuracy, with different coefficients involving varying degrees of secret loss. The decoding accuracy will be further described in the following section.

Dropout   Cropout   Crop   Gaussian   JPEG   Pepper   filtering Mixed

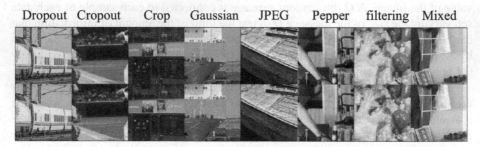

Fig. 6. Trained carrier density images for each noise

The findings of this research paper demonstrate that combining the RS-GAN model with the noise layer yields results that are almost identical to those perceived by the human perceptual system. Both the specific and mixed noise can be adjusted according to the image being used, without compromising visual quality. This suggests that introducing specific or mixed noise during the encoding process of dense images can help these images withstand noise attacks, without diminishing their visual appeal. Furthermore, to assess the quality of the carrier images, PSNR and SSIM were used to evaluate image quality.

Table 2. Carrier image quality assessment

	dropout	cropout	crop	gaussian	JPEG
PSNR	32.15	31.48	32.24	30.76	28.26
SSIM	0.93	0.94	0.92	0.91	0.89
	JPEG	pepper	mean filtering		mixing Noise
PSNR	28.26	29.38	30.24		31.62
SSIM	0.89	0.90	0.92		0.91

Based on the findings in Table 2, it is evident that the maximum PSNR and SSIM indices of the carrier image in Chapter 3 are 27.36 and 0.90 respectively, at a steganographic capacity of 0.6 bpp. However, the PSNR index of the noise-trained carrier image exceeds 27.36, and the SSIM index values are mostly above or equal to 0.90, except for JPEG compression. These results indicate that the RS-GAN model does not significantly reduce the PSNR and SSIM values; instead, it mostly enhances them. Therefore, noise training can contribute to improving the quality of the carrier image and obtaining a noise-resistant carrier image.

4.3 Decoding Accuracy

With the guarantee of good image imperceptibility, another important index is the accuracy of decoding, which is still guaranteed after the image has been attacked by noise, and the accuracy of evaluation of extraction is calculated using Eq. 11 [11].

$$acc = 1 - BER(W_t, W_{t'}) = 1 - \frac{\sum_{l=1}^{L_w} XOR(W_t(l), W_{t'}(l))}{L_w}, \quad (11)$$

where BER represents the BER, W_t represents the embedded secret message, $W_{t'}$ represents the decoded message, and L_w represents the length of the embedded secret message.

In image steganography, the accuracy of decoding is of utmost importance post transmission of confidential information. While designing the noise layer, Dropout noise and Cropout noise employ p-value to determine the carrier image's rate of pixel loss. The lost pixels of the carrier image are then substituted with the image itself. Consequently, we conducted a comparison of decoding accuracy for different p-values. Training by noise attack leads to loss of confidential information, and complete decoding accuracy cannot be achieved. Table 3 presents the decoding accuracy following the training.

Table 3. Decoding accuracy of Dropout and Cropout with different P values

ratio value	P = 0.1	P = 0.3	p = 0.5	P = 0.7	P = 0.9
no	95%	89%	82%	71%	61%
dropout	98%	98%	92%	71%	76%
cropout	99%	99%	93%	72%	74%
mixed	97%	97%	92%	69%	59%

From Table 3, the decoding accuracy of carrier-intensive images with Dropout and Cropout combined with noise training has not been reduced when p value = 0.3, and the decoding accuracy gradually decreases when p value is greater than 0.3, so the p value of image replacement ratio for both Dropout and Cropout is chosen at p = 0.3. Noise-free training is the carrier image obtained without combining noise layer, and then noise attack is performed on such carrier image. When p = 0.1, the decoding accuracy of carrier image without noise training has been reduced, and the decoding accuracy gradually decreases with the increase of carrier image loss ratio. In contrast, the decoding accuracy of the carrier image after combining noise training has improved compared with that of the carrier image without noise training, and the decoding accuracy of the carrier image remains above 95% after combining mixed noise training, indicating that the carrier image can resist noise attack after noise training and can still reach 95% decoding accuracy.

For the effect brought by the training crop operation on the decoding accuracy of the carrier image, the decoding accuracy is significantly reduced when the crop ratio k = 0.1 of the carrier image, and the decoding accuracy is only 70% after combining with the noise training, which is already impossible for the accuracy of the information transmission, so the value of the crop ratio can only be obtained experimentally in the direction of getting smaller and smaller, and the obtained crop The decoding accuracy related to the ratio value is shown in Table 4.

Table 4. Decoding accuracy of different P-value clipping noise

Ratio value	k = 0.01	k = 0.03	k = 0.05	k = 0.07	k = 0.1
no	90%	82%	73%	65%	56%
crop	98%	98%	89%	82%	71%
mixed	97%	97%	92%	69%	59%

From Table 4, the crop ratio of the laden secret image has a large impact on the decoding accuracy of the secret information. At k = 0.1, the decoding accuracy is still below 80%, far from the usable requirement, regardless of whether noise training is used or not. When the k value is reduced to 0.03, the decoding accuracy after training for the specific crop operation is at 98%, and the result of mixed noise is also at 97%, which has reached the decoding accuracy did not change even when the k value was further reduced, indicating that the k value was already the maximum value that could be trimmed.

The difference of Gaussian blurred noise lies in the value of standard deviation σ. With different values of σ, the blurring degree of carrier image is different. Gaussian noise has a greater impact on the visual effect of carrier image, but less impact on the decoding accuracy. During the experiment, the initial value of σ is determined at 1 according to the experience of researchers, and then the boundary value of σ is found from both sides. The relevant taking data are shown in the table.

Table 5. Decoding accuracy of Gaussian noise with different σ values

Ratio value	$\sigma = 1$	$\sigma = 1.5$	$\sigma = 2$	$\sigma = 2.5$	$\sigma = 3$
no	82%	80%	71%	62%	58%
gaussian	97%	98%	98%	93%	89%
mixed	97%	97%	92%	69%	59%

From Table 5, it can be concluded that at $\sigma = 2$, the influence of Gaussian noise on the decoding accuracy of the carrier image gradually increases and the decoding accuracy gradually decreases, so the value of σ is taken as 2. Comparing the decoding accuracy of the carrier image trained by Gaussian noise with that of the carrier image without noise training, at $\sigma = 1$, the decoding accuracy of the carrier image without noise training has been to 82%, which is already lower than 95% of the usable standard, while after Gaussian noise training, the decoding accuracy at $\sigma = 2$ is still at 98%, which meets the usable steganographic requirement.

The remaining noise does not have the problem of determining the coefficients and is also used directly in the training process, and the decoding accuracy is shown in Table 6.

Table 6. Decoding accuracy of each noise

	No	JPEG	No	Mean filtered	No	Pepper
Ratio value	47%	78%	76%	98%	73%	96%

From Table 6, it can be seen that the decoding accuracy of the carrier image without noise training is generally not high, especially in JPEG compression, the decoding accuracy of the carrier image without noise training is only 48%, but when trained with the noise incorporated into JPEG compression, the decoding accuracy increases by 31%, but overall, the decoding accuracy of JPEG compression is much lower than that of other noise The reason for this is that when the noise layer is designed, JPEG compression has a non-differentiable quantization process, which can only approximate the JPEG compression process and has a large impact on the decoding accuracy, which is only 78%, and this is also the direction that needs to be researched subsequently.

4.4 Steganography Security

The StegExpose steganalysis tool is used to detect the carrier images, and the carrier images trained with different noise layers are selected for detection, and the results are shown in Table 7:

Table 7. Detection rate of steganalysis for each noise at different embedding capacities

	0.4 bpp	0.5 bpp	0.6 bpp
no	0.54	0.57	0.61
dropout	0.40	0.45	0.49
cropout	0.42	0.44	0.48
crop	0.41	0.43	0.47
gaussian	0.43	0.44	0.40
JPEG	0.52	0.56	0.61
pepper	0.42	0.41	0.47
mean filter	0.41	0.40	0.44

As can be seen from Table 7, from the overall results, compared with the detection results of the steganalysis resistance of the model in Chapter 3, the steganalysis resistance of the carrier image after the noise layer training has improved compared with the previous one, but the results after the JPEG compression training have only improved by about 2%, especially when the steganographic capacity reaches 0.6 bpp, the detection rate of the steganography tool has exceeded 60%, and the reason for this is that when simulating the JPEG compression The reason for this is that when simulating JPEG compression, JPEG compression training cannot be fully performed, and only approximate simulation operations can be performed. This point needs to be improved later. The detection rate of steganalysis does not exceed 50% for the other carrier images, which means that the carrier images can effectively resist the detection of the steganalysis tool at this time.

One of the main features of the image steganography algorithm based on generative adversarial networks is that it can embed the secret information in complex regions of the image texture, making the impact on the image generation smaller and the embedding location hidden. In image steganography, the network responsible for information steganography continuously tries to embed the secret information in different regions of the image, while the steganalysis network analyzes different regions of the image to find the location of the secret information embedding. As the network is trained, the steganalysis network gives feedback to the steganalysis network, which makes the steganalysis network begin to optimize, and the steganalysis network gradually selects the embedding location in the complex area of image texture, currently the steganalysis network seems to be incompetent, and gradually it is difficult to find the embedding location of the carrier image, and the distinction between the carrier image and the carrier image is balanced.

In order to verify whether the embedding position of the secret information is in the complex region of the image texture, in this paper, the embedding position is observed using the residual map of the carrier image and the carrier image [12], and the results are shown in Fig. 7:

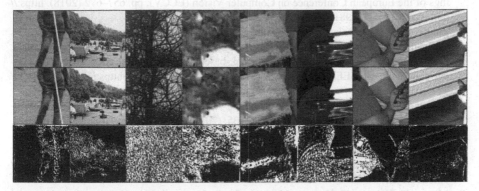

Fig. 7. Analysis of the embedding position of the carrier image

As can be seen from the figure, the white part indicates the embedded information points, which are the markers of the altered image. The secret information is embedded in the complex area of the image texture or in the darker area of the image color, making the impact on the carrier image smaller.

5 Conclusion

In this study, we present a secure steganography scheme called RS-GAN that is designed to resist noise attacks. RS-GAN includes a noise layer between its encoder and decoder to mimic noise attacks, and utilizes the COCO dataset to train the carrier image with noise attack resistance. To stabilize the discriminator during training, spectral normalization is added to the middle of the discriminative network. Our experimental results demonstrate that carrier images generated by the RS-GAN model show robustness against noise attacks, and exhibit decoding accuracies above 95% for each noise layer at a steganographic capacity of 0.6 bpp, except for JPEG compression. Furthermore, the detection rate of other noise-trained carrier images is less than 60% when subjected to steganographic analysis using the tool StegExpose. These findings suggest that detecting these steganographic images is only slightly more effective than random guesses. In future studies, we will explore better optimization methods for JPEG compression to improve overall performance.

References

1. Volkhonskiy, D., Nazarov, I., Borisenko, B., et al.: Steganographic generative adversarial networks. arXiv preprint arXiv:1805.06798 (2018). https://doi.org/10.48550/arXiv.1703.05502

2. Li, C., Liu, X.Y., Yang, Y.: Spatial image steganography based on generative adversarial network. IEEE Access **7**, 26004–26012 (2019). https://doi.org/10.48550/arXiv.1804.07939
3. Hayes, J., Danezis, G.: Generating steganographic images via adversarial training. Adv. Neural Inf. Process. Syst. 1954–1963 (2017). https://doi.org/10.48550/arXiv.1703.00371
4. Zhu, J., Kaplan, R., Johnson, J., et al.: HiDDeN: hiding data with deep networks. In: Proceedings of the European Conference on Computer Vision (ECCV), pp. 657–672 (2018). https://doi.org/10.1145/3219819.3220123
5. Zhang, L., et al.: Imbalanced data enhancement method based on improved DCGAN and its application, pp. 3485–3498 (2021). https://doi.org/10.3233/JIFS-210843
6. Ploshikhin, V., Paramonov, I., Kober, V.: Rank-based estimation of the covariance matrix under gaussian noise. IEEE Signal Process. Lett. **27**, 481–485 (2020). https://doi.org/10.1109/TIT.2011.2147320
7. Ahani, S., Ghaemmaghami, S.: Colour image steganography method based on sparse representation. IET Image Process. **9**, 496–505 (2015). https://doi.org/10.1049/iet-ipr.2014.0351
8. Iqbal, N., Ali, S., Khan, I., Lee, B.M.: Adaptive edge preserving weighted mean filter for removing random-valued impulse noise. Symmetry **11**(3), 163–169 (2019). https://doi.org/10.3390/sym11030395
9. Miyato, T., Kataoka, T., Koyama, M., et al.: Spectral normalization for generative adversarial networks. In: International Conference on Learning Representations (2018). https://doi.org/10.48550/arXiv.1802.05957
10. Liu, Z.W., Deng, C.H., Liu, J.: Target detection algorithm based on asymmetric hourglass network structure. Comput. Appl. **40**(12), 3526–3533 (2020). https://doi.org/10.11772/j.issn.1001-9081.2020050641. (in Chinese)
11. Pan, Y., et al.: Hiding image within image based on deep learning. In: Journal of Physics: Conference Series, vol. 2337, no. 1 (2022). https://doi.org/10.1088/1742-6596/2337/1/012009. (in Chinese)
12. Liu, R., Li, G., Jia, B.: Adaptive steganography model for images based on improved generative adversarial networks. Comput. Eng. Des. **42**(06), 1551–1561 (2021). https://doi.org/10.3390/math8091394

SR-GNN: Spectral Residuals with Graph Neural Networks for Anomaly Detection in ADS-B Data

Xiaolei Zhang$^{(\boxtimes)}$ and Jiasheng Li

University of Electronic Science and Technology of China, Chengdu, China
xiaolei_zhang@std.uestc.edu.cn

Abstract. The Automatic Dependent Surveillance–Broadcast (ADS-B) system is an essential component of the air traffic system. However, its protocol lacks data encryption and authentication, making it highly vulnerable to various deceptive attacks. ADS-B data represents typical multivariate time series, and existing solutions have limitations as they fail to capture relationships between features. In this paper, we propose a new self-supervised framework called SR-GNN. It leverages spectral residual (SR) to identify and remove point anomalies and utilizes two graph neural networks to capture relationships between time series. Finally, the model is jointly optimized using prediction and reconstruction. To address this issue, we create an evaluation dataset using commonly used trajectory modification methods. Through extensive experimentation, we demonstrate that the proposed method significantly outperforms other models.

Keywords: Anomaly Detection · Multivariate Time Series · Graph Neural Networks · ADS-B · Air Traffic Security

1 Introduction

Automatic Dependent Surveillance–Broadcast (ADS-B) is a surveillance technology in which an aircraft determines its position via satellite navigation and periodically broadcasts it, enabling it to be tracked [1]. ADS-B significantly enhances the efficiency and safety of air traffic control (ATC). Compared to traditional radar surveillance technology, ADS-B costs less, has fewer errors, and can provide more accurate data. The technology enables real-time surveillance and seamless coverage and is suitable for various aviation applications, such as flight monitoring, air traffic control, and flight safety management. ADS-B has digitalized and automated flight surveillance on a global scale, gained recognition for its accuracy and efficiency, and has been widely used in many flight and navigation systems.

However, due to the unencrypted broadcast method used by the ADS-B system, it is subject to a series of security threats, such as information spoofing, location deception, and interference. Attackers can mislead other aircraft or ground control systems, and even cause serious air accidents, by tampering with ADS-B messages or injecting false information [2, 3].

H. Yang and R. Lu (Eds.): FCS 2023, CCIS 1992, pp. 503–516, 2024.
https://doi.org/10.1007/978-981-99-9331-4_33

Therefore, ensuring the security of the ADS-B system has become one of the critical issues in the field of ADS-B research, and a hot topic in related technologies. The academic and industrial communities are continually exploring and researching how to improve the security of the ADS-B system. In existing solutions, some classic anomaly detection methods are distance-based, such as One-Class Support Vector Machines (OCSVM) [4], while others evaluate whether the data is anomalous based on reconstruction errors, such as AutoEncoder (AE) [5] and Variational AutoEncoder (VAE) [6]. However, ADS-B includes multiple sensor information, such as latitude, longitude, speed, altitude, heading, etc., which are interrelated, and these schemes do not consider the correlation between multiple variables. Recent advances in Graph Neural Networks (GNN) [7]in anomaly detection, including Graph Convolutional Networks (GCN) [8], Graph Attention Networks (GAT) [9], and Multi-Relation Networks [10], have effectively overcome this limitation by applying GNN to the anomaly detection of ADS-B. This paper uses a Graph Neural Network model combined with spectral residuals [11] to predict and reconstruct ADS-B data for anomaly detection. The contributions of this paper are as follows:

1. To the best of our knowledge, this is the first time that the graph attention mechanism has been applied to anomaly detection of ADS-B data.
2. By amplifying anomaly information through spectral residuals and combining prediction and reconstruction, we perform anomaly detection on ADS-B data.
3. We use a complete data framework with existing tools, including data cleaning, feature extraction, and model training data serialization. Emphasis is placed on reproducibility through the open code repository.
4. Through comparative experiments with different existing machine learning anomaly detection models, our method performs well in ADS-B detection.

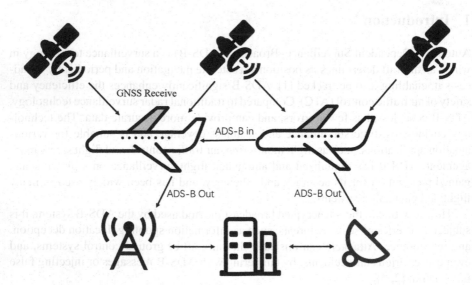

Fig. 1. The Automatic Dependent Surveillance–Broadcast (ADS-B) system

2 Background

2.1 ADS-B Protocol Overview

The ADS-B system is illustrated in Fig. 1. Aircraft are equipped with ADS-B transmitters, which acquire the aircraft's specific location information through the Global Navigation Satellite System (GNSS). The transmitter then continuously broadcasts ADS-B messages comprised of a series of aircraft state information. The ADS-B system includes two subsystems: ADS-B IN and ADS-B OUT.

ADS-B IN receives ADS-B messages broadcast by surrounding aircraft, and then displays the received information on the cockpit traffic information display to enhance the awareness of the surrounding situation. On the other hand, ADS-B OUT broadcasts the aircraft's ADS-B messages at a fixed transmission frequency to surrounding aircraft and ground stations.

2.2 Main Risks of the ADS-B

Due to the lack of security measures, ADS-B is highly susceptible to various types of cyber attacks. For instance, the mobile application, Plane Finder AR, can provide real-time information about any flight; at the Black Hat Conference in 2012, Costin and Francillon proved that a counterfeit aircraft could easily be incorporated into real-time monitoring screens using a low-cost ADS-B transmitter [3]. The International Civil Aviation Organization (ICAO) has become aware of the vulnerabilities of ADS-B and has recommended research into the security of ADS-B to find possible security solutions. This section will discuss active attacks in ADS-B.

Active attacks in ADS-B represent a method of creating chaos and terror in the air. The adversary in active attacks attempts to affect flight operations, including altering ADS-B messages or generating false assertions. The types of active attacks are as follows:

- **Denial-of-Service (DoS) Attacks:** DoS attacks can inundate ADS-B receivers by emitting sufficient power on the 1090 MHz frequency in Mode S. Interference can disrupt specific aircraft, specific ground stations, or even entire areas covering ground stations and aircraft. In this way, all ADS-B message traffic in the affected area can be effectively invalidated. Although DoS attacks are common problems in wireless communications, due to the complexity of airspace and the importance of communication, the impact of DoS attacks on aircraft communication is particularly severe. DoS attacks are low-difficulty attacks. Schafer et al. demonstrated this attack by continuously sending white noise to a ground station, resulting in denial of service [12]. Due to high power interference, it is challenging to cause a blackout in an area with a variety of ADS-B receivers. A powerful jamming attack can devastate a high-density area if the interference leads to collision avoidance failure. Due to the high-speed maneuverability of aircraft, it is relatively difficult to interfere with aircraft in flight.
- **Message Injection:** Since ADS-B messages are not authenticated, attackers may inject illegal ADS-B messages into the ADS-B system without being detected. For example, this attack could create phantom aircraft visible to both pilots and ATC, causing pilots to interact with these fake aircraft or ATC to unnecessarily guide the fake aircraft to land or deny the real aircraft landing. As fake valid messages also have

the correct message format, it is hard to distinguish fake messages from real ones, so any ADS-B receiver will consider these fake messages as legitimate information. Because phantom aircraft are difficult to separate from real aircraft, countless phantom aircraft will flood the sky in case of an attack, causing ATC services to completely break down. Schafer et al. demonstrated the feasibility of phantom aircraft injection using software-defined radio connected to a computer flight simulator [13].

- **Message Deletion:** This type of deletion attack uses constructive or destructive interference to make ADS-B messages disappear from the radio frequency medium. Destructive interference overlaps the original ADS-B signal with a reverse signal synchronously to cancel or significantly attenuate the legitimate signal. This attack requires precise and complicated timing, making it extremely challenging in practice. Constructive interference doesn't require precise timing synchronization and causes errors in the transmitted messages. As 1090ES can correct up to 5 bit errors for each message, messages that exceed this limit will be automatically discarded by the ADS-B receiver as damaged, effectively deleting the message. This attack requires careful positioning of the interfering transmitter to successfully delete messages from a distance of 100 km [13]. In addition, the attacker can combine the deletion of information with injection to change the position of the aircraft. The attacker first deletes all messages on the aircraft and then injects a message seemingly from the aircraft that changes position. For a successful attack, the injected message has a higher transmission power than the deleted message. Apart from modifying the position, this attack might also inject information, indicating an existing aircraft is in an emergency or being hijacked. False emergencies or hijackings will severely mislead air traffic controllers.

- **Message Modification:** Message modifications at the physical layer include masking and bit flipping. Masking uses a high-power signal to replace all or part of the target information. Bit flipping overlaps a signal onto the original signal and flips multiple bits from 0 to 1, and vice versa. In both cases, arbitrary data can be injected without the participant's knowledge. This effect can also be achieved by combining message deletion with injection. However, because the manipulated message was initially legitimate, modifying messages might be more dangerous than injecting entirely new messages. Existing work also proves the feasibility of this message modification [14, 15].

2.3 Adversarial Model

Given the actual flight conditions of the aircraft, this paper considers two types of anomalies. The first type is self-failure anomalies of the aircraft, i.e., when the aircraft suffers a failure, it cannot navigate as specified by Air Traffic Control (ATC). The second type of anomaly is the one caused by an attacker's attack.

Since there is no security mechanism in the ADS-B protocol and the messages are not encrypted broadcasts, any individual with an ADS-B receiver can use the device to obtain data from the ADS-B messages. Particularly, one can now purchase ADS-B transmitters abroad, and these devices can be used to inject ADS-B information into the airspace to execute flood attacks, or ghost aircraft injection, etc. Therefore, it is reasonable to assume that attackers will have the capability to eavesdrop and forge, to obtain ADS-B messages within the reception range, and to inject false data using Software Defined Radios (SDR).

Understanding the adversary's capabilities is very helpful in analyzing which anomaly needs to be targeted. Adversaries can be divided into the following two types:

- **External adversaries.** External adversaries are those who can carry out simple attacks with ADS-B transmitters, such as attackers on the ground, passengers on aircraft, or drones. It's quite possible for external adversaries to perform such attacks, as transmitting ADS-B messages doesn't require any authentication information. Therefore, external adversaries can receive and transmit signals, and carry out DoS, eavesdropping, and deception attacks, etc.
- **Internal adversaries.** Internal adversaries typically have access to core system components and can affect system behavior through certain operations (mainly including ATC crew members and aircraft maintenance personnel, etc.). Internal adversaries can manipulate data processing behaviors, sabotaging the ADS-B system.

After acknowledging the adversary's capabilities, we can determine the type of anomalies that adversaries can achieve. Firstly, the adversary can cause the ADS-B message signal to disappear for a period through flooding or certain means. Another ability is to tamper with the message content, causing the aircraft to send anomalous data inconsistent with the real ADS-B data. Considering the series of anomalies mentioned above, the types of anomalies that this paper eventually considers are as follows:

- **Speed anomaly:** The speed changes, which may be caused by an aircraft accident, or it could be a result of an adversary maliciously tampering with ADS-B messages.
- **Altitude anomaly:** The altitude changes, this anomaly may also be caused by an aircraft accident, or it could result from an adversary tampering with the real ADS-B messages.
- **Location anomaly:** This type of anomaly may be caused by an attacker's attack on the one hand, with the attacker injecting information that does not conform to the aircraft's flight path into the ADS-B messages, thereby changing the original flight path. On the other hand, it might be due to an aircraft accident, where the aircraft deviates from its original trajectory in an unusual way.

3   Related Work

For the security challenges posed by the ADS-B protocol, current solutions can roughly be segregated into six categories. However, for the sake of brevity, these can be synthesized into two primary categories. The first category pertains to cryptographic encryption protection schemes, whereas the second relates to feature-based anomaly detection techniques.

3.1   Encryption Protection Schemes

Valovage et al. implemented symmetric encryption using Message Authentication Code (MAC) for identity verification in the Universal Access Transceiver (UAT) data link used in general aviation aircraft, and employed Public Key Infrastructure (PKI) for encrypting ADS-B messages [16]. Baek and colleagues proposed an identity-based signature scheme to address the security issues of ADS-B, simplifying public key management in PKI systems [17]. He et al. utilized a Three-level Hierarchical Identity-based Signature (TLHIBS) framework for data authentication, enhancing batch certification and reducing computational complexity [18]. Due to the signature length reaching thousands of bits, the communication cost of the ADS-B system increases correspondingly. However, the available data bits of the ADS-B system are limited, and the high communication cost is not consistent with the original intention of ADS-B design. Yang et al. conducted an in-depth study of online ADS-B data streams. The authentication method adopted the Timed Efficient Stream Loss-tolerant Authentication (TESLA) protocol, used MAC encryption, and employed delayed key transmission for ADS-B data authentication. Format-preserving encryption was used for the Aircraft Address (AA) field in ADS-B, with the reserved fields in the message used to transmit authentication information, thus achieving lightweight authentication of ADS-B data [19]. Wu et al. put forward a certificate-less short signature scheme for ADS-B, where the user's private key is jointly generated by the Key Generation Center (KGC) and the user [20].

3.2 Anomaly Detection

The aforementioned solutions often require modifications to the current protocol architecture (e.g., adding encryption or authentication mechanisms). However, with the ADS-B system already deployed in most aircraft, such modifications to the existing protocol are not practical at this stage.

Sampigethaya and Kovell have proposed a solution that uses Kalman filter and group verification techniques to detect significant deviations in trajectory data [21, 22]. Habler et al. suggested the use of a seq2seq model of Long Short-Term Memory (LSTM) for determining ADS-B anomalies. By partitioning the extended ADS-B time sequence into multiple window blocks using a sliding window, the trained network predicts the value at the next moment, with anomalies identified based on cosine similarity [23]. Akerman proposed the use of a ConvLSTM encoder-decoder to detect anomalies in image streams formed by aircraft ADS-B information within a specified range. Their VizADS-B anomaly detection model also provides relevant operational information for pilots [24]. Melnyk et al. adopted an unsupervised model framework, which uses a Vector Auto-Regressive model with eXogenous variables (VARX) to represent each flight. They computed a distance matrix between flights and used the Local Outlier Factor (LOF) method to identify anomalous flights [25]. Das et al. developed MKAD, which can effectively detect significant anomalies in heterogeneous sequences containing discrete and continuous variables. Based on kernel functions and One-Class Support Vector Machine (OC-SVM), MKAD can identify operational conditions in Flight Operational Quality Assurance (FOQA) data, such as round-trip operations, unusually high-speed flights, gust-affected flights, and abnormal approaches [26]. Churchill et al. proposed a hierarchical clustering method for grouping the spatiotemporal trajectories of aircraft on the airport surface [27]. Olive et al. introduced a method based on autoencoders to analyze flight trajectories, detect unusual flight behaviors, and infer Air Traffic Control (ATC) actions from past Mode S data [28].

Such methods analyze at the data level. Without changing the original system architecture and standards, they achieve the goal of anomalous ADS-B data determination with minimal cost.

4 Methodology

4.1 Problem Formulation

The multivariate time series is composed of multiple univariate time series from the same entity. ADS-B messages are a quintessential example of this, where a single time series encompasses sequential sensor data, collected with uniform time interval stamps. We define the problem as follows:

The input of the multivariate time series is represented as $\mathbf{X} = \{\mathbf{x}_1, \mathbf{x}_2, \ldots, \mathbf{x}_N\}$, where $\mathbf{X} \in R^{M \times N}$. Here, N is the length of the time series, representing the time series of continuous N timestamps, and M denotes the number of features. $\mathbf{x}_t \in \mathbf{x}$ is an M-dimensional vector, with $\mathbf{x}_t = [x_t^1, x_t^2, \ldots, x_t^M]$. For long time series, they are generated through a sliding window of length T, and $\mathbf{W_T} \in R^{M \times T}$ is a set of time series of length T, which consists of $\{\mathbf{x}_{t-T+1}, \ldots, \mathbf{x}_t\}$ from time $t\text{-}T + 1$ to t.

The task of anomaly detection is to generate an output vector $y \in R^n$, where $y_i \in \{0, 1\}$ signifies whether the ith th timestamp is anomalous or not.

4.2 Model Architecture

The overall network structure of SR-GNN is depicted in Fig. 2:

The first layer initially employs the single-variable anomaly detection method, Spectral Residual (SR) [11], to replace point anomalies in the training data with the normal values surrounding that timestamp. We posit that point anomalies in aerial flight are generally system noise. Subsequently, a one-dimensional convolution is used to extract features from each time series, where the convolution operation demonstrates excellent performance in terms of local features within the sliding window.

The second layer processes the output from the previous layer through two graph attention layers, which emphasize the relationships among features and among timestamps, respectively.

The third layer concatenates the outputs from the first two layers and feeds them into the RNN [29] and VAE [30], respectively. The RNN is employed to achieve the prediction results, while the VAE is used for data reconstruction.

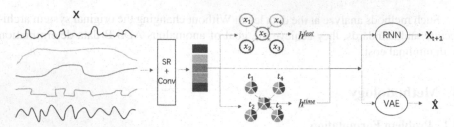

Fig. 2. The SR-GNN of Architecture of for Anomaly Detection in ADS-B Data

4.3 Graph Attention Networks

GAT is capable of modeling relationships between any nodes within a graph. Given a graph of n nodes $\{v_1, v_2, \cdots, v_n\}$, where v_i represents the feature vector of each node, the GAT layer calculates the output representation of each node as follows:

$$h_i = \sigma\left(\sum_{j=1}^{L} \alpha_{ij} v_j\right) \tag{1}$$

Here, h_i denotes the output representation of node i, which has the same shape as the input v_i; σ represents the sigmoid activation function; α_{ij} is the attention score, measuring the contribution of node j to node i, where j is one of the neighboring nodes of i, and L represents the quantity of neighboring nodes. The formula is as follows:

$$e_{ij} = \text{LeakyReLU}\left(w^\top \cdot \left(v_i \oplus v_j\right)\right) \tag{2}$$

$$\alpha_{ij} = \frac{\exp(e_{ij})}{\sum_{l=1}^{L} \exp(e_{il})} \tag{3}$$

where $\oplus$ represents the concatenation of representations from two nodes, $w \in R^{2m}$ is a learnable column vector of parameters, where m is the dimension of the feature vector for each node, and LeakyReLU is a non-linear activation function [32]. In the context of multivariate time series anomaly detection, we employ two types of graph attention layers, namely, feature-oriented graph attention and time-oriented graph attention.

Feature Oriented Graph Attention Layer
Each feature is considered as a node, and each edge represents the relationship between features. The relationships between neighboring nodes are captured by the feature graph attention layer. Each node $x_i = \{x_{i,t} \mid t \in [0, n)\}$, where n is the total number of timestamps. Figure 1 displays a relationship graph of a node.

Time Oriented Graph Attention Layer
Each feature vector at timestamp t is considered as a node, with neighboring nodes being other feature vectors within the same time window. In this way, the time-dependency of the sequence is captured by the time graph attention layer.

4.4 Training Model

Loss Function of Prediction

The prediction-based model employs an RNN model comprised of Gated Recurrent Units (GRU) to predict the value at the next timestamp. The loss function is calculated using the Root Mean Square Error (RMSE):

$$LOSS_{pre} = \sqrt{\sum_{i=1}^{k} \left(x_{n,i} - \hat{x}_{n,i}\right)^2} \tag{4}$$

x_n represents the input $x = (x_0, x_1, \ldots, x_{n-1})$; $x_{n,i}$ represents the ith feature in x_n, and $\hat{x}_{n,i}$ is the output value of the prediction model.

Loss Function of Reconstruction

The reconstruction-based model uses VAE, which provides a probabilistic means to describe the latent space. Given an input x, the conditional distribution of the output is $p_\theta(z \mid x)$:

$$p_\theta(z \mid x) = p_\theta(x \mid z)p_\theta(z)/p_\theta(x) \tag{5}$$

$$p_\theta(x) = \int p_\theta(z)p_\theta(x \mid z)dz \tag{6}$$

Calculate the above equation is challenging, so we introduce an inference model $q_\phi(z \mid x)$ to approximate the posterior distribution. The loss function based on reconstruction can be calculated as follows:

$$\text{Loss}_{rec} = -E_{q_\phi(z|x)}\left[log p_\theta(x \mid z)\right] + D_{KL}\left(q_\phi(z \mid x) \| p_\theta(z)\right) \tag{7}$$

Loss Function of Model

The loss of the model is the sum of two loss functions.

$$\text{Loss} = \text{Loss}_{pre} + \text{Loss}_{rec} \tag{8}$$

4.5 Threshold Calculation and Exception Score

The model produces two outputs for the input, one is the predicted value and the other is the reconstruction probability. Finally, an anomaly score s_i is calculated for each feature, and the sum of all anomaly scores constitutes the final score. The threshold is automatically selected using the Peak Over Threshold (POT) method [31].

$$Score = \sum_{i=1}^{k} s_i \tag{9}$$

$$s_i = \frac{\left(\hat{x}_i - x_i\right)^2 + \gamma \times (1 - p_i)}{1 + \gamma} \tag{10}$$

5   Experimental Setup

5.1   Data Collectiom

OpenSky Network is a non-profit flight tracking and aviation data sharing platform [32]. The project utilizes Automatic Dependent Surveillance-Broadcast (ADS-B) signals collected by volunteers worldwide to provide open-source aviation data for research, analysis, and innovation. This platform allows participants to view and analyze flight data, contributing to improving the efficiency and enhancing flight safety in the aviation industry.

Traffic is an open-source tool based on Python that allows users to query and download historical data from the OpenSky Network [33]. It simplifies the data collection process by aggregating different types of ADS-B information such as position, velocity, and identification, making data cleaning less cumbersome. Sun et al. implemented a clustering algorithm that separates raw data composed of a series of messages into well-defined flights once decoded [34]. The ADS-B message transmitters receive position and velocity information every half-second and identification information every five seconds. The short intervals between these receptions result in a significant amount of data redundancy that cannot be ignored.

Traffic enables downsampling and concatenation of different information, transforming the original time series from several messages per second to one message per second. This approach offers an evident advantage of reducing the size of the dataset. Additionally, reducing the amount of information has another benefit, as it affects the amount of information contained within a time window. This greatly improves the time-dependency of the RNN layer, leading to significant improvements in training time and accuracy.

5.2   Data Preprocessing

The training data consists of normal data, while the test data is generated by applying simple modifications to the normal data to create abnormal test data. The methods for generating abnormal test data are as follows:

Altitude+: Increase the altitude information of certain time periods in the data.
Altitude−: Decrease the altitude information of certain time periods in the data.
Speed+: Increase the speed information of certain time periods in the data.
Speed−: Decrease the speed information of certain time periods in the data.

To enhance the robustness of the model, we normalize each univariate time series by scaling it using the maximum and minimum values in the data. This normalization process involves standardizing the time series using the maximum and minimum values present in the data.

$$\tilde{x} = \frac{x - \min(X_{\text{train}})}{\max(X_{\text{train}}) - \min(X_{\text{train}})} \tag{11}$$

5.3 Experimental Method

In the experiment, we utilized complete data from 100 flight routes throughout the entire flight phase as the training data, consisting of a total of 915,339 message data. Additionally, modified data from 12 flight routes were used as the test data. The model was implemented using the PyTorch library with the Adam optimizer. A sliding window size of 64 was employed, and the learning rate was set to 0.001.

5.4 Experimental Evaluation

We evaluate the anomaly detection performance of the model using Precision, Recall, and F1 score.

$$Precision = \frac{TP}{TP + FP} \tag{12}$$

$$Recall = \frac{TP}{TP + FN} \tag{13}$$

$$F1 = 2 \cdot \frac{Precision \cdot Recall}{Precision + Recall} \tag{14}$$

In the evaluation, TP represents true positives, FP represents false positives, and FN represents false negatives.

To demonstrate the performance of SR-GNN, we compare it with five other methods used for ADS-B anomaly detection. These methods are LSTM-AE [23], IForest [35], VAE-SVDD [36], K-Means [37], and OC-SVM [4]. The evaluation results, as shown in Table 1, indicate that SR-GNN outperforms all other models in terms of anomaly detection across all abnormal data samples.

Table 1. Experimental Result.

Methods	Altitude+			Altitude−		
	Prcision	Recall	F1	Prcision	Recall	F1
LSTM-AE	**0.9987**	0.7235	0.8627	**0.9999**	0.8814	0.9369
IForest	0.4630	0.7344	0.5629	0.6593	0.9069	0.7479
K-Means	0.5654	0.6264	0.5981	0.659	0.6424	0.6504
OC-SVM	0.6664	0.8264	0.6764	0.6684	0.7359	0.6949
SR-GNN	0.9588	**0.9999**	**0.9790**	0.9391	**0.9999**	**0.9686**

(*continued*)

Table 1. (*continued*)

Methods	Speed+			Speed−		
	Prcision	Recall	F1	Prcision	Recall	F1
LSTM-AE	**0.9999**	0.8814	0.9369	0.0783	0.0809	0.0798
IForest	0.2939	0.7384	0.4196	0.3939	0.9681	0.5599
K-Means	0.4899	0.5629	0.5227	0.6107	0.6639	0.3359
OC-SVM	0.3112	0.8224	0.4505	0.3925	0.9999	0.5637
SR-GNN	0.9461	**0.9999**	**0.9695**	**0.9487**	**0.9999**	**0.9699**

6   Conclusion and Future Work

In this study, we propose a multivariate time series anomaly detection approach that combines SR with GNN models to detect injected false data in ADS-B messages. To address the multivariate nature of ADS-B data, we utilize feature-based graph attention layers to capture relationships between features. Furthermore, to capture the time-dependent characteristics of ADS-B data, we employ time-based graph attention layers to capture temporal dependencies. The prediction and reconstruction models are jointly optimized. Experimental results demonstrate that the proposed model achieves excellent performance across various evaluation metrics. Future work will focus on fully exploring the characteristics of ADS-B data and incorporating additional features during training to further enhance the model's performance.

References

1. Mccallie, D., Butts, J., Mills, R.: Security analysis of the ADS-B implementation in the next generation air transportation system. Int. J. Crit. Infrastruct. Prot. **4**(2), 78–87 (2011)
2. Magazu, D., Mills, R.F., Butts, J.W., Robinson, D.J.: Exploiting automatic dependent surveillance-broadcast via false target injection (2012)
3. Costin, A., Francillon, A.: Ghost in the air (traffic): on insecurity of ADS-B protocol and practical attacks on ADS-B devices (2021)
4. Schlkopf, B., Williamson, R.C., Smola, A.J., Shawe-Taylor, J., Platt, J.C.: Support vector method for novelty detection. In: Advances in Neural Information Processing Systems, NIPS Conference, Denver, Colorado, USA, 29 November–4 December 1999, vol. 12 (1999)
5. Zhou, C., Paffenroth, R.C.: Anomaly detection with robust deep autoencoders. In: The 23rd ACM SIGKDD International Conference (2017)
6. An, J., Cho, S.: Variational autoencoder based anomaly detection using reconstruction probability (2015)
7. Defferrard, M., Bresson, X., Vandergheynst, P.: Convolutional neural networks on graphs with fast localized spectral filtering (2016)
8. Kipf, T.N., Welling, M.: Semi-supervised classification with graph convolutional networks (2016)
9. Velikovi, P., Cucurull, G., Casanova, A., Romero, A., Liò, P., Bengio, Y.: Graph attention networks (2017)

10. Schlichtkrull, M., Kipf, T.N., Bloem, P., Berg, R., Titov, I., Welling, M.: Modeling relational data with graph convolutional networks. In: Gangemi, A., et al. (eds.) ESWC 2018. LNCS, vol. 10843, pp. 593–607. Springer, Cham (2018). https://doi.org/10.1007/978-3-319-93417-4_38

11. Ren, H., Xu, B., Wang, Y., Yi, C., Huang, C., Kou, X., et al.: Time-series anomaly detection service at microsoft. ACM (2019)

12. Schäfer, M., Lenders, V., Martinovic, I.: Experimental analysis of attacks on next generation air traffic communication. In: Jacobson, M., Locasto, M., Mohassel, P., Safavi-Naini, R. (eds.) ACNS 2013. LNCS, vol. 7954, pp. 253–271. Springer, Heidelberg (2013). https://doi.org/10.1007/978-3-642-38980-1_16

13. Strohmeier, M., Schfer, M., Lenders, V., Martinovic, I.: enabling next-generation airborne communications realities and challenges of nextgen air traffic management: the case of ads-b (2015)

14. Pöpper, C., Tippenhauer, N.O., Danev, B., Capkun, S.: Investigation of signal and message manipulations on the wireless channel. In: Atluri, V., Diaz, C. (eds.) ESORICS 2011. LNCS, vol. 6879, pp. 40–59. Springer, Heidelberg (2011). https://doi.org/10.1007/978-3-642-23822-2_3

15. Wilhelm, M., Schmitt, J.B., Lenders, V.: Practical message manipulation attacks in IEEE 802.15.4 wireless networks. In: MMB & DFT 2012 (2012)

16. Samuelson, K., Valovage, E., Hall, D.: Enhanced ADS-B research. In: Digital Avionics Systems Conference (2007)

17. Baek, J., Byon, Y.J., Hableel, E., Al-Qutayri, M.: An authentication framework for automatic dependent surveillance-broadcast based on online/offline identity-based signature. Secur. Commun. Netw. 8(5), 740–750 (2015)

18. He, D., Kumar, N., Choo, K.K.R., Wu, W.: Efficient hierarchical identity-based signature with batch verification for automatic dependent surveillance-broadcast system. IEEE Trans. Inf. Forensics Secur. 12(2), 454–464 (2016)

19. Yang, H., Zhou, Q., Yao, M., Lu, R., Zhang, X.: A practical and compatible cryptographic solution to ADS-B security. IEEE Internet Things J. 6, 3322–3334 (2018)

20. Wu, Z., Guo, A., Yue, M., Liu, L.: An ADS-B message authentication method based on certificateless short signature. IEEE Trans. Aeros. Electron. Syst. 56(3), 1742–1753 (2019)

21. Sampigethaya, K., Poovendran, R., Bushnell, L.: A framework for securing future e-enabled aircraft navigation and surveillance. AIAA J. (2009)

22. Kovell, B., Mellish, B., Newman, T., Kajopaiye, O.: Comparative analysis of ADS-B verification techniques (2012)

23. Habler, E., Shabtai, A.: Using LSTM encoder-decoder algorithm for detecting anomalous ADS-B messages. Comput. Secur. 78, 155–173 (2017)

24. Akerman, S., Habler, E., Shabtai, A.: VizADS-B: analyzing sequences of ADS-B images using explainable convolutional LSTM encoder-decoder to detect cyber attacks (2019)

25. Melnyk, I., Matthews, B., Valizadegan, H., Banerjee, A., Oza, N.: Vector autoregressive model-based anomaly detection in aviation systems. J. Aeros. Inf. Syst. 13(4), 1–13 (2016)

26. Das, S., Matthews, B.L., Srivastava, A.N., Oza, N.C.: Multiple Kernel learning for heterogeneous anomaly detection: algorithm and aviation safety case study. In: ACM Sigkdd International Conference on Knowledge Discovery & Data Mining (2010)

27. Churchill, A.M., Bloem, M.: Clustering aircraft trajectories on the airport surface. In: Proceedings of the 13th USA/Europe Air Traffic Management Research and Development Seminar, Chicago, IL, USA, pp. 10–13 (2019)

28. Olive, X., Grignard, J., Dubot, T., Saint-Lot, J.: Detecting controllers' actions in past mode S data by autoencoder-based anomaly detection. In: SESAR Innovation Days (2018)

29. Chung, J., Gulcehre, C., Cho, K.H., Bengio, Y.: Empirical evaluation of gated recurrent neural networks on sequence modeling. Eprint Arxiv (2014)

30. Kingma, D.P., Welling, M.: Auto-encoding variational bayes. arXivorg (2014)
31. Siffer, A., Fouque, P.A., Termier, A., Largouet, C.: Anomaly detection in streams with extreme value theory. In: ACM Sigkdd International Conference (2017)
32. Schafer, M., Strohmeier, M., Lenders, V., Martinovic, I., Wilhelm, M.: Bringing up OpenSky: a large-scale ADS-B sensor network for research. In: IPSN-14 International Symposium on Information Processing in Sensor Networks, pp. 83–94 (2014)
33. Olive, X.: Traffic, a toolbox for processing and analysing air traffic data. J. Open Source Softw. 4(39), 1518 (2019)
34. Sun, J., Ellerbroek, J., Hoekstra, J.: Flight extraction and phase identification for large automatic dependent surveillance-broadcast datasets. J. Aerosp. Comput. Inf. Commun. 14(10), 1–6 (2017)
35. Liu, F.T., Ting, K.M., Zhou, Z.H.: Isolation forest. In: IEEE International Conference on Data Mining (2008)
36. Luo, P., Wang, B., Li, T., Tian, J.: ADS-B anomaly data detection model based on VAE-SVDD. Comput. Secur. 104(2), 102213 (2021)
37. Wong, J.A.H.A.: Algorithm AS 136: a K-means clustering algorithm. J. Roy. Stat. Soc. 28(1), 100–108 (1979)

Learned Pseudo-Random Number Generator Based on Generative Adversarial Networks

Xuguang Wu, Yiliang Han(✉), Shuaishuai Zhu, Yu Li, Su Cui, and Xuan Wang

College of Cryptography Engineering, Engineering University of People's Armed
Police, Xi'an 710086, China
hanyil@163.com

Abstract. Pseudorandom number generators (PRNGs) are fundamental components of modern cryptography and information security. Due to the inherent complexity and unpredictability of neural networks, they have become an attractive alternative for designing PRNGs. In recent years, several PRNGs based on Generative Adversarial Networks (GANs) have been proposed, which is an end-to-end generation approach. However, current GAN-based PRNGs have been found to suffer from several limitations. For instance, their input length is often too short to resist exhaustive attacks. And the randomness tests of NIST are not always met under recommended parameter settings, indicating the need for further improvement in the design of GAN-based PRNGs. To address these issues, this paper proposes a practical and secure PRNG designed based on GANs. Specifically, we rationalized the input and output parameters by setting the input to 32 8-bit unsigned integers and the output to 256 8-bit unsigned integers in a single iteration, ensuring that the input data space reaches 2^{256}. We also optimized the GAN network architecture and incorporated the GELU activation function to ensure that the generated output passes all randomness tests of NIST under the recommended parameter settings.

Keywords: Adversarial neural networks · Pseudo-random number generators · Neural cryptography

1 Introduction

Random number generators(RNGs) have a wide range of applications in the fields of cryptography [1], secure communication [2], and computer simulation [3]. According to the different generation methods, they can be divided into two types: true random number generators(TRNGs) and pseudo random number generators(PRNGs). TRNGs mainly utilize the inherent randomness of physical phenomena, chemical phenomena, or biological characteristics to generate

This work is supported by The National Defense Innovation Project(No. ZZKY20222411), National Natural Science Foundation of China (No. 61572521), and Natural Science Basic Research Plan in Shaanxi Province of China (No. 2021JM252).

random numbers. Although TRNGs can generate sequences with high randomness and good distribution properties, they still rely on the inherent randomness of a specific phenomenon in reality, which poses certain limitations and adds complexity to their implementation.

In contrast, PRNGs [4,5] use deterministic algorithms with a seed as input to generate a large pseudo-random number sequence, which apparently has a length greater than the input. Moreover, this output distribution cannot be truly random, but is pseudorandom, which means it is indistinguishable from the uniform distribution. Compared to TRNGs, PRNGs typically only use software methods, making them easier to implement on a computer. The algorithms of PRNGs usually include the square median method, linear congruence method [6], and linear feedback shift register method [7].

Recently, deep learning has gradually emerged in the design of PRNGs. Due to the weak explanatory power of neural networks, their use in PRNGs design can result in unpredictable randomness. Additionally, neural networks possess numerous parameters, and a single training can generate a PRNG algorithm automatically. The existing PRNGs designs based on deep learning can be categorized into two types: (1) utilizing deep neural networks as a component to develop complex PRNG algorithms, such as those based on recurrent neural networks (RNNs) [8], hierarchical neural networks (HNNs) [9], long short-term memory (LSTM) networks [10], and so forth; (2) training end-to-end PRNG generators [11–14] using generated adversarial networks (GANs) [15].

This paper focuses on the pseudo-random number generator based on GAN. Numerous challenges exist in this field, including the limited input space for pseudo-random numbers, output data lengths not exceeding input data lengths, and the need for further improvement in the results of NIST randomness testing [16].

To address the aforementioned issues, this paper proposes a more practical and secure pseudorandom number generator. The input and output parameters are rationalized, with the input set to 32 8-bit unsigned integers and the output to 256 8-bit unsigned integers in a single iteration, such that the space for input data reaches 2^{256}. Additionally, the output length meets the requirement of a pseudorandom number generator being greater than the input length. The network structure is optimized, and the GELU activation function [17] is utilized to ensure that the output data passes the randomness tests of NIST Test under the recommended parameter settings.

The specific contributions are as follows.

- We propose a novel GAN-based pseudorandom number generator (PRNG). In comparison to prior work, our PRNG boasts a significantly longer input data length of 256 bits, which surpasses the generally accepted safe limit of 128 bits and effectively mitigates the risk of malicious attacks. Additionally, our PRNG outputs 256 × 8 bits in a single iteration, which is considerably larger than the input length of 256 bits, thus meeting the prescribed pseudo-random number length criteria. Particularly, our proposed PRNG exhibits superior randomness, input sensitivity, and predictable performance.

– We carefully design the model structure and set the appropriate network parameters, which guarantees that pseudorandom number generators have good performance. In particular, we have found that the GELU activation function is more effective in generating pseudo-random numbers. Furthermore, we leverage the BCE loss function to optimize our model and accurately measure both true and pseudo random numbers.
– We deploye the designed PRNG onto the paddlepaddle platform and conducted rigorous experimental tests. The implementation code can be found at https://aistudio.baidu.com/aistudio/projectdetail/5716463.

The remainder of this manuscript is structured as follows. In Sect. 2, we provide an overview of the prerequisite knowledge, including PRNGs, GANs and PaddlePaddle code implementation frameworks. In Sect. 3, we review related work and analyze their shortcomings while identifying areas for improvement. The proposed GAN-based PRNG implementation is presented in Sect. 4. In Sect. 5, we evaluate the experimental results, including randomness testing, sensitivity testing, and predictive testing. Finally, we conclude in Sect. 6.

2   Preliminaries

This section delves into the fundamental principles of PRNG and GANs, and then provides an overview of the PaddlePaddle platform, which is utilized for implementing the codes.

2.1   Generative Adversarial Networks

The introduction of generative adversarial networks can be traced back to the seminal work by Ian Goodfellow in 2014 [15]. Since its inception, GANs have garnered significant attention and interest from the academic community, as evidenced by the proliferation of GAN variants and architectures. Notable examples of such innovations include Conditional GAN (CGAN) [18], Deep Convolutional GAN (DCGAN) [19], Information Maximizing GAN (InfoGAN) [20], and Sequence Generative Adversarial Networks (SeqGAN) [21].

This section utilizes the generation of images as a case study to elucidate the concept of GANs. As depicted in Fig. 1, GAN comprises two neural networks, namely, the generator network (G) and the discriminator network (D). The former is responsible for learning the distribution of real data, while the latter functions as a binary classifier tasked with distinguishing between real and generated data.

The genuine data samples x follow the distribution $P_r(x)$, while the latent space variables z conform to the distribution $P_z(z)$, such as Gaussian or uniform distribution. In the generator G, data samples $y = G(z)$ are generated by sampling from z. The discriminator D then evaluates both the real data samples x and the generated samples y to produce binary classification results. In the original GAN framework, the discriminator D performs binary classification. The

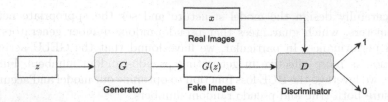

Fig. 1. GAN model.

fundamental idea of GAN involves using binary cross entropy as the loss function. Specifically, the real data samples are labeled with 1, whereas the generated samples are labeled with 0. The generator G aims to synthesize data samples such that the discriminator D is tricked into labeling them as real data samples with a label of 1. The objective function of GAN can thus be defined as follows:

$$\min_G \max_D V(D, G) = \mathbb{E}_{x \sim P_r} [\log D(x)] + \mathbb{E}_{z \sim P_z} [\log (1 - D(G(z)))] \quad (1)$$

2.2   Deep Learning Framework PaddlePaddle

Although several deep learning platforms and frameworks exist, including TensorFlow and PyTorch, this paper centers on PaddlePaddle, another popular deep learning platform. PaddlePaddle provides a powerful and scalable environment for developing deep learning models, boasting comprehensive model libraries, end-to-end development kits, advanced tool components, and deep learning training and reasoning frameworks. The platform's extensive capabilities and cutting-edge features make it an alluring option for researchers and practitioners alike.

3   Related Works

This section aims to provide a comprehensive review of current GAN-based PRNG schemes, as well as an in-depth analysis of their underlying issues.

In 2018, Bernardi et al. [11] proposed two GAN-based models that focus on discriminative and predictive patterns in PRNG, as illustrated in Fig. 2. In the discriminative mode, G functions as a pseudo-random number generator, with seed and internal state s_i as input parameters. The discriminator D, on the other hand, utilizes a combination of a randomly extracted true random number and a pseudo-random number generated by G to distinguish between the two. The discriminator D undergoes continual adversarial training with G, ultimately improving the pseudo-random number generation capability of G. In the predictive mode, G is again utilized, with the predictor P acting as the opponent instead of the discriminator D. P predicts the last element of an output sequence generated by the first $n-1$ elements of G's output; continual adversarial training ensues until there is no further room for improvement.

In this research, two 16-bit unsigned integers are used as input data for the generator G, which then outputs eight 16-bit unsigned integers. The research specifies a direct binary conversion of the eight generated integers to obatin the binary random number. The proposed models offer a promising direction for improving PRNG using GAN and provide insight into potential applications in cryptography and information security.

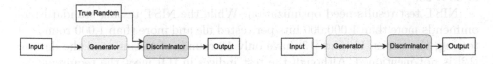

Fig. 2. The discriminative mode (left) and predictive mode (right)

In 2019, Oak et al. [12] presented a novel approach to pseudorandom number generation that employs a three-layer fully connected neural network with random input matrix. However, the literature lacks specific input parameter definitions. As for the output, Oak et al. specified a matrix size of 256×1 in a single iteration. In terms of binarization, the researchers normalize the floating-point data before rounding to the nearest integer values of either 0 or 1.

In 2021, Kim et al. [13] introduced a novel predictive mode PRNG that utilizes a GAN-based architecture with four fully connected layers and LeakyReLU and sigmoid activation functions. The generator process involves the incorporation of 64 bits of input data, resulting in an output of 137400, which is a substantial amount of data that necessitates significant computational resources for processing. To perform binary conversion, the authors proposed a method that relies on determining the nearest binary value based on the output of the sigmoid activation function.

In 2022, Okada et al. [14] introduced a novel PRNG that is based on the Wasserstein GAN [22] with gradient penalty algorithm. The generator architecture comprises a single fully connected layer, with input data of 36×1 floating-point numbers and output data of the same size. To perform binarization of the output data, the researchers employed the mantissa method, which involves extracting the mantissa within the floating-point numbers in the output data to generate binary random numbers. The authors argue that the mantissa within the floating-point numbers possesses a considerable degree of randomness, which can be utilized for generating secure and unpredictable random numbers.

However, several issues and challenges exist in the current state of the art that require further attention and investigation.

Most considered PRNGs have insufficient input space due to the simplification of the internal state s_i by Bernardi et al. The input sizes of manuscripts [11,13] and [14] are 32, 64, and 1152 bits floating point, respectively. Research indicates that PRNGs with less than 128 bits may be vulnerable to exhaustive attacks.

The parameter settings employed by Gan and Okada in their work [14] do not conform to established criteria for designing PRNGs. Their generator architecture uses a 36×1 floating-point number as input and produces a 36×1 floating-point number as output. The authors compute the output pseudorandom number as the mantissa of a floating-point number, which occupies only 23 bits of memory compared to the full floating-point number (32 bits). Consequently, the input space in their generator exceeds the maximum output space of 36×23.

NIST test results need optimization. While the NIST testing standard recommends more than 1,000,000 bits per tested file and more than 1,000 rounds of testing, the works [11] and [13] have only 10 rounds of testing, and the data in [12] is not mentioned. Although the test indices in [14] meet the requirements, its input and output length fail to satisfy the definition of PRNG.

4   Proposed Method

In this section, we provide a detailed description of the design and architecture of PRNG based on GAN, along with the specific techniques employed for their integration during training, which facilitates the generation of superior-quality pseudo-random numbers.

4.1   Generator Model Design

The generator G can be represented as a function :

$$G(s_0) : \mathbb{U}^{32} \to \mathbb{U}^n \tag{2}$$

where s_0 is a random seed, n is a very large number, $\mathbb{U}$ is represented as an 8-bit unsigned integer, which takes values in the range $[0, 255]$. And the output of PRNG is a sequence of pseudo random numbers.

The traditional PRNG is a structure $(S, \mu, \mathcal{U}, f, g)$, where S is a finite set of states, μ is a probability distribution on S used to select the initial state s_0(or *seed*), $f : S \to S$ is the transition function, $\mathcal{U}$ is the output space and $g : S \to \mathcal{U}$ is the output function. As illustrated in Fig. 3, we conducted an adaptive transformation based on neural networks, where G's input $\mathbb{U}^{32}$ are used as s_{i-1}, and G's output $\mathbb{U}^{256}$ are divided into two parts, with the first $1/8$ serving as s_i and the latter $7/8$ serving as random number u_i output. For individual iteration, our PRNG can be expressed mathematically as follows:

$$G^\nabla(s_{i-1}) : \mathbb{U}^{32} \to \mathbb{U}^{256} \tag{3}$$

Generally, to ensure security against brute force attacks, a safe input length is typically 128 bits. In our work, we have set the input length to 256 bits to increase the input data space of G.

At the same time, we represent functions f and g using neural networks. The generator G consists of four Dense layers, which are deeply interconnected. A Dense layer is a fully connected layer where each neuron is linked to every neuron. The parameters for the four Dense layers are (32,100), (100,200), (200,400), and (400,256) respectively. During the training process, the four Dense layers progressively increase the dimensionality from 32 to 400 before decreasing it to 256.

The GELU activation function [17] is utilized in the initial three layers of Dense. In comparison to other commonly employed activation functions, such as ReLU and Sigmoid, GELU boasts a stronger non-linear characteristic that augments the model's efficacy and enhances the randomness of the output sequence. The output of the last layer of Dense is a 256-dimensional floating-point number. To convert it to a binary sequence, we apply the Mod activation function, which executes modular operations on data, yielding integer portions.

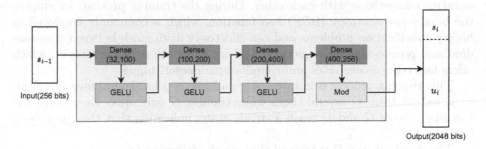

Fig. 3. Architecture of the generator

4.2 Discriminator Model Design

The discriminator D can be represented as a function :

$$D(input) : \mathbb{U}^{256} \rightarrow p, p \in [0, 1] \tag{4}$$

D takes as input 256 8-bit unsigned integers, which can be either a pseudo-random sequence generated by G or a random sequence with true randomness. D processes the input sequence and produces a probability value p that indicates the likelihood of the sequence being true randomness. The ideal output of D for a true random sequence is 1, while the ideal output for a non-random sequence is 0.

The structure of the discriminator D is illustrated in Fig. 4. We have adopted a network architecture similar to that of previous studies [11]. The network comprises Conv1d (1D Convolution Layers) and Dense layers. Each Conv1d layer has a filter value of 4, a kernel size of 2, and a stride value of 1. The parameters for the two Dense layers are (1004,4) and (4,1), respectively. All activation functions utilized are GELU, except for the output layer which employs Sigmoid.

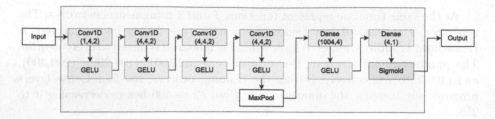

Fig. 4. Architecture of the discriminator

4.3 Train Design of Our PRNG Based on GAN

This paper proposes a novel method for enhancing the quality of PRNG by leveraging the adversarial game idea of generative adversarial networks. The approach involves optimizing both the generator G and the discriminator D through an iterative competition with each other. During the training process, we employ the binary cross-entropy (BCE) loss function, which is commonly employed in binary classification problems and can effectively distinguish between true random and pseudo-random sequences. And we select the Adam optimizer, which offers fast convergence rates and simplifies parameter tuning.

This training process is iterated over multiple epochs. To improve D's accuracy, we can train D several times while training G only once. Eventually, the loss functions of G and D reach a steady state, indicating that they have been optimized.

The discriminator D is trained through the following process:

- Input the random numbers into G to obtain a generated pseudo-random sequence.
- Input the generated pseudo-random sequence into D to determine the probability p_{fake} that the sequence is a true random sequence.
- Input the true random sequence into D to determine the probability p_{true}.
- The goal of D is to minimize p_{fake} and maximize p_{true}, aiming to enhance its ability to discern between true random and pseudo-random sequences.
- The binary crossentropy loss function $loss_D = bce(p_{fake}, 0.0) + bce(p_{true}, 1.0)$ is used to evaluate D's performance.
- Adam optimizer is employed to perform gradient descent for parameter updates, enhancing D's performance in identifying true randomness.

The primary objective of G is to maximize D's inaccuracy, thereby minimizing the probability that D assigns to a pseudo-random sequence. The detailed training procedure is as follows:

- Feed the random seed s_0 into G to produce a pseudo-random sequence;
- Input this pseudo-random sequence into D, and D calculates p_{fake}.
- Calculate the binary crossentropy loss function $loss_G = bce(p_{fake}, 1.0)$.
- Perform gradient descent using Adam so that the sequence generated by G is increasingly random. Adam optimizer is employed to perform gradient descent

to update G's parameters, influencing the generated sequence's randomness positively.

5   Evaluation Study

This section offers a comprehensive account of the experiments conducted to assess the effectiveness and efficiency of the proposed algorithm. In addition, the implementation of the proposed algorithm, including the proposed details of the experiment, can be accessed through the following link: https://aistudio.baidu.com/aistudio/projectdetail/5716463.

5.1   Experiment Settings

For our experiments, we utilize the PaddlePaddle platform, which hosts a Tesla V100 GPU graphics card with 16GB of memory. Python version 3.7.4 and PaddlePaddle-GPU 2.4.0 are used in the program environment. Notably, the training of the model did not demand an excessive amount of resource consumption, thus enabling the possibility of training it on a CPU as well.

To evaluate the performance of our proposed PRNG based on GAN, we meticulously test and select the network's hyperparameters. The system's hyperparameters are specified as follows:

- **Input Data**: To optimize the input data space, our model employs 32 8-bit unsigned integers as its input. The model's output is composed of 256 8-bit unsigned integers in a single iteration. During training, these 32 8-bit unsigned integers are randomly generated by PaddlePaddle. We aspire for the input data to be as random as possible, and through training, the output data should also exhibit a high level of randomness, in order to achieve the desired final trained model. During the evaluation phase, the input data is truncated from the first eighth of the output data. By continuously recursing in this manner, longer pseudo-random sequences can be generated.
- **Batch Size**: In the training phase, a batch size of 32 is selected to allow D to optimize its ability to discern true random and non-random data. Conversely, during the evaluation phase, a larger batch size of 512 is set to facilitate the generator's production of as much data as possible at once. With a batch size of 560 inputs, the PRNG can generate a sequence of random data of length 1,003,520 bits.
- **Initialization**: The Gaussian distribution is applied to determine the initial weight values of the Conv1d layers, with a mean value of zero and a variance of 0.02. As for the Dense layers, uniform distribution is utilized to initialize their weights and biases, with the weight range spanning from $[-1, 1]$ and the bias range being $[-2, 2]$.
- **Number of Iterations**: This parameter denotes to the number of training steps, which is set to 10,000.
- **Optimizer**: The Adam optimizer is employed in PaddlePaddle, with a learning rate of 0.001.

– **Evaluation Data**: With the aforementioned parameters in place, evaluation was carried out 1000 times, producing a random sequence of 1,003,520,000 bits.

5.2   NIST Tests

The National Institute of Standards and Technology (NIST) has developed a series of information security standards that, while not formally adopted as official standards, are widely recognized by the international community for their practical application. NIST SP800-22 is dedicated to testing the randomness of numerical sequences. This standard encompasses 15 distinct tests that evaluate the quality of randomness based on various criteria. Achieving success in all of these tests is indicative of high-quality random numbers.

The following are different tests for evaluating the randomness of a sequence:

– **Frequency Test** evaluates the proportion of 0s to 1s in the sequence to determine if its distribution is comparable to that of a truly random sequence.
– **Frequency Test within a Block** evaluates the percentage of "1" codes in M-bit subblocks, with the purpose of checking if the frequency of "1" code approaches $M/2$ as predicted by random assumptions. M is a fixed value of 9.
– **Runs Test** evaluates the total number of runs, which are sequences of identical numbers that are continuous and do not contain any gaps, either consisting of "1111" or "0000". The purpose of this test is to ascertain whether the number of "1" runs of varying lengths and the number of "0" runs in the sequence conform to the expected distribution of an ideal random sequence.
– **Longest Run of Ones in a Block Test** evaluates the length of the longest "1" run within a sub-block of M bits. The aim of this test is to ascertain whether the length of the longest run of "1" in the sequence under examination corresponds to that of a random sequence.
– **Binary Matrix Rank Test** evaluates the rank of the partition matrix of the entire sequence to detect any potential linear dependencies between substrings of fixed length in the source sequence.
– **Discrete Fourier Transform (Spectral) Test** evaluates the magnitude of the peak obtained after performing a sequential Fourier transform on the sequence. The aim of this test is to identify any periodicity in the sequence, revealing the extent to which it differs from a corresponding random sequence.
– **Non-overlapping Template Matching Test** evaluates the frequency of occurrence of a predetermined target string in the sequence, with the purpose of detecting generators that produce an excessive number of non-periodic patterns.
– **Overlapping Template Matching Test** evaluates the frequency of occurrence of predetermined target modules in the sequence.
– **Maurer's Universal Statistical Test** evaluates the number of bits between matching modules to determine whether the sequence can be compressed substantially without the loss of information.

- **Linear Complexity Test** evaluates the length of the linear feedback shift register to determine whether the complexity of the sequence is sufficient to consider it as a random sequence.
- **Serial Test** evaluates the frequency of all possible overlapping m-bit patterns in a given sequence, aiming to determine whether the number of $2m$ overlapping m-bit overlapping patterns is approximately equal to what would be expected in a random sequence.
- **Approximate Entropy Test** evaluates the frequency of all possible overlapping m-bit patterns in the sequence and compares the frequency of two adjacent overlapping sub-blocks of length m and $m+1$ with what is expected in a random sequence.
- **Cumulative Sums Test** evaluates the maximum offset of random excursions to determine whether the cumulative sum of the sequence is too large or too small compared to what is expected.
- **Random Excursions Test** evaluates the number of cycles with K nodes in a cumulative sum random walk to determine whether the number of nodes corresponding to a particular state within a loop deviates from what is expected in a random sequence.
- **Random Excursions Variant Test**: evaluates the total number of special states encountered in a cumulative sum random walk. The objective of the test is to determine the degree of deviation between the actual number of states encountered in the random excursion and the expected value.

The NIST SP800-22 standard mandates a minimum sequence length of 10^6 bits for the purposes of testing. To meet this requirement, our proposed pseudo-random number generator produces 1000 sequences, each comprising 1,003,520 bits, for evaluation. Each of these sequences serves as a test instance. The NIST SP800-22 test utilizes default settings from the test suite. For each test, the algorithm generates a P-value and a corresponding minimum pass rate based on the sequence number. A generated sequence is deemed to have passed the test if its P-value is greater than 0.01 and its actual pass rate for each test exceeds the specified minimum pass rate.

Table 1 presents the results of the Nist Tests. The minimum pass rate for each statistical test with the exception of the random excursion (variant) test is approximately $= 980$ for a sample size $= 1000$ binary sequences. The minimum pass rate for the random excursion (variant) test is approximately $= 633$ for a sample size $= 648$ binary sequences. In every test instance, the P-value exceeds 0.01, and the actual pass rate has exceeded the minimum acceptable threshold, indicating that the generated sequences are statistically random. Therefore, all statistical tests for randomness have been successfully passed.

Table 1. NIST Tests results

No	Test	P-value	Proportion	Accepted/Rejected
1	Frequency Test	0.583145	988/1000	Accepted
2	In-block Frequency Test	0.564639	993/1000	Accepted
3	Runs Test	0.353733	991/1000	Accepted
4	Longest Run of Ones in a Block	0.566688	991/1000	Accepted
5	Binary Matrix Rank Test	0.920383	992/1000	Accepted
6	Discrete Fourier Transform (Spectral) Test	0.473064	995/1000	Accepted
7	Non-overlapping Template Matching Test	0.521642	990/1000	Accepted
8	Overlapping Template Matching Test	0.881662	994/1000	Accepted
9	Maurer's Universal Statistical Test	0.181557	987/1000	Accepted
10	Linear Complexity Test	0.516113	989/1000	Accepted
11	Serial Test	0.655393	991/1000	Accepted
12	Approximate Entropy Test	0.887645	992/1000	Accepted
13	Cumulative Sums Test	0.646179	988/1000	Accepted
14	Random Excursions Test	0.521913	640/648	Accepted
15	Random Excursions Variant Test	0.416916	641/648	Accepted

6 Conclusion

In this study, we propose a secure and practical approach for generating pseudo-random numbers. To ensure that the input data space is greater than 2^{128} and that the output length exceeds the input length for the PRNG, we rationalized the input and output parameters by assigning 32 8-bit unsigned integers to the input and 256 8-bit unsigned integers to the output in a single iteration. Furthermore, our proposed method improves the GAN network and employs the GELU activation function to guarantee that the output data generated satisfies the randomness tests defined by the NIST Test.

Despite the promising performance of our proposed PRNG, it is imperative to note that additional true random numbers are still required for its training. Additionally, the theoretical analysis of the safety of PRNGs warrants further attention and repetition. In light of these considerations, we propose future research into the integration of prediction models from [11] and [13], which could potentially yield a PRNG solution that does not rely on true random numbers. Such research could also enable the evaluation of the interpretability of deep learning in conjunction with PRNG safety analysis.

References

1. Pandit, A.A., Kumar, A., Mishra, A.: LWR-based quantum-safe pseudo-random number generator. J. Inf. Secur. Appl. **73**, 103431 (2023)
2. Hobincu R., Datcu O.: A novel chaos based PRNG targeting secret communication. In: 2018 International Conference on Communications (COMM), pp. 459–462. IEEE, Romania (2018)

3. Miyamoto, K., Shiohara, K.: Reduction of qubits in a quantum algorithm for Monte Carlo simulation by a pseudo-random-number generator. Phys. Rev. A **102**(2), 022424 (2020)

4. Katz, J., Lindell, Y.: Introduction to Modern Cryptography. CRC Press, Boca Raton (2020)

5. The joy of cryptography. https://joyofcryptography.com/. Accessed 30 May 2023

6. Faure E, Fedorov E, Myronets I, et al.: Method for generating pseudorandom sequence of permutations based on linear congruential generator. In: 5th International Workshop on Computer Modeling and Intelligent Systems, pp. 175–185. Zaporizhzhia, Ukraine (2022)

7. Lewis, T.G., Payne, W.H.: Generalized feedback shift register pseudorandom number algorithm. J. ACM **20**(3), 456–468 (1973)

8. Desai, V., Patil, R., Rao, D.: Using layer recurrent neural network to generate pseudo random number sequences. Int. J. Comput. Sci. Issues **9**(2), 324–334 (2012)

9. Hameed, S.M., Ali, L.M.M.: Utilizing hopfield neural network for pseudo-random number generator. In: 15th International Conference on Computer Systems and Applications (AICCSA), pp. 1–5. IEEE, Aqaba (2018)

10. Jeong, Y.S., Oh, K.J., Cho, C.K., et al.: Pseudo-random number generation using LSTMs. J. Supercomput. **76**, 8324–8342 (2020)

11. De Bernardi, M., Khouzani, M.H.R., Malacaria, P.: Pseudo-random number generation using generative adversarial networks. In: Alzate, C., et al. (eds.) ECML PKDD 2018. LNCS (LNAI), vol. 11329, pp. 191–200. Springer, Cham (2019). https://doi.org/10.1007/978-3-030-13453-2_15

12. Oak, R., Rahalkar, C., Gujar, D.: Poster: using generative adversarial networks for secure pseudorandom number generation. In: Proceedings of the 2019 ACM SIGSAC Conference on Computer and Communications Security, pp. 2597–2599. ACM, London (2019)

13. Kim, H., Kwon, Y., Sim, M., Lim, S., Seo, H.: Generative adversarial networks-based pseudo-random number generator for embedded processors. In: Hong, D. (ed.) ICISC 2020. LNCS, vol. 12593, pp. 215–234. Springer, Cham (2021). https://doi.org/10.1007/978-3-030-68890-5_12

14. Okada, K., Endo, K., Yasuoka, K., et al.: Learned pseudo-random number generator: WGAN-GP for generating statistically robust random numbers. Research-Square, Preprint (2022)

15. Goodfellow, I.J., et al.: Generative adversarial networks. arXiv preprint arXiv:1406.2661 (2014)

16. Rukhin, A., Soto, J., Nechvatal, J., et al.: A statistical test suite for random and pseudorandom number generators for cryptographic applications. Booz-allen and hamilton inc mclean va (2001)

17. Hendrycks, D., Gimpel. K.: Gaussian error linear units (gelus). arXiv preprint arXiv:1606.08415 (2016)

18. Mirza, M., Osindero, S.: Conditional generative adversarial nets. arXiv preprint arXiv:1411.1784 (2014)

19. Radford, A., Metz, L., Chintala, S.: Unsupervised representation learning with deep convolutional generative adversarial networks. arXiv preprint arXiv:1511.06434 (2015)

20. Chen, X., Duan, Y., Houthooft, R., Schulman, J., Sutskever, I., Abbeel, P.: Info-GAN: interpretable representation learning by information maximizing generative adversarial nets. In: 30th Conference on Neural Information Processing Systems (2016)

21. Yu, L., Zhang, W., Wang, J., et al.: Seqgan: sequence generative adversarial nets with policy gradient. In: Proceedings of the AAAI Conference on Artificial Intelligence, pp. 2852–2858 (2017)
22. Gulrajani, I., Ahmed, F., Arjovsky, M., Dumoulin, V., Courville, A.C.: Improved training of wasserstein GANs. In: Advances in Neural Information Processing Systems. Curran Associates, New York (2017)

An Intrusion Detection System Using Vision Transformer for Representation Learning

Xinbo Ban$^{(\boxtimes)}$ (ID), Ao Liu, Long He, and Li Gong

The Second Research Institute of CAAC, Chengdu 610042, China
banxinbo@gmail.com, {liuao,helong,gongli}@caacsri.com

Abstract. Intrusion Detection System (IDS) is important in safeguarding cybersecurity by identifying and responding to malicious activities. Traditional IDSs filter the abnormal traffic through rules or learn the behaviors of normal and abnormal network data. Nevertheless, these methods utilize the manually designed feature set that introduces limitations in this field. Machine learning shows advantages in the traffic classification domain but still faces challenges of computing resource consumption and a high false positive rate. This paper presents an innovative approach to lightweight IDS using vision transformer techniques for feature representation learning in the context of network intrusion detection. Specifically, our IDS uses a self-attention mechanism to process network traffic, which flattens the splitted network flow to images for training the model. It utilizes Natural Language Processing techniques to capture temporal-spatial information from network traffic. We conduct several experiments to show the effectiveness of our proposed method. The results show that our approach can achieve high accuracy in intrusion detection tasks and keep the false positive rate very low at the same time. The findings highlight the potential of vision transformers in IDS and contribute to the development of robust network security solutions for critical domains like civil aviation.

Keywords: Intrusion detection system · Vision Transformer · Representation learning · Network anomaly detection · Traffic classification

1 Introduction

Intrusion detection plays a vital role in ensuring network security by identifying and mitigating malicious activities that could compromise the integrity and confidentiality of critical systems. With the increasing reliance on digital infrastructure in various domains, including the civil aviation sector, the need for robust intrusion detection mechanisms becomes even more paramount [1]. Within the realm of civil aviation, the importance of a robust intrusion detection system (IDS) cannot be overstated. The aviation industry heavily relies on

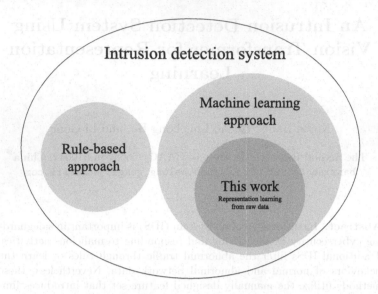

Fig. 1. IoT Taxonomy

interconnected systems, such as air traffic control, flight operations, passenger data management, and surface guide system, which are all vulnerable to cybersecurity threats. A successful breach in any of these systems could have far-reaching consequences, including compromised flight safety, data breaches, disruption of services, and damage to the reputation of airlines or airports. Therefore, deploying effective IDSs is imperative to maintain the integrity and security of critical aviation infrastructure.

A taxonomy from Artificial Intelligence is shown in Fig. 1. Rule-based IDS used pre-defined rules to filter the network traffic, achieving high effectiveness but low efficiency. Machine learning approaches extract patterns from empirical data using a manually selected set of features to classify network traffic. While these classic approaches overcome certain limitations of rule-based methods, such as high computational costs, they face a new challenge of feature design, prompting recent studies to focus on this issue [2]. In recent years, representation learning has emerged as a rapidly evolving machine learning approach that automates the process of feature extraction from raw data, partly addressing the problem of manual feature engineering [3]. Notably, deep learning, a prominent method in representation learning, has exhibited impressive performance across various domains, including image classification and vulnerability detection [4–6].

In the context of civil aviation, not only is the accuracy and reliability of IDSs crucial, but the rate of false positive reports must also be minimized. False positives in intrusion detection systems within the civil aviation context can have significant consequences beyond disruption and increased operational costs. A high rate of false positive reports can lead to unnecessary investigations, diverting resources and attention away from legitimate security concerns [7]. False positives occur when a system incorrectly identifies normal network activities as malicious, leading to unnecessary disruptions and resource wastage. On the other hand, the increasing complexity and size of detection models pose a significant burden on computational resources, making it challenging to deploy them in real-world scenarios with limited processing capabilities [8,9]. Large models demand extensive computational power, memory, and storage, hindering their practicality and scalability [10]. Therefore, striking a balance between minimizing false alarms and developing lightweight detection models is crucial to ensure the efficiency, effectiveness, and feasibility of IDSs in various domains, including civil aviation [11].

This necessitates the development of lightweight and efficient artificial intelligence models that can effectively analyze network traffic and identify genuine security threats while minimizing false alarms. The adoption of vision transformer techniques in IDS holds promise for addressing these requirements. Vision transformers have demonstrated their effectiveness in capturing intricate patterns and contextual information from visual data, making them a potential asset for analyzing network traffic in civil aviation systems. Attention-based approach is currently a popular representation learning approach in Natural Language Processing (NLP) domain. Vision transformers have demonstrated their efficacy in feature representation for images by leveraging a unique approach that treats images as natural language.

In this paper, we address the aforementioned challenges by exploring the application of vision transformer techniques for the representation learning approach in the IDS domain. By leveraging the potential of vision transformer models, we contribute to the advancement of IDS in civil aviation by proposing a vision transformer-based approach that prioritizes both accuracy and the low rate of false positives. Rather than extracting features from traffic statistics, our approach utilizes raw traffic data as images to capture temporal-spatial information. This innovative method allows us to leverage the inherent characteristics of the data in a more direct manner. In order to showcase the scalability of our proposed approach, we conducted a series of experiments. Remarkably, the final average accuracy achieved an impressive 92.41%, meeting the threshold required for practical applications. This result underscores the effectiveness and reliability of our method. Our work makes several key contributions as follows:

- We propose the utilization of vision transformer techniques as a novel approach for detecting intrusions in network traffic, by leveraging the powerful capabilities of vision transformers in capturing complex patterns and contextual information.
- We address the specific requirements of civil aviation by focusing on minimizing false positive reports. We design and implement our IDS to achieve a low rate of false positives, thereby reducing unnecessary disruptions, operational costs, and delays in the provision of services.
- We endeavor to strike a balance between model complexity and performance, ensuring that our vision transformer-based IDS remains computationally feasible in real-world scenarios with limited processing capabilities.

2 Related Work

In terms of different detection techniques, IDS has two main categories: rule-based and anomaly-based (machine learning approach). Rule-based IDS heavily relies on pre-defined signature knowledge bases, leading to the challenges of detecting new intrusions. Anomaly-based IDS has gained significant attention from researchers and developers, which focuses on detecting abnormal behaviors and issuing alarms when the observed behaviors significantly deviate from benign behaviors. Machine learning recently has been widely applied in many domains, including intrusion detection. It leads to the emergence of the application of machine learning on IDS, as highlighted in recent studies [12,13].

Hadem et al. [14] introduced an IDS for a software defined network based by using selective logging and support vector machines. Prasad et al. [15] suggested an IDS using a clustering center initialization approach. Bhati et al. [16] utilized XGBoost to construct an ensemble approach, which demonstrates improved performance by combining multiple classifiers. However, this approach has higher event complexity compared to general machine learning models, making it challenging to manage the balance. Furthermore, deep learning techniques have shown promise and efficiency in IDS. Otoum et al. [17] proposed an IDS that utilized a deep learning algorithm. The author extracted features by using the spider monkey optimization and identified optimal features by using a stacked-deep polynomial network. Xiao [18] presented a simplified residual network for IDS, while Li et al. [19] applied the random forest with automated coding, resulting in reduced time and space complexity. Wang et al. [20] also proposed a deep learning method but performed poorly on small datasets. Another approach by Wang et al. [21] involved a data augmentation solution and a self-supervised approach for an IDS. However, it achieved less accuracy compared to supervised approaches. Long short-term memory (LSTM) and convolutional neural network (CNN) gain popularity in recent years. A model proposed by [22] utilized LSTM and CNN to analyze temporal and spatial features. Gupta et al. [23] developed an IDS based on LSTM classifiers, improving the handling of frequent and infrequent network intrusions using an improved one-to-one technique. Yao et al. [24] introduced an IDS using the cross-architecture combination of CNN and LSTM, effectively considering global and temporal intrusion characteristics. However, this approach is time-inefficiency and exhibits many false positives, falling short of expectations.

Traditional machine learning techniques are considered shallow, making it difficult to reach the desired level of research. Additionally, deep learning methods involve complex training processes, capturing more information from raw data. Attention mechanism has demonstrated remarkable effectiveness in various domains, including NLP, and vulnerability analysis. In this paper, we propose a IDS that utilizes raw traffic data. We exploit the strengths of the attention mechanism to handle the temporal-spatial information of network packets, considering them as images for representation learning. This approach enables us to effectively capture and analyze the intricate characteristics of network traffic, leveraging the power of the attention mechanism for improved detection performance.

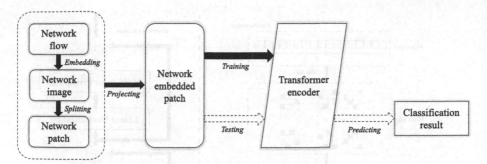

Fig. 2. A Flowchart illustrates the workflow of the proposed method. The network flow undergoes pre-processing to generate network patches (sub-images). Subsequently, a projection function transforms the patches into vectors that conform to the requirements of the Transformer encoder. The trained model identifies intrusions whenever an abnormal sample is introduced.

3   Methodology

In this section, we present details of our proposed IDS framework. As shown in Fig. 2, it first converts flow bytes into flow images. Afterward, the flow image is split into separated network patch images. We use a linear projection of flattened network patches for mapping patch images into a constant latent vector. The flattened vectors are composed of position embeddings to carry positional information. We refer to the output of this projection as the network patch embedding. Next, we feed them into Transformer encoders and extract the learned features.

3.1   Traffic Granularity

The scope of network traffic includes various levels of granularity, such as TCP connection, flow, session, service, and host [25]. Each level of granularity presents distinct units of traffic for analysis. In this study, our focus revolves around the utilization of flows, a commonly employed approach in the research community. Specifically, a flow as a group of packets shares the same 5-tuple, consisting of the source port, source IP, destination port, destination IP, and transport-level protocol. To provide a formal description, the definition can be precisely stated as follows:

Raw Data: Given n packets $P = \{p^1, \cdots, p^n\}$, each packet is $p^i = (x^i, b^i, t^i), i = 1, 2, \cdots n$. x^i represents a 5-tuple, and b^i indicates packet size $b^i \in [0, \infty)$ in bytes The third one t^i represents the start time of traffic transfer $t^i \in [0, \infty)$.

Network Flow: Given a set of raw network data P, multiple subsets are available through splitting the flow. Packets are relevantly sorted by time, e.g.

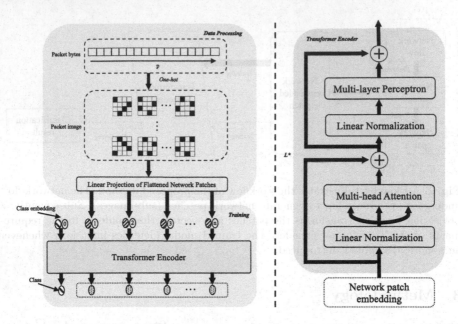

Fig. 3. The architecture of the proposed method. Transformer encoder can contain more than one encoder block to enhance the fitting ability.

$\left\{p^i = \left(x^i, b^i, t^i\right), \cdots, p^n = \left(x^n, b^n, t^n\right)\right\}, t^1 < t^2 < \cdots < t^n$. A flow is a subset and defined as $f = (x, b, d_t, t)$. The first element is 5-tuple of raw traffic, e.g. $x = x_1 = \cdots = x_n$. The second one represents the size of total packets. The third element indicates the flow duration $d_t = t^n - t^1$. t is the time where the packet transfers. Consequently, the flows are obtained from raw traffic $F = \left\{f^1, \cdots, f^n\right\}$.

3.2 Flattening Network Patches

The operational procedure of the proposed IDS is depicted in Fig. 3. The initial phase involves transforming raw traffic data into a network patch. To achieve this, the raw traffic is initially adjusted to a consistent length. If the file size exceeds or falls short of a predefined size, it is trimmed or padded with 0x00 to ensure the uniform length is maintained. Subsequently, the processed data is divided into discrete traffic units. Finally, the resulting files of equal size are converted into gray images.

The entire flow is converted into a q dimension vector by splitting the flow, resulting in an $p \cdot q$ grey image. The input of the Transformer encoder is processed on a per-patch basis, with each flow consisting of n network patch images. The aforementioned steps enable the conversion of network flows into $2D$ images. The network patch images are then flattened into a D vector using a linear projection, in order to meet the fixed vector size requirement of the Transformer encoder, as shown in Eq. 1.

Table 1. USTC-TFC2016 datasets.

Normal		Abnormal	
BitTorrent	Outlook	Cridex	Nsis-ay
Facetime	Skype	Geodo	Shifu
FTP	SMB	Htbot	Tinba
Gmail	Weibo	Miuref	Virut
MySQL	WoW	Neris	Zeus

$$z_0 = \left[x_{class}; x_p^1 E; x_p^2 E; \cdots ; x_p^n E\right] + E_{pos},$$
$$E \in R^{\frac{p \cdot q}{n} \times D}, \ E_{pos} \in R^{(n+1) \times d} \tag{1}$$

The result of the linear projection is referred to as network embedded patch. When using supervised learning algorithms, labeled data is compulsory and the data labels are used to update the model. In this work, a learnable encoding ($z_0^0 = x_{class}$) is added to the front of the embedded sequence, which represents the subsystem class y of data flow, that is output after being processed by the Transformer encoder (z_0^L), as shown in Eq. 2. y represents the labels of different subsystems labeled during the data collection phase.

$$y = LN\left(z_0^L\right) \tag{2}$$

3.3 Transformer Encoder

The order of patch images in a flow is important as the relative positional information is representative. Therefore, a learnable positional embedding is added positional information to embedding. The results are used as input to the Transformer encoder that is used as the deep learning model. As shown in Fig. 3, network embedded patch is fed into several encoders. The MSA and MLP blocks are stacked and interacted with LN for the normalization of each sample, and residual connections are used to stabilize the training process of the deep learning.

The final output has two parts: the label y is used to update the model, and the rest is the features extracted by the deep learning model. We save the trained model for processing incoming network traffic into learned features that can be used as input to the intrusion detection model.

4 Experiment

4.1 Datasets

Progress in IDS is hindered by the lack of diverse and shareable trace datasets for testing, as emphasized by Dainotti et al. [25]. Many IDS research relies on

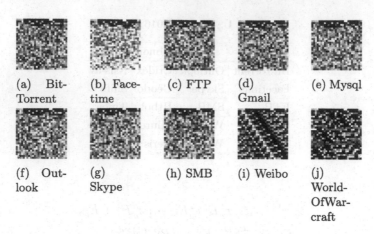

(a) Bit-Torrent (b) Face-time (c) FTP (d) Gmail (e) Mysql

(f) Out-look (g) Skype (h) SMB (i) Weibo (j) World-OfWar-craft

Fig. 4. Normal

private datasets from security institutes, which is not available and appliable in other work. Additionally, The limitation arises partly from the situations in which the feature selection process highly relies on knowledge basis from experts. Consequently, publicly available traffic datasets tend to be skewed toward flow features rather than raw traffic data. For instance, well-known datasets like KDD CUP1999 and NSL-KDD [26] offer only a limited range of traffic classes and do not adequately capture the characteristics of contemporary networks due to technological advancements. As a consequence, these datasets fall short of meeting the requirement for analyzing raw traffic, posing challenges in the development of robust IDS models. Additionally, in the realm of civil aviation, complex systems are composed of multiple interconnected subsystems, each contributing to crucial functionalities. Many datasets contain the limited number of categories which fails to fit the requirements of data preparation.

To address these problems, we use USTC-TFC2016 as our experimental dataset, consisting of labels, as shown in Table 1, involving normal traffic of 10 types of the common application and 10 types of abnormal traffic from public websites. Totally, USTC-TFC2016 contains 272,708 samples including 245,437 training samples and 27,271 testing samples. In experiments, the pre-defined size of flow is specified as 784. Consequently, the first 784 bytes of each flow are used. Each flow is transformed to a gray image with 28×28 size. We then split images into 7×7 patches which are 49 4×4 images out of a single flow image. The gray images are visually presented in Fig. 4 and Fig. 5. Each gray image has a size of 784 bytes (28*28). It is evident that they are distinguishable from one another, with only a few images displaying similarities, such as FTP and SMB.

4.2   Experiment Setup

For conducting the experiments, the PyTorch framework is utilized as the software framework, operating on an Ubuntu 16 64-bit operating system. The exper-

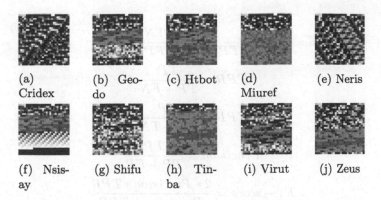

(a) Cridex   (b) Geo-do   (c) Htbot   (d) Miuref   (e) Neris

(f) Nsis-ay   (g) Shifu   (h) Tin-ba   (i) Virut   (j) Zeus

Fig. 5. Abnormal

imental setup comprises an Intel(R) Xeon(R) W-2223 3.6 GHz CPU with 32 GB of memory, while an Nvidia GeForce RTX 3090 GPU serves as the accelerator. During training, a fixed mini-batch size of 256 is employed, and the cross entropy loss function is utilized. The optimizer and classifier utilized are Adam and Softmax, respectively. To control the learning process, a learning rate of 0.005 is set. The experiments encompass exploring the impact of different numbers of encoder blocks. Each experiment involves training the model for a total of 100 epochs, allowing for a thorough analysis of the model's performance and convergence patterns.

4.3 Evaluation Metrics

To evaluate the effectiveness of the proposed IDS, we employed standard information retrieval metrics. In this study, we assigned the positive class label to abnormal traffic and the negative class label to normal functions.

Positives (abnormal traffic) and Negatives (normal traffic): Let's consider an abnormal flow denoted as V and the normal class as NV. The classifiers' outputs determine whether V belongs to NV or not. To evaluate the classifier outputs, a widely-used approach is to utilize the following measures: TP (true positive), FP (false positive), TN (true negative), and FN (false negative). These measures can be defined as follows:

- TP - Abnormal flows of class V correctly predicted as elements of V.
- FP - Abnormal flows not belonging to class V incorrectly predicted belonging to class V.
- TN - Abnormal flows belonging to class NV predicted as flows that belonging to class NV.
- FN - Abnormal flows of class NV incorrectly predicted belonging to class NV.

This work reports Accuracy, F1-score, Precision, False Positive Rate (FPR), and True Positive Rate(TPR), defined as:

$$Acc = \frac{TP + TN}{TP + TN + FP + FN} \tag{3}$$

$$TPR = \frac{TP}{TP + FN} \tag{4}$$

$$FPR = \frac{FP}{FP + TN} \tag{5}$$

$$Precision = \frac{TP}{TP + FP} \tag{6}$$

$$F1 - score = \frac{2 * Precision * TPR}{Precision + TPR} \tag{7}$$

4.4   Results and Discussion

In this section, we present the experimental results and relevant discussion. The results are shown in Fig. 6.

The loss metric reflects the discrepancy between the predicted outputs and the actual outputs during training. In our evaluation, we measured the loss values for five different blocks as shown in Fig. 6a. Overall, the decreasing trend in the loss values across all blocks suggests that the model is effective in learning and improving its predictive capabilities. This is a positive indication of the model's performance, as lower loss values correspond to better accuracy and alignment with the actual data. Additionally, experiments of 5 blocks exhibit a fluctuating pattern in the loss values, ranging from 2.71 to 2.19. Although the fluctuations are present, the overall trend showcases a loss reduction, indicating the model's ability to improve its predictions.

The increasing trend in accuracy values suggests that the model is learning and improving its classification performance. Higher accuracy values indicate better overall performance and a stronger ability to correctly classify instances in the dataset. Experiment of 5 blocks shows an upward trend in accuracy values, appearing highest results compared to others. It suggests that the model is becoming more accurate in its predictions. However, it is worth noting that there may be variations in accuracy values across different blocks. This could be due to variations in the complexity or distribution of the data in each block. Further analysis is required to understand the specific factors contributing to these variations.

The results of 3 blocks present over 0.92, indicating a consistent improvement in the model's ability to detect positive instances. The results of 5 blocks show a fluctuating trend in TPR values, with values ranging from 0.39 to 0.90. Although there are variations, overall, the model demonstrates a reasonably high ability to detect positive instances.

A high TPR and low FPR are desirable for an effective intrusion detection system. The results of the 2 blocks show an apparent decrease trend, with FPR values ranging from 0.76 to 0.16. This suggests that the model is becoming more

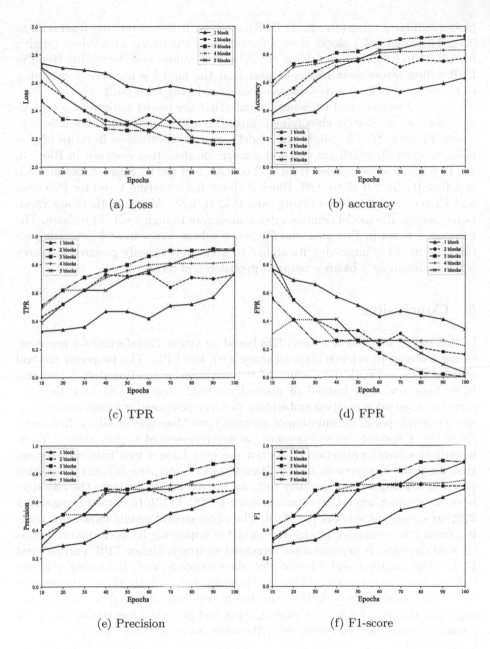

(a) Loss

(b) accuracy

(c) TPR

(d) FPR

(e) Precision

(f) F1-score

Fig. 6. Results

accurate in identifying negative instances correctly. In the experiment of 3 blocks, the FPR values decrease significantly from 0.56 to 0, indicating a substantial improvement in the model's ability to avoid false positives. The results of 4 blocks exhibit a relatively stable FPR trend, with values ranging from 0.22 to 0.41. The results of 5 blocks show a fluctuating FPR trend, with values ranging from 0.03 to 0.86. The increasing trend in TPR values and decreasing trend in FPR values across most blocks suggest that the model is improving its ability to correctly identify positive instances while reducing false positives.

A high Precision and F1 Score indicate that the model achieves a good balance between accurately classifying positive instances and minimizing false positives. These metrics highlight the model's overall effectiveness in terms of precision and recall, which are crucial for intrusion detection systems. In Block 3, the Precision values increase from 0.42 to 0.88, and the F1 Score values increase significantly from 0.43 to 0.89. Block 5 shows a fluctuating trend for Precision and F1-score, with values ranging from 0.32 to 0.88. Although there are variations, overall, the model demonstrates a moderate to high level of precision. The increasing trend in Precision and F1 Score values across most blocks suggests that the model is improving its ability to accurately classify positive instances while maintaining a balance between precision and recall.

5   Conclusion

In this paper, we present a novel IDS based on vision Transformer for representation learning to achieve high accuracy with low FPR. The proposed method processes the network data using NLP techniques, extracting deep-learnt features from raw data instead of manually selected features. Besides, the proposed method adds position embedding to carry positional information, capturing temporal-spatial information of network flow. More specifically, it first splits the network flow into several network patches represented as gray images. Then, it utilizes a linear projection to flatten the gray images into fixed-size vectors that meet the requirement of the Transformer. Lastly, the network embedded patch is fed into several encoders to train the model. To evaluate the effectiveness, we conduct several experiments using USTC-TFC2016 datasets containing 272,708 samples of network raw data. The experimental results show that, ranging from 1 to 5 encoder blocks, the model is improving its performance across multiple metrics. It demonstrates increased accuracy, higher TPR, and reduced FPR. The precision and F1-core also show improvement, indicating a better balance between precision and recall. These findings indicate the effectiveness in the context of the IDS task. However, the fluctuations observed in some metrics highlight the need for further investigation and potential fine-tuning to ensure consistent and reliable performance. We leave these for future work.

References

1. Ghosal, S.K., Mukhopadhyay, S., Hossain, S., Sarkar, R.: Application of Lah transform for security and privacy of data through information hiding in telecommunication. Trans. Emerg. Telecommun. Technol. **32**(2), e3984 (2021)

2. Dhote, Y., Agrawal, S., Deen, A.J.: A survey on feature selection techniques for internet traffic classification. In: 2015 International Conference on Computational Intelligence and Communication Networks (CICN), pp. 1375–1380. IEEE (2015)
3. Bengio, Y., Courville, A., Vincent, P.: Representation learning: a review and new perspectives. IEEE Trans. Pattern Anal. Mach. Intell. **35**(8), 1798–1828 (2013)
4. LeCun, Y., Bengio, Y., Hinton, G.: Deep learning. Nature **521**(7553), 436–444 (2015)
5. Ban, X., Chen, C., Liu, S., Wang, Y., Zhang, J.: Deep-learnt features for Twitter spam detection. In: 2018 International Symposium on Security and Privacy in Social Networks and Big Data (SocialSec), pp. 208–212. IEEE (2018)
6. Ban, X., Liu, S., Chen, C., Chua, C.: A performance evaluation of deep-learnt features for software vulnerability detection. Concurr. Comput. Pract. Exp. **31**(19), e5103 (2019)
7. Hubballi, N., Suryanarayanan, V.: False alarm minimization techniques in signature-based intrusion detection systems: a survey. Comput. Commun. **49**, 1–17 (2014)
8. Bakhtiar, F.A., Pramukantoro, E.S., Nihri, H.: A lightweight ids based on J48 algorithm for detecting dos attacks on IoT middleware. In: 2019 IEEE 1st Global Conference on Life Sciences and Technologies (LifeTech), pp. 41–42. IEEE (2019)
9. Fenanir, S., Semchedine, F., Baadache, A.: A machine learning-based lightweight intrusion detection system for the Internet of Things. Rev. d'Intelligence Artif. **33**(3), 203–211 (2019)
10. Chen, Y., Li, H.: SMALE: enhancing scalability of machine learning algorithms on extreme scale computing platforms. Technical report, Yiran Chen/Duke University (2022)
11. Yu, Y.-T., Lin, G.-H., Jiang, I.H.-R., Chiang, C.: Machine-learning-based hotspot detection using topological classification and critical feature extraction. In: Proceedings of the 50th Annual Design Automation Conference, pp. 1–6 (2013)
12. Ray, B., Mukhopadhyay, S., Hossain, S., Ghosal, S.K., Sarkar, R.: Image steganography using deep learning based edge detection. Multimed. Tools Appl. **80**(24), 33475–33503 (2021). https://doi.org/10.1007/s11042-021-11177-4
13. Drewek-Ossowicka, A., Pietrołaj, M., Rumiński, J.: A survey of neural networks usage for intrusion detection systems. J. Ambient Intell. Human. Comput. **12**, 497–514 (2021). https://doi.org/10.1007/s12652-020-02014-x
14. Hadem, P., Saikia, D.K., Moulik, S.: An SDN-based intrusion detection system using SVM with selective logging for IP traceback. Comput. Netw. **191**, 108015 (2021)
15. Prasad, M., Tripathi, S., Dahal, K.: Unsupervised feature selection and cluster center initialization based arbitrary shaped clusters for intrusion detection. Comput. Secur. **99**, 102062 (2020)
16. Bhati, B.S., Chugh, G., Al-Turjman, F., Bhati, N.S.: An improved ensemble based intrusion detection technique using XGBoost. Trans. Emerg. Telecommun. Technol. **32**(6), e4076 (2021)
17. Otoum, Y., Liu, D., Nayak, A.: DL-IDS: a deep learning-based intrusion detection framework for securing IoT. Trans. Emerg. Telecommun. Technol. **33**(3), e3803 (2022)
18. Xiao, Y., Xiao, X.: An intrusion detection system based on a simplified residual network. Information **10**(11), 356 (2019)
19. Li, X.K., Chen, W., Zhang, Q., Lifa, W.: Building auto-encoder intrusion detection system based on random forest feature selection. Comput. Secur. **95**, 101851 (2020)

20. Wang, Z., Liu, Y., He, D., Chan, S.: Intrusion detection methods based on integrated deep learning model. Comput. Secur. **103**, 102177 (2021)
21. Wang, Z., Li, Z., Wang, J., Li, D.: Network intrusion detection model based on improved BYOL self-supervised learning. Secur. Commun. Netw. **2021**, 1–23 (2021)
22. Jianwu Zhang, Yu., Ling, X.F., Yang, X., Xiong, G., Zhang, R.: Model of the intrusion detection system based on the integration of spatial-temporal features. Comput. Secur. **89**, 101681 (2020)
23. Gupta, N., Jindal, V., Bedi, P.: LIO-IDS: handling class imbalance using LSTM and improved one-vs-one technique in intrusion detection system. Comput. Netw. **192**, 108076 (2021)
24. Yao, R., Wang, N., Liu, Z., Chen, P., Sheng, X.: Intrusion detection system in the advanced metering infrastructure: a cross-layer feature-fusion CNN-LSTM-based approach. Sensors **21**(2), 626 (2021)
25. Dainotti, A., Pescape, A., Claffy, K.C.: Issues and future directions in traffic classification. IEEE Netw. **26**(1), 35–40 (2012)
26. Tavallaee, M., Bagheri, E., Lu, W., Ghorbani, A.A.: A detailed analysis of the KDD CUP 99 data set. In: 2009 IEEE Symposium on Computational Intelligence for Security and Defense Applications, pp. 1–6. IEEE (2009)

PaBiL-Net: Parallel Bidirectional LSTM Network for Mobile Encrypted Traffic Classification

Bin Cheng, Fushan Wei, and Chunxiang Gu[✉]

Henan Key Laboratory of Network Cryptography Technology, Zhengzhou, China
gcx5209@126.com

Abstract. With the rapid popularity of smart handheld devices, the demand for the classification of mobile encrypted traffic is growing quickly. The data feature selection strategy is an important factor affecting classification performance. However, most classification models in recent years have used a fixed feature selection strategy, making it difficult for the models to adapt to new datasets and application scenarios. We propose an end-to-end classification model called parallel bidirectional LSTM network (PaBiL-Net) to address this issue. The model arranges similar neural networks in parallel and processes different features separately in each parallel path, thus it is more flexible in feature selection and can easily adjust the type and number of features computed by the model. We compare PaBiL-Net with 3 baseline methods by conducting mobile encrypted traffic classification experiments on 2 publicly available datasets. The results of 5-fold cross-validation show that PaBiL-Net outperforms the baseline models with an increase in accuracy of 4.0939% and 2.2061% on the 2 datasets respectively. Additionally, the macro F1 increased by 3.9029% and 2.2933%, respectively.

Keywords: Deep Learning · Encrypted Traffic Classification · Mobile Application · LSTM · Parallel

1 Introduction

Traffic classification is widely used in network access control, anomaly detection, behavior analysis, and quality of service assurance. However, encryption technology has led to an increase in encrypted network traffic, which protects user privacy but poses potential security threats. Additionally, the growing popularity of mobile Internet and smart handheld devices has resulted in a greater need for classifying and identifying encrypted mobile traffic. Some researchers employ machine learning techniques to enhance the classification accuracy of encrypted mobile traffic. Nevertheless, complex and time-consuming feature engineering [1] has prompted researchers to explore deep learning approaches, which can automatically extract data features [2].

Deep neural networks' classification performance heavily relies on the training data, and effective feature selection can significantly enhance classification accuracy. However, current methods face the following issues. Firstly, most studies employ a fixed feature selection strategy, where specific features are selected during model design and cannot be modified based on evolving requirements. This restricts the model's adaptability and its ability to meet new demands. Secondly, certain researchers select only a single or a limited number of data features [3–6] during the feature selection process. This might hinder the model's ability to capture the complete data pattern, consequently impacting its performance.

To address these problems, we propose PaBiL-Net, an end-to-end mobile encrypted traffic classification model. PaBiL-Net utilizes a parallel arrangement to effectively leverage information from each feature and offers enhanced flexibility and adaptability in feature selection for different datasets and application scenarios. In this approach, the traffic's feature sequence is treated as text, with data being analogous to words. Applying word embedding techniques commonly used in Natural Language Processing (NLP), the data is transformed into vector representations. These representations are then inputted into PaBiL-Net to learn the relationships between each data in the feature sequence. Ultimately, this parallel structure constructs the model.

The contributions of this paper are summarized as follows:

(1) We combine the word embedding approach of NLP with encrypted traffic classification and propose an end-to-end classification model called PaBiL-Net to improve classification accuracy.
(2) To validate the classification performance of PaBiL-Net, we conducted experiments on 2 publicly available datasets comparing PaBiL-Net with 3 baseline methods. 5-fold cross-validation results show that PaBiL-Net outperforms the baseline methods on all 4 metrics.
(3) Since PaBiL-Net has high flexibility in feature selection, this paper explores the impact of various types of features on the performance of mobile encrypted traffic classification. And the ranking of the contribution of each type of feature to the performance is roughly given.

2 Related Work

In this section, we provide an overview of existing methods for encrypted traffic classification, including traditional methods, traditional machine learning-based methods, and deep learning-based methods.

2.1 Traditional Methods

Traditional traffic classification methods encompass port-based techniques and deep packet inspection (DPI) techniques. However, with the prevalence of dynamic port assignment in applications, the effectiveness of port-based classification techniques diminishes. DPI examines packet header fields and payload, identifies matching rules, and stores them in a feature library. While DPI can achieve high classification accuracy [7–9], it requires frequent updates to the protocol fingerprints in the feature library. Additionally, encrypted data poses challenges for accurate classification. Subsequently, researchers have introduced machine learning methods to classify encrypted traffic in later studies.

2.2 Traditional Machine Learning

Machine learning methods excel in processing vast amounts of data with speed and accuracy. Qazi et al. [10] introduced Atlas, enabling fine-grained classification of mobile apps. Wang et al. [11] utilized side channel leakage information as data features and employed the Random Forest algorithm to analyze packet-level traffic and classify apps. Alan et al. [12] employed the Jaccard coefficient and Naive Bayesian algorithm to classify Android apps. Shbair et al. [13] proposed a two-level hierarchical traffic classification framework utilizing the C4.5 algorithm and Random Forest for classifying services on HTTPS connections. Taylor et al. [14] proposed an app fingerprint recognition framework that extracts a 54-dimensional sequence of features from packet length sequences, subsequently recognized using Random Forest. Although traditional machine learning methods exhibit high classification accuracy, feature engineering necessitates expert experience and extensive computations, rendering real-time classification challenging. Additionally, the extracted features are highly abstract, posing difficulties for machine learning algorithms to learn fine-grained features.

2.3 Deep Learning

Neural networks demonstrate strong feature learning capabilities, making them highly effective in handling complex and extensive datasets. Aceto et al. [15] introduced MIMETIC, a multimodal framework utilized for mobile app classification. Wang et al. [16] addressed the challenges of mobile traffic classification and proposed the App-Net multimodal framework, which exhibits impressive performance in app classification. Aceto et al. [17] discussed the disparities between traditional machine learning methods and deep learning methods and proposed a generic deep learning-based framework for encrypted traffic classification. Montieri et al. [18] developed a packet-level feature-based framework, showcasing superior performance when compared to traditional machine learning methods. Jiang et al. [19] designed FG-Net, an APP fingerprint recognition algorithm based on graph neural networks (GNNs), effectively transforming encrypted traffic fingerprint recognition into a graph representation learning task. However, the existing works have the following limitations:

(1) Most works use only a small portion of features from the data, which may lead to the loss of important information and thus reduce the classification performance.
(2) Most classification methods in recent years have used multimodal neural networks including CNNs. However, CNNs have difficulty capturing temporal features of traffic data.
(3) Due to a limited number of public datasets in the field of mobile traffic and the early collection time [20], most existing works choose private datasets for experiments, which makes it difficult to reproduce the research results.

3 Methodology

This section describes the proposed PaBiL-Net in detail. The general architecture of PaBiL-Net is first introduced, and then each part is elaborated. The structure of PaBiL-Net is shown in Fig. 1. The first part is the feature extraction. Each input feature is a set of attribute data of a biflow, such as packet transmission direction sequence, etc. Next is the word embedding layer. The feature data are input into different embedding layers separately to learn the deep semantic information and the relationship between the data. Then, the embedding of each feature is passed through different Bi-LSTMs respectively to fully mine the contextual relationships of the sequences. Finally, the outputs of all Bi-LSTMs are concatenated and then successively passed through the fully connected layer, the dropout layer, and the softmax function to obtain the final probability distribution. Each part of PaBiL-Net is described in detail below.

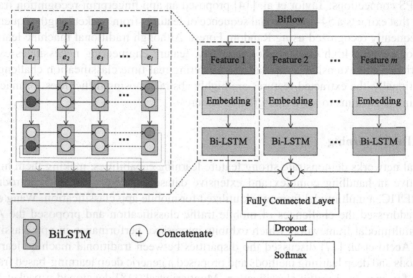

Fig. 1. The General Framework of PaBiL-Net

3.1 Feature Selection

In the real world, datasets and classification tasks often require models to learn different features that may change dynamically. PaBiL-Net uses a parallel structure that facilitates the addition and deletion of features. For example, network traffic data often involves multiple features, such as a sequence of packet lengths, a sequence of packet arrival intervals, and a sequence of packet transmission directions. In this case, there are 3 features, so the model needs to process 3 feature sequences in parallel. As requirements and data evolve, the feature selection strategy can be effortlessly changed by adding or removing the number of parallel channels.

3.2 Embedding Layer

Our work introduces the word embedding method commonly used in NLP into PaBiL-Net. This method can map words into a vector space, thus mining the potential relationships between words. Similarly, we treat the data in a sequence as a vocabulary in natural language and represent the deep connections between the data by embedding layers.

The essence of the embedding layer is a lookup table that can be used to store the embedded representation of a fixed-size dictionary. Given an index value, the embedding layer returns the embedding vector corresponding to this index, and the embedding vector reflects the semantic information of the corresponding data to some extent. Lookup tables, as an efficient data structure, can effectively reduce the computation time for mapping from elements to vectors. Consider a set S of elements with the number of elements L and the dimension of the embedding vector of each element is d. The total embedding can be regarded as a matrix $S \in R^{L \times d}$, where S will be continuously updated during the training process. Given an element E and an embedding matrix S, the embedding vector corresponding to E is the E-th row of the matrix S, i.e., S_E.

In PaBiL-Net, the input to each embedding layer is a set of feature sequence data containing n elements f.

$$f = [x_1, x_2, ..., x_n] \tag{1}$$

where f is the sequence data of a feature of the biflow and each element $x_i, I \in \{1, 2, 3, ..., n\}$ is converted into a d-dimensional vector S_i according to the lookup table S. The output of the embedding layer is the vector after the transformation of each element.

$$\text{Embedding}(f) = [S_1, S_2, ..., S_n] \tag{2}$$

3.3 Bidirectional LSTM

Considering each data packet as a sentence composed of word vectors, then the whole biflow is considered as a text sequence. Encoding this text sequence by an LSTM [21] model results in a high-dimensional vector representation. This representation captures the temporal relationships between the data.

The bidirectional LSTM (Bi-LSTM) structure in [22] is used to compute the feature data after the embedding layer, as shown in Fig. 1. The input of the Bi-LSTM layer is the sequence data $[S_1, S_2, ..., S_n]$. The computation process is divided into sequential computation ($\overrightarrow{\text{LSTM}}$) and inverse sequential computation ($\overleftarrow{\text{LSTM}}$). The detailed computation process is as follows.

$$\overrightarrow{h_t} = \overrightarrow{\text{LSTM}}\left(S_t, \overrightarrow{h_{t-1}}\right), t \in \{1, 2, 3, ..., n\} \tag{3}$$

$$\overleftarrow{h_t} = \overleftarrow{\text{LSTM}}\left(S_t, \overleftarrow{h_{t+1}}\right), t \in \{1, 2, 3, ..., n\} \tag{4}$$

where $\overrightarrow{h_t}$ and $\overleftarrow{h_t}$ are the outputs of the sequential and inverse-order calculations at time t, respectively, and the very first $\overrightarrow{h_0}$ and $\overleftarrow{h_{n+1}}$ are both initialized to 0. Finally, the Bi-LSTM sequential and inverse-order outputs are concatenated together to obtain the final output o.

$$o = \text{Concatenate}\left(\overrightarrow{h_n}, \overleftarrow{h_1}\right) \tag{5}$$

To provide better modeling capability, a two-layer Bi-LSTM is used in PaBiL-Net. Compared with a single-layer network, a multilayer network not only adapts better to complex data patterns but also avoids prematurely forgetting the information and effectively passes on long-term memory. Equation (6) shows the output form of Bi-LSTM.

$$o = \text{Concatenate}\left(\overrightarrow{h_n^1}, \overleftarrow{h_1^1}, \overrightarrow{h_n^2}, \overleftarrow{h_1^2} \right) \tag{6}$$

h_i^j is the output at moment i in the j-th LSTM layer.

3.4 Classification Layer

The structure of the classification layer is divided into 4 parts. First, the output vectors of all parallel Bi-LSTM layers are concatenated to obtain a summary of all features. Then, the feature representation is further compressed by a fully connected layer. Next, a dropout layer is added after the fully connected layer to prevent overfitting. Finally, by feeding the data into a softmax function, the probability distribution for each category is output and the model's classification results are derived based on the index of the maximum probability value.

4 Evaluation

This section first introduces the datasets used in the experiments, including the data source, collection process, and content of the dataset. Then, the experiment setup is elaborated, including the experiment environment, the hyperparameter settings, and the training strategy. Next, the baseline methods used in the experiments and the evaluation metrics are described. Finally, the results of the experiments are presented.

4.1 Datasets

MIRAGE-2019. We choose MIRAGE-2019 [23] as the dataset for the experiment. It was collected by researchers from the ARCLAB laboratory of the University of Naples "Federico II", Italy. They collected data containing 20 different APPs and 3 different brands of smartphones by recruiting more than 280 volunteers.

MIRAGE-2019 is released in JSON format and provides multiple features, including packet-level features, flow-level features, and metadata, for each 5-tuple feature that is identical for a biflow. Specifically, the packet-level features include some characteristics for the first 32 packets of a biflow. The flow-level features include statistical and distributional features of packet length and packet inter-arrival time. The metadata includes the number of packets, the length of the payload, and the duration of a biflow. Table 1 shows the details of MIRAGE-2019.

Table 1. Name, category, and number of biflows of each APP in MIRAGE-2019

Index	APP	Category	Biflows
1	Waze	Maps & Navigation	11755
2	OneFootball	Sports	10810
3	AccuWeather	Weather	10695
4	Duolingo	Education	8319
5	Subito	Lifestyle	8188
6	Wish	Shopping	6519
7	Spotify	Music and Audio	6447
8	FourSquare	Travel and Local	6420
9	Youtube	Video Players	6364
10	Comics	Comics	5519
11	Facebook	Social	5441
12	Dropbox	Productivity	4815
13	Twitter	News and Magazines	4746
14	Pinterest	Social	4078
15	Messenger	Communication	4059
16	TripAdvisor	Travel and Local	3578
17	Slither.io	Games	3088
18	Viber	Communication	2740
19	Trello	Productivity	2308
20	Groupon	Shopping	1995

MIRAGE-COVID-CCMA-2022. MIRAGE-COVID-CCMA-2022 [24] (hereafter MIRAGE-2022) collected traffic data generated by more than 150 experiment participants communicating and collaborating over 3 mobile devices using 9 mobile APPs. MIRAGE-2022 focuses on data about people's use of mobile devices for telecommuting, meetings, classes, and social activities during the Covid-19 pandemic. Table 2 shows the details of these APPs.

4.2 Experiment Settings and Hyperparameters

Our experiments were implemented on a server equipped with an Intel Xeon Gold 5218R CPU and accelerated with Nvidia Tesla V100 GPUs. The software runs on an Ubuntu 20.04 operating system using the Python 3.9.7 programming language and Pytorch 1.10.2 deep learning framework. The training batch was set to 64 and the learning rate was set to 0.001, which gradually decayed by a factor of 0.8 per round. Adam was used as the optimizer and an early stopping mechanism [25] was used to prevent overfitting.

Table 2. Name, category, and number of biflows of each APP in MIRAGE-COVID-CCMA-2022

Index	APP	Category	BiFlows
1	Microsoft Teams	Business	6541
2	Skype	Communication	6373
3	ZOOM Cloud Meetings	Business	5126
4	Webex Meetings	Business	4789
5	Messenger	Communication	4463
6	Discord	Communication	4337
7	GotoMeeting	Business	3695
8	Slack	Business	2988
9	Google Meet	Business	2252

To avoid the interference of random factors and ensure the accuracy of the experimental results, 5-fold cross-validation was used in all experiments.

In the experiments, we made many attempts to adjust the hyperparameters of the model. This includes feature selection, embedding vector dimension, and hidden state dimension of Bi-LSTM. First, in terms of feature selection, after many experiments, 5 features are finally determined, which are the sequence of transmission directions of the first 32 packets (0 indicates upload and 1 indicates download), the sequence of transport layer payload length of the first 32 packets, the sequence of inter-arrival time of packets (in seconds), the sequence of TCP window size (the value is 0 in case of UDP), and the first 128 bytes of transport layer payload (decimal sequence). Second, when determining the embedding vector dimension, if the size of the embedding dictionary is less than 1024, then the embedding vector dimension is equal to the size of the dictionary because a larger size of the embedding vector leads to unnecessary information redundancy. If the dictionary size is greater than or equal to 1024, then the embedding vector dimension is set to 1024. Although a larger dimension can lead to a richer information representation, it will also greatly increase resource consumption. Note that an embedding layer in a parallel branch is not necessarily required. For example, the value of the inter-arrival time of packets is continuous rather than discrete, so it is impossible to quantify the number of its embedding dictionary, so the embedding layer is not used in the branch where this feature is located. Next, the hidden state dimension of Bi-LSTM needs to be set reasonably. Considering computational resources and efficiency, it is set to 128. The number of neurons in the fully connected layer is the number of categories, i.e. 20 or 9. The random deactivation rate of the dropout is set to 0.4.

4.3 Baseline Methods

In our experiments, the performance of PaBiL-Net is evaluated by comparing it with 3 other baseline methods (RF, App-Net, and MIMETIC) that focus on mobile encrypted traffic classification.

(1) **RF.** A traditional machine learning-based mobile APP fingerprint detection model is proposed by Taylor et al. in [14]. The model first extracts 54-dimensional statistical features for packet length sequences, and then feeds these features into a random forest classifier to classify mobile encrypted traffic.

(2) **MIMETIC.** The model was proposed by Aceto et al. in [15]. It inputs the first 576 bytes of the transport layer payload to CNN and fully connected layer, while the number of bytes of the transport layer payload, the TCP window size, the inter-arrival time of the packets, and the direction of the first 12 packets are input to Bi-GRU. These 2 outputs are combined and then input to the softmax function to obtain the classification results.

(3) **App-Net.** This model was proposed by Wang et al. in [16]. It inputs the first 1014 bytes of the transport layer payload into CNN for feature extraction after one-hot coding, while the packet length sequence is input into Bi-LSTM for extracting the temporal relationships after the embedding layer. Finally, the outputs of the 2 networks are combined and the probability distribution of each category is obtained by the softmax function.

4.4 Metrics

In this paper, we choose Accuracy, macro Precision, macro Recall, and macro F1, which are widely used in deep learning, to evaluate the overall classification performance of each model. The specific formulas are as follows.

$$\text{Accuracy} = \frac{n_{correct}}{n_{all}} \tag{7}$$

where $n_{correct}$ denotes the number of correctly classified data and n_{all} is the number of all data in the dataset. Suppose there are c categories in the dataset and the formula of the F1 score for category i is as follows.

$$\text{Precision}_i = \frac{TP_i}{TP_i + FP_i} \tag{8}$$

$$\text{Recall}_i = \frac{TP_i}{TP_i + FN_i} \tag{9}$$

$$F1_i = \frac{2 \cdot \text{Precision}_i \cdot \text{Recall}_i}{\text{Precision}_i + \text{Recall}_i} \tag{10}$$

where TP_i (True Positive) indicates the amount of data in category i that are correctly classified. FP_i (False Positive) indicates the number of data not in i but incorrectly classified in i. FN_i (False Negative) indicates the amount of data in i that are classified into other categories. TN_i (True Negative) indicates the number of data that are not in i and are also classified as not in i. $F1_i$ is calculated from the harmonic average of Precision_i and Recall_i. The macro Precision, macro Recall, and macro F1 are obtained by averaging each category's Precision, Recall, and F1 scores, respectively.

$$\text{Macro\_Precision} = \frac{1}{c} \sum_{i=1}^{c} \text{Precision}_i \tag{11}$$

$$Macro\_Recall = \frac{1}{c} \sum_{i=1}^{c} Recall_i \qquad (12)$$

$$Macro\_F1 = \frac{1}{c} \sum_{i=1}^{c} F1_i \qquad (13)$$

4.5 Experiment Results

The experiment results of mobile encrypted traffic classification using each of the 4 models are given below.

Table 3. Classification performance of 4 models on MIRAGE-2019. **Bolded** indicates the best performance.

Metrics/Methods	RF [14]	MIMETIC [15]	App-Net [16]	PaBiL-Net
Accuracy	74.2133%	75.6348%	77.0164%	**81.1103%**
Macro-Precision	71.0807%	69.8155%	74.9011%	**78.5262%**
Macro-Recall	68.0366%	68.6161%	71.8995%	**76.1381%**
Macro-F1	69.0149%	68.7413%	73.0922%	**76.9951%**

Table 4. Classification performance of 4 models on MIRAGE-COVID-CCMA-2022. **Bolded** indicates the best performance.

Metrics/Methods	RF [14]	MIMETIC [15]	App-Net [16]	PaBiL-Net
Accuracy	90.8466%	90.2133%	91.2791%	**93.4852%**
Macro-Precision	92.3667%	91.1617%	91.5447%	**94.7965%**
Macro-Recall	91.2156%	90.3743%	91.3125%	**93.3709%**
Macro-F1	91.5112%	90.6051%	91.4945%	**93.8045%**

Table 3 and Table 4 show the results of the classification experiments of PaBiL-Net and the 3 baseline methods on the 2 datasets. The experiments show that all the 3 baseline models show good performance. Compared to RF and MIMETIC, App-Net shows better performance in all 4 metrics on MIRAGE-2019, while on MIRAGE-2022, the performance gap between the 3 baseline models is not significant, probably due to the small amount of data in this dataset. The proposed PaBiL-Net achieves the best performance among all models. Specifically, PaBiL-Net achieves 81.1103% and 93.4852% accuracy on the 2 datasets, which were 4.0939% and 2.2061% better than the best-performing baseline method, App-Net. In addition, the macro F1 of PaBiL-Net was 76.9951% and 93.8045%, which were 3.9029% and 2.2933% better than the best baseline models (App-Net and RF), respectively. Overall, it seems that PaBiL-Net outperforms the 3 baseline methods in all 4 metrics and shows excellent classification performance.

Nowadays, more and more multimodal frameworks are widely used in encrypted traffic classification. Many researchers expect to achieve better performance by combining different network structures. However, the results of this paper show that using multiple structures does not necessarily lead to the best results.

5 Ablation Study

In this section, we take MIRAGE-2019, which contains a larger amount and variety of data, as an example. We investigate the influence of the first 2 components (feature selection strategy and embedding layer) in PaBiL-Net on the performance. First, the feature selection strategies using different numbers and types of features are compared separately. A ranking of the contribution of the 5 features to performance is provided. Second, the performance of the model with the embedding layer removed is compared with the original model.

5.1 Feature Selection Strategy

Since PaBiL-Net has a high degree of freedom in feature selection, i.e., the number of parallel channels in the model can be adjusted according to the actual needs, we attempt to investigate how the number of features or the type of features affects the classification performance. The experiment results are shown in Fig. 2.

In Fig. 2, PB is the number of transport layer payload bytes. Iat is the inter-arrival time of packets. Dir is the transmission direction of packets. Win is the TCP window size. First, a single feature is selected for the experiment, as shown in Fig. 2(a). Only one path in PaBiL-Net is used to try each of the 5 features. The results show that the best performance is achieved by the model selecting PB as a feature, followed by payload, win, and dir in that order. The model choosing iat performs the worst with an accuracy of only 34.39%, possibly because the channel containing this feature cannot use the embedding layer.

Among the experimental results for a single feature, the feature with the best result (i.e., PB) is selected as the basis and combined with each of the other 4 features to obtain 4 comparative results, as shown in Fig. 2(b). The model combined with win achieves the highest accuracy rate, but the macro F1 is not the highest. On the contrary, the model combined with payload achieves the highest macro F1. This proves that the fusion of multiple features does lead to a better performance than a single feature.

In classification tasks, the macro F1 usually indicates the overall performance more than the accuracy, so in the next experiments, we constructed 3 models based on PB and payload for comparison. This is shown in Fig. 2(c). The results show that the model combined with win obtains the best performance, followed by iat and dir. This implies that TCP window size is important for encrypted traffic classification, but most existing studies ignore this feature. Instead of increasing, the macro F1 obtained after adding dir and iat decreased. This may be because the feature itself contains less information, or

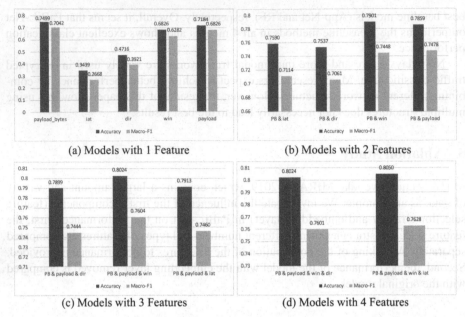

(a) Models with 1 Feature

(b) Models with 2 Features

(c) Models with 3 Features

(d) Models with 4 Features

Fig. 2. Performance comparison of PaBiL-Net using different feature selection strategies

because other features have already covered its contribution. Therefore, more features do not necessarily mean better performance for classification models.

Following the same principles, 2 models were constructed for comparison, as shown in Fig. 2(d). The results show that the model combined with iat performs better, while the model combined with dir does not improve.

Combining the above results and analysis, we explored the contribution of each feature to the classification performance. Equation (14) gives the ranking of the contributions of the 5 features.

$$payload\_bytes > payload > TCP\_window\_size > iat > dir \tag{14}$$

First, the number of transport layer payload bytes and the transport layer payload are the key features that affect the performance. Very good performance can be achieved by using only these features. Second, TCP window size also plays an important role in classification, and the performance is still greatly improved by adding this feature. Compared with the first 3 features, inter-arrival time and transmission direction contribute less to the performance.

5.2 The Necessity of Embedding Layers

Our study is inspired by the NLP approach to applying the embedding layer to PaBiL-Net. To thoroughly investigate the influence of the embedding layer, we performed the same experiments on the model after removing the embedding layer. The results are compared with the original model.

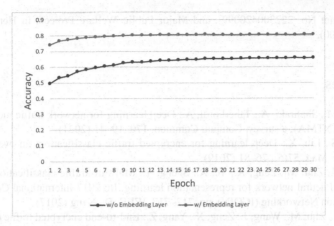

Fig. 3. Comparison of accuracy of PaBiL-Net with and without embedding layer

Figure 3 shows the accuracy comparison of the 2 models with a line graph. The blue line represents the model without the embedding layer. The red line represents the original model with the embedded layer. Each point represents the accuracy of the validation set after each training epoch. The results show that the performance of the model without the embedding layer degrades severely. On the other hand, the original model shows a clear advantage. In particular, at the end of the first training epoch, the accuracy of the original model has reached a high level, higher than the highest level of the other model. Eventually, the difference between the accuracies of the 2 models reached 14.9025%. This indicates that the embedding layer is crucial to improve the classification performance.

6 Conclusions

In this paper, we present PaBiL-Net, an end-to-end classification model aimed at enhancing the performance of mobile encrypted traffic classification. PaBiL-Net utilizes a parallel similarity structure to handle diverse data features, offering greater flexibility in the feature selection strategy. We conduct experiments on 2 publicly available datasets and compare the performance of PaBiL-Net against 3 baseline models (RF, MIMETIC, and App-Net). The 5-fold cross-validation results demonstrate that PaBiL-Net surpasses the baseline models across all performance metrics. Moreover, the inclusion of the embedding layer further enhances performance. Additionally, we assess different feature selection strategies and rank the contributions of 5 feature types to the classification performance. These findings contribute to the refinement and optimization of PaBiL-Net, with practical implications for real-world applications. We hope that this model and the conclusions drawn in this paper provide valuable insights and aid future research in the domains of cyberspace security and network management.

Acknowledgement. This work was supported by the National Natural Science Foundation of China (Grant No. 61772548), the Science Foundation for the Excellent Youth Scholars of Henan

Province (Grant No. 222300420099), and Major Public Welfare Projects in Henan Province (201300210200).

References

1. Abbasi, M., Shahraki, A., Taherkordi, A.: Deep learning for network traffic monitoring and analysis (NTMA): a survey. Comput. Commun. **170**, 19–41 (2021)
2. Rezaei, S., Liu, X.: Deep learning for encrypted traffic classification: an overview. IEEE Commun. Mag. **57**(5), 76–81 (2019)
3. Wang, W., Zhu, M., Zeng, X., Ye, X., Sheng, Y.: Malware traffic classification using convolutional neural network for representation learning. In: 2017 International Conference on Information Networking (ICOIN), pp. 712–717. IEEE, Da Nang (2017)
4. Wang, W., Zhu, M., Wang, J., Zeng, X., Yang, Z.: End-to-end encrypted traffic classification with one-dimensional convolution neural networks. In: 2017 IEEE International Conference on Intelligence and Security Informatics (ISI), pp. 43–48. IEEE, Beijing (2017)
5. Aceto, G., Ciuonzo, D., Montieri, A., et al.: Mobile encrypted traffic classification using deep learning: experimental evaluation, lessons learned, and challenges. IEEE Trans. Netw. Serv. Manage. **16**(2), 445–458 (2019)
6. Lotfollahi, M., Jafari Siavoshani, M., Shirali Hossein Zade, R., et al.: Deep packet: a novel approach for encrypted traffic classification using deep learning. Soft. Comput. **24**(3), 1999–2012 (2020)
7. Antonello, R., Fernandes, S., Kamienski, C., et al.: Deep packet inspection tools and techniques in commodity platforms: challenges and trends. J. Netw. Comput. Appl. **35**(6), 1863–1878 (2012)
8. Bujlow, T., Carela-Español, V., Barlet-Ros, P.: Independent comparison of popular DPI tools for traffic classification. Comput. Netw. **76**, 75–89 (2015)
9. Xu, C., Chen, S., Su, J., et al.: A survey on regular expression matching for deep packet inspection: applications, algorithms, and hardware platforms. IEEE Commun. Surv. Tutor. **18**(4), 2991–3029 (2016)
10. Qazi, Z.A., Lee, J., Jin, T., et al.: Application-awareness in SDN. In: Proceedings of the ACM SIGCOMM 2013 Conference on SIGCOMM, pp. 487–488. ACM, Hong Kong (2013)
11. Wang, Q., Yahyavi, A., Kemme, B., et al.: I know what you did on your smartphone: inferring app usage over encrypted data traffic. In: 2015 IEEE Conference on Communications and Network Security (CNS), pp. 433–441. IEEE, Florence (2015)
12. Alan, H.F., Kaur, J.: Can Android applications be identified using only TCP/IP headers of their launch time traffic?. In: Proceedings of the 9th ACM Conference on Security & Privacy in Wireless and Mobile Networks (WiSec), pp. 61–66. ACM, Darmstadt (2016)
13. Shbair, W.M., Cholez, T., Francois, J., et al.: A multi-level framework to identify https services. In: NOMS 2016-2016 IEEE/IFIP Network Operations and Management Symposium (NOMS), pp. 240–248. IEEE, Turkey (2016)
14. Taylor, V.F., Spolaor, R., Conti, M., et al.: Robust smartphone app identification via encrypted network traffic analysis. IEEE Trans. Inf. Forensics Secur. **13**(1), 63–78 (2017)
15. Aceto, G., Ciuonzo, D., Montieri, A., et al.: MIMETIC: mobile encrypted traffic classification using multimodal deep learning. Comput. Netw. **165**, 106944 (2019)
16. Wang, X., Chen, S., Su, J.: App-net: a hybrid neural network for encrypted mobile traffic classification. In: IEEE INFOCOM 2020-IEEE Conference on Computer Communications Workshops (INFOCOM WKSHPS), pp. 424–429. IEEE, Toronto (2020)
17. Aceto, G., Ciuonzo, D., Montieri, A., et al.: Toward effective mobile encrypted traffic classification through deep learning. Neurocomputing **409**, 306–315 (2020)

18. Montieri, A., Bovenzi, G., Aceto, G., et al.: Packet-level prediction of mobile-app traffic using multitask deep learning. Comput. Netw. **200**, 108529 (2021)
19. Jiang, M., Li, Z., Fu, P., et al.: Accurate mobile-app fingerprinting using flow-level relationship with graph neural networks. Comput. Netw. **217**, 109309 (2022)
20. Dainotti, A., Pescape, A., Claffy, K.C.: Issues and future directions in traffic classification. IEEE Netw. **26**(1), 35–40 (2012)
21. Hochreiter, S., Schmidhuber, J.: Long short-term memory. Neural Comput. **9**(8), 1735–1780 (1997)
22. Graves, A., Schmidhuber, J.: Framewise phoneme classification with bidirectional LSTM and other neural network architectures. Neural Netw. **18**(5–6), 602–610 (2005)
23. Aceto, G., Ciuonzo, D., Montieri, A., et al.: MIRAGE: mobile-app traffic capture and ground-truth creation. In: 2019 4th International Conference on Computing, Communications and Security (ICCCS), pp. 1–8. IEEE, Rome (2019)
24. Guarino, I., Aceto, G., Ciuonzo, D., et al.: Classification of communication and collaboration apps via advanced deep-learning approaches. In: 2021 IEEE 26th International Workshop on Computer Aided Modeling and Design of Communication Links and Networks (CAMAD), pp. 1–6. IEEE, Porto (2021)
25. Prechelt, L.: Early stopping-but when? In: Orr, G.B., Müller, K.R. (eds.) Neural Networks: Tricks of the Trade. LNCS, vol. 1524, pp. 55–69. Springer, Heidelberg (2002). https://doi.org/10.1007/3-540-49430-8_3

A General Source Code Vulnerability Detection Method via Ensemble of Graph Neural Networks

Ciling Zeng[1], Bo Zhou[2], Huoyuan Dong[3], Haolin Wu[2], Peiyuan Xie[2], and Zhitao Guan[3]([✉])

[1] State Grid Hunan Electric Power Company Limited, Changsha, China
[2] Hunan SGIT Technology Co., Ltd., Changsha, China
[3] School of Control and Computer Engineering, North China Electric Power University, Beijing, China
guan@ncepu.edu.cn

Abstract. Deep neural networks have been recently utilized in source code vulnerability detection methods due to their automated feature learning capabilities. However, current deep vulnerability detection models heavily rely on fixed code static analysis tools, limiting their applicability to a single programming language. Furthermore, the existing models often fail to fully extract semantic features from the source code, leading to limited generalization capabilities. To address these challenges, this paper proposes a language-agnostic code vulnerability detection framework based on ensemble of graph neural networks. Our approach considers the source program as a linear token sequence and constructs an initial graph representation by capturing the co-occurrence relationships between tokens. The model's hidden layers leverage a combination of graph convolutional module and gated graph neural networks to extract semantic features from vulnerable code. To adaptively learn the importance of each vulnerability feature, we introduce a self-attention layer after the hidden layer. Additionally, to enhance model stability and prevent overfitting, we incorporate residual connections and flooding regularization techniques. Experimental results on real-world vulnerability datasets demonstrate our approach surpasses previous SOTA approaches by a margin of over 2.37% in terms of detection accuracy.

Keywords: Vulnerability detection · Source program · Graph neural network · Deep learning · Self attention · Code augmentation

1 Introduction

The complexity of computer software systems has increased due to advancements in computer hardware and the evolving demands of application scenarios. This complexity is evident in functional design, code size, and the technology stack used in development. Consequently, there has been a significant rise in software security vulnerabilities, posing increased risks of unauthorized access and compromise of information systems [1]. In the first half of 2022, the China National Vulnerability Database of Information Security (CNNVD) reported 12,466 new general vulnerability information items, including 1,927 highly critical vulnerabilities (15.46% of the total) [2]. Detecting vulnerabilities proactively is crucial to prevent their exploitation and enhance the security of information systems.

Vulnerability detection methods for source code vulnerabilities can be classified into two types: static detection and dynamic detection, depending on whether the program is running or not. Static detection aims to establish an ideal model of the program's state and analyze how it transitions between different states [3]. Existing static analysis methods primarily include lexical analysis techniques, data flow analysis, and control flow analysis techniques. Lexical analysis methods slice the program and compare each fragment with a security vulnerability library. If a match is found, it is considered a security vulnerability [4]. However, these methods often lack generalization since they only consider surface-level information from the source code fragments, resulting in a higher rate of missed vulnerabilities. Data flow and control flow analysis rely on experts to determine the presence of security vulnerabilities based on data flow or control processes, such as buffer overflow and unauthorized access [5]. Nonetheless, these methods heavily depend on human experts, leading to a higher probability of overlooking vulnerabilities.

Dynamic analysis methods primarily employ fuzz testing [6] and taint analysis [7]. Fuzz testing utilizes automated tools to generate diverse input data, which are then fed into the software system. Potential vulnerabilities are detected based on the system's output results. Taint analysis determines whether the system has produced data leaks or performed dangerous data operations by assessing whether the tainted source has propagated. The drawback of these approaches is that the analysis results from a single execution may be incomplete, necessitating multiple executions of the source program.

Traditional machine learning approaches based on manually annotated features [8] are also employed in vulnerability detection. However, these methods rely heavily on prior knowledge and human experts, and the manually defined features struggle to adapt to the iterative development of software programs. As a result, deep learning has gained significant popularity in recent years for source code vulnerability detection due to its ability to automatically learn features and patterns.

Existing source program vulnerability detection methods based on deep neural networks differ primarily in two aspects: the representations of the source program and different network architectures. Li et al. [9] treat program slices involving the same function call as sequential processing units and utilize word2vec vector representation to depict each symbol within the sequence. These vectors are then interconnected to construct the vector representation of the source code. Subsequently, a bidirectional long short-term memory network is employed to extract vulnerability features and train the model, effectively addressing code dependencies in both forward and backward directions. Building upon this approach, another study [10] introduces a code attention mechanism to further

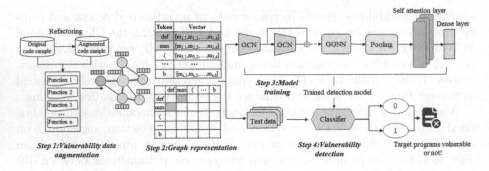

Fig. 1. Workflow of our proposed vulnerability detection framework.

enhance the detection performance of the model. On the other hand, Wu et al. [11] represent the source program at the function level as a program dependency graph, where each node corresponds to a line of source code. They employ three centrality analysis strategies - "degree centrality", "Katz centrality", and "adjacent centrality" - to assess the importance of each line of source code. The vulnerability detection is then performed using a convolutional neural network (CNN). Additionally, the abstract syntax tree (AST) is commonly utilized as the initial representation of the code [12]. Pre-trained language models, such as BERT, have demonstrated promising performance in downstream tasks like vulnerability detection, benefitting from their pre-training on extensive data. However, the attention layer's interconnection between every position in the source code restricts the network's ability to capture local information within the code [13]. Overall, existing methods employ sequence and tree representations for code, resulting in the loss of significant structural features. Graph representations, while capturing structural information, often rely on source code analysis tools like Joern [14]. Nonetheless, some studies have revealed challenges in parsing source code or third-party libraries in different programming languages using such tools, leading to internal compilation errors or anomalies [15]. In terms of model structure, CNNs, recurrent neural networks, and Transformer-based architectures [16] are commonly employed to handle sequence data but face limitations in directly handling the graph structure information inherent in variable-length source code, such as variable-function and function-function calling relationships.

In response to the aforementioned challenges, this paper presents a novel code vulnerability detection model that combines graph convolutional neural networks (GCN) [17] and gated graph neural networks (GGNN) [18], as shown in Fig. 1. By leveraging the specific strengths of GCN in capturing local information in source code and GGNN in capturing long-range dependencies and global graph information between nodes, our model effectively integrates the advantages of these two models. Notably, we design the hidden layers of our model by concatenating GGNN after the graph convolutional layer. This strategic configuration allows the model to simultaneously extract both local and global information from the source program, consequently enhancing the accuracy of the vulnerability detection model. Additionally, drawing inspiration from ResNet [19], we introduce residual connections between the hidden layers to mitigate the issue of gradient vanishing commonly encountered in deep graph neural networks. This structural enhancement ensures stable and effective information flow throughout the model. Moreover, prior to reaching the output layer, we incorporate a self-attention mechanism that allocates greater attention weights to key features. This mechanism facilitates the embedding representation of the source program to pass through the fully connected layer for precise graph-level prediction. In terms of the loss function design, we employ the flooding regularization technique to smoothen the model's loss and prevent overfitting to the training set. This regularization strategy promotes robust learning and generalization of the detection model.

Regarding the representation of the source program, this paper draws inspiration from Nguyen et al. [15] and leverages a pre-trained program language model. The model effectively splits the source program sequence into a linear sequence composed of individual tokens, excluding duplicate tokens. We treat distinct tokens as nodes in the initial representation graph, where the edges of the graph reflect the co-occurrence relationships between tokens within a moving window. To obtain the initial feature representation of the nodes, we utilize the embedding layer of the pre-trained program language model, ensuring informative and meaningful node representations. Furthermore, due to the scarcity of labeled data with vulnerabilities, we adopt six code refactoring methods to generate augmented code samples that maintain same labels with the original data. This augmentation approach substantially expands the training set of the detection model and significantly improves its generalization performance during the testing phase. Importantly, our proposed approach does not rely on language-specific tools such as Joern [14] for extracting program dependency graphs from the source code. Thus, it offers broad applicability for program vulnerability detection across various programming languages.

To verify the effectiveness of our proposed approach, we conducted extensive experiments on a popular real-world vulnerability dataset CodeXGLUE. The results unequivocally demonstrate that our method surpasses other strong baselines.

In summary, this paper contributes in the following key aspects:

- We introduce a novel graph neural network-based model that effectively combines graph convolutional module and gated graph neural networks for precise source code vulnerability detection. By incorporating a self-attention layer, the model strategically focuses on crucial node correlations, resulting in improved detection accuracy.
- To address the challenge of overfitting to the vulnerability training set, we employ code augmentation strategies and flooding regularization techniques, which significantly enhance the model's generalization capability and alleviate the risk of overfitting.

– Importantly, we evaluate the performance of our model on a more realistic vulnerability dataset called CodeXGLUE, encompassing highly complex source code data, instead of relying solely on artificially generated data. Through rigorous experimentation, we demonstrate that our model achieves superior detection accuracy compared to other prevailing models.

The structure of this paper is outlined as follows: Sect. 1 provides backgrounds and existing research in the field. Section 2 defines vulnerability detection and introduces code refactoring strategies. In Sect. 3, we present a comprehensive description of our model. The experimental outcomes, obtained from real-world vulnerability datasets, are presented in Sect. 4. Finally, Sect. 5 summarizes our conclusions.

2   Preliminaries

In this section, we begin by presenting the formal definition of the problem, establishing a clear foundation for our subsequent discussions. Additionally, we describe the preprocessing and augmentation techniques employed on the vulnerability dataset to facilitate effective training of our proposed model.

2.1   Problem Definition

We address the issue of source code vulnerability detection by framing it as a binary classification problem, using a deep learning-based classifier F to effectively identify whether a given source program sample contains vulnerabilities or not. To facilitate analysis, we consider functions as the fundamental unit and define a sample as $\{(x_i, y_i) \mid x_i \in X, y_i \in Y\}_{i=1}^{n}$, where X represents the input data space and n denotes the size of the sample set. The label set $Y = \{0, 1\}$ is defined such that 1 denotes a vulnerability and 0 denotes no vulnerability. To implement the classifier F, we adopt a graph neural network structure that characterizes each source program x_i as a graph $g_i(V, M, A) \in G$. In this representation, V denotes a collection of s nodes within the graph, $M \in R^{s \times d}$ denotes the feature matrix of the nodes, and each node $v_i \in V$ is represented by a real-valued vector $m_i \in R^d$. The adjacency matrix $A \in \{0, 1\}^{s \times s}$ indicates the existence of edges between nodes v and u, with $A_{v,u}$ being set to 1 when there is a connection and 0 otherwise. We then utilize the classifier F to learn a mapping based on the constructed graph g_i. To optimize the mapping function $f(x)$, we define the objective function $\mathcal{L}$ with a regularization term $\Omega(\theta)$ that penalizes overfitting and a parameter λ that adjusts the regularization strength as shown in Eq. (1):

$$\min \sum_{i=1}^{n} \mathcal{L}\left(f\left(g_i(V, M, A), y_i \mid x_i\right)\right) + \lambda\Omega(\theta) \tag{1}$$

Table 1. Various refactoring methods used in our work to augment vulnerability datasets.

Refactoring method	Operation	Example
Method renaming	Rename a method using a synonym	*def remove(m) → def delete(m)*
Arguments renaming	Rename an augment using a synonym	*def func(length) → def func(size)*
Duplication	Duplicate an assignment	*m = 1 → m = 1; m = 1*
Print adding	insert a print statement	*add: print (1)*
Dead if adding	insert an unreachable if statement	*add: if(0 == 1): print(1)*
Local variable adding	Add an unused local variable	*add: tmp = 1*

2.2   Preprocess of Code Data

For a source program vulnerability detection model, the training data is crucial. However, obtaining high-quality real-world vulnerability code data is challenging, as it typically requires manual annotation by human experts. Therefore, in this paper, to enhance the model's generalization, we performed data augmentation on a real-world vulnerability dataset from CodeXGLUE [20]. Specifically, we employed six simple yet effective code refactoring strategies [21,22] to generate new code samples while preserving the semantic features and labels of the original samples. Table 1 provides examples of these code refactoring methods and their corresponding transformations.

3   Proposed Model

This section presents our proposed program vulnerability detection model, which utilizes an ensemble of graph neural network. The model comprises four main components: 1) Source program representation: This component focuses on reasonably representing the vulnerability source program. 2) Feature extraction: A hybrid network structure with residual connections is designed to integrate graph convolutional layer and gated graph neural network to capture code features comprehensively. 3) Feature aggregation: To enhance robustness and reduce the risk of overfitting, a weighted pooling strategy is proposed, which incorporates both global and local information of vulnerability features. 4) Model output layer: We employs batch normalization and dropout techniques to achieve graph-level prediction. Additionally, we introduce a self-attention layer that helps the model focus on important relationships within the input, further enhancing its predictive capabilities. By incorporating these four components, our proposed model demonstrates enhanced accuracy in detecting program vulnerabilities.

3.1   Build Graph of the Source Code

Previous studies have relied on programming language parsers to extract semantic graph information from source code [10,27]. However, these parsers often

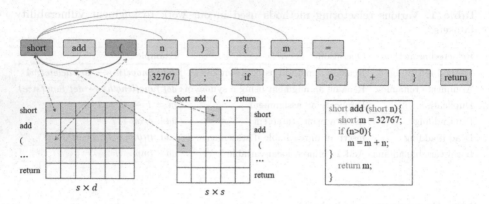

Fig. 2. Structure of graph for a vulnerability sample. We set sliding window of length $2p = 2$ for the node "*short*". The node feature matrix has a size of $s \times d$, while the adjacency matrix has a size of $s \times s$.

struggle with parsing code from various programming languages without encountering internal compilation errors and exceptions, which limits their practical applicability [15]. In contrast, this paper leverages a language-independent graph construction method that is both simple and effective. Specifically, the proposed method treats source code as a token sequence and initializes each token as a d-dimensional vector, which is continuously updated during training. The method then removes duplicate tokens, keeping only the unique ones that serve as nodes in the code representation graph. The co-occurrence of different tokens in a fixed window is captured as edges in the graph, as depicted in Fig. 2. Using the following Eq. (2), we can define the graph representation of the source program in this manner.

$$\begin{cases} N = \{r_v | v \in [1, s]\} \\ E = \{A_{v,u} | v \in [1, s], u \in [v - p, v + p]\} \end{cases} \quad (2)$$

where N and E denote the collection of nodes and edges, respectively, s denotes the total length of the preprocessed token sequence, p denotes half of the length of the sliding window, and $A_{v,u}$ denotes the undirected edge between token v and token u. In accordance with previous literature [15], self-loops are neglected in the construction of the graph in this paper as they do not improve model performance.

To initialize the node feature vectors in the graph, we leverage a pre-trained programming language model CodeBERT or GraphCodeBERT [23,24] and integrate its token embedding layer into our model design, following the approach used in prior research [15].

3.2   Combined Novel Graph Neural Network Structure

We introduce the hidden layers that serve as feature extractor in our proposed vulnerability detection model. The feature extractor incorporates a hybrid architecture that combines graph convolutional module and gated graph neural networks, utilizing residual connectivity. The feature extraction process begins with the graph convolution layer, where the attributes of neighboring nodes are merged with their own attributes. This enables the current node to update its representation by incorporating local information relevant to the analyzed vulnerability. Following the GCN module, the GGNN module updates the node embeddings using a gated update mechanism. The GGNN layers consist of linear transformations and gating operations, which enable the network to capture complex dependencies within the graph. To enhance the model's representation capacity and overcome challenges like gradient vanishing or exploding during training, we integrate residual connectivity into the feature extraction component. This ensures the stability and effectiveness of the feature extraction process, ultimately enhancing the model's performance in vulnerability detection tasks.

The graph convolution layer updates the feature vector of node v at the $(k+1)$-th iteration by combining the feature vectors of its neighboring nodes at the k-th iteration. This transformation is expressed as the following Eq. (3):

$$h_v^{k+1} = \phi \left(\sum_{u \in N_v} a_{v,u} \boldsymbol{W}^{(k)} h_u^{(k)} \right), \forall v \in V \tag{3}$$

where $a_{v,u}$ represents the edge constants between node v and u in the Laplace renormalized adjacency matrix $\boldsymbol{D}^{-1/2}\boldsymbol{A}\boldsymbol{D}^{-1/2}$ [15]. Here, $\boldsymbol{D}$ refers to the diagonal node degree matrix of $\boldsymbol{A}$. $\boldsymbol{W}^{(k)}$ represents the weight matrix, and ϕ denotes a nonlinear activation function used in the transformation.

The gated layer takes the node feature matrix processed by the convolutional layer as input. In the gated neural network, the gating mechanism computes new features for each node. This mechanism has two steps: firstly, the update gate is calculated, which determines whether the node should update its features or not. Secondly, a reset gate is computed, which determines which historical information the node needs to forget. Finally, the new node features are computed from the current node's information and that of its neighboring nodes. The update gate and reset gate are computed using the sigmoid activation function. To compute the hidden state, we first obtain a "forgetting vector" by multiplying the reset gate and the input node feature matrix, and then multiply it with the adjacency matrix to obtain $\boldsymbol{A}$. We then perform an activation function on the result to obtain the updated hidden state $\boldsymbol{H}$. The computation process of the gating layer is shown in the following Eq. (4, 5, 6, 7, 8):

$$a_v^{(k+1)} = \sum_{u \in N_v} a_{v,u} h_u^{(k)} \tag{4}$$

$$z_v^{(k+1)} = \sigma \left(\boldsymbol{W}^z a_v^{(k+1)} + \boldsymbol{U}^z h_v^{(k)} \right) \tag{5}$$

$$r_v^{(k+1)} = \sigma \left(W^r a_v^{(k+1)} + U^r h_v^{(k)} \right) \tag{6}$$

$$\widetilde{h_v^{(k+1)}} = \phi \left(W^o a_v^{(k+1)} + U^o \left(r_v^{(k+1)} \odot h_v^{(k)} \right) \right) \tag{7}$$

$$h_v^{(k+1)} = \left(1 - z_v^{(k+1)} \right) \odot h_v^{(k)} + z_v^{(k+1)} \odot \widetilde{h_v^{(k+1)}} \tag{8}$$

where z and r denote the update gate and reset gate, respectively. W and U are trainable weights. $\odot$ denotes multiplication by elements, while σ and ϕ denote nonlinear activation functions.

We connect the residuals of the graph convolution layer and the gated GNN layer separately to deepen the capacity of proposed model, so the relationship between hidden GNN layers can be simply shown in the following Eq. (9):

$$H^{k+1} = H^k + GNN(A, H^k) \tag{9}$$

3.3 Mix of Pooling Layer

The pooling layer transforms the feature representation of the hidden layer into a one-dimensional graph embedding vector. Sum pooling has been shown to improve the generalization performance of graph neural networks [25]. However, maximum pooling is more suitable for capturing the typical semantic features of source code vulnerabilities. To leverage both methods, this paper proposes a weighted pooling approach. Specifically, for each node v, its final vector is obtained as follows Eq. (10):

$$e_v = \sigma \left(w^T h_v^{(K)} + b \right) \odot \phi \left(W h_v^{(K)} + b \right) \tag{10}$$

where $\sigma \left(w^T h_v^{(K)} + b \right)$ represents the soft attention applied to node v in the last layer of the gating layer. The hyperparameters α and β are used to weight the contributions of sum and max pooling, respectively. The final graph-level embedding for the source code program can be formulated as Eq. (11):

$$e_g = \alpha \sum_{v \in V} e_v + \beta \, \text{MaxPool} \{e_v\}_{v \in V} \tag{11}$$

3.4 Output Unit

The graph embeddings obtained from Pooling layer are fed into the output layer to be transformed into predicted probability vectors. The feature vectors of the graph pass through a linear layer, then through a batch normalization layer, followed by a nonlinear transformation using the ReLU activation function, and then through a Dropout operation to reduce overfitting. As Fig. 3 shows, the output module also utilizes a self-attention mechanism, which helps the model attend to important relationships within the input. It is worth noting that the Q, K, and V vectors used in the attention layer are all graph embedding vectors

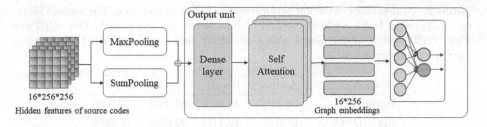

Fig. 3. Pooling unit and output unit in our detection model.

themselves. To fully capture the source code features, we employ two output layers in parallel. The batch normalization operation normalizes the data within each batch, resulting in a smoother semantic distribution of exploit codes. This reduces the internal covariance shift, speeds up the training convergence, and enhances the stability of the network, mitigating issues such as gradient vanishing or exploding.

3.5 Design of Training Loss

In our study, we adopt the binary cross-entropy loss with logits as the loss function, which is applied to the predicted probabilities and their corresponding labels. To mitigate overfitting and improve model robustness, we employ the flooding regularization technique [26]. This technique involves setting a flooding value and encouraging the loss to remain in proximity to this value, effectively constraining the loss from becoming excessively small. The mathematical representation of this approach is shown in Eq. (12). By employing flooding regularization, we promote a more balanced and controlled optimization process, leading to improved model performance and generalization capabilities.

$$\tilde{\mathcal{L}}_{CE} = |\mathcal{L}_{CE} - b| + b \tag{12}$$

4 Experiments and Analysis

4.1 Experimental Settings

Datasets. In this paper, we use real benchmark data from CodeXGLUE [20] to evaluate our model. This dataset was originally curated by Zhou et al. [27] from two popular open-source projects written in the C language, namely QEMU and FFmpeg. We expanded the training set of this dataset to 22,180 instances using the code refactoring method mentioned in Sect. 2.2. The development and test set consist of 2,732 instances, aligning with prior research [20]. Note that the vulnerable codes in CodeXGLUE dataset are highly complex and not generated artificially, making the detection process more challenging.

Table 2. Vulnerability detection performances of various methods. The highest scores are indicated in **bold**, while the second highest scores are underlined. "Our_CB" and "Our_GCB" refers to our model with CodeBERT and GraphCodeBERT embedding layer, respectively.

Method	Accuracy	Recall	Precision	F1
Devign	59.22%	44.46%	57.23%	50.04%
ReGCD_GCN	61.90%	42.31%	62.62%	50.50%
ReGVD_GGNN	62.12%	46.61%	61.58%	53.06%
Our_GCB	63.98%	**61.35%**	60.68%	**61.01%**
Our_CB	**64.49%**	51.08%	**64.29%**	56.93%

Strong Baselines. ReGVD [15]: A method that considers the co-occurrence relationship between tokens to construct a code graph and utilizes residual connections in GNN layers for vulnerability detection. The ReGVD method offers two models, GCN and GGNN, which we evaluate separately to gauge their individual performance. Devign [27]: A method that operates on a code property graph and employs 1-D convolution pooling for predictions based on GGNN.

Implementation Details. During the model training process, we utilized a batch size of 16 and trained for a total of 42 epochs. The Adam optimizer was employed, starting with a learning rate of $5e-5$. To enhance regularization, we set the Flood level value to 0.4. The model was trained on a system equipped with an NVIDIA 3090 GPU and an Intel(R) Core(TM) i9-10900K CPU at 3.70 GHz. To encourage community comparisons and facilitate the reproducibility of our findings, our code and dataset slices are available at: https://github.com/sullendhy/vul_detection_gnn.

4.2 Detection Performance of Our Model

We evaluate the performance of various methods using accuracy, recall, precision, and F1 score. Table 2 presents the detection performances of our model alongside other prevailing models. The reported results are based on the best model checkpoint, which corresponds to the model achieving the highest accuracy on the validation set. Notably, our model consistently outperforms other methods using the exact same parameter and data settings. Specifically, our approach achieves a detection accuracy of 64.49% on the CodeXGLUE dataset, establishing a new state-of-the-art (SOTA) value. We also observed that the detection performance of our model varies when using different pre-trained models to initialize the node embeddings.

4.3 Ablation Study

We conduct an ablation study to empirically evaluate the impact of key components in our model, including the code refactoring process of the dataset, the

Table 3. Accuracy and precision with different settings. "Our_CB" denotes our original method, "-DA" represents that we did not perform data augmentation on the training set, "-RES" indicates that we removed residual connections between hidden layers, "-Flooding" denotes that we did not utilize flooding regularization technique, and "-SA" signifies the removal of self-attention layers in our model.

	Our_CB	-DA	-RES	-Flooding	-SA
Accuracy	**64.49%**	63.29%	63.98%	64.35%	61.24%
Precision	**64.29%**	62.00%	63.59%	61.96%	59.84%

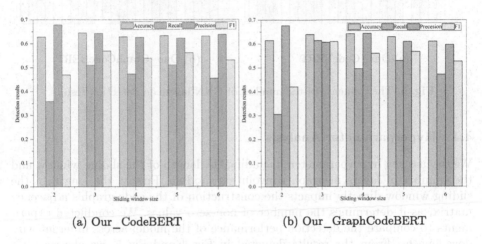

(a) Our_CodeBERT   (b) Our_GraphCodeBERT

Fig. 4. Impact of different sliding window lengths on model performance.

presence of residual connections between GNN layers, the utilization of flooding regularization, and the inclusion of the self-attention layer, on the overall detection performance. From Table 3, we observe notable variations in the model's generalization performance when these components are modified or excluded. Specifically, when data augmentation is not applied, when residual connections are removed, when flooding regularization is not utilized, or when the self-attention layer is omitted, the model's effectiveness in detecting vulnerabilities experiences a noticeable decrease. Notably, the self-attention layer has the greatest impact on the detection model's effectiveness. We believe that including the self-attention layer allows the model to prioritize essential code feature, leading to enhanced accuracy in vulnerability detection. This observation further emphasizes the importance of the self-attention mechanism in our proposed model and validates its role in bolstering the model's detection capabilities.

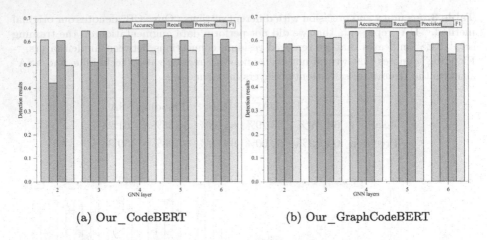

(a) Our_CodeBERT   (b) Our_GraphCodeBERT

Fig. 5. The influence of the number of GNN layers on detection results.

4.4 Hyperparameter Analysis

We discuss key hyperparameters including the length of the sliding window and the number of layers in graph convolution module. Firstly, the length of the sliding window directly impacts the construction of the code graph's adjacency matrix, as it determines the number of non-zero values. We conducted experiments to compare the detection performance of the model across different window lengths. From the results depicted in Fig. 4 and Fig. 5, we observe that the highest detection accuracy is achieved when the window length is set to 3. This optimal window length strikes a balance between capturing sufficient global information in the code sequence and avoiding excessive noise introduced by longer associations between nodes. When the window length is too small, the model fails to capture comprehensive global information. Conversely, when the window length is too long, noise features stemming from associations between distant nodes can interfere with the identification of critical features.

Additionally, we explored the impact of the model's depth by varying the number of hidden layers in the graph convolution, specifically considering values in {2, 3, 4, 5, 6} [27]. Surprisingly, our experiments revealed that the number of layers in the GNN does not significantly affect the model's performance. Based on these findings, we default to employing three layers for the GNN, with both the GCN module and the GGNN module set to three layers.

5 Conclusion

In this paper, we have proposed a novel vulnerability detection model based on graph neural networks and self-attention mechanism. Our model effectively captures local and global semantic features of source code by incorporating graph convolution modules and gated GNN layers. Additionally, the integration of a self-attention layer allows the model to identify and emphasize the relatively important vulnerability features, thereby facilitating accurate classification. To further enhance the model's generalization performance, we introduce Flooding regularization technique and data augmentation strategies based on code refactoring. These techniques have proven to be instrumental in improving the model's ability to detect vulnerabilities. Experimental results on the real-world vulnerability dataset CodeXGLUE demonstrate that our model achieves the best detection performance, with a detection accuracy higher than other prevailing methods by at least 2.37%. We believe that our approach can serve as a new general and language-agnostic benchmark for real-world source code vulnerability detection.

Acknowledgements. This work is supported by the Science and Technology Project of State Grid Corporation of China (Research on key technologies of automatic security protection for new business applications, No. 5108-202218280A-2-154-XG).

References

1. Lin, G., Wen, S., Han, Q., Zhang, J., Xiang, Y.: Software vulnerability detection using deep neural networks: a survey. Proc. IEEE **108**, 1825–1848 (2020)
2. CNNVD Homepage. https://www.cnnvd.org.cn. Accessed 10 June 2023
3. Engler, D.R., Chen, D.Y., Chou, A.: Bugs as deviant behavior: a general approach to inferring errors in systems code. In: Proceedings of the 18th ACM Symposium on Operating System Principles, pp. 57–72 (2001)
4. Russell, R.L., et al.: Automated vulnerability detection in source code using deep representation learning. In: 17th IEEE International Conference on Machine Learning and Applications, pp. 757–762. IEEE, Orlando (2018)
5. Chakraborty, S., Krishna, R., Ding, Y., Ray, B.: Deep learning based vulnerability detection: are we there yet? IEEE Trans. Software Eng. **48**(9), 3280–3296 (2022)
6. Huang, H., Guo, Y., Shi, Q., Yao, P., Wu, R., Zhang, C.: BEACON: directed grey-box fuzzing with provable path pruning. In: 43rd IEEE Symposium on Security and Privacy, pp. 36–50. IEEE, San Francisco (2022)
7. Karim, R., Tip, F., Sochurkova, A., Sen, K.: Platform-independent dynamic taint analysis for JavaScript. IEEE Trans. Softw. Eng. **46**(12), 1364–1379 (2020)
8. Shin, Y., Meneely, A., Williams, L., Osborne, J.A.: Evaluating complexity, code churn, and developer activity metrics as indicators of software vulnerabilities. IEEE Trans. Software Eng. **37**(6), 772–787 (2011)
9. Li, Z., et al.: VulDeePecker: a deep learning-based system for vulnerability detection. In: 25th Annual Network and Distributed System Security Symposium, San Diego, California, USA (2018)
10. Zou, D., Wang, S., Xu, S., Li, Z., Jin, H.: μ VulDeePecker: a deep learning-based system for multiclass vulnerability detection. IEEE Trans. Dependable Secure Comput. **18**(5), 2224–2236 (2011)
11. Wu, Y., Zou, D., Yang, W., Xu, D., Jin, H.: VulCNN: an image-inspired scalable vulnerability detection system. In: International Conference on Software Engineering, pp. 2365–2376 (2022)
12. Lin, G., et al.: Cross-project transfer representation learning for vulnerable function discovery. IEEE Trans. Industr. Inf. **14**(7), 3289–3297 (2018)

13. Nguyen, D.Q., Nguyen, T.D., Phung, D.Q.: Universal graph transformer self-attention networks. In: Companion of The Web Conference 2022, pp. 193–196. Virtual Event/Lyon, France (2022)
14. Yamaguchi, F., Golde, N., Arp, D., Rieck, K.: Modeling and discovering vulnerabilities with code property graphs. In: 2014 IEEE Symposium on Security and Privacy, pp. 590–604. IEEE, Berkeley (2014)
15. Nguyen, V., Nguyen, D.Q., Nguyen, V., Le, T., Tran, Q.H., Phung, D.: ReGVD: revisiting graph neural networks for vulnerability detection. In: 44th IEEE/ACM International Conference on Software Engineering: Companion Proceedings, pp. 178–182. ACM/IEEE, Pittsburgh (2022)
16. Ashish, V., et al.: Attention is all you need. In: Conference on Neural Information Processing Systems, pp. 5998–6008 (2017)
17. Kipf, T.N., Welling, M.: Semi-supervised classification with graph convolutional networks. In: 5th International Conference on Learning Representations, Toulon, France (2017)
18. Li, Y., Tarlow, D., Brockschmidt, M., Zemel, R.S.: Gated graph sequence neural networks. In: 4th International Conference on Learning Representations, San Juan, Puerto Rico (2016)
19. He, K., Zhang, X., Ren, S., Sun, J.: Deep residual learning for image recognition. In: 2016 IEEE Conference on Computer Vision and Pattern Recognition, pp. 770–778. IEEE, Las Vegas (2016)
20. Lu, S., Guo, D., Ren, S., et al.: CodeXGLUE: a machine learning benchmark dataset for code understanding and generation. In: Proceedings of the Neural Information Processing Systems Track on Datasets and Benchmarks 1. Virtual (2021)
21. Kaur, A., Kaur, M.: Analysis of code refactoring impact on software quality. In: MATEC Web of Conferences (2016)
22. Dong, Z.M., Hu, Q., Guo, Y.J., et al.: MixCode: enhancing code classification by mixup-based data augmentation. In: IEEE International Conference on Software Analysis, Evolution and Reengineering, pp. 379-390. IEEE, Taipa (2023)
23. Feng, Z., Guo, D., Duan, N., et al.: CodeBERT: a pre-trained model for programming and natural languages. In: Findings of the Association for Computational Linguistics: EMNLP 2020, pp. 1536–1547. ACL, Online Event (2020)
24. Guo, D., Ren, S., Lu, S., et al.: GraphCodeBERT: pre-training code representations with data flow. In: 9th International Conference on Learning Representations. Virtual Event (2021)
25. Xu, K., Hu, W., Leskovec, J., Jegelka, S.: How powerful are graph neural networks? In: 7th International Conference on Learning Representations, New Orleans, LA, USA (2019)
26. Ishida, T., Yamane, I., Sakai, T., Niu, G., Sugiyama, M.: Do we need zero training loss after achieving zero training error? In: Proceedings of the 37th International Conference on Machine Learning, pp. 4604–4614. Virtual Event (2020)
27. Zhou, Y., Liu, S., Siow, J.K., Du, X., Liu, Y.: Design: effective vulnerability identification by learning comprehensive program semantics via graph neural networks. In: Advances in Neural Information Processing Systems 32: Annual Conference on Neural Information Processing Systems 2019, Vancouver, BC, Canada, pp. 10197–10207 (2019)

Federated Long-Tailed Learning
by Retraining the Biased Classifier
with Prototypes

Yang Li and Kan Li[(✉)]

School of Computer Science and Technology, Beijing Institute of Technology,
Beijing 100081, China
likan@bit.edu.cn

Abstract. Federated learning is a privacy-preserving framework that collaboratively trains the global model without sharing raw data among clients. However, one significant issue encountered in federated learning is that biased classifiers affect the classification performance of the global model, especially when training on long-tailed data. Retraining the classifier on balanced datasets requires sharing the client's information and poses the risk of privacy leakage. We propose a method for retraining the biased classifier using prototypes, that leverage the comparison of distances between local and global prototypes to guide the local training process. We conduct experiments on CIFAR-10-LT and CIFAR-100-LT, and our approach outperforms the accuracy of baseline methods, with accuracy improvements of up to 10%.

Keywords: Federated learning · Long-tailed data · Prototype learning · Privacy protection

1 Introduction

Federated learning is a novel methodology that trains a single model among multiple clients without raw data, which tackles the challenges posed by data silos and label scarcity in various domains, including Recommended Systems [14,17] and Computer Vision [4,9]. General Data Protection Regulation (GDPR) [25] and California Consumer Privacy Act (CCPA) [24] impose stringent restrictions on the use and transmission of data. Currently, the numerous open-source federated learning frameworks are growing rapidly, including FATE [13], PySyft [18], TFF [1], FedML [6], and more. In a centralized federated learning framework [15], each client copies the parameters of the global model and trains the model on local data. Then, the client transmits its trained model parameters to the server, which aggregates these local models to update the global model. This iterative process continues until the model convergence. The goal is that the performance of the global model in federated learning approximates the performance of the model trained on centralized data.

Various approaches [2,28] explore the problems of long-tailed data distribution, including instance-level re-weighting and class re-weighting, resampling,

H. Yang and R. Lu (Eds.): FCS 2023, CCIS 1992, pp. 575–585, 2024.
https://doi.org/10.1007/978-981-99-9331-4_38

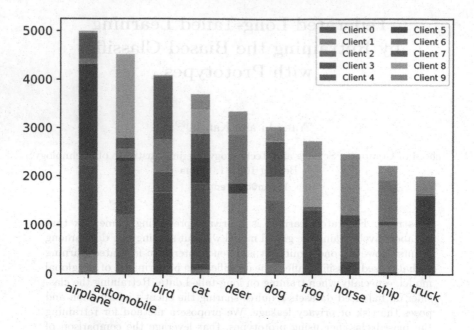

Fig. 1. The illustration of CIFAR-10-LT in 10 clients

and cost-sensitive learning. However, some of these methods can't be directly applied in federated learning due to the inherent agnostic and different data distribution across clients. To mitigate these challenges, Zhang et al. [29] allocate different weights to each class according to training samples, shaping an efficient decision boundary to classify images. However, setting weights based on the instances becomes impractical and infeasible when the number of classes is large (as shown in Figure 1).

The performance degradation in federated learning can be attributed to two key factors: biased classifiers and inconsistent gradient updates from different clients. Additionally, the low performance of tailed classes and the lack of robustness in the softmax function. The solutions to improve the accuracy of the model include re-training the classifier and designing a new loss function. Yang et al. [8] decouple the model into multiple components, emphasizing the significant impact of biased classifiers on the classification performance of long-tailed recognition and exploring various re-balancing strategies. CReFF [20] compares the impact of different layers on accuracy in ResNet-8, dividing the model into four blocks and one classifier, and retraining the biased classifiers using the federated feature. Furthermore, Yang et al. [27] propose the robustness of convolution neural networks (CNNs) affected by softmax function and design a prototype loss (PL) to improve the intra-class compactness of the feature representation. Recent studies [16,26] use prototypes to augment feature extractors. The prototypical network [22] learns a metric space that reflects potential features, in which classification can be performed by computing distances to prototype representations of each class. Fedproto [23] keeps the generated local prototypes close enough to the corresponding global prototype to normalize the training of local models.

In this paper, we use prototypes to retrain the biased classifier, using global prototypes to guide local training and mitigate the detrimental impact of bias. Our contributions are listed as follows:

- We focus on the long-tailed problem of federated learning, and train an efficient global model when averaging gradients doesn't reflect local characteristics.
- We decouple the model into the feature extractor and the classifier, and utilize a prototypes-based federated learning method to retrain the biased classifier on long-tailed data.
- We conduct some experiments on CIFAR-10-LT and CIFAR-100-LT using LeNet-5 and ResNet-8, and analyze the impacts of multiple factors on accuracy.

The rest of this paper is as follows. We describe the related works on federated long-tailed learning in Sect. 2. Section 3 conducts the formulation of the problem and describes our proposed method in detail. Section 4 provides the experimental results, followed by the conclusion in Sect. 5.

2 Related Work

Federated learning is a popular distributed framework that protects user privacy while aiming to train efficient models. However, the performance is influenced by the data distribution and model structure. The distribution of input characteristics from different clients is heterogeneous, averaging local models trained on different data neglects the distinction of each local model and leads to performance degradation. For instance, ref [3] uses synthetic data for pre-training to decrease the gap between local models and global models in federated learning. FedProx [12] adds the regularization term to measure the distance between the global and the local model and helps model convergence. MOON [11] utilizes the similarity between model representations to correct local training on non-independent and identically distributed (Non-IID) data.

The long-tailed distribution highlights the importance of the class attributes, but it increases the uncertainty of the model when training. Chu et al. [5] augment feature and sample space to the problem of bias towards majority classes. In federated learning, long-tailed data includes imbalance-like distributions at the local and global levels, as well as unbalanced sample sizes. Training on long-tailed data from different clients decreases benefits in federated learning, such as increasing communication costs and degrading performance, which needs to trade off privacy and performance. From a novel data perspective, the model can be optimized by re-weighting and re-sampling to increase the ratio of tailed classes [4]. In addition, refs [19,20] focus on decoupling feature extractor and classifier, retraining the biased classifier to improve performance.

3   Methodology

3.1   Formulation

Suppose there are K clients in the federated learning framework. The overall distribution represents $D = \cup_i D_i(x, y)$ and the sample size is n. The local distribution of i-th client is $D_i(x, y)$, x represents feature space, and y denotes corresponding label space, the sample size is n_k. The model is $\theta = \{X_j^p; Y_j^p\} = [f_{j,1}, \cdots, f_{j,s}]$, $f_{j,i}$ denotes model layer and X_j^p represents feature extractor, and classifier Y_j^p is a mapping from feature space to label space. The optimization objective is formulated as:

$$arg \min_w f(w) = \sum q_k F_k(\theta; D_k)$$

$$F_k(w^k) = \frac{1}{n_k} f_i(w^k; D_k; \theta)$$

where $F_k(\cdot)$ is local objective function of k-th client, $q_k = \frac{|n_k|}{|n|}$, $f_i(w^k) = l(x_i, y_i; w^k)$ represents loss function on samples n_k made with weight parameters of local model w^k.

Prototype is a mean value of each class with a representative feature vector. Local prototype is $p_k = [p_k^1, \cdots, p_k^m]$, m represents the number of class prototypes.

$$p_k^j = \frac{1}{|D_i^j|} \sum f_i(f_i; D_i) \tag{1}$$

where f_i is embedding function and $|D_i^j|$ represents the number of samples of i-th client of j-th class. Global prototype of j-th is

$$P^j = \frac{1}{K} \sum_k p_k^j \tag{2}$$

3.2   Our Method

In our proposed approach, we decouple the model to the feature extractor and the classifier, augmenting the feature space, mining underlying knowledge from different prototypes locally and capturing different representations to improve the robustness of tailed classes. Our approach consists of three main components: local training, prototypes generation, and re-training the classifier (see Fig. 2).

Local Training. The model is trained on local long-tailed data. We compute cross-entropy loss function between the hard labels and the soft targets.

$$L_{CE} = -\sum_{i=1}^{N} \sum_{m=1}^{M} I(y_i) log(p_i^m(x_i)) \tag{3}$$

where I is an indicator function, $p_i^m(x_i)$ is the prediction of the model.

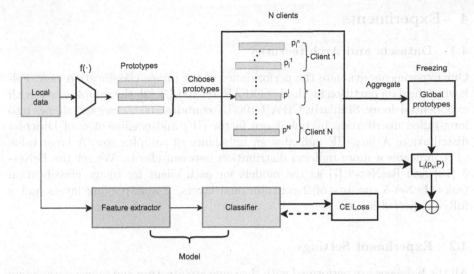

Fig. 2. The framework of our method. Client send local model and class prototypes selected to the server, server aggregates prototypes and freeze global prototypes.

$$w_t^k \leftarrow w_{t-1}^k - \eta \nabla L(w, D_k) \tag{4}$$

Prototypes Generation. Prototypes include potential representation and augment representation ability across clients. In round t, client trains local model and generates class prototypes p_k on local data by Eq. 1. We randomly aggregate local prototypes p_k as global prototype P, and set to freeze global prototypes, which freeze operation means one aggregation between local prototypes from clients.

$$P = freeze(\sum_k p_k) \tag{5}$$

Retraining Classifier. We measure the distance between local prototypes and global prototypes and use it to guide local training. We use global prototypes to retrain the classifier and describe it as follows:

$$L(p_k, P) = \|p_k - P\|_2 \tag{6}$$

The objective function is as follows:

$$L = L_{CE} + \lambda \sum_i L_i(p_k, P) \tag{7}$$

where λ is a balance factor.

4   Experiments

4.1   Datasets and Architectures

Our experiments evaluate the performance of the image classification task. Following the data partition method of CIFAR-10/100-LT [2], the sample size is with exponential decay. Similarly, CIFAR-100-LT contains 100 classes and shapes into long-tailed distribution by imbalance factor (IF) and coefficient α of Dirichlet distribution. A large IF indicates an imbalance of samples size. A large value of α indicates a more uniform distribution between clients. We set the LeNet-5 [10] and ResNet-8 [7] as the models for each client for image classification tasks. LeNet-5 consists of 2 convolutional layers, 2 max-pooling layers and a fully-connected layer.

4.2   Experiment Settings

All the baselines are performed with the same architecture and hyper-parameters as ours. For CIFAT-10-LT and CIFAT-100-LT, we set $IF = \{10, 50\}$ and $\alpha = 0.5$. We set 10 clients and 80% of clients participate in each round. We implement our experiments by PyTorch with NVIDIA GeForce RTX 2080 GPUs. We set local epoch E = 5, batch size B = 64 and the learning rate is 0.01. For the long-tailed problem, we compare four centralized FL algorithms which include FedAvg [15], FedProx [12], Fedproto [23] and BalanceFL [21].

- FedProx uses a proximal term incorporated into the objective function to reduce the adverse influences of data heterogeneity on the convergence stability.
- FedAvg is that the server aggregates and averages the gradient and then sends these updated gradients back to the clients.
- Fedproto aggregates local prototypes collected from different clients and then sends global prototypes back to all clients to normalize the training of local models.
- BalanceFL robustly learns both common and rare classes and addresses both the global and local data imbalance at the same time.
- Our method is based on prototypes and offers a guide to local training. Freezing global prototypes and measuring the distance between global prototypes and local prototypes to retrain local classifiers.

4.3   Main Results

We evaluate the performance of various methods on the CIFAR-10-LT and CIFAR-100-LT using different CNNs under same conditions, aiming to provide a fair comparison. The results are in Tables 1 and 2.

Table 1. The accuracy of multiple methods using ResNet-8.

Methods	CIFAR-10-LT		CIFAR-100-LT	
	IF = 10	IF = 50	IF = 10	IF = 50
FedAvg [15]	67.23	61.18	34.18	29.05
FedProx [12]	60.44	55.07	32.45	27.77
FedProto [23]	41.16	46.87	13.91	13.72
BalanceFL [21]	58.34	45.89	31.22	28.47
Our method	**77.11**	**67.70**	**35.64**	**30.37**

Table 1 describes the results obtained from our experiments on the CIFAR-10-LT and CIFAR-100-LT using ResNet-8, we observe that the degree of imbalance has an impact on the accuracy of the models when the IF = {10, 50}. The performance degradation becomes more pronounced as the degree of imbalance increases. However, it's interesting to note that in the case of the FedProto approach, when comparing different IFs, the accuracy of the model trained with IF = 50 is higher than that of IF = 10. Furthermore, we observed that the number of label classes also influences the accuracy of CIFAR-10-LT and CIFAR-100-LT when IF and α are the same.

Table 2. The accuracy of multiple methods using LeNet-5.

Methods	CIFAR-10-LT		CIFAR-100-LT	
	IF = 10	IF = 50	IF = 10	IF = 50
FedAvg [15]	63.93	52.37	33.36	26.06
FedProx [12]	51.02	41.46	24.39	18.43
FedProto [23]	57.73	61.07	17.63	18.52
BalanceFL [21]	50.87	39.75	23.49	18.10
Our method	**67.89**	**64.07**	**34.22**	**26.75**

Table 2 presents the results on CIFAR-10-LT and CIFAR-100-LT using the LeNet-5, we found the performance is influenced by the model complexity, LeNet-5, being a relatively simpler model compared to ResNet-8, possesses limited representation capabilities, which can result in lower accuracy. Meanwhile, the accuracy is also affected by class imbalance and data heterogeneity. From the Tables 1 and 2, we found that our method outperforms the existing algorithms in all settings.

4.4 Analysis

The objective of federated learning is to train a high-quality global model for image classification tasks, particularly when dealing with long-tailed problems.

However, simply averaging the model parameters from different clients with the same initial can't achieve optimal performance, and averaging gradients can't reflect local characteristics on long-tailed data, resulting in biased classifiers. We compare the impact of different parameters and try to identify the underlying reasons for the long-tailed problem.

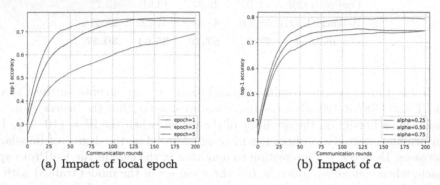

(a) Impact of local epoch   (b) Impact of α

Fig. 3. The accuracy of our method using ResNet-8 on CIFAR-10-LT with different parameters.

Impact of Epoch. We compare the impact of local training epochs on the performance of the model (see Fig. 3(a)), the result indicates that higher accuracy is achieved when the number of local epochs is relatively small. One possible explanation for this phenomenon is that the long-tailed distribution is unknown the absence of guaranteed distribution similarity between clients. When the number of local epochs is large, the local model becomes more inclined to fit the local data, potentially resulting in a drift during the model aggregation process. We found a novel case in which there is an overlap in accuracy between epochs 3 and 5. We think that this overlap is influenced by the underlying distributions of the data.

Impact of α. In our comparison of different values of the coefficient α in Fig. 3(b), which controls the uniformity degree of the classes. The result demonstrates the more uniform the distribution, the accuracy of the model is generally higher and the convergence is faster. The similarity of class prototypes tends to be higher when the distribution between clients is more uniform and the number of classes is similar. This indicates that the model has learned to capture and represent the common characteristics of different classes more effectively. Our proposed scheme performs well on CIFAR-10-LT, maintaining stable convergence and robustness. We also found that uniformity had a large impact with fluctuations of up to 10% observed.

Security. Federated learning enables clients to collaboratively train models and protect user privacy without transmitting data between clients. Model complexity affects the ability of the feature extractor which depends on data quantity, distribution difference, and model structure. In our scheme, the use of class prototypes instead of transmitting features, gradients, or other information, which greatly reduces the transmission of redundant information and reduces the risk of information leakage.

5 Conclusion

In this paper, we propose a federated learning method on long-tailed data, decoupling the model into a feature extractor and a classifier, which re-trains the biased classifier using both global prototypes and local prototypes. To address the issue of model drift, we highlight the impact of classifier and the features of inner classes. We freeze the global prototypes as general knowledge and allow the local models to learn from them. In the experiments, we compare the performance of our method and other methods and analyze the impacts of epoch and uniform coefficient α to understand the method and principle. In the future, we will consider the generalization ability of class prototypes in federated learning frameworks on other datasets or real-world scenarios.

Acknowledgments. This work is supported by Beijing Natural Science Foundation (No. 4222037, L181010) and the BIT Research and Innovation Promoting Project (Grant No. 2023YCXY036).

References

1. Bonawitz, K.A., et al.: Towards federated learning at scale: system design. CoRR abs/1902.01046 (2019)
2. Cao, K., Wei, C., Gaidon, A., Arechiga, N., Ma, T.: Learning imbalanced datasets with label-distribution-aware margin loss. In: Advances in Neural Information Processing Systems, vol. 32 (2019)
3. Chen, H.Y., Tu, C.H., Li, Z., Shen, H.W., Chao, W.L.: On the importance and applicability of pre-training for federated learning. Arxiv. 2206.11488 (2022)
4. Chen, Z., Liu, S., Wang, H., Yang, H.H., Quek, T.Q., Liu, Z.: Towards federated long-tailed learning. ArXiv:2206.14988 (2022)
5. Chu, P., Bian, X., Liu, S., Ling, H.: Feature space augmentation for long-tailed data. CoRR abs/2008.03673 (2020)
6. He, C., et al.: FedML: a research library and benchmark for federated machine learning. CoRR abs/2007.13518 (2020)
7. He, K., Zhang, X., Ren, S., Sun, J.: Deep residual learning for image recognition. In: 2016 IEEE Conference on Computer Vision and Pattern Recognition (CVPR), pp. 770–778 (2016)
8. Kang, B., et al.: Decoupling representation and classifier for long-tailed recognition. ArXiv:1910.09217 (2019)
9. Karimireddy, S.P., Kale, S., Mohri, M., Reddi, S., Stich, S., Suresh, A.T.: SCAFFOLD: stochastic controlled averaging for federated learning. In: International Conference on Machine Learning, pp. 5132–5143. PMLR (2020)
10. Lecun, Y., Bottou, L., Bengio, Y., Haffner, P.: Gradient-based learning applied to document recognition. Proc. IEEE **86**(11), 2278–2324 (1998)

11. Li, Q., He, B., Song, D.: Model-contrastive federated learning. In: 2021 IEEE/CVF Conference on Computer Vision and Pattern Recognition (CVPR), pp. 10708–10717 (2021)

12. Li, T., Sahu, A.K., Zaheer, M., Sanjabi, M., Talwalkar, A., Smith, V.: Federated optimization in heterogeneous networks. In: Dhillon, I., Papailiopoulos, D., Sze, V. (eds.) Proceedings of Machine Learning and Systems, vol. 2, pp. 429–450 (2020)

13. Liu, Y., Fan, T., Chen, T., Xu, Q., Yang, Q.: FATE: an industrial grade platform for collaborative learning with data protection. J. Mach. Learn. Res. **22**(1), 0320–10325 (2021)

14. Luo, S., Xiao, Y., Song, L.: Personalized federated recommendation via joint representation learning, user clustering, and model adaptation. In: Proceedings of the 31st ACM International Conference on Information & Knowledge Management, CIKM 2022, New York, NY, USA, pp. 4289–4293 (2022)

15. McMahan, B., Moore, E., Ramage, D., Hampson, S., y Arcas, B.A.: Communication-efficient learning of deep networks from decentralized data. In: Artificial Intelligence and Statistics, pp. 1273–1282. PMLR (2017)

16. Mu, X., Shen, Y., Cheng, K., Geng, X., Fu, J., Zhang, T., Zhang, Z.: FedProc: prototypical contrastive federated learning on non-IID data. CoRR abs/2109.12273 (2021)

17. Qiang, Y.: Federated recommendation systems. In: 2019 IEEE International Conference on Big Data (Big Data), p. 1 (2019)

18. Ryffel, T., et al.: A generic framework for privacy preserving deep learning. CoRR abs/1811.04017 (2018)

19. Shang, X., Lu, Y., Cheung, Y.M., Wang, H.: FEDIC: federated learning on non-IID and long-tailed data via calibrated distillation. In: 2022 IEEE International Conference on Multimedia and Expo (ICME), pp. 1–6 (2022)

20. Shang, X., Lu, Y., Huang, G., Wang, H.: Federated learning on heterogeneous and long-tailed data via classifier re-training with federated features. In: Proceedings of the Thirty-First International Joint Conference on Artificial Intelligence, IJCAI-22, pp. 2218–2224 (2022)

21. Shuai, X., Shen, Y., Jiang, S., Zhao, Z., Yan, Z., Xing, G.: BalanceFL: addressing class imbalance in long-tail federated learning. In: 2022 21st ACM/IEEE International Conference on Information Processing in Sensor Networks (IPSN), pp. 271–284 (2022)

22. Snell, J., Swersky, K., Zemel, R.: Prototypical networks for few-shot learning. In: Proceedings of the 31st International Conference on Neural Information Processing Systems, NIPS 2017, pp. 4080–4090. Curran Associates Inc., Red Hook (2017)

23. Tan, Y., et al.: FedProto: federated prototype learning across heterogeneous clients. arXiv e-prints arXiv:2105.00243 (2021)

24. de la Torre, L.: A guide to the California consumer privacy act of 2018. Available at SSRN 3275571 (2018)

25. Voigt, P., Von dem Bussche, A.: The EU general data protection regulation (GDPR). A Practical Guide, 1st edn., vol. 10, no. 3152676, pp. 10–5555. Springer, Cham (2017). https://doi.org/10.1007/978-3-319-57959-7

26. Xu, X., Wang, Z., Fu, Z., Guo, W., Chi, Z., Li, D.: Flexible few-shot class-incremental learning with prototype container. Neural Comput. Appl. **35**(15), 10875–10889 (2023)

27. Yang, H.M., Zhang, X.Y., Yin, F., Liu, C.L.: Robust classification with convolutional prototype learning. In: 2018 IEEE/CVF Conference on Computer Vision and Pattern Recognition, pp. 3474–3482 (2018)
28. Yang, W., Chen, D., Zhou, H., Meng, F., Zhou, J., Sun, X.: Integrating local real data with global gradient prototypes for classifier re-balancing in federated long-tailed learning. ArXiv. 2301.10394 (2023)
29. Zhang, Y., Kang, B., Hooi, B., Yan, S., Feng, J.: Deep long-tailed learning: a survey. IEEE Trans. Pattern Anal. Mach. Intell. 1–20 (2023)

Internet of Things and System Security

Ensuring SLA Compliance of Edge Enabled Cloud Service for IoT Application: A Dynamic QoS-Aware Scheme

Xiang Li[1], Peng Xiao[2], Qixu Wang[3(✉)], Xingguo Li[1], and Yi Zhu[3]

[1] Informatization Construction and Management Office, Sichuan University, Chengdu 610065, China
{xiangli_icmo,lxg}@scu.edu.cn
[2] Information Center, China Southern Power Grid Yunnan Power Grid Co., Ltd., Kunming, China
xiaopeng03@yn.csg.cn
[3] School of Cyber Science and Engineering, Sichuan University, Chengdu 610065, China
{qixuwang,zhuyi20}@scu.edu.cn

Abstract. The synergy and convergence of edge, cloud and Internet of Things (ECoT) has increasingly become a promising service paradigm. It provides a wide variety of benefits for IoT applications deployed at the edge of the network to serve end users. However, the open connectivity, complex heterogeneity, and flexible mobility of the ECoT environment bring the challenging issues of service level agreement (SLA) compliance to various IoT applications. To this end, a dynamic QoS-aware based SLA compliance verification model is proposed. Considering the dynamic uncertainty of QoS attributes of edge service in ECoT context, the model presents a QoS consistency detection method to enhance its fault tolerance for QoS violation. Moreover, the model adopts an objective weight assignment method for dynamic QoS to improve the accuracy of SLA compliance verification. Finally, the simulation experiments conducted using a real-world dataset show that our scheme can effectively ensure SLA compliance of edge enabled cloud service for IoT applications.

Keywords: Edge cloud computing · SLA compliance model · QoS violation detection · IoT application

1 Introduction

Cloud computing (CC) is a novel utilization of computing resources, which provides individuals and organizations a promising service paradigm with dynamic scalability, ubiquitous network access, on-demand self-service resource sharing and measurability [4,27]. Unfortunately, CC has inherent shortcomings in supporting Internet of Things (IoT) oriented application scenarios with location

H. Yang and R. Lu (Eds.): FCS 2023, CCIS 1992, pp. 589–601, 2024.
https://doi.org/10.1007/978-981-99-9331-4_39

awareness, low latency, geographically distributed and mobility [19], which usually need to be deployed close to network edge for end users [2,9,31]. Moreover, since the lack of sufficient computing, network and storage resources dedicated to the processing and transmit of huge volumes of data generated by various IoT devices [11], it resorts to employ cloud service to address the issues of resource constraints [23]. Obviously, bridging the gap between cloud and IoT has become an inevitable challenge [20,21]. The emergence of edge computing (EC) paradigm not only makes up for the deficiency of CC and greatly expands its service boundary [28], but also enables IoT devices access cloud service ubiquitously [1,3,5]. The synergy pattern of integrating CC, EC and IoT can be well adopted to different application scenarios and provide a wide variety of services for users with different demands, as shown in Fig. 1. The innovative paradigm provide various benefits to our daily lives in many ways, ranging from individual applications (e.g., smart wearables and smart home) to enterprise business (e.g., smart factory and smart city) [33,34]. Therefore, the edge enabled cloud of things (ECoT) architecture has been a promising and emergent service paradigm [18]. In addition, it has became a leading trend in IT service marketplace and attracted more and more traditional cloud service providers to develop edge services based on cloud resources in specific IoT scenarios and provide them to different users.

As with many new technologies, there are several challenging issues when it comes to achieving success in ECoT context [37]. The biggest concern is quality of service (QoS) consistency and SLA compliance of edge service [17]. The amalgamated paradigm of ECoT not only enriches the system functions, but also extremely increases the complexity of software and hardware. The dynamic and complex ECoT architecture will inevitably impact on the QoS of edge platform/service, and in turn affect the stability of applications (e.g., traffic and security monitoring in smart city, product quality inspection in smart factory and virtual/augmented reality in smart home) deployed on it. Hence, the challenging issue for edge application developers (EADs) is how to ensure that the QoS of edge services can continuously satisfy the performance requirements of their IoT-oriented applications so as to provide high quality experience for end users. Fortunately, the traditional QoS based service level agreement (SLA) violation detection for the cloud service provides a feasible solution, which can be well improved and employed into the ECoT context to address the issue. In cloud context, SLA is considered to be a legally and valid agreement or contract on the QoS of cloud service between a cloud customer and a cloud provider. It stipulates that when the customer is using the cloud service, the QoS should satisfy the service level objective (SLO) promised by the provider [8]. Thus, the SLA provides a strong guarantee for customers to adopt cloud service with confidence.

However, in ECoT context, it is very difficult for EADs to rely solely on edge service providers (ESPs) to consciously realize the promised SLO agreed in SLA for edge service. On the one hand, the agreed SLOs regrading the QoS attributes of edge service in the SLA are deterministic and constant, which are usually not frequently modified. Nevertheless, in the actual edge context for IoT oriented application, the changes of computing resources and system

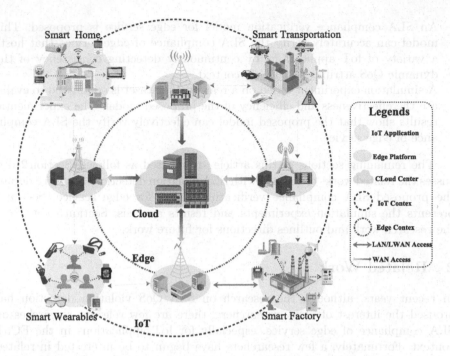

Fig. 1. The edge enabled cloud service paradigm for IoT applications

functions of edge platform (e.g., function optimization of components, system update, capacity expansion and reduction) will definitely lead to the QoS of edge service continuous fluctuation. It makes the traditional SLA violation detection methods based on the constant SLO no longer adopted well to the edge service. For instance, the smart wearables shown in Fig. 1, EAD and ESP agreed that the SLO of *latency* on the edge service (i.e., a QoS attribute of network) of VR system is 100 ms. In a certain period of time, the *latency* fluctuates around 100 ms due to network jitter caused by increased connection or congestion. In this case, sometimes the *latency* may exceed its SLO, but it should not be considered violations, while the traditional detection methods have a certain probability of identifying it as violations.

On the other hand, an ESP may be driven by benefit to oversell the virtual computing resources of edge and cloud in order to obtain more profits. It also has an impact on the QoS of IoT applications deployed on edge platform. Moreover, the failure of guaranteeing a service leads to negative consequences such as penalty payments, loss of revenue, customer churn and service interruptions [35]. It would further reduce the reputation and competitiveness of the ESP, which in turn may cause irreversible losses to both parties [16].

To address the aforementioned challenges, we propose a promising solution that can ensures SLA compliance of edge enabled cloud service for IoT application in dynamic QoS scenario. The major contributions of our work are summarized as follows.

- An SLA compliance verification model for edge service is proposed. This model can accurately verify the SLA compliance of edge service that hosts a variety of IoT applications by continuously detecting consistency of the dynamic QoS attributes in ECoT context.
- A simulation experiment based on a real-world dataset is conducted to evaluate the effectiveness and efficiency of the proposed model. The experimental results show that the proposed model can effectively verify the SLA compliance of edge service.

The remaining sections of this article are devised as follows. Section 2 discusses the related works concerned with SLA violation detection. Section 3 details the proposed SLA compliance verification model for edge service. Section 4 presents the simulation experiments and results analysis. Section 5 concludes the research work and outlines directions for future work.

2 Related Work

In recent years, although the research on SLA/QoS violation detection has aroused the interest of many researchers, there are few relevant researches on SLA compliance of edge service, especially for IoT applications in the ECoT context. Fortunately, a few researchers have begun to be interested in related fields and try to make efforts. Nawaz et al. [18] proposed an approach to detect in real-time external events of interest related to the SLOs of the formed SLA by monitoring tweets, and using this information to proactively ascertain the chances of SLA violation and evaluate its impact on cloud of IoT (CoT) applications. In [22], a scalable anomaly-aware approach was proposed to address the challenge that the dynamicity of distributed service environments and communication networks in CoT environments causes anomalies in calculating QoS values.

However, most researchers tend to focus on studying SLA/QoS violation detection in cloud environment from the perspective of QoS monitoring of cloud service [12]. They have carried out numerous researches on the existing issues in this field and gained some achievements, which have contributed a promising solution for ensuring SLA compliance of edge service in ECoT context. Emeakaroha et al. [6] presented an infrastructure architecture of SLA violation detection, named as DeSVi, which senses SLA violations through resource monitoring. The DeSVi allocates computing resources for a service requested by user and deploys it on a virtualized environment. Resources are monitored by mapping low-level resource metrics to user-defined SLA. The detection of SLA compliance relies on the predefined SLOs to manage and prevent possible violations. In [32], a hierarchical architecture for monitoring and evaluating of the compliance of SLA was proposed. In this architecture, a data collection service is deployed in the intranet of each cloud provider. Metrics data is first collected and analyzed by local data collection service. When SLA violations are detected, related data is packed, signed and sent to the evaluation center located on the internet. Schubert et al. [24] presented a solution to ensure trustworthy measurement and arbitration of metrics to detect SLA violations in the cloud. It allows monitoring detailed application-level details instead of only generic system-level metrics. A hybrid approach combining measurement software with aspect-oriented programming and a trusted third party component were proposed to handle high-volume data and automatically transforms SLA requirements. Floricu et al. [7] implemented a solution for monitoring SLA violations of web service in cloud context. It facilitated cloud users to verify the functionalities of service in comparison with metrics defined in the SLA contract signed with CP. The solution examines the extent to which the SLA is complied with through a series of specific reports and graphs. In [26], a new metric in SLA representing the maximum completion time of all jobs submitted to the cloud was introduced, named as makespan. In addition, a framework of SLA violations detection was proposed to mathematically calculates the makespan at the time of SLA definition. The time period, for which SLA is violated, can be estimated from the comparison of simulation results. Upadhyay et al. [30] presented a fuzzy logic-based mechanism for predicting submitted tasks which are likely to encounter SLA violations. It may assist CPs to design corrective interventions in terms of additional resource allocation to prevent SLA violations and improve the QoS experience of CUs. Additionally, some researchers are working to study SLA compliance issues in cloud, IoT, and edge environments from the perspectives of security and trust assessment [10,13–15,25,29]. In summary, the most of the above researches adopt the constant threshold based comparison method to detect SLA/QoS violations for cloud service. However, the traditional SLA violation detection methods can not be adopted to the more complex ECoT environment.

3 The Proposed SLA Compliance Verification Model

3.1 Problem Formulation

We consider a scenario that there is an edge service deployed on an edge platform supported by a cloud to provide application accessing close to edge network for multiple IoT devices. Let $T = \{t_i \mid 1 \leq i\}$ represent the set of time periods for the SLA compliance verification of edge service, where t_i represents that an SLA compliance verification is performed at the i-th moment. The collected monitoring data of QoS attributes will be used for the next SLA compliance verification of edge service at the t_{i+1} moment. Let $A = \{a_j \mid 1 \leq j \leq J\}$ represent the set of QoS attributes of the edge service hosting the IoT application. Let $S(A) = \{s(a_j) \mid a_j \in A\}$ denote the set of SLOs specified in the SLA for the QoS attributes of edge service. Let B and C denote the set of benefit QoS attribute (i.e., the larger value of the QoS attribute, the higher its performance or capability) and cost QoS attributes (i.e., the larger value of the QoS attribute, the lower its performance or capability) respectively. Then, A can also be represented as $A = \{B, C\}$. Let $D = \{d_k \mid 1 \leq k \leq K\}$ denotes the set of IoT devices accessing the application hosted by the edge service. Let $M_k^i(a_j) = \{m_k^i(a_j)_z \mid z \leq 1\}$ denote the set of monitoring values for the QoS attribute a_j of edge service collected by monitoring the kth device, where $m_k^i(a_j)_z$ denotes the monitoring value of a_j collected by monitoring the transaction data of the kth IoT device for the z time during the time between t_{i-1} and t_i.

In the practical ECoT context, the QoS attributes A of edge service would continuously fluctuate during its operation. It makes the monitoring values of these QoS attributes A dynamic and uncertain, but their SLOs $S(A)$ specified in the SLA are deterministic and constant. Based on this premise, we assume that each QoS attribute $a_j(a_j \in A)$ of the edge service will fluctuate within a certain range around its SLO $s(a_j)$ during its operation. Moreover, the acceptable fluctuation degree of a QoS attribute is determined by the tolerance of an EAD, which is defined as *fluctuation factor* in SLA. Consequently, the EAD should clearly claim the *fluctuation factor* for each QoS attribute of edge service. Once the monitoring value of a QoS attribute exceeds its fluctuation range, it is considered as one violation.

Algorithm 1. Fluctuation Interval Construction

Require: The SLOs set $S(A)$, monitoring values set $M(A)$ and fluctuation factor set *beta* of QoS attributes A

  1: **procedure** FLUCTUATION INTERVAL CONSTRUCTION
  2:    Create arrays $B, C, F(B), F(C) \leftarrow \emptyset$;
  3:    Create variables $i, j, k, n \leftarrow 0$;
  4:    $n \leftarrow$ Get the number of A;
  5:    $B, C \leftarrow$ Divide A into two categories according to benefit-type and cost-type;
  6:    $S(B), S(C) \leftarrow$ Divide $S(A)$ into two categories according to B and C;
  7:    **for** $i = 1$ to n **do**
  8:        $F(B_j) \leftarrow$ Calculate fluctuation interval of B_j according to $beta_i$ and $S(B_j)$;
  9:        j add 1;
 10:        $F(C_k) \leftarrow$ Calculate fluctuation interval of C_k according to $beta_i$ and $S(C_k)$;
 11:        k add 1;
 12:    **end for**
 13: **end procedure**

3.2   Fluctuation Interval Construction

Let $\beta^i(a_j)$ denote the *fluctuation factor* of the j-th QoS attribute at the t_i moment, and $\beta^i(a_j) \in [0, 1]$. According to the $\beta^i(a_j)$ and the specific type of a_j (i.e., $a_j \in B$ or $a_j \in C$), the fluctuation interval of a_j can be constructed. Let $F^i(a_j) = \left[f^i(a_j)^L, f^i(a_j)^U \right]$ denote the fluctuation interval of a_j. Algorithm 1 illustrates the process of fluctuation interval construction.

3.3   QoS Consistency Calculation

The consistency of the QoS attribute a_j with its SLO $s(a_j)$ can be determined by detecting whether its monitoring value came from the k devices is within its fluctuation interval $f^i(a_j)$ at the t_i moment. Algorithm 2 illustrates the QoS consistency calculation.

As described in Algorithm 2, the average monitoring value of each IoT device d_k about the QoS attribute a_j in the time period between t_{i-1} and t_i is calculated firstly. Then, the consistency of a_j can be detected according to its $F^i(a_j)$ and $\bar{M}_k^i(a_j)$, which is denoted as $r_k^i(a_j)$. It can be obtained in accordance with the type of a_j.

Algorithm 2. QoS Consistency Calculation

1: **procedure** QoS CONSISTENCY CALCULATION$(n, M(A), F(B), F(C))$
2:     Create arrays $R(B), R(C), E(A) \leftarrow \emptyset$;
3:     Create variables $i, j, k \leftarrow 0$;
4:     **for** $i = 1$ to n **do**
5:         $E(A_i) \leftarrow$ Calculate average value of $M(A_i)$;
6:     **end for**
7:     **for** $i = 1$ to n **do**
8:         $R(B_j) \leftarrow$ Calculate consistency value of B_j according to $E(A_i)$ and $F(B_j)$;
9:         $R(C_k) \leftarrow$ Calculate consistency value of C_k according to $E(A_i)$ and $F(C_k)$;
10:    **end for**
11:    **return** $R(B), R(C)$;
12: **end procedure**

3.4 Dynamic Weight Assignment

In order to objectively determine weights for different QoS attributes of the edge service during the time between t_{i-1} and t_i, we adopt a weight assignment method based on entropy [14]. The weight of a QoS attribute at t_i moment can be obtained according to its consistency, which is denoted as $\omega^i(a_j)$.

3.5 SLA Compliance Verification

As aforementioned, the SLA compliance verification is an ongoing process, a *time factor* is introduced in the model to realize the strong coupling relationship between the compliance verification results at adjacent moments. Algorithm 3 illustrates the process of SLA compliance verification for the edge service.

As described in Algorithm 3, the SLA compliance value of edge service can be calculated on the basis of the consistency values of its QoS attributes and weights. The g^i and g^{i-1} denote the SLA compliance value of the edge service at the t_i and t_{i-1} moment respectively. They are within range $[0, 1]$ $0 \leq g^i \leq 1$. The closer g^i is to 1, the more compliant the SLA of edge service is, and vice verse.

Algorithm 3. SLA Compliance Verification

Require: The consistency set $R(A)$ and $\Omega(A)$ of QoS attributes A, time factor α,
   compliance threshold λ, SLA compliance value $g(t-1)$ at $t-1$ moment
 1: **procedure** COMPLIANCE VALUE CALCULATION$(A, R(A), \Omega(A), g(t-1), \alpha)$
 2:     Create array $R(A) \leftarrow \emptyset$;
 3:     Create variable $g(t), n, m \leftarrow 0$;
 4:     $n \leftarrow$ Get the number of A;
 5:     **for** $i = 1$ to n **do**
 6:         $sum \leftarrow$ Calculate the cumulative sum of $R(A_i)$;
 7:         $s\bar{u}m \leftarrow$ Calculate average value by sum/m;
 8:         $g(t) \leftarrow$ Calculate cumulative sum $R(A_i) \times \Omega_t(A_i)$;
 9:     **end for**
10:     $g(t) \leftarrow$ Obtain SLA compliance value by $g(t-1)$ and α;
11:     $G(T) \leftarrow$ Add $g(t)$ to the set of SLA compliance;
12:     **return** $G(T)$;
13: **end procedure**

---

4   Simulation Experiment and Results Analysis

In this section, simulation experiments based on a real-world web service dataset
are conducted to demonstrate the effectiveness and efficiency of the proposed
model.

Table 1. Parameters setting in SLA compliance verification experiment

QoS attribute	Dataset	Verification Period T	Monitoring Frequency	Initial Fluctuation Factor β_0	Time factor α	Threshold λ	SLO
Response Time	RT	64	117	0.35	0.7	0.85	3 s
Throughput	TP	64	117	0.25	0.7	0.85	0.5 kbps

4.1   Experimental Setup

The simulation experiments are conducted on a desktop computer with the following configuration: an Intel Core i5 2.7 GHz CPU, 8 GB RAM. The real-world
web service datasets [36], namely *WSDream dataset 2*, are utilized to simulate
the the monitoring values of QoS attributes of edge service. It records the real-
world monitoring data of QoS attributes from 142 users of 4,500 web services
over 64 different time slices (with the step size of 15 min). Each web service has
two QoS attributes (i.e., response time and throughput).

   The data are selected from dataset 2 to represent the monitoring values
of the QoS attributes (i.e., response time and throughput) of edge service,
denoted as RT and TP. The *Time Slice ID* is used as the time period (i.e.,
$T = \{t_i \,|\, 1 \le i \le 64\}$) for the SLA compliance verification of edge service.
Accordingly, each monitoring dataset of RT and TP in different moments can be

obtained, denoted by $RT = \{rt_i \mid 1 \leq i \leq 64\}$ and $TP = \{tp_i \mid 1 \leq i \leq 64\}$. The *User ID* is used to represent the number of IoT devices accessing the application of edge service, denoted as $d(rt_i)$ and $d(tp_i)$.

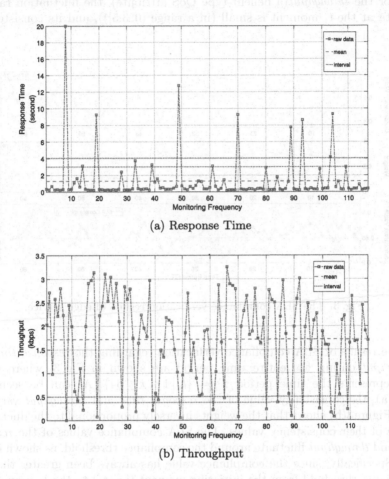

(a) Response Time

(b) Throughput

Fig. 2. The data and fluctuation interval at t_1

In this simulation experiment, *Service ID* = 1 is taken as an example. The parameters used in the experiment are shown in Table 1. The number of IoT devices (i.e., $d(rt_i)$ and $d(tp_i)$) of response time and throughput respectively refer to the number of user who feedback the web data.

4.2 Effectiveness Analysis

We take the data of RT and TP at the t_1 moment as an example (i.e., rt_1 and tp_1) to construct their *fluctuation interval*, namely $d_1(responsetime)$ and $d_1(throughput)$, as shown in Fig. 2. It can be seen from Fig. 2(a) that for the *response time*(a cost-type QoS attribute), although the data fluctuates widely (in a range $(0, 20]$) at the t_1 moment, it can be determined based on the mean that its consistency is relatively high. Similarly, as can be seen from Fig. 2(b) that for the *throughput*(a benefit-type QoS attribute), the fluctuation range of its data at the t_1 moment is small (in a range $(0, 3.5]$)), and its consistency is high.

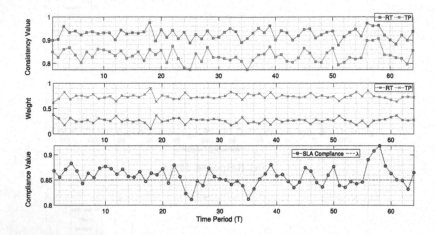

Fig. 3. The SLA compliance verification results of edge service.

The results of SLA compliance verification regarding the *response time* and *throughput* during the entire time period are shown in Fig. 3, where the x-axis represents the time period $T = \{t_i \mid 1 \leq i \leq 64\}$. As can be seen from Fig. 3(a), the consistency value of the *response time* and *throughput* vary over time. Figure 3(b) shows that the weights inversely proportional to the fluctuation degree of their consistency values. The SLA compliance values of the *response time* and *throughput* fluctuate around the compliance threshold, as shown in Fig. 3(c). Specifically, since the compliance value has always been greater than the compliance threshold from the initiating moment (i.e. t_1) to the t_5 moment. In other words, the SLA of edge service is compliant. Therefore, we can conclude that the SLA compliance value is directly proportional to the consistency of its QoS attributes, and can accurately reflect the current operation situation of edge service.

5   Conclusion

In this work, we propose a promising solution in ECoT contex that ensure continuous SLA compliance of edge service during its operation. Firstly, an SLA compliance verification model is proposed. This model uses the SLOs of QoS attributes of an edge service specified in the SLA to construct their fluctuation intervals. The consistency values of QoS attributes are calculated by combining their monitoring values and fluctuation intervals for violation detection. It enhances the fault tolerance of the model for QoS violations. Then, the model employs an objective method based on entropy to determine weights of dynamic QoS attributes, which improves the accuracy of SLA compliance verification. Finally, simulation experiments based on a real-world web service dataset verify the effectiveness and accuracy of the model.

In the future, the security features of ECoT services will be considered as metrics to be incorporated in the model for ensuring security of ECoT service continuously.

Acknowledgements. Please place your acknowledgments at the end of the paper, preceded by an unnumbered run-in heading (i.e. 3rd-level heading).

References

1. Abbas, N., Zhang, Y., Taherkordi, A., Skeie, T.: Mobile edge computing: a survey. IEEE Internet Things J. **5**(1), 450–465 (2018). https://doi.org/10.1109/JIOT.2017.2750180
2. Abdullah, M.N., Bhaya, W.S.: Predication of quality of service (QoS) in cloud services: a survey. In: Journal of Physics: Conference Series. vol. 1804, p. 012049. IOP Publishing (2021). https://doi.org/10.1088/1742-6596/1804/1/012049
3. Botta, A., de Donato, W., Persico, V., Pescapé, A.: Integration of cloud computing and internet of things: a survey. Future Gener. Comput. Syst. **56**, 684–700 (2016). https://doi.org/10.1016/j.future.2015.09.021, https://www.sciencedirect.com/science/article/pii/S0167739X15003015
4. Buyya, R., et al.: A manifesto for future generation cloud computing: research directions for the next decade. ACM Comput. Surv. (CSUR) **51**(5), 1–38 (2018). https://doi.org/10.1145/3241737
5. Cao, K., Hu, S., Shi, Y., Colombo, A.W., Karnouskos, S., Li, X.: A survey on edge and edge-cloud computing assisted cyber-physical systems. IEEE Trans. Industr. Inf. **17**(11), 7806–7819 (2021). https://doi.org/10.1109/TII.2021.3073066
6. Emeakaroha, V.C., Netto, M.A., Calheiros, R.N., Brandic, I., Buyya, R., De Rose, C.A.: Towards autonomic detection of SLA violations in cloud infrastructures. Futur. Gener. Comput. Syst. **28**(7), 1017–1029 (2012). https://doi.org/10.1016/j.future.2011.08.018
7. Floricu, A., Buzatu, R., Negru, C., Pop, F., Castiglione, A.: Implementing a solution for monitoring SLA violations in cloud. In: 2020 IEEE 6th International Conference on Dependability in Sensor, Cloud and Big Data Systems and Application (DependSys), pp. 80–86 (2020). https://doi.org/10.1109/DependSys51298.2020.00020
8. Girs, S., Sentilles, S., Asadollah, S.A., Ashjaei, M., Mubeen, S.: A systematic literature study on definition and modeling of service-level agreements for cloud services in IoT. IEEE Access **8**, 134498–134513 (2020). https://doi.org/10.1109/ACCESS.2020.3011483
9. Sabireen, H., Neelanarayanan, V.: A review on fog computing: architecture, fog with IoT, algorithms and research challenges. ICT Express **7**(2), 162–176 (2021). https://doi.org/10.1016/j.icte.2021.05.004

10. Halabi, T., Bellaiche, M.: A broker-based framework for standardization and management of cloud security-SLAs. Comput. Secur. **75**, 59–71 (2018). https://doi.org/10.1016/j.cose.2018.01.019

11. Hassija, V., Chamola, V., Saxena, V., Jain, D., Goyal, P., Sikdar, B.: A survey on IoT security: application areas, security threats, and solution architectures. IEEE Access **7**, 82721–82743 (2019). https://doi.org/10.1109/ACCESS.2019.2924045

12. Hussain, W., Hussain, F.K., Hussain, O.K., Damiani, E., Chang, E.: Formulating and managing viable SLAs in cloud computing from a small to medium service provider's viewpoint: a state-of-the-art review. Inf. Syst. **71**, 240–259 (2017). https://doi.org/10.1016/j.is.2017.08.007

13. Junior, F.M.R., Kamienski, C.A.: A survey on trustworthiness for the internet of things. IEEE Access **9**, 42493–42514 (2021). https://doi.org/10.1109/ACCESS.2021.3066457

14. Li, X., Jin, X., Wang, Q., Cao, M., Chen, X.: SCCAF: a secure and compliant continuous assessment framework in cloud-based IoT context. Wirel. Commun. Mob. Comput. **2018** (2018). https://doi.org/10.1155/2018/3078272

15. Li, X., Rui, Y., Xingshu, C., Yaolei, L., Qixu, W.: Assessment model of cloud service security level based on standardized security metric hierarchy. Adv. Eng. Sci. **52**(3), 159–167 (2020). https://doi.org/10.15961/j.jsuese.201900429

16. Li, X., Wang, Q., Lan, X., Chen, X., Zhang, N., Chen, D.: Enhancing cloud-based IoT security through trustworthy cloud service: an integration of security and reputation approach. IEEE Access **7**, 9368–9383 (2019). https://doi.org/10.1109/access.2018.2890432

17. Mubeen, S., Asadollah, S.A., Papadopoulos, A.V., Ashjaei, M., Pei-Breivold, H., Behnam, M.: Management of service level agreements for cloud services in IoT: a systematic mapping study. IEEE Access **6**, 30184–30207 (2018). https://doi.org/10.1109/ACCESS.2017.2744677

18. Nawaz, F., Hussain, O., Hussain, F.K., Janjua, N.K., Saberi, M., Chang, E.: Proactive management of SLA violations by capturing relevant external events in a cloud of things environment. Futur. Gener. Comput. Syst. **95**, 26–44 (2019). https://doi.org/10.1016/j.future.2018.12.034, https://www.sciencedirect.com/science/article/pii/S0167739X18318065

19. Ometov, A., Molua, O.L., Komarov, M., Nurmi, J.: A survey of security in cloud, edge, and fog computing. Sensors **22**(3) (2022). https://doi.org/10.3390/s22030927

20. Prokhorenko, V., Babar, M.A.: Architectural resilience in cloud, fog and edge systems: a survey. IEEE Access **8**, 28078–28095 (2020). https://doi.org/10.1109/ACCESS.2020.2971007

21. Ranaweera, P., Jurcut, A.D., Liyanage, M.: Survey on multi-access edge computing security and privacy. IEEE Commun. Surv. Tutor. **23**(2), 1078–1124 (2021). https://doi.org/10.1109/COMST.2021.3062546

22. Razian, M., Fathian, M., Wu, H., Akbari, A., Buyya, R.: SAIoT: scalable anomaly-aware services composition in CloudIoT environments. IEEE Internet Things J. **8**(5), 3665–3677 (2021). https://doi.org/10.1109/JIOT.2020.3023938

23. Ren, J., Zhang, D., He, S., Zhang, Y., Li, T.: A survey on end-edge-cloud orchestrated network computing paradigms: transparent computing, mobile edge computing, fog computing, and cloudlet. ACM Comput. Surv. **52**(6), 1–36 (2019). https://doi.org/10.1145/3362031

24. Schubert, C., Borkowski, M., Schulte, S.: Trustworthy detection and arbitration of SLA violations in the cloud. In: Kritikos, K., Plebani, P., de Paoli, F. (eds.) ESOCC 2018. LNCS, vol. 11116, pp. 90–104. Springer, Cham (2018). https://doi.org/10.1007/978-3-319-99819-0_7

25. Sharma, A., Pilli, E.S., Mazumdar, A.P., Gera, P.: Towards trustworthy internet of things: a survey on trust management applications and schemes. Comput. Commun. **160**, 475–493 (2020). https://doi.org/10.1016/j.comcom.2020.06.030

26. Shivani, Singh, A., Singhrova, A., Kumar, J.: A makespan based framework for detection of SLA violations in cloud computing environment. In: Pant, M., Sharma, T., Verma, O., Singla, R., Sikander, A. (eds.) Soft Computing: Theories and Applications. Advances in Intelligent Systems and Computing, vol. 1053, pp. 503–512. Springer, Singapore (2020). https://doi.org/10.1007/978-981-15-0751-9_47

27. Tabrizchi, H., Rafsanjani, M.K.: A survey on security challenges in cloud computing: issues, threats, and solutions. J. Supercomput. **76**(12), 9493–9532 (2020). https://doi.org/10.1007/s11227-020-03213-1

28. Taleb, T., Samdanis, K., Mada, B., Flinck, H., Dutta, S., Sabella, D.: On multi-access edge computing: a survey of the emerging 5G network edge cloud architecture and orchestration. IEEE Commun. Surv. Tutor. **19**(3), 1657–1681 (2017). https://doi.org/10.1109/COMST.2017.2705720

29. Ud Din, I., Guizani, M., Kim, B.S., Hassan, S., Khurram Khan, M.: Trust management techniques for the internet of things: a survey. IEEE Access **7**, 29763–29787 (2019). https://doi.org/10.1109/ACCESS.2018.2880838

30. Upadhyay, P.K., Pandita, A., Joshi, N.: Fuzzy logic based detection of SLA violation in cloud computing-a predictive approach. Int. J. Next-Gener. Comput. **11**(3) (2020)

31. Verma, R., Chandra, S.: A systematic survey on fog steered IoT: architecture, prevalent threats and trust models. Int. J. Wirel. Inf. Netw. **28**, 116–133 (2021). https://doi.org/10.1007/s10776-020-00499-z

32. Wang, Q., Liu, M.W., Chen, K.Q., Zhang, Yu., Zheng, J.: A hierarchical framework for evaluation of cloud service qualities. In: Zhu, L., Zhong, S. (eds.) MSN 2017. CCIS, vol. 747, pp. 45–54. Springer, Singapore (2018). https://doi.org/10.1007/978-981-10-8890-2_4

33. Wang, Q., Chen, X., Jin, X., Li, X., Chen, D., Qin, X.: Enhancing trustworthiness of internet of vehicles in space-air-ground integrated networks: attestation approach. IEEE Internet Things J. 1 (2021). https://doi.org/10.1109/JIOT.2021.3084449

34. Wang, Y., et al.: ContainerGuard: a real-time attack detection system in container-based big data platform. IEEE Trans. Industr. Inform. 1 (2020). https://doi.org/10.1109/TII.2020.3047416

35. Zeng, X., et al.: Detection of SLA violation for big data analytics applications in cloud. IEEE Trans. Comput. **70**(5), 746–758 (2020)

36. Zheng, Z., Zhang, Y., Lyu, M.R.: Investigating QoS of real-world web services. IEEE Trans. Serv. Comput. **7**(1), 32–39 (2014). https://doi.org/10.1109/TSC.2012.34

37. Zhou, J., Cao, Z., Dong, X., Vasilakos, A.V.: Security and privacy for cloud-based IoT: challenges. IEEE Commun. Mag. **55**(1), 26–33 (2017). https://doi.org/10.1109/MCOM.2017.1600363CM

A Regenerating Code Based Data Restoration Scheme in Active RFID System

Feng Lin[1,2](✉), Guodong Peng[1], Liping Ma[2], and Yu Liu[1]

[1] Yunnan Traffic Science Research Institute Co., LTD., Kunming, China
[2] Yunnan Transport Engineering Quality Inspection Co., LTD., Kunming, China
fenglinytsr@sina.com

Abstract. Due to the complex and uncontrollable operating environment of high dynamic active RFID systems, the risk of individual loss of RFID tags occurs from time to time, resulting in the loss of important data. On the other hand, the storage capacity of RFID tags is limited, such that the storage space of a single RFID tag cannot meet the storage needs. Therefore, how to achieve reliable cooperative storage of active RFID systems in complex and even hostile environments is extremely important. To solve the above problems, this paper studies the efficient cooperative storage of key data in active RFID system. Specifically, a data restoration scheme is designed by using regenerating code against individual loss for active RFID systems. Moreover, the optimization of scheme parameters is studied according to different application scenarios to ensure that key data can be successfully recovered under different RFID tag loss probabilities. Finally, the simulation platform is designed to verify the performance of our data restoration scheme.

Keywords: Data Restoration · Regenerating Code · RFID System

1 Introduction

With the the development of Internet of Things technology (IoT) [1–3], RFID systems have been widely used in terminal identification and positioning [4–6]. Radio Frequency Identification (RFID) is a non-contact automatic identification technology, which automatically identifies the target object through the radio frequency signal and obtains relevant data [7]. It consists of RFID label and RFID reader. RFID labels are classified into active labels and passive labels based on whether they are equipped with batteries [8]. Passive tags can convert part of the microwave energy into direct current for their own operation after receiving the microwave signal emitted by the card reader. The operating power of active RFID is completely supplied by the internal battery, and the battery's energy is converted into the radio frequency energy required for communication between the RFID tag and the RFID reader, which usually supports remote

© The Author(s), under exclusive license to Springer Nature Singapore Pte Ltd. 2024
H. Yang and R. Lu (Eds.): FCS 2023, CCIS 1992, pp. 602–612, 2024.
https://doi.org/10.1007/978-981-99-9331-4_40

identification. Passive RFID costs are relatively low, while active RFID costs are relatively high. But the active RFID function is more rich, which can achieve displacement, alarm, inspection and other functions. For the management of high-value fixed assets, active RFID tags are required, such as the displacement of fixed assets or leaving a certain location [9].

In this paper, data restoration scheme based on regenerating code in active RFID system is studied. The mainstream data fault tolerance and repair technology is multi-copy technology, which is based on the idea of creating multiple copies of a block of data and storing multiple backups in different ones. The system can take any copy of the required data and access the nearest copy as needed to improve data access efficiency. When a data failure is encountered, the system can use any surviving copy to recover the failed data, and only when there are at least two surviving copies can the complete data be correctly obtained. Specifically, the reader evenly divides all the data into k data blocks and randomly selects r data blocks to store [10]. However, with the increasing amount of data, the disadvantages of low storage space utilization of multi-copy technology are becoming more and more obvious.

Since the storage capacity of RFID tags is limited, and the storage space cannot meet the storage needs. Cooperative storage is an alternative solution, which divides large data into small data blocks and stores them on each label by means of distributed assistance. However, due to the complex and uncontrollable operating environment of active RFID systems, RFID tags are vulnerable to all kinds of attacks [11–13], which leads the result that the risk of individual loss of RFID tags occurs from time to time [14–16]. As a result, the storage important data of a single RFID tag may be lost frequently. Therefore, how to achieve reliable cooperative storage of active RFID systems in complex and even hostile environments is extremely important. Based on this, this paper studies the efficient cooperative storage of key data in active RFID system. Specifically, a collaborative storage and data restoration scheme against individual loss is designed for active RFID systems. Moreover, the optimization of scheme parameters are discussed according to different application scenarios to ensure that key data can be successfully recovered under different RFID tag loss probabilities. Finally, a simulation platform is presented to verify the performance of the designed cooperative storage and data restoration scheme in active RFID system.

2   Related Work

Network coding technology is a distributed storage technology suitable for active RFID systems [17]. Distributed storage technology uses distributed storage nodes to reliably store data objects. Because of the advantages of distributed storage in reliability, scale and performance, it is more and more widely used in cloud computing, wireless sensors and P2P storage networks.

In [18], Dimakis et al. introduced the idea of network coding into the field of failure repair of erasure Codes and proposed a method of erasure codes based on network coding, called Regenerating Codes (RC codes). At the same time, they also proved that there are two critical cases of regenerating code from two aspects of storage utilization and repair cost, i.e., Minimum-Storage Regenerating Codes (MSR Codes) and Minimum-Bandwidth Regenerating Codes (BR codes) [19–21]. Among them, MSR code adopts the data storage mode similar to the traditional MDS code, that is, the minimum storage space overhead. However, MSR code reduces data downloads during the failed node repair process in two ways: the segmentation of data blocks and the addition of provider nodes. The subdivision of the data block refers to the subdivision of the data block stored in each node into multiple symbols in the coding process of MSR code, and the coding calculation is carried out in symbol bit units. The increase of provider nodes refers to the increase in the number of provider nodes in the MSR code during the repair process. In contrast, the MSR code allows more nodes to participate in the repair process of the failed node, while the amount of data downloaded by each node is smaller than the size of the data block. Through the combination of the two technologies, MSR code reduces the repair cost of failed nodes without increasing the storage cost. Compared to MSR, BR offers a smaller additional storage space overhead in exchange for less repair overhead [21]. That is, the amount of data stored in each node of BR is more than that stored in MSR code, and the total amount of data downloaded by BR is smaller than that of MSR in the repair process. MSR and BR can well represent the two extremes of regenerating code: minimum storage overhead or minimum repair bandwidth overhead [21].

Shah et al. proposed a method of Interference alignment to reduce repair bandwidth consumption [22]. In the field of communication, there are many ways to eliminate interference, among which interference alignment is a common interference management method. It overlaps the interference signal and the expected signal at the receiving end through pre-coding technology, thus reducing the influence of interference. Different from the traditional interference processing methods such as decoding/eliminating interference and orthogonal access, interference alignment makes the system obtain higher degrees of freedom by compressing the dimensions of the interference to the signal, thus improving the system capacity and reliability. It is a very excellent solution. In order to reduce the repair efficiency of the storage system, the researchers tried to apply the interference alignment method to the data calculation and placement during the coding process. Through clever design, the repair process can minimize the amount of data read, while completing the data repair. However, this method is limited by the size of the finite field and only applies to specific parameters. Therefore, this method has not been widely used.

Nihar et al. in [23] proposed a Repair by Transfer (RT) method without coding calculation and constructed an accurate BR coding. Specifically, RT uses a clever coding algorithm to store the generated coding symbols redundantly in the nodes. During the repair process, RT completes the repair directly by accessing all online nodes and downloading corresponding symbols without any coding calculations. However, the computation-free repair mode of RT method is realized with large extra space overhead and specific coding parameters, so the generality of this method is poor [24].

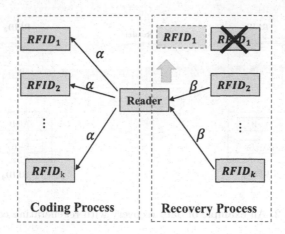

Fig. 1. The data coding process and recovery Process with regenerating codes in active RFID systems.

Regenerating code provides a new research direction for reducing the repair cost of erasure codes. The existing methods also explore the feasibility of regenerating code from many aspects, and put forward the corresponding coding algorithm and repair algorithm. However, in order to meet certain coding requirements, such as accurate repair, the finite field where the coefficient is located must be large enough to ensure the existence of the coefficient. Moreover, the selection method of the coding coefficient is irregular and not easy to implement.

3 Regenerative Code Architecture in RFID Systems

When an RFID tag fails, its data needs to be restored and repaired, and then a new tag can be used to store the data. Due to an active RFID system may be highly dynamic, one of the most important problems is how to complete data repair with the minimum amount of data transferred. In [25], it has been proved that the repair process of erasure codes is not optimal. The network coding methods were introduced to improve erasure codes, and combined these two methods to propose regenerating codes. The process of data encoding and data repair of the regenerating code is shown in Fig. 1. Compared to erasure codes that only store and forward, each of the regenerating codes can transmit data, greatly increasing the repair bandwidth consumed to repair a single fault label. A set of regenerating codes can be described by parameters (n, k, d). Specifically, in the data encoding process, k data blocks are mapped into n coding blocks for storage. The reader connects k tags and transmits alpha data to each tag. When something is lost, the system automatically connects at least d assists to recover the lost code block. The aid first uses its own data to perform a linear operation, and then transmits the operation results to the reader, the transmission amount is β.

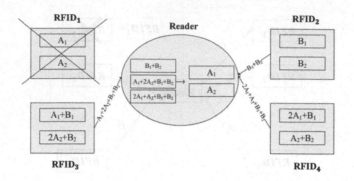

Fig. 2. An example of data recovery with regenerating code.

Figure 2 shows an example of regenerating code for data encoding and data failure repair. Assuming that the pre-stored data is (A_1, A_2, B_1, B_2), the regenerating code can be encoded into $(4, 2, 3)$ regenerating code. and $RFID_1$, $RFID_2$, $RFID_3$, and $RFID_4$ are four storage labels, where each RFID tag needs to store $k = 2$ data. Specifically, $RFID_1$ stores (A_1, A_2), $RFID_2$ stores $(A_1 + B_1, 2A_2 + B_2)$, $RFID_3$ stores (B_1, B_2), and $RFID_4$ stores $(2A_1 + B_1, A_2 + B_2)$. Assume that when $RFID_1$ fails, and other RFID tags are normal. $RFID_2$, $RFID_3$, and $RFID_4$ becomes the assist tag, transmitting the calculated data to the reader. The data is recovered by the reader to decode the values of A_1 and A_2 and transmitted to the alternative RFID tag. This method only needs a simple XOR operation to complete the data recovery.

The minimum cut analysis of the information flow graph of the regenerated code in the process of data restoration of RFID system can be carried out. It is assumed that the regenerating code is to store the original information S of size B into n RFID tags, each of which has a storage size of α. X_{in}^i and X_{out}^i are stored in $RFID_i$, where X_{in}^i represents the acquired information and X_{out}^i represents the output information. The weight α on the directed side represents the capacity stored in the memory RFID tag, and the weight β represents the repair bandwidth of the recovery of RFID label information. The lower limit of the repair bandwidth of the failed label is obtained by calculating the minimum cut of the information flow diagram. The regenerating code is on the optimal curve of the storage cost α and the repair bandwidth β. Codes that reach the minimum extreme point of Storage are called Mini-mum Storage Regenerating Codes (MSR). The Codes that reach the minimum extreme point of repair Bandwidth are called Mini-mum Bandwidth Regenerating Codes (MBR).

4   The Proposed Scheme

The repair strategy can be divided into the following two types.: 1) functional repair: the repair strategy does not require that the RFID tag data after repair is the same as the RFID tag data before failure; and 2) accurate repair: the RFID tag data after repair is the same as the RFID tag data before failure. Because of the small bandwidth required by the minimum bandwidth regenerating code, it is more suitable for high dynamic RFID tag system. In this paper, the minimum bandwidth regenerating code is precisely repaired coding strategy. The minimum bandwidth regenerating code is represented as a matrix, and the data matrix is a symmetric matrix containing the data itself. The matrix consists of data matrix and repair matrix. The data matrix and the repair matrix are stored in the RFID reader and each RFID tag in advance. In this paper, $[n, k, d]$ minimum bandwidth regenerating code C is adopted, where the storage cost α is set to d, the amount of data uploaded on a single node $\beta = 1$, and the total repair bandwidth overhead of a single node failure is $\gamma \, (= d \cdot \beta)$.

The original data $M = [M_1, M_2, ..., M_s]$ is reorganized into a data matrix $D(M)$ with $d \times d$ dimension as follows.

$$D(M) = \begin{bmatrix} X & Y \\ Y' & 0 \end{bmatrix} \tag{1}$$

where matrix X is a symmetric matrix of $k \times k$ dimension, and matrix Y consists of the remaining $k \times (d - k)$ data elements. Therefore, the data matrix $D(M)$ is a symmetric matrix.

Take $[6, 3, 4]$ minimum bandwidth regenerating code encoding as an example. Let $M = [M_1, M_2, ..., M_s]$. The matrix X and Y in the data matrix $D(M)$ are

$$X = \begin{bmatrix} M_1 & M_2 & M_3 \\ M_2 & M_4 & M_5 \\ M_3 & M_5 & M_6 \end{bmatrix} \quad \text{and} \quad Y = \begin{bmatrix} M_7 \\ M_8 \\ M_9 \end{bmatrix}$$

respectively. Therefore, we have

$$D(M) = \begin{bmatrix} M_1 & M_2 & M_3 & M_7 \\ M_2 & M_4 & M_5 & M_8 \\ M_3 & M_5 & M_6 & M_9 \\ M_7 & M_8 & M_9 & 0 \end{bmatrix} \tag{2}$$

The data collector RFID reader connects any k tags $RFID_1, RFID_2, ...,$ $RFID_k$. A data repair matrix R is stored in advance in RFID reader with $n \times d$ dimensions. Specifically, $R = [W, Z]$, where W is a matrix of dimension $n \times k$, Z is a matrix of dimension $n \times (d - k)$, and any s rows of the repair matrix R are linearly independent of any t rows of the matrix W. The repair matrix is adopted as the $(6, 4)$ Vander Monde matrix in the finite field F_7, and set $a_i \ (i = 1, 2, ..., 6)$, then the repair matrix R is

$$R = \begin{bmatrix} 1 & a_1 & a_1^2 & a_1^3 \\ 1 & a_2 & a_2^2 & a_2^3 \\ 1 & a_3 & a_3^2 & a_3^3 \\ 1 & a_4 & a_4^2 & a_4^3 \\ 1 & a_5 & a_5^2 & a_5^3 \\ 1 & a_6 & a_6^2 & a_6^3 \end{bmatrix} = \begin{bmatrix} 1 & 1 & 1 & 1 \\ 1 & 2 & 4 & 1 \\ 1 & 3 & 2 & 6 \\ 1 & 4 & 2 & 1 \\ 1 & 5 & 4 & 6 \\ 1 & 6 & 5 & 6 \end{bmatrix} \tag{3}$$

The minimum bandwidth regenerating code $C = R \times D$, which is call the minimum bandwidth regenerating code matrix of (n, d, k). If the message sequence is $(w_1, w_2, \cdots w_9)$, the matrix construction of the minimum bandwidth regenerating code

$$
C = R \times D = \begin{bmatrix}
w_1 + w_2 + w_3 + w_7 & w_2 + w_4 + w_5 + w_8 & w_3 + w_5 + w_6 + w_9 & w_7 + w_8 + w_9 \\
w_1 + 2w_2 + 4w_3 + w_7 & w_2 + 2w_4 + 4w_5 + w_8 & w_3 + 2w_5 + 4w_6 + w_9 & w_7 + 2w_8 + 4w_9 \\
w_1 + 3w_2 + 2w_3 + 6w_7 & w_2 + 3w_4 + 2w_5 + 6w_8 & w_3 + 3w_5 + 2w_6 + 6w_9 & w_7 + 3w_8 + 2w_9 \\
w_1 + 4w_2 + 2w_3 + w_7 & w_2 + 4w_4 + 2w_5 + w_8 & w_3 + 4w_5 + 2w_6 + w_9 & w_7 + 4w_8 + 2w_9 \\
w_1 + 5w_2 + 4w_3 + 6w_7 & w_2 + 5w_4 + 4w_5 + 6w_8 & w_3 + 5w_5 + 4w_6 + 6w_9 & w_7 + 5w_8 + 4w_9 \\
w_1 + 6w_2 + w_3 + 6w_7 & w_2 + 6w_4 + w_5 + 6w_8 & w_3 + 6w_5 + w_6 + 6w_9 & w_7 + 6w_8 + w_9
\end{bmatrix}
\tag{4}
$$

Tag $RFID_i$ section stores C_i $(i = 1, 2, \ldots, 6)$, e.g., $RFID_1$ storage $(w_1 + w_2 + w_3 + w_7, w_2 + w_4 + w_5 + w_8, w_3 + w_5 + w_6 + w_9, w_7 + w_9 + w_8)$. Now assume that the $RFID_1$ fails, and the stored data of $RFID_1$ can be regenerated through the remaining viable RFID tags. The reader connects any 4 of the 5 viable RFID tags (such as $RFID_j$ $j \in \{2, 4, 5, 6\}$), and obtains the matrix Λ as

$$
\begin{bmatrix}
w_1 + 2w_2 + 4w_3 + w_7 & w_2 + w_4 + w_5 + w_8 & w_3 + w_5 + w_6 + w_9 & w_7 + 2w_8 + 4w_9 \\
w_1 + 2w_2 + 4w_3 + w_7 & w_2 + 2w_4 + 4w_5 + w_8 & w_3 + 2w_5 + 4w_6 + w_9 & w_7 + 4w_8 + 2w_9 \\
w_1 + 3w_2 + 2w_3 + 6w_7 & w_2 + 3w_4 + 2w_5 + 6w_8 & w_3 + 3w_5 + 2w_6 + 6w_9 & w_7 + 5w_8 + 4w_9 \\
w_1 + 6w_2 + w_3 + 6w_7 & w_2 + 6w_4 + w_5 + 6w_8 & w_3 + 6w_5 + w_6 + 6w_9 & w_7 + 6w_8 + w_9
\end{bmatrix}
\tag{5}
$$

Then, the reader get the active submatrix R_{active} from matrix R, which corresponds to rows 2, 4, 5, and 6 of the matrix R. Here,

$$
R_{active} = \begin{bmatrix}
1 & 2 & 4 & 1 \\
1 & 4 & 2 & 1 \\
1 & 5 & 4 & 6 \\
1 & 6 & 1 & 1
\end{bmatrix}
\tag{6}
$$

The next, the reader computes the inverse matrix R_{active}^{-1} of R_{active}. Finally, the reader can calculate

$$
R_{active}^{-1} \Lambda \lambda = \begin{bmatrix}
w_1 + w_2 + w_3 + w_7 \\
w_2 + w_4 + w_5 + w_8 \\
w_3 + w_5 + w_6 + w_9 \\
w_7 + w_8 + w_9
\end{bmatrix}
\tag{7}
$$

where $\lambda = [1, 1, 1, 1]^T$, so as to realize the data repair of the failed $RFID_1$.

5   Experimental Verification

In this section, we test the repair bandwidth cost and storage cost respectively for the multi-copy algorithm, erasure code and the minimum bandwidth regenerating code algorithm used in this paper under the same repair rate or the same file size, and compare the three schemes.

The experiments are conducted on a PC of CPU with Intel(R) Core(TM)i5-8265H CPU@1.60 GHz2.30 GHz, Memory with 8G, Hard disk with 20GB, Operating system Ubuntu 18.04, Build environment python 3.7, and Virtual machine with VMware® Workstation 14 Pro. Moreover, [10, 5, 7] minimum bandwidth regenerating code C is leveraged in our experiments. The regenerating code parameter indicates that there are 10 RFID tags in the entire RFID tag group, and the original file can be recovered by connecting any 5 RFID tag nodes. When a single point RFID tag fails, the new RFID tag can be connected to any 7 of the remaining RFID tags to accurately recover the data on the original faulty RFID tag.

In the first experiment, we simulate the independent repeated experiment of RFID tag loss for 20 times, in which the failed RFID tag serial number is randomly generated by the pseudo-random number function. Using the control variable method, the experiment is carried out under the condition that the file size is 500$bits$ and the recovery rate is 90%. The result of Repair method bandwidth cost comparison is shown in Table 1.

Table 1. The comparison of Repair method bandwidth cost.

Number	Regenerating Code	Erasure code	Multiple Copies
1	0.518bits	0.701bits	0.800bits
2	0.517bits	0.705bits	0.801bits
3	0.511bits	0.702bits	0.793bits
4	0.509bits	0.707bits	0.793bits
5	0.500bits	0.703bits	0.795bits
6	0.512bits	0.692bits	0.798bits
7	0.507bits	0.693bits	0.802bits
8	0.499bits	0.687bits	0.805bits
9	0.486bits	0.703bits	0.809bits
10	0.497bits	0.719bits	0.809bits
11	0.498bits	0.694bits	0.799bits
12	0.501bits	0.702bits	0.798bits
13	0.502bits	0.685bits	0.804bits
14	0.500bits	0.698bits	0.804bits
15	0.510bits	0.703bits	0.802bits
16	0.494bits	0.704bits	0.791bits
17	0.502bits	0.700bits	0.789bits
18	0.498bits	0.699bits	0.800bits
19	0.499bits	0.689bits	0.802bits
20	0.482bits	0.701bits	0.809bits

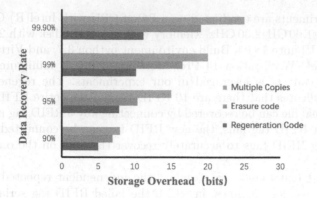

Fig. 3. The comparison of the storage cost under different recovery rates.

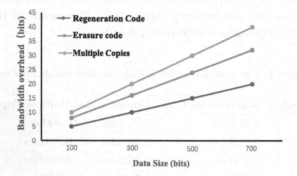

Fig. 4. The comparison of the storage cost under different data sizes.

Figure 3 is a comparison of the storage cost of the three repair methods after averaging under different recovery rates. It can be observed that when approaching 100%, the minimum bandwidth regenerating code algorithm used in this paper is almost 1/3 of the multiple copies and 1/2 of the erasure code. It can be concluded that under the same recovery rate, the storage cost required by the proposed scheme is much less than that of the multi-copy algorithm and the erasure code algorithm.

The second experiment is conducted to study the storage cost of the three repair methods under different data size, in which the recovery rate is set to be 99%, and the data sizes are set to be 100bits, 300bits, 500bits and 700bits. We independent repeat the experiment 20 times, in which the failed RFID tag serial number is randomly generated by the pseudo-random number function. Figure 4 shows the comparison of the three repair methods after averaging the bandwidth overhead test data under the same file size. It can be observed that the bandwidth overhead increases uniformly with the file size, and at close to 100%, the minimum bandwidth regenerating code algorithm used in this paper is much smaller than the previous two. It can be concluded that under the same file size, the repair bandwidth required by the proposed scheme is much smaller than that of the multi-copy algorithm and the erasure code algorithm.

6 Conclusion

Because of the high dynamic environment of active RFID systems, the risk of individual loss of RFID tags occurs from time to time, resulting in the loss of important data. Collaborative storage can be used to solve the problem of the limitation storage capacity of RFID tags. However, it is still a challenge how to achieve reliable collaborative storage of active RFID systems in complex and even harsh environments. In view of the above problems, this paper studied the efficient collaborative storage of key data with regenerating code in an active RFID systems. Specifically, for the active RFID system, a regenerating code based collaborative storage scheme for individual losses is designed. Then we discussed the optimization of the scheme parameters for different application scenarios to ensure that key data can be successfully recovered under different RFID tag loss probabilities. Finally, the simulation platform is designed to verify the performance of the proposed scheme. The experiment results show that the proposed scheme has good performance in communication cost.

Acknowledgements. This work is supported by Research on the construction of intelligent full-process laboratory system based on RFID (Radio frequency identification) technology (No. YCIC-YF-2022-05).

References

1. Farahsari, P.S., Farahzadi, A., Rezazadeh, J., et al.: A survey on indoor positioning systems for IoT-based applications. IEEE Internet Things J. **9**(10), 7680–7699 (2022)
2. Chen, D., Wang, H., et al.: Privacy-preserving encrypted traffic inspection with symmetric cryptographic techniques in IoT. IEEE Internet Things J. **9**(18), 17265–17279 (2022)
3. Yang, Y., Wang, H., Jiang, R., et al.: A review of IoT-enabled mobile healthcare: technologies, challenges, and future trends. IEEE Internet Things J. **9**(12), 9478–9502 (2022)
4. Zhang, N., Yang, P., et al.: Synergy of big data and 5G wireless networks: opportunities, approaches, and challenges. IEEE Wirel. Commun. **25**(1), 12–18 (2018)
5. Ale, L., Zhang, N., et al.: Online proactive caching in mobile edge computing using bidirectional deep recurrent neural network. IEEE Internet Things J. **6**(3), 5520–5530 (2019)
6. Chen, D., Mao, X., Qin, Z., Wang, W., Li, X.-Y., Qin, Z.: Wireless device authentication using acoustic hardware fingerprints. In: Wang, Yu., Xiong, H., Argamon, S., Li, X.Y., Li, J.Z. (eds.) BigCom 2015. LNCS, vol. 9196, pp. 193–204. Springer, Cham (2015). https://doi.org/10.1007/978-3-319-22047-5_16
7. Tan, W.C., Sidhu, M.S.: Review of RFID and IoT integration in supply chain management. Oper. Res. Perspect. **9**, 100229 (2022)

8. Gayatri Sarman, K., Gubbala, S.: Voice based objects detection for visually challenged using active RFID technology. In: Gupta, N., Pareek, P., Reis, M. (eds.) IC4S 2022. LNICST, vol. 472, pp. 170–179. Springer, Cham (2022). https://doi.org/10.1007/978-3-031-28975-0_14

9. Hsu, Y.F., Cheng, C.S., Chu, W.C.: COMPASS: an active RFID-based real-time indoor positioning system. HCIS **12**(07), 1–19 (2022)

10. Wang, Y., Wang, Q., Chen, X., et al.: ContainerGuard: a real-time attack detection system in container-based big data platform. IEEE Trans. Industr. Inf. **18**(5), 3327–3336 (2020)

11. Chen, D., Zhao, Z., Qin, X., et al.: MAGLeak: a learning-based side-channel attack for password recognition with multiple sensors in IIoT environment. IEEE Trans. Industr. Inf. **18**(1), 467–476 (2020)

12. Sun, J., et al.: A privacy-aware and traceable fine-grained data delivery system in cloud-assisted healthcare IIoT. IEEE Internet Things J. **8**(12), 10034–10046 (2021)

13. Qin, Z., Zhao, P., et al.: A survey of identity recognition via data fusion and feature learning. Inf. Fusion **91**, 694–712 (2023)

14. Dobrykh, D., Filonov, D., Slobozhanyuk, A., et al.: Hardware RFID security for preventing far-field attacks. IEEE Trans. Antennas Propag. **70**(3), 2199–2204 (2021)

15. Ai, X., Chen, H., Lin, K., et al.: Nowhere to hide: efficiently identifying probabilistic cloning attacks in large-scale RFID systems. IEEE Trans. Inf. Forensics Secur. **16**, 714–727 (2020)

16. Hosseinzadeh, M., Ahmed, O.H., Ahmed, S.H., et al.: An enhanced authentication protocol for RFID systems. IEEE Access **8**, 126977–126987 (2020)

17. Bassoli, R., Marques, H., Rodriguez, J., et al.: Network coding theory: a survey. IEEE Commun. Surv. Tutor. **15**(4), 1950–1978 (2013)

18. Dimakis, A.G., Godfrey, P.B., Wainwright, M.J., et al.: The benefits of network coding for peer-to-peer storage systems. In: Third Workshop on Network Coding, Theory, and Applications, pp. 1–9 (2007)

19. Rashmi, K.V., Shah, N.B., Kumar, P.V., et al.: Explicit and optimal exact-regenerating codes for the minimum-bandwidth point in distributed storage. In: IEEE International Symposium on Information Theory, pp. 1938–1942 (2010)

20. Goparaju, S., Fazeli, A., Vardy, A.: Minimum storage regenerating codes for all parameters. IEEE Trans. Inf. Theory **63**(10), 6318–6328 (2017)

21. Jiekak, S., Kermarrec, A.M., Le Scouarnec, N., et al.: Regenerating codes: a system perspective. ACM SIGOPS Oper. Syst. Rev. **47**(2), 23–32 (2013)

22. Suh, C., Ramchandran, K.: Exact-repair MDS codes for distributed storage using interference alignment. In: IEEE International Symposium on Information Theory, pp. 161–165 (2010)

23. Shah, N.B., et al.: Distributed storage codes with repair-by-transfer and nonachievability of interior points on the storage-bandwidth tradeoff. IEEE Trans. Inf. Theory **58**(3), 1837–1852 (2011)

24. Shah, N.B.: On minimizing data-read and download for storage-node recovery. IEEE Commun. Lett. **17**(5), 964–967 (2013)

25. Lin, W.K., Chiu, D.M., Lee, Y.B.: Erasure code replication revisited. In: Fourth International Conference on Peer-to-Peer Computing, pp. 90–97 (2004)

Lightweight Privacy-Preserving Medical Diagnostic Scheme for Internet of Things Healthcare

Yanghuijie Tang[✉], Ling Xiong, Mingxing He, and Liangjiang Chen

School of Computer and Software Engineering, Xihua University, Chengdu, China
yqh13108418018@163.com

Abstract. Remote medical diagnosis is an emerging trend in technological development. Retrieving diagnostic reports is crucial in remote medical diagnosis systems. However, patients' medical records are highly sensitive and valuable for accurate disease diagnoses. Additionally, timely and accurate diagnostic reports are vital for efficient medical services. Therefore, timely and accurate diagnosis by healthcare professionals, while respecting patient privacy, is a challenging yet promising task. Hence, this work proposes a lightweight and efficient privacy-preserving medical diagnostic scheme based on Bloom filters and oblivious transfer protocol. The Bloom filter is employed in this scheme to compress the search space, thereby enhancing query speed. Additionally, the oblivious transfer protocol and polynomial encoding techniques are integrated to safeguard user query privacy and database privacy. Based on experimental results, our proposed solution significantly reduces matching time to the millisecond level and decreases communication overhead by 60%. Therefore, the proposed scheme is more suitable for medical diagnostic systems in the Internet of Things environment that require high time and privacy requirements.

Keywords: Lightweight privacy-preserving medical diagnostic scheme · Bloom filter · Oblivious transfer · Remote medical diagnosis

1 Introduction

With the rapid development of intelligent sensor technology and Internet of Things healthcare, the healthcare industry is undergoing a transformative shift towards intelligent healthcare. Intelligent healthcare services refer to the integration of new-generation intelligent technology into the traditional healthcare services industry, providing patients with more convenient, flexible, personalized, and diversified healthcare services [1,2]. Among these services, intelligent healthcare diagnostic systems are an important technology in the field. Patients

Supported by the National Natural Science Foundation of China (No. 62171387, No.62202390).

can measure their own vital signs such as heart rate, blood pressure, pulse, BMI index, and other vital signs data through self-service medical devices. Intelligent doctors analyze these parameters to achieve efficient and convenient medical services, providing patients with more efficient and convenient medical services [3–5]. In general, smart healthcare services can effectively improve the health of the population by increasing the efficiency and quality of healthcare services. In this context, intelligent healthcare diagnostics are an unstoppable trend in the future of the healthcare field [6–8].

However, there are still some problems and challenges in the present intelligent healthcare diagnostic system [9]. In medical field, previous patients' cases are extremely private as well as significantly valuable for disease diagnosis [10]. Due to the security vulnerability of healthcare information systems, medical information leakage occurred at any time owing to the security vulnerability of healthcare information system, since malware is more and more difficult to detect and resist [14,15]. For example, in the largest healthcare breach to date, Anthem announced on January 29, 2015, that records of 78 million patients had been stolen, including highly sensitive data. Furthermore, the screening of hospital disease databases one by one can result in high computational costs and time consumption, which is not suitable in the current Internet of Things (IoT) environment. Therefore, how to establish an efficient and secure intelligent healthcare diagnostic system has become a crucial research direction in the field of intelligent healthcare. This article aims to explore the use of Bloom filters [16] and oblivious transfer protocol to address the problems of disease retrieval and patient privacy protection in the intelligent healthcare diagnostic system.

1.1   Our Contribution

Inspired by Sun's privacy-preserving medical record searching scheme [10], we have designed a lightweight and privacy-preserving smart medical disease diagnosis scheme based on Bloom filters and oblivious transfer protocols. While performing medical diagnosis on patients, the scheme protects both patient privacy and hospital disease database privacy. Compared with previous smart medical schemes, we have made the following contributions:

- LPMDS realizes intelligent self-helped medical diagnosis by IoT data privately. There is no need for the participation of real doctors or any centers.
- LPMDS is more lightweight compared to previous approaches, reducing the computational burden on the hospital's server by approximately 70%. Cloud doctor use patient's Bloom filter to screen the entire disease database, filtering out most disease information that is of no help in diagnosis. During the protocol process, there is no need for encryption and transmission of all disease information. This improves the timeliness of information acquisition, meets the requirements of high-speed information sharing, especially in the future 5G device-to-device (D2D) communication.
- LPMDS has achieved effective privacy protection. Regardless of whether the matching process is successful or not, the scheme can protect the privacy and security of patients and the disease database.

2 Related Work

Data encryption technology is presently the most popular avenue among privacy protection technologies for medical privacy. Data encryption technology primarily employs specific algorithms to encrypt data, ensuring the prevention of patient privacy information theft or leakage. For example, the Fully Homomorphic Encryption (FHE) algorithm processes encrypted data and produces an output that can be decrypted to yield the same result as processing the original unencrypted data using the identical method [17–19]. However, the substantial computational cost of FHE renders these solutions impractical for large-scale application scenarios. [20] introduced a scheme that relies on the AES algorithm and elliptic curve cryptography. This scheme enhances the security of medical data by integrating symmetric and asymmetric encryption techniques. However, these schemes exhibit a higher matching delay and solely concentrate on protecting the privacy of hospital disease data, limiting their effectiveness in achieving smart healthcare. [21] introduced a secret sharing scheme based on AES, where all cycle keys can be calculated on demand, resulting in a 25% reduction in running time. However, it employs an Sbox structure with a complexity less than 32, rendering it susceptible to linear crypt analysis and algebraic attacks. In addition, numerous researchers [22] have suggested RSA-based solutions. However, these schemes entail demanding prerequisites and intricate key generation processes, rendering one-time encryption unfeasible and unsuitable for the current medical setting. Searchable encryption [23], a novel cryptographic primitive, seeks to encrypt data files and store them on cloud servers. The encrypted data can be searched using keywords, enabling robust search capabilities while maintaining user privacy throughout the entire process. By this way, it effectively safeguards user privacy while significantly enhancing retrieval efficiency with the aid of the cloud server [24]. However, it is challenging to prevent the involvement of the cloud service provider in partial decipherment, and the cloud becomes vulnerable once compromised. In conclusion, the aforementioned solutions typically suffer from drawbacks, including high computational costs and inadequate security, making them unsuitable for the current IoT healthcare scenario.

Arecent study by [10] introduced a medical case retrieval scheme that utilizes the ElGamal Blind Signature. This scheme ensures privacy protection for both patients and hospital databases during the medical diagnosis process, while also reducing the matching delay in case retrieval. However, this scheme is unsuitable for the current IoT scenario, especially when dealing with avast disease database, as encrypting all disease information using ElGamal is not feasible. Moreover, patients have the potential to retrieve the keys of other disease information and compromise the security of the hospital's disease database through bruteforce traversal attacks. Therefore, based on this idea, Our scheme incorporates a Bloom filter during the disease matching phase, significantly reducing the server's computational cost. Additionally, it employs Oblivious Transfer to safeguard patient and database privacy during transmission.

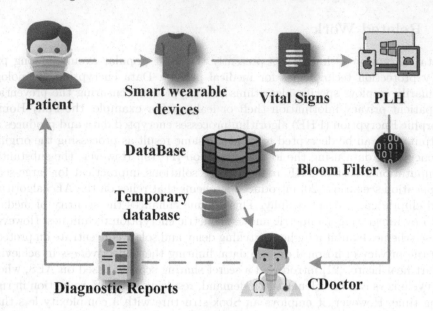

Fig. 1. The Framework

3 Preliminaries and Notations

3.1 Bloom Filter

Bloom filters were introduced by Bloom [11] as an efficient representation of data sets.

A Bloom filter, $\mathbf{BF} = (\mathbf{BF}[0], \ldots, \mathbf{BF}[j], \ldots, \mathbf{BF}[m-1])$ with a length of m that encodes a set S with a size of at most n into a bit string with a length of m bits. This is achieved by using k randomly selected hash functions, $(h_1, h_2, ..., h_k)$, where $h_i : \{0,1\}^* \rightarrow [0, 1, ..., m-1]$. In order to insert S into a Bloom filter, first initialize all indicators to 0. Then, for each x in S, set the indicators $h_1(x), h_2(x), ..., h_k(x)$ to 1. If an indicator is already 1, do nothing. Any party can verify whether an element is stored in a Bloom filter through a simple check process. Bloom filters have no false negatives error, as they are deterministic; when an element is represented in a Bloom filter, its indices are all set to 1 during the query phase.

Definition 1 (Represented element). *We say that an element, e, is represented in the Bloom filter, $\mathbf{BF}$, if we have that*

$$BF[h_i(e)] = 1, \quad \forall i \in \{1, \ldots, k\}$$

where $\{h_1, ..., h_k\}$ are the hash functions used in conjunction with $\mathbf{BF}$. We say that the set S is represented by $\mathbf{BF}$ if every element $e \in S$ is represented in $\mathbf{BF}$.

3.2 Oblivious Transfer

The oblivious transfer protocol was first proposed by Rabin [12] in 1981. Later, [13] improved the protocol and proposed the 1-out-of-n oblivious transfer protocol. In this protocol, the sender S has n secret messages $m_1, m_2, ..., m_n$. The receiver R selects the α-th message it wants to receive, and the S sends message m_α to R based on R's choice. During the entire process, the sender does not know which message R is searching for, and R does not know any information about the messages other than m_α. The 1-out-of-n oblivious transfer protocol is as follows:

Setup: The system generates a large prime number p to guarantee that the discrete logarithm problem is difficult to solve on G_p, G_p is a p-order subgroup of Z_p^*.

Input: The sender input $(m_1, m_2, ..., m_n)$, and R input α.

Output: The receiver output m_α, $1 \le \alpha \le n$.

1. Step 1: R generates a random number $r \in_R Z_p$ and calculates $y = g^r h^\alpha$. Then, the y is sent to the S.
2. Step 2: S generates a random number $k \in_R Z_p$ .Then, S sends $a = g^k$ and $c_i = m_i \oplus H((y/h^i)^k, i)$ to R, $i = 1, ..., n$.
3. Step 3: R computes $m_\alpha = c_\alpha \oplus H(a^r, \alpha)$ by a and c_α.

This is an efficient protocol: 2 modular exponentiations are required by R to compute y and a^r; 3 modular exponentiations are required by S to compute a, y^k, and h^k, and a and h^k can also be precomputed.

4 LPMDS

In this scheme, we have achieved a lightweight medical diagnosis scheme while protecting the privacy of patients and the hospital's disease database. Patients can match medical diagnosis reports with their physical condition based on their own vital signs. This chapter is mainly divided into two parts: system model and proposed solution, which introduce the composition parts of the protocol and detailed process.

4.1 The System Model

In this system, here are two key participants: the patient with their patient's local host (PLH) and the cloud doctor (CDoctor) with access to the disease database that contains treatment plans and vital sign information for each disease. PLH can collect vital sign information through sensor devices. PLH encrypt and upload these parameters to the CDoctor to obtain professional diagnostic results and achieve private self-diagnosis. It introduces oblivious transfer to protect the information between patient and CDoctor so that CDoctor gets no idea about the patient's vital signs and the patient has no information about CDoctor. In short, the proposed scheme can not only prevent CDoctor from disclosing, but also protect the patient's health date, personal privacy and their queries efficiently. With the introduction of a Bloom filter, cdoctor can directly filter out a temporary database containing the patient's diagnostic report using the patient's Bloom filter, which reduces computational and communication costs. The framework of the whole process is illustrated in Fig. 1. Regarding some detailed parameters in the system, we have provided supplementary information in Table 1.

Table 1. Notations

Notations	Description
PLH	patient's local host
CDD	Cloud Doctor's disease database
n	the number of disease information in the disease database
M^*	the query vector for the current patient
m_j^*	the j-th parameter in the current user's query vector
BF^*	the Bloom filter corresponding to the user's query vector M^*
D_i	the i-th disease in the Cloud Doctor's disease database
M_i	the feature vector of the i-th disease
m_j^i	the j-th parameter in the feature vector of the i-th disease
BF_i	the Bloom filter corresponding to the i-th disease
c_i	the disease diagnostic report of the i-th disease

4.2 The Proposed Scheme

Our scheme is mainly divided into two parts: the **initialization phase** and the **query phase**. The initialization phase involves generating system parameters and grouping disease information. In the query phase, the main task is to diagnose the patient's medical condition based on the patient's vital signs, which is also the most important phase. Throughout the entire query and diagnosis process, we must not only avoid revealing any patient's life characteristics but also accurately determine the patient's medical condition and provide a diagnosis report to the patient. This is a very challenging and conflicting task, however we have completed it using Bloom filters, polynomial encoding, and oblivious transfer.

To visualize the entire process of our scheme, we illustrate the grouping process of the initialization phase in Fig. 2 and the disease information query process in detail in Fig. 3.

4.3 System Initialization

During the initialization process, there are two main tasks: parameter generation and grouping disease information. Diseases with equal Bloom filter values will be

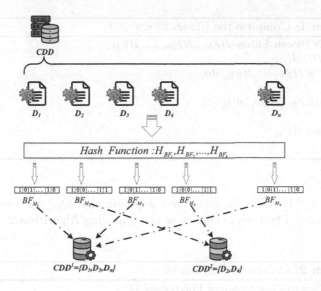

Fig. 2. Group Phase

grouped into a new temporary database, each temporary database is represented by a Bloom filter, The specific steps are as follows:

1. parameter generation
   - *Step 1:* The CDoctor randomly selects k hash functions, $H_{BF_1}, \ldots, H_{BF_k}$, to be used as the hash functions for the Bloom filter and generates n Bloom filters, each with an initial value of 0.
   - *Step 2:* The CDoctor selects a large prime number p to guarantee that the discrete logarithm problem is difficult to solve on G_p. It also chooses a generator $g \in G_p$ and a random number $h \in G_p$. The random numbers p, g, and h are public parameters that remain constant throughout the entire process.
   - *Step 3:* Select the secure hash function $H(.), H_2(.)$.

2. grouping of disease
   - *Step 1:* CDoctor compute the Bloom filters BF_{M_i} corresponding to disease information $D_i = \{M_i, d_i, i\}$ in the disease database, where $M_i = \{m_1^i, m_2^i, \ldots, m_v^i\}$. The pseudo code is as the following Algorithm 1.
   - *Step 2:* The CDoctor divides the disease information in the disease database into groups and generates several temporary disease databases $CDD^{(1)}, CDD^{(2)}, \ldots, CDD^{(u)}$. Bloom filter corresponding to each disease information in each temporary disease database is equal. For example, assuming a temporary database $CDD^{(\alpha)}$ containing m pieces of disease-related information it follows that $CDD^{(\alpha)} = \{D_{\alpha_1}, D_{\alpha_2}, \cdots, D_{\alpha_m}\}$ where $BF_{M_{\alpha_1}} = BF_{M_{\alpha_2}} = \cdots = BF_{M_{\alpha_m}}$.

Algorithm 1: Compute the Bloom filters

Result: N Bloom Filters $BF_{M_1}, BF_{M_2}, ..., BF_{M_n}$
1 Input: $CDD, H_{BF_j}, j = 1, ..., k$;
2 **for** $H_{BF_j} = H_{BF_1} \to H_{BF_k}$ **do**
3   **for** $t = 1 \to v$ **do**
4 | $let BF_{M_i}[H_{BF_j}[m_j^i]] = 1$
5   **end**
6   Output: BF_{M_i}
7 **end**

- *Step 3:* The CDoctor constructs a polynomial $Q(.)$ for each temporary database. The pseudo code is as the following Algorithm 2.

Algorithm 2: Construct Polynomial

Result: Newton Interpolating Polynomial $Q(.)$
1 Input: $CDD^{(\alpha)} = D_{\alpha_1}, D_{\alpha_2}, ..., D_{\alpha_m}$;
2 **for** $i = 1 \to m$ **do**
3 | $Q[i] = H(M_{\alpha_i})$
4 **end**
5 **for** $j = 2 \to m$ **do**
6   **for** $k = m \to jm$ **do**
7 | $Q[k] = (Q[k] - Q[k-1]/(\alpha_i - \alpha_{k-1}))$
8   **end**
9 **end**
10 **for** $i = m - 1 \to 0$ **do**
11 | $Q(x) = Q(x) * (x - \alpha_i) + Q[i]$
12 **end**
13 Output:$Q(.)$

After system initialization, each temporary database will have several disease information entries, one representing its Bloom filter and one interpolation polynomial $Q(.)$. For example $CDD^{(\alpha)} = \{\{D_{\alpha_1}, D_{\alpha_2}, ..., D_{\alpha_m}\}, Q(.), BF_\alpha\}$.

4.4   Query Phase

The query phase mainly consists of two phase: the filtering phase and the oblivious transfer phase. In the filtering phase, the PLH collects the patient's vital signs and processes them into vector form. The CDoctor filters out the temporary disease databases related to the patient's condition based on the patient's vital signs. In the oblivious transfer phase, the patient and CDoctor use the oblivious transfer protocol for the patient to obtain their diagnosis report. The specific steps are as follows:

1. *Filtering Phase*
    - *Step 1:* PLH collects the patient's physical parameters and processes them in the form of vectors to generate the patient's query vector $M^* = \{m_1^*, m_2^*, ..., m_v^*\}$.
    - *Step 2:* PLH calculates the Bloom filter BF^* that represents the patient's query vector M^* ,and sends it to CDoctor.
    - *Step 3:* The CDoctor obtains a Bloom filter BF^* and filters out the temporary disease database $CDD^{(\alpha)}$, where $BF_\alpha = BF^*$.
2. *Oblivious transfer phase*
    - *Step 1:* The CDoctor sends $Q(.)$ in $CDD^{(\alpha)}$ to PLH.
    - *Step 2:* After receiving the polynomial $Q(.)$, PLH calculates

$$\beta = Q(H(M^*)),$$

    where $1 \leq \beta \leq m$. PLH generates a random number $r \in_R Z_p$, calculates $y = g^r h^\beta$, and sends y to the CDoctor.
    - *Step 3:* The CDoctor receives y and selects a random number $k \in_R Z_p$ to calculates $\mu = g^k$. Then, the CDoctor encrypts each diagnostic report d_i to

$$c_i = d_i \oplus H_2((y/h^{\alpha_i})^k, \alpha_i)$$

    and sends both μ and $\{c_1, c_2, ..., c_m\}$ to PLH.
    - *Step 4:* PLH compute $d_\beta = c_\beta \oplus H_2(\mu^r, \beta)$ to obtain diagnostic report.

From the entire filtering phase, it can be seen that the patient's vital signs are calculated and uploaded to CDoctor in the form of a Bloom filter. CDoctor can determine which temporary database the patient's queried disease information is in, thus filtering out most of the data. In this process, CDoctor has no way to infer any information about the patient's vital signs from the Bloom filter uploaded by PLH. And the patient cannot infer any information about the disease database from the polynomial $Q(.)$. During the OT phase, the user will submit their selected index to CDoctor in the form of a commitment. CDoctor encrypts and sends each piece of information in the temporary database to PLH. In this process, the patient can only solve their own d_α, and CDoctor cannot obtain any information from the commitment value y.

5   Analysis

We consider a two-party secure computing model consisting of one Patient and a CDoctor, both of whom are honest and curious, and will not attack the system, however may attempt to gain more information from the information they have. CDoctor has a disease database and needs to provide secure computing services to patient.

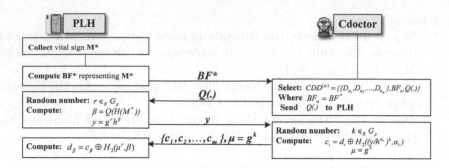

Fig. 3. Workflow of LPMDS

5.1 Security Analysis

Correctness: Since the disease database is a repository that includes all disease information, if there is a disease information D_β whose feature vector matches the patient's vital signs M^*, then after the filtering phase, the selected temporary disease database will definitely include the disease information D_β. Therefore, based on the correctness of the 1-out-of-n oblivious transfer protocol, the goal can be achieved if CDoctor and PLH correctly execute the protocol.

Patient Privacy Security: After the entire query process is completed, both CDoctor and any potential attacker can only learn about the patient's privacy information through the transmitted Bloom filter BF^* and y. However, it is known that attackers cannot break the BF^* and y due to the irreversibility of the Bloom filter and the one-way property of the discrete logarithm.

Disease Database Privacy Security: After the entire query process is completed, the patient can obtain information about the hospital's disease database through the polynomial $Q(.)$ and the ciphertext set $\{C_1, C_2, ..., C_m\}$. The polynomial $Q(.)$ is constructed from a set of points $\{(x_1, y_1), (x_2, y_2), ..., (x_m, y_m)\}$, and there are multiple sets of points $(x_1', y_1'), (x_2', y_2'), ..., (x_m', y_m')$ that construct the same polynomial. Therefore, even if the patient has unlimited computing power, they cannot learn any information about the disease database through the polynomial $Q(.)$. Furthermore, the ciphertext set $C_1, C_2, ..., C_m$ is secure based on the security of the 1-out-of-n oblivious transfer protocol, ensuring disease database privacy security (Table 2).

5.2 Performance Analysis

Our schedule has been implemented in Java and ran experimental programs on a computer with an AMD Ryzen 5 5600 6-Core Processor 3.50 GHz configuration, the performance of our schedule will be compared with several previous related schemes PMRSS [10], MPSI [19], SPA [21]. Because our protocol involves the participation of patients and cloud doctors, this section focuses only on the computational efficiency and communication overhead of the user and server.

Table 2. Communication Complexity Comparisons

Scheme	Number of Message Required	Number of Bite Required
PMRSS [10]	2 Message	15618
MPSI [19]	4 Message	8448
SPA [21]	4 Message	1368
Our	4 Message	5784

5.3   Computation Analysis

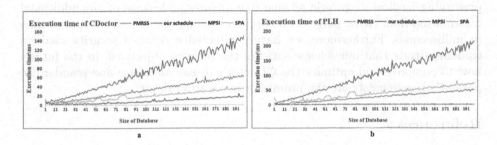

Fig. 4. Execution time

We selected 10,000 diseases as experimental data to ensure accuracy and representativeness. We randomly generated the health data of 10 patients as test samples and compared the computational efficiency of three protocols. As shown in Fig. 4a, our scheme has a higher computational efficiency than other schemes because we introduced a Bloom filter, which eliminates the need for the cloud doctor to encrypt all disease information in the disease database. This advantage will be significantly enhanced with the increase in data volume.

On the user side, the main task of the patient is to decrypt the ciphertext and obtain their own diagnostic report. Compared with other schemes, in our scheme, the patient only needs to decrypt one ciphertext to obtain the diagnostic report, while other schemes need to decrypt all the ciphertexts in the database, as shown in Fig. 4b. In terms of computational efficiency, our scheme is far superior to [10,19,21], both on the user and server side.

5.4   Communication Analysis

In this section, we will compare communication efficiency of our schedule with several previous related schemes [10,19], We set up a disease database containing ten thousand disease records, the bit length of disease record (d_i, M_i), (y, μ), bloom filter (BF^*), hash (H_1) output, and hash (H_2) output are 128,128, 32, 256, 256 bits. To make convincing comparisons, we analyzed a temporary database of 20 diseases, for which we constructed a 20-degree polynomial consisting of 21 coefficients, resulting in a size of 336 bits per polynomial. In our proposed scheme, the sizes of the information BF^*, $Q(.)$, y , and $(c_1, ..., c_m, \mu)$ were 32, 336, 128, and (20*258+128)=5288 bits, respectively. Adding these four values, the total communication cost of our schedule is 5784 bits.

6   Conclusion

In this scheme, we consider the problem of how to securely search a medical diagnosis report from CDoctor in IoT healthcare while protecting the security of both current patient's privacy and the hospital's disease database. By applying bloom filters and oblivious transfer protocols, we proposed a lightweight privacy preserving medical diagnostic scheme that ensures no leakage of any additional information from either party, while also controlling the system's response time in milliseconds. Furthermore, we have conducted a detailed security analysis to demonstrate that our scheme satisfies the security objectives. In the future, how to compress and optimize the CDoctor's disease database and standardize patient's requirements are the promising issues to work on.

References

1. Batista, E., Moncusi, M.A., López-Aguilar, P., Martínez-Ballesté, A., Solanas, A.: Sensors for context-aware smart healthcare: a security perspective. Sensors **21**(20), 6886 (2021)
2. Chen, Y., Zhang, L., Wei, M.: How does smart healthcare service affect resident health in the digital age? Empirical evidence from 105 cities of China. Front. Public Health **9**, 2423 (2022)
3. Zhang, Y., Chen, M., Huang, D., Wu, D., Li, Y.: iDoctor: personalized and professionalized medical recommendations based on hybrid matrix factorization. Futur. Gener. Comput. Syst. **66**, 30–35 (2017)
4. Yu, K., Tan, L., Shang, X., Huang, J., Srivastava, G., Chatterjee, P.: Efficient and privacy-preserving medical research support platform against COVID-19: a blockchain-based approach. IEEE Consum. Electron. Mag. **10**(2), 111–120 (2020) **17**(12), 8523–8530 (2021)
5. Yu, K., Tan, L., Aloqaily, M., Yang, H., Jararweh, Y.: Blockchain-enhanced data sharing with traceable and direct revocation in IIoT. IEEE Trans. Industr. Inf. **17**(11), 7669–7678 (2021)
6. Zhang, C., Lei, X., Strauss, J., Zhao, Y.: Health insurance and health care among the mid-aged and older Chinese: evidence from the national baseline survey of CHARLS. Health Econ. **26**(4), 431–449 (2017)
7. Barbosa, W., Zhou, K., Waddell, E., Myers, T., Dorsey, E.R.: Improving access to care: telemedicine across medical domains. Annu. Rev. Public Health **42**, 463–481 (2021)
8. Alnoman, A., Anpalagan, A.: Towards the fulfillment of 5G network requirements: technologies and challenges. Telecommun. Syst. **65**, 101–116 (2017)
9. Nilashi, M., Ahmadi, H., Shahmoradi, L., Ibrahim, O., Akbari, E.: A predictive method for hepatitis disease diagnosis using ensembles of neuro-fuzzy technique. J. Infect. Public Health **12**(1), 13–20 (2019)

10. Sun, Y., Liu, J., Yu, K., Alazab, M., Lin, K.: PMRSS: privacy-preserving medical record searching scheme for intelligent diagnosis in IoT healthcare. IEEE Trans. Industr. Inf. **18**(3), 1981–1990 (2021)

11. Bloom, B.H.: Space/time trade-offs in hash coding with allowable errors. Commun. ACM **13**(7), 422–426 (1970)

12. Rabin, M.O.: How to exchange secrets with oblivious transfer. Cryptology ePrint Archive (2005)

13. Tzeng, W.G.: Efficient 1-out-of-n oblivious transfer schemes with universally usable parameters. IEEE Trans. Comput. **53**(2), 232–240 (2004)

14. Vasan, D., Alazab, M., Venkatraman, S., Akram, J., Qin, Z.: MTHAEL: cross-architecture IoT malware detection based on neural network advanced ensemble learning. IEEE Trans. Comput. **69**(11), 1654–1667 (2020)

15. Sriram, S., Vinayakumar, R., Sowmya, V., Alazab, M., Soman, K.: Multi-scale learning based malware variant detection using spatial pyramid pooling network. In: IEEE INFOCOM 2020-IEEE Conference on Computer Communications Workshops (INFOCOM WKSHPS), pp. 740–745. IEEE (2020)

16. Davidson, A., Cid, C.: An efficient toolkit for computing private set operations. In: Pieprzyk, J., Suriadi, S. (eds.) ACISP 2017. LNCS, vol. 10343, pp. 261–278. Springer, Cham (2017). https://doi.org/10.1007/978-3-319-59870-3_15

17. Gentry, C.: A fully homomorphic encryption scheme. Stanford University (2009)

18. Rajan, D.P., Alexis, S.J., Gunasekaran, S.: Dynamic multi-keyword based search algorithm using modified based fully homomorphic encryption and Prim's algorithm. Clust. Comput. **22**, 11411–11424 (2019)

19. Bay, A., Erkin, Z., Hoepman, J.H., Samardjiska, S., Vos, J.: Practical multi-party private set intersection protocols. IEEE Trans. Inf. Forensics Secur. **17**, 1–15 (2022)

20. Das, S., Namasudra, S.: A novel hybrid encryption method to secure healthcare data in IoT-enabled healthcare infrastructure. Comput. Electr. Eng. **101**, 107991 (2022)

21. Laur, S., Talviste, R., Willemson, J.: From oblivious AES to efficient and secure database join in the multiparty setting. In: Jacobson, M., Locasto, M., Mohassel, P., Safavi-Naini, R. (eds.) ACNS 2013. LNCS, vol. 7954, pp. 84–101. Springer, Heidelberg (2013). https://doi.org/10.1007/978-3-642-38980-1_6

22. Rivest, R.L., Shamir, A., Adleman, L.: A method for obtaining digital signatures and public-key cryptosystems. Commun. ACM **21**(2), 120–126 (1978)

23. Bellare, M., Boldyreva, A., O'Neill, A.: Efficiently-searchable and deterministic asymmetric encryption. Cryptol. ePrint (2006)

24. He, W., Yan, G., Da, X., L.: Developing vehicular data cloud services in the IoT environment. IEEE Trans. Industr. Inf. **10**(2), 1587–1595 (2014)

Windows Fuzzing Framework Based on Dynamic Tracing and Process Cloning

Wei Long(✉)

University of Electronic Science and Technology of China (UESTC), Chengdu, China
longwei@std.uestc.edu.cn

Abstract. Existing security and fuzzing techniques for Windows operating systems have garnered substantial interest, but suffer from issues such as low efficiency, poor stability, challenges in circumventing the graphical user interface (GUI), and complicated interface framework construction. This paper introduces a method for creating a Windows platform Fork-Server based on process cloning technology, which improves fuzzer performance and stability. This method resolves the problems of low efficiency and unstable execution that are characteristic of existing fuzz testing methods. Moreover, This paper present a method for automating the construction of Fuzz Harness, which employs dynamic tracing technology to test the program's core code and bypass GUI and related code logic. This technique decreases the development threshold and testing costs of fuzz testing while tackling the challenges of difficult GUI bypass and interface framework construction. This paper designed and implemented a fuzz testing framework named LQSWIN, which we evaluated against WinAFL in six categories and eight Windows applications. Experimental results demonstrate that LQSWIN performs significantly better than WinAFL, executing an average of 9.42 times faster with a maximum speed increase of 22.25 times. Additionally, LQSWIN detected an average of 3.30 times more basic blocks.

Keywords: Fuzz testing · Fuzz Harness · Dynamic tracking · Process Cloning

1 Introduction

Fuzz testing is a testing method based on random inputs, which simulates unexpected user inputs by injecting data with randomness into the software. Through fuzz testing, various defects and vulnerabilities in the software can be discovered, including crashes, memory leaks, and security vulnerabilities. Compared with other testing methods, fuzz testing has advantages such as a high automation level, high test coverage, and high test efficiency. In the past few decades, various fuzzers [1–3] have discovered thousands of bugs in different fields [4, 5].

Currently, there is limited research on fuzz testing methods for Windows operating systems. The majority of fuzz testing techniques and methods are tailored toward Unix-like systems, making them challenging to direct translate to Windows systems. Recent reports indicate that Windows dominates the global desktop operating system market with a market share of 74.14%, surpassing other operating systems [7]. Meanwhile, the exploitation and discovery of software vulnerabilities on Windows has always been an area of great interest to malicious attackers, who invest a lot of effort in it [8, 9]. As such, fuzz testing for Windows software programs is of the utmost importance not only in academic research but also in industrial and practical network defense and attack fields.

In this paper, we employ the fuzz testing technique to detect security vulnerabilities in Windows applications. To design an effective fuzz testing method, we must address the following challenges:

1. Lack of stable and efficient fuzz testing methods for the Windows platform. Popular fuzzers under the Linux system adopt the architecture of Fork-Server to clone and run target programs, which greatly improves the execution speed of AFL [6] and other fuzzers on Linux by more than 2 times [10]. However, the Windows platform lacks a similar process cloning mechanism. Existing Windows fuzzers typically use re-execution mode and persistent mode [11, 12] to test programs, which suffer from low efficiency and unstable execution.
2. Windows GUI seriously impedes the fuzz testing process. Windows applications heavily rely on GUI to realize user interaction and rarely provide a command-line interface (CLI) for execution. Therefore, when conducting program testing on the Windows platform, it is a big challenge to avoid GUI-related code logic and focus on testing core code.
3. High cost of constructing interface programs. In practice, to conduct fuzz testing on closed-source Windows programs, corresponding interface programs need to be developed. This program does not have a strict name, "fuzz harness", "fuzzing harness", "fuzz driver", "harness", and "test harness" are all common names, with "fuzz harness" being the most frequently used [24]. However, writing an effective and reliable interface program is relatively difficult, requiring experienced security professionals to consume a lot of time and effort in program analysis.

To overcome the challenges outlined above, this paper proposes LQSWIN, a fuzz testing framework for Windows closed-source programs. The framework makes the following contributions:

- This paper presents a method for constructing a Fork-Server on the Windows platform using process cloning technology. This method can effectively avoid restarting and various initialization work, mitigate the problem of high resource consumption under the re-execution mode, and speed up the fuzz testing process, thus improving the efficiency of the fuzz testing. Meanwhile, this method restricts the execution impact of each test case to a single process by constantly copying and running the target program, avoiding the problem of mutual interference among multiple test cases under the persistent mode, which can effectively improve the stability of fuzz testing.
- LQSWIN reduces the manual effort required for program analysis and test code development by automating the construction of Fuzz Harness. This approach significantly lowers the development barrier and testing cost of fuzz testing, while improving the testing efficiency.

In summary, the main contributions of this paper are as follows:

1. A method for constructing a Windows platform Fork-Server is proposed, which enables the fuzzer to run efficiently and stably on the Windows platform.
2. A method based on dynamic tracing technology for automating the construction of Fuzz Harness is proposed. This method can effectively bypass GUI restrictions, significantly lower the development threshold and testing cost of fuzz testing, and make fuzz testing more automated.
3. The prototype framework called LQSWIN is designed and implemented, and its effectiveness is demonstrated through experiments.

2   Background and Motivation

2.1   Research on the Construction of Interface Frameworks

During the actual fuzz testing process, developers must create a corresponding program or interface framework, referred to as "Fuzz Harness" program in this paper. "Fuzz Harness" is a small program that contains processing functions for parsing external data. Its primary purpose is to simulate the operating environment and interface of the target program so that the test cases generated during the fuzz testing can be passed to the target program and the information, such as crash logs, memory leaks, and performance bottlenecks, can be collected during the program's runtime [15, 24]. An effective Fuzz Harness program can effectively bypass the GUI limitation, enable testing of the target program without any user interaction, and help the Fuzzer better explore the code path of the application program, thereby improving the efficiency of vulnerability detection [25].

The interface framework can be implemented using two primary methods: manual coding and automated construction. Manual coding is a complex method that necessitates developers to have an in-depth knowledge of the target program's internal structure and operational mechanism. Subsequently, relevant code must be added to create the Fuzz Harness. Automated construction is a quicker and more efficient method that can facilitate automated fuzz testing. Currently, some schemes automatically generate interface code, such as FUDGE [18] and FUZZGEN [19], which essentially automatically construct interface code by extracting API calls from source code, but only for open source software and cannot be applied to closed source programs. APICraft [20] and WINNIE [21] propose an interface code automatic generation scheme for closed source programs, which infers the API call relationship by collecting the program's runtime trajectory to complete the automatic construction of the Harness program.

2.2 Research on Fuzz Testing Method for Windows System

All major fuzzers under the Linux operating system employ the Fork-Server mode for conducting fuzz testing. Fork-Server's implementation primarily depends on the fork() function of the Linux system. it eliminates repetitive tasks such as loading target files and libraries, and resolving symbol addresses, thus speeding up the running speed of AFL and other fuzzers on Linux by more than two times. Moreover, Fork-Server enhances the testing process's stability by confining the execution impact of each test case to a single child process. This configuration precludes mutual interference between multiple test cases, thus minimizing errors and ensuring better test coverage [22, 23].

Unfortunately, Windows systems do not have a similar fork function or any suitable equivalent. Therefore, traditional fuzzing tools generally use a repeated execution method, that is, continuously launching new processes through the CreateProcess() function for testing. Distinct from Linux systems, Windows systems require multiple initialization operations to initiate an application, which results in lower testing efficiency using this approach.

To address the aforementioned issues, WinAFL [13] uses the persistent mode to test programs by looping through the target function, avoiding the repetitive process of starting the application. Compared with the traditional repeated execution method, the persistent mode can improve the efficiency of fuzz testing, saving ample time and system resources. However, the persistent mode also has some drawbacks. Firstly, since the target process does not terminate in the persistent mode, problems such as memory leaks and changes to global variables may arise. Secondly, continuous operation of the target process in persistent mode may have potential implications on system stability and security.

3 Design and Implementation

3.1 Overview

This paper proposes and designs a fuzz testing framework called LQSWIN for Windows closed-source programs. The basic workflow and primary components of LQSWIN, including the construction of Fuzz Harness and Fork-Server, are shown in Fig. 1.

1. Construction of Fuzz Harness: based on dynamic tracing technology, the Harness interface program is automatically generated by collecting dynamic behavioral information during program execution. The program contains the entire code logic of how the target program handles input data.
2. Construction of Fork-Server: based on process cloning technology, the Fork-Server for Windows platform is constructed to effectively avoid the problem of excessive resource consumption under the repeated execution mode and the mutual influence of multiple test cases under the persistent mode, thereby improving the efficiency and stability of the fuzz testing.

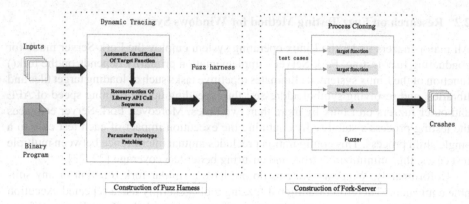

Fig. 1. Overview of LQSWIN

3.2 Automated Fuzz Harness Construction

This paper presents an automated method for constructing Fuzz Harness that applies dynamic execution tracing technology to overcome the limitations of traditional harness construction methods. By applying API monitoring and Hook techniques, execution traces are recorded automatically, and program dynamic behavior information is collected during application runtime. This automated approach to constructing Harness programs removes the requirement for manual program analysis and writing testing code, thus reducing the development threshold and testing cost associated with fuzz testing, while simultaneously enhancing testing efficiency. The automated Harness construction process consists of three main steps: automatic identification of the target function, reconstruction of library API call sequence, and parameter prototype patching, as shown in Fig. 2.

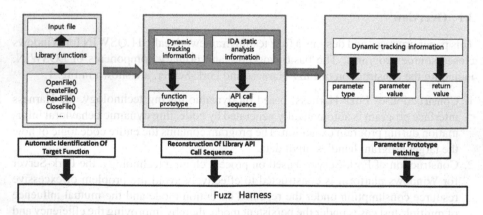

Fig. 2. Construction method and process of fuzz harness

Automatic Identification of Target Function
An ideal fuzzing target should possess several key characteristics [14]. To identify such targets, this paper adopts a feature-matching approach to search for potential target library functions. Specifically, this paper examines whether each library function call's parameter points to the input data file path, such as "C:\test\inputs.txt", and performs Hook operations on common file operation APIs such as OpenFile(), CreateFile(), ReadFile(), WriteFile(), etc., to record the callers of relevant APIs. If a library function takes the data file path as a parameter or calls APIs related to file operations, this paper determines it to be a file parsing function and considers it a potential testing target.

Reconstruction of Library API Call Sequence
Once the target function has been identified, a series of library APIs used by the function need to be dynamically loaded and called. This paper uses Hook technology to trace the execution process of the target function, record all function calls and register states to construct the API call sequence. Moreover, a hybrid analysis approach is employed, which combines the static analysis data provided by IDA Pro and the specific information recorded in dynamic tracing to deduce the prototype of the function, including function name, declaration type, number, and types of parameters.

Parameter Prototype Patching
When calling an API function, it is essential to accurately enter the parameter types, values, and return values. To obtain these key pieces of information, this paper uses dynamic tracing to record detailed information about the API function's pre-entry and post-exit parameters and return values, including all register states, stack space, and thread ID. Then, the function's parameter values and return values are dumped recursively. For output parameters, this paper first identifies whether a parameter is a pointer, and if so, monitors whether the content pointed to by the pointer changes before and after entering and exiting the API function. If there is a change, the parameter is considered an output parameter.

3.3 Stable and Efficient Windows Fork-Server

This paper proposes a method for constructing a Windows Fork-Server based on process cloning technology, which can effectively reduce the cost of restarting and various initializations, and avoid the problem of excessive resource consumption in repeated execution mode, thereby accelerating the process of fuzz testing and improving the efficiency of fuzz testing. Furthermore, by constantly copying and running the target program, the execution impact of each test case is limited to a single process, avoiding the problem of multiple test cases affecting each other in persistent mode, and effectively improving the stability of fuzz testing.

Windows Process Cloning
Currently, there are many studies on manual process creation, and the existing solutions are relatively mature. However, these solutions suffer from instability during runtime and high overhead, which cannot meet the requirements of efficient and low-cost fuzz testing. Therefore, to build a stable and efficient process cloning mechanism on Windows, this

paper proposes a method that utilizes the CSRSS (Client/Server Runtime Subsystem) to implement process cloning. This method provides a stable and efficient process cloning mechanism, which avoids frequent loading of target programs and dependent libraries, reduces the resource consumption of fuzz testing, and improves the efficiency of fuzz testing.

The CSRSS program essentially uses LPC (Local Procedure Call) for inter-process communication [16]. This paper mainly clarifies the roles of several key global variables in the communication process. These variables describe some basic memory mapping information provided by the CSRSS program to the client, such as server-side base address and view size, and the mapping relationship of shared memory heap, which are crucial for data exchange. Since these global variables are stored at a fixed (relative) address in the NTDLL library and this address changes with the version, they cannot be obtained using hardcoded methods. To address this issue, this paper parses the code part of NTDLL to find the instructions that reference these global variables and uses the reference to find their absolute addresses.

Specifically, NtCreateUserProcess() is the last function accessible in user mode, and by directly calling this function, the program can run normally with minimal effort, reducing system overhead in user mode [17]. Figure 3 shows the main implementation steps of process cloning. This paper creates a suspended process using the NtCreateUserProcess() function by using a specially constructed PS_CREATE_INFO structure parameter. Then, the absolute addresses of several global variables are found by analyzing the code part of NTDLL. A specific BASE_API_MSG structure parameter is constructed and the ntdll!CsrClientCallServer() function is called to send a message to the CSRSS process to notify it of the existence of the new process. Finally, the NtResumeThread() function is called to resume the process execution.

```
1   /* set Structure parameters of CreateInfo and  AttributeList , call NtCreateUserProcess */
2   NtCreateUserProcess(
3       &hProcess,
4       &hThread,
5       MAXIMUM_ALLOWED,
6       MAXIMUM_ALLOWED,
7       NULL,
8       NULL,
9       PROCESS_CREATE_FLAGS_SUSPENDED, /* suspended flag */
10      THREAD_CREATE_FLAGS_CREATE_SUSPENDED,
11      ProcessParameters,
12      &CreateInfo,                    /* PPS_CREATE_INFO struct */
13      &AttributeList                  /* PPS_ATTRIBUTE_LIST struct */
14      );
15
16  /* get the address of a global variable and return its address ( CsrPortHandle,
    /*CsrPortBaseTag, CsrPortHeap, CsrPortMemoryRemoteDelta, CsrProcessId ) */
17  find_csr_global_variable( GlobalNmae, &Address );
18
19  /* set  Structure parameters of ApiMsg , Connect to the CSRSS via CsrClientConnectToServer */
20  CsrClientCallServer(
21      &ApiMsg,                        /* PBASE_API_MSG struct */
22      captureBuffer,
23      CSR_MAKE_API_NUMBER( BASESRV_SERVERDLL_INDEX, BasepRegisterThread ),
24      sizeof(BASE_API_MSG) - sizeof(PORT_MESSAGE) );
25
26  /* resume */
27  NtResumeThread() ;
```

Fig. 3. Main implementation steps of process cloning

Agent-Based Application-Level Fuzzer

Currently, most fuzzing tools on the Windows platform are function-level and require knowledge of the target program's source code or reverse analysis to isolate functions for testing. However, this method is time-consuming and limits the development and extension of the fuzzer. This paper proposes a Fuzzer design that lowers the entry barrier for testers, enhances extensibility, and reduces testing costs by developing a Fork-Server based on WinAFL, as shown in Fig. 4. This Fuzzer has the following features: automated Fuzz Harness construction, stable and efficient process cloning, integration of other auxiliary tools and automated testing result analysis, etc. Through these steps, the Fuzzer can directly conduct fuzz testing on the entire application program, improve testing efficiency and stability, and greatly reduce testing costs. The Fuzzer in this paper mainly includes the following three objects:

- Fuzzer: The Fuzzer is the main process of fuzz testing, which is responsible for initializing the seed queue, generating test cases, analyzing code coverage, analyzing test results, handling crash events, etc.
- Agent: The automatically constructed Harness program is injected into the target program as an agent. The agent first performs Hook operations on the program entry and target function to detect the program execution status and check all basic blocks to collect code coverage. it is responsible for controlling the execution of the target program, analyzing where to insert tracking code in the target program, repeatedly copying the target function to run, and transmitting the input data generated by the Fuzzer to the agent for testing through a bidirectional pipeline. The agent reports the status to the Fuzzer after the target function execution is completed.
- Target function: Refers to the function or API in the tested program that needs to be fuzz tested.

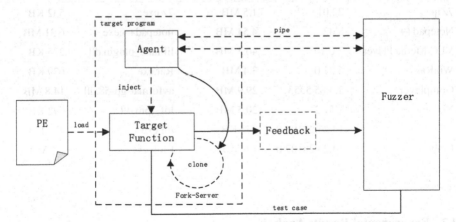

Fig. 4. Framework of agent-based fuzzer

4 Evaluation

This paper presents LQSWIN, a prototype fuzz testing framework designed for Windows closed-source software based on the existing fuzz testing platform WinAFL. The chapter aims to investigate and compare the applicability and effectiveness of LQSWIN and WinAFL in practical applications. The experiments in this paper are designed to answer the following questions:

- Q1: Applicability of LQSWIN: Does LQSWIN have the ability to test a wide range of Windows applications under real-world conditions?
- Q2: Effectiveness of LQSWIN: Can LQSWIN enhance fuzz testing performance, and if so, what degree of improvement can be achieved?

4.1 Experimental Design

This paper selected eight Windows closed-source applications, as shown in Table 1, for experimental analysis. The chosen programs represent six categories, including image processing, video processing, file compression, document processing, compiler, and linker. These programs have varying software sizes, spanning between 475 KB to 40.5 MB. Additionally, the experiments were conducted on a virtual machine running Windows 10–64 and a 2-core Intel(R) Core(TM) i7-7700 processor. WinAFL was set to persistent mode and compared with LQSWIN for testing. Each program was executed for 24 h, and three experiments were conducted for each program to collect average data.

Table 1. Program list

Program	Version	Program Size	Target	Target Size
7Zip	22.01	1.5 MB	7z.exe	532 KB
Notepad++	8.42	4.54 MB	notepad++.exe	6.31 MB
VLC Media Player	3.0.10	40.5 MB	libfaad_plugin.dll	275 KB
WinRar	6.21.0	3.4 MB	Rar.exe	629 KB
Gomplayer	2.3.85.5353	29.9 MB	avformat-gp-58.dll	14.8 MB
XnView	2.51.2	20.5 MB	ldf_jpm.dll	692 KB
ML	14.23.28107.0	475 KB	ml.exe	475 KB
Link	14.23.28107.0	1.6 MB	Link.exe	1.6 MB

4.2 Experimental Results Analysis

Table 2 presents the experimental analysis results, which primarily compare the applicability, running speed, and basic block count of the two tools to examine their performance difference. The experimental results indicate that LQSWIN is superior to WinAFL in terms of applicability and detection efficiency.

Table 2. Experimental analysis results

Program	Input	Size	Speed (exec/sec)		Coverage (BBs)	
			WinAFL	LQSWIN	WinAFL	LQSWIN
7Zip	.7z	1.5 MB	8.2	47.3 (5.76 × ↑)	1421	2106 (1.47 × ↑)
Notepad++	.txt	4.54 MB	✗ (time out)	44.7	✗	1035
VLC Media Player	.mp4	40.5 MB	5.4	25.8 (4.77 × ↑)	873	1721 (1.97 × ↑)
WinRar	.rar	3.4 MB	7.8	38.4 (4.92 × ↑)	1217	2915 (2.39 × ↑)
Gomplayer	.mp4	29.9 MB	1.2	26.7 (22.25 × ↑)	187	1384 (7.40 × ↑)
XnView	.jpg	20.5 MB	✗ (crash)	23.9	✗	16672
ML	.asm	475 KB	✗ (crash)	43.1	✗	2399
Link	.obj	1.6MB	✗ (time out)	36.5	✗	3257
Total				**(9.42 × ↑)**		**(3.30 × ↑)**

Q1: According to Table 2 and Fig. 5, LQSWIN supports more Windows applications than WinAFL. Specifically, LQSWIN first generates an effective Fuzz Harness program for all applications to perform fuzz testing. In contrast, WinAFL only tests four of the listed programs. Notably, XnView and ML crashed, while Notepad++ and Link timed out, rendering them unable to undergo effective testing. The reason for this failure is due to the persistent mode used by WinAFL, which is not stable enough and frequently terminates unexpectedly due to memory leaks, handle exhaustion, variable tampering, and other issues, resulting in crashes or timeouts.

Q2: According to Table 2 and Fig. 6, when a program can be tested by both LQSWIN and WinAFL at the same time, LQSWIN has faster execution speed and higher basic block coverage than WinAFL. Specifically, for the 4 programs that can be fuzz tested by both LQSWIN and WinAFL, LQSWIN has an average testing speed that is 9.42 times faster than WinAFL, with the highest improvement being 22.25 times faster. In addition, LQSWIN has discovered an average of 3.30 times more basic blocks than WinAFL. The results demonstrate that LQSWIN can effectively improve the efficiency of fuzz testing compared to WinAFL.

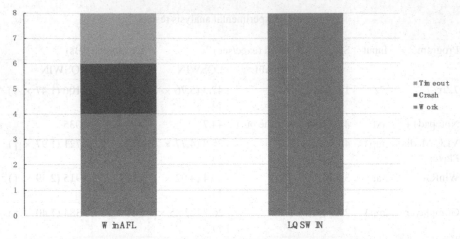

Fig. 5. Applicability of LQSWIN and WinAFL

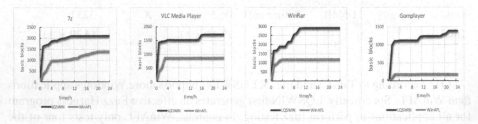

Fig. 6. Comparison of basic block coverage

5 Conclusion

This paper proposes LQSWIN, a fuzz testing framework for Windows that leverages dynamic tracing and process cloning. It is shown to be more suitable for testing a wide range of applications and has superior testing efficiency and coverage compared to the traditional fuzz testing tool, WinAFL. LQSWIN has a significantly broader range of applicability, reducing the need for manual analysis and code writing. The testing efficiency and coverage of LQSWIN were tested through a set of experiments consisting of eight applications, varying in file size and type. The results revealed that LQSWIN had an average testing speed of 9.42 times greater than that of WinAFL, with a maximum speed increase of 22.25 times. Additionally, LQSWIN discovered an average of 3.30 times more basic blocks.

References

1. Google. OSS-Fuzz (n.d.). https://github.com/google/oss-fuzz. Accessed 20 Apr 2023
2. Google. honggfuzz (n.d.). https://github.com/google/honggfuzz. Accessed 20 Apr 2023
3. LLVM. libFuzzer–a library for coverage-guided fuzz testing (n.d.). https://github.com/llvm-mirror/llvm/blob/master/docs/LibFuzzer.rst. Accessed 21 Apr 2023

4. Google. OSS-Fuzz: Five months later, and rewarding projects. Google Security Blog (2017). https://security.googleblog.com/2017/05/oss-fuzz-five-months-later-and.html. Accessed 20 Apr 2023
5. Rashid, M.: A collection of vulnerabilities discovered by the AFL fuzzer (afl-fuzz) (n.d.). https://github.com/mrash/afl-cve. Accessed 20 Apr 2023
6. Zalewski, M.: American fuzzy lop (n.d.). https://lcamtuf.coredump.cx/afl/. Accessed 20 Apr 2023
7. StatCounter Global Stats. Desktop Operating System Market Share Worldwide (n.d.). https://gs.statcounter.com/os-market-share/desktop/worldwide. Accessed 20 Apr 2023
8. Cyclonis. Advanced Persistent Threat (APT) (n.d.). https://www.cyclonis.com/threats/advanced-persistent-threat-apt/. Accessed 20 Apr 2023
9. Trellix. Feb 2023 Threat Report (n.d.). https://www.trellix.com/en-us/advanced-research-center/threat-reports/feb-2023.html. Accessed 20 Apr 2023
10. Kaminsky, M.: Fuzzing random programs without execve(). Michael Kaminsky's Blog (2014). https://lcamtuf.blogspot.com/2014/10/fuzzing-binaries-without-execve.html. Accessed 20 Apr 2023
11. AFL++. AFL++ Persistent mode (n.d.). https://github.com/AFLplusplus/AFLplusplus/blob/stable/instrumentation/README.persistent_mode.md. Accessed 20 Apr 2023
12. Zalewski, M.: New in AFL: Persistent mode. Michael Kaminsky's Blog (2015). https://lcamtuf.blogspot.com/2015/06/new-in-afl-persistent-mode.html. Accessed 20 Apr 20 2023
13. Google Project Zero. A fork of AFL for fuzzing Windows binaries (n.d.). https://github.com/googleprojectzero/winafl. Accessed 20 Apr 2023
14. Google Project Zero. How to select a target function (n.d.). https://github.com/googleprojectzero/winafl#how-to-select-a-target-function. Accessed 20 Apr 2023
15. Bishop Fox. Fuzzing (aka Fuzz Testing) (n.d.). https://bishopfox.com/blog/fuzzing-aka-fuzz-testing. Accessed 20 Apr 2023
16. j00ru. Windows CSRSS Write-up: Inter-Process Communication (Part 2) (2010). https://j00ru.vexillium.org/2010/07/windows-csrss-write-up-inter-process-communication-part-2/. Accessed 20 Apr 2023
17. Microsoft. Using process creation properties to catch evasion techniques (2022). https://www.microsoft.com/en-us/security/blog/2022/06/30/using-process-creation-properties-to-catch-evasion-techniques/. Accessed 20 Apr 2023
18. Babić, D., et al.: Fudge: fuzz driver generation at scale. In: Proceedings of the 2019 27th ACM Joint Meeting on European Software Engineering Conference and Symposium on the Foundations of Software Engineering, pp. 975–985 (2019)
19. Ispoglou, K., Austin, D., Mohan, V., Payer, M.: FuzzGen: automatic fuzzer generation. In: Proceedings of the 29th USENIX Conference on Security Symposium, pp. 2271–2287 (2020)
20. Zhang, C., et al.: APICraft: fuzz driver generation for closed-source SDK libraries. In: 30th {USENIX} Security Symposium ({USENIX} Security 21), pp. 2811–2828 (2021)
21. Jung, J., Tong, S., Hu, H., Lim, J., Jin, Y., Kim, T.: WINNIE: fuzzing windows applications with harness synthesis and fast cloning. In: Proceedings of the 2021 Network and Distributed System Security Symposium (NDSS 2021) (2021)
22. Smetsers, R., Moerman, J., Janssen, M., Verwer, S.: Complementing model learning with mutation-based fuzzing. arXiv preprint arXiv:1611.02429 (2016)
23. Tong, S.: Efficient Windows Application Fuzzing with Fork-server (2021)
24. Dissanayake, S.J.: Fuzz Driver Generation. Dissertation (2022)
25. Lakshminarayan, S.: Fuzzing: A Comparison of Fuzzing Tools. University of Twente (2023)

Meta-HFMD: A Hierarchical Feature Fusion Malware Detection Framework via Multi-task Meta-learning

Yao Liu(ID), Xiaoyu Bai(ID), Qiao Liu(✉)(ID), Tian Lan(ID), Le Zhou, and Tinghao Zhou

University of Electronic Science and Technology of China, Chengdu 610054, Sichuan, China
{liuyao,qliu,lantian1029}@uestc.edu.cn,
{202121090126,202222090440,202222090441}@std.uestc.edu.cn

Abstract. With the proliferation of malware, malware detection techniques have become more critical to protect the security and privacy of users. While existing malware detection techniques have achieved superior accuracy and detection rates, most of these techniques require a large number of labeled samples for training. In general, assembling a large amount of reliable data is still expensive, time-consuming, and even impossible. These malware detection techniques do not achieve good results on a small number of labeled samples and do not have the capability to detect new or variant malware. Therefore, it is necessary to investigate solutions for detecting malware in the few-shot scenario. This paper proposes a hierarchical feature fusion malware detection framework based on multi-task meta-learning, namely Meta-HFMD. The proposed framework first adopts a hierarchical feature fusion approach to learn hierarchical spatial traffic features from packet-level and flow-level. Then, it constructs an efficient multi-task malware detection model based on model-agnostic meta-learning (MAML), which can detect malware with tiny labeled samples. Experimental results demonstrate that Meta-HFMD achieves satisfactory results in the few-shot malware detection task, both in single-platform and cross-platform environments, and its performance metrics outperform other baseline models.

Keywords: Malware detection · Meta-learning · Hierarchical feature fusion · Few-shot learning

1 Introduction

Malware is defined as "a generic term that includes viruses, trojan, spyware and other intrusive code", any software that intentionally executes a malicious load on a victim machine (computer, mobile device, etc.) is considered malware [26].

At present, the mainstream malware detection methods are machine learning-based and deep learning-based. (i) Machine learning methods first extract manually designed features from network traffic and then use traditional machine learning algorithms for classification. MLDriod [17] uses four different machine learning algorithms in parallel to achieve a 98.8% detection rate. Liu et al. [3] extracts features from network traffic, reduces the dimension of features, and uses an improved SVM algorithm to detect malware. While machine learning approaches can achieve great results in some specific scenarios, it is undeniable that current machine learning approaches are data-driven statistical methods that rely heavily on feature engineering and extensive prior expert knowledge. (ii) Deep learning methods use neural networks to automatically extract features from the raw bytes of traffic. For example, IMCEC [25] uses a CNN architecture to convert network traffic into images for malware detection. The performance of deep learning depends on the size of the dataset, hence deep learning usually requires a large amount of data as support, which otherwise often leads to overfitting.

In view of the problems described above, the technique of few-shot learning has been proposed, which aims to learn a solution to a problem from few-shot samples. Meta-learning is one of the essential branches in the field of few-shot learning, which uses prior knowledge to quickly generalize to new tasks [33]. Using meta-learning for malware detection is a novel direction. Currently, ConvProtoNet [35] is a modified prototypical network architecture for few-shot malware detection, which achieves an average accuracy of over 70% with only 5 examples per class. Bai et al. [34] proposes a method based on Siamese network. The above two methods can effectively solve the few-shot learning problem, but the limitations are also evident. They used a technique based on the Windows PE file dataset, which is a static malware detection method. Static detection is performed without the malware being executed. It is not suitable for malware detection in real-world network environments. Dynamic detection is typically carried out by performing malware in a controlled environment, such as extracting the deep features of network traffic for classification (flow-level [4] or packet-level [16]). The limitation of the existing few-shot malware dynamic detection technology is that they only extract the deep features of a single level (flow-level or packet-level), ignoring the correlation between the features of each level, resulting in a waste of information to a certain extent.

To address such issues, in this paper, we propose a hierarchical feature fusion malware detection framework, namely Meta-HFMD, which is based on multitask meta-learning. It is a meta-learning based framework for few-shot malware detection. Experimental results show that Meta-HFMD is capable of performing malware detection tasks with elevated accuracy when new malware variants appear in early stages and the number of samples is limited, and it achieves satisfactory results on cross-platform malware detection tasks.

The main contributions of our research can be summarized as follows:

- We design a hierarchical features fusion method for few-shot malware detection, which can automatically exploit more abundant spatio-temporal features from large-scale unlabeled network traffic. The hierarchical convolutional layers extract flow-level and packet-level traffic features, respectively, and then concatenate them to obtain flow-packet-level features. This approach can effectively combine the advantages of flow-level and packet-level traffic features to significantly improve the few-shot malware detection metrics.

- We develop an efficient multi-task meta-learning malware detection framework (Meta-HFMD) based on MAML model. This few-shot malware detection framework updates the temporary model parameters in the inner loop and the meta-learning algorithm parameters in the outer loop, so that the current task can obtain a large amount of prior knowledge formed by the existing tasks. In other words, our framework can quickly detect emerging unknown malware from large-scale network traffic with few-shot or even one-shot labeled training data.

- We compare the performance of Meta-HFMD with the other start-of-the-art frameworks based on few-shot learning. In both single-platform and cross-platform experiments, Meta-HFMD outperforms the others by a large margin. The ablation studies verify that the hierarchical flow-packet-level hybrid features can help the framework to detect malware more efficiently and accurately than the single packet-level and flow-level features in the few-shot scenarios.

The remainder of the paper is organized as follows. We first present related work on few-shot malware detection in Sect. 2. Second, the implementation details of the Meta-HFMD framework are elaborated in Sect. 3. Then we the experimental results and analyze the results in Sect. 4. Finally, Sect. 5 summarizes the paper and looks forward to future work.

2   Related Work

2.1   Malware Detection

In the early years, signature-based detection methods were the dominant approach for malware detection. These methods compare various monitored or collected data with existing signature databases. Malicious behavior is determined when activity is observed that matches the signature database [9]. Uddin et al. [24] proposed a new model called Signature-based Multi-Layer IDS using mobile agents, which can detect imminent threats with extremely high success rate by dynamically and automatically creating and using small and efficient multiple databases. These signature-based method have fast detection speed, but it fails to detect unknown malware without an existing signature.

In recent years, malware detection methods based on machine learning and deep learning are on the rise. The malware detection technology based on machine learning firstly extracts multi-dimensional features from the original files (Windows PE, PCAP, etc.), and then inputs them into the machine learning algorithm for detection. Yang et al. [32] proposed an Android malware detection model based on Decision Tree (DT) and Support Vector Machine (SVM) algorithm (DT-SVM), which uses n-gram model to generate feature vectors of samples. Khammas et al. [13] proposes a ransomware detection method based on static analysis, which uses frequent pattern mining to extract 1000 features from raw bytes and uses Random Forest classifier for detection. Compared with machine learning based methods, complex feature engineering and domain expert knowledge are not required for methods based on deep learning, which uses neural networks that consider raw bytes as input and embed them in a high-latitude feature space. Nataraj et al. [19] first proposed to visualize malware binaries as grayscale images, and they used GIST descriptor [20] to extract global image attributes as input features for KNN. Vu et al. [27] proposes the AdMat framework, which builds adjacency matrices for each app, and these matrices act as input images for the CNN. Wang et al. [28] proposed a new intrusion detection system. It is called the hierarchical spatial-temporal features-based intrusion detection system (HAST-IDS). The system uses CNN and long short-term memory (LSTM) networks to learn the low-level spatial features and high-level temporal features of traffic to complete the classification task, respectively. The success of deep learning based methods also has obvious limitations [18]. For example, successes have largely been in areas where vast quantities of data can be collected or simulated, and where huge compute resources are available [10]. They are not suitable for some scenarios where data is intrinsically rare or expensive [1], or compute resources are unavailable [12].

2.2 Meta Learning

A promising paradigm for few-shot learning is meta-learning. Meta-learning is defined as "learning how to learn" [23]. Meta-learning aims to improve the learning algorithm itself, given the experience of multiple learning episodes. For example, this objective could be the generalization performance or the learning speed of the inner algorithm [10]. Various meta-learning methods have been proposed. Finn et al. [6] introduced a meta-learning category called model-agnostic meta-Learning(MAML). The idea is to learn an initial set of parameters that can be sufficiently generalized to allow the model to converge quickly with only a few steps of gradient descent.

Meta-learning techniques have also been used in the field of malware detection. ConvProtoNet [35] is an improved prototypical network architecture for few-shot malware detection. To prevent overfitting, ConvProtoNet designs a convolutional induction module to replace the insufficient prototype reduction in most few-shot models. With only 5 samples per class, it can achieve an average accuracy of more than 70%. Bai et al. [34] introduces a malware detection model based on Siamese network, which trains an effective multilayer perceptron network for embedding malware applications into a real-valued, continuous vector space to determine whether they belong to the same or different classes of malware. Chai et al. [5] proposes a dynamic prototype network based on sample adaptation for few-shot malware detection (DPNSA). DPNSA uses dynamic convolution to achieve sample-based adaptive dynamic feature extraction. Other similar research works include UMVD-FSL [4], AMDetector [15], CSNN [8], etc. While these aforementioned malware detection models achieve excellent results, most of them are based on metric-based meta-learning, which relies on similarity measures between unseen tasks and previously learned models. The prerequisite is that the unseen task shares the similarity structure with the previous tasks. Otherwise, unseen tasks are not identifiable under the framework of similarity-based meta-learning methods. In this paper, we want to design a more flexible framework based on MAML that is applicable to vastly different tasks. MAML provides fast and accurate generalization of deep neural network models without imposing any model assumptions. In other words, MAML is applicable to any learner model optimized with stochastic gradient descent. In addition, current malware detection models use single-level features from packets, flows, or sessions. We design a hierarchical feature fusion approach adopted in our framework, which is able to capture more layer-wise spatial features from both packet and flow levels and leads to better performance.

3 Multi-task Malware Detection

In this section, the problem definition of meta-learning based malware detection is first introduced in Sect. 3.1. Secondly, the overall framework of Meta-HFMD and its specific implementation details are elaborated in Sect. 3.2.

3.1 Problem Definition

Meta-learning is divided into two phases: meta-training and meta-testing. Different from traditional machine learning/deep learning, the training unit of meta-learning is "task". As shown in Fig. 1, each task can be divided into support set and query set. Specifically, N classes are randomly selected from the meta-training dataset or the meta-testing dataset, and K samples are selected from each class without replacement. A total of $N \times K$ samples constitute the support set. Then select Q samples from each class (N classes in the support set) to form the query set. It is worth noting that although the support set and query set share categories, the samples do not coincide.

In meta-training phase, the algorithm parameter ω is specified in advance, and ω is usually referred to as cross-task knowledge or meta-knowledge [10]. The dataset is denoted as $\mathcal{D}$ and assuming that meta-training has M tasks, $\mathcal{D}_{train} = \left\{ \left(\mathcal{D}_{train}^{support}, \mathcal{D}_{train}^{query} \right)^{(i)} \right\}_{i=1}^{M}$.

Meta-training can be formalized as bi-level optimization:

$$\omega^* = \arg\min_{\omega} \sum_{i=1}^{M} \mathcal{L}^{meta} \left(\theta^{*(i)}(w), \mathcal{D}_{train}^{query(i)} \right) \tag{1}$$

$$\text{s.t.} \quad \theta^{*(i)}(w) = \arg\min_{\theta} \mathcal{L}^{task} \left(\theta, \omega, \mathcal{D}_{train}^{support(i)} \right) \tag{2}$$

where $\mathcal{L}^{meta}$ and $\mathcal{L}^{task}$ refer to outer loop loss function and inner loop loss function (e.g. cross-entropy for classification problems), respectively. Here, ω can also refer to the initialization parameter of the few-shot learning model. Parameter ω does not change during each task training.

Task

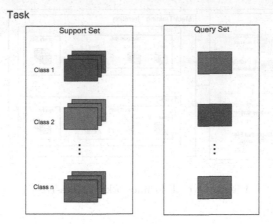

Fig. 1. Task in Meta-Learning

In the meta-testing phase, suppose that there are J tasks, then $\mathcal{D}_{test} = \left\{ \left(\mathcal{D}_{test}^{support}, \mathcal{D}_{test}^{query} \right)^{(i)} \right\}_{i=1}^{J}$. We first train on the support set, i.e., fine-tune ω^*. Meta-testing for new task j can be formalized as:

$$\theta^* = \arg\min_{\theta} \mathcal{L}^{task} \left(\theta, \omega^*, \mathcal{D}_{test}^{support(j)} \right) \tag{3}$$

Finally, we use the parameter θ^* after fine-tuning to make predictions on $\mathcal{D}_{test}^{query(j)}$.

3.2 Meta-HFMD Framework

The overall framework of the proposed Meta-HFMD is shown in Fig. 2, which contains two parts: the data preprocessing step and the malware detection step.

The first step is data preprocessing. The first 784 bytes of each flow are converted into flow-level grayscale images of $1 \times 28 \times 28$. The first six packets of each flow are considered, the first 100 bytes of each packet are converted into grayscale images of $1 \times 10 \times 10$, that is, six grayscale images of $1 \times 10 \times 10$ (see Sect. 3.2 for details). This paper proposes a hierarchical features fusion technique (see Sect. 3.2 for details). Hierarchical CNNs are used to extract the local spatial features from packet-level images and the overall spatial features from flow-level images, respectively. After concatenation, the flow-packet-level features are input to the fully connected layers for malware detection.

The second step is malware detection based on meta-learning. We use MAML as meta-learning model (see Sect. 3.2 for details), meta-training trains a model f_θ with strong generalization. After several fine-tuning on the support set of the meta-testing task, the classification model f_{θ^*} for this new task can be obtained, then the malware detection in the query set is finished.

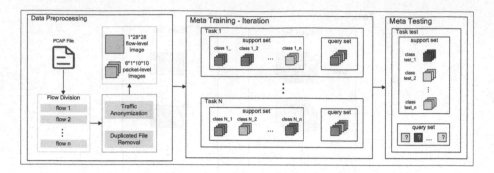

Fig. 2. Overall Framework of Meta-HFMD

Data Preprocessing

Flow and session are the basic units that are often used to segment traffic data in the field of traffic classification. Flow is defined as a set of packets with the same 5-tuple (source IP, source port, destination IP, destination port, transport protocol). Session consists of a bidirectional flow between two communication objects, which contains more interactive information compared to a single-directional flow. In this paper, the session is chosen as the traffic splitting unit. Because session is a bidirectional flow, the "session-level" is also called "flow-level".

Essentially, the network traffic processed in a computer can be regarded as a time series, and accordingly, this series can be overlaid in the space and time and visualized as an image. An advantage of visual representation is that it can be used to efficiently observe the overall situation corresponding to network traffic [31].

Data preprocessing is divided into the following three steps.

(1) Flow dividing. The "bidirectional flow" (hereinafter referred to as "flow") is used as the traffic division unit. Because session is a bidirectional flow, the 5-tuple (source IP, source port) and (destination IP, destination port) are interchangeable when dividing flows. Unlike other similar malicious detection works, only flows with at least six packets are retained and flows with less than six packets are discarded in this paper. When a flow contains more than 6 packets, only the first 6 packets are retained.

(2) Traffic cleaning. First, traffic anonymization is performed, which means that MAC and IP addresses are randomized. In LAN (Local Area Network), there is a strong correlation between MAC/IP address and label, if it is used for training, the accuracy will be very high in LAN, but it is not feasible in WAN (Wide Area Network). Second, removing duplicated files is carried out, that is, remove PCAP files with the same content to avoid training bias [4].

(3) Traffic images generating. The first 784 bytes of flow (less than 784 bytes are filled with 0x00 to 784 bytes) are extracted firstly to form a $1 \times 28 \times 28$ flow-level grayscale image, and each byte of the original data represents a pixel. Second, the first 100 bytes of the first 6 packets in one flow (less than 100

bytes are filled with 0x00 to 100 bytes) are used to form $1 \times 10 \times 10$ packet-level grayscale images, respectively, i.e., there are six $1 \times 10 \times 10$ packet-level grayscale images per flow.

Hierarchical Feature Fusion

Network traffic has a clear hierarchical structure, i.e., byte-packet-flow. Multiple traffic bytes are combined to form a network packet, and multiple network packets communicated between two sides are further combined to form a network flow [28].

URLNet [11] receives URL strings as input and extracts Character-level and Word-level features using Character-level CNNs and Word-level CNNs, respectively. Both Character-level and Word-level CNNs are optimized to learn the URLNet prediction model. HAST-IDS [28] is an intrusion detection model using spatial-temporal features of flows. The hyper-parameter experiment of HAST-IDS shows the best performance is achieved when (i) the first 784 bytes of each flow are selected, (ii) the first 6 packets are selected per flow, (iii) the first 100 bytes of each packet are selected.

Inspired by the aforementioned two works, a novel hierarchical features fusion technique is designed in this paper, as shown in Fig. 3. Hierarchical CNNs are used to learn the hierarchical spatial features from the packet-level and flow-level images. For a flow, a grayscale image of $1 \times 28 \times 28$ is obtained from the data pre-processing phase, flow-level CNNs (5×5 Conv2d, 8 filters$\rightarrow ReLU \rightarrow$ Batch Normalization$\rightarrow 2 \times 2$ MaxPool2d$\rightarrow 5 \times 5$ Conv2d, 16 filters$\rightarrow ReLU \rightarrow$ Batch Normalization$\rightarrow 2 \times 2$ MaxPool2d) are used to extract the overall spatial features from the flow-level image, namely flow-level features. For each packet in this flow, we use packet-level CNNs (3×3 Conv2d, 5 filters$\rightarrow ReLU \rightarrow$ Batch Normalization$\rightarrow 2 \times 2$ MaxPool2d) to extract the local spatial features from $1 \times 10 \times 10$ images, resulting in six packet-level features after this step. Six packet-level features and one flow-level features are concatenated to obtain flow-packet-level fussion features, namely hierarchical features.

Training Strategy

The training strategy of Meta-HFMD is shown in Algorithm 1.

In meta-training, the model parameters θ are first randomly initialized. We sample a set of tasks T from meta-training set $\mathcal{D}_{train}$. For each task $\mathcal{T}_i$ in T, we perform base learner optimization, which uses an inner loop (shown in line 5 of Algorithm 1) to obtain optimal parameters $\theta_i{}'$ for $\mathcal{T}_i$. It is crucial to note that inner loop does not change the model parameters θ. After the inner loops of all tasks, the outer loop in line 7 of Algorithm 1 is carried out to update the model parameters θ.

In meta-testing, we sample a task $\mathcal{T}_{test}$ that never seen before from $\mathcal{D}_{test}$. Then, we fine-tune parameters on support set with gradient updates in just a few steps. After that, the optimal parameters θ^* for $\mathcal{T}_{test}$ are obtained. Finally, the fine-tuned model f_{θ^*} is used to evaluate the performance of malware detection on query set.

Algorithm 1. Meta-HFMD

Input:

$\mathcal{D}_{train}$, $\mathcal{D}_{test}$: meta-training dataset, meta-testing dataset

α, β: meta learning rate, inner learning rate

f_θ: hierarchical features fusion malware detection model with parameter θ

1: **Meta-training:**

2: Randomly initialize θ

3: Sample batch of meta-training tasks $\mathcal{T} \sim \mathcal{P}(\mathcal{D}_{train})$

4: **for** $\mathcal{T}_i \in \mathcal{T}$ **do**

5:    **Base learner optimization:**

   Obtain the optimal parameters θ_i' for task $\mathcal{T}_i$:

$$\theta_i' = \theta - \beta \nabla_\theta \mathcal{L}_{\mathcal{T}_i^{support}}(f_\theta)$$

   where $\mathcal{T}_i^{support}$ indicates support set of $\mathcal{T}_i$

6: **end for**

7: Update $\theta \leftarrow \theta - \alpha \nabla_\theta \sum_{\mathcal{T}_i} \mathcal{L}_{\mathcal{T}_i^{query}}(f_{\theta_i'})$

8: **Meta-testing:**

9: Sample a meta-testing task $\mathcal{T}_{test} \in \mathcal{D}_{test}$

10: Obtain the optimal parameters θ^* for task $\mathcal{T}_{test}$:

$$\theta^* = \theta - \beta \nabla_\theta \mathcal{L}_{\mathcal{T}_{test}^{support}}(f_\theta)$$

11: Evaluate the model on $\mathcal{T}_{test}^{query}$ using f_{θ^*}

Output: Evaluation indicators in meta-testing stage

---

4 Experiment

4.1 Dataset

In this section, we describe the datasets used in our experiments. Windows PE files are the dataset used by literature [5,34,35], these methods belong to static malware detection. In contrast, dynamic malware detection is typically performed by executing malware in a controlled environment, which is more representative of malware behavior. We used a total of three traffic datasets: CICAndMal2017 [14], MCFP [22] as the malware dataset source, and BEN-1 [2] as the benign software dataset source. These three traffic datasets used in this paper are PCAP files captured in real-world environments with malicious/benign software dynamic running. The overview of CICAndMal2017, MCFP and BEN-1 dataset is shown in Table 1.

CICAndMal2017 is an Android malware dataset published by the University of New Brunswick. Malware samples in the CICAndMal2017 dataset are divided into four categories: Adware, Ransomware, Scareware, and SMS Malware. There are several malware families within each category. For example, Ransomware includes: Charger, Koler, etc. There are 42 malware families in CICAndMal2017. MCFP (Malware Capture Facility Project) is a sister project of the Stratosphere IPS Project. MCFP dataset has many malware families, Refer to [4], from which

Table 1. Overview of CICAndMal2017, MCFP and BEN-1 Datasets

Category	Dataset	Number of Classes	Number of Samples
Malicious	CICAndMal2017	42	470376
	MCFP	36	881761
Benign	BEN-1	20	13576

we select 36 malware families, such as Andrometa, Barys, Zeus, etc. As the source of the benign software dataset, BEN-1 has 20 benign software families such as baidu, taobao, amazon, etc. See Table 2 for details of the three datasets.

Table 2. Details of CICAndMal2017, MCFP and BEN-1 Datasets

Category	Dataset	Software Name									
Malicious	CICAndMal2017	Youmi	Koler	Jisut	RansomBO	Dowgin	FakeJobOffer	FakeTaoBao	Biige	PornDroid	WannaLocker
		Pletor	koodous	Simplocker	AVpass	fakenotify	jifake	Mobidash	Gooligan	Charger	AVforandroid
		Beanbot	Svpeng	fakeinst	Feiwo	fakemart	AndroidSpy.277	FakeAV	Nandrobox	FakeApp	zsone
		Penetho	mazarbot	LockerPin	Selfmite	FakeApp.AL	VirusShield	plankton	AndroidDefender	Shuanet	Ewind
		Kemoge	smssniffer								
	MCFP	Andrometa	Artemis	BAB0	Barys	Bundled	Bunitu	Cerber	Cobalt	CoreBot	Downware
		Dridex	Emotet	Geodo	Htbot	Kazy	Kelihos	Magic Hound	Locky	MediaGet	Miuref
		Ncurse	ReImage	OpenCandy	PUA	Razy	Ammyy	Shifu	Stlrat	TrickBot	Trickster
		Trojan	Ursnif	WannyCray	Worm	Yakes	Zeus				
Benign	BEN-1	amazon	baidu	bing	douban	facebook	google	imdb	instagram	iqiyi	jd
		neteasemusic	qqmail	reddit	taobao	ted	tieba	twitter	weibo	youku	youtube

4.2 Implementation Details

All experiments in this paper were run on the server, the hardware and software information are listed as follows: Operating System: Ubuntu 20.04.4 LTS, CPU: i7-c8700k@3.70 GHz, Memory: 46 GB, GPU: 2 × NVIDIA GeForce RTX 3090. Hyper-parameter settings are shown in Table 3. *meta_ learning_ rate* means the learning rate of the outer loop in MAML, namely α in Algorithm 1 line 7. *inner_ learning_ rate* means the learning rate of inner loop in MAML, namely β in Algorithm 1 line 5 and line 10. *meta_ batch_ size* means the number of tasks in a batch, can also be interpreted as the number of inner loops in a batch. *adaptation_ steps* specifies how many steps of gradient descent/gradient update are required in an inner loop. *query_ shots* means the number of samples of each class in query set. *num_ test_ task* means the number of tasks in meta-testing. And we use Adam as *optimizer* of our frame.

As for the neural network part, we design flow-level and packet-level CNNs to extract the spatial features at the corresponding levels, and then concatenate the flow-level and packet-level features. This is called hierarchical features fusion technique, also called flow-packet-level features extraction technique. The structure of convolutional layers is shown in Fig. 3. Specifically, the parameters of flow-level CNNs are listed below: *5 × 5 Conv2d, 8 filters→ReLU→Batch Normalization→2 × 2 MaxPool2d→5 × 5 Conv2d, 16 filters→ReLU→Batch Normalization→2 × 2 MaxPool2d*. The parameters of packet-level CNNs are listed below:

Table 3. Hyper-parameter Settings

Hyper-parameter	Value/Name
meta_learning_rate	0.001
inner_learning_rate	0.05
meta_batch_size	32
adaptation_steps	1
query_shots	10
num_test_task	1000
optimizer	Adam

3×3 Conv2d, 5 filters→ReLU→Batch Normalization→2×2 MaxPool2d. Finally, we input flow-packet-level features to the fully connected layer for classification. There are three hidden layers in the fully connected layer with the number of units 256, 128, 64 respectively.

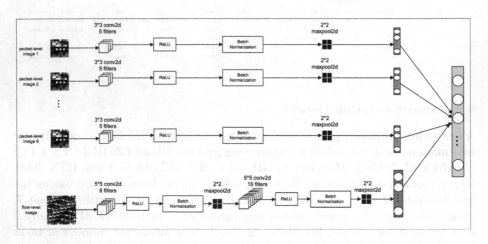

Fig. 3. Architecture of Hierarchical Features Fusion

4.3   Results and Discussions

Baseline Models

To validate the superiority of the proposed Meta-HFMD on the few-shot malware detection task, we select the following baseline methods to compare with Meta-HFMD.

XGBoost [21]: Using XGBoost algorithm to detect malicious traffic.

RF [7]: Using RandomForest algorithm to detect malicious traffic.

CNN [29]: A conventional CNN is used to detect the traffic data.

CNN+LSTM [28]: CNN and LSTM are used to extract the spatial-temporal features of traffic, so as to perform malicious traffic detection.

ProtoNet [4]: The session-based grayscale image is extracted and detected using prototypical network.

SiameseNet [30]: Siamese network is used for few-shot malware detection.

Malware Detection Experiment

Distinguishing malware and benign software from traffic is an important application in the field of cyber security. We randomly select 10 benign software labels from BEN-1, put all their corresponding data into the training set, and put the data corresponding to the remaining 10 benign software labels into the testing set. For the CICAndMal2017 dataset, we randomly sample 32 malware tags, place their corresponding data in the training set, and place the data corresponding to the remaining 10 tags in the testing set. For the MCFP dataset, we randomly sample 26 malware tags, put their corresponding data into the training set, and put the data corresponding to the remaining 10 tags into the testing set. In other words, it guarantees that the labels corresponding to the data in the meta-test phase are never seen by the meta-training. We draw several samples from the training set to form a task in the form of N-way K-shot, 5 and 10 for N, 1 and 5 for K in this experiment. The remaining parameters are given in Table 3.

To determine the value of parameter *adaptation_ steps*, we conducted 5-way 1-shot and 5-way 5-shot experiments on MCFP and CICAndMal2017 datasets, respectively. As shown in Fig. 4, the horizontal axis represents the number of fine-tuning on support set, and the vertical axis represents the value of loss. In this paper, "CrossEntropyLoss" is selected as the loss function. As can be seen in Fig. 4, when the adaptation step is 0, that is, without any fine-tuning, the loss value on the testing set is very large, and the detection effect is not good. After one adaptation step, the loss on the test set immediately decreases and the detection performance improves significantly. When the adaptation step is larger than one, although the loss is also decreasing, the overall change is not large. Considering the time efficiency of the model, *adaptation_ steps* in this paper is set to 1.

The experimental results on CICAndMal2017 and MCFP datasets are shown in Table 4 and Table 5. A discussion of the experimental results is given below.

(1) The proposed Meta-HFMD performs significantly better than other models on malware detection task. In CICAndMal2017 dataset, the accuracy of 5-way 1-shot, 5-way 5-shot, 10-way 1-shot and 10-way 5-shot can reach 95.59%, 98.26%, 94.62% and 94.83%, respectively. F1 score can reach 95.04%, 95.55%, 94.22%, 94.26%, respectively. In MCFP dataset, the accuracy of 5-way 1-shot, 5-way 5-shot, 10-way 1-shot and 10-way 5-shot can reach 96.64%, 99.23%, 94.39% and 95.25%, respectively. F1 score can reach 95.88%, 96.59%, 92.20% and 94.12%, respectively. It is worth noting that the proposed model in this paper can also

Table 4. Results(%) of Benign and Malicious Software Detection Experiment Conducted on CICAndMal2017 (Ac Means Accuracy and F1 Means F1 Score)

Models		5-way				10-way			
		1-shot		5-shot		1-shot		5-shot	
		Ac	F1	Ac	F1	Ac	F1	Ac	F1
ML-based	XGBoost [21]	49.24	45.73	54.23	49.29	44.20	50.02	48.29	51.24
	RF [7]	52.09	49.23	53.87	48.37	45.34	47.69	47.98	50.03
DL-based	CNN [29]	57.32	45.82	63.82	46.67	52.24	31.93	55.49	39.75
	CNN+LSTM [28]	60.24	59.89	65.28	49.42	55.90	49.32	57.25	42.71
FSL-based	ProtoNet [4]	90.83	89.15	92.06	90.44	86.24	85.16	89.24	88.37
	SiameseNet [30]	91.15	91.61	92.93	92.24	85.19	84.52	87.24	90.08
	Meta-HFMD	**95.59**	**95.04**	**98.26**	**95.55**	**94.62**	**94.22**	**94.83**	**94.26**

achieve high accuracy and F1 score when shot is set to 1, which means that Meta-HFMD can also be competent for malware detection when data is extremely scarce without training on a large amount of data.

Table 5. Results(%) of Benign and Malicious Software Detection Experiment Conducted on MCFP (Ac Means Accuracy and F1 Means F1 Score)

Models		5-way				10-way			
		1-shot		5-shot		1-shot		5-shot	
		Ac	F1	Ac	F1	Ac	F1	Ac	F1
ML-based	XGBoost [21]	50.02	52.09	55.94	49.12	39.48	42.59	39.46	44.04
	RF [7]	49.21	48.58	57.10	50.53	40.90	41.25	42.81	48.49
DL-based	CNN [29]	68.41	59.43	69.42	60.98	60.84	49.29	65.23	55.57
	CNN+LSTM [28]	69.94	60.24	72.49	64.42	59.47	48.84	66.39	52.33
FSL-based	ProtoNet [4]	90.04	89.25	91.66	90.26	83.80	84.07	88.91	88.94
	SiameseNet [30]	89.20	85.90	90.93	89.78	85.38	79.72	87.96	88.98
	Meta-HFMD	**96.64**	**95.88**	**99.23**	**96.59**	**94.39**	**92.20**	**95.25**	**94.12**

(2) The whole experiment can be divided into 3 series: (i) Machine Learning-based (ML-based) models consisting of XGBoost and RF. (ii) Deep Learning-based (DL-based) models consisting of CNN and CNN+LSTM. (iii) Few-Shot Learning-based (FSL-based) models consisting of ProtoNet, SiameseNet and Meta-HFMD. It can be observed that FSL-based models perform significantly better than ML-based and DL-based models as a whole. When the sample size is small, DL-based models cause severe overfitting due to insufficient data, that is, they have high accuracy on the training set but low accuracy on the testing set. The ML-based model proceeds as follows. First, the statistical features of traffic are extracted and input to the machine learning classification algorithm after preprocessing. Because the categories of benign software and malware (0 and

1) come from many different software families, it is difficult to learn the characteristics of their respective categories, especially the value of "way" is large and the "shot" is small. In addition, the software families in the testing set have never been seen in the training set, and thus, it is very difficult for traditional ML-based and DL-based models to learn their features. Meta-HFMD can obtain a model with generalization after meta-training phase, and can perform well on new tasks with only a few steps of fine-tuning.

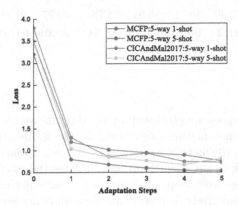

Fig. 4. Impact of Adaptation Steps on Meta-HFMD

Cross-Platform Experiment

In addition, the cross-platform experiments have also been conducted in this paper. N is set to 5, and K is set to 1 and 5. (i) Train on CICAndMal2017, test on MCFP. (ii) Train on MCFP, test on CICAndMal2017. Section 4.3 shows that ML-based and DL-based models do not perform well on a single dataset, so it is meaningless to conduct cross-platform experiments. Therefore, only FSL-based models are used for the cross-platform experiment. The experimental results are shown in Table 6.

Experimental results show that although the accuracy and F1 score of Meta-HFMD in cross-platform experiment are lower than those of single dataset, they still reach more than 90%, which is significantly higher than the other two FSL-based models. Since CICAndMal2017 collected Android mobile software traffic and MCFP collected traditional Internet software traffic, it can be concluded unambiguously that Meta-HFMD also performs well in cross-platform few-shot malware detection.

Table 6. Results(%) of Cross-Platform Experiment (Ac Means Accuracy and F1 Means F1 Score, Tr Means Training Dataset, Te Means Testing Dataset)

Models	Tr:CICAndMal2017 Te:MCFP				Tr:MCFP Te:CICAndMal2017			
	5-way				5-way			
	1-shot		5-shot		1-shot		5-shot	
	Ac	F1	Ac	F1	Ac	F1	Ac	F1
ProtoNet [4]	84.50	83.74	86.59	88.38	82.10	80.24	85.97	85.03
SiameseNet [30]	82.40	80.71	85.91	83.78	80.77	79.26	82.69	81.34
Meta-HFMD	**91.23**	**90.85**	**94.43**	**91.51**	**90.06**	**91.87**	**93.19**	**92.25**

5   Conclusion

In this paper, we propose a meta-learning based framework with hierarchical feature fusion for few-shot malware detection. In the framework of Meta-HFMD, MAML is selected as the meta-learning method, which updates the model parameters specific to task in the inner loop and updates the model parameters with generalization in the outer loop. Malware detection experiments are conducted on two datasets, respectively. Experiments show that the accuracy and F1 score of CICAndMal2017 dataset are 98.26% and 95.55% respectively, and the accuracy and F1 score of MCFP dataset are 99.23% and 96.59% respectively when 5-way 5-shot is set, it is significantly higher than other malware detection models. The 10-way experiment also achieves better results than the other models. Notably, in the 5-way 1-shot, where only one sample per class is used for training and the testing set contains previously unseen classes, the accuracy and F1 score on both datasets can reach more than 94%, meaning that in the extreme lack of labeled data for malware variants, Meta-HFMD also performs well in malware detection. Cross-platform experiments show that the model trained by Meta-HFMD is transferable even for two different Internet platforms. In the future work, we will try to design more deep learning models to be embedded in MAML, and improve existing meta-learning methods to implement the multi-class classification of malware to complete fine-grained few-shot malware detection.

Acknowledgements. This work is jointly supported by the National Natural Science Foundation of China (U19B2028, U22B2061), the National Science and Technology Major Project of the Ministry of Science and Technology of China (2022YFB4300603), the Sichuan Science and Technology Program (2023YFG0151) and the Development of a Big Data-based Platform for Analyzing the Coupling Relationship of Strip Production Processes Project.

References

1. AltaeTran, H., Ramsundar, B., Pappu, A.S., Pande, V.: Low data drug discovery with one-shot learning. ACS Cent. Sci. **3**(4), 283–293 (2017)
2. Bill, K.: Dataset 20 D2 (2020). https://drive.google.com/drive/folders/1-I3a3lM6v_ANU6uu_AUmpNYt7rGu3kzt
3. Bo, L., et al.: An approach based on the improved SVM algorithm for identifying malware in network traffic. Secur. Commun. Netw. **2021**, 1–14 (2021)
4. Rong, C., Gou, G., Hou, C., Li, Z., Xiong, G., Guo, L.: UMVD-FSL: unseen malware variants detection using few-shot learning. In: 2021 International Joint Conference on Neural Networks (IJCNN), Shenzhen, China, pp. 1–8. IEEE (2021)
5. Chai, Y., Du, L., Qiu, J., Yin, L., Tian, Z.: Dynamic prototype network based on sample adaptation for few-shot malware detection. IEEE Trans. Knowl. Data Eng. **35**(5), 4754–4766 (2023)
6. Chelsea, F., Abbeel, P., Sergey, L.: Model-agnostic meta-learning for fast adaptation of deep networks. In: Proceedings of the 34th International Conference on Machine Learning, Sydney, Australia, pp. 1126–1135. PMLR (2017)
7. Chen, R., Li, Y., Fang, W.: Android malware identification based on traffic analysis. In: Sun, X., Pan, Z., Bertino, E. (eds.) ICAIS 2019. LNCS, vol. 11632, pp. 293–303. Springer, Cham (2019). https://doi.org/10.1007/978-3-030-24274-9_26
8. Conti, M., Khandhar, S., Vinod, P.: A few-shot malware classification approach for unknown family recognition using malware feature visualization. Comput. Secur. **122**, 862–887 (2022)
9. Einy, S., Oz, C., Navaei, Y.D.: The anomaly-and signature-based ids for network security using hybrid inference systems. Math. Probl. Eng. **2021**, 1–10 (2021)
10. Hospedales, T., Antoniou, A., Micaelli, P., Storkey, A.: Meta-learning in neural networks: a survey. IEEE Trans. Pattern Anal. Mach. Intell. **44**(9), 5149–5169 (2021)
11. Hung, L., Quang, P., Doyen, S., Steven, C.: URLNet: learning a URL representation with deep learning for malicious URL detection. arXiv preprint arXiv:1802.03162 (2018)
12. Ignatov, A., et al.: AI benchmark: all about deep learning on smartphones in 2019. In: 2019 IEEE/CVF International Conference on Computer Vision Workshop (ICCVW), Seoul, Korea, pp. 3617–3635. IEEE (2019)
13. Khammas, B.M.: Ransomware detection using random forest technique. ICT Express. **6**(4), 325–331 (2020)
14. Lashkari, A.H., Kadir, A.F.A., Taheri, L., Ghorbani, A.A.: Toward developing a systematic approach to generate benchmark android malware datasets and classification. In: 2018 International Carnahan Conference on Security Technology (ICCST), Bangalore, India, pp. 1–7. IEEE (2018)
15. Li, W., Bao, H., Zhang, X.Y., Li, L.: Amdetector: detecting large-scale and novel android malware traffic with meta-learning. In: Groen, D., de Mulatier, C., Paszynski, M., Krzhizhanovskaya, V.V., Dongarra, J.J., Sloot, P.M.A. (eds.) ICCS 2022. LNCS, vol. 13353, pp. 387–401. Springer, Cham (2022). https://doi.org/10.1007/978-3-031-08760-8_33
16. Liu, J., et al.: Deep anomaly detection in packet payload. Neurocomputing **485**, 205–218 (2022)
17. Mahindru, A., Sangal, A.: MLDroid-framework for android malware detection using machine learning techniques. Neural Comput. Appl. **33**(10), 5183–5240 (2021)

18. Marcus, G.: Deep learning: a critical appraisal. arXiv preprint arXiv:1801.00631 (2018)

19. Nataraj, L., Karthikeyan, S., Jacob, G., Manjunath, B.S.: Malware images: visualization and automatic classification. In: Proceedings of the 8th International Symposium on Visualization for Cyber Security, pp. 1–7 (2011)

20. Oliva, A., Torralba, A.: Modeling the shape of the scene: a holistic representation of the spatial envelope. Int. J. Comput. Vision **42**(3), 145–175 (2001)

21. Sharan, A., Radhika, K.: Machine learning based solution for detecting malware android applications. Mach. Learn. **4**(3), 664–668 (2020)

22. Stratosphere: Stratosphere laboratory datasets (2015). https://www.stratosphereips.org/datasets-overview

23. Thrun, S., Pratt, L.: Learning to learn: introduction and overview. In: Thrun, S., Pratt, L. (eds.) Learning to Learn, pp. 3–17. Springer, Boston (1998). https://doi.org/10.1007/978-1-4615-5529-2_1

24. Uddin, M., Rahman, A.A., Uddin, N., Memon, J., Alsaqour, R.A., Kazi, S.: Signature-based multi-layer distributed intrusion detection system using mobile agents. Int. J. Netw. Secur. **15**(1), 79–87 (2013)

25. Vasan, D., Alazab, M., Wassan, S., Safaei, B., Zheng, Q.: Image-based malware classification using ensemble of CNN architectures (IMCEC). Comput. Secur. **92**, 731–748 (2020)

26. Vasudevan, A., Yerraballi, R.: Spike: engineering malware analysis tools using unobtrusive binary-instrumentation. In: Proceedings of the 29th Australasian Computer Science Conference, Hobart, Australia, vol. 48, pp. 311–320. ACM (2006)

27. Vu, L.N., Jung, S.: AdMat: a CNN-on-matrix approach to android malware detection and classification. IEEE Access **9**, 39680–39694 (2021)

28. Wang, W., et al.: HAST-IDS: learning hierarchical spatial-temporal features using deep neural networks to improve intrusion detection. IEEE Access **6**, 1792–1806 (2017)

29. Wang, W., Zhu, M., Zeng, X., Ye, X., Sheng, Y.: Malware traffic classification using convolutional neural network for representation learning. In: 2017 International Conference on Information Networking (ICOIN), Da Nang, Vietnam, pp. 712–717. IEEE (2017)

30. Wang, Z., Tian, J., Qin, J., Fang, H., Chen, L.: A few-shot learning-based siamese capsule network for intrusion detection with imbalanced training data. Comput. Intell. Neurosci. **2021**, 1–17 (2021)

31. Xu, C., Shen, J., Du, X.: A method of few-shot network intrusion detection based on meta-learning framework. IEEE Trans. Inf. Forensics Secur. **15**, 3540–3552 (2020)

32. Yang, M., Chen, X., Luo, Y., Zhang, H.: An android malware detection model based on DT-SVM. Secur. Commun. Netw. **2020**, 1–11 (2020)

33. Wang, Y., Yao, Q., Kwok, J.T., Ni, L.M.: Generalizing from a few examples: a survey on few-shot learning. ACM Comput. Surv. (CSUR) **53**(3), 1–34 (2020)

34. Yude, B., ZhenchangXing, XiaohongLi, Zhiyong, F., Duoyuan, M.: Unsuccessful story about few shot malware family classification and siamese network to the rescue. In: 2020 IEEE/ACM 42nd International Conference on Software Engineering (ICSE), Seoul, South Korea, pp. 1560–1571. IEEE (2020)

35. Zhijie, T., Peng, W., Junfeng, W.: Convprotonet: deep prototype induction towards better class representation for few-shot malware classification. Appl. Sci. **10**(8), 28–47 (2020)

Privacy-Preserving Cloud-Edge Collaborative K-Means Clustering Model in IoT

Chen Wang[1], Jian Xu[1,2](✉), Shanru Tan[1], and Long Yin[1]

[1] Software College, Northeastern University, Shenyang 110169, China
xuj@mail.neu.edu.cn
[2] State Key Laboratory of Information Security, Institute of Information Engineering, Chinese Academy of Sciences, Beijing 100093, China

Abstract. A growing number of smart devices collect data and store it in the cloud for clustering services. K-means outsourcing cloud services not only brings benefits, but also brings privacy issues for sensitive data and clustering models. At the same time, entrusting computing to the cloud for processing can bring computational bandwidth issues. In order to achieve secure and efficient data collection and application, we propose a new system employing a Privacy-Preserving Cloud-Edge Collaborative K-Means Clustering Model (PPCCKCM) based on multi-Key fully homomorphic encryption (multi-key FHE) in IoT. Firstly, we first propose a cloud-edge collaborative training scheme, in which the edge node shares the computing task of the cloud and securely trains the K-Means model in the interaction between the two parties. We further design secure protocols to support multi-key FHE of multi-smart devices, complete the basic operation of K-Means operation, and satisfy the semi-honest security model in cloud computing outsourcing. Finally, the model is analyzed and evaluated, and the results show that PPC-CKCM can protect data and model privacy, and share 41.91%–42.75% communication and 47.52%–53.01% computation overhead.

Keywords: Multi-key FHE · Cloud-edge · Privacy-Preserving Computing · Data Privacy

1 Introduction

Internet of Things (IoT) brings greatly benefits for smart city to a variety of fields (e.g., smart transportation systems [1], 5G [2], and virtual reality [3]). Its rapid development has brought more convenient, efficient and personalized services to urban residents, and improved the quality of life and competitiveness of cities. However, the amount of data generated by the IoT has increased dramatically [4], placing higher demands on computing and storage resources. Storing and processing mass data only by cloud servers will bring serious bandwidth and power consumption problems [5,6]. By using edge nodes, a portion of computing tasks can be moved from the central data center to edge nodes to reduce

© The Author(s), under exclusive license to Springer Nature Singapore Pte Ltd. 2024
H. Yang and R. Lu (Eds.): FCS 2023, CCIS 1992, pp. 655–669, 2024.
https://doi.org/10.1007/978-981-99-9331-4_44

latency, save bandwidth, and improve data privacy [7,8]. Edge nodes are usually used to support some special application scenarios, such as smart city and IoT applications.

In smart city, machine learning is used to analyze complex data and industrial predictions by IoT. Due to its simplicity and easy implementation, K-Means has become one of the most common machine learning models, and has been widely used in the fields of image segmentation, social network analysis, medical diagnosis and risk assessment [9]. In brief, clustering algorithm can obtain useful knowledge from a large amount of data and find out the potential relationship between data. When sufficient training data is collected, the model can better learn the relationships and rules between data, so as to improve its generalization ability and accuracy [10].

Outsourced K-Means services can be trained by uploading data to the cloud for remote machine learning service providers. These service providers often have powerful computing and storage resources and can provide specialized algorithms, model optimization, and parameter tuning services to better train high-quality models. When using outsourced machine learning services, users need to pay attention to data security and privacy protection to avoid the disclosure of sensitive data [11]. Moreover, data in the edge can easily be stolen and tampered with, resulting in loss and damage to the industrial system. It is therefore necessary to improve security during data processing and introduce an encryption mechanism. However, due to resource constraints, this means that the data collection framework must not only maintain security and privacy, but also ensure low energy consumption.

In outsourced machine learning, homomorphic encryption (HE) can be used to protect data privacy while also allowing calculations and analysis without exposing the original data [12,13]. For example, data can be encrypted and uploaded to the cloud, and the cloud provider can encrypt and calculate the data, and then return the result to the user. In this way, requirements such as data sharing and outsourcing computing can be realized.

The main advantage of homomorphic encryption is that calculations can be performed without exposing the original data, thus protecting the privacy and security of the data. However, homomorphic encryption technology also has two problems. First of all, HE assigns computing tasks to cloud services, and users need to participate in the computing process. In the outsourcing machine learning method proposed by Kim [14], most technologies of computing and data processing require the use of cloud computing resources for processing and analysis, resulting in the burden of cloud servers. In Mandal [15], users need to participate in the calculation process, such as data encryption, decryption, calculation and other operations, which need to use local computing resources for processing. Second, existing schemes [16,17] use the same public key for encryption, which leads to the risk of data leakage. In HE, it is not secure to encrypt data using the same public key.

To trains the K-Means model of multi-smart devices, we further propose a Privacy-Preserving Cloud-Edge Collaborative K-Means Clustering Model (PPC-CKCM) based on multi-key FHE for training and clustering in IoT. In our scheme, the smart devices generate different keys, and the trained K-Means model is encrypted and outsourced to edge nodes and industrial clouds. Our contributions are as follows:

- Firstly, we design a privacy-preserving cloud-edge collaborative K-Means clustering model based to expand the data volume of the IoT. Compared to single cloud server computing, by assigning data and computing tasks to different computing nodes, larger scale data and models can be processed simultaneously, improving the accuracy and efficiency of clustering models.
- Second, we designed three secure communication protocols based on multi-key FHE, *Selection*, *Comparison* and *getMin*. Aboved three protocols, we further completed the clustering process based on multi-key FHE. It also provides a security analysis to protect data and models, and prevent collusion between IoT devices.
- Finally, we conduct an evaluation with our scheme and Privacy-Preserving K-Means Clustering Model (PPKCM), showing our scheme securely trains the K-Means clustering model under multiple party, while sharing 41.91%–42.75% communication and 47.52%–53.01% computation overhead of the cloud.

2 Related Work

2.1 Privacy-Preserving K-Means Problems

There has been a lot of work on privacy-preserving K-Means problem. Baby et al. [14] used the code-based threshold encryption sharing scheme as a privacy protection mechanism, and processed it separately on different servers. Compared with the existing protocol, the number of iterations was less and the computing burden was reduced. Qian et al. [15] encrypt the sensitive data of users to prevent the privacy leakage of external analysts and clustering service providers, and fully support the selection clustering function of online user behavior analysis, while ensuring the differential privacy. Keith et al. [18] designed a ciphertext aggregation model for high-dimensional data. The server calculates ciphertext data vectors held by large users from mobile devices to evaluate the efficiency of the model, and the server has low communication overhead. Qiu et al. [19] solved addition and multiplication operations in ciphertext aggregation, designed three-party communication protocols, used differential privacy to process sensitive data, and supported selective aggregation function of online user behavior analysis.

2.2 Privacy-Preserving Edge-Cloud for IoT Problems

Several prior works have proposed the use of edge computing to aid the training of the industrial clouds. An edge node is composed of network devices that can be deployed anywhere over a network connection. Edge nodes have certain computing, storage and autonomous capabilities that can reduce the data processing load on resource-constrained IoT equipments. Previous studies were based on the semi-honest model [9], in which the computing participant would calculate according to the requirements of the computing protocol during the calculation process, but might try to obtain the calculation result by analyzing the information flow in the protocol process, rather than directly tampering with the information in the protocol process. In [20], solution was designed a privacy protection edge intelligent data aggregation solution was designed to ensure data confidentiality, integrity, and real-timeness. In [21], they propose a secure and smart communication solution for pervasive edge computing in infrastructure that supports IIoT. In the proposed scheme, the IIoT device detects adversary's counterfeit identity and shares it with the edge server to prevent the upstream transmission of its malicious data. In [22], they propose a device-oriented anonymous privacy protection scheme with identity verification for data aggregation applications in a fog-enhanced IoT system.

2.3   Multi-key Outsourcing Problems

Users cannot fully trust industrial clouds run by third parties, meaning that conducting privacy-preserving machine learning for cloud data from different data providers becomes a challenge. The work [23] accordingly proposed a new scheme that use the different public keys with double decryption algorithm to encrypt data sets of different providers. The work [10] proposed a distributed deep learning scheme, which implements transform keys servers by using homomorphic re-encryption in asynchronous stochastic gradient descent, which is applied to deep learning to prevent collusion between learning participants and servers. The work [24] and [25] proposed a multi-key outsourcing scheme in cloud computing, which combined double decryption algorithm with an MK-FHE scheme to solve the problem of collaborative deep learning over ciphertext with different public keyskeys. More specifically, [24] implements a deep learning scheme, while [25] implements a k-means clustering scheme. However, the cost of computation and communication is high, which complicates the implementation of an FHE scheme in an actual machine learning.

3   System and Security Model

3.1   System Model

Our system consists of four entities in total: smart device (SD), edge node (EN), industrial cloud (IC) and user (U), is shown in Fig. 1. Smart devices (such as sensors, mobile phones and vehicles) collect a large number of user (such as residents) data, use edge and cloud computing to train models (such as automatic management of industrial plants, intelligent traffic control and medical care), and provide clustering services. Clustering is mainly divided into two processes: cluster allocation and cluster center movement: First, calculate the euclidean distance between the encrypted sample point and the cluster center, find the minimum value and complete the cluster allocation process according to the minimum value; Then the new cluster center is recalculated to complete the cluster center moving process. The above process is analyzed to extract the basic operation, and the secure communication protocol corresponding to the basic operation is designed. The IC side and the EN interact through the communication protocol. The clustering process is mainly carried out in the EN, and the IC assists the calculation, which reduces the calculation pressure of the IC. The trained model contains sensitive information and knowledge from the training data, so it should not be accessible or usable by unauthorized entities. These entities may try to use the information for malicious activities or gain commercial benefits, which may lead to serious consequences, including disclosure of personal privacy and infringement of intellectual property rights. Similar multi-server architecture has been studied and applied [8,9].

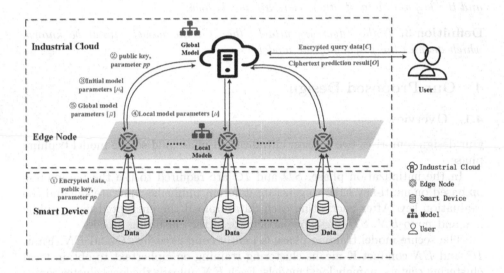

Fig. 1. The PPCCKCM architecture.

A Privacy-Preserving Cloud-Edge Collaborative K-Means Clustering Model (PPCCKCM) based on Multi-Key FHE can be described by the following tuples $\{SD, EN, IC, Selection, Comparison, getMin\}$.

- *Selection*: Secure selection protocol, inputs encrypted data $[[x]]$ and $[[y]]$ to obtain the selection result of encrypted data $[[x \oplus y]]$;
- *Comparison*: Secure comparison protocol, which uses encrypted data $[[x]]$ and $[[y]]$ as input, and calls *Selection* to obtain the encrypted comparison result $[[z]]$;
- *getMin*: Secure get minimum protocol takes the *Comparison* result $[[z]]$ as input, and uses *getMin* to calculate the minimum;

3.2 Security Model

All participants in PPCCKCM are assumed to be semi-honest, which means that all participants are threatened by a semi-honest attack, that is, an attacker may eavesdrop and view messages, but cannot modify or forge them. Consider an adversary who wants to obtain user data, and give the following security definitions:

Definition 1. *PPCCKCM guarantees input privacy through multi-key FHE, unless adversaries attack SD and IC. In multi-key FHE, SD encrypts each data under different keys, providing confidentiality.*

Definition 2. *If the adversary attacks the SD and the decryption key is leaked, PPCCKCM can ensure that only the key and data of the single user are leaked, and the key and data of other users are not known.*

Definition 3. *If the adversary attacks the IC, the model cannot be known, which ensures the privacy of the model.*

4 Our Proposed Design

4.1 Overview

Our design comprises two phases: initialization phase and secure model training phase.

In the initialization phase, SD and IC are required to use the parameters pp based on multi-key FHE to generate different public key, private key and the evaluation key. After encrypting each data, upload the encrypted data, public key and pp to EN. SD does not participate in the clustering process.

The secure model training phase is jointly completed by IC and EN. First, IC and EN conduct K-means clustering training on ciphertext to obtain local clustering centers, namely local models. Each EN uploads the local cluster center to the IC, and the IC aggregates the local cluster center to get the global cluster center, that is, the global model, and returns it to each EN. Each EN repeats the encrypted clustering process until the goal is completed, which the global model is better.

4.2 Initialization Phase

In the initialization stage, there are three stages: key generation, data upload and key conversion.

- Key generation: Each smart device independently generates its own key pair $\{pk_{l,i}, sk_{l,i}\}$ according to the public parameter pp, where L is the maximum circuit depth. IC generates its own key pair independently, $\{pk_{l,IC}, sk_{l,IC}\}$.

$$\{pk_{l,i}, sk_{l,i}\} \leftarrow MK.KeyGen(pp, i) \tag{1}$$

IC generates an evaluation key $\{Evk_{sk_{l.IC}}\}$ to refresh the ciphertext.

$$\{Evk_{sk_{l.IC}}\} \leftarrow MK.SKeyGen(pp, sk_{l,IC}, pk_{l-1,IC}) \tag{2}$$

- Data Upload: Each smart device encrypts their data, and upload encrypted data, evaluation key $\{Evk_{sk_{l.SD}}\}$ and pp to edge nodes; Industrial cloud IC then uploads its evaluation key $\{Evk_{sk_{l.IC}}\}$ to EN;
- Key Conversion: In the key conversion sub-algorithm, "fresh" ciphertext $[m_i]$ that can only be decrypted by the private key of each smart device will be converted to "fresh" ciphertext $[[m_i]]$, which can only be decrypted under the EN private key. Each edge node executes the key conversion sub-algorithm to generate the evaluation key $\{Evk_{sk_{l.EN}}\}$ required for the conversion encrypted data.

$$\{Evk_{sk_{l.EN}}\} \leftarrow MK.SKeyGen(pp, sk_{l,SD}, pk_{l,IC}) \tag{3}$$

EN runs the key exchange sub-algorithm to convert $[m_i]$ to $[[m_i]]$.

$$[[m_i]] \leftarrow MK.SKey(Evk_{sk_{L.EN}}, [m_i]) \tag{4}$$

4.3 Secure Model Training Phase

Secure model training phase is primarily engaged in edge node and the industrial cloud. This training phase includes secure protocol construction phase and secure clustering process phase.

Secure Protocol Construction Phase. Analyze the operation of logical regression and extract the basic operations, such as comparison and get the minimum value. Design corresponding secure communication protocols, including secure *Selection* protocol, secure *Comparison* protocol and secure *getMin* protocol.

Secure *Selection* protocol, it will complete the selection operation between the two values, corresponding to the IF-ELSE selection expression, as shown in Protocol 1.

The secure *Comparison* protocol compares the value of two encrypted data by calling the *Selection* protocol. If $t = 1$, then $a < b$; if $t = 0$, then $a \geq b$. Protocol 2 is shown below.

The *getMin* protocol is to compare m encrypted data and obtain an ascending ciphertext sequence. Taking the minimum value adopts the idea of divide and conquer, and the whole iterative process is equivalent to a binary tree. m represents the length of the array, $\lceil \log_2^m \rceil$ represents the depth of the tree, and the number of comparisons is $num/2$.

Protocol 1 *Selection* protocol over encrypted data

Input EN: $[[a]], [[b]], [[c]]$;
Input IC: private key $sk_{l-1,IC}$;
Output EN: result $[[res]]$
1: EN:
2: $r \xleftarrow{R} \mathbb{Z}_N$
3: $[[a']] \leftarrow [[a]] \oplus [[r]]$
4: send $[[a']]$ to IC
5: IC:
6: $a' \leftarrow MK.Dec([[a']], sk_{l-1,IC})$
7: send a' to EN
8: EN:
9: **if** $r = 0$ **then**
10:     $[[a]] \leftarrow a'$
11: **else**
12:     $[[a]] \leftarrow r \odot a'$
13: **end if**
14: $[[res]] \leftarrow ([[a]] \cdot [[b]] \oplus [[c]])) \oplus [[c]]$
15: EN output $[[res]]$

Secure Clustering Process Phase. Secure clustering process mainly includes two parts: cluster class assignment and cluster center movement. After analyzing the calculation process, it is found that MKFHE has three problems in the application process, namely, the distance measurement problem, the minimum problem for finding the minimum distance centroid, and the division problem for calculating the average value of data points.

IC provides two parameters, the number of clusters K and the number of iterations T, to control the end of the clustering process. These two parameters are not encrypted.

The clustering process of PPCCKCM is as follows:

5   System Analysis

This section analyzes the security of the communication protocol and PPC-CKCM under the semi-honest model. Both EN and IC are semi-honest participants. They faithfully follow the implementation of the protocol and allow inference from the data obtained during the implementation of the protocol. Its input data is private data and can only be known by individuals.

In *Selection* protocol, the view of EN is $V_{EN} = ([[a]], [[b]], [[c]], pk; r, [[a']], [[res]])$. Because MKFHE is semantically safe, Party EN cannot extract clear text from it, thus ensuring data privacy. EN encrypts the random number r. In order to add noise, the processed data $[[a']]$ is sent to IC and decrypted by IC. Then send it to EN to remove the noise and get the true value. The view of IC, because r is a number evenly and randomly selected from it, represents the information space of MKFHE. Unless brute force cracking is used, IC finds

---

Protocol 2 *Comparison* protocol over encrypted data

Input *EN*: $[[a]]=[[a_n]],[[a_{n-1}]]...[[a_0]]$, $[[b]]=[[b_n]],[[b_{n-1}]]...[[b_0]]$, the number n of bits;

Input *IC*: private key $sk_{l-1,IC}$;

Output *EN*: comparison result $[[t]]$

1: **for** $i \in \{0, \ldots, n\}$ **do**
2:   EN:
3:   $[[p]] \leftarrow 0, [[e]] \leftarrow 0$
4:   **if** $r = 0$ **then**
5:     $[[p]] \leftarrow [[a_i]] \oplus [[b_i]] \oplus 1$
6:   **end if**
7:   EN,IC:
8:     $[[e]] =$ Selection$([[p]], [[e]], [[b_i]])$
9: **end for**
10: EN:
11: $[[res1]] \leftarrow ([[a_n]] \otimes (([[b_n]] \oplus 1))$
12: $[[res2]] \leftarrow ((([[a_n]] \oplus [[b_n \oplus 1]] \otimes [[e]])$
13: $[[res]] \leftarrow [[res1]] \oplus [[res2]]$
14: $r \xleftarrow{R} \mathbb{Z}_N$
15: $[[res']] \leftarrow [[res]] \oplus [[r]]$
16: send $[[res']]$ to IC
17: IC:
18: $res' \leftarrow MK.Dec([[res']], sk_{l-1,IC})$
19: **if** $res' = 0$ **then**
20:   $[[c]] \leftarrow 1$
21: **else**
22:   $[[c]] \leftarrow 0$
23: **end if**
24: send $[[c]]$ to EN
25: EN:
26: $[[t]] \leftarrow [[r]] \odot [[c]]$
27: EN return $[[t]]$

---

it difficult to get real value from the data of decryption data, so as to ensure the data confidentiality.

In *Comparison* protocol, the view of the *EN* is $V_{EN}= ([[a]], [[b]], n, r, pk, [[res]]; [[p]], [[res']])$. Because MKFHE is semantically safe, the *EN* side cannot extract the clear text a, b, res, t, res' from $[[a]], [[b]], n, r, [[res]]$. The view of the *IC* is $V_{IC} = ([[res']], sk; [[e]])$, and the private key $sk_{l-1,IC}$ of the FHE owned by the *IC* side can decrypt to obtain the plaintext res, but the random value r is randomly obtained from a large number, stored locally, and is the private data of the *EN* side, which is random. Unless it is cracked by force, it is difficult to obtain r, and the violent cracking consumes time and computing resources. Random values usually generated by cryptographic techniques such as encryption or hash functions and are highly random and unpredictable. Even if an attacker

Protocol 3 *getMin* protocol over encrypted data

Input EN: $[[t_0]], \ldots, [[t_{n-1}]]$;

Input IC: private key $sk_{l-1,IC}$;

Output EN: $[[t_{min}]]$

1: EN:
2: **for** $i \in \{0, \ldots, n\}$ **do**
3: $\quad [[t_i']] \leftarrow [[t_i]]$
4: **end for**
5: $num \leftarrow n$
6: **for** $1 \leq i \leq \lceil \log_2^n \rceil$ **do**
7: $\quad$ **for** $1 \leq j \leq \lfloor num/2 \rfloor$ **do**
8: $\quad\quad EN, IC$:
9: $\quad\quad f = EncCompare \left([[t'_{2^i(j-1)}]], [[t'_{2^i(j-1)+2^{i-1}}]] \right)$
10: $\quad\quad r_1 \overset{R}{\leftarrow} Z_N, r_2 \overset{R}{\leftarrow} Z_N$
11: $\quad\quad [[t_1]] \leftarrow [[t'_{2^i(j-1)}]] \oplus [[r_1]]$
12: $\quad\quad [[t_2]] \leftarrow [[t'_{2^i(j-1)+2^{i-1}}]] \oplus [[r_2]]$
13: $\quad\quad$ send $[[t_1]] \; [[t_2]]$ to IC
14: $\quad\quad IC$:
15: $\quad\quad$ **if** $f = 1$ **then**
16: $\quad\quad\quad$ refresh $[[t_{min}]] \leftarrow [[t_1]]$
17: $\quad\quad$ **else**
18: $\quad\quad\quad [[t_{min}]] \leftarrow [[t_2]]$
19: $\quad\quad$ **end if**
20: $\quad\quad$ send $[[t_{min}]] \; [[t_f]]$ to EN
21: $\quad\quad EN$:
22: $\quad\quad [[t'_{2^i(j-1)}]] \leftarrow [[t_{min}]] \oplus ([[f]] \odot [[1]]) \otimes r_2 \odot [[f]] \otimes r_1$
23: $\quad\quad [[t'_{2^i(j-1)+2^{i-1}}]] \leftarrow [[0]]$
24: $\quad$ **end for**
25: **end for**
26: $num \leftarrow \lceil num/2 \rceil$
27: **return** $[[t_{min}]] \leftarrow [[t_0']]$

---

can obtain some information about random values and encryption algorithms, it is difficult to derive the original values from them.

In *getMin* protocol, the view of the EN is $V_{EN} = ([[t]], pk, r, [[A]], [[min]], [[A']] \; [[M]], [[c]])$, where r is a uniformly randomly selected number. IC and EN first compare the encrypted data $[[t]], [[min]]$ of the EN side by calling the *Comparison* protocol of the encrypted data, and EN obtains the comparison result $[[M]]$. Because of the security of the *Comparison* protocol of the encrypted data, the privacy of the data during the comparison between IC and EN is guaranteed. Then EN sends the encrypted data $[[A']]$ after the random interference to IC, because $[[A']]$ is the encrypted data with the random interference value, Therefore, even if the IC can use the MKFHE private key to decrypt, it is difficult to extract the true value from the plaintext A', thus ensuring the privacy of the data to be compared in the IC. Due to the semantic

---

Protocol 4 Secure clustering process algorithm

Input EN: encrypted training data $[[x]]$;

Input IC: the number of clusters K and the number of iterations T, private key $sk_{l-1,IC}$;

Output IC: Cluster center μ_k

1: IC:
2:   initialization parameters $E(A[i][k])$ and sent it to EN
3: **for** $i \in \{0,\dots,K\}$ **do**
4:     $E(\mu_k) = E(x_k)$
5:     **for** $j \in \{0,\dots,T\}$ **do**
6:       **for** $i \in \{0,\dots,m\}$ **do**
7:         **for** $k \in \{0,\dots,K\}$ **do**
8:           EN,IC:
9:           $E(dis[k]) = \|x_i - \mu_k\|_1$
10:           $E(A[i][k]) \leftarrow getMin(E(dis),E(A[i][k]))$
11:         **end for**
12:       **end for**
13:       **for** $k \in \{0,\dots,K\}$ **do**
14:         EN:
15:         $E(\overline{\mu_k}) \leftarrow E(\mu_k)$
16:         $E(\mu_k) \leftarrow 0$
17:         **for** $i \in \{0,\dots,m\}$ **do**
18:           $E(\mu_k) \leftarrow E(\mu_k)+Selection\,(E(A[i][k]),E(x_i),E(\overline{\mu_k}))$
19:         **end for**
20:       **end for**
21:       $E(\mu_k) \leftarrow {E(\mu_k)}/{m}$
22:       send $E(\mu_k)$ to IC
23:       IC:
24:       compute $\bar{\mu}_k \leftarrow \sum_{t=1}^{T} \frac{m_t}{m}\mu_k$
25:       send $\bar{\mu}_k$ to EN
26:     **end for**
27: **end for**

---

security of MKFHE, the EN side cannot extract the value of plaintext A' from the ciphertext data.

PPCCKCM constructed based on *Selection* protocol, *Comparison* protocol and *getMin* protocol is also safe in the semi-honest model.

6 Experiments

6.1 Simulation Settings

All experiments are performed on a Lenovo laptop: Ryzen 9 5900HX with Radeon Graphics @ 3.30 GHz single-threaded with 32 GB memory, compiled with C++ on Ubuntu 18.04.2. This paper uses the same environment to simulate EN and IC for collaborative K-Means model training. The paper builts *Selection*,

Comparison, *getMin* protocols based on the multi-key FHE proposed by Chen et al. [26]. We evaluated the performance of the CIFAR-10 dataset [28], which consists of 15000 samples. Among them, 10000 samples are used for training, and the rest are used for testing. This section describes the performance of PPCCK-MeasCM, where the maximum data transfer and computing cost are used for training evaluation of EN and IC.

6.2   Performance Evaluation

This section evaluates the performance of the edge nodes and industrial cloud in terms of the maximum data transfer and computing cost.

Edge Nodes. The communication and computation cost of EN in PPCCK-MeasCM training phase on 0 to 50 devices are shown as Fig. 2. The communication cost including receive encrypted data, IC and SD security parameters pp and exchange of local clustering center. Figure 2(a) shows the maximum data in EN needs to transmit. The computation cost of EN is positively related to the number of devices in the training phase, with more devices increasing the communication cost, shown as Fig. 2(b).

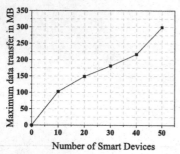 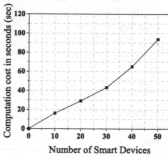

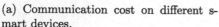

(a) Communication cost on different smart devices.

(b) Computation cost on different smart devices.

Fig. 2. Communication and computation evaluation in edge nodes.

Industrial Cloud. The communication and computation overhead of the PPC-CKCM in this paper is compared with that of the scheme PPKCM without edge-assisted, as shown in Fig. 3.

The communication cost of the industrial cloud includes receiving encrypted local cluster centers and encrypted data in secure protocols. The cost of industrial cloud computing is positively correlated with the number of edge nodes. As the number of edge nodes increases, so does the computing cost of industrial cloud. Compared with PPCCKCM, PPKCM is only completed by industrial

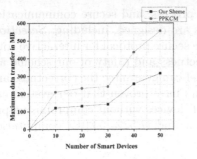

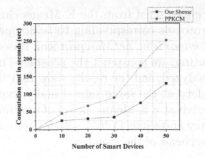

(a) Comparison of communication cost.   (b) Comparison of communication cost.

Fig. 3. Communication and computation evaluation between our sheme and PPKCM.

cloud and smart devices. Therefore, EN shares 41.91%–42.75% computational and 47.52%–53.01% computational overhead. Experiments show that the PPC-CKCM method can reduce the computational cost of cloud.

Model Performance Evaluation. The silhouette coefficient is used to measure the clustering effect. Table 1 shows the comparison of the silhouette coefficient of plaintext K-Means and PPCCKCM when T is selected with different values. When $T = 5$–15, the silhouette coefficient increases rapidly, which means that the clustering performance is obviously improved. When $T = 15$–30, the silhouette coefficient has little change. After 15 rounds, no further iterations are required.

Table 1. Silhouette coefficient comparison of plaintext and PPCCKCM

	$T = 5$	$T = 10$	$T = 15$	$T = 20$	$T = 25$	$T = 30$
Plaintext	0.704	0.716	0.729	0.724	0.727	0.726
PPCCKCM	0.667	0.681	0.688	0.690	0.692	0.687

According to the data analysis in Table 1, the silhouette coefficient of PPC-CKCM is 2.9%–5.8% lower than that of the plain-text K-means algorithm, and the silhouette coefficient of PPCCKCM is above 0.6, which is within the acceptable range.

7 Conclusion

This paper proposes a PPCCKCM scheme suitable in IoT based on Multi-Key FHE, which allows multiple smart devices to outsource encrypted data to industrial clouds and edge nodes to share compute. Firstly, basic operations are extracted from the K-Means clustering process, and secure communication protocols corresponding to basic operations are designed, including: *Selection, Comparison, getMin* protocol. Based on the secure protocol for interactive computing, we construct the scheme; The correctness and safety of our scheme are analyzed, and the results show that the model can guarantee the correctness and safety at the same time. Finally, experiments have proven that our system can arrive at a K-Means model of multiple smart devices without compromising privacy and share 41.91%–42.75% communication and 47.52%–53.01% computation overhead of the cloud.

References

1. Wang, Z., Hu, J., Min, G., Zhao, Z., Wang, J.: Data augmentation based cellular traffic prediction in edge computing enabled smart city. IEEE Trans. Industr. Inf. **17**(6), 4179–4187 (2021)
2. Lin, K., Xu, X.L., Gao, H.H.: TSCRNN: a novel classification scheme of encrypted traffic based on flow spatiotemporal features for efficient management of IIoT. Comput. Netw. **190**, 1–11 (2021)
3. Shanmuganthan, V., Khari, M., Dey, N., Crespo, R.G.: Enhanced resource allocation in mobile edge computing using reinforcement learning based MOACO algorithm for IIOT. Comput. Commun. **151**, 355–364 (2020)
4. Ren, S., Kim, J., Cho, W.S., Soeng, S., Kong, S., Lee, K.H.: Big data platform for intelligence industrial IoT sensor monitoring system based on edge computing and AI. In: 2021 International Conference on Artificial Intelligence in Information and Communication, Korea. IEEE (2021)
5. Jiang, Z.L., Ning, G., Jin, Y., Lv, J., Fang, J.: Efficient two-party privacy preserving collaborative K-means clustering protocol supporting both storage and computation outsourcing. Inf. Sci. **518**, 168–180 (2020)
6. Shamsabadi, A.S., Gascon, A., Haddadi, H., Cavallaro, A.: PrivEdge: from local to distributed private training and prediction. IEEE Trans. Inf. Forensics Secur. **15**, 3819–3831 (2020)
7. Zhou, Z., Chen, X., Li, E., Zeng, L., Luo, K., Zhang, J.: Edge intelligence: paving the last mile of artificial intelligence with edge computing. In: Proceedings of the IEEE, pp. 1738–1762. IEEE (2019)
8. Zhou, J., Cao, Z., Qin, Z., Dong, X.L., Ren, K.: LPPA: lightweight privacy-preserving authentication from efficient multi-key secure outsourced computation for location-based services in VANETs. IEEE Trans. Inf. Forensics Secur. **15**, 420–434 (2019)
9. So, J., Guler, B., Avestimehr, S.: CodedPrivateML: a fast and privacy-preserving framework for distributed machine learning. IEEE J. Sel. Areas Inf. Theory **2**(1), 441–451 (2021)
10. Tang, F., Wu, W., Liu, J., Wang, H., Xian, M.: Privacy-preserving distributed deep learning via homomorphic re-encryption. Electronics **8**(4), 1–21 (2019)
11. Sharma, V., You, I., Jayakody, D.N.K., Ayiquzzaman, M.: Cooperative trust relaying and privacy preservation via edge-crowdsourcing in social internet of things. Futur. Gener. Comput. Syst. **92**, 758–776 (2019)
12. Bonte, C., Vercauteren, F.: Privacy-preserving logistic regression training. BMC Med. Genomics **11**, 13–21 (2018)

13. Kim, A., Song, Y., Kim, M., Lee, K.: Logistic regression model training based on the approximate homomorphic encryption. BMC Med. Genomics **11**, 1–13 (2018)

14. Baby, V., Chandra, N.S.: Distributed threshold k-means clustering for privacy-preserving data mining. In: International Conference on Advances in Computing, Communications and Informatics, India. IEEE (2016)

15. Qian, J., Qiu, F., Wu, F.: A differentially private selective aggregation scheme for online user behavior analysis. In: Global Communications Conference, USA. IEEE (2016)

16. Phong, L.T., Aono, Y., Hayashi, T., Wang, L., Moriai, S.: Privacy-preserving deep learning via additively homomorphic encryption. IEEE Trans. Inf. Forensics Secur. **13**(5), 1333–1345 (2018)

17. Shokri, R., Shmatikov, V.: Privacy-preserving deep learning. In: 2015 53rd Annual Allerton Conference on Communication, Control, and Computing (Allerton), USA. IEEE (2015)

18. Keith, B., Vladimir, I., Ben, K.: CCS-practical secure aggregation for privacy-preserving machine learning. In Proceedings of the 2017 ACM SIGSAC Conference on Computer and Communications Security, USA, pp. 1175–1191. IEEE (2017)

19. Qian, J., Qiu, F., Wu, F.: Efficient and private scoring of decision trees, support vector machines and logistic regression models based on pre-computation. IEEE Trans. Comput. **66**(2), 217–230 (2016)

20. Xiong, J.B., et al.: A personalized privacy protection framework for mobile crowd-sensing in IIoT. IEEE Trans. Industr. Inf. **16**(6), 4231–4241 (2020)

21. Khan, F., Jan, M.A., Rehman, A., Mastorakis, S., Alazab, M., Watters, P.: A secured and intelligent communication scheme for IIoT-enabled pervasive edge computing. IEEE Trans. Industr. Inf. **17**(7), 5128–5137 (2021)

22. Guan, Z.T., et al.: APPA: an anonymous and privacy-serving pre data aggregation scheme for fog-enhanced IoT. J. Netw. Comput. Appl. **125**, 82–92 (2019)

23. Li, P., Li, T., Ye, H., Li, J., Chen, X.F., Xiang, Y.: Privacy-preserving machine learning with multiple data providers. Futur. Gener. Comput. Syst. **87**, 341–350 (2018)

24. Li, P., et al.: Multi-key privacy-preserving deep learning in cloud computing. Futur. Gener. Comput. Syst. **74**, 76–85 (2017)

25. Zhou, Y., et al.: Highly secure privacy-preserving outsourced k-means clustering under multiple keys in cloud computing. Secur. Commun. Netw. **2020**, 1–1 (2020)

26. Chen, L., Zhang, Z., Wang, X.: Batched multi-hop multi-key FHE from ring-LWE with compact ciphertext extension. In: Kalai, Y., Reyzin, L. (eds.) TCC 2017. LNCS, vol. 10678, pp. 597–627. Springer, Cham (2017). https://doi.org/10.1007/978-3-319-70503-3_20

27. Zheng, Y., Duan, H., Wang, C., Wang, R.: Securely and efficiently outsourcing decision tree inference. IEEE Trans. Dependable Secure Comput. **19**(3), 1841–1855 (2020)

28. CIFAR-10 DataSet. https://www.cs.toronto.edu/kriz/cifar.html

Author Index

Author index

Printed in the United States
by Baker & Taylor Publisher Services